THE LONG ROAD TO THE SOMME

VOLUME I:
EPISODES
1870 TO 1915
SEDAN TO CHANTILLY

ALAN MACDONALD

IONA BOOKS

Copyright © Alan MacDonald 2024

British Library Cataloguing In Publication Data
A Record of this Publication is available from the British Library

ISBN 978-0-9558119-3-7

Published 2024 by Iona Books
and printed by Lightning Source, Milton Keynes

The right of Alan MacDonald to be identified as Author
of this work has been asserted by him in accordance with
the Copyright, Designs and Patents Act 1988

All rights reserved.
No part of this book may be reproduced or transmitted in any form or by any means, electronic or mechanical including photocopying, recording or by information storage and retrieval system, without permission from the Publisher in writing

Cover design by Nigel Soper
www.nigelsoper.com

Cover: C.R.W.Nevinson: *Returning to the Trenches*, 1916, Dypoint (detail), Courtesy of *Osborne Samuel, Modern & Contemporary Art*
www.osbornesamuel.com

Maps by Paul Hewitt
www.battlefield-design.co.uk

In memory of my mum
Ollie
Olwen Jean MacDonald MacCormick
&
My mother-in-law
Chris
Christine Anne Purnell

"We will forget. The veils of mourning, like dead leaves, will fall. The vision of the missing soldier will slowly fade from the consoled hearts of those they loved so much. And the dead will die for a second time."

Roland Dorgelès
Les Croix de bois, Chapter XVII, *'Et c'est fini'*

Also by Alan MacDonald:

Pro Patria Mori:
The 56th (1st London) Division at Gommecourt, 1st July 1916

"This is a wonderful book and is an example which others with the time and dedication need to follow."
Col. Bob Wyatt, *Stand To!* Western Front Association

*

A Lack of Offensive Spirit?
The 46th (North Midland) Division at Gommecourt, 1st July 1916

"This well recorded and well-argued book is one of the best titles I have read for some time and the author deserves our congratulations on the work."
Col. Bob Wyatt, *Stand To!* Western Front Association

*

Z DAY, Saturday, 1st July 1916,
The Attack of the VIII Corps at Beaumont Hamel and Serre

"Read Martin Middlebrook's influential *First Day on the Somme*? Think you all know about the day? I've read the book a number of times and thought I had a real handle on 1 July 1916 until reading Alan MacDonald's 700–odd pages of *Z Day*. Now I know better."
David Filsell, *Stand To!* Western Front Association

*

The Affair at Lagarde
10th-11th August 1914
Published April 2024

*

The Long Road to the Somme
Volume II: Planning the Big Push
Published September 2024

*

Liberating Elsaß
The French Invasions of Alsace, August 1914
(due 2025)

For more information go to:
www.billmacccormick.co.uk

CHAPTERS

Introduction: What this book is not i
Acknowledgements ix
Part One: A War Foretold xii
Priming the War Pump 1
1. Prophets without Honour 25
Part Two: France – The Tactics of Revenge 77
2. Defeat, Dreyfus and War Plans 78
3. *Offensive à Outrance*: Tactic of Inferiority 146
4. The French Artillery Debate 208
Part Three: A Second-Class Army? 310
5. Wars and Rumours of Wars 311
6. Class, Cash or Competence 355
7. *Plus ça change, plus c'est la même chose* 425
8. More warnings: Manchuria and the Balkans 531
9. The Army and Change in Edwardian Society 575
Part Four: The Western Front 608
Trial and, Mainly, Error 608
10. Prologue 609
11. The Making of the New Armies 627
12. The British Armaments Failure 640
13. A Very British Shell Crisis 680
Part Five: Action and Reaction 704
15. From Mulhouse to the Marne 705
16. French Tactical Tinkering 730
17. Sir Douglas Haig takes over 775
Glossary 842
Appendix 1: The Virginia Campaigns 1864-5 845
Appendix 2: The Franco-Prussian War 1870-1 845
Appendix 3: 2nd South African War 1899-1902 847
Appendix 4: Russo-Japanese War 1904-5 848
Appendix 5: First Balkan War 1912-3 848
Bibliography 849
Index 858

PHOTOGRAPHS

1. Alfred Harmsworth, the 1st Viscount Northcliffe 11
2. 'Two men to eighty' 17
3. Jean de (Jan Bogumił) Bloch, Russia 33
4. Bertha *Freifrau* von Suttner, Austria 33
5. Reginald Brett, Viscount Esher, Britain 33
6. Lt. Col. Émile Mayer, France 33
7. Heinrich Gotthard von Treitschke 65
8. Generalfeldmarschall Wilhelm Leopold Colmar *Freiherr* von der Goltz 65
9. Generalfeldmarschall Helmuth Karl Bernhard Graf von Moltke (the Elder) 80
10. Emperor Napoleon III 80
11. Maréchal de France Marie Edme Patrice Maurice de Mac Mahon 80
12. Maréchal de France François Achille Bazaine 80
13. Général de Division Antoine Eugène Alfred Chanzy 80
14. Général de Division Charles Denis Sauter Bourbaki 80
15. Gen. Victor-Constant Michel 104
16. Capt. Alfred Dreyfus 108
17. George Clemenceau 141
18. Aristide Briand 141
19. Ernest Monis 141
20. Joseph Caillaux 141
21. Raymond Poincaré 141
22. Louis Barthou 142
23. Gaston Doumergue 142
24. Alexandre Ribot 142
25. René Viviani 142
26. Maurice Berteaux 142
27. Gen. François Goiran 142
28. Adolphe Messimy 143
29. Alexandre Millerand 143
30. Albert Lebrun 143
31. Eugène Étienne 143
32. Joseph Noulens 143
33. Théophile Delcassé 143
34. Gen. Joseph Gallieni 144
35. Gen. Pierre Roques 144
36. Col. Charles Jean Jacques Joseph Ardant du Picq 152
37. Gen. François-Jules Loyzeau de Grandmaison 181
38. The *28e Régiment d'Infanterie* with the Detaille/Scott uniform and helmet 198
39 Krupp 15-cm schwere Feldhaubitze 1893 211
40 10.5-cm leichte Feldhaubitze 98/09 212
41 15-cm-schwere Feldhaubitze 13 at Arras 1917 215
42 77-mm Feld Kanone 96 219
43 Général de division Louis Henri Auguste Baquet 229
44 Capt. Joseph Jules Ducros 229
45 Lt. Col. François Léon Emile Rimailho 229
46 Général de division Charles Étienne Sainte-Claire Deville 229
47 Lt. Col. Joseph-Albert Deport 229
48 Col. Louis Jean François Filloux 229
49 Canon de Campagne de 75-mm modèle 1897 230
50 Charles Timothée Maximilien Valérand Ragon de Bange 231

51 Lt. Col. Henry-Jules-Frédéric-Antoine Périer de Lahitolle 231
52 Gen. Frédéric Georges Herr..233
53 Henri Schneider 246
54 Pierre-Louis-Adrien de Montgolfier-Verpilleux 246
55 Gen. Alexandre Percin..262
56 Gen. Hippolyte Langlois 269
57 Gen. Edmond Buat..269
58 10-cm Kanone 04 at full recoil..275
59 Obusier de 120-mm C modèle 1890 Baquet..287
60 Obusier de 155 mm CTR modèle 1904 Rimailho..287
61 Canon de campagne de 90-mm modèle 1877 de Bange 293
63 Canon de 120-mm L modèle 1878 294
64 De Bange howitzers: 'swan-necked' 155-mm Canon Court, Mortiers 220 and 270 296
65 Albert Thomas 299
66 Mortier de 370-mm Filloux 304
67 Canon de 194 GPF sur affût chenilles Saint-Chamond 305
68 Mortier de 280 sur affût chenilles Saint-Chamond...305
69 Renault FT tank in 1918...306
70 Lt. Gen. Sir George Stuart White 332
71 General Sir Redvers Henry Buller...332
72 Lt. Gen. Paul Sanford Methuen,...332
73 Lt. Gen. Sir William Forbes Gatacre 332
74 Lt. Gen. Sir Charles Warren 332
75 British dead at Spion Kop, 23–24 January 1900..334
76 Rt. Hon. Aretas Akers-Douglas MP 363
77 Gen. Sir Henry de Beauvoir de Lisle 398
78 Col. George Francis Robert Henderson 442
79 Lt. Gen. Sir Launcelot Edward Kiggell...462
80 Brig. Gen. Norman Reginald McMahon..462
81 General Sir Horace Lockwood Smith-Dorrien..493
82 Gen. Aleksey Nikolayevich Kuropatkin 541
83 Gen. Anatoly Mikhaylovich Stoessel 541
84 Gen. Konstantin Nikolaevich Smirnov...541
85 Lt. Gen. Alexander Viktorovich Fok...541
86 Lt. Gen. Roman Isidorovich Kondratenko 541
87 Col. Nikolai Aleksandrovich Tretyakov 541
88 Field Marshal Prince Ōyama Iwao,..542
89 Gen. Viscount Kodama Gentarō 542
90 Gen. Count Nogi Maresuke 542
91 Gen. Count Oku Yasukata 542
92 18-pdr. QF Mk I field gun..646
93 4.5-in. QF Field Howitzer 649
94 4.7-in. BL QF Gun...650
95 A 60-pdr BL Mk I Field Gun at full recoil, Cape Helles, June 1915 652
96 6-in. BL Mk VII Field Gun 653
97 6-in. 30 cwt BL Siege Howitzer in service with the Greek Army 654
98 6-in. 26 cwt BL Siege Howitzer 654
99 8-in. BL Siege Howitzer on the Somme 655
100 9.2-in. BL Mk I Siege Howitzer..657
101 12-in. BL Siege Howitzer 658
102 15-in. BL Siege Howitzer, Polygon Wood, September 1917...658
103 Rt. Hon. David Lloyd George 702
104 Gen. Sir John Philip Du Cane...702
105 Rt. Hon. John Fletcher Moulton 702

106 Sir Eric Campbell Geddes ... 702
107 Maréchal de France Joseph Joffre ... 727
108 Général d'armée Augustin Dubail ... 727
109 Général d'armée Noël Édouard de Castelnau ... 727
110 Général de division Pierre Ruffey ... 727
111 Général de division Fernand de Langle de Cary ... 727
112 Général d'armée Charles Lanrezac ... 727
113 Mortier de 58 T (Tranchée) No. 1 ... 732
114 Mortier de 58 T (Tranchée) No. 2 ... 732
115 Artillery modern: the Mortier de 280 TR (modèle 1914) ... 751
116 Artillery old: the 95-mm modèle 1888 de Lahitolle ... 752
117 A pair of Canon de 32 cm modèle 1870-93 sur affût à glissement Schneider ... 754
118 *Brutale*, 1er Batterie, Cannonières Fluviales de 14 cm modèle, Paris 1917 ... 755
119 Field Marshal Sir John French ... 838
120 Gen. Sir Douglas Haig ... 838
121 Gen. Sir Archibald James Murray ... 838
122 Lt. Gen. Sir William Robert Robertson, CIGS, ... 838
123 Lt. Gen. Sir George Mark Watson Macdonogh, ... 838
124 Brig. Gen. John Charteris ... 838

MAPS

Map 1 French territory ceded to Germany, Treaty of Frankfurt ... 84
Map 2 The Franco-German border 1907 ... 91
Map 3 Michel's deployment plan 1911 ... 104
Map 4 Joffre's Plan XVII deployment plan and the German Schlieffen Plan ... 131
Map 5 The South Africa campaign, 1899 ... 324
Map 6 Lord Methuen's advance on Magersfontein, ... 325
Map 7 The siege of Ladysmith and the Natal Field Force's advance ... 326
Map 8 The War in Manchuria 1904-5 ... 533
Map 9 Nanshan to Port Arthur ... 539
Map 10 The Siege of Port Arthur ... 540
Map 11 First Balkan War: Western theatre ... 563
Map 12 First Balkan War: Eastern theatre ... 564
Map 13 The Invasion of Lorraine, August 1914 ... 711
Map 14 The retreat from Morhange and Sarrebourg, 20th to 24th August 1914 ... 712
Map 15 The opening attack of the 2nd Battle of Artois, 9th May 1915 ... 737
Map 16 Joffre's plan for the autumn offensives in Artois and Champagne ... 741
Map 17 The Second Battle of Champagne, advance from 25th to 29th September 1915 ... 744
Map 18 First day advance Third Battle of Artois and Battle of Loos, 25th September 1915 ... 745
Map 19 Battle of Neuve Chapelle, 10th March 1915 ... 802
Map 20 Plan for the attack on Aubers Ridge, 9th May 1915 ... 811
Map 21 Dispositions and initial advance in the attack on Loos, 25th September 1915 ... 821

TABLES

Table 1 British Colonial wars 1857-1906 61
Table 2 Relative casualties in selected British Colonial wars 1857-1906 61
Table 3 Strength of peacetime and mobilised European Armies 1912 95
Table 4 Mobilisation of the French Army 1914 97
Table 5 Growth of the German Active Army 1875-1914 97
Table 6 French military war deaths 1914-1918 203
Table 7 Types of artillery available on the outbreak of war 241
Table 8 Characteristics of French & German guns/howitzers, August 1914 242
Table 9 French gun and shell supplies 2nd August 1914 296
Table 10 Increases in German munitions production August 1914 to December 1915 297
Table 11 Performance of British Rifles 1871 onwards 312
Table 12 Allocation of examination marks, Sandhurst 1901 374
Table 13 1910 Cadet intake - Father's occupation 411
Table 14 Strength and casualties, major battles of the Russo-Japanese War 1904-5 549
Table 15 Increase in percentage casualty rates 1866-1905 572
Table 16 Population changes in British cities and towns 1851-1911 576
Table 17 Proportion of the workforce in agricultural employment 577
Table 18 Recruitment figures August 1914 to July 1915 627
Table 19 The raising and training of Kitchener's New Armies 634
Table 20 Deployment of New Army Divisions to the Western Front by date of arrival 639
Table 21 Guns available to the Army, August 1914 and June 1915 644
Table 22 Guns ordered before and delivered by 30th June 1915 644
Table 23 Guns and howitzers available to the BEF, June 1915 669
Table 24 Numbers of guns required by the BEF, June 1915 671
Table 25 Estimated shortfall in gun/howitzer deliveries March & September 1916 671
Table 26 Gun Programme A, July 1915 672
Table 27 Gun Programme B, 28th July 1915 672
Table 28 Gun Programme C1, 26th August 1915 674
Table 29 Gun Programme C, 8th September 1915 675
Table 30 Deliveries under Gun Programme C 675
Table 31 Companies building guns for Gun Programme C 676
Table 32 British shells supplies on the outbreak of war 680
Table 33 BEF daily shell requirements and supply, December 1914 681
Table 34 Percentage of high explosive shells received by BEF, December 1914-May 1915 684
Table 35 Shells requested and allowed 1914-1915 684
Table 36 Shells requested by CinC BEF, 10th May 1915 685
Table 37 Shells ordered, delivered and due 29th May 1915 (Main natures) 689
Table 38 18-pdr. shrapnel and HE use Sept. 15 to Jan. 16 690
Table 39 Maximum weekly requirements for shells under the various programmes 691
Table 40 Delivery of explosives 1914-6 698
Table 41 German, French and British artillery, Artois, 9th May 1915 731
Table 42 French casualties in major actions 1915 to early 1916 765
Table 43 British casualties in major actions 1915 766
Table 44 Guns/howitzers used for trench bombardment British offensives 1915 797
Table 45 Bombardment groups Neuve Chapelle and Aubers Ridge 809
Table 46 British artillery at Festubert, 15th May 1915 814

INTRODUCTION: WHAT THIS BOOK IS NOT

THIS BOOK IS NOT A HISTORY of, an explanation of, or an interpretation of all of the events which led to the outbreak of the Great War. It is, rather, an attempt to understand and explain the social, political, military, and technical reasons why the British and French found themselves manning their front-line trenches in the early hours of 1st July 1916 with such different plans, tactics, objectives – and outcomes.

By social and political I mean issues relating to class, education, training, intelligence, character, experience, motivation, and relationships.

By military and technical I refer to arms, equipment, munitions, training, tactics, doctrine, strategic considerations, and practice on the battlefield itself.

A separate volume – *The Long Road to the Somme: Planning the Big Push* – describes the British and French planning of the campaign, as well as the impact of related events: Verdun, and the Austrian Trentino and Russian Brusilov offensives.

This book attempts to address, if not answer, several questions, e.g.:

Why were the Generals and officers of all the combatant nations so completely caught by surprise by the siege tactics employed on the Western Front after the opening weeks of manoeuvre warfare? I would suggest all prior military experience, and the advice of both military and civilian experts over the preceding decades, clearly shown this was the likely outcome of an industrialised European war with technology in its 1914 state.

Why was the British Army, the only Western European army with recent direct experience of war, so peculiarly ill-equipped both technically and tactically to fight a prolonged war on the continent?

How well trained and educated for such a conflict were the commanding and junior officers who led the Regular Army into war?

How did the French obsession with revenge, and the return of Alsace and Lorraine lost in 1871, lead them into strategic and tactical decisions which led to the catastrophic casualties of the opening weeks of the war?

Why did the French Army go to war so reliant on a single artillery piece, the *Canon de Campagne de 75-mm modèle 1897*, when all the evidence pointed to the need for heavier, indirect fire and long-range howitzers and guns?

Then, how did the commanders of the BEF and the French Army adapt to the conditions of siege warfare and to what effect?

Why was the Army of one of the three great industrial powerhouses of the world, Great Britain, so lamentably supported and supplied with armaments and ammunition for so long?

How did France, which lost a large part of its steel and coal production within weeks of the outbreak of war, not only supply its Army with more guns and shells in a quicker time, but also support the air forces of itself and its allies with aircraft and aero-engines, and design and produce innovative tracked artillery, split-trailed guns and the first 'modern' tank?

And, finally, how did the preceding impact on the planning and conduct of the opening phase of the Battle of the Somme, up until then, the largest offensive ever undertaken by the British Army in its entire history?

THIS BOOK DOES NOT ATTEMPT to take the reader in a smooth and continuous line from events on Date A to those on Date B. Rather, it is a series of separate 'episodes' which this writer believes help explain some of the reasons underpinning the British approach to the Battle of the Somme.

It examines how and why 'war fever' was spread across the population by militarists, nationalists, and imperialists of all political persuasions.

It examines the warnings given that any war would descend into a prolonged period of grinding, miserable and hugely expensive siege warfare.

It then moves on to the reaction of the French to the loss of the Franco-Prussian War of 1870-1 and how it adapted militarily to the defeat.

It reviews the development of its various war plans, defensive arrangements, and tactical theories, most especially the concept of the *offensive à outrance*, and how these impacted on the opening weeks of the 1914-18 war.

It examines in detail at how the development of one brilliantly conceived and revolutionary artillery piece, the 75-mm field gun of 1897, nearly led to France's defeat in the dreadful opening Battles of the Frontiers.

It looks at the state of the Victorian Army from which most British senior officers were drawn between 1914 and 1918. Its initially woeful performance in South Africa between 1899 and 1902 is reviewed as are the tactical and technical lessons learned (and unlearned) in the years before 1914.

The impact on military thinking and tactics of the conduct of the Russo-Japanese War of 1904-5, the Italian-Turkish War of 1911-2, and the First Balkan War of 1912-3 are investigated and some time is spent exploring these three conflicts.

It looks in some detail at the social, educational, and professional background of the British Officer class, and the frankly lamentable intellectual level of rather too many amongst its ranks.

It touches upon the social and political attitudes which undermined some senior officers' confidence in the commitment and resilience of the huge citizen army raised in 1914-5, attitudes which, perhaps, allowed politicians and senior Army officers to find the huge physical and economic costs of the war acceptable.

Moving on to the war itself, the book reflects on the problems Britain had in absorbing, training, and equipping the huge and immediate influx of men who wished to join the Army and then, later, the problems it faced when this manpower well ran dry.

It also looks at how the government sought to solve the armaments crisis which existed beyond even 1916 and how their failures to do so by 30th June 1916 impacted on British hopes for the opening of the Battle of the Somme.

It further examines the tactical changes brought about by the catastrophes of the Battle of the Frontiers and, in 1915, the various attempted 'breakthrough' battles in which both the French and British indulged themselves.

It then moves on to examine how some, like Ferdinand Foch and Henri Pétain, drew timely and useful lessons from this fighting, whilst others, like Joffre, Sir John French and Douglas Haig, did not. It explores the development of Foch's tactical ideas which would briefly bear fruit on 1st July and examines why, in many respects, British tactical thinking went into reverse during the same period.

Finally, it looks at the trials and tribulations of the BEF in 1915 which led to the appointment of Sir Douglas Haig as CinC and it reviews his ore-war and wartime experience and his suitability as commander of British and Empire forces on the Western Front.

THE PARTNER VOLUME, *The Long Road to the Somme – Planning the Big Push*, is a detailed narrative of the events which led from the Chantilly Conference in December 1915 to the beginning of the Battle of the Somme on 1st July 1916. It is an account of the planning of the Somme campaign from the time the French Commander in Chief, Joseph Joffre, proposed a joint Franco-British offensive for the mid-summer of 1916 as part of a set of concentric and simultaneous attacks on the Central Powers on all Allied fronts. What, perhaps, makes this account different from most others is its equal focus on the part played by the French in this process. This is based on French-language sources, most especially the enormous and well-documented official history, the 107-volume *Armées françaises dans la Grande Guerre*. This is essential as, firstly, the *Somme* offensive was a French idea and, furthermore, until but a few weeks before the attack, more French troops would have gone 'over the top' in Picardy than British and Empire ones. The reason this balance was altered was the heavy French losses suffered at Verdun since the opening German attack on 21st February 1916. The impact of the fighting around this city is, therefore, a significant and somewhat ignored element in the telling of the story of the planning of the Battle of the *Somme*. Nothing which happened subsequently on the Western Front can be sensibly considered and understood without a genuine appreciation of the impact of what became the longest battle of the 'War to end all Wars'.

IT IS THIS WRITER'S VIEW that rather too many Generals down the millennia have spent their time planning to re-fight the last war in which their country was involved rather than look into the future and assess how the next war might be fought. With the Maginot Line, the French planned to re-fight the Great War in 1940. In 1914 many officers on all sides anticipated a souped-up and super-sized version of the Franco-Prussian War. In the 1790s, the monarchies of central Europe expected a continuation of the 'cabinet wars' on the mid-18th Century when they attacked Revolutionary France, only to be overthrown by the 'nation in arms' concept of the *levée en masse* and the flawed genius of Napoleon. And so on.

It takes a man of personality, vision, and imagination, but who also sees how modern technology and industry might be applied in war, to make the great strategic and tactical leap forward to a new form of warfare. They are few and far between: Alexander, Julius Caesar, Genghis Khan, Gustavus Adolphus, Marlborough (at times), Napoleon, Ulysses S Grant (perhaps)… There are others who have shown flashes of tactical genius adapted to the prevailing forms of warfare but whose overall careers are too chequered to place them in the Premier League of great commanders: Frederick the Great, for example, who, though revered by Bonaparte, lost too many battles and saw Berlin occupied too many times to be placed shoulder to shoulder with the greatest of Generals. He, perhaps like Charles XII of Sweden, showed that what glittered in the military firmament was not necessarily all 24-carat gold.

No Great War General comes close to this standard because too many ignored, failed to understand, or were simply ignorant of, the enormous technological and industrial leaps made in the forty or so years between the Franco-Prussian War and 1914.

Armies, and the men who run them, are essentially conservative organisations designed to protect, i.e. conserve, the *status quo*, and a large part of the problem in the Victorian/Edwardian era was the lack of intellectual curiosity engendered in an organisation in which discipline, tradition, obeying orders, and not making waves were the essential elements.

This was, perhaps, because, in the main, the intellectual *élites* of most industrial countries towards the end of the nineteenth century did not join their country's Army. In Britain, if serving the nation in a military capacity was one's calling, one *might* join the Royal Navy. It did, at least, rule the world's oceans. It was the 'Senior Service', and had a history, ignoring one or two embarrassments, wreathed in glory. Normally, though, thoughtful, creative, industrious, ambitious men were to be found administering the country or Empire, running increasingly complex businesses, developing new ideas in science, technology, and medicine, exploring the lesser-known parts of the world, or investigating new ideas in politics and social policy. They were not to be found on the parade ground, training reluctant, barely adequate, and mostly illiterate volunteers, or sitting with their feet up on the veranda of some officer's mess in the over-heated tropics, sipping a brandy and soda, or astride a horse and either sticking some unfortunate pig with a long lance or chasing a ball around a polo field. Some men, of course, through family tradition, a determination to enhance the Empire, or even a genuine interest in soldiering, decided voluntarily upon an Army life. But rather too many, at least in the British Army, saw it as path towards a decent social and sporting life, a relatively pleasant way of occupying time between school and retirement, and a chance to continue in the same exclusive social *milieu* as at their Public School. All with the added thrill of being able to travel to some foreign and perplexing country, there to kill ill-equipped natives, preferably at long range, and usually in uncountable numbers.

This is not to say everyone in the Army was dim or lazy. There were brilliant minds within its ranks – as well as some with good, mediocre, and some with downright empty brains. And, with (for a long time) commissions based on purchase and promotion founded on simple seniority, there was a horrible inevitability that more than a few mediocre and empty-headed officers would find a way into positions of importance. Their influence and decision making could then undermine the development of an Army already constrained by the ultra-conservative social and political values of its upper hierarchy.

ARMIES SERVE THREE ESSENTIAL FUNCTIONS: conquering foreign lands; defending such territories; and the protection of the homeland from enemies, both external and domestic. Men who seek to command in such an organisation must, therefore, put the interests of the nation/empire and the survival of its *élite* and establishment above all other interests. It matters not what form of government it protects – monarchist, capitalist, democratic, communist, fascist – its overriding duty is to protect the *status quo*. There is an inevitability, therefore, that Army officers are of a conservative bent. After all, to conserve is to protect. And, here I mean real 'conservatives' and not the 'revolutionaries' of the radical right or radical left or ultra-nationalists seen in politics at the turn of the twentieth century and even more so now.

Conservatives seek the maintenance of hierarchy, demand stability, want people to 'know their place', to be disciplined, and quiescent. Otherwise, troops are ordered onto the streets to shoot people, as was too often the case in pre-Great War Britain, France, Germany, Russia, the USA, and many other countries. But conservatism is essentially unimaginative. It tends to hark back to former, supposedly, better times rather than looking forward to embrace change and innovation. Such conservative attitudes were widely shared within the British and European Armies at the *fin de siècle*. Radical ideas about the nature of modern warfare in the face of new powerful, long-range, and quick-firing weaponry, especially if generated from outside the military world, were dismissed as alarmist and erroneous, much as many modern conservatives dismiss the prospects of climate change. This, both before the outbreak of the *War to End All Wars* and during it, contributed significantly to the horrendous casualties and the drawn-out nature of the conflict.

Britain's experience was the most alarming. The prolonged fiasco of the Second Boer War caused such a stir back home that Parliamentary commissions and inquiries were launched to find out the reasons for the repeated failures and inept performance of too many of the Empire's senior and junior Army officers. These revealed a culture of amateurism amongst a widely ill-educated and anti-intellectual officer class which harboured an arrogant antagonism towards military thought, work, and learning which staggered the country and its political leadership. Broadly, rather too much of the British Army was a playground for the wealthy, and inherently lazy, younger offspring of the nobility, the landed gentry, and those of the *nouveau riche* who aspired to mix in such circles. The *élite* regiments in particular, the Guards and the Cavalry, were the province of the moneyed but dim upper class because they were the only ones who could afford the expensive lifestyle these exclusive units demanded of its officers.

Efforts were made to change the culture of the Army in the light of the revelations of the post-South Africa *Elgin Commission*, and the investigations into the education and training of Army officers, and the costs of becoming an Army officer. The unfortunate point is that the majority of senior and middle ranking officers who took command in the British Expeditionary Force in France and Flanders in 1914, and those deployed in other parts of the eastern Mediterranean and Middle East, came through the ranks of the Army prior to the Boer War. It was a time when scant regard was taken of native intelligence, general and military education, the quality of the performance of one's duties, and any ongoing learning and development of military skills. Officers who dedicated themselves to self-improvement, unless on the back of a polo pony or some other sporting past-time, were viewed as swots, poor companions, and lacking in essential regimental *ésprit*. Such men could be driven out of their unit, or even the Army, if they were found to be more interested in a history book than riding to hounds. Sadly, as this book suggests, this aspect of the culture of the Army did not rapidly change after the South African War. Nor, generally, did the intellectual and educational quality of the officers who later passed out of Sandhurst.

Although lessons were learned from South Africa, particularly in the areas of infantry tactics and field artillery, much else was either ignored or put down to the peculiarities of warfare on the hills and plains of Natal, the Orange Free State, Transvaal, and the Eastern Cape. There were many good intentions, but rather too many fell by the wayside in the intervening years.

Later wars, Manchuria, Libya, and the Balkans, were more, or less, closely observed, dissected and, rather too often, misinterpreted either by error or design. In the meantime, the British Army debated the application of the lance on the modern battlefield, the design of the cavalry sabre, and how trumpets and drums might assist attacking troops across the battle zone and into the enemy's positions. Some lonely voices argued that additional mobile firepower such as a light machine gun, of which many examples existed before the *Lewis Gun* was belatedly adopted after the outbreak of war, might better cover the advance of the infantry over what was known as the 'Fire Swept Zone' or, later, No Man's Land. The fact the *Lewis* went into mass production *after* the war started shows how little impact such arguments had on tactics and equipment.

British (and French) Army manoeuvres seemed steadfastly to ignore the impact of modern inventions such as the machine gun, replicated outmoded direct fire artillery tactics, witnessed the odd mass cavalry charge, and reinforced the notion that no junior officer should embarrass his senior by displaying superior competence in such rehearsals for fear of damaging his future job prospects.

Nor were matters much better across the Channel within the ranks of the French Army. Undermined by the Republican and Radical Socialist response to the deep social, political, and religious divisions of the Dreyfus Affair; hamstrung by a policy of outright and often reckless attack – the *offensive à outrance*; and limited by a decision to make the ground-breaking 75 mm field gun of 1897 almost the only artillery piece to be involved in the fighting with Germany, the French went to war tactically and materially ill-equipped to deal with the more sophisticated German arsenal of weapons, better communications, and (occasionally) enhanced tactics. Further hampered by the decision to send its troops to war wearing blue uniforms and bright red trousers and *kepis*, and the catastrophes of the Battles of the Frontiers were disasters impatient to happen.

Neither the British nor the French, or the Germans for that matter, accepted the need for some original thinking in how the great clash of infantry might turn out. The British, it can be said, dramatically improved their defensive capabilities prior to the war but, as with all the other combatant nations, little or no creative or productive thought was given to the execution of the great crisis of a battle – the advance of the infantry into the enemy's lines: the charge. All that was accepted was that, because of the enhanced firepower of automatic weapons and quick-firing artillery, casualties inevitably must be heavy. The 'eggs and omelettes' mentality was widespread in all armies, thus the emphasis placed by many General Officers on aggression, *élan*, and high morale as the means by which at least some of the attacking troops might overcome the rapid fire of the machine gun in order to launch the battle-winning attack with the bayonet, another old-fashioned 'up and personal' weapon wielded by the 'Other Ranks' and much loved by senior officers who had never, ever, used one in battle.

AS SET OUT ABOVE, Armies, both through the inclination of their leadership and their *raison d'être*, i.e. the protection of the apparatus of the state against enemies foreign and domestic, are inherently conservative in nature, social attitudes, and political instinct. Thus, 'little people' tend not to matter in the grander scheme of things. Such attitudes made the ordinary soldiers, the 'Other Ranks', as disposable as the bullets and shells fired to kill them. Acceptance that many would become casualties, and a failure to address ways this might be avoided, resulted in percentage casualty rates higher than any previous war, while the enormous numbers of troops deployed resulted in higher real casualties than ever before. The previously inconceivable quantities of bullets and shells manufactured and fired put strains on the combatant nations' economies in a way no previous war managed. And, as was predicted fifteen years before the war started, the consequences for the Empires, monarchies, governments, and peoples of the combatant nations would be profound, often disastrous and are still felt today.

And yet, despite conscious efforts by politicians, the military, the media, and self-interested industrialists to prime the masses for an inevitable major European war through repeated speeches, books, pamphlets, articles, and campaigns designed to stir up feelings against the competing nations, all the countries involved in August 1914 were, in their different ways, ill-prepared strategically, tactically, industrially, and in terms of equipment. No-one, despite the warnings by people like the Polish Jew, Jean de Bloch, and the evidence of the wars in Manchuria and the Balkans, foresaw the static carnage of the nearly four years of siege warfare which scarred the Western Front. And amongst the most relentlessly blinkered were the most senior officers of the various Armies.

When the predicted war erupted, some within their various armies learnt lessons, some more quickly than others. Some, after months of futile and costly fighting, adapted to the new forms of warfare and adopted new tactical ideas which attempted to avoid throwing large numbers of men against well-prepared positions and well-armed troops. New technologies, such as the tracked and armoured 'tank', which, with some creativity and foresight, might have been in place pre-war, were eventually made available, and new forms of warfare slowly became possible. But, for all that, old methods and assumptions were still too well engrained amongst those in command for change to be either rapid or widespread.

For the two nations of the *Entente Cordiale* – Great Britain and France – the results of different ways of thinking about the war were revealed in the varying fortunes of the two Allied Armies engaged on the Somme on 1st July 1916. The difference in size of the two Armies casualty lists hint at this: Great Britain and Newfoundland 59,000 dead, wounded and missing; France 2,500 dead, wounded and missing. The British barely 40% successful in achieving their day's objectives, the French c. 99% successful.

This book and *Planning the Big Push* seek to explain and understand how these wildly divergent figures came about. The answers provided here (if answers they are) are not simply rooted in the war-time experience. I believe we must go back to events and actions from well before the war. Furthermore, the impact of institutions, politics, economics, and other factors are of significance. As a result, this book touch upon events which took place over forty years before the 1914-18 war started, as well as looking in detail as to how each Army developed its tactical ideas, skills and equipment in response to what had gone before, whether good or bad.

Alan MacDonald
July 2024

Acknowledgements

First of all, it must be said that the French government, national and local, and the French people have embraced remembrance of the 1914-18 War in a far more full-hearted and generous manner than is the case in Britain. I say this if nor no other reason than that the enormous volume of data which has been collected, collated, digitised, and placed online for free far outweighs anything available to the serious student of the Great War in the UK.

Therefore, I must first thank the French Government for allowing free access to the enormous official history of the war, *Les armées françaises dans la grande guerre*. The eleven *Tomes* comprising some 24 narrative volumes plus appendices and maps, some 107 volumes in all, can be downloaded in its entirety from:

http://www.memoiredeshommes.sga.defense.gouv.fr.

The website *www.memoiredeshommes.sga.defense.gouv.fr* also contains a database of casualties and another with details of the official burial sites of members of the French armed forces.

Furthermore, I must thank the French Government for allowing free on-line access to the *Journaux de marche*, i.e. unit war diaries, which cover the actions of French headquarters, the *Grand Quartier General*, down to trench mortar batteries, ambulances, *aerostier* (balloonist) companies, as well as naval and aerial units of all types. Unlike the penny-pinching British government, which has chosen to charge historians and the public alike for access to British official records even during the 100th Anniversary commemorations of the Great War, France decided to open its records to all for free. For this they are to be congratulated.

Further congratulations are due to the *Bibliothèque nationale de France* (*http://www.bnf.fr/fr/acc/x.accueil.html*) and *Gallica* (*https://gallica.bnf.fr/accueil/*), its online presence. They have made available, again for free, hundreds of regimental and unit histories along with large numbers of French military journals, books, etc., all scanned and downloadable. In parallel to this is a private initiative which has links to over 500 downloadable unit histories. This can be found at:

Guerre 1914 - 1918 Les Historiques de Régiments en ligne
(*http://jeanluc.dron.free.fr/th/historiques.htm*).

Then, the opening up of official files relating to the recipients of the *Legion d'Honneur* allows one detailed access to the personal and career details of the French Army officers and politicians mentioned in the text. These can be found at the *Base Leonore* (*http://www2.culture.gouv.fr/public/mistral/leonore_fr*).

The numerous departments in France are also to be congratulated for the huge task of scanning and indexing the *Fiches Matricule* which record the personnel records of every French member of the military since the 1860s. In most cases these provide details of the record of a serviceman's career, sometimes including details of awards, citations, wounds, etc. The job of indexing these records fell, I gather, to a huge team of volunteers who gave up their time so that these records might be available to all. They should be profusely thanked for undertaking such a time-consuming but valuable role.

Much, if not yet all, of this data is brought together at another government website entitled the *Grand Mémorial* (*https://www.culture.fr/Grand-Memorial/*) where many of these records can be queried from one central site.

Mémorial GenWeb (*https://www.memorialgenweb.org/index.php*) is another private initiative which records the personal details of French casualties from both World Wars and other conflicts, as well as where and how those casualties are memorialised in France. Again, hundreds, perhaps thousands, of ordinary French citizens have scoured memorials, monuments, cemeteries, churches, yearbooks, annuals, etc., etc., to link these records to the serviceman listed.

GERMAN INFORMATION IS MUCH LESS COMPLETE, partly because of the destruction of the Prussian Government's records stored around Berlin during World War Two. Initiatives both public and private have, however, provided an enormous quantity of detailed information on-line.

It is, for example, possible to download the official German account of the war, *Der Weltkrieg*, and the official history of the Austro-Hungarian Army free from the *Die digitale Landesbibliothek Oberösterreich* (*The digital State Library of Upper Austria*). They, and many other WWI related books, can be found here:

https://digi.landesbibliothek.at

Several German state libraries have also developed a programme for the digitisation of hundreds of regimental histories which, normally, are lengthy and very detailed. These again are available as free downloads. One such is the *Württembergische Landesbibliothek* (*https://www.wlb-stuttgart.de*).

At *GenWiki* (*https://wiki.genealogy.net/Hauptseite*) one can find two invaluable databases. Through its *Militär* portal one can access several databases about the armed forces of pre- and post-unification Germany from the era of Napoleon onwards. These include the forces of the *Norddeutscher Bund* involved in the campaigns against Denmark and Austria in the 1860s, the Franco-Prussian War, the First and Second World Wars, the Weimar Republic, and the German army since 1945. (*https://wiki.genealogy.net/Portal:Milit%C3%A4r*). The specific address for the First World War is:

https://wiki.genealogy.net/Milit%C3%A4r/Formationsgeschichte/Deutschland/Erster_Weltkrieg.

The second resource is the scanned and indexed *Verlustlisten* which provide details of the casualties – dead, wounded and missing – of the German and Bavarian Armies between 1914 and 1918 and which are searchable by a variety of criteria (*http://des.genealogy.net/eingabe-verlustlisten/search*). Another database for casualties from the Austro-Hungarian Army is also on-line.

For those with an interest in the personnel of the German air force between 1914 and 1918 there is a privately published but comprehensive on-line database at *Frontflieger* (*http://www.frontflieger.de*).

Another private initiative is the *Denkmalprojekt* which, amongst other things, has digitised and made available the casualty lists drawn from numerous German regimental histories covering infantry, cavalry, artillery, *Landwehr*, *Landsturm*, etc., units This can be found at:

http://www.denkmalprojekt.org/covers_vl/vl_wk1_index_heer.html#I

At a state level, the *Landesarchiv* of Baden-Württemberg have scanned the *Kriegstammrollen* of the regiments from this area (*https://www2.landesarchiv-bw.de/ofs21/olf/struktur.php?bestand=13908&sprungId=3473836&letztesLimit=suchen*). These are the effective equivalents of the French *Fiches Matricule* in that they provide the service records of all other ranks and some officers who served during the war in units raised in Baden and Württemberg. They are not indexed but usually come with an alphabetic list from which it is possible to identify where on the regimental roll a soldier's name might be. These have proved invaluable in the somewhat painstaking work of determining the number of casualties suffered by regiments from these two states and which feature heavily in other books. Similar records for Bavarian units can be found on *Ancestry*

(*http://www.ancestry.de/cs/de/bayern-erster-weltkrieg-stammrollen*).

FURTHER CONGRATULATIONS are due to the US-based *Field Artillery Journal* (now called *Fires Bulletin*) which prior to, during and after the Great War, printed many important articles and book excerpts by writers from all of the combatant nations. These, too, are available for free from *http://sill-www.army.mil/firesbulletin/archives/*. Again, one must compare unfavourably this approach to that of the UK where important journals, such as those of the *Royal United Services Institution, RUSI,* are mainly available only from behind a paywall.

I AM ALSO GRATEFUL, at least in this one respect, to live in the London Borough of Bromley where membership of the Library Service provides one with free access to *The Times Digital Archive 1785-2006*, the *Oxford Dictionary of National Biography, Who Was Who* and several other useful on-line archives.

BELATEDLY, IN RECENT YEARS, more British historians are paying attention to the actions of the French Army during the Great War. It is, perhaps, ironic, that this move towards an understanding of the role played by our major Ally has, in the main, come after an also long-overdue focus on the German Army, the enemy against which both Britain and France fought between 1914 and 1918. There has for far too long been a one-sided, insular, Anglo-centric approach to the war amongst military historians which has only recently started to change thanks to the efforts of people like Jack Sheldon, Ralph Whitehead, Johnathan Krause, David O'Mara, Terence Zuber, Simon House, the late Elizabeth Greenhalgh, and Bill Philpott, even if the latter two could not agree on many things. One should also acknowledge the ground-breaking work of historians such as Douglas Porch, Leonard Smith, Robert Doughty, Alistair Horne, and others in bringing to our attention the issues affecting France and her armies before and during the war.

PART ONE: A WAR FORETOLD

"Military science has from time immemorial been a book with seven seals, which none but the duly initiated were deemed worthy to open. Institutions of the Army, like those of the Church, were taken under the protecting wing of the State and flourished all the more luxuriantly in the shade... It is hardly credible, and yet it is a historic fact, that no priestly caste, since the days of the Pharaohs, has managed to remain so exclusive, so powerful and so secret as the men whose profession it is to kill or be killed."

Jean de Bloch

1. PRIMING THE WAR PUMP

"Men, it has been well said, think in herds; it will be seen that they go mad in herds, while they only recover their senses slowly, one by one."

Charles MacKay,
*Extraordinary Popular Delusions
and the Madness of Crowds*, 1841

ORDINARY MEN AND WOMEN in Europe and beyond have, for centuries, been primed and prepared for war by a non-stop barrage of speeches and books, magazine and newspaper articles, and now social media and on-line 'news', all predicting dire consequences for any country if it failed to arm itself to excess in readiness for imminent hostilities with one neighbour or another. Since the Industrial Revolution, such non-stop propaganda has helped fuel the enormous growth, and huge profits, of the international arms trade, *aka* the Military-Industrial Complex, first so described by U.S. President Dwight D. Eisenhower in his final address to the nation on 17th January, 1961. There is more than enough evidence to show that businessmen and politicians exploit the mood engendered by these prognostications and publications to force governments into massive 'defence' spending whether a 'threat' is genuine or not.

Then there is evidence to show some of these 'threats' are manufactured to fill empty order books, to generate profits, and to pay dividends to those who can afford to invest spare cash in arms companies. One such 'invention' was the Anglo-German Naval Arms Race started, at least in part, by the self-interested British businessman Herbert Hal Mulliner in 1908, and helped on its way by Conservative politicians and newspapers such as the *Daily Mail*, The resulting 'arms races' prove economically and politically expensive, generate tensions where none need be, and make war an inevitable result of the 'threats' thus invented.

'Arms races' are an excellent way of transferring money from ordinary non-shareholding taxpayers to those who can afford to invest in the companies which not only profit from such races, but which work hand-in-hand with those promoting the arms race in the first place. The few benefit, the many suffer.

In Victorian Britain 'invasion scares' were the common currency of those seeking to ramp up spending on armaments. They have had a long and damaging history down the years. After the Napoleonic-era, these fears manifested themselves in several scares which, until the Franco-Prussian War, involved a French invasion. The comprehensive defeat of France by Prussia and its allies in 1871 allowed these concerns to briefly subside, only for them to re-emerge but with the Germans and the Russians now added into the mix. After the signing of the *Entente Cordiale*, however, the focus of Edwardian Britain was almost entirely on fears of a German invasion as their military power and their navy grew.

There is very little new under the sun, and this includes 'invasion scares'. One does not doubt that, even in the ancient world, unfounded rumours and 'fake news' about the aggressive intentions of near neighbours were commonplace in Babylon, or Athens, or Rome. Nowadays, in the absence of a direct military threat to these shores, we have the 'threat' of invasion by penniless, desperate refugees fleeing from political or environmental catastrophes for which the industrialised nations are mainly responsible. All unscrupulous politicians need a scapegoat. And somewhere there is an equally unscrupulous businessman making a profit from the crisis thus created. In modern terms where did this all start?

One early 'invasion scare' was the work of an influential if, today, little-known Welsh soldier of fortune: Henry Humphrey Evans Lloyd (born c. 1718, died 19th June 1783). Lloyd attended Jesus College, Oxford, but lacking the funds to purchase a commission in His Majesty's Army, took a more circular route, joining the army of France. Serving as an engineer, he fought in the War of the Austrian Succession, being present at the Battle of Fontenoy on 11th May 1745 where Marshal Saxe defeated the Duke of Cumberland. He then accompanied the Young Pretender on his unsuccessful attempt to remove the Hanoverian monarchy in the Jacobite rebellion of 1745-6. Lloyd managed to avoid the disaster at Culloden – crushing ragged and poorly-armed Highlanders was more within Cumberland's military abilities. He was off surveying the south coast of England in hopes of a French invasion. Our hyper-active, if not especially loyal, Welshman then served the French, the Prussians, then spied again in Britain for the French, then joined the Austrian Army in the early stages of the Seven Years War, before seeing the light and switching sides to re-join the Prussians. His attempt to join the Portuguese Army in 1763 was only spoiled when the conflict between the two nations of the Iberian Peninsula ended before he arrived. His peregrinations were not at an end, however, as before his death in 1783 in The Hague, he worked for the British in Corsica, and he commanded Russian troops in the latter part of the Russo-Turkish War of 1768-74.

Between times, in the odd spare moment, Lloyd wrote. First, in 1766, *The history of the late war in Germany between the king of Prussia and the empress of Germany and her allies*. A second edition in 1781 included a section entitled *Reflections on the principles of the art of war*. Translated into multiple editions in both Germany and France, this work is reported to have influenced Washington, Patton, and J F C Fuller. In the early 1770s he broadened his outlook producing *An Essay on the English Constitution* and *An Essay on the Theory of Money*. Then, in 1779, emerged *A Rhapsody on the Present System of French Politics; on the Projected Invasion, and the Means to Defeat It. Illustrated with Plans, on three copper plates. By ... a Chelsea Pensioner*, (London: W. Faden, 1779). Mainly directed at those in power, any hopes of generating some income failed when the book was effectively suppressed by the Government. Well after his death, however, and with the effects of the French Revolution resounding across Europe, it was twice reprinted in the 1790s under the title of *A Political and Military Rhapsody on the Invasion and Defence of Great Britain*. Having twice surveyed the south coast for the French with a view to an invasion, Lloyd was uniquely well placed to argue how a hostile landing might be defeated. His principle means for defeating the French, however, was to prevent them landing in the first place stating that:

"A powerful fleet and thirty thousand marines... will save us from destruction, and nothing else."[1]

Thus, was set the scene for 'invasion scares' for the next 120 years. If the Royal Navy failed, so failed the country. It was a recurring theme exploited for all it was worth by conservative politicians, naval officers and, later, ambitious, not to say greedy, industrialists.

THE FIRST VICTORIAN INVASION SCARE occurred in the 1830s after Charles X of France was forced to abdicate on 2nd August 1830. He was replaced by Louis Philippe (1830-48) and, at least initially, there was a dip in the cordiality of Anglo-French relations. Britain responded by re-arming and repairing the Martello Towers on which work first started in 1805 and of which 101 been built. As Louis Philippe was keen on maintaining good relations this scare subsided. In 1848 Louis Philippe was overthrown and a republic declared. The election of Louis Napoleon prompted renewed fears of Gallic intentions. Palmerston suggested an expansionist French foreign policy globally and within Europe (newly created Belgium being a possible target) might lead to a confrontation with Great Britain.

In 1851, an anonymous author penned the alarmist *A history of the sudden and terrible invasion of England by the French, in the month of May, 1852*. It proved the forerunner of numerous 'invasion scare' books written over the next sixty or so years (now replaced in the public's mind by *'The War against Terror'* and the 'threat' of immigration). The British press added to the agitated atmosphere and, in January 1852, *The Times* 'reported' on the prospects of 40,000 Frenchmen descending on the south coast. This led to a flurry of anxious letters to the Editor concerning *'National Defence'*. In response, in 1853, the building of five large forts to protect the naval base at Portsmouth began around Gosport[i]. None ever saw action, but their construction kept building and armaments contractors contentedly busy for the next decade.

It was only the increasing friction between Russia and Turkey resulting in the Anglo-French involvement in the Crimean War which calmed things down. Soon thereafter, with France taking the side of those seeking Italian independence from Austria, concerns about French intentions again grew. In 1859 a *Royal Commission on the Defence of the United Kingdom* concluded Britain's coastal defences were inadequate, especially if the main Royal Navy fleet was not able to defend the Channel. Another round of expensive and eventually redundant military building took place with a massive programme of eight forts and redoubts occupying Portsdown Hill above Portsmouth, amongst other works. Again, however, national nervousness about a French invasion subsided and evaporated completely in 1871, at least for a while.

From that date, the new concern was the unified Germany and this fear was reflected in a new series of stories and books. Initially, the 'invaders' came from an unnamed country (where coincidentally they spoke German). Later they directly specified Germany as the source of any likely attack.

The first and most important of these books was *The Battle of Dorking* written in 1871 by Lt. Col. George Tomkyns Chesney[ii]. He viewed the rapid and total defeat of the French by Prussian Armies in 1870 with dismay and wrote an

---

[i] Fort Gomer (started 1853), Fort Elson (started 1855), Fort Grange (started 1858), Fort Rowner (started 1858), and Fort Brockhurst (started 1858).

[ii] Gen. Sir George Tomkyns Chesney, KCB, CSI, CIE, was born in 1830 and died in 1895. Chesney was a product of the Indian Army and served with the Bengal Engineers during the Indian Mutiny. He set up the Royal Indian Civil Engineering College at Coopers Hill, Englefield Green, Egham, later known as Cooper's Hill or ICE College.

anonymous piece for *Blackwood's Magazine*. *The Battle of Dorking* is a dire warning of the consequences of both military and political complacency as well as of Britain being over-reliant on the Royal Navy to both patrol the world's sea lanes *and* keep Britain safe from foreign invasion.

In the story the British Army is struggling with the aftermath of the Indian Mutiny and is spread far and wide to deal with an apparent threat from the USA towards Canada, as well as Fenian uprisings in Ireland. The Navy is also split into squadrons patrolling the Caribbean, the Pacific, and the China Sea. With a growing threat from a new European power, attempts to increase recruiting for the Army at home are ham-strung by a sudden need to produce more naval ships with a consequent demand for workers. The unspecified enemy, which has just added Holland and Denmark to its newly conquered lands in France, then requisitions every available ship along the North Sea coast and starts to embark troops. What is left of the Channel Squadron (half were despatched to the eastern Mediterranean on a false scent) is then destroyed by some 'fatal engines' of which the public knew nothing but of which the British Government had been warned (politicians are always letting the side down in these stories).

The story of the subsequent invasion is told by a survivor – a civil servant and a member of a volunteer regiment based near Dorking. His unit, as with Kitchener's volunteers in 1914, did not have enough rifles, such that one half trained with them in the morning and the other in the afternoon, the rifles swapped between them over lunch. Under threat of imminent invasion, obsolete smooth-bore muskets are distributed from the Tower of London as panic grips the City and the economy collapses. The storyteller recalls how the enemy lands in the south-east and his regiment is entrained for Dorking before moving towards Horsham where the sounds of fighting are heard. His unit then withdraws to a defensive line about Dorking, Reigate, and the North Downs where they line up next to three battalions of the Guards. Otherwise, the British forces are mainly made up of poorly trained and poorly armed volunteers, like the troops of Antoine Chanzy's soundly defeated *Armée de la Loire* at the Battle of Le Mans in mid-January 1871 (see page 82). Now, between Leith Hill and Box Hill, the British Army is attacked and routed by the anonymous, (suspiciously Prussian) blue-clad invaders. They retreat towards the Thames and, near Surbiton Station, the fighting resumes and the invaders again are victorious against the ill-equipped, ill-trained and poorly officered volunteers. In the aftermath, Britain becomes a province of the conqueror and the Empire is looted wholesale and dismantled.

This awful warning about the perils of unpreparedness struck an immediate chord with the general public and continued to do so right up to the outbreak of war in 1914, with six re-prints of the original and a new edition being published as late as the autumn of 1914.[2] Its timing was apposite, however, as German success in France was the kick up the *derrière* the country needed to more actively pursue the Army reforms recommended by the Royal Commission which reported in 1862 on the failings of the Crimean War, and on which a start was made in 1869 by Edward Cardwell, Gladstone's Secretary of State for War.

Chesney's article was the foundation of a fast-growing genre of 'invasion literature' which the British public devoured. Similar stories were told in various other European countries and, across the continent, it has been estimated some 400 books on this theme were written in the years between the end of the Franco-Prussian War and the start of the First World War[i].

More than a dozen responses to Chesney's book appeared including, in 1876, *The Invasion of 1883*, a story which reversed the outcome of Chesney's gloomy publication because of presumed reforms to the British Army. But nearly every new book had a specific axe to grind about failed government policies and/or concerns about a particular foreign power:

Railing against the vulnerabilities created by the prospect of a Channel Tunnel were *Submarina* (1882), *The Battle of the Channel Tunnel and Dover Castle and forts* (1882), *The Surprise of the Channel Tunnel (*1883), *London's Peril* (1900), *Pro Patria* (1901) and *The Tunnel Terror* (1907);

Worries about Britain being starved into submission because of its failure to maintain the fleet and a too great reliance on foreign food were found in *The Great War and Disastrous Peace of 1885* (1885), *The Sack of London in the Great French War of 1901* (1901) and Clarke's *Starved into Surrender* (1904) where, again, the enemy was the French with Russian help;

Irish independence featured in *The Battle of the Moy: Or How Ireland Gained Her Independence in 1892-1894* (1883), and *The Great Irish Rebellion of 1886, Retold by a Landlord* (1886); and

Fears about Russian naval and military power appear in *The Russia's Hope* (1888) and, along with the perceived threat from France, represent the most common theme before the end of the century. Even noted naval historians such as Sir William Laird Clowes, revered writer of *The Royal Navy, A History from the Earliest Times to 1900,* wrote such a book in 1894 - *The Captain of the Mary Rose* – which described a naval war between France and Britain.

There were even books suggesting a wide-ranging war between the USA and Britain such as *The Battle of the Swash* by S Barton (1888), *The Great Anglo-American War of 1900* by C V Anson (1896), which results in the loss of Canada, and *The Unpardonable War* by J Barnes published in 1904.

After the end of the South African War, however, the most common books by far were those involving conflicts between Germany and Great Britain, and these appeared regularly in both countries. Some, such as *Sink, Burn, Destroy: Der Schlag gegen Deutschland* (1905) and *The Battle of the North Sea* written in 1914 by Rear Admiral S M Eardley-Wilmot[ii] (1913), or the German *Deutschlands Flotte im Kampf* (H G von Bernstorff, 1909) and *Die 'Offensiv-Invasion' gegen England* (K Bleibtrau, 1907) described mainly naval events. Others are more typical 'invasion scare' books such as *The Writing on the Wall* written in 1906 by someone using the pseudonym of *'General Staff'*, *The Invasion of England* by R H Davis, and *Great was the Fall*, written under the *nom de plume* of '*A Naval Officer*', both published in 1912.

Not quite so usual was *Modern warfare: or, How our soldiers fight* by Brig. Gen. Frederick Guggisberg under the pseudonym *Ubique* (1903)[3]. Guggisberg was an uncommon man. Born in Ontario, he was educated in England and was

---

[i] A very long list of such books can be found at *http://www.theriddleofthesands.com/*.
[ii] He wrote *The Next Naval War* in 1894 only this time the enemy was the French.

commissioned into the Royal Engineers from the RMA, Woolwich, in 1889. For five years he was an instructor in fortifications at the RMA (1897-1902), before spending several years in West Africa. During the war he became the Commander, Royal Engineers, of the 8th and 66th Divisions. He also, if briefly, commanded an infantry brigade, the 170th. After the war he spent eleven years as the Governor of the Gold Coast and then British Guyana. Surprisingly, as a representative of the colonial power, a statue of him was erected in Accra in 1974 to commemorate his founding of the *Korle Bu Teaching Hospital* in 1923. He also founded the *Prince of Wales College and School,* Achimota (later *Achimota College*) at which various leaders of Ghana and other African states were educated. His enlightenment did not stop there. His first marriage to Ethel Emily Hamilton Way ended in divorce after nine years but he then went on to marry the also divorced actress and singer Lilian Decima Moore. She started her career in Gilbert and Sullivan operas with the *D'Oyly Carte Opera Company*. Moore was also a social activist founding the *Actresses' Franchise League* and the *Actress' Freedom League* and being active in the cause of women's suffrage. During the war she founded the *Women's Emergency Corps*, and was Director-General of the *British Navy, Army, and Air Force Leave Club*. For her war work she was awarded the CBE. As Lady Moore-Guggisberg she continued to perform charity work on behalf of servicemen during WW2. When she died in 1964, she was the oldest surviving originator of a Gilbert and Sullivan role.

Guggisberg was a man of unusually liberal instincts for an officer and was fond of putting pen to paper. His first work was a history of *'The Shop'*, i.e. the Royal Military Academy at Woolwich. His second, in 1903, was *Modern Warfare*. This was not an 'invasion scare' book as such. No Germans (or French or Russians for that matter) landed in Sussex or Norfolk or anywhere else on the mainland. Instead, its preliminaries explain in somewhat condescending terms to modern eyes, the structure of the post-Boer War British Army and how it fought. It draws some lessons from South Africa, even though Guggisberg did not serve there. Part one, therefore, runs to some 70 pages. The rest of the book, 400 pages and more, describes the results of a British Army being sent to Belgium in 1903 to confront an invasion of that country by Germany, in support of another German attack on France in the area between Belfort and Nancy. It therefore pre-dates all the inter-Army planning instituted a few years later after the *Entente Cordiale* linked the futures of Britain and France against the mutual threat of Germany.

War is declared by Britain on Germany on 1st July 1903 after German troops cross the Belgian border. Guggisberg then describes the process of mobilisation, taking the 2nd Lincolnshire Regt., 3rd Division, based at Aldershot as his exemplar. The four-division Expeditionary Force comprising the I Corps (1st-3rd Infantry Divisions and a Cavalry Division) is commanded by Sir John French and its units land at Blankenberge, Oostende, and Nieuwpoort Bad then advance towards Brussels through Gent and Kortrijk. Guggisberg describes this, and the organisation of the infrastructure put in place, in huge detail. It is more of a lecture than a novel. On the fall of Liège, Kitchener is appointed commander in chief of the British and Belgian forces opposing the Germans who are now advancing on Namur, whilst other troops march through the Ardennes into Northern France.

The complete BEF concentrates around Brussels sixteen days after the declaration of war and Gen. French is tasked with relieving besieged Namur. Guggisberg composes imaginary orders to all units involved, painstakingly explains the purpose and composition of cavalry screens, gives details of how a cavalry unit patrols and, indeed, goes into every excruciating detail about how an Army plans, organises, deploys, and fights. There are maps, some in colour, sketches, and organisational charts. Our author loves detail.

Then there is the fighting. The artillery of both sides repeats Colenso: direct fire at ranges of 1,500 yards or less, the gunners shot down by rifle fire. Cavalry lurks in hollows and behind woods and repeatedly justifies their continued existence by crashing into the flanks of unsuspecting infantry. It culminates in a five-day second battle of Waterloo fought over the old battlefield but extending far beyond. Guggisberg's fellows in the Engineers have done sterling work and numerous defensive positions allow brave British troops to defend against overwhelming odds. Repeatedly the writer states the near impossibility of defeating troops in well-concealed defensive positions supported by artillery and machine guns. The Germans are repelled at appalling cost but, by sheer numbers, seem likely to prevail as they outflank French's men. But wait! Where is Kitchener you ask? He is advancing with the British 2nd and 3rd Corps which have, miraculously, been mobilised and transported to Belgium within 21 days of the declaration of war. Facing calamity, the Germans retreat. The war is won.

Modern Warfare is a strange book. It takes the failed tactics of South Africa and applies them to a European war as if Colenso, Magersfontein, *Modder River* and Spion Kop never happened (see Chapter 1). But it suggests the defence now had the upper hand, an idea which would have appalled most infantry and cavalry officers in the British and French Armies. It makes no other great points, suggests no great insights concerning tactics, equipment, technology, etc. It becomes something of a 'Boys' Own' yarn in which the plucky under-dog prevails against the playground bully. Unlike other books, it does not make a point about preparedness, about conscription, about military spending. Indeed, it is not a 'scare' story. After all, the British win. But, at least Guggisberg identified the right enemy, invading the right country, and, exceptionally, accepted the murderous impact of artillery, automatic weapons and rifles on troops attacking an enemy concealed and protected by trenches.

A FEW 'INVASION SCARE' BOOKS REACHED the standards of genuine literature. One such was Erskine Childers' *The Riddle of the Sands* (1903). More of a spy story than a true 'invasion scare' novel, it concerns two British friends' attempts to find out what the German Navy and Army are up to behind the dreary barrier of the mud flats and shallow inlets of the East Frisian Islands between the *Ems* and *Jade Rivers*. The book proved an essential element in sustaining the widespread view amongst conservative-inclined politicians and civilians and the military that Britain was ill-prepared for what was viewed as an increasingly certain European war.

As reinforcement, Rudyard Kipling's poem *The Dutch in the Medway*, written in 1911 about one of the worst disasters to befall the Navy, the Dutch incursion up the Medway in 1667, more than hints at the danger of a lack of preparedness. One need simply substitute 'German' for 'Dutchmen' to understand the reference:

If wars were won by feasting,
Or victory by song,
Or safety found, by sleeping sound
How England would be strong!
But honour and dominion
Are not maintained so,
They're only got by sword and shot
And this the Dutchmen know![4]

The audience for these books was predominantly the educated middle and upper class. Literacy rates amongst the urban and rural working class significantly increased after the *Elementary Education Act* of 1870 and was further enhanced by the *Education Act* of 1902. But books and magazines were not for the *hoi polloi*[i]. It needed the actions of a populist and cheap newspaper to extend the fear of invasion and dislike and distrust of the likely German invaders. Conveniently there was one such proprietor only too keen to move into this market – Alfred Harmsworth, the 1st Viscount Northcliffe of the Isle of Thanet in the County of Kent, and the owner of the *Daily Mail*, first published in 1896 and sadly still with us. He applied himself vigorously to the task. The *Daily Mail* was an imperialist, nationalist, xenophobic, populist, down market rag (no change there then) and, perhaps more than any other British newspaper, whipped up anti-German sentiment before the war. In this respect, its virulent dislike of foreigners is an editorial policy which has stood it in good stead down the years. The newspaper was, according to Lord Salisbury, Tory Prime Minister between 1895 and 1902, 'a newspaper produced by office boys for office boys'[5] but, by 1902, one million 'office boys' were reading the *Mail*.

Northcliffe, it would seem, disliked all of foreigners indiscriminately. If he wasn't whipping up public sentiment against Germany (until Hitler came to power, then he was an admirable example of how to run a country), his attention might rapidly switch to another objectionable nation – the French, for example.

In November 1914, Northcliffe ordered a writer at the *Mail*, who rejoiced in the name John Twells Brex[ii], to collect and publish a collection of articles from the newspaper to be published under the title: *'Scaremongerings' from the Daily Mail, 1896-1914: The paper that foretold the war*. Though the title gave the start date of its 'dreadful warnings' about the Teutonic threat as 1896, the date the *Mail* was founded, its coverage was still broader, with Brex's brief introduction stating that:

> "This collection of extracts traces the beginning of Prussian hostility to the British Empire from 1864, pointing out how it was accentuated by England's neutrality in 1870, and by her attitude in 1875."[6]

---

[i] *Hoi polloi* – ancient Greek for 'the masses' or majority. It is a phrase since used in a derogatory sense by the *hoi oligoi* ('the few' and the derivation of 'oligarchs') to describe the lower classes, 'plebs' or 'proles'.

[ii] John Twells Brex (1870-1920) was a journalist and author who published, amongst other books, *The Civil War of 1915* (C Arthur Pearson, 1912) and *Adventures on the Home Front* (Methuen and Company, 1918).

There ensues a series of brief, highly selective, quotes from the *Mail* from 1896 to 1914 designed to place Northcliffe on a pedestal of far-seeing omniscience, and to disparage and insult all (mostly Liberal and Labour) politicians, journalists and newspapers who had, in any way, dared to suggest war with Germany was not inevitable. Some of it is laughable. Typical complaints about German clerks taking British jobs (9th November 1896); about carrier pigeons released from places adjacent to ports like Dover (19th July 1897 and again, in a rush, on 9th, 11th and 12th August 1898); and German 'spies' collecting Ordnance Survey maps over a period of 18 years, (4th January 1900). There were efforts at playing the 'the enemy within' card by, for example, attempts to denigrate the industrialist and Liberal MP Sir John Brunner when the *Mail* described him as 'the son of an alien school master'[i] (March 1908. Brunner's father was Swiss). The rest was simply and relentlessly anti-German, anti-*Kaiser*, anti-Liberal, and anti-Socialist. And pro-war.

Certain items went conveniently missing, however. Like the Leader of the Conservative Party's conciliatory response to the speech of Sir Edward Grey on 27th November 1911, in which the Foreign Secretary commented on the resolution of the Agadir Crisis by the Franco-German Accord of 4th November. Andrew Bonar Law had only become the Tory leader two weeks earlier and was very much the third choice of the Parliamentary Party. Only the simultaneous withdrawal of the two front runners, Walter Long and Austen Chamberlain, ensured his election on 13th November. Nevertheless, he now gave a thoughtful speech about Germany when called to respond to Grey's address to the Commons. His words must have had Northcliffe grinding his teeth in frustration:

> "We are all thinking a great deal about our relationship with Germany. It is an idea prevalent, especially on the Continent, that there is in this country a feeling of hostility to Germany. In my opinion that belief is entirely unfounded. So far as I am concerned… I never had, and certainly have not now, any such feeling. During my business life I had daily commercial intercourse with Germany. I have many German friends, I love some German books almost as much as our favourites in our own tongue, and I can imagine few, if any, calamities which would seem so great as a war,

---

[i] Sir John Tomlinson Brunner, 1st Baronet, DL (1842–1919), was born in Everton, Liverpool, son of John Brunner, a Swiss teacher who founded St George's House, a Pestalozzi school in Everton, and Margaret Catherine Curphey. With Ludwig Mond, he founded *Brunner, Mond & Co.* in 1873. By the end of the century it was the largest chemical company in the country, its workers enjoying shorter working hours, sickness and injury insurance, and holidays with pay. Elected Liberal MP for Northwich, 1885, he supported the disestablishment of the Church of England, the reform of property laws, and Irish Home Rule. He lost his seat in 1886, regaining it in a by-election in 1887. He held it at each subsequent election until he retired in January 1910. Although he argued for a peaceful resolution of tensions between Britain and Germany, he fully supported the war and his company provided chemicals for explosives. A disused *Brunner Mond* caustic soda factory at Silvertown, West Ham, was taken over by the War Office and, despite the company's opposition, used to purify TNT. It blew up on 19th January 1917 killing 73 people and wounding 400. *Brunner Mond* became part of *ICI* in 1926 and was taken over by the Indian *Tata Chemicals* in 2006.

whatever the result, between us and the great German people. I hear it also constantly said – there is no use shutting our eyes or ears to obvious facts – that, owing to divergent interests, war some day or other between this country and Germany is inevitable. I never believe in these inevitable wars. Prince Bismarck once said, and said truly, that no man can overlook the hand of Providence. I am myself old enough to remember that twenty-five or thirty years ago the same thing was said far more persistently about our relationship with Russia. It is never said now. Why? For one reason, because the whole perspective of the world has changed. It is constantly changing, and I see no reason to think that ten or fifteen years hence it may not completely change again. If, therefore, war should ever come between these two countries, which Heaven forbid! it will not, I think, be due to irresistible natural laws; it will be due to the want of human wisdom. But neither men nor nations are always wise, and in my belief the best, perhaps the only absolute security for peace, is that each country should realise always the strength of the other, and should realise, too, that whatever may be the domestic differences, from whatever party in either country the Government may come, each nation is prepared to defend to the last her rights and her honour."[7]

What more is missing? Well, the *Daily Mail's* previous view of France for one. Whilst Brex happily quotes any anti-German material he can lay his hands on, he neglects two remarks from *Mail* editorials in late 1899, both pro-German and anti-French. On 9th November 1899, the newspaper shrieked:

"The French .... have succeeded in thoroughly convincing John Bull that they are his inveterate enemies, and that all his attempts at conciliation are useless. There will be no more such attempts. England has long hesitated between France and Germany. But she has always respected the German character, whereas she has gradually come to feel a contempt for France. A country where the most monstrous injustice can be perpetrated with impunity (i.e. Dreyfus), a nation whose beloved heroes are the forgers of the French General Staff, can never be a British ally. Nothing like an *entente cordiale* can subsist between England and her nearest neighbour, ... Enough of France; she has neither courage, foresight, nor sense of humour."

And then, three weeks later, on 1st December:

"If they cannot cease their insults, their colonies will be taken from them and given to Germany and Italy – we ourselves want nothing more – France will be rolled in the blood and mud in which her Press daily wallows."

And, between the two, where in the *Mail's* grubby little booklet is their headline and article from 11th November 1899?

"A Friend In Need Is A Friend Indeed
The *Kaiser* is fully alive to the fact that a bond of concord is to the material advantage of both Germany and England in the world-wide career that lies before these two great nations."[8]

Then the enemy was France. Five years on it was beastly, ambitious Germany.

1. Alfred Harmsworth, the 1st Viscount Northcliffe
of the Isle of Thanet in the County of Kent

Thus, in 1906, the *Mail* commissioned William Tufnell Le Queux (1864-1927) to write *The Invasion of 1910*. Le Queux was one of the best known 'invasion scare' authors. His first book, *The Great War in England in 1897*, saw a Britain beset by Russian and French foes bailed out by Germany, but the devious Hun was the enemy in *The Invasion of 1910*. An enormous success for le Queux and the *Mail*, it was published in 27 languages, sold one million copies, and was made into a film, *If England were Invaded*, in 1912. In the meantime, it served its purpose of spreading through the lower middle and working classes the fear and distrust of German intentions which lay at the heart of the widespread enthusiasm for war in 1914.

Invasion scare stories even made it onto the London stage in the form of Maj. Guy du Maurier's[i] play *An Englishman's Home* which made a considerable impact in 1909. Its opening coincided with a campaign to increase the numbers enlisting in the newly formed London Territorial battalions. It was supported by an aggressive campaign of agitation in Northcliffe's rag which, to quote *The Times* military correspondent, set out 'to thrust down the throat of its many readers' the need for more Army recruits both in London and beyond.[9] Not that *The Times* disagreed with the premise of du Maurier's work. It was, as ever, a Conservative journal, as its critique of liberal Edwardian England makes clear:

> "It is obvious, though Major du Maurier appears to be guiltless in the matter, that the conclusion of his play is inartistic, illogical and absurd; but, whatever the blemishes may be, the play synthesizes in a manner as forcible as truthful the careless confidence of modern Englishmen that security can be obtained without sacrifice; it satirizes with unsparing scorn the crass

---

[i] Lt. Col., Guy Louis Busson du Maurier, DSO, was born on 18th May 1865, son of Emma Wightwick and George Louis Palmella Busson du Maurier, a cartoonist for *Punch* and author of the novel *Trilby*. Marlborough and Sandhurst. Commissioned, Royal Fusiliers, 1885. Burma and South Africa, commanding 20th Battalion, Mounted Infantry. Assistant Commandant, School of Instruction for Mounted Infantry. Killed at Kemmel on 9th March 1915, CO 3rd Royal Fusiliers. Buried in Kemmel Chateau Military Cemetery, grave L. 4.

indifference of our people to their most elementary duties, and presents a living picture, in the fashion best suited to captivate the public mind, of what many have been thinking but no one has been able to express so well. No more scathing indictment of the debilitating literature, the frivolous occupations, and the debasing pleasures, which have become the gods of modern middle-class England[i], could well have been penned."[10]

Army officers 'hurrahed!' at such statements and, as well as the public, flocked to see their fellow officer's play. Amongst them was Douglas Haig:

"It is extraordinary how the play draws crowded houses every night and how impressed the audience seem to be with the gravity of the scenes. I trust that good may result and 'universal training' may become the law of the land."[11]

In this last thought Haig and his allies such as Lord Roberts, desperate to see universal service introduced in Britain, were disappointed. A Liberal government with many of its leading lights striving for peace would never introduce such an unpopular militaristic policy. Nor would socialists and Trades Unionists have welcomed the militarisation of the general public. But the clamour for its introduction from senior Army officers and many of influence in the Conservative Party was loud and remained insistent[ii].

DEREK LINNEY'S EXCELLENT WEB SITE *The Riddle of the Sands.com: Victorian and Edwardian Invasion Literature* provides a downloadable database of 190 invasion scare books/articles published from 1851 to 1914. They are described variously as *'Invasion/General', 'Speculative Science Fiction', 'Espionage', 'Future War Technology', 'Future Fantasy', 'Parody/Spoof/Satire'* (as from 1906), and *'Insurrection'* (involving Ireland).

Analysis is revealing.

The 'enemy' goes in phases. From 1871 to 1876, i.e. during and immediately after the Franco-Prussian War, there are 14 books with Germany attacking Britain. The odd two are *The Commune in London* by S B Hemyng ('socialists'), and *The British Federal Empire* by *'Octogenarian'* with Russia the protagonists. Thereafter, it is mainly France and, on occasion, Russia which appear most regularly, although a few of these titles are written from a foreign perspective. That is until Germany

---

[i] In the aftermath of the disasters of Jena-Auerstedt in 1806, Prussian officers complained in the same way about the state of society. Maj. (later *Generalfeldmarschall*) August Wilhelm Antonius *Graf* Neidhardt von Gneisenau, staff officer to Frederick Louis, Prince of Hohenlohe-Ingelfingen, the Prussian General defeated at Jena, wrote: 'Our long garrison life has spoiled us, and effeminacy and desire for and love of pleasure, have weakened our military virtues. The entire nation must pass through the School of Misfortune, and we shall either die in the crises, or a better condition will be created, after we have suffered bitter misery, and after our bones have decayed'. (quoted in Balck, W, *Entwickelung der Taktik im Weltkriege* [*Development of Tactics in the World War*], R. Eisenschmidt, 1922)

[ii] In the January 1910 General Election, forty (15%) of the 273 Conservative and Unionist Party's MPs declared a rank in the Army or Navy.

embarked upon a major naval expansion with the passing of the first of five Naval Acts (or *Flottengesetze, Fleet Laws*) in 1898[i]:

Year – Enemy
1882 – France (5), Russia (2), Germany (2)
1883 – France (2), Germany (1)
1884 – Russia (1)
1885 – France (1)
1887 – France (2)
1888 – France (1), Russia (1)
1889 – Russia (3), Germany (1)
1892 – France (2)
1893 – France (2)
1894 – France (3)
1895 – France (3)
1896 – France (1)
1897 – France (2)
1898 – France (2), Russia (2), Germany (1) (N.B. First German naval law)
1899 – France (1), Germany (1)
1900 – Russia (3), France (2), Germany (1)
1901 – France (8)
1902 – Germany (1)
1903 – France (1), Germany (1)
1904 – France (2), Germany (1) (N.B. *Entente Cordiale* agreed)
1905 – Germany (4), France (1)
1906 – Germany (7)
1907 – Germany (6), France (1), Russia (1) (N.B. *Anglo-Russian Convention*)
1908 – Germany (3)
1909 – Germany (7)
1910 – Germany (3)
1911 – Germany (3)
1912 – Germany (4)
1913 – Germany (4)
1914 – Germany (2)

Many books were written by serving or recently retired officers[ii]. In 2011, A M Matin suggested ten essential ingredients for any invasion scare book:

"(1) near-future settings, usually the present to five years, for hostilities or narrowly averted hostilities (although the time of narration may be many years later) and corresponding displays of the wisdom of hindsight;

---

[i] The others followed in 1900, 1906, 1908, and 1912.
[ii] Those written by 'civilians' were often criticised by officers sympathetic to the message but annoyed by a lack of 'proper' military knowledge. Col. F N Maude, RE, for example, criticised Le Queux's first invasion scare book *The Great War in England in 1897* (published 1894) [*Source*: Matin, A. M. *The Creativity of War Planners: Armed Forces Professionals and the Pre-1914 British Invasion-Scare Genre*, ELH 78, no. 4 (2011), page 806].

(2) demonstrations of the vulnerability of the territories of the British Empire in addition to that of England or Great Britain;
(3) depictions of invading or occupying troops and/or subversive foreigners (spies, saboteurs, terrorists, or disguised soldiers) on British soil;
(4) blendings of documented fact with fiction (enhancing the verisimilitude and plausibility of the fiction);
(5) denunciations of incompetent (usually Liberal) British politicians, including exposures of their mismanagement of the armed forces and of foreign policy;
(6) governmental and public underestimations of the capabilities and nefariousness of Britain's enemies;
(7) appeals to the reader's senses of patriotism and shame;
(8) failures to support strategic and tactical innovations, including those associated with technological advancements;
(9) geographical specificity and depictions of familiar local detail, such as English national landmarks (monuments of power and national pride that are usually damaged or destroyed);
(10) decisive conclusions to events with Britain either defeated and the British Empire dismembered, or the nation and empire strengthened by the experience of actual or threatened invasion."[12]

This writer would draw the reader's attention to number 5. All bar one of the major invasion/naval scares took place with Liberal Governments in power: Gladstone 1868-74, Gladstone 1880-5, Salisbury 1886-92, Gladstone 1892-5, Campbell-Bannerman/Asquith 1906-10. There was almost always a Conservative-linked inspiration behind these scares, culminating in attempts to interfere with the January 1910 election result with the Mulliner naval scare of 1908/9.

Mind, there is considerable irony that these books suggest a failure to embrace tactical and technical change was a root cause of repeated 'defeats' by invading powers. And yet, pre-war, several senior Army officers showed themselves peculiarly resistant to tactical and technical change on a range of vital issues.

NORTHCLIFFE WAS NOT CONTENT with publishing scare stories about invasions and non-existent German naval superiority. In early 1909 *The Aerial League of The British Empire* was formed[i], at 'the initiative of very highly placed naval and military men whose names are guarantees of good faith' according to *The Times* (bought by Northcliffe in 1908). The names given are: James Edward Hubert Gascoyne-Cecil[ii], 4th Marquess of Salisbury; Archibald FitzRoy George Hay, 13th Earl of Kinnoull, the Viscount Dupplin and Lord of Kinfauns[iii]; Rear Admiral the Hon. Thomas Seymour Brand[iv] (second son of Henry Bouverie William Brand, 1st Viscount Hampden); Maj. Gen. Harry Ashley Vane Cummins; Vice Admiral Sir

---

[i] Now simply called *The Air League*.
[ii] Previously Lord Cranborne, he was the son of the late Conservative Prime Minister and had been Conservative MP for Darwen in Lancashire, 1885-1892.
[iii] Grandson of Henry Somerset, 7th Duke of Beaufort.
[iv] Fought Hastings (1886) & Eastbourne (1892, 1895, 1900) for the Liberal Party.

Charles Campbell[i]; Sir Horatio Gilbert George Parker, MP[ii]; Edward Carr Glyn, then the Bishop of Peterborough (ironically given events to come); and 'other well-known men'. Amongst these unnamed 'other well-known men' was a certain Alfred Charles William Harmsworth, 1st Viscount Northcliffe.

The Times, describing the purpose of the *League*, declared it sought:

"… to do propagandist work, in order that the British Empire may secure and maintain its supremacy in the air… It is, in effect, a counterpart of the *Navy League*; but it has a far more difficult task before it, as we are yet without an aerial fleet, and the public has not fully recognized its necessity. Thus the *League* must educate the public…"[13]

In a remarkable coincidence of timing, given the need to 'educate the public', the early Spring of 1909 saw articles appear in the *Mail* (and other newspapers) about the dramatic appearance in the skies over London and the South East of objects similar to the airships recently designed and built by *Graf* von Zeppelin. The *Mail* reported the first sighting on 23rd March near Peterborough. If so, the airship had travelled some 1,000 miles on its round trip from its base at Friedrichshafen on the northern shore of Lake Constance on the border between Switzerland and southern Württemberg. No mean feat if one takes into account a Parliamentary exchange during Questions on 24th March, one day later, in which the Liberal MP for St Pancras East, Mr Hugh Cecil Lea, remarked on how a German *Zeppelin 1* managed to fly just over 150 miles in one go as if this were something remarkable.[14] Indeed, a trip from Friedrichshafen to Munich some months later was greeted as a great step forward for the future of the airship. The distance between the two places is c. 200 kms or just 125 miles. *Zeppelins* over Peterborough eight times further away, one must suggest, was just one of the thousands of stories made up in the editorial rooms of the *Daily Mail*, a 'creative tradition' it has maintained ever since and an early indicator of the *'Alt-Right's'* pervasive system of 'Fake News'.

During May, 49 airships sightings were reported in the skies above England, Wales and even Northern Ireland. Some of the more sensationalist newspapers[iii] were full of the potential threat these posed, a threat which played on fears generated by such little understood new technology and exacerbated, no doubt, by H G Wells' 1908 story *The War in the Air*, serialised in *The Pall Mall Magazine*.

This was then reinforced by wild statements made in July 1908 by Rudolf Martin[iv], an ultra-nationalist official in the *Staatssekretäre des Reichsamts des Innern des*

---

[i] Contested Northern Monmouthshire for the Conservatives in 1906.

[ii] Tory MP for Gravesend, 1900-1918. A prolific novelist, during the war he was a propagandist on behalf of Great Britain with his work targeted at the USA.

[iii] Others, mainly regional newspapers, were openly sceptical of the reports and treated them as the imaginings of either manipulative or credulous individuals.

[iv] Rudolf Emil Martin had 'previous' on airships and German expansion. In 1907 he published *Berlin-Bagdad; Das deutsche Weltreich im Zeitalter der Luftschiffahrt, 1910-1931* (*'Berlin-Baghdad: The German World Empire in the Age of Airship Travel, 1910—1931'*) in which Germany defeats Russia and occupies the Middle East. In 1909 came *Der Weltkrieg in den Lüften* in which German airships defeat Great Britain.

Deutschen Kaiserreichs (the German *Interior Ministry*). These were gleefully reported in the *Daily Mail* on 11th July 1908. Martin asserted that a fleet of 3,500 *zeppelins* would land a German Army of 300,000 men and more in Kent within half an hour of leaving the coast at Calais[i].[15] These troops would then march on London putting an end to Great Britain and its Empire. This same Martin also wrote how:

> "The future of Germany demands the absorption of Austria-Hungary, the Balkan States, and Turkey, with the North Sea ports. Her realms will stretch towards the east from Berlin to Baghdad, and to Antwerp on the west."[16]

His expansionist timetable was 'from twenty to thirty years hence', i.e. between 1928 and 1938, which latter year saw the *Anschluß* or annexation of Austria. Statements such as those by Martin, amplified and exaggerated by the Yellow Press, did nothing to calm the British public's fears about German intentions and encouraged the hysteria which greeted the reports of sinister airships hovering over Great Britain in the spring and early summer of 1909.

Some journals gave Martin the 'respect' he deserved. *The Illustrated London News* of 19th December 1908 has an illustration to underline the seriousness with which they took his suggestion Germany would build 50,000 aircraft (cost £50 million). These would take off from Calais, each with two soldiers on board, allowing an invading Army of 100,000 to land in East Kent within thirty minutes.

A tongue-in-cheek illustration shows some archetypal sleepy Kentish village, its church surrounded and its roads and green covered in aircraft nose to tail whilst dozens more fly forlornly overhead desperate for somewhere to land. Treating the concept with all due 'seriousness', the magazine calculated that the space required to land and park such a quantity of aircraft would be that normally occupied by an army of 4 million lined up shoulder to shoulder, as each aircraft would occupy the space required for eighty soldiers!

The Illustrated London News summed up such nonsense nicely:

> "*Herr* Martin's lecture, it need hardly be said, has been received as a welcome contribution to the gaiety of nations."

---

[i] In a 1913 letter to *The Times*, John Leyland recites the fate of the 16 (not 3,500) airships built by the *Zeppelin Company*. LZ No. 1 was dismantled after three flights, 1902. Count Zeppelin's company, *Gesellschaft zur Förderung der Luftschiffahrt (Society for the Promotion of Airship Flight)*, was then liquidated due to lack of funds. *No. 2* was destroyed in a storm at Kissleg during her second flight, January, 1906. *No. 3* was built for the Army but failed a 24-hour endurance trial. *No. 4* was destroyed in bad weather at Echterdingen, August, 1908, and also failed the Army's 24-hour endurance trial. Public donations allowed Zeppelin to setup the *Luftschiffbau Zeppelin GmbH (Airship Construction Zeppelin Ltd.)*. *No. 5*, Army airship *Z 2*, was destroyed in a gale at Weilburg, April, 1910. *No. 6*, a passenger vessel, burned at Oos, September, 1910. *No. 7*, the passenger vessel *Deutschland*, was destroyed in a bad landing in the Teutoburger Wald, 1910. *No. 8*, was dismantled after three flights after being damaged coming out of her hangar at Dusseldorf. *No. 9* was an Army airship, *No. 10* a passenger vessel *Schwaben*, and *No. 11* also a passenger vessel. *Nos. 12* to *15* were: naval airship *L1*, Army airship *Ersatz Z1*, a passenger vessel, and Army airship *Z 4 (No. 15)*. *No. 16* was undergoing tests [*Source: The Times, Zeppelin Airships*, John Leyland, 5th May 1913, page 7].

2. 'Two men to eighty'
The impossibility of finding landing-room and cover for an army of aeroplanes
Illustrated London News, 19th December 1908

On 17th May, the Conservative MP for Great Yarmouth, Arthur Fell[i], asked Haldane, Secretary of State for War, about the numbers of *zeppelins* under construction in Germany. The answer was seven built and five under construction (i.e. 3,488 to go if *Herr* Martin's suggestion was to come to fruition). The Liberal MP for Lambeth North, Horatio Myer, joined in the fun by asking:

"…whether there was any truth in the reports circulated in regard to the presence of a certain dirigible on the East Coast?"

Myer's witty description of the overweight Member for the Norfolk coastal constituency drew laughter from others in the chamber but, from Haldane on the front bench, 'no answer was returned'. None was required.[17]

Then, on 21st May, the *Daily Mail*, called for an end to the mania for spotting cigar-shaped aerial phantoms. The mass delusion of the 1909 *Zeppelin* Scare was almost at an end though there were similar outbreaks of '*zeppelin* hysteria' in Sweden, Australia, New Zealand and, at the end of 1909, parts of New England.). But the pressure was now on the Government to ensure Britain mount an effective response to these ghostly threats from the air. Northcliffe's work here was done.

---

[i] Fell was the subject of an election petition by his Liberal opponent concerning bribing voters in the 1906 election. Its dismissal was described by *The Times* as a 'curious conclusion'. Two judges had to agree on the charge but ex-Tory MP and friend of the previous Great Yarmouth MP, Sir William Grantham, found for Fell. Grantham, previously involved in petitions for Bodmin and Maidstone, was subject to a Commons' motion supported by 347 MPs demanding his removal but the Attorney General intervened. Fell, by now knighted, lost to a Liberal in 1922.

ADDING FURTHER FUEL TO THESE ALARMIST FIRES were books written by German officers in which war was not just predicted but celebrated as overdue and essential. One was penned by a previous member of the *Großer Generalstab* and a recent *Armeekorps* commander. *General der Kavallerie* Friedrich Adolf Julius von Bernhardi, who saw action on the Western and Eastern Fronts in the coming war. He was born in St Petersburg in 1849 but his family moved to Silesia two years later. He entered the Prussian Army, joining the *2. Hessische Husaren-Regiment Nr. 14* with which he served in the Franco-Prussian War and he was given the signal honour of leading the victorious troops through the *Arc de Triomphe* in the victory parade in Paris at the end of the war. After three years at the *Kriegsakademie* he joined the *Großer Generalstab* before spending time as the military *attaché* in Berne. He then took command of the *1. Badischen Leib-Dragoner-Regiment Nr. 20*. In 1898 he became director of the *Kriegsgeschichtliche Abteilung (War History Department)* of the *Großer Generalstab* and, while there, was involved in the development of the *Schlieffen Plan*. He was then, successively, the commander of *30. Kavallerie-Brigade* in Straßburg; of *7. Division* in Magdeburg; and of *VII. Armeekorps* in Munster before he retired in 1909 to dedicate his time to writing on military matters.

His most influential work was 1912's *Germany's Next War (Deutschland und der Nächste Krieg)*. 200,000 copies of its translation were printed for distribution in the UK by the end of 1914.[18] The impression created by the book can easily be gained by reading the sub-headings of the opening chapters, for example:

Chapter I – *The Right to Make War*: The Biological Necessity of War, The Duty of Self-Assertion, The Right of Conquest, War a Moral Obligation, Beneficent Results of War, Destructiveness and Immorality of Peace Aspirations;

Chapter II – *The Duty to Make War*: The Duty to Fight;

Chapter IV – *Germany's Historical Mission*: Grounds of the Intellectual Supremacy of Germany, Germany's role as a Spiritual and Intellectual Leader, The Necessity of Colonial Expansion, etc.

Bernhardi, like almost every military man, derided the idea of peace – especially universal peace. Moltke the Elder once wrote 'universal peace is a dream, and not even a beautiful dream', but Bernhardi, a convinced social Darwinist, went further:

"War is a biological necessity of the first importance, a regulative element in the life of mankind which cannot be dispensed with... the efforts directed towards the abolition of war must not only be termed foolish, but absolutely immoral, and denounced as unworthy of the human race."[19]

And, lest one imagine that such attitudes were peculiar to Teutonic militarists, in 1913 the Liberal MP, John Robertson[i], quoted Lord Roberts as saying in 1904:

---

[i] John Mackinnon Robertson (1856-1933), rationalist and secularist Liberal MP for Tyneside, 1906-18. Beaten by a *National Democratic and Labour Party (NDP)* candidate in Wallsend, 1918. Robertson believed in free trade, votes for women, payment for MPs, and the abolition of the House of Lords. The *NDP* was a right-wing, pro-war Labour Party splinter group based on the *British Workers League* formed 1916. The ten MPs elected in 1918 joined Lloyd George's National Liberal Party in 1922.

"Without war – at any rate without the vigilance and discipline which prepare for that stern emergency – a nation is in risk of running to seed. And where a war is a just one – where it is waged as an act of self-defence, as in the case of the Japanese, who are now fighting for their very life[i] – its benefit to the nation is great. It is an appeal to the manhood and the virtue of a people. It prevents decadence and effeminacy. It corrects the selfishness and querulousness which are inevitably bred by a long peace. Without the preparation for an armed defence of its boundaries or the vindication of its honour, an empire would slip into habits dangerous for itself and dangerous for the whole of humanity. Even in the Anglo-Saxon race, which is as vigorous as any in the world, we find that a long peace breeds a complaining and luxurious spirit, to which every hardship and every little inconvenience becomes an intolerable injustice.
Fortitude and the cheerful bearing of adversity are apt to fall out of the category of human duties in a long and luxurious peace. And since character is tried by sorrow and affliction, this querulous antipathy to hardship and exertion is bad for the individual, and consequently for the State. We are all tried by fire, are we not? And the test of a man's character is his ability to bear gallantly the sorrows and afflictions of his life; so, too, I think, a nation needs to be tried by fire – needs to be put upon its trial every now and then, and tested by the laws which govern this planet – the law, I mean particularly, that only the efficient survive."[20]

Who were Roberts's 'decadent, effeminate' people enjoying 'a luxurious peace'?. Such a description can, at best, only fit the wealthier, educated elements of the middle and upper classes, i.e. Roberts' peers. As would be clear to anyone who knew anything about the working class, life for the overwhelming majority of men toiling in factories, mines, and fields or who made up the rank and file of the Regular Army, as well as the women who supported them, was anything but 'luxurious'. For them, an Edwardian life was one of long hours, poor pay, poor housing, poor food, and the poor health which led to 40% of volunteers for the South African War being rejected on medical grounds (see page 583 onwards).

John Robertson's retort was withering:

"I can imagine a working man, familiar all his life long with hardship and exertion, giving Lord Roberts a very plain opinion on this tissue of simple sentimentalism. Millions of men and women bear hardship and exertion daily, over all the earth, in the ordinary course of peaceful toil; and the spectacle of Lord Roberts, the man who is always in a state of apprehension, prescribing drill or fighting for them in the name of a prophylactic against querulousness, is enough to move them to Homeric laughter. It may be that some men of Lord Roberts's caste need hardship to rouse them to a serious realization of life; but the solemn assertion that the wholesale slaughter of private soldiers (who can have a sure sufficiency of hardship and exertion all their life-long in peace) will alone supply the

---

[i] An interesting interpretation of the Manchurian War, started by Japanese attacks on Russian naval units before declaring of war. A 'trick' repeated in 1941 at Pearl Harbor.

required conditions, is sufficient to evoke the question whether Lord Roberts is capable of a serious realization of life under any conditions."[21]

With such militarist, nationalist and imperialist material being pumped out of Germany (and Britain and the rest of Europe too) it is no wonder its neighbours looked nervously in the direction of Berlin and wondered when, and not if, such attitudes might lead to war on a scale unknown. And with the British public primed for the fight by the growing hysteria of 'invasion scare' publications such as *The Invasion of 1910* it can be of little wonder war was greeted by so many with such enthusiasm. Equally, in Berlin the threat of encirclement and of the growing military and naval power on its western and eastern borders persuaded even the most unaggressive citizen the future of their country and its burgeoning imperial prospects were in dire peril from historic enemies and current trading competitors.

DISTRIBUTED ACROSS EUROPE, these militaristic publications which threatened national disaster if extra cash was not found for more, bigger and more powerful weapons of war were all grist to the mill of the development and maintenance of the burgeoning military-industrial complex of which companies like *Krupp, Rheinmetall, Schneider, Vickers, Beardmore* and *Armstrong Whitworth* were a growing, powerful and influential part.

Some, like Bertha von Suttner, a supporter of Jean de Bloch and ardent pacifist (see Chapter 2), recognised how militaristic texts and alarmist invasion fiction worked hand in glove with politicians, industrialists and army officers of all nations to prevent peace and disarmament. During this time of rising tension, Suttner corresponded with Alfred Nobel, the Swedish chemist who, through *Alfred Nobel Industries* founded the *British Dynamite Factory* in 1870 at Ardeer in Scotland[i]. Nobel was responsible for the development of the high explosives *dynamite* and *gelignite* and the low explosive propellant *ballistite*; owned the Swedish arms and steel manufacturer *Aktiebolaget Bofors-Gullspång (Bofors)* from 1894; and was responsible in his will for the creation of the peace prizes awarded annually in his name.

It is ironic that Nobel hoped the invention of these powerful high explosives would help bring about the end of war. In a letter to Bertha von Suttner he wrote:

"Perhaps my factories will put an end to war sooner than your congresses: on the day that two army corps can mutually annihilate each other in a second, all civilised nations will surely recoil with horror and disband their troops."[22]

No doubt some of the scientists involved in the Manhattan Project held out similarly hopes after the invention of the atomic bomb but, sadly, there will always be some sociopath ready to use any weapon made available to them whatever the cost. Nobel died in 1896 but Suttner carried on her work and was one of the first to be awarded the Nobel Peace Prize. In her acceptance speech made on 18th April 1906 in the Hals Brothers Concert Hall in Oslo, she identified invasion scare books and the active lobbying by both industry and the military for more and more powerful weapons as feeding the frenzy for armaments and the drive for war:

---

[i] Later absorbed by *ICI* and later sold to *Inabata*. The site is no longer in use.

"… we have distrust, threats, sabre rattling, press baiting, feverish naval build-up, and rearming everywhere. In England, Germany, and France, novels are appearing in which the plot of a future surprise attack by a neighbour is intended as a spur to even more fervent arming. Fortresses are being erected, submarines built, whole areas mined, airships tested for use in war; and all this with such zeal – as if to attack one's neighbour were the most inevitable and important function of a state."[23]

Agreeing in a speech made on 21st December 1905 in the Albert Hall, the new Liberal Prime Minister[i], Sir Henry Campbell-Bannerman, declared that:

'A policy of huge armaments keeps alive and stimulates and feeds the belief that force is the best if not the only solution to international differences…'[24]

And yet, in Britain, these fears manifested themselves in a huge investment in the Royal Navy and a vastly expensive arms race with Germany triggered by the launching of the revolutionary battleship *HMS Dreadnought*. The lemming-like rush towards the precipice seemed unstoppable. The problem for the Army in Britain was that the investment made in armaments was concentrated on the part of the military best suited to stopping an invasion – the Royal Navy – rather than the fighting of a land campaign on the continent. And with the German *Hochseeflotte* growing annually it was on the Senior Service most new money was spent.

Another leading pacifist, the journalist and politician Norman Angell[ii], noted the fundamental flaw of this naval arms race – and arms races in general – in the opening paragraph of his 1909 booklet *Europe's Optical Illusion:*

"It is pretty generally admitted that the present rivalry in armaments with Germany cannot go on in its present form indefinitely. The net result of each side meeting the efforts of the other with similar effort is that at the end of a given period the relative position of both is what it was originally, and the enormous sacrifices of both have gone for nothing. If it be claimed that England is in a position to maintain the lead because she has the money, Germany can retort that she is in a position to maintain the lead because she has the population, which in the end must mean money."[25]

---

[i] He assumed office on 5th December 1905.
[ii] Later Sir Ralph Norman Angell (1872–1967). Born Ralph Norman Angell Lane, he was educated in England, France, and Switzerland before moving to California. He wrote for British, French, and American newspapers and was Paris editor of the *Daily Mail* 1905-12. In 1914, with Sir Charles Philips Trevelyan, Liberal MP for Elland, Yorkshire, and James Ramsay MacDonald, Labour MP for Leicester, and Chairman of the Parliamentary Labour Party, he founded the *Union of Democratic Control* which sought to reduce the influence of the military over foreign policy. Angell was elected Labour MP for Bradford North, 1929-31, was knighted in 1931, and awarded the Nobel Peace Prize in 1933. He actively campaigned against the aggressive foreign policies of what would become the Axis Powers in the late 1930s.

Angell commented that the normal consequence of such an arms race was 'armed conflict' which led to a greater or lesser period of relative calm before the whole process started again. Such conflict was, according to Angell:

"... on the whole, accepted as one of the laws of life; one of the hard facts of existence which men of ordinary courage take as all in the day's work."[26]

It was, he wrote, all part of the Social Darwinist philosophy which emerged in the second half of the nineteenth century and from which:

"We are reminded of the survival of the fittest, that the weakest go to the wall, and that all life, sentient and non-sentient, is but a life of battle."[27]

To reinforce this point, he later quoted from an article in *Blackwoods' Magazine* of May 1909 in which the phrase 'survival of the fittest', so recently coined, was used to suggest there never was, and never would be, an alternative to war, an idea with which Angell fundamentally if, as experience has since shown, optimistically disagreed. The *Blackwoods'* piece declaimed:

"We appear to have forgotten the fundamental truth – confirmed by all history – that the warlike races inherit the earth, and that Nature decrees the *survival of the fittest* in the never-ending struggle for existence ... Our yearning for disarmament, our respect for the tender plant of non-conformist conscience and the parrot-like repetition of the misleading formula that the 'greatest of all British interests is peace' ... must inevitably give to any people who covet our wealth and our possessions ... the ambition to strike a swift and deadly blow at the heart of the Empire – undefended London."[28]

Angell argued, perhaps naively, war should be prevented by economic and financial self-interest as, so closely were trade, credit and finance linked, the destruction of one country inevitably damaged the economy of the victor. His was not a lone voice in arguing this case. Winston Churchill, recently converted Liberal MP[i] and now President of the Board of Trade, made essentially the same argument in a speech to Welsh miners in Swansea on 15th August 1908:

"I say ... there is no collision of primary interests – big, important interests – between Great Britain and Germany in any quarter of the globe. Why, they are among our very best customers, and, if anything were to happen to them, I don't know what we should do in this country for a market (*Cheers*). While there is no danger of a collision of material interests, there is no result which could be expected from any struggle between the two

---

[i] Churchill was elected Conservative MP for Oldham in 1900. He crossed the floor to join the Liberal Party on 31st May 1904. He was elected Liberal MP for Manchester North-West in 1906. Appointed President of the Board of Trade in 1908 he fought a by-election (as did all newly appointed Cabinet members) and lost. He then fought and won a by-election in Dundee which seat he held until 1922. He was defeated by Edwin Scrymgeour, the only Prohibitionist MP ever elected. Remarkably, Scrymgeour won another three General Elections before losing in 1931. Dundee was a two-seat constituency and one of the successful candidates in 1931 was the Liberal Dingle Foot, brother of the late Michael Foot.

countries except a destruction of a most appalling and idiotic character (*Cheers*). People said it would be well worth their fighting for the sake of our trade. Gentlemen, it is never worth fighting for the sake of trade. In a month of fighting you would destroy more wealth than the successful trade of five years would produce if everyone worked 12 hours a day… What remains as a prize to be fought for by two great countries? Nothing but tropical plantations and small coaling places scattered here and there about the world."[29]

Churchill praised the good sense of the 'working classes' and damned owners of newspapers and politicians in their London clubs who would not do the fighting but who 'liked to stay at home and read about it'. There were but '15,000 persons' in Germany and Britain desiring 'to make war on one another' but, he went on:

"Even if those persons were as influential as one would think from the noise they make and the clatter they keep up, what about the rest of us? What about the 100 millions of people who dwell in these islands and Germany? Are we all such sheep? Is democracy in the 20th Century so powerless to effect its will? Are we all such puppets and marionettes to be wire-pulled against our interests into such hideous convulsions? (*Cheers*)."[30]

Sadly, the answers to Churchill's questions were: the 'rest' do not count; the views of '100 millions of people' were irrelevant; the masses were, and are still, sheep too easily manipulated and deceived; democracy was (and is) powerless against the actions of a powerful minority; and the 'puppets and marionettes' too easily led into war. By August 1914, the peoples of all countries were persuaded armed conflict was the only answer to whatever the question might be, even if most did not know what that question was.

Of course, Angell's and Churchill's words on the economic and social impact of war, which so closely echoed those of Bloch from a decade earlier, were born out by the collapse of the German Mark after the war and the general world-wide economic instability which led to crash of 1929 and the Great Depression. But the power of competitive nationalism, militarism and imperialism drove such considerations to the margins, and the accepted solutions to the international disputes between the competing European powers were seen as only being resolvable at the point of the bayonet.

It was also widely accepted that, because of the huge economic costs of a European war, the conflict must be swift. It was for this reason that Schlieffen devised his sweep through neutral Belgium. The war must be, and would be, won quickly, a view shared by most of the leading military minds of the day.

But they were wrong. And a number of men with more imaginative, if more pessimistic, minds told them so.

ENDNOTES:
[1] Lloyd, H, *A Rhapsody on the Present System of French Politics; on the Projected Invasion, and the Means to Defeat It*, W. Faden, 1779, page 14-5.
[2] Chesney, Gen. G T, *The Battle of Dorking*, Grant Richards Ltd., London, 1914.
[3] Guggisberg, F E, *Modern Warfare or How our Soldiers Fight*, Thomas Nelson & Sons, 1903.
[4] The first of five verses of Kipling's *The Dutch in the Medway (1664-72)*, one of fifteen poems written for C R L Fletcher's *A History of England* (1911).
[5] Wilson, A N, *The Victorians*, W W Norton, New York, 2003, page 590.
[6] *Daily Mail, Scaremongerings' from the Daily Mail, 1896-1914: The paper that foretold the war*, 1914.
[7] Hansard, House of Commons debates, Sir Edward Grey's Statement, 27th November 1911, Vol. 32, cc 67-8.
[8] All quotes from *The Star, The Daily Mail and the liberal press: a reply to Scaremongerings and an open letter to Lord Northcliffe*, 1915.
[9] *The Times, The London Territorials*, 15th February 1909, page 6.
[10] Ibid.
[11] *Haig Diary*, 3rd February 1909.
[12] Matin, A. M. *The Creativity of War Planners: Armed Forces Professionals and the Pre-1914 British Invasion-Scare Genre*, ELH 78, no. 4 (2011): 801–31. http://www.jstor.org/stable/41337555.
[13] *The Times, Aeronautics*, 8th February 1909, page 17.
[14] *The Times, House of Commons*, 25th March 1909, page 7.
[15] de Syon, G, *Zeppelin!: Germany and the Airship, 1900–1939*, Johns Hopkins University Press, 2007, page 72.
[16] Angell, N., *Europe's Optical Illusion*, Simpkin, Marshall, Hamilton, Kent & Co., 1909, page 18.
[17] *The Times, House of Commons, 17th May* 18th May 1909, page 7.
[18] Weber, Thomas, *British War Propaganda and the Thesis of German Militarism. Friedrich von Bernhardi's Germany and the Next War reconsidered*. Unpublished thesis quoted in Rose. Andreas, *Waiting for Armageddon? British Military Journals and the Images of Future War (1900–1914)*, 2011, Veröffentlichungen des Deutschen Historischen Instituts, page 321.
[19] Bernhardi, Gen. F von, *Deutschland und der nächste Krieg* (Germany and the next war), op. cit., pages
[20] Robertson, J M, *Superstitions of Militarism*, in *Essays Towards Peace*, Rationalist Peace Society, Watts & Co., 1913, page 26.
[21] Ibid., page 28.
[22] The Nobel Prize, *Alfred Nobel's Thoughts about War and Peace*, https://www.nobelprize.org/alfred-nobel/alfred-nobels-thoughts-about-war-and-peace/
[23] Haberman, F W, ed., *Nobel Lectures, Peace 1901-25*, Nobel Foundation, 1995, pages 87-8.
[24] *The Times, Sir H. Campbell-Bannerman at the Albert Hall*, 22nd December 1905, page 7.
[25] Angell, op. cit., page 1.
[26] Ibid., page 2.
[27] Ibid.
[28] Ibid., page 16.
[29] *The Times, Mr. Churchill at Swansea*, 17th August 1908, page 7.
[30] Ibid.

2. Prophets without Honour

'It is easy to be 'wise after the event'; but I cannot help wondering why none of us realised what the most modern rifle, the machine gun... would bring about... The modern rifle and machine gun add tenfold to the relative power of the defence... and has driven the attack to seek covered entrenchments after every forward rush of at most a few hundred yards.'

Sir John French
1914, page 11

IN 1904, LORD ESHER DESCRIBED SIR JOHN FRENCH as 'The best soldier we have got'.[1] With hindsight, he might have wished to review that opinion had he read the quote above from French's 1919 book *1914*. Nevertheless, based on such admiration and support, French became the Commander in Chief of the British Expeditionary Force in France and Flanders for some sixteen unproductive, and increasingly costly, months.

Ironically, though a politician and courtier, Esher, with several others, clearly divined the likely nature of the next European war in a manner seemingly beyond the recently ennobled but clearly baffled Field Marshal Viscount French. Brett and others, both military and civilian, made clear, accurate, and well publicised, assessments of the way in which technology would impact the modern battlefield and the way in which the next war would be fought. The failure of professional soldiers to listen then contributed hugely to the dreadful and protracted war and the millions of casualties which resulted. Perhaps, had monarchs and governments been advised by their Generals of the nature and consequences of the next war, they might have been so appalled it might not have happened. We cannot tell. But warnings there were – and they were studiously ignored.

So, who were these 'Prophets without honour' who forecast the static, grinding misery of the Western Front? And why were their warnings not treated seriously?

IN 1899 A SIX-VOLUME BOOK originally entitled *Budushchaya Voina* was published in France as *La Guerre Future; aux points de vue technique, economique et politique*. Its author was the variously named Jan Bogumił (Gotlib) Bloch, Ivan Stanislavovich Bloch or, as he is best known in the West, Jean de Bloch.

A Jew, he was born on 24th June 1836, the seventh of nine children of Selim and Fryderyka Bloch. His father was a minor textile producer and the family lived in the city of Radom in modern central Poland. At fourteen he moved to Warsaw to work in the bank of the Jewish family Toeplitz. In the space of six years Bloch converted from Judaism to join the Reformed Calvinist Church and then, aged twenty, to Catholicism. In the same year he moved to the Russian capital, St Petersburg, for eight years during which time he laid the foundations of his considerable fortune by investing in new technologies, most especially the underdeveloped railways of the Russian Empire. In his mid-20s, this remarkable young man became a sub-contractor for the construction of the Warsaw to St Petersburg railway line alongside a Russian industrialist, Ryszard Skvorcov. He began to move in increasingly elevated circles, earning the soubriquet 'King of the Railways', and was soon within the orbit of the Tsar himself. Perhaps his key achievement was the building of the railway which connected the main Russian/Polish textile centre of Łódź, 100 kms west of Warsaw, to the Polish, Russian and European rail network via a line to Koluszki which linked into the Warsaw to Vienna line. Bloch was just 29 when the first trains arrived in the brand new Łódź station.[2] Unusually for an ethnic Jew in anti-Semitic 19th Century Russia, he became a Russian Councillor of State and, in 1876, was appointed Chairman of the Committee of Representatives of Railroads of the Empire and the Kingdom of Poland.

He married Emilia, niece of another Jewish businessman, Leopold Stanisław Kronenberg from Warsaw. He later broke with his father-in-law over Polish nationalism. Kronenberg helped finance the bloody and crippling 1863 Polish uprising. Bloch, on the other hand, favoured an accommodation with the Russian Empire over a romantic restoration of the links between Poland and Lithuania first forged in 1386 when Grand Duke Władysław II Jagiełło of Lithuania married Queen Jadwiga of Poland. In this, Bloch's antipathy to the concept of solving disputes through conflict was an indicator of things to come.

In 1878, Bloch's multi-volume work entitled *The impact of railways on the economic conditions of Russia (Wpływ dróg żelaznych na stan ekonomiczny Rosji)* won 1st Prize at the *Geographical Congress* in Paris. In 1891, a second multi-volume work was published: *A Social History of Russo-Polish Jewry in the Late Imperial Period* though most were lost in a fire. A leading investor, along with Kronenberg, he helped found the *Bank Handlowy w Warszawie* in 1870 which, by 1914, was the largest privately-owned bank in Poland and a major player in commerce and trade between the Russian Empire and Western Europe. According to Michael Howard in *Men Against Fire*, Bloch was no mere financier but a global financial player and 'an entrepreneur almost on the scale of the Rothschilds in Western Europe or Carnegie in the United States', although Kronenberg was by far the wealthier of the two.[3]

Bloch was also a philanthropist, helping to found and fund the *Emperor Nicolas II Technology Polytechnic (Instytut Politechniczny im. Cara Mikołaja II)* in Warsaw in 1897[i] (now part of the *Politechnika Warszawska*), a children's hospital and a Jewish library amongst other charitable acts. Although a convert to Catholicism, Bloch continuously supported the Jewish communities of Poland and Russia, even as discrimination against Jews steadily increased across the Russian Empire after the elevation of the reactionary Tsar Alexander III in 1881, whose reign was scarred by several vicious pogroms not only in Russia-proper but also in Warsaw.

A banker and a railroad man, Bloch helped develop the railway systems of both Russia and his Russian-occupied homeland of Poland and, as President of the Kiev-Brest[ii] Railway Company, he was involved in the transportation of troops, military supplies and even the Tsar during the Russo-Turkish War of 1877-8. Although he never gained direct military experience, his indirect involvement in this war gave him an insight into both military logistics and the military mind. This latter experience proved most instructive:

---

[i] Bloch joined a 5-man commission in creating a Polytechnic in October 1897. It opened in the old Union tobacco factory at *Marszałkowska Street 81* in 1898.

[ii] Brest-Litovsk, now Brest, Belarus. The railway from Kiev to Brest-Litovsk was completed in 1873. It west via Bialystok to Grajewo then on the East Prussian border.

"I entered into conversation with the Generals *à la suite*, and amongst other topics we discussed the prospects of the future war. The Generals foresaw its course, consummation and duration distinctly. 'Well, and what are you going to do,' one of them asked me, 'after you have escorted us to our destination?' 'I shall go off to Karlsbad and take the waters there,' I answered. 'You surely don't mean it! Why we shall be coming back to St. Petersburg too soon to permit of your going so far away. We shall return in two or three weeks from now.' 'What?' I exclaimed, 'you already foresee the moment of your return?' 'Certainly we do. You see our expedition will resolve itself into a mere military promenade'. Less optimistic than the Generals, I repaired to Karlsbad without present hesitation or subsequent regret, for events showed me that I was not mistaken in my forecast.

I was not surprised that the campaign should have lasted a twelve month. What was far more astonishing to me was the belief fondly cherished by specialists who had facts, figures and reasoning powers to guide them, that they would decide the issue by a simple military walk over. For the mobilised forces amounted to no more than one third of what was absolutely indispensable. There were other unpleasant surprises in store for them, which forethought and freedom from bias would have enabled them to foresee and ward off. Thus they paid a terrible price for the needless repetition of the lesson taught by the 48,000 Germans of the Franco-Prussian Campaign, that entrenchments impart a power of resistance to the defence out of all seeming proportion to numbers[i].

That lesson had not been lost on Osman Pasha. This general was no carefully trained nursling of a great military academy, no scientific strategist; he was, in fact, a mere barbarian as compared to his opponents. But, on the other hand, he was a man with open eyes and unbiased mind. He profited by the painful experience of the French troops in 1870, constructed an entrenched position around Plevna, and for four months held in check a Russian force four times more numerous than his own. The first onslaught against this common-sense soldier cost the attacking force 36 per cent of the men engaged. That result should have sufficed to prove the point and render further trials superfluous. But it is easier to kill than to convince, and a second effort was made, which ended in 26 per cent of the Russian assailants being cut down. And, as if that proved nothing in particular, a third time our soldiers were led to the attack and left 20 per cent of their number on the field. And the chiefs who thus ignored the advantages of entrenchments, had not a single spade or other trenching tool in the army. Bayonets had to take their place.

This appalling loss of life was not the result of miscalculation or of belief in a mistaken theory. It was the outcome of narrow prejudice, and of an irrational faith in worthless traditions."[4]

---

[i] Bloch is referring to the Battle of the Lisaine (also known as the Battle of Héricourt or the *Lizaine* in France) 15th-17th January 1871.

Plevna's garrison which, at its maximum, totalled 40,000 men, resisted 150,000 Russian and Rumanian soldiers for over twenty weeks (19th July – 10th December 1877) in spite of the Russian forces having an overwhelming preponderance of artillery. This was predominantly field artillery, however, and had little appreciable effect, either on the entrenched Turkish troops bottled up in Plevna or on their far inferior but well protected batteries:

> "The Russian artillery seldom found an opportunity to fire on troops not under cover; the fire was mostly directed against lines of infantry under natural cover, against rifle trenches or more or less regular entrenchments, and the fire had hardly any effect."[5]

Four assaults on the town resulted in a casualty ratio of 4:1 in favour of the Turks[i]. After each assault, the Turks increased the quality and complexity of their defences. The first attack on 19th-20th July saw the Russians repulsed with a loss of 2,900 officers and men, nearly a third of those involved. The second, ten days later, against a reinforced and better fortified Ottoman Army, cost 7,500 troops or c. 25% of those involved. Turkish losses are estimated at between 1,500 and 2,000. The third attack, during which the combined Russian-Rumanian Army held a numerical advantage of four to one, cost the attackers at least 20,000 men against Turkish losses of c. 5,000. Thereafter, commanded by the German-born Russian General Franz Eduard *Graf* von Tottleben, who led the defence of Sevastopol during the Crimean War, the town was surrounded and invested and, after a failed break-out on 9th December, Osman Pasha surrendered the town and his army.

Although defeated, the Turks' gallant resistance at Plevna rallied Western European sentiment behind them when the war ended. The survival of the garrison, however, pointed out the need for the plunging fire and heavier shells of the howitzer, a point taken on board by the German Army. Others, especially France, responded to this development with surprising sloth.

From exposure to such blinkered military obstinacy Bloch quickly developed a low opinion of the intelligence and ability of the average army officer and of the conduct of their preferred 'profession':

> "Military science has from time immemorial been a book with seven seals, which none but the duly initiated were deemed worthy to open. Institutions of the Army, like those of the Church, were taken under the protecting wing of the State and flourished all the more luxuriantly in the shade. It was the duty of the masses to pay the bill in men and money, and the privilege of governments or monarchs to spend or misspend both, according to the lights of their reason or the vagaries of their will. Criticism of the means employed and discussion of the ends aimed at were alike forbidden to the outsider. It is hardly credible, and yet it is a historic fact, that no priestly caste, since the days of the Pharaohs, has managed to remain so exclusive, so powerful and so secret as the men whose profession it is to kill or be killed."[6]

---

[i] 40,000 killed and wounded Russians/Rumanians against 10,000 Turks (excludes Turkish PoWs, many of whom died in the snow when taken into captivity).

The actions of this 'priestly caste' then pre-occupied Bloch for the rest of his life as his concerns turned to the growing likelihood of a major European war triggered by the competing interests of the various empires which currently ruled most of the continent and large tracts of the world.

IN 1894, RUSSIA FORMALLY ENTERED into an alliance with France[i] intended to counter the strength of the central European Triple Alliance of the German and Austro-Hungarian empires and Italy. Its main purpose was to ensure mutually supportive action should any member of the Triple Alliance mobilise its army. If such an event occurred then each country undertook to attack Germany, seen as the strongest partner of the Alliance.

Bloch was certain Poland, part of the Russian Empire, would be a major battlefield in a war between the Triple Alliance and Double Entente. Warsaw might be besieged and, with his expertise as an economist and statistician, he investigated how long the city might resist. His investigations then included not just the fate of Warsaw but the countries involved – Russia, France, Germany, and Austro-Hungary. It became a five volume, all-embracing work about a European war, covering strategy and tactics, armaments, industry, transport, the civilian population, food supply, the economy and, finally, how such conflicts might be peacefully resolved. He read widely, consulted military men of all sides as well as politicians, government officials, economists and others and set up a research institute at *Marszałkowska Street 154* located near its junction with *Królewska Street* in the heart of old Warsaw.[ii]

Bloch was a firepower theorist. He believed modern high-powered, quick-firing weapons would overwhelm the human element on the battlefield. Thus, the threat of mutual destruction created by the power of modern armaments, i.e. the quick-firing, smokeless rifle and field artillery piece, *should* make war between the major European states impossible as the casualty rates, economic and social dislocation, and sheer ruinous cost would bring about the destruction of the regimes of the losers and the bankruptcy of those who 'won'. This latter point was a fact previously noted by *The Times* in 1898 when discussing the planned manoeuvres of that summer:

---

[i] A secret German/Russian Re-Insurance Treaty of June 1887 lapsed in 1890. The treaty had two main conditions, i.e. if Germany was attacked by France, or Russia by Austria-Hungary, then the other would remain neutral in spite of existing treaty arrangements. Were Germany or Russia to instigate military action then existing treaty arrangements would hold good. Germany also agreed to remain neutral if Russia undertook any actions against the Ottoman Empire as far as control of the Bosphorus and Dardanelles were concerned. A Russo-French Rapprochement followed in 1891. Formalised in 1892, it included a military convention agreeing on mutual military aid were either attacked by Germany.

[ii] Named after Grand Marshal of the Crown Franciszek Bieliński (1683–1766), it was destroyed during the 1944 Warsaw Uprising as was *Królewska* (Royal) *Street*. It is one of the main thoroughfares of modern Warsaw [*Source*: Mandeles, M D, *The Future of War: Organizations as Weapons*, Potomac Books, 2005, footnote page 37].

"Ask any candidate in a military examination to forecast the general course of modern war, and he will in his reply lay stress on the fact that owing to the cost wars must be short, otherwise national bankruptcy will result."[7]

In addition to the longer-term results of war, Bloch noted that the conscription of mass, citizen armies, a replica of the emergency *Levée en masse* mobilised by Lazare Carnot[i] in 1793 to defend revolutionary France against the First Coalition and continued by Napoleon in the raising of the large armies needed to conquer Europe and then defend France, changed the nature of war and threatened the societies and economies of both the combatants as well as those countries with which they habitually traded:

"A relatively short time ago an army was a body of men set apart for a special purpose; it was not the entire adult male population. The pursuit of arms was a career to which a man devoted his whole life, not one of the many burdens of citizenship… All these conditions are now radically changed. The romance of war has vanished into thin air with its gaudy uniforms, unfurled banners, and soul-stirring music. Military operations have become as prosaic as ore-smelting, and far less respectable. Armies of today are not composed of gallant, jovial cavaliers, but of entire peoples who curse the fate that compels them to abandon their trades, industries and professions, thus depriving their families of help and throwing an enormous extra burden upon the State which has to maintain them in idleness at a time when the sources of public revenue are drying up and the necessities of life are more costly than before. The economic aspect of the matter has become formidable, because international. The belligerents suffer more than their neighbours; but all other nations are likewise affected by the stagnation of trade and the slackness of industry."[8]

Unless, like the USA, one stands aloof and, instead, profits from supplying, at inflated cost, often sub-standard arms, and ammunition. Then wars fought by others become rather profitable for the private sector, as is the case now.

Waiting in the wings to take advantage of the ensuing military, social, economic, and political collapse were the socialists, anarchists, and revolutionaries whom Bloch clearly feared – men who offered simplistic and, invariably, totalitarian solutions to the new world order thus created. If, therefore, war was not in the interests of any current government then, Bloch suggested, the huge and growing sums of money currently being spent on arms development and purchase, and on the maintenance of enormous armies and navies, could be better spent on the social and economic development of the various countries, before

---

[i] Lazare Nicolas Marguerite, Count Carnot (1753-1823), an Army engineer elected to the *Committee of Public Safety* in 1793 with France threatened with invasion by the First Coalition. He increased the size of the Revolutionary Army to 645,000 in mid-1793 by means of quotas imposed on each *département*. The *Levée en masse* was declared on 23rd August. This required all unmarried able-bodied men to join the army which increased in size to 1.5 million. Carnot had a major impact on training, tactics, and supply of the Revolutionary and Napoleonic armies. Minister of the Interior during the 100 days in 1815 and a brilliant mathematician, he instituted compulsory education for all citizens.

the strains placed on these economies caused by this late 19th Century Arms Race started to create social and political problems of their own. It is a thesis as appropriate to the modern world as it was to *fin de siècle* Europe.

Towards the end of the 1890s Bloch's ideas found their way to the court of Tsar Nicholas II and they struck a chord with the Tsar and Tsarina, as well as several Russian political and military leaders. Russia had fallen behind in the development of quick-firing weapons, e.g. the revolutionary French 75-mm field gun, and, as a result, the nation's leaders were interested, if only for reasons of expediency, in finding some means of slowing down the rate of development of the armed forces of its competitors. The result of such self-interest was that Nicholas proposed an international peace conference be convened at The Hague in the Netherlands. Held over ten weeks in the summer of 1899 (and attended and addressed by Bloch), the conference, conducted in an atmosphere of general if not universal good will, resulted in *The Hague Convention* of 1899 signed on 29th July.

The international agreement came under six main headings:

1. Pacific Settlement of International Disputes;
2. Laws and Customs of War;
3. The Adaptation to Maritime Warfare of the Principles of the Geneva Convention of 1864; and declarations on the
4. Launching of Projectiles and Explosives from Balloons;
5. Use of Projectiles the Object of which is the Diffusion of Asphyxiating or Deleterious Gases; and the
6. Use of Bullets which Expand or Flatten easily in the Human Body.

The first four items were agreed by Great Britain, France, Germany, Austria-Hungary, Italy, Spain, Russia, Japan, China, and the United States. The last two were *not* ratified by the United States. Germany, though it voted for these initiatives, was a reluctant attendee. Peace-making was not part of their programme for global aggrandisement as the ease with which they abandoned Items 5 and 6 listed above early in the Great War rather indicate.

Prior to the Conference, Bloch wrote to the Austrian writer and pacifist Bertha *Freifrau* (Baroness) von Suttner[i], a friend, supporter and, later, author of *La Thèse*

---

[i] Bertha Felicitas Sophie *Freifrau* von Suttner (*née* Bertha Kinsky von Wchinitz und Tettau) was born in 1843 and died on 21st June 1914. In 1889 she published a pacifist novel *Die Waffen nieder!* (*Lay Down Your Arms!*), re-printed in 37 editions and twelve languages. She edited a journal of the same title (later *Die Friedens-Warte*). She founded the Austrian (*Gesellschaft der Friedensfreunde*) and German Peace societies (*Deutsche Friedensgesellschaft* now the *Deutsche Friedensgesellschaft – Vereinigte Kriegsdienstgegnerinnen*). It is thought she persuaded Alfred Nobel, with whom she corresponded for 20 years, to include a Peace Prize amongst those funded in his will and she was awarded this prize in 1905. She married Arthur Gundaccar *Freiherr* von Suttner without his family's approval and lived in straightened circumstances in Kutaisi, Georgia, for a time, returning to Austria in 1885 once reconciled. In a sad irony, through her father, *Feldmarschall-Leutnant* Franz de Paula Josef *Graf* Kinsky von Wchinitz und Tettau, and the Duchess's mother, Wilhelmine Kinsky *Gräfin* von Wchinitz und Tettau, she was related to Sophie, Duchess of Hohenberg, the wife of the Archduke of Austria, Franz

de Jean Bloch published after Bloch's death. He set out his concerns that the 'powers that be' would hinder progress towards pacific solutions to international tensions and underlined his worries about the world 'revolution' which might then ensue:

> "Referring to the approaching Conference, he (i.e. Bloch) observes that it has chiefly met with the approval of political economists and *savants*, as well as that of the masses, while it is more or less openly opposed by the great majority of the diplomatic and military world.... M. de Bloch suggests that it should be decided to order a preparatory inquiry into the two following questions – first, whether the time has not actually arrived when war would result in the mutual destruction of the combatants; secondly, whether the existing balance of power would not remain the same after a war, with the difference that it would be no longer possible to prevent the Socialist movement from leading to a catastrophe."[9]

In a hotel in nearby Scheveningen, Bloch was interviewed for *The Times* on 21st May 1899. The report reveals a humble man[i] keen to see international disputes resolved through arbitration rather than war:

> "M. de Bloch seemed to me anxious to keep his own individuality in the background, and makes very sparing use of the personal pronoun. He evidently looks upon his book as a Bible to serve as the foundation of the peace worship of the future. However, there is no trace of vanity about him. He is an enthusiast, but, in propagating his idea, proceeds by practical, business-like methods seldom employed by exponents of a new faith. He does not advocate immediate disarmament. What he seeks to show, before dealing with arbitration, is that a great war is no longer possible with annihilation on one side and ruin on the other...
> Later on he said that the continuation of the present state of things would bring about the triumph of Socialism in Germany, Communism in France, and would result in *'la misère'* for Russia herself."[10]

Before the conference, Bloch's *Budushchaya Voina*, was published in Russian and Polish, followed by French and German versions. An English edition, entitled *Is War Now Impossible? The Future of War: In its Technical, Economic and Political Relations*, is a condensed version of the first five volumes but still runs to over 350 pages. It is an extraordinary work full of tables and charts and startling statistics, even if the provenance of some is misted in obscurity.

Bloch died from an aneurism on 25th December 1901. Nominated in 1901 for the Nobel Peace Prize, he died before the decision was made, though a later prize went to his fellow pacifist Bertha von Suttner. His first memorial was the *Museum of War and Peace* founded in Lucerne and opened by his son, State Councillor

---

Ferdinand, assassinated in Sarajevo on 28th June 1914, seven days after Bertha's death. Bertha's likeness appears on the German 10 *Euro* coin and the Austrian 2 *Euro* coin.

[i] *The Times* described Bloch, 'little known before the Conference met', as having 'already won the respect and sympathy of them all (i.e. the 120 or so delegates)... Nobody speaks with more authority and impartiality on all matters connected to the Peace Conference' [Source: The Times, The Peace Conference, 21st June 1899, page 7].

Henryk Bloch on 7th June 1902. Ironically, after the most devastating war in human history, it closed in 1919 due to a lack of visitors (it is now a school). More lasting is the *Fundacja Jana Blocha*, the Jean de Bloch Foundation, based in Warsaw.

PROPHETS WITHOUT HONOUR

3. Jean de (Jan Bogumił) Bloch, Russia

4. Bertha *Freifrau* von Suttner, Austria

5. Reginald Brett, Viscount Esher, Britain

6. Lt. Col. Émile Mayer, France

There are aspects of Bloch's predictions about the nature of warfare which, by 1914, were wrong, but he wrote before the advent of the aeroplane or modern submarine, without knowledge of the impact of motor transport, and prior to the use of massed machine guns and the tank in a war between industrialised states. Although he foresaw the war as being long, slow, hugely costly and fought from trench to trench, even he did not envisage two lines of complex fortifications stretching unbroken from the English Channel to the Swiss border and resulting in a unique and appallingly costly form of siege warfare lasting for four years.

In addition, the enormous material and tactical impact of the indirect fire of field and medium howitzers was a lesser-known quantity at this time, although their use in attacking entrenched troops he previously forecast:

"In a work which has since appeared, the German artillerist, General Hauschild, studies this question (i.e. the use of artillery against trenches), and I have already cited what he said: 'Nothing remains for the attacker but to have recourse to trenches and earthworks. But it is obvious that for this the attack is in a much less favourable position than the defence. As a prelude to assault an attempt must be made to destroy the structures sheltering the troops in reserve, and this cannot be done without howitzers and heavy siege guns…'"[11]

Had Bloch survived to learn of the Russo-Japanese War, the siege of Port Arthur with its trenches, mines, electrified barbed wire, machine guns and heavy howitzers; 123,000 dead, missing, died of disease or wounded; the 12-day Battle of Liaoyang fought over three sets of Russian trenches at a cost of 42,000 combined casualties; the inconclusive 13-day Battle of Shaho fought on a front of 37 miles (60 kms) at a total cost of 61,000; or the climactic three-week long Battle of Mukden fought over a 90 mile (140 km) front in which 25% of the 620,000 combatants became casualties, then his views on the next European war might have been even more precise.

IN BRITAIN ANOTHER HIGHLY PLACED CIVILIAN interested in the military foresaw a similar future. Reginald Baliol Brett[i], later 2nd Viscount Esher, was a man who preferred to work, and gossip, behind the scenes. Though a Liberal MP for five years he was more courtier than politician and, by 1899, had been secretary of Her Majesty's Office of Works for four years. He was a *confidant* of Victoria and the Prince of Wales and a man who preferred power rather than responsibility (except to the Royal family)[ii]. He had, however, a long-term interest in the British Army and played a vital, if controversial, role in the reforms of this organisation after the shambles of the war in South Africa.

When news of the first two defeats of 'Black Week' (10th-15th December 1899) arrived in Britain Brett wrote to his younger son, Maurice Vyner Baliol Brett[iii], on

---

[i] Reginald Baliol Brett, 2nd Viscount Esher, GCVO, KCB, PC, DL, was born on 30th June 1852, son of Eugénie Mayer and William Baliol Brett, 1st Viscount Esher, Solicitor General, Lord Justice of Appeal, Master of the Rolls, and Conservative MP for Helston, Cornwall. Educated at Eton and Trinity College, Cambridge, BA, MA, and honorary LLD, Brett was Liberal MP for Penryn & Falmouth, 1880-1885. Appointed secretary of HM Office of Works, 1895. Involved in Victoria's funeral and Edward VII's coronation. He edited three volumes of *The Letters of Queen Victoria, 1837–1861*. Fell out with St John Brodrick, Conservative Secretary of State for War, over defence reform after 1900. Served on the Elgin Commission, dissenting from some findings. Offered but refused Brodrick's job by Balfour. Chaired the *War Office Reconstitution Committee*. Chaired the *Territorial Army Committee* in 1906. He acted as an unofficial liaison between Britain and France during the war. He died on 22nd January 1930.
[ii] He turned down, *inter alia*, the editorships of the *Daily News* and *New Review*, the jobs of Under Secretary for the Colonies, Under Secretary and Secretary of State for War, the Governorship of Cape Colony and the Viceroyship of India.
[iii] Lt. Col. Hon. Maurice Vyner Balliol Brett, MVO, OBE, Coldstream Guards and 6th Black Watch. ADC, Sir John French 1902-1912, and ADC, Lt. Gen. Sir J S Ewart,

13th December about the state of the campaign and bemoaning the death of Maj. Gen. Wauchope of the Highland Brigade (see page 327) at Magersfontein on 11th December. Five days later he told his son that, though the men fought splendidly, 'the tactical errors (in South Africa) have been awful'.[12] The paragraph which follows, however, is the revealing one, and one which showed that a few educated and intelligent civilians then had a far better grasp of the future of war than many supposedly professional soldiers:

> "This war will do two things – change our whole military system in England, and alter military tactics throughout the world. The old war of 'sieges' will begin again. It is clear that a direct attack, with modern weapons, against good and brave men entrenched, is impossible."[13]

More famous than either Bloch or Brett was H G Wells whose novels and other writings contained numerous prognostications on the future of the world and of war. In 1902 Wells produced a book entitled *Anticipations of the Reaction of Mechanical and Scientific Progress upon Human Life and Thought*. *Anticipations* for short. It starts by saying:

> "It is proposed in this book to present in as orderly an arrangement as the necessarily diffused nature of the subject admits, certain speculations about the trend of present forces, speculations which, taken all together, will build up an imperfect and very hypothetical, but sincerely intended forecast of the way things will probably go in this new century."[14]

Chapter 6 is entitled *War*. Drawing on the experiences of South Africa and on Bloch's earlier writings, it rehearses Bloch's opinion on the impact of the combination of the high-powered, long-range rifle and smokeless powder. This rifle Wells sees rapidly developing into an automatic, multi-shot weapon akin to a one-man, lightweight Maxim (i.e. the Lewis Gun of 1914), a weapon which would dominate the battlefield making both advance and manoeuvre slow and hugely expensive to the attacking forces.

He sees the battlefield expand until it reaches some natural border at which point the fighting becomes static, grinding, and impersonal:

> "… somewhere far in the rear the central organizer will sit at the telephonic centre of his vast front, and he will strengthen here and feed there and watch, watch perpetually the pressure, the incessant remorseless pressure that is seeking to wear down his countervailing thrust. Behind the thin firing line that is actually engaged, the country for many miles will be rapidly cleared and devoted to the business of war, big machines will be at work making second, third, and fourth lines of trenches that may be needed if presently the firing line is forced back, spreading out transverse paths for the swift lateral movement of the cyclists who will be in perpetual alertness to relieve sudden local pressures, and all along those great motor roads our first *Anticipations* sketched, there will be a vast and rapid shifting to and fro of big and very long range guns. These guns will probably be fought with

---

GOC, Scottish Command, 1914. MiD five times. He later edited his father's papers: *Journals and Letters of Reginald, Viscount Esher*, in 1934. Born in 1882 he died in 1934.

the help of balloons. The latter will hang above the firing line all along the front, incessantly ascending and withdrawn; they will be continually determining the distribution of the antagonist's forces, directing the fire of continually shifting great guns upon the apparatus and supports in the rear of his fighting line, forecasting his night plans and seeking some tactical or strategic weakness in that sinewy line of battle… there will be hundreds of little rifle battles fought up to the hilt, gallant dashes here, night surprises there, the sudden sinister faint gleam of nocturnal bayonets, brilliant guesses that will drop catastrophic shell and death over hills and forests suddenly into carelessly exposed masses of men. For eight miles on either side of the firing lines – whose fire will probably never altogether die away while the war lasts – men will live and eat and sleep under the imminence of unanticipated death.... Such will be the opening phase of the war that is speedily to come."[15]

Wells then explored Bloch's concerns about the impact this war of 'nations in arms' would have on government and society. Everything, private and public, must be devoted to the needs of the state and the war. State socialism, feared by Bloch and the ruling classes of Europe, would become the *de facto* form of government. Democracy would fade as the rights and lives of non-combatants be limited to supporting through their efforts the needs of politicians and Generals.

In detail, many of Wells' forecasts are unsurprisingly wrong. He heartily disliked the submarine, completely misjudging their use and impact[i]. His forecasts for aerial warfare, i.e. balloons attacking balloons, misjudge the timing of the arrival of the aircraft by decades:

"… long before the year A.D. 2000, and very probably before 1950, a successful aeroplane will have soared and come home safe and sound. Directly that is accomplished the new invention will be most assuredly applied to war."[16]

Barely a year later, on 17th December 1903, the Wright brothers made the first controlled, powered airplane flights near the Kill Devil Hills, four miles south of Kitty Hawk, Dare County, North Carolina. Otherwise, however, his view on the nature of war is positively Blochian and led, within a year, to his short story *The Land Ironclads* (*The Strand Magazine*, December 1903, see page 512) with its huge armoured fighting vehicles mounted on Bramah Joseph Diplock's pedrail wheel system over-running a traditionally-based army of hardy horseman and sharpshooters. Then, making up for lost time, Wells published in 1908 *The War in the Air: And Particularly How Mr. Bert Smallways Fared While It Lasted* (first serialised in *The Pall Mall Magazine*).

Writing at the same times as Wells in 1902, but with a focus more closely on the South African War, was one (or really, two) J-H Rosny, the pseudonym of two Belgian-born brothers who wrote together on a wide range of subjects but who, like Wells, often flirted with the *genre* of science fiction. Born Joseph Henri Honoré

---

[i] "My imagination… refuses to see any sort of submarine doing anything but suffocate its crew and founder at sea." [*Source*: Wells, H G, *Anticipations*, page 201].

Boex (1856-1940) and Séraphin Justin François Boex (1859-1948), they enjoyed joint Belgian and French nationality and, as from 1887, wrote prolifically, mainly novels, but also on science and history[i]. In 1902 they published: *La Guerre Anglo-Boër*. In their observations as to the impact of the fighting a key section reads:

> "When, later, European armies meet, it will perhaps be necessary to remember... two important points: the almost non-existent effects of (field) artillery against infantry entrenched in earthworks, and the difficulty of an attack in the open, even by dispersed infantry.
> The English (*sic*) soldier is brave. If he did not succeed in frontal attacks, if he let himself be demoralized, despite relatively low losses, shouldn't we conclude that all European troops would necessarily do the same? From then on, great generals will avoid all determined attempts (at frontal attacks). When the resources to outflank, to turn the enemy is lacking, fighting will take on the appearance of a patient siege..."[17]

THE IDEAS OF BLOCH, ESHER, WELLS AND ROSNY were not restricted to observant, educated civilians. Some military men took a similar view.

Chef de bataillon Charles Claude Joseph Nigote was born on 25th June 1833 in Ruffey-sur-Seille, *département du Jura*, and joined the *École Impériale Spéciale Militaire* as a volunteer in 1853. In 1856, he attended the *École d'application d'État-Major* and, thereafter, rotated between the infantry and the staff. In 1860 he resigned his commission, only returning in October 1870 to serve on the staff during the Franco-Prussian War, initially as an auxiliary lieutenant. By February 1871, he was the ADC to Gen. François Justin Paturel who, in 1870, commanded the *68e Régiment d'infanterie de Ligne* in MacMahon's ill-fated *Armée de Châlons* which surrendered at Sedan. Paturel later commanded a Brigade involved in the suppression of the Paris Commune. Nigote was promoted *Chef de bataillon* in the *58e Régiment d'Infanterie* in 1882 and, from 1884, spent four years on the staff of the *3e Corps d'Armée* before joining the *119e Régiment d'infanterie*.

Coming to the end of his professional career (he was placed in reserve in 1894 and died in 1902), Nigote published *La Bataille de la Vesles* four years before Bloch's book appeared. Its remarkable tone is set early on. On Page 5 he writes:

> "But a day will come when all these cannons loaded to the muzzle and all these machines destined to vomit iron and lead will make their formidable voices heard, and then battles will be fought compared to which those of the greatest past wars will seem like simple skirmishes.
> Who can say today how long this struggle will last in which every man likely to carry a gun will take part?
> Are we supposed to agree with certain thinkers that it will be all the shorter and that the results will be all the more decisive as the masses engaged from the start of hostilities are greater?
> I do not think so.
> With the great range of the new weapons, their accuracy, the flatness of

---

[i] In 1908 they went their separate ways but continued to write, Joseph as J.-H. Rosny *aîné*, Séraphin as J.-H. Rosny *jeune*.

their trajectory, and the absence of smoke, the opposing troops will attack from a great distance and often will only be able to approach each other after efforts which will require a lot of time and work."[18]

His belief war was a way of solving international disputes had evaporated:

"If we now ask statisticians to evaluate in cash all the sacrifices that the united nations impose on themselves for their defence of land and sea, in order to give us an idea of the expenses which will be involved in these excessive armaments, he will answer us by a frightening number where the millions of past times will be represented by billions.

We will be told that it is the very importance of these colossal expenses that ensures peace by virtue of the adage: *si vis pacem para bellum* (If you want peace, prepare for war). To see what the *para bellum* costs today, we must recognize that never have nations more earnestly desired peace. But, if that is so, it would not be difficult, it seems to us, to put an end to a misunderstanding which exhausts us and threatens to devour all our resources by pushing us towards such expensive armaments and the end. Such provisions would allow us to use our billions for more useful and more humanitarian works."[19]

In his book, Nigote's imaginary battle along the banks of the *Vesle*, a small river running north-west from Châlons-en-Champagne through Reims and entering the *Aisne* just east of Soissons, takes fifteen days at a time which precedes by four years the arrival of the quick-firing 75-mm field gun and the other modern weapons which the likes of Bloch believed would paralyse the battlefield. Nigote wrote:

"… with weapons whose precision is constantly increasing, there comes a time when the maximum destructive power is reached on the battlefield, regardless of the number of combatants. Trying to increase their numbers, at this point, is a most serious error, completely contrary to the laws of humanity, and more, contrary to the very principles of war. It is useless to bring into the presence of the enemy masses of men who cannot fight.

… I no longer believe in the classic battle, which takes place between sunrise and sunset. Nor do I believe it possible for a general-in-chief to manoeuvre these great invisible masses on the immense battlefields of the future.

Combatants will soon realise that any man who holds a smokeless weapon in his hand, retains his moral strength, and is master of the ground to the limit range of his fire. Then they will seek a natural sanctuary, that is, cover provided by ground, and, if they do not find any, they will create some with their pioneer tools. The (enemy's) fire making no more smoke or so little that it is useless to take it into account, who will know what happens on the battlefield? Where reconnaissance will be impossible. Where binoculars will no longer discover anything. And where the tethered balloons themselves will often give only uncertain information.

Neither the generals nor their aides will see where the action is.

Try giving orders in such conditions! As the entire engagement escapes command, direction is no longer possible.

The art of the high command will consist in bringing to certain places concentrations of large, perfectly organized masses; but, once the action has begun, the real masters of the battlefield will be the commanders of lower units, because only those will see anything.
From then on, we cannot imagine how long and indecisive the engagements will be! ... The war will soon spread over vast areas and drag on..."[20]

Later, in a section entitled *Ce que sera la tactique nouvelle (What will be the new tactics?)*,[21] Nigote comes to the conclusion, later endorsed by Bloch, Brett, Wells, Mayer and others, that even with the reduced power of weapons as of 1894, each army would still resort to digging labyrinthine trench systems and that the attacking troops, in order to avoid catastrophic casualties and a breakdown of morale, would no longer be able to launch dramatic bayonet attacks over open ground from great distances. Instead, there would come the laborious and slow digging of saps and parallels in an effort to get close to the enemy so that a final bayonet attack might prove possible. And even then, and unless and somehow the opposition's artillery has been silenced at the crucial time, the enemy guns would be able to keep firing up to and during the charge, whilst those of the attacker must either cease fire or lengthen their range to avoid the added terror to the exposed, bayonet-wielding infantryman of losses through 'friendly fire'.

STILL ACTIVE WITHIN THE FRENCH ARMY and writing prolifically from this time forward was another colonel, a contemporary and critic of (amongst others) Ferdinand Foch and Joseph Joffre. A man whose clashes with military orthodoxy, extending over thirty years, blighted his career.

Émile Mayer was born in Nancy on 8th January 1851[i]. His family was Jewish though noted more for their devotion to Republican France than their religion.[22]

---

[i] Mayer was the son of Chailly Moyse *dit* Mayer, *Commissaire des Poudres et Salpêtres*, and Flora Goudchaux, from a Jewish banking family. Her uncle was Michel Goudchaux, twice *Ministre des Finances* in 1848, and a friend of *Baron* Jacob Mayer, *dit* James de Rothschild. He married Débora Gabrielle Anna Dalsème in 1881. Four children: Cécile Émilie, Éva, Raymond, a sergeant in the *228e régiment d'infanterie* killed aged 31 near Maricourt on the *Somme* on 25th October 1914 (buried in the *Nécropole Nationale*, Dompierre-Becquincourt, grave 541), and Paul, *Médaille militaire, Croix de guerre avec étoile de bronze*, a sergeant aged 27 in the *354e régiment d'infanterie*, who was reported shot by the Germans when summary executions took place after fighting at Fontaine-les-Cornus (now called Fontaine-Chaalis) near Senlis, 2nd September 1914. He is buried in the *Nécropole nationale Le Bois Roger*, grave 77. As a Lt. Col., Mayer commanded two Territorial artillery groups attached to *81e Division Territoriale* in Picardy in autumn 1914 and along the *Yser*. He was later *Commandant l'Artillerie du 6e Secteur du Camp Retranché de Paris*. He was 'retired' in 1916 having expressed admiration for the German Army in a letter to a prisoner of war friend, Lucien Nachin. He hoped such sentiments might make Nachin's life less harsh. The letter, dated 3rd January 1916, was seized by French censors and he was removed on the order of Gen. Roques, *Ministre de la Guerre* on 27th April 1916 [*Source: Jean Jaurès cahiers trimestriels No. 136, Société d'études jaurésiennes*, April 1995, pages 66-68]. Émile Mayer died on 28th November 1938.

And yet his Jewish connections saw him temporarily removed from the Army in 1899 over his support for Dreyfus. Mayer, however, was one of those rarities in *fin de siècle* European armies: a free thinker unfettered by convention. After 1918 he promoted the use of aircraft and armoured vehicles. One Charles de Gaulle became a disciple and attended Sunday morning discussions at the home of Mayer's older daughter, Cécile Emilie, and his son-in-law, Paul Grunebaum-Ballin[i], in *boulevard Beauséjour* in Paris's *16e arrondisement* near the *bois de Boulogne*.

His father, Chailly Moyse *dit* Mayer[ii], was a product of the *École Polytechnique* and he went on to become an *Inspecteur Generale 1ere Classe des Poudres* at Angoulême. Emile followed him into the *École Polytechnique* in 1871 but not before he attended the prestigious *Lycée Charlemagne* in Paris where he was in the same mathematics class as Joseph Joffre, and not before he volunteered for the Army on the outbreak of the Franco-Prussian War. He then entered the *École Polytechnique* where he met and befriended Ferdinand Foch, having prevented him from being bullied by older students. Although they came to disagree mightily on aspects of Foch's pre-war military teachings, their friendship endured.

Mayer joined the *2e régiment d'artillerie* in 1874, attending the *Ecole d'Application de Fontainebleau* in 1875, before experiencing a peripatetic lifestyle rotating through ten domestic postings including a time as the *professeur de balistique* at the artillery school at the *camp du Ruchard*, 25 kms south-west of Tours. Though a captain within five years of joining the army, it was another 17 before he was promoted *chef d'escadron*. It is thought that Mayer's iconoclastic ideas and independence of mind failed to attract the necessary support of rather more conservative higher authority when it came to promotion.[23] He is described as rejecting:

"… the spirit of routine and the intellectual mediocrity so common in the world of the officers."

As a result:

"His nonconformism must have bothered the servicemen of traditional mind who saw in him a troublemaker more than an officer likely to get promotion."[24]

His 'error' was to suggest that one could not foresee how, and with what, the next war would be fought and that flexibility and the ability to deal with the unexpected was essential. This did not sit well with the crude certainties espoused by many of his contemporaries as the Army became increasingly fixated on the *offensive à outrance*, and the superior *élan vital* of the French soldier. It was an idea he repeated in 1909 when he wrote a piece for the journal *L'Opinion* on 8th May, 1909:

---

[i] Paul Grunebaum-Ballin: lawyer; socialist deputy for Saint-Étienne from 1902; to 1904, secretary general, *Parti socialiste français*; Chief of Staff to Prime Minister Aristide Briand. Briand, with Grunebaum-Ballin, was central to the secularization of France as *rapporteur* of the law on the separation of church and state (*Loi du 9 décembre 1905 concernant la séparation des Églises et de l'État*), fall-out from the Dreyfus affair.

[ii] The use of '*dit*' indicates an alternative but legal surname (as in 'Moyse also known as Mayer'). A mainly French practice, it died out towards the end of the 19th Century.

"We should teach the future leaders of our armies...that they will enter the field without knowing according to what rules the war will be fought.... Certainly, it must seem strange to refuse to foresee what the war will be like and to base on ignorance the education of the army, the command and the troops... To prepare for something well determined is relatively easy, but it is a question here of working with a view to a dark result, to a mysterious work, and by uncertain means."[25]

Initially, Mayer's written output was tepid and technical, but he also wrote under various pseudonyms such as *commandant* Émile Manceau, Abel Veuglaire, Anna Déborah d'Alsheim, Colonel Héricourt d'Adam, and Milès. Some of these were used as cover for works published outside France such as in the *Bibliothèque universelle de Lausanne, la Revue scientifique*, and *la Revue militaire Suisse*. Indeed, in 1898 he became columnist for the latter publication.

Things started slowly. In *la Revue scientifique* in 1882-3, he tentatively questioned the whole historic basis of the 'offensive' being the only means by which wars were won, a view not widely popular with his colleagues. In 1888 he got into deeper water by suggesting that the concept of the *offensive à outrance*, allied to the conviction the next European war would be one of movement, were both fundamentally wrong. Then, in February 1891, in an article entitled *Evolution de la Tactique* in the *Bibliothèque universelle de Lausanne,* which Mayer later suggested may well have influenced Bloch's research, he argued that the power of modern artillery and the complexity and strength of field fortifications meant officers must now learn the process of the defensive in warfare. They would not fight manoeuvre wars but 'wars of immobility' with the troops so extensively 'dug-in' it would be as if they were 'nailed to the soil'. Fighting from trench to trench, it would be more like urban house-to-house fighting but would take place in the apparently wide-open spaces of the countryside. As a result, he argued, what was needed was:

"... a general reorganization of the army, a different distribution of combat arms, a complete overhaul of equipment, a radical transformation of the means of command used to this day."[26]

This was tantamount to heresy in the prevailing climate of French military thinking. His article ended with an obscure reference but a baleful warning:

"Asked about the troubling secrets of the future, the sibyl could only utter unintelligible words; but these riddles are full of threats. We feel something terrible is brewing, and we know, alas! that the word of the enigma will only be found in the blood of numerous human victims."[27]

Matters came to a head in 1899. Despite having permission from the *Ministre de la Guerre,* Mayer published several articles on technical issues and about the organisation of the Army. Deeply embroiled in, and increasingly embarrassed by, the Dreyfus affair, and with Mayer closely aligned with the *Dreyfusard* cause, neither the Army nor right-wing politicians were about to take a relaxed view. In a debate in the *Chambre des Députés* on 16th May 1899 he was viciously attacked by Joseph Lasies, a virulently anti-Semitic, anti-Dreyfus deputy from Gers in the far south-west of France. Elected in 1898 as part of a 29-strong contingent described as the *Groupe antijuif* (most joined *Action libérale* after 1902), he accused Mayer, a Jew, of slandering the French Army. The conservative *Républicain progressiste* Camille Krantz who was, even by French standards, extremely briefly *Ministre de la Guerre* (6th May-22nd June 1898) in the fifth and last administration of Charles Dupuy[i], duly took note and Mayer was sacked. At age 48, with only a small pension on which to survive, Mayer was now at a loose end – but also free to say and write what he liked. He could, therefore, afford to be even more controversial. And, whatever his domestic and financial problems Mayer still had many contacts in high places: i.e. Joffre, Foch, Percin, d'Amade, Lanrezac, Sarrail and Gallieni.

Like Bloch and Esher, Mayer's view of the conduct of another European War was totally at odds with most senior French officers. In 1902, under the name Emile Manceau, knowing he would not find a technical military publication in France willing to carry the article, he published in *la Revue militaire Suisse* a piece entitled *Comment on pouvait prévoir l'immobilisation des fronts*, or *How we can predict the immobilisation of the fronts*. Re-published by *Le Temps* on 7th April 1915 and re-printed in a special monograph by *la Revue Militaire Suisse* in June, it became something of a sensation. In its introduction it explained why Mayer was so out of line with French military policy not only in 1902 but also in 1915:

> "… this officer became our collaborator in 1898, first under the pseudonym Abel Veuglaire, then under that of Emile Manceau… (in 1914) recalled to the flag, (he) sometimes stood out for the severity of some of his judgements and for the audacity of some of his proposals.
> Some of the ideas he developed were in flagrant opposition, in fact, with the dogmas of official orthodoxy, with the teachings of the *École supérieure de guerre* and the *Centre des Hautes Études Militaires*, with the doctrine followed by the General Staff of the Army, both in France and abroad, so it is not surprising that they were not welcomed by General Joffre, his classmate from the *Lycée Charlemagne*, nor by General Foch, his comrade in promotion at the *École Polytechnique*, although both remained in fairly close and fairly intimate relations with him."

The key section of Mayer's article reads:

> "This is the character of the defensive battle of the future. We see it as putting two human walls in contact face to face, separated by no man's land, and this double wall will remain almost inert despite the will to advance on both sides, despite all the attempts made to succeed.
> Unable to succeed head-on, one of these lines will seek to out-flank the other. The latter, in turn, will extend its front, and it will be a competition to which will extend the most, to the extent that its troops allow it. Or, at least, that would happen if we could grow indefinitely. But nature presents obstacles. The line will stop at a point of support, a sea, a mountain, the border of a neutral nation…

---

[i] Dupuy led five administrations totalling 22 months between 1893 and 1899. The briefest was No. 2 which lasted from 30th May to 25th June 1894. Blink and you'd have missed it. Dupuy was so large his nickname was *le pachyderme*, i.e. the elephant.

It is therefore due to external circumstances that the purely defensive war of the future will end. For example, one will be forced by the state of finances or by politics to ask for peace or to accept it, even without having won significant advantages or without having suffered decisive defeats. When we think of the daily cost of the Transvaal War to the English, let us assume the expense of maintaining this threefold, fourfold, fivefold! State credit is running out fast; war treasuries are emptied; on the other hand, all families will be grieving and worried... They will tire of seeing the armies getting nowhere, but still suffering painful losses. And that's what will end the campaign, rather than the great victories like those of yesteryear."[28]

Mayer drew a clear parallel with this new form of warfare and that of sieges, both historic and modern. But there were also differences:

"The comparisons with siege warfare, as I said earlier, are obvious to anyone who studies this new conception of military art. We see the assailant advancing slowly, digging his parallels and extending them, seeking to envelop the front chosen for the attack.
There are, however, differences which are considerable.
A defender surrounded and cut-off in such a place must exhaust his resources; he is neither in contact with the mass of the armies, nor with his sources of supply.
The lines that face each other are curved in an arc, not straight. He is therefore in a situation of manifest inferiority.
In the hypothesis which we have just considered, on the contrary, if there is equality in the armament, in the strengths and in the moral value of the troops present, it is obvious that there is also equality in their tactical condition. There soon ceases to be one party that attacks, another that is attacked. The two enemies soon find themselves, in a way, in the same boat. They are immobilized..."

In other words, Mayer foresaw siege warfare not in the sense of Metz in 1870, Paris in 1871, or Plevna in 1877, when each city was surrounded and entirely cut-off from sources of food and ammunition supply and manpower. The nine-month siege of Petersburg in the American Civil War (see page 52) was perhaps a better example. There, though the entrenched positions of both the Union and Confederate Armies extended further and further, eventually reaching thirty miles in length, Robert E Lee's position was, at least technically, never cut-off from what remained of the Confederacy.

Closer to 1914, the successful Turkish defence of Constantinople against determined and costly Bulgarian attacks in the First Balkan War along the 42 km long Catalça Line between Karaburun on the Black Sea coast and Büyükçekmece on the northern shore of the Sea of Marmara (just 35 kms from the *Hagia Sophia* and the *Golden Horn*) was an excellent example of Mayer's ideas (see Chapter 9).

After his enforced retirement in 1916, Mayer was free to criticise the conduct of the war, even if only privately, and his view was one of acute frustration. The succession of large-scale offensives designed to gain limited, and perfectly useless, ground instigated by both French and British CinCs, he saw as simply a means of frittering away men to no tangible advantage. He shared Rawlinson's view, learnt the harsh way from Neuve Chapelle onwards and which Rawly tried to employ on the *Somme* before being over-ruled by Haig, that the only sensible strategy was to kill as many Germans as possible with the least loss to the Allies, unless, and until, the 'immobilisation of the fronts' was brought to an end by some combination of new technology, overwhelming firepower, and collapsing enemy morale.[29] This latter objective, both at the front and domestically in Germany, was to be gained by killing disproportionate numbers of young Germans, to the increasing dismay and despair of the family and friends of the dead. whilst the war otherwise went nowhere. But, whilst *territory* remained an objective, as it did up to 11 a.m. on 11th November 1918, such an imbalance in casualty rates was never to be achieved.

Writing after the war, Mayer fulsomely praised Nigote's pioneering work:

"*The Battle of the Vesle* and *The Great Questions of the Day*, by Commandant Nigote, are writings worth remembering, for they contain many original insights and forecasts whose accuracy has been demonstrated by the facts when no one believed in them at the time he issued them. I want to take advantage of the opportunity offered to me to pay homage to the foresight of this bold spirit, the value of which was overlooked by his contemporaries and which subsequent generations ignored."[30]

EVEN ARDENT SUPPORTERS of the *offensive à outrance*, the philosophy which led to such carnage in the opening months of the war, foresaw the likely nature of a war between France and Germany. Col. Jean-Baptiste Montaigne was an advocate of the offensive and, in 1913, published a three-volume work entitled *Vaincre: esquisse d'une doctrine de la guerre basée sur la connaissance de l'homme et sur la morale (To win: sketch of a doctrine of war based on the knowledge of man and on morality)*. In Volume 2, *Enseignements et Conclusions, V – Les moments matériels de la bataille de demain (Lessons and Conclusions, V – The essential elements of tomorrow's battle)* one reads:

"… the battle of the future, using the speed and processes of siege warfare where the perfection of technique, the power of weapons, and the abundance of supplies, with the perseverance and tenacity of the combatants playing the main role, will no longer last for days and weeks, but for whole months.

The war of Engineers! The triumph of scientific warfare!

… the belligerent nations will cause all the levies of the country to move onto the selected battlefield. In other words, the wars of the future will be resolved in a single and gigantic battle, which will be fought near the frontier or on the frontier itself, and in which all the armed forces of the two adversaries will compete.

And this battle, decisive or indecisive, will bring the end of the war, because the combatant states will be unable to renew or even sustain the colossal effort.

And the murderous action will extend over vast regions; and the field of battle, if one designates by these words the total extent of the front… will encompass even the entire territories of the contending peoples. Because the battle will be in full swing in the Vosges and on the *Meuse*, but the reserves which will decide the victory will still be on one side in Brest and Bordeaux, on the other in Posen and Danzig.

... This unheard-of extension of the battlefields will no longer permit the energetic, constant and regular direction of the action; and the battle will resolve itself into an infinity of combats more or less important, determined by local circumstances and carried out almost independently of each other.

... So that it is quite possible that this great battle of the nations will degenerate into a barbarous battle of attrition where the victory will go to the people best able to fuel the fight, to those who will be able to throw the last soldier into the furnace. The battle will be decided by exhaustion. In fact, the tactics of siege warfare, to which we must compare the next field war, try to reduce the enemy to surrender by the progressive ruin and systematic destruction of all its resources.

And I am afraid that this brutal conception does not yet reveal itself to the minds of our high command in an encounter of this kind: twenty French army corps shoulder-to-shoulder along our north-eastern frontier, engaging head-to-head with about equal numbers of German corps, and straining and exhausting themselves in a series of dire struggles."[31]

OVERALL, THE INSIGHTS OF BLOCH, Esher, Nigote, Mayer and Montaigne into the nature of the next war were startlingly accurate. Bloch's assessment was that any war between the major states of Europe would be of long duration, slow moving, extremely costly in human and economic terms, and full of indecisive battles which favoured the defender. With labour and food shortages on the home fronts, the war would prove hugely disruptive socially, economically, and politically, and would, whatever the result, so devastate the combatants they would be forever changed. Such a war, in fact, would bring about the end of empires.

Bloch's tone, however, tended towards the didactic. He brooked no argument against his contention that disputes *must* be settled by arbitration as the alternative was the annihilation of the loser and ruin of the victor. Furthermore, as he argued early and often for a negotiated peace in South Africa, the initially somewhat favourable attitudes of British newspapers such as *The Times* when he came to prominence at The Hague in mid-1899 soon changed to irritation and downright antipathy. As a Jew and a Russian at a time when relations between Britain and Russia were not ideal, his policies and personality were all too easy to attack in the eyes of his opponents.

Having said that, one cannot argue with the final element of his analysis as it pertained to empire. By war's end, the German, Austro-Hungarian, Russian and Ottoman Empires no longer existed. The British Empire teetered on the brink of bankruptcy. Victorious France was morally shattered and financially devastated, partly by huge loans borrowed from both Britain and the USA, and partly because of the enormous financial losses French banks and its *rentier* class suffered when the new Bolshevik Government in Russia repudiated all international loans made to the Tsarist government. This default hit France especially hard as, since the 1894 Alliance, its banks had invested hugely in the Russian armaments industry, the more so after the disaster of the Russo-Japanese War which required the rebuilding of its entire navy and the re-equipping of its army with modern hardware.

It was, post-1918, the re-establishment of a capitalist regime in St Petersburg which partly lay at the heart of western intervention in the Russian Civil War[i].

Alone of the major powers, the USA thrived, profiting hugely from the supply of arms and munitions to the Allies and having seen all its major industrial competitors ruined[ii]. It saw the British Empire brought nearly to its knees, a job completed to American satisfaction by 1945.

Meanwhile, there was a revolution, a vicious civil war, and the breakaway of parts of the Russian Empire such as Bloch's precious Poland. Extreme political forces were at work in Germany and Italy. Their extreme right-wing leaders would, within a generation, take the world into an even more cataclysmic conflict than 'the war to end all wars'. The Austro-Hungarian Empire dissolved into its various ethnic components, leaving Austria a powerless and irrelevant minor nation soon to be absorbed by its resurgent northern neighbour. The Ottoman Empire was reduced to its Anatolian heartland. Domestically, the growth of organised labour and socialism in Great Britain saw the election of the first but short-lived Labour Government within a few years of the end of the war (1924), a brief General Strike in 1926 and the destruction of the Liberal Party, one of the old established political parties but the one which took the country to war in 1914.

After 'Bloch's war', politics everywhere changed, and nowhere for the better.

---

[i] This was an issue with long legs. In the mid-1990s the Russian government agreed to pay France €330 million to settle outstanding loans. This was in addition to Russian assets seized by the French after the war. This was not the end of the story. Many ordinary citizens were persuaded to buy Russian Government Bonds between 1880 and 1917. As recently as 2018, representatives of some 400,000 bond holders claimed they were owed €30 billion by Russia, a debt the Russians dismissed. Britain had, on the other hand, compensated British holders of Russian bonds after the war. [*Source*: Russia Beyond: *French still waiting for multi-million imperial debt payout from Moscow*, 15th January 2018. *https://www.rbth.com/lifestyle/327261-french-still-waiting-for-debts-payment*].

[ii] The USA had long taken a cynical economic interest in foreign wars. They greeted with *faux* concern the Russo-Turkish War, deploring 'the carnage and waste of battle', but then expressed a view that 'the greater the waste, the more there will be for us to do, and the more for us to sell'. Moreover, they wished the war to start ASAP: 'If Russia and Turkey were aware of the very great service they could do the United States by expediting their impending war, hostilities would probably begin at once'. *The Times* accused the USA of 'taking a purely commercial view of a war which threatens with incalculable miseries a good deal more than a hundred millions of the human race' [*Source*: *The Times*, 30th April 1877, page 9]. The Russo-Turkish War (24th April 1877- 3rd March 1878), saw the deaths by battle or disease of c. 300,000 Russian, Rumanian, Bulgarian, Montenegrin, Serbian and Turkish soldiers. The impact on civilians was greater still: 250,000 to 400,000 Turkish non-combatants died with 1-1.5 million displaced. 15,000 Bulgarian civilians were massacred at Stara Zagora by Turks between 31st July and 2nd August 1877. It is thought 10,000 Bulgarian females were sold as slaves. In the Caucasus, many Armenians were murdered by Turks and Kurdish irregulars and 300 Cossack PoWs massacred on 19th June 1877 after the Turks re-captured the town of Bayazid (now Doğubayazıt, Ağrı Province, Turkey), a town destroyed by the Turks in 1930 after a Kurdish uprising.

BUT WHAT OF THE BATTLEFIELD ITSELF? In what ways did Bloch envisage the next war being different to the last great European War – the brief and yet devastating Franco-Prussian War of 1870-1 which broke out on 19th July 1870 and which lasted a mere nine months and three weeks? In this war, at least initially, great masses of men in dense formations were blasted by rifle volleys and massed artillery fire. Cavalry roamed the battlefields making gallant attacks costly to both man and beast. Artillery was pushed up close to the fighting line to give the attacking infantry close support even at the cost of the men and horses who serviced the guns. Clouds of smoke obscured large parts of the field but showed from where guns were firing. The final victorious charge was still delivered with a few inches of cold steel stuck on the end of the infantryman's rifle. But battlefields were still relatively compact and might be overseen by a single commander, manoeuvre was still an option, it was possible to flank an enemy and send them in to helter-skelter retreat. Other than the new technology, it was warfare recognisable to a Napoleon, a Wellington, or a Marlborough.

Bloch's vision of the 20th Century battlefield was totally different to all of this. To start with, he believed attacking troops would see little or nothing of their enemy. They would face, as did the British in South Africa, an apparently empty battlefield. Bloch believed the defending force would no longer stand in large masses ready to give and receive volleys of rifle fire but would be entrenched, revealing only as much of themselves as was needed to fire their quick-firing, long-range weapon. With smokeless powder in use, the location of a rifleman would not be revealed after he fired. Bloch paid close attention to the South African War believing it provided concrete evidence for how a major European war would be fought. He foresaw large conscript armies locked in grinding, prolonged battles spread over huge areas in which the advantage lay with the defender. Trenches and redoubts would be essential as the more poorly trained the conscript the more they needed the confidence bolstering protection of such fieldworks. And, once secure in their trenches, and with a parapet on which to rest their rifle to fire accurately rather than shoot wildly from a standing position, even relatively green troops would be able to scour clean of attacking infantry 'the fire swept zone' between the two armies. They would inflict massive, one-sided, casualties on troops seeking to advance. Casualties would be enormous[i], the economic, political, and social costs huge and the impact on all sides ruinous.

This issue of the entrenched Boer in the early part of the war was partially the subject of a talk he gave at the *Royal United Services Institution* in Whitehall on 24th June 1901. The meeting was chaired by Maj. Gen. Sir John Frederick Maurice,

---

[i] Bloch's fears about the nature of wounds inflicted were challenged early in the South African War. A letter in *The Times* by Frederick Grenfell Baker (a photographer) described a small, high velocity bullet as 'comparatively harmless' as it 'creates no shock – that is, it has no 'stopping power' – and gives rise to but little pain or haemorrhage'. Also dismissed were Bloch's concerns about bullets, diverted by a bone, tumbling through the body. Instead, Grenfell Baker averred from the safety of his studio in Cheyne Walk, Chelsea, concerns about 'the deadly nature of modern weapons of precision' could be quietly put from one's mind [*Source: The Times,* Letters: *'Is War Now Impossible'*, 26th January 1900, page 14].

KCB, RA, then the commandant of the Woolwich District, and it was attended by an august gathering of senior Army and Navy officers and several ex-military politicians, amongst them three Generals (two with VCs[i]) and three full Admirals.[32] The title of Bloch's talk was *The Transvaal War: Its lessons in regard to militarism and Army re-organisation.* The talk, read by Col. Lonsdale Hale because of Bloch's concerns about his English, and the resulting discussions were not brief[ii].

One concern Bloch was keen to, as it were, 'shoot down' was the continental accusation that South Africa revealed a peculiarly British military shortcoming, i.e. a failure properly to reconnoitre the enemy's position. This was an allegation Bloch was keen to disprove even though sadly true in the early months. Indeed, such an opinion was reinforced by the early commander of the troops in South Africa, Gen. Sir Redvers Buller. In a despatch to the Secretary of State for War dated 28th December 1899 Buller commented on a small action at a bridge at *Zoutspans Drift* (*Drift* = ford) when some British troops came across (blundered into?) a group of Boers, with the British suffering several casualties including the commander, Capt. William Edmond John Bradshaw[iii] of the South-Eastern Company, Mounted Infantry, who was killed. Commenting on a report from the local CO, Col. Herbert Miles[iv], Buller advised the Marquess of Lansdowne:

---

[i] Gen. Sir Harry North Prendergast, VC, and Lt. Gen. Sir James Hills-Johnes, VC.

[ii] The initial talk went on so long a second meeting was convened on 1st July for Bloch to complete his presentation and for questions. The volume of questions required another meeting, on 15th July, for Bloch to reply. Maurice then summed up (mainly in favour of the attending Army officers and despite Bloch's detailed and sensible answers). It is fair to say that, though the mass of attendees disagreed with his thesis, the issues raised were taken with due seriousness.

[iii] Bradshaw was born in 1868 and joined the York and Lancaster Regt. He served in the Soudan in 1898 and was at the Battles of Atbara and Khartoum.

[iv] Col., later Lt. Gen., Sir Herbert Scott Gould Miles, GCB, GCMG, GBE, CVO, was the commander around De Aar and Belmont. Born in 1850, he joined the 101st Regiment of Foot (Royal Bengal Fusiliers) which, in 1881, became the Royal Munster Fusiliers. He became a barrister at the Inner Temple in 1880 before re-joining the Army, becoming DAQG, War Office, in 1889. AAG, Aldershot Command, 1893, and Commandant of the Staff College, 1898. Post-war he was the Army's Director of Recruiting and Organisation and, in 1908, Quartermaster-General to the Forces. In 1913 he was made Governor of Gibraltar. He retired in 1919 and died in 1926. His report stated: "For some days information had been received that a party of Boers was at Dalton's Pont, some 20 miles up river, and a guide informed us … another party was at *Zoutspans Drift* (the next above Orange River Bridge). Other parties of Boers were believed to be moving on the north bank of the river, from 20 to 30 Boers in each, all… from a Boer *laager* at Goemansberg… it was deemed advisable to strengthen the ordinary patrol which proceeds daily from here to the *drift*. Half the company of Mounted Infantry (South-Eastern Company), under Captain Bradshaw (54 men) and a party of Remington's Guides (16 men), under Lieutenant Macfarlane. were detailed for the duty, and Captain Bradshaw was instructed to proceed to the *Drift* to reconnoitre carefully, and to report the strength and position of the enemy. The party appears to have come upon the enemy somewhat suddenly… it appears that their

"I suppose our officers will learn the value of scouting in time, but in spite of all one can say, up to this, our men seem to blunder into the middle of the enemy and suffer accordingly."[33]

In the light of the Buller's previous failures on this score in the shambolic 1898 manoeuvres (see page 315), his comments were picked up by an outraged writer to *The Times* who described them as 'casual and irresponsible'.[34] Another critic of the war, Capt. Cairnes, wrote in his book *An Absent-Minded War*:

"And who is more to blame for this than Sir Redvers Buller himself who, as Adjutant General of the army for several years, had every opportunity of seeing that our officers were being instructed on proper lines, and were being made to appreciate the importance of scouting and the best manner in which it should be performed."[35]

Bloch, however, pointed out that his book, published before the outbreak of the war, forecast the near impossibility of closely approaching entrenched riflemen who could not be seen even after firing their rifles. He scoffed at European critics' notions the British should have sent cavalry squadrons forward as scouts. Bloch responded with a comment by Lord Methuen who:

"… declared from personal observation that 'it is impossible to sit on horseback at less than 2,000 yards from the enemy'."[36]

Of course, it was also impossible to see the man firing at you.

Bloch started by asserting that such problems being experienced in South Africa were not due to 'defects in the British Army'. Rather, and this would apply to all armies anywhere, they were caused by the 'impossibility of determining the enemy's positions'. Given the Boers' increasingly expert use of entrenchment[i] and the accuracy of their smokeless rifle fire, Bloch posed this question:

"…(if) another nation under compulsory service had fought the Boers, (would) the results have been different, and the war… over long ago'?"[37]

Bloch added into this query the question as to what might happen were the fighting to be transposed to the European sphere:

"For this reason I am forced to study this question from two points of view: at first, whether it can really be believed that a European Army, such as that of Germany, which has the best reputation, would have obtained more decisive results than the British Army; and, secondly, whether in case of an invasion, say of Germany by France, the invader would not meet with still greater difficulties than the British Army had to meet in South Africa."[38]

---

attack was in the nature of a surprise. The attack was pushed on very rapidly, and, unfortunately, Captain Bradshaw was killed early in the action… Captain Bradshaw was an energetic and valuable Officer, and I deeply regret his loss." [*Source: London Gazette*, No. 27517, 26th January 1900, page 512].

[i] Initially, the Boers dug trenches on the tops, or slopes of, *kopjes* (hills). Their fire was less accurate as they were aiming at men on a different level. Moving them to the base of hills allowed more accurate use of the high muzzle velocity, flat trajectory *Mauser* rifle and helped conceal their positions, making them less vulnerable to artillery fire.

Bloch went on to describe the consequences of the enemy's invisibility, quoting evidence from the Battles at Stormberg and Magersfontein where British infantry suffered heavy casualties by advancing 'blind' on Boer positions, and Colenso where, as was the common Europe-wide practice, field gun batteries deployed in close support of the infantry. There the gun crews and horses were shot down by long-range rifle fire and ten guns lost.

If this was the case in South Africa then what might be the outcome in a major European war? Bloch concluded that continental terrain allowed for even greater concealment of the defence and, with a far greater number of troops involved, the volume of defensive fire which could be poured into an advancing mass of infantry would render such attacks catastrophically, even prohibitively, expensive. In Bloch's view, the result of such a European conflict would be a war of trenches, both defensive and offensive, separated by a 'fire swept zone' (or No Man's Land) just as was later witnessed in Manchuria in 1904-5, the Balkans in 1912-3 and across France and Flanders from the autumn of 1914 to 1918. Even the availability of large amounts of space seemed not to have an effect. The war between Italy and the Ottoman Empire in 1911-12, for example, might have expanded into the vast open desert tracts of Tripolitania (modern Libya) but instead rapidly degenerated into trench warfare around the main towns and cities punctuated by appalling atrocities committed by both sides.

In the introduction to a 1914 US edition of Bloch's book there is a prefatory interview conducted more than a dozen years earlier by an English journalist, the late William T Stead[i]. In it, Bloch set out his understanding of the new battlefield:

"What do you mean by a fire-zone?"

"A fire-zone is the space which is swept by the fire of the men in the trench."

"But you assume that they are entrenched, M. Bloch?"

"Certainly, everybody will be entrenched in the next war. It will be a great war of entrenchments. The spade will be as indispensable to a soldier as his rifle. The first thing every man will have to do, if he cares for his life at all, will be to dig a hole in the ground, and throw up as strong an earthen rampart as he can to shield him from the hail of bullets which will fill the air."

"Then," I said, "every battlefield will more or less come to be like Sebastopol[ii], and the front of each army can only be approached by a series of trenches and parallels?"

---

[i] William Thomas Stead was a investigative journalist who edited the *Northern Echo* and the *Pall Mall Gazette*. This latter magazine was instrumental in the creation of a Royal Commission into slum conditions in London, and an investigation into child prostitution which resulted in the raising of the age of consent from 13 to 16. A pacifist, he attended the Hague Peace Conferences of 1899 and 1907. He was nominated several times for the Nobel Peace Prize. He was on his way to a Peace Conference in New York but drowned when the *Titanic* sank in April 1912.

[ii] The Siege of Sebastopol, September 1854-September 1855. British/French deaths from action/disease: 128,000. Russian losses c. 102,000 dead and wounded.

"Well, that, perhaps, is putting it too strongly," said M. Bloch, "but you have grasped the essential principle, and that is one reason why it will be impossible for the battle of the future to be fought out rapidly. All digging work is slow work, and when you must dig a trench before you can make any advance, your progress is necessarily slow. Battles will last for days, and at the end it is very doubtful whether any decisive victory can be gained."[39]

Bloch was not the first man to predict that in the next war troops would spend much of their time burrowing underground to preserve themselves from the new weaponry available. Maj. Gen. Sir Cornelius Francis Clery, KCB, KCMG, of the 32nd Regiment of Foot[i], was a veteran of the Zulu War and later fought in the 2nd South African War. He was also the commandant of the Staff College between 1888 and 1893. In 1875, while a professor of tactics at Sandhurst, he wrote a book entitled *Minor Tactics*. A comprehensive handbook for officers at all levels, it took under especial consideration the tactical impact of the Franco-Prussian War. The dramatic enhancement in firepower was the most obvious point and he remarked upon the destruction of the Prussian *38. Infanterie Brigade* at Mars le Tour on 16th August 1870 in this context.[ii] 'Fire', he pronounced, 'has become… the soul of the defence'.[40] The purpose of defensive fire was now to prevent the attackers from ever reaching the defensive position and not just defeating the bayonet charge. This fire was to be delivered from a trench which was now 'an almost indispensable provision for troops on the defensive'. In short, therefore, the then Capt. Clery as early as 1875 was suggesting digging-in would be one of the soldier's first actions on the battlefield and that, as Bloch states above, 'The spade will be as indispensable to a soldier as his rifle'.

Of course, one need look back no more than half a dozen years from the Franco-Prussian conflict to understand that temporary field fortifications would play a major role in the immediate future of war though, during the American Civil War and previously, it was 'Field fortifications' rather than 'trenches' to which Armies resorted to protect their troops. These temporary defences were usually breastworks constructed of timber and earth with no great depth of trench behind them as the relative lack of power of the musket and field artillery made this sufficient to protect the troops manning such defences. This would soon change with significant implications for both the offence and the defence.

The American Civil War provided numerous examples of the uses of temporary field fortifications as an effective defensive system, but none more so than the campaigns in Virginia waged between Ulysses S Grant's Union Army and the Confederate Army under Robert E Lee. These became known as the Overland

---

[i] As from 1881 part of the Duke of Cornwall's Light Infantry.

[ii] *38. Infanterie Brigade, 19. Division,* was supposed to take part in a joint attack with *20. Division* but orders for the latter division failed to arrive. The *38. Brigade, Infanterie-Regiment Freiherr von Sparr (3. Westfälisches) Nr. 16* and *Infanterie-Regiment Herzog Ferdinand von Braunschweig (8. Westfälisches) Nr. 57,* attacked over a long distance through a defile opposite Grenier's Division, *IVe Corps*. Casualties caused by the *Chassepot* rifle amounted to two-thirds of the brigade's officers and over 2,500 of its 4,500 other ranks.

(or Wilderness) Campaign and the Siege of Petersburg which together ran from early May 1864 to 25th March 1865 and cost, in total, some 160,000 casualties. The fighting started on 5th May 1864 around the Wilderness Tavern, the area from which Stonewall Jackson's *II Corps* launched its attack on the right wing of Hooker's *Army of the Potomac* on 2nd May 1863 during the Battle of Chancellorsville, and near where Jackson was fatally wounded by his own men[i]. Now, Grant was bringing his much larger force south to take the Confederate capital, Richmond, and to either destroy or severely erode the power of Lee's *Army of North Virginia* (full details of the actions of the Overland and Petersburg campaigns are in Appendix 1, page 845).

In every major battle (there were fourteen actions during the 50-day Overland campaign in which only six days were without fighting of some severity) earthworks and/or trenches were employed, none being more infamous than the *'Bloody Angle'*, part of a Confederate salient called the *'Mule Shoe'*, which saw ferocious fighting on 12th May 1864 during the two-week Spotsylvania Court House campaign. As Grant sidestepped south-east towards the scenes of the Seven Days Battle and the Peninsula Campaign of March-July 1862, the fighting continued, with large scale actions along the crossings of the *North Anna river* (23rd-26th May) before the two armies met at Cold Harbor, a battle which dragged on from 31st May to 12th June but is perhaps best known for the disastrous Federal attack on 3rd June during which Northern casualties outweighed Lee's by a factor of c. four to one. Cold Harbor was Lee's last tactical victory and Grant's reputation suffered badly when the casualty lists from this battle (c. 13-14,000 men were lost) and the entire campaign (55,000 Federal versus c. 33,000 Confederate) became known. Grant, however, won the strategic victory and was now able to besiege Richmond and the important town of Petersburg to the south.

The siege of Petersburg lasted over nine months during which field fortifications, mainly breastworks, over thirty miles long were constructed by both sides. Apart from 'position warfare' interspersed with various attempted attacks, there was also an example of a form of war which became commonplace on the Western Front – mining. On 30th July 1864, in an effort to shorten the siege (Grant had bad memories of the prolonged seven-week siege of Vicksburg on the *Mississippi* in May-July 1863), a large mine was blown under a section of Confederate trench to the south-east of the town. A division of Black troops, *4th Division* of *Ninth Corps*, was trained to assault the resulting crater but political sensitivities got in the way, with concerns about heavy Black casualties leading Grant to countermand the order they should lead. Instead, the advanced division was drawn by lot by Gen. Ambrose Burnside (the man who led the *Army of the Potomac* to crushing defeat at the Battle of Fredericksburg in December 1862) and *1st Division* was chosen. Their commander, Brig. Gen. James H. Ledlie, failed to

---

[i] He and his staff were mistaken for Union cavalry by men of the 18th North Carolina Infantry and he was hit by three bullets though none of them need have been fatal. His left arm was broken and was amputated. He then contracted pneumonia and died on 10th May 1863. With him died any lingering hopes of some sort of Southern victory or any form of favourable settlement of the war.

brief his men as to their course of action (though given little time do so) and he was later accused of being drunk behind the lines along with Brig. Gen. Edward Ferrero the commander of the Black troops who were now one of the follow-up units. The mine was successfully blown taking with it some 2-300 Southern soldiers and *1st Division* advanced slowly (they waited for ten minutes in their trenches concerned about falling debris from the explosion. This fell to earth within a few seconds. A similar delay, with similar consequences, occurred on the *Somme* at Hawthorn Ridge on 1st July 1916) and, instead of skirting the rim of the crater and either spreading out laterally or pushing through, descended into it. There they were later joined by men from two more Divisions and eventually Ferrero's men and what then ensued was, in Grant's description, 'the saddest affair I have witnessed in the war'. Confederate troops under Maj. Gen. William Mahone lined the perimeter of the crater, bringing up artillery too, and, in what he described as a 'Turkey shoot', proceeded to slaughter the white and black troops milling aimlessly around the bottom of the crater. Nearly 4,000 Union troops were killed, wounded, missing, or taken prisoner, against some 1,500 Southern soldiers lost. Burnside and Ledlie were both removed from command, though Ferrero, somehow, survived.

The American Civil War, along with the Franco-Prussian War, was the war most studied and researched by officers of the Army interested in such pursuits (the important military theorist Col. George F R Henderson and the Official Historian, Brig. Gen. Sir James E Edmonds, both wrote accounts of all or part of the Civil War). To anyone who attended the Staff College or Sandhurst, knowledge of events such as the Overland and Petersburg campaigns would, or rather, *should* have been widely known and appreciated. Apparently not.

A leading German theorist, Gen. Colmar von der Goltz, author of the seminal *Das Volk in Waffen (The Nation in Arms)*, also believed entrenchment a key feature of the modern battlefield and the spade an essential piece of infantry equipment. Furthermore, he foresaw battles lasting for days with the attacker attempting to wear out the defence and suffering heavy casualties as he did so, a view with which Schlieffen agreed, and the attempted avoidance of which was the *rationale* behind his gigantic flanking movement which was the basis of German strategy in 1914.

Such thinking persuaded Bloch that battles would be fought by huge, unwieldy conscript armies in which the abilities of junior officers and senior NCOs would be of vital importance as no senior officer could possibly have oversight over the whole battlefield. Inevitably, to lead and encourage inexperienced, under-trained conscripts into battle, these officers must expose themselves to the murderous fire of entrenched defenders. As was the case between 1914 and 1918, casualties amongst platoon, company, and battalion officers were appallingly high, making command and control of attacking troops difficult and even impossible. According to Bloch, young officers in the German and Austro-Hungarian Armies accepted this brutal fact of life and death even if, as yet, French battalion officers did not. It was his view they would learn the hard way. He also believed this reduction in experienced junior officers would lead to problems with discipline, to confusion on the battlefield, and to an inexorable increase in casualties and a concomitant decrease in morale. It is a reasonable approximation of the state of the French Army in 1917 when troops mutinied after the horrors of the Nivelle spring offensive.

As Esher too predicted, the battlefield would necessarily become the scene of protracted siege warfare where offensives proceeded slowly as trenches and saps were advanced towards the defenders' lines to minimise the gap between the opposing forces. For Bloch, however, the power of massed machine guns to dominate the 'fire swept zone' was not yet clear and other weapons, such as quick-firing field and medium howitzers, would have a huge but not yet fully appreciated impact on the conduct of the fighting on the modern battlefield.

The primary example of this latter gun type was the German *10.5-cm leichte Feldhaubitze* (*lFH* or light field howitzer). First introduced in 1898, as Bloch was putting the finishing touches to his book, it was developed partly in response to the artillery problems encountered by the Russian Army at the siege of Plevna during the Russo-Turkish War of 1877-78. It was at Plevna that the defending Ottoman soldiers dug actual trenches with a small parapet meaning a man could shelter below ground whilst under the fire of increasingly higher-powered rifles and artillery. These protected the defenders admirably from the flat-firing field artillery of the Russian/Rumanian Army which besieged the town for 145 days in 1877. Writing after the war, Clery stated that General Franz Eduard *Graf* von Tottleben, who was brought in to lead the siege of Plevna after the unsuccessful and costly attacks, calculated that each Russian field battery managed to kill just one Turkish defender after a whole day's firing.[41]

In the absence of practical knowledge about how this high-firing gun might impact the battle, the key weapon for Bloch was the modern rifle which, he believed, would scour the 'fire swept zone' of most of an attacking force as in many actions during the Boer War[i]. This war, however, was viewed by nearly all European military 'experts' as anomalous in the context of a continental conflict and any lessons learnt were almost studiously ignored.

Some eminent military minds, however, admitted to being perplexed by the likely nature of the next war. Bloch quoted the German military theorist Colmar von der Goltz in support of this contention:

"The future battle is a sphinx whose riddle nobody has yet solved."

But the voices of Bloch, Brett, Mayer, and the others were lonely voices in an international military wilderness populated by Generals convinced a new European war would be bloody but swift and decisive. Perversely, however, this belief in a rapid outcome was based on an agreement with Bloch's views on the devastating economic and social impact of a major war. It was a widely held opinion that the war would be over quickly because it had to be. No government or nation could afford an extended conflict. All the planning was, therefore, for another Sedan, a decisive early engagement, a crushing victory. Most thinking extended no further.

---

[i] A Bloch 'statistic' was that 400 men attacking across a 300-metre wide 'fire zone' would lose 336 men to 100 entrenched men armed with quick-firing rifles [Jean de Bloch, *The Future of War*, The World Peace Foundation, Boston, 1914, page xxvii].

For a time, however, some British military opinion seemed to accept Bloch's basic thesis. One might note the comments made by a special correspondent of *The Times* in reaction to the 1901 French manoeuvres held around the *Marne*:

> "One nation rarely profits from the experience of another until it is forced to undergo similar experiences. Last year I pointed out that France, far from profiting from our bitter experiences in South Africa, was so conservative that the French officers maintained that we were wrong and they were right and that there would ever be but one factor in the determination of a modern battle. That factor would be the superior weight of infantry driven wedge-fashion against the enemy... My claim was then, as it is now, that it will be impossible to get civilized men satisfactorily to face 2,000 yards of shambles (N.B. 'shambles' used in the historic sense of the old term for a butcher's slaughterhouse) and it is now at 2,000 yards that the shambles will commence. If savages, goaded into the attack by the fanatical belief that death on the battlefield will result in Paradise, cannot face a thousand yards of shambles, then civilized troops never will."[42]

What the writer then failed to suggest was by what method an attacking force might cross the 'shambles' of the fire swept zone to launch the final attack. Assuming he arrived at the answer eventually assumed by all armies immediately prior to and during the Great War, i.e. the digging of numerous lengthy trenches, parallels, and saps, then crossing the 2,000 yards of 'shambles' must inevitably be slow, painful, and involve an awful lot of digging. Within a few years such opinions faded as the idea re-asserted itself that high morale and discipline would get enough men across the 'shambles' to get to grips with the enemy. In this respect, Britain did not profit from its experience in South Africa, nor would it profit from the appalling experience of others in Manchuria in just three years' time.

During his 1901 *RUSI* presentation, Bloch lamented the blinkered approach Europe's soldiers displayed in the planning of their autumn 1901 manoeuvres. His talk raised laughter amongst the assembled officers when he referred scathingly to the 'Gorgeous uniforms with showy lace... and aberrations performed by the military tailor with cloth, leather and steel' on display at the German Army's manoeuvres.[43] But, more importantly, in these manoeuvres no account whatsoever was to be taken of the defensive methods employed in South Africa.

In addition, for fear of stifling promotion prospects, no senior General was to be embarrassed by a subordinate showing initiative or any degree of creativity:

> "The most striking features of the Transvaal war were the invisibility of the Boers and their entrenchments, neither of which will figure in the approaching manoeuvres. They will take place on ground where there is no trace of fortifications and which is well known to the combatants. The enemy will never thwart the plans of a general who has anything to say in the question of promotion. The formations will be the same as they were at a time when the range of rifles was but a 100th part of what it is now."[44]

In an interview with *The Times* Bloch recited what Lord Roberts and his Director of Intelligence, Col. George Henderson, learnt in South Africa and which would not then be applied in military exercises:

- dispersal in the line of attack was essential. Roberts ordered this to be six, ten and, eventually, twenty paces apart with lines 200-400 yards distant. *At the European manoeuvres attacking formations were 80 times denser*;
- an upright man in an attack invited 'certain death'. *'They had to advance crouching (but) this fact will not be taken into account'*;
- a man firing from a trench could not be discerned at distances greater than 150 yards (according to Lord Roberts) but, *in the manoeuvres, 'decisive volleys' (prior to a charge) were fired at distances approaching 900 yards*;
- again, according to Lord Roberts, battles would be resolved by firing at short ranges *and no longer by the bayonet charge*;
and, finally,
- Because defensive firepower now allowed troops to defend a greater area, Roberts argued an army deploying 65,000 men would occupy an area twenty kilometres square (c. 400 square kms.). *Given the size of European conscript armies, which were ten or more times this size, the scale of the battlefield would mitigate against centralised command and control.*[45]

He then quoted various estimates as how long it might take to conduct attacks on these enormous battlefields. The Prussian General Rudolf von Janson[i] reckoned two days, the Frenchmen Langlois five, and Nigote up to fifteen. But, as Bloch pointed out, attacks during manoeuvres were completed in hours by dense masses of troops led by officers on horseback and, at least with the French, to the accompaniment of bands, and with flags waving. It was still thus in 1913 and beyond into the opening weeks of the war.

THE GRIMNESS WITH WHICH CONSERVATIVE ELEMENTS clung to outdated methods of resolving conflict also came in for criticism. Again, Bloch was able to draw upon the comments of distinguished soldiers, none more so than Count Dmitry Alekseyevich Milyutin, the last Field Marshal of Imperial Russia who served for twenty years as Minister of War (1861-81), instituting sweeping reforms in the Russian Army in the aftermath of the Crimean War. For a 19th century Russian noble, he held remarkably liberal and progressive instincts. He left the government when the reactionary Alexander III took power after the assassination of his predecessor, Alexander II, the Tsar who liberated the serfs in 1861. Milyutin was a supporter of Bloch's work and, in 1899, wrote that his book was of:

"… immense and beneficial importance if it could exercise any influence on … the men who conduct the politics of states… But, unfortunately, there is no hope of it. The terrible consequences of the catastrophe which is to be foreseen will not make the stubborn fanatics of militarism swerve from the path they have traced."[46]

This is all, in many ways, a reflection of the dire warning given nine years' earlier by none other than Helmuth von Moltke, the man who directed the creation of the German Army and led it through it through three successful wars in the

---

[i] *Gen. der Infanterie* Rudolf August von Janson (1844-1917). Joined *2. Ostpreußischen Grenadier-Regiments Nr. 3*, 1861, and wrote a dozen books on military history and theory.

1860s and 70s. A member of the *Reichstag* since 1871, he gave his final speech on 14th May 1890 at the age of 89 (he died in Berlin on 24th April 1891). Ever since the Franco-Prussian War he had grappled with the conundrum of how the *next* war would be fought, as nation battled nation to the death. It was more than just an issue of two-front wars, or pre-emptive strikes, of encirclement and *Vernichtungsstrategie* (annihilation strategy), it was about the very existence of nations in an age of total war:

> "If war should break out, this war which has now been hanging like a sword of Damocles over our heads for more than ten years, no one can estimate its duration or see when it will end. The greatest powers of Europe, which are armed as never before, will fight each other. None can be annihilated so completely in one or two campaigns that it would declare itself vanquished and be compelled to accept hard conditions for peace without any chance, even after a year's time, to renew the fight. Gentlemen, it might be a seven, or even a thirty years' war - but woe to him who sets Europe alight and first throws the match into the powder-barrel!"[47]

Despite this, European Governments and Generals vilified Bloch and his fellow pacifists, their views were trivialised and ignored and two generations of European citizens paid the price. Our prescient Polish banker knew this was likely to happen. If there was a man professional soldiers disliked and distrusted more than a politician, it was a Jewish banker with ideas above their station:

> "The civilian who is free to ask questions about military matters does so at the risk of his political good name, and with the certitude that he will not be vouchsafed an answer. However patriotic his motives, he is frowned down as an impertinent busybody, and perhaps talked of as a friend of his country's foes. Even the citizen who has devoted himself with success to the study of military science, without any *arrière pensèe*, is rudely told that the ground he treads is holy and reserved for the initiated. It is thus that the Army is wrapped up in swaddling clothes and protected from the light of day."[48]

It was in this mood of blinkered indifference to the fate of the peoples of Europe the continent blundered blindly into war.

Post-war, Bloch's opinions were re-examined in a more favourable light. Basil Liddell-Hart remarked in his book *'The British Way in Warfare'* (1932):

> "...the only ground for surprise is that so few believed him (i.e. Bloch). For even he was thirty years late in his discovery."[49]

Ex-staff officer, British fascist, occultist, and military historian Maj. Gen. John Frederick Charles Fuller[i], in the final volume of *Decisive Battles of the Western World*, was more directly complimentary:

---

[i] Maj. Gen. John Frederick Charles 'Boney' Fuller was a military writer and theorist, a fascist, anti-Semite, Hitler supporter, and early advocate of the use of tanks. He served at the *Machine-Gun Corps' Heavy Branch* HQ, later the *Tank Corps*. Post-war he argued for the mechanisation of the British Army. He spent some years at the Staff College and was promoted Major-General in 1930, retiring in 1933. His later writing, for

"... among the many military theorists who appeared during these years (1870-1914) one was outstanding, namely I. S. Bloch, because he got down to the roots of the war problem."[50]

Going further, in *The Dragon's Teeth* in 1932, Fuller described Bloch as the:

"Only man of note (who) took the trouble to examine war scientifically and who made remarkable prophecy as regards the next great war in Europe."[51]

Tragically, Bloch's assessment that war in Europe should be 'impossible' because it was a direct route to economic, social, and political ruin was twice proved incorrect within 40 years of his death. But it must be noted he was saying war *should* not, rather than *could* not, happen. His books explained the nature of any war and its social, military, political and economic impact. He concluded it was illogical and against all self-interest for a leader to voluntarily expose their country to such enormous and devastating costs and risks. His analysis of the impact and outcome of such a war proved remarkably correct, but his faith in the judgement of politicians and the military to appreciate his analysis and act prudently was, and still is, sadly misplaced.

In the years after his untimely death international affairs and hardening national attitudes dragged Europe closer and closer to war. Indeed, between the publication of his book and the start of the Great War in August 1914, there were five wars involving European states: Britain fought in South Africa, Russia fought Japan, Italy attacked the Ottoman Empire, and two wars were fought in the Balkans involving, at one time or another, Greece, Serbia, Montenegro, Bulgaria, Rumania, and Turkey. There were also five major foreign policy crises which very nearly led to wars: the two Moroccan crises of 1905 and 1911 which might have pitted France against Germany and with Britain perhaps involved through the Royal Navy; the Austro-Hungarian annexation of Bosnia in 1909 during which both Russia and Austria started to mobilise their armies; another Russian-Austrian crisis of 1912 in which both Britain and Germany acted as peacemakers; and, during the Italo-Turkish War of 1911-12, the possibility of an Austrian invasion of Italy as advocated by certain leaders of the Austrian military. Several of these crises were averted simply because one or other side was not yet ready to fight. France, in

---

example the three-volume *Decisive Battles of the Western World*, displays sympathies for such as Mussolini and Hitler, anti-Slav racism, anti-Semitism, virulent anti-Bolshevism, and a dislike/distrust of such as China and Japan. He loathed politicians and democracy. A senior member of Oswald Mosley's *British Union of Fascists*, he was a member of the *Nordic League*, an extreme, organisation which, from 1935-9, promoted fascism and anti-Semitism in the most rabid terms. He was a guest at Hitler's 50th Birthday military parade. His commentary on both World Wars, especially his vicious criticisms of Churchill and Roosevelt, should be read in this context. One of the *Nordic League's* supporters, Capt. Archibald Henry Maule Ramsay, Unionist MP for Peebles and Southern Midlothian, was interned for four years (1940-44). Several others were interned/arrested when war broke out. Ramsey sued the *New York Times* for libel in 1941 and was awarded a farthing and had to pay prosecution *and* defence costs. Fuller was also a friend of the occultist Aleister Crowley, editing some of his books. He wrote *The Star in The West: A Critical Essay Upon the Works of Aleister Crowley* in 1907.

1905, recognised its current weakness and was dragged into conciliation and negotiation; Russia, in 1909, had not yet recovered from the devastating effects of the war with Japan in Manchuria in 1904-5; and Germany realised its navy was nowhere near the equal of the Royal Navy when Lloyd George's Mansion House speech in 1911 made clear Britain's support for France in the Agadir crisis. But, as the socialist writer Henry Noel Brailsford[i] made clear in his 1914 book *The War of Steel and Gold: A Study of the Armed Peace*, sometimes governments misjudged either their own or the opposition's strength and wandered complacently into wars:

> "A Power which has been forced by the deficiency of its own armaments to accept a diplomatic reverse, at once sets to work to beggar itself in the effort to recover its lost prestige. Nor does it always happen that a Power is able to gauge, before the decisive moment, either its own weakness or its enemy's strength. Nicholas II no more foresaw Tsushima than Louis Napoleon foresaw Sedan. A moment of national vanity, a passing caprice in which fashion amuses itself by despising the enemy, as the Russians despised the Japanese and our own Imperialists derided the Boers, suffices to make a war."[52]

Nevertheless, the Anglo-German Naval Race, the re-armament of Russia by British and French companies paid for with mainly French money, the friction over colonial interests in Africa, the continuing disintegration of the Ottoman Empire, and the rise of Balkan nationalism all contributed to the increasingly fevered political, diplomatic, and military atmosphere.

To many, a new war seemed inevitable. To some, it was desirable.

WHEN WAR CAME IN 1914 it was the culmination of two tensions, the first generated by the process of competitive northern European imperialism which dominated the nineteenth century, and the second the longstanding ethnic and military rivalries which had riven Europe over many centuries. The empires of the countries of the Mediterranean littoral were either gone or fast fading. The Spanish American War saw the end of the Spanish Empire in 1898. The Ottoman Empire was in rapid decline. After the loss of Greece in 1830, it progressively lost its Balkan provinces, with the major reduction in its European territory coming after the Russo-Turkish War of 1877-8 when the Balkans were carved up at the Congress of Berlin. Here, Serbia, Montenegro and Rumania were all recognised as independent states; Bosnia and Herzegovina were occupied by Austro-Hungary; and the autonomous principality of Bulgaria was formed. It declared full independence in 1908. Albania was, by 1912, semi-independent leaving the Ottomans with just Macedonia and Thrace of its erstwhile European territories.

---

[i] Henry Noel Brailsford (1873-1958) was a left-wing journalist and prolific writer who wrote for the *Manchester Guardian*, the *Morning Leader*, and *The Daily News*. He joined the *Independent Labour Party*, helped form the *Men's League for Women's Suffrage* in 1907, was opposed to the war and joined the *Union of Democratic Control*. Post-war he twice visited the Soviet Union, edited the *New Leader*, the *ILP's* newspaper, and wrote for *Reynolds News* and the *New Statesman*. He was a vigorous critic of both Hitler and Mussolini and denounced Stalin when Russia attacked Finland in 1939.

The major parts of these provinces were then divided between Greece, Serbia, and Bulgaria after the First Balkan War of 1912-3.

Great Britain, that Victorian imperial colossus, bestrode the globe, its worldwide empire based on the power of its navy. It is ironic that Britain would enter the war based on a treaty obligation to defend the 'freedoms' of tiny Belgium[i] when its own enormous wealth and power were based on the invasion of other countries and the spilling of copious quantities of native blood. Any pretence Britain was a benign presence in its far-flung colonies would have been robustly disputed by locals who survived the appearance of the numerous white, Christian, and well-armed invaders who took over their institutions, plundered their wealth and oppressed their families and neighbours. But, at the turn of the century, an image was created, at least at home, that god-fearing British men and women were leading benighted savages into a new era of economic well-being, peace, and progress, all under the benevolent eyes of the Queen Empress and a Christian god. Tosh, but still, apparently, widely believed in certain quarters in modern Britain.

Below is a list of all the British colonial wars, expeditions, and campaigns from the Indian Mutiny to the beginning of the war. It does not include multi-national operations such as the Boxer Rebellion in China.

Second Opium War	8th October 1856 – 24th October 1860
Indian Mutiny	10th May 1857 – 1st November 1858
First Taranaki War, New Zealand	17th March 1860 – 18th March 1861
Second Taranaki War	April/May 1863 to November 1866
Invasion of the Waikato, NZ	12th July 1863 – April 1864
Duar War, Bhutan	1864–1865
East Cape War, New Zealand	13th April 1865 to 12th October 1866
British Expedition to Abyssinia	4th December 1867 – 13th May 1868
Titokowaru's War, New Zealand	June 1868 – March 1869
Te Kooti's War, New Zealand	July 1868 – May 1872
Perak War, Malaysia	1875-6
Anglo-Zulu War	11th January – 4th July 1879
Second Anglo-Afghan War	1878–1880
Basuto Gun War	1880-1881

---

[i] Belgium became a constitutional monarchy in 1831 after the 'Belgian Revolution' of 1830 when French-speaking Walloons split with the United Kingdom of the Netherlands (created in 1815). Britain, France, Russia, Prussia, and Austria imposed Leopold I of Saxe-Coburg as King of the Belgians. Fighting between the Dutch and Belgians continued, the Dutch taking Antwerp in 1832 before its recovery by a French Army. The final geographic make-up of Belgium was resolved in the Treaty of London, 1839 (*aka* the First Treaty of London, the Convention of 1839, the Treaty of Separation, the Quintuple Treaty of 1839, or the Treaty of the XXIV Articles). The independent Grand Duchy of Luxembourg was formed from the majority German-speaking areas. Other parts became a province of Belgium. Both new states were to be neutral in all future conflicts. Luxembourg's neutrality was guaranteed by Britain, Austria, France, Italy, Prussia and the Netherlands, Belgian neutrality by Britain, Austria, France, the German Confederation/Prussia, Russia, and the Netherlands.

First Boer War	20th December 1880 – 23rd March 1881
Mahdist War	1881–1899
Anglo-Egyptian War	July–September 1882
North-West Rebellion, Canada	26th March – 3rd June 1885
Third Anglo-Burmese War	7th November – 29th November 1885
Hazara Expedition, Pakistan	October 1888 – November 1888
Mashonaland	1890
Hunza–Nagar Campaign, Pakistan	1891
Anglo-Manipur War, Burma	31st March – 27th April 1891
First Matabele War	October 1893 – January 1894
Mat Salleh Rebellion, N. Borneo	1894-1905
Chitral Expedition	1895
Second Matabele War	March 1896 – October 1897
Anglo-Zanzibar War	27th August 1896
Benin Expedition	9th–18th February 1897
Siege of Malakand	26th July – 2nd August 1897
Mohmand campaign	1897 to 1898
Tirah campaign	3rd September 1897 – 4th April 1898
Six-Day War, Hong Kong	14th–19th April 1899
Second Boer War	11th October 1899 – 31st May 1902
Somaliland campaign	1900-1920
Anglo-Aro War	November 1901 – March 1902
Tibet Expedition	December 1903 – September 1904
Bambatha Rebellion, Natal	1906

Table 1 British Colonial wars 1857-1906

The one-sided nature of most of these wars can be seen from the following sample numbers which include both military and civilian casualties:

	British fatalities	Native fatalities
Indian Mutiny	6,000	800,000
Second Opium War	170	2,800
British Expedition to Abyssinia	2	700
Anglo-Zulu War	1,900	7,000
First Matabele War	100	10,000
Second Matabele War	400	50,000
Mahdist War	48	12,000
Second Boer War	23,000	47,500
Bambatha Rebellion, Natal	36	4,000

Table 2 Relative casualties in selected British Colonial wars 1857-1906

While Britain busily pillaged the Indian sub-continent, the Antipodes, Africa and elsewhere, the now unified Germany joined Britain, France, and Russia in an urgent drive to expand its territorial ambitions, the principle focus of the first three being on the 'Scramble for Africa'[i]. Continental imperialists, jealous of British pre-

---

[i] So relentless was the European occupation of Africa that, by 1914, only Ethiopia (Abyssinia) and Liberia (which declared its independence from the USA in 1847, a

eminence, sniggered openly when Victoria's army failed to quell the insubordinate Boers in 1899. Prior to 1871, Britain's only genuine military concerns, beyond native rebellions and rumoured Russian threats to the North-West Frontier of India via Afghanistan, were intermittent fears of French invasion. These fears were replaced by deeper worries about German intentions as their *Hochseeflotte,* the High Seas Fleet, grew in size and power at the turn of the century. As a result, the Anglo-Russian-French *Triple Entente* had to overcome long-standing and conflicting imperial ambitions in the face of a greater threat from the militaristic industrial powerhouse which was Wilhelmine Germany.

Standing aloof from the unseemly colonial scramble of the imperialists from the old world was the 'great democracy' of the United States. Hypocritical then as now, the USA was busily extending its own imperial ambitions with the brief war with Spain in 1898 bringing with it the rewards of Cuba, Puerto Rico, Guam, and the Philippines[i]. Not all the Filipino population embraced the US takeover, however, and this latter territory was only eventually secured after a three-year war which cost the civilian population losses of, perhaps, as many as one million. Fighting with some of the more remote ethnic groups such as the Moros and Tagalogs continued until the battle of Bud Bagsak on 15th June 1913 which saw Pershing wipe out the final rebel elements.

To add to this world-wide white, Christian-driven, imperialist tidal wave, the relatively recently united Italy (Rome was finally added to the Kingdom of Italy in 1870) decided it too wanted a piece of the action. The Horn of Africa was its initial target, with Eritrea and the Somaliland being occupied between 1889 and 1899, although an attempt to conquer Ethiopia in 1895-6 was humiliatingly repulsed at the Battle of Adwa on 1st March 1896. Then, when Italy felt it was missing out on further African land grabs, it fought the Turks over the future of Libya (Tripolitania) in 1911, gaining most of the country and subjecting it to harsh rule until Italy was defeated in 1943 and the country fell under Allied control[ii].

Even little Belgium demanded an empire. Thus, the horrors of the Belgian occupation of the Congo Free State in 1885 at the instigation of Leopold II, whose *Force Publique* murdered and abused their way across the country. Finally exposed by the work of the anti-imperialist, and later Irish Republican, Roger Casement in 1904, the Congo Free State was properly absorbed as a colony of Belgium in 1908 after which time life for its sorely tried native inhabitants marginally improved. In 1919, however, a Belgian Commission estimated that the population of the country was now half of that of 1879.

---

claim accepted by Congress in 1862) were still independent countries. In 1870 only 10% of the landmass had been under European domination.

[i] As testament to the relentless progress of US imperialism, Daniel Immerwahr in his book *How to Hide an Empire* gives the following figures for overseas bases as of 2018: Britain and France thirty between them, Russia nine, various other countries one each, and the USA 800 [*Source*: Immerwahr D, *How to Hide an Empire: A Short History of the Greater United States*, Bodley Head, 2019].

[ii] Libya declared independence in 1951.

Generally, therefore, most of the major countries of Europe, along with their cousins across the Atlantic, were busy trying to grab any area in which the benighted local population was unable to resist modern military technology. The inevitable tensions when European powers faced one another along the new borders of lands stolen from the local population were a growing source of friction. This friction translated itself into an increasing sabre-rattling nervousness along those same countries' European borders.

Within Europe, both Central Powers proved adept at growing their continental territories through land seizures of one sort or another. Against Russian opinion Austria formally annexed Bosnia-Herzegovina in 1908; while Prussia gained by battle the Duchy of Schleswig from Denmark in 1864, Hannover, Nassau, Hesse-Kassel, Frankfurt, and part of Hesse-Darmstadt as a result of the Austro-Prussian War of 1866, and large chunks of the French regions of Alsace (*Elsaß*) and Lorraine (*Lothringen*) in the Franco-Prussian War of 1870-1. These latter conquests remained a festering wound between the French and Germans nations.

To resolve the resulting tensions and vaulting ambitions, the view was that there was but one solution: war, the true test of the virility of a nation. If one could not fight and win one did not deserve an empire or, indeed, a country.

Bloch was, in one essential and tragic respect, wrong: war was *not* impossible. War was not only probable, it was inevitable, even, to many people like Bernhardi, desirable. The competing interests and the increasing tensions generated in a world of imperial militarism rendered war the only available solution to those politicians and military leaders bound by the political theories and social attitudes of the early twentieth century. And with Europe in turmoil, it was not a case of *if* war broke out, it was a case of when.

Bloch, however, was not so starry-eyed about the prospects for peace. As he stated unequivocally during a presentation made at the *Royal United Services Institution* on 24th June 1901 (see page 352):

> "He knew that, unhappily, war might break out any day, and he had no delusions on that point. When he said war was practically impossible on the Continent of Europe, it was not because he put any faith in the desire for peace. The basis of his argument was that under the military, social and economic conditions of Europe at the present day, though it was possible that war might break out, it was almost impossible for it to be waged successfully; and that in any case it must be waged in an entirely different way from that of the past."[53]

MEANWHILE, THE EUROPEAN DIPLOMATIC and military pot was close to boiling over. Irrespective of cultural, social, and trading relations, the conservative political leaders of Germany loathed Britain for its pre-eminent Imperial position which it thought its own true destiny. Across the North Sea, Britain feared expansion of the German *Hochseeflotte* and could not countenance the idea of the German Navy operating from ports directly threatening the Channel and Atlantic trade routes. Furthermore, the vigour of German industry and its need for a global outlet for its trade must inevitably threaten Britain's position as one of the three leading industrial and mercantile powerhouses[i]. France's resentment over the loss of Alsace and Lorraine and its defeat in 1871 festered and revenge against its eastern neighbour was high on its agenda. Italy and Austria were at loggerheads over the Balkans into which mix could be added the small but thorny problem of aggressive little Serbia. By 1913 Bulgaria was embittered and frustrated by its defeat in the Second Balkans War and sought revenge, especially on the Serbs. The Ottoman Empire, though severely weakened, still looked longingly at its recently lost European territories and, to the south, at its fast-eroding position in North Africa. Russia, although seriously weakened by the Japanese defeat in Manchuria and the attempted revolution of 1905, was now re-arming and presented a growing threat to both the German and Austrian eastern borders.

Russia, the self-declared champion of the Slavic nations (especially the Serbs), represented, for German nationalists and imperialists, an alliance of their oldest and greatest enemies which inflicted on the Teutonic Knights two of their greatest military defeats: at Lake Peipus in 1242[ii] and at Tannenberg[iii] in 1410. Until its catastrophic defeat by a Polish-Lithuanian Army in 1410, the Teutonic Order devoted its existence initially to the destruction or enslavement of the old pagan Baltic Prussians. This achieved, their defeat at Lake Peipus by Alexander Nevsky of Novgorod stopped any further advance into the heartland of modern Russia. They then focussed on a 200-year war with the still pagan Lithuanians before turning on the Poles. It was the eventual baptism of the Grand Duke Władysław II Jagiełło of Lithuania and his marriage to Queen Jadwiga of Poland which formed the alliance which eventually crushed the Teutonic Order at Tannenberg. It is interesting to note the defeat at Tannenberg in 1410 was, like the end of the First World War, blamed on a 'stab in the back', this time by a renegade Polish knight, Nikolaus von Renys, who was subsequently executed without trial along with all his male relatives. The antagonism between the 'new' East Prussians of the Teutonic Order and neighbouring Poles, Lithuanians, Letts, Estonians, and Russians was, therefore, of long and bitter standing.

The history of the Teutonic Order, the *Ordo domus Sanctæ Mariæ Theutonicorum Hierosolymitanorum* (The Order of the House of St. Mary of the Germans in Jerusalem), became an integral part of the semi-mystical belief of German nationalists in their 'manifest destiny' to rule large eastern territories and to purge the area of the Slavs. This destiny, later aggressively pursued by Hitler, would, they

---

[i] Paul Kennedy in *The Rise and Fall of the Great Powers* (Random House 1988, page 202) estimates the percentages of world manufacturing in 1913 as: USA 32%, Germany 15%, Britain 14%, Russia 8%, France 6%, Austria-Hungary 4%. Thus, at the beginning of the war Germany's manufacturing production was more than the combined total of France and Russia and France lost a large proportion of its coal, iron and steel production within the first few weeks of the war. The USA enjoyed huge trade surpluses until its 'defence' commitments (or military/industrial colonialism) rapidly expanded during and after the Korean and Vietnam wars. It now has the largest national debt of any country.

[ii] 'The Battle on the Ice' was famously re-created in Sergei Mikhailovich Eisenstein's 1938 film *Alexander Nevsky* with a soundtrack by Sergei Prokofiev.

[iii] Also known as the Battle of Grunwald (Polish) or Žalgiris (Lithuanian).

believed, take them to the leadership of Europe and beyond, thus giving Germany its rightful place with a global empire. It would also lead to the final subjugation and, possibly, elimination of the troublesome Slavs on its eastern borders. Perhaps, then, a permanent answer to the historically persistent 'Jewish question' might be found by the rabid anti-Semites who infected central Europe.

7. Heinrich Gotthard von Treitschke
Ultra-nationalist, Anglophobe, and prominent anti-Semite

8. Generalfeldmarschall Wilhelm Leopold Colmar *Freiherr* von der Goltz
Author of *Das Volk in Waffen* (*The Nation in Arms*)

The influential historian Heinrich Gotthard von Treitschke[i] (1834–1896), ultra-nationalist and later a member of the *Reichstag*, described the actions of the Teutonic Order against its eastern neighbours in language chillingly reminiscent of that used to justify the mass slaughter of Poles, Jews, and Russians in the Second World War. In *The Origins of Prussianism*, 1864, Treitschke described the knights' murderous actions as part of a 'pitiless racial struggle' between the Germanic peoples and the Slavs. Moltke the elder became a firm friend of Treitschke[ii] when he was elected to the *Reichstag*, and Treitschke's *History of Germany in the Nineteenth Century* was on a list of Moltke's favourite books revealed in 1890.[54] What if Moltke's unfulfilled plan to destroy France in 1871 meant that, by removing the traditional western threat to Germany, the nation might focus on its longer standing enemy in the east. The eventual outcome of such thinking was the destruction of Nazi Germany in 1945, and the occupation of their capital by the dreaded Slavs. 'Be careful what you wish for' was, perhaps, not a well-known saying in Wilhelmine Germany.

There are those who, before the war and since, have argued this long-term concern about the Russian threat to Germany's eastern border was exacerbated by the enthusiastic way French banks and British and French arms manufacturers helped Russia re-build its navy and army after the Russo-Japanese War. The size of the planned Baltic Fleet – sixteen Dreadnoughts – must have caused genuine concern as Germany already faced the far larger Grand Fleet in the North Sea.

---

[i] He was appointed the Professor of History at the University of Berlin in 1874.

[ii] As was *Großadmiral* Alfred Peter Friedrich von Tirpitz.

The idea a fleet of modern battleships might emerge out of the Skagerrak to help crush the High Seas Fleet cannot have been reassuring. And Anglo-French involvement in enlarging and modernising Russia's armaments industry at such places as the *Putilov Works* in St Petersburg, and the large Tsaristsyn[i] weapons factory in which *Vickers* was the driving force, suggested a growing threat on land from both west and east.

Treitschke was to become an influential figure in German politics and society in the last quarter of the nineteenth century. He, like Moltke, was revolted by the idea of continual peaceful co-existence with which he associated both liberals and socialists and which he adjudged displayed weakness, sentimentality, and cowardice. Such people deserved to 'perish, and perish justly'. 'War', he declared, 'was the one remedy for an ailing nation'.[55] In this he echoed the views of Joseph-Marie, *comte* de Maistre, whose writings on the inevitability and rightness of war came to influence many such as Ferdinand Foch on the other side of the Franco-German border towards the end of the 1800s (see page 156).

Treitschke believed Germany was entitled to foreign colonies and regarded Britain's pre-eminent colonial position as one of the greatest blocks to his country's rightful 'place in the sun'. This 'colonial right' was not based solely on Germany's desire to expand its trade, wealth, and influence, it was also a crude expression of the rampant social Darwinism which swept military and political circles in the second half of the nineteenth century:

'Every virile people has established colonial power. All great nations in the fullness of their strength have desired to set their mark upon barbarian lands and those who fail to participate in this great rivalry will play a pitiable role in time to come. The colonising impulse has become a vital question for every great nation.'[56]

Treitschke was also a raging anti-Semite responsible for one of the most infamous, miserable, and sadly far-reaching pronouncements in the German language. In 1880, he published a pamphlet entitled *A Word about Our Jews* (*Ein Wort über unser Judenthum*). Coming as it did from the prestigious position allowed him as Professor of History at Berlin University, it carried a weight and resonance far beyond the statements of mere politicians or journalists. '*Die Juden sind unser Unglück!*' he declaimed, 'The Jews are our misfortune!', a phrase adopted and run as a banner on every edition of the war criminal Julius Streicher's rabid Nazi rag *Der Stürmer* from 1923 to the end of the war.

Just how firmly established anti-Semitism was in mainstream 19th Century German society (as it was in France[ii]) can be shown by the fact that it was officially represented in the German *Reichstag*. In the 1887 General Election, Otto Böckel was elected to represent Marburg (Hesse) on the platform '*Gegen Junker und Juden*' (*Against Barons and Jews*), having published a pamphlet, *Die Juden - die Könige unserer Zeit* (*The Jews - the kings of our times*), attacking the place of Jews in Germany. He formed the *Antisemitische Volkspartei* which, in alliance with Max Liebermann von

---

[i] Later Stalingrad, now Volgograd.
[ii] France too had anti-semitic Parliamentary representation. In 1898 28 deputies led by Édouard Drumont were elected as the *Groupe antijuif* or *Groupe antisémite nationaliste*.

Sonnenberg's *Deutschsoziale antisemitische Partei* (or *Deutschsoziale Partei* or *DSP*) fought the 1890 General Election, gaining five seats. In 1893, under the name of the *Deutsche Reformpartei* (German Reform Party or *DRP*), it gained eleven seats with other anti-Semites taking five. In 1892, however, the *Deutschkonservative Partei*, the *DkP*, officially adopted anti-Semitism as part of its programme at the Tivoli Congress, named after the Tivoli Brewery on the Kreuzberg in Berlin, and the other smaller anti-Semitic parties found progress more difficult. The *DkP* won 72 seats in the 1893 General Election. In the last pre-war General Election in 1912, the combined overtly anti-Semitic parties, the *DkP* and the *DRP*, took 46 seats (down from 76 in 1907) out of the 397 up for election, their seats coming mainly from Prussia, Saxony, and Hesse. Their popular vote ranged from 17% (in 1893) to 10% in 1912. Post-war, Hitler was ploughing already fertile anti-Jewish soil.

The seeds of Nazism were not just sown in the years after the war, the weeds were well established and guided much of thought and policy, especially foreign policy, in Wilhelmine Germany. To pursue such an expansionist foreign policy required a large, well-trained, and well-equipped army and navy. Furthermore, the entire nation needed to support the sacrifices required to make Germany the leader of Europe and a world colonial power. Prussian military prowess, which faded badly after the mid-eighteenth century exploits of Frederick the Great, were firmly re-established by wars against Denmark, Austria, and France between 1864 and 1871 and the German General Staff, the *Großer Generalstab*, developed an enviable reputation for efficiency, professionalism, and tactical *nous*. Military writers such as *Generalfeldmarschall* Colmar von der Goltz[i] were widely read and hugely influential both inside and outside Germany, and his seminal 1883 work, *Das Volk in Waffen (The Nation in Arms)*, was a classic text for all aspiring Generals throughout the world. The title of this work is self-explanatory: Germany needed all its resources, including all its young men, devoted to the task of protecting and expanding the German Second Reich and of creating a German Empire which was to vie with, and then exceed, that of Britain as the world leader.

Steps down the path towards Empire were made with *Deutsch-Westafrika*, formed from a series of 'protectorates' which developed into a full-blown colony after 1884 and comprised parts of modern Cameroon, Nigeria, Chad, Guinea, Ghana, Togo, the Central African Republic, Gabon, and the Congo. Further acquisitions followed, with *Deutsch-Ostafrika* being formed in 1891 after initial

---

[i] *Generalfeldmarschall* Wilhelm Leopold Colmar *Freiherr* von der Goltz, one of the most widely read military theorists of the 19th and early 20th Centuries, was born in 1843 and died in 1916. He joined *Infanterie-Regiment 'von Boyen' (5. Ostpreußisches) Nr. 41* in 1861, serving in the Austro-Prussian and Franco-Prussian Wars. In the historical section of the *Kriegsakademie* he wrote a series of books about the latter war. He was seconded to the Ottoman Empire to reorganise their Armies after defeat by Russia in 1878. *Das Volk in Waffen* was regarded as a classic and widely translated. Promoted Field Marshal, 1911, when he retired. Returned 1914 and appointed Governor of Belgium. He dealt ruthlessly with *franc-tireurs* and saboteurs. Shootings, of the innocent as well as guilty, were widespread. He went to Turkey, commanding 5th Army. He stopped Townsend at the Battle of Ctesiphon in Mesopotamia in November 1915, and then besieged him at Kut-al-Amara. Von der Goltz died two weeks after Townsend surrendered.

claims were filed in 1885. This new colony consisted of territories now comprising Burundi, Rwanda and much of mainland Tanzania. According to Bernhardi in *Germany and the Next War*, these territories, along with the Belgian Congo and the Portuguese colonies (Angola and Mozambique) were to form German *Mittelafrika* to go along with *Mitteleuropa*, a continent-dominating entity created from the German and Austro-Hungarian Empires and the Balkans.[57]

There followed the annexation of *Deutsch-Südwestafrika* (now Namibia) in 1890 after its initial development as a trading post was turned into a colonial land grab. Its first *Reichskommissar* was one Heinrich Ernst Göring, the father of Hermann Göring of Nazi notoriety. There, between 1904 and 1908, the German authorities conducted what was later described as 'the first genocide of the 20th Century' against the Herero, Nama, and San tribes. As many as 100,000 tribesmen, women and children were killed or starved to death, first in the Namibian desert and later in concentration camps where some were used for medical experiments. The actions of the local commander, Lt. Gen. Lothar von Trotha, were known and approved of by the *Großer Generalstab* including Alfred von Schlieffen[i].

In addition, small territories were scattered in the Far East and Pacific: *Deutsch-Neuguinea* (*Kaiser-Wilhelmsland*)[ii], *Deutsch-Samoa* and the Chinese concessions of Kiautschou Bay (*Tsingtao*) and Tianjin (*Tientsin*). These colonies, especially those in Africa, were ruthlessly and, in *Deutsch-Südwestafrika,* bloodily exploited, but, in truth, Germany's foreign possessions were 'small potatoes' compared not only to Britain but also, gallingly, to France. Nothing in Germany's 'empire' matched the majesty of India, Britain's Jewel in the Crown, a cause of great resentment amongst imperialists within the German ruling class. Expansion, therefore, was not just a question of the destruction of the Slavs, it needed the defeat of its two western European competitors for colonial power: France and Britain.

The First World War was, therefore, not just a war between Empires, it was a war about the future of those Empires.

BUT LET US NOT PRETEND that aggressive, Empire-building intent was uniquely German. Also, in reference to the previously described 'invasion scare' mania, let it not be thought that Britain (or France) were the only countries to feel threatened. Germany, too, had its concerns: a war on two fronts, an invasion by a Slavic horde from the steppes of Central Russia, the strangling of trade and its fast-growing economy by a powerful Anglo-French naval blockade, or a re-appearance of a Napoleon-like military messiah within France. After all, part of the justification for the German seizures of territory on the west bank of the *Rhine* after the Franco-Prussian War was to block yet another French invasion of German territory, invasions which took place with relentless regularity over the previous 250 years and more: French invasions of German territory took place, often more than once, in the Thirty Years' War 1618-48, the Nine Year's War

---

[i] Germany recognised the atrocity in 2004 but refused compensation. In May 2021, they agreed to pay €1.1 billion over 30 years [*Source*: Oltermann, P, *Germany agrees to pay Namibia €1.1bn over historical Herero-Nama genocide, The Guardian,* 28th May 2021.
[ii] Also including the Bismarck Archipelago, Caroline Islands, Palau Islands, Nauru, (northern) Marianas Islands, (northern) Solomon Islands, and the Marshall Islands.

1688-97, War of the Spanish Succession 1701-14, War of the Polish Succession 1733-5, War of the Austrian Succession 1740-8, Seven Years' War 1756-63, and the Wars of the First, Second, Third, Fourth, Fifth and Sixth Coalitions during the French Revolutionary/Napoleonic era, 1793-1815.

Thus, while Britain, France and others looked with concern at German Laws which were increasing the size of an already powerful army and navy, Germany looked askance at the dramatic increase in manpower generated by the effect of the *loi de trois ans* passed through the French legislature in 1913 and which, overnight it seemed, added over 100,000 men to the Armies of Metropolitan France.

On 7th April 1913, the *Reichskanzler*, Theobald Theodor Friedrich Alfred von Bethmann Hollweg, addressed the *Reichstag* about the new Army Law, and the Taxation Law designed to underpin the former financially. In it, he made specific reference to certain attitudes in France which might threaten European peace, attitudes which, as we shall later see, infected much of the upper echelons of the French Army. A certainty of the innate superiority of the French soldier with their belief in his natural *élan vital* and revolutionary *ésprit*, allied to the presumed material superiority of the ground-breaking French 75-mm field gun, and all topped off with the growth of *Revanchism*, of revenge for the indignities of 1870-1, produced, in certain quarters. a toxic cocktail of attitudes which would hurry France to war on a tide of mis-placed enthusiasm. These ideas the *Reichskanzler* ascribed to a rise of 'Chauvinism' in France, a mixture of blinkered nationalism, racial superiority and extreme patriotism named after the probably apocryphal Napoleonic soldier and devotee Nicolas Chauvin. The section of Bethmann Hollweg's speech relating to France is, therefore, horribly prophetic in its way, not least in its comments about the manipulation of public opinion at a time when 'social media' existed only in the sense of newspapers, public speeches, and gossip:

> "Nobody could conceive the dimensions of a world-conflagration and the misery and trouble which it would bring upon the peoples. All previous wars would probably be as child's play, and no responsible statesman would be disposed lightly to set the match to the powder. On the other hand, the power of public opinion had increased, and within public opinion the driving force was the noisiest elements which in excited times tended to be not majorities but minorities the more democratic institutions became. He did not believe that the French people as a whole, with all its valour and courage and pride, with all its love of country and self-sacrifice, was pressing on to war, but, in certain circles, not only of Chauvinists, but of the quieter and thinking people, the situation had arrived which Bismarck feared. People in France believed that they were at least equal, if not superior, to Germany 'in confidence in the excellence of their own Army, in confidence in the Alliance with Russia, and perhaps also in the hope of England'. That was the dangerous side of the revival of French national sentiment. The French Army was good, according to military opinion, very good. It was the hope of the nation, and the whole people gave to it all that was possible. But a Chauvinistic literature had arisen which, when it spoke with justified pride of the Army, did so in order to display German

inferiority in a future war. They boasted of the superiority of French artillery, of the advantage gained by French aviation, and of the superior training of the French soldier, and they saw visions of Germany overrun by masses of Russian infantry and cavalry. The lively French spirit regarded the defeats of Turkey as defeats of the Germans, and assumed that both the Balkan States and Alsace-Lorraine would attach themselves to France. In this fantasy, France had already won the war."[58]

Such 'fantasies' were, indeed, widespread in certain sections of the French Army as we shall see later.

UNDERPINNING THE EUROPEAN-WIDE DESIRE for the power, prestige, and wealth which foreign conquests brought was the long standing and almost uniform belief in the innate intellectual, genetic, and moral superiority of the white European male. When allied, by people like the German proto-fascist Ernst Haeckel[i], to the development of theories surrounding what we now call Social Darwinism, these beliefs formed an unshakable certainty in the rightness of their actions in bringing 'discipline' (and, for some, the dubious benefits of Christianity) to those with darker or different coloured skin, wherever they were. Thus, white men of any class deemed themselves the betters and, therefore, the rightful masters of such people. Of course, they also deemed themselves the betters and, therefore, the rightful masters of all women of any colour. Unfortunately for the working and middle classes of Europe, the titled, the positioned and the wealthy of that continent also deemed themselves the masters of the fate of all white men and women (and any others) who ranked 'beneath' them socially. And, if that fate involved marching stolidly into the mincing machine of modern industrial war so empires and dynasties might survive, then so be it.

In Germany this white, male superiority was more precisely racial in tone with ethnic Germans perceived as 'more equal' than other white nations, an idea which would reach its apogee during the Nazification of the country. But, pre-1914, an assumed racial superiority over Celtic, Latin and Slav ethnic groups was widespread in Germany, bolstered by the publication of such books as *Die Grundlagen des neunzehnten Jahrhunderts* (*The Foundations of the Nineteenth Century*) written by the British-born but German naturalised philosopher Houston Stewart Chamberlain[ii]. Chamberlain was deeply paranoid, hysterically and rabidly anti-Semitic, loved Wagner (indeed he married Eva Maria von Bülow, the composer's daughter, also the granddaughter of Franz Liszt), and, from 1923, was a Nazi Party member who greatly influenced both Hitler and Goebbels. The book, published in 1899 by the publisher later responsible for *Mein Kampf*, held the 'Aryan race' as responsible for all the great advances of mankind and the Jewish People as the most destructive force in history. Every war or disaster was somehow the

---

[i] Ernst Heinrich Philipp August Haeckel (1834-1919) was a Prussian-born biologist, naturalist, and philosopher. His theories about race and racial purity underpinned much of Nazi ideology. For further information see Daniel Gasman's *Scientific Origins of National Socialism: Social Darwinism in Ernst Haeckel and the German Monist League* (1971).
[ii] Born in 1855 he was the son of Rear Admiral William Charles Chamberlain, RN, and Eliza Jane Hall, daughter of Captain Basil Hall, RN. He died in 1927.

responsibility of Jews who were, amongst many things, responsible for the Catholic Church and for foisting democracy on nations when autocracy and dictatorship were clearly the best forms of government.

Across the North Sea, the leading exponent of Social Darwinism in Britain was the philosopher, scientist and libertarian Herbert Spencer (1820-1903), the man who, in response to Charles Darwin's *On the Origin of Species*, coined the phrase 'survival of the fittest' in his book *Principles of Biology* (1864). Spencer, whose views were later reflected by Margaret Thatcher in 1987 with her quote 'there is no such thing as society'[59] (a view still popular within the Republican Party in the USA as well as with most British Tories), was not an imperialist or militarist but he most certainly was a vigorous opponent of social change as engineered by governments. He opposed almost every single social reform achieved by radicals and liberals in British politics in the nineteenth century and, in addition, was firmly against any extension of the vote to women. Land reforms, welfare reforms, compulsory education, etc., were viewed as dangerous elements of a creeping socialism. Although his influence was waning fast immediately prior to the outbreak of war, his views were widely read and hugely influential during the period in which the leading politicians and military leaders prominent in the war were born, raised, and educated. In many areas of upper class, conservative Britain many of Spencer's opinions were greeted with enthusiastic nods of approbation. They helped reinforce prejudiced attitudes towards those social classes which might benefit from such reforms and, as 'survival of the fittest' was slowly translated by them into the 'survival of the wealthy, powerful and well connected', the fate of these social classes became of less and less concern, except in as much as they continued to generate the wealth of their 'superiors' and populated the lower ranks of the armed forces. Indeed, if the masses wished to have pensions, education and some small modicum of health and safety at work then the least they could do was die, in whatever numbers necessary, for their country, its Empire, and its upper classes.

Another spin-off from Darwin's theories had time to run and great damage to do. Francis Galton was a half cousin of Darwin, a prolific author, statistician, psychologist, and anthropologist (amongst many other things)[i]. These three areas of interest, combined with Darwin's theories and Spencer's 'survival of the fittest' concept, led Galton down the path to the founding of a new 'science' – eugenics. Its aim was the 'improvement' of the human gene pool by the elimination of 'bad' genes. Galton and his subsequent followers (which included the Nazis) believed human traits, good and bad, were inherited. To 'improve' the human race it was necessary to remove those with 'bad' genes from the process of reproduction. This could be done in various ways but, with human males not renowned for sexual abstinence, this inevitably attracted ideas like castration for males, spaying for

---

[i] The grandson of Samuel John Galton, FRS, a somewhat hypocritical combination of Quaker and arms manufacturer, and the owner of one of Birmingham's largest gunsmiths, *Farmer & Galton* located in Steelhouse Lane. Tens of thousands of guns were supplied to the *Company of Merchants Trading in Africa* which, between 1752 and 1821, led the slave trade in West Africa. It replaced the *Royal African Company*, founded in 1660 by the Duke of York (later James II), which was reputed to have sent more slaves to the Americas than any other organisation in any country.

females or, in the case of the Nazis, simple eradication through mass murder.

Galton was, undoubtedly, a considerable polymath and seen by some as a progressive. But, to place properly this description into its Victorian imperial context, one needs to read, as an example, a letter to *The Times* of 5th June 1873, entitled *'Africa for the Chinese'*. A few excerpts will suffice:

> "My proposal is to make the encouragement of Chinese settlements at one or more places on the East Coast of Africa a part of our national policy, in the belief that the Chinese immigrants would not only maintain their position, but that they would multiply and their descendants supplant the inferior negro race… average negroes possess too little intellect, self-reliance and self-control to make it possible for them to sustain the burden of any respectable form of civilization without a large measure of external guidance and support… The Hindoo cannot fulfil the required conditions nearly so well as the Chinaman, for he is inferior to him in strength, industry, aptitude for saving, business habits and prolific power. The Arab is little more than an eater up of other men's produce; he is a destroyer rather than a creator…
>
> The history of the world tells a tale of the continual displacement of populations, each by a worthier successor, and humanity gains thereby. We ourselves are no descendants of the aborigines of Britain, and our colonists were invaders of the regions they now occupy as their lawful home."[60]

Galton's idea was roundly criticised two days later by Gilbert Sproat, a Scottish-born businessman who was, at the time, the Agent General for the newly formed province of British Columbia[i]. His reaction, however, was based mainly on his less than flattering opinion of the average Chinaman, although he found Black Africans to be decent servants, neighbours, and acquaintances. Thankfully, Galton's racist wishful thinking was quietly consigned to the dustbin of history.

Central to Galton's thesis was the idea that parenting, living conditions, diet, education, environment, etc., were irrelevant to the development of children as all personal traits were inherited. He thus coined the phrase 'nature not nurture'[61] to describe the fundamental premise of eugenics. By his definition, 'good' genes were found almost entirely amongst the white, Anglo-Saxon, middle and upper classes, i.e. the affluent, educated, well-fed and well-housed of society. Conversely, according to Galton 'bad' genes were endemic amongst the lower strata of society because, if they had the native wit and intelligence to remove themselves from their lowly position, they would not be lower class. They must, therefore, be inferior. 'Bad' genes were seen to result from the inter-breeding of the least intelligent, less physically prepossessing, poorest and most worthless in society and, looking globally, he posited that the darker the skin the worse were the genes. As suggested in his letter about the Chinese and Africa, the Dark Continent's indigenous population were people who, in his opinion, few would miss. In Europe, though, the classic example of such men or women was the 'village idiot', the unhappy product of generations of in-breeding in restricted and isolated societies.

---

[i] After whom Sproat Lake & Provincial Park, Vancouver Island, are named.

What appears to have escaped Galton is that he really had no further to look for people bred from a highly restricted gene pool than a large residence in central London – Buckingham Palace. Here, and in other obscenely opulent palaces across Europe, the members of the royal families of Britain, Germany, Russia, Austria, etc., busily inter-bred within a narrow circle of cousins, thereby condemning their off-spring to inherited conditions like haemophilia or producing several pathetic specimens with as many brain cells as their much-despised, remote, and rural 'idiot cousins'. Little appears to have changed in recent years.

Such was the in-bred nature of the royals of Europe Queen Victoria alone became the source of the haemophilia which spread rapidly throughout the families of the crowned heads of Europe. Her eighth and youngest son, Prince Leopold, died from the effects of haemophilia aged 30, but the impact of Victoria and Albert's children on the European gene pool was profound, with the royal families of at least three countries being affected by the *Haemophilia B* condition created by the defect on the X chromosome (and which thus impacted mainly male offspring of the carrier). The limited circles within which Europe's royal families married and bred can be seen from the details of Victoria's children's marriages and offspring:

The Princess Royal, Victoria Adelaide Mary Louisa, married Frederick, Crown Prince of Germany and Prussia, later, but for just 99 days, the German Emperor and King of Prussia Frederick III. Amongst their offspring was Kaiser Wilhelm II and Queen Sophia of the Hellenes, the wife of the Greek King, Constantine, who favoured the Central Powers during the war;

The Prince of Wales, Albert Edward, later King Edward VII, married Princess Alexandra of Denmark and amongst their children were King George V and Queen Maud of Norway. Known later as the 'Uncle of Europe', he was related to, *inter alia*, Kaiser Wilhelm II and Tsar Nicholas II (nephews) and King Haakon VII (nephew and son-in-law), one Empress, one Queen and three Crown Princesses (nieces), two Kings (sons-in-law), and four Kings (second cousins);

The haemophilia gene-carrying Princess Alice Maud Mary married Friedrich Wilhelm Ludwig IV, the Grand Duke of *Hessen und bei Rhein*. Amongst their children was Alix, later the Tsarina Alexandra Feodorovna, wife of Tsar Nicholas II, the last emperor of the Russian Empire. Her brother, Prince Friedrich of *Hessen und bei Rhein*, died aged three from the effects of haemophilia; her sister, Princess Irene was a carrier and helped pass the condition onto a junior part of the Prussian royal family; and the Tsarina's first son, Alexei, was diagnosed with the condition early in his life. He somehow managed to survive for thirteen years before being murdered by Bolsheviks in Yekaterinburg on 17th July 1918;

Prince Alfred Ernest Albert, Duke of *Saxe-Coburg and Gotha*, married Grand Duchess Maria Alexandrovna of Russia, daughter of Tsar Alexander II and Tsarina Maria Alexandrovna, previously Princess Marie of *Hessen und bei Rhein*, daughter of Ludwig II of *Hessen und bei Rhein*. One daughter was Queen Marie of Rumania. She persuaded her husband, Ferdinand I, to side with the Allies in 1916;

Princess Helena Augusta Victoria married Prince Christian of *Schleswig-Holstein*;

Princess Louise Caroline Alberta married John Douglas Sutherland Campbell, Marquess of Lorne and later 9th Duke of Argyll;

Prince Arthur William Patrick Albert, Duke of Connaught and Strathearn, married Princess Louise Margaret of Prussia, the daughter of Prince Friedrich Karl of Prussia and the great niece of Wilhelm I, King of Prussia and Emperor of Germany and the grandfather of Kaiser Wilhelm II. Arthur was the Governor General of Canada during the first two years of the war;

Prince Leopold George Duncan Albert, Duke of Albany, married Princess Helene Friederike of *Waldeck-Pyrmont* whose sister married William III of the Netherlands. Their second child was Charles Edward, Duke of *Saxe-Coburg and Gotha* (1900-1919). He became a leading Nazi being an *Obergruppenführer* in the *Sturmabteilung* (*SA* or Brown Shirts) in the mid-30s; and finally

Princess Beatrice Mary Victoria Feodore married Prince Henry of *Battenberg*, son of Prince Alexander of *Hessen und bei Rhein*, third son of Ludwig II of *Hessen und bei Rhein* (see Prince Alfred and Princess Alice above). Another haemophilia carrier, their daughter, Princess Victoria Eugenie of *Battenberg* (known as Ena), introduced it into the Spanish royal family after marrying King Alfonso XIII. Heir to the throne, HRH Alfonso, Prince of Asturias, inherited the condition, dying from internal bleeding after a minor car accident aged 31. Their youngest child, *Infante* Gonzalo Manuel María Bernardo Narciso Alfonso Mauricio of Spain, previously died in similar circumstances aged 19 in 1934. The revelation she introduced haemophilia into the royal family ruined Ena's and Alfonso's marriage.

But these were not the issues which exercised Galton and his ilk. Eugenics was not for the likes of royalty, however badly their gene pool was contaminated by relentless interbreeding amongst that tiny group of people deemed suitable for marriage into a monarchy. This was a class-based conceit which determined the lower classes from field, pit or factory or the black man of Africa, or wherever they were transported as slaves, were simply not capable of improving themselves because blood 'was all'. And good, pure Anglo-Saxon blood at that (even though there is no such thing as any DNA test will show).

IN LIGHT OF ALL OF THIS, IT WAS PERHAPS, OPTIMISTIC for Bloch to imagine peace might come to the continent of Europe. The toxic brew of imperialism, colonialism, nationalism, militarism, the arms race, anti-Semitism, racial conflict, political extremism and, through eugenics, the concept that the lives of many were of little consequence, was ready to boil over. It created a particular poison which, through a coincidence of timing and technology, allowed both for a multi-national war which would spread into the furthest reaches of the globe, and yet also helped create the peculiar and horribly intimate trench warfare of the Western Front, a war in which for four years, massive armies lived within a few hundred yards of one another with neither side having any real idea as to how to finish things.

Furthermore, despite Northcliffe's rabble rousing, Lord Roberts' conscription campaign, a massive expansion of the Navy and the maintenance of a huge armaments industry, the Army still went to war woefully ill-equipped for the type of war predicted. And, more bewildering still, the armaments industry was peculiarly ill-prepared to supply the needs of a 'nation in arms' about to fight a prolonged, industrialised war. Ill-prepared to the extent that shortages and failures of government the military and industry still affected tactics on 1st July 1916.

ENDNOTES:
[1] Brett, M V, ed. *Journals and Letter of Viscount Esher, Vol. 2, 1903-1910*, Ivor Nicholson & Watson, 1934, page 70-1.
[2] Bauer E, *Jan Gottlieb Bloch: Polish Cosmopolitism versus Jewish Universalism* in Miller, M L & Ury, S (eds), *Cosmopolitanism, Nationalism and the Jews of East Central Europe*, Routledge, 2016, pages 79-85.
[3] Howard, M, *Men Against Fire – Expectations of War in 1914*, International Security, Vol. 9, No. 1, Harvard University & MIT, Summer 1984.
[4] Bloch, Jean de, *Selected Articles*, U.S. Army Command & General Staff College, 1993.
[5] Trotha, Thilo von, *Tactical Studies on the Battles around Plevna*, trans. by 1st Lt. Carl Reichmann, US Army, Hudson-Kimberley Publishing Co., Kansas, 1896, page 223.
[6] Bloch, op. cit., page 4.
[7] *The Times, The Military Manoeuvres*, 22nd August 1898, page 6.
[8] Bloch, op. cit., page 7.
[9] *The Times, The Peace Conference*, 15th May 1899, page 7.
[10] *The Times, The Peace Conference, From our Special Correspondent, 23rd May, 1899*, page 3.
[11] Bloch, op. cit., page 77.
[12] Brett, M V, ed. *Journals and Letter of Viscount Esher, Vol. 1, 1870-1903*, Ivor Nicholson & Watson, 1934, page 251.
[13] Ibid., page 249.
[14] Wells, H G, *Anticipations of the Reaction of Mechanical and Scientific Progress upon Human Life and Thought*, Chapman & Hall, 1902, page 2.
[15] Ibid., pages 182-4.
[16] Ibid., page 191.
[17] Rosny, J-H, *La Guerre Anglo-Boër*, 1902, pages 312-3.
[18] Nigote, C C, J, *La Bataille de la Vesles*, Librairie Militaire de L. Baudoin, 1894, page 5.
[19] Ibid., page 4.
[20] Ibid., pages 6-7.
[21] Ibid., page 102 onwards.
[22] Lerner, H, *Le colonel Emile Mayer et son cercle d'amis*, Revue Historique, Tome CCLXVI, Presses Universitaires De France, 1981, page 75.
[23] Ibid
[24] Ibid., page 77.
[25] Mayer, Col. E, *Prophéties sur la guerre de 1914-1918*, Revue Militaire Suisse, 1935, page 394 onwards.
[26] Mayer under the name Manceau E, *Un vieil article du lieutenant-colonel Émile Mayer (Émile Manceau) sur la guerre actuelle.... 1915*, Revue Militaire Suisse, June 1915.
[27] Ibid
[28] Ibid.
[29] Lerner, H, *Le colonel Emile Mayer et son cercle d'amis*, Revue historique, July 1981, page 80.
[30] Mayer, E, *Prophecies about the 1914-1918 war*, Revue Militaire Suisse, 1935.
[31] Montaigne, Col. J-B, *Vaincre: esquisse d'une doctrine de la guerre basée sur la connaissance de l'homme et sur la morale*, Volume 2, Berger-Levrault, 1913, pages 159-161.
[32] It was reported in the *Journal of the Royal United Service Institution*, issue 45 (November 1901), pages 1316-44.
[33] *The London Gazette*, 26th January 1900, page 512.
[34] *The Times, The withdrawal of General Warren's force*, 27th January 1900, page 11.
[35] Cairnes, Capt. W E, *An Absent-Minded War*, John Milne, 1900, page 13.
[36] Bloch, *Selected Articles*, page 31.
[37] Bloch, *Selected Articles*, page 30.
[38] Ibid.
[39] Bloch, Jean de, *The Future of War: in its Technical, Economic and Political Relations*, Trans. by R C Long, The World Peace Foundation, Boston 1914, page xxvii.
[40] Clery, Capt. C F, *Minor Tactics*, 1875, page 107.

41 Ibid., but 1880 edition, page 318.
42 *The Times, The French Manoeuvres*, 1st October 1901, page 8.
43 *The Times, M. de Bloch on War*, 25th June, 1901, page 11.
44 *The Times, M de Bloch on the coming manoeuvres*, 12th September 1901, page 11.
45 Ibid.
46 Ibid.
47 Moltke, H *Graf* von, *Ausgewählte Werke*, Vol. 3. ES Mittler, 1925, page 345.
48 Bloch, *Selected Articles*, page 6.
49 Liddell Hart., B, *The British Way in Warfare*, London, 1932, p 123.
50 Fuller, J F C, *The Decisive Battles of the Western World*, London. 1956. Vol. 3, page 182.
51 Fuller, J F C, *The Dragon's Teeth: A Study of War and Peace*, London, 1932, pages 252-3.
52 Brailsford H N, *The War of Steel and Gold*, G Bell & Sons, first published 1914, 10th edition published in 1918, page 18.
53 *The Times, M. De Bloch on War*, 10th July 1901, page 14.
54 Gat, A, *The Development of Military Thought*, Clarendon Press, 1992, page 60.
55 Treitschke, H von, *Politics*, Vol. 1, 1898, pages 65-6.
56 Ibid., pages 115-6.
57 Bernhardi, op. cit., pages 132-55 and 207-8.
58 *The Times, Germany and her Army*, 8th April 1913, page 8.
59 Interview with Douglas Keay, *Woman's Own*, 31st October 1987, pp. 8–10.
60 *The Times, Africa for the Chinese*, Thursday, 5th June, 1873, page 8.
61 Galton, F, *On men of science, their nature and their nurture*, Proceedings of the Royal Institution of Great Britain, 1874 7: pages 227–236.

PART TWO: FRANCE – THE TACTICS OF REVENGE

"War is a series of catastrophes which result in victory."

Georges Clemenceau
Paris Peace Conference, 12th January 1919
The Macmillan Dictionary of Political Quotations,
page 689

3. Defeat, Dreyfus and War Plans

"Battles are mostly moral struggles. Defeat is inevitable as soon as the hope of victory ceases. Success thus comes not to the man who has suffered the least loss, but to the man whose will is the strongest and whose morale is most strongly tempered."

Règlement sur la conduite des grandes unites

THE CALAMITOUS DEFEAT OF FRANCE by Prussia and its allies in the North German Confederation in 1871 led to the ignominious end of the Second French Empire, the loss of most of two key provinces, Alsace and Lorraine, their people, their industry and, in the case of Alsace, some excellent vineyards, and to a huge reparations bill which loaded the new French Third Republic with an unprecedented national debt. Then, when the new German Empire was declared in the *Galerie des Glaces* (Hall of Mirrors) in Versailles on 18th January 1871, this confirmed that the balance of European power had shifted east to Berlin, perhaps irrevocably. French national morale was shattered. Its military reputation, based on the past glories of Napoleon Bonaparte, lay in ruins. Its economy was in ruins and, politically, it was in bloody pieces as the fall-out from the class-based bloodletting of the Paris Commune deepened divisions between royalists and republicans, catholics, and secularists, conservatives, and radicals.

But France recovered. Recovered sufficiently to start plan revenge on its old enemy. Its army found new beliefs, what it thought were new tactics and, in 1897, what it believed was a new war-winning weapon. How did this change take place? In what state were the armies of France, and why, in the opening years of the twentieth century? How did they recover militarily, materially, and morally from the catastrophe of the Franco-Prussian War?

But then: what then drove them to the strategy and tactics which resulted in the catastrophic casualties and loss of territory of the Battle of the Frontiers? Why did they spend 1915 throwing away huge numbers of men in one unproductive and costly offensive after another? And how did they adapt to these setbacks, as well as the prolonged and deadly conflict around Verdun, in time to produce such a successful opening phase of the Battle of the Somme as Foch and his Army commander, Fayolle, enjoyed in the first days of July 1916? And how, then, between 1st and 3rd July 1916, did strict adherence to the tactics employed prevent the exploitation of the first major rupture of the German lines which the Allies had achieved since the start of trench warfare?

These are some of the points addressed, if not necessarily conclusively answered, in this book and in *Volume II* of *The Long Road to the Somme*.

ONE MUST START IN 1870. Militarily, the Franco-Prussian War was lost because of French arrogance, incompetence, and because a poor army employed poor tactics. Mobilisation was chaotic, border defences obsolete and ineffective, reserves untrained, Generals barely competent. Battles were lost which might have been won and the forces of Prussia and her allies were able to crush the various French Armies in detail, occupying the north of the country within nine months.

One of the key questions facing the French Army in 1870, and one which returned to haunt them in 1914, was: what sort of Army should France have? Was it a mass, citizen Army conscripted along the lines of the *levée en masse* declared during the Revolution in August 1793 (and again in late 1870 when the regular army collapsed), i.e. one designed to protect France from external enemies *and* reactionaries within? Or should it be an *armée de métier*, professional, voluntary, and capable of effective military action at home and abroad? Republicans and socialists favoured the former, conservatives and monarchists the latter. This argument remained unresolved. The result was, in August 1914, an Army of barely trained, short-term conscripts and a dwindling, disillusioned professional officer corps. In 1870 it was even worse, but with added complacency.

The war started on 19th July 1870 and was a military catastrophe for France (the scale of the disaster can be seen on page 845). In a month, the regular armies of France were destroyed or neutralised. Having advanced to, and taken, Saarbrücken, French troops were forced to retreat after a series of damaging defeats: Wissembourg (4th August); Spicheren and Wörth (6th August); Borny-Colombey (14th August); and Mars-la-Tour (16th August). This left 59-year-old *Maréchal de France* François Achille Bazaine's[i] 113,000-strong *Armée du Rhin* west of Metz but a larger Prussian Army between it and either Paris or Verdun. Though inflicting heavier casualties, Bazaine was defeated at Gravelotte-Saint-Privat on 18th August 1870 and forced to retire into Metz to be besieged.

An attempt by Napoleon III and the *Armée de Châlons* to relieve Bazaine resulted in the surrender of 104,000 French soldiers, including the Emperor, at Sedan, on 1st-2nd September. This was a battle remarkable because three different Generals commanded the French Army at one time or another: *Maréchal de France* Marie Edme Patrice Maurice de MacMahon, *comte* de MacMahon, *1er duc* de Magenta, started the day in command before being wounded. He nominated *Général de division* Auguste Alexandre Ducrot, commander of the *1er corps d'armée*, as his successor until he was superseded by *Général de division Baron* Emmanuel Félix de Wimpffen on the previously issued written authority of the *ministre de la Guerre*, Charles Guillaume Marie Apoline Antoine Cousin-Montauban, *comte* de Palikao. Wimpffen only arrived at Sedan from North Africa the day before, knew nothing about the battlefield, countermanded Ducrot's sensible order to retreat, and signed the surrender document on 2nd September. This shambles of command and tactics summed up the overall French performance admirably.

---

[i] *Maréchal de France* François Achille Bazaine was born on 13th February 1811, the result of an affair between *général de corps d'armée* Pierre-Dominique Bazaine, a brilliant engineer who served in Imperial Russia for 24 years, and a haberdasher, Marie Madeleine Josèphe, *dit* Mélanie Vasseur. Having failed the 1830 *École polytechnique* entrance examination, François enlisted as a Private in *37e régiment d'infanterie de ligne* in 1831. He served in North Africa and Spain. Col. of the *55e régiment d'infanterie de ligne* in 1850. During the Crimean War he was promoted *général de division* in 1855, the youngest General in the French Army. He commanded the *3e Division d'infanterie* at the Battle of Solferino in 1859. He then served in Mexico, returning to command the *3e Corps d'Armée* in 1867 before taking command of the *Armée du Rhin* in 1870.

9. Generalfeldmarschall Helmuth Karl Bernhard Graf von Moltke (the Elder)

10. Emperor Napoleon III

11. Maréchal de France Marie Edme Patrice Maurice de Mac Mahon

12. Maréchal de France François Achille Bazaine

13. Général de Division Antoine Eugène Alfred Chanzy

14. Général de Division Charles Denis Sauter Bourbaki

Napoleon's surrender was the end of the monarchy in France in practice if not in law. The Second Empire was overthrown, a new Provisional Government formed, and a Third Republic and a *Gouvernement de la Défense nationale* declared on 4th September. Its leaders were Gen. Louis-Jules Trochu (President), Jules Claude Gabriel Favre (Vice-President and *ministre des affaires étrangère*), and Léon Gambetta (*ministre de l'Intérieur* and *ministre de la guerre*). Two days later, Favre declared 'no surrender'. The government called for a Revolutionary-style *levée en masse* which, by early 1871, nearly doubled the available manpower of the French Army. It announced a *'guerre à outrance'* – war to the death – against the invaders. In response, Moltke's forces invested Paris, and, on 17th September, its long siege began.

On 28th October, Bazaine and 142,000 French troops surrendered at Metz and, thus, after barely three months fighting, the regular forces of the French Empire were utterly defeated by the armies of the soon-to-be-formed German Empire[i]. According to conventional wisdom, France should now have asked for terms of surrender. That they did not, made a deep impression on the Prussian commander, Helmuth Karl Bernhard *Graf* von Moltke (the Elder)[ii]. He and other officers realised they were no longer fighting the organised armed forces of a foreign

---

[i] After the surrender of Metz, Bazaine's conduct was investigated by Gen. Raymond Adolphe Séré de Rivières and was unfairly blamed for all the disasters of the war. Court-martialled for treason, he was sentenced to death by a court presided over by Henri Eugène Philippe Louis d'Orléans, *duc* d'Aumale. The sentence was commuted to 20 years in prison by the then President, *Maréchal de France* Mac Mahon, who surrendered at Sedan before Bazaine surrendered at Metz. He escaped from the Île Sainte-Marguerite in August 1874 assisted by his wife and Angelo Hayter, an Englishmen with a familial connection. Living in straightened circumstances, the effect of numerous previous wounds and illness led to his death in 1888.

[ii] Helmuth Karl Bernhard *Graf* von Moltke was born in Parchim, Mecklenburg-Schwerin, in 1800, the son of a Danish *Generalleutnant*, Friedrich Philipp Victor von Moltke. He joined the *Oldenborgske regementet* in the Danish Army before switching to the *Leib-Grenadier-Regiment 'König Friedrich Wilhelm III.' (1. Brandenburgisches) Nr. 8* in the Prussian Army in 1822. He attended the *Allgemeine Kriegsschule* in Berlin (the *Königlich Preußische Kriegsakademie* from 1859), coming under the influence of Carl von Clausewitz, the Director since 1818. One of the Army's most brilliant prospects, he joined the *Großer Generalstab* in 1833. In 1835-7 he helped modernise the Ottoman Army. In 1838 he advised on the campaign against Muhammad Ali Pasha al-Mas'ud ibn Agha, founder of modern Egypt, who had declared independence from the Ottomans. His advice rejected, the Ottoman Army was routed at the Battle of Nezib on 24th June 1839 (modern Nizip north of the Turkish-Syrian border). He returned to Prussia suffering from ill-health, marrying an Englishwoman, Maria Bertha Helena Burt, in 1842. On the staff of *IV. Armeekorps* he was appointed Chief of Staff (1849-1855) and was ADC to Prince Friedrich Wilhelm Nikolaus Karl (Emperor Friedrich III for 98 days in the spring of 1888). In 1857 he was appointed Chief of the *Großer Generalstab* overseeing wars against Denmark, 1864, Austria, 1866, and France, 1870. Made a count (*Graf*) and promoted *GeneralFeldmarschall*, he served in the *Reichstag* for twenty years, retiring as Chief of the *Großer Generalstab* in 1888. He died in 1891. His nephew, Helmuth von Moltke (the younger) was Chief of Staff from 1906 until replaced on 25th October 1914 after the defeat on the Marne.

power but that power's entire population[i]. Moltke later described it as a return to the *Volkskriege* of the Revolutionary/Napoleonic era, i.e. entire nation versus entire nation, itself a transformation from what was termed *Kabinettskriege*, in which the relatively small army of one monarch faced that of another with limited objectives and limited opportunities for casualties. *Volkskriege* taken to its logical conclusion would lead, inevitably, to confrontations between mass, poorly trained, conscript armies with an attendant vast increase in both the economic and human cost in the face of the rapidly increasing firepower of industrially produced weapons and munitions.

Moltke's use of 110,000 troops, 25% of those available, to protect his lines of communication against French irregular *Francs-tireurs* and their guerrilla-style warfare cast another shadow. The German response was a foretaste of their violent, oppressive treatment of conquered peoples in both World Wars.[1] Still, with Paris besieged and much of the north and north-east of the country in the hands of troops from the Kingdom of Prussia and the North German Confederation, as well as their southern allies from Baden, Württemberg, Bavaria and Hesse-Darmstadt, the end seemed imminent.

Instead, French citizens flocked to serve under the *Tricoleur*. Poorly equipped, barely trained (if trained at all), with little or no artillery, and few experienced officers they were formed, at Gambetta's exhortations, into new Armies: the *Armée de la Loire, Armée de l'Est, Armée du Nord,* and *Armée de la Vosges*. Minor successes were achieved against Bavarian troops at Coulmier by the *Armée de la Loire* on 27th November, and at Hallue by the *Armée du Nord* just before Christmas but, in January, a series of disasters ensued. Orleans was lost and, at Le Mans on 12th January 1871, Antoine Chanzy's *Armée de la Loire,* a large but hopelessly ill-equipped and trained rag-bag of reservists and civilians, was utterly crushed[ii].

The *Armée de l'Est,* led by the tragically incompetent Gen. Charles Denis Bourbaki, was finally defeated on the *Lisaine* around Héricourt near Belfort on 17th January[iii]. In full retreat, its remnants were disarmed and interned when they fled

---

[i] Concern about this renewed resistance, especially in the Loire valley, generated several articles and books in Germany, e.g. von der Goltz, *Leon Gambetta und seine Armeen*, F. Schneider, 1877; Hoenig, F, *Der Volkskrieg an der Loire im Herbst 1870*, ES Mittler, 1893-1899; von Widdern, G C, *Der Krieg an den rackwartigen Verbindungen der deutschen Heer und der Ettapendienst*, R. Eisenschmidt, 1893-9.

[ii] Chanzy's 150,000 reservists and civilians outnumbered Prince Friedrich Karl of Prussia's 50,000-strong army, however his experienced, better equipped and trained troops inflicted 25,000 casualties on the French. 70,000 then deserted and fighting in western France ceased [*Source:* Katzenbach, E L, *Freycinet and the Army of Metropolitan France*, unpublished PhD thesis, Princeton University, 1952, page 129, quoted in Porch D, *The March to the Marne*, Cambridge UP, 1981, page 10].

[iii] Bourbaki's 152,000-strong *Armée de l'Est* tried to relieve Belfort but was defeated by 50,000 entrenched troops of Gen. August von Werder's *XIV Armeekorps*. Bourbaki retreated towards Besançon but, threatened with encirclement, moved on Pontarlier. Freezing weather caused enormous suffering and Bourbaki attempted suicide. The pistol ball deflected of his skull (he died in 1897). Led by Gen. Justin Clinchant (Commander of *20e Corps*. Captured at Metz and the only French General to escape

into neutral Switzerland on 1st February. The Swiss sold their weapons and equipment and were paid 12 million *francs* compensation. The last organised resistance, Gen. Louis Léon César Faidherbe's *Armée du Nord* was then soundly defeated at Saint Quentin on 19th January. Finally, Paris surrendered on 28th January 1871 under the terms of an armistice negotiated between Bismarck and Favre. In the meantime, Wilhelm I was acclaimed *Kaiser* of the new German Empire in the *galerie des Glaces* in the *Palais de Versailles* on the 18th January.

There followed the tragedy of the Paris Commune (18th March-28th May 1871) in which *bourgeois* French officers ordered their troops to slaughter working class French men, women and children. It laid waste to working-class neighbourhoods mainly in north and north-eastern Paris – Belleville, Menilmontant, La Villette, La Chapelle and Montmartre – as well as parts of its historic centre such as the *palais des Tuileries,* the Richelieu library next to the *Louvre,* and the *Hotel de Ville.* Atrocity was piled on atrocity, summary execution met with summary execution. By its end, some 10,000 Parisians were dead. Another 10,000 were deported or sent to prison.

Post-war, rather like many Germans in 1918, the French population refused to believe they had lost the war because their armies and officers were worse than those of Prussia or that they had simply been beaten by superior numbers and equipment. Someone had to be blamed and Bazaine became the chief scapegoat even though he had not been the first Army commander to surrender during the war. The need to spread blame continued and 71-year-old *Maréchal de France* and late-Napoleonic War veteran[i] Louis-Achille Baraguey d'Hilliers, 1st Comte Baraguey d'Hilliers, was appointed by the *Président de la République française,* Adolphe Thiers, to head a commission of inquiry into all of the reasons for the surrender of French garrisons during the war, e.g. Strasbourg, Toul, Metz, Soissons, and La Fère. It was conveniently the local commander's fault in every case.

The war was ruinous in other ways. Under the terms of the Treaty of Frankfurt signed in May 1871, the French province of Alsace (the *départments* of *Bas-Rhin* and *Haut-Rhin* including Strasbourg and Colmar but excluding Belfort) and a large part of Lorraine (three-quarters of the old *départment* of *Moselle,* including Metz and Thionville; the north-eastern third of the old *départment* of *Meurthe* containing the towns of Château-Salins and Sarrebourg[ii]; and a small part of the old *départment* of the Vosges around Saales and Schirmeck) became, respectively, the *Bezirk Unterelsaß,* the *Bezirk Oberelsaß* and the *Bezirk Lothringen*[iii], all part of the German *Reichsland Elsaß-Lothringen.* It is perhaps fortunate the territorial demands made on France were designed to suit mainly military and nationalistic, rather than economic, opinion in Germany. The gains made in Alsace provided a barrier in

---

and return to the Army), 87,000 men were disarmed and interned in Switzerland on 1st February 1871 under the terms of the *Convention des Verrières.*

[i] He fought at Leipzig in 1813 and at Quatre Bras in 1815.

[ii] Since combined as the new *départment de Moselle.*

[iii] *Lothringen* is named after Lothair II, great-grandson of Charlemagne. On the death of his father, Lothair I, in 855, Burgundy and Provence passed to Lothair I's youngest son, Charles of Provence; northern Italy went to his eldest son, Louis II, who was declared Holy Roman Emperor; and Lothair II inherited part of the Carolingian Empire called Lotharingia, i.e. the Low Countries, Lorraine and Alsace.

the form of the Vosges mountains and, further east, the *Rhine*. Their acquisitions in the *Moselle* and *Meurthe départments* helped protect routes towards Strasbourg and the valleys of the *Saar* and *Mosel* rivers. Furthermore, many of the inhabitants spoke Germanic dialects and this, in some nationalists' minds, made them prime contenders for integration into a 'Greater Germany'.

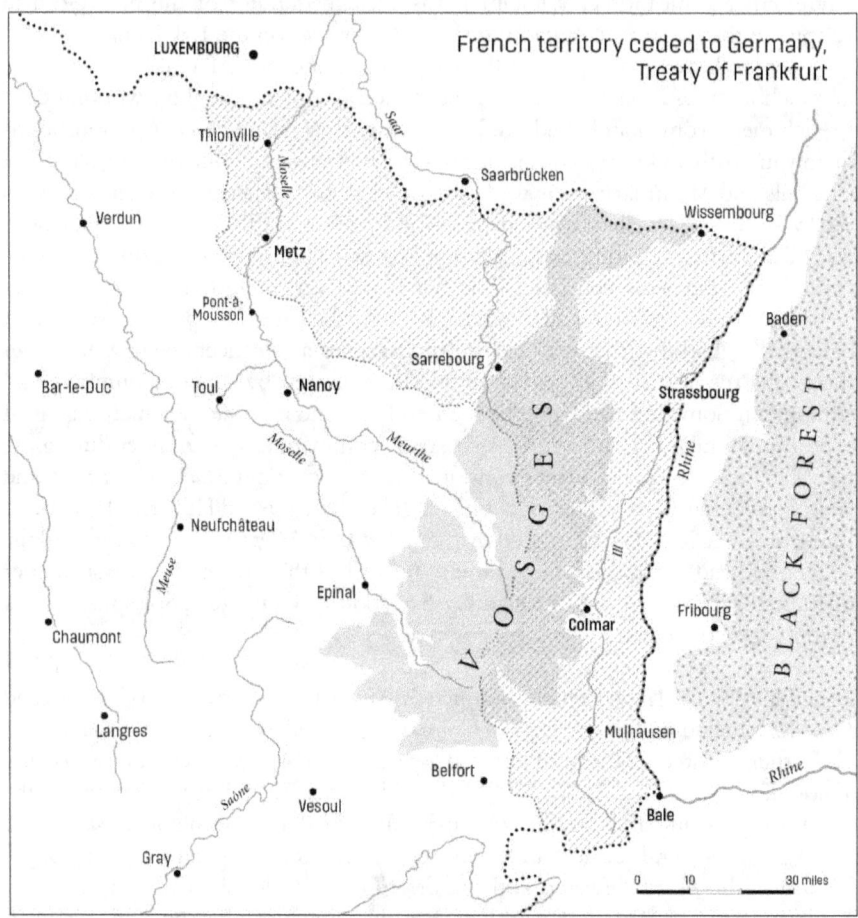

Map 1 French territory ceded to Germany, Treaty of Frankfurt

In terms of resources, the old *Moselle* department contained the French part of the Saar-Warndt coal mining basin centred on Saarbrücken in Germany and Forbach in France. It was the iron ore deposits of Lorraine which were more important, however, and here Bismarck and his government made an error when it came to its territorial claims. The area annexed contained large deposits of iron (two-thirds of Germany's immediate pre-war total) and, by 1913, it was supplying 74% of all Germany's iron ore, however, the western part of the region around Longwy and Briey, which remained with France, was later found to contain even more and held 90% of France's iron ore deposits which were a third larger than those in what was now *Bezirk Lothringen*[i].[2] Nevertheless, immediately pre-war, Germany's coal[ii], iron and steel production was, respectively, six, three and four times that of France.[3] There was an issue, however, with Germany's production of iron/steel which would raise its head once the allied wartime blockade was properly enforced. Though Germany possessed 25% of Europe's iron ore it still needed to import some 50% of the ore used in industry and, within three years, ore imports rose from 8 million tons a year to 11 million tons[iii].[4] This was because German ore was mostly phosphorus-rich and high concentrations of phosphorus in iron can make it extremely brittle (or 'cold short') in cold temperatures. Furthermore, Germany was almost entirely reliant on imports of manganese which, in 1856, was introduced as a means of producing much-improved steel and which, in 1882, Sir Robert Abbott Hadfield improved further with a 12% manganese steel (Hadfield steel or *mangalloy*) being later employed for armour-piercing shells and to manufacture the British *Brodie* helmet introduced in 1916[iv].

Of course, all these ore deposits and the foundries they supplied were lost in the opening months of the Great War, along with a large part of France's largest coalfields in the Nord-Pas de Calais Mining Basin. French industry had to show remarkable resilience in order to provide an adequate mineral and industrial base with which to supply her Armies between 1914 and 1918.

But Germany did not just take French land. Until a reparations bill of five billion[v] *francs* was paid, France, from Dijon to Dunkerque and Strasbourg to Orleans, was occupied by German troops. And, to rub Gallic noses in their defeat, the 60-metre high *Siegessäule*, the *Victory Column*, erected in the *Königsplatz* at the

---

[i] In 1914 there were c. 3,000 million tons of iron ore in the French *Meurthe et Moselle*, two-thirds around Briey. From 1890 to 1911 French iron production rose from 2.6 million tons to 14.8 million tons. Deposits of c. 700 million tons were discovered in Normandy. Some was bought by *Krupp* and *Stinnes* via a Dutch intermediary. *Stinnes* was a mining, steel-working and shipping company. It made large profits in the war and was later associated with the *Hamburg-American* and *North German Lloyd* shipping lines. Hugo Stinnes [1870-1924] supported right-wing parties post-war including the Nazis [*Source*: Bruneau, L, *Germany in France*, 2nd edition, Paris, 1914, page 5].

[ii] By 1913 Germany had 55% of Europe's coal reserves [*Source: Der Weltkrieg*, Vol. 1, page 44].

[iii] Imports of high-grade Swedish iron ore from Gällivare in the far north via the port of Luleå (ice-bound during the winter) became increasingly important. Attempts at blockading this trade were a continuous source of friction between Sweden and the Allies which nearly led to war. Sweden, however, also exported iron ore to Britain from the Kiruna ore fields (80 kms north of Gällivare) via the ice-free Norwegian port of Narvik using the *Malmbanan* (Swedish) and *Ofotbanen* (Norwegian) railway lines.

[iv] Germany was almost entirely dependent on imported tin, nickel and aluminium. 90% of its copper came from the USA. Materials for uniforms, equipment, etc., such as cotton, silk, flax, hemp, jute and leather were almost entirely imported. The munitions industry was much dependent on imported chemicals such as sulphur and nitrates and the medical services on imported chemicals and materials. Rubber was entirely imported [*Source: Der Weltkrieg*, op. cit., pages 44-6].

[v] Approximately £200 million in 1870's Sterling terms. Several billions now.

end of the *Siegesallee* in Berlin to celebrate Prussian victories over the Danes and Austrians, was decorated with French cannon captured during the brief war. And in human terms the cost was severe. During the fighting, the French Armies lost 250,000 men killed or wounded and nearly 500,000 as prisoners of war.

It was a shattering blow to French prestige and morale and, with the loss of key industries and raw materials, also to its economy. The resentment engendered by this humiliation festered for decades and the outbreak of war in August 1914 was seen by many *Revanchists* such as Georges Benjamin Clemenceau as a long overdue opportunity to wreak vengeance on the German Empire and to regain its lost territories straddling the *Meuse, Moselle*, and *Rhine*.

The peace imposed was that of Chancellor Bismarck and combined politics, economics, geography, security, and German pan-nationalism to varying degrees. But it could have been a great deal worse. Had Moltke had his way matters would have been far grimmer for France. He believed France needed to be utterly crushed once and for all and the myths and legends of Napoleonic France banished for all time. Once Paris fell, and the German Armies had destroyed the *ad hoc* forces still operating in the Loire valley and near the Swiss border, he believed they should then have marched into the south of France all the while enforcing the harshest of reprisals on anyone who stood against them, most especially the *Francs-tireurs*, whose guerrilla operations enraged Moltke and his men and for whom summary execution was the punishment if caught. *'Exterminationskrieg'* was the phrase used.[5]

From abroad, the war of 1870-1 was seen as a triumph for the Prussian Army and its renowned staff, the *Großer Generalstab*, led by Moltke the elder. Its efficiency and tactics honed by victories in the wars against Denmark in 1864 and Austria in 1866, the war confirmed the new pan-German Army as the strongest. best organised and trained in Europe. That is not to say its commanders proved an unqualified success during the campaign. Several early battles were 'lost' by the French rather than 'won' by the Prussians and their allies. Indeed, Bazaine's indecision snatched defeat from the jaws of victory in more than one of the opening contests in Lorraine.

But, leaving aside the qualities of the opposing commanders, this war was one where the modern *Chassepot* rifle, the *Fusil modèle 1866,* proved markedly superior to the elderly *Dreyse* needle rifle, the *leichtes Perkussionsgewehr Model 1841*. The *Chassepot,* a breech loading, bolt action rifle, could fire its 11-mm bullet to an effective range of 1,200 metres at a notional rate of between 8-15 rounds a minute. The breech loading *Dreyse* had a rate of fire of 10-12 rounds a minute but an effective range of just 600 metres. The essential point was the range of each weapon. Unless other factors came into play, the French infantry could stand off the Prussian infantry and slaughter them whilst out of range. These were essentially defensive tactics, and they were later blamed for the decisive defeats inflicted on the French Armies. In turn, this led to the conviction the 'offensive' was the only means by which the French should fight wars. The tendency to rely on a single superior weapon persisted, however, and the French went to war in 1914 equipped almost solely with the 75-mm field gun which many believed was the only artillery piece necessary to win the war.

The Prussians, of course, were aware of the shortcomings of their rifle (if not how effective the *Chassepot* was) and, thus, another factor came into play – their new artillery. They were equipped with c. 1,200 modern *Krupp*-built, steel, breech-loading cannon whilst the French had c. 900 bronze[i], muzzle-loading, rifled guns of the *Système La Hitte* of 1858[ii]. These weapons reversed the superiority between the two armies[iii]. The *Krupp* 4-pounder had longer range, a quicker rate of fire and greater accuracy than the equivalent *La Hitte* 4 pounder[iv] which tended to over-heat and could not be fired for sustained periods. There was another issue. Shrapnel, as in 1914, was regarded as the best anti-personnel weapon but the French fuzes for these shells had only two settings: 1,450 and 2,850 metres. Prussian troops outside these ranges were, therefore, safe from French fire.[6] As a result, once this superiority was recognised (but only after several costly battles in which German infantry suffered badly from the fire of the *Chassepot*), the massed Prussian guns demolished the French artillery, then battered the French infantry, before being used in close support in the final assault. But, whatever the role of these guns, battles still involved the use of massed infantry assaults, of artillery firing direct at the enemy and in full view, of artillery advancing with the infantry to act in close support, and of victory being assured at the point of a bayonet.

In addition, cavalry was still a prominent presence on the battlefield with

---

[i] Bronze because France relied on British and German supplies of high-quality steel until the end of the 1870s [*Source*: Buat, Gen. E, *L'artillerie de campagne: son histoire, son évolution, son état actuel*, Alcan, 1911, page 95].

[ii] Breech loading artillery was not introduced into the French Army until after the war by Gen. Jean-Baptiste Verchère de Reffye. Reffye was also responsible for the production at Meudon of the first French *mitrailleuse* (machine gun) in 1866. Originally designed by a Belgian Army officer, Capt. Toussaint-Henry-Joseph Fafchamps, and built at Fontaine l'Eveque by Joseph Montigny, the 25-barrel gun weighed in at 2 tons. 168 guns in 28 batteries were used in the war of 1870-1, and it could fire 100 rounds per minute out to some 2,000 metres. Horribly complicated to fire, its tactical applications were not properly appreciated, and it was mainly used ineffectively, at long range and in the open against German field guns. When concealed and employed against infantry such as at Gravelotte it was very successful but such events were few and far between. Those not lost in battle were either captured at Sedan and 72 were surrendered at Metz. Their final unhappy use was in the mass summary executions of *Communards* during and after the Paris Commune in the *jardin du Luxembourg, place d'Italie*, the *prison de la Roquette*, the *Bois de Boulogne* and *caserne Lobau* between 21st and 28th May 1871 and thought to include the final murder of 147 Communards in the *cimetière du Père-Lachaise* at what is now called the *mur des Fédérés*.

[iii] In *Age of Great Guns*, Frank Comparato, whilst reporting the failure of 200 *Krupp* guns because of breech defects, also gives examples of their effective range, accuracy, and rate of fire. He cites examples of an entire French battery destroyed at a range of 4,000 yards, and three Horse Artillery batteries wiped out before they could fire at the Battle of Sedan [*Source:* Comparato F E, *Age of Great Guns*, Stackpole Co., 1965, page 28].

[iv] *Canon de campagne de 4, modèle 1858 la Hitte* capable of firing two rounds of explosive shell a minute out to 1,850 metres. The heavier *Canon de 12 rayé de campagne modèle 1853-1859* had a range of 3,000 metres. The *Krupp 8cm-Stahlkanone C/64* could fire an explosive shell 3,450 metres and a shrapnel shell 1,800 metres.

several large-scale cavalry charges taking place, most notably at Mars le Tour on 16th August 1870. Here, Maj. Gen. Friedrich Wilhelm Adalbert von Bredow's *12. Kavallerie-Brigade* was ordered to charge the French guns to save the day. Now known as 'Von Bredow's Death Ride', two of his Brigade's regiments[i], the *Kürassier-Regiment 'von Seydlitz' (Magdeburgisches) Nr. 7* and the *Ulanen-Regiment 'Hennigs von Treffenfeld' (Altmärkisches) Nr. 16* successfully exploited the terrain and the cover of smoke to deliver their charge – but at a cost of 50% casualties. This action was regarded by some senior European military figures as confirmation the horse and its rider clutching his pennanted lance or sabre still had a place on the modern battlefield. Conveniently forgotten was the destruction of the *1re division de la réserve de Cavalerie*[ii] commanded by *général de division* Jean-Auguste Margueritte[iii] which was destroyed by rifle and the dominant Prussian artillery fire as they tried to lead a break-out from Sedan. As weapons and munitions improved, however, a significant body of officers believed the day of traditional cavalry was past. The argument persisted well into World War One[iv].

In terms of military *matériel* alone, the French were soundly beaten by modern German artillery. The French Army took this lesson to heart and, twenty-six years after their defeat, unveiled to a startled global military audience what was then, undoubtedly, the best modern field gun in the world, the *Canon de Campagne de 75-mm modèle 1897*. They even caught out the German High Command by delaying the announcement of the *75*, with its innovative hydro-pneumatic long recoil system and unprecedentedly high rate of fire, until after the Germans launched their new *77-mm Feld Kanone 96 (FK 96)*, a gun without a recoil system or a shield and which sacrificed range for mobility[v]. At a stroke, the French *75* rendered the German *FK 96* and all other field guns in the world obsolete. Potentially, here was the war-winning weapon the French Army craved. This was the edge which would bring victory over the Germans and the return of its lost provinces.

It could be argued that the focus on the excellent *75* nearly brought about the defeat of France in the opening months of the First World War. The military icon the *75* became did little to bring with it any significant changes in French military philosophy. Tactical thinking barely changed. The commitment to the '*offensive*', in

---

[i] The third, *Schleswig-Holsteinisches Dragoner-Regiment Nr. 13*, was not involved.

[ii] Made up of the *1er* and *3e régiments de Chasseurs d'Afrique*, the *1er régiment de hussards*, and the *6e régiment de chasseurs à cheval*.

[iii] Margueritte was hit in face by a bullet and died five days later on 6th September 1870 in the *château de Beauraing* in Belgium, home of the *Duchesse* d'Ossuna.

[iv] One is talking about cavalry in the traditional sense, i.e. mounted men armed with sword or lance charging *en masse* other cavalry, infantry, or artillery. Mounted men armed with a rifle or carbine who dismounted to fought on foot are not cavalry in this sense. Few disputed the need for mounted troops for screening the advance and reconnaissance (although the airplane undermined this case) but many considered the day of 'heavy cavalry' and 'shock action' by massed, knee-to-knee horsemen over.

[v] Its predecessor, the *C/73*, came in two variants: a 78.5-mm field gun and an 88-mm used by the Foot Artillery. The field gun underwent several upgrades to serve during WW1. The maximum range of the *FK 96* was c. 4,500 metres, 2,000 m. less than the *75* could fire shrapnel and c. 4,000 m. less than, technically, the *75* could fire HE shell.

which the *élan* of the French infantry would sweep away what was left of a German foe battered by the rapid fire of the 75, was, if anything, reinforced. War, it was thought, would be little different from the Franco-Prussian War except, this time, with the 75, France would win. Of the lessons of more recent wars, the Russo-Japanese War of 1904-5 in Manchuria and the First Balkan War of 1912-3, little note was taken or the wrong lessons learned. Men digging for their lives in labyrinthine trench systems swept by machine guns, protected by row upon row of barbed wire and pummelled by the plunging fire of powerful howitzers was not the form of war they recognised when scores were to be settled with the 'Boche'.

They were not alone in thinking this way. Many within the German High Command believed the next war, for which they planned and armed themselves so expensively, would be one of rapid manoeuvre and decided by the great clash of infantry. They planned for a war of movement, *Bewegungskrieg*, in which victory went to those achieving the battle of annihilation *à la* Sedan, *Vernichtungsschlacht*, through which the enemy's ability and willingness to wage war was destroyed. But there were certain tactical issues which forced them to develop a wider range of *matériel* for the battlefield than occurred to the majority of French Generals. Although hoping for the 20th Century equivalent of the French debacle at Sedan, there was also the necessity to reduce the fortified cities in eastern France and, for this, position war, *Stellungskrieg*, was required. In this eventuality, different tactics and high angle, heavy howitzers were needed. These tactical adaptations were incorporated into German planning and allied to more flexible thinking, gave the German Army a significant advantage when war finally broke out.

But in truth, neither of the two great armies of Western Europe, nor their allies, anticipated the grinding, miserable, costly years of siege warfare which scarred France and Belgium for more than four years – even if explicitly warned what to expect more than a decade before by Jean de Bloch, Émile Mayer and others.

DESPITE BLOCH AND MAYER'S WARNINGS, and the real-life experiences of the Manchurian and Balkans Wars, the strategic and tactical planning of all armies in August 1914 was predicated on the basis of a war of manoeuvre in which rate of fire and speed of action were of paramount importance. It was confidently expected the campaign would be fluid and fast moving, one in which the dictum of Nathan Bedford Forrest of American Civil War infamy about 'getting there the fastest with the mostest'[i] still held good.

In such warfare, infantry attacked and artillery supported. This artillery needed to be lightweight, quick to travel and rapid to fire. Ranges would be short and observation, in the main, direct. On such a battlefield large, long-range guns and heavy howitzers had no place. Their great weight and slow rate of movement meant they would be left far behind as the fighting moved swiftly across the disputed borderlands of France and Germany.

Or so thought the French. But this was not always the case.

Their initial response to the defeat of 1871 was defensive – and hugely expensive. The man responsible, military engineer Gen. Raymond Adolphe Séré de Rivières, was born in 1815. A graduate of the *École Polytechnique* (1835) and *École*

---

[i] Or, more prosaically: 'I always make it a rule to get there first with the most men'.

d'Application de l'Artillerie et du Génie in Metz[i], he joined the *2e régiment du Génie* (Engineers) in 1839. Prior to the Franco-Prussian War he was posted to various cities – Nice, Metz, Langres, and Lyon – where he worked on the construction and improvement of existing fortifications. By the beginning of 1871, with the French Armies everywhere else defeated, he was appointed commander of the *Génie* of the *24e Corps* in Gen. Bourbaki's *Armée de l'Est* just prior to its defeat on the *River Lisaine* in dreadful conditions in mid-January. At war's end he transferred to the *2e Corps* of the *Armée de Versailles* and was involved in the capture of three forts around Paris then held by the Communards. In 1874, as secretary of the newly formed *Comité de Défense*, he made proposals for the development of a system of defence along France's northern and eastern borders. He was promoted head of the *Service du Génie* at the Ministry of Defence and ordered to completely restructure French defences from Dunkerque all the way to the coastal boundary between France and Italy east of Nice. The key frontiers, however, were those with Belgium and, most especially, Germany, and this area was split into four sectors: the Jura, Vosges, *Meuse,* and from Montmédy to Dunkerque. Work started in 1874 and was accompanied, as from 1877, by the construction of a new network of railways connecting the north-east of France with Paris and other major French cities, a network which, subsequently enhanced, would be used effectively when the French Armies mobilised in August 1914. In 1880, aged 65, he was replaced by Gen. Louis-Pierre-Jean-Mamès Cosseron de Villenoisy who had previously fortified Grenoble.

The concept of Séré de Rivières' system was of twin rings of forts around Paris, certain ports, and the border cities of Verdun, Toul, Épinal and Belfort, with support from secondary fortifications and battery positions. When the main programme finished in 1885 (at a cost of c. 700 million *francs*) 196 forts, 58 smaller works, and 278 batteries had been built.[7] The strategy was to channel German troops into 'killing zones' between the heavily fortified cities where they could be destroyed by French Armies deployed initially on the defensive. The key zone was the *Trouée de Charmes*, or Charmes Gap. Charmes lies on the left bank of the *Moselle* in a gap in hills west of the river some 60 kms from the then Franco-German border. These hills run north-west via Toul to Verdun (the *Trouée de Spada* is smaller gap between the two) and south-east to Épinal and Belfort. The *Trouée de Belfort* lies between the south end of the Vosges and the northern edge of the Jura.

The areas from Toul to Verdun and Épinal to Belfort (both c. 65 kms, 40 miles) were heavily fortified but the *Trouée de Charmes* was left empty. The isolated *Fort de Manonviller*, 43 kms to the north-east and on the path of any German attack between Toul and Épinal, was the exception (for the fate of this fort see the footnote on page 240). North of the *Trouée de Charmes* lay the important French city of Nancy. The theory was a German invasion would be channelled into the apparently weak zone of the *Trouée de Charmes* where it could be attacked from three sides. This concept was predicated on the basis of a defensive campaign in which the Germans were drawn onto the comprehensive French fortifications.

---

[i] Moved to Fontainebleau after Metz was occupied in 1870.

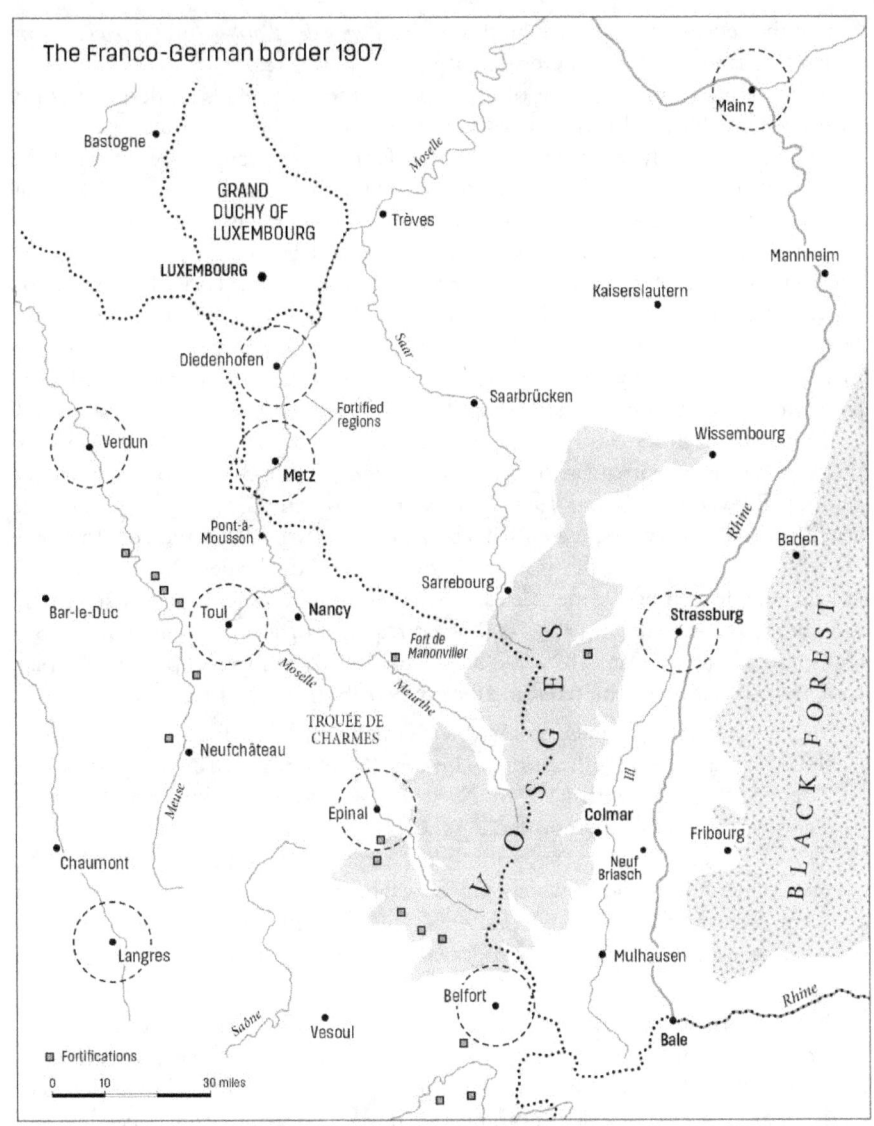

Map 2 The Franco-German border 1907
Circled cities are fortified regions. Small squares between Épinal/Belfort & Toul/Verdun indicate fortifications. The *Trouée de Charmes* between Nancy & Épinal was protected at a distance by the *Fort de Manonviller*.
N.B. Treves is now Trier, Diedenhofen is now Thionville

This was not the case in August 1914 when the French launched attacks *into* German territory under the provisions of *Plan XVII*. The concept of the original plan, in some ways, still held good as, after the heavy defeats at Morhange and Sarrebourg during the Battle of Lorraine, the defeated French armies of Castelnau and Dubail retired to positions along the *Hauts de Meuse* (east of Verdun), the *Grand Couronné* (protecting Nancy and Toul) and to the east of Charmes. Here were fought the successful defensive battles of the *Trouée de Charmes* and *Grand Couronné* which permanently stopped German offensives in this region.

Developments in the power of explosives in the early 1880s rendered masonry forts obsolete. Delayed-action fuzes, Paul Vieille's invention of smokeless powder, Eugène Turpin's advances on the German Hermann Sprengel's work on Picric Acid, and the development of the Picric Acid/guncotton explosive *Mélinite*, all contributed to making such fortifications highly vulnerable to artillery fire. This was demonstrated when, between August and October 1886, the Army fired 171 live 155-mm and 220-mm shells at the *fort de la Malmaison* near Laon. Its destruction proved that all the expensively constructed fortifications built since 1871 were obsolete. The ensuing panic was known as the *crise de l'obus-torpille*[i]. A decision was made, therefore, to improve some of the main fortifications with reinforced concrete, and iron, and then steel, cupolas for the guns. Others were downgraded.

Longevity in office has never been a trait of French government ministers and this was never truer than in the case of *Ministres de la Guerre* at the turn of the century. Between 1895 and 1900 there were ten changes of Minister. Just one lasted for over two years, *général* Jean-Baptiste Billot who left office on 15th June 1898. Six more occupied this hot seat before the end of the decade[ii]. But one was crucial, the four-time Prime Minister Charles de Freycinet[iii] (the first civilian *Ministre de la Guerre* ever in 1889-1890), who resumed office on 1st November 1898 and survived until 6th May 1899. On 24th February 1899 Freycinet presented a plan for a reorganisation of the fixed fortifications of France into three categories:

Première catégorie: Expected to resist a German attack, i.e. Paris, Lyon, Verdun, Toul, Épinal, Belfort, the forts *de Frouard* (6 kms north of Nancy), *Port Saint Vincent* (12 kms south-west of Nancy), *du Cognolet* (12 kms south-east of Langres), and *Manonviller* protecting the *Trouée des Charmes*;

Deuxième catégorie: in a support role. Armed and supplied according to governmental decisions which judged each case. Relegated to this category were, for example, Maubeuge, Besançon and Montmédy; and

Troisième catégorie: effectively abandoned, i.e. Lille, Laon, Reims, Hirson, Dijon, Langres and La Fère.

Not in office long enough to see his plan through, Freycinet was briefly replaced by Camille Krantz who demanded the immediate declassification of, amongst others, Lille, Longwy and Péronne as 'having no real value in defence'. Thus, apart from Maubeuge, nothing remained along the Belgian border, and Maubeuge was now a *Deuxième catégorie* fortification. The changes were voted through without debate but with a ringing declaration that:

---

[i] *Obus-torpille* - a shell which penetrated the ground or building before exploding.
[ii] *Général* Émile Zurlinden lasted 13 days, (5th-17th September 1898), and Camille Krantz five weeks, (6th May 1899-12th June 1899).
[iii] Louis Charles de Saulces de Freycinet, *Ministre de la Guerre* 1889-90, four-time *Président du Conseil des ministres français* 1879-1892, in 1878 introduced the *Plan Freycinet* for the industrial development of France through a vast expansion of railways, canals and other transport systems. The railway system was, in part, developed to underpin the French Army's mobilisation should war break out over Alsace and Lorraine.

"We dedicate ourselves to the principles of active defence of our frontiers, we rely above all on the value of our Army…."[8]

Afterwards, the elderly engineer and collaborator with Séré de Rivières, *général de division* Eloi-Théophile-Urbain-Félix Béziat, pointed out that the abandonment of the Belgian frontier defences meant:

"…violating Belgian neutrality is no longer just rational, it becomes fatal."[9]

As indicated, changes in French tactical thinking, as well as the burdensome costs, further undermined the basis for Séré de Rivières' fortifications. The focus shifted to just four main north-eastern cities, i.e. Verdun, Toul, Épinal and Belfort but, even here, modifications were not completed by 1914. Despite this, the fortifications along the *Meuse* and the Vosges persuaded the German war planner, *Generalfeldmarschall* and *Chef des Generalstabes* Alfred *Graf* von Schlieffen, that a direct westerly attack towards Paris from *Elsaß* and *Lothringen* was not practical. A great, neutrality-busting sweep through Belgium was the prerequisite for success in the next war. Meanwhile, in France, with the *Système Séré de Rivières* known in some circles as *'la grande muraille de Chine'*,[i] the mood was changing from the purely defensive, towards a more flexible, manoeuvre-based, and aggressive approach.

Other changes were made within the French Army in response to the defeat of 1870-1. Envious of the *Großer Generalstab's* exalted reputation, a complete overhaul of staffing arrangements and the education of officers was put in place. *général* Ernest Courtot de Cissey[ii] formed the *École supérieure de Guerre* in 1876 . Twice *Ministre de la Guerre* (5th June 1871-24th May 1873 and 22nd May 1874 to 15th August 1876) it was during his second term the decision was made to establish a Staff College which, for its first four years, was based at *Les Invalides*. In 1880 it moved to the old *École Militaire* founded in 1750 by Louis XV and based in Paris's *7e arrondissement*. Attendance at the *École supérieure* was based on merit rather than connections and rank. Previously, an atmosphere of anti-intellectualism had existed perhaps best embodied in a statement by *Maréchal* MacMahon (captured with the *Armée de Châlons* at Sedan on 2nd September 1870):

"I shall remove from the promotion list any officer whose name I read on the cover of a book."[10]

Now, in this new and progressive military era, young officers from the *École supérieure* then joined the *État Major de l'Armée*, the Army's General Staff, rotating between active units and staff positions as was the practice within the *Großer Generalstab*. It was these officers between 1876 and 1914 who developed the operational ideas with which France went to war when the opportunity presented itself to take revenge on the German nation.

---

[i] A General in the 1880s commented: 'On an open border the most powerful instrument of defence is a good rail network; it improves our ability to concentrate forces rather than a wall of China which will cost millions.' [*Source*: Loredan, J, *Lille et l'invasion allemande*, *La Nouvelle Revue*, April 1920, page 231].

[ii] Ernest Louis Octave Courtot de Cissey, a PoW at Metz, helped suppress the Paris Commune and was partly responsible for the *Semaine Sanglante*, 21st-28th May 1871, in which many *communards* were massacred or summarily executed.

The notion of *'revanche'* was fostered by such as right-wing nationalist Paul Déroulède and his *Ligue des patriotes* formed in 1882. They sought to teach children patriotism and militarism aimed, almost entirely, at the return of the lost provinces. *Revanchism* underpinned French attitudes towards Germany before, during and even after the war, most disastrously at Versailles.

AFTER 1871, FRANCE REPEATEDLY CHANGED its plans for what was regarded as an inevitable war against Germany. By 1898 the plans numbered fourteen, i.e. an average of one new plan every two years. *Plan XIV* was a defensive deployment based on border defence utilising Séré de Rivières' system of fortifications against a German attack. The guiding principle was to hold the lines of the *Moselle* and the *Meuse* whilst France's new Russian allies in the east mobilised. This was expected to take six weeks. Then, with Germany vulnerable on two fronts, the war would swing in France's favour. All French troops (five armies of nineteen Corps plus eight reserve divisions bar four reserve divisions around Ste Menehould), were located between Belfort and St Dizier. No significant quantity of troops was deployed on the Ardennes front or further west facing central Belgium.[11]

Russian help was crucial to France. Germany's population was over 60% larger than that of France and was growing at a faster rate. In 1872 the population of Metropolitan France was c. 36 million. By 1906 it was 39.25 million, a modest rate of growth of just 9%. In 1895, and twice since, the net annual birth rate slipped into the negative[i]. In addition, c. 500,000 native French lived in African and Asian colonies which had a native population of c. 33 million. Russia's population was 165 million. In the fifty provinces of Russia proper (excluding Siberia) where lived 70% of the population, this was increasing by c. 1.5 million annually. The population of Germany, however, stood at 65 million in 1910, up from 41 million in 1871, an increase of c. 58%[ii]. But, for various reasons, these numbers did not reflect in the size of the various armies with Germany possessing a large pool of able-bodied, if untrained men of military age.

By 1912 size of the various armies stood at:

France		Germany	
Peace Time establishment			
Metropolitan France	520,000		
Algeria	56,000 (1/3 native)		
Tunisia	20,000 (1/3 native)		
Colonial Army in France	28,000		
Total	624,000		665,000

[i] 1895 831,000 births against 852,000 deaths, 1900 827,000 births against 853,000 deaths and 1907 774,000 births against 794,000 deaths. Also note the steady decline in births [*Source: Whitaker's Almanack*, 1909, page 615].

[ii] It had grown to 67.8 million by 1914 but the rate of growth of the German population was slowing. In 1900 there were 2.06 million births from a population of 56.367 million. In 1910, 1.98 million births from a population of 65 million. In 1890 there were 38.25 births per 1,000. In 1910, 30.72 per 1,000 [*Source: The Times, The French and German Armies*, 18th February 1913, page 6].

Mobilised Field Army				
Ex. Reserves	725,000	Inc. reserves	1,165,000
1st Reserve	475,000		
Depot troops	625,000	Landwehr	600,000
Territorial (Organised)	550,000	Ersatz & Landsturm	2,000,000
Territorial (Unorganised)	700,000		
Total	3,075,000		3,765,000
Russia		Austria-Hungary	
Mobilised Field Army			
European/Caucasian Armies	1,500,000		895,000
West Siberian Army	250,000	Reserves	1,000,000
East Siberian Army	250,000		
Territorials Europe	700,000		
Total	2,700,000	Total	1,895,000
Entente total	5,775,000	Central Powers	5,660,000

Table 3 Strength of peacetime and mobilised European Armies 1912

After 1871 each country's Regular Army grew slowly in size. The 1912 French and German conscript armies (both involved a 25-year commitment from age 20 to 45) were based on the following terms of service:

France:
Active Army – Aged 20: 2 years (changed to 3 years in 1913);
Active Reserve – Aged 22: 11 years (2 training camps of 23 and 17 days);
Territorial Army – Aged 33: 6 years (one training camp 9 days);
Territorial Army Reserve – Aged 39: 6 years (one annual muster)

Germany[i]:
Active Army – Aged 20: 2 (infantry) or 3 years (cavalry);
Army Reserve – Aged 22/23: 4 or 5 years (two weeks' annual training);
Landwehr – Aged 27: 11 years (two weeks annual training for five years)
Landsturm – Aged 38: 7 years

The key difference was the relative lack of training of French reservists and it was because of this, and the disastrous experience with untrained militias in 1870-1, that the French were consistently reluctant to use reserves in the front-line.

Germany had fewer worries and, as in 1870, were prepared to mobilise active reserves on the outbreak of war and incorporate them into their plans for the offensives into Belgium and France. Another issue was the German Army for some time did not call up much more than a third of those young men liable for conscription in any one year. This meant that, by 1914, it had a large pool of several million untrained but men of military age to call up and this reserve of manpower saw the Army through the costly opening two years of the war.

---

[i] There was an alternative system in which the conscript joined the *Ersatz Reserve* for 12½ years, during which they attended three training sessions of 10, 6 and 4 weeks, then joined the *Landsturm* for the rest of their service up to age 45.

Universal military service was introduced in France in response to the defeat by Germany. Sponsored by *Général* Courtot de Cissey, *Ministre de la Guerre* in the first of four governments led by Jules Dufaure, the *loi de 27 Juillet 1872* required five years active service, four in reserve, five as a *Territorial* and six as a reserve *Territorial* – 20 years in all. Men were selected from the manpower pool by lottery. Draw a '*bon numéro*' and you were released from the initial five years' service after twelve months. A '*mauvais numero*' meant you served the whole term. It was also no longer possible to replace one man with another (a process which previously allowed the better off to avoid serving) but there were exemptions. These included, for example, if orphaned, being the oldest son; being a widow's only son or if the father was blind or over 70; if one had a brother already in the Army; students at the *École polytechnique* or the *École forestière*. There was a range of conditional exemptions involving teachers and students, those in holy orders, etc., but these exemptions still required attendance at a few training schemes. The *loi de 27 juillet* also created a reserve officer corps as well as training schemes for reservists.

This system was amended by the *loi du 15 juillet 1889* or the *loi Freycinet*. Previously both clergy and teachers were exempt from army service but in 1889 this exemption was removed and these men were required to serve for one year. More far reaching was the reduction of the active service period from five to three years. Overall length of service was, however, increased to 25 years: three on active service, seven in reserve, six as a *territorial* and nine as a *réserve territorial*. A minor change was made in the *loi du 19 juillet 1892* in which three years were added to the period served in the *réserve active* and three removed from time spent in the *réserve territorial*.

These conditions remained in force until 1905 when the Radicals in the French Government introduced the *loi du 21 mars 1905* or *loi Berteaux*. This dispensed with any exemptions except on health grounds in an effort to return to the Revolutionary concept of *le service universel et égalitaire pour tous*. The period of enlistment remained 25 years but time spent on *service actif* was reduced to two whilst that in the *réserve active* was increased to eleven, with six years each as a *territorial* and six as a *réserve territorial*. This did much to undermine the quality and training of recruits but remained in force until the controversial *loi du 19 juillet 1913*, the *loi des trois ans* (or *loi Barthou*), which re-introduced the three-year *service actif* period whilst extending the time spent in both sections of the *Territorials* by one year. This move increased the active Army by 200,000 men but all untrained (see page 127).[12]

As *The Times* pointed out, this meant 343,000 conscripts, arriving at depots in the autumn of 1913 all requiring training, 206,000 from the Class of 1912 and 137,000 from the Class of 1913. This represented c. 40% of the 'active' French Army in August 1914 and underlines how green were many of the troops thrown into battle. At most, they might have 'enjoyed' ten months training but, with a haemorrhage of experienced officers and NCOs, bringing these raw recruits up to military speed stretched available resources. Article 44 of the 1913 Law tried to staunch this loss of NCOs and experienced Other Ranks under 26 by providing financial incentives if they re-engaged for at least two years. By such means it was hoped the enlarged Army would, at the very least, reach its target mobilisation numbers by 1914, but how ready and well-suited these young conscripts would be was a serious question.[13]

The decision to increase the active service period tried to address a major concern: the surging population in Germany which allowed them to call up larger annual classes of conscripts than possible in France. As each year passed, Germany's Armies would become larger and better trained than those of France. By mid-August 1914 the French Army had at its disposal:

Formations	Numbers	Classes	Observations
Active	880,000	Classes 1911, 1912 & 1913 (Born between 1891 & 1893)	
Reserve	2,200,000	Classes 1900-1910 (Born 1880-90) Attached to active regiments	Called up 3rd to 12th August
		Classes 1908-10 Formed reserve regiments	Called up 3rd-4th August
		Classes 1904-07	Called up 4th-6th August
	(680,000)	In depots: Classes 1902-03	In anticipation of losses
Territorial	700,000	Classes 1893-99 (Born 1873-79)	Called up 3rd-13th August
Territorial Reserve		Classes 1887-92 (Born 1867-72)	Called up after 16th August
Voluntary enlistments 71,000 (including 26,000 foreign volunteers)			

Table 4 Mobilisation of the French Army 1914[14]

As Table 5 below shows, the German Active Army had doubled in size between 1875 and 1914 and when reserves were fully mobilised was considerably larger than their French equivalent. In addition, it had larger reserves and a far greater manpower pool on which to call.

Year	Strength	
1875	420,000	18 Active *Armeekorps*
1881	440,000	Army Law, April 1881. Improvements in training of Ersatz Reserve
1887	527,000	Army Law, 11th March 1887
1890	545,000	Army Law, January 1890. 20 Active *Armeekorps*; 20 Reserve divisions
1893	616,000	Colour service reduced from 3 to 2 years (except cavalry & artillery). Ersatz Reserve training discontinued
1899	632,000	Three new *Armeekorps* created
1905	642,000	Army Law, March 1905. 23 Active *Armeekorps*. Increased training for Reservists and Landwehr
1911	653,000	Army Law, 1911
1912	723,000	Army Law, 1912. 2 new Active *Armeekorps*
1913	870,000	Army Law, 1913
1914	900,000	25 Active *Armeekorps*: 21 German, 3 Bavarian; and *Garde Korps* 15 Reserve *Armeekorps*: 14 German, 1 Bavarian

Table 5 Growth of the German Active Army 1875-1914

Arguably, it was not in French interests to prolong the peace for too long. It was also in their interests to assist, so far as their finances allowed, in re-arming their Russian allies. This, however, was a considerable problem. The effect of the

1870-1 reparations (c. £200 million, £25 million more than France's entire Government revenues as of 1911) was that, by 1911, France had the largest national debt in recorded history. This exceeded £1.34 billion (up from £512 million in 1870) – nearly twice the size Britain's debt and more than five times that of Germany[i]. Re-arming its own forces *and* assisting its eastern ally threatened to impose enormous, even unsustainable, economic strains and, with governments of a manly radical/socialist hue, such costs were permanently under threat of review.

Germany had its own financial constraints, however, with spending on the *Hochseeflotte,* the High Seas Fleet, increasing by 120% between 1901 and 1911. Driven by *Großadmiral* Alfred Peter Friedrich von Tirpitz's grandiose vision for an Imperial Navy, new shipbuilding was running at £11 million a year[ii], compared to the £37 million[iii] annual cost of maintaining the Army. Because of concerns of the dominant Social Democrats in the *Reichstag* about military spending[iv] only 55% of Germans eligible to be conscripted each year joined up prior to the war, which explains why the German Army, relative to population sizes, was not significantly bigger than the French Army.[15]

The result of all this, according to *Der Weltkrieg,* was that the manpower balance between the Central Powers and the Allies of the mobilised armies was as follows:

German:	2,147 million troops
Austria Hungary:	1,400 million
Central Powers total:	3,547 million
France:	2,150 million[v]
Britain:	132,000
Belgium:	100,000
Western Front total:	2,384 million
Russia:	2,712 million (exc. 350,000 troops in Siberia, etc.)
Serbia:	285,000
Eastern Front total:	2.997 million
Allies total:	5.379 million

BECAUSE OF THE OBVIOUS FAILINGS of their reserves and Territorials during the Franco-Prussian War there was a long running dispute within French military circles about the employment of reservists in front-line action. The Prussian-led

---

[i] British National Debt in 1911 £685 million, down from a peak of £771 million in 1903-4. German Government debt amounted to £250 million in 1910.
[ii] 225 million Reichsmarks.
[iii] 750 million Reichsmarks.
[iv] In 1912 the Social Democrats took 35% of the vote (+6% from 1907), Centre Party (*Zentrum*, Catholic, centre/right) 16%, National Liberal Party (centre/right) 14%, Progressive People's Party (*FVP*, liberal) 12%, German Conservative Party (*DKP*, right) 9%, with 14% distributed amongst special interest/regional parties. The *SPD* received the largest vote (though not the largest number of seats) at every election from 1890 onwards, but only in 1912 did they become the largest party in the *Reichstag.*
[v] Not including 127,000 troops in North Africa.

coalition of 1871 relied significantly on reservists being deployed early and in large numbers (and did so again in 1914). French Generals were unconvinced as to their value and, in consequence, 1898's *Plan XIV* had no place for them in the fighting line. The Plan was based, however, on the Germans attacking France from the *Reichsland* provinces of *Elsaß* and *Lothringen* and not through Belgium.

In 1903 *Plan XV* emerged and again proposed Germany be invited onto the French defensive systems pending the mobilisation of Russia, when the French would move onto the offensive. One of the significant differences, however, was a role for reservists in the fighting, even if a subordinate one. The front to be defended was wider than in *Plan XIV*, with five French armies extending from north of Verdun and beyond Épinal. The Ardennes was again ignored, though more divisions would be within reach of Longwy and Sedan than previously.

The following year intelligence, an outline of the '*Schlieffen plan*', brought to light the prospect of a German advance through Belgium. The *Vengeur* documents, thought to be leaked by a disgruntled German staff officer, suggested German strategy was to have sufficient troops on the East Prussian front to hold up the Russians, whilst a large force drove through eastern Belgium, crossing the *Meuse* and the *Sambre Rivers*. Given German railway extensions were being laid between Aachen[i] (barely 40 kms from the Belgian fortress city of Liège), and Leuven[ii], 100 km to the west and just 25 kms from Brussels, and between the towns of Stavelot and Malmedy, this idea took root in certain circles, in particular with Gen. Louis André, the *Ministre de la Guerre* since 1900 (and about whom more later). Investigated by French Army intelligence within the *Deuxième Bureau*, it was concluded the Aachen rail network had a military rather than commercial purpose and they concluded that the Germans were planning to attack through Luxembourg and the Ardennes with as many as nine Army Corps.[16] It was thought, however, they would not cross the *Meuse-Sambre* line into central Belgium because of the need to reduce the various fortresses around Liège and Namur. According to the *Deuxième Bureau* analysis the front of this German advance would fall between Charleville-Mézières and Longwy, and then move into Champagne.

Others were not so convinced. Amongst them was Gen. Henri Joseph Brugère, an artillerist product of the *École polytechnique* and now the vice-president of the *conseil supérieur de la guerre*, which position, in the event of war, made him commander in chief designate of the French Armies facing the Germans. Brugère remained sceptical about the German Army's Belgian excursion, believing they did not possess enough troops to man the Franco-German border whilst providing an invasion force for eastern Belgium. Well, not unless German reservists were included in the front-line, something the French would not currently consider. Brugère would not entertain this idea and, in spite of the railway development near Aachen, he noted the main efforts in transportation improvement remained in the area between Metz and Diedenhofen[iii] which confirmed him in his belief the Germans would attack through Lorraine/*Lothringen*. Furthermore, should they

---

[i] Previously Aix-la-Chapelle. This line linked back to Köln.
[ii] Louvain to French-speaking Walloons.
[iii] Now Thionville.

indeed attack through Belgium this, without reservists in the front-line, could only be achieved by weakening their forces in Lorraine which, believed Brugère, played into French hands because that was where they were strongest.

The other issue facing France was that, even if the Germans had enough troops to cover the 550-kms between Aachen and Switzerland, the French did not. Brugère's only concession was to strengthen the troops available around Verdun in case of a German excursion through the Ardennes, and this was achieved by the creation of a new Army kept in reserve which, if necessary, could be directed towards the Charleville-Mézières/Longwy gap. Thus, the strategic and tactical principles enshrined in *Plan XV* held good.

Until 1907, that is, when work started on *Plan XVI* under the auspices of the 62-year-old infantryman Gen. Alexis Auguste Raphaël Hagron. This plan took more seriously the threat of German envelopment from the north but, in the meantime, *Plan XV* was replaced by an adapted version: *Plan XV bis* which came into being in May[i]. This reflected the concerns about the vulnerability of the Ardennes sector and, as a result, while the five armies still covered the *Moselle – Meuse* line, *Ve Armée* now occupied the line of the *Meuse* north of Verdun towards Mézières (i.e. south of the Ardennes), with the support of four reserve divisions in the area Laon – Rethel – Reims – Ste Menehould.

Plan XVI was finally introduced in 1909 and again showed French concerns about an attack through Belgium, concerns which were reinforced by an analysis of intelligence passed to the French on 2nd May 1908.[17] In the meantime, though, the expectation of military discussions resulting from the signing of the *Entente Cordiale* in 1904 led to the hope a British field army might be deployed in northern France in the event of war. These hopes were not immediate and, indeed, effective intervention by a British field army deployed to the European mainland was initially discounted in the aftermath of the Boer War.

Towards the end of 1904, however, Maj. Victor Huguet[ii] was appointed French Military *Attaché* in London. On the outbreak of war nearly ten years later, he was appointed Head of the French Military Mission to Sir John French's headquarters in France and Flanders. He came to Whitehall with no great confidence in the military prowess of the British Army, an attitude widespread amongst the French military. His predecessor, Lt. Col. Albert Gérard Léo d'Amade[iii], was appointed in

---

[i] A modification of *Plan XV* in 1906 allowed more divisions to concentrate near Verdun. The release of two Army Corps from the Italian frontier partially helped this deployment as well as an increase in numbers from the compulsory enlistment of all men except those unfit [*Source*: Zuber, T., *The Real German War Plan 1904-14*, page 65].
[ii] Gen. Victor Jacques Marie Huguet was born on 8th September 1858 in Boulogne sur Mer, Pas de Calais. He was the son of Auguste Victor Huguet and Julie Marie Grandsire. *École Polytechnique*, 1878. *École d'application de l'artillerie et de Génie*, 1880. Joined *26e régiment d'artillerie*, 1882. *École Supérieur de Guerre* 1889-1891. *État major de l'armée* (1891-4) then regimental and staff positions until appointed Head of the Mission to GHQ on 2nd August 1914 where he remained until 1st January 1916. He spent two years commanding the artillery of the *37e Corps*. He died in 1925 [*Source: Base Leonore*].
[iii] Gen. Albert Gérard Léo d'Amade was born in Toulouse on 24th December 1856. He attended *École Spéciale Militaire*, 1874. *Sous-Lt., 3e Régiment de tirailleurs algériens*, 1876.

early 1901 and spent some time in South Africa during the fighting and came away with a remarkably poor impression of the British forces employed there, considering them fit only for 'police duties or for minor colonial expeditions'.[18] Huguet, however, arrived at a time when the Army was trying to apply the lessons harshly learned and he was impressed by the changes in training and equipment which were instituted over the coming years. He shared, for example, Gen. Herr's concerns (see page 233) about the over-reliance of the French Army on the 75 and expressed approval of the provision of 4.7-in. and 60 pdr. guns to each British Division in addition to the normal field guns.[19] Towards the end of 1905 Huguet concluded the British might be able to field a well-equipped and well-trained European field army of some 150,000 effectives but few of these troops were likely to be deployed on the active front within the first thirty days of any new war.

He and the French Government were, as it turns out, pushing at an open door. Sir Edward Grey, later 1st Viscount Grey of Fallodon, was the new Foreign Secretary and he shared French concerns about German intentions, discussing them with Haldane during the General Election campaign in January 1906. The Prime Minister, Sir Henry Campbell-Bannerman, then explicitly instructed the War Office to enter discussions with the French on military mutual assistance.[20]

Prior to that, on 20th December 1905, whilst riding in Hyde Park, Huguet managed to 'run into' none other than the Director of Military Operations, the clever but overweight and unfit Maj. Gen. James Grierson[i]. With friction between Germany and France running high over Morocco, this meeting seemed either

---

Military *Attaché*, China, 1887-90. *2e Bureau, État Major de l'armée*, 1896. Military *Attaché*, London, 1901-4 when he requested a return to active service. Colonel, *21e* then *77e régiments d'infanterie*. Morocco until 1909. Commander, *9e Division*, then *13e* and *6e Corps*. *Conseil supérieur de la guerre*, April 1914. On 17th August 1914 he took command of a *Groupe de Divisions Territoriales* between Maubeuge and Dunkerque. He failed to distinguish himself and was replaced four weeks later. Military Governor of Marseille before being appointed commander of the *Corps expéditionnaire d'Orient* which was sent to Gallipoli in April 1915. Replaced the following month and returned to France. His last military service was commandant, *10e Région militaire*, Rennes. He died in 1941.

[i] Lt. Gen. Sir James Moncrieff Grierson, KCB, CVO, CMG, ADC, was born in Glasgow on 27th January, 1859, the son of George Moncrieff Grierson and Allison Walker. Glasgow Academy and RMA, Woolwich. Royal Artillery, 1877. He served in Egypt from 1882 and the Sudan and was on the staff in India. He then became the head of the Russian Section of the Intelligence Division in 1890 before serving as Brigade Major for the Royal Artillery at Aldershot. In 1896 he was appointed Military *Attaché* in Berlin which posting allowed him to gain 'an intimate knowledge of the German Army' according to Sir John French. He served in China during the Boxer Rebellion before taking part in the South African War where he occupied various staff positions. He was appointed AQMG and then Chief of Staff, II Corps, before being appointed Director of Military Operations in 1904. In 1906 he was given command of 1st Division, and made GOC, Eastern Command, in 1912. On the outbreak of war he took command of the II Corps but he died of an aneurism on a train near Amiens at 7:00 a.m. on 17th August 1914. He is buried in the Glasgow Necropolis, grave Primus. 38.

fortuitous or contrived depending on one's point of view. Huguet came away from this, and another official meeting with Grierson on 16th January, convinced of the utility of a British intervention in Belgium or the *Pas de Calais*, a plan which, it transpired, was already being studied by Grierson and the Staff. Not only might the British involvement be more substantial than believed in France but quicker too, with a British force being able to deploy far faster than Huguet's initial thirty day estimate.[21] Later, in March 1906, Grierson and Huguet, accompanied by 'Wullie' Robertson, toured Belgium in the area around Namur and Charleroi and further secret discussions continued between Huguet and Grierson whilst the British also conducted their own war games involving the commitment of an Expeditionary Force in northern France.

Unfortunately for these discussions, Grierson's removal to command 1st Division at Aldershot in July 1906 brought these high-level consultations to a temporary halt, even if lowlier officers continued to explore the various options and problems. Grierson's replacement as DMO was Maj. Gen. Sir John Ewart, KCB,[i] a man who 'rose without trace' and was so anonymous he barely rates a footnote in history. Described by Huguet as a man 'of a timorous nature (with) little liking for responsibility',[22] Ewart occupied his important position for four years and yet, throughout this time, he and Huguet never met. The French officer made do with lengthy and laborious meetings with more junior officers at the War Office and entered the building via the back door at Haldane's request so as not to upset too much the German ambassador.[23]

One of the key issues was the landing point for a British Expeditionary Force. Antwerp was favoured by the Army as it gave direct support to a threat to Belgian neutrality and because fear of Germany gaining access to the Channel via such an important port was a growing concern within government circles. The Navy's say was, however, final. They planned to close the English Channel on the line Dover to *Cap Gris Nez* should war break out and this meant the lines of communication by sea must be with French ports further south, i.e. Boulogne, Le Havre and Rouen. These landing points further dictated that the lines of communication with any likely Belgian front should run via Amiens towards Cambrai, Maubeuge and on to a line between Mons and Charleroi.

Such planning in Whitehall was, however, theoretical until such time as Ewart, the cypher masquerading as Director of Military Operations, was replaced by a character with a more urgent appreciation of the increasingly ominous military mood in Europe. That man was Brig. Gen., later Field Marshal, Sir Henry Hughes Wilson, 1st Baronet, GCB, DSO. Wilson, a controversial figure throughout his life, was appointed in 1910 having spent the previous three years as the Commandant of the Staff College in succession to his close friend Henry Rawlinson. A noted Francophile, Wilson nailed his colours to the mast at Camberley in late 1908 when he set his students the task of preparing an operational plan for the deployment

---

[i] Lt. Gen. Sir John Spencer Ewart, KCB, Queen's Own Cameron Highlanders, served in Egypt, the Sudan and South Africa. In 1910 he was appointed Adjutant General, resigning in 1914 over the Curragh Incident. He was GOC, Scottish Command, throughout the war. Born in 1861, he died in 1930.

of a British Expeditionary Force in northern France to counter a German invasion through eastern Belgium. When news of this exercise leaked it was the cause of some consternation amongst various Members of Parliament and others with a somewhat rosier interpretation of current German intentions. In consequence, the following year, when a similar scheme formed part of the College's curriculum, the enemy was not so precisely identified and the secrecy of the exercise was made robustly clear to those involved.[24] In December 1909 Wilson visited the *École Supérieur de Guerre* and its then commandant, Ferdinand Foch, with whom he struck up a close *rapport* even to the extent of agreeing where they believed the German thrust through Belgium would be located, i.e. in the Ardennes region between Verdun and Namur.[25] Wilson returned Foch's hospitality the following year taking him and Huguet to Camberley and then to visit his mentor, Lord Roberts, and the Secretary of State for War, Haldane.

The result of these discussions[i], allied to the continuing belief in a German attack through the Ardennes (though no further west)[ii], was *Plan XVI* which shifted the main troop concentrations to around Verdun with four armies (including a new reserve army and totalling twelve Corps) plus four reserve divisions deployed around Châlons, St Dizier, Verdun, Ste Menehould, Challerange and Rethel, with eight more at Laon and La Fère. Just two armies (six Corps) and four reserve divisions covered Toul to the Swiss border. There was great reluctance to cover more of the Belgian border as, by extending too far west, the centre was weakened, inviting a German attack between Verdun and Toul.[26]

This view that the Germans would attack through Belgium but not west of the *Meuse/Sambre* line was again reinforced in 1910 when the *Conseil supérieur de la Guerre*, under the vice-president Gen. Trémeau, determined Maubeuge should be a base for French troops ready to attack the 'outside flank' of any German troops attempting to enter France between the *Sambre* and the *Meuse* via the Belgian town of Philipville. The use of the phrase 'outside flank' clearly shows the French still did not believe the German breach of Belgian neutrality would extend west of the fortress cities of Liège and Namur.[27]

On 11th January 1911 a new vice-president, 61-year-old Gen. Victor-Constant Michel, took over the *Conseil supérieur de la Guerre*. He served in the Franco-Prussian War, was involved in the siege of Paris and in suppressing the Commune. A staff officer he was attached to the office of Gen. Billot, the *Ministre de la Guerre*, in 1882 and, the next year, joined the staff of the Military Governor of Paris. After battalion and regimental commands, in 1893 he was appointed Deputy Chief of Staff of the *Ministre de la Guerre*, Gen. Mercier. He received Brigade and Divisional commands before taking over *2e Corps*. Appointed to the *Conseil supérieur de la Guerre* on 22nd December 1907 he was replaced at *2e Corps* by Joseph Joffre.[28]

---

[i] Extended to regular exchanges of senior officers attending each Army's annual manoeuvres: Sir John French in France in 1908 and 1911 and Henry Wilson in 1912; Foch came to England in 1912 and de Castelnau in 1913. Joffre was due to attend the autumn 1914 manoeuvres [Huguet, *op. cit.*, page 26].

[ii] A view reinforced by an otherwise unnecessary German rail network in the Eifel region immediately east of the Luxembourg border [Zuber, T., *op. cit.*, page 101].

15. Gen. Victor-Constant Michel

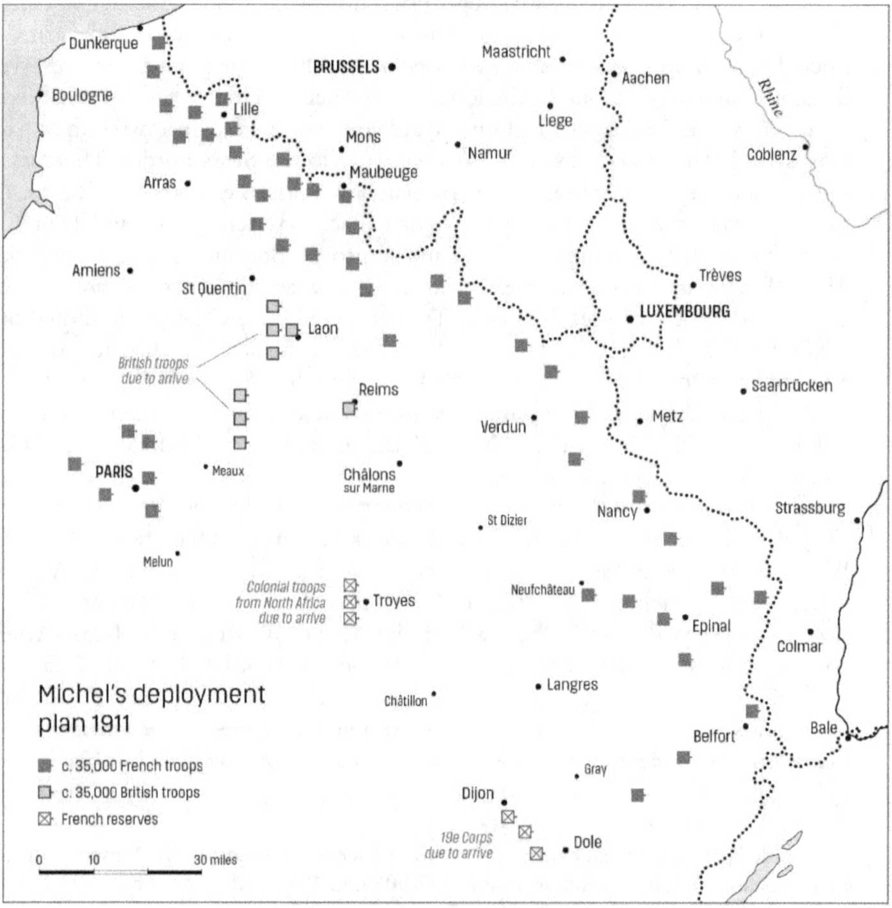

Map 3 Michel's deployment plan 1911
[*Source*: *AFdGG*, Tome I, Vol. I, Map No. 5]
Solid blocks are existing troops from Metropolitan France. Hatched blocks expected reinforcements

104

The successful deployment of the BEF in August 1914 later relied on Wilson's work. He had already met with the Belgian General Staff, with Ferdinand Foch, and the French Chief of Staff, Gen. Laffort de Ladibat, and had even been to Germany noting, on his way to Berlin by train, the large number of railway sidings being constructed on the Belgian-German border[i].

The conviction the Germans would attack through Belgium was now widespread. Indeed, as early as 1876, the French staff had planned for such an eventuality with the idea of a Belgium-facing army located on the line Laon-La Fère-Saint-Quentin. Notable French strategists such as Langlois and Bonnal envisaged a German holding action against the Russians in East Prussia while the main effort went through Belgium. This seemed to be the general consensus to which, according to German intelligence, 'there were no dissenting opinions' in either France, Belgium or Great Britain.[29] Whilst the majority still saw the attack coming through the Ardennes there was a growing sense amongst some, and this included Foch, the Germans would launch a surprise attack on Liège and cross the *Meuse/Sambre* line into central Belgium, the objective being as far west as Lille.

Wilson and Michel agreed that, in the event of war, Germany would leave as small a force as possible in East Prussia to face Russia whilst concentrating against France. They further agreed the Germans would not only avoid the fortified areas opposite *Lothringen* but also the difficult terrain of the Ardennes where there were 'only 13 roads' along which to advance.[30] The logical conclusion was they would outflank the left of the French deployment by crossing the *Meuse/Sambre* line and advancing through central Belgium. To achieve this required a surprise attack on Liège, which gave them the bridges across the *Meuse* they needed to move towards Brussels and beyond. Wilson even thought it possible they might violate Dutch neutrality by moving through the province of Limburg. Michel's solution was to suggest in February 1911 to the *Ministre de la Guerre*, Adolphe Messimy, that French forces between Belfort and Charleville-Mézières should stand on the defensive whilst the rest of the French Army launched 'a vigorous offensive in Belgium'[31] because, as he wrote to Messimy at the time:

"... the whole of Belgium would be the theatre of future operations between France and Germany."

And this would be, Michel suggested, because any forthcoming war would be triggered, not by friction between France and Germany, but by the growing naval and strategic competition between Germany and Great Britain[ii]. He claimed

---

[i] The location given by Wilson is Herstal, now a northern suburb of Liège and not on the border though the line from Aachen does pass through Herstal after leaving Liège. The Belgian-German border in 1914 was, however, very different from today. After 1918 Belgium gained territories known as the *Eastern Cantons* (French: *Cantons de l'Est*, Dutch: *Oostkantons*) comprising the mainly German-speaking areas around Eupen, Malmedy and Saint Vith. When Wilson and Foch visited the area the German border was c. 8 miles to the north close to the Dutch city of Maastricht.

[ii] His report opens with the words: "The conflict of interest between England and Germany is growing every day, and may at some point lead us into a war that would spread to many of the European nations" [*Source: AFdGG*, Tome I, Annexes Vol. 1,

Germany had, for a long time, harboured the intentions of seizing Antwerp in order to further their global maritime ambitions. This was something which Britain simply could not countenance if it wished still to dominate the Narrow Seas. German determination to seize the Belgian coast and British resolve to stop this meant that Belgium would become the main theatre of any war involving France and Germany. He stated Germany would employ 'without hesitation' 42 active and reserve Army Corps in an attack on France via Belgium. France could counter with forty Corps, if reserves were included, and, of these:

> "... a part can be devoted to the active defence of the entire region between Belfort and Mézières, and the rest to a vigorous offensive in Belgium. Antwerp, Brussels and Namur are, significantly, at an equal distance from both the French border and the German border."[32]

Michel then went on to discuss his concerns over the availability of staff and other officers of sufficient number and quality to take in hand the French reserve units he believed needed to be employed in any campaign. Changes to improve this situation were under way, and this was essential as Michel advocated reserve units being in the front-line alongside the current full-time active regiments of the Army. This was to be achieved by combining a currently active regiment with its reserve regiment into a new demi-Brigade commanded by a full-time Colonel. As it then stood, half of the reserve regiments would be put under the command of a Lt. Col. no more than five years past retirement. By this simple expedient, the effectives in every formation in the Army were doubled in number. The same applied to the artillery and, in addition, heavy artillery, the *artillerie lourde*, would be attached to each Army Corps as was currently the practice in the German Army.

The deployment of these reinforced Corps was also radically different from anything previously considered. Territorial units, made up of the most elderly men still considered fit for service, would defend important locations, e.g. Dunkerque, Maubeuge, Laon, Reims, the fortified cities of the east and the important ports on the Atlantic and Mediterranean coasts. Otherwise, the deployment was as follows:

25 divisions on the Franco-Belgian border between Dunkerque and Stenay south of the Ardennes. These c. 875,000 troops were not equally distributed. Three divisions, 105,000 men, were between the *River Lys* and the coast; three divisions were at Mézières, Sedan, and Stenay along the *Meuse* with one in reserve near Rethel; and eighteen, 630,000 troops, were concentrated around Lille, Valenciennes, Maubeuge, Avesnes and Hirson, i.e. within reach of the Belgian capital, Brussels, and the important river crossing at Namur. These were:

1er Corps between Dunkerque and Lille
8e, 9e, 10e, 11e, 12e and *13e Corps* between Lille and Avesnes-sur-Helpe
16e, 17e and *18e Corps* between Hirson and Rethel
2e Corps between Mézières and Montmédy

Annexe 3, page 7]. Bernhardi, in *Germany and the Next War*, repeatedly makes it clear that the fundamental conflict was between England (*sic*), the dominant colonial power, and Germany, the aspiring colonial power, and that the English (*sic*) Government wished to destroy Germany's fleet and thus frustrate its global colonial ambitions.

14 divisions (490,000 troops) faced the German border from Longuyon to Belfort, with eight close to the border and six in reserve:

6e, 20e and *7e Corps* between Montmédy and Belfort (to be reinforced by the *14e, 15e, 19e* and *21e Corps*)

Six divisions (i. e. *3e, 4e* and *5e Corps*, 210,000 men) formed a mobile reserve around Paris whilst the hoped for six divisions of the BEF were aligned from La Fère in the north down through Soissons and on to the north bank of the Marne. Three divisions of Colonial troops were in reserve around Troyes and the new *19e Corps* lay between Dijon and Dôle.

In total, nearly 2 million French and British troops of which eighteen divisions, 630,000 men, formed a floating reserve or a mass of manoeuvre.

Of these, *1er, 8e, 9e, 10e, 11e, 12e* and *13e Corps*, or 490,000 men, would enter Belgium between the coast and the line of the *Sambre/Meuse*. The *2e, 16e, 17e* and *18e Corps* (280,000 men) were to advance south of the *Sambre/Meuse* line in the direction Givet/Dinant to cover the right of the main force. This 'invasion' force amounted, therefore, to 770,000 men to which could be added 220,000 men of the three Corps in general reserve around Paris. The defence of the Montmédy to Belfort line was placed in the hands of the territorial garrisons of the fortified areas and 300,000 men of *6e* (Verdun), *20e* (Nancy), and *7e Corps* (Belfort). In addition, 200,000 men of the *14e* (to be formed at Lyon and Grenoble), *15e* (to be formed in Provence and south-east France), *19e* (Algeria) and *21e Corps* (to be formed at Épinal), could be later deployed for offensive action in *Elsaß* and *Lothringen*.[33]

What is clear from such a deployment is that:

1. Michel expected the main German attack to come through central Belgium;
2. There would be no *offensive à outrance* into the lost territories of Alsace/Lorraine; and
3. Michel still considered reasonable the prospect of 'offensive defence', i.e. drawing the Germans onto well-fortified and defended French positions in order to cause heavy casualties and enable counterattacks.

Michel's plan to incorporate reserve troops into the active front-line Corps was debated by the *Conseil supérieur de la Guerre* on 19th July 1911 and unanimously rejected.[34] The issue about the use of reserve troops and Territorials was a sore point within senior levels of the French Army and had been so for many years. It was exacerbated by the changes in the conscription system introduced in 1905 by Rouvier's left wing Government, changes which were part and parcel of the fall-out from the infamous Dreyfus Affair which tore apart both country and Army.

L'AFFAIRE DREYFUS OF 1894 exposed deep fault lines within the French Army, government and society, and exposed wide divisions between Catholics and secularists, between right-wing royalists and ultra-nationalists and republicans and socialists on the centre-left. Furthermore, it highlighted the vicious seam of anti-Semitism which ran through the country, again exposed for all to see when the Vichy Government co-operated so enthusiastically with the deportation of France's Jews after the German occupation in 1940.

Espionage in France was a constant concern in the years prior to the arrest of

Capt. Alfred Dreyfus on such a charge in 1894. Every year, it appeared, some French soldier or civilian was arrested and imprisoned for spying[i]. Then, in September 1894, the housekeeper at the German Embassy passed to the *Section de statistiques,* the section of the *Deuxième bureau* of the *État-major des Armées* responsible for counterintelligence, a torn up note which subsequently became known as the *'bordereau'*. The note was addressed to Colonel von Schwartzkoppen, German military *attaché* in Paris. It indicated important French military documents were to be passed over which related mainly to the technical details of the *Obusier de 120 mm C modèle 1890 Baquet*. This was a light field howitzer designed by Capt. Louis Henry Auguste Baquet between 1886 and 1890 and which utilised the first (and later shown to be inadequate) hydro-pneumatic recoil system[ii]. After a cursory investigation it was determined the culprit was a junior artillery officer seconded to the *État-major* – Capt. Alfred Dreyfus. Dreyfus was arrested on 15th October 1894, charged with treason, court-martialled in closed session between 19th and 21st December, unanimously found guilty, made subject to official and public *'degradation'* at the *École Militaire* on 5th January 1895 (his sword was broken in half and his uniform insignia and badges ripped off) before being deported for life to the notorious Devil's Island penal colony in French Guyana on 21st February. Many, including the soon-to-be-Prime Minister Clemenceau, believed he should have been executed, as did the socialist leader Jean Jaurès.[35] The only problem was Dreyfus was an innocent, if hugely convenient, scapegoat.

16. Capt. Alfred Dreyfus

Born in Alsace, his family left *Elsaß* after the German occupation of 1871. They were of Republican instincts and, as became rather more important, Jewish. The young Dreyfus joined the Army after leaving the *École polytechnique* in 1878. In 1890,

---

[i] Thomas (1888), Blondeau (1889), Boutonnet (1890), Triponé and Fassier (1891), Grenier (1892), and Marie Forêt ('the widow Millecamps') in 1893 were all imprisoned for espionage.

[ii] The gun, and its larger brother the *Canon de 155 C modèle 1890 Baquet*, were employed in WW1 but their limited range and slow rate of fire (1½ rounds per minute) rendered them ineffective on the Western Front.

he attended the *École de guerre,* being married in the same year. In 1893, he was attached to the *état-major de l'armée* at the Ministry of War.

When it came to finding the man responsible for the *'bordereau',* investigators did not look far. On the flimsiest of evidence, and with the use of a secret and falsified dossier none of which was seen by the defence, Dreyfus was convicted more because of his background, his politics, and his religion than because it was ever believed he was truly guilty. The secret dossier was a libel concocted by the head of the *Section de statistiques,* Col. Sandherr, but, when he fell ill in the summer of 1895, his replacement, Lt. Col. Marie-Georges Picquart, continued the investigation as a further incriminating document was retrieved from the German embassy in March 1896 known as the *'petit bleu'.* He reviewed the 'evidence', saw through it and, furthermore, rapidly discovered the name of the true traitor – Maj. Charles Marie Ferdinand Walsin Esterházy, a 47-year-old officer in the *Légion Étrangère* who failed in his previous effort to enter the *École spéciale militaire* at St Cyr but later exploited family connections to gain his commission in 1870. He was tried behind closed doors by a Military Tribunal in 1898 but found not guilty. Picquart, for his efforts, was first sent away to Tunisia to join the *4e régiment de tirailleurs algériens,* then accused of falsifying the evidence against Esterházy and sent to prison for a year and dismissed from the Army[i].

A full-scale scandal slowly emerged as the French Army and government, with aggressive support from right-wing, anti-Jewish nationalists, tried desperately to cover its tracks and justify its actions. Meanwhile, other politicians, artists, and writers, notably the author Émile Zola, tried to expose the lies, obfuscations, and prejudice at the heart of the Dreyfus prosecution.

It was a slow process and it was not until after Esterházy's exposure in 1898 that 'the good and the great' amongst French republicans (now including Clemenceau and Jaurès) demanded a re-trial. Famously, Zola penned a piece for the newspaper *L'Aurore* aimed at the President, Félix Faure, which, at Clemenceau's suggestion, was entitled *'J'accuse…!'.* The *Chambre de Deputes* voted that Zola be tried for libel and the country was thus ever more deeply split between nationalists, conservatives, royalists, and high Catholics and liberal, leftist, republican and secularist *'Dreyfusards'* who demanded a re-trial.

Zola was indeed tried for libel and found guilty but in a case rendered laughable by the President of the Court, Delegorgue, and his refusal to allow Zola's lawyer to call and/or question witnesses. The trial was characterised by riots outside the court predominantly organised by right wing agitators and, for some time thereafter, both the government and military intransigently defended their actions in a mood of increasingly rabid anti-Jewish sentiment. Zola only escaped imprisonment by fleeing to England.

In the midst of all this, legislative elections were held between 8th and 22nd May 1898. The 'moderate' Republican (*républicains modéré* or *républicains opportunistes*)

---

[i] Picquart was rehabilitated on the same day as Dreyfus in 1906. Promoted *général de brigade,* he was *Ministre de la Guerre* three months later in Clemenceau's first government (25th October, 1906 – 23rd July, 1909). In February 1910 he succeeded General Joffre in command of the *2e corps d'armée.* He died on 19th January 1914, aged 60.

government of Jules Méline staggered on to 28th June to be followed for 120 days by Henri Brisson and his *Radicaux indépendants* before Charles Dupuy led two more *républicains modéré* governments of 109 and 114 days' duration respectively. Only the *républicains modéré* administration of Pierre Waldeck-Rousseau (2 years, 346 days) brought some form of stability. But notably a new party gained representation in the *Chambre des députés*: the *groupe antijuif* or *groupe antisémite nationaliste*. Some 28 (or 23 depending on one's source) deputies were elected out of a total of 586 and they were led by the nationalist, anti-Semitic journalist Édouard Drumont, the founder of a newspaper *La Libre Parole* and the new deputy for Algiers. So, following on from Germany, France now officially, and equally shamefully, had explicitly anti-Semitic representation in its Parliament. Though the group disappeared in the 1902 elections, a dozen of its deputies joined the new Catholic, nationalist, ultra-conservative *Action libérale Populaire*, carrying forward their virulently anti-Semitic views into the new organisation formed to defend Catholicism from the *Parti républicain radical et radical-socialiste* government of Émile Combes.

'The truth will out' proved, at least in Dreyfus's case, to be an accurate, if long drawn out, aphorism. By 1899 the case against him appeared to have collapsed and a military re-trial was ordered which took place in Rennes. This hearing was even more of a shambles than either Dreyfus's first summary court-martial or the 'trial' of Zola with, at one point, Dreyfus's lawyer being shot and wounded in the street by a right-wing zealot. Confessions by the true culprit, Walsin Esterházy[i], and by Lt. Col. Henry, a French officer who forged documents to help prove Dreyfus's guilt were not considered and the two lawyers supposedly representing him fell out. Dreyfus was again found guilty on a majority, 5-2, decision and sentenced to ten years in prison. Dreyfus demanded another re-trial but was eventually persuaded to accept a pardon and a law was passed to allow this to be granted.

If France wanted to put the dreadful divisions behind them, they were not allowed to, not least by the international reaction to the second court-martial. Everyone in Europe, apart from the French government, courts, military, and the nationalist and anti-Semitic right, believed Dreyfus innocent. Those believing him innocent even included the *Kaiser* for whose country he was accused of spying!

It was the victory of the Left in the 1902 General Election which re-ignited the affair and, by 1903, yet another investigation was under way. This one started to reveal the enormous scale of the lies, fabrications and manipulations indulged in by official channels both within the Army and the Government. On 9th March 1905, the Attorney-General, Baudouin, demanded the Supreme Court quash Dreyfus's conviction without further delay but it still took another fifteen months before the military courts' decisions were set aside on 12th July 1906. Dreyfus was reinstated as a major in the Artillery the next day. He retired from the Army the

---

[i] Esterházy later fled France to live in Harpenden, Hertfordshire, where he died in 1923. During his exile he wrote articles for several anti-Semitic French magazines. Lt. Col. Henry was imprisoned in the *fort du Mont Valérien* on 30th August 1898 and committed suicide in his cell that night.

following year on the grounds of ill-health but was still the victim of an attempted assassination by an extreme right-wing journalist, Louis Grégori, in 1908. Dreyfus went on to serve as a reserve officer in the war and he was appointed an Officer of the *Légion d'Honneur* in 1919. He died in 1935.

The entire affair highlighted in the starkest terms the divisions between the republican left and the nationalist and catholic right in France and, in spite of severe setbacks in the 1890s, it was the republican and anti-clerical left which came out victorious. It also showed the widespread and profound nature of the vicious anti-Semitism which existed within France. Revenge on the *Dreyfusards* for their victory in 1906 would be taken on the Jewish communities of France after 1940.

The effects on France were profound. In 1904, the *Ministre de la Guerre*, Gen. Louis André, was implicated in the *Affaire des fiches*. The republican, anti-Catholic, Freemason André conspired to hold back the promotion of officers solely based on their catholic and conservative political beliefs. Simple attendance at Mass was sufficient to blight a career. Then, on 21st March 1905, a law was brought in by Henri Maurice Berteaux, a member of the *Parti radical-socialiste* and the *Ministre de la Guerre* between November 1904 and November 1905 in the governments of first Émile Combes and then Maurice Rouvier[i]. This law reduced the enforced period of Army service from three to two years, although the elimination of all exemptions except for physical unfitness served to increase the number of men available in the case of a general mobilisation. They would be less well trained, however, and this was an issue of great concern to professional officers already unhappy with the activities of André. It also meant that, as each recruit 'class' joined, there would be fewer experienced men to assist with their training. In addition, with the widening of the base from which men were drawn to include all but the medically unfit, the overall physical standards of the Army declined.

It was, however, regarded as a triumph of sorts for hard-line Republicans keen to see the Army become a replica of the Revolutionary Army of the 1790s. There was a clear political drive behind these changes. It was an attempt to widen the base of the Army; enforce equality between classes (as better educated, upper and middle-class men found it possible to avoid military service); and create a 'Citizen Army' more in line with radical republican thinking[ii]. One of its main effects, however, was to undermine morale amongst long service officers and NCOs, and reduce the effectiveness of the Army at a time of increasing political and diplomatic tension. The political mood also appeared to 'infect' the discipline of conscripts which now included nearly every man available whatever their physical or other attributes. Though no-one doubted their bravery and patriotism there were comments from both within the Army and from observers from Britain and Germany about the lax approach of the soldiers on the march and at the annual manoeuvres. Socialism was blamed for their less than immediate response to orders given by officers. Unfavourable comparisons were made between the rigid

---

[i] He then became the president of the *Commission de l'Armée*.
[ii] The assault on the Catholic Church continued with the *loi du 9 décembre 1905 concernant la séparation des Églises et de l'État*. This ended state funding of religion, closed most religious schools, and passed the property of the church to the state.

discipline and efficiency of the average German soldier, even though complacent French officers still held the view a single Frenchman was worth several Germans on the battlefield.[36] Clearly, the experience of 1870-1 had been forgotten by such men who, instead, cast their minds back to the glories of the Napoleonic era and its numerous French victories (whilst conveniently forgetting defeats such as Leipzig and Waterloo both of which involved German troops). French *élan* and *ésprit* were held to be more important than military efficiency, a view proved expensively wrong during the opening weeks of the war, and again in 1917 when Nivelle's absurd tactics induced the once resolute *poilus* to mutiny and refuse to leave their trenches for yet another pointless and ill-prepared attack.

IN CONSEQUENCE OF THESE TUMULTUOUS EVENTS, by 1911 the majority of senior officers were not prepared to contemplate any reliance in the front-line on inadequately trained and even less well-disciplined reservists officered by those deemed sub-standard by the regular army.[37] Furthermore, the increasingly influential advocates of the 'all-out attack' such as de Grandmaison (see page 178) were outraged that, in Michel's plan, there was no great offensive which might liberate *Elsaß* and *Lothringen*. As a result, Michel's ideas for a deployment opposite the Belgian border, although the most astute of any brought forward prior to 1914, were flatly rejected. In the face of such a fundamental disagreement between Michel, the putative commander in chief of the French Armies in the event of war, and the members of the supreme War Council of the Republic there could be only one outcome. Messimy sacked Michel and removed him from the *Conseil supérieur de la Guerre* on 28th July 1911[i]. In addition, the role of the vice-president of the *Conseil supérieur de la Guerre* as *de facto* CinC was removed and a new position of Chief of the General Staff (*chef d'état major*) created with that person to be CinC should war break out. With the fall of Michel so fell his deployment plan. The legacy of his brief time in charge of the French Army was, however, an agreement made on 20th July in Paris that the British would have available, by the 14th day of their mobilisation programme, a continental expeditionary force of six infantry divisions and one cavalry division plus two independent cavalry brigades.

Michel's replacement, named on 28th July, was *his* replacement as commander of *2e Corps* – Gen. Joseph Jacques Césaire Joffre, the man at whose door much of the blame for the catastrophe of the opening days of the war can justifiably be laid. Joffre was aged 62 on the outbreak of war. The son of Gilles Joffre and Catherine Plasa, he was born on 12th January 1852 amongst his family's vineyards in Rivesaltes just north of Perpignan, ten kilometres from the Mediterranean. He completed his preliminary studies at age 15 at the *lycée François-Arago* in Perpignan before attending the *lycée Charlemagne* in Paris in preparation for entry into one of the military schools. He joined the *École Polytechnique* in July 1869, but his studies were disrupted by the outbreak of the Franco-Prussian War. By September 1870 he was a *sous-lieutenant* in the artillery defending *Bastion 28* at the *Porte de la Villette* in the *19e arrondissement* during the Siege of Paris. On 3rd July 1871, he returned to complete his studies at the *École Polytechnique* from which he emerged as a *sous-*

---

[i] Michel became military Governor of Paris but was replaced by Gen. Gallieni on 26th August 1914. He did not receive another command. He died in 1937.

lieutenant in the *Génie* (Engineers), joining the *2e régiment de génie* in Montpellier. On his promotion to lieutenant, he was attached to the *École d'application de l'artillerie et du génie* at Fontainebleau and he met and married Marie-Amélie Pourcheiroux. It was a sadly short-lived marriage as she died within six months of the wedding.

In spring, 1874, Joffre joined the *1er régiment de génie* at Versailles and spent ten years engaged in the repair and construction of fortifications, first in Paris and then near Montlignon in the *forêt de Montmorency*, *département du Val-d'Oise*, before moving to the Jura region and, finally, closer to his family home, with work at Villefranche-de-Conflent and Mont Louis on the upper reaches of the *River Têt*.

In 1884, he went to French Indochina, leaving for Formosa in January 1885 before moving to Tonkin to organise the fortifications in the French 'protectorate' because of the tension in the area caused by the war between China and France ongoing since 1881. With peace established in June 1885, he carried on working on other fortifications in what is now Vietnam until he left at the beginning of 1888 to return to France via China, Japan, and the USA. On his return, he was attached to the office of the *directeur du génie* at the Ministry of War. He was then promoted *chef de bataillon* with the *5e régiment du génie* at Versailles. Here he became involved in the development of military railways, something which was of significance during the French mobilisation in the summer of 1914.

Rather like the naval movement of British troops to South Africa in 1899, the mobilisation and efficient transportation of the Armies to the killing grounds of north-eastern France was one of the few successes of the war. Outside Britain, the first railway was the 23 km line from Saint-Étienne to Andrézieux which opened on 30th June 1827. This was followed three years later by the 58 km route from Saint-Étienne to Lyon and, from 1832, the 67 km track from Andrézieux to Roanne. These lines employed either horse-drawn or fixed steam engine-powered rolling stock. The first steam locomotives were used from 1837 onwards between Paris and Saint-Germain-en-Laye. Tracks for proper steam-drawn trains then proliferated across France driven by the *loi relative à l'établissement des grandes lignes de chemin de fer* of 11th June 1842 with which it was intended to increase the existing 319 kms of railway track to match the railways of Britain where, in the same year, over 2,500 kms of line existed. The railway network was further enhanced by the creation, through the *loi du 17 juillet 1879*, of a plan to lay c. 8,700 kms of *voie ferrée d'intérêt local*, i.e. tracks linking smaller towns and rural parts of France to the national, strategic network. This was the *Plan Freycinet* named after the then Minister of Public Works, Charles de Freycinet. In all, 181 new lines were planned for construction. Much of this work was completed prior to 1914 and was promptly exploited in the movement of troops from around Metropolitan France and its North African colonies, with the double tracks between Paris and both Nancy and Belfort, and the routes connecting these lines, allowing for the speedy transportation of soldiers and equipment to the front in Lorraine and Alsace.

Ten major railway routes linked the military regions of France with the area where the fighting was expected, i.e. between Hirson and Belfort:

Line A, *14e corps*, from Lyon via Bourg-en-Bresse, and Besançon to Lure (30 kms west of Belfort) and Épinal;

Line B, *8e* and *13e corps*, from Clermont-Ferrand, Saint-Étienne, Bourges, and

Dijon, to the *trouée de Charmes* between Épinal and Nancy;
- Line C, *15e* and *16e corps*, from Marseille and Montpellier, via Mâcon, Dijon, Langres, and Mirecourt, to disembark at Pont-Saint-Vincent near Nancy. Also, the *19e corps* from North Africa via Marseille;
- Line D, *9e* and *18e corps*, from Bayonne, Bordeaux, Angers, and Châteauroux, via Tours, Orléans, Troyes, Chaumont, and Neufchâteau towards the region around Toul and Nancy;
- Line E, *12e* and *17e corps*, from Toulouse, Montauban, Périgueux, and Angoulême, via Limoges, Bourges, Auxerre, and Brienne-le-Château, to arrive at Commercy between Nancy and Verdun;
- Line F, *5e corps*, from Orléans, Melun, and Paris-Est, to disembark around Bar-le-Duc and Saint-Mihiel;
- Line G, *4e* and *11e corps*, from Vannes, Nantes, and le Mans, via Versailles, Choisy-le-Roi, and Reims to Verdun;
- Line H, *3e* and *10e corps*, from Rennes and Rouen, via Mantes, Pontoise, Compiègne, Soissons, and Rethel, to Vouziers, south of Sedan;
- Line I, *2e corps*, from Amiens, via Laon, Mézières, and Sedan to Stenay and Dun; and
- Line K, *1er corps*, from Lille via Douai, Valenciennes, and Avesnes, disembarking at Hirson and Rimogne (west of Charleville-Mézières);
- *6e corps* (Châlons-sur-Marne), *7e Corps* (Besançon), *20e corps* (Nancy) and *21e Corps* (Épinal) were already in the vicinity.

In 1891, Joffre became a lecturer at the *École d'application de l'artillerie et du génie* at Fontainebleau before, in 1892, going to *Soudan français* (now Mali) to build a railway between the provincial capital of Kayes across 500 kilometres of desert to the state capital, Bamako, on the *River Niger*. The governor of the *Soudan français*, Louis Albert Grodet, was under pressure from Paris to extend French influence and, under a pretext, troops were sent to Tombouctou. When the original commander was killed fighting with Touareg tribesmen, Joffre took command occupying Tombouctou in February 1894. This success saw him promoted Lt. Col. with control over the Kayes-Tombouctou area of what is now western Mali. 1895 saw him back in France attached to the *État-major du génie* before he left for Madagascar where he joined Joseph Gallieni in his brutal campaign to pacify the island. This, it is estimated, cost the lives of over 100,000 Malagasy over a fifteen-year period[i]. He was given responsibility for the fortification and facilities of the port of Diego Suarez, the scene of an attack by the British on Vichy forces in May 1942 designed to deny use of the port to Axis ships.

On his return in 1903 he was, for a time, commander of the *19e brigade de cavalerie* based at Vincennes but, at the beginning of 1904, he was appointed *directeur du génie* at the Ministry of War. The following year he married Henriette Penon, an old flame with whom he had an affair (and possibly a child) in the 1890s when she was still married. Promotion to *général de division* and command of *6e division d'infanterie* soon followed and, as his progress up the greasy pole accelerated, he

---

[i] France invaded Madagascar in 1883 and annexed the island in 1896. It became a colony the following year. The Malagasy royal family was exiled to Réunion in 1895.

was appointed the *inspecteur permanent des écoles militaires* but soon switched to take replace Michel in command of *2e Corps* at Amiens. In March 1910, he joined the *Conseil supérieur de Guerre* and started his involvement in the planning of the French Army's strategy for war with Germany. He was barely fifteen months from being placed in complete control of this work.³⁸

On 19th July 1911, Gen. Michel, the *chef d'État-Major* and *vice-président du Conseil supérieur de guerre*, presented his mobilisation and deployment plan. Nine days later he was sacked by Adolphe Messimy, the new *Ministre de la Guerre* [i]. Gallieni was approached to lead the Army but refused on grounds of age and ill-health. When asked who should be appointed, Gallieni is reputed to have replied: 'Castelnau'. When asked his second and third choices, the elderly general was consistent: 'Castelnau' he replied each time.

Gen. Noël Marie Joseph Édouard de Curières de Castelnau[ii], *vicomte* de Curières de Castelnau, was born on 24th December 1851 in Saint-Affrique, *département de l'Aveyron*. He was the son of Marie Mathieu Michel de Curières de Castelnau, a lawyer and mayor of Saint-Affrique, and Marie Antonine Léonie Barthe. It was an aristocratic family ruined by the Revolution and they lived in reduced circumstances in a house shared with his mother's clerical brothers.

He attended the *École Spéciale Militaire* in October 1869, joining the *31e régiment d'infanterie* on 14th August 1870. He was rapidly promoted during the Franco-Prussian War, starting as a *sous-lieutenant* in the *31e RI* he was an *Adjudant Major* in the *36e régiment d'infanterie de marche* by February 1871. After service with various regiments, he fulfilled staff appointments with *34e Division* and *17e Corps* in the 1880s. He was promoted *Chef de bataillon*, *139e RI*, in 1889, before joining the *1er*

---

[i] Adolphe Marie Messimy was twice *Ministre de la Guerre*: 27th June 1911 to 14th January 1912 and 13th June 1914 to 26th August 1914.

[ii] Castelnau commanded *IIe Armée* in Lorraine in 1914. After suffering heavy losses (including his son Xavier) at the Battle of Morhange, 19th-20th August 1914), he fought successful actions around Nancy at the *Trouée de Charmes* (24th-27th August 1914) and *Grand-Couronné* (31st August–13th September 1914) and was nicknamed *Sauveur de Nancy*. Involved on the Oise and in the Race to the Sea, in June 1915 he took command of the *groupe d'armées du Centre (GAC)*. The 2nd Battle of Champagne (25th September-9th October 1915) saw severe casualties and limited progress after a promising start. In late 1915, with Joffre promoted *Generalissimo*, he was made *Chef d'État Major* at *GQG*. Out of favour when Joffre was replaced by Nivelle at the end of 1916 he returned to command the *groupe d'armées de l'Est (GAE)* when Foch took overall command. Post-war, he was involved in catholic nationalist politics, being a Deputy of the *Bloc National*, President of the *Ligue des patriotes* and founding the *Fédération nationale catholique* in 1924. Vehemently anti-Masonic, he set up the *Comité d'études des questions maçonniques*, as well as writing pamphlets and newspaper articles attacking them. He opposed the Vichy regime in 1940. Active in the resistance, he encouraged his two grandsons, Urbain de la Croix and Gérald de Castelnau, to join the Free French. Gérald was seriously wounded on 16th October 1944 during the fighting in France and Urbain was killed on 31st March 1945 during the crossing of the *Rhine*. Two great nephews, Jean de Castelnau and Noël de Mauroy, were also killed in action in 1944. He died, aged 92 at the *château de Lasserre* at Montastruc-la-Conseillère (*Haut-Garonne*) on 18th March 1944.

Bureau of the *Etat Major* of the Army in 1893, being appointed its chief in 1897. As with Foch, de Castelnau's family were Jesuits and historically held royalist sympathies, a fact which undermined his standing with the mainly Republican and secular governments in power after *l'affaire Dreyfus*. In 1900, the career of the *le Capucin Botté* ('The Capuchin in boots'[i] or The Fighting Friar as he was later dubbed by Clemenceau) was profoundly set back when the aggressively republican and anti-clerical *ministre de la Guerre* Gen. Louis André sought to have him sacked. Though removed from the *Etat General*, the soon-to-resign *Chef d'Etat Major*, Gen. Alfred Louis Adrien Delanne, refused to sack him, instead appointing Castelnau commander of the *37e RI*. André's revenge was to keep Castelnau in post for an unusually extended five years and then not promoting him. André, however, was forced to resign over the *affaire des fiches* in early 1906 (see page 261). Back in favour, he was promoted *général de brigade* and given command of the *24e Brigade* at Sedan and then the *7e Brigade* at Soissons.

On 21st December 1909 he was promoted *général de division* with *13e Division* at Chaumont. He now encountered Joffre, commanding *2e Corps*. Castelnau was clearly highly thought of by Gallieni and many of his peers but was not of sufficient seniority to be effective head of the Army. Anyway, a 62-year-old infantryman, Paul Pau[ii], also a devout Catholic, was widely favoured by the Army and was offered the job. He turned it down on similar grounds to Gallieni, although his demand that he should select senior Generals counted heavily against him. This left Joffre as the last candidate standing, even if Castelnau's junior in years of service. He was appointed on 28th July 1911. Joffre then called on Castelnau's services and he re-joined the *Etat Major* as Joffre's deputy in which role he would be a driving force behind the mobilisation plan, *Plan XVII*, with which France went to war in August 1914.

Joffre was an engineer by 'trade'. Porch describes him as 'an amiable self-effacing man, the Eisenhower of the Western Front'.[39] His experience was based mostly in French colonies and his specialism fortifications and railways. He admitted no great knowledge of, or experience in, the planning or conduct of a European war.[40] Furthermore, though being offered the position of Chief of Staff, he had little or no experience of staff work.[41] But he was now in control of the planning and conduct of any war with Germany, an event which, in the light of ongoing events in North Africa, many regarded as imminent.

CONCENTRATING MINDS THROUGHOUT the summer of 1911 were events in Morocco known as the Agadir crisis. Events at this remote and, at the time, tiny Moroccan port[iii] led to a sudden and substantial surge in continental military

---

[i] Described by Charles Debierre, President, *Grand Orient de France*, the oldest French Masonic Lodge. Castelnau was virulently anti-Masonic. The nickname appeared in the satirical magazine *Le Lanterne* on 18th October 1913. The *Ordo Fratrum Minorum Capuccinorum* (*Order of Friars Minor Capuchin*), a Franciscan order founded in 1525 aimed at returning the order to its fundamental purposes of poverty, solitude, and penance.
[ii] Pau commanded the *armée d'Alsace* (11th - 28th August 1914) until *VIe Armée* (Gen. Manoury) was formed. He performed diplomatic missions during the war.
[iii] It had a population of c. 1,000 in 1913.

spending and, within France, were the trigger to what became known as the Nationalist Revival. It was the Nationalist Revival which swept the politicians of the centre-left coalition which dominated French politics from 1881 into the same camp as the nationalist right. This, in turn, led in 1913 to the Presidency of the conservative anti-German Raymond Poincaré, about whom more later.

France had long since claimed an interest in Morocco and their pre-eminent position was confirmed five years earlier at the Algeçiras Conference designed to settle the previous crisis in 1905. This earlier crisis, caused by the unilateral French declaration of its intentions to take control of certain trade, customs, and policing activities within the Sultanate of Morocco in breach of the 1880 Treaty of Madrid[i], led to the German Chancellor von Bülow threatening France with war in June 1905[ii]. In many respects such a declaration came as a bolt out of the blue. Only a year earlier the thoughts of a major European war were far from the minds of every major nation. They all had other worries to concern them.

France was struggling with the political, social, and military fall-out from the *l'affaire Dreyfus* which wrecked morale within the Army and exposed deep fault lines in French society. In addition, in 1905 a radical new government reduced the period of conscription for the Army from three to two years with significant effects on both its training and numbers[iii]. Britain was slowly coming to terms with the embarrassment and enormous cost of the South African War and, through the *Entente cordiale*, was trying to build bridges with European and other nations to end its diplomatic isolation[iv]. Russia was embroiled in the war in Manchuria which would expose the hollowness of Russian military power and fragility of Russian society when the 1905 Revolution broke out[v]. Italy's Army was yet to come to

---

[i] An agreement guaranteeing the territorial integrity of Morocco which gave Germany the right to be consulted on any changes in the status of the Sultanate.

[ii] A war Germany would almost certainly have won. Germany would have been able to mobilise some 36 Corps against just 21 for France. France's 'allies' would have been of little use as Russia was embroiled in Manchuria and Britain had no commitment to send troops to the continent at this time.

[iii] 60 infantry regiments lost their fourth battalions amongst other consequences.

[iv] This included an alliance with Japan in 1902 which allowed several ships of the China Squadron to return to the UK, as well as less formal arrangements with the USA which had a similar effect on naval ships in the Caribbean and elsewhere.

[v] In practice the unrest started in December 1904 with a strike at the giant St Petersburg *Putilov Works* (since 1934 the *Kirov Plant*) which built railway rolling stock and artillery including the new 7.62 mm field gun. By the end of January, the city was at a standstill with no electricity and c. 150,000 workers on strike. On 22nd January 1905 a large demonstration was fired on outside the Winter Palace killing anything between 200 and 1,000 striking civilians. Within days strikes broke out across the Russian Empire with mutinies in the navy including the famous one aboard the battleship *Potemkin*. By the end of the uprisings in December 1905, 14,000 people had been executed, some 13,000 killed on the streets and 75,000 imprisoned. Despite attempts at constitutional change, political violence and government repression escalated. A degree of calm returned before 1914 but another lost war triggered the 1917 Revolution, the overthrow of the Tsar and the Russian Civil War.

terms with its humiliating defeat in Ethiopia at the Battle of Adwa in 1896, the worst ever defeat of a European colonial force by native troops. Now, under the Prime Ministership of the liberal Giovanni Giolitti, the country was more interested in domestic reform than rebuilding its armed forces.

Within the Central Powers the focus, too, was on matters other than their armies. Germany embarked on a major naval building programme the costs of which were putting enormous pressures on Government spending and taxation. With the Social Democrats (*SPD*) dominating the 1903 Reichstag elections in terms of the popular vote[i] there was a clear nervousness within the German government about how far and how fast military spending could grow. The Austro-Hungarian Empire, its ally and neighbour, was, meanwhile, riven with disputes between the two main ethnic components – the German speaking Austrians and the increasingly nationalistic and independence-minded Hungarians. Such was the nature of these disputes the Army Class of 1903 from the Hungarian regions reported seven months late, in May 1904, and debates about increases in military spending invariably ended up deadlocked.[42]

In short, none of the combatant nations of 1914 either sought, or were ready for, a major conflict in 1904-5. But the 1905 Moroccan crisis, and the brief and almost certainly empty sabre-rattling threats of Germany, changed attitudes and, from that date, international relations moved only in a negative direction. Great Britain's understanding with France, solidified in 1904 with the *'Entente cordiale'*, was extended to include their erstwhile Russian protagonists through the Anglo-Russian Convention of 1907 signed in St Petersburg. This resolved several major outstanding issues affecting Persia, Afghanistan, and Tibet. Set alongside the growing momentum of the naval arms race between Britain and Germany, triggered by the launching of the game-changing *HMS Dreadnought* in 1906, this served to increase the nervousness of the German Government as the coalition surrounding it grew.

Tension increased further with Austria-Hungary's decision to annexe Bosnia-Herzegovina (previously part of the Ottoman Empire) on 6th October 1908, the day after Bulgaria formally declared its complete independence from the Ottoman Empire. The annexation had the effect of further uniting the *'entente'* as France, Russia and Britain which all objected to the Austrian action. In this they were joined by Italy, previously allies of Austria and Germany, in what was the first step in the break-up of this tri-partite arrangement and which eventually led to Italy joining the *'entente'* in 1915. The Serbian and Russian Governments, meanwhile, mobilised their armies. This threat to European peace was eventually negotiated away but not before the Austrians, too, started to mobilise. The outcome was, overall, unsatisfactory to almost all concerned and, with the Russians effectively

---

[i] The *SPD* gained 31.7% of the vote in 1903 but only 81 seats in the Reichstag. The Catholic Centre Party, part of the government, achieved just 19.8% but took 100 seats. The *SPD's* vote had steadily grown from a low of 6.1% (12 seats) in 1881. Their vote fell to 29% in 1907 and they lost nearly half of their seats (down to 43 seats) but in 1912, with 34.8% of the popular vote, they won a plurality of the seats in the Reichstag, taking 110 seats, 19 more than the Centre Party.

having to back down on their confrontation with Austria, this somewhat soured relations between the *entente* nations, most especially France and Russia.

Relations, especially between the Serbs and Russians on one hand and the Central Powers on the other, significantly deteriorated and sowed the seeds for the tragic events in the Bosnian capital, Sarajevo, on 28th June 1914 which led directly to war. Russia's enforced climbdown opened a temporary distance between it and its Western European allies and it embarked upon a significant, if belated, enhancement of its arms[i] and munitions supplies and production capability as well as a review of its mobilisation plans in the event of another and even more serious crisis. And were one to occur, the Russian Empire made clear it would not back down again. Italy, too, concerned at the threat on its north-eastern border from its erstwhile Austrian ally reviewed its military position and spending, even if the results were less than satisfactory by the time it joined the war in 1915[ii].

Now, a few weeks before Joffre was appointed, a rebellion in the Moroccan hinterland threatened the stability of the Sultanate and, at the end of April 1911, France sent a military force towards Fez to help with its suppression. Given the sensitivities of the area, Germany responded by sending a gunboat, the *SMS Panther*, to the Moroccan port of Agadir to 'protect German interests'[iii]. This vessel arrived on 1st July, followed four days later by a modern German light cruiser, the *SMS Berlin*[iv]. The British response was to hint at sending warships in a display designed not only to underscore the effectiveness of the *'Entente cordiale'* but also Britain's determination to deny Germany any form of Atlantic naval base.

The issue was partially resolved by another unseemly division of central Africa. This temporarily cooled the over-heated relations between France, Germany, and Britain, but led to another proto-colonial nation, Italy, demanding 'compensation', i.e. territory on the southern Mediterranean littoral. This led to the Turco-Italian War of 1911-12 fought in modern-day Libya (see footnote page 249) and the Ottoman defeat encouraged a Greek/Slav coalition to embark on the First Balkan War of 1912-3. Every cloud has a silver lining and a happy benefit for the French was that the diversion of 100,000 Italian troops to North Africa, along with increasing tension between Italy and Austria, allowed Joffre to add the *14e* and *15e*

---

[i] By 1909 the entire Russian Army was supplied with *76.2 mm field guns model 1902* developed at the *Putilov Works* in St Petersburg. Orders were placed with *Schneider* for the *107 mm gun Model 1910*, *152 mm howitzer M1910*, *152 mm siege gun M1910* and *122 mm howitzer M1909*, versions of which were also provided by *Krupp*.

[ii] The major initiative was the adoption in 1912 of the French-designed *Cannone da 75/27 modello 11*, the radical brainchild of Col. Déport and which featured a split trail and a dual recoil system. Delays in production meant it was not available to the Italian Army in significant numbers until 1915.

[iii] These 'interests' were a German salesman, Hermann Wilberg, sent to Agadir by the German Foreign Office. Unfortunately, he arrived in the port three days after the *Panther* dropped anchor. He arrived, therefore, too late to be 'protected'.

[iv] The *SMS Berlin* was a *Bremen*-class light cruiser, launched 1903, commissioned, 1905. She was one of six light cruisers retained by Germany under of the Treaty of Versailles and was scuttled in the Skagerrak in May 1947 with a load of chemical weapons.

Corps, currently covering France's Alpine border with Italy, to the potential deployments in north-east France should war break out with Germany.

The French Prime Minister during the early part of this period[i] was Antoine Emmanuel Ernest Monis, briefly in office between 2nd March and 27th June 1911. When his *Ministre de la Guerre*, Berteaux, was killed in an accident on 21st May (see page 196) Monis appointed Gen. François Louis Auguste Goiran as his replacement. The Moroccan crisis was concentrating minds wonderfully in Paris and concerns were expressed about the command of the Army in the event of war. Currently, the vice-president of the *Conseil supérieure de la Guerre* took command of the Armies on the German border. The overall direction of the war, however, would be conducted by the *Ministre de la Guerre* and the Army Chief of Staff back in Paris. This arrangement was a result of reforms pushed through under André designed to give politicians and the government pre-eminence over the Army and its Generals and was, in part, a residue of the fall-out from *l'affaire Dreyfus*. Goiran was called before the *Sénat* to explain the current structure and its workings. The *Ministre de la Guerre* was forced to explain there was no such thing as a commander in chief of the French Army and the Army group commanders were answerable to his ministry which was in turn answerable to the Government.[43] In other words, in an effort to exert control over the Army in a post-Dreyfusian world, the Radical government of Émile Combes and Louis André, his *Ministre de la Guerre*, created an unwieldy system of independent commands in the field effectively directed centrally by politicians in Paris. Whilst this might have given the politicians a reassuring sense of control over the military in peace time, in war it was a recipe for disaster. Now, with the likelihood of war with Germany much increased, even the politicians realised this was unacceptable.

Monis and, therefore, Goiran were gone by 27th July, Monis succeeded by his *Ministre des Finances*, Joseph-Marie-Auguste Caillaux[ii]. It was a typically brief administration, lasting until 11th January 1912. Caillaux appointed the ex-soldier

---

[i] I.e. before *Panther* arrived at Agadir. The Moroccan issue began in April.

[ii] Joseph-Marie-Auguste Caillaux (1863-1944) from 1898 Deputy for Mamers, *département de la Sarthe*. He joined the moderate *Alliance républicaine démocratique*, 1901. *Parti Radical*, 1911. *Ministre des Finances* five times, three times before the war. The longest period in office was the first, 1899-1902, the briefest the last, 24 days in July 1926. *Président du Conseil des ministres français* and *ministre de l'Intérieur* 27th June 1911 to 14th January 1912. Unpopular with the nationalist right, the editor of *Le Figaro*, Gaston Calmette, launched a vicious campaign, including publishing private letters from Caillaux's wife, Henriette, written when she was his mistress. On 16th March 1914, she shot Calmette four times, killing him. Caillaux resigned as a Deputy to defend his wife now charged with premeditated murder, The jury decided it was a 'crime of passion' and she was acquitted. Re-elected, he 'fought' a duel with his opponent Louis d'Aillières in which they avoided harming one another. A leader of the peace movement, he was accused of high treason in 1917 for communicating with the enemy, arrested in 1918, tried and convicted in 1920. Granted amnesty in 1925 he twice served briefly as *Ministre des Finances* and once as *Vice-président du Conseil des ministers*.

Adolphe Messimy[i] as *Ministre de la Guerre* and it was left to Messimy, and his successor Millerand, to restructure the upper echelons of the Army. The role of Vice-President of the *Conseil supérieure de la Guerre* was abolished. All power was given to the Chief of the General Staff, the *chef d'état major*, who, after the sacking of Michel, was Joffre. And the phrase 'all power' is used deliberately, for Joffre became commander of all troops in France, not just those expected to confront the German Armies in *Elsaß* and *Lothringen*. His decision-making within the Army became virtually autonomous and, borne on a growing tidal wave of *revanchist* nationalism, those decisions formed the basis of the plans which led France to the brink of disaster in August 1914. He was, however, still constrained by the actions and decisions of the Government in terms of appointments, equipment (most especially artillery), munitions and strategy. Thus, for example, his demands for a new field howitzer, first voiced in 1910, fell on deaf ears. Millerand, when *Ministre de la Guerre*, summed up Joffre's position as one in which the government 'directs the war' whilst Joffre was responsible for the 'conduct of operations'.[44]

IT WAS IN THIS AGITATED, EXCITABLE ATMOSPHERE Joffre and Castelnau made significant changes to *Plan XVI* in September 1911. Prior to the details being confirmed, he outlined his thinking in a note dated 29th August 1911 in which he stated his intention to take the attack to the enemy on his territory. His new deployment plan would be underpinned by significant improvements in the rail network necessary to give him the widest range of options and routes for the movement of troops to the north-east of France in the event of war.

He was totally opposed to Michel's idea of retaining a 'mass of manoeuvre' in the rear around Paris. In language of which the more extreme French theorists such as de Grandmaison would have approved, Joffre made it clear he was there to 'organise a French offensive not just a response to a German attack'. To make his point even clearer he announced:

> "Maintaining a so-called army of manoeuvre, in fact a reserve behind the other armies, is not an answer to the idea of manoeuvre but is, in fact, a defensive concept. It is to be rejected in all cases."[45]

Plan XVI, Joffre wrote, did not take sufficient account of the prospect of the French left being outflanked through Belgium. His definition of the French left, however, was not the same as Michel's, i.e. the area between the Ardennes and the English Channel. Joffre's 'left' stretched no further west than the Ardennes and it was there, and towards the Swiss border, he planned to reinforce.

---

[i] Adolphe Marie Messimy (1869-1935) attended the *École Spéciale Militaire* and *École supérieure de guerre* before entering politics in 1899, being elected a Deputy in 1902. *Ministre des Colonies* under Monis then appointed *Ministre de la Guerre*. From 13th June 1914 he was briefly *Ministre de la Guerre* under Viviani (replaced by Millerand on 26th August 1914). Re-joining the Army, he was a staff officer in *14e Corps* then promoted Lt. Col. He was wounded commanding a unit of *chasseurs alpins* in the Vosges on 27th July 1915. Promoted Colonel, he commanded the *6e brigade de chasseurs à pied*. Wounded a second time, he was promoted *général de brigade*, commanding *213e brigade d'infanterie territorial* and *162e division d'infanterie*. Liberated Colmar in 1918. He lost in the 1919 elections but was elected a senator in 1923, serving until he died in 1935.

His proposed alterations weakened the centre in *Lothringen* and strengthened the wings opposite *Elsaß* in the south and the Ardennes in the north.⁴⁶ Now, the two armies (six Corps) which defended the line of the *Moselle* from about Toul to the south of Épinal were reinforced by three Corps and their front extended to include the southern Vosges and the fortress city of Belfort. Given French intelligence saw little signs of any major German attack in this region this was an offensive move by Joffre not a defensive one – and a sign of things to come. The centre, along the line of the *Meuse* between Toul and Verdun (i.e. opposite the German fortress city of Metz), behind which three Armies (ten Corps) and four reserve divisions were clustered in the original *Plan XVI*, was now reduced to two Armies totalling five Corps. Another reserve Army (*VIe Armée*) of four Corps was to be stationed between Reims and Ste Menehould. Finally, the French *Ve Armée*, previously to be held between Challerange and Rethel, was pushed forward to the *Meuse* at, and south of, Sedan, with two reserve Corps immediately to the west (north of Rethel). In essence, therefore, the balance of the distribution of forces changed from:

Vosges/Alsace – six Corps increased to nine;
Verdun-Toul – ten Corps (plus four divisions) decreased to five; and
Facing the Ardennes – two Corps (plus eight divisions) increased to eight.

These plans were based on French intelligence estimates that the Germans would deploy ten Corps opposite the Belgian/Luxembourg border ready to drive through the Ardennes; eleven Corps in *Lothringen* at and behind Metz, and ten Corps in *Elsaß* between Straßburg and Mülhausen.⁴⁷ The main German attacks were expected in the Ardennes towards Sedan and through *Lothringen* towards Verdun and Toul. Again, it was not anticipated the northern German attack would attempt to cross the *Meuse/Sambre* line beyond Liège and Namur.

In January 1912 Joffre repeated Michel's argument to the *Conseil supérieur de la Guerre* that the prospects for a French victory would be greatly enhanced if his armies were free to initiate offensive action in neutral Belgium and Luxembourg. The Government, however, was not prepared to sanction a deployment which threatened Belgian neutrality, though dispensation to attack through Luxembourg was given. At this point Joseph Caillaux's[i] seven-month administration collapsed

---

[i] Joseph-Marie-Auguste Caillaux (1863-1944) from 1898 Deputy for Mamers, *département de la Sarthe*. He joined the moderate *Alliance républicaine démocratique*, 1901. *Parti Radical*, 1911. *Ministre des Finances* five times, three times before the war. The longest period in office was the first, 1899-1902, the briefest the last, 24 days in July 1926. *Président du Conseil des ministres français* and *ministre de l'Intérieur* 27th June 1911 to 14th January 1912. Unpopular with the nationalist right, the editor of *Le Figaro*, Gaston Calmette, launched a vicious campaign, including publishing private letters from Caillaux's wife, Henriette, written when she was his mistress. On 16th March 1914, she shot Calmette four times, killing him. Caillaux resigned as a Deputy to defend his wife now charged with premeditated murder, The jury decided it was a 'crime of passion' and she was acquitted. Re-elected, he 'fought' a duel with his opponent Louis d'Aillières in which they avoided harming one another. A leader of the peace movement, he was accused of high treason in 1917 for communicating with the enemy,

when the *Ministre des Affaires étrangères,* Justin de Selves, resigned over the handling of the Agadir incident[i]. It was thus not until 21st February, after Raymond Poincaré formed a new government, that Joffre was able to pursue his arguments. Invited by the new Prime Minister to develop his ideas, Joffre, a devotee of the 'offensive' so popular amongst the French Army, explained:

> "…if we respect neutral territories, the existence near the Franco-German border of natural obstacles and fortified barriers confines our offensive to narrowly limited regions (thus any offensive in the direction of Strasbourg or in Lorraine would be blocked and threatened from the flank). The situation would be infinitely more advantageous if it were possible for us to extend our left beyond the borders of the Grand Duchy of Luxembourg and onto Belgian territory. On this flank we can deploy all our resources… Furthermore, the violation of Belgian neutrality gives us the means of involving the English (*sic*) Expeditionary Force, which would help provide a marked superiority over our adversaries. It is hoped that this consideration would be enough to persuade England to renounce its objections concerning the violation of Belgian territory. As they desire a result which can only be obtained by the definitive crushing of the common adversary, the British government will not be too scrupulous in the choice of means."[48]

What Joffre called for was the option of driving north into Belgium along a line between Namur and Liège starting from the area between Maubeuge in the west via Charleville-Mézières and down to Thionville south of Luxembourg.

Poincaré, Prime Minister and President of the *Conseil supérieur de la Guerre,* expressed concerns such action would generate huge ill-feeling towards France from the rest of Europe and, as Britain was the most dedicated guarantor of Belgian neutrality, it raised the risk of the British breaking existing military agreements with France. Making it clear this relationship trumped any strategic or tactical advantages gained by a pre-emptive strike into Belgium, Poincaré insisted any intervention must be in response to a positive intention of the Germans to invade that country.[49]

As a result, Joffre was left to ponder the now limited options for an offensive operational plan because, believing firmly in the power of the 'offensive', aggressive movement towards German troops, wherever they might be found, was the bedrock of any future action. Such thinking inevitably led to the strategy adopted in August 1914 of offensives first into the *Haut-Rhin* and beyond towards Straβburg in *Elsaβ* and then into *Lothringen* with the intention of fighting a decisive battle somewhere between Metz and Saarbrucken. After all, there was nowhere else France could advance gloriously, *tricoleurs* fluttering and the *Marseillaise* blaring out. National sentiment, as well as diplomacy and military opinion demanded it.

---

arrested in 1918, tried and convicted in 1920. Granted amnesty in 1925 he twice served briefly as *Ministre des Finances* and once as *Vice-président du Conseil des ministers.*

[i] Formed 27th June 1911, it fell on 14th January 1912. The previous administration of Ernest Monis was very brief, i.e. 2nd March 1911 to 23rd June 1911. Poincaré, succeeding Caillaux, managed 53 weeks (14th January 1912 to 21st January 1913).

Was there an alternative? Basically 'no' if one was committed to the *'offensive à outrance'* as espoused by the likes of Foch and Grandmaison. 'Yes', if you were a less exalted, somewhat troublesome, 54-year-old recently promoted artillerist by the name of *Général de Brigade* Marie-Georges Demange[i]. By 1914, Demange was the *Chef d'état-major* of Dubail's *1ère armée* which unit was charged with two essential roles in the opening weeks of the war: an invasion/liberation of *Elsaß* starting with Mülhausen in the south and then moving north to invest Straßburg; and, a week later, as part of an invasion/liberation of *Lothringen*, with some troops clearing the passes of the Vosges and others driving towards Saarburg and beyond. He, therefore, had a clear idea as to what was being demanded of his army and that of de Castelnau's *2e Armée* immediately to the north. And it was an idea with which he fundamentally disagreed. Like Michel, Demange envisioned a powerful and wide German sweep through Belgium and not, as Joffre planned for, a narrow drive through the south-east of that country. Like Michel, Demange believed it more sensible in this scenario to have the mass of the French Army ready and waiting along the Belgium/Luxembourg border rather wandering off into the blue in some vain hope they might easily re-take the lost provinces of 1871. Thus, he suggested that whilst two Armies defended the, as it would later prove, highly defensible line from Pont-à-Mousson via the *Grand Couronné* and Nancy to the *Trouée de Charmes* and Épinal and then south to Belfort, a third would sit to the rear ready to attack any German thrust out of Metz towards Verdun and Toul. Meanwhile, rejuvenating the much-derided Michel idea of a 'mass of manoeuvre', Demange suggested three Armies would lurk further west, ready to thrust into the left wing of any German drive through central Belgium, or within easy reach of the Ardennes or combat zones around Metz. Such a plan had the virtue of preserving Belgian neutrality until breached by Germany but also of utilising both geography and the heavily fortified border lands directly facing German territory as the defensive barrier they were designed all along to be. It's only flaw, and this a fatal one, was that such a strategy was one based on counterattack rather than on the 'offensive' and the concept of the counter-offensive was diametrically opposed to the widely held military wisdom in France. However sensible it might look to modern eyes, Demange's idea was foredoomed to fail. And for Joffre, there was no alternative to attacks into *Elsaß* and *Lothringen*, events for which the Germans had long since planned.

---

[i] Demange was born on 9th February 1860 in Einville-au-Jard, *département de Meurthe-et-Moselle*. *École d'application de l'artillerie et du Gènie*, 1882. *23e régiment d'artillerie*, 1884. From 1896 he filled several staff positions and, in 1899-1900, was an observer with the Boers in the Orange Free State. Lt. Col. in 1907 and Colonel in 1908, he commanded *46e régiment d'infanterie*. *Général de Brigade* in 1913. *Membre du Comité technique d'Etat-Major*, August 1914, he was *Chef d'état-major* of Dubail's *1ère armée*. On 17th September 1914 he took command of the *25e division d'infanterie*. *Général de Division*, 1915, he commanded *57e division d'infanterie de réserve*, the *groupement Demange*, the *Région fortifiée de Belfort* and, in October 1916, *34e corps d'armée* and *13e corps d'armée*. Removed by Franchet d'Esperey, he became deputy to the *Inspecteur général des Travaux et Organisations de la zone des armées*. In 1920, as *Inspecteur général de l'artillerie*, he was promoted *Général de Corps d'Armée*. He died on 23rd April 1941.

THE MOROCCAN CRISIS TRIGGERED more than just a review of France's military plans. It was also the point from which every mainland European nation dramatically increased their spending on arms and munitions. The German response was the most aggressive: a significant increase (though not as big as Moltke and Ludendorff wished) in spending and manpower enshrined in a new Army Law passed in May 1912, and a supplementary Naval Law passed the same month which provided for three new battleships and several smaller warships. The impact of the Slav/Greek success in the First Balkan War later that year added extra impetus to their, and Austria-Hungary's, military programmes. In July 1913, the *Reichstag* passed another Army Law, only opposed by the Social Democrats and Polish members. This increased the size of the Army by c. 15%, or approximately 135,000 officers and men. The costs were ruinous and indicative of the economic strains of a major war predicted by Bloch fourteen years earlier. Although an increase in naval spending was rejected, the enormous costs of the 1913 Army Law forced the government to introduce new taxes. These outraged the right, were not what the Government wanted, and were only passed with the support of the Social Democrats. The Army Law required c. £65 million (c. £8-25 billion in current prices depending on the index used) to be spent on the Army through to the end of 1915. To pay for this, a variety of taxes was employed. £50 million was to be generated by a levy on capital and higher incomes. The balance would come from permanent taxation. The levy proposed was 0.5% on all capital of £500 (i.e. between £50,000 and £200,000 depending on the index used generating between £250 and £1,000 per taxpayer at current prices). The problem was, pressed by the Social Democrats, most of the population were exempt. 56% of the approximately 15.7 million households fell outside the levy as their incomes were too low, or for other reasons. Another 38% had incomes of between £45 and £150 a year and so paid very little. The weight of this levy fell mainly on the middle and upper classes, i.e. just 6%, or c. 900,000 households and individuals. This was not the only new tax. A new *Vermögenszuwachssteuer*, or *Imperial Increment Tax*, taxed people (both Germans and non-Germans currently residing in the country) on a graduated scale on fortunes of £1,000 or more. This tax also applied to bequests from inheritances except those between married couples. According to *The Times*, conservatives complained this new system incorporated 'a property tax, an income tax and death duties' all in one Bill. Rather more acidly, the newspaper described the supposedly peace-seeking Social Democrats as having:

"... assisted to provide the sinews of war for the militarism they denounce."[50]

The Times then pointed out that:

"Germany, it must be remembered, is a country which trades largely upon borrowed capital, and for which the accumulation of capital is therefore of great economic importance... neither the levy nor the increment tax can tend to that accumulation. The last-named tax is indeed manifestly a tax upon savings... It is tolerably certain that attempts will be made at evasion, and it is credibly reported that large sums of German money have found their way to Switzerland since the Bills were introduced."[51]

That these taxes did not raise remotely enough revenue to pay for the growth demanded by the new Army Law was another portent of the profoundly damaging economic impact of European-wide conflict. Within the year, Hermann Kühn, Secretary of the Treasury, admitted the levy would not collect what was required and it must continue.[52] This was confirmed when official figures were released on 10th July 1914 showing the levy in Prussia raised £30.15 million against the hoped-for £50 million, whilst the non-recurring costs of the 1913 Army Bill were estimated at £53 million.[53] With Government debt mounting and an erosion in Germany's capital base, the economic prospects for the country looked challenging in all circumstances other than a swift and overwhelming victory.

Meanwhile, there was an exception to this wave of increased military spending: Britain. Its naval budget saw enormous increases because of the *Dreadnought*-based race with Germany, but spending on the Army was essentially flat and had been since 1904. By 1913 it was set at little more than a third of that being spent by Germany and was nearly equalled by that of both the Austrians and Italians[i].

In response to the moves made by Germany to increase its military power, Joffre further amended *Plan XVI* in April 1913, whilst the government, directed by the newly elected President[ii], the arch Germanophobe and *revanchist* Raymond Poincaré, introduced new laws to increase the size of the French Army. Joffre's changes were designed to further advance the jumping-off positions of several units in pursuit of his intention to take the fight into enemy territory as soon as possible. The major change was the advance of *VIe Armée* so it could either cross the *Meuse* between Verdun and Stenay or swing to face north between Dun-sur-Meuse and Sedan. To achieve this, the Army was to deploy on the line Grandpré – Varennes-en-Argonne – Clermont-en-Argonne. In addition, the *3e groupe de divisions de réserve*, due to occupy 50 kms of the *Hauts de Meuse* between Damvillers and Hattonchâtel, was to take up its initial positions to the north and south of Verdun along the *Meuse* from Dun-sur-Meuse in the north down to Troyon.

HAVING FIRST BEEN ELECTED PRIME MINISTER in January 1912, the 52-year-old lawyer Raymond Nicolas Landry Poincaré became President on 18th February 1913. Born in Bar-le-Duc[iii] on 20th August 1860, as a ten-year old he experienced his parents' house being occupied by the Prussians during the Franco-Prussian War, an experience he had never forgotten – nor forgiven. As a result, he was a committed *revanchist* writing:

"In all my years at school I saw no other reason to live than the possibility of recovering our lost provinces."[54]

---

[i] Army Estimates, 1905 to 1914, fluctuated between £29.8 million in 1905-6 to £28.5 million in 1914 being at their lowest in 1909 - £27.0 million. 1913 expenditure: Russia £67.8 million, Germany £80.9 million, France £37.2 million, Austria £24.1 million, Great Britain £28.2 million (*Source*: Hermann, D G, *The Arming of Europe*, page 237].
[ii] Poincaré was *Président de la République* 18th February 1913 to 18th February 1920.
[iii] In the *département de la Meuse* and, though not transferred to Germany in 1871, part of the historic area of Lorraine since the 15th Century.

He had already made it clear that, other than the recovery of the lost provinces, his primary objective was to limit Germany's global ambitions and, to achieve this, the alliance with Russia was to be re-affirmed and strengthened. This had been put under strain during the crisis precipitated by Austria's annexation of Bosnia-Herzegovina during which France failed to fully support Russia which was then forced into a humiliating climb down. Russia retaliated by being less than fulsome in support of France during the Agadir affair. Poincaré determined this situation should, indeed must, change and he visited the Tsar in St Petersburg in August 1912. Now, determined to make the Presidency more than a ceremonial role within Government, he supported a new government which was to answer German military expansion by expansion of its own. On 7th August 1913 the short-lived government of Jean Louis Barthou[i] (22nd March 1913 to 2nd December 1913), passed the '*Loi des trois ans*' which extended the initial full-time service in the Army from two back to three years and brought forward the age at which young men entered the Army from 21 to 20. Conscripts would now spend:

Three years in the *Armée d'active*;
Eleven years in the *Réserve de l'armée d'active* to provide men to top-up active regiments and form reserve regiments in the event of war;
Seven years in the *Armée territorial*; and
Seven years in the *Réserve de l'armée territorial* which provided additional men for Territorial regiments and others to guard lines of communication.

In some ways, this law, and the resulting increase in the numbers, if not the quality, available to the Army was a response to the development of *Plan XVII* in which Castelnau was heavily involved. His deployment plan required more front-line troops than were currently available, and the only solution was an extension of the period of service and, therefore, an extension in the service of men believing they were about to be released back into private life. This law, therefore, faced major opposition from those troops affected by the extension, by young men about to enter the Army for the newly extended period, and by such as Jean Jaurès and the *Section française de l'Internationale ouvrière*[ii] (*SFIO*). Significant demonstrations were held in Paris, Nancy, Mâcon, Châlons-sur-Marne and, generally, in the south of France especially the Languedoc, in the summer of 1913.[55]

---

[i] Barthou was a member of the *Parti républicain démocratique* and was previously Minister of Justice in Aristide Briand's 1st, 2nd , and 4th administrations (1909-10 and 1913).
[ii] Formed by a merger of the *Parti socialiste français* and *Parti socialiste de France*, it was the French Section of the *Workers' International*, founded in 1905 as part of the *Second International*. In 1906 it took 10% of the vote and 54 seats, 16.8% of the vote and 102 seats in 1914 (more seats than all the right-wing parties combined), making it the second largest party in the *Chambre des deputes*. Its most significant figure and leader was Jean Jaurès, a Marxist and anti-militarist assassinated by Raoul Villain, an unbalanced religious extremist and ultra nationalist, on 31st July 1914. War was declared three days later. The trial delayed, Villain was acquitted post-war but executed by Anarchists in Barcelona in 1936.

Castelnau[i], a catholic with a family with historic connections to the *Ancien Régime* and the right-wing catholic political party *L'Action libérale Populaire*[ii], was an easy and convenient target for their ire. He remained a *bête noire* of the *radicale-socialistes* for the rest of his life. Right wing and centrist deputies out-voted the *radicale-socialistes* and the *SFIO* in the *Chambre des deputes* by 358 votes to 204 on 19th July 1913 and the law was easily passed in the *Sénat* on 7th August. Like the 1913 German Army Law, the significant costs of this law were financed by a new progressive property tax and it was this tax reform which persuaded the Radicals, now led by Caillaux, to support the revocation of the Two-Year Law they helped pass back in 1905.

Although this law was a major theme of the election campaign in April and May 1914, it was not repealed and its net effect on the immediately available full-time French Army was considerable as it increased in size from just over 600,000 to over 700,000[iii]. Although this law produced a surfeit of men for the Army, it did little to increase the number of *trained* men immediately available. In fact, it had the effect of diluting what training was available. Since Dreyfus, there was a growing officer shortage in the French Army as well as one of trained NCOs. These shortages were in both absolute and, when the French Government passed the *loi de trois ans*, in relative terms too, as the ratio of officers and NCOs to the greatly increased number of conscripts fell sharply. This officer shortage was underlined further by the greater than 50% fall in applications to the officers' training academy, the *École spéciale militaire de Saint-Cyr*, and the training school, the *École Militaire d'Infanterie* at Saint-Maixent, at which NCOs were fast-tracked to commissions between 1900 and 1912.[56] As the proportion of officers and NCOs declined, it resulted in large numbers of barely trained troops entering the Army in time for the outbreak of war, a fact which may well have influenced some of the battlefield tactics employed at such cost in the opening weeks of the war.

One of the immediate effects of the additional troops generated by the *'Loi des trois ans'* was the permanent creation at the end of September of the *21e Corps* based at Épinal and of one of its component divisions, the *43e Division* based at Saint-Dié. In addition, over the nine months prior to the passing of the *'Loi des trois ans'*, a variety of new regiments were raised to augment the strength of the troops in Metropolitan France in response to the German Army Law of May 1912:

23rd December 1912, the *loi des cadres de l'infanterie* created ten infantry regiments;

---

[i] On 7th May 1914, Clemenceau, in his newspaper *L'Homme libre* described Castelnau as *le général de la Jésuitière*. The newspaper was renamed *L'Homme enchaîné* when banned by the Government on 29th September 1914.

[ii] Léonce de Castelnau, Édouard's older brother, was a Deputy elected for the Aveyron between 1902 and his death in 1909. He was the President of the Parliamentary group of *Action libérale*.

[iii] Troop number in Metropolitan France had been only 520,000. They were opposed by 782,000 German troops, increased from 646,000 the previous year as a result of new laws passed in January 1913. Prior to the *'Loi des trois ans'* it was thought a German attack might well succeed before reinforcements from North Africa could arrive.

19th March 1913, eight regiments of *Tirailleurs* and two of *Zouaves* were created; The *loi des cadres de la cavalerie* of 31st March 1913 added four new cavalry regiments; and a year later

15th April 1914, the day Joffre's new *Plan XVII* officially came into force, five new *régiments d'artillerie lourde* (equipped with 120-mm *Baquet* or 155-mm *Rimailho* howitzers and attached to the Armies) were brought into being as well as fourteen batteries of *75s* attached to the cavalry.

Taking the first three of these changes into account, a final minor tweak was made to *Plan XVI* in the autumn of 1913 but, by now, the major work of the French Staff was in developing the now notorious *Plan XVII* with which the French Army went to war in August 1914.

Joffre presented the details of *Plan XVII* to the *Conseil supérieur de la guerre* on 13th April 1913 at which it was approved. Joffre then took the plan to the *Ministre de la Guerre* Eugène Étienne, who endorsed it on 2nd May 1913. The details of the plan were then completed over the ensuing months with the results being sent to the five Army commanders on 7th February 1914. The final piece of the jigsaw of the plan was, in fact, in position as of December 1913 after the formation of the *21e Corps* based at Épinal. As mentioned, *Plan XVII* officially superseded *Plan XVI* on 15th April 1914 and this detailed plan for the mobilisation and concentration of the various Armies and other units was approved by Joffre on 28th May 1914.

Plan XVII was formulated on the basis most German forces would deploy on the French border in *Lothringen* and none would cross the *Meuse* in Belgium to threaten western Belgium, the Channel ports, and Paris. Effectively, the plan removed all French troops between Hirson and the coast leaving this sector to the BEF. These dispositions were based on a fundamental and repeated misjudgement of German intentions. As Jack Snyder shows in his 1984 book *The Ideology of the Offensive* French intelligence interpretations of, and Joffre's suppositions about, German war plans were horribly wide of the mark.[57] Neither believed Germany would use more than 65 divisions (actual number 76), because they did not believe they would risk employing large numbers of reserve divisions (French estimates c. 20, actual number 32). Furthermore, they generally did not believe many, or any, of these reserve units would be combined into discreet *Reservekorps* with attendant supporting artillery (26 of the 32 divisions were in *Reservekorps*) and, crucially, even if they were, they believed few, if any, would see much/any action. Most then did. Then there was the issue of actual deployments and routes of march. No-one thought German troops would cross the *Meuse-Sambre* line to enter western Belgium, and few thought that more than 22-26 divisions might enter any part of Belgium, and then no further west than Dinant to threaten Charleville-Mézières and the rear of French troops facing Metz. In fact, 34 divisions entered Belgium, of which 26 crossed the *Meuse* to drive west to threaten the Maubeuge-Mons front. It was a calamitous misjudgement and ignored repeated evidence to the contrary.

Plan XVII, however, was a mobilisation and concentration plan and *not* an operational one which determined the Armies' subsequent tactical application and objectives. Such was the centralisation of authority in the French Army that only one man would decide how, when, where, and why these troops were to be employed – Joseph Jacques Césaire Joffre, *chef d'État-Major* and *vice-président du*

Conseil supérieur de la Guerre. Post-war. Joffre was questioned about the 'operational plan' for August 1914. This exchange between Maurice Viollette, the *président de la commission d'enquête parlementaire*,[i] took place on 4th July 1919:

> "*President*: Shall we move on to the plan of operations? Was the plan of operations discussed at the *Conseil supérieur de la guerre*?
> *Joffre*: No, it was not the business of the *Conseil supérieur de la guerre*.
> *President*: So how was this plan of operations drawn up?
> *Joffre*: The concentration plan is a function of the operations plan.
> *President*: By whom was the plan of operations drawn up?
> *Joffre*: By the general staff of the army under my direction.
> *President*: General de Castelnau testified that as deputy chief of staff, he had been unaware of this plan of operations.
> *Joffre*: I am not able to comment.
> *President*: Who drew up the plan of operations and who collaborated with you in this work if the deputy chief of staff did not take part in it?
> *Joffre*: I don't remember.
> *President*: It seems that you could remember the officers with whom you worked: is that indeed something that must have caused you a lot of worry?
> *Joffre*: But the whole staff took part in it. An operations plan is an idea that you have in your head but that you don't put on paper.
> *President*: I would want to make this clear. An operations plan, you tell me, is a design that cannot be put on paper.
> *Joffre*: We put notes on paper if we want to say such and such a thing to such an officer, such and such a thing to another. But there was no elaborate plan like a concentration plan, for example.
> *President*: So there is nothing on paper. There is no documentation at the *ministère de la Guerre* which contains the plan of operations.
> *Joffre*: I don't think so. What exists are guidelines on concentration."[58]

The main objective of Joffre's plan was to concentrate troops opposite Lorraine and Alsace, pushing deployments up against the German border to enable attacks between Metz and Straβburg, and Mülhausen and Colmar, and bringing the mass of the German Armies to battle east of the heavily fortified city of Metz. The guiding principle was the *offensive à outrance*. The key manual which guided this concept was *Règlement sur la conduite des grandes unités* (*Regulations for the conduct of large units*), written by a thrusting officer by the name of de Grandmaison (see page 178 onwards). This document made it clear that, as the Commander in Chief could not direct minutely the actions of each Army, Corps or Division, liaison officers from *GQG*, the *Grand Quartier Général* (the French version of the British GHQ) would monitor the actions of subsidiary commanders, potentially circumscribing their discretion and the flexibility of their actions if they did not fulfil the CinC's overall operational plan. These liaison officers then rapidly produced recommendations for who to sack as Joffre's plans went pear-shaped.

---

[i] Chair of the Parliamentary commission of inquiry into the conduct of the war.

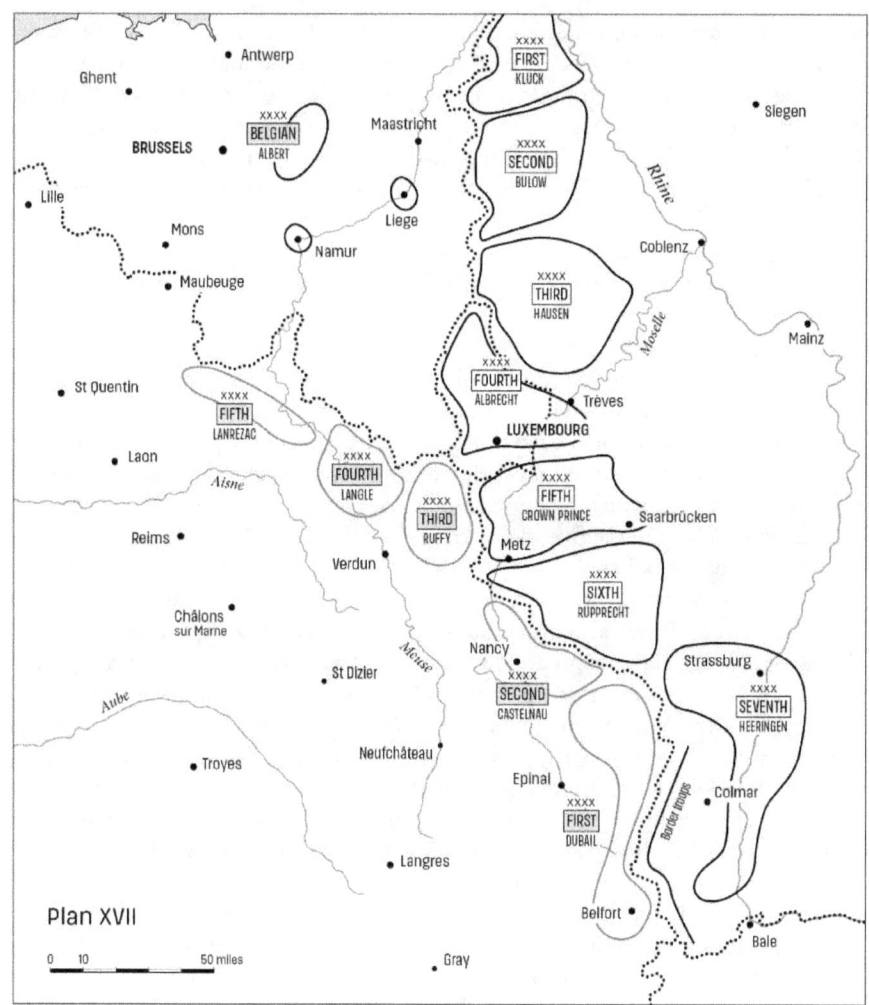

Map 4 Joffre's Plan XVII deployment plan and the German Schlieffen Plan
[*Source: AFdGG*, Tome I, Vol. I, Maps]
Note the complete absence of French troops around Maubeuge, Lille and the Channel Coast

To fulfil Joffre's strategic thinking, most of Dubail's *Ire Armée* and de Castelnau's *IIe Armée* were to drive north-east from between Épinal and Nancy towards Saarburg and Morhange respectively, thus cutting links between Metz and the heavily fortified area around, and in front of, Straßburg. At the same time, *7e Corps*, detached from Dubail's army, was to attack out of Belfort in the direction of Mülhausen. Together, these two armies consisted of 600,000 men. After taking their first objectives, each army was to continue north-east, *Ire Armée* along the *River Saar* to Saargemünd (now Sarreguemines) at the confluence of the *Rivers Saar* and *Blies*; while *IIe Armée* attacked towards Saarbrücken.

To the north, Ruffey's *IIIe Armée* was to move from Verdun north-west of Metz to invest the city's outer fortifications and pin German troops to this area. It would also threaten Diedenhofen (Thionville). Langle de Cary's *IVe Armée* was in reserve in the Argonne, west of Verdun. It had no pre-defined role but was to be available to attack either to the north or south of Metz as circumstances dictated. *Ve Armée* too had options: either attack towards Diedenhofen and into Luxembourg or, if the Germans threatened through the Ardennes, move towards Neufchâteau in Belgium. Protecting the extreme left wing of Joffre's armies was Sordet's *Corps de cavalerie* initially based around Mézières.

Except for two reserve divisions attached to *Ve Armée*, all units involved in these movements were active divisions. The reserve divisions were not to be called upon to be in the immediate front-line and were split into four *groupes de divisions de réserve* and were to hold various lines and be in reserve to *Ire, IIe, IIIe* and *Ve Armées*. Another 216,000 troops, mainly reserves and Territorials, were to be deployed either around Paris or around Lyons and 160,000 were to defend the four fortified cities of north-eastern France, Verdun, Toul, Épinal and Belfort, or were on coastal or frontier duties. Again, these were reserves or Territorials. In total, the entire deployment encompassed c. 1.9 million men of which 1.25 million were active soldiers in the five main armies and the *Corps de cavalerie*.

The strategy employed after mobilisation was, therefore, offensive, unlike previous ones which invited German Armies onto French fortifications in the *Meurthe-et-Moselle*. It was also based on the notion German troops would not cross the *Meuse* at Liège and Namur and drive into central Belgium before turning south towards Maubeuge and, finally, Paris. But this was a key point: whilst German strategy threatened the capital of France *and* the rear of the French Armies by its flanking movement through Belgium, Joffre's strategy threatened little except territory. It would not interfere directly with German lines of communication and, however far it went, the French would still need to deal with the triangle of fortresses blocking their advance towards the *Rhine*: Metz, Straßburg and Mainz[i]. And all without a siege train of any significance.

Having grossly misjudged the enemy's intentions there was not yet anything inherently disastrous (though quite a lot pointless) about the essentials of Joffre's *Plan XVII*. His subsequent deployments, however, assumed everything would run to plan and that the Germans would roll over and played dead. They did not. Opposing the French between Luxembourg and the Swiss border were four Armies: *7. Armee* (Heeringen) in *Elsaß*, *6. Armee* (the Crown Prince of Bavaria) on the *Saar*, *5. Armee* (Crown Prince of Prussia) around Metz and *4. Armee* (Duke of Württemberg) north of the Mosel. The other three armies – *3. Armee* (Hausen), *2. Armee* (Bülow) and *1. Armee* (Kluck) – were aligned opposite the Belgian border ready for their neutrality-busting invasion. Optimistically, the ideas behind the mobilisation activated by *Plan XVII* envisaged the four German Armies in *Lothringen* and *Elsaß* being beaten before any enemy troops further north could intervene. These remaining armies would then be defeated in detail. If you truly believed French soldiers were super-human, then anything seemed possible.

---

[i] *Festung Mainz* described by Baedeker (1864) as one of the strongest fortresses in the German Confederation, having three defensive lines around the citadel and town.

During the immediate pre-war period, French attitudes to another war with Germany progressively changed and the prospect was now viewed with increasing confidence by both public and military. The Russo-Japanese war saw the German-trained Japanese victorious over the French-influenced Russians but the defeat of the German-trained and equipped Ottoman Army by the mainly French-equipped and trained Greek/Slav alliance in the First Balkan War seemed to many an excellent omen for the conflict to come.

In addition, increasing tension between Italy and Austria during the period of the fighting in the Balkans finally undermined any prospect of the Italians joining with the two Central Powers in the event of war. Relations were so bad, indeed, there was, for a time, considerable agitation at the highest levels of the Austrian Army for a pre-emptive strike against Italy through the Alps and across the *River Isonzo*[i]. Such a breakdown between the two states is, perhaps, unsurprising. Italians, after all, fought three wars of independence to rid themselves of their Austrian overlords[ii]. The first war, 1848-9, was unsuccessful but the second, and very brief, war of 1859[iii] was, with French assistance, transformative. The Kingdom of Sardinia gained Lombardy and the central Italian states of Tuscany, Parma, and Modena. France took Savoy and Nice leaving Austria with the Veneto. 1860 saw the demolition of the Kingdom of the Two Sicilies (Naples and Sicily) by Garibaldi and his insurgents which left only Rome and the Papal States, and the Austrian-controlled Veneto outside the new Italy. This situation was resolved by the Third War of Independence in 1866 when, allied to the Prussians who were themselves at war with Austria, the Italians seized the Veneto despite a military reverse at Custoza (24th June) and a naval defeat at Lissa (20th July). The severity of the Austrian Army's defeat at Königgratz (aka Sadowa, 3rd July 1866) and the subsequent terms of the Peace of Prague saw Prussia annexe Hanover, Holstein, Schleswig, Hesse-Kassel, Nassau, Frankfurt and some parts of Bavaria and Hesse-Darmstadt, whilst Italy was given the Veneto and parts of Friuli (capital: Udine) in the far north-east. Rome became the final piece of the puzzle in 1870 when it fell after the briefest of sieges after the withdrawal of a French garrison re-called because of the Franco-Prussian War. Italy and Austria, therefore, had been at loggerheads for much of the previous sixty years and leading figures in both

---

[i] *Genoberst*. Friedrich von Beck-Rzikowsky, then Austrian Chief of Staff, suggested this in 1904. His successor, and later commander of the Army, *Feldmarschall* Franz Xaver Joseph Conrad *Graf* von Hötzendorf, proposed attacking Italy in April 1907 (with a coup in Budapest to overthrow the troublesome Kingdom of Hungary). The operation was to start in July and measures to ensure sufficient ammunition were to be put in place. He hated the Italians. In 1902, he commanded 55. *Infanteriebrigade* in Trieste where he helped suppress a large-scale pro-Italian uprising. Hötzendorf was the prime mover in the declaration of war on Serbia in July 1914.He actively argued and planned for an attack on Serbia in 1909 after the Austrian annexation of Bosnia-Herzegovina the previous autumn [*Source*: Hermann, D G. *The Arming of Europe*, pages 107-125].
[ii] World War One was regarded by some as Italy's 4th War of Independence.
[iii] 26th April-12th July 1859 with two major Austrian defeats, at Magenta (4th June) and Solferino (24th June).

nations wanted either revenge for previous humiliations (Austria) or, amongst Italian nationalists, further expansion into the *terre irredente*[i].

This change in allegiance by Italy helped Joffre by releasing troops used to cover the Italian border. These changes, allied to what the French believed to be their tactical superiority and, of course, the brilliant 75 field gun, contributed to a conviction amongst senior French officers this was a very winnable war. What was needed, especially south of Metz, was speed, aggression, and vigour on the part of both Generals and their troops. Then, it was believed, Straßburg would again be Strasbourg, Mülhausen Mulhouse, and Diedenhofen at long last Thionville.

The oddity about France's chosen strategy – one of outright attack – was that there was little need for it. Germany was the nation in a hurry to defeat its western enemy before it turned to repel and defeat the Russian bear in the east. The French, as in *Plans XIV* and *XV*, only needed to wait for the mobilisation of the Russian Armies before it became useful to go over to the attack. In the interim, absorbing the energy of the German offensive whilst exacting as high a price as possible from the enemy, was surely their best option.

Progressively though, the smothering embrace of the '*offensive*' had an increasing impact on the underlying philosophy of the war plans formulated after 1871. *Plans I* to *VII* (1875 to 1886) were fundamentally defensive as they were framed in the context of a bilateral Franco-German war. Thereafter, as relations with Russia improved to be sealed by their Alliance of 1892, the plans for the late-1880s took on a more aggressive tone, with *Plans VIII* and *IX* of 1887 and 1888 respectively indicating a willingness to go on the offensive rather than await a German attack. There were also clear signs the huge investment in Séré de Rivières' fortifications was now regarded as a mistake, in scale if nothing else, which tied the French Armies to fixed positions rather than adopt the Napoleonic principles of speed, manoeuvre and the economy of force. This was reflected in the general nature of the Plans developed between 1889 and 1895, *Plans X* to *XIII*, and culminated in *Plans XIV* (drafted by Bonnal) to *XVI* (1898, 1903 and 1909) in which several Armies along the borders of *Elsaß* and *Lothringen* screened a large reserve, a 'mass of manoeuvre', which the French commander could deploy wherever and whenever opportunity arose. Joffre's *Plan XVII* changed all of that and, during its introduction, this was reinforced by the three publications each of which institutionalised 'the offensive' in French theory and all of which exhibited the malign influence of de Grandmaison on French tactical thinking.

There were critics of *Plan XVII*. Joseph Gallieni resigned as commander of *Ve Armée* in April 1914 rather than implement what he knew of its post-deployment activities (no Army commander was given a total overview of his campaign ideas by Joffre) and his successor, Charles Lanrezac, once highly thought of by Joffre, tried belatedly and unsuccessfully to persuade his CinC to change his deployment plans just as war broke out. Both were concerned about a massive German

---

[i] Parts of the Alps, the area around Trieste, and parts of Dalmatia. Guglielmo Oberdan, an *irredentist* from Trieste (born Wilhelm Oberdank), failed to assassinate Emperor Franz Joseph there in 1882. He was executed. Declared a martyr by Italians favouring further re-unification, there is a *Piazza Oberdan* in the centre of Trieste.

incursion through Belgium which would outflank the mass of the French forces which, by then, would be busily driving north-east by-passing Metz to the south.

These concerns were not exactly put to rest but were well and truly undermined by a faked document concocted by an artillery officer, Lt. Col. Edmond Alphonse Léon Buat, whose mother, Marie Poincelet from Magny near Metz, instilled in him a great determination for the 'liberation' of Lorraine from German control.

Buat[i] was highly regarded and entered the *École supérieure de guerre* in 1895 where he was taught by Bonnal, Foch and, ironically, Lanrezac before passing out second in his class in 1897. In 1912 he was attached to the office of the *ministre de la Guerre* Alexandre Millerand and, by 1914, he was an assistant professor of tactics at the *École supérieure*. Miraculously, Buat, whilst travelling on a train in Germany, claimed (but only later) to have found a copy of the German deployment plan. This forgery was published anonymously in the *Journal des Sciences militaire* in February 1914 under the title *La Concentration allemande d'après un document trouvé dans un compartiment de chemin de fer*.[ii] It indicated that, while the right-wing of the German forces would indeed breach Belgian neutrality, they would not then cross the *Meuse* at or south of Liège and move on Brussels, but would drive south-east towards Givet and the Ardennes in order to attack the flank of the French assault on Lorraine. The left-wing of the German invasion force based in Lorraine and Alsace would act as the pivot for this grand out-flanking movement. It also suggested that, while 25 divisions of reservists and of *Landwehr* were to be mobilised, they would not be in the front line which, given the attitude of the senior command to French reservists and their reluctance to put them anywhere near the front line, came as a relief.[59]

Such a report proved only too attractive to the French Staff and coincided with fondly held beliefs underpinned by real, physical evidence. For example, there were various railway lines either emanating from, or linked to, lines within Germany which suggested an intention to attack through Belgium and Luxembourg. Mainly, however, they pointed to the Ardennes as a route. By 1909, four lines ran from the *Rhine* through to the area between Namur and the *River Chiers* c. 90 kms south, a river which rises near Differdange in Luxembourg before

---

[i] Buat was born on 17th September 1868 in Châlons-sur-Marne (now Châlons-en-Champagne), the son of Léon Aubin Celestin Buat and Marie Poincelet. *École polytechnique*, 1887. *École d'application de l'Artillerie et du Génie*, 1889. *Sous-Lt.*, *121e régiment d'artillerie*, 1891. *École Supérieure de Guerre*, 1895, passed out 2nd to Pierre des Vallières. He married Jeanne Louise Caroline Bubbe, the daughter of *Général de Brigade* Henri Bubbe (*Directeur de la Fonderie à canons à Bourges*), 1893. Various staff jobs then attached to Gen. de Lacroix, member of the *Conseil supérieur de la guerre* in 1906, and its *vice-président* 1907-09. Commanded, *3e groupe*, *25e régiment d'artillerie* 1909-1912. Attached to the *ministre de la Guerre*, Alexandre Millerand, 1912. Professor of tactics, *École supérieure de guerre*, 1914. *Chef d'état-major*, *Armée d'Alsace*, August 1914. *Chef de cabinet* to *ministre de la Guerre*, Alexandre Millerand. Commanded *245e Brigade*, November 1915. GQG, January-May 1916. Commanded *7e Brigade* and *121e Division* until January 1917. Commander, *réserve générale d'artillerie*. Commanded *33e Division*, *17e Corps d'armée* February 1918, and *5e Armée*. GQG, July 1918 to October 1919. *Chef de l'État-Major général des armées françaises*, January 1920, he died suddenly on 30th December 1923.

[ii] Buat was not punished for his forgery to which he later admitted.

wandering westwards just south of the southern edge of the Ardennes via Longwy, Montmédy and Carignan before it joins the *Meuse* near Remilly-Aillicourt, 6 kms south-east of Sedan.

The first route from Köln via Aachen and Eupen avoided Liège, taking a long loop to the east and south of the city via Montjoie (Monschau), Malmedy, Stavelot and Comblain before running south-west via Marche and Jemelle to Dinant, less than 70 kms from Sedan, Hirson and Maubeuge.

The second line ran from Sankt Vith (now Saint Vith in Belgium) via Ulflingen (now Troisvierges, Luxembourg), Gouvy, Bastogne, Libramont to Bertrix in the heart of the Ardennes and just 28 kms from Sedan.

The third route started at Wasserbillig, the junction of the rivers *Moselle* and *Sauer*, running across Luxembourg towards Ettelbruck before turning west and running via Arlon and Virton to Montmédy. Virton is 5 kms from the Franco-Belgian border, 46 kms from Verdun and 115 kms from Reims.

The fourth line started at Coblenz, travelling south-west via Trier and Luxembourg to Longwy, 47 kms from Verdun.

In addition, another line from Luxembourg via Ettelbruck to Ulflingen linked the last three lines laterally.

The potential front line this created, Dinant-Bertrix-Virton-Longwy, broadly represented the area of the Ardennes facing France between Hirson and Verdun. To the south of the Dinant-Longwy line lie the open chalk down lands of Champagne or, in the east, the forests of the Argonne.

The railways in and through Luxembourg were mainly run by two companies: the *Société royale grand-ducale des chemins de fer Guillaume-Luxembourg* founded in 1857 which controlled lines up to the border towards Diedenhofen, Arlon, Trier, and Aachen to Köln. The company later developed the line to Ettelbruck and Ulflingen. After the Franco-Prussian War *Guillaume-Luxembourg* lost its connections to France and their railways were increasingly dominated by the *Kaiserliche Generaldirektion der Eisenbahnen in Elsaß-Lothringen* which had taken over the French railway system of *Lothringen* and *Elsaß* and, in 1902, it effectively lost control of its operations to the German authorities. The other company was the *Société anonyme luxembourgeoise des chemins de fer et minières Prince-Henri* which controlled a series of secondary, connecting routes. Finally, the company which lost out to the Germans after 1871, the French *Compagnie des chemins de fer de l'Est*, effectively was left with control of a short stretch of line which linked Rodange in southern Luxembourg with Mont-Saint-Martin just across the border. As a result, Germany, or German interests, controlled a network of railway lines which ran from the *Rhine* through Luxembourg and eastern Belgium towards the sensitive Ardennes area. This made it rather too easy to imagine that this sector was a key objective for any German invasion of France and conveniently allowed some to ignore the threat further west should a mass of German armies cross the *Meuse* at Liège and drive westwards towards Brussels before turning south towards Paris.

It has been suggested that Buat's forgery helped confirm Joffre's plans to attack towards Saarburg and advance Langle de Cary's *IVe Armée* from a reserve position about Bar-le-Duc where they might have intervened either in *Lothringen*, north towards the Ardennes, or even to the west about Maubeuge. Instead they moved into the gap between Lanrezac's *Ve Armée* and Ruffey's *IIIe Armée* and then on into the Ardennes where they were defeated piecemeal with heavy casualties, especially about Rossignol where the *Corps d'armée colonial* was all but destroyed.

Thus, the reckless and/or ill-informed advances of the French into German and Belgian territory played into the hands of the more tactically astute, better equipped and better trained German Armies. It quickly became apparent the *75* was not the only gun needed on a modern battlefield and *élan* plus gallantry but minus tactical acumen and the correct equipment was an equation which led to massive casualties, chaos and headlong retreat. In particular, the fire of German howitzers they could neither see nor reach wreaked havoc amongst both the French infantry and the frantic gun teams of the *75s*. Whatever the high opinion of themselves, the French had not learnt the correct lessons of recent wars.

One previously professionally-isolated 59-year-old Alsatian General, Frédéric Georges Herr (see page 233), currently the artillery commander of *6e Corps d'Armée*, was, however, proved to have been right all along but, in the meantime, he ploughed a long, lonely furrow with the powers that be in the French Army.

Buat's made-up piece was the culmination of a series of articles in newspapers and military journals all of which pointed to the Ardennes as the site of the expected German outflanking movement after the much-anticipated breach of Belgium's neutrality. Belgium had for thirty years accepted that, in a war between France and Germany, she would be invaded by Germany. After all, the German General Bernhardi stated as much in 1904[i]. Not that the opinions of a German General counted for much amongst the French Staff:

> "The apostles of the *offensive à outrance* did not believe in an attack on Belgium: 'The violation of Belgian neutrality by Germany', exclaimed one, 'can only lead to the complete destruction of its army. General Bernhardi, if he is a brilliant cavalry general, is a very mediocre strategist; if we were in the place of his compatriots, we would strongly invite him to return to the benches of the School of War to read his Clausewitz again… As for us, we, with our Belgian friends, can only ardently desire the adoption of his ideas by the great German general staff; victory will never have been so easy for us'."[60]

Nevertheless, in Belgium the only question was how would the Germans invade and with what final objective? The key was what happened when their forces reached the *Meuse*. Would they turn south and advance down the right (i.e. eastern) bank of the river towards the Ardennes or would they cross the river and advance on its left (western) bank past Namur and along the *Sambre* towards Maubeuge? Opinion in Belgium was divided – but only on the tactical details. The strategic German movement through Belgium was a *fait accompli* in the event of war. In 1913, the Belgian government sought belatedly to improve its defences and increase its military manpower. Pointing out in a secret session of the Belgian Parliament that the German Army Law of 1912 provided a regular army 300,000 larger than the French equivalent, the Belgian Prime Minister, Charles Marie Pierre Albert, 1st Comte de Broqueville, stated that:

---

[i] He also considered an invasion of France through Switzerland.

"During the last summer we learned that these increased numbers had as their objective an advance across Belgium."[61]

Within a day of the start of war, Broqueville asserted, the Germans could have 50,000 troops outside Liège. It was, in fact, 32,000 men of the *2. Armee* reinforced by 380 and 420-mm *Skoda* and *Krupp* siege howitzers but still the city and its forts held out from 5th-16th August (and Namur, further south, from 16th to 23rd August). This, it is thought, delayed the German advance through Belgium by up to five days. To paraphrase Napoleon, you can regain territory but you cannot regain time, and the time lost was crucial in the overall development of the war.

Prior to this, however, there were somewhat inflated ideas in wide circulation as to the potential resistance which might be put up by the fortified cities of Liège and Namur on the *River Meuse*, These suggested the Germans would not seek a crossing. *Général de brigade* Charles-Arthur Edouard Xavier Maitrot was, by 1911, the *chef d'état-major* of the *6e corps* based at Châlons-sur-Marne (now Châlons-en-Champagne). He had been attached to the *106e régiment d'infanterie* in 1880 (in 1914 *24e Brigade, 12e Division, 6e Corps*) and first joined the *Etat-major* of the *6e corps* in 1881 when a captain. He was rotated in and out of staff jobs whilst progressing to Colonel in 1902 before being appointed *chef d'état-major* at *6e corps* in 1907. Maitrot was, after 1911, a prolific writer producing nine volumes on military matters between that year and 1921. Thus, his comments on the state of Belgian defence, first written in 1911 as *Nos frontières de l'Est et du Nord* (Berger-Levrault 1911 and 1914) but which re-surfaced in 1914, were given due (or undue) weight. He expected 'effective resistance' from the Belgians along the *Meuse* and anticipated a 'long and vigorous defence' of Liège. Although the old fortifications and the citadel had no modern defensive value, Maitrot thought the twelve new forts an entirely different kettle of fish. At Namur, the forts numbered nine and were of similar 'quality'. With their supporting field troops, Maitrot did not believe the Germans would risk sending an Army towards these places. Instead, he believed German forces would drive through the Ardennes towards a line between Sedan and Stenay, arriving there sixteen days after war was declared, while another force would maintain a watching brief on the Belgians in the area around Malmedy and Saint Vith.[62]

At the same time as Maitrot was writing, on 4th December 1911 a letter from Gen. Langlois was published in *Le Soir*, a French language daily based in Brussels, suggesting that an attack through Belgium was inevitable and that it would be launched from around Trier and Saint Vith through Luxembourg and the Ardennes towards the *River Chiers* between Longwy and Sedan.[63] And this was the received wisdom in French military circles. A series of books and articles reinforced this view, amongst them: *La Doctrine de la défense nationale* (1912) written anonymously by a Capt. Sorb; *France et Allemagne* (1913) by Lt. Col. Grouard; and *Mission de couverture du 3e corps d'arméee* (1913), another anonymous piece by *Une Sentinelle de l'Est*.

In 1911, Col. Eugéne Arthur Boucher, an infantryman born in 1847, published the first of a series of four 'what if' books. The first of his *Etudes stratégique* was the optimistically titled *La France victorieuse dans la guerre de demain. L'Allemagne en péril* in which he suggested that, with the aid of Russia and Great Britain and, interestingly, with basically a defensive strategy in Lorraine, France would defeat Germany (but not, as actually happened, after more than four years and with over 30 million dead and wounded soldiers and c. 8 million dead civilians world-wide).

More in tune with modern French strategy, *L'Offensive contre L'Allemagne* was published the same year. In it he envisaged a French offensive starting twelve days after mobilisation in which French armies attacked between Metz and the Vosges with, as would be the case in August 1914, the objective of Sarrebourg. Within four days, Germany would be in retreat after a victory of which Napoleon would have been proud. Writing before Joffre's *Plan XVII* was envisaged, Boucher complained that, although: '… all of the regulations proclaim the advantages of the offensive' it was impossible to find in any military library a study of such an event into *Lothringen*. And yet, he asserted in an echo of Ferdinand Foch, was it not true that:

> "… history is there to remind us a thousand times that the offensive suits remarkably the character of the French soldier, doubling his moral value."⁶⁴

Such were the depths of delusion within the ranks of the Army of France.

Part III of this short work was entitled *Violation par les Allemands de la neutralité de la Belgique et du Luxembourg* and, in this Boucher explicitly envisaged a German attack through the Ardennes. This stratagem was confirmed in his *La Belgique à jamais indépendante* (1913). Not only French officers noted Boucher's slim volume with approval. German ones did too, and this volume was translated as *Die französische Offensive gegen Deutschland* (Éditions Stalling, 1911). So impressed were the German authorities by its contents that, in May 1912, they organised an exercise involving troops from Metz and Straßburg, the *XVI Armeekorps* and *8. Bayerisches Infanterie Brigade*, around Morchingen (Morhange), the place which became the high-water mark of the French advance of August 1914 and the final resting place of many a brave Frenchmen whose morale had been briefly doubled by their assault into old Lorraine. Apparently, though the exercise did not go well, lessons were clearly learned. Forewarned is forearmed as they say.⁶⁵

The last, and longest, of his publications was *L'Allemagne en péril* written in the late summer of 1913 though not published until 1915. He reiterated his opinion about Germany's invasion of Belgium and foresaw that Germany would seek to knock France out of the war before turning east to take on Russia. He again raised the issue as to how numerically inferior France would cope with the numbers and *material* available to Germany and, as seemed the only available recourse for elderly officers contemplating the next war, the answer was with the lives of its young men. Discussing the change from two to three years' service he wrote:

> "… this measure alone will not be enough, taking into account the numerical inferiority of the French, it will be necessary to remember that in war it is not the number nor the force which procures the victory, but that it is, above all, the superiority of courage."⁶⁶

Boucher was a student of ancient Greek military history and wrote several books on subjects such as the *Anabasis* of Xenophon. He now equated the courage and fighting abilities of the 10,000 Greek hoplites and their campaign in Persia with the modern and outnumbered French troops, although failing to note that the Persians did not possess machine guns and howitzers in 400 BC. And as was ever the case at this time, no statement on the prowess of French soldiers was complete without a reference or two to Napoleon and his morale versus *material* ideas. Mind, the same caveat about *l'Empereur* and the absence of automatic weapons c. 1806 applies.[i]

One officer begged to differ although, in his case, it might have been possible to dismiss his arguments as special pleading given his close connections to the city – Lille – whose effective disarmament he argued against. In *Considérations sur la défense de la frontière du Nord* published in 1912-3 in the *Journal des sciences militaires*, Gen. Gabriel Jean Herment[ii] argued that the Germans would try to occupy the Belgian coast to prevent Britain intervening in the war. The development of a railway system east of Luxembourg and Liège over the previous ten years could, he suggested, have no other purpose than to enable an attack into eastern Belgium and the Ardennes, *and* one further west to threaten Lille, Maubeuge, the route to Paris, as well as Dunkerque, Calais, and Boulogne. The argument that it would take eight days of marching (let alone fighting) to reach the French border opposite Belgium was true, he wrote, but mobile units, cavalry, etc., could reach into western Belgium in 3-4 days, well before French units might arrive, let alone the BEF. A concentration of German forces around Mons was to be expected, he believed.[67]

He was right.

---

[i] Boucher's last book, written aged 83 and three years before his death, is entitled *L'Infanterie sacrifiée* (1930). He seeks to place the role of the infantry above the artillery in the war and spends time denigrating Gen. Herr, describing him sarcastically as the 'Great Master of Artillery'. He points out that infantry casualty rates were (unsurprisingly) five times higher than that of the artillery (most of those casualties, of course, would have been caused by artillery) but spends little time analysing the changes in casualty rates as the war, and the role and power of artillery, developed. Broadly, he disagreed with Foch's statement: 'artillery conquers, infantry occupies'.

[ii] Gen. Gabriel Jean Herment was born in 1848. A veteran of the Franco-Prussian War and the suppression of the Paris Commune, he served with the *15e régiment d'artillerie*. By 1900 he was the director of the *atelier de construction de Douai* where he experimented with new types of shells. Commander, artillery, *1er corps d'armée*, Lille, 1903. In 1906 he was involved in the suppression of the widespread strikes which broke out after the *Catastrophe de Courrières* on 10th March 1906 (Courrières is 8 kms east of Lens) in which 1,099 French coal miners were killed in an explosion at mines owned by the *Compagnie des mines de houille de Courrières*. It remains Europe's worst ever mining disaster. Reserve 1910. Governor of Lille, 20th August 1914. *Limoged* on 10th September 1914, taking command of the artillery depots of the *1re Région*. He retired on 1st February 1917.

'AN INSTABILITY OF PRIME MINISTERS' - OCTOBER 1906-MARCH 1917

17. George Clemenceau
(Independent)
25th October 1906-24th July 1909
16th November 1917-20th January 1920

18. Aristide Briand
(Républicain-socialiste)
24th July 1909-2nd March 1911
21st January 1913-22nd March 1913
29th October 1915-20th March 1917

19. Ernest Monis
(Parti radical et radical-socialiste)
2nd March 1911-27th June 1911

20. Joseph Caillaux
(Parti radical et radical-socialiste)
27th June 1911-14th January 1912

21. Raymond Poincaré
(Parti républicain démocratique)
14th January 1912-21st January 1913
President of the Republic, 18th February 1913-18th February 1920

22. Jean Louis Barthou
(*Parti républicain démocratique*)
22nd March 1913-9th December 1913

23. Gaston Doumergue
(*Parti radical et radical-socialiste*)
9th December 1913-9th June 1914

24. Alexandre Ribot
(*Parti républicain démocratique*)
9th June 1914-13th June 1914
20th March 1917-12th September 1917

25. René Viviani
(*Républicain-socialiste*)
13th June 1914-29th October 1915

A Merry-Go-Round of *Ministres de la Guerre*, March 1911-December 1916

26. Maurice Berteaux
2nd March 1911-27th May 1911

27. Gen. François Goiran
27th May 1911-23rd June 1911

28. Adolphe Messimy
27th June 1911-11th January 1912
13th June 1914-26th August 1914

29. Alexandre Millerand
14th January 1912-12th January 1913
25th August 1914-29th October 1915

30. Albert Lebrun
12th January 1913-18th January 1913

31. Eugène Étienne
21st January 1913-2nd December 1913

32. Joseph Noulens
9th December 1913-3rd June 1914

33. Théophile Delcassé
9th June 1914-13th June 1914
(then Messimy, then Millerand)

34. Gen. Joseph Gallieni
29th October 1915-16th March 1916

35. Gen. Pierre Roques
16th March 1916-12th December 1916

ENDNOTES:

[1] Howard, M, *The Franco-Prussian War: The German Invasion of France 1870–1871*, Rupert Hart-Davis, pages 277-278
[2] Berglund, A, *The Iron-Ore Problem of Lorraine*, The *Quarterly Journal of Economics*, Vol. 33, No. 3 (May, 1919), pages 531-554.
[3] Gat, A, *The Development of Military Thought in the Nineteenth Century*, Clarendon Press, 1992, page 74.
[4] Bruneau, L, *Germany in France*, 2nd edition, Paris, 1914, page 2.
[5] Foley, R T, *Attrition: Its Theory and Application in German Strategy, 1880-1916*, PhD Thesis, King's College, London, 1999, page 30.
[6] Langlois, Col. H, trans. by Gibson, Lt. W, *Shrapnel for Field Artillery*, Journal of the United States Artillery, Volumes 2-3, 1894, footnote page 599.
[7] Le Hallé, G, *Le système Séré de Rivières ou le témoignage des pierres*, Ysec Editions, 2001.
[8] Loredan, J, *Lille et l'invasion allemande*, La Nouvelle Revue, April 1920, page 233.
[9] Ibid., page 234.
[10] Quoted in Horne, A, *The Price of Glory*, 1962, page 16.
[11] Zuber, T., *The Real German War Plan 1904-14*, The History Press, 2011, map, page 24.
[12] Musée du Génie, *Le redressement militaire de la France 1871-1914*, pages 1-2.
[13] *The Times, Europe's Armed Camp*, 21st August 1913, page 3.
[14] Musée du Génie, *Août 1914 - La mobilisation et la concentration des forces*, page 3.
[15] Zuber, op. cit., page 30.
[16] Tanenbaum J K, *French Estimates of German Operational War Plans* in May, Ernest R, *Knowing One's Enemies*, Princeton Legacy Library, 1986, page 154.
[17] *Les Armées Française dans La Grande Guerre* (then *AFdGG*), Tome I, Vol. 1, page 37.
[18] Huguet, Gen. V, *Britain and the War: A French Indictment*, Cassell & Co., 1928, page 3.
[19] Ibid., page 4.
[20] Dunlop, op. cit., page 239.
[21] Huguet, op. cit., page 5.
[22] Ibid., page 7.

[23] Ibid., page 16.
[24] Jeffrey, K, *Field Marshal Sir Henry Wilson: A Political Soldier*, Oxford University Press, 2006, page 73.
[25] Wilson Diary, 2nd-3rd December 1909 quoted in Jeffrey.
[26] *AFdGG*, Tome I, Vol. 1, page 37.
[27] Ibid.
[28] *Base de données Léonore* (*www.culture.gouv.fr/public/mistral/leonore_fr?*).
[29] Zuber, T., op. cit., page 123.
[30] *AFdGG*, Tome I, Vol. 1, page 37.
[31] Ibid., page 38
[32] *AFdGG*, Tome I, Annexes Vol. 1, Annexe 3, page 8.
[33] Ibid., page 11.
[34] Ibid., Annexe 4, page 17.
[35] Gorce, P-M de la, *La République et son armée*, Fayard, 1963.
[36] Herrmann, D G, *The Arming of Europe and the Making of the First World War*, Princeton University, 1996, pages 81-6.
[37] A problem highlighted by Macbean, Col. W A, *The French Plan of Concentration and the Collapse of 1914, The Journal of the Royal Artillery*, April 1923, page 2.
[38] *Base de données Léonore.*
[39] Porch, D, *The March to the Marne*, Cambridge University Press, 1981, page 217.
[40] Joffre, J, *The Memoirs of Marshal Joffre*, trans. Capt. Bentley-Mott, Geoffrey Bles, 1932, page 11.
[41] Messimy, A, *Mes Souvenirs*, 1935, page 70.
[42] Herrmann, op. cit., page 33.
[43] Langlois, H, *Le Haut Commandment, Revue des deux mondes*, 1st September 1911, page 56.
[44] Millerand Papers quoted in Porch D, *The March to the Marne*, page 175.
[45] *AFdGG*, Tome I, Vol. 1, page 40.
[46] *AFdGG*, Tome I, Annexes Vol. 1, Annexe 5, page
[47] Zuber, T., op. cit., pages 103-5.
[48] Quoted by Pedroncini, G. in *Remarks on the Major French Strategic Decisions from 1914 to 1940*, http://www.institut-strategie.fr.
[49] *AFdGG*, Tome I, Vol. 1, page 41.
[50] *The Times, The German Army Bills*, 4th July 1913, page 9.
[51] Ibid.
[52] *The Times, The German Army 'Levy'*, 7th May 1914, page 7.
[53] *The Times, Yield of German War Levy*, 11th July 1914, page 7.
[54] Quoted in McMeekin, S, *July 1914: Countdown to War*, Basic Books, 2014, page 66.
[55] Smith, L V, *From Mutiny to Obedience*, Princeton Legacy Library, 1994, page 26.
[56] Ibid., footnote page 37
[57] Snyder, J, *The Ideology of the Offensive*, Cornell University, 1984, page 100.
[58] Quoted in servant, P, *Le complexe de l'autruche: pour en finir avec les défaites françaises 1870-1914-1940*, Tempus, 2013.
[59] Palat, Gen. B E, *La Grande Guerre sur le front occidental II: Liège, Mulhouse, Sarrebourg, Morhange*, Librairie Chapelot, 1917, page 72-3
[60] Loredan, op. cit. page 239.
[61] Ibid., page 235.
[62] Palat, Gen. B E, op. cit., pages 66-70
[63] Ibid., page 70.
[64] Boucher, Col. A, *L'Offensive contre L'Allemagne*, Berger-Levrault, 1911, page 5.
[65] *Le Journal*, 19th May 1912.
[66] Détrie, J-F, *Le général Arthur Boucher (1847-1933): une carrière atypique, une oeuvre erudite*, Unpublished PhD thesis, Université Paul Valéry - Montpellier III, Page 257.
[67] Herment, Gen. G, *Considérations sur la défense de la frontière du Nord, Journal des sciences militaires*, 1st January 1913, page 5 onwards.

4. *OFFENSIVE À OUTRANCE*: TACTIC OF INFERIORITY

"Strength in the face of danger does not plunge ahead but bides its time, whereas weakness in the face of danger grows agitated and has not the patience to wait."

5. Hsü/Waiting, I Ching
Translated by Richard Wilhelm

TO ACHIEVE THE MUCH-NEEDED RAPID VICTORIES, the French embraced the theory of the *'offensive à outrance'*, or all-out attack, which started to emerge in the 1880s but which took some time before being fully incorporated into French military planning. Flimsily based on Napoleonic concepts, it granted to the French soldier a superiority of spirit, of *élan*, which would see him overcome the material and human advantages of their eastern enemy as, without such an intangible and spiritual advantage, the 'big battalions' of modern Germany must surely win. As an insurance policy against Gallic *élan* proving insufficient, however, allies were essential. Thus, Russia and even the historic enemy, Britain, were recruited to their cause.

Prior to this, French strategy was based on defence, thus the immense expenditure of money and manpower on Séré de Rivières' fortifications. Military attitudes were changing, however, in part led by a new intellectual ferment amongst officers triggered by the defeat of 1870-1. One of its leaders was a Col., later *général de division* and, very briefly, *Ministre de la Guerre*, Jules Louis Lewal[i]. Lewal was 47 years old in 1870 and joined the staff of Bazaine's *Armée du Rhin* in July 1870 in time to participate in the defeats which saw the army bottled up in Metz and surrender on 28th October. Previously in charge of the *2e Bureau* of the *Dépôt de la Guerre* (the office of military cartography, now the *Institut géographique national* [*IGN*], and archives, now the *Service historique de la défense* [*SHD*]), he had campaigned in Italy and Mexico. A prolific writer, his most important publication appeared with the war barely over: *La Réforme de l'Armée*, published by J. Dumaine in 1871. At more than 600 pages, it was an argument for a comprehensive overhaul of training, education, and organisation. In 1877, he presided over the creation of the *École militaire supérieure* (later the *École supérieure de guerre*) before returning to field command. It was a first step in broadening and deepening the professionalism and expertise of officers now keen to learn from military theorists and practitioners everywhere, but most especially Germany. A series of military journals appeared[ii]. One, the *Revue militaire de l'étranger*[iii], introduced officers to translations of foreign publications. The most influential was by a Prussian officer named Clausewitz. Its title: *Vom Kriege*.

CLAUSEWITZ'S INFLUENCE IN FRENCH MILITARY CIRCLES was not great until several officers rather tripped over him in the 1880s, nearly half a century after *Vom Kriege's* first publication. This influence increased in the remaining years of

---

[i] 3rd January to 5th April 1885 in the soon-to-fall administration of Jules Ferry.
[ii] *Revues d'artillerie* & *militaire française*, 1875, *Revue de Cavalerie*, 1885, *Revues d'infanterie* & *du génie militaire*, 1887. The *Journal des Sciences Militaires* started 1824.
[iii] Later *Revue militaire des armées l'étrangères*.

the century but it was the second translation of *Vom Kriege* (*On War*) in 1887 which accelerated the shift in French opinion on Clausewitz. Published under the title of *Théorie de la Grande Guerre* it was translated by a Lt. Col. de Vatry. It contained a brief preface written by Gen. Édouard Pierron, taken prisoner at Sedan in 1870 and later the Director of Studies at the *École supérieure de guerre*, a member of the *Conseil supérieur de guerre*, and the commander of the *7e Corps*. As tended to be the case, Pierron selectively quoted:

> "First, Clausewitz, showed how false was the theory, still in place today, of strong defensive positions. There is, in fact, no position, however strong it may seem, which is not compelled to yield under a concentric attack. Positions are nothing; directions (of attack) are everything. If we make our forces act in converging directions, if we act *en masse*, we have all the elements of success."[1]

On the other hand, however, Clausewitz had also written that the:

> "… defensive form of warfare is intrinsically stronger than the offensive."[2]

Pierron's comment was, however, a reaction to the essentially defensive tactics of the Franco-Prussian War and a harbinger of things to come where the offensive, by frontal attack rather than astute manoeuvre, became the guiding principle of certain influential French officers. Clausewitz, on the other hand, was pointing out the strength, and therefore the dangers to the imprudent attacker, of properly organised defensive positions and this some eighty years before the deployment of automatic weapons and barbed wire, etc. He was not advocating that armies stay permanently on the defensive but underlined the power of defence and its use as a springboard to the offensive.

Growing support for the 'offensive', and the moral superiority of the victor, was enhanced by lectures given by Maj. Lucien Cardot[i] at the *Ecole de Guerre* in 1885. Cardot was inspired by reading von der Goltz's *Das Volk in Waffen* published in 1883 and was then moved to study and lecture on Clausewitz in 1884. As with almost all French (and many British) students of Clausewitz, Cardot picked selectively at his mentor's ideas whilst, almost all the while, ignoring his proposition that the defence had, on occasions, strength greater than that of the offensive. And that, furthermore, when such defence proved disproportionately costly to the attacker, it offered great opportunities for a transition from defence to attack:

---

[i] Maj., later *Général de Brigade*, Lucien Cardot was born on 19th October 1838 in Roville-devant-Bayon, near Nancy, *département de Meurthe*. He joined the *98e régiment d'infanterie de ligne* in 1859. Attended St Cyr, 1860, passed out 53rd in a class of 239 in 1862. *98e régiment*, 1863-80. Taken prisoner, 19th August 1870, having been wounded at the Battle of Gravelotte-Saint Privat the day before. After his release on 6th April 1871, he attended the *École normal de tir* where he was awarded the 2nd Prize for Special Theory and passed out 5th out of 98 students. *Chef de bataillon, 141e RI*, in 1882 he was attached to the *État Major* between 1884-6 during which time he lectured at the *École de Guerre*. He was promoted Colonel in 1890, commanding the *111e RI*, and in 1900 he was given command of the *40e Brigade*. He died in 1920.

"A sudden powerful transition to the offensive – the flashing sword of vengeance – is the greatest moment for the defence."[3]

For Cardot, Gilbert and, later, Foch and Grandmaison, high morale and the essential power of the offensive were the key lessons gleaned… and little else.

Clausewitz's star blazed for a time in the French military firmament (even if he was a mere German!) and lessons lingered in the upper echelons of the French Army which were adopted, adapted, and made their own. *Vom Kriege* provided a veritable *Smörgåsbord* of delights for those willing to read and understand it, and even more for those happy to selectively quote which ever piece of self-serving sub-editing in which they cared to indulge. Of course, when one adds into the mix the issues of translation and all the opportunities of mistake, misunderstanding, misinterpretation, and misuse this may cover then Clausewitz's great work can, in some areas, become all things to all people depending on their needs or point of view. Broadly, and pursuing the Nordic foody theme, *Vom Kriege* covered the rollmops of 'moral forces' and the dour rye bread of 'defensive tactics', the *lutefisk* of 'absolute war' to the stewed cabbage of 'limited war'. And all washed down with copious quantities of the mis-labelled or mis-translated *akvavit* of 'total war'.

Carl Philipp Gottfried von Clausewitz was born on 1st June 1780 in Burg bei Magdeburg, 100 kms west of Berlin. By 1792 he was an officer cadet in the Prussian Army, just in time for the opening engagements of the French Revolutionary Wars. As a result, he was involved in the *Rhine* campaign of 1793-4 including the successful siege of Mainz (*aka* Mayence, 14th April to 23rd July 1793). According to Donald Stoker, over the next 22 years, Clausewitz or his unit came under fire on 36 occasions.[4] When adjutant to Prince August von Preußen he was captured by the French at the disastrous joint battles of Jena-Auerstedt in 1806; was with the Russians at Borodino in 1812; and was Chief of Staff to Thielmann's *III Armeekorps* at the Battle of Wavre on 18th June 1815. Clausewitz was not, therefore, some idealistic and remote military academic and philosopher but rather a practical soldier with vast and intimate first-hand knowledge of Napoleonic warfare (unlike Foch *et al* who heard stories at their grandfathers' knee and then studied the Emperor's campaigns in books).

Clausewitz was also, first and foremost, a patriot. After the disasters of 1806 and the defeat of Prussia's Russian allies at the Battle of Friedland (14th June 1807) Prussia was forced to sign the punitive Treaty of Tilsit the following month. Apart from costing territory which saw, *inter alia*, the creation of the new Kingdom of Westphalia governed by Napoleon's youngest brother, Jérôme Bonaparte, Prussia was also placed under an obligation to provide Napoleon with troops if required. This cheque was cashed in 1812 when he demanded Prussian support for the invasion of Russia under the terms of the Treaty of Paris signed on 5th March 1812. Prussia thus supplied some 21,000 men, half of the Army Prussia was allowed under the terms of the Tilsit Treaty. So appalled were many of the Prussian officer corps that they resigned, left the country or, in the case of Clausewitz volunteered to join the Russian Army. Others notable for their impact on reforming the Prussian Army followed suit: Gerhard Johann David von Scharnhorst, the Prussian Chief of Staff, resigned his position; August Wilhelm Antonius *Graf* Neidhardt von Gneisenau went to England having savagely criticised the King, Frederick William III of Prussia, for his supine response to French demands; and the hero of Waterloo, Gebhard Leberecht von Blücher, resigned his commission.[i]

Clausewitz eventually joined the Russian-German Legion, a unit made up of non-French soldiers taken prisoner or deserted from Napoleon's *Grande Armée* which invaded Russia. It was a motley crew made up of Prussians, Dutch, Belgians, and others and fought across northern Europe before the German elements were absorbed into the Prussian Army to become part of Thielmann's Corps during the Waterloo campaign. But, before then, Clausewitz played an important role in negotiating on behalf of the German-born Russian commander, Hans Karl Friedrich Anton *Graf* von Diebitsch, the Convention of Tauroggen, signed on 30th December 1812, which effectively neutralised the Prussian contingent of Napoleon's forces commanded by *Generalfeldmarschall* Johann David Ludwig *Graf* Yorck. This led to the Prussian break with France and an alliance with Russia formalised with the Treaty of Kalisz signed on 28th February 1813. This, in turn, led to the War of the Sixth Coalition in which all the major powers of Europe aligned themselves against Napoleon and which, in 1814, resulted in the fall of Paris and his exile to Elba.

In the meantime, Clausewitz courted and, in 1810, married a Prussian noblewoman, Marie Sophie *Gräfin* von Brühl[ii]. Marie was educated, multi-lingual, artistic, and well-connected. She was lady-in-waiting to the Queen dowager Frederika Louisa of Hesse-Darmstadt (the widow of Frederick the Great's son, Friedrich Wilhelm II); Princess Friederike Luise Charlotte Wilhelmine of Prussia (later Alexandra Feodorovna Romanova, Empress Consort of the reactionary Russian Emperor Nicholas I); and Princess Augusta Marie Luise Katharina of Saxe-Weimar-Eisenach, Queen and then Empress consort of the first German emperor, Wilhelm I. She was also tutor to the young Prince Friedrich Wilhelm Nikolaus Karl, later Emperor Friedrich III, who reigned for 99 days in 1888.

The marriage seemed a genuine love match and one of intellectual equals. Childless, Marie devoted herself to preparing her husband's manuscripts, helping with research, and organising his notably disorganised paperwork. It was she, after Clausewitz's untimely death from cholera in Breslau on 16th November 1831, who

---

[i] Perhaps fortunately for Clausewitz's image he was the only one of this group *not* to have a capital ship named after him in Hitler's *Kriegsmarine*. *Scharnhorst* and *Gneisenau* were 11-inch gunned battleships commissioned in 1939 and *Blücher* one of three completed *Admiral Hipper*-class heavy cruisers. *Scharnhorst* was sunk at the Battle of the North Cape on 26th December 1943. *Gneisenau* was severely damaged in a bombing raid in dock in Kiel on 26th February 1942. Decommissioned in July 1942 she was sunk as a blockship on 27th May 1945 in *Gotenhafen* harbour (now Gdynia). *Blücher* was sunk by Norwegian coastal batteries in the Battle of Drøbak Sound, 9th April 1940, leading a task group to seize Oslo in the invasion of Norway. Its predecessor was sunk at the Battle of Dogger Bank, 24th January 1915.

[ii] She was the daughter of Carl Adolph *Graf* von Brühl and a British woman, Sophie Gomm. Gomm was the aunt of Field Marshal Sir William Maynard Gomm, GCB, who served during the Peninsular War, the Waterloo campaign, as Governor of Mauritius, as CinC, Bombay Army and, in 1851, as CinC India.

organised the publication of *Vom Kriege*, writing a preface, and editing and making alterations to the final publication. Her health then broke down and, not helped by inadequate and often counter-productive medical treatment, she died on 28th January 1836, aged 56. Her and her husband's legacy was one of the most influential treatises on the nature and conduct of war of the past 200 years, even if *Vom Kriege* was somewhat late in its widespread discovery outside Germany.

We should be clear that *Vom Kriege* is not an early nineteenth century version of *Field Service Regulations*. It is not a tactical handbook for Army officers which they might quickly thumb through when an especially thorny battlefield problem presents itself. Indeed, it is explicitly *not* such a publication. It is a book about the nature of war and about its possible outcomes. Post-war, some tried to blame Clausewitz for the excessive casualties and the huge economic damage caused. Amongst them were Basil Liddell Hart and J F C Fuller. Whilst Fuller later mainly reconciled himself with Clausewitz's opinions and judgements, Liddell Hart continued to point the finger of blame in an increasingly perverse and unreasonable fashion. He conflated Napoleonic and Clausewitzian theories of war until they were one and the same. He blamed the concept of *Total War* for the disastrous results imposed on both victor and vanquished. He suggested that *Total War* was a Clausewitzian concept but the phrase never appears in the original *Vom Kriege* and only in some anglicised translations.

Henry Spenser Wilkinson was, perhaps, the *doyen* of pre-war British military writers. A prolific author, he was appointed the first *Chichele Professor of Military History* at Oxford University in 1909. Between 1882 and 1914 he wrote for the *Guardian*, until 1892, and the *Morning Post*, covering, increasingly, wars and military matters. In 1927, the *Army Quarterly* published Wilkinson's attack on Liddell Hart's new book *The Remaking of Modern Armies* in which he sets out his understanding of Clausewitz's theories. Wilkinson's comments are worthy of extensive quotation as they provide a useful, simplified digest of Clausewitz's core thesis:

> "He (i.e. Clausewitz) explicitly disclaims the intention to formulate a system or to give rules or precepts for the guidance of generals; what he tried to do was to think out the nature of war both in its general aspect and in its various phases.
> He begins by asking what is war? It is, he says, action by force for the purpose of compelling the enemy to do our will. Force is the means; to constrain the enemy's will is the object. To attain that object we must disarm the enemy; this is the military aim. The enemy will meet force by force, so that if we are to overpower him we must grapple with his strength. This consists in his armed forces, his country with its population, and his allies. The natural order would be first to destroy his armed forces and then to conquer his country in which otherwise he might raise up fresh forces. But the war will not be ended until the enemy's will has been overcome, that is, until his Government and his allies have signed a treaty of peace or his people have made their submission. By the destruction of the enemy's armed forces is meant putting them into a condition in which they cannot continue to fight – the word 'destruction' being understood not merely in a physical but rather in a moral sense.

This, says Clausewitz, is the theory of war in the abstract; what it would be if all the world were always guided by pure logic; it is war fought out to a finish – absolute war. The reality comes very far short of it. In practice the State which finds itself outmatched agrees to its adversary's terms long before its strength is exhausted. It is induced to do so by two considerations, either because it sees little or no prospect of turning the scales in its own favour, or that the price of success will be too great. To produce one or both of these frames of mind, the adversary need not make the extreme effort required for crushing blows. Once he has proved his superior strength he will have shown that the prospect of a change of luck is small, and he can raise for his opponent the price of success by wearing him out, by occupying parts of his territory, not with a view to annexation, but merely to injure the weaker side, or may use any other means of damaging him. All these are military aims, but in every case the military means is fighting – battle. From an enemy ready to fight nothing can be gained except by fighting. The paramount military aim, the destruction of the enemy's armed forces, has for its obvious counterpart the preservation of our own."[5]

Despite the various conditions Clausewitz attached to the conduct of war, it is the final sentence, or at least the first half, to which rather too many Army officers of all countries became unreasonably attached at the turn of the century. When added to his comment that 'Blood is the price of victory'[6] one begins to see how simplified, not to say simplistic, interpretations might lead to the French passion for the '*offensive à outrance*'. Thus, Foch later wrote in *Principes de la Guerre*:

"To seek out the enemy's armies – the centre of the adversary's power – in order to beat and destroy them; to adopt, with this sole end in view, the direction and tactics which lead to it in the quickest and safest way: such is the whole mental attitude of modern war."[7]

And thus, Foch endorsed Clausewitz when he wrote about:

"… the omnipotence of *mass* multiplied by *impulsion*, with the object of breaking, in a battle sought from the outset of the war, the moral and material forces of the adversary."[8]

'Mass multiplied by impulsion' – as accurate a description as one might hope for when describing the reckless French attacks of the opening weeks of the war. Add 'morale' to the mix and one gets the Napoleonic formula:

"The strength of an army, like the momentum in mechanics, is evaluated by the mass multiplied by the speed. A brisk march increases the morale of the army, it increases its means of victory."[9]

From this comes the equation: if speed increases morale, and offensives demand speed then, hey presto!, offensives increase morale.[10] Simple.

FURTHER INFLUENCING FRENCH THINKING was a posthumously published work by Col. Charles Jean Jacques Joseph Ardant du Picq, a Crimean War veteran taken prisoner during the storming of the Malokoff redan at Sevastopol on 8th September, 1855, and later commander of the *10e régiment d'infanterie*. He died in

Metz on 18th August 1870 having been severely wounded by a shell at Longeville-les-Metz three days earlier. Before his death, du Picq published *Combat antique*. Expanded after his death and entitled *Etudes sur les combat: Combat antique et modern*,[11] another edition was published in 1903[i].

36. Col. Charles Jean Jacques Joseph Ardant du Picq

Du Picq's work was hijacked by advocates of the *offensive* to bolster their arguments, even though his views were far more circumspect. He was not in favour of the helter-skelter form of attack later advocated by people like Grandmaison and Marie-Robert Altmayer. Before the experience of the Franco-Prussian War, he was aware of, and concerned by, the growth of firepower and saw the intelligent use of terrain and manoeuvre as essential. Defensive fire needed to be supressed as far as possible up to the moment the attacking infantry entered the enemy position.

His main concern, however, was the psychology of the soldier on the battlefield and he undoubtedly influenced Foch's views about the importance of 'moral force' in war:

"With equal or even inferior power of destruction he will win who has the resolution to advance… who, in a word has the moral ascendancy. Moral effect inspires fear. Fear must be changed to terror to vanquish."[12]

---

[i] To this writer's eye the book is full of assertions and assumptions, lacks objective evidence or is otherwise provably wrong. It contains glib generalisations about the 'characteristics' of various nations which influence their military abilities. The British, for example, are 'stolid and unimaginative' which traits allowed them to withstand the attacks at Waterloo for so long. The French made better skirmishers because of their temperament, an argument the Light Division in the Peninsular War might dispute. There are absurd generalisations e.g.: 'French infantry has always been defeated by English infantry' but 'The English have always fled before our cavalry' which are simply not true. The latter point would certainly be disputed by the officers and men of Milhaud's IV and Kellermann's III reserve cavalry corps and Lefebvre-Desnoëttes' light and Guyot's heavy cavalry divisions of the Imperial Guard, some units of which lost c. 50% of their strength whilst attacking the British infantry squares at Waterloo.

He was not, however, a man who subscribed to the view that superior morale was generated simply either by mass or by greater enthusiasm to attack. Discipline and training were his key words, especially on a battlefield on which the means to kill and maim were ever improving. He was not, therefore, an enthusiast for conscripts in the front line of battle.

He was not a firepower theorist but a man who subscribed to the Napoleonic view that the Army which achieved moral supremacy underpinned by discipline would be the victor, a view perhaps best encompassed by Bonaparte's previously quoted saying 'The moral is to the physical as three to one', a sentiment ever popular with Generals of all armies at the turn of the 20th Century irrespective of the nature of their troops. By 1914, this view had widespread, if not unanimous, support amongst French officers but most especially amongst the group known as *'Les Jeune Turcs'* of which Grandmaison, Laure, Altmayer, Montaigne, and others were leading lights. Their views were expressed with a semi-religious fervour as if members of some obscure yet influential cult which existed on a higher plain to the rest of a society which scurried around in some materialistic, hedonistic dirt.

31-year-old Lt. Émile Laure[i], later a failed General in 1940 and a close supporter of Pétain and Vichy, wrote in *L'Offensive française* in 1912:

"The progress of science and the ideas which develop in the most civilised nations are but the microbes of utopias and the germ of the failure of character."[13]

Laure would also call upon his fellow officers to adopt the war cry:

"We want to conquer!"[14]

To which was to be added what he described as 'the corollary':

"*L'Offensive!*"

In other words, to conquer, one advanced. And broke through:

"*Vive la percée! Vive l'Offensive Française!*"

Because Joffre was also an advocate of such crude simplicity, this demand for the 'breakthrough' lingered within the higher ranks of the French Army to the end of 1915 despite the horrendous casualties suffered for the first seventeen months of the war. It raised its ugly head again with Nivelle's costly and botched offensive in 1917. Mind, the BEF took a similar line throughout that period.

Lt. Col. Jean-Baptiste Montaigne[ii], a fervent if misguided admirer of the Japanese soldier in Manchuria, was equally opposed to science and logic, a theme

---

[i] Lt., later Gen., Auguste Marie Émile Laure (1881-1957). He was attached to Pétain at *GQG* in 1917. Commanding *VIIIe Armée* in 1940 he was taken prisoner on 22nd June 1940. Released at Pétain's request, he was appointed *Secrétaire général du cabinet*. Arrested by the Gestapo in 1943, he was acquitted of collaboration after the war.

[ii] Lt. Col. Jean Baptiste Montaigne was born in Arlanc in 1856. *Ècole Spéciale Militaire*, 1875. Capt., *4e régiment de Zouaves*, 1889. Served, Tunisia and Algeria. *Chef de bataillon, 123e RI*, 1899. Lt. Col., *143e RI*, 1907. *École supérieure de guerre* 1884-1886, he came under the influence of Lucien Cardot to the extent that, in 1911, in *Ètudes sur la guerre* he wrote: *"Et la parole du commandant Cardot assura ma foi."* ('And the words of Commander Cardot assured my faith'). Montaigne somehow stretched his views on war and morale

which has repeated itself in the modern era with anti-vaxxers, global warming sceptics and idiots like Michael 'people have had enough of experts' Gove. Writing in his numbingly long three-part 'epic' *Vaincre*, Montaigne wrote in 1913:

"Salvations lies in the revolt of the will against reason."[15]

Reinforcing this view, 41-year-old Capt. Marie Marcel André Billard[i] in *Èducation de l'Infanterie* stated in Part 1: *Éducation morale et intellectuelle de l'infanterie*:

"In war, it is even less about being clever than it is about courage; science will always give way to dedication and solidarity. So it will be necessary above all to imbue every last man with this spirit of superior sacrifice which will be revealed immediately, by the offensive, by the push towards the border... by disdaining the safety of the trench which might save individuals but which is surely the coffin of nations."[16]

What was needed, he went on, were:

"...*des gens qui veuillent bien se faire tuer.*" (Men who want to be killed).[17]

To give these men some sort of comfort, he claimed that:

"... in war, the offensive – its perfect and victorious expression – often leads on the battlefield to more losses for the victor than for the vanquished, this sacrifice, like all sacrifices, finds its reward. The country is saved and glorious..."[18]

OK, lots of men on the victorious side are dead but Billard then made the highly dubious claim that, anyway, in the two largest most recent wars:

"... the attacker and winners, Germany in 1871 and Japan in 1905, lost far fewer people than the vanquished French and Russians."[19]

In fact, in 1904-5, Japanese battle fatalities exceeded Russian, being some 12% higher (58,900 versus 52,623) according to various sources. Japanese deaths from disease were also 50% higher than for the Russian Army. But who needs accurate statistics when glory (and death) beckons?

No matter because, as Billard explained, he was talking about the special qualities of the French soldier, not some useless Turk, Russian or German. Thus, in an extraordinary statement on the *Poilu's* behalf, Billard claimed:

"... *il veut bien être tué, mais autant que possible utilement et intelligemment.*"
('... he wants to be killed, but, if possible, usefully and intelligently')[20]

---

into a 693-page, work: *Vaincre - Esquisse d'une Doctrine de la Guerre basée sur la Connaissance de l'Homme et de la Morale*, Berger-Levrault, 1913 (*Conquer - Outline of a Doctrine of War based on the knowledge of Man and Morale*). Its three volumes were: I: *Preparation for the study of war. Man and fear.* II: *Study of the war. Facts and Doctrines.* III: *The War. War in its form and in its essence.* Won the *Académie Française's Prix Marcelin Guérin*, 1913.

[i] Capt. Marie Marcel André Billard (1872-1963) *École Spéciale Militaire*, 1892. Sous-Lt., *8e bataillon de Chasseurs à Pied*, 1894. *École supérieure de Guerre*, 1904. *État-Major, 40e Division*, 1907. Capt., *150e RI*, 1908. Staff positions at Belfort and Poitiers from 1911. *État-Major, 52e Division*, 2nd August 1914. *Chef de bataillon, 291e RI*, in November. *Chef d'État-Major, 52e Division*, January 1915. *Chef de bataillon, 245e RI*, July 1916. *Chef d'État-Major, 87e Division*, 1917. Gassed on 25th October 1917. Lt. Col., 1918.

This is *not* an error of translation. On Page 28, under the heading: *Chapitre III: Éducation morale et intellectuelle du soldat*, Billard is equally explicit:

> "*Il s'agit toujours de transformer boutiquiers, paysans, ouvriers, en gens qui veuillent, puissent et sachent se faire tuer utilement...*"
> ('It is always a question of transforming shopkeepers, peasants, workers, into people who want, can, and know how to be usefully killed.')."[21]

And, again, on page 38:

> "We will stick essentially to our own task of training people of heart who want and know how to be killed properly and usefully."

It must be said that, even by the standards of the time, one is not dealing with a totally rational person here. With such men in command in August 1914, it is easy to see why casualties were so appalling and defeat so widespread. As Billard sets out in *Axiomes de combat*, the two essential yet simple principles for him were:

> "1. To win is to attack, to plant your bayonet in the belly of the enemy.
> 2. Victory belongs to those who best accept death."[22]

The tactics of the abattoir if one is the animal to be slaughtered.

This mystical, semi-religious belief in the unique nature of the French soldier grew in importance. As the tangible elements of a future war – manpower, material, money, industrial power – increasingly favoured Germany, so the belief in, and the reliance on, the intangible elements of morale, *ésprit* and *élan* – and of self-sacrifice – became fundamental to any chance of French victory. This latter element would lead Cardot to write in *Hérésies et apostasies militaires de notre temps*, published in 1908:

> "We have to find a way to lead people to their deaths, otherwise, no war will be possible. The means by which we do it is familiar to me; it lies in the spirit of sacrifice, and nowhere else"[23]

Self-sacrifice is a theme of Jesuit teachings, and without over-egging this religious pudding, it is not surprising certain key military figures were raised or educated within that religious environment. Foch, Fayolle and Castelnau attended Jesuit colleges and Grandmaison came from a strongly Jesuit family.

The need for 'sacrifice' was a recurring and increasingly hysterical theme amongst certain French officers. This, for example, from a *'Cdt. Cébro'* to be found in an article entitled *Les Conditions de l'offensive* in the pages of the March 1914 edition of the *Journal des sciences militaires*:

> "An execution of the offensive requires on the part of the troops great cohesion and very thorough training. It was because they possessed neither of these qualities that the Boer militiamen in the Transvaal, the Russian reservists in Manchuria and the Ottomans in Thrace and Macedonia failed to succeed in almost any attack.
> Finally, the offensive requires a spirit of sacrifice that only a deep and passionate national feeling can generate: either the racial hatred which inflamed the Japanese against the Russians and the Balkan peoples against the Ottomans; either the thirst for expansion which animated the French of 1805 and 1806, the Prussians of 1866 and the Germans in 1870; or finally

the patriotic exaltation which uplifted the French of the Revolution and the Prussians of 1813."[24]

Cardot was not alone in proposing the need for a spirit of sacrifice amongst the soldiers of France and he, like Foch, drew inspiration from the writings of Joseph-Marie, *comte* de Maistre, another with a Jesuit education. Maistre was born on 1st April 1753 in Chambéry[i] in the Duchy of Savoy, at that time part of the Kingdom of Piedmont-Sardinia. He studied law at the University of Turin, was a member of the Savoyard Senate, and a mason. Maistre was a monarchist, believing in the 'Divine Right of Kings', the belief which got Charles I into so much trouble and eventually cost him his head outside the Banqueting Hall in Whitehall in 1649. With the coming of the French Revolution, Maistre became a strident counter-revolutionary, living a peripatetic life in Switzerland, Venice, Cagliari, and St Petersburg (where he was ambassador to Russia from 1802), to avoid the French Revolutionary and then Napoleonic Armies. Maistre wrote prolifically and his most relevant work is *Considérations sur la France*, published in 1797.

Maistre held a grim view of society. And *society* here is, to this writer at least, the important word because 'societies' have leaders – political, military, industrial, financial and within the media – and it is they, for the most part, who control and direct the route of travel of public opinion, especially when it comes to whipping up resentment, xenophobia, racism, antagonism, jealousies and, eventually, war between nations or communities. We see this often enough at the current time. Maistre, however, then takes it to the individual level, suggesting violence is an innate characteristic of mankind. Thus, in his world, peace and cooperation are the outliers of human behaviour and their results damaging to the development of society at large. War and violence are the natural conditions of mankind, as he spells out in a chapter entitled *On the Violent Destruction of the Human Species*:

> "… if you go back to the birth of nations, if you come down to our own day, if you examine people in all possible conditions from the state of barbarism to the most advanced civilization, you always find war. From this primary cause, and from all the other connected causes, the effusion of blood has never ceased in the world. Sometimes blood flows less abundantly over some larger area, sometimes it flows more abundantly in a more restricted area, but the flow remains nearly constant."[25]

As Moltke the Elder, von der Goltz and Bernhardi and others would suggest 100+ years later, according to this philosophy, war was good for society. Maistre suggested a parallel with the *vigneron* who ruthlessly prunes leaves and poorer fruit from the vine to improve the final vintage. Maistre puts it more brutally still:

> "… when the human soul has lost its strength through laziness, incredulity, and the gangrenous vices that follow an excess of civilization, it can be re-tempered only in blood."

Some (this writer) might suggest that lower levels of human violence are mainly either domestic or random and arbitrary – triggered by rage, drugs, alcohol, jealousy, etc., and involving individuals or small numbers. They might further

---

[i] Now in the *département de la Savoie* in the region *Auvergne-Rhône-Alpes*.

argue that large scale violence is organised – by autocrats, governments, religions (in the case of Crusades/Jihads), politicians or criminal gangs (though it is sometimes difficult to tell the difference between the latter two). It does not seem to this writer to be the case that large numbers of people wake up one morning and independently decide to sweep away the 'trappings of materialism' or the 'gangrenous vices that follow an excess of civilization' or a neighbouring state, for that matter. Such movements are organised and led, usually by one or more of the population who displays sociopathic or psychopathic tendencies and who care not a jot for the impact the ensuing violence will have on their own supporters, let alone the opposition/enemy. And one does not just talk about military men here, politicians, religious leaders and, for example, the CEOs of major corporations are all likely members of this dangerous club[i]. Unless the proverbial 'red mist' has descended, most ordinary people, even if inclined to violence, are likely to weigh the possible costs against the potential benefits – or the even greater losses which might be incurred – before indulging in such action. And here, research suggests, most people are 'risk averse'. Only if they appear likely to lose by a failure to resist are they more likely to resist violently. Ordinary people tend not to fight to gain something, they fight to protect, to defend, which is, perhaps, one of the reasons why such as Clausewitz credited the defensive with such power.[26]

Nevertheless, military men found the words of Maistre inspiring if for no other reason that such thinking guaranteed their jobs. Officers from all countries, Britain included, fulminated against the liberalism, reformism, and socialism of an increasingly comfortable, materialist, *fin de siècle* Europe. They believed the threat of war, and war itself, would sweep away these corrupting influences, to the long-term benefit of the nation and mankind as a whole. With this mindset, it clearly did not seem remotely absurd for officers to demand their men sacrifice themselves for the 'greater good'. And, when you were a French General Officer looking with increasing alarm at the growing 'imbalance of power' between your country and its main and traditional enemy, then grasping at the straws of psychological intangibles: *ésprit, élan* and sacrifice, was a better option than drowning in a *material*-driven despair at German superiority.

Cardot was not the only Frenchman to talk directly or circumspectly about the need for the French soldier to sacrifice himself for the good of *La Patrie*. Indeed, it might be argued that anyone who gave credence to the argument that 'morale' trumped 'firepower' in the modern age was taking this point of view. Therefore:

> Gen. Hippolyte Langlois: 'War has always paid for itself dearly and it is with morale that we fight, with morale that we gain, by attacking';[27]

---

[i] A 2016 Australian study led by forensic psychologist Nathan Brooks found 21% of CEOs displayed psychopathic tendencies. Other studies suggest 1% of the population are psychopaths and 4% display sociopathic tendencies (i.e. c. 3.3 million people in the UK). Recent studies of those resisting Covid-linked restrictions and precautions in Brazil (*State University of Londrina*, 2020) and Poland (*Adaptive & maladaptive behaviour during the COVID-19 pandemic: The roles of Dark Triad traits, collective narcissism, and health beliefs*, Nowaka, Brzóska, Piotrowski, Sedikides, Żemojtel-Piotrowska & Jonason, 2020) suggest psychopathic or sociopathic tendencies in up to 25% of the population.

Capt. Jean-Francois-Georges Gilbert: '… finally and above all it [war] demands the constant, total, absolute sacrifice of the individual to the community';[28]

Gen. de Castelnau: '… you have to know how to die. The death of a soldier should not be a vain sacrifice, a sort of passive act reminiscent of the resignation of the fallen gladiator, offering himself to the knife… When there is nothing left to do but die, there is still to die powerfully';[29]

And again, Cardot: '… let us affirm strongly to the enemy that our contempt of danger and death, that our spirit of sacrifice prevails,'[30] because 'Losses – this is the price we pay for each step forward… it is the brave men lost on the way forward who open it to others…'.[31]

Et encore une fois Cardot: "…war is sacrifice; victory belongs to the bravest, to the most determined, to the one who knows best how to be killed, to the one who wins in the sublime escalation of sacrifice."[32]

By this thinking, men's lives were a commodity to spend on the battlefield at a General's whim. Or to put it another way, and paraphrasing the Gospel of John, Chapter 15, Verse 13: 'Greater love hath no General than this, that he lay down his men's life for his victory'. Three of the four officers quoted above retired from active service well before 1914 (of whom one, Gilbert, died in 1901) and were at no risk of being asked to sacrifice themselves for any cause. Castelnau was an Army commander, and thus ensconced in comfortable security, well away from any dangerous front-line action in 1914. His direct experience of sacrifice was vicarious: three of his sons were killed in the war.

As it turned out, from their own accounts rather than spiritual ecstasy, what soldiers needed to motivate them to leave their trenches seems to have been matters more mundane: camaraderie, solidarity, a fear of letting their mates down. That, and the dread of being shot by the Battle Police if they failed to leave the trench or, later, by their own colleagues as a deserter. One does not read too much from soldiers desperate to sacrifice their lives for *La Patrie* or *Blighty*, either because such idealists/lunatics (take your choice) were amongst the first to be shot down and had no chance to record the motivation for their glorious demise or, perhaps, because few if any went into battle with such thoughts.

Cardot and Foch were much influenced by the Russian General and theorist Mikhail Ivanovich Dragomirov, the leading military Russian figure in in the last quarter of the 19th Century. His family, the Dragomirecki, were originally Polish but, being ennobled, moved to Russia proper[i] in the middle of the 18th Century. He started his career in the *Dvorianskii polk* (*Noble Regiment* or *Regiment of the Nobility*) formed in 1808 to train army cadets from the nobility. He then moved to the *Semyonovsky leyb-gvardii polk* (*Semyonovsky Lifeguard Regiment*) before attending the Nikolaev Academy to train as a staff officer. There he passed out first in his class, being awarded a rare gold medal for his work. Highly intelligent and, for the time, remarkably liberal, he wrote a lengthy report and lectured on the Austro-Prussian War of 1866, having been present at the decisive Battle of Königgrätz. He was, perhaps, too liberal for some of his senior colleagues as, in 1869, he was shunted off to Kiev though, by now, a Major General. In 1873 he took command of the

---

[i] To Konotop, now in the Sumy Oblast in northeastern Ukraine.

14th Division which, as part of Lt. Gen. Radetzky's VIII Corps, he led through the Russo-Turkish War of 1877-8 with conspicuous success, leading the way with the crossing of the Danube at Zimnitza[i] on 27th/28th June 1877. He later fought at, and was badly wounded in, the defence of the Shipka Pass[ii] on 12th August 1877 which injuries prevented him from returning to active service. Instead, he assumed the important position as head of the Nikolaev Academy (1878-89) where he exposed staff officers to the ideas and literature of the leading military theorists from around Europe. One of these was Clausewitz whose work he partly translated and interpreted in 1888.[33]

Cardot twice attended the Russian Army's manoeuvres (1882 and 1895) and was impressed and influenced by Dragomirov's ideas. The Russian drew on the career of his successful predecessor, Alexander Vasilyevich Suvorov (1730-1800), an officer who, reputedly, never lost a battle and who was regarded as Napoleon's tactical equal, if not superior, before his death in Saint Petersburg on 18th May, 1800. Suvorov was, arguably, Russia's greatest soldier. Present at Frederick the Great's shattering defeat at Kunersdorf on 12th August 1759, and part of the army which raided Berlin in October 1760, Suvorov made his name in wars against the Poles (War of the Bar Confederation 1768-1772) during which he captured Kraków; against the Turks (1768-1774 and 1787-92); and the Poles again (the Kościuszko Uprising of 1794). After Napoleon's successes in Italy in 1796-7, Suvorov went to Italy, Bonaparte having left for the Egyptian campaign in 1798, where he took Turin and Milan and defeated the French in a series of battles – Cassano d'Adda, Trebbia, and Novi – finishing with his masterly extrication of this troops from nearly being surrounded by French forces in Switzerland in 1799.

Suvorov based his success on a belief in training, high morale, initiative at all levels, speed and mobility. And the power of the bayonet. Thus, his is known for two famous aphorisms: 'Train hard, fight easy' and 'The bullet is a mad thing; only the bayonet knows what it is about'. Dragomirov based his approach along nearly identical lines including his continuing belief in the effectiveness of the bayonet even at a time of long-range and automatic weapons. War, for Dragomirov, was a combination of willpower, morale, and intelligence, and uppermost of these was the will of the soldier to confront and defeat his enemy face to face with the bayonet. He was, however, firmly in favour of the use of field fortifications and the training of soldiers in the use of the spade as much as the rifle after his experiences of the Austro-Prussian War of 1866.[34] The experience of the Russians in the siege of Plevna, however, suggested that they were just as slow as any other Army to adopt and adapt new ideas to the reality of warfare.

Dragomirov lived (just, he died on 28th October 1905) to see the outcome of the war in Manchuria. One wonders whether the huge casualty lists of both armies might have persuaded him of the error of his ways as the war was fought under the guidance of a 1904 Field Manual for which he was largely responsible. On the other hand, he was a man, like Cardot and the others, who believed in laying his

---

[i] Now Zimnicea, Rumania.
[ii] Now part of the Kazanlak Municipality, Stara Zagora Province, Bulgaria.

soldiers' lives down on Abraham's sacrificial altar as in Wilfred Owen's poem *The Parable of the Old Man and the Young* [i]:

> "If every soldier was imbued with the thought that he is chosen as a bloody sacrifice for the good of the entire people; that he is a representative of the great principle that 'you cannot have more love than that you lay down your soul for your friends'; if this were remembered constantly, a different structure of thought ... would arise"[35]

Following this line of thought, 37-year-old Capt. Marie-Robert Altmayer[ii] wrote a piece in 1912 entitled *Je Veux'* for Langlois's *Revue militaire Générale*.[36] The introduction by Gen. Henri de Lacroix would have left no-one in any doubts as to the direction of travel of Altmayer's article:

> "Captain Altmayer has confidence and is right. His study is suffused with a breath of invigorating patriotism. He is an apostle of the 'will' and the offensive 'will'. But this 'will' is not enough; we also need material and moral strength. He says it and proves it with the sharp insights of a believer. France can have these two forces united. It is also a matter of will and faith in our traditions and our destinies."[37]

And, to make his point, Altmayer (selectively) quoted Ardant du Picq:

"*R (résolution), et R, et toujours R > que tous les MV²*."
(R (Resolution) and R, and always R, is greater than all the MV squared[iii] in the world)."

And this Altmayer more than generously interpreted as:

"... *c'est-à-dire: l'impulsion morale > les moyens matériels.*"
(That is to say: the moral impulse is greater than the material means)

Never mind that du Picq is describing the collision of two cavalry forces, thus his formula is preceded by the words: 'The formula of the cavalry is R (Resolution) and R etc.'. No matter, Altmayer wished to gather to himself the approval of the dead colonel from the Franco-Prussian War. It is, perhaps, unfortunate that

---

[i] *So Abram rose, and clave the wood, and went, And took the fire with him, and a knife.*
And as they sojourned both of them together, Isaac the first-born spake and said, My Father,
Behold the preparations, fire and iron, But where the lamb for this burnt-offering?
Then Abram bound the youth with belts and straps, and builded parapets and trenches there,
And stretchèd forth the knife to slay his son.
When lo! an angel called him out of heaven, Saying, Lay not thy hand upon the lad,
Neither do anything to him. Behold, A ram, caught in a thicket by its horns;
Offer the Ram of Pride instead of him.
But the old man would not so, but slew his son, And half the seed of Europe, one by one.

[ii] Gen. Marie-Robert Altmayer (1875-1959) was the son of *général de division* Victor Joseph Altmayer. A cavalryman, he served in North Africa before WW1. He commanded the cavalry in Algeria in 1929 and, as *général de corps d'armée*, was *inspecteur général de la Cavalerie*, 1932-6, when he retired. He took command of *10e Armée* on 24th May 1940 and was taken prisoner four weeks later, on 19th June 1940.

[iii] M(mass) times V(velocity)² refers to the Kinetic energy of an object which is the energy it possesses due to its motion.

Altmayer and Grandmaison, in their anxiety to 'fly at the throats of the enemy' wherever they were to be found, did not also give due weight to du Picq's admonishment that:

> "There is always mad impatience for results, without considering the means. A general's ability lies in judging the best moment for attack and in knowing how to prepare for it."

In other words, for du Picq, and to paraphrase Grandmaison, 'imprudence was *not* the best security'. Superior French morale, the *élan* and *ésprit* with which the French credited themselves was, on its own, not enough to ensure victory according to du Picq. Grandmaison and his ilk ignored this stricture at their country's peril.

To achieve this 'moral supremacy' du Picq believed the men of an Army needed discipline, training, and obedience and to be part of a cohesive unit in which the men acted as a single, even if dispersed, organism rather than as a disparate group of individuals concerned solely for their own fate. Battle, though, was still the *raison d'être* of any Army and bringing the enemy to combat was its primary objective. Later, this latter concept was isolated, hijacked and distorted into the concept that the offensive battle was the *sole* objective of an Army and should be sought *whenever* and *wherever* opportunity presented itself, and irrespective of the relative tactical and strategic positions of the forces involved. Du Picq would have been appalled.

WHY MIGHT THESE CONCEPTS BE SO POPULAR, especially in France? It might well be associated with four important 'Ps': Passivity, People, Pride and Purpose. And, later, underpinned by another 'P' popular in France – Philosophy.

'Passivity' – because passive, reactive tactics lacking aggression is how the Army was perceived as having acted in the Franco-Prussian War, and overly defensive tactics were believed to have led to the swift and crushing defeat by Prussia. This reactive approach was damned by von der Goltz:

> "It became an article of faith to the French army that you must utilise to the utmost the power of armament and keep to an absolute defensive. They thought that the offensive strength of the Prussian army would fail to break a defence relying on their new and terrible firearms. Our adversaries did much more in developing this system than had previously been done by any other army, and yet failed to secure victory.
> They ruined by that doctrine the spirit of their own army. External form, the increase of material power actually attained, replaced neither the moral strength lost nor the confidence shaken by a defensive doctrine. It was tis that turned the scales. Whatever is done within an army must always aim at increasing and strengthening its moral force."[38]

'People' – because the fast-growing discrepancy between the populations of metropolitan France and greater Germany made some fear France might never again be able to take on its increasingly powerful neighbour and the lost provinces might never be returned. If numbers were inadequate then something else, something intangible, almost spiritual, needed to flow through the ranks of the Army: the *élan vital* which some French officers and politicians thought unique to

France, and which would allow them to overcome the enemy's greater numbers and 'miraculous machines'.

Ferdinand Foch, like others, was devoted to the idea of the innate superiority of the French soldier over the German:

"We, the French, possess a fighter, a soldier, undeniably superior to the one beyond the Vosges in his racial qualities, activity, intelligence, spirit, power of exaltation, devotion, patriotism... If we are beaten, it will be due to the weakness of our tactics. Let us then find, and provide our soldiers with, those tactics which get the better of numbers and valour as at the Pyramids[i]; which will doubly enable us to get the better of an army the individual valour of which is inferior to our own."

'Pride' – in the reputation of its Napoleonic Army and its charismatic leader whose tactics, strategy, and ethos they wished to see re-invigorate the Armies of France so that, whatever the difference in numbers and even weaponry, the *élan* and *ésprit* for which its soldiers were famed might again defeat the German threat. For some twenty years after the Franco-Prussian War and the traumas of the Paris Commune a close connection between people and the Army was re-established but was then seriously and nearly fatally undermined by *l'affaire Dreyfus*. It was in the process of being re-built when war broke out; and

'Purpose' – the growth of *revanchism*, a determination to get back lost lands and a willingness, by some, to make almost any sacrifice to achieve this end.

Lastly *'Philosophy'*. If Britain had the baleful influence of the Social Darwinist Herbert Spencer to deal with then, for France, it was the Spencer-reading Henri-Louis Bergson (1859-1941) who, though not attempting to interfere with political and social matters, had a profound effect on French national morale and, oddly, military tactics.

Bergson was the proponent of the *élan vital* as expressed in his 1907 book *Creative Evolution* for which he was awarded the Nobel Prize for Literature in 1927. The *Élan vital* encompassed action, instinct/intuition, will, and force rather than reason and was the 'added extra', France's *Unique Selling Proposition*, which would enable them to overcome Germany's many material, financial and physical advantages in the struggle to come. After all, the supply of money, guns and manpower could run out, but a resilient spiritual France would be sustained by the inexhaustible depths of its vital spirit, its *élan vital*. Until 1940, that is, when that reservoir ran dry.

According to some, the influence of Bergson went beyond the *élan vital*. In 1923 Jean de Pierrefeu published a volume entitled *Plutarque a menti (Plutarch Lied)*.

---

[i] A reference to Napoleon's defeat of the Ottoman Mameluke Army at the Battle of the Pyramids, 21st July 1798, part of France's invasion of Egypt. In the battle c. 20,000 French troops defeated 25,000 Mamelukes suffering just 300 casualties to estimated Ottoman casualties of c. 20,000 [*Source*: Nakoula El-Turk, *Histoire de l'expédition des français en Égypte*, M. Desgrandes Aîné]. On the 1st August 1798 the French fleet was destroyed by Nelson at the Battle of the Nile leaving Napoleon's army stranded. French efforts to occupy the Holy Land were finally defeated at the Siege of Acre, March-May 1799.

Pierrefeu[i] worked under Joffre, Nivelle and Pétain at *GQG* from November 1915 to November 1918 writing the official Army communiqués. A prolific and controversial writer after the war, his books included *L'offensive du 16 avril. La vérité sur l'affaire Nivelle* (1919), *GQG. Secteur I. Trois ans au Grand Quartier Général par le rédacteur du communiqué* (2 volumes, 1920) and then *Plutarque a menti*.[ii] By now, Pierrefeu was an outspoken critic of senior Army officers both before and during the war, castigating them for their luxurious lifestyles at Chantilly, for their desperate ambitions for promotion, and for their attachment to out-moded traditions and ways of thinking. He believed Joffre a decent man misled by his staff, Nivelle a mediocrity who promised what others wanted to hear, and unsurprisingly given his background and future actions, Pétain to have been the saviour of France.

In *Plutarque a menti* there is a chapter entitled *Plan XVII in application, or Bergson versus Lanrezac*. It refers to the infamous mobilisation plan which Joffre then used to launch French Armies on full-scale attacks into *Lothringen* and *Elsaß* whilst ignoring the well-known German outflanking attack through central Belgium, *aka* the *Schlieffen Plan*. The sub-heading, *Bergson versus Lanrezac*, refers to what he believed to be the unreality of a French Army staff driven by Bergsonian intuition as opposed to the more realistic, prudent voice of Gen. Charles Lanrezac, the commander of the French *5e Armée* in August 1914 and sacked by Joffre in early September, who opposed the '*offensive à outrance*' and warned of the German 'right hook' through Belgium. Pierrefeu wrote:

"Before 1914 France had a General Staff worthy to be called Bergsonian. Its doctrine eroded intelligence in favour of a cult of intuition. This statement is stupefying and incredible: at first sight it is positively staggering. But after due examination, it emerges as a perfectly truthful assertion. This General Staff of ours drove its conviction to the ultimate limits. It went far beyond Bergson himself, who would never have dared to admit that intuition was possessed of a power marvellous enough to prepare the revenge for 1870: Bergson would at least have invited intelligence to collaborate in that difficult task. You would hardly believe it, but our Joffre, so comfortably established as a physical entity, and so completely attached, by good health and a good appetite, to the world of solid things which the Bergsonian professes to despise, identified himself with this theory, fit only for the somnambulist and the medium. He came

---

[i] Jean de Pierrefeu was born in 1883 in Paris. In 1905 he became a journalist, joining the staff of *L'Opinion*, a nationalist political weekly, in 1908. A reservist, he was mobilised on 1st August 1914 as a sergeant major. Wounded early, he joined the Information Section at *GQG* on 23rd November 1915, drafting communiqués before switching in 1916 to perform the same function for the army in Salonika (still based at *GQG*). He continued writing for *L'Opinion* and *L'éclair*. He was a supporter of Pétain in 1940 and edited *Les Cahiers de la Jeune France - organe de la rénovation nationale* a part of Vichy's *Révolution nationale*. He died the same year.

[ii] Buoyed by the success of *Plutarque a menti*, Pierrefeu followed it up with *Anti-Plutarque* (*Anti-Plutarch*, 1925) and *Nouveaux mensonges de Plutarque* (*New Lies by Plutarch*, 1931).

to adhere to a doctrine which counted on intangible things as well as on regiments, and which hoped to achieve a victory of the 'unconscious' in battle by making use of the *élan vital* of the troops: which *élan* was to be produced by a deep-rooted instinct of success. The office table of the General Staff on which was drawn up *Plan XVII* was, if I may say so, the sort of table which is 'turned' by a pseudo-spiritualist."[39]

ON A MORE DIRECTLY PRACTICAL, if linked, level, theorists such as the above-quoted Capt. Jean-Francois-Georges Gilbert[i] emerged. Their analysis of the failure of 1870-1 concluded it was the passive, defensive French tactics which handed victory to Prussia and its allies. Not only were the tactics incorrect, suggested Gilbert, they did not exploit the dashing and aggressive nature of the French soldier who, when unleashed, was irresistible. This opinion of the innate superiority of the French soldier became a common theme amongst French theorists – Foch, Cardot, Négrier, etc., etc., – irrespective of whether they were supporters or critics of the cult of the offensive and was especially costly when put to the test.

Like the majority of British officers prior to the war, Gilbert believed battles were won by the Army with superior morale, the greater 'will to win', and an absolute commitment to 'the offensive'. Perhaps in this he was influenced by Maistre's elegant if absurd notion that:

"…a lost battle is a battle we believe we've lost."[40]

For Gilbert and others, only through 'the offensive' could the initiative be grasped, exploited, and victory gained. Gilbert was one of the first generation of officers to emerge from the *École supérieure de Guerre* and was a conditional admirer of Clausewitz, reviewing *On War* for *La Nouvelle Revue* in 1887. This book drew many French officers back to a study of the Napoleonic methods of war of which both Foch and Haig were so enamoured, if in different ways. Increasingly, however, French theorists came to see Clausewitz as not especially revolutionary in his ideas which were, they believed, a crude and simplified Prussian version of the Emperor's strategy and tactics. Espousal of these fundamental ideas was, however, a 'return to basics' for the French Army which many thought had lost contact with its roots during the middle of the nineteenth century. The result of this loss of focus, concluded Gilbert, was the defensive fiasco of 1870-1, conveniently forgetting all the while that Napoleon lost too. It just took him rather longer than six months until, in quick succession, came the Russian campaign, Leipzig and Waterloo.

Others took a similar view. Maj. (later *Général de Brigade*) Louis-Adolphe Goujat *dit* Maillard (1838-1901) was appointed Professor of Applied Infantry Tactics at

---

[i] An artillerist, Capt. Jean-Francois-Georges Gilbert attended the *École polytechnique* with Joffre in 1869 and was involved in the Siege of Paris. Illness forced his retirement in 1884 but he wrote articles in the *Nouvelle Revue* between 1887 and 1898. He died in 1901. His maternal grandfather was *Général de division* Pierre François Joseph Durutte, *1er comte Durutte et de l'Empire*, who fought in the Revolutionary and Napoleonic Wars and commanded the *4e Division* at Waterloo, losing his right eye to a sabre wound.

the *École supérieure* in 1881, staying nine years. Amongst his students were four future *maréchals de France*: Franchet d'Esperey (1882-4), Foch (1885-7), Pétain (1888-90), and Fayolle (1889-90). His formative experiences were as a Captain in the *98e RI*, part of the *4e Corps d'armée* of Bazaine's *Armée du Rhin* and all involved Bazaine's indecision and failure and the surrender of Metz on 28th October. Maillard's regiment first fought at the Battle of Borny-Colombey (14th August 1870), 5 kms east of Metz[i], where Bazaine should have defeated the outnumbered Karl Friedrich von Steinmetz's *1. Armee*. Foch later described the battle as:

> "…opening in an entirely unforeseen manner, and was conducted in a completely unpremeditated way by the Germans. It might have been disastrous for them, as General von Moltke has acknowledged since."[41]

Two days later, on 16th August, between Mars-la-Tour and Rezonville (17 kms west of Metz), the 30,000 men of Reimar Constantin von Alvensleben's *III. Armeekorps* held off Bazaine's 127,000 strong army for seven hours as it tried to retire westwards. Reinforced in the evening, and despite losing c. 17,000 men, Alvensleben's defence (which included Von Bredow's 'Death ride', see page 87) prevented Bazaine's escape. The Battle of Gravelotte-St Privat on 18th August, just 8 kms to the east, sealed Bazaine's fate when the Prussian *1. Armee* and the North German Confederation's *2. Armee* defeated the heavily outnumbered *Armée du Rhin*. It retreated into Metz, surrendering *en masse* on 28th October.

Maillard's analysis of this campaign for students at the *École supérieure de Guerre* was to be one of the more influential contributions to French military thought. He determined that the successful German offensive tactics could be traced back via Moltke to Clausewitz and from the Prussian to its (naturally French) source: Napoleon. He and his successors, Bonnal, Langlois and Foch, were happy to confirm the two Prussians as mere imperfect copycats of the French master. Thus, though it was prudent to study the 1870-1 war as a source of salutary lessons, more essential still was the study of the campaigns and ideas of the 'Little Corporal'.

Maillard commanded *5e brigade d'infanterie* and later was appointed commandant of the *École spéciale militaire* (1896-1900) and was thus able to directly influence the future officers of the Army. He was also a member of the *Comité technique de l'infanterie*. In 1891, having left the *École supérieure de Guerre*, he published *Eléments de la Guerre*, a book based on his lectures. In it, he unequivocally stated:

> "The destruction of the enemy is the aim; the offensive the means."[42]

These ideas were established in official documents with the Infantry Field Regulations of 1884 which demanded battle should culminate in a decisive bayonet assault 'with no attention to losses'. Furthermore, and directly linking him to *Les Jeunes Turcs*, Maillard believed in a 'higher power', in '*la puissance morale*', a power:

> "… as old as the world, though always young, more formidable than the cannon and the rifle, capable of giving rise to surprises; it animates the masses and prepares them for the great sacrifices victory demands."[43]

Post-war some French officers did not see, or did not accept, that Maillard's thinking was in any way responsible for the events of 1914[44]. In their view, it was

---

[i] Now, essentially a suburb of Metz.

only a younger, clique of officers such as Grandmaison who distorted his thinking into the calamities of the *offensive à outrance*. One begs to differ.

Following Maillard was Henri Bonnal appointed Professor of Military History, Strategy and Applied Tactics (1892-6). It was Bonnal who borrowed from Germany the idea of the war game (*Kriegspiel*) but, like Maillard, Bonnal was a Napoleonist who saw both the past and the future through the little Emperor's eyes. A lieutenant in the *41e régiment d'infanterie* he was taken prisoner at Sedan on 1st September 1870. He too regarded the war as one from which one learnt lessons from the Germans and then filtered them through the experiences of Napoleon in order to apply them to the future. Like Gilbert he was later highly critical of the British performance in South Africa between 1899 and 1902, but he spent the 1890s lecturing budding staff officers and, between 1901 and 1912, he produced books analysing in detail several of Napoleon's campaigns, as well as three volumes describing the Battle of Gravelotte–St. Privat in 1870. He sought a return to Napoleonic 'first principles' of flexibility, speed of thought and movement, manoeuvre and the 'economy of force' with which one Army concentrated overwhelming power on an exposed element of the enemy.

His influence was felt in the 28th May 1895 edition of the French *Règlement sur le service des armées en campagne* (effectively the equivalent of the British *Field Service Regulations*). These regulations were designed for the purpose of advising units such as a *Corps d'Armée* and subsequently it was determined that the principles which might guide smaller units, i.e. Division-sized and smaller, were fundamentally different to those for Corps and, more especially, armies.

Soon after the Franco-Prussian War a commission of officers prepared a new version of the infantry regulations which was submitted to the *Ministre de la Guerre* on 12th June 1875. Its conclusions were stark:

"An indisputable fact has occurred in the improvements made over a number of years to the armament of the infantry and that of the artillery which have profoundly modified the physiognomy of combat. Effects due to increased range, accuracy and speed of fire have exceeded all expectations. The experience of the last wars proves it abundantly and the facts which occurred there in the most profound manner provoked studies whose conclusions are already adopted in almost all the foreign armies."[45]

As a result, they proposed the four following principles:

1. The preponderant importance of fire as a mode of action;
2. The impossibility of a considerable force to move and to fight in close order in the effective zone of the enemy fire, either in line or in column;
3. The consequent need to divide the troops in the front line, and to adopt dispersed order;
4. The line of skirmishers was now the main combat line, whereas formerly they were responsible only for the preparation of the attack.

The 1895 regulations, however, although stating that preliminary fighting was to be conducted by a strong skirmishing line in extended order, then declared that the decisive bayonet attack was to be delivered with the attacking troops concentrating some 400 metres from the enemy. After a further advance to within

200 metres, covered by as much fire as could be brought to bear, the charge was signalled by bugles and drums. Then the mass was launched with typical French *élan* to rout the enemy at the point of *'la baionette'*.[46] What these troops were supposed to do as they milled around well within range of the quick-firing German *Gewehr 88* rifle[i] (used widely by the Boers in the South African War) the sights of which were ranged up to 2,000 metres, is an open question. Die, perhaps.

The 1895 regulations were superseded by a provisional set in 1901 but these concentrated on the infantry to the detriment of the artillery with little about inter-arm cooperation. The steady erosion of the principle of dispersal can be seen from the sections below and these regulations were savagely criticised by Gen. François Oscar de Négrier[ii] in an anonymously penned article in the *Revue des Deux Mondes* in February 1904, one of six he wrote after 1st September 1901 and which were attributed to '*XXX*':

> "Title V., Article 52: The assault troops approach gradually and are placed in front of the chosen objective. Each of their battalions is arranged in one or two lines, the companies in deployed lines or lines of sections by four, or in company columns separated by the intervals and distances which best suit the circumstances.
> Article 53: The march continues in this way, up to an assault distance, and by this time the assault troops must have arrived at 200-300 metres from the skirmishing line. Their leader then orders the charge which is, for the skirmishers, the signal of repeated fire and, for the assault troops, the order for the uninterrupted march on the adversary."[47]

The regulations go on to say:

> "Title VII, Article 16: When the preparation is deemed sufficient by the general of the division, the assault troops set off on his order, irrevocably and without second thoughts, having only one goal, that of approaching at all costs the adversary."[48]

Négrier observed, and at considerable length, that, in the light of the British experience in South Africa, this return to the concept of mass plus impulsion was only a recipe for heavy casualties and disaster. He commented on how the German Army, since its 1902 manoeuvres on the Tempelhof exercise ground, trained in dispersed order, using ground as cover, approaching the enemy in short rushes with one line covering the next as it advanced before the main assault went in, preferably from the flanks. And he quoted no less an authority than Colmar von der Goltz in support of his view:

> "'The lessons of the South African war have more profound consequences than those which appear on superficial examination. The Boer War, in one

---

[i] The *Gewehr 88* was the German response to the smokeless, small bore French *Lebel* rifle of 1886. It was superseded by the *Mauser Gewehr 98*.

[ii] He also previously suggested the use of khaki for the uniform as a means of concealment for attacking troops. It would be another twelve years, and c. 80,000 fatal casualties in August 1914 alone, before the *Horizon bleu* uniform replaced the blue jacket and *pantalon rouge* [*Source*: Négrier, *Quelques enseignements de la guerre sud-africaine*, *Revue des Deux Mondes*, 1902, Livraison du 15 juin, page 761].

sense, will mark an era in the history of warfare. For the first time, this war did away with the belief that victory can be obtained using troops *en masse*, a belief bequeathed to us by the campaigns of Napoleon.

At that time, the guns were crude, imperfect, and one soldier was as good as another. It was mainly a question of gathering as many as possible in a small space, to be the strongest there. Napoleon's mastery in the art of generalship was evident in the rapid gathering of numerous battalions and hundreds of cannons at one point on the battlefield.

Since then, we have tried to imitate him in this way of doing things. The battles of 1870 prove it, and, in theoretical exercises, in staff rides, in war games, we run the risk of relying on a simple count of the forces present, to give the preponderance to one of the parties. This error is also attributable to the unjustifiable phases in which we wanted to divide the battle, phases which are already decided before having started.

All of that is changed.

The South African war taught that the mere mechanical grouping of troops has no effect on the battlefield today. This is perhaps the most important result, the most striking revelation brought to us, and will probably exert the greatest influence on the development of the art of war in Europe.

The bullet from the current infantry rifle, with its flat trajectory, can easily pass through four or five men who would be deep behind each other. The man who precedes is no longer a protection for the one who follows him, nor is the latter a support for the former.

Infantry in close order and in deep formation will often have less chance of seizing an enemy position than a well-led line of skirmishers advancing deftly and resolutely."[49]

But Négrier was still, at heart, a 'morale' man who believed in the power of the offensive. His complaints were not so much about the importance of these aspects but more about the developments of French battlefield tactics and an apparent return to their Napoleonic roots of mass plus morale and impulsion.

Intriguingly, Négrier had something in common with three leading WW1 Generals who, whilst professors at the *École supérieure de Guerre* and though 'morale' men of one shade or another, also believed in the principles of dispersal, of decentralised command, and were against the idea of the massed frontal attack. Maud'huy, Pétain and Debeney, along with Négrier, had all, at one time or another, served in the *3e bataillon de Chasseurs à Pied*, one of the first battalions created by the Duc d'Orléans in 27th October 1840. This unit served extensively in Algeria, the Crimea, Italy and as part of the unhappy *Armée du Rhin* in 1870. The *BCP* were *élite* light infantry, trained specifically in independent fire and movement. Such training undoubtedly influenced these senior officers' views about the battlefield.

Négrier was not alone in criticising the Bonnal-inspired return to mass/impulsion concepts and tactics contained within the 1895 and 1901 Regulations. *Général de division* Charles Kessler was eight years older than Bonnal (Kessler was born in 1836) and, like Bonnal had been taken prisoner at Sedan. He saw this campaign from a somewhat more elevated position than Bonnal, then a lieutenant in the infantry. Kessler, having volunteered in 1855 was, by 1870, a staff captain attached to Auguste Alexandre Ducrot's *1er Corps d'Armée*. By 1899, Kessler was a senior officer in the French Army: commander of the *6e Corps* and a member of the *Conseil Supérieur de la Guerre*. Writing in 1902 in his brief book *Tactique des Trois Armes*, his perspective on the new regulations and the theories behind them was damning. Describing infantry tactics, he explained that to get the troops into position two conditions needed to be met: troops should avoid losses as they advanced, but yet be in a position to unleash concentrated fire on defenders once the initial advance stopped in order to prepare for the final assault. To limit what he described as 'the murderous effects of the new weapons'[50] in training and manoeuvres it had been deemed necessary to change formations either by widening the interval between each man in the skirmish line and/or by widening the distance between each line. He suggested, however, that whatever formations were adopted, the targets they would present to the enemy's modern artillery would be such as to decimate the attackers, and in such a short time that the losses might well undermine the morale of even the most spirited *Poilu*. Indeed, he suggested that a single battery of modern field guns firing at a range of 3,000 metres would cause 25% casualties in a battalion in combat formation, and that in but a few minutes.[51]

Referring then to the current Regulations and their application in the annual manoeuvres he went on:

"If the infantry combat formations, recommended by the regulations, offer such vulnerability at long distances, what should one think of the procedures used in large manoeuvres where one frequently sees attacks made by dense lines several men deep and supported at a short distance to the rear by battalions in column!

It must be stated that the great manoeuvres cannot give a faithful impression of war...The troops, their thinking dominated by practice on the exercise grounds, remain close to one another in such a way as to preserve intervals, distances and directions, and in order to see each other well, and thus they show themselves (to the enemy), in spite of the most express recommendations made to them, every year, to advance only under cover of the ground."[52]

This tendency to revert to something akin to the close order which characterised the Napoleonic battlefield Kessler put down to the influence of younger officers amongst whom 'lessons of war are quickly lost'. Thus, he concluded, 'in an army that no longer makes war, it is the dogmatic teaching that ends up taking over'. Taking a swipe at the likes of Foch, who both before and during the war had a tendency towards making war formulaic, he went on:

"After 1870, young officers devoted themselves with ardour to the study of Napoleon's campaigns, which their predecessors were reproached for having ignored; seduced by the successes of this great era, they adopted its tactical forms without taking sufficient account of the difference in armament, and little by little a new school was created, advocating dense formations, not only for marches and manoeuvres preceding the action, but also for the fight itself.

A whole military technology has been implanted in modern education which now claims to find formulas guaranteeing success, and which takes pleasure in the use of terms with effect such as: shock troops, mass of manoeuvre, etc. The influence of these innovations has been felt even in the transformations that our regulations have undergone."[53]

Reflecting on changes in infantry Regulations since 1871 he commented:

"The regulations of 1875, drawn up by officers who had served in the war, took care to banish any compact formations from the 'beaten zone' (i.e. the area across which men must advance to make the final assault); they affirmed the impossibility of moving in close order under fire... The regulations of 1884, amended in 1894, took a new path; it recommended the use of small columns as the formation to be used by the troops of the third line who were to make the assault.

Today the lessons of the past are completely forgotten, and certain treatises on infantry tactics, reviving old methods, recognized as impracticable by the experience of recent wars, now consider the column as a possible combat formation for the so-called shock troops, called upon to lead the decisive attack.

Fire, in its brutal reality, would very quickly bring everything into focus, and would send all those fine theories about the employment of the masses up in smoke."[54]

Finally, in another swipe at the advocates of the all-out offensive who had gained such influence over the Army, Kessler remarked that:

"Officers who have not served in war believe that an energetically commanded force must overcome all obstacles; they are unaware that fire, in addition to the losses it causes, now exerts a depressing action (on troops) all the more intense as the losses undergone occur more rapidly."[55]

In the end, however, the ultra-conservative and nationalist-minded Kessler was, like most of his younger colleagues, a man who believed the offensive gave the attacker the moral advantage over the defender:

"The power of the new armaments has increased the value of the defensive, but it has not changed the moral conditions of inferiority in which the defender finds himself.

The assailant imposes his will on the enemy; he dominates the situation, the defender submits to it. The great weakness of the defender is to live in permanent uncertainty about the direction and the nature of the blows that will be dealt to him, and he is very clearly aware that, even by parrying all the attacks, his success remains incomplete because he has only the immediate prospect of preventing the assailant from advancing.

The superiority of the offensive rests on moral factors which cannot be held in check by the perfection of the weapons of war, from which the attacker benefits as much as the defender."

Kessler's view on who gained the real advantage of the new long-range, rapid-fire arms was a half-way house, a somewhat soggy compromise between Foch's position that the attacker had the advantage, and that of Mayer and Bloch, who stated that the defence now held the upper hand. What Kessler was really arguing for was a degree more tactical prudence to be displayed by the commanders of attacking troops to minimise, where and when possible, casualties. In this respect, he was out of line with both other current French theorists (and British ones such as Maude) and the existing Regulations with their call for 'bloody sacrifice' in the final assault. And even more so with the 'Young Turks' such as Grandmaison for whom the idea of prudence in the offensive had no place whatsoever. Kessler died on 13th December 1916, the end of the year of Verdun and the Somme. It is not known whether his views about the power of the defensive changed in the light of real experience of modern weapons over the previous 28 months.

In 1904, an update of the *Règlement pour l'infanterie* was almost immediately rendered obsolete by reports from Manchuria and, no doubt to Kessler's relief, changes were made to take account of the need for dispersion and concealment. Then, in the new *Règlement sur le service des armées en campagne* issued on 2nd December 1913, the principle of fire and movement before the final charge was made specific but, with artillery relegated to the role of supporting the infantry rather than preparing the way. The final charge was still the key point of the battle. By 1914 these regulations went on to describe the bayonet as the 'supreme weapon' of the infantry.[56] Obviously this was a weapon only of use at close quarters but it was with this short pointy thing French Generals (and several British ones, notably Kiggell) believed the decision would be won with the enemy forced from their trenches by the glittering steel and the superior moral force of the charge. How many men would survive the crossing of the 'fire swept zone' to deliver this battle-winning onslaught was another question, and the French had as little answer to Bloch's conundrum as did the commanders of every potential combatant nation.

For the French, however, there was another issue. The idea of a dispersed skirmishing line preparing the way for the charge was all very well, but it depended on well-trained and *experienced* troops able to deliver this aspect of the battle, not a mass conscript army that trained only briefly before reverting to the reserve where they underwent little training. Hew Strachan in *European Armies and the Conduct of War* estimates 70% of the army of August 1914 were first year conscripts or reservists unsuited to the technically complex role of a skirmisher.[57] They might form the 'mass' for the charge but on a battlefield where the preparation for that charge was inadequate because the elements necessary to its success did not exist.

And there was another issue about the well-spaced lines of skirmishers aligned both laterally and in depth with which the British and Russians, for example, and, for a while, the German Army, now attempted to advance. This slow creep forward using the terrain to provide cover from defensive fire lacked the drama and aggression so beloved of the French *'à outrance'* enthusiasts. Britain learnt this prudent technique from their experiences in South Africa and combined this approach with a great commitment to a significant improvement in the accuracy and rate of fire of its riflemen. Russia adopted similar infantry tactics after the calamities of the Manchurian campaign though, again, in 1914 the huge influx of reservists rendered such tactics well-nigh impossible. The French, however, regarded the British volunteer soldiers as more akin to mercenaries when compared to their own conscripts (who had no alternative but serve but should have regarded their time in the Army as a welcome patriotic duty), and for them this form of attack lacked the necessary aggressive desire to get amongst the enemy with cold steel which underpinned French tactics. The key point, however, evaded them. The British and the Russians alone of the major European combatants had fought wars in which modern, long-range, and quick-firing weapons dominated the battlefield. Their tactics and training were a direct response to first-hand experience, not ideas dreamed up in a classroom by officers who fantasised about old glories and revenge against an historic enemy.[58] Perversely, however, this learning experience was forgotten by the British once the fighting on the Western Front took hold but, belatedly, discovered anew by the French.

Nonetheless, the commitment to 'the offensive' grew, encouraged by officers like Ferdinand Foch. Foch and Joffre are the two most important French military figures of the war and they share responsibility for the devastating defeats suffered in the opening weeks of the war. Foch, however, went on to adapt and thrive, ending the war as *de facto* commander in chief of the Allied armies on the Western Front. Joffre survived the initial calamities to be acclaimed as the 'victor of the Marne' (though Foch shared in the kudos of victory), but then oversaw a series of costly, unproductive offensives in 1915 as well as the titanic struggles at Verdun and the Somme in 1916. By the end of these battles both Joffre and Foch lost their positions, Joffre permanently and Foch temporarily. Foch, though hardly error free, proved the more adaptable and forward thinking once the original tactics of 1914 and 1915 proved to be inappropriate to modern industrial siege warfare.

Ferdinand Foch was a product of the far south-west of France, being born in Tarbes in the *département des Hautes-Pyrénées* on 2nd October 1851. He was the son of the appropriately named Bertrand Jules Napoleon Foch, a civil servant and Secretary General of the local Prefecture, and Marie Sophie Jacqueline Dupré. His maternal grandfather, Jacques Romain Dupré, was an officer in the Revolutionary and Napoleonic Armies and this veteran of Austerlitz's stories about his experiences inspired the young Foch to pursue a military career. In addition, the godmother of his sister, Jenny, was the wife of Gen. Antoine Noguès[i] who, aged 15, had enlisted in the *2e bataillon volontaires pyrénéens* and rapidly risen through the ranks. In 1815, he commanded the *1re Brigade* of Marcognet's *3e Division* of d'Erlon's *I Corps* during the 100 Days, fighting at Quatre Bras and Waterloo where he was wounded. The military tradition ran strong in the Foch household.

Foch was educated at the *Lycées de Tarbes* and *de Rodez* where he excelled in geography, mathematics, and religious studies, as well as Latin and the classics. His family were devout Roman Catholics, something which caused him professional problems during his military career. He now attended a Jesuit seminary at Polignan some 60 kms east of Tarbes. Following his father's civil service postings, he then attended the Jesuit *collège St-Michel* at Saint-Étienne not far from Saint-Chamond

---

[i] His older brother, Gen. Jean-François Xavier Noguès, fought at Marengo and campaigned in the West Indies. Taken prisoner by the British at St Lucia in 1802, he died, 1808 (*Source: Bulletin de la Société académique des Hautes-Pyrénées*, 1951, pages 17-20].

where many of France's artillery pieces were manufactured during the war[i]. There he passed his BA degree. In 1869, he attended the Jesuit College of *Saint-Clément* in Metz to train for the examinations for entry into the *École Polytechnique*. Here he witnessed the entry into the city of the exhausted Emperor Napoleon III in the summer of 1870 and, while he and others toiled over their final exam essays, nearby the French Army was going from defeat to defeat: Wissembourg on 4th August 1870, Spicheren on 5th August and, worst of all, Wœrth on 6th August.

On 24th January 1871, he enlisted in the *4e régiment d'infanterie* but the war was all but lost and he was not involved in any fighting. Demobilised seven weeks later (on 14th March), he returned to Metz to complete his studies in higher mathematics needed for entry into the *Polytechnique*. Metz was now occupied by German troops as part of the new province of *Lothringen*. Sharing the college were, according to Foch, the '37th Pomeranian Regt.'[ii] Their behaviour served only to reinforce his enthusiasm for another war which would return the lost provinces to France.

Having completed the entrance examinations in Nancy, Foch entered the *École Polytechnique* on 1st November 1871. He moved to the *École d'application de l'artillerie et du génie* at Fontainebleau at the beginning of 1873 and, on 16th October 1874, he became a *sous-lieutnant* in the *24e régiment d'artillerie* before serving in several regiments prior to being promoted full Captain in 1884. He married Julie Ursule Louise Bienvenue[iii] of St Brieuc in the *Côtes du Nord* in 1883[iv] and in 1885 he was sent to the *École supérieure de Guerre* coming under the influence of such as Cardot, for whom the outcome of an engagement did not depend on the balance of physical forces but on the balance of moral forces, the offensive-minded Maillard and, most particularly, Maj. Charles-Ferdinand Millet. Millet was taken prisoner at Metz in 1870 and interned in the fortress at Graudenz[v], then in East Prussia. On his return he saw service in Algeria and Tunisia before being appointed Professor of Applied Infantry Tactics at the *École supérieure*. Millet believed firepower to be the essential factor on the battlefield and this was a position which would grow stronger as technology improved the range and firepower of rifles and guns. Establishing superiority of fire over the enemy was, to him, an essential prerequisite of any successful attack. Even so, once the infantry was committed, casualties were bound to be heavy and the success of any one unit or any one

---

[i] The college was also attended by Emile Fayolle who commanded *VIe Armée* during the Battle of the Somme. Fayolle was a year behind Foch.

[ii] This title is given in *'The Memoirs of Marshal Foch'*, page xxvii, and is presumed to be *Füsilier-Regiment von Steinmetz (Westpreußisches) Nr. 37*.

[iii] A niece of Fulgence Bienvenue. With Edmund Huet, he was the 'father' of the *Metro*.

[iv] They had four children: Marie (1885-1972), whose husband Capt. Paul Marie Joseph Bécourt (*Chevalier de la Légion d'Honneur, Croix de guerre avec palme, 1re compagnie, 26e bataillon de Chasseurs*) was killed at Joppécourt, *Dept. Meurthe-et-Moselle*, on 22nd August 1914 (their son Cdt. Jean Bécourt-Foch, *Armée de l'Air, Groupe de Bombardement II/63* died in an accident in Algeria on 15th August 1944); Anne (1887-1981); Eugène (born and died 1888); and Germain Jules Louis, an *aspirant* in the *131e régiment d'infanterie*, also killed on 22nd August 1914 at Ville-Houdlémont, *Dept. Meurthe-et-Moselle* and buried in the *Nécropole Nationale Gorcy*, communal grave 22.

[v] Now Grudziądz in Poland.

attack did not guarantee overall victory. Supporting attacks needed to be pre-planned and committed one after the other until the enemy gave way.

Passing out fourth in his year at the *École supérieure* after 1887 Foch performed a variety of staff duties before, in 1891, he joined the *3e Bureau* (Operations) of the *État Major des armées* (General Staff) under Gen. Joseph de Miribel[i]. This gave Foch access to the planning process of French War Plans, at this stage based on *Plan XI* introduced in April 1891. Foch's concern was the plan was too defensive and switching an Army deployed thus onto the offensive was a difficult and potentially dangerous manoeuvre. His view was that without 'forward movement' there could be no victory and, therefore, the current plans were fraught with danger.[59] Foch's antipathy towards the defensive would only grow based on the view later expressed in his book *Des Principes de la Guerre:*

"In tactics, *action* is the *governing rule* of war.
'To make war always means attacking' (Frederick [the Great]).
Of all faults, only one is ignominious, *inaction.*"[60]

Miribel, aged 62, died suddenly in 1893 before he could resolve this particular and thorny military problem. Between 1895 and 1901 Foch was again lecturing in military history, strategy, and tactics at the *École supérieure* and was propagating the ideas taught him by the now *général de brigade* Millet who was also the Director of Infantry at the Ministry of War. It was the lectures given by Foch which became the basis of his two key books: *Des Principes de la Guerre* and *De la Conduite de la Guerre*. These lectures were described by one of his students as being delivered:

"… with authority and conviction, in a grave, somewhat monotonous voice, invariably appealing to logical process, and even having recourse to mathematical metaphors. He was sometimes difficult to follow through the exuberant wealth of ideas that lay behind his words…"[61]

Foch's Jesuit background caught up with him in 1901. He was 'purged' from the staff by the Republican, anti-clerical *ministre de la Guerre*, Louis André. He returned to regimental life as second in command, *29e régiment d'artillerie*, and, as a Colonel in 1903, as commander of *35e régiment d'artillerie* at Vannes in Brittany.

Further experience was gained as the Chief of Staff to his mentor Gen. Millet with *5e Corps* at Orleans. By 1907 he was a *général de brigade*. Then, somewhat to his surprise, when the position of commandant of the *École supérieure de Guerre* became vacant with the removal of Gen. Bonnal in 1907, he was given the job by Clemenceau who nonetheless commissioned a police investigation into his beliefs and background before confirming him in the job.[62] In 1911 Foch was promoted *Général de Division* and given command of *13e Division* at Chaumont (succeeding de Castelnau) and briefly the following year *8e Corps d'armée* before transferring to *20e Corps d'armée* based at Nancy on 23rd August 1913. His two divisions, the *11e* and *39e Divisions,* were later heavily involved in the Battles of the Frontiers, leading Castelnau's *2e Armée* advance into Lorraine during which *39e Division* was so badly hit at Morhange on 20th August 1914 it was withdrawn from the front line.

---

[i] Miribel was twice *Chef d'État-Major des armées*: 1878-9 and 1891-3.

In the years before this he published two theoretical works: *Des Principes de la Guerre* (*On the Principles of War*) in 1903, and *De la Conduite de la Guerre* (*On the Conduct of War*) in 1904. These two books became the foundations of the theory Foch was the arch-advocate of the 'cult of the offensive' and was, therefore, in many ways responsible for the havoc of the opening weeks of the war. In truth, Foch was a less significant pupil of the various theorists who had gone before: Cardot, Bonnal, Langlois, Gilbert, Maillard, Millet and others, but he just happened to be in place when war break out whilst the others were all either dead or long since retired. As Azar Gat points out, had war broken out in late 1915 Foch might well have been retired and some other French advocate of the offensive would have become the target of the criticism of people like Liddell Hart post-war. Furthermore, Foch's elevated position at the end of the war has tended to inflate his pre-war importance in the eyes both of his critics and his advocates.[63]

Whilst Foch advocated that defeating the enemy required an army to attack, he was also in favour of prudence and against the reckless throwing of troops against a resolute opponent uncowed by superior firepower. But he, like so many others, was a man who believed victory went to the morally superior General and warfare was, fundamentally, about one commander imposing his military and moral will on another because, as he wrote in 1898:

"Generals, not soldiers win battles; and a general who has been defeated is one who has not understood the task of leadership."[64]

In his brief biography of Foch contained in the Marshal's *Precepts and Judgements* published in 1919, the prolific military historian Maj. Alphonse Grasset puts this theory of moral superiority thus:

"... there will come, almost fatally, a certain moment of crisis when the nerves of a force will be strained to their utmost, when human capacity will seem to have reached its limit, and when the dangers and obstacles present will appear insurmountable. That is the moment when we must fall back upon the conception that spirit always dominates matter; that in spite of the most crushing weight of apparent circumstance, in spite of the most formidable effects of the most modern instruments of destruction, it is always (in the long run) the moral effort which triumphs over the material one. It is always the spiritual side which impresses the whole.
Victory resides in the will, and a battle won is a battle in which one has not admitted oneself defeated."[65]

Foch, like Clausewitz, talked of the destruction of the enemy's army. Though they both meant the destruction of the enemy's *will to fight*, in certain quarters this idea was taken at face value. Too many Generals harbour fantasies of achieving a great victory which might establish their reputation for all time. The destruction of an entire Army such as Hannibal achieved at Cannae or, far more recently, the triumph of the German Confederation at Sedan for example. Both battles were great victories but neither ended their respective wars. Carthage *lost* the war with Rome and was destroyed after Scipio Africanus defeated Hannibal at Zama in 202 BC, and it was not until the fall of Paris five months after Sedan the Franco-Prussian War ended. Despite this, certain officers, especially in France and taught by Foch, became unreasonably enamoured at the prospect of a rapid destruction of Germany' Armies. But the Great War was not to be concluded with the 'destruction' of the German Army on the Western Front within a few weeks, crushed by the irresistible exuberance of the French *Poilus* and the wonderful 75. Instead, and after more than four years, while still a coherent fighting force, German troops would conduct a heavily contested withdrawal under severe pressure from the Allies whilst proving capable of inflicting heavy casualties on their enemies. It is estimated that, during the famous '100 Days' advance between 18th July and 11th November 1918, Allied casualties amounted to nearly 1.1 million and German just short of 1.2 million (not all battle casualties which have been estimated at 710,000-760,000).[66] This was no Sedan. Rather, the Armistice was caused by a realisation at all levels in the German Army and government that the forces to which they were opposed, both military and economic, were overwhelming. This knowledge generated a growing reluctance amongst German soldiers to die for a cause clearly lost, further underpinned by an awareness that, back home, their parents, wives and children were starving as the Allied naval blockade strangled the German economy. Meanwhile, politically, Germany was falling apart, riven by the political dissension between the extremes of left and right which Bloch so accurately forecast twenty years earlier.

But the fantasy of a swift and glorious victory persisted and grew. Foch as a teacher was a powerful theorist. But a theorist only. He had no practical experience of war. Nevertheless, he talked a good game even if his talk was about the past rather than the future. Foch's analysis of the effects of increased firepower supported his belief this gave the advantage to the attacker. He took the not uncommon view that new, quick-firing weapons improved the prospects for the offensive as the sheer weight of fire would so dominate a static defence the attacking troops would be on the cowering enemy and amongst them with the bayonet before they could respond. He tried to explain this in *Des Principes de la Guerre* through both historical references and mathematical formulae:

> "Any improvement of firearms is ultimately bound to add strength to the offensive... History shows it, reason explains it. For, if rational tactics have always finally consisted, on the offensive, in assembling on a given spot more rifles and more guns than the enemy, it cannot be denied that such tactics would assemble to-day on that spot better rifles and better guns, and that the advantage of the assailant would thereby be increased."

He then explains this by a simple mathematical calculation of a contest between two battalions (2,000 men) against a defending battalion (1,000 men). Unsurprisingly, were the 2,000 able to fire simultaneously at the defenders then they should be able to fire twice as many rounds in a given time as the defenders. Thus, as weapons fired more quickly, the numerical difference between the number of rounds fired by attacker and defender increased. Foch cites a rifle firing 10 rounds a minute. Thus, in a minute, 2,000 men will fire 10,000 more rounds (20,000 versus 10,000) than the defender. According to Foch, therefore:

> "As you see, the material superiority of fire quickly increases in favour of the attack as a result of improved firearms. How much more quickly will

grow at the same time the ascendancy, the moral superiority of the assailant over the defender, of the crusher over the crushed."[67]

This staggeringly simplistic analysis makes one wonder just how far intelligent men will go to support a point of view however much it runs counter to contemporary experience. If one was talking about 2,000 men standing and firing at another group of 1,000 men also standing and firing *à la* Napoleonic warfare one might just understand Foch's point. But those days were long since gone. Now we are talking about 2,000 men firing from necessarily exposed positions as they advance to the eventual assault (because, if they are not advancing why bother?) on the positions of 1,000 men firing from entrenchments, rifles stabilised by a parapet and able to fire more accurately than a nervous man exposed to a torrent of bullets fired by men he cannot see let alone get at because of the long effective range of the modern gun. This is what had happened to the British in the opening months of the war in South Africa, four years before *Principes* was published.

The crude nature of this analysis is reinforced by Foch later in *Des Principes de la Guerre*. We are in the chapter entitled *Modern Battle* and the section *Decisive Attack* – the climax of any battle. The assaulting troops are faced with Bloch's 'fire swept zone'. What is the answer? More. Simply more. Of everything – men, guns, ammunition. Simple numbers because now, it is numbers, not the special spirit of the troops, which 'imply a moral superiority in our favour':

"In front, there is a, so to speak, 'impassable' zone; no defiladed ways of access are left; a hail of bullets sweeps the ground in front of the first line. Success is not yet secured; 'nothing is done so long as something remains to be done' (Frederick [the Great). The laurels of victory are on the point of the enemy's bayonets. They must be plucked *there*; they must be won by a hand-to-hand fight, if one means to conquer…

To run away or to fall on, such is the unavoidable dilemma. To fall on, but to fall on in numbers and masses: therein lies salvation. For numbers, provided we know how to use them, will allow us, by means of the physical superiority placed at our disposal, to get the better of that violent enemy fire. Having more guns we will silence his own; it is the same with rifles, the same with bayonets, if we know how to use them all.

Numbers imply a moral superiority in our favour, owing to the feeling of strength connected with numbers, a feeling we shall increase by means of formation. Numbers create surprise in the enemy's ranks, as well as the conviction that he cannot resist; a conviction caused by the sudden appearance of danger, by the speed and proportions of an attack he neither has the time, nor the means to parry."[68]

To be fair, this was not to say that Foch wanted French Armies simply to charge at the enemy everywhere and anywhere. The attack still must be prepared by fire, the enemy's weaknesses probed and then overwhelming force brought to bear on them. A General should be circumspect but always be looking for the chance to attack and to move his reserve to the point of greatest effect by employing the 'economy of force' of which Napoleon was such a great exponent. But, from this distance, Foch's remedies all seem so simple, especially given the enemy he assumes France will fight, i.e. Germany. Germany, after all, had a larger population and would, therefore, bring more men to the fight. And more guns, as their industry was more powerful. No matter. As Foch blithely predicts:

> "A quarter of an hour's quick fire by a mass of artillery on a clearly determined objective will generally suffice to break its resistance, or at any rate to make it uninhabitable and therefore uninhabited."[69]

Or not, as it would turn out, especially as the French Army went to war armed almost entirely with shrapnel-firing 75-mm field guns which would prove useless at demolishing field fortifications in the war to come. It is as if in *Des Principes de la Guerre* Foch is preparing the way for battles long since passed. It is as if the machine gun had never been invented. Which, given that the phrase does not appear once in the book seems almost to have been the case. The word 'trenches' appears once in reference to the campaign around Dijon in January 1871. Of modern warfare, the 'empty battlefield', automatic weapons, howitzers, indirect fire, etc., there is no mention.

'Moral', however, is referenced 54 times. Moral force, the strength of will of the commander communicated to his soldiers, the refusal to accept defeat ('A battle won is battle in which one will not confess oneself beaten'[70]) were to Foch and many others the essence of warfare:

> "War = the domain of moral force. Victory = moral superiority in the victor; inferiority in the defeated. Battle = a struggle between two wills."[71]

The cost in human terms was irrelevant. But then Foch had no experience of 'the cost'. He was a theoretician. A man who had not seen the effects of war on the human body and mind but read all there was to read about the great Napoleon and the failures of the Franco-Prussian War. As he taught his expectant students about the means of imminent French victory, the iron tang of blood, the stink of human excrement, the screams and moans of the wounded were absent from the hushed lecture theatres of the *École supérieure*.

FERDINAND FOCH WAS AMONGST THE OFFICERS to be inspired by Cardot's interpretation of the significance of the superiority of morale which, when allied to the fundamental importance of the offensive spirit, allowed for the imposition of one will over another. His views became more sophisticated and complex as time drew on but his influence was wide if shallow. Others sought to apply the principle with brutal and, therefore, costly simplicity.

The major baleful proponent of this latter perspective was François-Jules Loyzeau de Grandmaison[i]. Grandmaison came from an ancient noble family

---

[i] *Général de Division* François-Jules Louis Loyzeau de Grandmaison was born on 21st January 1861 in Le Mans, the son of François Philippe Loyzeau de Grandmaison and Jeanne Marthe Stephanie Ravot. *École Spéciale Militaire*, 1881 *Sous-Lt.*, *20e bataillon de chasseurs à pied*, 1883. Captain, 1892. *1er régiment étranger* in Sidi-Bel-Abbès, Algeria, before detachment to Tonkin, 1894, where he was posted to Đồng Đăng on the Chinese border. *131e régiment d'infanterie*, 1896, Orléans. In the same year he married Marie Julie Virginie Gillet. *École supérieure de guerre*, 1898. Rotated through *25e, 5e, 144e* and *110e RI* over the next two years. *Chef de Bataillon*, 1900, he spent some time with

dating from the fifteenth century and the family's base was between Angoulême on the *River Charente* and Poitiers. Traditionally royalist and, like Foch, Jesuitical (his brother, Septime Léonce Ludovic Loyzeau de Grandmaison, was a prominent Jesuit theologian) he was commissioned in 1883. Grandmaison attended the *École supérieure de guerre* in 1898 where he studied under Foch, graduating from his class in second place.[72] He then joined the *3e Bureau* of the *État Major* in 1905 after serving in French Indochina and then qualifying as a staff officer and, in 1908, he was appointed the *3e Bureau's* head. Here he had significant involvement in the defence of the French frontier as well as being responsible for the organisation of the French annual manoeuvres through which he repeatedly attempted to promote his extreme views on the offensive and undermine others of a different and more conservative (or realistic) opinion.

It was the belief of one senior artillerist, Gen. Alexandre Percin, that the resulting manoeuvres were highly damaging in the long run and gave the infantry a false idea as to the nature of the modern battlefield. This, in turn, lead to men having no realistic concept of the effect of the enemy's weaponry, as well as to numerous examples of French casualties from 'friendly fire', something he believed persisted throughout the war. The problem was, organising these manoeuvres were officers who would brook no argument about their interpretation of the nature of war. In 1907, Gen. Percin met Grandmaison during the annual exercises and the Lt. Col. made the position of *Les Jeunes Turcs* remarkably clear:

"We are a certain number of young officers very convinced of the correctness of our ideas, of the superiority of our theories and our methods, and determined to make them prevail against all."[73]

Percin would later write:

"Under the undoubted influence of the *offensive à outrance* ideas which reigned in the highest military spheres, the leaders of small units affected a regrettable contempt of the precautions to be taken under fire.
Appointed several times during my career to perform the duties of umpire for the autumn manoeuvres, and appointed in 1910 to perform the duties of chief umpire, I was struck by the lack of concern that the infantry showed to the use of the land, and, in all my reports, I had said that, if war broke out, our infantrymen would suffer appalling losses on the battlefield through the fault of their leaders.

---

the *État Major* of *14e Corps* in Lyon then *30e RI* in Annecy, 1902. *3e Bureau, État major des armées*, Boxing Day 1905. Lt. Col., June 1908. *Chef, 3e Bureau*, 1st December 1908. Colonel, *153e régiment d'infanterie, 39e Division, 20e Corps*, 13th July 1911. Wounded, 20th August 1914. Commander, *53e Division*, January 1915. Temporary commander, *5e groupe de divisions de réserve*. He was killed by a shell just north of Soissons on 19th February 1915. He has no known official grave. After the death of his wife in 1909, Grandmaison married Germaine Delambre, widow of Eugène Sellier (Capt., *65e RI*), and daughter of the late Gen. Philippe-Alfred Delambre, formerly professor at the *École de Guerre*, the *directeur du Génie*, and the *inspecteur de la Défense des Côtes en France, Afrique et Indochine*.

Everyone was of my opinion, but no one had succeeded in changing the habits which the infantry had acquired during the autumn manoeuvres of doing in fifteen minutes what must have taken two hours on the battlefield... What, in fact, most appealed to the public, eager for military excitement, and what most appealed to the civilian authorities who were invited to follow the autumn manoeuvres every year, was not what the troops were doing well but, on the contrary, what they were doing badly – intrepid marches, executed under fire, in insane formations, followed by furious hand-to-hand combat."[74]

Nothing changed by 1913 when, according to Percin, in the last manoeuvres before the war, they ended:

"... with a theatrical performance offered to members of the Government... Our statesmen are very guilty of having gone into ecstasies at the autumn manoeuvres, at Longchamp, at Vincennes and at Satory[i], witnessing exercises which do not resemble at all what would happen in war, which only compromise the training of the troops and result in disastrous massacres."[75]

So, whilst these supposed high points of the military training year indulged in elaborate but misleading displays for astonished spectators, basics were let slip. In 1910, Percin asked the commanders of 59 artillery units whether they were in direct contact with the infantry unit they were supposed to support. Just 23 gave what he deemed adequate or better answers. He reported this to the *Ministre de la Guerre*: Gen. Jean Jules Brun, himself an artillerist product of the *École polytechnique* and the *école d'application de Metz*. Nothing was done.[76]

By 1911 Grandmaison was in a position of great influence on French thinking. His 1906 book *Dressage de l'infanterie en vue de l'offensif* (*Infantry Training for the Offensive*) established him as the leading proponent of the outright attack. It was a book endorsed by one of France's most eminent military teachers who wrote its preface: *général de division* Hippolyte Langlois, the commandant of the *École supérieure de guerre* from 1898 to 1901, and a member of the *Conseil supérieur de la guerre*. Langlois was not some thrusting younger officer keen to make his mark. He was a 67-year-old veteran of the siege of Metz in 1870 who graduated from the *École polytechnique* in 1856. He, like Foch, believed the power of modern weapons possessed such a 'material and moral effect' they enabled the success of the offensive.[77] Clearly, the currents of the *offensive à outrance* ran deep within the veins of the French military.

In 1911 two lectures given to *élite* staff officers at Foch's recently created *Centre des hautes études militaires*,[ii] the contents of which were distributed under the title

---

[i] Army exercise grounds around Paris: Longchamp on what, since 1857, has been the racetrack in the *bois de Boulogne*; Vincennes to the east of the centre of Paris with its *château* and grounds; and Satory, a military camp near Versailles.

[ii] Set up by Foch by Ministerial decree on 21st October 1910, the *Centre des hautes études militaires* started work in January 1911. It ran six-month courses for c. 25 Lt. Cols. to train them in the operational work of Armies and Army groups. Staff rides and involvement in the autumn manoeuvres were part of the course. It was closed during the war, re-opening in 1919 and is still in operation.

Deux conferences faites aux officers de l'état-major de l'armée, established, *sans doute*, that Grandmaison's philosophy was the dominant force in French military thinking. With Joffre now in charge and with the offensive now at the heart of the planning for the coming war, Grandmaison's belief in the *élan vital* – or the will to conquer – became pre-eminent in French strategic and tactical thinking and the *'offensive à outrance'* was established as being central to any successful war against Germany.

37. Gen. François-Jules Loyzeau de Grandmaison

Grandmaison's preference was for a smaller, long service Army in which training by repetition instilled reaction by reflex amongst the men. In other words, he sought by discipline and training to overcome the natural human instinct for self-preservation. Of course, such soldiers were not the material with which he was dealing but, nonetheless, he believed this approach could work with the short service conscripts available. He, like Hamilton, referenced the performance of the Japanese soldier in Manchuria as being the epitome of military prowess, dedication, and discipline. In this analysis, the Japanese Army was seen as significantly influenced by a modern militaristic interpretation of the semi-mystical, semi-religious concept of *Bushidō* which, by 1904, it was suggested, was centred on the Emperor. It was an ethos which demanded loyalty and self-sacrifice above almost all other virtues. Later, it was *Bushidō* which led, during the Second World War, to the idea of the *kamikaze*, the preference of death to surrender, and of the appalling ill-treatment of the enemy's soldiers and civilians by Japanese soldiers of all ranks. It was now suggested it was the spirit of *Bushidō* which made possible this description of the Russo-Japanese War's Battle of Liaoyang[i] written by Maurice Baring[ii], a journalist attached to the Russian Army:

---

[i] The Battle of Liaoyang, 25th August to 5th September 1904, resulted in a tactical Japanese victory at a cost to the victors of over 24,000 men or 19% of those involved. Russian casualties are given as c. 18-19,000 or 8% of those involved.
[ii] Maurice Baring, OBE, was born in 1874 and was the 5th son (and 8th child) of Edward Charles Baring, 1st Baron Revelstoke. He was educated at Eton College and Trinity College, Cambridge. He covered the war in Manchuria for the London *Morning Post*. He served in the RFC and RAF during the war and was a prolific author of books and poetry after the war. He died in 1945. His father ran Baring's Bank which later and

"All through the night of the 31st (August) the Japanese attacked the forts; a Cossack officer, who was in one of those forts, told me that the sight was beyond terrible; that line after line of Japanese came smiling up to the trenches to be mown down with bullets, until the trenches were full of bodies, and then more came on over the bodies of the dead. An officer who was in the fort he described went mad from the sheer horror of the thing. Some of the gunners went mad also."[78]

Many European soldiers, amongst them Grandmaison and Hamilton, were not appalled but encouraged by such accounts. Even Baring sensed some sort of 'silver lining' in such carnage:

"… I thought that war is perhaps to man what motherhood is to woman, a burden, a source of untold suffering, and yet a glory."[79]

Another French officer inspired by such behaviour was the aforementioned Lt. Col. Montaigne who believed that, because of their loyalty to the Emperor, devotion to the motherland, and *Shintō* religious convictions, the average Japanese soldier welcomed death on the battlefield:

"In his patriotic fanaticism, he does not dream of triumphant returns and enthusiastic ovations, he dreams of dying for the homeland."[80]

Modern commentators take issue with this thinking, suggesting that several of the more influential observers of the war interpreted actions and events for their domestic market in the way most likely to support their existing thoughts on strategy, tactics, and the argument of morale versus firepower. Dr Stewart Lone, then a Senior Lecturer in Modern East Asian History at the *Australian Defence Force Academy*[i], has depicted some of the descriptions of the dedicated militarism of the Japanese people in 1904-5 as a 'myth' partly 'sponsored by foreign commentators'.[81] These mythical images:

"… included a Japan which was militarily powerful and, in the reading of Western observers, aggressive for territory; also a society which was imbued with the values of the military and ready to forfeit everything in support of war."[82]

Dr Lone continues:

"…any examination of civil society shows how flimsy and unpersuasive are the myths of Japanese popular militarism."

Furthermore, he suggests the idea of a 'powerful, aggressive *Bushidō* Japan' was popularised by 'superficial observers of Japan' with an axe to grind.

As to the idea of *The Honourable war death* (*meiyo no senshi* in Japanese) on which this was based, this seems to have been an *ex post facto* rationalisation of the heavy casualties perpetuated by self-interested Japanese political and military parties to

---

infamously collapsed in 1995. 105 years earlier, Revelstoke oversaw another, not quite terminal, collapse of the Bank's fortunes which caused the Panic of 1890, one of the worst economic crises of the nineteenth century and which was especially devastating in South America.

[i] Now an associate professor at the ADFA.

encourage militarism and nationalism. Furthermore, there was a strong German influence on Japanese training, methods, and ethos. Between 1885 and 1888 Gen. (then Major) Klemens Wilhelm Jacob Meckel was special adviser to the Imperial Japanese Army, having been personally selected by Helmuth von Moltke to fill this role. Meckel was a firm Clausewitzian and, whilst in Japan, he trained its leading soldiers in the theories and practice of his German hero. Meckel also preached the principle that Japan's army officers should display the same unswerving loyalty to their sovereign as did German officers to their *Kaiser*, the *Obersten Kriegsherrn* (Supreme Warlord). So strongly did he pursue this line that Articles XI to XIII of the Meiji Constitution introduced on 29th November, 1890 (which remained in force until May 1947) formalised and codified this requirement. Meckel, however, proved a man of inflexible tactical opinions and some held his belief in the power of massed infantry and the threat of the bayonet was responsible for the painfully long Japanese casualty lists which resulted from the war in Manchuria.

Modern research shows Japanese soldiers were no different to those from any country. They did their duty but did not accept *death* as their *duty* to their Emperor. Research by historians such as Naoko Shimazu, Senior Lecturer in Japanese History at the *School of Classics and Archaeology* at Birkbeck College, shows Japanese soldiers feared death as much as any man. They thought of their families before going into battle and wished to return alive, not as ashes in an urn.[83] Prof. Shimazu describes *The Honourable war death* as '...a rhetorical invention of the Russo-Japanese War'.[84] Contrary to the image presented by Ian Hamilton, and exalted by Grandmaison and Montaigne, the true picture was not of the 'death-defying Japanese soldier' but of a man who desired:

"... desperately not to die in battle, because of their love for their families, underlined by a strong sense of filial piety. ... What mattered most was the family.'[85]

Whatever its actual hold over the public and military in Japan nothing like the *Bushidō* existed in Europe even though society was certainly far more religious than now. However, whip up a confection of militant Catholicism, ultra-nationalism, authoritarianism with a dash of social Darwinism and one has a recipe which comes close to that which Hamilton, Grandmaison and Montaigne suggested provoked Japanese soldiers to run headlong into their own barrages to get at Russians cowering in their trenches.

Grandmaison's public statements increasingly took on the tone of a hysterical military mystic. According to him the actions of the enemy were of no interest. All that was needed was for the army to locate the enemy and attack them. Fixing bayonets, they were to charge, pressing the advance irrespective of casualties. In an orgy of self-immolation, the brave and resolute *poilus* were to 'fly at the throats of the enemy'.[86] By their very nature, such strictures took away control of the campaign from the commanding General. If every junior officer felt impelled, indeed obliged, to attack the enemy wherever and whenever he found them and without reference to 'higher authority' then fighting would break down into a series of uncontrolled battles disconnected from any plan and strategy and without any objectives other than to kill the enemy. Grandmaison wrote:

"It is more important to develop a conquering state of mind than to cavil about tactics"

It was as if, Liddell Hart declared in his biography of Foch:

"The strategy of the bull had replaced that of the matador."[87]

Grandmaison's statement borrowed from Frederick the Great *'Vaincre, c'est avancer'* ('to win is to advance'),[88] mirrors Haig's response to Rawlinson's original conservative Somme plan 'to kill Germans at the least cost to ourselves'. Haig wanted the Germans out of their trenches so they could be fought in the open and, as a result, sacrificed security to ambition.

Like almost every other officer, whatever his strictures about exploiting the lie of the land and gaining fire superiority, he saw that the advance eventually came down to 'men versus fire'. This was the moment for the attack to be pressed 'without concern for casualties, without economy', and all this because the war in Manchuria 'revealed' to him 'the frontal attack is necessary and possible'.[89]

In his 1911 lectures he went further. Whilst Foch urged a degree of caution and prudence in the advance, and the likes of Pétain, Maud'huy, Fayolle and Debeney placed strong emphasis on the importance of firepower in defence and attack, Grandmaison dismissed such prevarication, declaring:

"… in the offensive, imprudence is the best security."

His lectures were aimed squarely at Michel's deployment plan which focussed on the Belgian border and not Alsace and Lorraine, and on the counter-offensive not all out attack. Instead, Grandmaison demanded France attack the lost provinces, without hesitation and with no concern for loss. With Michel's plan rejected and Joffre, an adherent of the philosophy of the all-out offensive, in place, Grandmaison now sought a command to lead in this glorious fight to the death.

The unit concerned, the *153e régiment d'infanterie*, *39e Division* of Foch's *20e Corps* ran into German troops on 19th August 1914 near Château Salins and were involved in a 'violent combat' during the afternoon and evening in which the regiment suffered 'serious losses'. Grandmaison was amongst the wounded, suffering a head wound but remaining in command. The following day, ordered by Foch to attack at 6 a.m., the move was pre-empted by a violent attack by the German *6. Armee* at 5 a.m. in the Battle of Morhange. Within days, all French troops were ejected from *Lothringen*. On 19th August 1914 Grandmaison's regiment had 61 officers and 3,055 other ranks. In two days, after losses of 45%+, it was reduced to 32 officers and 1,684 other ranks. Grandmaison was wounded again and evacuated by ambulance. Commanding *53e Division*, Grandmaison died the day after being wounded in the trenches near Soissons on 18th February 1915[i].

---

[i] He is remembered on the *Plaque commémorative 1914-1918 de la paroisse Saint-Étienne, Toul*, *Plaque commémorative, église Saint-François-Xavier, Paris*, *Plaque Commémorative* & the *Monument aux Morts, Charroux, département de la Vienne*, *Plaques commémoratives pour les 20 arrondissements de Paris*, *Plaques commémoratives des écrivains (Panthéon)* & *Mémorial des Généraux 1914-1918, Hôtel des Invalides*. His funeral took place in the *église Saint-François-Xavier*, in what is now the *Place du Président Mithouard, Paris*.

THE CONSEQUENCE OF ALL THIS THEORISING, philosophising and of Grandmaison's semi-religious fervour was that France went to war essentially governed by three set of regulations:

La Conduite des Grandes Unites of 28th October 1913;
Le Decret sur le Service des armées en campagne of 2nd December 1913; and
Le Règlement de manuever de l'infanterie of 29th April 1914.

None was more influential than the first: *Règlement sur la conduite des grandes unités* (*Regulations for the conduct of large units*). Under Grandmaison's guiding hand this document demanded of the Army repeated attacks without any second thoughts, with victory only coming at 'the cost of bloody sacrifice'.[90] The intention was set out in paragraph two of the first chapter entitled *'Généralités sur la conduite de la guerre'* (*General information on the conduct of the war*):

"*Les opérations militaires visent l'anéantissement des forces organisées de l'ennemi* (Military operations aim at the annihilation of the enemy's organized forces)."[91]

One should note the word 'annihilation'. The means of this 'annihilation' was the 'decisive battle' which led to the 'destruction' of an enemy's armies:

"The decisive battle, exploited thoroughly, is the only means to collapse the will of the opponent, by the destruction of its armies. It constitutes the essential act of war."[92]

Occupying the enemy's territory and capturing his fortresses were not enough as they did not produce the definitive result according to the Regulations. No, only battle could achieve the necessary defeat of the opposition and this required:

"... the attacks pushed all the way, without a second thought; (victory) can only be obtained at the price of bloody sacrifices. Any other idea must be rejected as contrary to the very nature of war."[93]

And only the offensive could bring success:

"The offensive alone leads to positive results. Success in war has always been won by generals who wanted and sought out battle; those seeking to avoid it have always lost."[94]

If one equates 'avoidance' with the defensive, then, leaving to one side the Battle of Waterloo at which the attacker, Napoleon, was soundly defeated by Wellington's defensive tactics and Thielmann's defence of Wavre; and Napoleon's invasion of Russia (or, more recently and focussing on the success of the defence, Fredericksburg and Gettysburg); the simplistic ideas propounded were attractive to an officer corps bereft of any proper tactical doctrine but for whom gallantry and the glory of the advance were alluring prospects. Foch, on the other hand (but after the war), described Grandmaison's regulations as 'a donkey's guide'.[95]

Paragraph 8 on page 6 perhaps best links the tactical theory with the eventual and costly outcome not just of France's opening battles of the war but of the war in general as practised by all the participants. It is social Darwinism military-style in which great leaders deploy mass armies of anonymous men whose loss is inconsequential as long as victory is gained.

It is clearly closely linked to Foch's pronouncements in *Principes*:

"Battles are mostly moral struggles. Defeat is inevitable as soon as the hope of victory ceases. Success thus comes not to the man who has suffered the least loss, but to the man whose will is the strongest and whose morale is most strongly tempered."[96]

The 'decisive battle' was brought about by 'the offensive alone'. This was because 'passive defence is doomed to certain defeat' and was 'absolutely precluded'. The reason for the urgent need to 'annihilate' the enemy's armed forces was because:

"… the great numbers which are employed, the difficulty of re-supplying them, the interruption of the social and economic life of the country, all urge that a decision should be sought within the shortest possible time so as to promptly end the fighting."[97]

Clearly, and whether consciously or unconsciously, the French Staff had absorbed Bloch's warnings about the immense dislocation of economic and social life which would be caused by enormous citizen armies fighting one another over any extended period. What they failed to grasp, however, was Bloch's warnings about the slow, grinding, enormously costly nature of a new European war. Like the British, the French still held optimistically if grimly to the 'over by Christmas' idea with which they went to war in August 1914.

La Conduite des Grandes Unites then made this boastful statement:

"Of all nations, the military history of France offers the most striking examples of the great results produced by a war of attack… Developed by us almost to the point of perfection, the doctrine of the offensive has won the most glorious successes and, by a cruel counter-test, on the day we have misunderstood it, it has precisely provided our adversaries with the weapons with which they have defeated us… The first duty of the commander is to seek battle. To win it is necessary to break by force the armies of the opponent. This destruction demands attacks pushed until the end without second thoughts; it can only be obtained at the cost of bloody sacrifices.

The teachings of the past have borne fruit: the French Army has returned to its old traditions, and no longer recognises any Law in the conduct of operations but that of the offensive…"[98]

It has to be said that the basis for the French claim of martial success can only be founded on the performance of Napoleon (until such time as he started to lose). Though successful with their allies in the Crimea and in the Second Italian War of Independence in the 1850s, the French displayed little flair or imagination in the grinding costly battles fought, the last of which, at Solferino on 24th June 1859, so horrified the Swiss Jean-Henri Dunant he founded the *International Red Cross* and the Geneva Conventions. Prior to the Revolutionary and Napoleonic Wars France was on the losing side in the eighteenth century almost everywhere it came up against continental opposition and, during the Seven Years War, its colonial holdings were savaged by the British in North America, the West Indies and India. Nevertheless, buoyed by their newly revealed *élan vital*, they now claimed a tactical genius close to 'perfection'. No wonder they launched themselves into *Lothringen* and *Elsaß* with such confidence. But, tragically for the junior officer and ordinary soldier, military pride too often comes before a fall.

The French further reinforced their absolute commitment to the offensive by dismissing out of hand Britain's South African experience which suggested frontal attacks were dangerously expensive and sometimes impossible. They then re-interpreted the huge casualties suffered in massed frontal attacks by both sides in Manchuria as a 'striking denial to the dangerous theories' concerning the 'inviolability of fronts'.

Thus, the offensive became the 'be all and end all' of French military strategy and tactics with the defensive being relegated to a single purpose: 'the necessity to economise troops at certain points with a view to providing greater forces in the attacks'. In other words, any defensive stance was to be subsumed into the offensive and was but a temporary affair before the *poilus* continued their relentless and victorious advance.

Titre V 'Le Combat' of the *Le decret sur le Service des armées en campagne* of 2nd December 1913 reinforced this point:

"The two regulations (i.e. 1895 and 1913) affirm that only the offensive can break the will of the adversary and that defence never gives victory."[99]

The writers of the 1913 *Decret*, however, then went on to disagree fundamentally with the authors of the 1895 regulations. In the 1895 version the defensive was viewed as a means of 'attracting the enemy to ground where one believes it possible to fight under favourable conditions'. An eminently sensible concept one would have thought. But no, not in 1913 and not under the influence of Grandmaison, Foch and others. Now, the very idea that a position might determine tactics was viewed as a step away from a commander determining a defensive posture preferable to an offensive one, and this was unacceptable to the enthusiasts for the *'offensive'*. The only justification for troops taking up a defensive posture now was to release more troops for the offensive. Thus, 'the defensive is, strictly speaking, no more than an auxiliary to the offensive', even though those on the defensive had, like those attacking, to fight until, if necessary, they made the ultimate sacrifice and were wiped out. And, as for the attackers, whether in the main or a diversionary assault, all must advance 'with the firm resolution to tackle the enemy and to destroy it'. There is, the regulations insisted, no other way of fighting.

This section on *'Le Combat'* finishes with a hearty endorsement of Article 138 of the 1895 regulations:

"The text of article 138 of the 1895 decree relating to 'the duty of officers and soldiers' has been reproduced almost literally. It was impossible to give a higher or truer idea of military duty under fire, and of the amount of energy and self-sacrifice one must spend in battle to secure victory from the enemy."[100]

The relevant section reads (highlights are this writer's):

"All the qualities of the troops, discipline, instruction. marksmanship, march training, manoeuvring skills, and above all moral qualities, are the most essential elements for success.

It is the value of the troops that decides matters in the last resort:
Whatever their number, whatever the skill of the leader's tactics, it is always necessary, on certain points, *to resist to the end and to be killed on the spot rather than to abandon the flag*; on others, to march at all costs to the enemy and drive him from his position.

The morale of armies untrained by recent campaigns can be shaken in the first battles. It is therefore important, during times of peace, to elevate to a maximum the spirit and heart of the soldier, and to persuade him that the salvation of *'La Patrie'* will depend on his ability to bear manfully the fatigue and privations of war with tenacity, bravery, and an enthusiasm for fire."

Finally, the burden this placed on young officers who were to advance with their men was made explicit and explains the foolhardy and too often fatal activities of these young men and their attendant disproportionate casualties:

"Finally, officers must be well imbued with the idea that their first and most beautiful mission is to set an example for their troops.

Nowhere is a soldier more obedient and more devoted than in combat. His eyes are constantly fixed on his leaders. Their bravery and coolness passes into his soul; and make him capable of energy and sacrifices."[101]

This obsession with 'forward movement' meant that, pre-war, little attention was paid to the defensive let alone the withdrawal, be it tactical or strategic. There was, however, one experienced officer liberated by early retirement from the army who was able to voice his support for such heresy. 70-year-old Auguste Antoine Grouard had been a Lt. Col. in the artillery having attended the *École Polytechniquq* in 1863 and the *École d'Application* two years later. He served with the *7e régiment d'artillerie* during the Franco-Prussian War being engaged in the bitter fighting at Bazeilles on 1st September 1870 during the Sedan campaign. After various regimental and staff attachments he became the *Directeur d'artillerie* at Bastia on Corsica in 1894. He retired in 1900 to write on military matters, dying in 1929. He wrote a series of books on Napoleon's later campaigns of 1813 and 1815, and on the Franco-Prussian War, focussing much more than his colleagues on strategy rather battlefield tactics. In this he was unusual as he shied away from the concept of the *offensive* and the great climactic battle with which any brief war would be won (or lost).

In 1913 he published *France et Allemagne; la guerre éventuelle*. In this, he assessed not only the abilities of the French Army but also that of Germany. Given the basis of conscription in France, the short time spent with the colours of the average ranker, and the reliance of even front-line units on an influx of recently discharged men to bring them up to war-time strength, he believed the modern French Army was, basically, an army of reserves. Such an army was far better suited to the defensive than on the fast-moving, hyper-aggressive offensives wished for by people like Grandmaison. After all, had not Grandmaison himself suggested a preference for a smaller, long service, better-trained, army more able to achieve the results he desired? Grouard then addressed the strategic needs of each country were war to break out, considering the problem for Germany of a war on two fronts. His conclusions were radical in 1913 France. He harked back to early War Plans based on defensive deployments which absorbed the power of the German Army whilst giving the Russian forces time to deploy and invade East Prussia. He even took this a step further, suggesting the French Armies should withdraw in the face of German attacks rather than attempt the great war-winning battle such as Jena. Indeed, his view was that Germany's need for a quick victory which necessitated invading neutral Belgium, even knowing it would bring Great Britain into the war (and negatively impact on public opinion around the world), was so desperate that even a result as tactically indecisive a battle as Valmy on 20th September 1792[i] would be a huge strategic setback:

> "It would be a grave mistake to try to end the war in one battle. To break the first shock of the Germans, by forcing them to retreat, would already be a result which would produce a great moral effect because, on the side of our adversaries, we can be sure that they will only engage in the hope of 'getting it over with all at once', and if the first great battle were only indecisive, it would undoubtedly have the same consequences for them as a defeat."[102]

Though forced into it by the dreadful losses of the Battles of the Frontiers and the failure to stop the German offensive through Belgium, one can see that the Battle of the Marne was far closer to Grouard's representation of the way the war would develop than that of any of the advocates of the *offensive à outrance*. He was, however, a lonely voice in the proverbial military wilderness of pre-war French strategic and tactical thinking.

Perhaps wise after the event, Lt. Col. Pascal Marie Henri Lucas, writing in 1923, was hugely critical of the attitudes within the French Army which led to the almost religious devotion to the *offensive*. Lucas was born in 1874 and called up in 1894 before attending the *École spéciale militaire* the following year. He was commissioned into the *30e régiment d'infanterie* in 1897. He started to serve in staff positions from 1907 (*8e Corps*) and by 1918 was the head of the *3e Bureau* of the *10e Armée*. In 1919 he was appointed professor of General Tactics at the *École supérieure de guerre*. After his time there he joined the *503e régiment de chars de combat* based at Versailles. Postwar Lucas devoted himself to a large work analysing the tactical developments of the French and German armies throughout the war. His opinions of the French Army before and during the early parts of the war are scathing. It includes comments about the problems confronting any officer who might wish to debate anything to do with defence or withdrawals. Such concerns could stifle a promising career:

> "Sometimes we took up the delicate question of retrograde movements, but we must acknowledge the word 'defensive' had such a bad sound to

---

[i] The Battle of Valmy, *aka* the Cannonade of Valmy, involved a counter-revolutionary coalition army led by the Duke of Brunswick of Prussians, Austrians, Hessians, and royalist French, and two French armies combining the old, royalist, army and thousands of citizen volunteers. The armies, each c. 35,000 strong, faced one another between Valmy and Sainte Menehould and the French artillery proved superior. Demoralised, Brunswick's army withdrew to the east. Total casualties for both armies did not exceed 500. Strategically it was a major victory for Revolutionary France.

our ears we would not have dared to present a defensive situation in a map exercise, much less in a manoeuvre on the terrain... anyone who might have attempted to make a closer study of this important question... would have put himself in an unfavourable light."[103]

And the reason for this?

"Our corps of officers had absorbed the theory of the *offensive* to the point where it had become a disease; it was the *offensive* in every case and in spite of any situation, the *offensive* blind and to the limit, which was to give a solution in every situation."[104]

Because it had been determined that the war needed to be over rapidly to avoid the social, economic and political dislocation referred to earlier, everything done was to be done quickly:

"As a result, we did not pay enough attention to the effect of fire, we went on using formations which were too dense, we neglected liaison; all this was done in order to make speed, for, according to our way of thinking, once the attack was started the question of its progress being stopped was not to be considered.

And it was with these general ideas and habits that the French Army was thrust into battle; it threw itself into battle with an ardour which was superb, but with a disdain for fire for which it had to pay dearly."[105]

This is not to say the French Army had nothing in print about how to defend. The handbook of the *Génie*, the Engineers, gave plenty of advice on trench location and depth, on concealment and *points d'appui*, etc., etc. There was advice on the echeloning of troops: an advanced line, the main defence, and the reserve ready to counterattack. Then came cheery comment on a 'principle which is *absolute*', i.e. defending troops must cling on until wiped out:

"They will resist to the end; each man will die rather than give ground."[106]

Easy for a General to say. Furthermore, all ground lost was to be regained by immediate counterattack (a costly German tactic early on during the Somme, and one which might have been even more disastrous had Haig allowed Rawlinson's initial 'bite and hold' proposal). And that, broadly, was that.

Advice on the offensive was far more comprehensive. So comprehensive, in fact, that Lucas did not have the time or space to consider it all. He restricted himself, therefore, to five headings:

Fire effect
Artillery support
Liaison (i.e. communications)
Field works
Precautions against aerial observation

French Regulations explicitly recognised the great increase in the rate of fire of modern weapons. This applied to both the defensive and the offensive and, in particular, to the essential importance of fire and movement, with movement being 'alone... decisive and irresistible, and which alone is capable of producing victory'.[107] The Regulations noted, however, that the volume of fire which a defensive line could produce 'makes any attack in dense formations delivered in daytime over open terrain impossible'. True and sensible advice. Attacking infantry, therefore, needed to deploy in skirmish formation as was eventually adopted by the British in South Africa and used by the Japanese in Manchuria. Were the enemy to be dug-in then an attack needed to be methodical, with the enemy position minutely inspected before troops were committed. *Tres bon, mais...*

La conduite des grandes unités was followed by *Règlement sur le service des armées en campagne* of 2nd December 1913. Finally came *Règlement de manœuvre d'infanterie* of 20th April 1914, which set out the actions of the infantry in the attack. The objective was hand-to-hand bayonet fighting in which the 'naturally superior' (according to Foch in *Principes*) French *ésprit* and *élan* overwhelmed the enemy. Initially dispersed, troops would advance without firing for as long as possible then, through a combination of fire and movement, approach a position from which the bayonet charge could be delivered. Finally, led by the exhortations of officers and NCOs: *'en avant à la baïonette!'*, the now unified and compact force would rout the terrified enemy with cold steel.[108] Victory would, nevertheless, come at a cost of: 'an enormous expenditure of physical and moral energy and with bloody sacrifices'.[109] All well and good but, as Leonard Smith points out, this triumph of moral over material forces was somehow to have been instilled in that untrained and untried third of the Army only recently inducted under the provisions of the *'Loi des trois ans'* passed the previous August, and who had then spent the intervening period mainly learning drill and doing route marches.[110]

The job of the artillery was simply to support the infantry. And that was it. The explanation given showed how badly Gen. Herr lost the arguments about the use of artillery as based on the First Balkan War (see page 233 onwards):

"Until a few years ago, it was considered that the first duty of the artillery in battle was to gain fire superiority over the hostile artillery... Today it is recognised that the primary role of the artillery is to support the infantry attacks by destroying everything which opposes the progress of attacks."[111]

The main reason for this was it had been concluded artillery was of little use against entrenched and sheltered troops. Only the bayonet-wielding infantry could get the enemy out of its fieldworks and into the open, much as Douglas Haig told Henry Rawlinson when responding to the latter's conservative initial plan for the Somme. The French Regulations concluded:

"The artillery no longer prepares attacks, it supports them."[112]

Liaison between commanders and units was generally considered a very good thing. Liaison between the infantry and the artillery a jolly good thing. Telephones, as a means of liaison, a terrifically good thing. But aircraft? No. They were only useful for long-range reconnaissance (even if the Germans thought differently) and avoiding being spotted by enemy aircraft was simply a matter of hiding in nearby bushes and woods when on the march (as Grierson managed in the 1912 manoeuvres much to the discomfort of his opponent Gen. Haig). So far so good.

Field works were divided into two: light (i.e. temporary trenches, etc.) which were the province of the infantry; and heavy with which the *Génie* concerned themselves. Captured enemy positions were to be immediately fortified. If threatened, defensive fieldworks should be thrown up. But essentially, everything needed to be geared to the advance, to the offensive. No sitting around in trenches between glorious advances enjoying a *Gauloise* and a *verre de vin rouge* for the tired but happy *Poilu*. *Non! En avant* and on to Berlin.

Sadly, however, as with the British Army (which laid tapes to indicate trenches during manoeuvres), field works were sometimes discussed but little practised. And for this there were two reasons:

> "It was asserted that once a man was dug in behind an even more or less hasty shelter, it would be difficult to get him to go forward again under fire."[113]

Ah, that pesky sense of self-preservation rears its ugly head again. But then, economics (and laziness) got in the way too:

> "We usually did not have the land which troops could be permitted to dig up at will; and when by chance such land was available, the necessity for refilling the trenches after having dug them, was excuse enough never to dig them."[114]

Lucas then went to analyse how these Regulations impacted on early French tactics. The French, as explained previously, were in a hurry to win but seemed to have little idea as to how much heavy enemy fire slowed down the whole process of battle (as Bloch predicted). Rather:

> "… our regulations… seemed to be absorbed with the rapidity of movements, as if above all, everything which might restrict the natural dash of the French temperament must be avoided… (and) that in battle, rapidity takes precedence over order."[115]

Or, again, as Grandmaison stated before the war: 'in the offensive, imprudence is the best security'. This, according to Lucas, resulted in:

> "Poorly considered attacks, often totally lacking in co-ordination in which everything was sacrificed to rapidity of execution."[116]

Lucas's other criticisms show how little the Regulations, however worthy, were followed. Honoured in the breach, perhaps? Attack formations were too dense; artillery support inadequate; liaison between the infantry and artillery absent; knowledge of, and aptitude for, the digging of fieldworks lacking. Oh dear.

Lucas excuses some of this by suggesting that every new war brings with it surprises. He remarks on how Moltke failed to appreciate the impact of the range and rate of fire of the *Chassepot* until after the first battles of the Franco-Prussian War (Wissembourg, 4th August 1870 and Spicheren, 6th August 1870). More fool Moltke, this writer would suggest. 'Surprises' are surely those things which emerge but were previously unknown, for example the tank in WW1 (though numerous opportunities were given to various armies to adopt and adapt the idea before 1914). The effectiveness of quick-firing long-range rifles and automatic weapons, of trenches and barbed wire, of howitzers and high-explosive shells, and even of aerial reconnaissance and bombing was more than adequately displayed in various wars prior to 1914. And yet they apparently came as a 'surprise' to senior officers of all armies and most especially the French in the opening weeks of the war. This is not a failure of 'intelligence; in the sense of gathering information, it is a failure of 'intelligence' in an intellectual sense. A failure of imagination, of lateral thinking, of creativity, *of concern for one's men* which seems the hallmark of rather too many who pursue a military career and seek to become Generals.

As Bloch wrote in 1898:

"It was the outcome of narrow prejudice, and of an irrational faith in worthless traditions"[117]

Thus, what Gen. Lanrezac called after the war the 'extreme fetish of the headquarters staff for the offensive' was enshrined in what passed for French doctrine.[118] Not only was it enshrined, it was done so without consultation with other senior Army officers. At the *Ècole supérieur de guerre*, however, were officers who fundamentally disagreed with these concepts. Men who were fearful of the power of the new weapons available to the contending forces. Men who would bring to bear, when given the chance to lead, far greater sophistication, awareness and tactical sense than was currently the case. Men who exhibited at least some concern for the lives of their troops whilst accepting war was, essentially, about killing. Men like Henri Philippe Benoni Omer Joseph Pétain, Marie Émile Fayolle, Louis Ernest de Maud'huy and Marie-Eugène Debeney. But for now, no-one could speak of the defensive without fearing dismissal and ridicule, for the *'offensive à outrance'* was now not just a military philosophy, it was military policy.

OTHER THAN THE TACTICS EMPLOYED, an additional and avoidable reason for such heavy casualties early in the war was the French uniform: a dark blue coat, a bright red *kepi* and bright red trousers, the infamous *pantalon rouge*[i]. Only the French went into battle in August 1914 dressed so horribly conspicuously.

But, *les pantalons rouge* were not the French soldiers only problem. In 1902, an officer of the *Chasseurs à Pied*, Émile-Charles Lavisse[ii], published a work critical of the current uniform and its various accoutrements such as the *havresac* and its large, bright and shiny cooking utensil perched on the top. As someone who came up through the ranks over eight years, Lavisse knew whereof he wrote as he wore the uniform and other kit throughout that period. The book, *Sac au dos. Études comparées de la tenue de campagne des fantassins des armées française et étrangères*, (Backpack: Comparative studies of the campaign dress of infantrymen of French and foreign armies)[119] was followed in 1913 by another, briefer, volume by the same author though on the same subject: *La tenue de campagne de l'infanterie. Comment l'améliorer?*.[120] In this latter

---

[i] The dye used is known as *garance*. Derived from the Common Madder plant (*Rubia tinctorum*, part of the family *Rubiaceae* which also includes the coffee plant *Coffea*), it was the dye used for the red coats of the British Army.
[ii] Émile-Charles Lavisse (1855-1915) volunteered in 1873 and worked his way up the ranks until he attended the *École Militaire d'Infanterie* in 1881. He served in various *BCP* until moving to the infantry in 1899. Commandant of the *École Militaire de Saint-Maixent* (1907-1910). He was made Col., *54e RI*, in 1910 and took command of the *12e brigade d'infanterie* in 1914 with the rank of *Général de brigade*. He died from illness on 28th June 1915 in the hospital at *134 rue Blomet*, Paris, (now the *Clinique Blomet - Ramsay Santé*) whilst in charge of the *15e Région Militaire* and is buried in the *Cimetière communal*, Le Nouvion-en-Thiérache, *département de l'Aisne*.

book, because nothing had been done in the meantime, Lavisse again pointed out the numerous flaws in the *Poilu's* clothing and equipment.

The problems perceived by Lavisse were not just the colour combinations of the French uniform. The knapsack, the *havresac* or, simply, *le sac*, was an unpopular item 'worn' by the infantry. Barely changed since the Second Empire, the 1914 model was the 1893/14 and known as the *Azor* (originally made from dog skin, the knapsack was nick-named after the French version of 'Fido') or the *As de Carreau*, the Ace of Diamonds. *Le sac* weighed c. 2 Kgs (4 lbs) and had eight straps. Putting it on was a labour of itself. Its contents weighed c. 13 Kgs (28 lbs) including cooking utensil and digging tool. The uniform, rifle, ammunition, etc., weighed 17 Kgs (37 lbs), for a total of some 69 lbs/31 kilos.[121] As an experiment, a battalion of the *51e RI* used a new *havresac* design in the 1906 manoeuvres. *The Times* wrote:

> "This experiment represents a serious endeavour to reduce the excessive weights carried by the infantry which run to 66 lbs in war."[122]

It was rejected. On the subject of the *havresac* Lavisse was scathing, pointing out that, compared to the German version, it was bigger, heavier, more visible and more complicated to put on. Then, mounted on the *havresac* in various ways, was a soldier's cooking equipment. He again pointed out that these were larger and heavier than those in use in any other army and then produced a table to prove it which gave the weight, volume and material of the cooking utensil, the *marmite*, of thirteen different armies. Made of steel the French version was three times the size and weight of the lightest (Russian and aluminium) pot. He calculated that a company of 250 men would, between them, carry 212 Kgs of cooking pots whilst a Russian company of the same size enjoyed a load of just 65 Kgs. A German company's aluminium cooking utensils weighed some 114 Kgs whilst the British and Austrian steel pots weighed in at 158 Kgs and 160 Kgs respectively.

In fact, Lavisse pointed out, nearly every piece of equipment carried by the infantry or by the regimental transport was unnecessarily heavier, larger and more cumbersome than their European equivalents. And shiny. Shiny enough to be visible to the enemy at a distance. Such complaints had a practical purpose. Other than their transportation to their mobilisation areas by train, all other movements were likely to be conducted on foot. It was bad enough for the regulars to have to carry significantly heavier and more awkward weights than their potential enemy but, for the one third of every regular regiment who would be recent reservists called up at short notice, these weights would be more exhausting as these men would lack the necessary route march strength, experience, and resilience. They might either fall out *en route* or be exhausted when called to action. Which, as we shall see, they were.

Let us now deal with the uniform. Lavisse's thesis was simple – it should reflect the widespread use of camouflage in nature:

> "Visibility. Nature has given a large number of animals fur or plumage that conceals them in the environment in which they live, which makes them perhaps less visible and protects them from a hunter; we must imitate nature and give our soldiers a garment the colour of which will approach that of the battlefield in order to conceal him as much as possible from the

sight and bullets of his adversary. This idea has become more imperative with the development of weaponry. Reducing the visibility of the troops has been the main concern of nations since the wars of the Transvaal and Manchuria in particular. From these wars, in fact, we have drawn very clear lessons and the following is a summary:

The colour to be given to uniforms must be such as to blend best and most often with the general appearance of the terrain on which the troops may be called upon to fight;

Colour contrasts between clothing and equipment or between different parts of clothing should be avoided;

The shiny accessories of the outfit and, in general, anything that can project bright reflections is to be avoided; and

Officers should be dressed in the same attire as the troops."[123]

As he explained in his 1913 book, khaki was adopted by the British Army during the South African War and by the Japanese in Manchuria (they had previously worn blue). Russia used a variety of dull grey colours in the war against Japan, officially adopting a grey-green uniform in 1909. Initial attempts to persuade the *Kaiser* to move away from Prussian Blue were unsuccessful but, after 5 or 6 years of studies involving several colour options – dark grey, dark blue and dark green – he was persuaded to allow the use of *feldgrau* in 1909, with a grey-green kit approved for the *Jäger* and machine gun teams. Austria adopted *hechtgrau* (or 'pike grey') as used by their Tyrolean *Jäger* troops by 1907 though it took some time to provide all soldiers with the new uniform. Italy changed to a grey-green colour by 1908 as a result of tests which showed their previous blue uniform attracted seven times the number of hits compared to the new colour.[124] Even the neutral Dutch adopted such colourings.

The French infantry uniform was essentially that worn by troops of the Second Empire resoundingly thrashed in 1870-1. From 1898, efforts made to change to something less conspicuous met resistance from conservative military and political opinion. Some even viewed the change to duller, grey-green colours as likely to undermine the martial spirit and morale of the troops which, in turn, would erode the hoped-for impact of the *offensive à outrance*. Nevertheless, with a study showing the blue/red colour combination attracted more hits than a blue-grey one, efforts continued. The first experiments were started in 1903 ('ten years ago!' as Lavisse complained) when, after South Africa, a blue/grey uniform (called 'Boer') was tried by the *8e compagnie* of the *28e Régiment d'infanterie* during the 14th July parade at Longchamp. They led the march past of the infantry in a new blue/grey uniform and sporting a large-brimmed felt hat. In an absurd nod to tradition, large and gaudy red epaulettes adorned their shoulders. Designed by a committee, and looking like it, the uniform was rejected.

In the 1906 autumn manoeuvres between the *Rivers Aisne* and *Marne* a dark grey/blue uniform was tried by a company of the *72e RI*. It was described scathingly in *The Times*:

"… a dark grey-blue uniform with a single-breasted great coat to match, a colonial pattern helmet of the same colour with a red pom-pom stuck on, as though inadvertently, in front. A section of this company wore the beret of the Alpine troops. The beret apart, it would be difficult to discover a more hideous garb, and the colour did not confer any advantage so far as invisibility is concerned."[125]

It was also rejected, apparently because it reminded people of the clothing issued to men in hospital.[126]

In October 1910, the then *Ministre de la guerre*, Gen. Jean Brun, announced that, after long deliberations and numerous experiments, a new uniform of either khaki, grey or some other colour, was to be adopted and that definite proposals would be brought forward 'at an early date'.[127] Unfortunately, Brun then died suddenly, aged 61, on 23rd February 1911.

On 2nd March 1911, he was succeeded in the short-lived Monis administration by Henri Maurice Berteaux (previously *Ministre de la Guerre*, November 1904 to November 1905)[i]. Berteaux, too, wanted to change the uniform to a grey-green one, *la tenue réséda*[ii], more suited to modern warfare, and this was announced at the beginning of April with the news that two battalions would be so dressed in the year's autumn manoeuvres. Ten weeks later Berteaux was then killed, and Monis injured, when the aircraft of Louis Émile Train hit the crowd at the start of the Paris-Madrid air race on 21st May 1911. Train, flying a plane of his own design, had engine trouble after take-off and decided to return to the airfield. Whilst trying to avoid a *peloton* of *Cuirassiers* trotting across the runway, he stalled and crashed into a crowd of VIPs. Berteaux died almost immediately; his arm severed by the propeller.

When the Monis administration fell a month later, Berteaux's replacement, Messimy, pursued his predecessor's attempt to modernise the uniform, with three regiments trialling the new kit during the autumn manoeuvres. Many conservative and nationalistic-minded senior officers and politicians were appalled. A right-wing newspaper, the *L'Écho de Paris,* described it as being against 'French taste and military function'. More extreme still, Eugène Étienne, a lawyer and *Ministre de la Guerre* throughout most of 1913 (but a man who never served in his country's Army), exclaimed histrionically:

"*Jamais! Le pantalon rouge c'est la France!*"

Others tried to provide a reasoned tactical explanation why the retention of *les pantalons rouge* was acceptable: the red trousers would make it easier to identify friend and foe on the battlefield and even from those new-fangled flying contraptions – aeroplanes. Then there was a financial implication. Vast quantities of the old uniform were stored across the country in depots awaiting the arrival of the reservists who would swell the army's ranks in their hundreds of thousands when mobilised. So, there was also a degree of parsimony in certain government quarters with ministers and civil servants reluctant to spend what would be serious money on making a change.

---

[i] Five men occupied the role between 23rd February 1911 and 27th June 1911: Brun, Briand (for five days), Berteaux, Goiran (less than a month) and Messimy.
[ii] Also known as *Mignonette. Mignonette* is a garden herb part of the genus *Reseda* of the family *Resedaceae*.

According to Lavisse, change was essential, and not just to the basic colours. He also believed there need be some differentiation between a new uniform and that of other armies in order to avoid 'friendly fire' errors on the battlefield. His suggestion was akin to the blue-grey which became the *Bleu Horizon* of September 1914. Beyond that, his other essential changes were:

1. Getting rid of the red *kepi* which, in a sad irony, he described as being:

"... very visible by itself, like a poppy in a wheat field."[128]

2. Getting rid of *le pantalon rouge* for reasons with an excellent recent precedent:

"... after the Spanish-American war, the Spaniards, the only infantry who wore red trousers as with ours, energetically demanded the suppression of this colour which constituted, they said, a real danger because of its visibility. This is a lesson from war that must be learned; it is more compelling than all the arguments in the world."[129]

3. Getting rid of any shiny accessories. As he pointed out, in Germany, they had done away with shiny metal buttons on the uniforms, something the French Army needed to do urgently:

"I will emphasize once again the danger to which all this tinsmithing exposes us, made up of the collective utensils and the individual's cooking bowl, which we persist in carrying on the *havresac*; this is the first suppression to be done and to be done immediately."[130]

4. Insisting on the same uniform for officers and men.

As far as officers were concerned, he wanted them to remove or change any items which reflected light or which were contrasts to the basic uniform. Varnished straps and pistol holsters reflected light over great distances. Black holsters or binoculars cases or brightly coloured map cases were also easily visible. Map cases without a leather cover were a particular cause of concern because the shiny mica face which protected the contents reflected light over long distances like a mirror.

Lavisse believed these changes not just useful but urgently necessary. They were changes of 'paramount importance' to the infantry and his frustration with the inaction of politicians and senior officers was palpable:

"We are full of good intentions, we have been experimenting for twenty-five years, but we do not succeed: we want to do too well, and we do nothing."[131]

He was not alone in his frustration with the lack of change. In a front-page article on 16th July 1912 in the French military daily newspaper, *La France Militaire*, an anonymous writer, '*H*', expressed his anger, describing the lack of action as 'Criminal impotence!'. He wrote how, along with several hundred thousand Parisians, he watched the Army parade at Longchamp on 14th July. A special feature of the parade was that the *28e RI* (now based in and around Paris) was dressed in various experimental uniforms designed by the specialist in military painting Édouard Baptiste Detaille[i] at the request of the *Ministre de la Guerre*, Adolphe Messimy. This contract was announced in November 1911 and Detaille and a pupil, Georges Scott, set to work on the designs. The assignment covered every uniform from dress, through off-duty, to active service. An article in the illustrated daily newspaper, *l'Excelsior*, included an article *Deux peintres militaires vont habiller l'armée française (Two military painters to dress the French Army)*. It explained how, on 3rd November, Detaille and Scott were called to the *Ministre de la Guerre* there to meet Messimy, Generals Michel and Dubail and a Cdt. Bertrand who made up a commission exploring new uniforms. Scott described how Messimy requested 'two new, elegant, and dapper outfits' which, in this writer's view, seem strange criteria on which to base a modern military uniform fit for a war.

38. The *28e Régiment d'Infanterie* with the Detaille/Scott uniform and helmet Longchamp, 14th July 1912.

The colour of Detaille's tunic and greatcoat would be blue/grey. Extraordinarily, the red trousers were not to be eliminated completely but instead of being full-length they were to be replaced by red *culottes* and dark *puttees*. Neither was the red (and blue) *kepi* to completely disappear but it would be augmented by a *bourguignotte*-style helmet, a development of a 15th Century Burgundian metal helmet, described as likely to be 'an elegant model... practical, light, solid, perhaps in burnished steel', though the original model was rejected as one of the Commission suggested it would not be possible to fire lying down whilst wearing it. Messimy seems to have absorbed a minimum of Lavisse's ideas with a further demand all shiny ornamentation be removed, but this was but scratching at the surface of what Lavisse demanded.

---

[i] Born in 1848, the nationalist, *Boulangerist, anti-Dreyfus* Detaille was well-known for his paintings of the Franco-Prussian War and especially for the explicitly *revanchist* 1888 painting entitled *Le Rêve*. He died on 24th December 1912.

As an alternative, when first revealed to the public at Longchamp on 14th July 1912, the previously tried grey/green uniform, *la tenue réséda,* was also displayed, though the shade was slightly different. Those so dressed also wore the *bourguignotte* helmet rather unflatteringly described in *The Times* report as:

"... a helmet which, to judge from the comments of the crowd, is unlikely to satisfy public opinion. It is of a low coal scuttle shape with a hollow ridge."[132]

'H' watched the soldiers 'model' the fruits of Detaille and Scott's labours from the grandstand wondering:

"... if any other country in the world would be capable of exhibiting an impotence of achievement similar to that embodied, at the head of the infantry, by the almost carnival mix of experimental outfits presented to the public."[133]

Not that the public seemed unduly bothered by the:

"... ridiculous, if not macabre, comedy that comes at the cost of the blood of our valiant little *pioupious*[i]."[134]

Everyone, it seemed, agreed that *la tenue réséda,* an alternative blue-grey version, and the *bourguignotte* helmet were 'perfectly ugly'. Even the writer did not like the look but near him an elderly lady summed up the situation aptly:

"I don't see," she said, "why so many fuss. If the soldiers need a new outfit for war, give it to them. Bravery has no uniform. And when our little soldiers have fought well with *la tenue réséda* or blue-grey trousers, then these trousers, too, will become glorious."[135]

For *'H'*, the solution was clear. Immediately make this lady *Ministre de la Guerre*, if only for a day, because, in that time, she would have correctly answered the key question:

"... yes or no, can the French army safely enter the field in its current uniforms?"[136]

Whilst he hoped the new occupant of that key ministry, Millerand, would be able to agree that the answer was 'no', this was, for *'H'*, a matter of doubt, if only because of the prejudiced, bureaucratic conservatives who surrounded him and who had either forgotten, or chosen to ignore, the recent lessons of real wars. And these lessons were clear:

"Three peoples, the English, the Japanese and the Russians, operating in regions of climate and cultures of diverse and infinitely varied aspects, have, from the first engagement, recognized that their uniforms, very similar to ours, were incompatible with the conditions of modern warfare. To avoid massacres, all three changed these uniforms; and they made this change in the middle of an active campaign.
This is the lesson that has been lost by us. If it had been lost by the others,

---

[i] A 17th Century word used to describe the cry of chicks. Used in 1838 by the playwright Antoine-François Varner in *Le Pioupiou ou la gloire et l'amour* to describe a young soldier.

there would be only partial harm. But we are the only ones who have not taken advantage of it: Germans, English, Austrians, Italians, etc., all have adopted uniforms similar to our *la tenue réséda*, whose visibility is minimal on all backgrounds and in all light."[137]

He could not determine whether the decisions made (or not made) were simply 'ridiculous or just plain heart-breaking'. Whatever the answer, Detaille and Scott's work did not come to fruition despite a government announcement on 8th November 1912 that a new uniform, based as far as possible on the invisibility of troops in the field, was to be adopted. It would comprise a grey/blue tunic and great coat; the red *kepi*, but now covered with a waterproof material of the same colour as the tunic; *le pantalon rouge*, to be mainly concealed by the great coat (though who would wear these in the heat of August 1914?); epaulettes to be covered by a less visible material; and an improved soft *havresac* similar to one used by the British Army. The cost was c. £32,000 (£13-30 million in current values). The issue of shiny buttons, etc., was ignored as it was thought they would grow dull and less visible on campaign. Little of this happened, as can be judged from the section below. The use of the old Empire uniforms continued into the war.[138]

In June 1914, less than two months before the outbreak of war, an article appeared in the *Revue militaire Générale* written by Capt. Abel Jean Ernest Clément-Grandcourt who, after leaving St Cyr in 1895, spent five years with the *11e bataillon de Chasseurs Alpin*[i]. It was an article endorsed by Gen. de Lacroix, the *vice-président* of the *Conseil supérieur de la guerre* as recently as 1909. Lacroix wrote in his preface (emphasis below is this writer's):

> "He (Clément-Grandcourt) tells us today that the complete transformation of clothing is not possible. He gives the reasons for this, and he seeks, 'not the ideal solution, but the improvements possible immediately or at short notice'. He successively examines campaign dress and peacetime dress, in all the details they entail, and he does so with his experience as a troop officer, knowing the soldier and his needs well. He posits in principle that the question of visibility, *if it is important*, must be dominated by that of convenience, strength, and lightness. He is concerned with elegance and he is right."[139]

One need hardly stress the significance of the phrase 'the question of visibility, *if it is important*,' in the light of the complete lack of decisive action by the authorities and the disasters about to unfold within a few weeks. At least, as comfort to their widows and orphans, the soon-to-be-dead soldiers would be 'elegantly' dressed.

Clément-Grandcourt's article starts hopefully but misleadingly:

> "The improvement of the clothing of our infantry, an improvement often tried but which has never succeeded, will be postponed again.
> However, the French infantry are the worst dressed in Europe, at least in Western Europe. No need to dwell on this painful truth and try to

---

[i] Formed as the *11e BCP* in 1854, surrendered at Metz 1870, re-formed 1871 and was renamed the *11e BCA* in 1889. It was based at Annecy. The future *président de la République*, Raymond Poincaré, was an officer in the battalion in the late 1890s.

understand why France, which has remained the arbiter of women's fashion, so ridiculously adorns the great grandsons of the prestigious soldiers of the *Grande Armée*."[140]

Then the dampener:

"However, a complete transformation of clothing is impossible. The enormity of the expense required, the immense quantity of the present type accumulated in the stores, obliges us to seek, not the ideal solution, but the best possible improvement, immediately or at short notice."[141]

And, finally, the almost literal killer:

"It is this we propose to study but by noting, first of all, that the concern for invisibility in the field must, as Mr. Millerand has well understood during the last test attempted by the Paris garrison, to be overtaken in precedence by other more urgent considerations: convenience, solidity and lightness first; differentiation from the probable enemy secondly; and finally, elegance and respect for traditional colours."[142]

So, when it came to uniforms, the French officer's priority was: convenience, differentiation, elegance and tradition. In the light of the latter two considerations, it is not very surprising that so many officers were then killed wearing white gloves with cassowary plumes in their head gear.

Clément-Grandcourt first spends some time discussing such head gear. Immediately dismissed was the concept of the *bourguignotte*. As mentioned above, such a thing had previously been tested but, despite '…the very effective protection it provided to the head', this rather fancier (and undoubtedly more expensive) precursor to the iconic *Casque Adrian* was:

"…definitively condemned, for the infantry at least. By its massive form and weight, it is not suitable for our infantry composed of generally small men who are called upon to make long marches in the heat."[143]

His greater concern was how to waterproof the *Kepi* and what colour it should be! He suggested the *bleu ciel tirant sur le gris* (sky blue tending to grey) worn by the officers of the *cavalerie légère* e.g. the *Chasseur à cheval* (and, nowadays, still part of their dress uniform. Along with their red trousers) as:

"This very distinctive, very French colour (which) is very elegant and extremely inconspicuous."[144]

But not yet suitable for the 'poor, bloody infantry's' main uniform.

Eventually, on page 796, we get to the two paragraphs about *le pantalon rouge*. They are quoted, in full, below. Read them and weep:

"Trousers: for the line infantry, the only one studied here, we should retain the madder (i.e. red) colour – solid, traditional, and shows up, beyond 800 metres, as a kind of useful flicker, since it prevents confusion much feared at the current combat distances. Modify its cut during manufacture, giving it a shape a little wider at the legs, a little tighter at the instep."[145]

'You cannot be serious', to quote John McEnroe.

The result of the prevarication and stupidity of the old men in Paris was that the French Army was the only one *not* dressed in a khaki or grey uniform. Instead, it marched through the ripening crops of August wearing brightly coloured and highly visible uniforms of blue coats and bright red trousers and *kepis*, providing a target which Messimy later described as having 'cruel consequences'.

Realism dawned too late, and a law proposed the previous year by Messimy's successor, Millerand[i] (who succeeded Messimy again in August 1914) to adopt the *bleu horizon* uniform was eventually adopted on 18th July 1914. A debate on the proposal was opened by Messimy on 9th July. Given what had gone before, and even more so, what was to come, *'H's'* 1912 accusation against the government of 'Criminal impotence!' rings still more horribly true. *The Times* reported it as follows:

> "French Army's New Uniform, Value of the Change, Paris, July 9
>
> The Government's intention to dress the army in a new blue/grey uniform on account of its 'invisible' quality was discussed in the Chamber this afternoon. M. Messimy, Minister of War, stated that the English in the Transvaal were the first to realize the danger of bright uniforms, and had substituted khaki. In the Balkan War the Bulgarians and Servians had come to the same conclusion. In France successive experiments had been carried out with different kinds of clothing. At 1,500 yards the old cloth was as visible as the new at 550 yards. It was necessary to authorize the change at once, in order that cloth in sufficient quantities for the active army and the reserve should be supplied in four and a half or five years. This was the time taken by the Germans to effect a similar change. Aesthetic considerations ought not to weigh in the matter. In giving soldiers a uniform which strengthened their moral, one augmented their confidence and fighting capacity."[146]

Too little, too late.

Ironically, one of Messimy's last acts during his brief tenure as *Ministre de la Guerre* between June and August 1914 was, on 17th August 1914, to select the precise blue shade to be employed from several proposed by Roger de la Selle, the executive director of the *Établissements Balsan* of Chateauroux,. The new uniform was a wool blend of white (35%), dark blue (15%), and light blue (50%). The first new uniforms were delivered in September, just after the appalling losses of the Battle of the Frontiers, but it was 1915 before all the men were so clothed.[147] It was too late for tens of thousands of dead, though elegantly dressed, Frenchmen.

GIVEN THE APPALLING LOSSES ENDURED between 1914 and 1918 it is not at all surprising great thought was given post-war to the response to another war with Germany. As Robert Doughty points out in *Seeds of Disaster*, France suffered nearly 5 million casualties out of a total mobilised Army of 8.4 million, of which 16.4%, or 1.382 million, were dead. This latter figure represents 1 in 10 of the 'active' male population of France, i.e. of those eligible for some form of military service.

---

[i] Alexandre Millerand, 1859-1943, a socialist lawyer elected as a Deputy, 1885. Introduced industrial reforms as Minister of Commerce, 1899. Minister of Works, 1909, he used troops to suppress a 1910 railway workers' strike. *Ministre de la Guerre* under Briand and Viviani, 1914-5. Prime Minister of post-war and elected President, 1920. Escaped an anarchist's assassination attempt, 1922. Resigned, 1924.

The dead, and the far more numerous physically and psychologically damaged survivors, would have been the fathers of the next generation of Frenchmen who, aged between 21 and 25, would have fought in the next war. But, these potential fathers were dead, at the front and/or, perhaps, physically or psychologically incapable of siring children. Thus, France's population fell by 3 million between 1914 and 1918 as, because of a plummeting birth rate[i], the dead were not replaced.

French strategic and tactical thinking dramatically changed after 1918 but in response to technical and tactical changes which had taken place before August 1914 not those hinted at by the 'all arms' successes of the summer and autumn of 1918. Perhaps one of the reasons for this was that 1918, had it run for the full twelve months, would still have been the third most costly year of the war in terms of deaths (i.e. 269,000 if annualised, see table below). Despite the Allies military success, the power of the defence was still strong. Indeed, after the war, Culmann calculated that across all the combatant armies on the Western Front the offensive was nearly twice as expensive as the defensive. Consequently, the pre-war rhetoric concerning morale and *élan* was now replaced with *'puissance du feu'*, firepower. Thus, war was no longer a struggle between two opposing wills or competing moral forces but about who could deliver the greatest volume of fire on the enemy's troops because now, and too late for the millions of dead and maimed *Poilus* (and Tommies) it was accepted that *'le feu tue'* – fire kills. From a distance a statement of such blinding obviousness one can but wonder why it took soldiers and politicians from across Europe four years or more to realise it.

War years	Deaths	Average/month	Average/day
1914	301,000	60,200	1,974
1915	349,000	29,100	954
1916	252,000	21,000	688
1917	164,000	13,700	449[(1)]
1918	235,000	22,700	744
1914-18	1,301,000	21,200	695

Table 6 French military war deaths 1914-1918

[*Histoire militaire de la France*, tome III: Main report & *Service Historique*, Vincennes - 6N58]

[1] c. 30,000 French soldiers were killed in the opening ten days of the Nivelle offensive on the Chemin des Dames (16th-25th April 1917). The average monthly losses for the rest of 1917 were, therefore, c. 11,300.

The tactics and philosophy of 'the offensive' were widely blamed for these horrific numbers. It might be possible to suggest that only the appalling losses of the opening months of the war can be clearly blamed on this idea (e.g. 51,000 French dead in the week 19th-25th August 1914 including 21,000 dead on 22nd August alone, and 84,419 dead between the 9th and 31st August) and that, thereafter, the move into the tactical 'unknown' of trench warfare, the shortage of suitable artillery, the shortage of shells, etc., all contributed to the high casualty rates. Clearly, though, had senior officers anticipated the need for such things in response to the war in Manchuria, for example, then much might have been

---

[i] c. 120,000-200,000 French people died during the Spanish Flu pandemic of 1918-9.

different. Even more to the point, Joffre's and Haig's obsession with breakthrough tactics (resurrected by Nivelle in the spring of 1917) were an adaptation of *offensive à outrance* to the new paradigm of trench/siege warfare, which approach was maintained throughout the three middle years of the war by both armies.

The irony of the Great War was that France spent the next twenty years planning to re-fight it. The elaborate defences of the Maginot Line were championed by men scarred by experiences of the Western Front: Joffre and Pétain. The opinions of Emile Mayer (again, ahead of his time) and Charles de Gaulle that France, instead, should invest in the mobility of tanks, self-propelled artillery and aerial power were ignored and so, as in the 1870s with the *Système Séré de Rivières*, France resorted to a strategy of fixed defence and counterattack should Germany again invade. Even vigorous critics of the post-Franco-Prussian War policy of the 'offensive defence' such as *Gen. de Brigade* Frédéric Culmann supported a defensive stance *vis-à-vis* Germany. By 1930, he was head of the secretariat of the *Commission d'organisation des régions fortifiée* (CORF), the organisation which decided upon the construction of the Maginot Line and other fixed defences. In May 1940 they were hopelessly caught out by the speed, power and urgency of German *Blitzkrieg* tactics which avoided frontal attacks, attacked points of weakness, drove around the flanks, and attacked troops, communications, and supply lines from the air. 1940 was, as in 1870 and again in 1914, not at all what France expected in modern warfare, a fact which, sadly, is a poor reflection on those who led France's Armies in the years before all three disastrous wars.

ENDNOTES:

[1] Clausewitz, C von, trans. by Lt. Col. de Vatry, *Théorie de la Grande Guerre*, Libraire Militaire de L Baudouin et Cie, Paris 1886, Vol. 1, page vi.
[2] Clausewitz, C von, trans. by Howard, M, & Paret, P, *On War*, David Campbell Publishers Ltd., 1993, page 428.
[3] Clausewitz, *Vom Kriege*, page 434.
[4] Stoker D J, *Clausewitz: His Life and Work*, Oxford University Press, 2014.
[5] Wilkinson, S, *Killing No Murder: An Examination of Some New Theories of War*, *Army Quarterly*, v.14, 1927.
[6] Quoted in Foch, *Principles*, op. cit., page 34.
[7] Ibid., page 42.
[8] Ibid., page 44.
[9] *Anthologie des classiques militaires francais. Textes choisis et présentés par le Général L.-M. Chassin*, Charles-Lavauzelle & Cie, 1950, page 181. This refers to *The officer's manual: Napoleon's maxims of war* by Gen. Burnod, 1827.
[10] d'Andurain, J, *Verdun, ou le tournant de la doctrine française*, Revue Défense Nationale 2016/2 (No. 787), pages 37-45.
[11] Du Picq, Col. C J J J A, *Etudes sur les combat: Combat antique et moderne*, Hachette, 1880.
[12] Ibid.
[13] Laure, Gen. A M E, *L'Offensive française*, Berger-Levrault, 1912.
[14] Ibid.

[15] Montaigne, Lt. Col. J-B, *Vaincre - Esquisse d'une Doctrine de la Guerre basée sur la Connaissance de l'Homme et de la Morale*, Berger-Levrault, 1913
[16] Billard, Capt. breveté, *Éducation de l'infanterie*, Librarie Chapelot, 1913, page 1.
[17] Ibid., page 3.
[18] Ibid., page 4.
[19] Ibid.
[20] Ibid.
[21] Ibid., page 28.
[22] Ibid., page 30.
[23] Cardot, L, *Hérésies et apostasies militaires de notre temps*, Berger-Levrault, 1908, page 89.
[24] Cebro, Cdt,, *Les Conditions de L'offensive, Journal des sciences militaires*, March 1914, page 35.
[25] Maistre J-M de, *Considérations sur la France*, 1797, page 62.
[26] See Kahneman and Tversky's *Prospect Theory*, 1979 as explained in Kenneth Payne's *Prospect theory and the defence in Clausewitz's On War*, Paper presented to the annual meeting of the International Studies Association, 16th March 2016, Atlanta, Georgia.
[27] Langlois, Gen, H, *Enseignements de deux guerres récentes: Guerres Turco-russe et Anglo-Boer*, Lavauzelle, 1904, page 148.
[28] Gilbert, Capt. G, *La Guerre sud-africaine*, Berger-Levrault, 1902, page 502.
[29] Gras, Gen. Y, *Castelnau ou l'art de commander*, Denoël, 1990, page 143.
[30] Cardot, op. cit., p. 104.
[31] Ibid., page 452.
[32] Ibid., page 457.
[33] Dragomirov, Gen. M I, *Uchenie o voine Klauzevitsa - osnovnye polozheniia*, in the journal *Voennyi sbornik*.
[34] Persson, G, *The Russian Army 1859-1871*, PhD thesis, London School of Economics and Political Science, 1999, page 97.
[35] Dragomirov, *Manuel de préparation des troupes au combat, Préparation de la compagnie*, Librairie militaire de L. Baudoin et Cie, 1885, page 137.
[36] Altmayer, Capt. M-R, *Je Veux, Revue militaire générale*, tome XII, 1912, pages 417-446.
[37] Ibid., page 417.
[38] Foch, *Principles*, op. cit., page 33.
[39] Pierrefeu J de, *Plutarch Lied*. 1924, page 316 quoted in Loboda Y O, *French Military Strategy of the End of XIX – First Half of XX Centuries: between Descartes and Bergson?* University of North Carolina at Greensboro, 2016.
[40] Maistre, *The Evenings of St. Petersburg or Talks on the Temporal Government of Providence*, 1821, reprinted 2017.
[41] Foch, F, trans. by Bentley-Mott, T, *The Principles of War*, Henry Holt & Co., 1920, page 235.
[42] Maillard, Maj. L A G d, *Éléments de la Guerre*, Paris 1891.
[43] Ibid.
[44] See Baillot, Capt. R, *Le Général Maillard et les Origines de la Doctrine de Guerre Actuelle, Revue militaire Générale*, November 1923, page 852 onwards.
[45] Quoted in Négrier, Gen. F O, *L'évolution actuelle de la tactique, Revue des Deux Mondes*, 1904, livraison du 15 février, p. 855.
[46] Strachan, H, *European Armies and the Conduct of War*, Routledge, 1983, page 115.
[47] Quoted in Négrier, op. cit, page 856-7.
[48] Ibid.
[49] Goltz, Gen. C v d, writing in the *National Review*, November, 1903, quoted in Négrier, op. cit, pages 876-7.
[50] Kessler, Gen. C, *Tactique des Trois Armes*, Libraire Militaire R Chapelot, 1902, page 22.
[51] Ibid.
[52] Ibid., pages 22-3.
[53] Ibid., pages 23-4.
[54] Ibid., page 24.
[55] Ibid.

⁵⁶ Doughty, R. A, *Pyrrhic Victory: French Strategy and Operations in the Great War*, Harvard University Press, 2008, page 28.
⁵⁷ Strachan, op. cit., page 115.
⁵⁸ See Hermann, op. cit., pages 96-7.
⁵⁹ Foch, F, trans, Bentley Mott, Col T, *The Memoirs of Marshal Foch*, W Heinemann Ltd., 1931, page xxxii.
⁶⁰ Foch, F, trans. Belloc, H, *The Prnciples of War*, Holt & Co., 1920, page 284
⁶¹ Foch, F, trans. by Belloc, H, *Precepts & Judgements*, Chapman & Hall Ltd., 1919, page 3.
⁶² Earle, E M, *Maker of Modern Strategy*, Princeton, 1948, page 220.
⁶³ Gat, A, *The Development of Military Thought*, Clarendon Press, 1992, page 133.
⁶⁴ Foch, *Precepts*, op. cit., page 9.
⁶⁵ Foch, *Precepts*, op. cit., page 8.
⁶⁶ Tucker, S, & Zabecki, D, (ed.). *Germany at War: 400 Years of Military History*, 2014, page 634.
⁶⁷ Foch, *Principles*, op. cit., page 32.
⁶⁸ Foch, *Principles*, op. cit., page 341.
⁶⁹ Ibid., page 343.
⁷⁰ Ibid., page 286.
⁷¹ Ibid., page 287.
⁷² Seltzen, J A, *The Doctrine of the Offensive in the French Army on the Eve of World War One*, PhD dissertation, University of Chicago, 1972, page 83.
⁷³ Percin, Gen. A, *1914*, Albin Michel 1919.
⁷⁴ Percin, Gen. A, *Le massacre de notre Infanterie*, Albin Michel, 1921, pages 199-200
⁷⁵ Ibid., page 201.
⁷⁶ Ibid., page 203.
⁷⁷ Langlois, Gen H, preface to Grandmaison, Cdt. L, *Dressage de l'infanterie en vue du combat offensif*, Berger-Levrault, 1908, page viii.
⁷⁸ Baring, M, *With the Russians in Manchuria*, Methuen, 1905, page 132.
⁷⁹ Ibid., page 133.
⁸⁰ Montaigne, *Vaincre, Esquisse d'une doctrine de la guerre basée sur la connaissance de l'Homme et sur la Morale*, Berger-Levrault, 3 volumes, 1913, page 125-6.
⁸¹ Lone, Dr S, *The Japanese Military during the Russo-Japanese War, 1904-05: A Reconsideration of Command Politics and Public Images* in *Aspects of the Russo-Japanese War*, The Suntory Centre, LSE, London, 1998, page 18.
⁸² Ibid.
⁸³ Shimazu, N, *Japanese Society at War: Death, Memory and the Russo-Japanese War*, Cambridge University Press, 2009, Chapter 3.
⁸⁴ Ibid., page 98.
⁸⁵ Ibid., page 118.
⁸⁶ Sanders, C W, *No Other Law: The French Army and the Doctrine of the Offensive*, Rand, 1987, page 11.
⁸⁷ Liddell Hart, B, *Foch: The Man of Orleans*, Vol. 1, Penguin, 1931, page 74.
⁸⁸ Grandmaison, Cdt. L, *Dressage de l'infanterie*, op. cit., page 5.
⁸⁹ Ibid.
⁹⁰ Ministère de la Guerre, *Règlement sur la conduite des grandes unites*, 1913, page 5.
⁹¹ Ibid., page 4.
⁹² Ibid.
⁹³ Ibid., page 5.
⁹⁴ Ibid., para. 6, page 5.
⁹⁵ Bugnet, Cdt. C, *En écoutant le Maréchal Foch*, Grasset, 1929, page 60.
⁹⁶ *Règlement sur la conduite des grandes unites*, op. cit., page 6.
⁹⁷ Lucas, Lt. Col. P, trans. Kieffer, Maj. P V, *The Evolution of Tactical Ideas in France and Germany during the war of 1914-1918*, first published by Berger-Levrault, 1923, page 4.
⁹⁸ *Règlement sur la conduite des grandes unites*, op. cit., page 5.

[99] Ministère de la Guerre, *Le decret sur le Service des armées en campagne*. 2nd Decembre 1913, pages 13-16.
[100] Ibid.
[101] Ibid.
[102] Grouard, A, *France Allemagne. La guerre éventuelle*, Chapelot, 1913, pages 196-7.
[103] Lucas, op. cit., page 6.
[104] Ibid.
[105] Ibid.
[106] Ibid., page 8.
[107] Ibid., page 9.
[108] Ministère de la Guerre, Article 313, *Règlement de manœuvre d'infanterie*, 1914.
[109] Ibid., page 126.
[110] Smith, L V, op. cit., pages 30-1.
[111] Lucas, op. cit., pages 8-9.
[112] Ibid., page 10.
[113] Ibid., page 12.
[114] Ibid.
[115] Ibid., page 13.
[116] Ibid.
[117] Bloch, J de, *Selected Articles*, U.S. Army Command & General Staff College, 1993.
[118] Lanrezac, C., *Le plan de campagne français et le premier mois de la guerre (2 août-3 septembre 1914)*, Paris, Payot, 1920, page 285.
[119] Lavisse, É, *Sac au dos, études comparées de la tenue de campagne des fantassins des armées française et étrangères*, Paris, Hachette, 1902
[120] Lavisse, E, *La tenue de campagne de l'infanterie. Comment l'améliorer?*, Chapelot, Paris, 1913.
[121] http://www.151ril.com/content/gear/uniforms/6
[122] *The Times, The French Manoeuvres of 1906*, 17th September 1906, page 6.
[123] Ibid., page 44-45.
[124] Hermann, op. cit., pages 70-3.
[125] *The Times, The French Manoeuvres of 1906*, 17th September 1906, page 6.
[126] Lavisse, op. cit, page 46.
[127] *The Times, New Uniform for the French Army*, 29th October 1910, page 12.
[128] Ibid.
[129] Ibid.
[130] Ibid.
[131] Ibid., page 48.
[132] *The Times, The Longchamp Review*, 15th July 1912, page 5.
[133] H, *Les Uniformes de l'Armée, Criminelle Impuissance, La France Militaire*, 16th July 1912, page 1.
[134] Ibid.
[135] Ibid.
[136] Ibid.
[137] Ibid.
[138] *The Times, The Uniform of the French Army*, 9th November 1912, page 7.
[139] Clément-Grandcourt, Capt. A J E, *La Question de l'uniforme de l'infanterie, Revue militaire Générale*, June 1914, page 791.
[140] Ibid., page 792.
[141] Ibid.
[142] Ibid.
[143] Ibid.
[144] Ibid., page 793.
[145] Ibid., page 796.
[146] *The Times, French Army's New Uniform*, 10th July 1914, page 7.
[147] Descols, L, *La Genèse du drap Bleu Horizon*, Eguzon, Point d'Ancrage, 2014, page 40.

5. THE FRENCH ARTILLERY DEBATE

"Question one hundred officers of all ranks drawn at random from all arms: What is heavy artillery? What is it used for? How is it employed? To whom is it attached? How is it deployed? The odds are 100 to 1 on that you will not get an answer or that they will reply by asking the same questions in return."

'General D' in an article *Une doctrine pour l'artillerie lourde*
Revue d'artillerie, March 1914

FOR THE FRENCH, HEAVY ARTILLERY was only seen as useful during sieges. As, except for Metz and its defences, they did not anticipate besieging anywhere during the fighting to come, heavy artillery was, thus, irrelevant to their war planning. On the other hand, as France and Russia[i] had heavily fortified frontiers opposite Germany, the Germans invested seriously in such equipment. Whilst mainly for use in traditional sieges of forts, observers of their effective employment during the Russo-Japanese War suggested such heavy guns had an application in open battle[ii]. The French took a contrary view and went to war in 1914 lacking any howitzers with which to demolish the hurriedly extemporised German defences which appeared after their defeat on the Marne or long guns with which to reach into rear areas or defiladed positions.

Whilst the absence of a French siege train might be explained by their conviction the war would be fast moving and fluid, the lack of siege guns on certain parts of the front is peculiar. Surrounding the French-held cities of Verdun, Toul, Nancy, Épinal, and Belfort were numerous traditionally pentagonal forts usually built in two rings as part of Séré de Rivières' defensive programme. But it was not only the French who fortified their vulnerable eastern cities both before and after the Franco-Prussian War. The Germans did not sit back and observe this building programme. After the occupation of *Lothringen* and *Elsaß* in 1871, the German Army busily constructed a similar series of fortifications around three key cities: Metz, Straßburg (Strasbourg) and Diedenhofen (Thionville). Where possible

---

[i] Russia constructed three lines of fortifications from the Baltic through Poland, Belarus and the Ukraine during the 19th Century though several fortresses had been abandoned by 1914. Others were given expensive (and useless) upgrades. Defending Warsaw were the Modlin Fortress (Novogeorgievsk now Nowy Dwór Mazowiecki) on the *River Narew* some 50 kms north of the capital, and the Warsaw Citadel (Cytadela Warszawska). Novogeorgievsk was the subject of a major upgrade starting in 1912 but the Warsaw Citadel was deemed obsolete and was to have been demolished. To the south was the Ivangorod fortress at Dęblin which lay at the confluence of the *Vistula* and *Wieprz rivers* near Lublin. Further east was another line of defences running along the *Bug River* which included the massive fortress at Brest-Litovsk (Brestskaya krepost) in Brest, Belarus. The third line ran from modern day Latvia through Belarus and into the Ukraine, with major fortresses at Dinaburg (Daugavpils, Latvia), Babruysk (Babruysk, Belarus) and Kiev (also known as the Pechersk Fortress, Kyiv, Ukraine) although all of these had no great military significance by 1914.

[ii] The German Army knew heavy plunging fire was of use in sieges but was also annihilating against exposed field batteries if fighting a normal battle.

they utilised existing French works and, around Metz, four forts (*Festen*) begun in 1867 by the French were adapted and completed after 1871[i]. Another twelve '*Festen*' defending Metz were constructed between 1872 and 1913, thus eight '*Festen*' comprised the outer and eight the inner ring of city defences. In addition, there were c. 70 open battery positions, 65 '*Raum*' (protected bunkers)[ii], and, after 1900, six *Infantriewerk* or infantry strongpoints. Diedenhofen to the north was protected by three post-1871 '*Festen*': Feste *Ober-Gentringen*, Feste *Illingen* and Feste *Königsmackern*[iii], as well as numerous battery positions, etc.[1]

The defences between Metz and Diedenhofen were known as the *Moselstellung* and, in places, work was still ongoing on the outbreak of war. Its purpose, other than defending the two cities, was to help protect the left wing of the German *Schlieffen Plan* thrust through Belgium and Luxemburg to the north. Further to the south-east were two more fortified areas around the town of Mutzig and the city of Straßburg. These two positions were designed to block access to the Rhineland to French forces advancing north in *Elsaß*. Festungsgürtel *Straßburg* comprised a ring of fourteen forts built between 1874 and 1882[iv], as well as five *Zwischenwerken* (intermediate works) added in 1889-90 and designed and built from 1873 to 1884 under *Generalmajor* Hans Alexis von Biehler, the *Chef des Ingenieurkorps und der Pioniere* and *Generalinspektor der preußischen Festungen* (Chief of the Corps of Engineers and Pioneers and Inspector General of Prussian Fortresses).

The fortress at Mutzig, *Feste Kaiser Wilhelm II*, was an altogether different beast. Built to block the valley of the *River Bruche*, which runs eastwards out of the Vosges Mountains to enter the *Rhine* at Straßburg, it was started in 1893 and was made up of three separate forts covering an area of 254 hectares (630 acres). Underground lay rooms and tunnels extending over some 40,000 square metres (400,000 square feet). It was equipped with twenty-two turrets containing either 10 or 15-cm. howitzers as well as numerous smaller calibre guns. Although not complete in 1914 it was still one of the most formidable fortifications anywhere in Europe. Together, *Feste Kaiser Wilhelm II* and *Festungsgürtel Straßburg* made up a German defensive barrier known as the *Breuschstellung* (*Bruche River* position).

In any successful French attack in Alsace-Lorraine the reduction of these fortifications was a necessity, especially around Metz and Diedenhofen, but the means by which it might be achieved were grossly inadequate. In the original plan Gen. Ruffey's *IIIe Armée* was to hold the line opposite the *Moselstellung*. Its secondary role was to attack the defences of Metz, a task for which a siege train was essential. The heaviest guns available were a *groupe* of *155 CTR*, and one each

---

[i] Fort de St-Julien (later *Feste Manteuffel*), Fort de *Queuleu* (*Feste Goeben*), Fort de *Plappeville* (*Feste Alvensleben*) and the *Groupe Fortifié de St Quentin* (*Feste Friedrich-Karl*).
[ii] *I-Raum* for infantry, *A-Raum* for artillery and *M-Raum* for munitions.
[iii] Renamed *Fort de Guentrange*, *Fort d'Illange* and *Fort de Koenigsmacker* when occupied by the French post-war. Incorporated in the Maginot Line in the 1930s.
[iv] *Festungs Kirchbach, Bose* and *Blumenthal*, were on the right bank of the *Rhine* defending the eastern end of the bridges at Kehl. Two infantry works were built at Marlen and Kinzig between 1911 and 1913. By August 1914, additional defences around Straßburg consisted of: 9 *Infanterieräume*, 32 *Postenstände*, 9 *Artillerieräum*, 6 *Munitionsräum*, 4 *Artilleriestellungen* and 1 *Unterstand* (a shelter for a searchlight).

of *120 C* and *120 L*, all wholly inadequate to the task of reducing Metz's fortifications[i]. But this did not matter because the German field armies were the prime target of the *offensive à outrance*. Destroy these armies and the remaining German defences would collapse. Or so went French thinking.

Attitudes were different in Germany. The war correspondent of the *'Kolnische Zeitung'*, a First Lieutenant Ullrich, witnessed the effectiveness of high trajectory, heavy guns in Manchuria and not just in set-piece sieges:

> "The heavy artillery of the army has become, far more than the field artillery, an important weapon for the preparation of the infantry attack... (Japanese) Heavy artillery was the most destructive of material and far surpassed the accomplishments of the field artillery, even if the varying character of the targets for the two types is taken into consideration."[2]

Having absorbed the lessons of Plevna, Germany noted the effectiveness of Japanese 12, 15, and 28-cm howitzers at Port Arthur and Mukden. The defeated Gen. Kuropatkin acknowledged the 'powerful effect' of these high-angle weapons on trenches and covered positions,[3] and the Japanese and Russian Armies subsequently increased the number of battlefield howitzers within their armoury[ii].

After the Battle of Nanshan on 25th May 1904, a piece in a 1908 edition of the *Großer Generalstab's Vierteljahreshefte für Truppenführung und Heereskunde* commented[iii]:

> "The battle at Nanshan shows convincingly the uselessness of field guns against fortifications, how entrenched infantry can confidently await an attack even by greatly superior forces. It shows that without special means – high-angle fire and heavy guns – the most active and resilient troops will fail to take a fortified, energetically defended position by frontal attack."[4]

In consequence, the argument within the German Army about whether field and medium howitzers should accompany the advancing infantry was confirmed in favour of the high-angle, indirect fire weapon:

> "The necessity of introducing high-angle fire into the field artillery was brought about by the extensive use of field fortifications and cover of all sorts (in the Russo-Japanese War). In firing on targets on the same level (field) guns failed utterly. In the opinion that, in the future we have to deal with like conditions, the much-discussed howitzer question has been decided by us in the affirmative."[5]

Whilst France and Britain regarded heavy artillery as a hindrance to manoeuvre, the Germans regarded it as an enabler. With fortified zones in eastern France and Belgium and *'forts d'arrêt'* on key strategic routes, heavy and super-heavy howitzers would allow the Army to break into the open terrain Champagne and Flanders.

---

[i] Instead, *IIIe Armée* and neighbours, *Ier* and *IIe Armées*, were defeated in the third week of August. Within days, *IIIe Armée* was 70 kms to the west, trying to hold Verdun.
[ii] Japan: the *Type 38 12* & *15-cm* howitzers introduced 1905 & *Type 45 24-cm* howitzer 1912. Russia: 122-mm M1909 (*Krupp*) & M1910 (*Schneider*), and 152-mm M1909 (*Krupp*) & M1910 (*Schneider*) howitzers & 152-mm *Schneider* M1910 siege guns (built from 1912 at the *Putilov Plant* but not delivered until 1915).
[iii] *'The Quarterly Journal for Leadership and Military Studies'* issued from 1904 to 1914.

39 Krupp 15-cm schwere Feldhaubitze 1893

In the 1880s 12 and 15-cm howitzers were tested but proved barely mobile and, needing platforms, useful only during sieges. In 1888 the *General-Artillerie-Komitee* was asked to investigate what calibre might be needed to deal with infantry dug-in with reasonable head cover. After testing by the *Artillerie-Schiessschule* 12 and 13.5-cm guns were discounted either because the shell's explosive charge was inadequate (12-cm) or, to fit a suitable charge (a 40 Kg shell containing 10-12 Kgs of explosive), the shell was too long to be accurate (13.5-cm). In May 1891 a 15-cm calibre was decided upon and, later that year, *Krupp* was awarded a contract for its design and testing which was to weigh no more than 2,800 Kgs 'on the road' and have a range of at least 5,000 metres. The specification fell on the desk of *Krupp Direktor* Wilhelm Gross who, using nickel steel, provided a gun which came in 75 Kgs 'underweight'. The results which did not require a fixed platform, proved acceptably manoeuvrable. The *1893* model, though, lacked a recoil system and managed two rounds a minute with a maximum range of just 6,000 metres. Despite this, after witnessing live-firing by the *Garde-Fussartillerie-Regiment* during X. *Armeekorps'* manoeuvres near Münster in August 1900, it was endorsed by the *Kaiser*. Thus was born the *15-cm schwere Feldhaubitze 93*[i], so named officially in September 1900. The *Kaiser* subsequently announced that any commander who failed to use these guns would 'make himself guilty of neglect of duty'.[6]

Within a few years, a lighter, faster moving, but similar high-angle gun was deemed necessary for divisional attachment. There was a concern, however, that, based on experiments in the Saxon Army in 1889, a 12-cm howitzer was too heavy and too slow moving for it to be the ideal calibre for a howitzer attached to the infantry. In 1898, the fruits of discussions between *Krupp* and the *Artillerieprüfungskommission* commanded by the handily-named Bavarian

---

[i] 870 *15-cm SFH 93s* were available in 1914 and were deployed in the field when losses amongst more modern guns became heavy. They stayed in use until 1918.

Generalleutnant Otto Reinhold Michael Dietrich *Freiherr* Fuchs von Bimbach und Dornheim was the *10.5-cm lFH 98,* a fixed recoil, light field howitzer, 24 of which were attached to each of 23 *Armkeekorps,* i.e. 552 in total.

40 10.5-cm leichte Feldhaubitze 98/09

This light howitzer had a rate of fire of 6 rounds per minute but, with no recoil system, this was only achieved if one did not re-aim the gun after each round. This rate of fire was, therefore, purely 'notional'. Furthermore, for a relatively short-range gun, there was no protective shield for the crew. This made them vulnerable to both long-range rifle fire and the shrapnel of the *75* which had a similar range of c. 6,000 metres. Its main form of defence was, therefore, to fire from defiladed positions which the flat-firing *75* could not reach. There was, however, a widespread sense of disillusionment within the German Army with the performance of the *10.5-cm lFH 98* especially when compared to the *75.* Between 1902 and 1904, *Krupp* extensively re-designed the gun adding a recoil system, a new carriage and 200 Kgs in weight. Or, put another way, when modernised, the only element from the *98* variant in the *10.5-cm-leichte Feldhaubitze 98/09* was the barrel. The conversion of existing guns was completed in 1912 and the new *material* added to each *Armeekorps* increasing the total to 36. In total, 1,402 were available in 1914 of which 1,068 were with active or reserve units and the rest in general reserve. They were built by several companies until a new *lFH 16* was introduced.

There would always be circumstances when a heavier howitzer was needed to deal with defences the 16 Kg shell of the 10.5-cm could not destroy and a new *Krupp* 15-cm heavy howitzer replacing the *sFH 93*, the *schwere Feldhaubitze 1902* or *sFH 02,* was adopted by the Army in June 1903. This was an upgrade of a weapon the *Artillerie-Prüfungskommission* asked *Krupp* to develop in 1897, the requirements being a recoil system and 7,000+ metre range. The result was the inadequate *15-cm-Versuchshaubitze*[i] *99* or *V.H. 99.* Ordered in 1899, with 24 delivered in 1900, a total of 42 guns were built. They were tested against the old 15-cm material by *4.*

---

[i] Experimental howitzer.

Batterie, Fußartillerie-Regiment von Dieskau (Schlesisches) Nr.6 at the Thorn[i] firing range. Their range was 7,450 metres, but they were too heavy, 2,335 Kgs in battery, and had no traversing mechanism, i.e. the whole gun and carriage had to be moved to change target. In addition, the short recoil (340-mm) caused problems. The barrel was retained (still with a range of 7,450 metres), and various changes included in the new *sFH 1902*: a long hydro-spring recoil (lengthened to 650-mm.), weight reduced to 1,994 Kgs, and a 4° traverse. 416 were available in August 1914.[7] This new howitzer was further enhanced by the provision of a new 40.5 Kg shell, the *15-cm 04*, which contained 4.8 Kgs of explosive, had a delayed-action fuze, and was more effective against fortified positions with a degree of reinforced head cover.

If possible, the *Kaiser* was even more enthusiastic about his heavy artillery than before. Like Napoleon, he was devoted to the modern equivalent of Bonaparte's 'beautiful daughters'[ii]. On 8th August 1906, he attended the firing exercises on the *Schießplatz Wahn*[iii] and afterwards told his heavy gunners:

> "There is no doubt that the infantry and field artillery… today will breathe a sigh of relief when your heavy shells first smash between the enemy lines, and that the spirit to advance and a feeling of gratitude towards the heavy artillery will flow through them."[8]

Every year in the *Kaiserpreis-Schiessen* (The *Kaiser's* prize shoot, for those thinking it meant something else) his *15-cm sFH 02's* showed off their skills. Put in battery in c. 17 minutes they fired 100 rounds each at an enemy 'battery' 5,000 metres distant and a 'trench' 4,500 metres away. All excellent practice for the destruction of French infantry and *75s* in the war to come.

In 1907 the *Artillerie-Prüfungskommission* suggested an upgrade of the 15-cm howitzer was needed, with a shield to protect the crew, amongst other enhancements. At the same time, testing of an upgrade of the *10.5-cm lFH 98* was on the go and would, eventually result in the recoil-equipped *lFH 98/09*, and there were those within the army who argued that this, of itself, was the answer to any questions about improvements to the *15-cm*. There were those in the *Generalstab* who wished to see battlefield howitzers simplified into one, intermediate, *13.5-cm* weapon. Arguments continued within the German Army about the use of heavier howitzers in the field army but, with the *Kaiser's* support and their repeated appearance in the annual manoeuvres, their existence and tactical application was maintained and then confirmed when fighting broke out in August 1914.

In 1908 *Krupp* put forward a new *15-cm sFH* but, at 3,400 Kgs, it proved far too heavy and, instead, the *Artillerie-Prüfungskommission* and the *Generalinspekteure der Fussartillerie*, Gen. der artillerie Otton von Dulitz, called for a single piece howitzer weighting no more than 2,100 Kgs[iv]. In December 1908, the *Artillerie-*

---

[i] Now Toruń, Poland.
[ii] Napoleon described *Canon de 12 Gribeauval* cannon as his *'Belles Filles'*.
[iii] The Wahn shooting range, just south of what is now the *Flughafen* Köln/Bonn.
[iv] The French equivalent, the *155-mm CTR Rimailho*, was broken down into two sections for transportation purposes and weighed, in total, 5,250 Kgs. On 20th

Prüfungskommission, Krupp and the *Rheinische Metallwaren- und Maschinenfabrik* were asked to design such a gun suitable for field warfare with a range of 8,000 metres, a travelling weight of 2,700 Kgs, a 3-mm thick shield, an elevation of 45°, a minimum traverse of 2°, and an independent sighting device for indirect fire. In February 1909 test howitzers from *Krupp* and *Rheinmetall* were ordered and *Rheinmetall* was first in the field on 23rd February 1910. Its gun was generally within the parameters set. *Krupp* had a weight problem, however, and built four experimental models before one was chosen by the *Artillerie-Prüfungskommission* on 23rd January 1911 even though Professor Friedrich Heinrich Rausenberger, the designer of the *42-cm Kurze Marine-Kanone 14 („M-Gerät")* or *Dicke Bertha*, and, since July 1910, the *Direktor* of the *Dezernat für Artilleriematerial (Department for artillery material)* at *Krupp*, announced that they had started on a new design.

The *Artillerie-Prüfungskommission* started testing the two prototypes (its own having been already discounted) and, in general, the Ehrhardt/*Rheinmetall* material appeared superior. Both weighed in slightly over the 2,100 Kgs spec and both used a hydro-spring recoil rather than the hydro-pneumatic system preferred for lighter calibres[i]. They both had a range of c. 8,250 metres. Initially the advantage seemed to lie with the Ehrhardt design but given the late arrival of the *Krupp* models, the testing season was extended into the spring of 1912. In May a test battery was ordered from each manufacturer with *Krupp* building their No. 6 design and *Rheinmetall* their No. 2 design. In 1913, the guns were sent to the *Badisches Fußartillerie-Regiment Nr. 14* based at Straßurg for testing and then went to the autumn manoeuvres. Weight still seemed to be the issue and the *Krupp* was lighter by 45 Kgs – 2,160 Kgs in battery to 2,215 Kgs for the *Rheinmetall* gun. As a result, on 22nd November 1914 the *Krupp* gun was announced as the new *15-cm sFH 13*. But so desperate was *Krupp* for the order, they had cut corners to reduce weight and it was now found that their gun was unsuitable for mass production. Instead, the weapon became a joint venture between *Krupp* and *Rheinmetall* going into production in time for the first battery to be available in August 1914. By May 1915 there were 252 at the front to be added to the 840 upgraded *sFH 02* of which 416 were with active army units, 400 with reserve units and 24 in general reserve.[9]

These upgraded *sFH 02s* were adapted in 1913 with a longer barrel mounted on the existing carriage and became the *15 cm sFH 13/02*. These two models were, by common consent, amongst the most effective medium howitzers of the war. Known as the '5.9' and, because of the black smoke emitted when the shell exploded, as a 'Black Maria', 'Jack Johnson'[ii] or 'Coal Box', it was heartily disliked by British front-line troop. In addition to the 840 *sFH 13/02s*, some 3,409 *sFH 13s* were built by *Krupp* (2,676) and *Rheinmetall* (733) by war's end.

February 1913 it was decided to modify the *155-mm CTR* so it could be transported in a single piece. This work was not completed.

[i] This changed after war-time experience and multiple spring failures. Most new guns were fitted with a hydro-pneumatic recoil. A pneumatic recuperator prepared for the *sFH 02* was added from Spring 1915 [*Source*: Schirmer, op. cit., page 66].

[ii] Jack Johnson was a black heavyweight boxer from Texas who held the World Title between 1908 and 1915.

In the original specification for the *15-cm SFH* it was laid down that a key function of these guns was the destruction of enemy artillery as the shrapnel shells of the *77-mm FK 96 n/A* were thought to have little effect. This was tested on the firing range at Jüterbog, a garrison town 65 kms south-west of Berlin, in October 1910. Live firing showed both field and medium howitzers effective against enemy batteries though the *15-cm sFH* obtained more hits and covered a greater area.

41 15-cm-schwere Feldhaubitze 13 at Arras 1917
[Source: Bundesarchiv, Bild 183-S36048]

In the meantime, however, and as an indication that the German Army was not entirely devoted to a war of continuous manoeuvre, the 1906 *Feldbefestigungsvorschrift (Field Fortification Regulations)* now recommended defences protected by double layers of steel rail with earth and logs above them.[10] It was, therefore, determined that extensive tests of existing shells, such as the *15-cm 04*, needed to be conducted as well as those of 13.5 and other 15-cm shells and these took place at the Kummersdorf firing range. It was rapidly shown that the *15-cm 04* with its 4.8 Kgs of explosive would not penetrate the protection required by the 1906 Regulations. Then, as had been the case around 1890, trying to fit a larger charge of 6-7 Kgs into a 13.5-cm shell resulted in a shell too long to be accurate. The 15-cm calibre was, therefore, confirmed as the best size for the purposes required. This was not, however, the end of testing of howitzer shells against fortified positions as the process carried on from 1908 until 1910. The results were revealing. When a 15-cm shell with an explosive charge ranging from 5.5 to 8.2 Kgs was fired at one of six differently constructed concrete, reinforced concrete or gravel concrete fortifications ranging from 0.5 to 1.08 metres thick they had no effect. To penetrate such cover required a 21-cm *Mörser* shell. Beyond 1 metre and one was looking at a 30.5 or 42-cm *Mörser* shell. These tests then formed the basis on which the effectiveness of all high-angle guns were subsequently judged.[11]

By comparison, the pre-war French equivalent, the *Obusier de 155 mm CTR modèle 1904 (Rimailho)*, had a maximum range of 6,300 metres, weighed 3,200 Kgs against the *1913's* 2,250 Kgs, and, in August 1914, there were just 104 in the entire Army. In addition, there were 84 obsolete *Obusier de 120 mm C modèle 1890 Baquet* with a range of just 5,800 metres. Facing them, each German *Armeekorps* was equipped with 18 *15-cm sFHs* (Corps) and 36 *10.5-cm lFH* (Divisional).

In addition, experience in Manchuria and South Africa suggested long-range, flat-firing, guns with which to interdict the enemy's rear areas and supply lines were of use. Japan used the *Krupp*-designed *Type 38 10 cm cannon*, Russia invested in the *Schneider*-designed *107-mm gun M1910*, the British in the (12.8-cm) 60 pounder and the Germans in nearly 950 *10 cm Kanone 04* and later *13.5 cm Kanone 09*. These were guns with a range of 10,400 to 16,400 metres but, because of the fixation on the *75*, such guns again had little place on French battlefield. Opposed to this mass of long-range guns were eighty obsolete, slow-firing, difficult to install de Bange-era *canon de 120 mm L modèle 1878* with a range of less than 9,000 metres.

The French, the nation most dedicated to the offensive, ignored the growing evidence for the need for variety in gun types. Instead, they pinned their hopes on the pride of army – the *Canon de campagne de 75-mm modèle 1897*, *'notre glorieux 75'*, the *'soixante-quinze'* – the rapid-firing field gun whose introduction changed the rules of the battlefield and left other nations scrambling for upgrades and clever designs for new field guns. Thereafter, no significant artillery capability was added to the Army's arsenal and, as far as guns were concerned, it was the *75* or bust.

AS IRONY AND HISTORY SEEM FOREVER INTERTWINED, it is ironic that the key feature of the ground-breaking French *75*, its hydro-pneumatic long recoil, was, in its initial conception, a German invention. It is also ironic that the German heavy artillery adopted a heavy howitzer with a modern recoil system, the *V.H. 99*, before their brethren in the field artillery embraced the same technology. It seems the more technically/scientifically and more open-minded (more intelligent?) gunners of the heavy artillery in both Germany and Britain were well ahead of the game in this sphere of military development. Prussian and German army officers were as inherently conservative as those from other nations and conservatism resists change and innovation. Thus, in the 1850s, as William Armstrong was beginning to produce rifled cannon at *Elswick*, *Generalleutnant* Karl Friedrich Ludwig von Hahn, head of the Prussian *Generalinspektion der Artillerie* from 30th March 1854 to 19th December 1864, was stating that most Prussian artillery officers remained in favour of smooth bore cannon.[12]

In 1888, Konrad Haußner, a young *Krupp* engineer, invented a gun in which the carriage remained static while the barrel's recoil was absorbed and returned to the firing position using an oil/compressed air, long-recoil system. This invention, the Holy Grail of all artillery engineers, brought with it the prospect of a field gun firing without re-aiming at a rate ten times greater than existing guns. So transformative was such a weapon it was, if brought to fruition, almost the 1880's equivalent of the atomic bomb. It was the game changer France craved.

Haußner learnt his trade as an engineer and draftsman in the mechanical-technical department at the *Technischen Hochschule* in Munich, graduating in August 1883. He was first employed by *Dinglersche Maschinenfabrik* in Zweibrucken, a small town 30 kms east of Saarbrücken, where he mainly worked on steam engines[i]. He also took an interest in powered flight and airships. In 1884 he moved to *Maschinenfabrik L A Riedinger* in Augsburg, a major constructors of gas works across Germany and Europe[ii], where he worked on pumps and turbines before leaving in September 1885, having answered an advertisement in the *Zeitschrift deutscher Ingenieure* (*German Engineers' Magazine*) to join the *Artilleriekonstruktionsbureau* in Spandau, near Berlin. His work was not directly connected to the development of artillery but, whilst working there, he accompanied a colleague, *Artilleriehauptmann* Keppel, to the *Schiessplatz Kummersdorf* of the *ArtilleriePrufungskommission* (the firing range of the *Artillery Testing Commission*). There he saw, for the first time, a current model of a large calibre cannon being fired:

> "The enormous stress during the shot, which manifested itself in the gun jumping and running backwards considerably… and the lifting of the rear part of the barrel from the aiming pad made such an impression on me that I returned from that day obsessed with the shooting process and tried to find a solution to master this recoil."[13]

Money was always a problem for the young Haußner and his salary of 150 marks/month was not enough on which to live in Spandau next to the expensive capital, Berlin. He therefore returned to Augsburg, becoming an *Assistentenstelle fur Maschinenbau* (mechanical engineering assistant) at the *Koniglichen Industrieschule*. There he spent twenty hours a week teaching technical drawing in the workshops, and, in his spare time, he worked on the problem of recoil in artillery pieces. In early 1888 he answered two job advertisements, one again with *Artilleriekonstruktionsbureau* in Spandau, and the other as an assistant designer for artillery vehicles with *Friedrich Krupp* in Essen. He was offered the job at Spandau but was also invited for an interview in Essen and, clutching the acceptance letter from Spandau, was immediately employed to work in the artillery department of the huge enterprise. Starting work in May 1888, his first job was to work on reducing the weight of artillery limbers. He had, however, over the years refined his ideas for a long recoil system based on the barrel's recoil being resisted and then returned to position by compressed air. In November 1888 he submitted a 14-page memorandum to the head of the *Krupp Kannonressort* (*Gun Factory*), *Direktor* Wilhelm Gross, which included the details, drawings, and calculations of just such a gun. *Krupp*, by this time, was a comfortable, semi-monopolistic industrial leviathan populated by senior managers resistant to change. It enjoyed a symbiotic relationship with the government which helped maintain its huge profitability and, it seems, now and over the next fifteen years, it saw no reason to change its existing

---

[i] Until recently *Tadano Demag GmbH*, a subsidiary of a Japanese crane company. *Demag* filed for bankruptcy in December 2020 and now trades under the name: *Tadano*.

[ii] From 1888, August Riedinger, the son of company founder Ludwig August Riedinger, with his partners August von Parseval and Rudolf Hans Bartsch von Sigsfeld designed military balloons and dirigibles known as *Drachens*. Later, twenty-two *Parseval* airships were constructed between 1909 and 1919 and used in the war. The company is now part of *MAN SE*, *Maschinenfabrik Augsburg-Nürnberg*, the heavy vehicle and bus manufacturer.

practices and, more importantly, its existing artillery designs. After a few weeks' consideration, *Direktor* Gross rejected Haußner's idea out of hand[i], stating no such recoil system could possibly be built.

Firmly put in his place, but still believing in his idea, Haußner resigned and was employed as a foreman at the *Bayerisches Geschutzgießerei* (Bavarian artillery foundry) in Ingolstadt. He continued his work and, with the permission of the *Bayerisches Kriegsministerium*, was granted patent No. 61224, Class 72c, Group 9 on 29th April 1891. The design was also later patented in France. In this refined version it was clear Haußner had in mind a fluid/compressed air recoil system.

Having built a 17-mm version with the encouragement of the authorities, he entered into an agreement with Hermann August Jacques Gruson of Magdeburg whose company, *Grusonwerk AG Buckau*[ii], had a background in railways and was a minor player in arms manufacture. Going back to the authorities, they were invited to build two test models. Unfortunately for Haußner, and the German Army, later in 1891 Gruson, then aged 70, retired from the board and it was promptly taken over by *Krupp* in 1893 and re-named *Friedrich Krupp AG Grusonwerk*. The test models had been constructed, however, and the *Krupp* hierarchy could not avoid sending them for testing by the *Artillerie-Prufungskommission*. These tests were conducted in March 1894 at Meppen near the Dutch border under such conditions that an appendix in Haußner's 1928 book *Das Feldgeschütz mit langem Rohrrücklauf: Geschichte meiner Erfindung* (*The long recoil field gun: history of my invention*) suggests the tests were rigged, perhaps because the idea was too radical for the *Krupp* hierarchy.[14] The tests were disastrous and a senior officer and 'expert' on field artillery present, one *Oberst* von Reichenau[iii], is said to have demanded 'away with the monstrosity!'.[15] According to *Generalleutnant* Hermann Schirmer in 1937:

> "The unusual appearance of the new guns undoubtedly played a role in the decision by the military authorities. The trained military eye was still too used to the image of the previous field guns, and was captivated by their simple construction and operation… The process shows how difficult it is to gain access to new ideas and how disadvantageous it is to make a negative judgment after the first unsuccessful attempts."[16]

---

[i] Wilhelm Gross, director of the *Kannonressort* since 1888, was replaced in 1895, partly, according to Ralf Stremmel in *Friedrich Alfred Krupp: ein Unternehmer im Kaiserreich*, because he was 'not sufficiently committed to advancing the technical development of rapid-fire cannons' [*Source*: Stremmel, R: *Friedrich Alfred Krupp: Handeln und Selbstverständnis eines Unternehmers* in *Friedrich Alfred Krupp: ein Unternehmer im Kaiserreich*, ed. Epkenhans, M, & Stremmel, R, published by C H Beck, 2010, pages 33-4].

[ii] Gruson founded *Maschinen-Fabrik und Schiffsbauwerkstatt H. Gruson* in 1855, specialising in chilled cast iron for railways, etc. He moved into arms and military equipment, becoming *Grusonwerk AG Buckau* in 1886. A 10 km firing range was constructed at Tangerhütte, 100 kms west of Berlin, which, in the German Democratic Republic after 1945, was part of *Schwermaschinenbau-Kombinat Ernst Thälmann* (*SKET*). Thälmann was a Communist Party (*KPD*) leader shot in Buchenwald in 1944.

[iii] Author of *Studie über die kriegsmässige Ausbildung der Feldartillerie* (*Studies on war training of field artillery*), Berlin 1895.

Krupp dropped the project, returned the patent inherited from *Gruson* and, instead, went on to foist on the German Army the inadequate *77-mm Feldkanone 96* which, within seven years, was subject to a massive upgrade using Haußner's recoil system which cost the government 100 million marks in addition to the 140 million marks paid out for the original contract[i].

42 77-mm Feld Kanone 96

It was not, however, the end of Haußner's military odyssey as there was an upstart competitor of *Krupp's* ready to exploit errors of judgement committed by the somewhat arthritic giant of Essen. This irritant resided just 35 kms to the south in Dusseldorf – Heinrich Ehrhardt and his company: *Rheinische Metallwaaren- und Maschinenfabrik AG*, or *Rheinmetall AG* for short. Ehrhardt was a self-made man, a brilliant engineer and self-publicist *par excellence* (he would later, and falsely, claim Haußner's invention as his own[ii]). He was also keen to rub *Krupp's* nose in the dirt whenever possible and now, just such an opportunity arose. Although he had never previously built an artillery piece, he employed Haußner[iii] and built an improved version of his gun tested on his small shooting range near Zella St. Blasii[iv]. This was tested by the *Artillerie-Prüfungskommission* in the Spring of 1897, or at about the time the French *75* was nearing final testing and approval for mass construction. By all accounts the new gun performed well, but France and Britain were not the only nations infested by short-sighted military conservatives and the observers from Berlin failed to grasp the gun's importance. With a decision about a new field gun imminent, the power and influence of *Krupp* was overwhelming. The *77-mm FK 96* was selected and, within months, rendered obsolete by the *75*.

---

[i] At least €1.5 billion in current prices, probably several multiples more.
[ii] In a book entitled *Hammerschläge. 70 Jahre deutscher Arbeiter und Erfinder* (*Hammer Blows: 70 year a Geran worker and inventor*), K F Koehler Verlag, Leipzig, 1922.
[iii] They fell out. Haußner moved to Argentina being replaced by Carl Völler, who became chief engineer, designer, and manager at *Rheinmetall*, Düsseldorf. Völler died in an accident in 1916 at the company firing range in Unterlüß, Celle, Lower Saxony.
[iv] Merged in 1919 with Mehlis to form Zella-Mehlis, Thuringia.

Ehrhardt was not too dismayed and continued to develop Haußner-based guns. His breakthrough came when the Director-General of Ordnance, Gen. Sir Henry Brackenbury, on behalf of the British government, bought 108 *Rheinmetall* 76.2-mm QF field guns for use in South Africa in 1901. Then Norway, after testing nine different models, ordered 138 *Ehrhardt 7.5-cm Model 1901* field guns[i] and suddenly *Krupp* was faced with the embarrassment of having tested twice and rejected twice the type of gun which was now the industry standard worldwide. A legal attempt to claim Haußner's original patents as their own – after all, had he not he been a *Krupp* employee back in 1888 and again in 1893? – failed in the German courts but it was left to the German taxpayer to pick up the tab when the programme of upgrading the *Krupp FK 96* started in 1904.

IN 1886, INVESTIGATIONS STARTED in France into a new range of *matériels de campagne à tir rapide* with a focus on 57-mm quick-firing guns for the Army. *Etablissements Hotchkiss*, at Saint-Denis, had developed 37, 47 and 57-mm guns for the Navy and they, along with the *Fonderie de Bourges* and the *Atelier de Construction de Puteaux* (*APX*), were invited to look at similar weapons for use in the field.

In 1887, the *Directeur de l'Artillerie* at the *Ministère de la guerre*, Gen. Charles Philippe Antoine Mathieu[ii], authorised the investigation of a new generation of field guns for the French Army to replace the aging de Bange 80 and 90-mm guns from 1877/8. Though the 90-mm gun had a range of 7,000 metres and was accurate once laid, its rate of fire was just two rounds per minute or, as was pointed out in an appendix in Konrad Haußner's book, a rate of fire half that of Gustavus Adolphus's Swedish 4-pounder smoothbore cannon in the Thirty Years' War.[17]

On 23rd August Mathieu sent a note to the Directors at *Bourges*, *Puteaux* and the *Atelier de Tarbes* requiring they make these investigations a priority so as 'not to be left behind by foreigners'.[18] Not wishing to circumscribe their research or their imaginations, Mathieu wrote:

"The greatest latitude is left to the officers who will deal with this question, either for the determination of the calibre, or for the layout of the system (barrel and mounting)."[19]

What was required, he went on, was maximum power, minimum recoil and minimum weight allied to a high rate of fire and good manoeuvrability. They were given to 31st December 1888 to come up with their ideas.

---

[i] Known in the Norwegian Army as the *7.5 cm feltkanon m/01*. They were used in the German invasion of 1940 and some went to Finland in their war against Russia. Captured models were integrated into the German Army.

[ii] Born in Vouziers, *département des Ardennes*, on 2nd November 1828, the son of Antoine Mathieu and Charlotte Joséphine Roulez. *Ecole Polytechnique*, 1848. *Direction d'artillerie de Strasbourg*, 1858. Italian campaign, 1859. *Dépôt central*, 1861. *Bureau du matériel, Direction de l'Artillerie*, 1866. Set up the *Atelier de Puteaux*. *Chef d'escadron*, Head, *Bureau du matériel, Direction de l'Artillerie*, 1873, staying until 1881. Col., *27e Régiment d'artillerie de campagne*, Douai. *Général de brigade*, 1883. Commanded the artillery, *6e Corps*. *Directeur de l'Artillerie*, 1887. *Général de Division*. He died on 11th January 1912 [*Source: Base Leonore*].

Work was already ongoing involving guns of 52 and 57-mms and conducted by *Etablissements Hotchkiss*; by Capts. Baquet and Sainte-Claire Deville at the *Fonderie de Bourges*; and Capt. Joseph Jules Ducros[i] at the *Atelier de Puteaux*, and all came up with prototypes over the next four years. The Director at Tarbes, however, decided not to be involved in the process.

Capt. Charles Étienne Sainte-Claire Deville[ii] developed at Bourges experimental 52 and 57-mm guns employing advances in technology to the full: smokeless powder[iii], a combined shell and brass-encased propellant charge, a short hydro-pneumatic recoil system designed by Capt., later *Général de division*, Louis Henri Auguste Baquet[iv], and a Nordenfelt-designed rotating screw breech.

In the meantime, interest developed in larger, longer-range 75-mm field guns and, by the end of 1891, two models were being developed, one by Baquet at *Bourges* and the other, under Ducros, at *Puteaux*. At the beginning of 1892, Gen. Mathieu concluded that a decision must be made on one or other gun and a special committee was formed to oversee the process. The remit of the committee was to produce a field gun which (amongst various more technical items):

Was common to Corps and Divisional artillery and to the cavalry;
Weighed no more than 1,000 Kgs deployed and 1,700 Kgs when transported;
Had a steel tube, screw breech, and rear spade; and
Could fire shrapnel and high explosive shells of 7 to 7.5 Kgs with a muzzle velocity of 600 metres/second.

---

[i] Capt. Joseph Jules Ducros was born in Saint-Satur, *département du Cher*, on 29th July 1853. The son of Joseph Ducros, *Ingénieur des Ponts-et-Chaussées*, and Françoise Éléonore Desmonts. *Ecole Polytechnique*, 1873. *Ecole d'application de l'artillerie et du Gènie*, 1875. *22e Régiment d l'artillerie*, 1877. *Atelier de construction de Puteaux*, 1883. Tonkin, 1884-5. Attached, *16e bataillon d'artillerie de forteresse* before returning to Puteaux in 1888, serving there until 1897. *Chef d'escadron*, *11e* then *29e Régiment d l'artillerie*, 1897. He died in a riding accident on 18th March 1901 in Saïgon, French Indochina [*Source: Base Leonore*].

[ii] *Général de division* Charles Étienne Sainte-Claire Deville was born in Paris on 3rd May, 1857, the youngest of four sons of Étienne Henri Sainte-Claire Deville, a professor at the *Ecole Normale Supérieure*, and Jeanne Françoise Cécile Girod de l'Ain, the daughter of Gen. Jean-Marie-Félix, *4e baron* Girod de l'Ain. *École Polytechnique*, 1874. Tunisia 1881-3. *Fonderie de Bourges*, 1886. *2e bataillon d'artillerie de forteresse* and *1er Régiment d'artillerie*, 1887-90. *Section technique de l'artillerie des etudes sur less bouches à feu*, 1891. *Chef d'escadron* and *Sous directeur de l'atelier de Construction de Puteaux*, 1897. *Inspecteur de matériel de 75*, 1900. Lt. Col., *39e Régiment d'artillerie*, 1903. *Directeur de l'atelier de construction de Lyon*, 1906. Col., 1908, then *Section technique*. *Général de brigade*, 1912. President, *Commission des Poudres de Guerre*, Versailles. *Inspecteur des Etudes et Expériences techniques de l'Artillerie*. As President, *Commission des poudres*, he tried to solve the 1914 French shell crisis. *Général de division*, 1915. *Inspecteur général du matériel aux Armées*. Placed large calibre guns onto tracked *chassis* to create the *canon automoteur Saint-Chamond 1917*, forerunner of modern self-propelled guns. He died on 29th March, 1944. [*Source: Base Leonore*].

[iii] Paul Marie Eugène Vieille invented smokeless nitrocellulose-based powder in 1884 at the *Laboratoire Central des Poudres et Salpetres* in Paris.

[iv] This system was also used on the *Canon de 120 C* and *155 C modèle 1890 Baquet*, the first guns to utilise a hydro-pneumatic recoil system.

This latter requirement was important as it was closely linked to the way the French expected, and wanted, to fight the next war, i.e. rapid, offensive manoeuvres, high rates of fire at not especially long ranges, and not involving in any significant way, trench or 'position' war. Thus, the French, and later the British, preferred the speed and agility of their *material* on the battlefield rather than flexible tactical positioning through indirect fire and defilade.

The importance of high muzzle velocity to French tactics is explained in Col. Bethell's 1910 book on field artillery *'Modern Guns and Gunnery'*:

"MUZZLE VELOCITY.

The object of a high muzzle velocity is not to increase the range of the gun... it is to decrease the angle of descent. The steeper the angle of descent, the less the distance which the shrapnel bullets will cover before they are stopped by striking the ground. Modern infantry tactics, and the Q.F. artillery tactics which have been devised to meet them, require the power of covering a large area with bullets without sacrificing intensity of effect; and this is most economically achieved by increasing the effective depth of the shrapnel cone without reducing the number of bullets or the angle of opening. The French gun is a good example of a successful combination of angle of opening and angle of descent. It is reported to have a M.V. of 1740 ft/sec. with a 15.95 lb. shell. This, with an angle of opening of 16½°, gives at 3000 yards, a cone 330 yards deep with a maximum width of 95 yards, containing some 250 (out of 300) effective bullets of 38 to the lb."[20]

In other words, they wanted a rapid-fire gun capable of smothering either large masses of enemy infantry or field artillery batteries in the open (or not seriously concealed/protected) with huge volumes of shrapnel in a very short time. As shrapnel was regarded as the anti-personnel weapon *par excellence* then a high muzzle velocity gave both a deep and wide spread of the shrapnel bullets because of the resulting shallow angle of the descent of the shell when the bursting charge behind the balls was detonated[i]. And, with artillery personnel unprotected by shields at this time, and guns likely to be deployed either in the open or in only partially covered positions, these volumes of shrapnel would not only disable large numbers of infantry but devastate the gun crews too.

The weight of the equipment and its manoeuvrability was also important and the current assessment was Ducros' gun was too heavy and Baquet's mobile but under-powered. Nevertheless, if these issues were addressed then complete batteries would be built of one, or both, models, for further rigorous testing. Another difference was that Baquet's had a recoil system, the short hydro-pneumatic recoil system he developed for the *120 C,* whilst Ducros' did not. Baquet's came in two variants:

No. 1, first built in 1888, was light, 1,050 Kgs, but only fired a 6.5 Kg shell at an initial speed of 500 metres/second; and

---

[i] At 4,000 metres, 75-mm shrapnel had an angle of descent of 10° 36', the *Krupp 77-mm FK n/A* one of 13° 31'. The cone along which the shrapnel balls of the 75-mm spread was longer and wider than that of the 77-mm [*Source*: Bethell, op. cit, page 364].

No. 2, started in 1889, managed a muzzle velocity of, first, 575 metres/second and then 630.

Version No. 1, tested in late 1890, proved to have serious defects but No. 2, tested early in 1892, provided accurate fire and a very flat trajectory. Meanwhile, Ducros' gun was also tested and it, too, had some serious shortcomings and was 100 Kg 'overweight'. It could, however, fire a 7.8 Kg shell with a muzzle velocity of 600 metres/second. For a time, it was the preferred model pending testing in the field and, in 1893, a new, lighter version, 980 Kgs, was built, able to fire a 7 Kg shells with a muzzle velocity of the required 600 metres/second.

But now, another idea was to upset the artillery apple cart.

On 22nd February 1892, Haußner's two patents (nos. 21/1.618 and 216.2/10 of 1891) were examined by the *Président du Comité d'artillerie*, Gen. Ernest Louis Charles Ducos de La Hitte[i], the son of the *vicomte* de La Hitte who designed the French artillery so unsuccessful in the Franco-Prussian War. La Hitte was going to send the details of the patents to the Directors of the *Fonderie de Bourges* and the *Atelier de Puteaux* in Paris but was pre-empted by Gen. Mathieu. Mathieu asked the Directors of the two establishments if a similar system might be designed which did not infringe Haußner's patent, although it appears Haußner's rights to the French patents had lapsed as he had not kept up payments of the necessary fees.[21] The Director at *Bourges* demurred but, after three days' consideration, Lt. Col. Joseph-Albert Deport[ii], the director at *Puteaux*, gave a verbal undertaking to study the project.[22] By June 1892, Deport's initial thoughts were with La Hitte and Matthieu. La Hitte, not knowing that *Bourges* had passed on the project, wanted them to develop a prototype with a maximum weight of 1,000 to 1,100 Kgs even if this meant reducing the weight of shell from 7.5 Kgs to 7 Kg and the muzzle velocity from 600 metres/second to 570. Mathieu, meanwhile, ordered Deport to produce a long recoil 75-mm cannon while testing the recoil on existing field guns.

---

[i] Born in Paris on 8th November 1828, the son of Gen. Jean Ernest Ducos, *vicomte* de La Hitte, and Jane Cécilia Cotter, daughter of Rogerson Cotter, MP for Charleville, County Cork, in the Irish House of Commons 1783-1800. *Ecole Polytechnique*, 1848. Crimea, 1854. ADC to his father, then *Président du Comité d'artillerie*, 1856, ADC to Gen. Le Boeuf, Italy, 1859. *Military attaché*, Berlin, 1860-1. *Garde Impériale*, 1863. Lt. Col., 1868, *Sous-Chef, Etat-Major General de l'artillerie de l'Armée du Rhin*, surrendering at Metz, October 1870. *Général de brigade* commanding artillery, *11e Corps*, 1877. *Général de Division* and *Inspecteur Général*, 1885. Member *Comité technique d'artillerie* 1888, *Président*, 1889. Member, *Conseil supérieur de la guerre*. Died, 27th October 1904 [*Source: Base Leonore*].
[ii] Lt. Col. Joseph-Albert Deport was born in 1846 in Saint-Loup-sur-Semouse, *département de la Haute-Saône*, the son of Romain Deport and Augustine Cornibert. *École Polytechnique*, 1866. *École d'application de l'artillerie et de Génie*, Metz, 1868. Wounded, Franco-Prussian War. *8e regiment d'artillerie*. Adjutant, Director at Bourges. *Atelier de construction d'artillerie de Tarbes*, 1877. Director, *Atelier de construction de Puteaux*, 1888. Resigned, 1894. Director, *Compagnie des forges de Châtillon et Commentry*, Montluçon. Châtillon-sur-Seine, *département de la Côte-d'Or*. In 1897 the company took over the *Société metallurgique de Champigneulles et Liverdun* and was renamed *Compagnie des forges de Châtillon, Commentry et Neuves-Maisons*. Neuves Maisons is in the *département de Meurthe-et-Moselle* and its seven blast furnaces were lost in August 1914. He died in 1926.

Thus, in 1892, three, and then four, designs came under consideration:

75 A, an adapted short-recoil Baquet design (*No. 1 bis*);
75 B, a second variant of Ducros' gun (*No. 2*);
75 C, the Deport model incorporating Haußner's long recoil; and
75 D, another long recoil version designed by Maj. Locard.

On 8th February 1893, Deport was ordered to build a prototype *75 C* as soon as possible whilst new versions of Ducros' and Baquet's guns were to built in case Deport's efforts came to nought. Deport's experiments were, however, subject to the greatest secrecy as they held out the hope of providing the French Army with a field gun so superior in rate of fire and accuracy that it would render all other field guns instantly obsolete. Furthermore, it was known the Germans were working on a 77-mm field gun replacement for the aging *9 cm Kanone C/73* and they did not wish to alert them to the huge potential the Deport design offered.

On 22nd November 1893, Deport's gun was ready for testing. This took place at the *fortresse de Mont Valérien*, just south of *Puteaux*, initially in the presence of Gen. Julien Loizillon, briefly *Ministre de la guerre* (11th January-25th November 1893), and then Gen. Auguste Mercier, his successor (3rd December 1893 to 15th January 1895). By March 1894, the new *Président du Comité d'artillerie*, Gen. Michel Arsène Victor Ladvocat[i], was able to send to the Minister results of tests conducted on the *A, B* and *C* designs. In addition, it was decided to test all three designs first at Bourges and then Calais. There were, however, problems with Baquet's gun, the *75 A*, and this was not available. Locard's *75 D* version was also far behind in development and took no part. In December the results were made available to Gen. Ladvocat and, since 1893, the *Directeur de l'Artillerie,* Gen. Denis Francois Felix Deloye[ii]. It reinforced Deloye's view Deport's gun was what was needed to the extent that he had already investigated the manufacture of many of the key components.

But every silver lining has a cloud and the cloud was that Deport expected a promotion and, when not forthcoming, he resigned and joined the private sector becoming a far better paid director of the *Société des forges de Châtillon et Commentry*. He was replaced as Director by Maj. Paul Emile Gustave Ply who had an excellent

---

[i] Born 18th August 1830, in Le Havre, *département de la Seine-Inférieure*, the son of Placide Léon Ladvocat and Louise Eglé Clementine le Cellier. *Ecole Polytechnique*, 1850. Wounded in the Crimea, 1855. Capt., 1859, *Direction du Havre* and *Ecole de Pyrotechnie*, then *Commssion d'experience* at Châlons. In 1870, he commanded a battery of *mitrailleuses*. Promoted Lt. Col., 1871. Colonel, 1878, *Directeur d'artillerie*, Douai. *Général de brigade*, 1883 and *Directeur d'artillerie* to 1887. *Général de division*, 1888. Commander, Place de Paris, 1891. *Président du Comité d'artillerie*, 1893. He died on 1st February 1903.

[ii] Deloye was born on 30th September 1837 in Sérignan-du-Comtat, *département de Vaucluse*, the son of Alexis François Esprit Pascal Deloye and Marie Louise Josephine Coste. *Ecole Polytechnique*, 1856. Etat-Major Général de *l'artillerie*, 1870. Bureau du matériel, 1873, becoming its head in 1884. *Général de brigade*, 1892, commanding the artillery, *7e Corps. Général de division* and *Directeur de l'Artillerie, Ministère de la Guerre,* 1893. Member, *Comité d'artillerie*, 1900, and *Président*, 1901. He died on 26th June 1909.

reputation as an expert in the efficient manufacture of weapons[i]. His place on the *75 C* project was taken on 12th December 1894 by Capt. Sainte-Claire Deville who moved from *Bourges* to *Puteaux* where he was joined on 5th January 1895 by Capt. François Léon Émile Rimailho[ii].

The test reports on the *75 C* from *Bourges* were a revelation. Though, at 530 metres/second, the muzzle velocity was shy of the 600 metres/second demanded, the gun proved remarkably stable and, using the combined shell/propellant, produced a rate of fire of an extraordinary 28 rounds per minute under test conditions, though it was accepted that, in real life, this was unlikely to be achieved if for no other reason than the exhaustion of the gun crew. There was, however, an issue: the long recoil leaked oil, even if the tank which contained it allowed for the firing of 200 rounds before needing a refill. There were other relatively minor issues, one being its weight which, though only 994 Kgs once deployed, was 1,800 Kgs when transported. The *Commisssion de Bourges* was able to say, however that:

> "Lieutenant-Colonel Deport has proved that it is possible to organize rapid-fire and powerful field equipment. This achieved result marks an important stage in the progress of the Artillery."

Ducros' *75 B*, on the other hand, though having a muzzle velocity of 600 metres/second, was a more rudimentary gun capable of firing only 4 aimed rounds per minute. These conclusions were then endorsed by the *Commission de Calais*.

The special committee examined the results in February 1895 and reviewed the data on the Baquet gun, the *75 A*. This gun was dismissed as not being worthwhile to test and, anyway, was only an 'accelerated fire' gun, as was the *75 B* (and, later, the new German *77-mm FK 96*). It only remained to build test models of the simple, robust 'accelerated fire' *75 B* and the more complex, delicate, rapid and accurate firing *75 C* before a decision was made, as there were still concerns about the long recoil and the 530 metres/second muzzle velocity of the *75 C*.

Changes required to the *75 C* led to the development of *C1* and *C2* variants. The *C1* was essentially the basic *75 C* with minor modifications. It weighed 1,100 Kgs deployed and 1,850 Kgs transported, had no shield, carried 36 rounds in the limber and had caissons which required the removal of the cartridges from the top

---

[i] His *Etude sur l'organisation du Service technique dans les Manufactures d'armes*, published in 1888 in the *Revue d'artillerie*, was still regarded as 'authoritative' in 1935 [*Source*: Challeat, op. cit., footnote, page 345].

[ii] Lt. Col. François Léon Emile Rimailho was born in Paris on 2nd March 1864, the son of Jean Marie Rimailho and Marie Ernestine Léontine Crolley. *École Polytechnique*, 1884. *École d'application de l'artillerie et de Génie*, 1886. *31e regiment d'artillerie*, 1888. *Atelier de Construction de Puteaux*, 1895. *16e bataillon d'artillerie à pied*. *Inspecteur permanente de fabrication de l'artillerie*, 1904. Commanded a battery of his *155 C TR*, *13e régiment d'artillerie*, Vincennes, 1906-8. Took early retirement 1913 and followed Deport to be a director of *Compagnie des forges de Châtillon*. Technical director, *Saint-Chamond* being involved in artillery development and the 75-mm armed *Saint Chamond* tank of 1917. Post-war he was administrator of the *Compagnie Générale de construction et d'entretien du matériel de chemin de fer (CGCEM)* and President of the IT-based *Compagnie des Machines Bull*, part of *Atos SE*, whose subsidiary *Atos Healthcare* is widely loathed in the UK. He died in 1954.

which slowed down the rate of fire. The *C2* was lighter to provide a 5-mm thick chrome/steel shield to protect the gun crew. There were 18 rounds in the limber but the caisson was designed to be reversed and tipped to present an armoured *'derrière'* to the enemy. The cartridges were also available horizontally rather than vertically thus speeding loading and maintaining a rapid rate of fire. In addition, Sainte-Claire Deville had improved the seals in the hydro-pneumatic recoil to reduce the loss of fluid and to increase the internal air pressure.

1895 was a year of rigorous testing of the new guns. A battery of six of the *C1* variant was put into production in May 1894 and it was the first to be sent on a round of experiments and exercises: to the *Commission de Bourges*, to the annual manoeuvres at Châlons, to the *15e Brigade d'artillerie* at Nîmes, and then back to *Bourges* at the end of the year. The designs of each variant were continually tweaked by Sainte-Claire Deville and, by mid-summer, he was suggesting that the very high rates of fire and accuracy achieved by the guns meant that, with no loss of relative firepower, it might be possible to reduce the current six-gun batteries to just four whilst 'facing an adversary equipped with slow-firing weapons of the current type'. The *Commission de Bourges* was asked to investigate such a change. The arithmetic was simple. In a minute a battery of four *75 Cs* could fire 60 to 80 shells whilst a battery of six *77-mm FK 96s* might manage only 48 and those less accurately.

The tests at the manoeuvres at Châlons proved so satisfactory that the *Président du Comité d'artillerie*, Gen. Ladvocat[i], proposed that three complete groups of *75 Cs* be built, i.e. 54 guns, in order test the issues surrounding the mass manufacture of the guns. Indeed, so content were the authorities with the progress of the *75 C*, and also being aware of the imminent launch of the new German field gun, that the *Ministre de la Guerre*, Gen. Émile Zurlinden[ii] (who had been on the committee looking into 75-mm guns in 1891-2) approved the process on 24th August 1895.

At the beginning of 1896, the existing battery of *C1* guns was sent to the *8e Brigade d'artillerie* for further testing; a new battery of *C1s* went to the *18e Brigade* at Tarbes; and a battery of *C2s* was nearing completion with a section of two guns being despatched to *Bourges* for preliminary investigation. It was then planned that all three batteries would attend manoeuvres at Châlons in June along with a battery of Ducros' *75 B*, if ready, and other batteries of older 80 and 90-mm field guns.

The major issue still affecting the *75 C* was fluid leakage from the hydro-pneumatic recoil, the details of which were still so secret that even Ladvocat had not seen the plans. Work on an improved version of the system, the *Modèle II* or *'frein à tige pleine'* (*full rod brake*), started at *Puteaux* on 20th February 1896 and a working version was sent to the *Commission de Bourges* on 6th August where it was tested for a month.

With the Germans having launched the 'accelerated fire' *77-mm FK 96* Zurlinden had asked the committee in April 1896 whether the most recent version of the *75*, the *C2* with its shield and other changes, was likely to be the best choice for a new field gun. The committee's response was to say:

---

[i] Gen. Paul Arthur Nismes succeeded Ladvocat as the new *Président du Comité d'artillerie* in late August 1895.
[ii] Previously the commandant at the *Ecole Polytechnique*.

1. the rate of fire of the *75 C* far exceeded expectations set in 1892;
2. the muzzle velocity of 530 m/s was less than hoped but still acceptable;
3. its weight was greater than planned but, again, acceptable;
4. the caisson was too heavy but that the *Atelier de Puteaux* was developing one nearly 200 Kgs (10%) lighter; and
5. the hydro-pneumatic recoil had generally worked well in 1895 though some issues were revealed with greater use towards the end of the year but that the new design seemed to solve these problems.

In summary, the committee advised Zurlinden that:

"The experiments carried out up to now allow us to hope that we are in the presence of equipment capable of fulfilling all the conditions of good war service and constituting, at the same time, in relation to the artillery in service in foreign armies, a most considerable progress.

But these experiments are not yet complete enough for us to be able to come to a definite conclusion.

While recognizing the importance attached to a prompt decision, an incomplete and premature solution must not risk placing us in a state of inferiority *vis-à-vis* other powers which, as soon as our decision taken, will endeavour to imitate us and to perfect what we have adopted.

It is therefore essential to continue and hasten the completion of the commissioning experiments.

In the meantime, it seems possible to prepare the way for large-scale construction, to provide the facilities that will be required for the manufacture of the equipment, especially that of the metal casings.

Finally, the barrel has so far given rise to no criticism. The elements (tube and jacket) which compose it can therefore be considered as finalised; it would be possible to put a number of them on order."[23]

By May 1896 the newest variant of the Ducros gun, the *75 B3*, was ready for testing and Gen. Paul Arthur Nismes[i] now *Président du Comité d'artillerie* sent it to Bourges, along with the *C2* and the *90-mm* used for testing against existing hardware. The following month, following tests at Calais, Nismes selected a pale blue-grey paint rather than an olive green for the new guns.

Zurlinden enquired again in July and asked whether elements of the *C2* variant were ready for production. On 27th October the committee was able to report on the results of the comparative testing of the three guns at Bourges – *75 B3*, *75 C2* and the *90-mm* – as well as the continued testing of *C1* variants by the *8e* and *18e Brigades*. The results from Bourges were conclusive:

---

[i] Nismes was born 30th July, 1834, in Barbaste, *département de Lot-et-Garonne*, the son of Pierre Nismes and Elizabeth Delclou. He entered the *Ecole Polytechnique* 1854. Italian campaign 1859. Capt. 1863, he served in Mexico 1865-7. Franco-Prussian War 1870-1. 1871, *Direction de l'artillerie, Ministerie de la Guerre*. Lt. Col., 1876 and Col., 1880. Commanded, *6e régiment d'artillerie*. *Général de brigade*, 1880, and *Directeur d'artillerie*. Commanded *2e brigade d'occupation du Tonkin et Annam*, 1887-8. Commanded *19e Brigade d'artillerie*, Vincennes, 1888. *Général de Division*, 1890, and member *Comité technique d'artillerie*. *Président du Comité d'artillerie* 1895 to 1899. He died 27th May 1912.

"A battery of *75 C* with 4 or 6 guns will put out of action in c. 3 minutes a battery of 6 guns of *90* or *75 B*, and suffer losses about three times less.
A battery of *75 C*, with 4 or 6 pieces, will fight with advantage against a group of two batteries of *80* or *90*; in about three and a half minutes, it will put out of action half of their strength and will lose only a third of its own. These conclusions had been obtained by means of double-action fire, with specially organized knockdown silhouettes. The superiority of the *75 C* therefore constitutes a real increase in power, subject to examining up to what point we are sure of remedying the defects still reported."[24]

In addition, heavy testing of the *Modèle II* recoil system revealed significant improvements. The gun was able to fire more than 200 rounds before fluid was needed to top-up the reserve tank and this process was considerably easier with the new design. The committee was thus able to assure Zurlinden the *75 C* constituted a significant increase in firepower, and that production of its components was already, or would soon be, in hand. Throughout 1897 testing continued with the recoil system proving reliable. Tests were also conducted on various shell types to be used and batteries were sent out to various artillery brigades and regiments for familiarisation and final tests. The *Commission de Poitiers* was given the task of developing regulations for the use of the guns.

On 28th March 1898, the *Ministre de la Guerre*, now Gen. Jean-Baptiste Billot, told Gen. Nismes that the *75 C2* model was, from now on, the *matériel de 75 modèle 1897*. In addition, now that the full capabilities of the *75* relative to the *77-mm FK 96* were known, it was decided to reduce the battery size from six to four guns with no loss, indeed a net gain, in firepower. Thus, after five years' work, the *75* emerged, initially led by Lt. Col. Deport[i] and then by Capts. Sainte-Claire Deville and Emile Rimailho, the two officers who finally resolved the hydraulic fluid leakage problem which had beset Haußner's and the initial French designs.

In France, an initial order for 600 *75 C2* guns was placed with state-owned factories. The tubes were built at the arsenals at Bourges and Tarbes, the carriages at Tarbes and Tulle, the ammunition caissons at Saint-Étienne and Châtellerault, and the recoil system at Puteaux and Saint-Étienne. The entire operation was overseen by two *présidents* of the *Comité technique de l'Artillerie*: Gen. Nismes until 1st August 1899, and Gen. Basile Gras[ii], who occupied the role until 1st January 1901.

---

[i] Lt. Col. Joseph-Albert Deport was born in 1846 in Saint-Loup-sur-Semouse, *département de la Haute-Saône*, the son of Romain Deport and Augustine Cornibert. *École Polytechnique*, 1866. *École d'application de l'artillerie et de Génie*, Metz, 1868. Wounded, Franco-Prussian War. *8e regiment d'artillerie*. Adjutant, Director at Bourges. *Atelier de construction d'artillerie de Tarbes*, 1877. Director, *Atelier de construction de Puteaux*, 1888. Resigned, 1894. Director, *Compagnie des forges de Châtillon et Commentry*, Montluçon. Châtillon-sur-Seine, *département de la Côte-d'Or*. In 1897 the company took over the *Société metallurgique de Champigneulles et Liverdun* and was renamed *Compagnie des forges de Châtillon, Commentry et Neuves-Maisons*. Neuves Maisons is in the *département de Meurthe-et-Moselle* and its seven blast furnaces were lost in August 1914. He died in 1926.

[ii] Gras (1836-1901) designed the *Gras* rifle which replaced the *Chassepot* in 1874, and was also involved in the design of the *Lebel* rifle.

43 Général de division Louis Henri Auguste Baquet

44 Capt. Joseph Jules Ducros

45 Lt. Col. François Léon Emile Rimailho

46 Général de division Charles Étienne Sainte-Claire Deville

47 Lt. Col. Joseph-Albert Deport

48 Col. Louis Jean François Filloux

It was unveiled to the French public in the Bastille Day military display along the *Champs-Élysées* on 14th July 1899. Most French generals believed the *75* the best gun in the world and, moreover, the *only* gun they would need when scores were settled with Germany. France sat smugly on a dwindling artillery advantage until confronted by harsh truths about the technical/tactical development of German artillery as from 1904 by which time it was nearly too late to re-dress the balance.

At 1,140 Kgs the *75* was lightweight and quick to manoeuvre. With its groundbreaking hydro-pneumatic recoil system it could fire, but for brief periods, 15-20 rounds a minute with surprising accuracy and with no need to re-aim. A 7.24 Kg shrapnel shell could be despatched over 6,800 metres (4¼ miles). The French looked at the shield-less, slower and, essentially, direct-firing *77-mm FK 96* and believed their *75s*, concealed on gentle reverse slopes, would be able to swamp both the German guns and infantry with an unanswerable hail of shrapnel and high explosive delivered at a rate of fire more than twice that of the German field gun. Even the upgraded *77-mm FK 96/04 (n/A)* was not seen as much of a threat.

But, with a maximum elevation of 18° and with a high initial muzzle velocity of 530 metres/second making it extremely flat firing, it could not fire *over* anything of any size. As current French artillery tactics dictated targets needed to be seen by an officer observer positioned close to, or at, the gun[i], this was not a problem. Furthermore, even experienced French artillery officers such as Gen. Alexandre Percin (see page 260), who set up the initial tests for the tactical application of the gun believed, right up to the start of the war, the *75's* manoeuvrability would allow it to switch positions rapidly in order to take under fire defiladed German guns before those guns could locate the position of the *75* batteries. His utter devotion to the weapon proved miserably misplaced, not that he would ever admit it.

49 Canon de Campagne de 75-mm modèle 1897

---

[i] The French did not use field telephones for observers when the war began despite their use by the Serbs in the First Balkan War. Commanders, observers, and guns were kept close together. The officer was provided with a ladder to gain a better view.

Other, heavier, weapons existed: obsolete field guns or heavy fortress and coastal protection guns. After the catastrophe of 1870-1, when Prussian *Krupp* steel breech-loading guns wreaked such havoc amongst French artillery and infantry, great efforts were made over the next fifteen years to bring French artillery up to date. In 1875, Lt. Col. Henri Périer de Lahitolle (later director of the *établissements militaires de Bourges*), the *inspecteur des études à l'École Polytechnique*, designed the first steel, screw breech cannon, the *Canon de campagne de 95-mm modèle 1875 de Lahitolle*[i]. Then came the *'Barrière de Bange'* designed and constructed between 1877 and 1885 the guns of which ranged from 80-mm field guns to 270-mm siege *mortiers*.

INSTIGATORS OF THE POST-FRANCO-PRUSSIAN WAR ARTILLERY REVIVAL

50 Charles Timothée Maximilien Valérand Ragon de Bange

51 Lt. Col. Henry-Jules-Frédéric-Antoine Périer de Lahitolle

The appropriately named Charles Timothée Maximilien Valérand Ragon de Bange was born in 1833 in the tiny village of Balignicourt, *département de l'Aube*[ii]. The son of two other mouthfuls: Maximilien Antoine Barnabé Ragon de Bange and Bathilde Charlotte Louise Edmée de Fadate de Saint-Georges, he attended the *École Polytechnique* in 1853 and the *École de application* in 1855 before joining the *8e régiment d'artillerie* in 1856. He fought in the Battles of Palestro and Solferino in 1859 during the Second Italian War of Independence against the Austrians. His involvement in artillery design began in 1860, first at the Brest arsenal, then at the *Forges du Centre* at Nevers, then, in 1864, with the *Manufacture d'armes de Châtellerault*. After two-years as adjutant of the *9e régiment d'artillerie* he joined the *Atelier de Précision du dépôt central de l'artillerie* in Paris, serving in the defence of the capital against the Prussians. In 1871 he designed the first effective obturator system[iii] for breech-loading artillery, one later adopted by the British and US Navies.

---

[i] Upgraded in 1888 this obsolete weapon, without a recoil system, went into service in the autumn of 1914. Over 200 were still in use at the end of the war. Some tubes survived until 1940 being used in parts of the Maginot Line.

[ii] He died a few days before the outbreak of war, on 9th July 1914.

[iii] An obturator seals the breech when an propellant charge ignites. Now known as an *O-Ring*, it prevents the blow back of hot gasses and maintains the power of the propellant charge by ensuring the expanding gas stays in the tube to drive the shell.

In 1873 he was appointed Director of the *Atelier de Précision* and, over the next twelve years, the last three as Director General of the *Société Anonyme des Anciens Etablissements Cail*, he designed a range of guns from 80-mm to 270-mm, all of which were still in use in one form or another throughout the coming world war.[25]

The guns in the de Bange range were[i]:

Canon de campagne de 80-mm Modèle 1877
Canon de campagne de 90-mm Mle 1877
Canon de 155 Long Mle 1877
Canon de montagne de 80-mm Mle 1878
Canon de 120 Long Mle 1878
Mortier de 220-mm Mle 1880
Canon de 155 Court Mle 1881
Canon de 240 de côte Mle 1884
Mortier de 270-mm Mle 1885

Although the tubes of these guns were well made, they lacked recoil systems (and thus slow firing), had limited range, and were unsuited to the war envisaged by most French officers in 1914. It is significant that 120-mm or larger guns were described as *'de siège et de place'* (for siege purposes and fixed fortifications), i.e. not battlefield guns. These guns were adapted, and others became available in small numbers during the 1890s, but the stellar *75* in 1897 was, for the French military, the game changing moment in their struggle for superiority over the Germans.

As war seemed increasingly inevitable, there were some concerned that, with the *75*, they were putting all their eggs into one small, if beautifully designed, basket. Military doctrine, however, was clear: in battle, speed of manoeuvre and *élan* in attack trumped firepower. Infantry were Kings of the battlefield and the role of the gunner was to support them as they advanced. It was enshrined in the *Règlement sur le service des armées en campagne*, the equivalent of the British *Field Service Regulations*, issued on 2nd December 1913. Paragraphs 96 and 97 stated the position:

> "Only the offensive breaks the enemy's will. Once begun, combat is pushed to the end; success depends more on vigorous and tenacious execution than on the perfection of the plan. Infantry is the principal arm. It conquers and holds the terrain. It pushes the enemy from his strong points. It acts by fire and by movement; only the advance, pushed to hand-to-hand fighting, is decisive and irresistible, although generally fire must prepare the way."[26]

This absolute certainty in the virtue of 'the offensive' is excellently expounded by a French officer, Capt. Edmond Dosse[ii], in an article entitled *'Tactical Studies'* in

---

[i] *'Canon de campagne'* = flat-firing field gun; *'Canon long'* = flat-firing medium range field gun; *'Mortier'* = high-angle heavy howitzer; *'Canon court'* = medium field howitzer; and *'Canon de côte'* = long-range fixed position gun for coastal protection or frontier forts.

[ii] Capt. Edmond Louis Dosse originally *6e bataillon de chasseurs à pied*. A staff officer with *20e Corps* he was a professor at the *École Militaire d'Artillerie et du Génie* and, in 1912, at the newly formed *École Militaire d'Artillerie* at Fontainebleau. On the outbreak of war, he joined the staff of *IIe Armée*. He served in Salonika after 1917. Later military governor of Lyon and commander *14e Région*. He died in 1949.

the January-March 1914 edition of the US Military magazine the *Field Artillery Journal*. Under the heading of *'General Principles – Moral Doctrine'* this fundamental principle of French military doctrine is explained:

> "The purpose of war is to destroy the enemy, materially and morally. The only means of attaining this result is to attack from the start with the resolution to push forward at any cost, no matter what losses may result. To proceed in any other manner is sure to result in a certain and inevitable check, and would be against common sense and the French spirit. To act on the defensive is only the role of a weak force on the battlefield. It should only be resorted to by a definite order or through absolute necessity. In these cases, the force which takes the defensive should continue to be aggressive and attack at every opportunity."[27]

These views were reproduced and reinforced in the *Règlement de manœuvre d'infanterie* of 20th April 1914. The role of the 75 batteries, and that of the German 77-mm batteries, was to support the infantry come what may. Their function, expressed by an anonymous German writer in a *Field Artillery Journal* article about artillery in the Russo-Japanese War of 1904-5, was that the men of the field artillery should 'sacrifice yourself if you must and save yourself if you can'.[28] Close support meant direct fire from positions obvious to, and well within the range, of the enemy's rifle fire, let alone artillery. Casualties, if necessary heavy, were worthwhile if the success of the infantry was assured.

52 Gen. Frédéric Georges Herr

ONE ARTILLERY OFFICER TO DISAGREE with the idea the 75 was all France required was Frédéric Georges Herr, the son of Jacques Georges Herr, a medical doctor, and Marguerite Emylida Cabanet. Born in what was then the French town of Neuf-Brisach[i] near Colmar in Alsace in 1855, Herr was a graduate of the *École Polytechnique* and *École d'application*. He served with various artillery units before joining the *9e Bataillon d'artillerie de fortresse* at Besançon in 1883. In the same year, he married Anne Caroline Hélène Peugeot, part of the family of the now well-

---

[i] Neuf-Brisach is one of the best examples of a 17th Century Vauban fortification and listed by UNESCO. It was part of greater Germany after the Franco-Prussian War.

known car manufacturer. He, like Joffre, was involved in the campaign in Madagascar under Gen. Gallieni. In 1896 he was on the staff of *7e Corps* and then, briefly, oversaw the artillery at Besançon. After four years as a *chef d'escadron* in the *32e régiment d'artillerie* based in Orléans he worked on the staff of the *3e Corps*, being promoted Lt. Col. in 1902. He then took command of the *32e régiment d'artillerie* spending some time in charge of the artillery at Lorient. He was promoted *Général de Brigade* on 23rd March 1911 and made commandant of the artillery of *6e Corps*.[29] Given command of *12e Division* in September 1914, he went on to command *6e* and *2e Corps* and, on 9th August 1915, he took charge of the *Région fortifiée de Verdun (RfV)* which he commanded until 26th February 1916, five days after the German assault was launched. Then, exhausted both by the work to prepare the salient and by the enormous pressure once the fighting started, he was relieved[i].

His work was not done and his successor at Verdun, Pétain, set up a new organisation to study the Army's use of artillery. At the beginning of June 1916, Herr was appointed *Président* of the *Centre d'études d'artillerie aux Armées* based at Vitry-le-Francois[ii]. Initially serving Pétain's *Groupe d'Armées du Centre (GAC)*, within three weeks it was taken over by *GQG* and was opened to officers of every Army Group. Its purpose was not to teach theory and practice but to absorb and disseminate best practice and innovation from wherever it came.

Herr was, therefore, an experienced artilleryman, but his selection as *Président* of the *Centre d'études* was as much because of his pre-war thinking about artillery methods and material, thinking totally at odds with the prevailing French doctrine of the power of manoeuvre, direct fire and the essential nature of the advance, as it was his war-time experience. His battles with pre-war orthodoxy left him somewhat exposed but, since then and in almost every respect, he had been proved correct in his damning analysis of the existing shortcomings and urgent needs of the artillery arm of the French Army and of its tactics.

Pre-war, Herr was a witness to the French Army's annual exercises in which a mass of blue-jacketed and red-trousered infantrymen triumphantly took their objective at the point of the bayonet to cries of *'en avant!'*:

> "In peace-time exercises, though the advance could be taught, the effects of fire could not be replicated. Our grand manoeuvres, the high point of annual training, consisted of a few days of marching, ending in a great military spectacle where dense infantry formations with drums beating and flags flying, advanced with superb disdain of the enemy's fire on a position to be taken. In the critiques, discussions were only about things which could be seen: for the attacker, the direction of attack, the routes followed, and the pace of the final assault; for the defender, the counterattack with the bayonet; its timing and vigour. The cannon and machine gun, only effective when stationary, were almost forgotten… Few thought of commenting on the method of artillery and machine gun employment and

---

[i] Appointed *Inspecteur général de l'instruction de l'Artillerie*, 2nd October 1917. He retired, aged 64, on 24th October 1919 and died in Paris on 27th October 1932. He is buried in Pont-de-Roide on the *River Doubs*, the birthplace of several of his wife's family.
[ii] It carried on functioning after the war having moved to the now liberated Metz.

of the influence of these in the final success. It was from this conception of combat that our doctrines of artillery employment were drawn."[30]

Such absurdity drew this scathing comment in *The Times* on the French 1913 manoeuvres (and predicted the conduct of the Battle of the Frontiers) thus:

"Today the French Army manoeuvres came to a spectacular end with furious bayonet charges, heavy artillery duels, and the usual impossible attack upon strongly held positions."[31]

The key point for Herr was that senior French commanders believed artillery was only truly effective against human targets in the open. Were they sheltered, i.e. in a trench, then it was the role of the infantry to attack to force the enemy into the open, a view still expressed by Douglas Haig in the spring of 1916 when responding to Sir Henry Rawlinson's first and cautiously conservative 'bite and hold' plan for the Somme offensive[i].[32]

Indeed, this limited view of the application of artillery was enshrined in the French version of *Field Service Regulations*. With interpretations of the causes of death and injury in recent wars indicating the majority were caused by rifle bullets rather than artillery shells, it was but a small step before artillery was relegated to a supporting and secondary role[ii]. Artillery was thought to be useless against sheltered troops or artillery. Artillery duels were, therefore, pointless. Preparing the way for the infantry was, equally, a waste of time. This view was, in fact, a

---

[i] Haig's diary, 5th April 1916: "His intention is merely to take the enemy's first and second system of trenches and 'kill Germans'. He looks upon the gaining of three or four kilometres more or less of ground as immaterial. I think we can do better than this by aiming at getting as large a combined force of French and British as possible across the *Somme* and fighting the enemy in the open!"

[ii] Herr gives figures for the causes of casualties in the Franco-Prussian and Russo-Japanese Wars. In the former, 90% of Prussian and 70% of French casualties were caused by rifle bullets. 25% of French casualties were caused by artillery but just 5% of Prussian. French casualties are estimated at 280,000, with c. 70,000 caused by Prussian artillery [Nolte, Frédérick (1884). *L'Europe militaire et diplomatique au dix-neuvième siècle, 1815–1884*. E. Plon, Nourrit et ce. p. 527]. German casualties are estimated at 117,000 of which c. 6,000 were killed/wounded by French artillery [Michael Howard: *The Franco–Prussian War: the German invasion of France, 1870–1871*. New York City: Macmillan, 1962, p. 453]. The war was won by the Prussians who, coincidentally perhaps, inflicted by far the higher number of artillery casualties.

In the Russo-Japanese War, according to the *Vierteljohshefte für Truppenfuhring und Heereskunde*, 1908, Vol. 1, quoted in Lt. W Neuffer, *3. Bayerische Feldartillerie Regt.*, *What lessons in the employment of field artillery should be deduced from the experiences of the russo-japanese war?* (*Artilleristische Monatshefts*. No. 35, November, 1909, and *Field Artillery Journal*, April-June 1911, page 202) figures for bullet-caused casualties were c. 80%. Artillery caused 14% of Russian casualties and 8.5% of Japanese. The highest recorded casualties (28%) from artillery were inflicted on the *1st Battalion, 4th Japanese Guards Regt.*, Battle of the Shaho (5th-17th October 1904). These figures are disputed. A Dr Schafer and two Russian doctors in a 1906 edition of the *Archiv für Klinische Chirurgie*, estimated at least 22% of Russian casualties were caused by artillery. Coincidentally or not, the Army which inflicted the larger number of casualties using artillery won both wars.

change from that of the 1890s, a time when the artillery duel prior to the infantry attack was a prescribed part of the preparation for battle. But now, with the *75* expected to dominate the battlefield, this was no longer the case. Furthermore, the *75* was expected to be so dominant no other form of artillery was required.

The introduction to the 1910 *Field Artillery Regulations* made it clear how the role of the artillery had changed since the *75* became available:

> "It has been assumed until recently that the first mission of the field artillery in combat was to gain superiority of fire over the enemy field artillery and that then its rôle consisted of preparing the infantry attacks by bombarding the objectives assigned to these attacks before the infantry came into action. To-day it is recognized that the essential rôle of the field artillery is to support the infantry attack by destroying everything which can oppose these attacks; seeking superiority over the enemy field artillery has no other object than to insure its ability to act with maximum power against the infantry objectives … as for the artillery preparation of attacks, this cannot be made independent of the infantry action, because artillery fire has only limited effect against a sheltered adversary, and, to lead this adversary to uncover himself, it is necessary to attack with infantry… *Artillery does not prepare the attacks, it supports them.*"[33]

And, when a French General or a military Regulation talked about 'field artillery', or indeed any type of artillery, this meant just one weapon. Post-war, Herr quoted a telling sentence from an Official military document:

> "The 75-mm. gun suffices for all the missions which can be entrusted to artillery in field warfare."[34]

Such was the emphasis on field artillery that it is telling that *all* the artillery graduates of 1913 from the *École polytechnique*, the training school for gunners and engineers, went into the *artillerie de campagne*.[35]

The next, inevitable step in this single-minded thinking was to question the need for long-range or high angle guns. If artillery was to support infantry its effective range need be no more than the range of the best binoculars and telescopes available, i.e. c. 5,000 metres. Technically, the *75's* high explosive shell at maximum elevation had a range of 8,000 metres but, according to Herr, 'the carriage and the sighting mechanisms were conceived and constructed for a maximum range of 6,500 metres' and shrapnel fuzes for a distance of 5,500 metres[i]. In practice, according to Herr, *75s* were not to be used much beyond 4,000 metres as it was not envisaged fighting would extend beyond these ranges.[36]

Limiting the use of artillery and the natures needed, allied to the quasi-mystical adherence to the power of the infantry and the offensive, resulted in tactical theories which help explain the catastrophic casualties the French suffered in the first six weeks of the war. Herr summed this theory up thus:

> "The war will be a short one with quick changes of position in which manoeuvre will play the principal rôle; it will be an open warfare.

---

[i] Test results for the *75* and American 3 in. Model 1905 gun in the *Field Artillery Journal*, gave a maximum range of a shrapnel shell for the *75* as 6,014 yards/5,500 metres.

The battle is essentially an infantry fight, in which victory will be on the side of the greater number of battalions; the army must be an army of effectives (i.e. infantry) and not an army of *matériel* (i.e. artillery).

Artillery will be a dependent arm with one mission: to support infantry attacks. For this it will need only a limited range and its main quality must be rapidity of fire in order to be susceptible of action on the numerous and fleeting objectives which will be put up by the infantry.

Obstacles met in open warfare will not be very important; light artillery will have sufficient power to overcome them.

The *matériel* must be light, flexible and easy to manoeuvre, so as to be able to follow the infantry which is to be supported as closely as possible. The usefulness of heavy artillery will not be felt very often; it will, of course, be wise to have some batteries, but these batteries must be comparatively light in order to have sufficient mobility and this fact precludes the use of large calibres and powerful *matériel*.

As a battery of four 75-mm. guns has absolute efficacy on a front of 200 metres, the concentration of fire of several batteries is not necessary. It would be unwise to be overloaded with too much artillery. The number of batteries which large units should have in their ranks may be calculated according to the normal front of engagement contemplated for the unit."[37]

Interestingly, German tactical theories did not diverge too much but they invested more time understanding the power of the machine gun and the application of indirect fire as provided by the *10.5-cm leichte Feldhaubitze* and other high angle and long-range guns. But more on that later.

The consequences of this absolute faith in the *75* can be seen in the artillery immediately available to the French Field Army in August 1914[i]:

3,680 *Canons de 75 Mle 1897* [ii]
128 *Canons de montagne de 65 Mle 1906*
120 *Canons de 120 L Mle 1878 de Bange*
84 *Canons de 120 C Mle 1890 Baquet*
104 *Canons de 155 C Mle 1904 TR Rimailho*
24 *Mortiers de 220 mm modèle 1880*

Of these guns, the *75s*, the 65-mm *Canons de montagne* and the *155 Cs* were quick-firing at a maximum of 15, 15 and 6 rounds per minute respectively. The *Canons de 120 C Mle 1890 Baquet* might manage two rounds per minute and the others one round per minute if severely pushed but not for any extended period.

---

[i] According to *Les Canons de la Victoire 1914-1919'*, Touzin & Vauvillier, *Histoires et Collections*, Paris, 2006. Herr gives different figures: 3,840 *75s*, 120 *65s*, 308 'heavy guns for mobile units' (i.e. the *120 L, 120 C* and *155 C* above) and 380 various de Bange guns. Baquet confirms the figures for 120-mm and above [Baquet, Gen. L H, *Souvenirs d'un directeur d'artillerie*, Charles-Lavauzelle, 1921, page 118].

[ii] There were 4,986 *75s*. 364 were in fortresses (e.g. 88 in casemates in eastern forts and 146 *75-mm R* [*raccourci* or cut-down] *modèle 1905* in rotating/retractable gun turrets). The rest were used for training or deployed in the colonies [*Source: Les armées françaises dan la grande guerre*, Tome I, Vol. 1, page 521].

The *M220s* could fire a rate of one round every three minutes. The real problem was that there were only 188 *Canons court*, or medium field howitzers, in the entire army. Command of this artillery was shared between Corps and Division. There was no commander of artillery at an Army HQ. Co-ordination between Corps therefore depended on the willingness of the commanders at Corps and Divisional level to co-operate.

In addition to these field/medium guns there were siege guns which might be able to add heavy firepower to the Army. In the main, however, they were of limited range and needed time to emplace, thus making them unsuitable for the early days of the war and thus they were not available or useable until the 'war of position' started. These were weapons of the era 1880-85 adapted and improved since 1890. Of these there were:

108 *Canons 155 C modèle 1881-1912 (modification Filloux)* with a range of 6,000 metres (extended to 7,000 metres by the end of 1915);

96 *mortiers de 220 modèle 1880-91* (metal platform), range 7,000 metres; and

32 *mortiers de siège de 270 modèle 1885*, range 4,300 metres (65 Kg shell) or 7,000 metres (35 Kg shell).[38]

There were, however, very large numbers of obsolete guns (Herr's estimate: 7,000 de Bange-era and earlier heavy guns) in the fortified zones of Verdun, Toul, Épinal and Belfort; or used for coastal protection. Gen. Baquet talks of large numbers of un-adapted *90 modèle 1877*, *95 modèle 1878*, *120 L. modèle 1878* and *155 L. modèle 1877* guns in fixed positions as well as c. 350 *155 C modèle 1881* and 230 *mortiers de 220 modèle 1880*. The totals were in fact:

778 *80 mm modèle 1877*
3,994 *90 mm modèle 1877*
1,524 *95 mm modèle 1875*
2,296 *120 mm L modèle 1878*
1,392 *155 mm L modèle 1877*
331 *mortiers de 220 mm modèle 1880* (and 1880 modified 1891)
32 *270 mm modèle 1885* and *modèle 1889* [39]

AT BATTERY LEVEL HERR ACCEPTED officers and men were excellently trained for the methods of fighting anticipated by French military doctrine. Quick to move and deploy, they were well used to acting as independent artillery support to the infantry, bringing fire to bear on large forces and targets of opportunity. The move to trench warfare, however, brought totally new and unexpected challenges for which none of their training prepared them.

Equally perplexed were the commanders and men of the heavy artillery. They were not trained to co-operate with infantry and were ignorant of the tactical methods employed by the army in the war of manoeuvre of the opening months of the war. Trained in the arts of siege warfare or in coastal defence there was little crossover of tactical or technical information between the heavy and field artillery. They each trained and studied in a tactical vacuum, expert in their own fields but ignorant of the others special concerns and problems.

That it was a singularly unhealthy position for an army setting out on the greatest challenge it had ever faced is underlined by this account drawn from the brief history of the *3e regiment d'artillerie à pied* (*3e RAP*), i.e. foot, or heavy, artillery. This regiment started the war with its batteries involved in coastal defence around Cherbourg, Brest, and la Rochelle. When Britain and its navy entered the war and effectively undertook the role of coastal protection, the personnel of a number of batteries were released and sent variously to Maubeuge and Toul. The men of eight batteries went to Maubeuge on the evening of 8th August where they were introduced to a variety of field/medium guns: *80, 90, 95, 120 L* and *155 L*. Unfortunately, as their history records:

> "... the men, coming from a regiment of coast artillery, were ignorant of the manoeuvres of the siege guns and the construction of the batteries."[40]

An enforced and rapid learning curve was needed as men who serviced heavy guns in fixed emplacements learnt how to construct the necessary dugouts, magazines, gun positions as well as emplace, load, aim and fire a motley collection of elderly guns they had not previously seen. And this just as the town was about to come under the concentrated artillery fire of Gen. Hans von Zwehl's *VII Reserve Armeekorps* equipped with some of the *Škoda 30.5 cm Mörser M.11s* and *42cm kurze Marinekanone L/12s* (or *Gamma-Gerät/Gamma Mörser*) which had recently demolished the forts at Namur in Belgium. Though some escaped, many of the *3e RAP's* officers and men were amongst the 49,000 soldiers who surrendered the town on 7th September after a two-week siege[i].

As previously mentioned, the tactical assumptions of speed and manoeuvre were shared by the staffs of the French and German Armies. They shared an unshakeable belief in the power of the offensive and believed the next war would be brief, as was at barely seven months, the previous war. Just how brief might be indicated by the quantities of ammunition provided for the field guns of the opposing armies in 1914. The French went into action with an initial supply of 1,300 shells per *75*, though not all of these were with the guns. Some were in reserve and others in depots. Heavy rates of fire soon meant these numbers rapidly and dangerously diminished. Just 500 per gun remained at the end of the Battle of the Marne[41]. In the German 77-mm field batteries supply did not exceed 987 rounds[ii] (and 973 for the *10.5 cm lFh*) and, as in intense fighting, the small numbers of shells with the guns might be used within a day it was not long before the invading forces faced their own shell crisis. Even with Germany's undoubted industrial might, this took time, energy, and organisation to resolve and, for a time, French production exceeded that of Germany with 7,000 77-mm shells per day being produced through to October 1914 at which point the demands of the Army were increased to 15,000 a day and then, from 21st December, 42,000 a day![42]

---

[i] Later in the war *3e RAP* was able to respond 'in kind' as they were equipped with super heavy guns of the *ALGP* and *ALVF* ranging in size from 270 to 400 mm.

[ii] This is surprising given the plentiful evidence of high shell consumption by field artillery during the Russo-Japanese War. Numerous articles in German military publications such as *'Artilleristische Monatshefte'*, *'Vierteljohshefte fur Truppenfuhring und Heereskunde'* and *'Militar-Wochenblatt'* record daily rates of fire for Russian field guns of anything between 200 and 400 rounds. Supplying their own guns with only between two and four-days' worth of ammunition seems a strange decision.

But, and crucially, the Germans studied and developed defensive aspects of the battlefield. The use of the machine gun, the need for improvised field fortifications, the addition of the *10.5-cm leichte Feldhaubitze 1898/09* and *15-cm-schwere Feldhaubitze 1902* or *1913* added facets to their tactics the French simply could not match. Knowing of the forts built around key border cities and towns in Belgium and north-eastern France, they did not ignore the need for a relatively mobile yet powerful siege train. Thus, they went into action with *21-cm Mörsers* as well as 10-cm and 13-cm long guns (*Kanone*), and super heavy *30.5-cm* and *42-cm Mörsers* which reduced the forts around Liege, Namur, Antwerp and Maubeuge[i], and the isolated *fort de Manonviller*[ii] near Lunéville.

The 10.5-cm howitzer was of particular significance. Mobile and quick-firing, the 10.5-cm could lob a shell of 16 Kg the same distance as the *75* was equipped to fire the majority of its shells with any real accuracy – 6,400 metres. The difference was the *10.5-cm lFH* could fire over obstructions – woods, hills, steep ridges – and onto the lightly fortified gun positions of the *75s* or troop concentrations thought to be out of reach of the flatter firing 77 mm field gun. As the German *Artillery Regulations* of 1912 stated:

> "The light howitzer accomplishes the same missions as the field gun. It has a much greater efficacy than the gun against defiladed artillery, objectives protected by overhead cover, against localities, and against troops placed in heavy woods."[43]

German tactical theories included, unlike the French who discarded it, the idea of the artillery duel as a necessary aspect of the battle before the infantry advance. German exercises involved the deployment of the heavier guns, not just the field artillery, and showed heavy howitzers and long guns to be of great benefit in the infantry battle. Firing from beyond the maximum range of the *75s*, these heavy weapons could not only destroy the French guns but also break up troops assembling behind the front-line. German tests showed how effective a heavy howitzer could be against an enemy battery, i.e. 80-100 rounds of 15-cm howitzer shell dropped into a zone around an enemy battery some 400 metres deep and twice the width of the battery position could cause the incapacity of 30-50% of the battery personnel and the destruction of 60-65% of the guns and equipment.

Having covered the deployment of the field guns and howitzers, these heavier weapons, sent forward with the leading elements of any advance, were thus tasked with the methodical destruction of the enemy artillery. Once achieved, their fire

---

[i] Forts built of concrete and rapidly reduced by *42-cm Mörsers*. French forts were built of reinforced concrete and better resisted the power of super heavy howitzers.

[ii] The *fort de Manonviller* east of Lunéville blocked the route to Nancy. Part of the *Système Séré de Rivières*, work started in 1879, being completed in 1882. It was extensively re-built and re-armed on four occasions. It was surrounded and heavily bombarded from 25th-27th August 1914 with a battery of *42-cm Krupp Mörsers* joining in on the afternoon of 26th August. The fort surrendered the following day. Amongst the 5,868 heavy calibre shells fired at the fort were: 159 42-cm, 134 30.5-cm, 4,594 21-cm, and 979 15-cm. In total, some 17,000 shells from 77-mm upwards were fired at the fort [*Source:* Cédric & Julie Vaubourg, *http://fortiffsere.fr/trouedecharmes/index_fichiers/Page4590.htm*].

was to be turned on the attacking and supporting infantry. Thus, and under cover of their expertly located machine guns, their infantry could proceed with the destruction of the enemy force. Because of this tactical thinking, the German Army went into battle in August 1914 with:[44]

5,068 *77 mm FK n/A*
1,260 *10.5-cm lFH 98/09*
416 *15-cm sFH 02*
216 *21-cm Mörser 10*

In addition, there were significant numbers of elderly 10-cm and 13-cm guns (range 13-16,000 yards), as well as less high powered (and obsolete) 9-cm guns and some 15-cm 1893 era *Krupp* howitzers. This added c. 1,400 long-range guns and short-range howitzers to the German arsenal. In addition to each Corps' sixteen 15-cm howitzers, several batteries of *21-cm mörsers* were attached to most Armies and some had 30-cm and 42-cm super heavy pieces. Direct command of many of these guns was assigned to Divisions which were able to make immediate local use of this great enhancement to their normal firepower. Crucially, given the terrain over which the early fighting took place, the Germans possessed more aircraft and balloons, and a better trained cadre of observers with considerable experience of working with troops and artillery. This despite the fact France was the European leader in the development of aircraft technology in the years before the war.

As the table shows, the German Army had 1,900 field, medium and heavy howitzers in August 1914 (some in East Prussia) against 443 for the combined French and British Armies. The French suffered greatly as a result. The direct artillery comparison between the Central Powers and the Entente was:

	Germany	Austria	Total	France	Gt Britain	Russia	Total
Field Guns	5068	1934	7002	4780	897	6278	11955
Field How.	1260	420	1680	84	169	512	765
Med. How.	416	112	528	104	86	164	354
H'vy How.	216	0	216	0	0	0	0
Total	6960	2466	9426	4968	1152	6954	13074

Table 7 Types of artillery available on the outbreak of war
Source: *German Artillery of World War One*, Herbert Jager, The Crowood Press, 2001.

It would be instructive to further breakdown the performance of the guns and howitzers available to the two protagonists in August 1914 (and soon after) as the detail underlines just how superior was German artillery in terms of numbers, range, rate of fire and weight of shell (see below).

Only the *75* exceeded the rate of fire of its German equivalent and, in every category, German guns outranged the French. The numbers were similarly one-sided. A French *Corps d'armée* deployed 120 75-mm field guns, but its German equivalent had 108 77-mm field guns, 36 10.5-cm field howitzers, and 16 15-cm medium howitzers. To put this into some rough, hypothetical context this meant that, with every gun firing for a minute, a French Corps could fire 2,160 shrapnel or high explosive shells versus a maximum of 1,512 for the German guns. But the Germans would fire more shrapnel balls/minute (568,800 to 540,000 French) and a far greater weight of high explosive. In addition, the *75s* could only reach the

77s, and, if within range, any *15-cm sFH*, and *10.5-cm lFH* unwisely deployed in the open. If the German medium guns fired from behind cover of any size they would be as invulnerable as the other, longer range, German guns.

Field and Medium guns	Rounds/ min.	Range (metres)	Type/weight of shell (Kgs) Shrapnel	HE
French				
Canon de 75 modèle 1897	12-18	6500	7.2	5.5
Canon de 90 modèle 77	1-2	6800	8.6	8
Canon de 95 modèle 75	1	6400	12.3	11
Canon de 120 L modèle 78	1	8900	18.7	19.2
Canon de 155 L modèle 77	1	9600	40.8	41
German				
7.7 cm FK 1896 n.A.	10-12	8400	6.8	6.8
10 cm K 1904	10	11000	18.7	17.8
13 cm K 1909	2	16500	40	40
Field and Medium howitzers				
French				
Canon de 120 C modèle 90	2	5700	19.2	18.7
Canon de 155 CTR modèle 1904	5-6	6300	40.8	41.3
German				
10.5 cm lFH 1898/1909	4	6300	12.8	15.7
15 cm sFH 1902 or 1913	4	8800	39	40.5
Heavy and Super Heavy howitzers/guns				
French				
Mortier de 220 modèle 80	1 in 3	7100	-	c. 100
Mortier de 220 mle 80/01	1 in 2	7100	-	c. 100
Mortier de 270 mle 85 & 89	1 in 3	7900	-	149.5
German				
21 cm Mörser L/12	2	9400	-	119
28 cm Mörser L/12		11000	-	338
30.5 cm schwerer Küstenmörser 1896 or 1909	1 in 2	8800/11900	-	335/410
42 cm Kurze-Marine-Kanone 1912 (M-Gerät)	1 in 6	12500/14100	-	795/930/1160

Table 8 Characteristics of French & German guns/howitzers, August 1914

BEFORE THE OUTBREAK OF WAR, the expansion of the German medium and heavy artillery capability was much discussed in French circles. Some, like Herr, advocated replicating these developments as they might find themselves at a serious disadvantage when fighting broke out. In its most basic form, the argument effectively came down to this rather simplistic question: which was more effective, ten 5 Kg shells from a *75* or one 50 Kg shell from a heavier gun. In these debates, most French officers favoured the former. In these discussions, much reference was made to various conflicts since the Franco-Prussian War. Of relevance was the previously mentioned siege of Plevna in the summer of 1877, the campaign which led the Germans to develop their original field howitzers in the 1890s. Much was made of the Russian artillery's failure to destroy Turkish trenches and earthworks and of the improved Turkish morale when their troops realised they were relatively safe from the noisy but ineffective field artillery shells. Nevertheless, the reported failures of heavy guns in more recent wars in South Africa, the Russo-Japanese War of 1904-5 and the First Balkan War of 1912-3 were also cited as reasons to stick almost entirely with the *75*.

The dispute between the opposing opinions in the Army eventually caused official intervention by the General Staff which received intelligence reports of the development and deployment of the German light and medium howitzers, medium guns, and heavy howitzers which came on stream from the late 1890s onwards. The *77 mm FK 96* was a botched attempt to match the French *75* but, since then, various new weapons rolled out of the *Krupp* and *Rheinmetall* factories:

- *10.5-cm leichte Feldhaubitze* (light field howitzer) *98/09 (lFH 98/09)*, a 1898 *Rheinmetall* design updated and improved by *Krupp* from 1902 to 1904 and officially accepted into the German Army in 1909;
- *15-cm schwere Feldhaubitze 1902 (sFH 02)*, a *Krupp*-designed medium and mobile howitzer; and the
- *21-cm Mörser 10,* a *Krupp/Rheinmetall* developed heavy howitzer which succeeded the 1899 variant.

The French response was a 155-mm QF howitzer, the *155 C TR 1904* designed by Capt. François Léon Emile Rimailho, a designer of the *75*. This used the *155 C 1881 de Bange* tube and shared its less than impressive ballistic properties. Its maximum range was 6,300 metres (compared to the *15-cm sFH 02* with a range of 7,400 metres) but it could fire six rounds a minute at a pinch. By the outbreak of war 104 were available. There were, however, concerns about its mobility. The Rimailho came in two sections – tube and platform – and each weighed over 2,500 Kgs. It was regarded as a siege weapon rather than one to be used in open warfare.

By now, the French *Conseil supérieur de la Guerre* wanted a small and lighter field howitzer and, in 1909, the development of a 120-mm howitzer was demanded. This move was, however, opposed by senior elements within the Army and, in particular, the *Comité technique de l'artillerie*. Their belief was the German *10.5-cm lFH* was only developed to make up for the deficiencies of the *77 mm FK 96 n/A* but the increasingly heated argument now found its way into the French Parliament. Here grave concerns were expressed about the German developments of modern, mobile guns and howitzers and the view amongst the politicians was the French Army needed similar weapons if they were to compete effectively on the battlefield. Eventually, in September 1911, a commission to investigate new *matérial* was set up to enquire into the options for new guns and howitzers and, within a month, Gen. Léon Jean Benjamin de Lamothe, the *Président du Comité technique de l'artillerie,* proposed to the Minister of War a programme for the development and testing of a light field howitzer and a long gun with a range of 12,000 to 13,000 metres.

Previously, there had been a reluctance amongst the Republican and Socialist members of successive governments to give contracts to private arms manufacturers, not least because they did not wish to feather the nests of capitalists some of whom, like Eugène Schneider, were active, elected members of the opposition or, at the very least, their paymasters. Now, for the first time, private industry was allowed to tender for these entire weapon systems rather than just parts[i]. *Schneider* and *Saint-Chamond* were the dominant private enterprises involved in the production of French heavy armaments although, initially, these were mainly made either for the Navy or for export. Their headquarters and chief production centres were both in eastern France, *Schneider* at le Creusot in Burgundy (*région Bourgogne-Franche-Comté*), some 35 kms due west of Chalon-sur-Saône, and *Saint-Chamond* (more properly known as the *Forges et Aciéries de la Marine et d'Homécourt* or *FAMH*) in the Department of the Loire (*région Auvergne-Rhône-Alpes*), 50 kms south-west of Lyon.

Schneider et cie was founded in 1836 by the brothers Adolphe and Eugène Schneider and was based on coal mines and forges around le Creusot[ii]. The finance was provided by the private *Banque Seillière*[iii] for which Adolphe Schneider had previously worked on the recommendation of his cousin, Gen. Antoine Virgile, *chevalier* Schneider[iv]. The *Banque Seillière* was given to job of supplying logistical support for the 1830 French campaign in Algeria and this was successfully handled by François-Alexandre Seillière and Adolphe Schneider. In 1833 François-Alexandre Seillière became interested in buying an ironworks at Le Creusot. This was based on the coal deposits in the north-west of the *départment de Saône-et-Loire*, and the first French blast furnace using coke was established there in 1782 by

---

[i] The *Loi sur la fabrication et le commerces des armes de guerre* of 14th July 1860, effectively made arms manufacture a state monopoly based at the arsenals at Saint-Étienne and Tulle, for firearms, and Châtellerault, firearms/edged weapons. This changed under a law promoted by Jérôme Eugène Farcy, deputy for the *15e arrondissement* of Paris. The *loi de 14 Aout 1885* liberalised arms manufacture and export and allowed the emergence of private arms manufacturers such as *Schneider* and *Saint-Chamond* which then exported their weapons all over the world. It thus contributed mightily to the world arms' race which has carried on ever since.

[ii] Now dominated by companies such as *ArcelorMittal*, *Schneider Electric*, and *Alstom*.

[iii] Later the *Banque Seillière-Demachy* originally founded in 1807 by Florentin Seillière and his son François-Alexandre Seillière. They helped fund Florentin's nephew, Aimé-Benoît Seillière, with the creation of a network of textile factories in the Vosges, Reims, and Beauvais. In 1858 Charles-Adolphe Demachy joined the bank and in 1873 a new bank – *la Société Demachy, R. et F. Seillière* – was formed, becoming *la banque Seillière-Demachy* in 1884. In 1911, the Seillière family withdrew their capital and the bank was taken over by the de Wendel steel group. Ironically, the forebears of the de Wendels were the previous owners of the *Société du Creusot* taken over by the Schneider brothers with the help of the Seillière family in 1836.

[iv] Gen. Schneider (1778-1847) fought in Poland, Spain and Russia during the Napoleonic Wars. He was involved in the Spanish campaign of 1823 and went to Greece in 1825 where he led the French campaign in the Peloponnese to expel the Turks during the eight-year Greek War of Independence (1821-9). Promoted Lt. General in 1831 he was elected deputy for Sarreguemines in 1834. He was appointed *ministre de la Guerre* in 1839, serving for 9½ months.

François Ignace de Wendel with the assistance of the English forgemaster William Wilkinson.[45] It was their *Société du Creusot* the Schneiders took over in 1836 with Seillière's help and which formed the basis of their industrial empire. The company *Schneider frères et Cie* was formed with Adolphe Schneider became the financial and commercial director and Eugène Schneider was appointed factory director. Further developments of the company's capabilities took place under the guidance of Eugène's son, Henri Schneider (1840-98) and his son, also called Eugène.

One problem for European steel producers was a high phosphorus content in most iron ore, resulting in low grade steel. Sidney Gilchrist Thomas and his cousin, Percy Carlyle Gilchrist, developed a variation of the Bessemer Process at the *Blaenavon Ironworks* which solved this problem. It was patented in 1878 as the Thomas and Gilchrist process. With the help of Henri de Wendel, great-grandson of François Ignace de Wendel, and Sidney Thomas, plant for the 'Basic Bessemer Process' was established at le Creusot and then at Joeuf, a small town[i] 17 kms north-west of Metz in the *département de Meurthe-et-Moselle*. Here, by 1914, were eight blast furnaces which all fell into German hands in the opening weeks of the war. Other expansions included the purchase of the *Forges et Chantiers de la Méditerranée's* artillery workshops constructed by Gustave Canet in Le Havre in 1897[ii].

Eugène Schneider the second was an excellent example of how the armaments industry, finance and politics were indelibly mixed, with all the potential for vested interests it suggests. Before the war he became a director of *Crédit lyonnais* and the *Banque de l'Union parisienne*[iii] as well as the *Compagnie des chemins de fer de Paris à Lyon et à la Méditerranée*. He was also the somewhat low-key Parliamentary Deputy for le Creusot between 1898 and 1910, representing the right-wing Catholic party *Action libérale* after 1902.

Although *Schneider* was, by French standards, a major industrial concern it was, next to *Krupp* on the Ruhr, 'small potatoes'. According to David Stevenson in *'Armaments and the Coming of War: Europe, 1904-1914'* pre-war investment in plant and machinery at le Creusot was barely a tenth of that invested in *Krupp's* vast factories at Essen.[46] Expanding production with new buildings, machine tools, the training of employees, etc., was a costly business which left the likes of *Schneider* and *Saint-Chamond* seriously disadvantaged when competing with the German industrial leviathan. *Krupp* grew at an extraordinary rate after the breakthrough of its steel cannon in the 1850s. In twelve years from 1861 the size of the works increased twentyfold and, between 1853 and 1887, the workforce increased by the same proportion and then more than doubled by 1902. It was estimated that, in 1889, the *Krupp* works at Essen contained 73 kms of railways lines, served by 28 locomotives pulling the best part of 1,000 wagons[47]. By 1914 it was larger still.

---

[i] Its population grew from 236 in 1872 to 9,589 in 1911. The de Wendel family built two large *chateaux* overlooking the enormous plant on the *River Orne*, a tributary of the Moselle, the *Château de Wendel* built for Henri de Wendel in 1895 and the *Château de Brouchetière* built for his youngest son, Maurice, in 1905.

[ii] Previously owned by the *Société Nouvelle des Forges et Chantiers de la Méditerranée* and located at Graville-Sainte-Honorine.

[iii] A bank formed in 1904 and which merged to form *Crédit du Nord-BUP* in 1973.

Leaders of the French Military-Industrial Complex

53 Henri Schneider   54 Pierre-Louis-Adrien de Montgolfier-Verpilleux

The *Forges et Aciéries de la Marine et d'Homécourt*[i] at Saint-Chamond was a merger in 1854 of four companies based along the banks of the *River Gier*, a small tributary of the Rhone (the companies involved were: *Pétin-Gaudet de Saint-Chamond et Rive-de-Gier, Établissements Jackson frères de Assailly, la société Neyrand-Thiollère, Bergeron et Compagnie de Lorette*, and *la société Parent, Schaken, Goldsmidt et Compagnie de Paris*). Here the first French foundry for the refining of cast iron was established in 1820 and was quickly followed by plants for steel casting and wrought iron. These companies, iron and steel foundries and coal mining, utilised France's first railway line, the Saint-Étienne to Lyon railway opened in 1833, and the local coal resources of the Loire coal mining basin of which Saint-Étienne was the centre. Originally based in both Rive-de-Gier and Saint-Chamond the merged company moved to Saint-Chamond in 1871. Under the guidance of an engineering graduate of the *École Polytechnique*, Pierre-Louis-Adrien de Montgolfier-Verpilleux[ii], the company quadrupled its turnover in the 34 years during which he was Director General from 20 to 80 million *francs*. New plant constructed at Saint-Chamond enabled the production of heavily armoured naval gun turrets as well as the iron, and then steel, cupolas of the numerous fortifications of the *Système Séré de Rivières*.

---

[i] Originally called the *Compagnie des hauts-fourneaux, forges et aciéries de la Marine et des Chemins de fer*. In 1903 two blast furnaces of *société Vezin-Aulnoye* at Homécourt (north-west of Metz) in the *département de Meurthe-et-Moselle* were bought and two more added in 1904 and 1905. Homécourt was therefore added to the company name. The *département de Meurthe-et-Moselle* was a new French *département* created out of the remains of the old *Moselle* and *Meurthe départements* otherwise occupied by the Germans in 1871. Foundries at Hautmont-sur-Sambre (south-west of Maubeuge), owned by the Belgian *Société Anonyme des laminoirs, forges, fonderies et usines de la Providence*, were also bought at the same time. Both foundries and those at Homécourt were lost to the Germans during the opening weeks of the war.

[ii] The grandnephew of Jacques-Étienne Montgolfier, the first balloonist.

Thus when, in February 1912, the *Atelier de Construction de Puteaux's*[i] 120-mm howitzer design proved inadequate, *Schneider et Cie* put forward two guns designed for the Bulgarian and Russian Armies. The Bulgarian weapon was the *Schneider-Creusot* 105-mm howitzer and, although it proved highly successful in the 1912 manoeuvres taking on infantry 75-mm guns were unable to reach, it was rejected in the following year[ii]. The gun designed for the Russian Army was, however, accepted after a minor re-design reduced it from 106.7 mm to 105-mm. This became the *Canon de 105 L modèle 1913 TR Schneider* of which 24 were available on the outbreak of war and 100 at the start of the Somme battle. Progress on the development of other weapons was, however, painfully slow.

Ideas were mooted for ways the *75* could become a multipurpose gun. The designers and engineers at *APX* constructed a double calibre gun, the *75/120* which was rejected at the same time as their 120-mm howitzer. Proposals were put forward for adaptations to allow the *75* to act as a field howitzer (and as an anti-aircraft gun). One idea was the *Plaquette Malandrin*. By attaching a ring to the nose of 75-mm shells the flight of the shell affected causing them to fall more sharply, as if a plunging howitzer round. The genesis of this idea shows the lengths to which politicians (in this case supported by certain army officers) will go to save money in the short-term only to lose far more in the medium/long term.

The system was designed by a Capt., later Lt. Col., Michel Hippolyte Malandrin of the *27e régiment d'artillerie*. Born in 1868, he entered the *Ecole Polytechnique* in 1889 and, in 1900, was ordered to China with the *15e batterie, 20e régiment d'artillerie* as part of the Expeditionary Force sent to suppress the Boxer Rebellion. There, on 31st October 1900 at the Che Maën pagoda near Beijing occupied by Boxers:

> "… he opened a rapid fire with his section of *75s* which demoralised the enemy and led to them evacuating the position."[48]

It was the first use of the *75* in action. On his return, he was attached to the *Atelier de construction de Douai* serving for five years before rejoining the *27e régiment*. While training gunners there was an issue on the shooting ranges concerning the safety of nearby properties. The *75* was often deliberately fired to ricochet before its shell exploded, a technique made possible by its flat trajectory. These ricochets sometimes left the range in an unpredictable fashion. Malandrin devised a simple iron ring which, attached to the nose of the shell, slowed the shell, gave the trajectory a greater curve, reduced its range to 4,000 metres, and stopped shells disappearing into the unknown. It was, first and foremost, a safety device.

Then, in 1911, made nervous by the crisis in Morocco, the French government voted through a budget of 500 million *francs* with which to re-equip the army with modern heavy artillery. There were, from both government and private factories, several types to chose from. As the ripples caused by the Moroccan crisis

---

[i] Puteaux lies on the left bank of the *Seine* near Nanterre in western Paris and now includes the area known as *la Défense*.

[ii] A brief report in the *Field Artillery Journal* (October-December 1913 edition, page 619) remarked: "These episodes of the manoeuvres, all entirely unpremeditated, seem to demonstrate beyond question the utility of the light howitzer, either to support an infantry attack or engage artillery."

disappeared, however, the government was less keen to spend such an enormous sum of money and, out of the blue, the *Plaquette Malandrin*, seemed to offer a solution by turning the flat-firing *75* into some sort of pseudo-howitzer. In debates and discussions in 1913 on the state of French artillery the *Plaquette* was seized on by the *Minstre de la Guerre*, Eugène Étienne (the man who declared *'Le pantalon rouge c'est la France!'* in the debate on the French uniform. See page 196), as a magical way with which to supply a field howitzer capability whilst saving 85 million *francs*. A light field howitzer was therefore abandoned and, instead, large numbers of incredibly cheap *Plaquettes* were produced. They came in two types:

Plaquette P, diameter 68 mm, weight 50 grams, marked *'P'* for *'Près'*; and
Plaquette L, diameter 58 mm, weight 34 grams, marked *'L'* for *'Loin'*.

The result was a maximum range of 4,000 metres and a significant reduction in accuracy. It worked with all fuzes except the *IA, instantanée allongée*, which was later found to be the best means of cutting barbed wire.

The system's limited range meant guns firing these shells would be outranged by the German *lFH 98/09*. It was a cheap, quick, poor quality, and short-term fix. But politicians were only too keen to adopt it, even if Lamothe and his commission were opposed. Nevertheless, a delighted Étienne instantly promoted the now Cdt. Malandrin[i] to Lt. Col., crediting him on 20th March 1913 as the:

"…inventor of the marvellous mechanism which makes it possible to transform the *75* gun into a howitzer and thus save 60 million."[49]

Thirteen days earlier, the idea of a light field howitzer for the French Army was rejected and was, instead, to quote Gen. Herr:

"… replaced by a crude expedient which the war judged mercilessly."[50]

Then, when the *Plaquette Malandrin* proved worse than useless on the battlefield, the poor man responsible found himself the target of abuse and derision from his fellow artillery officers. Life is never fair.[51]

Another option, rather than face up to the costs of a suitable field howitzer, was to use a reduced-power cartridge, the *cartouche réduite*. This had a similar effect as the *Plaquette* with a similar maximum range of 4,000 metres, over 2,000 metres less than the German light field howitzer. That these ideas were adopted exhibits a considerable lack of foresight by senior officers which, allied to the politicians' penny-pinching approach, meant the French Army went to war in August 1914 without a proper field howitzer with which to oppose the *10.5-cm lFH*.

In October 1913, further tests were carried out on three weapons either designed and built, or adapted, by *Schneider*. They were the:

Canon de 155 L modèle 1877/1914 sur affût Schneider – a *155 L de Bange* tube mounted on a new *Schneider* platform capable of firing 3 rounds a minute out to 13,600 metres;

---

[i] Malandrin later commanded the *2e groupe, 21e RAC* then *1er groupe de 95, 104e RAL*, 1914-16, then was at the *Commission d'experience de Calais* until 1918 [*Source: Base Leonore*]. The *Plaquette Malandrin* was still in use in 1936 and referred to in *Capt. d'artillerie* Anselme's *Organisation des matériels d'artillerie* from the *Ecole d'application d'artillerie*, Tome I, page 63. There was a version designed for use by tanks.

Canon de 105 L modèle 1913 TR Schneider mentioned above; and the *Mortier de 280 TR Schneider (modèle 1914)*, a super heavy howitzer firing a 275 Kg shell nearly 11,000 metres.

With a sudden realisation that large sums of money needed to be spent on new guns, the government agreed to find 163 million *francs* in February 1914, although the law giving financial approval for such expenditure was not passed until 13th July 1914, three weeks before war broke out. All the designs were accepted but, because of delays in manufacturing, none, except for small numbers of the *105 L*, were available before late summer 1916 and, by then, the *155 L* design was overtaken by new *Schneider* and *Saint-Chamond* designs. The delays were caused by a lack of domestic capacity and the demands of its Allies, most particularly Russia, for a share of French factories' production. After the huge losses of men and *matériel* of the Gorlice–Tarnów Offensive in May and June 1915, Russia sent repeated appeals to France in the autumn of 1915 for the supply of medium guns and heavy howitzers. In late October the Russian Government started to apply pressure for the delivery of 400 *105 L* guns to be manufactured by *Schneider* at le Creusot in Burgundy, even though this new quick-firing weapon was much needed by the French to replace obsolete *105* and *120 L de Bange* guns manufactured in 1878. To be in a French battery equipped with a new *105 L* by the end of 1915 was a rare privilege and yet here were the Russians demanding rapid delivery of 400 of these precious weapons. Joffre balked at the possibility, in spite of *Schneider* suggesting the financial impact of such an order would allow them to increase capacity such that they would not only be able to fulfil this order but speed up the completion of orders for other artillery, such as the *155 C*, also much needed by the French Army. Joffre did not believe their promises and the order for *105 L* guns was not completed in the time scale hoped for by the Russians.

THE CONFUSED THINKING and inevitable delays in artillery procurement were, in part, fed by contradictory reports from the First Balkan War of 1912-3. This pitted the Serbs, Montenegrins, Greeks, and Bulgarians against the failing Ottoman Empire and resulted in a decisive victory for the Slav/Greek alliance on both land and sea[i]. It also caused major concern to nearby major powers, with the Austrian Army twice starting to mobilise in the early winter of 1912 with the avowed intention of preventing the Serbs from gaining access to the Adriatic. Accordingly, the Russian Army also started its mobilisation process, an event deeply disturbing to, and closely monitored by, the German Government. The intervention of winter and a lack of activity on the part of the French somewhat defused the crisis, however all the major nations began busily to build up arms and ammunition stocks in anticipation of another and, possibly final, crisis.[52]

Other than a scramble for the Ottoman province of Rumelia (Eastern Rumelia [now southern Bulgaria], Thrace and Macedonia), the Balkan War became something of a contest between the French *Schneider* guns of the Serbs and Bulgarians, and the *Krupp*-equipped Turks. Several French officers made unofficial

---

[i] The Greek/Slav alliance was encouraged by the Turkish defeat in the Italian-Turkish War of 1911-12.

trips to the Balkans to observe the use and effectiveness of the artillery. Gen. Herr visited just prior to the armistice and he interviewed Serbian and Turkish artillery officers, focussing on the employment of the artillery in three major actions: Kumanovo, Monastir[i] and Çatalca (Tchataldja)[ii]. Three months later, another, this time official, delegation of French officers arrived in the Balkans. It comprised Col. Jean Frédéric Lucien Piarron de Mondésir[iii] of the *Génie* (Engineers) and a former professor of fortifications at the *École Supérieure de Guerre*, Capt. Louis Marie Joseph de Ripert d'Alauzier, *20e Bataillon de Chasseurs à Pied*, and Capt. Georges Bellenger, *Artillerie de campagne* (Field Artillery), a graduate of the *École Polytechnique* in 1898. Bellenger, too, visited the battlefields of Kumanovo and Monastir as well as several others involving both Bulgarians and Greeks (the others mentioned were Serbian battles). He also travelled to the city of Adrianople (now Edirne), the site of a four-month siege which ended with its capture by the Bulgarians on 26th March 1913[iv] (details of the land battles are on page 848). In this he was accompanied by Mondésir who later commented on the utility of the 38 Serbian 120 and 150-mm *Schneider-Canet* guns and howitzers brought up to bombard the defences immediately prior to the Bulgarian assault on 26th March 1913.[53]

Herr and Bellenger published reports in the February and November, 1913, editions of the *'Revue d'Artillerie'* (Mondésir wrote a book, *Siège et Prise d'Adrianople*, published in 1914). Herr's article appeared in the *Journal of the Royal Artillery* and the *Field Artillery Journal* (USA) and Bellenger's in the latter publication. Herr's piece, appearing first, championed the need for howitzers and long-range guns and caused such a stir great efforts were made by those favouring the 75 above all weapons to discredit and undermine the General's opinions. Adverse reaction to Herr's report sprang not only from his support for guns thought unnecessary by the '75ers' but also because he challenged the tactical use of artillery which underpinned French military thinking and, indeed, the entire basis of the *offensive*. The 75 was the weapon which allowed the ideas of de Grandmaison and Joffre to be translated into action. Slow-moving heavy guns had no place on their quick-moving battlefield. In fact, they would be a hindrance because their presence might persuade commanders to shy away from the all-out offensive envisaged by leading French theorists. There was, therefore, far more to this dispute than a simple debate on artillery tactics. It involved the soul of the French Army.

Herr first investigated the Serbian success at Kumanovo on 10th-11th November 1912[v]. Here, Ottoman troops under Zeki Pasha attacked the Serbs on both days despite being overwhelmingly outnumbered. Although casualties seem to have been relatively similar, the Turkish troops panicked and abandoned the

---

[i] Now in North Macedonia.

[ii] About 40 kms west of what is now Istanbul.

[iii] Later *Général de Division*, he commanded *30e Brigade, 16e Division, 8e Corps, 52e Division, 36e Corps* and *38e Corps* in the war. In 1915 he went to Albania to help reform the Serbian Army. Born in Russia, 1857, died 1943 [*Source: Base Leonore*].

[iv] Adrianople was re-taken by the Turks on 23rd July 1913 during the Second Balkan War when Bulgaria took on its old allies, the Turks, and Rumanians.

[v] 23rd-24th October 1912 in the Julian calendar used by Serbia, Russia, and Ottomans.

field in disorder, the situation not being helped by the attempted assassination of Zeki Pasha by a disgruntled Ottoman soldier.⁵⁴ They left behind 98 artillery pieces. According to Herr, the Serbian artillery played a crucial role, first by indulging in an activity thought unnecessary or unproductive by French Artillery Field Regulations. This was a preliminary artillery duel in which they destroyed many of the Turkish guns which deployed in the open to fire on the Serb infantry. Having eliminated the artillery threat, the Serbian gunners then turned on the infantry. Protected by inadequately built breastworks, the Serb artillery forced them from the field causing heavy casualties with shrapnel as they fled. Serb losses were not insignificant and *Morava Division I*, suffered badly from Turkish batteries firing obliquely. These were then destroyed by Serbian guns firing in the same manner.

Herr drew several conclusions, all contradicting current tactical theory:

- The Serbs showed an enemy's guns could be destroyed not just neutralised. Current thinking was that field gun shields would protect the gun team and allow them to operate even under heavy fire;
- Artillery caused more casualties than rifle fire. In addition, shrapnel wounds were more disabling than those caused by rifle bullets[i];
- The artillery duel was a necessity. By refusing such a duel and, instead, targeting the Serb infantry, the Turkish artillery allowed itself to be destroyed, at which point the Serb guns turned on the unprotected Ottoman infantry, routing them;
- Oblique fire from the flanks was highly effective. Isolated Turkish batteries firing thus on the *Morava Division I* caused severe casualties to the Serbs, and the Serbian Horse Artillery from the left flank caused similar casualties amongst the advancing Ottoman infantry;
- The damage caused by the Serb guns was achieved with a remarkably small quantity of ammunition, around 120 shells per gun; and, finally,
- Forward observers transmitting details of range and effect back to the battery commanders were crucial, both to their success and the economy of their shell consumption.

For Herr, the fighting at Monastir, 15th–18th November, highlighted the utility of long guns and 120-mm howitzers, even if slow firing and cumbersome. The Ottomans were mainly equipped with field guns and 120-mm howitzers. The Serbians, however, had eleven 120-mm long guns, five 150-mm mortars and four 120-mm howitzers as well as *Schneider-Creusot modèle 1907 75-mm TR* field guns[ii]. The

---

[i] A view supported in the publications *'Vierteljahreshefte für Truppenführung und Heereskunde'*, 1908 (page 169), and *'Schweiz Monatsschrift für Offiziere aller Waffen'* (1908 January to May). Both suggested artillery fire caused more serious *and* more fatal wounds than rifle fire, and by the article previously mentioned in the *'Archiv für Klinische Chirurgie'*, in 1906, which stated 'Statistics confirm the fact that artillery wounds with few exceptions caused a man's absence from his regiment a longer time' (page 986).

[ii] 120-mm *Schneider-Canet* guns 1897 pattern. Built by *Schneider-Creusot*, sixteen of these slow firing, recoilless guns were delivered to Serbia in 1902. They had a range of up to

longer guns allowed the Serbians to approach the Turks under artillery cover. In addition, the 120-mm long guns took on and silenced several poorly protected Turkish batteries and then, after the artillery took on and destroyed or neutralised other Turkish guns, the Serbian infantry, accompanied by mountain guns, drove the Turkish infantry from the field. For Herr, this battle reinforced his view about the essential nature of the preliminary artillery duel and the desirability of long-range guns, a factor confirmed in Serbian post-battle reports.[55] Their success in the artillery duel made it possible for Serbian infantry to advance across open country against a strongly held position. Previously, the long-range guns provided cover for the deployment of the Serbian forces and then helped destroy Turkish batteries outranged by the Serbian 120-mm weapons. When asked, the commander of the Serbian artillery made it clear to Herr they wanted the 120-mm long guns both for their range and the heavy weight of the shells. The flat trajectory, as with the *75,* was incidental.

From the fighting at Çatalca, one of the Turks' few successes and this against the Bulgarians, Herr drew conclusions not from what happened but from what failed to occur. On 17th November, the Turks occupied a ridge running along the peninsula between the Sea of Marmara and the Black Sea, the last line of defence in front of Constantinople. Their infantry was entrenched and the artillery dug in and protected, possibly because of the involvement of two German officers: *Oberst* Otto Hermann von Lossow[i], an adviser who commanded the 8th Division, and a Maj. Lehmann, commanding the artillery. With the Bulgarian field artillery unable to silence the Turkish guns, the advancing Bulgarian infantry was swept away and the remnants forced to ground where they dug trenches. Unable to move because of the Turkish artillery covering this terrain, they were eventually ejected by a Turkish infantry attack during the night of 19th November. Herr's complaint about the Bulgarian tactics was the absence of the artillery duel through which they might have removed the threat of the Turkish batteries. Although the Bulgarians fired numerous shells at the Turkish gun positions, they were mainly ineffective, long-range shrapnel from field guns. The absence of any Bulgarian long guns and howitzers firing high explosive proved crucial to the Turkish success in saving their capital and, by so doing, they inflicted the first major defeat on the Bulgarian Army since its formation in 1878.

Herr published his report in favour of howitzers and long-range guns in 1913. It immediately came under attack from those convinced of the supremacy of the *75*. Officers were found, amongst them Bellenger and another, Capt. Alvin, who challenged Herr's findings as well as his good faith.

8,400 metres. Bulgaria had 24 of these guns. 150-mm *Schneider-Canet* mortars, 1897 pattern.120-mm *Schneider-Canet* howitzers, 1897 pattern.

[i] Born in 1868 in Bavaria, Lossow commanded the *I. Königlich Bayerisches Reserve-Armeekorps* before returning to Turkey as military *attaché*. Promoted *Generalmajor* in 1916 he became *Militärbevollmächtigter* (Military Plenipotentiary) at the *Türkisches Hauptquartier*. Post-war he commanded *Wehrkreis VII* (Bavaria) in the *Reichswehr* and played a prominent part in the failed Beer Hall Putsch in Munich in 1923. Forced to retire, he returned to Turkey but died in Munich in 1938.

Bellenger's report was, initially, quite uncontroversial. Interestingly, or conveniently depending on one's interpretation, he was unable to verify Serbian claims of the destructive effect of their guns. In Thrace where mainly the Bulgarians fought the Turks, evidence of destructive effect was minimal. Here, he reported, the main effect of predominantly shrapnel fire was the neutralization of the enemy guns and the immobilisation of the infantry who, immediately on coming under artillery fire, dug themselves in. This desire to dig trenches applied to both sides. The Turks, on the defensive and with poor and inexperienced troops, did it as a matter of course; and the Bulgarians, even when advancing, dug in as soon as shells began to explode overhead.

Of course, it may be the lack of destructive effect caused by the Bulgarian guns on the Turkish artillery and entrenchments was caused:

By the Bulgarian tendency to fire at extreme range;
By the Bulgarian tendency to fire too high; and
The tendency to use flat-firing field guns firing shrapnel.

All of these factors were reported by Bellenger, as was the desire on both sides to entrench. The result: trench systems running from the front-line back to the reserve positions. Indeed, he complained:

"Numerous trenches were constructed solely for protection against artillery fire and without themselves affording any field of fire."[56]

Bellenger's view was:

"... both Bulgarians and Turks feared too much – quite too much – the enemy's artillery fire. But, be this fear well founded or not, the artillery's power of immobilization is considerable."[57]

Bellenger was either unaware of, or ignored, Jean de Bloch's prescient 1898 forecast about the nature of the modern battlefield and the essential importance of the soldier's spade (see *Volume I*), just as much as he was ignoring the potential uses of howitzers against men dug-in when judged against the poor effects of field artillery shrapnel fired on entrenched troops. He also reflected the French belief in the 'offensive' by suggesting trench digging should normally be for the purpose of launching an attack and not simply for protecting troops from the enemy's fire.

Bellenger noted there were few buildings or wooded areas in Thrace or Macedonia (commonplace along the Franco-German border), and thus there was no evidence of the effect of artillery fire on such places. But entrenchments were used by all armies, with the Serbian ones being the most complex. The Turkish trenches were, however, assaulted by the Bulgarians and Serbs in a different manner. The Bulgarians tended to keep the enemy's heads down with shrapnel during the day and attacked with the bayonet at night, whilst the Serbs attacked during the day with close cooperation between artillery and infantry. Close cooperation between these two arms was practised by the Japanese in Manchuria in 1904-5, with field artillery firing shrapnel sometimes up to the point at which their infantry arrived in the trench to be attacked. Friendly fire casualties were accepted as a necessary consequence of arriving at the enemy position with the enemy infantry still seeking protection behind their parapet.

According to Bellenger, however, the duel between concealed batteries (unconcealed batteries were invariably destroyed) was, in the view of both sides, useless and inconclusive. The point was made, though, that a complete lack of aerial observation made discovery of the locations of concealed batteries difficult if not impossible. Whether a different type of gun, i.e. a howitzer, might have been able to deal effectively with these concealed batteries was not, therefore, an issue he ever investigated. All of the combatant nations of the Slav/Greek Alliance were agreed on one thing: in contradiction of Herr's findings at Kumanovo far more rounds were expended than expected and re-supply proved an immense problem, to the extent that, after the battles of Lüleburgaz (see page 566) and Kumanovo (see also page 561), the winners had to wait for new shell supplies before continuing to advance[i]. Just under two years later, all the main armies on the Western Front found themselves short of field artillery ammunition which suggests military planners on all sides failed to understand the implications of this artillery aspect of the First Balkan War.

The next section of Bellenger's report set him in direct opposition to the views expressed by Herr. According to Bellenger neither the Serbs nor the Bulgarians felt the need to use the plunging fire of howitzers even though both armies possessed them. The Bulgarians only brought these guns into use, along with some long 120-mm *Schneider-Canet* guns, at the siege of Adrianople (and they were provided by the Serbs), during the fierce fighting at Pinarhisar (part of the Lüleburgaz campaign), and during the Çatalca attack when all available guns were needed. Post-war, various Bulgarian officers seemed to disagree fundamentally with Bellenger's observations and conclusions. The Chief of Staff of the *1st Bulgarian Army*, 48-year-old Col. (later Maj. Gen.) Asen Papadopov[ii], believed 120 and 150-mm howitzers essential for a successful attack on infantry in entrenched positions. Indeed, after considerable debate Bulgaria ordered 120-mm howitzers from *Schneider* in 1907 with these guns being delivered in 1912. One of the officers involved in the committee which ordered these guns was a Col. Stoyan Zagorski who had previously commanded the *1st Softyski Fortress Artillery Battalion*. It was he who, on examination of a 105-mm *Schneider* howitzer, determined it not powerful enough and thus an order was placed for the *Schneider-Canet Obusier de campagne à tir rapide de 120mm M 1909*. Zagorski would later describe lighter weight howitzers as 'toys'.[58]

For the Serbs, Bellenger asserted their long guns were only ever used at Monastir where long-range fire was needed to support the infantry advance. Bellenger's conclusion was:

> "The heavy artillery has, then, been of use in some special cases, but solely by reason of its range and power and not on account of the curvature of its trajectory. Do the services thus rendered compensate for the other inconveniences involved?"[59]

His answer was, effectively, no they did not. It did not matter whether the enemy infantry was entrenched or not, field guns should suffice, other than in

---

[i] It should also be said that the poor, wet winter weather allied to the general lack of any decent roads made movement for all armies a slow and tiresome activity.
[ii] Previously head of the Operations Department of the Bulgarian General Staff.

exceptional circumstances. Taking as his yardstick Napoleon's massed field guns of Jena and Austerlitz (though not mentioning the Grand Battery at Waterloo for some reason) rather than, for example, the far more recent siege of Port Arthur or the Bulgarian failure before the Turkish trenches on the Çatalca line in front of Constantinople, Bellenger concluded:

> "Napoleon always kept in hand a mass of artillery and the infantry reserves needed for the carrying out of his plans. By those means he won the battles of Jena and Austerlitz in a few hours. Modern means permit as quick a victory, if one has the necessary determination.
> So, if I have learned my lesson properly, the need of heavy artillery with an army does not proceed from technical improvements; it appears rather to be connected with the temperament of the commander. In operations which develop rapidly, and especially if there is much manoeuvring, the heavy artillery will rarely find employment; in operations in which it is sought to eliminate risk by prudent methods, it will more frequently play an important part."[60]

With current French doctrine based on fire, manoeuvre, and 'the offensive', this final statement suggested howitzers and other guns were irrelevant to the current plans on which the calamitous Battles of the Frontiers in the autumn of 1914 were based. Overall, Bellenger's report was written in support of current French thinking, i.e. the concentrated fire of field guns in support of the infantry would blast an opening in the enemy's ranks through which the soldiers advanced to victory. As a field artillery officer by training and profession he thought as a field artillery officer. The use of plunging howitzer shells fired from well concealed positions seems not have occurred to him as a means by which some of the thornier tactical problems facing the Serbs and Bulgarians might have been solved.

Capt. Pierre Alvin[i] was another field artillery officer to challenge Herr's heretical beliefs, although much of what he wrote appeared to be drawn from Capt. Bellenger's earlier report. Alvin started by explaining that, between 1903 and 1907, the various members of the Slav/Greek coalition tested and eventually selected the *Schneider-Canet Canon de Campagne de 75-mm Mle 1904* or *1906*. The Greeks and Serbs also tested guns from *Krupp*, *Skoda*, *Armstrong* and *Ehrhardt*. The *Krupp* gun was the *75-mm FK Model 1903*, built for export rather than domestic use, and only the Ottoman Army decided to adopt the weapon. When it came to the war it appears the *Schneider* gun was the better of the two and Alvin certainly repeatedly gives examples to support this idea. Perhaps even more importantly, the *Schneider* was in the hands of battery commanders and gun crews who knew

---

[i] Capt., later *Gen. de Division*, Pierre Hippolyte Scipion Isidore Alvin (1872-1950). *École polytechnique* and *École d'application* 1891-93. *13e régiment d'artillerie de campagne*, 1894. Professor, *École militaire d'artillerie at du génie*, 1903. *Chef d'escadron*, *61e régiment d'artillerie*, 1914. Fought on the *Marne*, Yser and in the Argonne and Champagne. In 1915 he joined the staff of the headquarters of the artillery and munitions. He went on to write the *'Manuel d'artillerie de tranchée'* with Capt Leon Lagay in 1917. In March 1918 he was given command of the *28e régiment d'artillerie de campagne* and, in August, command of the field artillery of *151e Division* fighting on the Aisne and in Champagne.

what they were about, trained, as many were, in France. Alvin quoted, and then attempted to rebut, some of Herr's points:

> "Was the superiority gained by the artillery of the Allies over that of the Turks obtained by a methodical duel between the two artilleries forming a definite phase of the battle and resulting in putting the Turkish batteries *hors de combat*? In other words, did every battle open with an artillery duel? From a detailed study of the battle of Kumanovo, Monastir and Tchataldja (Çatalca), General Herr thinks we should come to that conclusion. But this opinion is far from being shared by the belligerents. On the contrary, General Savov's[i] Chief of Staff thinks that the artillery duel, properly speaking, had no place in these battles. This point of view is held by many Bulgarian officers, who, in trying to make clear to one of our officers the character of the battles in which they participated, agreed that the artillery always sought to *'s'infanteriser'*, and that that was the only target to which it should devote itself. By the word *'s'infanteriser'* is meant that the first idea of artillery entering an action should be to occupy itself only with infantry; to try to destroy the enemy's infantry, and to break down obstacles which may stop the advance of its own infantry."[61]

Alvin claimed the Serbians were in agreement with Savov's Chief of Staff but, making reference to the determination with which both sides dug in as soon as the artillery opened fire, he went on to comment the best to be hoped for from the field guns was the neutralisation and immobilisation of the enemy infantry rather than its destruction. Overall, however, losses amongst the infantry to artillery fire were greater than those recorded in previous wars although the figures given for the various belligerent nations hover around the figure of 10-15% of total casualties being caused by shell and shrapnel fire. As a result, Alvin was able to state confidently it was the rifle which caused most injuries on the modern battlefield[ii]. If the rifle was 'king' of the battlefield then it meant the modern battle would still take place at relatively close quarters with both the infantry and the artillery initially facing one another at distances of no more than 4,000 metres. Alvin's conclusion was definite:

> "But it is probable that our infantry will be all the more sorely tried by artillery fire and it will be necessary for our artillery to increase their activity

---

[i] Gen. Mihail Savov was twice Bulgarian Minister of Defence and second in command during the First Balkan War. He ordered the Bulgarian attack on the Çatalca line resulting in the Bulgarian Army's first defeat since its formation. After the war, Savov initiated the Second Balkan War against his erstwhile allies, Serbia, and Greece, by attacking without a declaration of war. Savov was later dismissed as Commander in Chief. His action drew Montenegro and Rumania into the war on the side of the Greek/Serbian alliance, with the Ottoman Empire snatching back Eastern Thrace from the Bulgarians. Bulgaria lost most of its territorial gains from the First Balkan War as well as territory to Rumania.

[ii] Although he did accept these figures would be greater in a Franco-German conflict because of the far higher number of artillery pieces and the greater sophistication of the shells and fuzes available.

in order to compensate for this. They should be convinced that an attack cannot succeed unless the participants are willing to come to close quarters. In this regard the Turco-Balkan War has shown the uselessness of fire at long ranges, that is to say, beyond 4,000 meters, either for field or heavy mobile artillery."[62]

When it came to heavy howitzers, the *mortiers* of the French siege artillery, Alvin again disagreed with Gen. Herr:

"One may be tempted to expect from the experiences of the Balkan War some enlightenment on the question of the employment of the guns and mortars of heavy calibre. In spite of the opinion of General Herr, the facts borne to our notice do not permit us to decide either for or against the use of calibres greater than 75-mm."[63]

Expressing concerns about a howitzer's weight and immobility, Alvin mentions the difficult mountainous terrain over which the Serbs advanced and the generally lamentable state of the roads encountered everywhere without, at the same time, making allowance for the absence of such rugged terrain in the majority of northern France and the higher standard of both roads and railways within the two European super-powers. Eventually, though, Alvin hedged his bets over the employment of heavy howitzers, although he did state in his final paragraph:

"From the statements of officers who saw the campaign, it would seem the question of curvature of trajectories is an illusory one, and that heavy calibres are necessary only in an attack on strongly fortified positions."[64]

Another officer taking no note of Bloch's forecast that every infantryman would dig himself in during the next war, nor that this is what Alvin describes both sides in the Balkans doing as soon as the artillery opened fire.

Eventually, as this unseemly row rumbled on, the *Etat-Major* produced a document summarising the opinions of those opposed to heavy artillery. Within it, a detailed comparison was made of existing French and German field artillery and it concluded by deciding the small numbers of *120 L* guns, *155 C TR* howitzers and *105 L* guns would be more than adequate to take on the German heavy artillery on those rare occasions when the 75-mm field guns were incapable of undertaking the task themselves as:

"A manoeuvring artillery which knows how to use the terrain will be able to get within suitable distance of the enemy and will only rarely need a long-range gun."[65]

There were those other than Herr who voiced alternative opinions. Gen. Léon de Lamothe was President of the *Comité central de l'artillerie* and, in February 1913, he stated the Balkans War showed no reason for failing to adopt heavier calibres of guns and *mortiers*.[66] Joffre, too, previously called for a wider range of high angle guns and the *Conseil supérieur de la guerre* had been calling for such weapons since the *SMS Panther* appeared off Agadir in 1911. In addition, the elected Deputy for Aveyron, one Général Edouard de Curières de Castelnau, Joffre's Chief of Staff and later his right-hand man at *GQG*, also voiced his concerns about the lack of preparedness of the Army in a heated debate in the *Chambre des Députés* in 1913.

But, even had the weapons existed, was their use understood by Generals whose experience and training ignored these guns for so long? Apparently not. In the March 1914 edition of the *Revue d'artillerie* an anonymous artillery officer signing himself *General D* posed the following questions in an article entitled *Une doctrine pour l'artillerie lourde*:

> "We have heavy artillery," wrote *General D*, "Do we have a doctrine for the employment of this heavy artillery? It would seem not. Question one hundred officers of all ranks drawn at random from all arms: What is heavy artillery? What is it used for? How is it employed? To whom is it attached? How is it deployed?
>
> The odds are 100 to 1 on that you will not get an answer or that they will reply by asking the same questions in return. That, at least, is the impression given by the general uncertainty one sees during war games and small and large unit manoeuvres when it comes to the use of the heavy artillery."[67]

To underline this problem, an article written by an anonymous *General X* in the *Journal des sciences militaires* of 1st March 1914, entitled *Artillery in France and in Germany in 1914*, and sub-headed *'Confiance!'*, was an attempted rebuttal of criticisms of French artillery capability in a Paris newspaper which described the French position as one of 'heart-breaking inferiority'. 'We do not share this pessimism' it responded robustly before going on to make out that *every* French artilleryman offered the choice of a howitzer or a *75* would choose the latter even if the howitzer outranged the *75*. It posed the question: which artillery piece was more useful, one with a range of 6,000 metres (such as the *75*) or one with a range of 8,000 metres (such as the *15-cm schwere Feldhaubitze 1902* with a range of c. 7,500 metres). It asked:

> "Is the second more powerful than the first?"

The answer is, at least to this writer, extraordinary:

> "No. It is powerful in one area - between 6,000 and 8,000 metres - where the other is not. But since it only acquires this property at the cost of greater weight, and a piece less easy to service, etc. then between 0 and 6,000 metres it is less powerful than the first: *a priori*, for the reasons stated, it fires slower and launches, by unit of time, a lesser mass of explosive material."[68]

This makes sense in the context of the widespread French rejection of the 'artillery duel' in which one side sought to destroy or suppress the other's artillery before turning their guns on the infantry. If, however, the longer-range German howitzers, firing from defiladed positions, simply sat back and bombarded the French guns before causing havoc amongst the infantry then the point about landing 'a lesser mass of explosive material' over the shorter range becomes practically irrelevant. The rest of the article simply rehearses an increasingly fatuous series of reasons why the *75* is the answer to all known battlefield problems because, as it repeatedly argues, rate of fire is more important than range or weight of shell.

To make matters even worse, if that were possible, production capacity of new guns in diminished after the main part of the 75-mm field gun construction programme was completed. As with the British, skilled manpower at government armaments plants was allowed to run down alarmingly. Furthermore, experienced artillery officers such as Deport, Rimailho and Filloux, all involved in the design and construction of these guns, departed the government arsenals for better paid jobs in the private sector with companies like *Schneider* and *Saint-Chamond*.

The situation in the Army was not much better. French artillerists and engineers were supposed to be trained initially at the *École polytechnique* on the *montagne Sainte-Geneviève* in the *5e arrondissement*, part of the Latin Quarter of Paris. Their next step was the *École d'application de l'artillerie et du génie* at Fontainebleau[i]. This was the path of leading artillery officers like Foch and Fayolle. It was officers thus trained, however, who were leaving the Army in alarming numbers. In 1908, it was estimated half of the officers trained at the *École polytechnique* had resigned in search of better job prospects and enhanced pay. This situation then worsened such that the journal *France Militaire* calculated that, in January 1914, only a quarter of current artillery officers had been trained at the *École polytechnique*.[69]

Douglas Porch in *The March to the Marne* puts forward an argument that one of the problems in expanding the quantity of heavy artillery available to the French Army prior to 1914 was that there were simply not enough officers or men available to man the batteries proposed, and that this was a result of political decisions which had limited the size of the Army, e.g. the *loi du 21 mars 1905*, the *loi Berteaux*, which had limited conscripts to a two-year active period of service. The general malaise caused by the fall-out from the Dreyfus affair also undermined morale and enthusiasm amongst officers. Thus, in 1912, a plan to create an additional ten 155-mm batteries was rejected by the Army because there not enough trained artillerymen to man these guns without removing them from existing batteries of *75s*. The introduction of the *loi du 19 juillet 1913*, the *loi des trois ans* (or *loi Barthou*), which increased the period of active service to three years and the size of the army by c. 100,000 men more or less overnight, did allow for the creation of fifteen new heavy batteries and five new heavy regiments in early 1914.[70] But, and it is a big 'but', there was still a shortage of trained artillery officers; the guns with which these new units were to be equipped were still based on not very-recently-modified de Bange tubes, i.e. the Rimailho-adapted *obusier de 155 mm CTR modèle 1904*; and the existing officers and men attached to the *régiments d'artillerie à pied* manning the fortress and coastal defences, and the *régiments d'artillerie lourde* attached to the various armies still played no or little part in the annual French manoeuvres and thus operated in a tactical void with little or no connection to the tactical guidance which drove the infantry and the field gunners.

Porch also proposes the idea that the people at fault for the absence of sufficient heavy artillery in August 1914 were Republican politicians reluctant to spend the money necessary and not the supporters of the *offensive à outrance* some of whom believed heavy artillery would play no part in the rapid advances their strategic and tactical philosophy demanded. There was, however, a third group who acted as a brake on the development of new weapons and tactics: the officers who believed the *75* was the only gun required and who stated that the

---

[i] A separate *École d'application de l'artillerie* was formed in 1912.

introduction of new guns, for example a field howitzer, would only serve to cause tactical confusion on the battlefield and chaos in the supply of shells to a variety of guns once in action.

One of the leading proponents of this idea was the previously mentioned critic of Grandmaison, Gen. Alexandre Percin[i]. By 1914, Percin was 68 years old and, since July 1911, in the reserve[ii]. His last command, from 1907 to 1909, was the *13e corps d'armée* based around Clermont-Ferrand. Born in Nancy on 4th July 1846, he was the son of Nicolas Jules Percin, *Recteur de l'Académie de Nancy* and a mathematics teacher, and Joséphine Victorine *née* Blanpain[iii]. He attended the *École polytechnique* in 1865 and fought in the Franco-Prussian War being wounded twice. By 1882, he was a professor at the *École spéciale militaire de Saint-Cyr*. In 1890 he directed the *Manufactures d'armes de Saint-Etienne* and, by 1895, was *Inspecteur des Manufactures d'armes*. In the late 90s he was responsible for the development of the tactical application of the *75*. 1900 saw the most dramatic change in his career path when Gen. Louis Joseph Nicolas André became *Ministre de la Guerre* on 28th May 1900. André appointed fellow artilleryman Percin as his *chef de cabinet* and promoted him *Général de brigade*. André was a radical republican, vehemently anti-clerical, a Freemason, and a *Dreyfusard*. In the fevered atmosphere caused by *l'affaire Dreyfus*, he determined to change the French Army by promoting republican, anti-catholic officers, whether competent or not, at the expense of catholic 'reactionaries'. Ferdinand Foch, with his Jesuit background, was one such officer whose career was temporarily de-railed. According to Émile Mayer who knew them both, Percin became André's chief 'enforcer' in what became known as *'l'affaire des fiches*[iv].

André and Percin previously served together in Angoulême and, later, he would write of Percin that he was:

"A very intelligent general officer, very vigorous and active, with an exceptional capacity for work; diligent, methodical; wrote well with ease."

---

[i] Highly thought of, Percin was a Freemason and Radical Socialist. In 1914 he commanded the *1ere Region militaire* around Lille. Accused of abandoning 400 guns and 53,000 rifles in the city, he said he was simply obeying orders. In 1921 he published *Le Massacre de notre infanterie, 1914-1918*. He claimed 75,000 French troops were killed by 'friendly fire' (or c. 5% of the total French dead). In *Annex X* he lists every example of 'friendly fire' involving French infantry and artillery. It goes on for 75 pages.
[ii] Defeated as a *radical-socialiste* candidate for Deputy, Seine region, in November 1911
[iii] His three older brothers were: *Général de Brigade* Ferdinand Jules Percin, an Army engineer (1836-1900); Eugène Léon Percin, *Inspecteur Principal de la Compagnie des Chemins de Fer de l'Est* (1838-1919); and Prosper Henry Percin, *Chef de bataillon, 3e régiment de Zouaves* (1842-?).
[iv] André had a card (i.e. *fiches*) index of officers headed *'Corinth'* or *'Carthage'*. Other names were added by fellow Freemasons. The classical references were: for approved Republicans, Horace's quote *'non licet omnibus adire Corinthum'* (i.e. 'Not everyone can go to Corinth'). Corinth had a reputation for pandering to the wealthy with its thousand *hetairas* (temple prostitutes) at the Temple of Aphrodite, Acrocorinth); and, for 'reactionary' Catholics, the repeated phrase of Cato the Elder prior to the Third Punic War (149–146 BC), *'Delenda est Carthago'* ('We must destroy Carthage').

Despite his close association with André, Percin's career did not suffer when the *'l'affaire des fiches'* was exposed in 1904, bringing down not only André but the administration of the anti-clerical Émile Combes[i]. Percin, however, had already been promoted *Général de division* and taken command of the *7e Division* based mainly in Normandy. He went on to command the *13e Corps* in 1907 and to serve on the *Conseil supérieur de la guerre* between 17th October 1908 and 4th July 1911.

Percin was a clever man. The author of half a dozen books, mainly post-war, he was deeply affected by, and often highly critical of, the conduct of the war, and became an active proponent of the League of Nations, an opponent of the penal sanctions imposed on Germany in the Treaty of Versailles, and a pacificist in favour of 'moral disarmament' which views he expressed in his last book *La Guerre à la Guerre* published in 1927, a year before his death on 12th October 1928.

But, pre-war, he had a blind spot when it came to the *75* and the application of artillery generally, which is not surprising given his role in developing artillery tactics at the time the *75* was launched. In 1914, he published a work entitled *Le combat*.[71] It covers a host of areas: tactical, moral, the impact of new weapons, casualty rates[ii], fear on the battlefield, training, the involvement of reservists (in which he believed), all leavened with various examples taken from the Franco-Prussian War including the barely relevant Battle of Coulmiers near Orléans on 9th November 1870[iii], one of the very few French successes of the war.

He spends an inordinate amount of time discussing the benefits of the French 4-gun field battery versus its German 6-gun equivalent. He asserts, for example, that a 4-gun battery produces more hits on target than a 6-gun battery mainly, it seems, because the commander of the battery spends less time ensuring accuracy with each gun in the larger battery. In fact, it is the arithmetic which is rather simple: four *75s* fired 80 rounds a minute whilst six *77-mms* fired at most 60.

---

[i] Nevertheless, on 9th December with the *loi concernant la séparation des Églises et de l'État* was passed which turned France into a secular state.
[ii] He spends a lot of time persuading his readers, and perhaps himself, that new high-powered, long-range weapons only served to *decrease* battlefield casualties relative to, say, the Napoleonic wars. By the simple (simplistic?) method of dividing the number of casualties at, say, Mukden by the number of days over which the battle was fought he 'proves' it was less costly than Waterloo, for example. What he would have made of the casualties on 1st July and several other costly days in the war is unknown. But his horror at the casualties he witnessed in the Great War changed his attitude towards war as a means of settling national and international disputes [*Source*: Percin, Gen. A, *Le combat*, Alcan, *Nouvelle collection scientifique*, 1914, Chapter 3, page 17 onwards].
[iii] The *Armée de la Loire*, commanded by Gen. Louis Jean Baptiste D'Aurelle de Paladines, surprised the encamped *I. Bayerisches Armeekorps* under Ludwig *Freiherr* von und zu der Tann-Rathsamhausen. After heavy shelling, a bayonet charge routed the Bavarians. The exhausted, under-trained and inexperienced French failed to take advantage of the success and locked themselves up in Orléans. The city was re-taken during the Battle of Orléans, 2nd-4th December 1870, by the Prussian *II. Armee* commanded by *Prinz* Friedrich Karl von Preußen using troops released by Bazaine's surrender at Metz. During the fighting French casualties were nearly 20,000, killed, wounded and PoWs, against 1,700 for the Prussians.

55 Gen. Alexandre Percin

He then addresses the public concern that a French *Corps d'armée* with 24 batteries each of four guns, i.e. 96 in total, was at a severe disadvantage compared to a German *Armeekorps* with 24 batteries of six guns, i.e. 144 in total. Broadly, this amounted to four *75s* per 1,000 men in a French *Corps d'armée* against six *77s*, *10.5* and *15-cm* howitzers per 1,000 men in a German *Armeekorps*. This apparently did not matter because experiments conducted by Gen. Hagron in 1904, and by Percin himself with the *13e Corps d'armée* at Lorlanges, *département de la Haute-Loire*, on 12th September 1908, showed that it was well-nigh impossible to get all 96 French guns into a firing line on the front a Corps, let alone 144. All of which led to Percin stating, and advising an Army Commission set up in 1908 to enquire into this subject, that:

> "… if it pleased the Germans to further increase the number of guns in their army corps, we should be happy about it, and not imitate; it would be folly to encumber the columns and the battlefield with such a quantity of artillery there would be no room left for the infantry."[72]

The result was a somewhat soggy compromise. On 24th July 1909 a law was passed which kept the number of guns per battery at four but increased the number of batteries per *Corps' d'armée* to thirty, i.e. 120 guns, still 24 fewer than in the German army but raising the ratio of guns to infantry from 4:1,000 to 5:1,000. In 1910, manoeuvres with the increased number of batteries were in Picardy and Percin was a referee. There he was happy to find that that addition of a reserve brigade to each *Corps d'armée* had returned the ratio to the magical 4:1,000, or the 'happy medium' as Percin described it. But he was still critical of the Government:

> "Our leaders did not care. They said to themselves, quite simply:
> 'The more guns we have, the stronger we are. So let's increase the number of guns'.
> Then, almost immediately afterwards:
> 'The more battalions we have, the stronger we are. Let us therefore increase the number of battalions'."[73]

All very sensible to this writer's eyes but not to Percin who simply regretted the time taken getting back to (his) first principles. In the meantime, however, the

Germans played a nasty little trick. They increased the number of guns attached to each *Armeekorps* to 160 with the addition of extra 10.5-cm and 15-cm howitzers[i], both with a range 1-2,000 metres longer than the *75*.

No matter, according to Percin and, in his denial, he revealed the true state of mainstream French thinking about the use of artillery on the battlefield:

> "… what effect can we expect from ordnance firing at such distances because this firing is not observable? It would be, even more than in Manchuria, shooting 'at the unknown, at abandoned villages, unoccupied slopes, walls behind which nothing happens at all'.
>
> There is no possible liaison with the infantry, with an artillery which would be held six kilometres to the rear. Such artillery could only target the opposing guns, but then it would be a step towards the specialization of counter-batteries and infantry batteries, a specialization against which the regulation of 8th September 1910 quite rightly objects."

For Percin, the infantry was still *La Reine des batailles*, the Queen of the Battlefield, as, after all:

> "However brilliant the cavalry charges, however effective the artillery fire, until the infantry drives the enemy from their positions, nothing is done."[74]

Thus, the role of the artillery was to prepare the way for, and support, the infantry. Oddly, post-war, he complained bitterly about the number of men lost to French artillery fire when, to support the infantry until the last moment, the flat-firing *75s* almost inevitably must cause some friendly fire casualties amongst the on-rushing infantry. His complaint, however, was about heavy artillery. Thus his criticisms of, and antagonism towards, Gen. Herr.

Other than in an attack on field fortifications, heavy artillery, either long guns or howitzers, was of no immediate use. They moved too slowly, they got in the way both on the march and on the battlefield, and they fired too slowly. Furthermore, French Generals, however distinguished and experienced, apparently didn't know what to do with them anyway:

> "During the manoeuvres of 1912, the commander of the *armée de l'Ouest*, did not know what to do with a heavy artillery group (twelve guns) placed at his disposal. This group, according to the regulations, should have remained part of the army, but was passed, before any fighting, to one of his army corps commanders. He passed it to a divisional general. Finally, this group was used to support the attack on the village of Craon, on which four groups of *75s* were already firing, whereas one or two would have sufficed."[75]

The Army commander Percin is criticising here is none other than Joseph Simon Gallieni who, a year earlier, had been first choice as the *chef d'État-Major* and *vice-président du Conseil supérieur de guerre*, i.e. the *de facto* CinC of the French Army in the event of war.

---

[i] 21 batteries of six 77-mm field guns, three batteries of six *10.5-cm lFH* and four batteries of four *15-cm sFH*.

Of the more recent evidence of the efficacy of heavier guns on the battlefield Percin was at one with the younger officers such as Bellenger and Alvin who had talked to Serbian and Bulgarian witnesses of the First Balkan War. This put him in direct opposition to Gen. Herr, something which continued post-war with Percin directing heavily sarcastic comments at his colleague in his 1921 book *Massacre de notre infanterie, 1914-1918*. Percin took from Bellenger's reports that the only real use of howitzers by the Bulgarians was at the siege of Edirne (Adrianople), at the bloody five-day Battle of Lüleburgaz – Pinarhisar, 28th October to 2nd December 1912[i] and in the subsequent static fighting along the Çatalca lines in front of Constantinople. Furthermore, he argued that the only reason why these guns were used was because the severity of the fighting demanded all and any guns were involved and the curvature of fire and the heavier shells employed by the howitzers were not the reasons for their use.

Why, Percin asked, were the armies in the Balkans thus so encumbered with howitzers and long(ish) guns of 120-mm when their specific characteristics were neither required nor employed? It was, he stated, because the Serb and Bulgarian armies wished, 'without asking themselves if it was useful or not',[76] to emulate the German Army with its array of field guns and howitzers, medium howitzers and long guns all attached to their *Armeekorps*.

Percin then explained why he thought the Germans had, in the first place, adopted and added the *10.5-cm lFH* to their armoury. First, he quoted a piece taken from the journal *France Militaire* published on 27th July 1912:

> "The first objective of the German howitzers will be our artillery. It is by destroying this artillery, and not by being satisfied with neutralizing it, that the Germans intend to support their infantry: Their regulations lead them to consider the artillery fight as one of the essential acts of the battle.
> All the artillery will be in line, as soon as possible, and acting *en masse*. Such is the principle which seems to be adopted by the Germans."[77]

Leaving to one side the fact that such tactics would prove extremely effective in the Battle of the Frontiers in mid to late August 1914, Percin's explanation for the adoption of the *10.5-cm lFH* was that the high explosive shell of their 77-mm field gun was less powerful than that of the *75* and the German field gun generally inferior in all respects. The result was that, along with the adoption of the *15-cm sFH*, etc., the Germans would now have a cumbersome mix of weaponry on the battlefield, difficult to supply with ammunition and not necessarily deployed in the best locations to achieve the desired results. Thus, he argued, 'One would find cannon when one wanted howitzers, or howitzers when one wanted cannon'.[78] In his view, the simplicity and uniformity of the French artillery arsenal, i.e. almost entirely 75-mm field guns, would prove a distinct advantage, even if out-numbered and out-ranged by the enemy's *materiel*. In other words, Percin believed that the same tactical ignorance of the means of employing heavier guns which reached as high as the commanders of French Armies also obtained within the German Army. The fact they had been rehearsing the use of howitzers in the annual manoeuvres for several years appears to have passed him by.

---

[i] Total casualties on both sides were in excess of 42,000 out of 238,000 involved.

It was generally the case, both in France and Great Britain, that army officers and commentators believed German artillery tactics inferior to those of the French, partly because of the assumed superiority of the *75*. Germany was, however, moving in a contrary direction to that imagined by Percin and many colleagues. Percin believed the rapid firing *75s* would catch German batteries deploying in the open. But, several years earlier, Germany, with the introduction of its two howitzers able to fire from defiladed positions, aimed to prevent this. German artillery tactics were then simplified so that only two types of gun deployments were recognised: the *offene Stellung*, or open position, and the *verdeckte Stellung*, or covered position. The *offene Stellung* was, according to *The Times* in 1911, the exception not the rule as it exposed the gun and its personnel to fire from the enemy's field guns. It was still to be used at the key moment of the infantry assault, very much in the way of the Franco-Prussian War. The *verdeckte Stellung* was the norm. By *verdeckte* or 'covered' they did not mean the gun emplacements developed during trench warfare with reinforced head cover which protected both gun and crew. In 1911, and in the early months of the war, it referred to a defiladed position for both gun and crew, e.g. on the reverse slope of a ridge, or behind some other obstruction.[79] In this, the presence of the two howitzer types were useful. They could fire at the *75s* from beyond the maximum range of the *75* or from positions within its range but which the essentially flat fire of the *75* could not reach.

As *The Times* reported in 1911 whilst observing the German annual manoeuvres in Mecklenburg:

"Practically for the first time the covered position was the rule for all batteries in attack or defence, but at the crisis of an action the guns were usually run up to the crest by hand or galloped up by the teams and fired over the sights. In von der Goltz's attack upon the II Army Corps on September 13th the whole of his guns, so far as the writer could judge, were in the open when the Infantry prepared to assault... (but) the positions of German batteries were, as a rule, difficult to pick up with field glasses from the enemy's positions until the guns came up to the crest in the decisive phases of a fight."[80]

Despite this, Percin, nearly three years later, still harboured the hope that:

"Our masked batteries will demolish the enemy guns that let themselves be seen. The result will be, for our adversary, the superiority of their losses and not the superiority of their fire."[81]

In fact, in Lorraine and the Ardennes in August 1914, it was French Generals and artillery commanders who would complain they were constantly under fire from high-angle German howitzers they could not see, let alone reach. As the soon-to-be-*limogé* Gen. Émile Edmond Legrand-Girarde, commander of the *21e Corps d'Armée* of Dubail's *1re armée*, complained whilst fighting in the Vosges in August 1914, his troops relentlessly suffered under:

"... an incessant firing of howitzers which it is impossible to see and therefore to counter battery."

Broadly, Percin did not believe in the need either for counter-battery fire, *aka* 'the artillery duel', or, as he described it, for 'curved fire' in general. Instead, he fondly hoped that, whilst defiladed German guns tried to pinpoint the positions of the *75s*, the quicker moving and quicker firing *75s* would 'always find a site from where a *75* gun could reach the German howitzer'. If curved fire was ever needed then he believed the *Plaquette Malandrin* (see page 247) would suffice even if its use so reduced the range of the shell that the *75s* would be out-ranged by even the 77-mm field gun let alone both German howitzers.

There were others, typically younger, officers who fundamentally disagreed with Percin's opinions and, what is more, challenged the factual basis for his judgements. In January 1912, 44-year-old *Chef d'escadron* Jules Marie Joseph Challéat, wrote a piece for the *Revue d'artillerie* entitled *La question de l'obusier léger* in which he strongly argued in favour of the adoption of a 105-mm field howitzer and suggesting that the German *10.5-cm lFH* provided coverage of areas the *75* could not reach as well as a destructive power on field fortifications way beyond that of the HE shell of the *75*. He concluded that:

> "Our *Corps d'armée* therefore need light howitzers, if only to counteract enemy howitzers placed in conditions where the 75-mm (even assuming a certain reduction in initial speed for the high-explosive shell) would be powerless to reach them."[82]

The only remaining question for Challéat was: how many were needed and of what size? 105-mm was, he believed, the optimum size for manoeuvrability and weight of fire and 20-24 needed to be added to each *Corps d'armée* to adequately counter the 36 such guns now attached to each German *Armeekorps*.

In March 1912, an anonymous officer, O.B., published an article in the *Journal des sciences militaires*: '*The Question of the Light Field Howitzer*'.[83] He argued that the case for a light field howitzer had not been seriously studied within the army for 15 years, i.e. since the arrival of the *75*, and that 'an influential school' within the army had effectively blocked any debate on the development and application of such a weapon. Members of this 'school' were Percin, who developed the tactical use of the *75*, and the highly influential but recently deceased, Gen. Hippolyte Langlois, and two less elevated but still highly significant artillery officers: Lt. Col. Edmond Buat (the man who falsified the German war plans, see page 135), who was attached to Gen. Henri de Lacroix, the *vice-président* of the *conseil supérieur de la guerre* 1907-9 (and, therefore, commander in chief designate), worked for Alexandre Millerand, *ministre de la Guerre* in 1912, and, on the outbreak of war, was a professor in tactics at the *École supérieure de guerre*; and Gen. Jean Anatole Dumézil who was employed in *the section technique de l'artillerie* at the *Ministère de la Guerre* from 1904 to 1907 and then as Deputy and *président* of the *Commission d'étude pratique de tir* and as director of the *cours pratiques de tir* from 1907 to 1910. Dumézil had, therefore, overseen field artillery shooting training with Buat, for a while, assisting. Both would go on to play prominent roles in the war, Dumézil as commander of the artillery of *Xe Armée* from 6th November to 28th December 1914 then as *Inspecteur des études et expériences techniques de l'artillerie* from 8th June 1915 and finally, and ironically, as the Deputy and *Sous-secrétaire d'État de l'Artillerie et des Munitions* (for heavy artillery) from 3rd August 1915; and Buat as *chef d'état-major de l'armée d'Alsace* in August 1914 and then as the *chef de cabinet* of Alexandre Millerand, *ministre de la Guerre*. After time at *GQG* in 1916 he was, again ironically, appointed head of the *réserve générale d'artillerie*, again a role involving the build-up of French heavy artillery. Before the war, however, according to Émile Mayer:

> "They were virtuosos in the *75* gun; they knew how to play this instrument effectively; they knew the full range of its resources. So they were naturally inclined to attribute all merits to it, to believe it fit for all services, to entrust it with all tasks."[84]

But, in this time, perhaps no-one was as influential over artillery procurement and policy, and the resulting devotion to the *75*, as Gen. Hippolyte Langlois[i].

Langlois was born in Besançon on 3rd August 1839, the son of Marie Gabriel Hippolyte, a lawyer, and Thérèse Louise Turquin. He entered the *École polytechnique* 1856 and the *École d'application* in 1858 before being commissioned into the *12e régiment d'artillerie monté* in 1860. In 1864 he joined the *artillerie monté* of the *Garde Imperiale* and in 1866 the *19e régiment d'artillerie à cheval*, briefly being the adjutant of the *Manufacture d'armes de Saint Étienne*. Now with the *17e régiment d'artillerie à cheval* he was, for five years from 1870, an instructor in *Equitation et de conduit de voitures* in the horse artillery but this was interrupted when he was part of Bazaine's army which surrendered at Metz in October 1870, Langlois being interned in Coblenz from 29th October to 31st May 1871. Promoted Lt. Col. in 1885 he was appointed a professor of artillery tactics at the *École supérieure de guerre* which role he fulfilled for six years. Colonel of the *4e régiment d'artillerie* for three years he was then promoted *Général de Brigade* and commander of the artillery of the *13e Corps*. Three years as commander of the *17e Brigade d'infanterie* preceded his appointment as the commandant of *École supérieure de guerre* and elevation to *Général de Division*. As the commandant of the *École supérieure* he was extremely influential over the young officers in whom he imbued the spirit of the *offensive*. As a member of the *Comité technique d'état-major* he was also an important part of the process of the development of the *75* and its tactical application as part of the *offensive à outrance*. In 1901 he was given command of *20e Corps* based in the important border city of Nancy (subsequently commanded by Ferdinand Foch until 29th August 1914) and he joined the *Conseil supérieur de la guerre*. He retired in 1903 and became a prolific and influential writer on military matters until he died on 12th February 1912.

According to Mayer, Langlois produced the theory of rapid-fire equipment before Col. Deport[ii] created the *75*. This provoked Mayer to ask in 1918:

---

[i] Elected senator for *Meurthe et Moselle* 1906, a Member of the *Académie française* 1911. The author of various books, he founded the monthly *Revue militaire générale* in 1907.

[ii] Lt. Col. Joseph-Albert Deport was born in 1846 in Saint-Loup-sur-Semouse, *département de la Haute-Saône*, the son of Romain Deport and Augustine Cornibert. *École Polytechnique*, 1866. *École d'application de l'artillerie et de Génie*, Metz, 1868. Wounded, Franco-Prussian War. *8e regiment d'artillerie*. Adjutant, Director at Bourges. *Atelier de construction d'artillerie de Tarbes*, 1877. Director, *Atelier de construction de Puteaux*, 1888. Resigned, 1894. Director, *Compagnie des forges de Châtillon et Commentry*, Montluçon. Châtillon-sur-Seine, *département de la Côte-d'Or*. In 1897 the company took over the *Société metallurgique de Champigneulles et Liverdun* and was renamed *Compagnie des forges de Châtillon, Commentry et Neuves-Maisons*. Neuves Maisons is in the *département de Meurthe-et-Moselle* and its seven blast furnaces were lost in August 1914. He died in 1926.

"To what extent was he (i.e. Langlois) the instigator of the research which led to this creation? Was it just a coincidence? No matter. What is certain is that, in his course at the *Ecole de guerre* (published in January 1892 as *L'Artillerie de campagne en liaison avec les autres armes*) he fixed with extreme precision the essential characteristics that the technicians had to achieve".[85]

It is difficult to deny this assertion when one reads relevant parts of Langlois' book based on his lectures given before 1891:

"Entirely new equipment will soon become necessary, because the progress made since the creation of the latest models is considerable. The nation which adopts squarely a new principle will create a material against which the current artillery, even transformed, could not fight; it will force others to imitate it without delay and thus incur all the expense of a costly transformation, not to mention the danger of a delay of a few years perhaps[i]. This new principle leads to the creation of light artillery with rapid fire, fusing, and shields."[86]

He then went on to describe the basics of field artillery:

"Servicing the gun includes the following operations between the firing of two successive shots: 1. bringing the piece back into battery; 2. loading it; 3. aiming it. The purpose of the rapid-fire cannon is to minimize the time required for these three acts. 1. the resetting operation is eliminated by making the carriage stationary during firing; 2. re-aiming is eliminated or, at least, the time taken greatly reduced, by arranging that the gun barrel returns after each shot to its firing position; 3. the time required for loading is reduced by the use of a metal cartridge connected to the projectile."[87]

Stating that the gun shield would entirely protect the crew from bullets, shrapnel and splinters he then, according to one of his chief supporters, Edmond Buat[ii], set out:

"… the progress made by the metallurgical industries authorized, from 1890, to construct the equipment he dreamed of; he fixed the weight to be given to the different elements of the gun and carriage and detailed the type of shrapnel needed. Moreover, he knew how to foresee the methods of adjusting shooting and the use of fire which would be essential."[88]

Langlois accepted that artillery would have to fire from some sort of cover, i.e. reverse slopes, or other obstructions,[89] but, in essence, he had described the specification and performance and, thereby, to a great extent, the tactical use of the new field gun.

As far back as 1884, Langlois, then a *Chef d'escadron* with the *13e Régiment d'artillerie*, had been influencing artillery tactics, producing a report for the *Comité de l'artillerie* with reference to the new *Manuel de Tir* in which he underlined the need for field batteries to enter action as quickly as possible and to fire as quickly as possible. He wrote:

---

[i] The case when Germany re-designed the *77-mm FK 96* in response to the *75*.
[ii] Writing in 1911 and then a *Chef d'escadron* in the *25e régiment d'artillerie de campagne*.

"We see battery commanders - and there are many - who take 7 minutes or more between the command 'in battery' and the first gunshot and who do not fire a salvo in less than 4 to 5 minutes during registration."[90]

What was needed was both rapid action by battery and gun commanders and rapid fire from the guns (though ten rounds a minute at the time seemed 'rapid') and, to achieve the former, specific training was required allied to an agreed tactical application of such guns. Langlois, however, was a practical, not a technical, artillery officer, thus his 1892 book was written in ignorance of the progress made by Sainte-Claire Deville at *Bourges* with his 52 and 57-mm guns, let alone what Deport was up to at *Puteaux* with the *75*. Indeed, one of Langlois' main interests seems to have been in a quick-firing infantry support weapon based on the 37 and 40-mm *Canons-Revolver* built by *Hotchkiss* in 1879 and succeeded by the *Canons de 37* and *47-mm Mle 1885 Tir Rapide Système Hotchkiss*. In 1903, Langlois attempted to persuade the *Comité d l'artillerie* to invest in another 37-mm weapon but tests at *Bourges* proved it less effective than the *75* and the project was cancelled in 1908[i].[91]

ARCH-ADVOCATES OF THE *75*

56 Gen. Hippolyte Langlois

57 Gen. Edmond Buat

But a rapid-fire field gun, despite its apparent shortcomings against entrenched and defiladed enemy units, was the key to Langlois' ideas. Mayer's criticisms must be placed in the context of his belief, expressed in 1891 in *Evoluton de la Tactique*,

---

[i] A *Canon de 37-mm Mle 1916 TR* was produced by the *Atelier de Puteaux* as an infantry support weapon and used at Verdun in May, and on the Somme from 1st July 1916. Though not especially useful, it proved more effective in the open warfare of autumn of 1918. In 1914 Lt. George Nestler Tricoche wrote an article for the *Field Artillery Journal* of October/November 1914 in which he described a move away from the *75* to a rapid-fire 50-mm pom-pom: 'It is interesting to note that this proposal is nothing but an extension – not to say an 'adulteration' – of the ideas of that great French artillerist, General Langlois, who was the first to advocate the use of the pom-pom in his country, but who wished to add only two of these guns to each 75-millimetre battery.' [*Source*: Tricoche, G N, *French Artillery: The recent movement in favor of the Pom-pom (50-millimeter field gun)*, Field Artillery Journal, Oct-Nov. 1914, page 108 onwards].

that the next war would be dominated by immobile fronts and field fortifications.

Returning to O.B. and his thesis. His main point was that a flat-firing 75, the phrase used was 'tense trajectory', was useless against entrenched troops *and* defiladed artillery. He recited the current use of the 75 as advocated by Langlois:

> "Facing entrenchments or dugouts, field artillery should not aim to destroy cover: its role is to prevent the defender from using his weapons against our infantry, and to make it impossible to bring up food, ammunition and of, course, personnel. To this end, one or more batteries was to be placed overlooking the enemy's lines, on which they would carefully regulate their fire. This fire was to be executed in bursts as soon as the enemy gave any sign of activity either spontaneously or under the threat of friendly infantry moving to the attack. Other batteries were to take under their fire the ground behind the enemy line, to stop all movement. It was thought probable that, under these conditions, provided that the advance and fire of the friendly infantry was judiciously combined with the fire of the artillery, material and moral ascendancy would be gained over the defender which, if not complete, was at least serious enough to put him in a state of inferiority, whilst the attacking troops retained almost all their resources."[92]

That this was still the 'Langlois school's' opinion was made clear by Edmond Buat in his 1911 book *L'artillerie de campagne: son histoire, son évolution, son état actuel.* It was still the role of the infantry to uncover entrenched troops by advancing and, almost by definition, by suffering casualties:

> "Against infantry posted in a trench, the artillery will be without purpose unless the defenders of the field work reveal themselves to fire on the attacking infantry; only then can we strike them, and very effectively. This demonstrates that, in an attack on a fortified position, the long cannonades preceding the engagement of the infantry – the South African war provided numerous examples –uselessly waste ammunition. It is infantry advancing on the enemy which is then obliged to reveal itself to fire that brings about the artillery's intervention ... infantry which knows how to make judicious use of ground cover, to disperse in open areas, to concentrate in the parts which escape the observation of the enemy guns, will progress despite this guns, however quick-firing they may be, and will end up, without too much risk, coming to establish its line a few hundred metres from that of his adversary. From this moment on, rapid advances in quick bounds and lying down will be his only resources... with the support of his own cannon."[93]

This encapsulated the French (and British) belief that artillery *supported* an infantry attack but did not *prepare* the way for it. That the British in South Africa had neither the right sort of guns, i.e. howitzers, with which to bombard Boer trenches, nor the tactical acumen to work out such tactics, evaded Buat and his fellow 75-*ers*. Buat's description as to how to get infantry into position for a final assault of 'a few hundred metres' pre-supposes the enemy had no means of firing on troops in the apparently 'dead ground' across which French infantry hoped to approach relatively unscathed before the bayonet charge. And this is in a book written by a professional officer who knew full well that every German *Armeekorps* was equipped with numerous howitzers capable of achieving precisely that.

It was, nonetheless, generally accepted that the defenders under such an artillery attack would not suffer serious material or personnel losses as artillery support of the infantry involved firing shrapnel as an anti-personnel weapon. And this was because, as Buat admitted:

"Against entrenchments in the ground, the effects (of high explosive shells) are of little importance because of the weak charge in the shell."[94]

O.B. argued that, as these tactics were widely known, prudent defenders would only expose to French artillery fire those men needed to observe the progress of the French infantry. Then, because of the *75's* flat trajectory and the need to avoid 'friendly fire' casualties, the guns would be either forced to stop firing, or to lengthen their range once the attacking infantry was 3-400 metres from the defenders' lines. The attackers, now exposed and unsupported as they tried to get to close quarters, would thus come under fire from the entire garrison of the entrenched position and suffer serious, if not crippling, losses.

O.B. then pointed out another flaw in Langlois' tactics. The late General (he died on 12th February 1912, five weeks before the article appeared) had advocated the use of incendiary shells on places like fortified villages. Rather like the demands of Douglas Haig in 1916 for gas shells with which to render the German deep bunkers on the Somme uninhabitable (chlorine being heavier than air), the main problem in 1912, as in June 1916, was that such shells simply did not exist. Furthermore, O.B. argued, as both Langlois and Percin had argued in favour of one gun for all needs to simplify shells supplies on the battlefield demanding the use of a special shell for a special purpose rather contradicted their ideas.

In summary, O.B. argued that the *75* provided an incomplete answer to the problems of the modern battlefield. What it *could do* was neutralise enemy infantry by pinning them in their trenches, what it *could not do* was significantly erode their numbers or their defensive capability. As a result, he wrote:

"…infantry will pay with blood for insufficiently prepared attacks, whether or not it finds compensation for its sacrifices in success."

The solution was the 'curved fire' of the howitzer which allowed guns to attack defiladed positions and to drop either high explosive or shrapnel shells into or near trenches at such an angle that they would both proves effective. O.B. then entered into some arcane mathematical explanation as to why a howitzer is more accurate than a field gun which, with a Grade 6 Maths O-Level from 1967, this writer is in no position to understand, let alone challenge. He goes on to say that previous experiments with the elderly howitzers then available to the French Army which suggested otherwise should no longer be relied upon. After all, he pointed out, weapons were continually improving and the breech-loading artillery foolishly rejected by the French Army before 1870 was now the standard everywhere. With numerous major improvements to barrels, recoil systems, gun carriages, propellant charges, etc., there was every reason to believe that the accuracy of a modern howitzer had now vastly improved over the guns with which previous experiments had been conducted.

The fundamental question O.B. asked was: should the French Army rely on the simplicity of the *75* even if results in battle were inadequate and likely to lead to heavy infantry casualties; or should the Army invest in a lightweight, field howitzer which might increase the complexity of shell supplies and tactical control on the battlefield but which held out the hope of a more effective preparation of enemy positions prior to the assault by the gallant *poilus*?

O.B. then produced a 'concrete example' of the difference between the effectiveness of a battery of field howitzers, his material of choice being the 105-mm *Schneider* field howitzer (later used in the Army manoeuvres of 1912), and a battery of *75s* firing on a 200-metre long, two-metre-wide, trench manned by 200 troops. The battery of *105s* was supplied with 672 shells, half shrapnel containing 375 bullets, and half high explosive shells, containing 3 Kgs of explosive. The *75s* had 740 shells, half shrapnel (290 balls) and half high explosive (695 gms melinite). Each battery was to fire at a range of between 2 and 3,000 metres. The *105* battery fired 36 registration rounds and then 150 shrapnel and 150 HE rounds for effect. The *75* battery was to fire 40 registration shots and then all 700 rounds available.

O.B. argued that, in fifteen minutes, the *105s* would put eight HE shells into, or immediately next to, the trench and 36 shrapnel shells would explode overhead at an angle from which a proportion of the 13,500 shrapnel balls they contained would enter the trench[i]. He gave a low estimate that just 13%, or 50 bullets per shell, would do so but this still meant 1,800 shrapnel balls entering the trench at an average rate of c. nine per metre of front. He then gave an additionally low estimate that this combination of 24 Kgs of HE (plus the shards of the eight shell casings) and the 1,800 shrapnel balls would each cause a single casualty per shell, i.e. 44 deaths/wounded from a total out of 200 men. He then asked:

> "Can losses by fire amounting to 22% in a quarter of an hour cause moral and material wear and tear? We think the answer can only be yes."

But what of the *75s*? He argued that the flatness of the fire of the gun meant that if any of the 350 shrapnel shells caused a casualty it would be by chance. If the shrapnel shell detonated over the top of the trench, then the balls would be projected by the charge forward into the ground beyond the trench and, if it exploded in front of the trench, then any balls would be absorbed by the parapet behind which the enemy was hiding. Firing 75 shrapnel therefore only had the virtue of forcing the enemy into their trench. Of the HE, again fired flat, some twenty might land in or near the two-metre-wide trench. Those that landed in front of the trench would either bury themselves or ricochet over and beyond the trench. Others might have some material effect either through the explosive or shards from the shell case but then, even assuming half had a material effect, was the 6.95 Kgs of melinite likely to be anywhere near as effective as the 24 Kgs

---

[i] Bt. Col., later Brig. Gen., H A Bethell in *Modern guns and gunnery, 1910. A practical manual for officers of the Horse, Field and Mountain Artillery*, estimated that a 5-in. BL howitzer firing a HE Lyddite shell at a 20-yards by 10-yards casemate at a range of 3,500 yards would hit the target one time in six, i.e. a 16% success rate. Not dissimilar to O.B.'s figures [*Source*: Bethell, Col. H A, *Modern guns and gunnery, 1910. A practical manual for officers of the Horse, Field and Mountain Artillery*, F J Cattermole, 1910, page 178].

deposited into the trench by the *105s*? Thus, the effect of the *75* would be significantly less and the expenditure of ammunition more than double in terms of shells (but of a similar weight overall to the *105*).

O.B. called on the Army to conduct proper field howitzer experiments in order to judge objectively if one were needed and, if so, of what size and range.

By December 1912, O.B. published new evidence in the *Journal des Sciences Militaire* as *Questions d'artillerie d'actualité* (*Current Artillery Issues*). Even though the mainly French-equipped Slav/Greek coalition was advancing rapidly against the German-equipped and trained Ottomans it was, he suggested, too soon to draw conclusions from the First Balkan War which started on 8th October 1912. Instead, his evidence for the need for a light field howitzer (and other heavier, longer-range weapons) was drawn from the annual French manoeuvres which had taken place in western France the previous September and on which Percin had commented (see page 263) without once mentioning the role of the light field howitzer detachment added as an experiment to Gen. Marion's Red (or Eastern) Army.

The guns used were 105-mm field howitzers provided by *Schneider-Le Creusot* and attached to the *17e Division* of the *9e Corps*. These guns proved manoeuvrable, covering some 600 kms during the exercises in a manner comparable to that of the *75s*. O.B. then itemised the various occasions in which the *105s* had performed in a manner both helpful to the infantry and in a manner which the *75s* could not replicate. On 13th September[i], during an infantry attack on the tiny village of Vieillemont, whilst the *105s* were able to keep up a consistent 'fire' from a heavily defiladed position, the associated *75s* had to stop and move to another position from which to fire at Gallieni's Blue (Western) Army.

On the 16th September the guns were used in an attack near La Haye-Descartes. Their plunging fire was able to clear a valley through which the infantry needed to advance but which the flat-firing *75s* could not reach. Again, the following day, the *105s* swept an area the *75s* could not engage and 'demolished' fortifications and buildings on the edge of the village of Civray about to be attacked by the infantry all in a manner the lighter HE shells of the *75s* could not have achieved.

O.B. believed these actions displayed the advantages of the *105* to excellent effect. They supported the infantry and were able to take enemy *75s* under fire from positions the *75* could not reach. They deployed quickly not having the limitations of locations dictated by the flat fire of the *75*. They could continue to fire even when the enemy changed positions whereas often the *75s* needed to move to find their targets.

But, O.B. pointed out, the attacks on the field howitzer continued from those like Percin, who could see no further than the *75*:

> "Some come from resolute adversaries of the field howitzer, and the most obvious idea which seems to guide them has caused us a certain surprise. The introduction of a howitzer into our field crews seems by them an attack on the prestige of our *75* gun, which, in their opinion, suffices for all needs.

---

[i] On this day the unfortunate Gen. Marion, his staff, Corps artillery, and airplanes were captured by Blue cavalry under Gen. Dubois. The manoeuvres continued.

Without questioning either the high value of this piece, or the excellent training of our batteries, the examples cited above allow us to think that the cannon with flat fire is less suitable than the howitzer to carry out certain tasks... The two guns complement each other, such seems to be the truth, and the howitzer is the complement, the gun, the principal."[95]

O.B. then recited some of the other arguments levelled against the howitzer and in favour of the *75*, pointing out their contradictory nature. For example, if the need for curved fire was recognised by the *Plaquette Malandrin* or *cartouche réduite*, then why not use the plunging fire of the howitzer rather than reduce the range, power and effectiveness of the *75*?

Then there was the argument that the *10.5-cm lFH* had only been adopted to make up for the failings of the *77-mm FK*. These perceived failings were that the *77-mm* was essentially a direct fire gun unable to fire from defiladed positions and that it had a feeble amount of explosive (155 gms of Picric Acid) in its HE shell. O.B. made two points in rebuttal:

- The thin-walled *75* shell and thick-walled 77-mm shell were both, in slightly different ways, effective against troops in the open but neither was effective against field fortifications; and
- The Germans had adopted new aiming and ranging equipment and had been firing the *77-mm* from defiladed positions connected by telephone to observers for some years.

His conclusion was that the *10.5-cm lFH* was developed for a specific tactical purpose advantageous to the German Army and that France needed urgently to develop a weapon to counter its special characteristics.

But, in this article, O.B. went further, addressing the issue of heavier, longer-range guns available to the Germans such as the *10-cm Kanone 04* and *13.5-cm Kanone 09*. In April 1912, an article appeared in the *Revue d'Artillerie* written by a *Capitaine d'artillerie* Peloux[i] entitled *Matériels de campagne et de siège à tir rapide de gros calibres*.[96] It referenced the idea that long-range guns had been attached to the Revolutionary and the First and Second Empires armies in the form of Napoleon's *Belles filles*, the *Canon de 12 Gribeauval*[ii], and then the rifled, though muzzle-loading, *Canon de 12 La Hitte, Modele 1859*. Both, however, were Army guns, either used at long range or kept in reserve until the crucial moment on the battlefield. This concept of the 'artillery reserve' had persisted in the French Army and kept longer range guns (*120 L*) and heavier *220-mm mortiers* as well as the more mobile high-angle *155 C TR* well away from the fighting in August 1914.

Peloux then referred to the Boers' use of 155-mm guns in South Africa and by the Russians in Manchuria and their impact on the morale, if not physical well-being, of troops bombarded by 'invisible' guns. O.B. noted that the long-range, and often inaccurate, fire of the few Boer 155-mm guns delayed British advances

---

[i] Believed to be Capt., later Col., Peloux, *52e RAC*. Born 1876, he died 1957. *Section technique de l'artillerie* in 1911. *Etat-Major*, artillery, *5e Corps*, 1916. *Centre d'organisation d'artillerie lourde*, Arcis-sur-Aube, June 1917. Etat-Major-Général de l'Armée July 1917.

[ii] Developed by Jean Baptiste Vaquette de Gribeauval along with two shorter range cannons and a howitzer and first used in the American War of Independence.

or caused unnecessary deployments, all of which tired the already disconcerted troops. As a result, various countries adopted long-range guns:

Britain – from 1905 the *60 pounder BL* gun, range 9,400 metres;
Japan – from 1907 the *Type 38 10-cm cannon,* range 10,800 metres;
Germany – from 1905 the *10-cm Kanone 04* (range 10,400 metres) and, from 1909, the *13.5-com Kanone 1909* (range 16,500 metres); and
Russia – from 1910 the *107-mm gun M1910* with a range of 12,500 metres.

Peloux argued that the difference between the planned use of these guns and the attitude of the French Army towards them was that:

"… these guns are no longer intended, as in the past, to form an artillery reserve, but their role will be to force the enemy to deploy prematurely, to disturb the supply of ammunition, to prevent the approach of reserves, to extend, thanks to their 8 to 10 km range, the effects of the field gun beyond the limit of 4,000 metres where shrapnel quickly becomes ineffective."[97]

58 10-cm Kanone 04 at full recoil

In response to these developments, *Schneider* independently developed a *canon de 105-mm à tir rapide L/28,* capable of firing a 16 Kg shell 10,000+ metres for a fuzed shell (*tir fusant*), and a maximum of 11,800 metres for a percussion fuze (*tir percutante*). It had a maximum rate of fire of 12 to 14 rounds per minute. Critics, like Percin, complained such a gun complicated battlefield shell supply, that the gun would rarely be used, its results were invisible beyond 5-6,000 metres even in favourable terrain, and firing it at its maximum range was pointless as no-one would know what happened to the shells. This gun, too, was tested in the 1912 manoeuvres as part of Gallieni's *Armée de l'Ouest.* It proved as manoeuvrable as the *75s*, was quick to deploy, and proved its worth when called upon to support a crossing of the River Vienne near Pouzay. Defended by *Schneider 105* howitzers and a battery of elderly *120 L* guns firing at long range, the *75s* and *155C* howitzers available to Gallieni could not reach the *120 Ls*, let alone silence them. Eventually, a section of *canon de 105-mm à tir rapide* was ordered up, and covering 5 kms in thirty minutes, their range, 1,000+ metres longer than then *120 Ls*, did the trick.

O.B. thought the case was made for these guns and, in a sense, he was right. An order was placed in 1913 but just 24 were available in September 1914. As was almost inevitable with complex weaponry rushed into service there were problems with its manufacture and issues with the tube and thus, by May 1916, only 102 were with the Army. On the other hand, the 105-mm field howitzer was never ordered[i].

As *Generalleutnant* Hermann Schirmer wrote in the 1930s about German manufacturing problems both before and during the war:

> "Experience has taught that even the best arms factories cannot judge whether the proposed changes will hold up when fired live. It is not important to bring as many guns as possible to the front in a short time, but to deliver as many war-useable guns as possible to the front."[98]

Not content with addressing the issue of field howitzers and long guns, O.B. then moved on to heavy howitzers. Knowing of their use in Manchuria and that, since, the Germans had added a new 15-cm howitzer and other heavier high-angle guns to their arsenal, he commented that, though such guns would be used against *forts d'arrêt*, such as the *Fort de Manonviller* in the eastern approaches to Lunéville, they would also be in the forefront of any German advance and, therefore, able to bring down crushing, long-range fire from defiladed positions on any approaching French units. Opposing them, assuming they were deployed sufficiently far forward which, under current tactical theories, they would not, were elderly de Bange *mortiers* from around 1880 which would be easily outranged by the new German guns. Describing this generation of de Bange weapons O.B. stated that:

> "They may have been remarkable at the time and represented immense progress on their predecessors, but they have had their day and should have given way to more modern types. We have allowed ourselves to be overtaken by German artillery when we could easily have got ahead of it. It would be childish to deny it. The Germans introduced into their siege parks rapid-fire guns, firing without a platform: a 21-cm howitzer firing on wheels, against which our old equipment will cut a pretty bad figure."[99]

It was not that modern, quick-firing howitzers were unavailable because *Schneider* had developed for Russian, Bulgarian and Rumanian consumption the:

Obusier de siège de 15-cm à tir rapide Schneider L/15, with a rate of fire of 4-6 rounds per minute this gun fired a 40 Kg shell some 8,650 metres;

Obusier de siège de 21-cm à tir rapide Schneider L/13, with a range of 8,600 metres and a 98 Kg shell;

Mortier de siège de 24-cm à tir rapide Schneider L/12 with a 140 Kg shell and a range of 6,400 metres; and

Mortier de siège de 28-cm à tir rapide Schneider L/12 with a 275 Kg shell and an 8,300-metre range.

Neither the 21-cm nor 24-cm gun were adopted by the French but 22-cm variants *1915* and *1916* were ordered but not available until 1917. An order of 18 28-cm *mortiers* was placed in November 1913 but none had been started by mid-

---

[i] In 1915 Bulgarian *Obusiers de 120-mm modèle Schneider* were seized but sent to Salonika

1914. Instead, the French took over part of a Russian order for these guns and the first two came into service in autumn 1915. Twelve existed by May 1916.

O.B. then compared the characteristics of the de Bange *Mortier de 220 modèle 1880* and the *Obusier de siège de 21-cm à tir rapide Schneider*. It was not a happy picture:

	Mortier de 220 modèle 1880	Obusier Schneider de 21 cm T. R.
Shell weight, Kgs	98	98
Maximum range (metres)	5,200	8,500
Weight of gun, carriage etc., Kgs	12,180	7,765

And there were other drawbacks to the 1880 piece:
- simply building the *Mortier de 220's* platform took five hours;
- there was no shield to protect the *Mortier de 220's* gun crew;
- the *Mortier de 220* took hours to disassemble whereas the wheeled *Schneider* piece could be move more or less immediately; and
- the *Mortier de 220* fired, perhaps, one round every three minutes to the *Schneider's* two a minute.

As O.B. pointed out, it was no surprise guns designed thirty years earlier were less advanced, more cumbersome, fired more slowly, and had limited range[i]. Huge industrial, technical, and scientific advances were made between 1880 and 1912 of which the motor car (Carl Benz and his *Benz Patent-Motorwagen*, 1886) and powered flight (the Wright Brothers, 1903) were two prime examples. But, he said:

> "… let us not lose sight of the formidable consequences to which an artillery is exposed which tries to fight with ancient bombards against guns commensurate with the progress of their time. Let us remember the fate suffered by our fortresses in 1870 when our old bronze pieces collapsed before the steel artillery of our adversaries. We must hasten to modernize our siege artillery, and we can."[100]

In July 1913, as the clock rapidly ticked down to war, another heartfelt plea for the modernisation of French artillery was made by another, younger officer, 35-year-old Capt. Gabriel-Léopold Glück[ii]. It was of sufficient power and authority to be acclaimed, post-war, by none other than Émile Mayer as both 'remarkable' and 'truly prophetic'.[101] The piece was entitled *Obusiers de campagne et Artillerie lourde* and came in three parts (like Gaul) in the *Journal des sciences militaires*,[102] and emerged out of a conference held in Dijon on 18th January 1912. It had been updated to take account of the most recent developments and the First Balkan War which had finished on 30th May 1913.

---

[i] Another 'off the shelf' *Schneider* gun ignored by France was the *Canon de siège de 150-mm à tir rapide Schneider L/28* firing a 40 Kg shell 12,600 metres at 4-6 a minute.

[ii] Glück was born in 1878 and, in 1913, was an artillery captain based in Dijon. Post-war he was, by 1927, a Colonel commanding the Artillery of the French Army of the Levant. CO of the *62e régiment d'artillerie* in 1928, and commander of the artillery in Tunisia in 1931, of the artillery of the *17e Région* (Toulouse) in 1935, and the *3e Région* (Rouen) in 1938, retiring in 1940. He died in 1948.

Glück was forced to accept that disagreements about the future of French artillery had done little but confuse and worry the public:

> "Throughout the year, opponents and supporters of the field howitzer and heavy artillery have engaged in passionate and perhaps regrettable arguments, for we fear that they have not advanced a step and they have delayed the official solutions which all artillerymen recognize as urgent.
> During this time, the German artillerymen have perfected themselves in the use of their equipment.
> Public opinion today seems tired of these discussions, which it judges as almost byzantine. The tremendous increase in German military forces worries people."[103]

Furthermore, Glück expressed concern with the direction of German artillery tactics which was at odds with both British and French ideas that artillery's main function was to support the infantry attack:

> "The events of the Balkan war, and particularly the resistance experienced by the Bulgarians before Çatalça, seem to justify the importance and the credit accorded to heavy artillery by our adversaries across the *Rhine*, and to consecrate their doctrine, which aims at the destruction and not only to the neutralization of enemy batteries with shields."[104]

Then Glück provided a swift history lesson reminding his readers that Frederick the Great always marched with a mix of guns and howitzers, large and small. And, as with current German tactics, some heavier guns were always placed at the front of the line of march, ready to destroy any obstacle in his army's path. Then, progressively, heavier guns were placed in an Army's artillery reserve or used solely when sieges took place. But he also reminded his audience that Gen. Karl Wilhelm Friedrich August Leopold *Graf* von Werder, commander of the 45,000-strong *XIV Armeekorps* from Baden, defied Bourbaki and the 140,000-strong *Armée de l'Est* in the Battle of the Lisaine between 15th and 17th January 1871, in part by borrowing eighteen siege guns used in the siege of nearby Belfort. Then, whilst other countries abandoned heavy artillery for use in the field, the Germans, as from 1892, moved in the opposite direction, adding heavier guns like the *15-cm sFH 93* and incorporating them into the German Army's annual manoeuvres in a manner totally foreign to the French. Thus, the *Fußartillerie* (Foot or Heavy Artillery) learned their trade in the same tactical environment as the field gunners and the infantry. Then came the move to the improved *15-cm sFH 02* followed by changes to the regulations affecting heavy artillery such that, by 1908, they were fully integrated into each *Armeekorps*. Furthermore, the Germans had the *'forts d'arrêt'* and fortified zones of Verdun, Épinal, Toul and Belfort to deal with on the French border (and the forts of Liège and Namur in Belgium). Thus, heavy howitzers had the role not just of attacking these localities but of intervening on the battlefield as they would do in the Battles of Morhange and Sarrebourg on 21st and 22nd August 1914.

As in the French Army there were, initially, arguments about such moves. The difference was that the arguments were progressively won by those wishing to see heavy howitzers and long guns in the forefront of German Armies as Émile Mayer explained in 1918.[105] *General der Artillerie* and *Generalinspekteur der Fußartillerie* (1906-11), Otto Friedrich Franz von Dulitz wanted heavy guns deployed early so their greater reach could interfere with the advance of the enemy before each side came within field gun range:

> "… the proof has been made with certainty that, in the artillery struggle, (heavy artillery) furnishes a rapid result with a comparatively small expenditure of ammunition. Hence the conclusion that all the heavy artillery had to be brought into line early."[106]

With this statement he came into conflict with *General der Artillerie* Richard Theodor Ludwig Leopold von Schubert, the *Inspekteur der Feldartillerie* from 1907 to 1911, who represented a more conservative, not to say, French view of the use of heavy artillery:

> "Such a powerful weapon must be reserved for determined destruction. It would be wasting it to engage it before the situation is clarified. Moreover, it cannot be concealed that its presence at the head of the columns will cause congestion, and its intervention at the beginning of the engagement will only delay the entry into action of the field artillery.
>
> So, it is field artillery that will have to start the fight, and it is only when this fight is ongoing that the heavy cannon, brought forward at leisure and without having hindered the deployment of the troops, will usefully bring the support of its ballistic power and will help to open the gap through which the infantry will pass."[107]

With the *Kaiser* a firm believer in the howitzer, von Dulitz held the upper hand in this argument and the Regulations of 19th November 1908 confirmed the attachment of 15-cm howitzers to the field army for use on the battlefield and not just on heavily fortified positions. The regulations, however, contained compromises with which to satisfy both the *Fußartillerie* and the *Feldartillerie* and which ended up satisfying neither. So, whilst § 388 allowed long-range guns to be put into action early and it was stated that it needed to be able to intervene in combat as soon as circumstances allowed, § 365 placed the heavy guns behind the ammunition columns of the field artillery. It wasn't until the new regulations of 1912 were published that these inconsistencies were resolved, but resolved in favour of the heavy artillery (see page 286).

The French, however, had no plans to attack the fortified areas of Diedenhofen, Metz and Mutzig/Straßburg. The targets of the *offensive à outrance* were German Armies not their fortresses and this objective coloured not just French tactics but artillery procurement over an extended period.

Langlois not only influenced the design and use of the 75 he actively campaigned against the introduction of howitzers and heavier guns into the field army as, according to both Mayer and Glück, such guns 'seemed to him difficult to reconcile with our spirit of the offensive'.[108] Mayer wrote that it was Langlois:

> "…who led the campaign (against heavy artillery). He did so with his usual ardour and authority, speaking out forcefully against the principles adopted by the German army. He refused to admit that the defence could break the attack, or even that it would force it to stop…

'Let us never allow such a conception of war to penetrate our hearts, he wrote eloquently. 'After an appalling expenditure of ammunition on strongpoints perhaps occupied by insignificant forces, we would be no further forward than before, but our coffers would be empty'.

This is how he became the steadfast adversary of heavy artillery, the use of which seemed to him irreconcilable with our spirit of the offensive. Incidentally, he pointed out the disadvantages of using two different machines for two different jobs, particularly if you can cope with this dual role with a single machine. The main argument he invoked was based on this idea, that manoeuvre alone can bring victory, that manoeuvre implies flexibility, and that the possession of heavy equipment removes all flexibility from the troops who are provided with it."[109]

In this he was supported not only be Percin, Buat and Dumézil but also by acolytes such as Col. Henri Jules Paloque who, in 1904, was appointed Assistant Professor of tactics at the *École supérieure de guerre* and, in 1906, was put in charge of the course of applied artillery tactics for four years. In this role he published *Artillerie de Campagne*, a book which contained a lengthy history of French artillery and then comments and advice on the use of artillery in the modern age[110]. Broadly, unless needed for sieges, he viewed heavy guns and field and medium howitzers as an unnecessary encumbrance both in training and on the battlefield which is odd given that his history of French artillery contains numerous examples down the ages of the Army having a mix of heavy and light guns and howitzers at its disposal all the way up to 1897 and the arrival of the *75*. But now, according to the likes of Langlois, Paloque and Percin, the problems of re-supply, training, of tactics and command if there were multiple calibres on the battlefield were bordering on the insoluble. In addition, Paloque seems to suggest, as France could not compete with the industrial might of *Krupp* and *Rheinmetall* and produce a full range of artillery, it would be better to focus entirely on one gun and one set of tactics:

> "The problem arises, moreover, in a completely different way for countries which are excessively rich in men and horses and for those whose resources are strictly limited.
>
> For the former, it seems that there is every benefit in adding new, more powerful means to an already complete field artillery.
>
> For those on the opposite side, it is advisable to consider, with the most severe rigour, the services which batteries of heavy artillery can render, by comparing them with those one is deprived of, the field batteries which would have been formed with the same resources."[111]

Their main objection, according to Glück, was that heavier guns and howitzers consumed a far greater number and, therefore, weight of shell to achieve the same result as the *75*. Transporting more and heavier shells required more and larger transports and would inevitably slow down troops on the march and in the act of deployment. In the meantime, the *75s* would have opened rapid fire with shrapnel and high explosive to the great advantage of the French, i.e. the *offensive à outrance* in all its speed and vigour.

Howitzers, according to Langlois and Paloque, were inherently less accurate than the *75* and, according to experiments conducted at Bourges in 1907 with *155 Cs*, this had proved true. The numbers seemed conclusive:

> A gun would be destroyed either by a *75* or *15-cm* shell but to achieve this result with a *75* required no more than eight shells whilst with a howitzer the number would be as many as seventy. The difference was perhaps 10% of a caisson of *75* artillery shells against as many as three entire caissons of *15-cm* ammunition;

and

> Then, to destroy a 100-metre stretch of trench fired at from 3,000 metres would take 30-40 *15-cm* shells per metre, the equivalent of 150 caissons or as much as 200 tons of ammunition.

This allowed Langlois to state that:

> "Firing against a simple trench with a *15-cm* howitzer is like taking a club to kill a fly. Still, there is a great chance of missing it. In any case, the result is disproportionate to the goal to be achieved."[112]

Let us leave to one side the fact that German artillery tactics dictated firing from defiladed position unlikely to be reached by the flat-firing *75* and that, whilst destroying enemy trenches with howitzer fire might be a time-consuming activity it was, at least, achievable. Few would think it worthwhile trying to destroy a trench using a *75*. In response, Glück referred to O. B.'s article *La question de l'obusier léger de campagne* in the *Journal des Sciences militaires* of 15th April 1912, which had pointed out that artillery design had moved on significantly since Rimailho's *Obusier de 155-mm CTR modèle 1904* had first appeared. He also referred to O.B.'s figures suggesting howitzers now had far greater accuracy than previously thought.

Langlois then used the South Africa and Manchuria to further undermine the case for heavy artillery on the battlefield. Highly critical generally of the British performance, he was especially scathing about the handling of the 'heavy' artillery at the early battles of Colenso and Magersfontein[i], in particular suggesting that, at Magersfontein, Methuen's guns fired 15-20 tons of ammunition and managed to hit three Boers in the process.[113] Again, we shall leave to one side the miserable incompetence of Buller and Methuen and the fact that the British guns spent most of both battles firing at hillsides devoid of enemy troops.

Langlois declared evidence from Manchuria irrelevant even if heavy guns and howitzers were used extensively by both sides. A war in Europe would not consist of extended battles of position such as Mukden. It would be a war of manoeuvre. But he criticised their performance anyway, discounting both the physical and moral effect of even the heaviest howitzers used – the Japanese 28-cm coastal mortars employed against Port Arthur (though Col. Tretyakov whose Siberian troops came under their sustained fire on 203-Metre Hill would most certainly have disagreed). No, asserted Langlois, Manchuria proved heavy artillery in field armies was a waste of space, shells, and manpower.

---

[i] 'Heavy' is pushing it. Other than field guns, the artillery consisted of a variety of QF 12 pounder, 8 cwt (3-inch), converted 4.7-inch naval guns, and some 5-in. howitzers.

And yet… Glück then listed three examples from Mukden alone which showed the howitzers' usefulness:

2nd March – heavy artillery enabled the Japanese 4th Division to take the village of Ku-Chia-Tsu;

4th March – the 5th Division was supported by heavy mortars in the successful attack on Yui-Che-pu; and

5th March – 18 heavy howitzers shelled Kan-Kuan-Toun and Yang-Shi-Tun causing considerable damage in support of the 8th Division.

As Glück pointed out, these successful supporting roles were conducted by elderly equipment, not designed for battlefield action and all dating from the 1890s.

Despite these issues, Glück listed other reasons why advocates of the *75* believed it the best available weapon to serve the demands of the *offensive à outrance*:

1. Its rapid rate of fire and manoeuvrability made it the best weapon to use against infantry moving in the open;
2. The *75* would rapidly neutralise infantry in trenches or other light obstructions allowing troops to move forward to the assault;
3. The *75* would suffice against troops on the edge of woods and villages;
4. Against artillery either in the open or only in partial defilade the *75's* rapid and accurate fire was the best option;
5. Against fully defiladed artillery and infantry the use of heavier guns was pointless given the lack of observation and available shells;
6. Heavy guns were only of use against robust field fortifications presenting a reasonably sized target.

Against this he presented the case that few of these options would apply:

1. Knowing the abilities and shortcomings of the *75*, infantry would advance concealed by ground;
2. Enemy troops in trenches would only be neutralised up the point the *75s* had to stop firing to avoid 'friendly fire' casualties;
3. The *75* was almost useless against any enemy formations on reverse slopes and artillery in defilade; and
4. The *75s* HE shell was ineffective at ranges over 5,000 metres.

Then, to reinforce his point, Glück compared the current attitudes of the major military nations towards their use of heavy howitzers and long guns with the prevailing French idea of 'one all-purpose gun' as expounded by Langlois and others. He started with the two combatant nations in Manchuria: Japan and Russia. The Japanese Regulations of March 1911, as set out in the *Journal des Sciences militaires* of 15th September1911, explained the role of the new *Krupp*-designed 12-cm and 15-cm howitzers and *10.5-cm Arisaka* long guns as follows:

"This (i.e. heavy artillery) acts in combat in combination with other weapons. Its task is to destroy the objectives which the field artillery cannot overcome, and the obstacles which impede the march of the infantry, to shake the enemy, to undermine morale and thus bring about the end of the war."[114]

Russia, increasingly supplied with 12-cm *Krupp*, *Schneider* and *Obukhov-Putilov* howitzers, and a 15-cm howitzer and 12-cm cannon both from *Schneider*, attached groups of howitzers and batteries of long guns to each Army Corps.

Britain had added the 4.5-in. field howitzer and the 60-pdr long gun to the field guns which would accompany any expeditionary force to France.

By 1912 Austria-Hungary had proportionately more high-angle guns than any European army (1 in 3 batteries according to Glück, compared to 1 in 4 in Germany and just 1 in 30 in France). A law, passed on 5th July 1912, sanctioned a gradual increase in artillery with additions to both Corps and Divisions. One of Austria's problems was the multiplicity of models, partly because of the need to fight in the Carpathians or Alps, and because many guns were rather elderly. Several still had bronze or bronze/steel rather than steel barrels because of an issue with steel production in the Austrian empire. The bewildering array of guns is set out below (a dozen more designed and built during the war):

Mountain guns
Škoda 7 cm Gebirgsgeschütz M 1875 (bronze/no recoil)
7 cm Gebirgsgeschütz M 1899 (bronze/no recoil)
10 cm Gebirgshaubitze M 1899 (bronze/no recoil)
10 cm Gebirgshaubitze M 1908 (steel/hydraulic recoil)
Field artillery
9 cm Feldkanone M 75/96 (1898, bronze/no recoil)
8 cm Feldkanone M. 1899 (1901, bronze/no recoil)
8 cm Feldkanone M. 1905 (1907, bronze-steel, hydro-spring recoil)
Field howitzers
10 cm Feldhaubitze M 1899 (1903, bronze/no recoil)
Škoda 10 cm M. 1914 Feldhaubitze (steel, hydro-spring recoil)
Long guns
12 cm Kanone M 1880 (steel-bronze, no recoil)
15 cm Kanone M 1880 (steel-bronze, no recoil)
Howitzers
15 cm Mörser M 1880 (bronze, no recoil)
18 cm kurze Kanone M 1880 (steel-bronze, no recoil)
15 cm schwere Feldhaubitze M 1894 (bronze, no recoil)
Škoda 24 cm Mörser M 1998 (1900, steel, hydro-spring recoil)[i]
Škoda 305 mm Model 1911 (steel, hydraulic recoil)[ii]

Italy was starting to re-equip its army with modern artillery to include French-designed field guns and howitzers but its regulations stipulated that heavy artillery had a clear role to play on the battlefield:

"Heavy artillery, having the advantage of being employed from the start of the engagement, should never be kept in reserve in the offensive or too far back in the defensive.

It will therefore not be an exclusive organ of the army; the howitzers will

---

[i] Four were bought by Britain for South Africa as *Ordnance BL 9.45-inch Howitzer Mk I*. They fired one round before being sent to China where they were not used.
[ii] Eight were lent to the German Army and were first used against the Liège forts.

be assigned to the army corps. Only long guns will remain available to army commanders."[115]

Italian combat regulations stated that:

"Howitzers are intended to act against troops, even at great distances, in particular against those who are concealed in folds of ground or sheltered behind trenches, and against inhabited places organized defensively. They will also be very usefully employed in the final phase of the fight to continue the fire much later than the light artillery, without danger for the friendly infantry.

The guns will be used above all to counter the enemy artillery to facilitate the action of the friendly light artillery, to act at great distance on the troops discovered or even to destroy resistant material obstacles."[116]

Even less important countries had specified the use of heavier guns and howitzer within their field armies and Glück showed this to be the case in Switzerland, Sweden, Turkey, Serbia, Bulgaria, and Rumania.

But Germany was the key case and their artillery was described in detail:

"In 1911 the field artillery of an *Armeekorps* contains, in principle,:
21 x 6-gun batteries of 77-mm (126 guns);
3 x 6-piece batteries of 10.5-cm light howitzers (18 howitzers);
1 battalion of 4 batteries with 4 heavy howitzers of 15-cm (16 heavy howitzers);
A total of 160 pieces, including 34 howitzers.

It seems certain that the adoption of a new light howitzer determined the Germans to transform a group of guns into a group of howitzers, so that each division of the army corps will be equipped in the very near future with a group of light howitzers and that in total the *Armeekorps* will include: 108 guns, 36 light howitzers and 16 heavy howitzers.

It is also planned to mobilize as heavy artillery a certain number of *fußartillerie* battalions, to be assigned to the armies if necessary and which will have batteries of 15-cm howitzers, 21-cm *Mörsers* and 10 cm and 13-cm long guns.

The German *fußartillerie* comprised, on 1st April, 1912, 18 regiments with 2 or 3 battalions, i.e. 41 battalions, forming 170 batteries (27,000 men).

Three battalions only were to be employed in the defence of the coasts. Of the 38 others, 25 were assigned to the *Armeekorps* (howitzer batteries).
The other 13 formed the army heavy artillery.

In all, the *fußartillerie* called upon to cooperate in the field war comprised: 158 batteries serving 632 large-calibre guns.

The Army Law of 1912, covering the five-year period from 1911, determines a notable increase in foot artillery."[117]

Glück then described the possible impact of the updated *10-5-cm LFH 98/09* and the *15-com SFH 1903* on French artillery. Describing the potential effect of the *10.5's* shrapnel shell he wrote:

"... the large angle of fall of the shards makes this shell particularly suitable for hitting sheltered objectives and the even the best protected personnel of the shielded batteries.

The wide dispersion of the effective shards of a single projectile makes it possible to beat an area whose width (150-200 metres) is about twice that of the front of a 6-piece battery. It thus makes easier the fight against defiladed targets, the spacing of which cannot be fixed with certainty.

For these reasons, it is estimated in Germany that light howitzers, with systematic firing in an area 300 and 400 metres deep, can be highly effective against the personnel of masked and shielded batteries, and would give appreciable results without an exaggerated consumption of ammunition.

This explains the current of ideas which took shape in favour of increasing the number of batteries of light howitzers in the *Armeekorps*."

As for the *15-cm* howitzer, the German Army's heavy artillery regulations, updated on 21st March 1912, stated that:

"The lateral spray of this shell covers, under favourable circumstances, approximately the space occupied by a battery, i.e. width of 80 metres. Its depth is 25 to 30 metres. Shards are dangerous up to 40 metres on either side of the burst point and penetrate the thickness of a gun shield."[118]

The relevance of this was that German tactical advice meant the key role of the artillery was the destruction, not neutralisation, of the enemy's guns. With the shells of its two main howitzers able to smother and destroy entire battery positions (as, indeed, would happen in August 1914) whilst firing from concealed positions beyond the reach of the *75* this was now eminently possible and with little or no threat of retaliation from any French equivalent. The updated *fußartillerie* regulations in 1912 also showed that the first objective of 15-cm howitzers and 21-cm *Mörsers* was the enemy's artillery:

"§ 356: The heavy howitzer is superior to the light howitzer in the penetrative, destructive and dispersal power of its projectile. This is why it will be advantageously used against artillery and against strongly organized infantry positions.

§ 358: The surest way for *fußartillerie* to support infantry is to first crush the enemy artillery.

§ 416: The role of the heavy artillery is therefore to first supplement the action of the field artillery against the enemy artillery, then to remove the major part of the gun batteries of the enemy from the fight as soon as possible so that the field artillery can be used against enemy infantry."[119]

The artillery regulations were clear. So long as enemy artillery was firing it was the principal objective of the German howitzer batteries. Once they were silenced these guns could then turn their fire on fortifications and infantry concentrations. In many ways these were the tactics employed by Fayolle's *6e Armée* during the Somme bombardment. Then they were ordered that, unless tasked with a specific mission, they were to fire on any active German battery within range. Fayolle, too, believed in destruction not neutralisation whenever possible. The British did not accept this idea until well after the 1st July 1916.

He then went on to refer to the long guns available, whose shrapnel shells would be excellent at dealing with roads, railways, villages, balloons, etc., and the *28-cm Mörser*. This latter gun he felt unsuited to field warfare (or, at least, field warfare as currently envisaged) because of its weight and slow movement. They would, though, be brought forward to fire on the *'forts d'arrêt'* or other heavily fortified locations. But he had another thought. They might also be used to reinforce areas where Germany did not have similar fortifications with which to stop a French incursion. Somewhere like the *Nied* Line east of Metz where Édouard de Castelnau's *2e armée* would come seriously unstuck in the Battle of Morhange and where these *28-cm Mörsers* were emplaced for just such an event.

What would also emerge in the 'collision' battles in the early weeks of the war of movement, both in Lorraine and the Ardennes, was that the German belief in pushing forward heavy artillery with the advance guard was an effective and destructive tactic. In the 1908 regulations heavy batteries were inserted towards the front of the line of march. The amended regulations of 1912 stated:

"§ 417: If the army corps marches on a single road, the heavy artillery is attached, in principle, to the leading division... If we foresee its use early, we can push it further; in certain circumstances, it can even be placed in front of the main field artillery."

In these circumstances, § 370 declared that:

"Heavy artillery is subordinate to the general commanding the division with which it forms a column."

By comparison, the small numbers of heavier guns available to the French Army were kept under the hand of the Army commander and usually formed a reserve not a front-line component. Thus, as happened in several early battles of the war, French heavier guns, e.g. the *155 C TR Rimailho*, were so far from the front they were unable to contribute before the decision had been reached. And, wrote Glück, the *155 C TR* was not all that had been hoped for even amongst supporters of heavy artillery. The French Army previously possessed two high-angle guns in the shapes of the unsatisfactory compromises that were the *Canon de 120 C modèle 1890* and the *Obusier de 155 mm C modèle 1890*, both designed by Capt. Louis Henry Auguste Baquet. Rushed into service as stopgaps they had neither the range nor rate of fire required (though both were still in use during WW1).

The *155 C TR* was the brainchild of 34-year-old Capt. Émile Rimailho, working at the *Atelier de Puteaux*. He first suggested the piece to the army in a memorandum of 11th November 1898. The tube was to be based on the de Bange *155 C modèle 1881*, 'for reasons of economy' according to Raimailho[120], but it was to include several of the innovations present in the *75*, most especially the hydro-pneumatic recoil. The breech was also a new concept with which Rimailho hoped to be able to achieve a rate of fire of three rounds per minute. Mobility was also essential and the weight of the various components crucial. Nevertheless, each gun and its transport, at 5,250 Kgs, weighed nearly three times as much as a *75* and had to be broken down and transported in two parts in order to be moved (three including the ammunition caisson). More to the point, each gun in position and ready to fire, *en batterie*, weighed 3,200 Kgs, 50% more than the German *15-cm sFH 03*.

59 Obusier de 120-mm C modèle 1890 Baquet

60 Obusier de 155 mm CTR modèle 1904 Rimailho
[*Source*: Valvacher — Travail personnel, CC BY-SA 4.0, https://commons.wikimedia.org/w/index.php?curid=53955681]

Rimailho was told by Gen. Basile Gras, *président du Comité de l'artillerie*, to prepare a prototype of the *155 C TR* and, in 1900, also to produce a plan for a *obusier de 120-mm*. Gras only succeeded to the position of *président du Comité de l'artillerie* in July 1899 but was concerned that evidence already suggested the *75* had limitations against defiladed troops/artillery and field fortifications which a 120-mm field howitzer might solve. Others were not of the same view and the then *Directeur de l'artillerie*, Gen. Denis François Felix Deloye, called for experiments before committing to such a project whilst, at the same time, expressing the view that the

75 would suffice. In this he was supported by Baquet who felt that either a ricochet shot or a reduced-charge 75 shell could deal with enemy units concealed by reverse slopes. Gras was succeeded on 1st January 1901 (he died suddenly on 14th April 1901) by Deloye and support for the 120-mm gun rapidly waned although desultory experiments on a variety of gun types continued for four or five years[i].

The *155 C TR* was ready for testing by June 1901 but various delays meant that it was not finally tested at Bourges until the early summer of 1902 with Rimailho, now attached to the *16e bataillon d'Artillerie à pied*, in attendance. On 7th June 1902, Rimailho wrote that he now believed the *155 C TR* could do more than simply replace the *Obusier de 155 mm C modèle 1890*. Rimailho suggested that his gun's rate of fire and mobility meant that it could replace *all* the heavy artillery of the French Army. With the tests producing positive results, Rimailho now also suggested ambitious plans for the upgrading of the army's *120 L*, *155 L* and *mortiers de 220*.

On 4th November 1904, the *155 C TR* was recommended for adoption by the Army and yet, by 27th July 1905, the *Président du Comité*, Gen. Charles Ernest Borgnis-Desbordes, was placing limitations on its use:

"The *matériel* Rimailho can be of great service for attacking organized positions, but only used against troops in very exceptional cases."[121]

But Borgnis-Desbordes also expressed concerns about the flat fire of the *75* and the need for a light field howitzer. Again Baquet dismissed these concerns, reiterating his view the *155 C TR* was best suited for attacking heavily fortified areas and that the ricochet or reduced charge *75* shell would take care of lightly fortified areas or partially defiladed troops or artillery. These two guns, he wrote:

"... seem to satisfy all the missions which could be entrusted to the artillery on the battlefield."[122]

In this he was supported by Gen. Louis Pierre Parizot, commanding the artillery of the *8e Corps* and the *Président de la Commission de Bourges*, who added to Baquet's report the comment that:

"... the creation of a light field howitzer, likely to produce effects without a large consumption of ammunition, does not seem to be achievable in the short term, either in France or abroad."[123]

And this despite the existence of the *10.5-cm Feldhaubitze 98*. Thus Borgnis-Desbordes decided to:

"... abandon the idea of the immediate creation of a *matériel* of medium calibre, capable of an angle of fall of 30° at all distances, and to proceed immediately with verification of the curved fire of the *75*. Research relating to howitzers would only be continued... from a theoretical point of view."[124]

---

[i] Rimailho worked on a 120-mm, while, at the *Atelier de Tarbes*, a Capt. Luya designed a 95-mm and 120-mm gun and a Capt. Mourcet a 120-mm. Work was also done by Deport, and, separately, Capts. Bloch and Tournier [*Source*: Challeat, Gen. J, *L'Artillerie de terre en France pendant un Siècle, Histoire Technique (1816-1919), Tome Second (1880-1910)*, Charles Lavauzelle et Cie, 1935, pages 475-6].

The programme for the light field howitzer was then cancelled towards the end of 1905 by a combination of Gen. François Henry Oudard, *Directeur de l'artillerie*, and the *président du Comité*, Gen. Paul Peigné. Given the gestation period of the average piece of French artillery, i.e. the *155 C TR* had taken 7-8 years), thus died any real prospect of the French Army having a modern light field howitzer when they went to war. As Gen. Challéat wrote post-war:

> "Thus, before completing experiments on the proposed arrangements, we rejected, in principle, the light howitzer. However, tests relating to the curved firing of the *75* did not lead to a satisfactory solution[i] and delayed, from 1906, the search for a light howitzer, which was not resumed until after the period from 1900 to 1910."[125]

Meanwhile, the *Ministre de la Guerre*, Eugène Étienne, finally gave the *155 C TR* ministerial approval on 23rd June 1906. Once in use this gun proved to have drawbacks which undermined its use as an effective battlefield weapon. Gen. Percin, unsurprisingly, was not a fan:

> "This equipment does not have the qualities essential for field campaign equipment worthy of the name. It lacks the mobility to manoeuvre in mounted batteries; its usefulness is most debatable and disputed."[126]

But there were other issues as Glück pointed out. Rimailho's innovative breech caused problems officers thought beyond the average NCO to resolve. Then, the anticipated rate of fire of up to five rounds a minute proved unsustainable beyond, perhaps, ten minutes. Fatigue amongst the gun crew rapidly reduced the gun's output to one and two rounds a minute. There was also a profound lack of understanding about how these weapons might be used. In manoeuvres, the batteries were routinely attached to *Corps d'armée* thereby keeping them away from the front line. Glück then quoted 'a highly publicized lecture' from 1911 in which a senior artillery officer said:

> "There is hesitation and indecision in high places regarding the use of heavy artillery; and this is due to the inadequacy of the regulations (moreover very vague and very short) and to the ignorance of the results of the experimental commissions, in particular those of the Bourges Commission, which was called upon in 1907 to verify the projectile effect of 155.
> This said clearly: 'The use of heavy artillery against field fortifications would be a profound error. Artillery, even of large calibre, can only demolish earthworks at the cost of an exaggerated consumption of ammunition. It is necessary to act against the defenders of such works with high explosive shells fired at ricochet, and then the 75 is enough'."[127]

This begged the question: if the *155 C TR* was not to be used against field fortifications, then what on earth was it to be used for? New regulations in 1912 prescribed their use still further:

---

[i] A note from Bourges dated 26th April 1910 concludes: 'For these various reasons, the reduced charge of the *75* is abandoned. It will thus be necessary, during the following years, to try to bend the trajectory of the *75* a little by other means which will only be palliatives' [*Source*: Challeat, op. cit, footnote, page 481].

"It would be bad practice to use the *155* as a howitzer, using the curvature of its trajectory to hit live defiladed targets. Exceptions to this case can only be made when it is desired to reach very large concentrations of troops."[128]

Basically, it seemed that villages, farms, large woods, and heavily fortified positions were the only worthwhile targets and only in cases where the *75* might not be suitable. In other words, Glück observed, the *155 C TR* was now 'reserve artillery; an organ of the Army' or, as the regulations stipulated:

"… the batteries of *155* will first of all be held in reserve in a position judiciously chosen to ensure their rapid intervention on the various points of the battlefield."[129]

In other words, in a collision battle, as were so many of the early combats in the Battle of the Frontiers in 1914, whilst the German heavy guns would be 'front and centre' in their advance, the French heavy artillery would languish somewhere to the rear waiting for the Army or Corps commander to commit them. And, in August 1914, when sent forward it was probably already too late to make a difference. And all because, as even its designer, Col. Rimailho, stated at a conference at the *Centre des Hautes Etudes Militaires* in 1911:

"… the *155* is not a howitzer and should not be used as such."[130]

The tactical disadvantages under which the French Army would labour, as a result, seemed clear to our young Capt. Glück in 1913.

There was the issue of 'dead ground' which the *75s* could not reach, even with their *Plaquettes Malandrins* and *cartouche réduites*. Then, to support the infantry attack, the *75s* would need to be brought into the open and, even if the *155s* were brought up to try to help protect the exposed field batteries, they would be ineffective:

"The protection given to uncovered batteries by counter-batteries is illusory. These will, most of the time, be unable to discern where the blows come from which the former suffer. An exposed battery will be destroyed before the counter-batteries even have time to discover the enemy artillery. In addition, the batteries on the crest of a ridge will be easily taken to task by howitzers and long-range guns, and their long range will protect them from the *75* gun. Therefore, the artillery renouncing the protection of defilade to support certain infantry missions is playing into the hands of the German heavy artillery."

Then there was the problem of the German howitzers and long guns firing from heavily defiladed positions or from the protection provided by villages or woods against which the *75s* was useless?

France had been complacent, Glück argued. For ten years they had enjoyed the undoubted advantages provided by the *75* over the German *77-mm 96* which he described as an 'accelerated fire', i.e. not quick firing as the *75*, unshielded gun which needed to fire from open positions. This advantage had been eroded by the *77-mm 96 NA* which was now only slightly inferior to the *75* but could also now rely on the protection of howitzers and long-range guns. Glück betrayed his frustrations with the myopic attitudes of the 'one gun suits all' mentality such as those expounded by Gen. Percin:

"And yet, the opponents of the howitzer and heavy artillery are still legion in France. Their opposition is often more sentimental than scientific; for them the 75 cannon is always incomparable and they cannot admit that one thinks of having recourse to another piece of ordnance in view of certain special necessities of the field of battle.

Some ingeniously evade the problem: 'If the enemy howitzers, behind a wood or a village, or behind a large defile, are impossible to reach', says General Percin, 'the infantry takes the wood, the village or the ridge'[i]. The remedy is simple. We were accustomed to more rigour until now from the eminent artilleryman General Percin... in a letter recently sent to an artillery officer on the subject of the role of heavy artillery in major manoeuvres and communicated to us, he wrote. 'Will the bombardment of a village greatly hasten its fall? I doubt it. One more infantry regiment might do the trick better'. Obviously yes, if it is a question of the capture of the village itself; no, if it is a question of preparing it and shielding from the fire of the enemy howitzers the field artillery necessary to support the attack."[131]

Broadly, therefore, Percin was arguing for the use of men against fire. For flesh against steel. After the war he then had the gall to complain about the casualties he claimed French guns had caused amongst their own men whilst discounting the 95% caused by enemy action, much of it by German artillery.

Thus, not one of the modern guns and howitzers mentioned above was available to the French in August 1914. Other than a 370-mm howitzer, based on a prototype designed by Cdt. Filloux[ii] in 1912 and ordered in November 1914, no genuine progress was made on other projects pre-war. A belated proposal was put to the Government on 20th February 1913 by Gen. de Lamothe, President of the Commission of New *Matérials*, calling for:

A new 135-mm quick-firing (*TR* or *Tir Rapide*) gun;
A new carriage for the *155 L* gun to increase range;
The manufacture of the *Mortier de 370-mm Filloux*;
The manufacture of a *Mortier de 280*;
The modification of the *Canon de 155 C modèle 1904 TR Rimailho* so it could be transported in one piece; and
The modification of the *Canon de 155 C modèle 1881 de Bange* to increase its rate of fire (something already done by Cdt. Filloux with the *155 C Mle 1881-1912 de Bange-Filloux*).

By the outbreak of war some of these weapons were either in early production or final development stages, although the 135-mm (*TR*) never appeared. For many months, however, only small numbers were available and the lessons as to their application were, thus, yet to be learnt. The first *155 L Mle 1877/1914 sur affût*

---

[i] From an article by Percin in *Le Temps*, 5th February 1913.
[ii] Col. Louis Jean François Filloux was born in 1869 in Pontlevoy, Dept. Loir-et-Cher and died in 1957 at Vincennes. *École d'application de l'artillerie et du genie*, 1890. *30e regiment d'artillerie*, 1892. *Fondrie de Bourges*. *École de cannonage de la marine*, Toulon, 1907. *Chef d'escadron*, *12e regiment d'artillerie*, 1912. *Atelier de construction de Bourges*, 1914. *Atelier de construction de Puteaux*, 1916. Lt. Col., 1917.

Schneider appeared in April 1916. The first of ten *Mortier de 370 Filloux* was supplied in May 1915 but did not come into action until the autumn as there were no shells. The first *Mortier de 280 TR Schneider* arrived in June 1915. The modification of the *155 C Rimailho* did not happen but it began to be replaced by the new *Canon de 155 C modèle 1915 Schneider* in Spring 1916.

The consequence of these delays, and the infighting between those who supported the *75* as the only gun needed and those who demanded the development of more specialised weaponry, meant France went to war technically and tactically ill-equipped to deal with *any* of the circumstances the war might throw up, be they the open, fluid warfare anticipated by professional soldiers or the grim, static, entrenched siege warfare envisaged by Bloch, Brett, Mayer *et al*. Thus, when the *75* was conclusively proved *not* to be the only gun needed, the French Army first reached back into its arsenal of obsolete, recoil-less field guns, *canons court* and *mortiers* from the 1880s to fill the gaps, and then waited interminably for French industry to gear itself up for a huge expansion in gun and shell production, an exercise which took several years to complete. In the absence of these guns and shells, the infantry took the strain of a modern, industrial war being fought without modern industrial weaponry and it was the gallant red-trousered infantry who paid the price for this criminal short-sightedness.

WRITING AFTER THE WAR, GEN. HERR had every reason to feel satisfied with his pre-war contributions to the arguments about the balance of artillery a modern Army required. The devastating effect of modern artillery *en masse* showed the theory that manoeuvre and/or superior morale must always overcome firepower was simply wrong. That such theorists continued in positions of command throughout the war in certain armies was unfortunate, but it did not invalidate the fact their pre-war thinking was in error.

Secondly, as Bloch forecast, the war was not 'over by Christmas'. One reason was the artillery's power and rate of fire. Pre-war, Generals were certain the war would be brief but they failed to consider artillery's stopping power and the incredible volumes of ammunition required to maintain it. In 1914, the French allocated 1,300 rounds per *75*. During the Battle of the Yser, the climax of the race to the sea (16th-31st October 1914), *GQG* was only able to supply the guns by taking shells from all other parts of the front. Thankfully, the Germans were even more certain of a quick war, so their 77-mm field guns deployed with just 987 rounds per gun and these began to run out on the Marne[i]. Only the slow moving, heavy guns (with 4,000 rounds/gun), unable to keep up with the rapid changes of front in September and early October, had enough shells to last into November.[132]

---

[i] In 1911, Lt. W Neuffer, *3. Bayerische Feldartillerie Regt.*, warned about inadequate shell supplies in *What lessons in the employment of field artillery should be deduced from the experiences of the Russo-Japanese war?*: '… in a future war, we must expect a considerably increased use of artillery ammunition, especially for certain batteries. Our reserve of ammunition in Germany is far from sufficient, it should be largely increased.' [*Source: Artilleristische Monatshefts*. No. 35, November, 1909, reprinted in *Field Artillery Journal*, April-June 1911, page 206].

Notwithstanding this latter point, German heavy guns and howitzers achieved remarkable results. The 15-cm howitzers and 13-cm long guns proved especially destructive in all phases of the battle. There was only one way this fire could be disrupted – through effective counter battery work, the new name for the artillery duel which preceded battles of the 19th Century and which Herr argued back in 1913 was still essential. In this 'duel' the *75s*, outranged by the 10.5-cm and 15-cm howitzers[i] and 13-cm guns, were useless. Only against exposed 77-mm guns were they effective and the Germans learnt early on not to expose the *77s*. What was needed for effective counter battery work were long guns (155-mm/6-in. and upwards) and heavy howitzers, and these were the weapons still being developed, or in the early stages of production. The issues of observation and communication were others with which the French Army had to deal in a hurry, with their reluctance to use telephones on the battlefield between observation posts (OPs) and battery positions having been shown as short-sighted in the extreme.

In the absence of new *matériel* from Government and private factories there were three sources for the guns required. Joffre had already allowed the use of shells stored at fortresses in north-eastern France and, in mid-September, this was extended to include their guns and gunners. A few days later, this call was extended to coastal guns in forts and barbettes protecting French ports and naval bases[ii].

61 Canon de campagne de 90-mm modèle 1877 de Bange

Lastly, obsolete guns such as the *Canon de campagne de 90-mm modèle 1877 de Bange* replaced 15 years earlier by the *75* were brought out of mothballs and thrown into the fray. There were 3,994 in French arsenals and, by the end of November, 587 were in service[iii]. Apart from the breech loading mechanism, these were guns which would not have looked out of place at Waterloo, but the crucial thing was, elderly as they might be, shells and propellant existed, something in short supply

---

[i] Howitzers = '*steilfeuer*' weapons, i.e. steep firing. Guns = '*flachfeuer*', i.e. flat firing.
[ii] Guns were withdrawn from Langres, Besançon, Dijon, Lyon, Grenoble, Toulon, Brest, Paris, Verdun, Toul, Épinal and Belfort.
[iii] Use peaked in the 1st quarter of 1916 with 1,783 at the front. 144 were in use at the end of 1918. [*Source*: Touzin & Vauvillier, *Les Canons de la Victoire 1914-1919*].

for the *75s*. A drawback in using these elderly guns was that they used black powder propellant, making the guns visible in action. Work was urgently put in hand to replace this with smokeless powders.

By this means, hundreds of weapons, obsolete and requiring alteration to make them useable, were made available. From fortresses came 95, 120 and 155-mm guns, 155-mm howitzers and 220-mm *mortiers*. From coastal establishments came super heavy 270-mm *mortiers* and long 14 and 16-cm cannon, whilst the use of naval guns was also examined. Improvisation became the name of the game as they were placed on trucks and trains, on extemporised wooden or concrete platforms, on river boats and *péniches*[i].

62 Canon de 120-mm L modèle 1878

On 14th October 1914, this transformation of the heavy artillery was set out in a letter from Joffre who outlined how these unused resources might fill gaps in the current armoury or supplement existing guns. The result was the formation of:

100 batteries of *90-mm 1877 de Bange* guns, to cover the shortage of *75* shells;
Mobile groups of *95-mm 1888 de Lahitolle* and *120 L 1878 de Bange* guns;
Batteries of *155 L 1877 de Bange* guns, swan-necked *155 C 1881-1912 de Bange-Filloux* howitzers and the *Mortiers 220 1880* and *1901 de Bange*.

These were all heavy, cumbersome, slow-firing weapons with, at best, rudimentary recoil systems but, for the French, needs must. The advantage was there were lots of them scattered across the country, i.e.:

Field guns: 1,524 *95*
Long guns: 2,296 *120 L*, 1,392 *155 L*
Howitzers: 479 *155 C*
Mortars: 331 *M 220s*

---

[i] Steel-hulled canal barges initially built in Belgium and designed to fit the Franco-Belgian canal system. They were 38.50 m. (126 ft) long and 5.05 m. (16.6 ft) wide.

By early 1915, nearly 1,500 guns of all calibres had been altered for field service and sent to the front, and, by May 1916, this number grew to 3,500 (just as well as only 121 guns built since 1912 had arrived with the Army).

There was a problem. Finding officers who knew anything about these guns as most were trained on the *75*. Writing in 1918, a reserve artillery officer, 34-year-old Lt. Jules-Louis-Gaston (*58e régiment d'artillerie, 18e Corps*) was with Lanrezac's *5e Armée* near the Belgian border. At Charleroi (23rd August) and Guise (29th August) he came under fire from defiladed *15-cm sFHs* and was wounded. Later, he discovered his regiment was to form a battery of *120 L 1878 de Bange* guns. As the only officer with any knowledge of this *material* he took command. After several weeks training it was not until 18th November they went to Bourges to pick up the guns.[133] Pastre harboured doubts about the Army's over-reliance on the *75*:

"The commander... talks about the German heavy artillery which worries him a lot. We have stuck to the single calibre *75* gun, a good field gun, an excellent infantry gun, but which cannot claim to fulfil all missions. Napoleon wanted multiple, diverse calibres, employing each according to the circumstances; we have neglected his teaching...

He said we made a small effort in this direction, but to what end? The *155 C TR Rimailho*, excellent howitzers, but short range; and how many do we have? A tiny number. Our old de Bange guns are quite insufficient, not to mention that there are only a few *groupes* of them; then we had no time to create a doctrine, we do not know how to use heavy artillery.

But Captain V... interrupts and claims heavy guns are of no use: that against the large German masses with their early deployment and big guns, we will employ our flexible and mobile batteries, and manoeuvre in time and in space. He tells us what I believe he learned at the *École Supérieure de Guerre*. As I had already spoken of the German 105-mm howitzer, the commander brings the conversation back to the artillery and he asks me what I know of this *material*. My knowledge is minimal: it is a light howitzer which fires, from around 6,800 meters, an explosive shell from the *Ehrhardt* double-effect system. What makes this piece formidable is the weight of its projectile and the very great ease with which it can use large defilades which will be in the blind spot of our flat-firing cannon... The Germans are practical people; they not only offer a whole range of calibres, in each calibre they have a gun and a howitzer: thus they can face all eventualities... one of us asks our *chef d'escadron* several times what method we will employ to discover the enemy batteries, he replies angrily: 'I don't know'."[134]

De Bange's guns and howitzers designed in response to the calamity of 1870-1 now returned to save the nation when the *75* proved anything but a war winner. The result was that, by 27th November, every *Corps* had a heavy artillery group of 105, 120 or 155-mm guns. Though elderly they had a reach of c. 12,000 and 14,000 metres with which to combat the German 13-cm guns and others. It was a sea-change in attitudes towards artillery in the French Army.

It was another year, and 400,000 more French deaths, before a similar re-evaluation of infantry tactics. In the meantime, having put in place a short-term answer to the problem of the numbers and types of guns available, the Government and Army now had to grapple with an issue which beset every combatant nation in the opening period of the war – shell supplies.

63 De Bange howitzers: 'swan-necked' 155-mm Canon Court, Mortiers 220 and 270
Note the rudimentary recoil system: a hydraulic brake assisted by gravity as the gun recoiled up a slight slope

THE FRENCH ARMY WENT TO WAR with shell supplies set out below:

Gun type	Guns with the Army	Shells with the Army	Number per gun	Shells in forts/ interior	Number per gun
65 mm	128	169742	1326	0	1326
75 mm	3680	4460727	1212	905440	1397
80 mm	0	0	0	268160	346
90 mm	0	0	0	1068720	268
95 mm	0	0	0	655280	430
120 mm C	84	32600	400	885210	377
120 mm L	120	72000	600		
155 CTR	104	114400	1100	1373700	750
155 mm C/L	0	0	0		
220 mm	0	0	0	212720	643
270 mm	0	0	0	27000	844

Table 9 French gun and shell supplies 2nd August 1914
[Source: *AFdGG*, Tome XI, page 952]

The French laid plans for an industrial as well as a military mobilisation, one which involved thirty state and private organisations employing 50,000 male and female workers.[135] This system was supposed to supply daily:

13,600 shells for the 75-mm field guns (c. 410,000/month);
465 shells for the newer quick-firing *155 C* howitzers (c. 14,000/month);
2,470,000 rifle rounds (74 million/month); and
24 tonnes of explosive powder (720 tonnes/month)

Though these numbers seem impressive they pale in comparison to Germany's industrial power. In August 1914, Germany produced 41 tonnes of explosive powder per day (1,240 tonnes per month). By December this increased to 72 tonnes per day (2,170 tonnes per month) and, by December 1915, this rose to 163 tonnes per day (4,900 tonnes per month). Throughout 1915 Germany manufactured 43,300 tonnes of explosive powder for rifle bullets and artillery shells. Increases in German production of artillery shells and rifle ammunition were equally dramatic as Table 10 below shows.

Munitions type	Monthly production			Annual production 1915
	Aug. 1914	Dec. 1914	Dec. 1915	
Infantry ammunition	130 million	150 million	213 million	2,200 million
Field gun shells	170,000	1.2 million	2.1 million	21.5 million
Field howitzer shells	65,000	414,000	800,000	8.2 million
Heavy howitzer shells	26,000	266,000	684,000	6.5 million
Mörser shells	3,000	19,000	104,000	850,000
10 cm Canon shells	2,000	19,000	145,000	1.18 million

Table 10 Increases in German munitions production August 1914 to December 1915
[Source: *Der Weltkrieg 1914 bis 1918, Die Operationen des Jahres 1915*, Vol. 3, appendix 5]

It was clear, industrial production as much as men and *matériel* on the battlefield would dictate the course of the war over the next four years.

Because of the dominant philosophy that the *75* answered all battlefield questions, French industrial organisation was not designed to manufacture new equipment but to supply shells and bullets, and repair existing artillery pieces. This helps explain the grindingly slow process of manufacturing the new guns and howitzers ordered at the beginning of the war. In the meantime, it was essential French industry achieve the necessary output of shells and propellant for existing guns. The quantities of shells, bullets, and powder to be manufactured as listed above were not expected to be achieved immediately, but deadlines were set within which targets must be met. The timetable required explosive powder production be met within 61 days of the start of war and within 81 days for shells and bullets, although, after 49 days, the target for 75-mm shells was to be 11,800 a day. The immediate initial supply available to the *75s*, i.e. with the guns (the rest were held in reserve), was 240 rounds per gun (a total of 800,000) and this was to rise to 1,000 shells, not all available at the front but with some in the supply chain between the arsenals and the front.

In addition, there were material stocks for the manufacture of another 600,000 rounds for the *75s* (170 rounds per gun) with the resources for 60 days' manufacturing. Lastly, plans were put in place to ensure the manufacturing capacity and the supply of essential materials to the factories involved.

The availability of powder for the Army ran ahead of projections because the Navy cut its demands when it was realised how much the Royal Navy constituted the maritime front line. As a result, by 20th August 1914, powder available to the Army was running at 31 tonnes per day instead of the forecast of 10 tonnes per day. This was, however, the only area in which supply exceeded expectations.

At the beginning of September, as the French military position deteriorated north of Paris, the French Government was removed to Bordeaux. Even at this moment of crisis, the issue of arms and ammunition production was thought to be well under control. It was not. By 9th September 1914, reserves of 75-mm shells had nearly run out and an urgent call was made to increase production of shells, shell casings and explosives at the Government arsenals at Bourges, Lyon, Tarbes and Rennes. Meanwhile, deliveries of shells to the front-line were reduced. By 15th September there were just 20 rounds per gun stored in Army warehouses. Four days later, with the Artillery having used half of its opening day supplies of 75-mm shells, the warehouses stood empty. Frantic messages were sent by Joffre to the Government demanding new supplies of shells, with the CinC stating in a letter dated 20th September to the Minister of War, Alexandre Millerand, that the Army needed some 50,000 shells a day if operations were to be continued at the current rate.[136] The actual number of shells being produced was 12,000 which, it was hoped, would increase to 20,000 a day by the end of the month. Joffre urged the Government to approach foreign governments, the Americans, the British, the Italians and others, to help with supplies. In response, Millerand convened a meeting of the leaders of the various industries involved and, the following day, he phoned Joffre to advise him it was hoped to increase daily production of 75-mm shells to 30,000 per day 'in three to four weeks' time'. In the meantime, the rate of 12,000 rounds per day held good.

The Allied success on the Marne relieved the pressure on the French Army at least temporarily, which was just as well as, on 29th September, Joffre learnt the rate of 30,000 rounds per day promised for mid-October would not be reached. 20,000 rounds a day was the new target and that was not achieved until early November. It was this shortfall which forced Joffre to form the 100 batteries of *Canon de Campagne de 90-mm Modèle 1877 de Bange*. Such was the desperate need for artillery at Ypres and on the Yser Joffre was left with no alternative but to bring these obsolete weapons and their ammunition stocks into action.

Production of 75-mm shells hovered around 13,000 a day throughout October but the Government in Bordeaux promised to increase this rate to 33,000 by November. About the same value could be placed on the promises of politicians in 1914 as can safely be done at the current time and, on 3rd November, Joffre was informed daily production of 75-mm shells during the month would, in fact, be 23,000. Ten days later that number was revised again – down to 18,000 a day. And then, in December, the fact of the matter was admitted. The number was, and would be for some time, 13,000 a day, some 600 a day short of the figure which should have been achieved on 24th October, 81 days after the start of the war.

For Joffre the failures of government and industry were felt in only one way – economy in artillery ammunition had to be compensated for by the prodigal use of the infantry, and this production failure was paid for with his soldiers' lives.

To answer the multiple problems of munition supplies a 36-year-old member of the *Parti socialiste français* was returned from service with the *78e régiment d'infanterie territoriale* and appointed *sous-secrétaire d'État à l'artillerie et à l'équipement militaire* in the Viviani Cabinet on 26th August 1914. The impact of Albert Thomas on French armaments and munitions supply would be enormous.

64 Albert Thomas[i]

The problems Thomas faced were huge. Some crucial factories were closed and certain raw materials were in short supply, and these shortages were exacerbated by the fact that 77% of French metal production and 68% of coal output came from territories occupied by the Germans in the autumn of 1914. More specific to the manufacture of shells and guns, it was estimated in 1916 that these areas had previously contributed:

78% of coke production;
86% of iron production; and
70% of steel production[ii]

---

[i] Albert Thomas was born on 16th June 1878 in Champigny-sur-Marne. The son of Aristide Thomas, a baker from Poitiers, and Clémence Malloire. Aristide was involved in radical politics and imprisoned by the Prussians during the occupation after 1870. Albert was educated at the *lycée Michelet* at Vanves and, in 1899, the prestigious *École Normale Supérieure*. He won a scholarship and travelled in Russia. He also went to Berlin and the eastern Mediterranean. Between 1903 and 1905 he published half a dozen books and wrote for various socialist newspapers/periodicals: Jaures' *L'Humanité*, *L'Information*, and *Revue syndicaliste* (which he started in 1905). He became editor in chief of the *Revue socialiste*. In 1904 he was elected as a municipal councillor for Champigny where he was the Mayor in 1912. In 1910 he was elected to the Chamber of Deputies as the socialist deputy for the 2nd Electoral Division of Sceaux and was re-elected in 1914. After war was declared he was briefly attached to the *78e RIT* before being called back to Paris to serve first as *sous-secrétaire d'État à l'artillerie et à l'équipement militaire* under Viviani, then *sous-secrétaire d'État à l'artillerie et des munitions* under Briand (29th October 1915) and last as *ministère de l'Armement et des Fabrications de guerre* again under Briand (12th December 1915). He left the government on 12th September 1917 being replaced by his successor as *sous-secrétaire d'État à l'artillerie et des munitions* Louis Loucheur. After the war he was elected deputy for the Tarn in 1919 and in November was selected, *in absentia*, as Director General of the International Labour Office (ILO) which he led energetically until his sudden death on 8th May 1932, aged 53. Thomas suffered from diabetes. He is buried in Champigny-sur-Marne.

[ii] Post-war estimates were somewhat lower suggesting that 64% of pig iron, 58% of crude steel and 54% of finished steel production was lost in the opening months of

France started the war with 170 blast furnaces of which 90, most of them of modern design, were in the territories lost to the Germans in 1914. In January 1914, of those 170, the 131 which were active produced 434,000 tons of pig iron monthly. In July 1915, of the 81 still under French control, just 20 were producing a mere 46,000 tons per month. This figure tripled by July 1916 as more furnaces, 46, were put 'in blast' and not because of a significant increase in the total number of furnaces – 84.[137] Other steel-making facilities lost because of the German occupation of the north and north-east of the country were:

48 out of 164 open-hearth furnaces;
11 out of 24 electric furnaces;
53 out of 100 converters; and
38 out of 125 crucibles[138]

In addition, France lost over a third of its available steam horsepower which drove these mines and plants. To add to these huge problems, some 50% of the total workforce in these essential industries had been called up. Firmly believing in the idea that the war would be brief there had been no plan to protect essential workers in key armaments industries from being called up and sent to the front. In addition, another 21% of this key labour force was lost in the territories occupied by the Germans. This problem took some time to solve as, by August 1915, 42% of these key skilled workmen was still in the Army, however Thomas's efforts reduced this to 32% in two months. In the meantime, shortages of factories, raw materials and workers caused French munitions and armaments production to fall well behind the quantities needed at the front. [139]

JOFFRE'S DEMAND OF 19TH SEPTEMBER for 50,000 75-mm shells/day was eventually met in March 1915. The only problem was, on 2nd January 1915, he raised the necessary daily production rate to 80,000/day if the needs of the Army during the First Battle of Champagne were to be met. By the start of the Second Battle of Champagne and the Third Battle of Artois in the autumn of 1915, Joffre was asking for 150,000 shells a day but it was not until April 1916 the Army's daily requirement in 75-mm shells was achieved[i].

Ammunition supply on the Western Front was only one issue facing France. Russia, too, needed 75-mm shells and their factories in early 1915 were producing just 50% of the 40,000/day they required. France was the only other source of supply and, as one army had to do without, it was the Russian Army which suffered

---

the war [Source: Pinot, M, *Le Comité des Forges de France au Service de la Nation* quoted in Birkett M, *The Steel and Iron Trades during the War*, Journal of the Royal Statistical Society, Vol. 83, No. 3, May 1920, page 377].

[i] The French fired 1,387,370 75-mm shells from 22nd to 27th September 1915 in Champagne (the bombardment and opening attacks of the 2nd Battle of Champagne) at a rate of 231,000 a day or c. 210 shells per day for the 1,100 *75s* involved. The 872 heavier guns fired 295,800 shells (49,000/day) at a rate of 50 per gun per day [*Source:* Rhone, Lt. Gen., trans. by Spaulding, Col. O L, *Artillery Statistics from the World War, Field Artillery Journal*, Sept.-Oct. 1924, page 452, originally published in *Artilleristische Monatshepte*, Jan.-Feb., Berlin, 1924].

the effects of these shortages. The Serbian Army, too, went short of these essential munitions. Of course, the Allied excursions to the Gallipoli peninsula in the Spring of 1915 and the later Salonika expedition only made matters even worse.

In addition, pressure on the supply of 75-mm shell increased dramatically in early 1915 because of an experiment at the *Camp de Châlons* on 17th December 1914. Before then various methods were tried to cut the swathes of barbed wire the Germans were erecting in front of their trenches along the entire Western Front: machine gun fire and rockets, mechanical means like shears, and even grapnels to drag the wire out of the way. Nothing worked effectively. Barbed wire had been extensively used in both the First and Second Balkan Wars in large quantities and there it had been found difficult to deal with by any existing means. Indeed, Col. Pierre Victor Fournier, the French military *attaché* to Serbia and an observer of both wars, had noted in the fighting between the Bulgarians and Serbs the ubiquity of barbed wire in both armies' defences and then:

> "… the difficulty for artillery, whatever its calibre, to produce a material effect or to destroy field fortifications and barbed wire entanglements."[140]

His reports were forwarded to the *Ministere de la Guerre* in September 1913 and there, no doubt, filed beautifully and ignored resolutely. After all, there would be no use for barbed wire in the *offensive à outrance*.

But then, at Châlons, a 75-mm high explosive shell with an instantaneous graze fuse was tried. The shell's explosion immediately on contact with the wire or its support swept away the obstacle without leaving a large crater. *Trés bien*, the problem was solved. Or it might have been, were supplies adequate to use thousands of shells to cut the wire while the other field guns took on fortifications and troops.

Joffre, however, already knew the weight of shell of the *75* was inadequate to destroy or seriously damage the new, robust fortifications constructed by German engineers. In addition, the number of these guns available was steadily declining through wear, enemy action, and premature shell explosions, often caused by poorly manufactured war-time shells. Every major battle saw a rapid reduction in the number of *75s* guns available. By the end of the First Battle of Champagne in March 1915, 236 *75s* were out of action because of burst gun tubes. By 5th May that number more than doubled. In eight days, 9th to 16th May, the *Xe Armée* lost by this means the equivalent of 19 batteries of *75s*, i.e. 76 guns, in the fighting around Vimy Ridge[i]. Progressively, the French Army's supply of *75s* fell. On 22nd February 1915, there was a shortfall of 520 guns. By the end of March that rose to 609 and, by the middle of April, it shot up again to 805, the equivalent of 201 batteries, or a quarter of all 75-mm field gun batteries. By the end of the Second Battle of Artois, fully a third of the 3,680 *75s* with which started the war were lost to enemy action, wear, or accidents. Perversely, as shell supplies improved the number of guns available to fire them was in sharp decline. Throughout 1915, as new divisions were formed, they found their allocation of field artillery below the numbers prescribed by *GQG*. And, with every failure to supply guns and ammunition to the French Army, somewhere a *poilu* paid for it with his life.

---

[i] One unit lost twelve *75s* to prematures in one morning during the bombardment.

The problems for the French did not just lie with the guns and shells of the *75s*. All calibres, from 155-mm long guns and howitzers to heavy and super heavy *mortiers* of *220, 270* and *370*, were either not produced in the numbers required or not provided with sufficient shells. Indeed, the problems of shell supplies for these guns was not solved until the middle of 1917! One of the crucial weapons was the quick-firing 6-in. howitzer, the *155 CTR Rimailho*. Initial production of suitable shells was set at 365 a day. As trench warfare became the norm, on 24th December 1914 Joffre demanded an increase in production to 2,000 a day and, five days later, 3,000. Provision was only 300 per day and, of the 104 pieces of *155 CTR* with the armies, only 16 were ever in action during the December fighting. It got worse. During the battles of February 1915 not a single 155-mm shell was fired from a 155-mm howitzer. When, in preparation for the Second Battle of Artois in early May 1915, Foch asked Joffre for forty *155 CTR* with which to destroy the German defences at Vimy the CinC was unable to supply any.

Joffre demanded more and more 155-mm shells throughout the summer of 1915, rising from 7,000 a day in mid-June to 12,000 a day two weeks later. Deliveries amounted to 2,500 shells. Between 1st May and 20th June, the duration of the Second Battle of Artois, the French Army used 166,600 155-mm shells. During the same period, 95,000 were manufactured and a proportion were sent to Gallipoli. The daily rate Joffre demanded in anticipation of the autumn fighting in Champagne and in Artois was only eventually accepted in February 1916 after approaches were made to the USA for their fabrication. But it was not until June 1916 supplies of 155-mm shells reached the level Joffre required. By then, the rate needed was 20 shells a day per gun, a total of 18,000 a day, and eventually, 22 months after the start of the war, this production level was at last achieved[i].

Shells shortages had a direct relationship to infantry casualties. Post-war, in the *Revue Militaire Française*, a Col. Menu made a stark comparison between the casualty rates in Champagne, 25th September-15th October 1915, when 155-mm shells were in short supply, and the Somme, 1st July-30th November 1916, when production targets were at last met. In 21 days fighting in Champagne the French lost 81,500 dead and missing, an average of 3,880 men every day. In the 153 days on the Somme the total was 65,000 or 424 a day. Perhaps not the most robust use of statistics but a point well made, and it reflects Joffre's concern it was the infantry who suffered when the Army was forced to economise on the use of artillery.[141]

For the heavy *mortiers* things were not much better. In the winter of 1914-15 there were 330 *Mortiers de 220* and 56 *Mortiers de 270*. At the front there were 420 rounds for each *220* and 350 for the *270s*. In reserve, none. Thus, when the Second Battle of Artois started on 9th May 1915, Foch was limited to just eight *220s* and four *270s* with which to reduce the strongpoints on Vimy Ridge. Halfway through

---

[i] The extraordinary increase in shell production is clear In 1914 France produced 3.4 million shells of all types. This increased to 24.1 million in 1915 and to 80.3 million by 1916. Production peaked in 1917 when 101.3 million shells were produced [*Source*: Patrick Renoult, *Les munitions de l'artillerie française de la Grande Guerre* in Aubagnac, Berlemont, Boutet *et al.*, *Un milliard d'obus, des millions d'hommes: l'artillerie en 14/18*, Paris, Lienart éditions, 2016, page 108].

the battle, new supplies started to arrive and numbers increased to twenty *220s* and twelve *270s*, but the flow of shells was still slow and did not increase greatly by the opening of the Battle of the Somme. Daily production by then reached 1,200 for the *220s*, Joffre had demanded 3,000, and for the *270s* only 90 each day of the 1,000 required were manufactured. The required numbers for production for these guns was not met until December 1916 for the *220s* and April 1917 for the *270s*.

The sorry tale continued for the super heavy howitzers. Ten *Mortier de 370-mm Filloux* were ordered in October 1914 based on a 1912 prototype. The first monster 29 metric ton weapons came out of the factory in May 1915 and Joffre anticipated their use in the autumn battles. In the meantime, some 600 370-mm shells were manufactured but, without the required explosive, hardly any were fired in 1915.

Exacerbating these shortages was the necessity to supply arms and ammunition to France's European allies – Russia, Serbia, and Italy – and, later, the USA. Elizabeth Greenhalgh cites figures from French sources and the *History of the Ministry of Munitions* which presents the efforts of France in stark terms. During the war, France manufactured 300 million shells of which 25 million went to Russia. Britain, by contrast, sent Russia 2.7 million filled shells. France sent 20,000 machine guns to Russia (and provided a staggering 57,000 of these weapons to the American Expeditionary Force). Britain supplied Russia with 400. 1,300 French field guns went to the Eastern Front against 776 British artillery pieces (the AEF used 2,000 French 75-mm guns and 1,000 heavy guns and mortars as well as 200 tanks). To be fair, a very large proportion of the coal, iron and steel France needed to produce these items came from Britain, with, for example, 89% of its iron and steel imports in 1915 flowing across the English Channel.[142]

THE GREATEST IRONY OF THE FRENCH ARTILLERY DEBATE might have been witnessed had the war dragged on into 1919. Not only would France have been equipped with the first split-trail, long-range gun, the *Canon de 155 GPF (Modèle 1917 Filloux)* with a 16,300 metre range (17,825 yards/10 miles) and 3-4 rounds a minute rate of fire[i], but it would have had available a range of fully mobile, tracked, self-propelled guns and howitzers[ii] in the form of the *Canon de 194 GPF sur affût chenilles Saint-Chamond* and the *Mortiers de 220* and *280 sur affût chenilles Saint-Chamond*,

---

[i] Six captured *155 GPF* guns were thought to be emplaced at *Pointe du Hoc* between *Utah* and *Omaha* beaches in Normandy. The cliff-top position was assaulted by Coys D, E and F, 2nd Ranger Battalion, on 6th June 1944. The guns had been removed but they were found and the firing blocks destroyed. 50%+ of the 225-strong assault team became casualties.

[ii] The British Gun Carrier Mark I, designed by Majors John Greg and Walter Wilson and built by *Kitson & Co.*, Leeds, could carry a 6-in. 26 cwt. Howitzer or 60 pdr. Mk II gun and the guns could be fired from the carrier. 48 were built and first employed at Pilckem Ridge, 31st July-2nd August 1917. During 3rd Ypres a 6-in. howitzer was fired from the carrier but they were mainly used to move supplies and equipment, being used this way at Cambrai and extensively during the summer and autumn battles of 1918. The French weapons were proper self-propelled guns.

able to move across all terrains at between 2 and 5 kph and of which an arsenal of some 300 weapons was planned.[143] In addition, with the *Renault FT* tank, the French designed the first truly modern tank with its armament in a rotating turret. Designed by the *Société des Automobiles Renault* and armed either with a *Puteaux SA 1918* 37-mm gun or a *mitrailleuse Hotchkiss de 8 mm*, some 2,697 of these light tanks capable of 5 mph/8 kph were delivered before the end of the war. No other country could boast of such advanced *material*. Such was the change in attitudes and understanding in the field of modern artillery within the French Army it moved in four years from reliance on a single, lightweight field gun to the massive and mobile firepower these new weapons provided. It was a remarkable if belated transformation.

65 Mortier de 370-mm Filloux

66 Canon de 194 GPF sur affût chenilles Saint-Chamond

67 Mortier de 280 sur affût chenilles Saint-Chamond

68 Renault FT tank in 1918

ENDNOTES:

[1] Kaufmann H E and J W, *The Forts and Fortifications of Europe 1815-1945- The Central States,* Pen and Sword Military, 2014.

[2] Philpotts, Maj. A H C, RA, trans. *Activity of Field Artillery in the Russo-Japanese Campaign and the influence of the war experience on the use of artillery, Field Artillery Journal,* Vol. III, No. 4, Oct-Dec 1913, The United States Field Artillery Association, Washington, D. C., page 596.

[3] Ibid., page 587.

[4] Ibid., page 588-9.

[5] Ibid., page 588.

[6] Bruchmueller, G, *Die Deutsche Artillerie in den Durchbruchschlachten des Weltkrieges,* Mittler & sohn, 1922, page 8.

[7] Schirmer, *Generalleutnant* H, *Das Gerät der schweren Artillerie vor, in und nach dem Weltkrieg,* Vol 1, Bernard und Graefe, 1937, pages 52-55.

[8] Ibid., page 54.

[9] Ibid., page 64 onwards

[10] Ibid., page 57.

[11] Ibid., pages 57-8.

[12] Hohenlohe Ingelfingen, *General der Artillerie* Prince Kraft zu, *Aus meinem Leben* (*From my life*), Vol. II, pages 62/63 and 207.

[13] Haußner, K, *Das Feldgeschütz mit langem Rohrrücklauf: Geschichte meiner Erfindung,* R. Oldenbourg, 1928, page 4.

[14] Ibid., page 120.

[15] Menne B, *Blood and Steel - The Rise of the House of Krupp,* Menne Press, 2007.

[16] Schirmer, op. cit., page 9 onwards.

[17] Ibid., page 119.

[18] Challeat, Gen. J, *L'Artillerie de terre en France pendant un Siècle, Histoire Technique (1816-1919), Tome Second (1880-1910)*, Charles Lavauzelle et Cie, 1935, pages 316-7.
[19] Ibid.
[20] Bethell, *Modern Guns and Gunnery*, op. cit., pages 384-5.
[21] Haußner, op. cit., page 120.
[22] Challeat, op. cit., page 392 onwards.
[23] Ibid., page 350.
[24] Ibid., pages 352-3.
[25] *Base de données Léonore*.
[26] Reproduced from a translation of Gen. Frédéric-Georges Herr's book *L'Artillerie, ce qu'elle a été, ce qu'elle est, ce qu'elle doit être* (Paris, Berger Levrault, 1924) in *The Field Artillery Journal*, Vol XVII, No. 3, May-June 1927, page 222.
[27] Dosse, Capt. E., *Tactical Notes*, *Field Artillery Journal*, Vol. IV, No. 1, Jan-Mar 1914, page 97.
[28] Philpotts, op. cit., page 566, *Field Artillery Journal*, Vol. III, No. 4, Oct-Dec 1913,
[29] *Base de données Léonore*.
[30] Herr, op. cit., *Field Artillery Journal*, page 223.
[31] 'End of the French Army Manoeuvres'., *The Times*, 18th September 1913, page 5.
[32] Sheffield G & Bourne J, *Douglas Haig: War Diaries and Letters 1914-18*, Weidenfeld & Nicholson, 2005, page 184.
[33] Herr, op. cit. *Field Artillery Journal*, page 224.
[34] Ibid., page 224.
[35] Thooris, M-C & Billoux, C, *École polytechnique: une grande école dans la Grande Guerre*, Palaiseau, École polytechnique, 2004, page 43.
[36] Herr, op. cit.
[37] Ibid., pages 224-5.
[38] Baquet, Hen. L H, *Souvenirs d'un directeur d'artillerie*, Charles-Lavauzelle, 1921, page 120.
[39] *AFdeGG*, Tome 11, *La direction de l'arrière*, 1937, page 940.
[40] *Historique du 3e R.A.P.*, Paul Even, Metz, page 5.
[41] Rhone, Lt. Gen., trans. by Spaulding, Col. O L, *Artillery Statistics from the World War*, *Field Artillery Journal*, Sept.-Oct. 1924, page 451, originally published in *Artilleristische Monatshepte*, Jan.-Feb., Berlin, 1924.
[42] Ibid., page 452.
[43] Herr, op. cit. *Field Artillery Journal*, page 228.
[44] Jager, Herbert, *German Artillery of World War One*, Crowood Press, 2001, pages 23-29.
[45] Caron, Francois, *An Economic History of France*, Routledge, 2012.
[46] Stevenson, D., *Armaments and the Coming of War: Europe, 1904-1914*, Oxford University Press, page 30.
[47] *Baedeker* 1890.
[48] Malandrin, Lt. Col. M H, personal file, *Base Leonore*.
[49] *Le Courrier de l'Oise*, 20th March 1913.
[50] Herr, Gen. G F, *L'Artillerie, ce qu'elle a été, ce qu'elle est, ce qu'elle doit être*, Berger Levrault, 1924, pages 32-2.
[51] François, Gen. G as *ALVF*, *https://forum.pages14-18.com/viewtopic.php?t=51069*.
[52] Zuber, T., op. cit., pages 116-8.
[53] Mondésir, Col J F L P de, *Siège et Prise d'Adrianople*, Librairie Chapelot, 1914, page 202.
[54] Hall, R C, *The Balkan Wars, 1912–1913: Prelude to the First World War*, Routledge, 2000, page 47.
[55] Murray, N A A, *The Theory and Practice of Field Fortification from 1877-1914*, D. Phil Thesis, St Antony's College, Oxford, 2007, page 184.
[56] Bellenger, Capt. G., trans. by Maj. W S McNair, 6th Field Artillery, *Notes on the employment of artillery in the Balkan campaign*, *Field Artillery Journal*, Vol. IV, No. 1, Jan-Mar 1914, page 86.
[57] Ibid.
[58] Murray, op. cit., page 210

[59] Bellenger, op. cit., page 92.
[60] Ibid., page 93.
[61] Alvin, Capt. P, trans. by Lt. H R Odell, 3rd Field Artillery, *The Field Artillery in the Balkans*, Field Artillery Journal, Vol. IV, No. 2, Apr-June 1914, page 318.
[62] Ibid., page 322.
[63] Ibid., page 323.
[64] Ibid.
[65] Herr, op. cit. *Field Artillery Journal*, page 237.
[66] Porch, op. cit., page 236.
[67] General D, *Une doctrine pour l'artillerie lourde*, Revue d'artillerie, March 1914, page 431.
[68] *Journal des sciences militaires, Artillery in France and in Germany in 1914*, March 1914, page 1.
[69] Porch, op. cit., page 242.
[70] Ibid., page 244-5.
[71] Percin, Gen. A., *Le combat*, Alcan, Nouvelle collection scientifique, 1914.
[72] Ibid., page 252.
[73] Ibid., page 255.
[74] Ibid., page 115.
[75] Ibid., page 257.
[76] Ibid., page 258.
[77] Ibid., page 259.
[78] Ibid., page 261.
[79] *The Times, The German Army Manoeuvres: The Artillery*, 24th October 1911, page 5.
[80] Ibid.
[81] Percin, op. cit., page 261.
[82] Challéat, Chef d'escadron J M J, *La question de l'obusier léger*, Revue d'artillerie, January 1912, page 234.
[83] O.B., *The Question of the Light Field Howitzer*, Journal des sciences militaires, 19th March 1912, page 435 onwards.
[84] Mayer, E, *L'artillerie lourde de campagne avant la guerre*, Revue Militaire Suisse, LXIII, No. 8, August, and No. 9, September 1918.
[85] Ibid.
[86] Langlois, Gen. H, *L'artillerie de campagne en liaison avec les autres armes*, p. 113.
[87] Ibid., page 48.
[88] Buat, Gen. E, *L'artillerie de campagne : son histoire, son évolution, son état actuel*, F Alcan, 1911, pages 132-3.
[89] Langlois, op. cit., page 250.
[90] Quoted in Challeat, *L'Artillerie de terre en France pendant un Siècle*, op. cit.page 57.
[91] Ibid., page 296.
[92] O.B., *The Question of the Light Field Howitzer*, op. cit.
[93] Buat, op. cit., page 206.
[94] Ibid., page 210.
[95] O.B., *Questions d'artillerie d'actualité*, Journal des Sciences Militaire, December 1912, page 373.
[96] Peloux, Capt., *Matériels de campagne et de siège à tir rapide de gros calibres*, Revue d'artillerie, April 1912, page 5 onwards.
[97] Ibid., page 6.
[98] Schirmer, op. cit., page 71.
[99] O.B., *Questions d'artillerie d'actualité*, op. cit.
[100] Ibid.
[101] Mayer, E, *L'artillerie lourde de campagne avant la guerre*, op. cit.
[102] Glück, Capt. G-L, *Obusiers de campagne et Artillerie lourde*, Journal des sciences militaires, July 1913, page 76 onwards.
[103] Ibid.
[104] Ibid.

[105] Mayer, E, *L'artillerie lourde de campagne avant la guerre,* op. cit.
[106] Ibid.
[107] Ibid.
[108] Glück, op. cit.
[109] Mayer, E, *L'artillerie lourde de campagne avant la guerre,* op. cit.
[110] Paloque, Col. J H, *Artillerie de campagne,* Octave Doin et Fils, 1909.
[111] Ibid., page 207.
[112] Glück, op. cit.
[113] Langlois, quoting Devet, in Glück, op. cit.
[114] Glück, op. cit.
[115] Ibid.
[116] Ibid.
[117] Ibid.
[118] Ibid.
[119] *Revue militaire des armées étrangères,* December 1912.
[120] Rimailho, Lt. Col. E, *Artillerie de campagne,* Gauthier-Villars, 1924, page 72.
[121] Challeat, Gen. J, *L'Artillerie de terre en France pendant un Siècle, op. cit.* page 492.
[122] Ibid., page 481.
[123] Ibid.
[124] Ibid.
[125] Ibid.
[126] Percin, Gen. A, *L'Aurore,* 1st June 1912.
[127] Glück, op. cit.
[128] Ibid.
[129] Ibid.
[130] Ibid.
[131] Ibid.
[132] Herr, op. cit., *Field Artillery Journal,* page 243.
[133] Pastre, J.-L. G, *Trois ans de front: Belgique, Aisne et Champagne, Verdun, Argonne, Lorraine : notes et impressions d'un artilleur,* Berger-Levrault, 1918, page 33.
[134] Ibid., pages 8-10.
[135] This section is based on figures given in an article *'Le Fabrication de Guerre'* by Col. Menu in the *Revue Militaire Française,* October-December edition, 1933, pages 180-211.
[136] Joffre to the Minister of War, 6.284, 20th September 1914.
[137] Pinot, M, *Le Comité des Forges de France au Service de la Nation* quoted in Birkett M, *The Steel and Iron Trades during the War, Journal of the Royal Statistical Society,* Vol. 83, No. 3, May 1920, page 381.
[138] Ibid., pages 382-3.
[139] This section is drawn from an article *Manufacture and Consumption of Ammunition in France* which first appeared in the Austrian newspaper *Fremdenblatt* on 1st April 1916. It was translated and included in *The Field Artillery Journal,* April-June 1916, pages 331-2.
[140] Quoted in Murray, op. cit., page 212.
[141] Menu, Col. *'Le Fabrication de Guerre'* op. cit.
[142] Greenhalgh, E, *Errors and Omissions in Franco—British Co-operation over Munitions Production, 1914—1918, War in History,* Vol. 14, No. 2, April 2007, page 216.
[143] For more see Tauzin and Vauvillier, *Les Canons de la Victoire,* Tome I, pages 64-5.

PART THREE: A SECOND-CLASS ARMY?

"One class of men makes war and leaves another to fight it out."

Gen. William Tecumseh Sherman

6. WARS AND RUMOURS OF WARS

"Very characteristic... is the objection made by Colonel Graves when he says: 'The Boer fights to prevent his foe getting at him; while the British, I am proud to believe, fights with the view of getting at his foe'. Surely the question here is not who fights in the most chivalrous and romantic way, but who fights best with the object of gaining victory."

Jan Bogumił Bloch, 1901

THE OUTBREAK OF THE SECOND WAR with the Boers on 11th October 1899 found the Regular Army with just over 103,000 men (excluding officers) based in Great Britain. After the Transvaal and Orange Free State burghers invaded Natal and Cape Colony nearly two thirds of these troops were shipped to South Africa over the next six months[i]. In addition, nearly 43,000 of the approximately 80,000 reservists joined them. More reservists followed to replace casualties caused through fighting and illness and as the Army in South Africa grew.[1] It is fair to say their efficient transportation was one of the few British successes of the opening months of the war. Having said that, the *balance* of the troops sent out in the first waves of reinforcement was problematic as the overwhelming majority, 39,000 of the first 45,000, was infantry.[2] Such troops were sent out to combat an enemy which everywhere was mounted. Apart from the differences in speed of manoeuvre it also meant that, in the main, British forces were tied to the railways to move troops. Thus, thoughts of rapid outflanking movements were, in the short term, irrelevant.

The British started the war as if unaware of recent technologically driven tactical advances. As Bloch predicted, advancing *en masse* in the open proved suicidal against the rapid, long-range fire of the Boer's *Mauser Modell 1895* rifle. Using a smokeless cartridge, accurate shooting was possible out to 1,000 yards, with an effective range well beyond, and the well-practised Boer riflemen, firing from concealed positions, wreaked havoc amongst British troops and a shock to those on the receiving end. It should not have been as, the previous year, the Spanish inflicted severe losses on US troops at the Battles of San Juan Heights and El Caney in Cuba on 1st July 1898 in the Spanish-American War. At San Juan, c. 800 Spanish troops and their *Mauser 1894s* kept at bay 11,000+ US and Cuban troops causing casualties at a ratio of 9:1 before being overrun. At El Caney 520 Spanish troops held off 10,000 men before withdrawing, having inflicted 2½ casualties for every 1 suffered[ii].

Over the previous thirty years the rifle's performance dramatically improved. The bullet's calibre was reduced, its weight more than halved (allowing more ammunition to be carried), the muzzle velocity nearly doubled enabling a flatter

---

[i] The South Africa campaign area should not be underestimated, i.e. c. 650 kms north/south by 550 kms east/west (c. 400x350 miles). The Transvaal and Orange Free State superimposed on Europe covers eastern France (Côte d'Azur to Alsace), Switzerland, most of Austria, the west of the Czech Republic, Bavaria, and Germany north to Berlin and Hannover.

[ii] Casualties: San Juan 2,040 US/Cuban to 230 Spanish (39 PoWs), El Caney 440 US/Cuban to 176 Spanish (160 PoWs). Figures vary depending on the source.

311

trajectory, and the maximum range greatly improved. Changes from the single shot rifle, such as the British *Martini-Henry*, to the magazine rifles of the *Lee-Metford* and *Lee-Enfield* variants increased the rate of fire and, therefore, the volume of lead flying around the average battlefield.

The British were somewhat late in the field with the adoption of the *Lee-Metford*. The French finished arming their troops with the magazine-equipped *Fusil Modèle 1886*, the *Lebel*, in 1889 and, in response, Germany adopted the *Mauser Gewehr 88* in 1888. William Ellis Metford, meanwhile, developed a magazine version for his own rifle designs and, in 1888, the *War Office Small Arms Committee* adopted the basic *Metford* rifle with a bolt-action and magazine developed by James Paris Lee. There was resistance, however, within the higher echelons of the Army to the introduction of a rapid-fire rifle if for no other reason than the strains maintaining ammunition supplies on a battlefield would impose. There were other concerns about a loss of command and control over individual soldiers if they were no longer required to produce volley fire and could wander off to select their own firing position. There was also the question about its necessity when the British Army, in the main, faced poorly equipped and trained native insurgents or resisters to the delights of British imperialism. The prospect of facing continental adversaries at a significant firepower disadvantage eventually overcame the views of traditionalists and imperialists and the new rifle started to be manufactured at the *Royal Small Arms Factory* at Enfield Lock.

Table 11 shows the change in performance of the British rifle since 1871.

Rifle type (Year)	*Martini-Henry* (1871) Single shot	*Lee-Metford* (1888) Magazine	*Lee-Enfield* (1895)/ *SMLE* (1904) Magazine
Calibre	.45 (31gm)	.303	.303 (11.3 gm)
Powder type	Black powder	Black then smokeless	Smokeless
Muzzle velocity (ft/s)	1300	2040	2440
Effective range (yds)	400	800	550
Max range (yds)	1900	1800	3000
Rounds/minute	12	20	20-30

Table 11 Performance of British Rifles 1871 onwards

By comparison, the Boer *Mauser Modell 1895* had a muzzle velocity of 2,297 ft/s and an effective range of 550 yards and the model with which the German Army went to war in 1914, the *Gewehr 98*, a muzzle velocity of 2,881 ft/s, an effective range of 550 yards and a maximum range of 4,080 yds.

Equally suicidal in the face of such reach was the British tactic of deploying the artillery in the open to provide close support to attacking infantry. In the early battles of the South African war gun crews were mown down and guns lost as a result of a tactic adopted by the artillery in previous eras when relatively short-range muzzle-loading cannon still out-ranged the opposing infantry's muskets. More recently, they were the tactics so successfully employed by the steel, breech-

---

[i] Between 1887 and 1916 3.45 million *Lebels* were manufactured by the French State arsenals at the *Manufactures d'armes de Châtellerault*, *de St-Etienne* and *de Tulle*. An improved version was introduced in 1893: the *Fusil Mle 1886 M93*.

loading *Krupp*-equipped Prussian artillery in 1870-1 once the inferior French bronze muzzle-loading guns were silenced.

Thirdly, the experience of being shelled by even the few long-range *Krupp* and *Schneider* guns[i] the Boers possessed, but which British troops on the receiving end could not see, i.e. indirect fire, proved a hugely unnerving experience. Furthermore, when attempting to return this fire, the numerically superior artillery at the disposal of various British Generals proved singularly unable to locate the Boer positions. This artillery also proved rather useless when they attempted to bombard the positions from which it was thought, often incorrectly, the Boer riflemen fired.

IN THE PREVIOUS DECADE IT WAS HOPED that army manoeuvres of increasing size and a new *Drill Book* in 1896 might inform British officers on how best to conduct war against properly armed and trained armies. That they did not was highlighted by the comments made by the Duke of Connaught after the August 1895 exercises held in trying heat and thunderstorms around the New Forest. He:

> "…condemned the assailing force for having made 'an impossible frontal attack' and 'advancing in a succession of rigid lines' over ground bare and level as a billiard table; and at the same manoeuvres the umpires were censured for 'not taking the initiative' and stopping the advance or, at all events, decimating the infantry. The Senior Umpire, Sir Francis Grenfell, on one occasion gave 50 per cent casualties, remarking that 80 per cent would have been nearer the real loss… But… when each of the three brigadiers took his brigade to Pirbright for a day's field firing… the formations were so dense in two of them that the indispensable condition for success was that the weapons of the defenders should be bows and arrows only."[3]

In 1897 exercises were conducted around Arundel in Sussex. One of its less productive days was described by the Director, Maj. Gen. Sir William Butler, as a 'depressing' day of 'disappointments and surprises'.[4] But the greater criticism made of the six-day exercises was that, except for the senior and staff officers involved, no-one else learnt anything from their wearying days out near the South Downs.

Each day was devoted to a specific tactical situation:

Day 1. Woodland campaigning – after which the Military Correspondent of *The Times* could barely contain his anger and frustration in his report of 10th September. So inept was their performance he advocated, tongue in cheek (we assume), lynching the Generals and cavalry commanders. These were: invading *Blue Force*, Maj. Gen. (later Lt. Gen. Sir) Charles John Burnett, CB, 15th Regt. of Foot (East Yorkshires) commanding Eastern District and, here, 1st Division with Col. Charles Edward Beckett, CB, 3rd (the King's Own) Hussars, commanding 1st Cavalry Brigade; opposed by *Red Force*, Maj. Gen. (later Sir) Matthew William Edward Gosset, CB, 54th Regt. of Foot (Dorsetshires) commanding Dublin

---

[i] The Transvaal government bought four 155-mm *Schneider-Creusot* long guns and c. 9,000 shells the year before the war. They were used at the sieges of Mafeking, Ladysmith, and Kimberley as well as some of the earlier battles of the war.

District and, here, 2nd Division, with Lt. Col. Sir Simon MacDonald Lockhart of Lee and Carnwath, 5th Bart, MVO, 1st Life Guards, commanding 2nd Cavalry Brigade[i]. His secondary complaint was that 'no trees sufficiently high would have been found in North Wood to serve as gallows…'[5]. Then…

Day 2. Two supposedly opposed river crossings – the appalling conduct of the first attempt so gob-smacked Maj. Gen. Butler he admitted he had little to say so 'vast' was his surprise at the unfolding of events. But then he said it anyway in a typically polite and understated way:

> "That two distinct crossings of a rather formidable river obstacle should have been accomplished – one of them wholly without observation, and both without opposition – along a front of about two miles of river, entirely under the possible supervision of the enemy opposing such crossing is, I take it, a very remarkable incident."[6]

But that was not all. Having bridged the river, the commanding General then threw across four battalions, two batteries and two cavalry regiments. And then left them there. Alone. For two hours. Meanwhile, the rest of his force milled around on the wrong side of the bridge achieving nothing. The defending General, belatedly having woken up himself and his officers, then obligingly annihilated the isolated force on his side of the river.

Maj. Gen. Butler damned both Generals by talking about anything other than their conduct of the days' affairs:

> "Amid the events of an exceptionally depressing day, I think, Sir, we may recognize one brilliant feature in the manner in which the work of the bridging was done by the Royal Engineers."[7]

The second crossing was described simply in *The Times* as 'unreal', with *Blue's* troops apparently crossing the *River Arun* with ease during which time they caused 'dismay among the beautiful deer' and 'unsettled the inmates of the pheasanteries' of Arundel Park, only for the umpires to overturn the entire day's proceedings because some cunningly concealed *Red* batteries had sunk the RE's pontoons at short range.[8]

Day 3. Then came 'attack versus defence' on the open downs, a day of such apparent tedium *The Times* declined to 'take up valuable space… for their record' except to say:

---

[i] None of the above was held against them. Gosset and Burnett passed out of the Staff College. Burnett was born in Australia in 1843. He served in the Ashanti Wars and 2nd Afghan War. In 1900 he commanded the Poona District and was the senior observer with the Japanese in Manchuria 1904-5. He was GOCinC Western Command 1907-10. He died in 1915. Gosset was born in 1840 and served in the Indian Mutiny, the Kaffir and Zulu Wars, and 1st Boer War. He died in 1909. Beckett was born in 1849, served in the Sudan and 2nd Boer War and was, from November 1914 to November 1915, GOC, 66th (2nd East Lancashire) Division based in the UK. He died in 1925. Lockhart was born in 1849 and joined the 1st Life Guards in 1868 and served at Kassassin and Tel-el-Kebir (Sudan). He was ADC to the CinC 1899-1900 and commanded the cavalry at the Curragh, 1900-1901. He died in 1922.

"The only people who worked hard, and they had to work very hard, were those who had to find what are familiarly known as 'interesting points for comment'... the various arms either sat on the tops of the windy hills or walked around in the neighbouring valleys... But as soon as the leading brigade had been properly annihilated by a withering rifle fire, owing to the peculiar form of attack formation adopted... patience was exhausted and the very welcome 'Cease fire' was sounded."[9]

And finally...

Day 4. A fighting rear-guard across the Downs which included an 'attack' down one hill and up another, very much in the fashion of the 'Grand Old Duke of York', which found the position devoid of enemy troops because the intelligence on which the entire attack was made was more than two hours out of date and the 'enemy' was now on top of another hill some distance away. To make matters worse, the troops involved were also taken under heavy 'fire' from some RHA Batteries located on a nearby slope. At which point the 'Cease fire' ended these laughable proceedings but not before the cavalry, determined to show-off in front of the assembled public:

"... determined to subordinate the dictates of tactical judgement to the production of a good amount of spectacular effect."[10]

By now, the troops were so scattered that the anticipated 'march past' in front of the assembled 'good and great' was abandoned. But all was not lost, as a special *al fresco* luncheon was put on for both officers and the landowners, mainly the Duke of Norfolk, over whose land they had happily trampled for the previous week. Meanwhile, the troops trudged their way back to their various barracks and somewhat less exalted fare.

In 1898 the Army held extensive exercises and manoeuvres between July and early September in south Wiltshire and Dorset including the newly purchased 41,000 acres of Salisbury Plain. These were the first held since the passing of the *Military Manoeuvres Act* of 1897 (modified in 1911). This act came into force on Monday, 15th August 1898, and, theoretically, allowed the Army to train over an area of 1,500 square miles for up to three months. Thus, exercises of a scale similar to, though never as large as, those held in continental Europe became possible.

In total, some 53,600 men and 242 guns were involved in 1898, operating over some 48 square miles, making these the largest domestic exercises conducted to that date. They were also the last large-scale ones before the war in South Africa[i]. Nothing changed between 1895 and 1898 and the infantry tactics employed in South Africa were derived from these manoeuvres and concepts enshrined in the 1896 *Drill Book*. The 1898 manoeuvres, though by far the biggest ever held by the Army, were by general agreement worse than most. The French conducted similar exercises in the years immediately before the outbreak of the Great War.

---

[i] An exercise was conducted in Ireland in August 1899 involving a *Red Force* of one cavalry and two infantry brigades versus *Blue Force* comprising one cavalry and one infantry brigade. The Aldershot Command under Buller also conducted an exercise in September 1899.

Over a period of six weeks from 1st July ten cavalry regiments and two RHA batteries trained on Salisbury Plain (not all at the same time. Groups of regiments joined in every few weeks). From mid-August to the end of the month two Army Corps were to train separately before, between the 1st and 7th September, the two Corps manoeuvred against one another over southern Wiltshire and Dorset. These formations were a 'defending' *Northern (Red) Corps* (based on Aldershot Command[i] and commanded by Lt. Gen. HRH the Duke of Connaught[ii]) to train in Hampshire and on Salisbury Plain, and an 'invading' *Southern (Blue) Corps* (commanded by Sir Redvers Buller) which was based between Dorchester and Wareham. The Director and Umpire-in-Chief of the entire enterprise was the Commander in Chief Field Marshal, the Right Hon. Garnet Viscount Wolseley, KP, GCB, GCMG. A certain Lt. Col. John French commanded the 2nd Cavalry Brigade of the *Southern Corps*.

Even before it started the entire operation was viewed with some disdain by external commentators who pointed out that, unlike the regionally based Army Corps of France and Germany, no such bodies in principle or in practice existed within Great Britain. There was no body of staff officers who worked together to service such a unit. Indeed, to make up the numbers for the manoeuvres (some 60,000 men were involved) troops were brought in from all over the country including Ireland. And not just Regular ones, the Militia was involved too. Thus, the Divisions which made up the two Corps were not organised in the normal two Brigade, four battalion model (which was the case with the Division commanded by Willian Forbes Gatacre at Omdurman which battle took place at the same time as the actual manoeuvres on 2nd September 1898) but in two six-battalion brigades with four of the battalions being Regulars and the other two Militia, the Militia battalions appearing, as if an after-thought, just before the manoeuvres began. The Regular battalions previously organised in eight companies were re-organised into four. The Militia battalions had six. The Aldershot command cavalry which trained together just prior to the manoeuvres was then, for some reason, broken up with one regiment serving as 'Corps troops' to be replaced with another brought over from Ireland. In all, something of a dog's breakfast which necessitated the production of a special 107-page booklet to itemise the details of every unit's establishment and organisation.[11]

Then there were the commanders, a motley crew of active, half-pay and retired officers drawn from all over the country as were the units they commanded. The *Southern Corps*' divisional Generals came from Dublin (but took command of

---

[i] 1st, 2nd and 3rd Divisions, an independent cavalry brigade and associated field and horse artillery, engineers, Army Service Corps companies, balloon sections etc. The Southern Corps comprised the 4th, 5th and 6th Divisions and identical support troops, cavalry, etc.

[ii] Prince Arthur William Patrick Albert, Duke of Connaught and Strathearn and Earl of Sussex (1850-1942). 7th child and third son of Victoria and Albert. Trained as a Royal Engineer. Commanded, Bombay Army 1886-1890. Aldershot Command 1893-8. Field Marshal, 1902. Served variously as Commander in Chief, Ireland, GOC III Corps, Inspector General of the Forces and Governor General of Canada.

troops from southern England), York (but commanded the troops from Ireland) and Dover. Brigadiers were from training establishments at Hythe and Shorncliffe and the staff at Colchester while others were brought back from half-pay.[12] The *Northern Corps*, under the Duke of Connaught, had the virtue of being based on the Aldershot Command and some form of unified structure.

To add to the general air of unreality, the provisioning of this mass of men was left mainly to private enterprise (well, there was a Conservative government in power perhaps as reactionary as those of the 21st Century) and wagons bearing the names of grocer and tea merchant *Thomas Lipton*[i], and *William Whiteley*[ii], retailer of Westbourne Grove, amongst other more local suppliers to whom they then arbitrarily sub-contracted, were to be seen following, and sometimes blocking, the line of march of the troops. Their rather random distribution of over-priced and sub-standard food and drink to the troops was not then appreciated.[13]

Then there were the manoeuvres themselves. First, the apparent success of a preliminary frontal assault by Redvers Buller's troops on a well-defended position on 31st August was over-turned by Wolseley in his role as Umpire-in-Chief. He ventured that no such attack could possibly have succeeded. Optimistically, in the light of subsequent events in South Africa, *The Times* correspondent suggested:

"…it is hardly likely that in real warfare a frontal attack would be launched against such an enemy…"[14]

If only.

The slightly farcical nature of these manoeuvres was, in the main, a continuation of the worthless proceedings of the previous year.

An expected cavalry engagement failed to take place because orders given to each side were so open to interpretation and full of conflicting demands they managed to avoid one another, much to the disappointment of the watching worthies and crowds of excited locals. Redvers Buller then worryingly repeated his simplistic tactics of the preliminary attack two days earlier. Connaught's *Red* troops arrived at a key position (Charlton Down) and presented a formidable barrier to Redvers Buller's progress. He was given the option of simply pinning *Red* to this position as, according to the scheme, a completely imaginary *Blue Army* was advancing after landing at Bristol thereby threatening *Red's* rear? But Redvers Buller was not about to disappoint his audience a second time. Nor was he about to display any tactical acumen by anything fancy such as a flanking movement which might place his Corps between *Red* and their base at Salisbury. Given what *The Times* described as a choice between 'brute force pure and simple' or 'manoeuvring to a flank so as to obtain a decided tactical and strategical advantage' it is perhaps no surprise given later events in South Africa that Redvers Buller chose the former:

"… the *Blue* attack assumed the form of brute force… two-and-a-half of his divisions, supported by all his guns, were found when the 'Cease fire'

---

[i] Later Sir Thomas Johnstone Lipton, 1st Baronet, KCVO.
[ii] Shot dead, 24th January 1907, by Horace George Rayner claiming to be Whiteley's illegitimate son.

sounded hurling themselves against the right of *Red's* position... and without a chance of success... How could any attack succeed when... both the guns and the two-and-a-half divisions of infantry were exposed to, and to a considerable extent, enfiladed by, the fire of a powerful line of guns during their advance?"[15]

Day Three was another day of disappointments. Instructions from 'on high' were meant to result in a battle outside Shaftesbury. Again, vagueness and too many contradictory options led to Connaught deciding avoiding action was his best course. Perhaps it was just as well as one of Redvers Buller's divisions for reasons inexplicable 'lay down *en masse*' in a horribly exposed position, while two of *Red's* divisions got themselves all of a tangle a bit further north.[16] Generally, a day of shambles and confusion.

Day Four promised 'interest and amusement' as both sides rushed to cover the crossings of the *River Wylye* north-west of Salisbury but, just as affairs seemed about to get interesting, the 'cease fire' sounded and everyone trotted off to dinner.

Day Five, containing an egregious lapse of 'intelligence' (or lack thereof in all senses) by Redvers Buller, also highlighted a problem within the Army clearly not then rectified prior to South Africa. *The Times* described it thus:

"If there is one thing indispensable for forming the plan of an attack, it is reconnoitring the enemy's position; if there is one thing that can be, and constantly is, dispensed with in forming the plan for an attack on any position at our chief and almost only school of practical training, Aldershot, it is reconnoitring that position..."[17]

The correspondent then held out the baseless hope that:

"... during the next five years at Aldershot neglectors of reconnaissance will have a bad time of it."[18]

Or, be sent to South Africa as commander-in-chief. If only briefly.

Another problem the day identified was a tendency for senior commanders to meander off to inspect enemy positions or something else less productive. Here, the result was that one unit was taken by surprise as they twiddled their thumbs waiting for their General to return, and another failed to move when required because its commander disappeared off into 'the blue' and could not then be found.

Day Six revealed little except the fact HRH the Duke of Connaught had been dealt a somewhat more favourable strategical hand by Viscount Wolseley than his opponent. The benefit of Royal connections perhaps?

The Times was scathing in its criticism of the manoeuvres, describing the 'abnormal conditions' of the entire process. Broadly, it thought the £100,000 voted to enable them to take place a complete waste of government money and military time. Summing up, the newspaper wrote:

"As regards the general teaching from the manoeuvres, the fair summary is that we have learnt very much which we did not expect to learn, and of what we expected to have learnt very little."[19]

In other words, they learnt a lot about administration and very little about fighting. Furthermore, what the manoeuvres revealed was that slaughtering 'savages' in irregular warfare was in no way a sound basis on which to judge a General's ability to fight 'civilised' soldiers in regular, i.e. continental, warfare. In almost every respect Connaught came out ahead of Redvers Buller. The Duke's military experience came from large unit command: the 1st (Guards) Brigade in the Anglo-Egyptian War, fighting at the Battle of Tel El Kebir on 13th September 1882; the Bombay Army between 1886 and 1890; Southern District 1890-3; and Aldershot Command 1893-8.

That there was an awful lot of marching but little actual 'manoeuvring' (and precious little fighting) was generally accepted.[20] And, because only over-20s were despatched to India, the ranks of the two Corps were filled with young, inexperienced and not yet fully-formed lads of 18 years or less who struggled with the physical pressures of long and arduous marches in hot weather (as might apply in South Africa, for example). Both Wolesley and Connaught commented on this problem. Wolseley pointed out that, because Army was formed of volunteers, the rank and file could not be worked as hard in peace manoeuvres as were continental conscripts. Well, not without 'a very serious effect upon recruiting'.[21]

The Duke was similarly direct:

"... if such operations are to be carried out for several days in succession they should not be called upon to carry valises every day; if they do they are physically incapable of the rapidity of movement so often essential, they lose interest in the proceedings, and this loss of interest, fatal to valuable instruction, extends to the regimental officers who feel that their men's powers are being unduly strained."[22]

The Duke was generally scathing about the exercises, not least the time wasted in minor activities but also the numbers of officers attached to the various staffs and who would have learnt more had they been 'located where they could find a wider field for the discharge of their duties'.[23]

Wolseley's report, issued in early 1899, made wide-ranging comments on the various arms. The Engineers and Artillery were generally commended; and the cavalry criticised for their tendency to mass into bodies perhaps suitable for an *arme blanche*[i] charge but unsuited to the needs of proper reconnaissance and intelligence gathering. But, in the light of events to come later that year, it was the tactics of the infantry which were most worrying:

"(a) The manner in which battalions were frequently exposed to artillery fire in unsuitable formations...
(b) In attack formations the lines were often so close that two successive lines would have been struck by bullets from the same shrapnel... The final

---

[i] The *arme blanche* is a French term and refers to any use of edged weapons at close range, i.e. the bayonet by the infantry or the sword or lance by the cavalry. The *arme blanche* in cavalry terms, therefore, refers to its use in massed charges. This phrase in modern parlance is synonymous with cavalry armed with a sabre or lance but *not* carbine-equipped mounted infantry, e.g. the Imperial Yeomanry of the Boer War, or the Australian Light Horse of WW1.

assault and the supply of ammunition to the leading lines, as well as the withdrawal of beaten forces, are all exercises which it would have been of value to practise.

(c) The handling of machine guns was not always skilful or satisfactory…

(d) The extensions were in many cases premature and sufficient advantage was not taken of the ground to bring the troops into action under cover…"[24]

But then, priorities, priorities, most of his final comments were limited to criticism of the catering arrangements and the employment of tea merchants and other private contractors for such an essential task.

These exercises led to several highly critical newspaper articles and letters (they were much later described as a 'sad fiasco' in *The Times* in 1903[25]), not least the following to *The Times* from a correspondent calling himself *Onlooker*:

"There are Generals who would have to be employed in a great war, and who can hardly be said to have shown their ability to handle a brigade."[26]

The following year another letter writer, one *Majuba,* was equally critical:

"Your correspondent has made it abundantly clear that the art of handling any other than small units under modern conditions is but little understood in our home Army; that all combatant duties, including those of the Staff, are either unpractised or unfamiliar, and that the tactics of the three arms, when acting together, are of a crude description."[27]

IN THE LIGHT OF THE FOREGOING, it is of no great surprise the opening battles of the war in South Africa flashed danger signals for British forces in Natal, and gave notice of the potential for considerable arrogance, ignorance, error and stupidity amongst senior officers involved (details are in Appendix 2, page 845).

We need not delve too deeply into the reasons why the Boers of the Transvaal and Orange Free State declared war on 11th October 1899. Suffice to say the Cecil Rhodes-inspired Jameson Raid of early 1896, combining rampant imperialism with pure greed for the Transvaal's mineral wealth, was sufficient to de-stabilise a fragile peace between the Empire and the Boers, and helped cement a military alliance between the two Boer republics. The intervening period was simply an armed truce in which both sides prepared for a proper war, with President Kruger of the Transvaal purchasing 37,000 *Mauser Modell 1895* rifles, tens of millions of rounds of ammunition, and artillery from *Krupp, Schneider & Cie*, and twenty-five 37-mm quick-firing guns manufactured by the British *Maxim-Nordenfelt* company (which, in 1897, was bought out by *Vickers*). When negotiations between the two sides broke down in the late summer of 1899 war was inevitable and, with 33,000 men mobilised, the Boers significantly outnumbered the immediately available, and widely spread, British contingent of no more than 13,000 troops.

In the meantime, a British Field Force of three divisions was despatched from Britain to Cape Town to be commanded by Gen. Sir Henry Redvers Buller, VC, GCB[i], then the GOCinC of Aldershot Command. Buller was approaching his

---

[i] Later Knight Grand Cross of the Order of St Michael and St George (GCMG), November 1900. Rather more prosaically, a road in Aldershot is named after him.

sixtieth birthday when left for South Africa. After Eton, he joined the 60th Rifles (later the King's Royal Rifle Corps) and saw action across the globe: in the 2nd Opium War (1856-60); the Canadian *Red River* Expedition of 1870; the 3rd Ashanti Campaign of 1873-4 (in modern Ghana); the 9th Cape Frontier (or Xhosa) War in 1878; the Zulu War of 1879 (during which he won his VC for rescuing two officers and a trooper at the Battle of Hlobane); the 1st Boer War of 1881; and in the Sudan and the attempt to relieve Gordon in Khartoum (1884-5). For the next fourteen years he performed domestic administrative roles, becoming Quartermaster-General to the Forces in 1887 and Adjutant-General to the Forces in 1890. Thus, when appointed to command the troops in South Africa, Buller had not commanded in the field since 1879 as he had fulfilled staff and intelligence roles in South Africa and the Sudan. His only recent experience was his less than satisfactory performance as commander of the 'invading' forces in the heavily criticised 1898 Army manoeuvres. Neither his subsequent actions in South Africa, nor those of his subordinates, were to be blessed with great initial success.

Prior to his arrival, the Boer's immediate strategy was a quadruple-pronged invasion of British territory: around the small town of Mafeking[i]; to Kimberley, 330 kms/200 miles to the south (both towns lie on the railway line from Cape Town to Bulawayo); Ladysmith, on the railway out of Durban; and south across the Orange River towards the railway lines which link Cape Town, Port Elizabeth and East London. British troops garrisoned Mafeking (commanded by Robert Baden-Powell), Kimberley (George Kekewich), Ladysmith (Sir George Stuart White) and, 70 kms to the north-east, the small town of Dundee (Sir William Penn Symons). There were other, smaller, garrisons at various railway junctions on the lines to the south of the Orange River. Though the first action, the Boer success at the Battle of Kraaipan[ii] on 12th October, was along the Transvaal's western border, the main early action, once Mafeking and Kimberley were besieged, took place in Natal around Dundee and then Ladysmith.

The Battle of Talana Hill on 20th October 1899 (nine days after the Boers declared war) was a tactical British success – if occupying the enemy's position defines success. However, in driving the Boers of Lukas Meyer from the top of Talana Hill east of the small town of Dundee[iii], the British forces lost, *inter alia*, their commander, Lt. Gen. Sir William Penn Symons, KCB, fatally wounded whilst unwisely leading the attack, 51 killed, 203 wounded and over 250 prisoners. The casualties were caused by the decision to throw the 2nd Royal Dublin Fusiliers, 1st King's Royal Rifle Corps and 1st Royal Irish Fusiliers in a close order frontal attack up the slopes of Talana Hill, and the PoWs were lost through the perplexingly

---

[i] Now Mahikeng.
[ii] 60 kms south-west of Mafeking.
[iii] Except for the fact coal was mined there, occupying Dundee was an odd decision. It is 70 kms/39 miles north-east of Ladysmith on the main route of the three Boer columns invading Natal. Surrounded by hills, it was described by a French observer as *'un pot de chambre'*. a phrase previously used by Gen. Ducrot, *Ier Corps*, to describe the hopeless position of MacMahon's soon-to-surrender troops at Sedan in 1870 [*Source*: Anglesey, Lord, *A History of the British Cavalry*, Volume 4, 1899-1913].

incompetent behaviour of Lt. Col. Bernhard Drysdale Möller, CO of the 18th Hussars[i], in charge of his own regiment and some mounted infantry. Thoughtfully, these mounted troops positioned on the northern flank of the hill to be able to interfere with any attempts to either reinforce, or withdraw from, the Boer position. Instead, the bulk of them wandered off south, then east, then west, then split (two squadrons went back to Dundee) before trotting off northwards to the east of Mpati Hill which, being shrouded in mist, concealed the presence of *Assistant Commandant-general* S P Erasmus's Boer troops. Möller and his men were surrounded at Adelaide's Farm and forced to surrender[ii].

Penn Symons' successor, Brig. Gen. James Herbert Yule[iii], withdrew his troops into Dundee to be inaccurately bombarded by a Boer 155-mm *Schneider-Creusot* gun. On 22nd October they departed to amble about aimlessly for a couple of days before retreating into Ladysmith there to be besieged with the rest of Sir George White's garrison. They left behind large quantities of supplies, a bewildered population unaware of their departure, and the dying Penn Symons along with the rest of the wounded. Plus the Boer prisoners taken in the previous fighting.

In between, on 21st October, was a day which was, and for months to come, the best of the war for the British. At the railway stop at Elandslaagte, 15 miles north-east of Ladysmith, a Boer force of c. 1,000 under *Vecht-general* Johannes Kock was in position to cut-off Yule and his men from their base at Ladysmith. Troops under Sir John French and Ian Hamilton were despatched to see them off. Being uncharacteristically creative, the Boers were first pinned down by British artillery whilst the 1st Devonshire Regt. made a widely dispersed demonstration to their front. Meanwhile, Hamilton sent the rest of his men, 1st Manchester Regt., 2nd Gordon Highlanders and dismounted Imperial Light Horse, off to the right to attack the left wing of the Boers on their hilltop position. In the meantime, French split his cavalry, with four squadrons of the 5th Dragoon Guards and 5th Lancers sent to the west (left) of the Boers and one squadron of each regiment sent east to protect the outer flank of the infantry and Light Horse. Under the cover of a timely thunderstorm the infantry drove the Boers off the crest of their hill and mortally wounded Kock when he led a counterattack. The rest of his men attempted to ride off only to be intercepted by the Dragoon Guards and Lancers who passed through their ranks three times, causing heavy casualties. French's troops lost 55 dead and 205 wounded in the fight but, unusually, Boer losses were heavier and from a far smaller force. Forty-six died, including Kock a few days later in a British field hospital, 105 were wounded and another 181 became prisoners or were declared missing. This was roughly a third of their manpower.

---

[i] Möller joined the 18th Hussars in 1873 serving ten years in India and six in Ireland. He saw no action in 26 years' service and the 18th Hussars had not been in action since Waterloo. Möller was exonerated by a Board of Inquiry but was, nevertheless, removed from command and placed on half-pay the following year.

[ii] They were later paraded through the streets of the Boer capital, Pretoria, and the subject of some embarrassing cartoons back home.

[iii] A 52-year-old colonel in the 1st Devonshire Regt., and an old 'India hand' who had served in the 2nd Afghan War, in Burma and with the Tirah Expedition.

The promise of the victory was then squandered by Sir George White. First, on 24th October, fearing the retreating Yule might be cut-off from Ladysmith and safety, White led four infantry regiments, four cavalry regiments and two artillery batteries out to confront six Boer commandos commanded by Marthinus Prinsloo on hills near Rietfontein (*aka* Modderspruit). After desultory exchanges of fire and an unnecessary charge by some men of the 1st Gloucesters leading to a loss of 66 men including their CO, Lt. Col. Edmund Percival Wilford, White returned to Ladysmith having heard Yule was safe. White lost 114 men, Prinsloo c. 35.

Five days later, anticipating an attack on Ladysmith by c. 6-10,000 Boers under Joubert, White ordered a complicated attack requiring the co-ordination of two infantry brigades, a cavalry brigade under French, and an independent infantry detachment under Lt. Col. Frank Robert Crofton Carleton, 1st Royal Irish Fusiliers, all of which moved out during the night of 29th October. With units failing to arrive either in place or on time the day degenerated into a series of disparate and depressing skirmishes. A gun line of 24 15-pdr field guns was out-ranged by the Boer *Schneider-Creusots* and, mystified by the requirements of counter-battery fire, the gunners couldn't locate the enemy anyway. Yule's infantry brigade, now commanded by Lt. Col. Geoffrey Grimwood Grimwood[i], KRRC, came under heavy flanking fire attacking a position long since abandoned by the Boers and withdrew. French's cavalry simply did not arrive on time. The other infantry brigade, Ian Hamilton's men fresh from their success at Elandslaagte, could make no headway against the Boer *Mausers* this time and were forced to retire because isolated. Meanwhile, in error, Carleton's 1½ battalions of Gloucesters and Royal Irish Fusiliers climbed the lower of two neighbouring hills at Nicholson's Nek during the night. In an unhappy foretaste of the fighting at Spion Kop, De Wet's sharpshooters proceeded to pick them off from higher ground until, with casualties mounting, Carleton, 28 other officers and 898 of his troops surrendered. 200 lay dead or wounded. Meanwhile, White ordered an immediate withdrawal of the rest of his troops, a manoeuvre which degenerated into something of a panic in which only a stolid and disciplined performance by two Royal Field Artillery batteries prevented a rout. Total British casualties were c. 1,400. The Boers lost 200 men. The day became known as 'Mournful Monday'.

These British reverses in Natal and Cape Colony came to a climax when, after Ladysmith, Mafeking, and Kimberley were besieged, relief columns under Redvers Buller, Lt. Gen. Lord Methuen and Maj. Gen. William Gatacre came to grief between 10th and 15th December 1899 during 'Black Week'. Buller had arrived in South Africa with significant British reinforcements, including three British infantry divisions. These units he now split into three unequal forces, two to relieve the besieged towns and one to occupy a key area between them. Methuen commanded the western force ordered to relieve Kimberley and Mafeking, Gatacre commanded the smaller central force which was to occupy a key railway junction at Stormberg, and Buller lead the eastern force towards Ladysmith.

---

[i] Yule was ill after his precipitate retreat. G G Grimwood was the CO of the 1st KRRC. Born in 1851, he joined the regiment in 1872. He had served in the Manipore and Isazai Expeditions 1891-2 and the Chitral Relief Force 1895. He died in Malta in 1937.

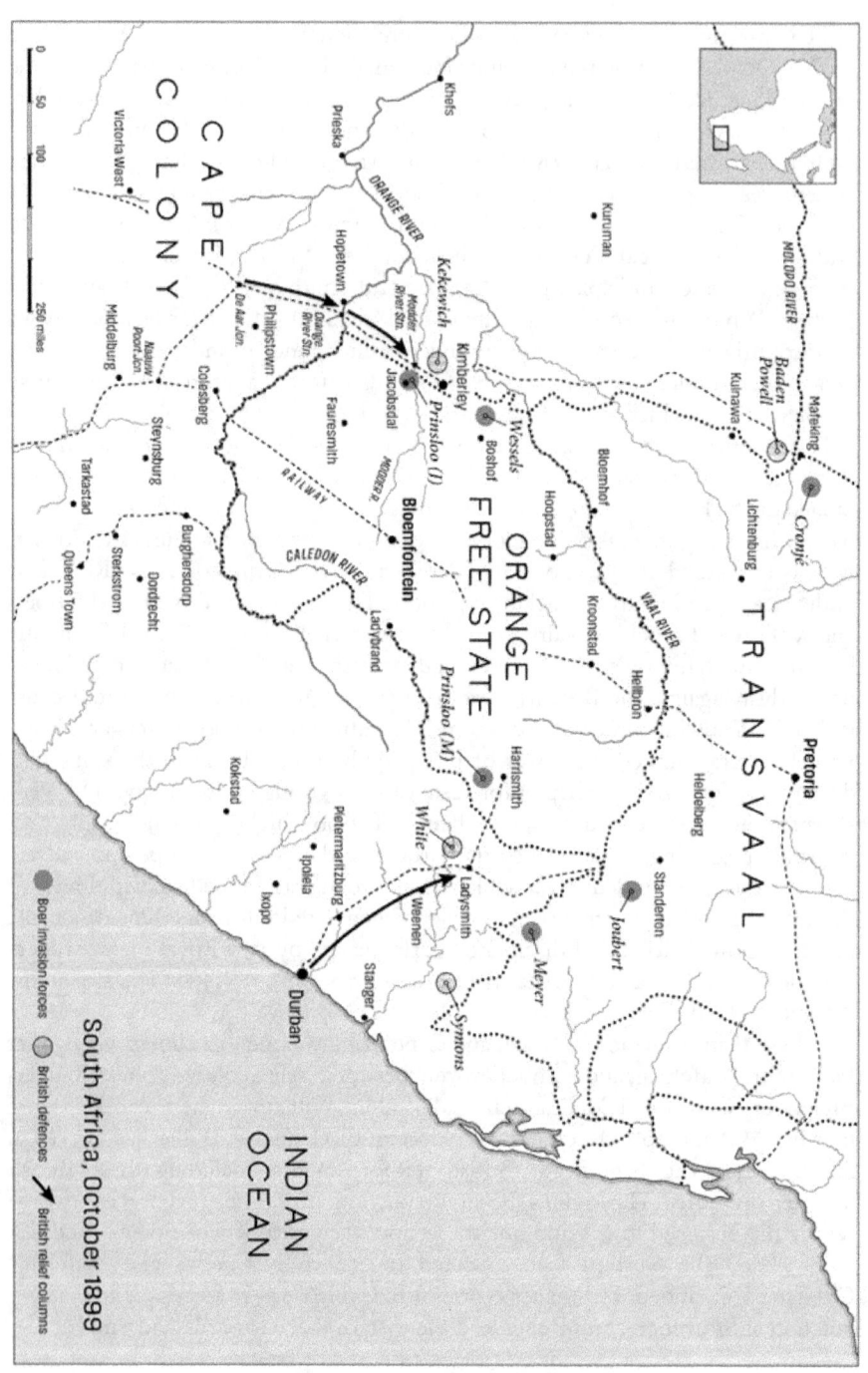

Map 5 The South Africa campaign, 1899
Redvers Buller advanced from Durban to relieve Ladysmith. Lord Methuen advanced along the railway line from Cape Colony to relieve Kimberley.

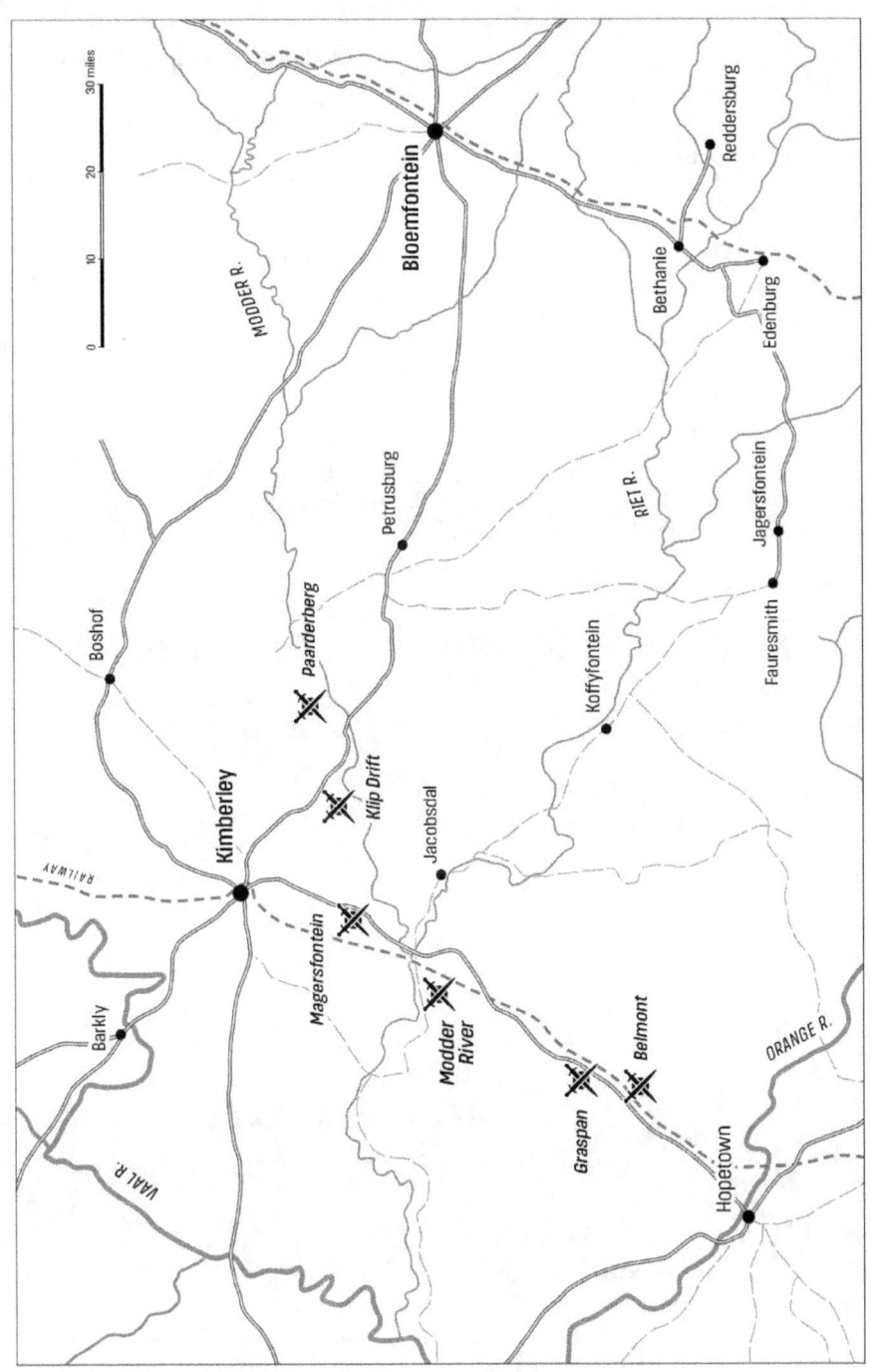

Map 6 Lord Methuen's advance on Magersfontein, the relief of Kimberley, and Robert's advance on Bloemfontein

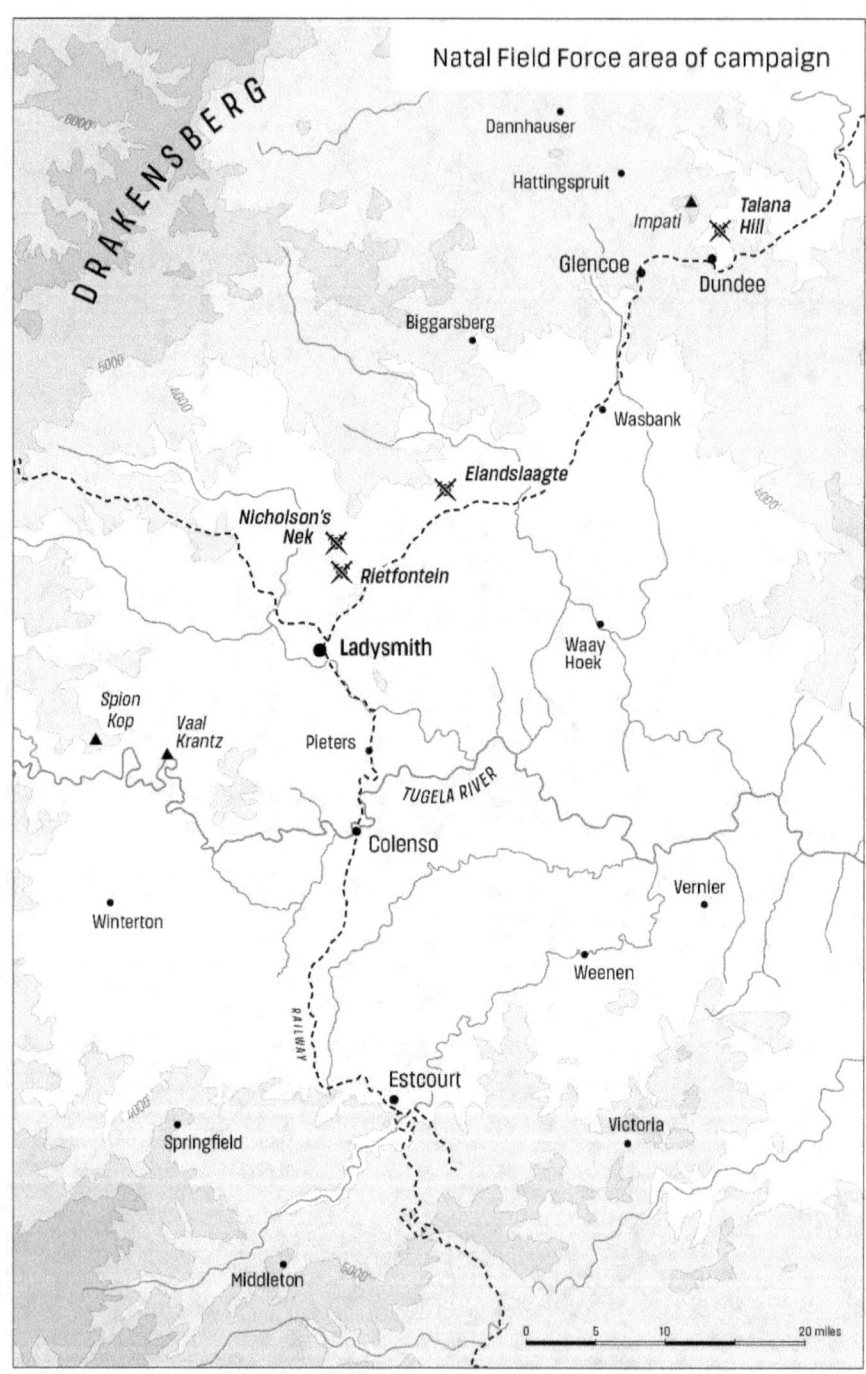

Map 7 The siege of Ladysmith and the Natal Field Force's advance
Redvers Buller fought battles at Colenso, Spion Kop, Vaal Krantz, and Pieters before Ladysmith was relieved

57-year-old Lt. Gen. Sir William Forbes Gatacre commanded the garrison at Colchester immediately before the war. He was an officer of previously high repute though, writing later, Conan Doyle wondered whether he 'possessed those intellectual gifts which qualify for high command'.[28] He served with distinction in India and, in 1898, he commanded the British division at Omdurman (its 1st Brigade being commanded by Brig. Gen. Wauchope, see below). But the Boers were not Mahdists armed mainly with spears and swords. Their *Mausers* gave them a range and accuracy which they exploited to the full.

He was the first to be defeated, at Stormberg on 10th December. There he lost 135 dead and wounded and saw nearly 600 men, mainly from the 2nd Royal Irish Rifles, taken prisoners of war, troops left on top of a hill and 'forgotten' in a somewhat abject retreat. To rub salt into the wounds two 15-pdr. guns were lost, and all at a cost to the Boers of barely thirty men. The root cause of this fiasco was Gatacre's decision to mount a night march against Boer troops which route he changed at the last minute. The new route was reconnoitred nor did adequate maps exist, and the one man who knew the ground was then left behind. After the exhausted column wandered into Boer pickets Gatacre's detachment dissolved. For reasons known only to himself, the CO of the 2nd Northumberland Fusiliers independently ordered a retreat and the unfortunate Irishmen were left behind.

Like Methuen, Gatacre was not summarily sacked. That decision was delayed until 10th April 1900 after three companies from 2nd Royal Irish Rifles and some mounted infantry were carelessly lost on 4th April during an unwise advance to, and retreat from, Dewetsdorp in the Orange Free State. 45 officers and men were killed or wounded and 546 taken prisoner. In a despatch to the War Office dated 16th April 1900, the new South African CinC, Lord Roberts (who arrived in Capetown on 10th January 1900), gave his reasons why he continued to employ Gatacre after Stormberg, but also why it was now necessary to remove him:

> "In my opinion, Lieut.-General Gatacre on this occasion (i.e. Stormberg) showed a want of care, judgment, and even of ordinary military precautions, which rendered it impossible for me, in justice to those who might be called on to serve under him, to employ him in any position where serious fighting might be looked for. I was, however, most anxious to avoid, if it were possible, the infliction on him of the slur which necessarily attaches itself to a General who is removed from his command while on active service. I, therefore, refused to supersede him at the time when I assumed the chief command in South Africa, believing that I might safely employ him on the lines of communication or in any position not actually in the front… I consider that in thus isolating a small detachment, Lieut.-General Gatacre[i] has shown a grave want of judgement which must necessarily shake the confidence of those under his orders and have a bad effect on the moral of his troops. I am therefore unable to retain him in command of his division and have given orders for his relief and return to England."[29]

The day after Stormberg, 11th December, Lord Methuen, a perennial staff officer with little field experience, came a cropper at Magersfontein in a fight

---

[i] Put on the retired list in 1904, he died at Iddeni in Abyssinia, 18th January 1906.

where 15,000 British troops and 29 artillery pieces were soundly whipped by just 8,500 Boers armed with five pieces of artillery and three machine guns.

That Methuen had been promoted well beyond his competence was hinted at in the weeks before, first at Belmont and Graspan and then, more clearly, on the *Modder River*. His route to relieve Kimberley ran north along the 120 kms between the Orange River and the besieged town lay alongside the railway from Cape Town, 850 kms to the south-west, from where they had been transported by train. On 23rd November 1899, Methuen and his three Brigades[i] (8,000 men) came across 2,000 Boers under *Vecht-general* Jacobus Prinsloo dug-in atop two lines of *kopjes* to the east of Belmont, a stop on the railway 90 kms from Kimberley. Convinced the sight of British bayonets approaching across the open *veldt* would be sufficient to send the Afrikaners packing, Methuen ordered a frontal attack over open ground. When it was suggested this might not be the best idea Methuen replied to the offending staff officer:

"My good fellow, I intend to put the fear of God into these people."[30]

298 British casualties later the Boers trotted off, losing 133 men.

British infantry tactics were worryingly variable as Lt. C W Barton of the 2nd Northamptonshire Regt. later suggested:

"The Grenadiers seem to have had some very hard fighting and had a terrible loss. A number of the 58th[ii] were with them but we had drummed it into the men that they must keep widely extended so that they kept about 6 or 10 paces apart while the Grenadiers were crowded to 1 pace apart & suffered accordingly."

Two days later Methuen came across another Boer force, this time commanded by *Vecht-General* Joos de la Rey, 13 kms to the north-east along the railway. They were, again, dug in on a hilltop at Graspan. The 9th Brigade and Naval Brigade[iii] attacked the entrenched Boers with the inexperienced sailors and Marines suffering badly (101 casualties from a strength of 365. Amongst the wounded was Capt. R C Prothero, RN, the captain of *HMS Doris*). Total British losses were 185 and, unusually, the Boers lost more heavily, some 220 killed, wounded and PoWs but Methuen would more than compensate for this imbalance just three days later.

On the *Modder River*, on 28th November, Methuen's men, reinforced by the Highland Brigade, blundered straight into a large Boer force commanded by Piet Cronje and Joos de la Rey concealed by wired trenches either side of the railway

---

[i] The Guards Brigade, 9th Brigade and the Naval Brigade.
[ii] The 2nd Northamptonshire Regt. had previously been the 58th Regiment of Foot.
[iii] Made up of Naval personnel and Royal Marine Light Infantry drawn from *HMS Doris* (an *Eclipse*-class protected cruiser launched in 1896 and the flagship of Vice-Admiral Sir Robert Harris, Commander-in-Chief, Cape of Good Hope Station. At least one of her six 4.7-in. guns was mounted on a carriage and attached to the Army) and *HMS Powerful* (a *Powerful*-class protected cruiser launched in 1895. Her sister ship, *HMS Terrible*, was captained by one Percy Scott and it was on his initiative that several 4.7-in. guns were mounted on a carriage of his design and employed in the war and beyond). Accompanied by four 12 pounder guns, the 'Naval Brigade' was not even of Regular battalion strength.

track to Kimberley[i], on the south side of what the maps described as the *Modder River* and, further east, the *Riet River* which flowed into it[ii]. Two British brigades, 9th on the left and the Guards on the right, advanced across the open *veldt* without any knowledge of the Boer positions because Methuen failed to conduct an adequate reconnaissance. Instead, he depended on a map drawn from memory after a previous visit five weeks earlier by a Royal Engineer and Staff College graduate, Capt. Walter Alfred John O'Meara. According to one account Methuen remarked to Maj. Gen. Sir Henry Edward Colvile[iii], GOC Guards Brigade, 'They're not here'. To which Colvile replied, 'They're sitting uncommonly tight if they are'.[31] Tight they were. The Boers opened fire pinning down the British troops 900 metres to their front. Whilst British guns banged away hopefully at empty positions north of the river, and the Northumberland Fusiliers targeted a bank 300 metres *behind* slit trenches occupied by the Boers[32], the Guards tried, and failed, to find a way around the enemy to the east. 9th Brigade, assisted by 1st Argyll and Sutherland Highlanders, then succeeded in crossing the river to the west but were again pinned down until an advance by the 2nd King's Own Yorkshire Light Infantry provoked a withdrawal by the Orange Free Staters. They withdrew (returning to collect their wounded and their guns overnight), retiring to the new position at Magersfontein where Methuen was given another chance to display his utter unfitness to command troops in the field. British losses on the *Modder River* were 4 officers and 93 men killed and 20 officers (including Methuen) and 362 wounded with the Highlanders suffering the heaviest casualties: 18 killed, 91 wounded and 2 missing.

Thirteen days later, at Magersfontein[iv] (11th December), Methuen succeeded in doubling these losses with another inept advance ignorant of *Assistant Commandant-general* Piet Cronjé's dispositions. Altogether it was an excellent example of the ability of British commanders (and, later, French and German ones too it turned out) to either ignore or to forget lessons supposedly learnt from earlier wars. After the Franco-Prussian War it was widely accepted the era of the attack in dense columns to within range of an enemy's rifles was now at an end. Citing the disastrous casualties of the Prussian *Gardekorps*[v] in front of the village of Saint Privat and the *VIII Armeekorps* of Gen. Karl Friedrich von Steinmetz's *1. Armee* in

---

[i] Two blockhouses from later in the war stand either side of the railway bridge on the southern side. Kimberley is some 40 kms further north.

[ii] It is now the other way round. The *Modder* is described as a tributary of the *Riet* which joins the *Vaal* 72 kms [45 miles] to the west. This enters the *Orange River* which runs into the Atlantic between the Namibian town of Oranjemund and the South African town of Alexander Bay. The battle was along the banks of what is now the *Riet River*.

[iii] Maj. Gen. Sir Henry Edward Colvile, KCMG, CB, was killed on 25th November 1907 when his motorcycle collided with Henry Rawlinson's motorcar at Bisley. Eton and the Grenadier Guards. Served in South Africa, the Sudan, Uganda and at Gibraltar. Commanded 9th Division, February 1900. The 13th (Irish) Battalion, a Yeomanry battalion under his command, was cut off and surrendered on 27th May 1900 and Colvile was sent home by Lord Roberts.

[iv] Another 10 kms up the railway line from the Modder River crossings.

[v] 8,000 out of 18,000 but with some units losing two-thirds of their men.

the Mance ravine during the Battle of Gravelotte[i] on 18th August 1870, the then Lt. J F Maurice stated unequivocally in 1872 'the impossibility of facing modern fire in any close formation whatever'.[33] He quoted three published German works to support this statement, all from officers who fought during the war[ii], and even drew references from a veteran of Waterloo and the Peninsular War – Col. George Gawler[iii] of the 52nd Light Infantry – who, writing as early as 1852, stated:

> "Under the immense increase which is now taking place in the length of range and accuracy in effect of small arms (Writer's note: at the time of writing c. 750 metres)… even columns and lines of infantry will now only be able to repel his (i.e. the 'accurate and distant infantry marksman') power of destructive annoyance by meeting him with troops in extended order."[34]

The recommended formation was skirmishing order (with attacks launched from the flank) but 3rd (Highland) Brigade advanced towards the foot of Magersfontein Kop in a block of 3,500 men 41 metres wide and 150 metres deep according to Pakenham.[35] The front rank was 370 metres from the Boer trenches when they opened fire. The body of the Brigade's GOC, Maj. Gen. Albert Gilbert Wauchope, was reputedly found 180 metres from the Boer lines.

One of the Scots present at this disaster is reported to have complained:

"(They) had been led into a butcher's shop and bloody well left there!"[36]

Another, simply known as Private Smith of the Black Watch, penned this bitter ode to Methuen's incompetence:

Such was the day for our regiment,
Dread the revenge we will take.
Dearly we paid for the blunder
A drawing-room General's mistake.
Why weren't we told of the trenches?
Why weren't we told of the wire?
Why were we marched up in column?
May Tommy Atkins enquire…[37]

---

[i] The Battle of Gravelotte (or Saint Privat or Amanvillers) was a battle lost by the French rather than won by the Prussians. Prussia lost c. 20,000 dead and wounded (from 188,000 troops) in a series of incompetently conducted infantry attacks at a cost to the French of just short of 8,000 dead and wounded and 4,400 missing/PoWs (out of 113,000 troops). A French counterattack during the latter part of the day might have swept Moltke's armies from the field but Marshal Bazaine instead withdrew into Metz to be besieged from 19th August to 27th October 1870 when he surrendered.

[ii] *Generalleutnant* Albert Karl Friedrich Wilhelm von Boguslawski (1834-1905) in his work *Tactical Deductions from the War of 1870-1871*, trans. by Colonel Lumley Graham, late 18th Royal Irish; an anonymous 'German General' in *Militarische Gedanken und Betrachtungen über den deutsch - franzosischen krieg denjahre 1870-1871*; and Field Marshal Wilhelm, Duke of Württemberg in *The System of Attack of the Prussian Infantry in the Campaign of 1870-1871*, trans. by C W Robinson, Garrison Instructor, Aldershot. 1871.

[iii] Lt. Col. George Gawler fought at Badajoz and Waterloo, was second governor of South Australia and an early proponent of homes for Jews in Palestine.

Perhaps if Methuen[i] taken up the place at the Staff College offered him in 1875 he might have known about 'recent' tactical developments. In short, however, he should never have been there. Neither Garnet Wolseley nor Lord Lansdowne thought him sufficiently competent to be given 'an almost independent command'[38] and, in spite of Lord Roberts' friendship, 'Bobs' removed the Highland Brigade from Methuen's command as 'it would not be safe to trust him in action with it'.[39] Hardly a ringing endorsement of a General Officer's abilities. Equally perplexingly, Colvile, the Guards Brigade commander, previously issued instructions to his officers and men stressing the need for dispersal, initiative amongst junior officers and NCOs, and fire and movement in the advance[40] none of which tactics then were employed by the troops under Methuen's command.

British casualties at Magersfontein, mainly amongst the Highland Brigade which lost 75% of the total, were just shy of a 1,000 against 236 suffered by the Boers, and Methuen was forced to withdraw by a force he believed twice as strong as was the case. Cecil Rhodes, besieged in Kimberley, commented:

"… we are exaggerating their numbers simply because by doing so we account for bad generalship without confessing it."[41]

Lord Lansdowne, the Secretary of State for War, wanted Methuen sacked but Redvers Buller was reluctant to make him a scapegoat, however richly deserved. A friend of his, Lord Roberts, was the next South African CinC and thus his place was secured, that is until he was wounded and taken prisoner at Tweebosch on 7th March 1902, making him the only British General to be captured during the war.

Unfortunately, these two shambles (or three, counting *Modder River*) were no 'one-offs'. The final calamity of 'Black Week' occurred on 15th December and was the crowning disaster. Somehow, Buller's 21,000 troops and 44 guns were one-sidedly thrashed by 4,500 Boers at Colenso. British losses of 1,500 men and ten ineptly handled guns were offset by just eight Boer dead and thirty wounded[ii].

---

[i] Remarkably, Paul Sanford Methuen, 3rd Baron Methuen, GCB, GCMG, GCVO, DL, became a Field Marshal. Born, 1st September 1845, he was the son of Frederick Methuen, 2nd Baron Methuen, and Anna Horatia Caroline *née* Sanford. Educated at Eton. A cornet in the Royal Wiltshire Yeomanry, he purchased a commission in the Scots Fusilier Guards (the Scots Guards since 1877). Wolseley's staff, 3rd Ashanti War, 1873. Berlin military *attaché*, 1878. Battle of Tel el-Kebir, Egypt, 1882. AA & QMG, Home District. Bechuanaland and DAG, South Africa. Commander, Guards Brigade, 1892. GOC, IV Army Corps (later Eastern Command), 1904. GOC, South Africa, 1908. Governor & CinC, Natal, promoted Field Marshal, 1911. Governor and CinC, Malta, 1915 which post he held for four years. Constable of the Tower, 1919, and deputy lieutenant of Wiltshire, 1921. He married (first) Evelyn, the eldest daughter of Sir Frederick Hervey-Bathurst, 1878 (died 1879), and (second) his cousin, Mary Ethel, the second daughter of William Ayshford Sanford. He died on 30th October 1932.

[ii] Amongst the dead was Lt. Freddy Roberts, only son of Lord Roberts soon CinC, South Africa. Roberts was killed trying to rescue twelve guns of 16th and 44th Batteries, RFA, abandoned by their crews. Two were recovered and four VCs awarded, one to Roberts. Another award went to Capt. Walter Norris Congreve, later appointed GOC, XIII Corps, in November 1915.

Idiots Abroad — The British in South Africa 1899-1900

69 Lt. Gen. Sir George Stuart White
Defeated at Ladysmith & Nicholson's Nek

70 General Sir Redvers Henry Buller
Defeated at Colenso, Spion Kop & Vaal Krantz

71 Lt. Gen. Paul Sanford Methuen,
Defeated at Magersfontein. PoW Tweebosch

72 Lt. Gen. Sir William Forbes Gatacre
Defeated at Stormberg. Sacked after Dewetsdorp

73 Lt. Gen. Sir Charles Warren
Defeated at Spion Kop

At Colenso it was the turn of Maj. Gen. Arthur Fitzroy Hart[i], commander of 5th (Irish) Brigade, to prove Wauchope was not the only gallant fool able to lead good men to their deaths. First, after accepting the directions of a non-English speaking guide (and against the advice of his own staff), he sent his troops into a loop of the *Tugela River* into which the Boers could fire from three sides. To compound the error, Hart insisted in a close order approach to a ford (of which no sign could then be found), going so far as to countermand an order given by the CO of the lead battalion, the 1st Royal Dublin Fusiliers, to deploy in open order. The result was 500 Irish losses and the third British defeat of 'Black Week'.

This was enough for the Government and a new South African CinC in the shape of Field Marshal Frederick Sleigh Roberts was despatched on the *Royal Mail* passenger ship *RMS Dunottar Castle* to take command[ii].

Buller remained south of Ladysmith and the disasters did not stop. On 23rd/24th January 1900, he crossed the *Tugela River* west of Ladysmith whilst Maj. Gen. Neville Lyttleton led a diversionary force to the east around *Potgieter's Drift*. The task of taking the high ground beyond the *Tugela* was given to 2nd and 5th Divisions, commanded by 59-year-old Royal Engineer, Gen. Sir Charles Warren. Some regard Warren as the worst of the Generals who ruined their reputations in South Africa and, on these two days, he did his level best to prove it.

His career was certainly varied. Born in 1840, the son of a Major General also called Sir Charles Warren, he was commissioned into the Engineers in 1857. His work took him to Gibraltar, the School of Military Engineering, Chatham, and Palestine as part of the survey of Jerusalem and other holy sites. He first visited South Africa in 1876 when he surveyed the Orange Free State border and was involved in one or two minor native actions. By 1880 he was Chief Instructor in Surveying at the School of Military Engineering though, in 1882, he was sent to the Sinai Desert. An archaeological expedition led by Professor Edward Henry Palmer had been robbed and murdered and Warren bought their killers to justice, an act which alerted the authorities in Whitehall to his 'policing' abilities. After a brief sojourn in Bechuanaland during which he brought 'law and order' to the border with Transvaal, he was appointed London's Commissioner of Police in 1886. A Liberal, he stood for election in Sheffield, Hallam in 1885, Warren immediately fell out with the Tory Home Secretary, Henry Matthews, and then managed to upset the Liberal-Radical press when his officers, supported by the army, caused numerous civilian casualties breaking up the 'Bloody Sunday' demonstrations of 13th November 1887 (see page 439). To ice the cake, in 1888 Jack the Ripper turned the spotlight's glare on Warren, fed up with criticism of the Met's failure to apprehend the murderer, resigned and re-joined the Army. He went to Singapore to command the local garrison, returning to command Thames District from 1895 to 1898, being promoted Lt. Gen. in 1897. With no previous experience, his selection for a field command was somewhat perplexing.

---

[i] Hart's other claim to 'fame' was that he took over the editing of *Hart's Army List*, started in 1840 by his father, Henry George Hart, which task Fitzroy Hart was still undertaking on the outbreak of war in 1914.

[ii] Ironically, the *Dunottar Castle* had also taken Buller to South Africa.

74 British dead at Spion Kop, 23–24 January 1900

Nevertheless, he was sent with 13,000 men and 36 field guns against 8,000 Boers equipped with four field guns and two Maxim-Nordenfelt machine guns. Starting out on 11th January, their ponderous approach was soon spotted by the alert Boers. It was probably difficult to miss given the size of the baggage train in part made necessary by Warren's insistence on travelling with a bathroom and fully equipped kitchen which his cavalry reconnaissance force under the Earl of Dundonald was recalled to protect. The weeklong approach allowed the Boers to entrench various *kopjes* including the 430-metre high Spion Kop. Warren sent Maj. Gen. Sir Edward Robert Prevost Woodgate's 11th Brigade to capture the hill and 1,000 men climbed it at night in a dense mist. They quickly dislodged a small Boer outpost and settled down to watch a few sappers try to dig in, not an easy task in the rocky ground. As dawn broke, the British realised they were not at the top of Spion Kop but on a smaller, lower outcrop overlooked on three sides by Boer positions and vulnerable to Boer artillery fire from the Tabanyama plateau to the west. An unusual infantry assault on the position by Boers from Pretoria resulted in a vicious hand-to-hand action on the crest of Spion Kop before the fight degenerated into a long slog in increasing heat. Morale on both sides suffered but casualties became one-sided as Boer rifle and artillery fire swept the British in their shallow trenches and scrapes which provided little protection.

With Woodgate killed early on 24th January, chaos, confusion, and procrastination ruled in Warren's command with officer after officer failing in their duty to act or even pass on basic information about the tactical positions of troops across a wide-spread battlefield. The Boers were in no better shape and, at one point, both sides withdrew from Spion Kop in ignorance of one another's actions. Eventually, the exhausted Boers were left in command of the battlefield as Warren took his defeated troops back across the *Tugela*. By the end of the second day the Battle of Spion Kop ended. British casualties were 1,500 of whom 243 were dead. The Boers lost 335 of whom 68 died.

Buller retreated before his troops rallied to resume the advance on Ladysmith. First came a pointless, half-hearted fiasco at Vaal Krantz where, over three days (5th-7th February), an attempt to cross the *Tugela* failed at a cost of 333 dead and wounded. Finally, after a week's fighting along the Tugela Heights (12th-19th February), the Boers were finally driven north of the *Tugela* around Colenso. Further advances north of the river were made slowly until another opportunity for idiotic generalship presented itself. On 23rd February, Maj. Gen. Fitzroy Hart, GOC of the long-suffering 5th (Irish) Brigade and the dunderhead of Colenso, managed to prove conclusively he was unfit for command when he threw his battalions one by one against a Boer hilltop position. 500 men were lost to add the 500 squandered at Colenso. It was not until 27th February, after a pontoon bridge was flung across the *Tugela* further north, that the British dislodged the Boers from the crucial Pieters Hill. Here, for the first time, a degree of co-ordination between infantry and artillery proved mightily effective. The road to Ladysmith was open and, with its liberation, the Natal field campaign was effectively at an end. Although a success, the cost to Buller's force was heavy, 2,300 casualties from 20,000 troops (12%) versus c. 200 Boers from 5,000 (4%), a ratio of eleven British soldiers to every Boer casualty.

These events were greeted with a knowing if saddened nod by Bloch[i]. Interviewed in his compartment on the Paris to St Petersburg express in early February 1900 for the Viennese *Neue Freie Presse* he expressed no surprise at the British failures, as well as those of the Boers when it came to the offensive. Entrenchments and long-range rifle fire meant:

> "... a very small number could successfully oppose a force of great numerical superiority, a fact proved at Ladysmith, Mafeking, and Kimberley, as well as at Magersfontein, Stormberg, and Colenso. Where the Boers departed from their defensive tactics, as in the first attacks upon Ladysmith, they were as decisively repulsed as were the British at Magersfontein... all attack had thus become impossible except at the cost of useless sacrifice of life... In reply to the question as to how long Ladysmith could hold out, M. de Bloch, assuming its capture by storm to be impossible, said that it would depend upon the supply of provisions and the health of the British troops."[42]

Ladysmith was relieved on 28th February, twenty days later.

Back home these setbacks were greeted with dismay if for no other reason that few, if any, official details reached London. There was no shortage in the private members' clubs of London of numerous recently retired officers ready and only

---

[i] Bloch's standing in Great Britain amongst politicians and the media fell because of his repeated calls for the British Government to enter into meaningful peace talks as the military tide appeared to turn against the Boers. His mouthpiece was often the *Neue Freie Presse* which had amongst its staff several leading and sympathetic Jewish journalists, one being their Paris correspondent and leading Zionist Theodor Herzl.

too willing to put pen to paper in letters to the editor of *The Thunderer*, aka *The Times*. One such, whose name will appear here from time to time, was the 65-year-old Col. Lonsdale Augustus Hale, RE, previously Professor of Fortification at Sandhurst, an Old Carthusian and the 1913 recipient of *RUSI's* Chesney Gold Medal, given to those responsible for 'especially eminent work calculated to advance the military sciences and knowledge', though it is not entirely clear from the list of his books appended below which one might have attracted such approval[i]. Now, however, he was amongst the thousands of perplexed Englishmen who wanted to give the benefit of the doubt to their erstwhile colleagues currently in command in South Africa but who feared the worst because of the 'extraordinary character' of the events which unfolding in the last quarter of 1899.

Bloch referred to the tendency for the weeds of incompetence to grow most luxuriously in the shade and now, according to Hale, the shadow of the censor's heavy hand was increasing the general gloom at home:

> "The present state of non-revelation of facts cannot last much longer. One hundred and ninety-one officers and 3,347 N.C.O. and men swept in a few weeks clean off the roll of our little Army, 259 officers and 3,416 of other ranks wounded, and *cui bono*? (i.e. who has benefited?) All we ask, and in patient resignation, is to be told how and why this appalling sacrifice has been caused."[43]

But there were other bad days – none more so than 'Bloody Sunday' on 18th February, 1900, when Kitchener ordered a madcap frontal attack and several uncoordinated flanking attacks on *Assistant Commandant-general* Piet Cronjé's entrenched Boers trapped at Paardeberg on the *Modder River*. Kimberley having been relieved after Sir John French took the cavalry on a rapid cross-country drive from the *Modder River*, Cronjé decided on a long withdrawal east from Magersfontein towards Bloemfontein. Slowed down by a large ox-drawn convoy he was eventually surrounded at a *drift* (ford) where his men dug in.

Having over-ruled Lt. Gen. Thomas Kelly-Kenny[ii], the commander of 6th Division, who wished to surround and destroy the 4,000 Boers with artillery,

---

[i] And author of, amongst many others, *Tactical Studies of the Battles of Columbey-Nouilly and Vionville* (1877), *What to observe and how to report it* (1883), *The Army and the Franchise* (1886), *The People's War in France, 1870-1871* (1904), *Awake, you Britishers, to your peril from over-the-way and hasten to face it* (1912), *The horrors of war in Great Britain. The miseries and sufferings of all non-fighters from crossing-sweeper to castle-dweller, were an invader in our island* (1914). Nailing his colours yet more firmly to the mast he also wrote the introduction to: *The Briton's First Duty, the case for conscription* (1902). He died in 1914.

[ii] Lt. Gen. Kelly-Kenny was senior in rank to the then Maj. Gen. Kitchener but Roberts supported Kitchener and demanded 6th Division and elements of 9th Division make these costly attacks. In December 1899 Kelly-Kenny issued *Standing Orders and Instructions* to his troops stressing the problems of smokeless powders which, allied to their mobility, increased the difficulty of identifying the locations of Boer troops. He further emphasised the need for low-level initiative because of increased dispersal and for flanking and turning manoeuvres rather than direct assault.

Kitchener insisted on sending troops, which again included the unfortunate Highland Brigade, across an 800-metre open *glacis* on which they were cut down by the Boer *Mausers*. Some mounted infantry, commanded by Col. Ormelie Campbell Hannay, Argyll and Sutherland Highlanders, was ordered, in spite of his objections[44], to launch a 'most gallant but impossible'[45] attack. Hannay was killed and his troops slaughtered. Horace Smith-Dorrien, recently arrived from Malta and commanding 19th Brigade, was horrified to see men from two of his units, 2nd Duke of Cornwall's Light Infantry and The Royal Canadian Regt., charge without orders. Well, without *his* orders at least. These troops, according to Smith-Dorrien:

> "… had been sent over by a higher authority to charge the Boer position… Of course, it was quite irregular that my troops should have been ordered to execute such an important movement, except through me, as any possibility of my supporting the charge with the rest of the Brigade was effectually prevented, for by the time I realised what was happening, the attack was over, since it only occupied a minute or two.
> It was a gallant charge, gallantly led, but the fact that not one of them got within 300 yards of the enemy is sufficient proof of its futility."[46]

His brigade, because of independent decisions by 'higher authority', lost 228 men including Lt. Col. William Aldworth, DSO, CO of the Cornwalls. Casualties overall were 1,270 against 100 Boers killed and 250 wounded, making it numerically one of the worst days of the war for the British. The following day Smith-Dorrien was asked by Roberts, in the presence of Kitchener, French and his divisional commander Colvile, whether his men could successfully assault the Boer position. Smith-Dorrien demurred, instead suggesting a continuous bombardment whilst his men sapped their way towards the enemy trenches. Kitchener applied some pressure, suggesting a successful attack would render Smith-Dorrien a 'made man'. Again, he refused saying he would 'only attack now if ordered to'.

The Boers surrendered on 27th February under threat of an all-out assault led by 19th Brigade. With the loss of over 4,000 prisoners, it was their biggest defeat of the war to date, but victory was almost thrown away by the idiotic frontal attack on the first day, and by the badly shaken Roberts and Kitchener coming close to abandoning their positions in the face of heavy casualties.

Paardeberg was, however, the beginning of the end of the traditional phase of the war. After the relief of the three besieged British towns and the loss of Bloemfontein, Johannesburg and, finally, Pretoria, the Transvaal capital, on 5th June, the war appeared to be over. With the fall of the main Boer cities, Roberts, thinking again in the traditional terms of warfare, declared the war won on 3rd September and the Boer republics were formally annexed and absorbed into the British Empire. The war was not over, however, as the Boer *'kommandos'* adopted guerrilla tactics to which the British eventually responded with a scorched earth policy, numerous block houses, vast quantities of barbed wire[i] and the brutal

---

[i] Barbed wire was patented by Lucien B Smith of Kent, Ohio, on 25th June 1867 and widely employed by farmers in the mid-West to keep cattle, etc., off their land. Another patent, lodged by Joseph Farwell Glidden from DeKalb, Illinois, in 1874, produced

employment of the insanitary and disease-ridden concentration camps for Boer and native civilians which so appalled liberal opinion back in Britain.

Again, caught unawares by this surprising change to asymmetric warfare, there were several embarrassing and costly British defeats. The first Boer hit and run attack was made as early as 31st March 1900 when 2,000 Boers (of whom 400 were directly involved) under *Chief-commandant* Christiaan De Wet surprised a 2,000-strong cavalry column commanded by Brig. Gen. Broadwood at Sanna's Post. Broadwood's force consisted of Q and U Batteries of the Royal Horse Artillery, a composite regiment of the Household Cavalry, the 10th Hussars, the New Zealand and Burma Mounted Infantry, and Roberts's Horse and Rimington's Guides. The British lost 155 men killed or wounded and 428 men, seven field artillery pieces and 117 wagons captured. The Boer force lost just three killed and five wounded.

Later, several setbacks involved the recently deployed Imperial Yeomanry. These were volunteer cavalry units drawn from the members of the Yeomanry in Britain, i.e. the partially trained reserve which formed part of the Auxiliary Forces which were to support the Regular Army in the case of overseas war or domestic invasion. The Imperial Yeomanry was formed after 'Black Week' when the Yeomanry was partially mobilised for overseas service. Officers and men already with these units were supplemented by volunteers, many with dubious military expertise, and units started to be sent out to South Africa in February 1900. By April, the first contingent of the Imperial Yeomanry, some 550 officers and 10,371 men, was formed into twenty battalions.

The Imperial Yeomanry spectacularly came unstuck on 27th May, the day before the Orange Free State was formally annexed to the Empire. At Lindley, a small town 100 kms north of modern Lesotho, the 13th (Irish) Battalion was ambushed losing 21 killed with 400 taken prisoner. The following week, around the town of Heilbron, north of Lindley, a series of successful Boer attacks caught British troops off guard. On Monday 4th June, 56 wagons and 160 Scots troops surrendered without a shot being fired. On 7th June, in three separate actions along the railway line between Kroonstad and Sasolburg, *Vecht-general* Piet de Wet's *kommando* caused 200 casualties and took 500 prisoners of a Militia battalion, the 4th Derbyshire Regt., and some Imperial Yeomanry at the *Renoster River* Bridge; took another 38 prisoners on the Vredefort Road; and, finally, caused thirty casualties and took another 180 prisoners at Rooiwal. This at a total cost of one Boer dead and seven wounded. More important still was the loss to the British of a vast quantity of supplies and ammunition, including a consignment of celebratory champagne due to be quaffed by Roberts and his staff in Pretoria. In all, the Boers caused over 1,500 casualties, 80% of them prisoners, in eleven days.

---

the style of barbed wire recognised today. Glidden's *Barb Fence Company* made him one of the richest Americans when he died in 1906. Its first military use is thought to have been by the Portuguese at Magul, Mozambique, on 8th September 1895 when 600 troops repelled an attack by 6,000 Tonga and Gaza tribesmen. A thorn bush and barbed wire fence helped the defence even though the two machine guns malfunctioned [*Source*: Stapleton, T J, *A Military History of Africa*, Vol. 1, Praeger, 2013, page 108].

These tactics continued throughout the autumn of 1900. A Boer high point was the Battle of Nooitgedacht on 13th December when 1,500 men and ten guns[i] under Brig. Gen. Clements were surrounded in an ill-advised camping position and lost nearly half their strength – 650 men killed, wounded and made prisoner[ii] – before the rest escaped, whilst the Boers gorged themselves on the plentiful supplies abandoned. The Boers lost just 78 men killed and wounded.

At Tweefontein, on Christmas Day 1900, 550 men, mostly of the 11th Battalion, Imperial Yeomanry, equipped with a 15-pdr. gun and a Vickers-Maxim 1 pdr. pom-pom, were isolated on a small hill. Attacked during the night, 57 officers and men were killed (including the commander, Maj. George Albanus Williams of the 1st South Staffordshires), 88 wounded and 206 taken prisoner. Boer losses were about 50.

The British answer to these raids was the building of hundreds of block houses, initially guarding road and railway junctions and bridges, but then built at regular intervals across Boer territory. These block houses were then connected by swathes of barbed wire and the areas of *veldt* thus partitioned the subject of intensive combing by British, Empire and Native troops. Boer farmsteads were torched, crops ruined, animals killed, and the mainly female, young and elderly Boer and native occupants forced into concentration camps where the accommodation was poor, sanitary conditions rudimentary, and the food dreadful and in short supply. Huge numbers, especially children, died from malnutrition and disease in yet another disgraceful episode in the Empire's history.

With the land now fenced-off, a series of sweeps, some involving as many as 9,000 troops, hoovered up 1,200 Boers, but missed the elusive de Wet who escaped to the Western Transvaal where fighting continued. In the autumn of 1901 attempts to attack British troops twice failed but still with the casualty balance of account notionally in the Boers' favour.

On 30th September, a British column[iii] commanded by Robert George Kekewich[iv], the military commander during the Kimberley siege, was attacked by

---

[i] 2nd Northumberland Fusiliers (560), 2nd KOYLI (279), 38th Field Company RE (24), P Battery, RGA (4 guns), 8th Battery, RFA (4 guns, a 4.7-in. gun from the Eastern Division, RGA, a Vickers-Maxim 1 pdr. Pom Pom), 2nd Mounted Infantry (242), Kitchener's Horse (211), and Imperial Yeomanry drawn from the Fife Yeomanry and Devon Yeomanry (199).

[ii] Mainly from the 2nd Northumberland Fusiliers commanded by Capt. Clement Yatman, GOC, 96th Brigade, 32nd Division, III Corps, on 1st July 1916.

[iii] Four companies of the 1st Derbyshire Regt., 4½ squadrons, Scottish Horse, 27th and 48th Companies, 7th Battalion, Imperial Yeomanry, three guns of the 28th Battery, RFA, and a Vickers Maxim 1 pdr. Pom Pom. About 800 men in total.

[iv] Maj. Gen. Robert George Kekewich, CB, was born on 17th June 1854, the second son of Trehawke Kekewich, of Peamore House, near Exeter, Devon. Educated at Marlborough. Commissioned 2nd Regt., Royal Cheshire Militia, in 1872 and The Buffs, 1874. Served in the Perak War of 1875-6 and the Sudan, 1884-5. DAAG, Sudan, 1888, then military secretary, Commander-in-Chief, Madras. Burma, 1892-3. CO, 1st Loyal (North Lancashire) Regt., in South Africa and commanded the Kimberley garrison during the siege. Lt. Col., The Buffs, 1909. GOC, 13th (Western) Division, 1914, but,

Boers commanded by Koos de la Rey whilst encamped in a poorly chosen position near the *Selous River* near Moedwil. Initial chaos within the British ranks was controlled and counterattacks drove the Boers off with a loss of 61 dead and 131 wounded, the latter including Kekewich. Casualties amongst officers were especially heavy with five dead and 21 wounded. Boer casualties were given as 46 killed or wounded and ten taken prisoner. On 24th October, de la Rey ambushed a detached column[i] commanded by Lt. Col. Stanley Brenton von Donop, RA. Although Boers got in amongst the hundred wagons and killed or wounded many of the gun crews, disciplined work by the Northumberland Fusiliers and action by the Yeomanry saw the attack repulsed. Casualties again appeared to favour the Boers – 139 on the British side versus fifty dead on the Boer – but the question was: who could afford to lose these men? It was not the Boers.

De la Rey was more successful in early 1902, surrounding and destroying a British column at Yzerspruit on 25th February. Despite brave resistance, 58 officers and men were killed, 129 wounded, and 194 made prisoner out of 490 who went into action. Boer casualties were admitted at 51. This was not the end of the disasters. On 7th March, de la Rey attacked the rear of a column of 1,200 men[ii] led by Lord Methuen near Tweebosch. Two hundred, including Methuen[iii], became casualties. Most of the column was taken prisoner and six guns lost.

Although an excellent tactical victory, the British response was to flood the Western Transvaal with troops led by two men to become 'famous' in the Great War – Ian Hamilton and Henry Rawlinson – as well as the now recovered Kekewich. In early April their columns tried to surround 3,000 Boers under de la Rey. Ironically, it was a foolhardy frontal attack by 1,700 Boers led by *Vecht-general* J C G Kemp against what they thought to be Kekewich's weakly held position at Roodewal which brought an end to set-piece warfare. Although some Imperial Yeomanry fled, disciplined rifle fire from entrenched troops broke the charge thirty yards from the British line. Routed and pursued, the Boers' flight marked the end of any serious fighting. Kekewich's column lost 87 dead and wounded whilst 127 Boers were killed or taken prisoner and another 100 wounded.

By now talks about peace talks were underway and, on 19th May, negotiations commenced at Pretoria and a treaty signed at Vereeniging on 31st May 1902. In nearly 32 months c. 22,000 British and Empire troops died (13,000 from disease), 23,000 were wounded and 75,000 evacuated sick.[47] Boer fatalities amounted to c. 6,000. In Kitchener's squalid and insanitary concentration camps, estimated to

---

suffering from gout, insomnia, and heart problems, and concerned about his ability to serve his country, he committed suicide on 5th November 1914.

[i] 5th Battalion, Imperial Yeomanry (680 men), 1st Northumberland Fusiliers (140 men), 1st Loyal North Lancashire Regt., (190 men), four guns 4th Battery, RFA, a 5-in. howitzer, 37th Battery, RFA, and two Vickers-Maxim 1 pdr. Pom Poms.

[ii] 5th & 86th Companies, Imperial Yeomanry, 1st Northumberland Fusiliers & 1st Loyal North Lancashire Regt., 4th & 38th Batteries, RFA plus two Pom Poms and various local Police/irregulars. 300 were Regulars, 300 Imperial Yeomanry, 600+ irregulars. Casualties were especially heavy amongst the Regulars and Artillery.

[iii] Although a prisoner, Lord Methuen, with a broken thigh, was sent to a British hospital, a humanitarian act which resulted in de la Rey being court-martialled.

hold over 116,000 Boer women, children, and the elderly, nearly 28,000 died, 85% of them under sixteen. Although ignorant of such appalling numbers, the policies of scorched earth and forced internment provoked the Liberal Party leader, Henry Campbell-Bannerman, into his famous and stinging 'methods of barbarism' speech of June 1901. Made to the National Reform Union at the Holborn Restaurant on 14th June 1901 it described the policy as 'unwise and unworthy':

> "What was that policy? ... we should... devastate their country, burn their homes, break up their very instruments of agriculture, and destroy the machinery by which food was produced ('Shame'). It was that we should sweep – as the Spaniards did in Cuba; and how we denounced the Spaniards – the women and children into camps in which they were destitute of all the decencies and comforts, and many of the necessities, of life, and in some of which the death rate rose so high as 430 in the 1,000 ('Shame')... A phrase often used was that 'war is war'... When was a war not a war? When it is carried on by methods of barbarism in South Africa. (Cheers)."[48]

In support of Campbell-Bannerman's contention, on 4th December 1900, Esher records a telegram from Lord Roberts which states:

> "... his 'young colonels' have overdone their job, and exceeded his orders by burning too many farms"[49]

These were not the only casualties. Some 15,000 Black South Africans died in internment and, perhaps, 6,000 as part of the British Army's ancillary forces, though no-one knew for sure, the numbers not being properly kept. Animals, most especially horses but also donkeys and mules, died in astonishing and horrifying numbers with approaching 400,000 dying or being killed[i].

Horses exported to South Africa from Britain had a life expectancy of just six weeks after arriving in the theatre of war[50], but that assumed the unfortunate animal was not one of the 16,000 which died in transit.[51] There were various issues which rapidly eroded the fitness of horses used by mounted troops. The Imperial Yeomanry, for example, attracted many gentleman volunteers undoubtedly well-used to being in the saddle and proficient in directing their mount. But, as Lt. Gen. John Wimburn Laurie[ii], the Conservative MP for Pembroke and Haverfordwest, pointed out in a letter to *The Times* on 19th January 1900, gentlemen did not put on saddles and harnesses, nor groom, feed and water their horses as, back home, there were staff for such menial tasks. On campaign, however, they had been rather left to their own devices and, as the General commented:

---

[i] It has been estimated that 326,000 horses, 51,000 mules and 195,000 oxen died during the war [*Source:* Evans, N, *From drill to doctrine: forging the British Army's tactics 1897-1909*, unpublished PhD thesis, King's College, London, page 160].

[ii] Lt. Gen. John Wimburn Laurie, CB, (1835-1912) served in the Crimea, India, South Africa, and Canada. Member, Canadian House of Commons (1887-91). Conservative MP for Pembroke and Haverfordwest, 1895. Defeated in 1906. His oldest son, Capt. John Haliburton Laurie, was killed in South Africa in 1901, and another, Col. George Brenton Laurie, 1st Royal Irish Rifles, killed at Neuve Chapelle, 12th March 1915. He was reputedly the first man to enter Neuve Chapelle on 10th March.

"Many of these men are drawn from a station in life where it is not usual for the rider to groom, feed and attend to his own horse, and if they are unable to care for their horses properly, they will soon lose them, and if the they do not understand how to fit a saddle, the horse will soon be non-effective with a sore back."[52]

The problem extended to the regular cavalry too with an article from a correspondent attached to John French's cavalry column explained:

"The English cavalry horses are doing none too well… Some observers say that the scale of forage allowance, though 2 lbs more than in England, is still insufficient to keep them in good condition with hard work. The newly arrived horses seem all to be troubled with bad colds, and the infectious illness, locally called 'new sickness', has made its appearance. The symptoms are dullness of eyes, running of the nose, swelling of throat and staring coat."[53]

Underfed and sick, it is of little surprise that, early in the war, the cavalry was hamstrung more by a lack of fit horses than by the action of the enemy.

Leaving to one side the political, diplomatic, and economic fall-out from the war, the impact on the British Army's organisation, training, equipment, armaments and tactics was significant. Not only were the Regular Army's infantry and artillery tactics shown to be grossly inadequate and naïve in the early months, major deficiencies were also exposed in the quality and training of the reserves sent out from the Militia and Yeomanry. Questions were asked about the training and, indeed, intelligence of many of the officers who took part. Overall, little was done right. Even in the care of horses and mules, the essential transport for both man and supplies, the Army was shown to be woefully ignorant and under-trained.

The cost of the war also proved immense, totalling some £201 million (somewhere between £20 and £70 billion at current prices), and the numbers of troops employed to suppress the small Boer fighting forces huge. The Elgin Commission, set up to take evidence about the conduct of the war, provided the following figures for the Empire's forces involved:

Regular Army 256,340
Militia, Yeomanry and Volunteers 109,048
Other Empire troops 30,633
Locally raised (native and white South African) 50-60,000[54]

In other words, at one time or another, the British Government committed c. 450,000 troops to defeat an estimated 88,000 Boers from the Transvaal, Orange Free State, and the Cape, and the foreign volunteers who supported them. The absurdity of the war was even further underlined when, in 1910, the Union of South Africa was formed and its first Prime Minister elected: Louis Botha, an Afrikaner who fought against the British in the First and Second South African Wars. He was succeeded in 1919 by Jan Christiaan Smuts, who led a Transvaal *kommando* during the second war, and by James Barry Munnik Hertzog, another Boer General. They were the first of nine Afrikaner Prime Ministers and one President who ruled South Africa until Nelson Mandela was elected on 10th May 1994. Looking back, it does not seem the Afrikaners lost the war at all.

THE WAR AGAINST THE BOERS WAS A SIGNIFICANT EVENT for the British Army and how the war was conducted and whether lessons were learned, forgotten, or ignored would be crucial to its development prior to 1914. This should have given the Army an advantage over its continental opposition as, unlike its western European allies and its potential enemies, the British Army had relatively recent experience of modern warfare, a position shared only by Russia, several Balkan countries, and the tottering Ottoman Empire. Furthermore, the British experience was gained from more than just a colonial enterprise involving the massacre with cannon and automatic weapons of poorly armed natives. But, between 1902 and 1914, there were other, later and even more relevant wars from which to learn if only one had a mind.

Two years after the end of the South African war, Russia engaged in a bloody 19-month war against Japan in Manchuria resulting in a combined total of c. 500,000 casualties (killed, wounded, prisoners of war, died of disease). It was a war characterised by the first use of many of the modern weapons and tactics which were commonplace on the battlefields of the Great War a decade later and, as a result, it was pored over by officers from all the opposing armies of 1914. The conclusions drawn, however, were neither consistent nor, often, correct.

Britain's war in South Africa between October 1899 and May 1902, although fought against 'irregular' Boer mounted riflemen, pitted the Army against modern equipment and this placed the conflict somewhere between their policing actions around the Empire and the 'proper' wars in Manchuria and the Balkans which followed. Although well-armed with newly purchased German *Mauser* rifles and *Schneider* and *Krupp* field guns, there were, before an influx of foreign volunteers and the raising of more men from the border areas of the Cape and elsewhere, no more than 40,000 members of the various *Kommandos* which made up the mainly irregular Boer Army. Its members were rugged farmers, excellent riders and expert shots who went to war equipped with their horse, a rifle and wearing their ordinary working clothes. They fought unconstrained by current European thinking on tactics, with concealment, dispersion and aimed, rather than volley, firing being the norm. The British commanders and their men were, therefore, exposed to a wholly new concept in warfare: Bloch's 'empty battlefield'. With modern rifles and artillery using the new smokeless propellants it proved almost impossible to spot the locations of the entrenched Boer marksmen who, from their concealed positions, targeted officers and NCOs of the British infantry as they advanced, and easily picked off the gun teams of any field artillery sufficiently unwise to advance too far in support of the attacking troops. The British infantry, too, proved poor marksmen and were regularly exposed by their Generals to costly frontal advances which proved horribly vulnerable to the modern Boer weaponry. Such weaponry also allowed the relatively small number of Boer troops to extend, and then successfully defend, their fronts well beyond anything thought sensible by European officers. Methuen was defeated on the *Modder River* by 3,000 Boer troops extended over 7,000 metres and 5,000 stretched over 10,000 metres at Magersfontein, and Buller by 4,500 spread thinly over 12,000 metres at Colenso.[55]

As for the artillery, British field guns firing shrapnel were altogether useless when there were no masses of troops to aim at, and any Boer hit by shrapnel whilst lurking in his trench must have counted himself singularly unlucky. Matters did improve tactically as the war went on and, post-war, the artillery was shown to have learned certain things from their experience in the wide-open spaces of Natal, the Cape Colony, the Transvaal, and the Orange Free State. Within a few short years, however, it became clear they had either then forgotten some of these hard-won lessons, re-interpreted them in the light of the Russo-Japanese War, or only partially disseminated them amongst the officers of the Royal Field Artillery.

If the artillery and the infantry underperformed what of the cavalry? Surely the open *veldt* should have been perfect terrain for their successful employment? Except for the artillery, the enemy army was entirely made up of mounted infantry armed with the new, accurate, long-range *Mauser* rifle. The British cavalry, however, still used the same weapons as in the Napoleonic Wars: the sabre and, after their experiences at Waterloo against French units so equipped, the lance.

In addition, they employed a carbine[i] giving them short-range mobile firepower. Except for Elandslaagte on 21st October 1899 the regular cavalry failed to thrive in South African conditions, as Roberts' decision to '*stellenbosch*'[ii] six cavalry Brigadiers and eleven out of seventeen regimental COs suggests. As the war developed, numerous *ad hoc* mounted infantry units were created to which was added the Imperial Yeomanry sent out from the UK. They were sometimes effectively used to counter the better armed, in terms of range and rate of fire, Boer mounted troops. On other occasions their lack of training was their undoing.

One long-term critic of the traditional role of the cavalry, Erskine Childers[iii], put the failure of these mounted troops in South Africa down to the 'profound

---

[i] The Lee-Enfield Cavalry Carbine Mk I (LEC) of 1896 was a cut down version of the Magazine Lee-Enfield (MLE), the standard Army rifle first issued in 1895. The infantry was armed with the Short Magazine Lee-Enfield (SMLE) in 1904 with the Mk III becoming the standard infantry weapon in 1907. It remained in service into WW2.

[ii] '*Stellenbosched*' was the South African equivalent of '*limoged*' for the French in WW1, i.e. somewhere, often notional, where officers were sent to 'enjoy' enforced retirement because of perceived incompetence and/or real failure.

[iii] Robert Erskine Childers (1870-1922) is, perhaps, best known as the author of the influential pre-war invasion scare novel *The Riddle of the Sands*' (1903). Son of an English father and Irish mother, his father was Hugh Culling Eardley Childers, Liberal MP for Pontefract, and a leading figure in several of Gladstones' administrations: First Lord of the Admiralty (1868-71), Chancellor of the Duchy of Lancaster (1872-3), Secretary of State for War (1880-2), Chancellor of the Exchequer (1882-5) and Home Secretary (1886). His mother was Anna Mary Henrietta Barton (the family own the Bordeaux *Deuxième Cru* Château Léoville-Barton and the *Troisième Cru* Château Langoa-Barton in the *Saint Julien appellation*). Erskine Childers was educated at Haileybury and Trinity College, Cambridge. He was a committee clerk in the House of Commons. A volunteer with the HAC he went to South Africa with the City Imperial Volunteers. Afterwards he was commissioned by L S Amery to write the fifth volume of *The Times History of the War in South Africa 1899-1902*. Childers was very anti cavalry and wrote a book (with a foreword by Lord Roberts) entitled *War and the Arme Blanche* (1910) followed by the *German Influence on British Cavalry* (1911). His views were attacked by Bernhardi and Sir John French. Sympathetic to Irish nationalism (he wrote

conservatism' of the arm in general and to the fact the officers' 'individual intelligence was not high enough for skilled skirmishing, much less for skilled reconnaissance'.[56] There will be more on the relative intelligence of the average cavalry officer later.

Field Marshal Lord Roberts, sent out to replace the incompetent Redvers Buller as CinC at the end of December 1899, became convinced the traditional weapons of the cavalry were now irrelevant on the modern firepower-dominated battlefield and, for a period, the lance was removed, at least partially, from service (see page 498 onwards). Other cavalrymen, e.g. French and Haig, later ensured British Lancer regiments went to war in 1914 equipped with this useless weapon and the concept of shock tactics delivered by the *'Arme Blanche'* in the face of massed firepower was retained throughout the war. This commitment to the traditional, some might say 'old-fashioned' while others, less kind, termed them obsolete, means of making war was reinforced by the Army's time and effort expended in designing a new cavalry sword in 1908, a 'thrusting' sword which, if used as intended, might lead to the disarming or even dismounting of the charging troops as the sword point became embedded in an enemy's body.

The major military powers scoffed at the British performance in South Africa and mainly ignored the way the war was conducted, especially the early and costly British defeats. For the British Army, however, it was to prove both a salutary and a perversely valuable, if costly, test of their tactics, armaments, and the organisation and leadership of their troops, even if one of the key questions raised by both the war and Jean de Bloch – how to get men across the 'fire swept zone' – was either ignored or never satisfactorily answered.

In the years immediately after the war many lessons were rapidly learned by the British Army, some only to be forgotten almost as quickly. Others were confused by the experience and analysis of officers who observed the fighting in Manchuria from both sides[i]. Overall, however, if the results of the twelve years' debate and reorganisation of the Army after South Africa are to be judged by the performance of the rank and file of the BEF in August and September 1914, then it appears the lessons learned significantly benefited the infantry, at least in terms of their defensive skills.

The Framework for Home Rule, 1911) he volunteered for the Royal Navy, learnt to fly and joined the RAF. Deeply affected by the Easter Rising (which employed rifles smuggled into the south aboard his yacht *Asgard* in 1914 in response to Unionist gunrunning in the north) he moved to Dublin to join *Sinn Féin*. Elected *Teachtaí Dála* (TD) for Kildare–Wicklow, 1921, along with his first cousin Robert Childers Barton. When the Irish Civil War broke out, he was a man 'wanted' by the Free State and was arrested, tried, and convicted by a military court in November 1922. He was executed whilst his appeal was pending. His eldest son, Erskine Hamilton Childers, elected TD 1938, was briefly the 4th President of Ireland (1973-4). He served in various ministerial positions, 1951-73.

[i] Some eccentric recommendations were made including such gems as that made by Col. J W G Tulloch, Indian Army, that re-arming infantry officers with swords might well be a good idea [*Source*: Various, *Reports from British Officers attached to the Japanese and Russian Forces in the Field*, Vol. II, HMSO, 1908, page 12].

The need to foster initiative amongst junior officers and other ranks was one important lesson from South Africa and this concept had already been promoted by Col. G F R Henderson before his untimely death (see page 441 onwards). As Leo Amery wrote in his 1903 book *The Problem of the Army* it was no longer enough for a soldier to respond automatically to 'orders which were shouted at him' and when 'The complete hypnotization of the soldiers by their officers was looked on as the ideal of training'.[57] Instead now the ideal was, according to Roberts:

> "... to encourage individuality amongst the men, and to make the company and section commanders understand that they must depend more upon themselves than has hitherto been necessary, because the moment a battalion now gets into action the companies are greatly spread out, and the commander loses all control over them."[58]

There was a determination thereafter that men of all ranks should be trained not to follow orders mindlessly but to develop individual initiative and the ability to take personal responsibility at times of crisis. Such thinking was made clear by a statement made by Brig. Gen. Michael Fredric Rimington of the Inniskilling Dragoons at a General Staff Conference held in early 1906. Rimington raised and commanded a group of irregular cavalry, Rimington's Guides (*aka* Rimington's Tigers), in South Africa. He was Mentioned in Despatches six times, made a CB and earned ten clasps to his Queen's and King's South Africa medals. No more clasps were possible[i]. Kitchener commended him for his 'independent raids' and 'exceptional services'[59]. This was an unusual man who knew about the importance of initiative and enterprise from his own first-hand experience:

> "The keynote to our training is always the same: develop the individual initiative of every officer, non-commissioned officer and man."[60]

The fostering of 'individual initiative' was a key objective identified by investigations into the failures in South Africa. It was determined to move the Army into a tactical environment where individuals could act more like the Boer burgher and select cover, chose targets, and fire and move independently rather than as a mass under centralised officer control. With the dispersal of advancing troops found to be essential because of the effectiveness of modern weaponry, it was recognised NCOs would take on an increasingly important role on a battlefield so large no officer could any longer control the actions of all of the men nominally under his control. In this respect, the 'section', and not the battalion or company,

---

[i] Lt. Gen. Sir Michael Frederic Rimington, KCB, CVO (23rd May 1858 – 19th December 1928) was commissioned into the 6th (Inniskilling) Dragoons in 1881. Post-South Africa he commanded the 3rd Cavalry Brigade (1903), the Secunderabad Cavalry Brigade (1907), and was Inspector-General of Cavalry, India (1911). He joined the Indian Expeditionary Force in 1914 as commander of the 1st Indian Cavalry Division and, in December 1914, took command of the Indian Cavalry Corps. When disbanded in 1916 he returned to England. He retired in 1919. He married Agnes Cunningham in 1887. Their son, Brigadier Reginald Gordon Ward Rimington, Royal Tank Regt., commanding 3rd Armoured Brigade, was seriously wounded and taken prisoner in Libya on 7th April 1941. He died in German hands on 10th April 1941 and is buried in Benghazi War Cemetery, grave 7. G. 5.

was now recognised as a key formation and the NCO in charge needed to be as well trained in tactics, techniques, objectives and methods as the subaltern, captain or major to whom he normally answered. As Leo Amery put it:

> "Every sergeant will have to be ... a tactician; similarly every captain will have to be something of a general. As for our generals and staff officers, we shall require of them qualities, especially of the intellect, which hitherto have only been very exceptional in their ranks."[61]

Giving evidence to the Elgin Commission, Col. Douglas Haig underlined this requirement stating:

> "The main lesson of the war is that modern conditions of warfare entail higher training of the individual."[62]

To further this an NCOs' school was set up at Salisbury Command in 1904. More would have been useful but, in spite of achieving good results, it fell victim to budget cuts just two years later, though some have suggested it was closed to maintain the same gap in status between officers and NCOs as there was between their originating social classes.[63] The long term impact of failing properly to educate and train Non-Commissioned Officers can, perhaps, be seen in the enormous losses suffered by junior officers which the British Army in particular deployed in large numbers during active operations in the absence of well-trained and educated NCOs. Ian Beckett in *A Nation in Arms* makes the point that, typically, more than half a battalion's officers would 'go over the top' during an attack. German snipers and others were trained to target 'leaders' and, even when officers stopped carrying a revolver and were armed as for the rest of their men, someone giving orders and directions would always be targeted when possible.[64] Officer casualties on 1st July 1916 were especially appalling with several battalions losing c. 100% of the officers involved. The Newfoundland Regt., managed to surpass even this awful number as some officers in reserve, hearing of the disaster befalling their unit, came forward to help and became casualties themselves. The Germans, on the other hand, tried to conserve officers and, because of their superior pre-war education, were happy to devolve responsibility to NCOs when required.

The impact on the officers of the BEF would prove especially harsh in the first twelve months of the war. Figures suggest that 42% of regimental officers became casualties in the twelve months between 1st October 1914 and 30th September 1915, of which 18% were killed or missing. The equivalent fatality figure for ORs was 26%.[65]

In spite of the talk by the likes of Amery, Rimington and Henderson about fostering initiative after the South African War it was regrettable that, when faced with a mass of enthusiastic volunteers in 1914, the Army reverted to the earlier principles of discipline, drill, order and control when it came to the training of the markedly different men who volunteered in the opening months of the Great War. And this despite their higher average education and intelligence when compared to many of the officers and private soldiers who formed the ranks of the pre-war Regular Army. That there was a sad inevitability about this was ensured by the temperament, training, and age of many of the officers and NCOs brought out of retirement to train this vast body of men. That the nature and potential of these new men should be so little understood was doubly unfortunate as the performance of the numerous Volunteer and Yeomanry units which fought in South Africa suggested to some that:

> "… general intelligence is so useful an element in the composition of a soldier that even a very short training will enable intelligent men to equal inferior men who have been trained on unintelligent and routine lines."[66]

A sharp division between Regulars and war-time volunteers widely remained in place through most of the war to come, irrespective of native wit or education. Cuthbert Headlam, then a captain in the Bedfordshire Yeomanry and a junior staff officer, railed regularly against the failure to reward the talented 'amateur' officer (including himself!) with promotion and responsibility whilst dimmer, less able Regulars achieved preferment because of their status and pre-war connections.

Writing to his wife in March 1917 he complained:

> "… we are all of us expected to bow down and worship the remnants of the Regular Army and look upon them as our Masters in the Art of War. It is ridiculous really when you come to think of it – for what man of the Regular Army ever anticipated this modern warfare or can claim to have any greater knowledge of its infinite scope than the men who have learnt their soldiering in it and devoted themselves to its understanding?"[67]

Post-South Africa it rapidly became clear some potentially valuable lessons were entirely lost on experienced, if supremely dim-witted, officers whose views about warfare were more to do with laughable notions of honour than the actual outcome of battle. Such an example comes from Bloch's rebuttal of criticisms made on his soon-to-be discussed *RUSI* presentation on 24th June 1901 (when the South African War was still in full swing), even if his expectations concerning the methods to be employed by the French Army in the opening months of the war proved well wide of the mark (perhaps because they attacked *'à outrance'* rather than 'defended their fatherland' in a more prudent fashion):

> "Very characteristic, but unfounded, is the objection made by Colonel Graves[i] when he says, to quote his own words: 'The Boer fights to prevent his foe getting at him; while the British, I am proud to believe, fights with the view of getting at his foe'. (Hear, hear). Surely the question here is not who fights in the most chivalrous and romantic way, but who fights best with the object of gaining victory. The question is merely which is the best way of fighting under modern conditions. Now, as Colonel Graves makes this comparison for the purpose of explaining British reverses, we must come to the conclusion that the unromantic Boer way is the best.

---

[i] Brig. Gen. Francis John Graves, commissioned, 20th Hussars, 1869. Adjutant of the Staffordshire Yeomanry, 1879. Promoted Lt. Col. he served in the Sudan in 1885, commanding the mounted troops of 2nd Brigade. He took command of the 20th Hussars in 1889 and the 83rd Regimental District (Royal Irish Rifles) between 1895 and 1901. He was appointed Assistant Adjutant General, Imperial Yeomanry, before transferring to Sierra Leone. He died in Freetown, Sierra Leone, in 1905, aged 56.

(Laughter). But if this is so, this is the method which will be adopted in a Continental war, in spite of all regulations and manœuvre drill. The French, for instance, are a very chivalrous and romantic race; but when it is a question of defending their fatherland, they will fight in the way that is most likely to gain victory, and not in the way that looks best in a picture. (Hear, hear). Therefore, if the Boers were most successful because they lay behind entrenchments, never exposed themselves, and crept instead of walking, they merely adapted themselves to new conditions of war, and did what Continental military men have often declared it was necessary to do. There is no use in accusing the Boers of fighting in an unromantic way.

Their object was to gain the victory; and if the so-called Boer methods, that is to say, ingenious entrenchments, creeping attacks, and a general preference for the defensive, are the best, we may be sure that they will be adopted in a future war. Colonel Graves says that, as a consequence of this differentiation, 'we find greater losses on the part of the British troops'. Exactly. But that the Boer method did not waste lives unnecessarily is its best justification. (Hear, hear)

To those who do not agree with this opinion, I will say that it is unworthy to regard war from the point of view of a sportsman, and to regard an Army as an instrument for seeking adventures, and showing address and audacity. Those who regard war in this light had better go hunting lions or competing in championships. The sacrifice of a single life merely in order to show heroism is nothing better than a crime. The sense for appreciating and admiring what Colonel Graves admires is probably lacking in me, but I fancy that all the mothers and all the wives and children will be on my side in this respect."[68]

Bloch's unromantic view of war was clearly not shared by military audiences across Europe. As many of the Generals who took the continent into war showed by both word and deed the feelings of 'all the mothers and all the wives and children' did not remotely register on their emotional Richter scale. As far as they were concerned, the male population of Europe existed so they might die for their country and the glory of their commanders, and all the be-medalled Generals of Europe, watching on far from the actual fighting, would ensure they did.

EUROPEAN MILITARY FIGURES were scornful about the competence of the British Army in South Africa after their failure to deal with what was seen as nothing more than a bunch of mobile, if well-armed, civilians. The French were especially scathing. Generals Henri Bonnal[i] and Hippolyte Langlois[ii] and *Capt.*

---

[i] Gen. Guillaume Auguste Balthazar Eugène Henri Bonnal, born Toulouse, 1844. *École spéciale militaire*. Served in Algeria. PoW at Sedan in 1870. Commanded the *École normale militaire de gymnastique* 1879-1884. Infantry instructor then professor of military history, tactics, and strategy at the *École supérieure de guerre* 1887. *Général de brigade*, 1899. Commandant *École supérieure*, 1901. Dismissed by Presidential decree, 1902. Died 1917. He wrote *La récente guerre sud-africaine et ses enseignements*.

[ii] Langlois wrote *Enseignements de deux guerre récente*.

d'artillerie Georges Gilbert[i] all wrote books highly critical of the British performance with Bonnal further arguing there was nothing new to learn from the war as the tactical errors committed by the British had long since been identified and corrected by continental armies, some as long ago as the Napoleonic Wars.

One experienced French senior officer fundamentally disagreed with this analysis. Gen. François Oscar de Négrier was born in Belfort in 1839, attending St Cyr in 1856. In 1859 he joined the *3e bataillon de Chasseurs à Pied* (BCP), serving in Italy and Africa. In 1870, his unit was attached to the *Armée du Rhin* and he became a prisoner of war when that army surrendered at Metz on 29th October, though he quickly managed to escape and joined Faidherbe's *Armée du Nord* in November. He was wounded three times. By 1881 he was a Colonel serving with the *Légion Ètrangère* in Africa then, in 1884, he commanded a Brigade in Tonkin, now Vietnam, where he was again wounded at the 2nd Battle of Lang Son, 28th March 1884. Returning to France he commanded the *11e Corps* at Nantes and the *7e Corps* at Besançon. A member of the *Conseil supérieur de la guerre*, he was placed in reserve in 1904.[ii] Having experienced it first hand and having been wounded on four of those occasions, Négrier was more impressed by firepower than many of his colleagues. Now, reflecting on the events in South Africa, he wrote four anonymous articles for the *Revue des Deux Mondes* concerning the power of the defensive displayed by the Boer riflemen and highly critical of current French thinking which still shied away from the dispersion of troops which proved necessary during the war. In this, he was swimming against the strong tide towards the *offensive* which was the main current in French military theory. He was also highly critical of people like Gilbert, Bonnal and Langlois who dismissed the South African experience as irrelevant to a European war and, furthermore, complained of their devotion to the study of Napoleon rather than modern wars involving modern weapons. Négrier, on the other hand, believed the war showed frontal attacks to be prohibitively expensive, that both heavy and field artillery were needed on the battlefield, and that massed cavalry was obsolete. He accused the professors at the *Ècole supérieure de Guerre*, such as Foch, of advocating:

> "… a system of human waves that will beat the rock until it is submerged. They forget that if a few thousand men thrown against a position see in a few moments 5 or 600 of their colleagues fall, then the rest become inert, lie down or disband."[69]

To counter this Négrier, like so many of his contemporaries, found refuge in the concept that high morale cultivated in peace time would somehow see the troops advance to victory. On a more practical level, however, he also suggested changing the current French uniform of blue jacket and bright red trousers to the khaki adopted by the British prior to the South African War.

---

[i] Gilbert's *Guerre sud-Africaine* was the first to be published, though posthumously, with a preface from Bonnal.

[ii] De Négrier died on 22nd August 1913 between Spitzbergen and Norway on a tourist ship *Kong Harald*. It operated between Trondheim and the North Cape. Twice captured by the Allies in WW2 she was nearly sunk twice by torpedoes and was bombed by the Allies in 1944. Part of the *Hurtigruten* fleet after WW2 she was broken up in 1954.

Similarly inspired, an Austrian observer, *Hauptmann* Robert Trimmel[i], the Austrian military attaché in South Africa, came away with firm but hardly radical ideas as to the new power of the defensive. In his view, frontal assaults were now all but impossible and what was needed was for some troops to pin the enemy to their front whilst others embarked upon out-flanking movements. In the absence of suitable high-angle artillery, Trimmel was of the view that artillery could do little to dislodge entrenched infantry. Its role was more to keep the enemy's heads down whilst the widely dispersed troops advanced having deployed several thousand yards from the opposition's trenches. But these troops were not advancing to deliver a bayonet charge rather they were to hold the enemy on their front whilst others sought a way around the flanks. And all because, from his experience, 'frontal assaults have become impossible' against entrenched troops.[70] Sadly for the Austro-Hungarian Army, Trimmel's opinions did not chime with those of the leading military thinker and later CinC of the Army, Conrad von Hötzendorf, a devotee of the offensive who believed the Boers lost because, after their initial forays into British territory, they fought a defensive war. It has been suggested that Trimmel's ideas were actively suppressed, presentations to fellow officers censored, and that others conspired to hinder interest expressed by Archduke Franz Ferdinand.[71] And all because Hötzendorf was not a firepower theorist but rather an 'eggs/omelette man' who believed success was gained by whoever smashed the largest number.[72] Victory went to the General with the moral courage to smash these eggs and, as a result, Austrian tactics went into reverse in several key areas. Fire superiority was to be gained by concentrating the firing line into dense groups vulnerable to counter-fire and the final charge could be delivered even in the absence of fire superiority. It is fair to say that the 1903 Regulations were more progressive than many of their European equivalents but when the driving force in the Army has their own fixed ideas as to the conduct of battle, such things counted for little.

In support of Trimmel's opinion, an article, penned by none other than Colmar von der Goltz for the London *National Review* in 1903, suggested the success of defensive fighting in South Africa was transformative as far as the future of warfare was concerned:

> "Infantry in close order and in deep formation will often have less chance of seizing an enemy position than a well-led line of skirmishers advancing deftly and resolutely... Previously, we tried to place as many rifles as possible on the combat front, so as to form dense lines of fire. This may still be justified in decisive moments. But, until then, we will do well to be moderate. The experience of Africa shows that by strengthening the line of fire to the extreme, there comes a time when the losses are so great, the position of each rifleman so inconvenient, that the increase in the number of rifles in line no longer corresponds to an increase in power."[73]

---

[i] Born in 1870, Trimmel was in South Africa from November 1899 until the fall of Pretoria in July 1900. He produced a brief book on what he witnessed entitled *Eindrucke und Beobachtungen aus dem Boerenkriege*. In 1914 he was the commander of *Infantrie Regiment Nr. 8* and he was later promoted Lt. Gen. He died in 1959.

Despite this, many senior Army officers in all countries took a contrary, Hötzendorf-inclined, view about the impact of the new weaponry. Modern quick-firing weapons were regarded by most as a means of breaking a defence. By the suppression of the entrenched infantry's fire with a heavy artillery bombardment, the attacking troops would cross the 'fire swept zone' and enter the enemy position where they would rout the defenders at the point of the bayonet. All that was needed was: accurate artillery fire and precise fuzes which exploded at the correct time and place; heavy small arms fire as the attackers approached the line to be taken; high morale and confidence in the advancing infantry... and the willingness of the attacking units to accept severe casualties. This latter point was not viewed as a problem. After all, Generals down the ages have convinced themselves their troops die willingly (or with only a little 'encouragement') and, given the enormous size of the continental armies generated by the 'nation in arms' concept espoused by men like Lord Roberts in Britain and Gen. von der Goltz in Germany, men were like ammunition – the same as any other expendable commodity on the battlefield. As a result, the heavy casualties suffered by the attacking Japanese infantry in the next war to come along, the Russo-Japanese War of 1904-5, were not greeted with any great concern by observers, though attitudes were, perhaps, rather different in Japan.

Endnotes:
1 Dunlop, Col. J K, *The Development of the British Army 1899-1914*, Methuen, 1938, page 78.
2 Stone J & Schmidl E A, *The Boer War and Military Reforms*, Atlantic Research and Publications Inc., 1988, p. 14-7.
3 *The Times, The Military Training Of 1903*, 15th April 1903, page 2.
4 *The Times, The Tactical Operations in Sussex*, 3rd September 1897, page 8.
5 *The Times, The Recent Tactical Operations in Sussex*, 10th September 1897, page 5.
6 *The Times, The Tactical Operations in Sussex*, 3rd September 1897, page 8.
7 Ibid.
8 *The Times, The Tactical Operations in Sussex*, 4th September 1897, page 8.
9 Ibid.
10 *The Times, The Tactical Operations in Sussex*, 6th September 1897, page 5.
11 *The Times, The Military Manoeuvres*, 17th August 1898, page 9.
12 *The Times, The Military Manoeuvres*, 25th August 1898, page 4.
13 *The Times, The Military Manoeuvres*, 31st August 1898, page 8.
14 *The Times, The Military Manoeuvres*, 1st September 1898, page 8.
15 *The Times, The Recent Military Manoeuvres:*, 6th October 1898, page 6.
16 Ibid.
17 Ibid.
18 Ibid.
19 *The Times, The Recent Military Manoeuvres*, 24th September 1988, page
20 *The Times, The Military Manoeuvres of 1898*, 28th January 1899, page 12.
21 Ibid.
22 *The Times, The Report on the Military Manoeuvres*, 7th February 1899, page 13.
23 Ibid.
24 Ibid.
25 *The Times, The Military Manoeuvres*, 14th September 1903, page 8.
26 *The Times, Letters: The Army Manoeuvres*, 11th October 1898, page 5.
27 *The Times, The Military Manoeuvres*, 1st April 1899, page 8.
28 Doyle, A C, *The Great Boer War: a two years' record, 1899–1901*, 15th ed., 1901, page 167.
29 Maurice, Maj. Gen. Sir F, & Grant, Capt. M H, *Official History of the War in South Africa 1899-1902*, vol. II, HMSO, p. 614.
30 Farwell, B, *Queen Victoria's Little Wars*, Harper and Row, 1972, page 342.
31 Kruger, Rayne. *Goodbye Dolly Grey: The Story of the Boer War*, Four Square Books, 1964.
32 Pilcher, T, *Some Lessons from the Boer War*, Isbister & Co., 1902, page 17.
33 Maurice, Lt. F., *The System of Field Manoeuvres Best Adapted for Enabling Our Troops to Meet a Continental Army*, Wellington Prize Essay, Blackwood & Sons, 1872, pages 29-31.
34 Gawler, Col. G, preface 2nd edition (1852) to *The Essentials of Good Skirmishing*, Savill & Edwards, originally published 1837.
35 Pakenham, Thomas, *The Boer War*, Johannesburg: Jonathan Ball, 1979.
36 Farwell, op, cit., page 344.
37 Quoted in Pakenham, op. cit., page 201.
38 Gooch, J, ed., *The Boer War: Direction, Experience and Image*, Routledge, 2000, page 62-3.
39 Ibid., page 154.
40 *Official Records of the Guards' Brigade in South Africa*, 1904, pages 11-20.
41 Farwell, op. cit., page 345.
42 *The Times, Our Own Correspondent. M. De Bloch On the Campaign*, 8th February 1900, page 5.
43 *The Times, Letters, Military Conundrums*, 11th January 1900, Page 10.
44 Smith-Dorrien, H L, *Memories of Forty Eight Years' Service*, page 152.
45 Conan Doyle, *The Great Boer War*,
46 Smith-Dorrien, op. cit., pages 152-4.
47 Spiers, Edward M., *The Late Victorian Army 1868-1902*, Manchester University Press, 1992, page 312.

⁴⁸ *The Times*, 15th June 1901, page 12.
⁴⁹ Brett, op. cit., page 270.
⁵⁰ Hayes, M H, *Horses on board ship: a guide to their management*, Hurst & Blackett, 1902, pages 213 to 214.
⁵¹ Spiers, op. cit., page 313.
⁵² *The Times, The Imperial Yeomanry*, 19th January 1900, page 4.
⁵³ *The Times, With General French's Force*, 19th January 1900, page 4.
⁵⁴ Spiers, op. cit., page 312.
⁵⁵ Fuller, J F C, *Decisive Battles of the Western World*, Vol. III, Cassell & Co., 1956, page 145-6.
⁵⁶ Childers, E, Amery, L S ed., *The Times History of the War in South Africa 1899-1902*, Vol V, Sampson, Low, Marston & Co., London, 1907, page 69.
⁵⁷ Amery, op. cit., page 181.
⁵⁸ Ibid., page 182.
⁵⁹ *The London Gazette*, 29th July 1902. No. 27459. pages 4835–4837.
⁶⁰ *Report on a Conference of General Staff Officers at the Staff College, 2nd-12th January 1906*, page 32.
⁶¹ Amery, L S, *The Problem of the Army*, Edward Arnold, 1903, page 192.
⁶² Ibid., footnote page 178.
⁶³ Ramsay, M A, *Command and Cohesion: The Citizen Soldier and Minor Tactics in the British Army 1870-1918*, Praeger, 2002, pages 56 & 64
⁶⁴ Beckett, I F W, Simpson, K & Keegan J, *A Nation in Arms, The British Army in the First World War*, Pen & Sword Military, 2014.
⁶⁵ Winters, J M, *Britain's Lost Generation of the First World War, Population Studies*, Vol. 31, 1977, page 458.
⁶⁶ Ibid., page 187.
⁶⁷ Beach J, ed., *The Military Papers of Sir Cuthbert Headlam*, Army Records Society, 2010, page 159.
⁶⁸ Bloch, Jean de, *Selected Articles*, page 80.
⁶⁹ de Négrier, Gen. F O, *L'évolution actuelle de la tactique, Revue des Deux Mondes*, 1904, livraison du 15, page 859.
février, p. 858
⁷⁰ Stone, J, & Schmidl, E A, *The Boer War and Military Reforms*, Atlantic Research and Publications Inc., 1988, pages 206-7.
⁷¹ Broucek, O, *Taktische Erkenntnisse aus dem russisch-japanischen Krieg und derer Beachtung in Österreich-Ungarn, Mitteilungen des österreichischen Staatsarchives 30*, 1977, Ergänzungsband, page 196, and Stone & Schmidl, op. cit., pages 189-221.
⁷² Sondhaus, L, *Franz Conrad Von Hötzendorf: Architect of the Apocalypse*, Brill, 2000, page 68.
⁷³ Goltz, Gen. C v d, writing in the *National Review*, November, 1903, quoted in Négrier, op. cit, pages 876-7.

7. CLASS, CASH OR COMPETENCE

"Only mediocrities rise to the top in a system that won't tolerate wave making."
Laurence J. Peter
The Peter Principle

"The British officer should be a gentleman first and an officer second."
HRH Prince George, 2nd Duke of Cambridge
Commander in Chief, British Army, 1856-95

THE FAILINGS IN SOUTH AFRICA PREDICTABLY drew attention to the quality and professionalism of the officers in charge as well as those at a more junior level. Perhaps the most scathing description of the average British Army officer was written by H G Wells in 1902. He saw them through the prism of the farces and failures of their most recent war in South Africa. Imagining an army of the illiterate and un-trained commanded by the carelessly ill-educated he wrote in *Anticipations*:

"And beside them, an absolute stranger to them, a stranger even in habits of speech and thought, and at any rate to be shot with them fairly and squarely, marches the subaltern – the son of the school-burking[i], shareholding class – a slightly taller sort of boy, as ill-taught as they are in all that concerns the realities of life, ignorant of how to get food, how to get water, how to keep fever down and strength up, ignorant of his practical equality with the men beside him, carefully trained under a clerical headmaster to use a crib[ii], play cricket rather nicely, look all right whatever happens, believe in his gentility, and avoid talking 'shop'."[1]

Then, in an unforgivingly acerbic footnote he suggests consigning the current army to a ceremonial role only, whilst proper professionals, dedicated to the military art, run a new army dedicated to excellence in war:

"And while the Private lives under these conditions, the would-be capable officer stifles amidst equally impossible surroundings. He must associate with the uneducated products of the public schools, and listen to their chatter about the 'sports' that delight them, suffer social indignities from the 'army woman', worry and waste money on needless clothes, and expect to end by being shamed or killed under some unfairly promoted incapable. Nothing illustrates the intellectual blankness of the British army better than its absolute dearth of military literature. No one would dream of gaining any profit by writing or publishing a book upon such a subject, for example, as mountain warfare in England, because not a dozen British officers would have the sense to buy such a book, and yet the British army is continually getting into scrapes in mountain districts. A few unselfish men ... find time to write an essay or so, and that is all. On the other hand, I find no less than five works in French on this subject in *MM. Chapelet & Cie.'s* list alone. On

---

[i] 'Burking': used in the sense of 'to avoid' or 'by-pass'.
[ii] Basically to cheat, as in an exam.

guerrilla warfare again, and after two years of South Africa, while there is nothing in English but some scattered papers by Dr. T. Miller Maguire, there are nearly a dozen good books in French... The British army not only does not attract ambitious, energetic men, it repels them. I must confess that I see no hope either in the rulers, the traditions, or the manhood of the British regular army, to forecast its escape from the bog of ignorance and negligence in which it wallows. Far better than any of projected reforms would it be to let the existing army severely alone, to cease to recruit for it, to retain (at the expense of its officers...) its messes, its uniforms, its games, bands, entertainments, and splendid memories as an appendage of the Court, and to create, in absolute independence of it, battalions and batteries of efficient professional soldiers, without social prestige or social distinctions, without bands, dress uniforms, colours, chaplains or honorary colonels, and to embody these as a real marching army perpetually *en route* throughout the empire – a reading, thinking, experimenting army under an absolutely distinct war office, with its own colleges, depôts and training camps perpetually ready for war."[2]

The grotesque and repeated shortcomings which afflicted rather too many British Army officers in South Africa was a subject of grave concern both politically and publicly and warranted extensive and detailed enquiry. The main investigation, starting even before the war ended (the issue had been previously internally flagged and publicly noted), was into junior officers, their education and training – or lack thereof. The 'crammer' Thomas Miller Maguire highlighted the scale of the problem in a letter to *The Times* on 6th March 1901, though his target, as part of a long running and very public spat, was the education provided by the country's leading public schools:

"That no system of education could well be worse is not my statement only... It is the deliberate opinion of the Headquarters Staff at Aldershot, who had charge last autumn of the most illiterate body of men of the social position of gentlemen who were ever gathered together in one place in a civilized country. They assert that they had to try and instruct in the art of war officers of 20 years of age whose intelligence was rudimentary and who were incapable of the efficient transmission of commands...

It was a matter of common knowledge that many of our young officers, especially of the Militia, know absolutely nothing about history, geography, sketching, sciences, or languages, or literature of any kind, and have never read any books on tactics. But some of your readers may be surprised to learn that they cannot write a legible letter or take down military details in proper spelling...

The whole system of the education of our officers is a national scandal of the worst kind."[3]

It must be said that, however accurate Miller Maguire's assessment was of the intelligence and education of young officers, he had a remarkable degree of self-interest in blaming the Public Schools for the problem. His income depended on young men coming to him to be 'crammed' for entry into Sandhurst or Woolwich.

Sensitive to the *nth degree*, only a few weeks earlier he erupted flamboyantly when someone dared to suggest that crammers and the young men who attended them were anything other than paragons of educational and personal virtue, even though there was, unfortunately, plenty of evidence to suggest otherwise[i].

But the argument between the interested parties – the Army, schools, crammers, the Government, and others – about the reasons for the poor quality of too many officers at all levels was one of longstanding. South Africa simply brought it to a head as here was visible and recorded evidence of incompetence, stupidity, ignorance and complacency. It could no longer be ignored.

In late 1900, with the war ongoing, there was a major confrontation between the Public Schools and the War Office over a proposed new Militia examination, one which filled the schools with such horror a motion was passed by the Headmasters Conference heavily critical of it. This examination was important as it was the pathway by which young men might enter the Regular Army without the need to pass through either Sandhurst or Woolwich. The schools were attacked for their opposition and they responded in kind. Annesley Ashworth Somerville[ii] was the Head of the Army Class at Eton, one of the main suppliers of cadets to the College and Academy which, over a five-year period from 1895-1900, supplied 150 candidates for cadetships of which 89 were immediately successful and others passed in later. In late December 1900 he responded to criticism of the schools' position in a lengthy letter to *The Times*. Apart from re-stating his objections to the exam (i.e. history, English composition, drawing, and tactics were excluded from the exam; there was no minimum pass mark in any subject; the candidate needed to attend two Militia training sessions in consecutive years before being eligible between which they were to return to school) Somerville also gave a robust retort to those who accused the Public Schools of simple self-interest in their objections:

> "The public schools need not hesitate to say to the War Office, 'We supply you with good material; what do you do with it when it reaches your regiments?' The regimental officers in South Africa have been conspicuous for the steadfast bravery with which they led their men, but also,

---

[i] There was an intemperate exchange of letters in *The Times* in mid-January 1901 between a certain 'A C.B.' and Miller Maguire who went off the deep-end attacking 'A C.B.' but not before stating '…the present war had the effect of so lowering the standard of education of officers that practically any person with sufficient means to buy a uniform can get a commission…' (*Source: The Times*, T Miller Maguire, *The Preliminary Education of Officers*, 15th January 1901, page 5]. An unfavourable commentary on crammers can also be found in J F C Fuller's *Memoirs of an Unconventional Soldier*, 1936.

[ii] Sir Annesley Ashworth Somerville was a graduate of Queen's College, Cork, and Trinity College, Cambridge. He was Assistant Master and then Head of the Army Class at Eton between 1885–1922 and commanded the Eton College Rifle Volunteer Corps between 1902 and 1906. A member of the Eton Board of Guardians (1892-1922) he commanded the 1st Battalion, Buckinghamshire Volunteer Regt. during the war. He was elected as Conservative MP for Windsor in 1922 and represented the seat until his death in 1942, aged 84.

unfortunately, for frequent ignorance of the rudiments of their profession. Their power of leading has been largely acquired in the playing fields of their schools; their ignorance of war is due to the neglect of the War Office to provide them with continuous intelligent instruction in their profession after they join their regiments. They learn, no doubt, the necessary elements of barrack-square drill, and the details of Court-martial procedure, but who instructs them in strategy and tactics, and teaches them to handle men in the open?"[4]

A teacher with some '15 or 16 years' continuous experience of teaching Army candidates in Public Schools then put his finger on two related problems:

"... Army candidates," he asserted, "are not, as a rule, clever, however sound and straightforward and gallant."[5]

They were then asked to study a wide range of subjects: mathematics, Latin, French, chemistry and heat, geometrical drawing, freehand drawing, essay and *précis* writing with the result that:

"The taught get but a smattering, a vague and inaccurate acquaintance with a number of subjects; none of the firm grip and sense of mastery that comes with a thorough knowledge; consequently they are disappointed and disgusted with their books and feel little inclination to take them up later on."[6]

If, as suggested by Miller Maguire and others, the schools were not up to the task of getting candidates through the RMC/RMA entrance examinations, then private crammers/tutors perforce must step in. It must be said the quality of 'crammers' varied markedly, but one of the best was the one to which Winston Churchill was sent after twice failing the Sandhurst entrance exam: *James, Carlisle and Gregson*[i] of 5, Lexham Gardens, South Kensington (just behind the Cromwell Hospital)[ii]. Known as *Jimmy's* to its students, its guiding light was Capt. Walter Haweis James[iii], RE, and it was used by those seeking entry to Sandhurst or

---

[i] Edward Carlisle, MA, a mathematician from Cambridge University, and Capt. Matthew Henry Gregson, RE, who passed out of the RMA in 1867 and served with James in the Public Works Department in India in 1871. He was promoted Capt. in 1879 and resigned in 1883.

[ii] The first crammer in Lexham Gardens was opened by the Rev. Dr George Frost in 1864. Capt. James took over in 1880 and there the business remained for some 90 years. In 1881, *Jimmy's* occupied Nos 5, 7, 19 and 21 Lexham Gardens [*Source*: Weekes, D, *The Origins of Lexham Gardens and Lee Abbey in London*. Gracewing, 1996].

[iii] Capt. Walter Haweis James (1847-1927) was the youngest son of H C James and his wife Elizabeth Jane *née* Page. He was commissioned into the Royal Engineers from the RMA in 1867. By 1871 was a Lt. in the Public Works Department in India. He passed through the Staff College in 1877 and was promoted Capt. in 1879 serving in the Intelligence Department of the War Office, and as DAAG during the Anglo-Zulu War. He then resigned his commission to start up his tutoring (as he preferred to call it) business initially in conjunction with Col. Edward Lynch. This partnership was dissolved in 1892 and James became the sole proprietor. James also had an interest in Trinity College, Stratford-upon-Avon, founded in 1872 and used as an Army tutors c.

Woolwich, serving officers faced with promotion exams, and others hoping to enter the Staff College[i]. Churchill writes of his time there in *My Early Life*. What is abundantly clear is that *Jimmy's* was a place where one passed exams *not* where one increased one's learning or expanded the mind:

> "It was said that no one who was not a congenital idiot could avoid passing thence into the Army. The Firm had made a scientific study of the mentality of the Civil Service Commissioners. They knew with almost Papal infallibility the sort of questions which that sort of person would be bound on the average to ask on any of the selected subjects. They specialised on these questions and on the answering of them... Thus year by year for at least two decades he held the Blue Ribbon among the crammers."[7]

Successfully entering Sandhurst in 1893 Churchill was pleased to tell his father that at least twenty other *Old Jimmies* gained entrance that year. Amongst other luminaries to grace the corridors of *Jimmy's* were Prince Arthur of Connaught, Bernard Marmaduke Fitzalan-Howard, 16th Duke of Norfolk, the Earl of Derby, Gen. Sir Hubert de la Poer Gough, Field Marshal William Edmund Ironside, 1st Baron Ironside, Field Marshal John Standish Surtees Prendergast Vereker, 6th Viscount Gort, and Maj. Gen. J F C Fuller, the noted military historian.

In 1896 *Jimmy's* proudly advertised the fact that their 46 staff (10 military, 36 civil service) had successfully helped negotiate the minefields of military examinations for:

25 Sandhurst candidates;
7 Woolwich candidates;
9 Staff College candidates; and
22 candidates for promotion

They helped a further 22 young men pass the Militia Literary examination and 42 the Militia Competitive examination.

Like Miller Maguire, Capt. James was no great fan of the public schools and the education they provided to anyone, let alone prospective soldiers. He entered vigorously and at length into arguments about the education of officers and the school versus crammer debate, though he chose to describe his business as tutoring. He was scathing about the tendency for Latin and Greek to be the pre-eminent public school subjects at the expense of more modern and sometimes technical subjects, but his concern, interestingly, was for the boys of average abilities, i.e. not those about disappear into a university or one of the grander

---

1904-8. Another Army tutoring business based in Bedford was dissolved in 1903. He was made a Major in the Reserve of Officers in 1901 and was promoted Lt. Col, in 1903 being appointed an assistant to the Permanent Under-Secretary at the War Office. He contested St Pancras West for the Conservative Party at the 1885 general election and was, for four years (1889-93), councillor for Kensington South representing the Moderate (basically Conservative) Party on London County Council. During the war he served in the Censor's Department. He was the author of two books: *Modern Strategy: An Outline of the Principles which Guide the Conduct of Campaigns*, Blackwood, 1908, and *The campaign of 1815: chiefly in Flanders*, Blackwood, 1908.

[i] One of the staff at *Jimmy's* was T Miller Maguire.

professions such as law or medicine[i]. These were the young men he sought to help gain access to the Army:

> "After spending eight or nine years in learning Latin and Greek the average youths know very little of the former and nothing of the latter."[8]

In his eyes, and with more than a little justification, he argued that if languages were to be learnt then why not German and French? These, at least, had the virtue of being spoken and written in the modern world (an argument this writer unsuccessfully made to his Latin master at a major public school in the early 1960s). For a soldier this had a double benefit: firstly, German and French military experts – Clausewitz, Von der Goltz, Jomini – wrote numerous books which an officer might beneficially study; and secondly, these were the two countries Britain might well go to war with, or be allied to, in the foreseeable future.

James then assaulted the public schools' exaltation of the athlete presumably because, with his premises being on a street in central London, there was no way his students could participate in organised sports, something which they could do at school and something to which many of *Jimmy's* students would return with more enthusiasm than for their studies once at Sandhurst or Woolwich.

But his main objective was to score points off the public schools:

> "In the meantime, tutors will continue to flourish because they teach better than the schools… to call us 'crammers' is foolish; any tolerably educated individual knows there is no such thing as cramming… Cramming is the name given by inferior teachers to a standard of imparting knowledge they are unable to attain themselves."[9]

Unfortunately for Capt. James, Winston Churchill saw at first-hand how they achieved their results. The education on offer from the public schools may have been narrow and archaic, that offered by the crammers/tutors was superficial and tailored towards just one thing: passing an exam. Neither benefited the genuine education of the average young man wishing to become an Army officer and, as James boasted, he had helped over 2,000 'average' young men enter Sandhurst and Woolwich, though how much this benefited either the country or them is open to question. Furthermore, James neglected to mention one point when he also argued for modern schooling along the lines of the *Musterschule*[ii] in Frankfurt am Main. In Germany, crammers were so frowned upon candidates for the Staff College, the *Kriegsakademie*, were fined 10% of their marks in the entrance exam if they admitted to using one. The German Army wanted the educated not the crammed.

---

[i] It is fair to say a robust rebuttal of James's claims was made by W M Baker, Head of the Military and Engineering Department at Cheltenham College on 1st February. He wrote: 'My experience is that a properly conducted' establishment (i.e crammer) is quite the exceptional thing'. There was little love lost between the two sides.

[ii] The *Musterschule* – a progressive co-educational school opened in 1803 based on the ideas of Johann Heinrich Pestalozzi. Its second headteacher was the influential educationalist Friedrich Wilhelm August Fröbel. It is now a *realgymnasium*, the highest tier of academically based high school in Germany.

To sum up the impact of the crammer, as Col. Henry Knollys, RA,[i] wrote in *Blackwood's Magazine* in 1895:

"… the parent can scarcely do better for his son's immediate success – he can scarcely do worse, save in exceptional circumstances, for his moral and mental training."[10]

But, whatever their competing financial and educational interests, the opinions of the schools and the crammers were as one on the deplorable current state of the education and intellectual development of the average Army officer.

SO, LET US RETURN TO THE OFFICERS themselves rather than arguments about their education between parties each with a clear vested interest. Miller Maguire later gave extensive evidence to the Akers-Douglas committee and he took the opportunity to criticise what he saw as a climate of anti-intellectualism in the Army:

"Up to the present the young officer has had every discouragement to fit himself for his post by study… Success at polo, or cricket, or tennis. Or theatrical, or billiards would have paid him in his career better than learning. I have heard Subalterns abused for reading, and for knowing modern treatises on Tactics… Learning and research do not 'pay' at all in our Army. No wise man in any walk of life works at things which are manifestly unprofitable."[11]

The consequences of this ignorance of their profession for the officers concerned when sent on active services were, too often, literally fatal:

"I have known boy officers fresh from my classes being sent on duty to the front without any knowledge of the Art of War, small or great, drill or theory. Most of these are dead. We had warned them and their parents against their folly in vain."[12]

Henderson, too, was severely critical of the education, training and professional development of young officers. Writing on the British Army in February 1903, shortly before his untimely death, he argued:

"…it is not to be denied that there were officers in the army of 1899 who had no thought beyond the mechanical performance of trivial duties… The educational machinery of the home army was far below that of any other profession. Instruction, in anything beyond drill, discipline, and interior economy, was not only limited in amount but carried on under the greatest difficulties."[13]

He was also critical of the way the Militia and the Army then failed to develop its officers once they left school or the RMC:

"…no further knowledge than an acquaintance with the routine of barracks was demanded from those who sought commissions from the Militia… At

---

[i] Later Col. Sir Henry Knollys, KCVO, he was the Private Secretary and Comptroller in Britain, 1896-1919, to Princess Maud of Wales (youngest daughter of Edward VII and, from 1905, Queen Maud of Norway) on her marriage to Prince Charles of Denmark (later King Haakon VII of Norway 1905-1957).

the depots it was even worse than with the regiments. The supervision of a few recruits, practising the most elementary exercises for a few hours daily, absorbed but little time, aroused less interest, and offered no opportunities for useful practice. In his two years of depot service, the officer, unless he chose to study in his own quarters, learnt nothing and forgot much. Time hung heavy on his hands, and it was often wasted."[14]

The result was an officer class which shied away from learning its profession and craft and was inclined solely to sports and other expensive forms of recreation:

"The result may be readily surmised. Theory, if it is to leave an impression on the mind, must go hand in hand with practice, and a system of instruction which overlooks this consideration is not only useless, but revolting to common-sense. Not a few, therefore, of the regimental officers, over-dosed with theory, and with theory forced upon them, it may be added, in the least attractive form, turned impatiently from the study of dull treatises, and sought an outlet for their energies in other directions. Nor was the path of knowledge made easy for the more active-minded. Generals and commanding officers were not held responsible for the intellectual advancement of their subordinates, but merely for their knowledge of the official textbooks and regulations. If an officer was inclined to read, there was no one to whom he could apply for advice as to what to read; his education in the higher branches of military science was no one's business but his own. He was even told that a knowledge of strategy – and strategy is at least one-half, and the more important half, of the art of war – was required from staff officers alone; and, in consonance with this extraordinary doctrine, military history was taught officially nowhere but at the Staff College."[15]

What underpinned this issue with the education of officers, however, was a more fundamental point about the essentially conservative, authoritarian, and hierarchical nature all military institutions. The previously mentioned *Navy League* proponent Henry Spenser Wilkinson was, perhaps, the *doyen* of British military correspondents and writers before the war. A prolific author, he was appointed the first *Chichele Professor of Military History* at the University of Oxford in 1909. Between 1882 and 1914 he wrote for the *Guardian*, until 1892, and the *Morning Post*, covering, increasingly, wars and military matters. On this subject, Wilkinson pointed out in his book *Brain of an Army* that:

"The intellectual advancement of every army is confronted by a peculiar difficulty. The foundations of all military institutions are authority and obedience - principles which appear to be directly opposed to the free movement of intelligence. Every army is constantly in danger of decay from mental stagnation. Free criticism is liable to undermine discipline, and the habit of unconditional obedience too often destroys the independence of judgement without which moral and intellectual progress is impossible."[16]

In an organisation such as an army there was always going to be friction between the forces of reaction and those of progress. In the British Army, the forces of reaction held the upper hand through the latter part of the nineteenth and a large chunk at least of the twentieth century. And to no good effect.

SO CALAMITOUS WAS THE PERFORMANCE of so many officers in South Africa, and so widespread the concerns voiced in Parliament and beyond, that St John Brodrick, Secretary of State for War, convened a Parliamentary committee, to be chaired by Aretas Akers-Douglas[i], Conservative MP for St Augustine's[ii], Kent. Its remit was to report on the state of Military Education. Its title was *The Committee on the Education and Training of Officers*. It first met on Thursday, 9th May 1901.

75 Rt. Hon. Aretas Akers-Douglas MP

It focussed on the education of young officers prior to entering the Army; their education and training whilst at either Sandhurst or Woolwich; and their professional development once assigned to their unit. The period of interest was after 1891, when cuts in military education budgets were first made by Lord Salisbury's Conservative administration. The findings of the report highlighted serious issues concerning the intelligence, attitudes, and education of junior officers within the infantry and, even more especially, the cavalry.

There was, however, no similar investigation into the abilities of the Generals and Colonels who led their subordinates so badly, even if Lord Kitchener advised the Elgin Commission[iii], which separately investigated the conduct of the war:

---

[i] Born in 1851. Eton and University College, Oxford. Called to the Bar, Inner Temple, 1875. Conservative MP, East Kent, 1880. 1st Viscount Chilton of Boughton Malherbe in the County of Kent, and Baron Douglas of Baads, in the County of Midlothian, GBE, PC, JP, DL. Home Secretary between 12th July 1902 and 5th December 1905.
[ii] The area around Herne Bay.
[iii] *The Royal Commission on the South African War* was chaired by the Earl of Elgin and Kincardine. Its members were: Viscount Esher; Sir John Edge, KC, previously Chief Justice, Allahabad High Court; Field Marshal Sir Henry Wylie Norman, Indian Army, previously governor of Jamaica and Queensland; Rt. Hon. Sir George Dashwood Taubman-Goldie, RE, previously Governor, *Royal Niger Company*, later President, *Royal Geographical Society*; Admiral Sir John Ommanney Hopkins, previously Commander-in-Chief, Mediterranean Fleet; Sir John Jackson, a civil engineer whose works included the Manchester Ship Canal; Donald Alexander, Lord Strathcona and Mount Royal,

"The junior officers were, in my opinion, better than the senior ones."[17]

Lord Roberts was even more scathing:

"The proportion of failures among commanding officers and brigadiers was considerably larger than that in the junior ranks."[18]

This was not the first Parliamentary committee to investigate the standards of education of prospective Army officers. Indeed, the British Army seems peculiarly adept at first investigating the causes of failure in war and then forgetting or ignoring some of the most crucial findings of such investigations. In 1855, i.e. during the Crimean War[i], so concerned were politicians about the abilities and training of officers that a *Select Committee on the Royal Military College, Sandhurst*, was convened. In addition, a special report on the war, known as the *Sebastopol Report*, was published, and debated in June 1855. *The Times* summed up well the general opinion of the conduct of the war and the state of the army which fought it:

"If any one grand inference is to be drawn from the *Sebastopol Report*, there is one at least the truth of which is almost undeniable, it is that scarcely anybody, if anybody, concerned in the war understood his business. There has been more or less of inexperience, obstinacy, presumption and other impractical qualities, but everybody has shown something of them... it seems to follow that one great cause of our calamities has been the want of military education in those who had to advise measures at home and conduct the war abroad.

Nor do we at all exaggerate the matter of fact when we assert, that for a long time past utter ignorance of tactics and of all military affairs has been the rule rather than the exception among the many thousands intrusted with Her Majesty's commission... The least symptom of professional zeal, as often as not, has been regarded simply as a piece of conceit, and as betraying a treacherous design to step over the heads of a man's fellows... under the existing system of the army it would never do an officer the least good to know more than the rest of his comrades... There is no denying the truth of all this, and it chimes in thoroughly with the English prejudice against professional education."[19]

The prejudice persists, as Michael Gove revealed on *Sky News* on 3rd June 2016 when he remarked: 'I think the people in this country have had enough of experts'.

High Commissioner for Canada; and Sir Frederick Matthew Darley, Lt. Gov. and Chief Justice of New South Wales. Its secretary was Bernard H Holland.

[i] Rather like many Australians believe Gallipoli was a solely Australian affair, this writer assumes most British people (with an opinion) believe the Crimean War to have been entirely fought in the Crimea and to have involved mainly/entirely British troops. There was, in fact, considerable activity in what is now Rumania, the Caucasus, the Baltic, the White Sea, and around the Kamchatka peninsula in the North Pacific. Also, nearly three times as many French troops were involved as British: i.e. 309,000 French to 108,000 British, and their losses were more than three times heavier: 135,000 v. 40,500. 53% of the joint 176,000 casualties died of disease and most of these were French: 75,400 v. 17,600 British.

Letters and articles in the newspapers reached a fever pitch of support or rebuttal of this criticism during the latter months of the war in the Crimea. One letter, signed by *'An officer of twenty-two years' experience'*, commented more precisely on the educational standards of young officers:

> "... there are several of the young gentlemen who have joined the army ... whose knowledge on almost every subject it would be dignifying to term even superficial and who have exhibited the most unpardonable deficiency in grammatical construction and orthography in the most commonplace notes and reports."[20]

The report on Sandhurst was damning and the Senior Department, from which the better educated and trained officers of the army were supposed to emerge, was found to be a hollowed-out shell with few students, just two professors (one of whom was nearly blind), no books in English on staff duties whatsoever, and nothing on tactics acceptable to the authorities at Horse Guards. The Senior Department was supposed to produce men equipped to be staff officers, instead, from amongst the few who attended, it produced men whose 'qualifications' were ignored by the 'powers that be'.[21]

As to the current education and professional development of army officers, however, it soon proved to be the case that little if anything improved in the intervening fifty years and attitudes towards these issues in the Army changed little in the period between 1855 and 1902. This was despite regular (if septennial can be regarded as regular) reports on the education of officers conducted by the Director General of Military Education. For example, the fourth of these reports emerged in 1889. Commenting on this report *The Times* gave an assessment of the previous state of officer education within the infantry and cavalry, i.e. the output of either Sandhurst or the Militia:

> "In the pre-Crimean days British officers did not necessarily receive any education, professional or other, before being granted commissions... the officers of cavalry and infantry received no preparatory military training, while as to a general education, there was no test whatsoever till 1849[i]. They were gentlemen, and it was therefore assumed that they had received a gentleman's education, the standard of which was by no means high... it was not the fashion to devote either thought or time to the acquirement of professional knowledge and any attempt to discuss technical matters in the mess-room was severely repressed by a cry of 'shop'. Moreover, there was no inducement to study, for proficiency in professional subjects did not advance an officer one whit...
>
> Already six years previous to the war with Russia (i.e. 1849) some suspicions had arisen that it was scarcely decent that commissions should be given to young gentlemen, many of whom could not write a short ordinary letter without half-a-dozen glaring errors in orthography and grammar..."[22]

---

[i] Thereafter candidates had to pass an examination covering Algebra and Euclid, history and geography, French and Latin, field fortifications, spelling and handwriting.

The article then went on to congratulate the Army for the changes since wrought in its system of education which, given the comments made about the generally dreadful state of officer education post-South Africa and the desperate need for a parliamentary investigation into the prevailing systems, seems, in retrospect, complacent in the extreme. Little changed.

This unhappy state of affairs was reinforced by the contents of a short book published not long after the early disasters in South Africa, and by the comments of a review of that book in *The Spectator* magazine. The book was entitled *An Absent-Minded War* written by '*A British Officer*' and published in September 1900. The 'British Officer' concerned was, in fact, the previously mentioned Capt. William Elliott Cairnes of the Royal Irish Fusiliers. Cairnes was born in Galway in 1862, the son of a professor at University College, London. Educated at University College School and the International College in Isleworth, he joined the Royal Irish Rifles (Militia) in 1882 before rapidly rotating through the 3rd Dragoon Guards and the South Staffordshire Regt., before joining the 2nd Royal Irish Fusiliers in 1884. He never saw overseas service, being appointed the adjutant of the 1st Volunteer Battalion, KOYLI, in Wakefield in 1897, which role he held until shortly before his premature death from pneumonia on 19th April 1902 aged 40.

His frustration at not joining his battalion in South Africa (it left for Natal in September 1899) must have been considerable. The outlet for his views were his books and journalism as the 'military correspondent' of the Liberal evening newspaper the *Westminster Gazette* between November 1899 and April 1901. There he wrote a near daily article, filling many column inches criticising the conduct of the war in South Africa[i]. In his obituary, *The Times* described him as 'a well-known and most promising writer on military subjects'.[23] *An Absent-Minded War* was a vicious (though not baseless) attack on the 'powers that be' – the War Office, the Staff College, the original commanders in South Africa (Redvers Buller and Methuen most especially), on the education and training of young officers, and on the shortcomings of their superiors. Unlike most of the other critics of a particular aspect of the Army, i.e. the feeble education and training of junior officers, Cairnes was later put in a position to help investigate and, in some respects, improve this failing facet of the British military. The review of Cairnes's short book in *The Spectator* seems almost a continuation of *The Times* article from eleven years' earlier:

> "His first complaint is the one which has been most often on our lips of late, the false attitude towards the Army which most of its members adopt. Soldiering is not sufficiently a profession; it is rather a graceful nominal calling to which young men of means habitually drift. And such a feeling is

---

[i] Other than *An Absent-Minded War*, he also authored *Social Life in the British Army* (1900), *The Army from Within* (1901), the adulatory *Lord Roberts as a Soldier in Peace and War* (1901) and the invasion scare book *The Coming Waterloo* (1901). He was secretary to the Akers-Douglas committee which reported in the month before his death, and to the Military Court of Inquiry in the Remount Department [*Sources:* Roger T. Stearn, 'Cairnes, William Elliot (1862–1902)', *Oxford Dictionary of National Biography*, Oxford University Press, 2004; online edn, May 2006 and his obituary in *The Times*, 22nd April 1902, page 10].

both a cause and an effect of the extravagant cost of living in the Army. 'Keenness' is bad form, and 'shop' is tabooed; a man who shows an interest in the science of arms has to undergo much snubbing, and support the reputation of one who is commercially eager for his own advancement. The popular officer is he who at the earliest opportunity hurries out of his uniform and for the rest of the day lives the life of a man of leisure, a good fellow, and a good sportsman, but one who knows nothing of his profession beyond the ordinary routine of barrack life. The mere cost of the thing effectually keeps out able young men who have their own way to make in the world."[24]

Getting down to 'brass tacks' Lord Wolseley advised the Elgin Commission:

"The great bulk of the young men in England do not come into our badly paid profession."[25]

He might well have inserted the word 'intelligent' before 'young men'.

THE COMMITTEE WHICH INVESTIGATED the education of officers was made up of three MPs, two exalted Public School Headmasters and two experienced Army officers. Apart from Akers-Douglas they were:

- Sir Michael Foster, KCB, the MP for London University, a professor of Physiology at Cambridge University and secretary of the Royal Society;
- Capt. Arthur Hamilton Lee[i], RA, Conservative MP for Fareham and late Professor of Strategy and Tactics, the Royal Military College, Canada;
- Rev. Dr. Edmond Warre, DD, MVO, the Headmaster of Eton College, Old Etonian, and graduate of Balliol College, Oxford, which he left with a double First in 1859;
- Mr Frederick William Walker, previously a barrister at Lincoln's Inn and the Headmaster of Manchester Grammar School, now High Master of St Paul's School with an MA from Corpus Christi College, Oxford;
- Maj. Gen. Richard Henry Jelf, CMG, RE., Old Etonian, Fellow of King's College, London, and Governor and Commandant of the Royal Military Academy, Woolwich; and
- Lt. Col. (later Maj. Gen.) Frederick Hammersley, yet another Old Etonian commissioned out of Sandhurst into the Lancashire Fusiliers in 1876 and who served in South Africa.

The committee's secretary was our Capt. Cairnes of the Royal Irish Fusiliers (already quoted on the previous page and on page 432).

Evidence was taken from some 73 serving officers, public school headmasters and civil servants including Mr William John Courthope, the First Civil Service

---

[i] Later Viscount Lee of Fareham. Lee bought Chequers in 1912 and gave the house and estate to the Nation in 1921 to be the official residence and country retreat of the Prime Minister. It was first used by Lloyd George for whom he was the Personal Military Secretary when L-G was Minister for Munitions. He was the Minister of Agriculture and Fisheries in the Cabinet from 1919 to 1921 and First Lord of the Admiralty, 1921-2, and enjoyed a hugely varied time in public life until his death in 1947.

Commissioner. In addition, 87 current commanding officers were written to and asked to respond to certain key points about the qualities and education of their younger officers. Amongst the officers giving evidence was one Field Marshal (the Rt. Hon. Earl Roberts), the Adjutant General of the Army (Gen. Sir Evelyn Wood), various Lt. Gens. (Lyttleton, Markham and Fryer), eight Maj. Gens. (including Sir Ian Hamilton), a bevy of Colonels and Lt. Colonels, the odd Major and a sextet of Captains, one being from the Royal Navy. Some of these were representatives from Sandhurst, Woolwich, Chatham, Hythe and various other military establishments.

From the great educational establishments came:

William Martin Baker, MA (Cambs), Head of the Military and Civil Department at Cheltenham College from 1888;

Rev. William Cookworthy Compton, MA (Cambs), Head of Dover College from 1892;

Prof. Henry Francis Pelham, MA (Oxon), President of Trinity College, Oxford, from 1897;

James Surtees Phillpotts, BA (Oxon), Head of Bedford School from 1875;

Rev. Bertram Pollock, BA (Cambs), Head of Wellington College from 1893;

Rev. Ernest Stewart Roberts, MA (Cambs), President of Gonville and Caius College, Cambridge, from 1894;

Rev. Archibald Robertson, Fellow of Trinity College, Oxford, and the Principal of King's College, London, since 1897;

Annesley Ashworth Somerville, MA (Cambs), an Assistant Master and Head of the Army Class at Eton since 1885; and

William Ashwell Shenstone, the Senior Science Master at Haig's *alma mater* Clifton College since 1880.

Others with an interest in education and representing other parts of the United Kingdom were:

Dr Anthony Traill, BA (Dublin), the Commissioner of National Education in Ireland; and

Rt. Hon. Sir Henry Craik, KCB, MA (Oxon), the Secretary of the Scotch Education Department in Whitehall since 1885.

First to give evidence on 9th May 1901 was 63-year-old Gen. Sir Evelyn Wood, a product of Marlborough College and the Royal Navy, which he joined as a midshipman in 1852.[26] Serving aboard *HMS Queen* off the Crimea in 1854 he went ashore with the Naval Brigade commanded by Capt. William Peel. Severely wounded in an attack on the Sebastopol Redan, he was invalided home and, still recovering, gained a commission into the 13th Light Dragoons. On his return to the Crimea, he contracted typhoid and, nursed by his mother in Florence Nightingale's Scutari hospital, returned to England to transfer to the 17th Lancers in 1857. With this regiment he went to India in time to be involved in the suppression of the Mutiny. In 1862 he passed the Staff College entrance examination but lost out because another 17th Lancers' officer achieved better marks and only one officer per regiment was allowed in each year. Showing commendable presence of mind, he transferred to the 73rd (Perthshire) Regiment of Foot, and graduated from the Staff College in 1864. Buying his way up the ranks (commissions were still purchased before the Cardwell Reforms put an end to this practice. Wood, sometimes, relied on relatives to stump up the cash), he served briefly in the Third Ashanti War before being appointed Superintendent of Garrison Instruction at Aldershot. He then fought in the Zulu and First Boer Wars, assuming command in Natal after the death of Sir George Colley at the infamous skirmish at Majuba Hill in May 1881. He was then obliged by the Government to sign terms with the Boers, an action which earned him the lasting *opprobrium* of Garnet Wolseley who, in 1894, was appointed Commander-in-Chief of the Forces. Wolesley believed Wood should have resigned rather than sign the treaty.

His career then took him to Egypt, where he became Sirdar of the Egyptian Army between 1882-5 and he was involved in the abortive expedition to extricate Gen. Gordon from Khartoum. He spent the rest of his career back in Great Britain, first in charge of the Eastern and the Aldershot commands then, from 1893, as Quartermaster-General to the Forces and, in 1897, as Adjutant-General to the Forces. In these latter years one of the younger officers to come under his wing was a certain Douglas Haig whose progress he smoothed with an appointment to serve with Kitchener in the Sudan in 1898.

Wood offered to serve in the second South African War but Wolseley, still unforgiving over the peace deal signed by Wood with Kruger in O'Neil's Cottage in March 1881, rejected his services and he continued his work at the War Office. Whatever one's view of the man, Haig thought him 'a capital fellow' whilst Wolseley described him as 'as cunning as a first-class female diplomatist… (but) a very second-rate general', his experience was undoubted and wide-ranging. He served with the infantry and the cavalry, in the Crimea, India, South and West Africa and along the Nile, as well as in numerous staff and administrative roles. His views, therefore, carried weight. His views on younger officers were damning:

> "*Akers Douglas*: Is there any difficulty in getting a sufficiency of officers for the Army?
> *Wood*: Yes, there is not only a difficulty in getting a sufficiency of officers, but there has been a greater difficulty in getting the officer we want for many years past."[27]

When combined with the sheer cost of being an officer, the consequence of this was that the entrance examination pass marks for Sandhurst for certain arms of the service were lamentably low and had been for some considerable time. Wood spoke from personal experience as a father whose three sons had been through Sandhurst in the 15 years before the outbreak of the Boer War (between 1886 and 1894).[i] Whereas one of his sons needed to achieve over 70% in his exam for the RMC to get into the infantry, this would have been just 50% for the cavalry and a laughable 25% for the Household Cavalry. The result was:

---

[i] Col. Evelyn Fitzgerald Michell Wood, DSO, Dragoon Guards, Lt. Col. Charles Michell Aloysius Wood, DSO, Northumberland Fusiliers, and Lt. Col. Arthur Herbert Wood, Cameronians (Scottish Rifles). All served in WW1.

"... only the boys who will not work as a rule go into the cavalry, and we are obliged to take them in, because there are no other candidates."[28]

And, as it turned out, standards had somehow deteriorated still further since Wood's lads entered the Army.

The Committee's report was published at the beginning of June 1902, over a year after the hearings began. A report in *The Times* of Monday, 9th June, 1902, described the report as:

"...a sweeping condemnation of the methods by which young officers are generally educated before joining the Army and technically trained after receiving their commissions."[29]

The article went on to say the contents of the report of the committee:

"... will come as a painful awakening to the public, who had been urged to believe that the numerous 'mishaps' and 'regrettable incidents' which occurred in South Africa were such as might normally be expected and were not owing to defective knowledge or faulty training on the part of the officers concerned."[30]

Responsibility for this problem was laid at the door of the mainly Conservative Governments whose 'desire for economy' resulted in significant cuts in the cash available for training and educating officers[i]. Paragraph 6 of the final report pointed out that, whereas £112,500 was set aside for the Military Education of an army of 143,533 officers and men in the Army Estimates of 1890-1, by 1898-9 the Estimates provided only £118,200 for an army 20% larger at 171,394 officers and men. Deducting the allowances made to Army schools (i.e. Sandhurst, Woolwich, Netley [medical] and Kneller Hall [music]) meant that, in 1898-9, only 0.22% of the Army budget, or £43,450, was spent on the continuing education of the Army.

And affairs were about to get worse. The Estimates for 1901-2 showed only 0.15%, or £40,630, available for education for an Army 209,911 strong. In other words, the 5 shillings and 9½ pence (c. £25 in modern money) per soldier education budget of 1890-1 was slashed to just 3 shillings and 9½ pence (c. £15) per soldier for 1901-2. Not only that, but the Military Education Department and its Director General were abolished and replaced by a single officer commanding a princely salary of just £800 (c. £65,000) a year.[31] The committee's comment:

"... economy appears to have been sought without sufficient regard to efficiency."[32]

Governments clearly never change, especially Conservative ones.

Under the heading of *The Antecedent Education of Army Candidates*, Part 1 of the report (paragraph 9) set out a general view expressed during the giving of evidence:

---

[i] After the Liberal Unionist split from the Liberal Party, Lord Salisbury's Conservatives won a large majority in 1886. They lost seats in 1892, and Salisbury lost a confidence motion in August. Gladstone then formed his last, minority, administration. In 1895 Salisbury won a massive majority over Lord Roseberry's Liberals. The belief the South African War was won helped win them the 'Khaki' Election in 1900. The war dragged on for another two years. The Tories, under Balfour, were then crushed in 1906.

"… the Committee have been impressed by the widespread dissatisfaction – a feeling expressed by practically all the witnesses – with the present state of education, both military and general, among the officers of the Army as a class. Officers are stated to be deficient in general education. The Commander in Chief has expressed himself as dissatisfied with both the general and technical education of the officer; and many witnesses have stated that it is no uncommon thing to find officers unable to write a good letter or to draw up an intelligible report."[33]

Other than the limited intellectual abilities of rather too many prospective officers some, as mentioned earlier, felt the core of these educational inadequacies lay with the superficial treatment of key subjects at Public Schools allied to rote learning of facts and figures done at the expense of understanding. The structure of the examination which, since 1870, officer candidates had to pass to enter the RMC/RMA was also blamed. Cramming for mathematics (50% of the total marks) and languages (40%) was held responsible for the generally dreadful standards of written English (10%). Writing to *The Times* in December 1903, Annesley Somerville, the Head of the Army Class at Eton, revealed just how weak candidates were in this latter subject. That year, Eton provided nine candidates for Woolwich and eleven for Sandhurst. In the Woolwich exam, the average mark for English composition was just 50%, a number reduced by two of the young men who barely surpassed 30%. For Sandhurst the average was 52% which, whilst not outstanding, was still better than the overall examination average mark of just 49%.[34] One explanation for the failure of Eton pupils in this part of the entrance examination might well be explained by a previous letter to *The Times* from a correspondent known only as 'X'. He was the father of a boy in the First Army Class at the school and noted English was not taught in the class at all![35]

The failure to teach the subject at school and to give it a proper priority in the entrance examinations was that the candidates' own language, as well as their country's history and geography, were neglected whilst they concentrated on the more lucrative subjects in the exam. Many officers displayed a 'lamentable ignorance' of written and oral English and, therefore, struggled to provide written or dictated orders to their men as well as reports for their superiors, as Miller Maguire's earlier comment: '(young officers) cannot write a legible letter or take down military details in proper spelling' made clear.

In a criticism of education which might have been written this century, the report declared 'cramming' and 'mark hunger' had replaced education, with the focus entirely on passing examinations or tests. Another consequence was that, once commissioned, officers then put aside their books, only studying them again when it was time to pass another exam in order to be promoted.

The existing testing was conducted by the Civil Service Commissioners who designed their exams in line with the curriculum of the Public Schools without considering whether this was the most suitable education for an Army officer. As a result, in what Capt. James might argue was a victory over the schools, the Akers-Douglas committee threw out the current system and drew up a syllabus they considered more suited to the needs of a young man entering Sandhurst or Woolwich. It consisted of four compulsory subjects:

English – to include composition, *précis* writing, and the history and geography of the British Empire (30% of marks);
Mathematics (30%);
A modern language (20%) though with less emphasis on grammar; and
Either Latin or science (20%).

Radically, the candidate had to achieve a minimum pass mark in *every* subject, not something which applied to Haig, Rawlinson, Allenby *et al.*

In addition, there was a choice of three voluntary subjects. Candidates for Woolwich had to select two and for Sandhurst one. It was also suggested there should be one common entrance examination and candidates for Sandhurst, Woolwich, the Militia and Yeomanry should all compete, with places being allocated strictly on the results of the examination. Finally, in this section, it was recommended to raise the age limits which currently stood at 16-18 for Woolwich and 17-19 for Sandhurst to 17-19 and 17½-19½ respectively.

Prior to this, however, the problem of inadequate education and its impact on the resulting output applied to all officers whatever their provenance – Sandhurst, Woolwich or the Militia. The CinC, Lord Roberts advised the committee:

"… the standard of education is not sufficiently high. I think there is a want of proper training. It is not so much deficiency in mental capacity as in training."[36]

Damning with faint praise a generation of Army officers with his statement it was 'not so much' a deficiency in their mental capacities, Roberts thus provided a less than overwhelming endorsement of the qualities of the men who would, in twelve years' time, lead the country's troops into war.

There were some whose opinion of the Army's young officers was far more savage. Miller Maguire's acerbic comment in 1902 'The younger officers are worse than for a generation' was not his first foray into the debate about the appalling state of the education of British Army officers (see page 440). In 1899, he wrote that suitability for admission to Sandhurst appeared to rest on:

"…the delusion that mere physique is the first qualification for a commission in the Army, and that next is money, the next still games of ball, the next horsemanship, the next good breeding and good manners, and the last general intelligence and culture."

He went on to describe the majority of the young men who came to him in an effort to enter Sandhurst and the Army as:

"… by far the most ignorant persons of their social class in Europe, Japan, our colonies or the United States."[37]

PART II OF THE REPORT LOOKED AT SANDHURST AND WOOLWICH in detail as well as at University candidates for a commission. The Army required an annual output of some 800 officers but the College and the Academy were only able to produce 510. The Militia was retained as another source of supply to which was added the Yeomanry, which saw extensive service in South Africa. In addition, it was recommended fifty commissions should be allocated to candidates from the Colonial Forces. It was also suggested up to 100 commissions be allotted to candidates educated at 'approved universities'. These candidates were to be aged 20 and over and were to have graduated or passed another acceptable form of examination. Radically, it was thought, if this system developed well, more commissions could be allocated to universities and the committee foresaw a time when it might be possible to do away with the RMC and RMA completely.

Which conclusion led to the committee's views on the two establishments. It was 'on the whole satisfied' with the RMA (no doubt a relief to committee member Maj. Gen. Jelf, the commandant of 'The Shop'). Their main criticism was that there was no clear link between officers teaching *'Command'* and those teaching *'Instruction'*. Sir Evelyn Wood remarked in a memorandum to the committee:

> "The importance of instruction and the ability to impart instruction are not sufficiently appreciated in the Army... I regard it as of great moment that young officers when they join their regiments should be qualified to instruct their men."[38]

Sandhurst was another matter entirely, as *The Times* made clear:

> "... the committee make remarks which are wholly unfavourable, and constitute a severe indictment of the college administration... There is a lamentable lack of supervision both of the indoor studies and of the outdoor work of the cadets."[39]

When Lt. Col. Johnston Stoney Talbot, King's Shropshire Light Infantry and the Assistant-Commandant since 1897, was asked why cadets were drilled and given practical training by staff sergeants he replied this was because:

> "There is not an officer at this college at the present moment who is fit to drill a squad."[40]

A revealing response from an officer in post for some four years.

The Times went on to say similar evidence was given by this officer and his superior, Lt. Gen. Sir Edwin Markham, about other aspects of the College, a position of 'almost incredible ineptitude' according to the newspaper. It was difficult to understand, the writer concluded, how such a situation could have continued unchecked for so long. Despite the fact only 20% of the cadets rode before entering Sandhurst, cavalry cadets received no more riding training than did infantry officers – a total of just 39 hours in their year-long stay at the college. Cadets received no training in rifle or revolver shooting. Cadets were never instructed in how to drill a squad or company of men. The Akers-Douglas committee remarked with a degree of incredulity:

> "Cadets are required to pipe-clay their own buff waistbelts... their rifles are cleaned for them. This is remarkable, for while a cadet might acquire a familiarity with the mechanism of the rifle from being required to clean it, the educational value of pipe-claying a belt is extremely slight."[41]

Furthermore, a cadet wishing to fire his nicely cleaned rifle was obliged to pay a £1 a term subscription (c. £100 at current prices) to join a shooting club.[42]

Underpinning this lamentable situation at Sandhurst was the fact that the role of instructor was regarded as a comfortable, unchallenging sinecure requiring neither great effort nor much skill at imparting wisdom to the educationally, and sometimes intellectually, challenged junior members of the upper class who filled the college. With the pay 'inadequate' and unlikely to attract the highflyer, officers who took up positions at Sandhurst were looked on as 'taking a step downhill' in their careers. The committee was predictably scathing:

> "The weight of evidence... leads to the conclusion that an instructional appointment is regarded in the Army generally as a shelf on which an officer may spend a few years comfortably, avoiding the monotonous routine of life in barracks and the constant changes of station, which constitute such a serious tax upon the pocket of the married officer."[43]

Technically, each instructor served a year's probation within which to prove himself worthy to teach the younger generation of officer cadets. In practice, the committee discovered, none ever reverted to regimental life because of their inadequacies. Markham[i], the Governor and Commandant of Sandhurst, seemed satisfied with this state of affairs but not Akers-Douglas and his colleagues:

> "The committee are, however, unable to share in the Governor's satisfaction with this fact or with the present method of selecting instructors."[44]

And the textbooks on which the instructors relied were also widely condemned as unfit for purpose, with one on topography being described by Capt. Lee as 'probably one of the worst books of its kind in the world'.[45]

The final nail in the coffin of the Sandhurst regime was the examination system and the priorities it revealed. The marks allocated to each subject are given below:

Subject	Senior Division	Junior Division
Military administration	300	300
Military law	300	300
Tactics	450	300
Military history & geography	150	150
Military engineering	900	300
Military topography	800	300
French or German	300	300
Drill	200	-
Riding	200	-
Gymnastics	200	-
Aggregate marks	3,800	1,950

Table 12 Allocation of examination marks, Sandhurst 1901[46]

---

[i] Lt. Gen. Sir Edwin Markham, KCB, was born in 1833. RHA, 1850. Served in the Crimea and Indian Mutiny. AAG, Woolwich, 1876. Commander, RA, Gibraltar, 1882-4. Director of Artillery Studies, Woolwich, 1885. DAG, RA Headquarters, 1887-1892. Lt. Governor of Jersey and, in 1895, Inspector-General of Ordnance. Governor of Sandhurst, 1898, leaving in 1902. He died in 1918. His younger son, 2nd Lt. Montagu Wilfrid Markham, 2nd Scots Guards, was killed on 29th August 1917 at the Third Battle of Ypres and he is remembered on the Tyne Cot Memorial, Panel 10.

The Junior Division was examined in seven and the Senior Division in ten subjects. The committee highlighted several anomalies, focussing on the 450 marks allocated to *Tactics* out of a 3,800 total in the Senior Division's final exam. This balance they found 'remarkable' in a Military College. They were also dismayed that, of those 450 marks, just 150 were available for practical work. Secondly, they noted both *Engineering* and *Topography* attracted double the marks, or nearly so, of *Tactics* and, after taking away the 150 marks for practical *Tactics*, the paper examination on this subject ranked equal to that of the modern language required. There was unhappiness that most of the marks on the three key military subjects, i.e. *Tactics*, *Engineering* and *Topography*, were awarded for written papers rather than practical work. The examination papers themselves came in for heavy criticism with many questions 'calculated to encourage 'cram''.[47] The *Engineering* paper, for example, required 'a minute knowledge of unimportant details' and the *Topography* paper was not far behind in its testing of irrelevant minutiae.

They did not, however, remark on the trivial 50 marks out of 300 for the colloquial use of French or German. That this might lead to potentially serious problems clearly did not occur to them. Problems such as the Commander in Chief of the BEF in France and Flanders, Sir Douglas Haig, not properly understanding discussions with his counterpart, Gen. Joffre, about the timing of the start of the Battle of the *Somme*. And this, barely four weeks before the offensive began.

In all, their conclusion was that the Sandhurst examinations were unsuited to the needs of the budding officer and, therefore, to the needs of the Army and Sandhurst was failing its cadets, its Army and, thereby, the country. Unsurprisingly, voices were raised to suggest it be closed.

After the publication of the report in June a debate on Military Education was held in the House of Lords on 17th July 1902 at the instigation of a Liberal Peer, the 2nd Baron Monkswell. His concern was that military education was 'worse than ever'. He quoted an unidentified 'Army coach' (Miller Maguire?) as saying:

> "…that there is no military training worthy of the name at Aldershot or at any other station; that the ordinary general education of officers is going from bad to worse, and that it is a public scandal that young officers sent to India have to be taught arithmetic by the regimental schoolmasters… I have met with men not Pedants nor particularly addicted to culture who have spoken in contemptuous terms of officers in the Army because they are so extremely ignorant. In this connection I should like to say that the chief complaint on the score of education, which is repeated over and over again in the evidence – and it is an extremely important one from a military point of view – is that a very large number of officers are unable to write an intelligent report."

The Earl of Cork opined that 'Many of them cannot even write a letter'[i]. Agreeing, Monkswell further commented that, with the great expansion of the

---

[i] There appears to have been a similar problem in the French Army but, worryingly, this applied to its higher ranks. In 1910, Gen. Alexandre Percin, a member of the *Conseil supérieur de la guerre*, was commissioned to conduct an inspection during which he noted: 'the training of the senior officers left much to be desired. At the

modern battlefield over which a commanding general could no longer keep a direct and personal eye, it was now 'absolutely necessary' officers:

"...should have sufficient powers of observation and be sufficiently intelligent and sufficiently master of the English language to write a report that can be understood by those to whom it is sent."

Which statement, unchallenged by his noble colleagues, suggests this was widely recognised as not being the case and the reason for this was:

"...there is absolutely no incentive to learning at Sandhurst... (and) having no incentive to learn, (officers) join more ignorant than they ought to be, and that when they are officers they have no inducement to keep up even the little knowledge they ever possessed."

The reasons for all of this were to be found in paragraph 93 of the Akers-Douglas committee report:

"The Committee regret to report that the general condition of education at the Royal Military College is far from satisfactory. In the first place, the cadets cannot be expected to derive much benefit from their instruction at Sandhurst, when it is clearly established that they have absolutely no inducement to work. This inducement is not afforded by the number of marks necessary to qualify for a commission, nor by the fact that those who fail to reach the low qualifying standard demanded are excluded from the Army. Indeed, there is too much reason to fear that even those cadets who fail to attain this standard have been commissioned none the less."

Sir Ian Hamilton, a literate, well-educated and, on certain subjects, a surprisingly liberal man for a senior Army officer, when asked about the quality of the officer now joining the Army told the committee:

"We want men of broader and better education."

Young officers were, he suggested, physically but not intellectually acceptable. Hamilton had more to say, however, and this reflected ill on the current crop of junior officers, their priorities and the regimental ethos and culture. When asked whether they displayed any great keenness for the profession he replied:

"No, it is not the correct 'form'; the spirit and form is rather not to have keenness... The idea is ... to do as little as they possibly can."

He went on to compare unfavourably the lack of keenness of the young Sandhurst cadets and Regular Army officer with the enthusiasm and interest of the Volunteers and Yeomanry, giving as an example an anecdote from the

---

manoeuvres, the orders were poorly given. The missions were poorly defined, sometimes not indicated at all. In these orders, there were improper terms, the meaning of which could give rise to different interpretations. It lacked essential details, such as the designation of the leader to whom a troop was to be subordinated, or that of the troops placed at the disposal of a leader for a specific mission. Out of the more than 500 orders that I collected, there were not 50 that were beyond reproach; there were more than 50 unintelligible.' [*Source*: Percin, Gen. A, *Le massacre de notre Infanterie*, 1921, page 201-2].

commandant at the Hythe School of Musketry (then Lt. Col. R L A Pennington) that the latter officers would:

> "…crowd round him and argue and dispute on points, and show the very greatest interest; whereas, on the other hand, Sandhurst boys who had been there did not at all display this interest, and the young officers in the regular Army were chiefly concerned in thinking very much of when the afternoon train went up to London."

Sir Evelyn Wood, quoted earlier, expressed himself 'absolutely dissatisfied' with the current state of education of young officers. These concerns were related to all stages of an officer's education with their schools also coming in for harsh criticism. There, too much emphasis was placed on sport and too little on intellectual development. Boys left their schools physically fit but academically unsuited to the professional, technical, and tactical demands of an Army officer's life. On the other hand, they were well prepared to play polo, cricket and rugby, a fact noted by several European commentators who suspected British officers to be more interested in sport than in war.

Col. Lonsdale Augustus Hale, a veteran of the Zulu War, suggested:

> "There is no incentive to the boy at Sandhurst to work, absolutely no incentive of any kind whatever."

Perhaps most damning of all was the observation made an Army 'crammer', Lt. Col. S Moores, when he suggested the fault lay not only with the young officer but with his superiors too. According to Moores, their excuses for their military failings were that they had:

> "…never looked at a military work or at the subjects since (they) joined the regular Army so many years ago; (they had) forgotten all the military subjects (they) knew on joining; no person (had) ever encouraged (them) to keep up (their) knowledge of the subjects, and, in fact, if (they) were to read or talk about reconnaissance, or field work, or strategy, or military history, the senior officers would not be pleased with (them), so (they) fell into the groove of doing only what the others did, which generally was playing billiards or cards, or smoking cigarettes or reading, or talking in the mess or quarters, for some hours daily when not on parade or at the orderly room."

The committee, according to Monkswell, had come to the extraordinary conclusion that the mass of the junior officers of the Army in 1901-2 not only lacked 'technical knowledge and skill' but also lacked the 'wish to study the science and master the art of their profession'.

It is disquieting to think that, fifteen years later, many of the young men so described would be up-and-coming officers in the BEF while their seniors, who had been through the same establishments offering an even worse quality of education, were commanding Brigades, Divisions, Corps, Armies and even the British Expeditionary Force.

In the Lords' debate Lord Monkswell went on to point the finger of blame for this sorry state of affairs squarely at the Conservative administration of Robert Arthur Talbot Gascoyne-Cecil, the 3rd Marquess of Salisbury, in power since 1895

and re-elected in 1900. Monkswell identified several key Government decisions which he believed undermined standards within the officer class of the Army:
- The 10% reduction in the required qualifying marks for entry into the Militia introduced in 1898;
- The reductions since 1895 in extra payments made to officers proficient in foreign languages;
- The abolition of the position of Director General of Military Education, a post which had existed for the 30 years since its establishment under the Dufferin Commission as part of the Caldwell Reforms, but which function was now relocated into the Military Secretary's Department and the position downgraded to the Assistant Military Secretary for Education; and
- The reduction in 1899 in the length of the officer cadet's training time at Sandhurst from 18 down to 12 months.

Of course, this latter point in part reflected the sudden need for new officers occasioned by the outbreak of the South African War.

The Government, as governments do, was having little or none of it. Replying to the debate, Lord Lansdowne, Secretary of State for Foreign Affairs but until 1900 and thus including the opening disastrous months of the war against the Boers, Secretary of State for War, suggested that if the material entering Sandhurst was poor then the producers of that material, i.e. the public schools, should look to themselves to rectify the problem. One of the critical contributors during the debate was the Lord Bishop of Hereford, the Liberal John Percival, previously the first headmaster of Clifton College, the President of Trinity College, and then headmaster at Rugby. For Lansdowne, a practised political passer of bucks, the Bishop and such as his schools were the scapegoats:

> "If the best lads we can get from the public schools are not good enough for us, that suggests to my mind the idea that there is something not quite right with the education given in the public schools themselves; and I trust that the learned headmasters who have given us so much valuable and admirable advice, which we shall take to heart, will turn their eyes towards matters nearer home, and consider whether they cannot do something in their own schools to bring up a race of lads better grounded for the great profession of arms."

But Lansdowne accepted another point: the process of continuous education once the officer entered the Army was almost entirely lacking and this was the key issue to be addressed by any reforms resulting from the Akers-Douglas inquiry.

THE *'MILITARY TRAINING OF OFFICERS'* after joining their unit was dealt with in Part III. According to *The Times*, it was 'a strongly worded condemnation of the present system'[48], and described as 'most unsatisfactory'.[49] The report declared:

> "The witnesses are unanimous in stating that the junior officers are lamentably wanting in Military knowledge, and what is perhaps even worse, in the desire to acquire knowledge and in zeal for the Military art."[50]

The majority of the 87 commanding officers contacted by letter confirmed this opinion even though *King's Regulations*, as *The Times* pointed out, placed a responsibility on these same commanding officers to instruct officers in their professional studies. The situation was, however:

"As long as their officers are punctual on parade, correct in the performance of their duties, and conduct themselves according to the regimental standard of gentlemanly decorum, they are left very much to themselves."[51]

Left to themselves, most of these officers turned to the sports field for entertainment and edification. These officers, it was claimed, only sought to see 'how much polo they can play and how soon they can get out of their uniform'.[52] Or, as *The Times* asserted, the main concern of a young officer in life was 'to get the *maximum* amount of amusement with a *minimum* of work'.[53]

The committee blamed this 'deplorable' situation on three things: poor organisation, which left no working role for junior officers in a regiment; the fact there was no 'inducement to self-improvement'; and the absence of any significant practice 'in the field' by which the:

"... officer can learn how best to take advantage of the accidents of ground, or how troops should be actually disposed to attain a desired result."[54]

The report stated the entire situation was now so absurdly out of balance:

"... the promotion of indolent officers is as rapid as – and may be more so than – that of their more industrious comrades."[55]

For the committee, the regimental system was to blame. Currently all matters pertaining to the running of a regiment were in the hands of either the Colonel or the Adjutant leaving nothing else for more junior officers to do. The result, according to *The Times* was:

"However ambitious a young officer may be, his professional duties offer no outlet for any talent which he may possess... British officers have been criticised all through the war for neglecting to take the initiative and assume responsibility on an emergency but they owe their inability to do so to the peace system which... compels them during the best years of their lives to be always in the position of waiting for orders."[56]

Sir Evelyn Wood expressed the view that the problem of the education and training of officers also affected the 'Other Ranks' as the current system rendered military training 'absolutely impossible'.[57] Superior officers were, in theory, responsible for the training and education of their juniors with captains, again theoretically, in charge of improving their subalterns and so on down the chain of command. In practice, however, this proved impossible as:

"Under the existing system the officer rarely sees the men for whose military efficiency he is supposed to be responsible."[58]

Unless this dire situation could be changed, warned the committee, then:

"... the training of the officer in the art of war must be mainly theoretical, with the inevitable result that in the opening stages of a campaign British troops must incur grave risks of disaster."[59]

The final recommendation of the committee and, as *The Times* described it, 'perhaps the most important of all' was all promotions should be by selection based on merit and not on simple seniority. As the report said:

> "It is useless to expect a spirit of keenness for self-improvement if promotion be accorded to the slothful and unintelligent and if the diligent and quick-witted find that they gain nothing by those qualities but are likely to be left behind by those possessing connexions (*sic*) and interest."[60]

In this respect, it was urgently necessary to reform the system of examinations by which officers were promoted. There were two examinations, the first known as '*A & B*' dealt with drill and 'interior economy' and the second, '*C, D and G*', covered military law, tactics, topography, engineering, organisation, and equipment. '*A & B*' was widely regarded as a joke. Its 'futility', according to the report, was 'notorious'.[61] The Board which oversaw and marked the examination was drawn from local officers in the District in which the examinee served and 'very possibly' belonged to the same regiment. In these circumstances, suggested the committee, it was unlikely these examining officers:

> "... would err on the side of severity and (would) probably frame such questions as the candidate may be expected to answer without more than superficial knowledge of the subject."[62]

The committee was not prepared to accept the continuation of a system so open to manipulation and abuse. Instead, they recommended COs, 'the officer responsible for the military training and efficiency of his officers', should put forward officers fit for promotion, even to the extent of seeking to promote a junior but more suitable officer over the head of his senior in years.

As to the second exam, '*C, D and G*', the committee stated it 'unduly exalted' theory 'at the expense of practice' but, as this was a written exam, this was inevitable.[63] As a result, this exam was not:

> "... a test of the candidate's real ability, but of his power to commit to memory and reproduce on paper facts from the text books."[64]

In fact, this exams' inadequacy had increased in recent times by the removal of the one practical element, a supervised sketch of an unknown piece of countryside. In general terms, therefore, the examination for promotion of officers in the practical and technical aspects of their profession were weak, impractical, and designed to benefit the assiduous 'crammer' of facts and figures. Practical soldiering in the field and in command was simply not tested.

RETURNING TO THE STATE OF EDUCATION of officers it is important to bear in mind that the Akers-Douglas committee's findings described the problems of an institution through which the majority of senior officers of the wartime BEF passed when the system was failing. In these circumstances, it makes little difference where in the rankings of any one year's candidates a particular cadet passed out when judging their fundamental qualities prior to this date. This was especially the case as it seems the position in which cadets passed out was based not just on their performance during their time at Sandhurst but on their marks in the initial examination for which the more one crammed the better one did.

The Letters Page of *The Times* was busy for some weeks after the report's publication, with correspondents voicing support for, or ire at, the members of the committee. One letter in the edition of 28th June 1902 was remarkable in its frankness about the nature of both Sandhurst and Militia officer candidates. Its author was George Minchin, the professor of Applied Mathematics at the Royal Indian Engineering College[i] at Cooper's Hill near Egham, Surrey. Minchin examined numerous officer candidates for the Admiralty, Woolwich, Sandhurst, and the Militia. His view was the Admiralty candidates were the best, closely followed by those for the RMA, Woolwich. His views about the Sandhurst and Militia candidates were distinctly less favourable:

"… of a large number of the Sandhurst candidates I could say only that the time which they had devoted to mathematics was utterly wasted. The Militia candidates were of a still lower type; and, from what I observed as regards spelling, composition, and an intelligent conception of the work before them I can appreciate the severe strictures of the committee on the literary incapacity of a very considerable number of military officers."[65]

Not only was the average Woolwich student better educated, the general training provided by the Academy was of a higher standard than at Sandhurst and there was more of it. The course at the RMA lasted two years, after which a newly commissioned Royal Engineer spent another two years at Chatham and an artilleryman two years at Shoeburyness. Clearly, their tasks in the Army were more scientific and/or technical and this longer instruction and training was appropriate but, as previously mentioned, prior to the end of the South African War, courses at Sandhurst appear neither to have stretched the intelligent nor to have taught the slackers or the duffers much either.

Amongst the graduates of Woolwich there was a hierarchy of preference when it came to which part of the Army was their favoured final berth. The Engineers paid more which was a simple attraction to many. The Royal Horse Artillery was the more flamboyant and prestigious home for the gunner who could afford the additional costs, whilst the Royal Field Artillery was an intermediate 'safe haven'. The 'poor boys' were the officers of the Royal Garrison Artillery, often sent to far flung parts of the Empire where little fun was to be had but where at least the costs were low. Ironically, when it finally came to the war, it was the officers of this latter 'Cinderella' arm whose job of killing the enemy and destroying his guns and fortifications became the most important of any on the Western Front.

EVEN AFTER THE DAMNING OF SANDHURST in Akers-Douglas's report it is clear standards did not rise quickly. Giving evidence to the Committee in 1901 Maj. Harold Goodeve Ruggles-Brise, Grenadier Guards and Brigade Major of the Home District, expressed trenchant views on the intellectual capabilities of a 'large percentage' of new officers, describing them as 'Dull and stupid and idle'. When challenged as to the proportion he suggested some 25% of the intake fell into this

---

[i] A civil engineering school also known as ICE (Indian Civil Engineering) College. Opened, 1872, closed, 1906. In the 1870s Cooper's Hill boasted one of the best Rugby Union teams in the country and produced nine international players.

category and this did not vary whatever the source: Sandhurst or the Militia.[66]

According to Col. Gerald Charles Kitson, appointed commandant of the College in 1902 and a graduate in 1875, every year a third of the intake might be described as 'intellectually challenged'. His actual words were:

> "… the standard of the last 60 is lamentably low. The Company Officers are constantly complaining to me of the crass stupidity of so many of their cadets."[67]

Kitson was no dullard. He was educated at Winchester and the RMC and commissioned into the 1st Regiment of Foot (later the Royal Scots) before transferring into the KRRC. He spent sixteen years in India in various staff appointments before, in 1896, becoming commandant of the Royal Military College of Canada at Kingston, Ontario, established some twenty years earlier. In a relatively short period, the RMC at Kingston became another military school desperately in need of reform and Kitson disposed of a high proportion of the staff and reduced the duration of the course from four to three years. Four years later he moved south to become the British Military *Attaché* in Washington before being appointed Commandant at Sandhurst in 1902 remaining there until 1907.

He was clearly not impressed by what he saw, stating in no uncertain terms 'Sandhurst wants waking up'.[68] As it stood, Sandhurst was not a place for the training and development of the brightest and the best hoping to become high flyers in the British Military establishment, but rather a finishing school for the sons of the upper classes and a continuation of their lives at their respective Public Schools of fagging, flogging and sports. A commission in, hopefully, a fashionable regiment would give lustre to the prospects of even the dimmest off-spring and what did it matter if he could not shoot straight (there was no instruction in musketry), ride a horse (a prospective cavalrymen saw a horse for less than an hour a week) or clean their rifle (a job undertaken by their servants). Nor was there previously any attempt made to judge a cadet's aptitude to command men.[69] One of Kitson's key recommendations when he took over at Sandhurst was that cadets must spend at least a term as an NCO and those who proved ineffectual in this role were either to be removed from the College or made subject to additional training. His efforts to raise the bar of the entrance examination and raise the pass mark in the final examination failed, however, and in 1904 Kitson was ordered to add marks to the results of this latter exam by which means it was ensured nearly every cadet, however stupid or lazy, passed.

Nor was Sandhurst especially good at identifying the potential military highflyer. As Bowman and Connelly point out in *'The Edwardian Army'*, a trio of cadets who passed out of Sandhurst in the years between the South African War and the Great War but then went on to achieve high rank and military success in World War Two – Montgomery, Alexander, and O'Connor – were all strangely anonymous at the RMC, with their results being moderate to average at best.[70]

Recollections of cadets' time at either of these two military establishments suggests that, for those with the budget and an appetite for sports, it was a pleasant diversion between leaving school and becoming a lowly subaltern. For many it came as a release from the greater discipline experienced at their Public School. As to teaching the young men about command, man management, and what it was to lead a company of men in battle it was, for some of those alive and able to write their memoirs, so much time wasted[i].

Indeed, a former cadet at Woolwich, Lieutenant General Frederick Morgan, later wrote about the 'futile absurdity' of the studies there[ii].[71] And the future Lord Ismay described Sandhurst as 'pleasant enough' but noted critically 'man management and the art of command found no place in the syllabus'.

AND THEN THERE WAS THE PROBLEM OF MONEY, especially in the *élite* regiments of the Army – the Guards and the cavalry. Whilst social class, geography, education, and connections were crucial determinants in accessing a commission and going on to higher rank (see page 409), underpinning all the issues which dictated the recruitment and training of officers was the availability of large amounts of cold, hard cash.

Training and living as an officer, especially in certain *élite* infantry and cavalry regiments, was no cheap affair. Just to become an officer was expensive. Fees at Sandhurst and Woolwich were high, except for the sons of an Army officer who received an 85% discount on the £150 a year fees (for estimates of current equivalent values see footnotes page 393). On joining a regiment some form of private income was a necessity as pay was not high but expenses could be. It was for this reason service in the Indian Army was popular, especially amongst the impecunious, as rates of pay were much higher although, as officers discovered on their arrival, expenses too were high[iii].

---

[i] It was not always thus. In 1862, with cadets beset by numerous petty rules and regulations, a battalion mutinied and occupied a training fortification for three days. Only the intervention of the CinC, HRH The Duke of Cambridge, brought an end to the disturbances. The RMC's reputation was so poor cadets regularly appeared in court accused of drunkenness and affray [*Source: The History of RMA Sandhurst*, MoD, 2009, page 3]. Further serious problems occurred in 1864 [*Source: The British Officer: Leading the Army from 1660 to the present*, Pearson Education Ltd., 2006]. There were complaints about the mutinous conduct of Woolwich cadets in a debate in the Commons on the Army Estimates on 13th March 1862 [*Source: Hansard*, Vol. 165, pages 1456-81].

[ii] Lt. Gen. Sir Frederick Edgworth Morgan KCB, RA, born 1894. Clifton College and the RMA, Woolwich, 1912. Commissioned, 41st Battery, 42nd Brigade, RFA, 1913. 84th Battery, 11th Brigade, RFA, India. Western Front, 3rd (Lahore) Division, October 1914. Staff Captain, 42nd (East Lancashire) Division, 1917. Post-war, Staff College, Quetta. War Office, then GSO1, 3rd Division, 1938. Commanded 1st Support Group, 1st Armoured Division, BEF, 1939. Involved in the planning of the Normandy invasion as part of COSSAC and then SHAEF as one the Deputy Chiefs of Staff. After the war he was involved with United Nations Relief and Rehabilitation Administration and later in the development of British nuclear weapons. He died in 1967.

[iii] The situation was, in some ways, worse in the French Army. Leonard Smith quotes a 1913 figure for the living costs and pay of a married lieutenant with a child living in unfashionable Verdun. Domestic and professional costs came to c. 4,800 *francs* per annum with pay just under 3,400 *francs*. Officers needed a CO's approval before getting married and, up to 1900, the prospective wife had to bring with her a dowry of 1,300 *francs* per annum. Though abolished in principle, the practice was neither stopped nor could be avoided. Promotion in France, therefore, depended not only on having no

Even if, since Cardwell's reforms, commissions could no longer be bought and sold[i], money, or the lack of it, still played a crucial role in a young man's entry, and progress through, the Army. Because of this, little changed in the social make-up of the officer class of the Army. An officer might no longer need to buy a commission but, if unable to purchase a decent hunter and a nippy polo pony, or unable to afford a certain standard of expenditure in the Mess, his prospects of either entering, or surviving, in certain regiments were minimal.

That money, status and living up to regimental etiquette were embedded in the culture of the Army was highlighted by a series of scandals, the first involving a young Grenadier Guards' lieutenant in 1903. Despite all the commissions and committees, and bold statements in the House of Commons and the Lords about reform and promotion based on talent and ability, matters were slow to change. Entrenched practices held back those unable, or reluctant, to conform to the standards of behaviour enforced by the backwards looking majority.

This first affair resounded across the Empire and beyond[ii]. It involved outrageous and barbaric practices within the senior infantry regiment of the British Army, the 1st Battalion, the Grenadier Guards. These were exposed by Rear Admiral Basil Edward Cochrane in a letter to *The Times* on 10th February 1903. Cochrane dropped a bombshell into the heart of the military establishment. His accusation was that the CO of the 1st Grenadier Guards, the experienced and well-connected Lt. Col. David Kinloch, either condoned, or failed to stop, the flogging of junior subalterns by their seniors as punishment for minor infringements of either military practice or regimental etiquette. These floggings, of between six and forty strokes on the bare backs of the officers, were administered after the young men were accused and judged at unofficial, 'kangaroo' courts martial[iii].

The story involved the treatment of Rear Admiral Cochrane's nephew (later named in the Commons by St John Brodrick as Mr John Henry Leveson-Gower[iv]).

---

post-Dreyfusian religious or political black marks against their name but also on the availability of personal, family or spousal cash [*Source:* Smith, L V. *Between Mutiny and Obedience: The Case of the French Fifth Infantry Division during World War I*, Princeton Legacy Library, 1994, footnotes pages 24-5].

[i] Purchase of commissions (up to Col.) in the infantry and cavalry was abolished by Royal Warrant in 1871. Promotion in the artillery and engineers were by seniority. A Royal Warrant was used rather than an Act of Parliament as it was probable vested interests in the Lords would have blocked any such legislation [*Source:* Fortescue, Sir J W, *The History of the British Army*, Vol. XIII, MacMillan, 1899, page 550].

[ii] It was, for example, reported in the *New York Times* on 11th and 12th February 1903 and in the *Chicago Tribune* the week before.

[iii] Such 'courts' were known of, but it was the non-military nature of the infringements and the severity of the punishments which lay at the root of the controversy. Lord Esher, writing on 10th March 1900 to his son Maurice (a Coldstream Guard's officer), recorded three instances of young Guards' officers being similarly treated though one case was for drunkenness and another involved behaviour of a degree Esher described as 'hopelessly unpardonable' [Brett., op. cit., page 259].

[iv] He was the son of John Edward Leveson-Gower and his second wife, Katherine Elizabeth Cochrane, daughter of Basil Edward Arthur Cochrane and Sally Caroline

Leveson-Gower resigned his commission because of the treatment meted out to him but Cochrane broadened his accusations to reference the treatment of other young officers, one of whom was brought to a state of collapse after being punished with forty strokes of the cane on his back. Leveson-Gower's 'crimes' were an error of protocol involving being granted leave and a disagreement over the completion of a report whilst on picket duty. According to the *Daily Express*, other young officers thought to have been similarly abused for failing 'to enter into any of the amusements and sports of the regiment' were the Master of Belhaven, and Marquis of Douro, the son of the then Duke of Wellington.

Eventually, the case arrived on the desk of Lord Roberts, the Commander in Chief, and his unsurprising judgement was that the flogging of subalterns was totally unacceptable and the battalion commander, Kinloch, derelict in his duty. He was immediately put on half pay and removed from command[i]. The issue rumbled on, with others writing to *The Times* both for and against Cochrane's initial complaint and Roberts' summary action. The affair reached the Lords and, eventually, was raised in the Commons on 11th March 1903 by Kinloch's brother-in-law (and the Conservative MP for Macclesfield) William Bromley-Davenport. A motion was proposed in support of Kinloch which was then soundly defeated after St John Brodrick spoke at length. During the month or so of argument and debate on the issue, other similar problems emerged, amongst them being one in which other subalterns were threatened with a thrashing unless they rode in the Grenadier Guards' drag hunt at Windsor. This latter case centred on the issue of the costs of being a member of an *élite* regiment of the Army and the attitudes of those officers who could afford to primp and play and those who came to soldier. It showed that, despite concerns raised by Robertson and Wyndham about the costs of being an Army officer in 1900 (see page 393), nothing much changed.

On the main issue of the beating of subalterns, however, other letters to *The Times* suggested the practices exposed within the Grenadier Guards were not only more widespread than imagined but also, in certain circles, condoned by higher authority. One correspondent, writing under the soubriquet of '*A Late Commanding Officer*', suggested that, had Col. Kinloch attempted to stamp out the abuse, he would have found himself out on his ear just as surely as he was after Lord Roberts learned of the problem:

> "In the Guards and in certain cavalry regiments", he wrote, "it would be difficult or impossible to interfere, and any determined action on the part of a colonel might lead only to his own removal".

FitzGerald. Leveson-Gower joined the Grenadier Guards from the 1st Volunteer Bn., Princess Charlotte of Wales's (Royal Berkshire) Regt., on 20th March 1901. He joined the 1st King's African Rifles in May 1903. He died in 1912 aged 32.

[i] Lt. Col., later Brig. Gen., David A Kinloch was reinstated after Roberts ceased to be CinC. Promoted Colonel he went on retired pay and was given command of 6th Brigade of 2nd London Division, Territorial Force, between 1908 and 1912. In 1912 he succeeded his father to the Baronetcy of Nova Scotia. He was given command of 70th Brigade of 23rd Division on the formation of this New Army division in the autumn of 1914. He was replaced in September 1915. He died in 1944.

Another letter writer, signing himself *'Witness'*, hoped Roberts's actions might 'put an end to a system which prevails in many regiments' and which, over the years, resulted in the 'virtual expulsion' of 'numerous' young officer who attempted to resist these arbitrary punishments:

> "What has always seemed to me intolerable is the fact that military officers practically claim a right to make regimental life intolerable for new officers whom at first sight they happen to dislike."[72]

The story also raised issues of a more fundamental nature concerning the Army. An editorial in *The Times* on 14th February 1903, supporting Lord Roberts in his sacking of Kinloch, reminded readers of the basic principle:

> "… the Army, for which the people of this country pay some thirty millions a year, belongs to the people of this country and not to its officers. Practical denial of this principle is unfortunately widely prevalent, notwithstanding the abolition of purchase. This country pays its thirty millions, more or less cheerfully, because it wants an efficient fighting machine to do its work in time of war. It has not yet obtained such a machine, and it never will obtain it so long as countenance is given to the pernicious theory that the Army belongs to the officers, and that they, in consequence, have vested rights in their appointments. Imperfect as our military arrangements are in practice, no one will, in theory, dispute that it is entirely with the competence of the Commander in Chief, at any time, to remove or supersede any officer, upon no other ground that he believes that officer's work can be better done by another."[73]

Clearly, not much had changed since an editorial in *The Times* of 14th February 1900 calling for the nation rather than its officers to be master of the Army. Nor did it change in the future if two other examples are any indicator.

In March 1906, an inquiry was opened at Aldershot into the 'ragging' of a new officer after an unofficial court-martial conducted by his peers in the Scots Guards. The victim was 2nd Lt. Arthur Robert Windsor Stuart Clark-Kennedy who, on returning from sick leave (he had contracted Scabies), was, at the colonel's suggestion, brought before a gathering of junior officers where he was accused of being generally dirty and afflicted by 'the itch'[i]. Against the Colonel's understanding of the disciplinary element of the resulting proceedings, Clark-Kennedy was made to strip, had cold water poured over him as well as a mixture of what seems to have been *'Keating's Bug Powder'* and motor oil, had the contents of his pillow emptied over him and jam smeared over his head. When the officers concerned later attempted to enter his room where was cleaning himself up, he escaped through a window wearing his pyjamas and an overcoat.

Clark-Kennedy joined the regiment in August 1905 from the Militia (4th West Yorkshire Regt.) but then found the expense of being a Guards' officer too much (his father was giving him £500 per annum) and put in his papers in January.

---

[i] Scabies, also known as the Seven Year Itch, is a contagious skin infestation caused by the mite *Sarcoptes scabiei*. It can be spread by prolonged contact with the skin of one already infected such as might occur during sex.

Though denied, there is some suggestion his failure to 'live up' to the financial and social standards of the regiment were in some way involved in what can only be described as an assault by nearly a dozen of his colleagues. As part of the ensuing investigation, the senior subaltern, Lt C F P Hamilton, was arrested and another ten officers involved called to give evidence. Oddly enough, the medical evidence given from outside the regiment about the officer's cleanliness and general health unanimously contradicted that given by the Surgeon Major of the Brigade of Guards and a regimental nurse. Suggestions his brother officers wanted him out of the regiment for non-medical reasons were, of course, strenuously denied even though Lord Robert Cecil, representing the officers, made it clear it was possible to drive out an officer such as Clark-Kennedy 'by perfectly legal means'. Clark-Kennedy resigned his commission on 19th May 1906 after being declared bankrupt. He later served in the war in the RNAS and the RFC and, by 1919, was a Captain in the RAF and a member of the Royal Aero Club.[74]

Nor was this last of such cases. The following year yet another Court of Inquiry was convened, this time at Chelsea Barracks, to investigate the complaints of Lt. Henry Charles Woods, 2nd Grenadier Guards[i]. Woods was an Old Harrovian. He passed out of Sandhurst 17th in a class of 120 or so candidates and was commissioned into the Grenadier Guards in August 1900, joining the 1st Battalion at Windsor.[75] Woods then served in the Army for seven years and was, according to *The Times*, a man 'of a studious disposition and of temperate habits'. And yet these two characteristics seem to have been enough to damn him in the eyes of his more 'sporting' fellows as he was hounded out of the Army by the end of 1907.

The Court of Inquiry was the culmination of a saga of antagonism towards Woods conducted by brother officers and superiors during which he resisted several attempts at forcing him to 'hand in his papers', i.e. resign his commission. The result was a high-profile hearing which was widely reported in the press, and which involved some of the leading legal and political minds in the country. His case was presented by two distinguished King's Counsels, Rufus Isaacs, MP[ii], and

---

[i] Henry Charles Woods (1881-1939) travelled in the Balkans and Middle East, acting as a correspondent for several newspapers including *The Times* in 1911. He covered the 1st Balkans War for the *Evening News*, becoming their Military and Diplomatic Correspondent, 1914-5. In October 1916 he contested the Winchester by-election as an Independent after the MP, Lt. Col. the Hon. Guy Victor Baring, 1st Coldstream Guards, was killed on 16th September, 1916, on the *Somme* (Result: Hon. D G Carnegie (Con) 1,218, H C Woods (Ind) 473). Lecturer at the Lowell Institute in Boston, 1917–18. Special correspondent, *Daily Telegraph* 1927-8. Fellow, Royal Geographical Society, 1905-1939. He was the author of five books such as *The Cradle of War: The Near East and Pan-Germanism*, *The Danger Zone of Europe* and *War and Diplomacy on the Balkans*. Twenty-three volumes of his diaries and notebooks are held by the National Archives.
[ii] Rufus Daniel Isaacs, 1st Marquess of Reading, GCB, GCSI, GCIE, GCVO, PC, KC, Liberal MP for Reading (1904-13). He served as both Solicitor General and Attorney-General and represented the Board of Trade in the *Titanic* inquiry. Lord Chief Justice in 1913, the Ambassador to the USA in 1918, Viceroy of India in 1921 and, briefly in 1931, Foreign Secretary in Ramsey Macdonald's National government.

Samuel Thomas Evans MP[i], and a certain Raymond Asquith[ii]. Their evidence commenced with the opinion of the then Governor and Commandant of Sandhurst, Lt. Gen. Markham, on the 19-year-old officer when he left the RMC. He described him as being:

> "… of exemplary character, of good ability, hardworking, steady, plodding, very good disposition, quiet, and popular, adding 'Does his best and will make a good officer'."

In 1901 Woods was recommended to Col. Henderson, then working on the official history of the South African War, 'as a young officer who could be trusted with confidential work'. Henderson was sufficiently impressed to involve him in his efforts which Woods combined with his regimental duties. A Gen. Trotter, the GOC of the District, believed Woods an officer 'anxious to get on'. The previously mentioned Col. Kinloch described him as 'fairly smart in performing his duties' and as a man of tact, judgement and self-reliance, keen to join in the various instruction classes and, overall, fit for promotion. There was a 'but', however, which was 'he did not mix with others of his rank as much as might be desired'.

Woods then moved to London where he commanded 150 men. No criticisms were made of his conduct or abilities. In early 1901, he went to South Africa where he commanded detachments holding blockhouses being constructed as part of the process of corralling the Boers on the *veldt*. Again, there were no complaints about his performance. His colonel (and later Brig. Gen.) Eyre Macdonnell Stewart Crabbe, CB, described him as 'an officer very anxious to do his work satisfactorily'. Other reports by superior officers stated the retention of Woods in the army was 'in every respect desirable and likely to be advantageous to the Army'. After a request to serve in Somaliland was turned down, Woods was sent to Aldershot where he served under Col. Gordon Gilmour in the 2nd Grenadier Guards. Woods served under Gilmour for longer than any other CO and the reports his superior made on the young lieutenant were uniformly good: he was 'fit in every respect for his present rank and employment; he was a very painstaking and hardworking officer who knew his drill well and was very energetic and keen'. Indeed, there were no adverse reports on Woods until March 1907.

The complaints though started on 21st July 1904. Although it was accepted Woods subscribed to all the regimental institutions, some officers objected to the fact he did not ride with the regimental 'drag', an echo of one of the complaints made in the Leveson-Gower case the previous year. A debate ensued with the Adjutant, Capt. Humphrey St. Leger Stucley[iii], after which Woods was ejected

---

[i] Sir Samuel Thomas Evans, GCB, PC, QC, Liberal MP for Mid Glamorgan (1890-1910). He was Solicitor General in 1908-1910 and was succeeded by Rufus Isaacs.

[ii] Raymond Asquith was a barrister and eldest son of Herbert Asquith. He joined the Queen's Westminster Rifles in December 1914 before, ironically, being transferred to the 3rd Grenadier Guards in 1915. Fatally wounded on 15th September 1916 during an attack on Ginchy, he is buried in Guillemont Road Cemetery, Plot I. Row B. Grave 3.

[iii] Capt., later Maj., Humphrey St. Leger Stucley, son of Sir George Stucley, 1st Baronet of Moreton. He was killed on 29th October 1914 commanding the King's Company, 1st Grenadier Guards. He is buried in Zantvoorde British Cemetery, grave VI. C. 3.

from the room by two other officers. Woods returned via the window at which point Stucley told him he was not fit to be in the regiment, using his temporary detachment to the 3rd Battalion as an excuse to say no-one in the regiment would have him. It was 'suggested', under the threat life would be 'made unpleasant for him', he should go to Uganda or join a Line regiment. Col. Gilmour, however, was having none of it and, for three months, Woods was given command of a company during which time his conduct drew no complaints from his superiors.

In October Woods took his promotion examinations for the rank of Captain, passing well. In early 1905, he attended the Hythe Musketry course and Col. Gilmour recommended him for employment as an ADC. Whilst on leave Woods prepared a report which was deemed 'of considerable service' by the Director of Military Intelligence. Woods then applied for the post of Military Vice-Consul, attracting a glowing reference from Maj. Gen. James Grierson and, in July 1906, he applied to attend the Staff College. This application required a certificate from his commanding officer stating he was suitable either to be an Adjutant or to serve on the CO's staff. It was now Major, later Lt. Col., the Hon. William Edwin Cavendish[i], soon to be the new CO of the 2nd Battalion, raised some concerns, even though he admitted he had no military complaint to raise against him.

Woods again went travelling, this time with a more specific location in mind. An attack on the Gallipoli peninsula to gain access to the Black Sea was already an item on the military agenda, with Jackie Fisher at the Admiralty, amongst others, looking at options either for forcing the Dardanelles or for a landing somewhere along the Aegean coast. Woods was invited by the British military *attaché* in Constantinople to investigate landing places as part of a shooting party and Woods obliged by reconnoitring the area between Eceabat on the Narrows side round to Gaba Tepe on the Aegean shore. Woods's report was sent on to Naval Intelligence which promptly proceeded to mislay it.[76] As Woods stated that, without complete surprise, any possible landing around Gaba Tepe (near where the ANZAC troops landed in 1915) in an effort to take the forts overlooking the Dardanelles from the rear would be stopped short of the hills behind the landing site it is, perhaps, doubly unfortunate Sir Ian Hamilton and his planners were not able to avail themselves of this report[ii]. Woods, though, had again shown his resourcefulness, intelligence and astute military mind, characteristics which now benefitted him not one whit mainly, it seems, because he did not play golf or choose to charge across the local farmland on horseback chasing some imaginary fox.

Matters came to a head in March 1907 when Woods went on company training with Nos 1 and 5 Companies under Maj. the Hon. John Gathorne-Hardy[iii]. Woods

---

[i] Lt. Col., later Brig. Gen., Hon. William Edwin Cavendish, MVO, son of the 2nd Baron Chesham.

[ii] With time on his hands after leaving the Guards, Woods published in 1908 a book entitled *Washed by Four Seas: An English Officer's Travels in the Near East* (T Fisher Unwin, 1908). Chapter Four, Part One, *The Defences of Constantinople* and Part Two, *The Dardanelles*, contain photographs of parts of the coast and the forts located there.

[iii] Maj., later Gen., the Hon. Sir John Francis Gathorne-Hardy, GCB, GCVO, CMG, DSO, Grenadier Guards. The son of the 2nd Earl of Cranbrook, he went to France in

unexpectedly found himself commanding No. 5 Company, his predecessor having handed in his papers. Furthermore, Woods had never previously met Gathorne-Hardy who had just returned from Camberley. Nonetheless, Gathorne-Hardy informed Woods he faced 'disappointment if he continued in the service' so dissatisfied was he in Woods's performance. On 15th March, there was a minor mutiny in No. 5 Company caused, it was alleged, by Gathorne-Hardy demanding more of the men than they thought reasonable. Woods appeared not to be involved nor was he asked to attend the court martial. Nonetheless, Cavendish, now in command, informed Woods he was unfit to command a company and a highly unfavourable report on him was to be submitted by Gathorne-Hardy in five days' time. Cavendish explained this was sufficient time within which Woods could send in his papers and leave the regiment. Gathorne-Hardy's report was, indeed, damning, finishing with the statement he saw 'no prospect of (Woods) ever becoming a satisfactory officer'. This opinion was endorsed by Col. Cavendish and Maj. Charles Edward Corkran[i] to whose company Woods was attached.

It was on this basis Woods asked for the Court of Inquiry. The reporting of the case went over seven editions of *The Times* (excluding letters). During evidence

---

1914 as GSO2 in Smith-Dorrien's II Corps, then GSO2, Second Army. 7th Division staff, March 1915 under Hubert Gough and then Thomas Capper. BGGS in Lord Cavan's XIV Corps, January 1916. To Italy as MGGS with Cavan in 1917, a fellow Grenadier Guard. Post-war, appointed Director of Military Training by Cavan who was then CIGS. Served in India, then Northern Command and Aldershot, 1933-1937. ADC to George V, Edward VIII, and George VI. He married Lady Isobel Constance Mary Stanley, daughter of Frederick Arthur Stanley, 16th Earl of Derby. His grandfather, Gathorne Gathorne-Hardy, 1st Earl of Cranbrook, was Secretary of State for War under Disraeli between 1874-8 and involved in the implementation of the Cardwell Army reforms. John Gathorne-Hardy died on 21st August 1949, aged 75.

Gathorne-Hardy was the brother-in-law of Cuthbert Headlam's wife Beatrice. Headlam served under Cavan and Gathorne-Hardy in 1916 and had a low opinion of the latter, writing: 'It is astonishing how universally loathed Gathorne-Hardy is. No-one has a good word for him. Apparently he is most unpleasant to work with' [*Source*: Beach J, ed. *The Military Papers of Sir Cuthbert Headlam*, Army Records Society, 2010, page 118]. Later, with a degree of *schadenfreude*, he describes how Gathorne-Hardy 'made a terrible mess' of the 1935 manoeuvres ruining any prospect of being appointed CIGS [*Source*: Ibid., page 299]. Just how much of a mess is clear from the opening paragraph of *The Times*' report: 'The Army manoeuvres ended late this afternoon, like most exercises, ahead of time. When they ended 2nd Corps (Westland) [Southern and Eastern Commands under Gen. Sir Cyril Deverell] had its somewhat larger opponent, 1st Corps (Eastland) [Aldershot Command under Gathorne-Hardy] in a highly uncomfortable position – penned into a narrow space with its right wing held and its left enveloped... the course of the operations formed a vivid demonstration of... exploiting finesse rather than of relying on strength' [*Source: Our Military Correspondent, End Of Army Manoeuvre, The Times*, 20th September, 1935, page 7].

[i] Maj. Gen. Sir Charles Corkran, KCVO, CB, CMG, commandant of Sandhurst in 1923, was the commander of the Brigade of Guards and GOC London District.

it emerged Woods, too, had been 'ragged' by two fellow officers but declined to take it further and the occasion of the argument with Capt. Stucley was based on an accusation he had withdrawn from participation in the Grenadier Guards' boat in the Brigade regatta at Maidenhead. It was further alleged Stucley claimed Woods was 'extremely unpopular' as he 'did not frequent the Guards' Club, did not play golf and did not go out with the Brigade draghounds'.

Despite the weight of evidence in favour of Woods, the opinions of two officers who barely knew him, Gathorne-Hardy and Corkran, counted heaviest and the Army Council, closing ranks, found against him and, in the process, criticised Col. Gordon Gilmour, the officer who knew Woods best, for not having pointed out earlier failings which Gilmour clearly did not perceive. Woods was told to resign and this he did, under protest, on Christmas Day 1907.

Woods's father, Col. William Woods, outraged by the outcome, distributed a pamphlet far and wide which included Rufus Isaac's address to the Court of Inquiry. A copy was sent to *The Times* with a covering letter which ended:

"… it will be a perilous thing for England if zealous, intelligent, high-charactered young officers are to be driven out the Army because they refuse to join in mere sports … useless to them as soldiers and likely to absorb time which might more profitably be devoted to the study of the military sciences."[77]

He also sent a letter to every MP writing:

"An Army in which intelligence is a curse, and games and the round of social life simply acceptable, would be, in Ruskin's fine phrase, 'a curse to itself and an opprobrium to the Empire.'"[78]

The issue did not go away. Woods took legal action against the Army Council which case was heard in the Court of Appeal on 15th June 1909 and dismissed two days later with the Law Lords saying it was a matter for Parliament. The matter still did not rest, with a Woods Re-instatement Committee pursuing candidates in the January 1910 General Election with demands they sign a pledge to have Lt. Woods brought back into the Army. The case clearly touched a sensitive nerve in Edwardian society which, after South Africa, was clearly more sensible to the shortcomings of its Army's younger officers and far less happy to see men of talent and dedication driven out of their profession because they took it too seriously.

What was made clear from the evidence gathered was that, in 1907, 'unpopular officers' were still the victims of 'ragging' by brother officers. This 'ragging' might be of a moderate or a more severe and daily nature depending on how unpopular an officer was within the mess. Furthermore, unpopularity seemed more to do with a failure to mix socially and participate in regimental sports than it did with military competence. It is interesting that, in Capt. Stucley's evidence, it was suggested Woods became more unpopular after being promoted.[79] A studious, hard-working officer whose explanation for his absence from the mess was the need to travel daily to London to attend foreign language lessons needed for an imminent examination, it seems his unpopularity might have had more to do with his devotion to learning his trade and a perception amongst his brother officers that, by such efforts, he was getting ahead of them in the promotion stakes, an attitude regarded as extremely bad form in the Edwardian Army. That this was still happening in 1907 suggests the rot of privilege and wealth still infected at least certain elements of the Army whose officers felt riding to hounds, golf, and polo more important than a proper military education.

On the day after the inquiry started (18th November 1907) Lord Esher confided in his diary his thoughts on the still lamentable state of education of Army officers and the still prevalent emphasis on sports and frivolity:

> "Politicians and others who are brought into contact with soldiers, notice the comparatively low standard of knowledge between the heads of the military profession and others: not in technique, but in general education. Men of fine natural abilities appear stunted. Exceptions there are, of course; but John Morley[i] and Knollys[ii], for example, are both struck by the comparative inferiority of our best Generals to men of equal standing in other professions, including the Navy…
>
> In the Army, a subaltern, during the first years of his life, and generally until he reaches middle-age, limits his efforts to acquiring such technical knowledge of his professions as can be absorbed between 9 and 1 daily. There is no inducement for him to educate himself, or to do more than he is obliged. Hence, during the ten most crucial years of his life, he acquires no habits of application, but devotes himself to sport, or sinks into indifference and idleness. Later on, when the responsibilities of the higher command begin to inspire prospective terror, an officer tries to make up for lost time, and regrets lost opportunities.
>
> No doubt some young officers read books, and improve their minds, but spasmodically, and without real incentive. A lad will think, for a week, that in order to be a General he must 'work at' strategy; so he will take real pains to master a campaign of Napoleon. The following week it strikes him that he cannot command armies until he is 40, and he falls asleep in the anteroom…"[80]

It is, therefore, of no surprise Woods failed to fit in with the culture of the Army's *élite*. It seems South Africa did little to change the atmosphere. Writing in 1899, William Cairnes, later the secretary of the Akers-Douglas committee, explained in his unintentionally hilarious book *Social Life in the British Army*:

> "… as soon as the name of the new subaltern appears in the (*London*) *Gazette*, the most anxious inquiries are made in the regiment as to whether he is a 'good sort', and likely to do the regiment credit. The lad who joins with a school reputation of being a fine cricketer or racket player is assured of a welcome which would possibly be denied to the lad who had passed at top of the list into the service."[81]

---

[i] John Morley (1838-1932), 1st Viscount Morley of Blackburn, OM, PC, Liberal MP for Newcastle upon Tyne 1883-95, Liberal MP for Montrose Burghs 1896-1908. Twice Chief Secretary for Ireland, twice Secretary of State for India, Lord President of the Council. Opposed the South African War and the Great War.

[ii] Francis Knollys, 1st Baron Knollys and later Viscount Knollys of Caversham, Private Secretary to Edward VII and George V from 1901 to 1913.

IF REGIMENTAL ETIQUETTE AND OBLIGATIONS lay close to the root of the Leveson-Gower and Woods cases, money, or its lack, was at the very heart of the matter in the cases itemised above. The issue was that officers in every cavalry regiment, the Horse Artillery, most of the Field Artillery, the Guards and many of the leading infantry regiments simply could not get by on their pay alone[i]. This was not because their professional costs were especially burdensome. Indeed, investment in their professional education was not something which bothered many officers unduly. It was in fulfilling non-military regimental commitments and participating in its sporting and social life that the true costs lay and this meant access to these more exalted and fashionable units was restricted to those with personal wealth or well-heeled families.

Concern at the failings of the South African War now exposed these elements of Army life to far greater scrutiny than before and the ensuing criticism was fierce. The problems within the ranks of officers had, however, been raised before, even as the shortcomings of many of them were being only too cruelly exposed on the *veldt* and in the hills of Natal.

On 13th February 1900, George Wyndham, the Tory MP for Dover and the Under Secretary of State for War, was 'enjoying' a somewhat torrid question time in the House when, in response to a backbencher's question, he touched upon the issue of the onerous costs involved in being an officer, especially in the cavalry:

"I think some effort should be made not to close the door of our cavalry to every man who does not enjoy an income of £150 a year[ii] in the one case

---

[i] A letter in *The Times* of 22nd March 1900 from '*AAH*' estimated a subaltern would make an annual loss of c. £20 a year (between £2,000 and £12,000 at current values depending on how you calculate these values. See footnote below) when his pay was set against the costs of his most basic mess bill (i.e. just food), and of his 'servant'. This left out: uniforms (i.e. ceremonial, working, mess and undress, estimated in a letter from a retired cavalry officer to *The Times* dated 11th March 1902 to cost c. £100), costs of moving and setting up barracks wherever he was sent as well as lighting and heating, wear and tear on equipment whilst on active service and manoeuvres, horse(s), stabling and forage, contributions to the running costs of the officers' and sergeants' mess, his drinks and smoking bills, sports, professional education, entertainment, etc., etc. [*Source: The Times*, 22nd March 1900, page 11]. As of 1912 a subaltern's daily rates of pay were: 6s 8d (Household Cavalry), 7s 8d (RHA), 6s 8d (Line Cavalry), 5s 7d (RFA/RGA/RE), 5s 3d (Guards/Infantry) [*Source: Whitaker's Almanac, 1912*, page 272]. An infantry subaltern therefore earned c. £96 a year.

[ii] There are problems about determining the current value of a sum of money from 1900. Based on the Retail Price Index £150 in 1900 is worth c. £15,000 at current prices. Other indices based on wages and income levels give figures of £55,000 and £91,000 respectively. If one takes the RPI-based figure and add the pay of a subaltern in the infantry (£96/annum) the figures suggest costs in pay and private income of a subaltern are the equivalent of £25,000 per year now. Hardly excessive. The pay of a 2nd Lt. is now 319 times greater than in 1900, however, which is a far larger multiplier than the 100 used as the RPI index for prices between 1900 and 2015. Based on a wages index, the current costs of pay plus private income needed is c.£90,000 per year and based on an income related index c. £150,000 per year. Given the concerns

and £500 in the other (Hear, hear). In view of this crisis it is nothing less than a scandal and a danger to the Empire that we cannot get young men into the cavalry unless their fathers or their friends are able to give them incomes to enable them to do so."[82]

Wyndham was responding to points raised by Edmund Robertson, Liberal MP for Dundee, who quoted a *Morning Leader*[i] article by the 'well known military expert', Mr Charles Williams, which estimated that, by the time the average officer attained the rank of Captain (reckoned to be on average ten years), he would have 'cost his relatives not far from £3,000 and in many cases much more'.[ii] Stating such costs denied opportunity to 'able bodied and able-minded young men' which meant the Army did not get 'the kind of officers wanted', Robertson went further:

> "The ideal British Army would be one which every young man physically, mentally and otherwise fitted should be encouraged to enter. From the time he entered it he should be able to support himself. Every kind of expensive amusement which, by custom, was now made obligatory on young officers in the Army should be stamped out with a firm hand. (Much laughter) Hon. Members laughed at this metaphor, and not at the substance of what he was saying. (Hear, hear) Expensive amusements should be discountenanced in the Army if they acted as a barrier against poor but otherwise suitable men seeking commissions."[83]

An editorial in *The Times* took an even sterner tone:

> "… a committee, over which General French presided, has taken evidence upon the scandal, for it is nothing less, that no man can hold the Queen's commission except under perfectly intolerable social conditions unless he can command a private income of from £150 to £500. The abolition of purchase was supposed to make the nation master of the Army. In practice, it has done nothing of the kind. Expensive habits, mostly connected with amusements of one kind and another, have made the Army a close corporation just as in the old purchase days. If this nation is to be recognised on a business footing, as Lord Roberts puts it, means must be found to remove a disability which is in every way injurious to the Army."[84]

Later letters to *The Times* suggested the estimates of costs made by Robertson and Wyndham were on the low side. On 15th February, a letter was published from Col. Amelius Lockwood, late of the Coldstream Guards and now the Conservative MP for Epping. Lockwood did not disagree with either of his fellow MPs' sentiments but disputed the figures given for the costs of being a cavalry officer. £600 per annum was nearer the mark, he suggested, and considerably more for the Household Cavalry. And where was this money spent?

---

expressed one would believe the latter figures provide totals closer to that which pay and private income figures represented in the Victorian/Edwardian era.

[i] The companion newspaper to *The Star*, an evening newspaper first published in 1888 which ceased publication in 1960.

[ii] On a simple cost of living index this amounts to £300,000 in current values. Based on wage/income relationships to GDP it is anything between £1.1 and £1.8 million.

"Principally in subscriptions to races, drags, polo, balls', stated Lockwood and spent by men 'who by the amount of their allowances and love of show set bad examples and are too often imitated.'"[85]

Lockwood's comments were not just about money but also social class. His hope was, by limiting costs, sons of impoverished 'country gentlemen' might again enter the cavalry rather than the sons of the urban *'nouveau riche'* who were viewed with scorn as effete show-offs without the 'character' necessary to be a 'proper' cavalry officer. Such class-based conceit was reinforced by the unidentified *'CO'* whose letter appeared on the same day as the *'General's'* mentioned below:

"As to the influx of the *nouveau riche*, to whom Colonel Lockwood very properly takes exception, he is always with us, always has been, and as long as he expects to consort with country gentlemen as brother officers, always will be."[86]

Class or, rather more, the perceived attributes of a proper English gentleman lay at the heart of *'CO's'* absurd notions. Raised amongst such attitudes and encouraged in them, it is perhaps no surprise Sir Douglas Haig and senior officers used the supposedly high standards of behaviour and character of an English 'gentleman' as a benchmark against which to judge the quality and ability of officers of Allied Armies during the war.

A week after Lockwood's contribution, an anonymous officer using the pseudonym *'General'* challenged even his high numbers and, in so doing, further exposed the rampant snobbery which infected cavalry regiments far less exalted than, say, the Blues and Royals or the most expensive Line Cavalry Regiment, the 10th (Prince of Wales's Own Royal) Hussars[i]:

"Only lately I was making inquiries on the subject with reference to a young friend who was anxious to join a well-known cavalry regiment, which is by no means looked upon as one of the fastest. I was told that he might 'rub along' on an allowance of £600 a year *but that the officers of the regiment did not like to have any officer who had less than £700 a year of his own*... In the first place, his pay does not cover his mess bill and, when one adds subscriptions to races, polo, drags, balls, etc., and takes in the fact that *an officer is considered 'a very poor fellow' and one not at all likely to do credit to his regiment* if he does not race and keep hunters and polo ponies, one may form a fair idea of what life in a cavalry regiment is and what it costs to keep it up."[87]

The emphases given to two parts of the quotation above are the writer's. They are indicative of an organisation and an environment where money and appearances were everything and ability counted for little. But *'General'* was not yet done with the issue:

---

[i] The 10th Hussars had a certain kudos. From 1798-1820 its Colonel was the Prince Regent and from 1863-1901 HRH the Prince of Wales. In 1899 it was said 'Officers have lived in the 10th with an allowance of only £500 a year in addition to their pay, but they have rarely lasted long' [*Source:* Cairnes, W E, *Social Life in the British Army*, John Long, 1900, page 27].

"The public suffers grievously. Nearly the whole of this expenditure goes to promote pleasure and amusements, and acts most detrimentally upon the efficiency of officers, who have neither time nor inclination for the serious study of their profession… It is by no means only in the cavalry that reform is urgently needed in this direction. In the Horse and Field Artillery the expenses of officers have enormously increased in the last few years, and there are few infantry regiments in which a subaltern's mess bill and regimental subscriptions do not absorb the whole of his pay.

The evil arises to a great extent from a spirit of emulation among officers to make their corps 'a good regiment'. This sounds well enough; but unfortunately the qualification does not rest upon efficiency and professional knowledge, but is derived from the amount which is spent on entertainments, in acquiring social success, and still more in gaining a reputation for sportsmanlike qualities, which certain persons still consider make themselves an efficient officer, but to which one of the critics, a well-known German General, lately ascribed, probably with some reason, the ignorance of the art of war which has been so unfortunately prominent in South Africa."[88]

The sports most expensive and most railed against were all equestrian – hunting, polo, point-to-point and drag racing. The sheer cost of simply buying and owing horses (one at least needed for each past-time), let alone of maintaining them, was enough to prevent many young men from ever contemplating seeking a commission not just in the cavalry but the Army in general. Polo, for example, had been played at Sandhurst since 1874 but, by 1894, it was banned along with hunting and racing as the costs were running out of control amongst some cadets.[89] Of course, there had been no such ban amongst the officers of the Army and, anyway, by 1900, when Robertson's, Wyndham's and Lockwood's complaints were voiced, the Sandhurst bans were relaxed.

Concerns about costs and the exclusion of suitable men without funds rumbled on. At length, in the Spring of 1902, a *Committee to Enquire into the Nature of the Expenses incurred by Officers* was formed under Lord Stanley, CB, eldest son of the 16th Earl of Derby, Conservative MP for Westhoughton, Lancashire, and Financial Secretary at the War Office. Other than Stanley, it comprised Col. J H E Hinde, CB, of the Border Regt., Mr R Chalmers, CB, the principal clerk of the Treasury, and Mr A Higgins, the Deputy Accountant-General at the War Office. Stanley who, as the 17th Earl of Derby, was the man responsible for the development of the Pals battalions on the outbreak of war, served in the militia, the Grenadier Guards and on the staff in South Africa, and was a man devoted to the interests of the Army. He was appointed Director-General of Recruiting in 1915.

The remit of his committee was to consider:

"… to what extent the expenses at present falling on officers are due to regulations or regimental customs, and whether it is possible to curtail such expenses; to report what are the legitimate expenses falling on an officer in the average Line or Cavalry regiment; and to suggest means of reducing expenses so as to bring commissions within the reach of men of moderate means."[90]

In addition to these subjects, the committee was also to look at other ways of reducing officers' costs such as the Army providing quarters, messes, horses (for solely military purposes) and uniforms. The committee reported in April 1903.

One of its main findings was that the principal burden of expense which fell on an officer was not due to the requirements of the Army. Rather, they were due to the need to keep up with: 'the style of living habitually adopted by the majority of their brother officers'. It was '… pursuits and amusements quite independent of their professional position…' which were '… mainly responsible for the high average of private incomes regarded as requisite in the Army generally'.[91]

The committee then looked in detail at the costs demanded by the Army of being an officer which, set against the remuneration, thereby determined the minimum levels of private income required. These were (not including the Household Cavalry or the Guards):

	Infantry	Cavalry
Initial expenses	£200	£600
Annual expenses	£155 16s 3d	£281 13s 4d
Annual pay	£95 16s 3d	£121 13s 4d
Private annual income required	£60	£160

'Annual expenses', however, only covered unspecified 'essentials'. After adding in other elements, the private income it was deemed necessary 'to live in comfort under present conditions' amounted to:

Infantry subaltern £100-150 per annum (£10,000-£60,000 at current prices)
Cavalry subaltern £260-300 per annum (£29,000-£105,000 at current prices)

Their estimate for the private income needed to subsist within a cavalry regiment in *actual*, not theoretical, terms was considerably higher, i.e. between £600 to £700 per year (i.e. anything from £66,000-£240,000 at current prices). It was thought advantageous to serve in India as pay rates were higher. A letter in *The Times* from *One who has tried it* (an infantryman) counselled against this. Apart from the dangers to health, expenses were even higher in India, with the pay of an infantry subaltern amounting to £171 per annum but their minimum costs being £325, thus demanding a private income of at least £160 a year. As such costs applied to a tee-total, non-smoking, non-sports playing, horseless hermit, the real figure was considerably more. *One who has tried it* advised staying at home and keeping one's health.[92]

To bring commissions into the orbit of men of talent who lacked the necessary finance, the committee looked at ways in which both necessary Army expenses might be reduced, as well as those associated with 'the style of living habitually adopted' by most officers. They listed eight recommendations which involved the Army supplying the basic needs in terms of accommodation and furnishings, the costs of regimental bands (currently paid by officers), chargers and accoutrements, uniforms, etc. In addition, regular changes of 'station' for each unit were to be avoided as moving and furnishing costs were a significant expense.

They then moved onto the 'lifestyle' costs. Limits were needed on regimental 'hospitality' – balls, dinners and the like – and no fees should be required of a new officer to join any regimental institution. Country-wide polo tournaments (popular with the cavalry but with infantry regiments and the Horse and Field Artillery too) were to stop and polo teams not to be allowed to play matches outside the military district in which they were based. Finally, all uniforms had to consist solely of authorised items and changes in uniforms were to be kept to a necessary minimum.

Their conclusions were that, whilst they hoped these economies might encourage suitable men whatever their circumstances to apply for commissions, they accepted that, amongst serving officers, these changes 'may conflict in many instances with individual predilection, and in some cases with established tradition'. Which, perhaps, begs the question yet again: to whom did the Army belong? The nation or the officers?

76 Gen. Sir Henry de Beauvoir de Lisle

That polo was highlighted by the committee reinforced the long-term concern about the pernicious impact of this hugely expensive sport. Polo exploded in popularity amongst Army officers, most particularly in the cavalry, at home and in India in the second half of the previous century. It was not, however, a sport restricted to cavalry officers. Those of the Horse and Field Artillery joined in with enthusiasm and the infantry were not left out. Indeed, the man regarded as one of the creators of 'modern' polo was an infantry lieutenant later Gen. Sir Henry de Beauvoir de Lisle, KCB, KCMG, DSO, the commander of the ill-fated 29th Division at Beaumont Hamel on 1st July 1916. In the mid-1890s de Lisle served with the 2nd Durham Light Infantry in India. Polo was his passion and he led his regimental team to victory in the *Indian Inter-Regimental Polo Tournament* three times between 1896 and 1898 and the *Indian Polo Association Championship* in 1898[i]. So good was he, and so radical his tactics (unlike on 1st July 1916), a book he wrote to assist his regimental teammates was later published under the title of *Hints to Polo Players in India*. In the 1930s, de Lisle trained polo players for the Maharaja of Kashmir. Although the victories of the 2nd Durham Light Infantry against the leading cavalry teams in India are remarkable, they were not isolated in terms of playing the game. There was, after all, an Infantry Inter-Regimental Polo

---

[i] 3rd Rifle Brigade also won the *Indian Inter-Regimental Polo Tournament*, in 1900 [Source: Laffaye, H A, *The Evolution of Polo*, McFarland & Co., 2009 page 61].

Tournament as well. In short, everyone who could afford it was at it. And those who could afford it looked down their noses at those who could not.

There were especial concerns about the great expense of being an officer in the cavalry or Guards. Despite previous efforts, the non-military costs of these units were still out of the reach of the vast majority of aspiring officers. As a result, the Akers-Douglas Committee found the Army was in something of a quandary when it came to filling the officer ranks of both these arms. In spite of the fact a disproportionate number of officers from these units went on to occupy elevated positions, the predicament was that, when it came to filling their ranks, such men could have money or they could have brains but they were unlikely to possess both.[93] Or, to put it another way, the continued financial exclusivity of the Guards and cavalry regiments meant their 'magnificence remained, undimmed by brains'.[94]

Such comments were reinforced by Lord Roberts' suggesting the names of prospective cavalry officers in the 1903 Sandhurst intake were most often to be found in the nether regions of the list of entrance examination results.[95] This also applied to the Guards and was certainly the case in 1902. In that year's first entrance examination there were thirty cadetships reserved for the cavalry and Guards (twenty and ten respectively) and 125 for the infantry. Far and away the top mark for the cavalry intake, 8,187 marks, was achieved by Geoffrey Vaux Salvin Bowlby, who went on to join the Royal Horse Guards[i]. He was followed by a J O Ewing (6,809), and the last placed cavalry candidate was Lord Hugh William Grosvenor (4,773), the son of the 1st Duke of Westminster, who joined the 1st Life Guards[ii]. There were only two successful candidates for the Guards, the rest having failed to achieve the necessary marks. In the infantry section the top mark was a whopping 11,394 and 71 of the infantry candidates achieved a higher mark than did the second placed cavalry candidate and all 125 achieved higher marks than all but seven of those seeking cadetships for the cavalry or the Guards.[96] Matters did not improve for those taking the entrance exam in July 1902. Just four of the ten places reserved for the Guards were taken and 114 of the infantry candidates received better marks than all but four of the 24 successful cavalry and Guards candidates, nineteen of which 'achieved' a lower mark than the lowest infantry candidate.[97]

---

[i] Capt. Geoffrey Vaux Salvin Bowlby, Royal Horse Guards, was born on 1st December 1883, the son of Mr Edward Salvin Bowlby and Mrs. Elizabeth Vans Bowlby of 56, Lowndes Square, London. He married the Hon. Lettice Annesley, the 5th child and 3rd daughter of the Rt. Hon. Arthur Annesley, the 11th Viscount Valentia and Conservative MP for Oxford. He was promoted Captain in 1907 and was ADC to the Commander in Chief in Ireland. Mentioned in Despatches for his conduct at Wytschaete in October 1914, he was killed on 13th May 1915. His body was never found and his name is inscribed on the Ypres (Menin Gate) Memorial, Panel 3. His wife had a memorial erected near where he fell at Gully Farm. His brother Lt. Lionel Henry Salvin Bowlby, 2nd Dragoons (Royal Scots Greys), was killed on 4th June 1916 and is buried in Bedford House Cemetery near Ypres.

[ii] Grosvenor was killed near Ypres on 30th October 1914. He too is remembered on the Ypres (Menin Gate) Memorial, Panel 3.

Concern about the quality of candidates for these *élite* units was voiced in the Akers-Douglas in a section in their report entitled *'Cavalry Expenses'*:

> "It has been stated by a number of competent witnesses (e.g. Field Marshal Earl Roberts and Gen. Sir Evelyn Wood) that there is no possibility, under existing circumstances, of exacting a high standard of education from candidates for Cavalry Commissions. In fact, the supply not being equal to the demand, the Military authorities have been compelled to accept almost any candidate."[98]

Until changes were introduced in 1903, it was the case candidates for either the Guards or the cavalry needed an entrance pass mark 3,000 less than the 8,000 demanded for the infantry. After this was changed to a flat pass mark of 8,000 for all entrants, a significant shortage of officers developed within two years in both *élite* parts of the Army.[99]

This was an issue highlighted in a debate on the Conservative Government's Army Reforms in the House of Commons on 24th February 1905 by the Rt. Hon. Sir Arthur Divett Hayter, the Liberal MP for Walsall. By this date, he reported, there was a shortage of 44 cavalry officers (the equivalent of two regiments' worth and up from 23 since 1903). The situation was even worse in the Guards:

Grenadier Guards 14 vacancies
Coldstream Guards 7 vacancies
Scots Guards 15 vacancies
Irish Guards 4 vacancies

There were, therefore, forty officer vacancies within the entire Brigade of Guards. To be fair, however, Hayter went on to report shortages of officers in other parts of the Army, as well as the Militia and the Volunteers, but nowhere were they proportionately as high as in the cavalry and the Guards.[100]

The seriousness of the problem of the supply of officers, and not just in the Regular Army, was highlighted even more starkly by Lord Roberts in his Mansion House speech of 1st August 1905 on the state of Imperial Defence, even if his analysis of its causes ignored the issues of expense and education mentioned above. Pursuing the idea that the training of 'Other Ranks' was no great problem but the training of officers most certainly was, Roberts gave details of the scale of officer shortages within the Army at home and abroad were war to break out:

> The Regular Army was short of 3,000 officers needed to get every unit up to strength and to replace existing officers called away on staff duties;
> 1,000 new officers were needed to train new recruits;
> 1,600 officers were needed to bring the Indian Army up to strength;
> 987 officers were needed to bring the Militia up to strength; and
> 2,770 officers were needed to bring the Volunteers up to strength.

This gave a minimum total of 9,357 officers required, a figure which excluded any 'wastage' caused by the 'war' itself. Against this total could be set the less than 2,000 reserve officers available, of whom many were either too old or too senior to carry out the tasks required. In short, therefore, the Army was short of more than 7,500 officers were a war to break out in which the British Army was involved.

Having set out the figures, Roberts then apportioned blame for this 'very dangerous state of affairs'. This problem was *not*, he asserted, the fault of either the Government or the Army (of which he was commander in chief between 3rd January 1901 and 12th February 1904). No. It was, somehow, the fault of:

> "… the people themselves whose lack of patriotism prevents them taking any interest in the condition of the armed forces of the country."

A statement betraying to an extraordinary degree how little personal and professional responsibility senior officers were prepared to accept both for the current situation and that which applied before the South African War.

THE PROBLEM OF A SHORTAGE OF OFFICERS and the concerns surrounding their education and intelligence were not issues easily resolved. On 7th September 1906 that serial correspondent Lord Esher wrote to the Duchess of Sutherland[i] on the issue of Britain's young officers and their continuing devotion to sports of all kinds, especially equestrian, to the detriment of their professional development:

> "I fear that proficiency in games, or in the hunting field, will not help our poor lads much when they have to face the carefully trained and highly educated German officers.
> Our difficulty is that our lawyers and physicians are professional men, but until quite lately, our soldiers have been amateurs – and soldiering a pastime and not a 'business'. Even now, it is the exception not the rule to find a clever and highly educated soldier."[101]

Some in the Army had radical, if reactionary, solutions to such shortages. Writing in the *RUSI Journal* in 1906, a Maj. Lord Douglas James Cecil Compton, 9th Queen's Royal Lancers and the 8th child and 4th and youngest son of Admiral William Compton, 4th Marquess of Northampton, and Eliza Compton, Marchioness of Northampton (herself the daughter of another admiral, Admiral Sir George Elliot, KCB), argued that one of the reasons for the paucity of officers, especially in the Guards and Cavalry, was the limitation in expenses on sports and social activities introduced in an attempt to widen the pool of prospective officer material. Unsurprisingly, under 'Recreations' in his *Who's Who* entry he stated: 'fond of almost all sports and most games'. Compton, not a poor man and thus happy to participate to the fullest in all activities, argued the Army should:

> "Avoid all interference with the way in which officers choose to spend their spare time and money; there are many easier and more unwholesome ways than playing polo, driving a drag, or even giving a ball."[102]

No doubt he also had in mind the general 'improvements' in the social class of officers which might result from such a decision. In Compton's opinion there was one way to increase numbers (of the right sort of individual):

> "There remains one remedy – which is never suggested – and that is to reduce the amount of work which officers now have to do, and to take other steps to make an officer's life in the Army as pleasant as it always used to be considered."[103]

---

[i] Millicent Sutherland-Leveson-Gower (*née* Lady Millicent Fanny St. Clair-Erskine).

An Army officer's ideal life: pleasant, untaxing and with numerous non-military diversions. Perfect! By 1914 our Old Etonian Lord Douglas was a full Colonel and had been on half pay for two years. He served in the war being awarded the CBE in 1918 for his otherwise anonymous service in the BEF. The final comment in his *Journal* piece may stand as his, and the Victorian/Edwardian Army's, epitaph:

> "Remember that change is in itself a bad thing in the Army, and that changes should only be made when the good to be gained distinctly outweighs the evils of changing."[104]

In March 1908, Secretary of State Haldane addressed the subject as part of a debate on that year's Army Estimates. Although re-organisation of the Army and its reserves and planning for an Expeditionary Force of six infantry divisions and four cavalry brigades appeared well in hand, Haldane was forced to admit of the:

> "… very formidable deficiency of officers in the Army… we (are) deficient in the quantity and also in the quality, because the training we give them is not in all respects satisfactory training."[105]

The overall shortage stood at c. 5,000 officers for home-based and colonial units (excluding India which was itself 3,000 short of the numbers needed). It was hoped to make up the numbers via a new reserve of officers, firstly made up of young men prepared to undertake a year's training but who then entered other professions, and secondly by the setting up of Officers' Training Corps in, at the time, 130 public schools and fourteen universities. By this means it was hoped to generate some 800 officers a year for the new special reserve of officers.

The issue of the shortcomings in the education and training of officers was, according to Haldane, still 'a serious one' in 1908. He was forced to accept that during an officer's schooling and his time at either Sandhurst or Woolwich their education was 'tolerably satisfactory' but between receiving his commission and his mid-30s:

> "… there is no adequate provision for his instruction at all… It is the period during which the officer has no opportunity… for making himself efficient in the science of war."[106]

The Akers-Douglas solution of relying on regimental and battalion commanders to oversee junior officers' training during this crucial period was not proving effective as the results were as variable as were the educational skills of the senior officers now responsible. Further reform was to prove necessary.

The previous month Lord Esher, who was so much involved in the restructuring and reorganisation of the Army both prior to and during the war, did not pull any punches in his comments about the state of officer education and intellectual ability in an article in the *United Service Magazine*. His comments were reported in *The Times* of 6th February 1908. He posed the question as to:

> "… whether the intellectual equipment of the average British officer of high rank and middle life is equal to that of men of the same standing in other professions, and, while admitting that many hold their own with their peers in other walks of life, he reluctantly concludes that, in the opinion of many competent judges, the average does not." [107]

Like Haldane, Esher blamed this on the years between 25 and 35 when, he suggested, 'the lives of young officers are to some extent wasted'. He blamed the lack of 'continuous education' for their failings. Of course, education and intellect are not one and the same thing. One might know a lot of things as a result of education but then, for want of intellect, be unable to apply reason and understanding in order to interpret and apply such learning. Esher, therefore, appears to suggest officers of a certain age were not as bright as one might have wished but thought 'continuous education' was a solution to a basic lack of brains.

The Times Military Correspondent commenting on Esher's article fell into the same trap by suggesting the below average intellect common within senior ranks of the Army was not the fault of the officers (they had the brains they were born with or, perhaps, without) but of a failure to educate them. Their continuous deployment around the Empire was simply not conducive to intellectual pursuits, 'even if the will to study is there', of which, in rather too many cases, it was not. There were (still) compensations for service in these remote and normally overheated locations for which time could always be found. The priorities so criticised by Akers-Douglas and his committee were still those of the average officer: '... hunting, shooting, polo, racquets, racing' with the result 'the average officer joins his average comrades and feeds the body while he starves the mind'.[108]

The consequences for the men under their command were:

"When chance flings an officer into a position of responsibility he too often realizes that he has neglected to study the higher branches of his profession and, for want of knowing what to do, only does what he knows."[109]

As before, the finger of blame was pointed at the education provided by the Public Schools. As Col. Gregory Fontenot, US Army, described them in his 1980 analysis of the social backgrounds of the 1914 crop of British Major Generals:

"The public schools were... English, because they taught Greek and Latin; public, because they were private; and schools, because they were devoted to the cult of athletics."[110]

Sir Ian Hamilton criticised 'The English system of educating the bodies and the characters rather than the minds of the upper classes'[111] without, apparently, wondering whether the basic intellectual equipment of the 'upper classes' might well be a problem as great, if not greater, than their lack of education or knowledge. According to Vivian Ogilvie, the Public Schools produced:

"Men who were sure of themselves and ready to assume responsibility, but devoid of imagination, sensibility and the capacity to criticize what they had been taught to accept, could conquer backwards countries – giving their lives if need be – and administer them conscientiously."[112]

The issue of education was again raised at the first General Staff conference at the Staff College between 7th and 10th January 1908. Chaired by Gen. the Hon. Sir Neville Gerald Lyttelton, GCB, Chief of the General Staff, it was attended, *inter alia*, by Haig, Rawlinson, Robertson, Haking, Haldane, Hunter-Weston, Edmonds and Kiggell. Haig introduced a paper on the final day concerning the education and training of officers for General Staff duties. After an explanation of the current systems for education and promotion, the discussion was opened to the floor.

Col. Aylmer Hunter-Weston commented that, whilst he hoped they might be able to do away with the examination/promotion system, to be replaced with one which considered the long-term performance and abilities of the officer candidate, he was of the view this 'time had not yet come'. The reason for this was:

> "The general standard of education in the Army must first be still further raised, and this might take the best part of a military generation."[113]

Col. Aylmer Haldane then blamed the Public Schools for the inadequacies of officers' 'slipshod' written English and an 'opportunity might be taken at the Staff College to pay some attention to writing'. The reason for this was clear to:

> "Anyone who had to wade through masses of illiterate staff diaries and war reports such as came to the War Office from South Africa and Manchuria and try to find out what the writers really meant to convey…"[114]

Edmonds, too, criticised the Public Schools for their focus on Classical languages and a failure to teach officers to write in their own language. He noted Napoleon had insisted some 100 years earlier French should be taught in France's schools, something not yet the case with the native language in the leading schools of Britain. He was also critical of the examination system for promotion and entrance into the Staff College, preferring instead the continental system of recording an officer's entire career performance and professional development. He further noted candidates for the *Kriegsakademie* had to declare whether they employed a crammer prior to the entrance examination. Those who answered in the affirmative could be penalised up to 10% of their resulting marks.[115]

Criticisms of the Public Schools' failure to educate pupils in French, German, history, and geography might have been partly historical but were also a response to the demands of the Army's own schools. This was underlined by a pointed letter written by Charles Hickson 'Cabby' Spence[i], Assistant Master and Head of the Modern Side at Haig's *alma mater* Clifton College:

> "The education of boys who wish to enter the Army is determined by the competitive examination for Woolwich and Sandhurst. Teachers do not ground their pupils in geography as no paper is set in that subject… No general knowledge of European history is required… very few of the successful candidates do history at all. Fewer still take German; in fact the present regulations have killed the study of German on Army sides[ii]. In the competitive examination held last December 36 boys entered Woolwich. Of these, 4 took German and 2 history. Of the 63 who gained infantry cadetships, 5 took German and 19 history. Of some 360 candidates in all, only 28 took German."[116]

In other words, Hamilton was wrong. The schools might fail to provide a suitably 'liberal' education, but the Army did not want students so educated. Even in 1908 the failure to attract suitably educated cadets still lay at the Army's door.

---

[i] Spence had an MA from Trinity College, Cambridge. He taught history, geography, and civics. His nickname 'Cabby' came from his unkempt appearance. He died in 1912.
[ii] Clifton College, founded in 1862, had a Classical Side (Greek and Latin were requirements for Oxbridge), a Modern Side and a Military and Engineering Side.

Given that note was taken of the lack of improvement in the quality, education and intellect of new officers in 1908, one must wonder what improvements were subsequently achieved? Few by 1909, according to our friend Thomas Miller Maguire, M.A., LL.D., Barrister-at-Law at the Inner Temple and inveterate critic both of the state of the Army and of the education and training of its officers. On 5th May 1909 he addressed the members of the *Royal United Services Institution* on the subject of *'Readiness or Ruin'*. Whilst railing heartily against the appalling living conditions of the poor from whom the rank and file of the Army were recruited[i], the aim of his ire was more directly targeted on the failures of the upper classes and their education:

> "Then what about the officer? Only to-day I heard from a young officer of the deplorable way in which he is treated. It is a great compliment for a man to volunteer to be an officer at all in our army; he gets little pay, little thanks, and has no legal rights and no status. A man who goes as an officer under such conditions is a highly estimable citizen. The officers are not properly instructed, indeed, it is officially reported that they are among the worst educated men of their rank in Europe or America. A non-instructed officer is, under modern conditions of life, nearly as little use in war as a weak or infirm soldier. He is a danger to himself and to the race."[117]

He went on:

> "I assure you that if I read out to you, had I the time, the state of education among the richer classes, the miserable and degrading reports about the fashion in which young men are prepared for the army – the very soul of our nation – the despicable way in which the young students are treated in the public schools, there is not a man here who is a father that would not join in league at once to mend these things."[118]

There was not much change the following year, according to a question asked of Haldane by the Tory MP for Woolwich, William Adam[ii], on 21st June 1910:

> "Major Adam asked the Secretary for War whether, in view of the deplorably low standard of education on the part of those endeavouring to

---

[i] This he blamed on the rise of industry and commerce: "In the Peace between 1815 and 1853 a terrible change took place. Mankind became, in the factories under the new commercial system, not the assets of the State, but the adjuncts of a machine. Nothing could awaken our rich people from their dream that opulence was everything, that manhood was nothing. Poor little children, as Dickens describes, and of whom Lord Shaftesbury was the champion, were brought out from the cradle to tend machines or furnaces; women were grovelling on the ground in mines, drawing after them waggons. Humanity was potted; no provision, no generosity, nothing good. Our land became one sink of level avarice and its victims." One might suggest Mr Miller Maguire was looking at life before the Industrial Revolution through rather rose-tinted spectacles.

[ii] Maj. William Augustus Adam, 5th Royal Irish Lancers, served in the South African and the Great War. He observed the Russo-Japanese War from the Japanese side. Born in 1865, he was elected the MP for Woolwich in the January 1910 General Election only to see it revert to Labour's Will Crooks in December 1910. He died in 1940.

qualify for commissions in the Army as revealed by the report of the Director of Military Training[i], he would take steps to procure a sufficient supply of candidates of the former standard of intelligence."[119]

By use of the word 'former' Adam, perhaps, bestows upon himself and his contemporaries a somewhat inflated estimate of their intellectual abilities if the previous reports and comments about officers both before and after the South African War are anything to go by. But, then again, Adam persists in confusing education with intelligence which reflects ill on him.

IN ADDITION TO THE EDUCATION/INTELLIGENCE of officer cadets the issue of the professional education of officers persisted well after the Akers-Douglas committee reported. In January 1910, Col. E M Perceval[ii] made a presentation at the General Staff conference under the title *Would it be Advisable to Prepare a Programme of a Suitable Progressive Course of Study of Military History and other Subjects for Junior Officers, together with a List of Books recommended?* His opening words hint at only muted confidence in the current crop of officers:

"I think we all agree that we are getting now a number of young officers who take their profession very seriously."[120]

'A number!' Faint praise indeed! That, by 1910, the Army was *still* debating (and failing to agree) whether its officers should make any sort of study of their chosen profession seems to this writer an extraordinary admission that the organisation was still too much regarded as a frivolous past-time for the younger sons of the peerage and gentry rather than as a serious undertaking for those determined to protect their country and Empire. Indeed, Perceval's further comment that, to start with, the idea should be 'to interest them in the subject' seems perfectly absurd when one considers just who he is talking about. He did not then seem to think young Army officers might regard the study of certain aspects of military history as being an essential element of their development. Apparently not, as he made it clear 'some inducement will be necessary' to persuade them away from the polo field or drag hunt and into a comfortable armchair with Col. Henderson's *Stonewall Jackson* on their laps and a whiskey and soda by their side. Perceval's suggestion was not entirely altruistic. As a member of staff at Camberley, an added benefit to having officers learn about military history was:

---

[i] Then Maj. Gen., later Gen., Sir Archibald James Murray GCB, GCMG, CVO, DSO, who was later Chief of Staff with the BEF for the first six months of the war, Deputy CIGS and briefly CIGS, and GOC, Egyptian Expeditionary Force.

[ii] Maj. Gen. Sir Edward Maxwell Perceval, KCB, DSO, RA (1861-1955). Royal Academy, Gosport, and RMA, Woolwich. Commissioned Royal Artillery, 1880. Served in India, Burma and South Africa. Staff College and an instructor at Woolwich in the late 1890s. He was a GSO1 at the Staff College between 1909 and 1912. In 1914 he was made Brig. Gen. of 2nd Division's artillery before being given command of 49th (West Riding) Division in September 1915, which unit he commanded during the attacks on Thiepval on 1st July 1916. He returned to England in October 1917 on health grounds, taking command of 68th Division. He retired in 1920.

"... we should then be able to assume the general knowledge of the strategy of certain campaigns on the part of all the officers who come here (i.e. the Staff College) as students."

Or, in other words, four years before the outbreak of the greatest war in the British Army's history it was still training as staff officers men with little or no knowledge of military history and the strategy and tactics then employed.

It was re-assuring to hear Col. Godley confirm Horace Smith-Dorrien, commanding at Aldershot, approved heartily of such additional education and, indeed, in that year, officers at Aldershot studied the Russo-Japanese War with lectures by specialists and the promotion exams including the subject. Edmonds (of the *Official History*), Col. Alexander Hamilton-Gordon, who succeeded Haig at Aldershot in 1914 and later commanded IX Corps, and Brig. Gen. Edward Sinclair May, a prolific author on tactics, former professor at the Staff College, and Adjutant General for Military Training and Education at the War Office, were all in broad agreement. May, indeed, regretted an earlier effort launched by Gen. Sir Henry John Thoroton Hildyard, whilst the Director General of Military Education when Roberts was CinC, came to nothing. Others were less certain. Col. Robert Arundel Kerr Montgomery, RA, put in a plea for the poor, over-worked young officer who 'has plenty to do and plenty of examinations'. In this plea he was supported by Brig. Gen. Aylmer Haldane and Col. Walter Pipon Braithwaite, later Chief of Staff of Sir Ian Hamilton's ill-fated Gallipoli Expeditionary Force.

After Henry Wilson stated French officers attending the *École Supérieure de Guerre* were assumed to have read widely on military history as 'they did not lecture on any campaigns, but they continually referred to them in every lecture at which I was present', the CIGS, Nicholson, made this remarkable contribution:

"... I think, taking people generally, there are few who for the love of it will study military history... People study... in the hope of professional advancement... I feel doubtful if any officer will study military history except it be to his advantage professionally."[121]

This from the most eminent soldier in the country. And, when the Australian representative on the Imperial General Staff, Col. William Throsby Bridges, suggested officers in the Dominions read 'for the sheer pleasure in military work... (seeking) knowledge because they find it interesting and instructive', he was met by the profoundly damning comment from Nicholson:

"Your experience is much more favourable than mine."

It should be noted that in France, although the process was hi-jacked and the result was the disastrous *offensive à outrance* of August 1914, the ongoing education of officers was expected and organised: there was a multiplicity of specialist and more general military journals, mainly developed after 1871; lectures, debates and the writing of articles was not just encouraged but demanded; and, by 1914, two hundred garrison libraries were in existence. The difference could not be starker.

Later in the day another discussion was held concerning *The System of Education and Training of Officers*. Broadly it was a plea from Col. William George Balfour Western to reduce the period of study for the next officers' examination in military history. It was currently set to cover the first two years of the American Civil War in Virginia and, suggested Western, 'officers... (were) really afraid of facing it'. Reflecting concerns expressed in previous years, it was felt officers tended to learn by rote, to cram 'certain comments and certain details which can be learned by heart', rather than absorbing and interpreting the tactical detail of the campaigns to be studied. In short, Western contended junior officers should study tactics rather than strategy. Du Cane, quoting Henderson in his *Science of War*, demurred. Furthermore, he made the rather obvious point that, however interesting were the tactical elements of a Bull Run or Antietam, these battles were fought at a level of technology and firepower but a fraction of anything likely to be utilised in a conflict in Europe or elsewhere at the end of the first decade of the 20th Century.

Maj. Maud replied on behalf of Murray, the Director of Military Training. The exam, he remarked, was in two parts: one on grand strategy, thus the extended period covered, the other on minor tactics and concentrating on Jackson's 1862 Shenandoah Valley campaign. The intention was:

> "... to encourage officers who have perhaps never read a military history book before in their lives to acquire a taste for this study... many officers who have been thus forced to study have been surprised to find how interesting the subject is..."[122]

To quote a modern Homer (i.e. not he of the *Odyssey* and *Iliad*): 'Doh!'

Maud conceded, however, 'many officers' did not find the subject of interest. Many contented themselves 'with the minimum amount of study... and some not even that'. This latter group resorted to crammers to help them through the exam and on to an unwarranted promotion. The results of such an approach were exposed in the promotion exams of November 1908 which focussed on Grant's 1864 Overland campaign. Several students regurgitated an interminable account of the conduct of the campaign rather than answer the questions relating to Grant's objectives and providing a critique of his strategy. These students, it was deemed, had 'not been studying profitably'. They failed to grasp:

> "It is the why and the wherefore, the wisdom after the event, the profiting by the experience of others which is the object of the study of military history."

That not much changed in the intervening months is indicated by a quote from a staff officer at the War Office, Capt. Charles Yate[i], when he addressed the

---

[i] Capt., later Maj., Charles Allix Lavington Yate, VC, 2nd King's Own Yorkshire Light Infantry, died on 20th September 1914, aged 42. He was the son of the Rev. George Edward Yate, Vicar of Madeley, Shropshire, and Prebendary of Hereford, and husband of Florence Helena. Served in South Africa. The VC citation in *The London Gazette*, No. 28985, 25th November, 1914, reads: 'Commanded one of the two Companies that remained to the end in the trenches at Le Cateau on 26th August, and, when all other officers were killed or wounded and ammunition exhausted, led his nineteen survivors against the enemy in a charge in which he was severely wounded. He was picked up by the enemy and has subsequently died as a prisoner of war'. The circumstances of his death are tragic. He escaped from Torgau PoW camp on 19th September. Cornered by some local workers he cut his throat to avoid recapture, dying the following day. He is buried in the Berlin South-Western Cemetery, grave II. G. 8.

General Staff conference in 1911. His subject, first on the agenda, was *The Desirability or otherwise of issuing an official manual of applied tactics*. Yate was a graduate of the Staff College and had been an official observer with the Japanese Army in Manchuria, being present at the siege of Port Arthur. He made numerous contributions to *Reports from British Officers attached to the Russian and Japanese Armies in the Field* published in 1908. Now, he was arguing, unsuccessfully as it turned out, for a manual which took actual examples of problems and gave answers to them, as opposed to the rather more generalised, some might even say vague, manuals such as *Field Service Regulations*. It was his comments about the continuing use of crammers with all of the drawbacks suggested above, which are of interest here:

> "At present, owing to the insufficient opportunities of instruction afforded in units, officers studying for promotion examinations go to crammers to an extent which I do not believe is realized everywhere. I recently heard one officer remark that if he was going to get a 'star' he must go to a crammer; he went and he got it."[123]

The concept of the manual was immediately shot down in flames by the now Maj. Gen. May for the reason that the sheer variety of environments in which an officer might serve prevented there being a 'one size fits all' approach to military quandaries. Others, such as Brig. Gen Davies, speaking on behalf of Smith-Dorrien, suggested officers of a lesser calibre might become over-reliant on such a book rather than using their brains, or what passed for them, in assessing and solving a particular problem. Du Cane, as he had suggested the previous year, proposed lectures given at the Staff College should be published and made available to officers, but Robertson, now in charge at Camberley, was far less keen and suggested instead interested officers might publish their own tactical advice which, as it was unofficial, could be ignored or accepted as anyone saw fit, all of which rendered his suggestion eminently pointless.

It is, therefore, unremarkable that it was not until mid-1912 some evidence of 'a marked improvement in military education' could be confidently reported.[124] All well and good for the subalterns who took the field in 1914 but not so for those more elevated and those under their command.

All of which rather begs the question: What was the leadership of the British Army like in 1914? With war comes opportunity for promotion, if only via 'dead men's shoes'. Thus, junior officer of 1914 might be commanding who knows what unit a couple of years later. What was the social status, background, and educational attainment of these actual and potential leaders?

The late Victorian and early Edwardian Army was *not* the home of the British intellectual *élite*. Men from the burgeoning middle class with education, ideas, and ambition did not head to Sandhurst, i.e. not into the Guards, the cavalry, or the infantry. They went into business, industry, politics, or diplomacy or, if the services beckoned, they opted for the Royal Navy[i].

---

[i] From 1841 to 1911, the numbers employed in eighteen 'professional' occupations (i.e. finance, law, medicine, religion, industry, the arts, teaching, clerking, etc.) increased from 173,755 to 951,232, an increase of c. 450%. The population in the same period

Those men of intelligence and education, the more technically or scientifically minded, who entered the Army tended towards the 'scientific branches' – the Engineers or Artillery. Indeed, it can be argued there was a military hierarchy of professionalism and education with, at its peak, the Royal Engineers[i], followed by the Royal Garrison Artillery, the RFA, the infantry, and then the cavalry in that order. Bringing up the rear were the often double and sometimes triple-hyphenated surnamed officers of the Horse and Foot Guards amongst whom wealth and position played a far greater role than any aptitude to a military career.

Consequently, some sections of the Army became the home of the non-inheriting second, or subsequent, son of the nobility, the landed gentry or, much more rarely, of the successful man of trade or industry. Allied to a leavening of the offspring of serving or retired officers and a sprinkling of sons of the clergy, and the officer class of the non-technical Army had a profile which was rural, upper class, public-school educated (though the word 'education' is used loosely), sporting and non-, perhaps even anti-, intellectual.

The Army was also dominated by 'gentlemen'. Even with the abolition of promotion by purchase, the Army was so structured as to ensure it was populated by an officer class with 'independent means'. A 'gentlemen' was one who did not have to work for a living and, with the expenses of being an officer so great, it made it practically impossible for someone without 'independent means' to join the Army's commissioned ranks. This was no accident. It was the way the landed classes – the aristocracy and the gentry – wished it to be, as it excluded those with whom they did not wish to mix, i.e. the sons of the middle class, of trade and commerce and, heaven forfend, anyone from the working classes.

Prof. Francis Michael Longstreth Thompson in his famous 1963 book *English Landed Society in the Nineteenth Century* defined a Victorian 'gentleman' as one who could depend on at least £1,000 per annum from his or his family's estates which, in current values, can best be estimated at anything between £100,000 and £1 million (or even more).[125] These figures alone helped define the sort of man who could sensibly aspire to becoming an officer in Her, or later, His Majesty's Army.

With purchase no longer possible, the rather horrid prospect of promotion by ability raised its ugly head. The sheer cost of maintaining one's position as an officer ruthlessly knocked this concept cold and it was not until the fiascos of the South African War that Government and Country started to demand the Army be rather more heavily populated by men of talent and intelligence irrespective of

---

grew by c. 125% [Source: Reader W J, *Professional Men, The Rise of the Professional Classes in Nineteenth Century England*, Weidenfeld & Nicolson, 1966, page 211].

[i] Being an Engineer or Gunner had the potential to open up alternative forms of employment. The *Ordnance Survey* (set up after the Jacobite rebellion of 1745-6 and the need for a detailed map of the Highlands with which to control the Clans) emerged from the *Principal Triangulation of Great Britain* which ran between 1783 and 1853 under the auspices of the *Board of Ordnance* and taken over by the War Office in 1855. It was effectively run by Engineers such as Maj. Gen. Thomas Frederick Colby, FRS, FRSE, FGS, FRGS, RE, Lt. Gen. Lewis Alexander Hall, RE, and Maj. Gen. Sir Henry James, FRS, MRIA, RE. Ex-Engineers also took on roles in the fast-growing railway industry and numerous technical posts within Government were filled by officers of both arms.

their background and social standing. But, even after this, there were those who argued against reducing the costs incurred by officers in maintaining their standing in the Officers' Mess or on the polo field. One such wrote in the *United Services Magazine* in 1902 that these enormous costs were an excellent way of keeping out:

> "... men of a class unsuited to the Army," thus shielding real gentlemen from having to rub shoulders "... day after day with a man whose habits and conversation continually jar on them and with whom they have nothing in common."[126]

That this exclusivity was slowly undermined is shown by the 1910 Sandhurst intake. Most were sons of 'gentlemen' and military families (64%) but a growing proportion came from families with ties to business or the professions. Nearly 50% of the Woolwich intake came from a business/professional background:

	Gentleman	Business/managerial	Military	Professional	Others
Sandhurst	20.5%	9.3%	43.8%	23%	3.4%
Woolwich	12.9%	12.2%	35.3%	36%	3.6%

Table 13 1910 Cadet intake - Father's occupation
[Otley, C B, *The social origins of British army officers, Sociological Review*, 18, 2nd July 1970, pp 213-40]

Demands to broaden the social and intellectual base of the officer class were already too late for the upper echelons of an Army in which, by 1914, there were 108 serving Major Generals. Depending on age, men of this rank might expect to be commanding Divisions and looking towards promotion to Corps command or, if the war developed over time, even an Army. These General Officers were born between 1850 and 1868 and were thus between 64 and 46 years old. Their years of service ranged from 43 to 26 years. The oldest was Maj. Gen. Sir Alexander Nelson Rochfort, KCB, CMG, RA, the Lt. Governor of Jersey from 1910 to his death in 1916. He served in the Sudan, South Africa, and Somaliland before being appointed Inspector of the Horse and Field Artillery in 1904. The youngest was Maj. Gen. George F Gorringe[i] who too served in the Sudan and South Africa and was commanding the Bombay Brigade in India on the outbreak of war. He later served in Mesopotamia with both Indian Divisional and Corps commands, and later commanded 47th (2nd London) Division in France. He survived to see the end of the Second World War, dying on 24th October 1945.

Between these two was an array of more or less distinguished officers, five of whom were promoted Field Marshal[ii]. They were men of a certain class, Public School educated, normally well-off and with excellent social and sporting connections. They enjoyed patronage from their seniors and bestowed the same on their friends and juniors as 'influence' still counted for more than basic talent, ability, and intellect.

They were also, usually, the non-inheriting sons of their fathers. The oldest son was groomed to take over, maintain and, preferably, expand the family estates.

---

[i] Later Lt. Gen. Sir George F Gorringe, KCB, KCMG, DSO, RE.
[ii] Allenby, Birdwood, Julian Byng, Robertson and Henry Wilson.

The brightest son was probably someone senior in the Government or Civil Service either in London or India. The rest, and Victorian families tended to numerous offspring, joined the Navy or Army and, in the latter case, wealth, and not ability or intelligence, dictated which regiment they then might join.[127]

Col. Fontenot, in his 1980 Master's thesis on the British Major Generals of 1914, estimated 32% of them came from amongst the landed classes – the aristocracy or gentry. Another 39% came from Army families (and 3% from Navy families) and 12% were sons of the clergy. Just 5% were from middle class (even if wealthy middle class) backgrounds and there was just one working class 'lad' amongst them: Sir William Robertson, soon to become the Chief of the Imperial General Staff. Of the sons of Army families, however, more than a few were born to the younger, non-inheriting, sons of the nobility or the landed gentry. Fontenot cites the example of Maj. Gen. Alexander Hamilton Gordon whose father was the second son of the 4th Earl of Aberdeen, the Prime Minister on the outbreak of the Crimean War. The same applied to some of the sons of the clergy, and then there those connected to landed families by marriage[i]. One such was Henry Rawlinson, the man who commanded Fourth Army on 1st July 1916. His full name was Henry Seymour Rawlinson and the middle name comes from his mother, Louisa Caroline Harcourt Seymour, who was the potentially wealthy heiress of Henry Seymour, previously the MP for Taunton and a nephew of the 8th Duke of Somerset (and whose mother was the Comtesse de Ponthon), and who held extensive estates in Somerset, Dorset and Wiltshire.

One way or another, therefore, the majority of senior officers of the Army had direct or indirect family connections to wealthy landowners. And they were geographically and, therefore, socially connected too. Over 70% of the English born Major Generals of 1914 (there were 56 or 52% of the total) came from rural areas south of a line from the mouth of the *Severn* across to the Wash. Another connection was their religious practice: they were almost uniformly Church of England.[128] They were, in short, WASPs – White Anglo-Saxon Protestants. And they were WASPs with connections, often at the highest level. Haig and Pulteney were friends of the King whilst several others prominent on 1st July 1916 were, or had been, in correspondence with him, for example Allenby (Third Army), Montagu Stuart Wortley (46th Division), Rawlinson (Fourth Army), Hunter-Weston (VIII Corps) and Lambton (4th Division).[129]

In terms of all senior officers from Colonel upwards it has been estimated that in 1914 42% of Generals and 33% of Colonels were sons of peers, baronets, or the gentry. About a quarter of both ranks were the sons of Army fathers. Perhaps surprisingly one colonel in eight was a son of the clergy.[130] Looking at those coming on behind, Bowman and Connolly, in their book *'The Edwardian Army'*, suggest little changed since these senior officers had themselves gone to Sandhurst or Woolwich in the 1880s. According to their research into cadets attending Sandhurst between 1910 and 1914 37% were the sons of soldiers and 33% were

---

[i] Fontenot states that 42% of the 1914 class of Major Generals (where the information was available) married into landowning families and 44% into existing Army families [*Source:* Fontenot, op. cit., page 102}.

described as 'gentlemen' or were the sons of peers. The rest were predominantly a mix of sons of the clergy, or of professional men and civil servants.[131]

Clearly, then, the officers of the BEF were mainly upper or upper middle class. Confirming this was the fact a small number of Public Schools predominated when it came to cadets at Sandhurst. Eton and Harrow, obviously, Wellington too, given its close military connections, and then Cheltenham, Clifton, Bedford, Haileybury and Marlborough[132] were amongst the small number of schools whose ex-pupils disproportionately trod the halls and parade grounds of Sandhurst in the years before the war[i].

In spite of serving officers' complaints to the likes of Elgin and Akers-Douglas about the poor and inappropriate quality of the education provided by Public Schools there had long been an almost symbiotic relationship between the two institutions. Writing in the 1960s and 70s, C B Otley, a sociology lecturer at Sheffield and then Lancaster Universities, emphasised this close connection which he went so far as to describe as the 'militarization' of the schools involved. This meant not only the introduction of departments, or 'sides', which were devoted to the education necessary to enter either Sandhurst or Woolwich[ii], but this also impacted on the ethos of the schools, with a glorification of all things martial and a special focus on the attributes deemed necessary to make a successful army officer: character, gallantry, sportsmanship. In other words, being a gentleman.

Although compulsion/conscription was not found acceptable to the British government or public before 1914 it is interesting to note the subject matter of a talk given in June 1900 by the Rev. Edmond Warre, the Headmaster of Eton, at RUSI. The talk was entitled *The Relation of Public Secondary Schools to the Orgnaization of National Defence*. Warre was a man much involved in the Volunteer movement which sprang up in 1859 in answer to a perceived threat from France. He had been involved in the formation of the Oxford University Rifle Corps in that year when a student at Balliol and, since then, in the Eton School Rifle Volunteer Corps. He was, at the time of the talk, the Hon. Col., 4th (Eton College) Volunteer Battalion, Oxfordshire Light Infantry.

Eton had been for some thirty years an active participant in the biennial Headmasters Conference of the Heads of most major and minor public and

---

[i] Not all Public Schools had strong links to the Armed Forces. Reader, in *Professional Men* (Appendix 2), gives the occupations of school leavers from six leading schools over a period from the early years of Victoria's reign to c. 1906/7. The variations are considerable. Whilst Winchester College (founded 1394) and Clifton College (founded 1862) saw approximately one in five of its leavers join the Army or Navy, with Marlborough College (founded 1843) and Merchant Taylors' School this figure fell to c. one in eight. At Mill Hill School (founded 1807) and Sedbergh School (founded 1525) these figures plummeted to barely 1%. The significant change in these schools was the rapidly growing proportion of the schools' output going into business. [*Source*: Reader W J, op. cit., page 212].

[ii] Otley suggests two-thirds of late-Victorian Public Schools offered classes, other preparation, or scholarships for entry into either the Army or Navy [*Source*: Otley, C B, *Militarism and Militarization in the Public Schools, 1900-1972*, The British Journal of Sociology, Vol. 29, No. 3 (Sept., 1978), pp. 321-339].

independent schools. Now, with the numerous failures in South Africa looming large in popular thinking, and with a shortage of suitable young men with even a modicum of military training having been exposed, Warre circulated a resolution to 100+ schools concerning military education. It was, in its way, tantamount to compulsion but only for a certain class of young man – those aged over 15 and still at school or at university (some 10-15,000 all told). In other words, not the working class. This cadre of middle and upper-class youth, according to Warre's idea, 'should be enrolled for the purpose of instruction in drill, manoeuvre, and the use of arms'. The Heads of 83 of the schools agreed with this approach and Warre took it to the War Office who asked that he prepare a memorandum for the Secretary of State. The first paragraph made clear what he intended: 'At the present time there is a golden opportunity for placing on a permanent footing, for the purpose of national defence, the training of a large portion of the educated youth of the country'. Warre wished an Act of Parliament to be passed to enshrine this requirement in law and for it to be done whilst public concern about the state of the Army was at its height. One reaching the age of 15 the name of each boy was to be passed to the Army officer commanding the local regimental district. Warre then went on to describe a three to four-year course of instruction and training, a system of promotion, a certification process and uniform with the objective of providing a permanently replenishing pool of prospective Army officers, better trained and equipped than anything which had gone before.

Warre's only concession to the general opposition to 'compulsion' was to replace the phrase that all pupils 'capable of bearing arms' be replaced with 'able and willing to bear arms'. This, he believed, maintained the 'voluntary principle' behind military service in Britain though, no doubt, knowing only too well that peer pressure in schools was of such a nature only the most resolute young man might withstand it. Bearing this in mind, Warre went on:

> "I believe that, as far as the Public Schools are concerned, the numbers that will take the patriotic view of their duty towards the defence of their country will not fall far short of those who are capable of bearing arms, and it is certainly better to maintain the voluntary principle until necessity compels us to conscription."

On this not all agreed. The Rt. Hon. Adelbert Wellington Brownlow-Cust, 3rd Earl Brownlow, GCVO, VD, PC, DL, JP, Eton and the Grenadier Guards, and previously Under Secretary of State for War in Salisbury's Tory administration, did not see why boys should be given the option of joining in military training, complaining that 'they were not asked whether they should learn Latin or Greek; they were ordered to do it'. So should it be for military education. Brownlow took it a step further, suggesting military training should apply in primary as well as secondary schools. His Lordship would clearly have loved to be alive and resident in certain US States in the modern era.

Warre's hope was that, over time, the functions and expertise of Woolwich would align closely with the universities and Sandhurst would disappear altogether to be replaced by a military university. Lastly, and in a swipe at the crammers, he dreamt of the day:

"... when the present system, by which a man has to cram in order to get into the Staff College, will have come to be thought monstrous and unnatural."

Militarization of these schools, as Otley would have it, was never far from the surface of the Public Schools.

Victorian Public Schools were a mixture of the old, historic and often charitably based schools and colleges and the more recently established independent schools with some, like Wellington College in Berkshire[i], being established entirely on the basis of supplying education to sons of military households. The term 'Public Schools' (which, as we all know, are in fact private) comes from the *Public Schools Act 1868* which sought to reform and to regulate the activities of, initially, nine ancient private schools. The Act gave these schools complete independence from the Crown, State or Church. Two of the schools, St Paul's (founded 1509 to serve children of 'all nacions (*sic*) and countries indifferently') and Merchant Taylor's (founded 1561) successfully argued they should be excluded from the provisions of the Act as they were already, in legal terms, private. That left seven schools for the Act to impact. They were all male, boarding schools:

Winchester College (founded 1382 for 70 poor scholars);
Eton College (founded by Henry VI in 1440 to provide free education to 70 poor boys);
Shrewsbury School (founded 1552 as a free grammar school);
Westminster School (previously a charitable school, re-founded in 1560);
Rugby School (founded 1567 as a free grammar school for the boys of Rugby and Brownsover);
Harrow School (founded 1572 as a free school for local boys); and
Charterhouse School (founded 1611)

The City of London School (founded 1834 though a school existed in 1442) was added to the list on appeal in 1887.

Perversely, as mentioned, many of these schools were founded to the benefit of 'poor scholars' but, by the mid to late-Victorian period, they became the fee-paying educational home for the sons (and only the 'sons') of the upper and the wealthier middle classes.

By 1914, the term Public School had become generic. 782 endowed grammar schools were examined by the Taunton Commission after the 1868 Act. The result was the *Endowed Schools Act 1869*, passed by Gladstone's first administration, which produce the basis for a national network of secondary schools. To counter this process, Edward Thring, the Head at Uppingham, convened annual meetings to consider and counter the impact of the *Endowed Schools Act* on the private school sector, meetings which became the basis of the *Head Masters' Conference* (HMC)

---

[i] Wellington College opened its doors in 1859 and much of its intake was the orphaned sons of Army officers. Its first Master was Edward White Benson, later Archbishop of Canterbury. Otley states it was the single biggest contributor to the ranks of Army officers over the 100 years prior to 1970 [Otley: op. cit.].

representing now some 296 independent schools. These independent schools often maintained very close links to the Army and, where possible, aligned their curriculum with the needs of Sandhurst or Woolwich entry. Thus, there was a proliferation of military-related 'sides' of which Otley cites: the Military and Engineering sides at Cheltenham and Clifton, the Army Division at Haileybury, The Army House at Bradfield and the Civil and Military side at Bedford. There were also, for example, Army Classes, or sides, at Eton, Harrow, Radley and Dulwich. It was from such schools that many army officers came and, during the 1890s, some 180 boys a year were sitting entrance examinations for Sandhurst and Woolwich from the ten top schools. Overall, Otley estimated that by 1900 43% of *HMC* schools had an Army side/class, 24% indicated that they offered some form of 'preparation for the services', and 5% provided some form of incentive for those seeking to join the military.[133]

Amongst already senior officers the concentration in certain schools was still narrower. Fontenot's study shows that 91 of 108 Major Generals whose education he could then identify, ten were educated privately and of the remaining 81 (all educated at either major or minor public schools) some 62% were educated at just six schools: Eton 12, Cheltenham 11, Wellington 10, Harrow 7 and Clifton and Marlborough five each.

GIVEN THESE BOOKS' FINAL FOCUS on the preparations for the attack on the *Somme* on 1st July 1916, it is worthwhile looking rather more specifically at the background and education of the GOCs of the Armies, Corps, Divisions and Brigades involved. The 'occupations' of the fathers of 65 of the 82 GOCs have been ascertained and, of these, 34 (52%) were themselves in the Army. If one adds in fathers from the Navy and Peers/landowners then 66% of GOCs came from such backgrounds. Seven (11%) had clergymen for fathers. Another seven came from a broadly business or professional background, though only one from 'trade', and that was Sir Douglas Haig. Four more had a legal background and the rest from miscellaneous professions (Pilcher's father being the curator of an art museum in Rome and Charteris's a university professor). What is also notable is all bar one (Congreve) of the officers coming from the peerage/landowning background were second or later sons, i.e. they would not automatically inherit. None of the sons of those in business or trade were first sons and likely to take over the running of the business and Sir Douglas Haig, the youngest surviving child in his family, was fifth in line to inherit the Haig whiskey empire.

As far as education is concerned, an analysis (where possible) of the schools of British GOCs on 1st July 1916 shows a heavy bias towards a select group of public schools. The leading ones, representing 53% of the total, were: Haileybury/USC 11, Harrow 9, Charterhouse 9, Eton 8, Wellington 8, Clifton 5, Marlborough 4, Winchester 4 and Cheltenham 4. At least another thirteen came from other public schools, meaning at least 65% of the General Officers involved on 1st July 1916 were public school products. This figure is certainly an under-estimate.

The formation of Officer Training Corps (OTCs) as part of the 1908 Haldane Reforms gave an even greater impetus to the concentration of public schools as the source of most Army officers. First mooted in 1906, when approved two years later, OTCs were formed as a Junior Division (Public Schools) and a Senior Division (Universities). Some of the senior OTCs were based on pre-existing Volunteer units. The Oxford University OTC, for example, was born out of the 1st (Oxford University) Volunteer Battalion of the Oxfordshire Light Infantry. The Cambridge University Rifle Volunteers became the University OTC. In all 23 Senior Division OTCs and an Inns of Court OTC were created between 1914-18.

Some 166 Junior Divisions were formed because of the 1908 changes of which, by 1914, just a third were *not* formed in Public Schools. Looked at another way, 80% of Public Schools had an OTC by 1914. Their effect was to widen the range of schools which supplied cadets to Sandhurst and officers to the Army with no school being as dominant as was Eton which supplied 11% of the officers involved in the South African War. This changed by 1914 such that Wellington and Cheltenham supplied the largest groups out of the 4,000 young men commissioned out of OTCs but each school *only* supplied some 8% of the total.[134] During the war itself, of the 2,223 cadets at Sandhurst and Woolwich up to 29th October some 797, or 35%, came from just twelve schools with Eton (114), Wellington (105) Cheltenham (104) providing 15% on their own.[135]

Spiers, in *The Late Victorian Army*, shows there was a consistent geographical bias within the Officer Corps. Throughout the late Victorian and Edwardian eras and up to 1914 two-thirds of Colonels and Generals came from families living in rural communities, i.e. towns and villages with fewer than 5,000 inhabitants. This heavy rural bias was, of course, one of the reasons why field sports were so popular within the ranks of officers brought up in households where horse-riding, shooting and hunting generally were the norm. These were an expensive set of past-times and influenced the final determinant of the characteristics of many officers, i.e. the availability of substantial sums of family cash. Up to and including 1914 there was also a regional bias amongst officers with Ireland and Scotland heavily over-represented amongst the ranks of Colonels and Generals relative to each country's population. Spiers calculates 30% of Generals came from Scotland and Ireland and another 30% from the Home Counties[i], the South and South-West[ii]. By 1914, in contrast, the more heavily industrialised West and East Midlands provided just 3% of Generals and 5% of Colonels.[136]

The financial and intellectual costs of access to a commission explained the popularity of the other pre-Haldane route to a full-time commission: the Militia. Via this route a prospective officer might avoid the costs, as well as the entrance and final exams, of either Sandhurst or Woolwich. As a result, about one third of all officers entered the Army from the Militia prior to the reform of the system post-1902. Indeed, prior to the findings of the Akers-Douglas committee on the education of officers, Militia officers entered the Regular Army via an examination which the committee roundly condemned, highlighting, for example, the complete absence from a military examination of anything to do with tactics[iii].

---

[i] Kent, Sussex, Surrey, & Middlesex.
[ii] Counties west & south of Hampshire, Berkshire, Wiltshire, & Gloucestershire (inc.).
[iii] 16 of 108 Major Generals in 1914 came via the Militia [*Source*: Fontenot, op. cit., page 50].

The recommendation of the Akers-Douglas committee was that candidates from the Militia should now either take the same examination as that sat by cadets at Sandhurst or Woolwich or, indeed, an even more specifically military exam on purely military matters. This latter recommendation was adopted in 1904 and immediately gave a more attractive path to a commission for those who failed the more academic entrance examinations of the two officer training schools. None of the ex-Militia officers mentioned below received their commission by way of the more rigorous examination then instituted.

It was, however, through the previous and far less rigorous process some 19 (16%) of the 118 General Officers involved in the opening day of the *Somme* (or in close reserve) gained their commissions, and all of them via the examination thought by the Akers-Douglas committee to be inadequate. This figure, however, underestimates the numbers of purely infantry and cavalry officers who entered via the militia as every GOC drawn from either the artillery or engineers went through Woolwich. These 19 militia GOCs therefore represented 23% of those commanding an infantry or cavalry Corps, Division or Brigade. They were:

Corps commanders (1): Pulteney (III Corps);
Divisional commanders (8): Watts (7th Division), Pilcher (17th Division), Wanless O'Gowan (31st Division), Ingouville-Williams (34th Division), Nugent (36th Division), Stuart-Wortley (46th Division), Hull (56th Division) and MacAndrew (2nd Indian Cavalry Division);
Brigade commanders (10): Prowse (11th Brigade), Compton (14th Brigade), Shoubridge (54th Brigade), Jackson (55th Brigade), Rawling (62nd Brigade), Steavenson (90th Brigade), Ingles (93rd Brigade), Rees (94th Brigade), Withycombe (107th Brigade) and Adlercron (148th Brigade)[i].

Finally, Fontenot suggests, in the long term, it paid to be in the cavalry. Of the 108 Major Generals in 1914: 43 came from the infantry, 28 from either the RA or RE, 17 from Indian infantry regiments, and seven each from the cavalry and the Indian cavalry. Of the five Major Generals who were promoted to Field Marshal, four came from either the cavalry or Indian cavalry, and one from the infantry. This means 29% of the cavalry Major Generals of 1914 were elevated to this supreme rank and just 2% of their infantry equivalents. Not one Guards, RA or RE officer achieved Field Marshal rank and, furthermore, not one RA or RE officer reached the rank of full General (all the cavalry officers who reached full General became Field Marshals). Furthermore, the average time in service needed to reach the rank of Major General in either the RA or RE was six years longer than that of a cavalry officer (i.e. 35 years against 29). 71% of British cavalry Major Generals from 1914 (5 out of 7) and 66% of Guards Major Generals (4 out of 6) were at least promoted to Lieutenant General as opposed to just 30% of infantry and 21% of RA/RE Major Generals.[137]

These numbers are reinforced by an analysis of officers who commanded either an Army/Expeditionary Force or Corps during the war. Of the 22 officers who on one or more occasion commanded one of the five BEF Armies or three

---

[i] Brig. Gen. Reginald Shuter, 109th Brigade, was commissioned out of the local military forces of Victoria, Australia.

Expeditionary Forces eleven were infantrymen, nine were cavalrymen and two artillerymen (neither of them from the RGA). These commanders were drawn from the 58 officers who on one or more occasion commanded a Corps. Of these, 28 were infantrymen, 13 cavalrymen, 9 artillerymen (none from the RGA) and two from the Royal Engineers (Harper and Hunter-Weston). Once again, it shows being from the cavalry appeared to smooth one's path to promotion at the highest level with two-thirds of the cavalrymen given Corps command then going on to an Army command later. The respective figures for the other branches of the Army were: infantrymen 40%, artillerymen 22%, engineers 0%.

IT WAS NOT JUST IMPECUNIOUS GENTLEMEN who struggled to enter the officer class. Another side-effect of the need to be financially, if not intellectually, well-endowed was that it was well-nigh impossible for a ranker to aspire to such exalted heights[i]. There were many in the Army who regarded this as excellent news and their condescending views were admirably summed up by a letter to the editor of *The Times* from the previously quoted '*AAH*' which mainly describes the huge costs to be incurred by young officers in the Army. On the subject of 'promotion from the ranks', however, he was quite clear (although taking great care not to upset someone like William Robertson, the ex-ranker now Deputy Assistant Adjutant-General to Lord Roberts in South Africa). '(Promotion from the ranks) is not,' he averred, 'except in very rare instances, a good thing'. He justified this sweeping statement on the basis that any commissioned NCO must inevitably be older than, but more junior in seniority to, officers emerging from Sandhurst or Woolwich. Furthermore, he suggested, a man promoted from the ranks did:

"... not as a rule (of course, there are brilliant exceptions) carry the power of 'leading men' in the same way that the veriest youngster from Sandhurst or the Militia does. This to the civilian may appear strange and improbable, but it is a well-known fact all the same."[138]

Such attitudes ensured promotion from the ranks was a highly unusual occurrence and, indeed, the numbers thus promoted declined throughout the Edwardian era[139]. In 1913, for example, just seven men (1% of the 625 newly commissioned officers) were permanently commissioned into the Regular Army from the ranks[140], all of which makes Sir William Robertson's climb from Private soldier to Field Marshal even more remarkable[ii].

---

[i] Not so in 'egalitarian' Republican France. The *École Militaire d'Infanterie* at Saint-Maixent, *département des Deux-Sèvres*, provided a year-long course by which NCO's trained as officers. Smith in *From Mutiny to Obedience* (page 37) states that 60% of the lieutenants mobilised for *5e Division* in August 1914 were commissioned out of the ranks. The introduction of the *élèves officiers de reserve* programme, introduced 1905, allowed conscripts after one year to enter a 12-month reserve officer training programme to become the equivalent of a 2nd Lt (*Sous-Lt.*). For the first six months they were given the rank of *aspirant* [*Source*: Smith, op. cit., footnote page 38].

[ii] Of the remaining, 461 (74%) came from either the RMC (6 from the RMC, Canada) or RMA, 78 (12%) from University OTCs, 76 (12%) from the Special Reserve/Territorial Force and 3 (0.5%) from the Colonies. Between 5th August 1914 and 1st December 1918, of the 16,544 newly permanently commissioned 2nd Lts, 6,713

There were various problems for the man of talent who climbed through the ranks of non-commissioned officers (NCOs). As previously mentioned, whether a man was considered a 'gentleman' was an essential issue in the Victorian and Edwardian eras and Sir Douglas Haig made regular references in his diaries to various Allied officers not being 'gentlemen'. These comments were normally reserved for the French, and their Commander in Chief, Joseph Joffre, was so described, but it was equally applied to officers of other nations, most especially the Italians, and was normally accompanied by comments about their lack of trustworthiness and/or grasping nature.

Within the Army family background and status was an issue which, for some, could not be ignored. Robertson, despite a favourable marriage to the daughter of a General in the Indian Army, was not regarded in some quarters as a *real* 'gentleman'. Gen. Sir William Nicholson, for example, referred to Robertson's 'want of breeding' prior to the latter's appointment as commandant at Camberley.

Of course, being a 'gentleman' had nothing to do with native wit or intelligence, hard work or dedication to one's profession, and everything to do with bloodline, connections, the ownership of land and property – and money. But, ideally, not money from 'trade'. As men like Amelius Lockwood and the anonymous *'CO'* made clear, the peerage and the gentry were always suspicious of the motives of the *'nouveau riche'* whose wealth came after success in business or industry rather than from inheritance and land.

Money was an obvious brick in the wall which blocked promotion on merit and performance from the ranks, and might also prevent the upward movement of the bright and motivated young officer keen to get on professionally. Without cash a man could be isolated, unable to dine in an expensive officers' mess and pay for all of the other expenses which came with being an officer. It is clear from earlier references that a failure, or inability, to participate in the social life of the regiment made junior officers vulnerable to the snobbery and arrogance of the financially better endowed and connected. A private income was essential unless you were an unusually, almost perversely, driven, self-sufficient and self-contained man like Robertson, of which type few joined the lower ranks of the British Army, or unless one was an officer in a regiment which did not look down its nose at those who put their military career and professionalism before a gilded lifestyle.

The results of such restrictions and attitudes was a self-perpetuating, socially exclusive, unprofessional officer class barely fit to the purpose of making modern war. For too many officers an Army commission was as much, if not more, a lifestyle choice not a profession and significant numbers were no more than ill-educated, upper-class *dilettantes*. Furthermore, the Army, like Britain even now, was

---

came from the Ranks (41%), 7,113 (43%) from the RMCs and RMA, 1,109 (7%) were Temporary commissions and the rest, 1,609 (10%) came from the Special Reserve, TF, the University OTCs, and the Colonies. In all, 229,316 war-time commissions were granted including the above: 30,376 from the Special Reserve, 60,044 from the Territorial Force and 107,929 from OTCs (not including the RAMC, RAF, Royal Defence Corps, Veterinary Corps, and other units) [*Source: Statistics of the Military Effort of the British Empire during the Great War 1914-1920*, HMSO, 1922, page 234-5].

not a meritocracy. Promotion was based on connections: who one knew, who one went to school with, who one hunted or shot with, who one knew at Court. Almost every leading soldier, be it Wolesley, Kitchener or Roberts or, later, French and Haig, had a coterie of junior officers hanging grimly to their coat tails hoping for preferment and recognition just as their benefactors had done before. The most exalted surrounded themselves with people they knew, who shared their opinions (or, at least, never voiced a contrary one), and who acted as an echo chamber to decisions made and statements uttered. Haig was no more guilty than other senior officers when he selected a motley group of friends and connections to be his staff, however badly equipped some were (e.g. Kiggell and Charteris) to fulfil the essential positions to which they were appointed. It was the way of the Army down the generations. Equally, if one fell foul of the high and mighty then not only could one's career stall badly, it might even be over as the dismissal of Smith-Dorrien by Sir John French in May 1915 shows. Theirs was a relationship which festered for some years and 'Orace' got his undeserved comeuppance when the opportunity arose during the Second Battle of Ypres (see page 495).

War winnowed out the wheat and the chaff within the senior ranks of the Army though not all the wheat fell to a German scythe, some was cut down by British hands because of perceived or genuine disagreements on tactics, strategy, and policy. Sadly, some of the chaff lingered for years, occupying space far better used by the brighter and more vigorous shoots emerging from the lower ranks of the Army's pre-war professional and war-time amateur officers.

ENDNOTES:
1 Wells, H G, *Anticipations*, op. cit., page 207.
2 Ibid., footnote, page 209.
3 *The Times*, T. Miller Maguire. *The Aldershot Staff on Education*, 6th March 1901, page 2.
4 *The Times*, *The War Office and the Public Schools*, 29th December 1900, page 10.
5 *The Times*, Emeritus, *The Preliminary Education Of Officers*, 22nd January 1901, page 11.
6 Ibid.
7 Churchill, W A, *My Early Life*, Fontana, 1957, pages 36-7.
8 *The Times*, James, W H, *The Preliminary Education Of Officers*, 26th January 1901, page 3.
9 Ibid.
10 Knollys, Col. H, *Public Schools and Army Competitive Examinations*, *Blackwood's Magazine*, July 1895, page 67.
11 Akers Douglas, *Report* op. cit., Appendix XV, page 79, para 27.
12 Ibid., para 28.
13 Henderson, G F R, *The Science of War*, page 393.
14 Ibid.
15 Ibid., pages 397-8.
16 Wilkinson, S, *The Brain of an Army*, Constable & Co., 1913, page 191.
17 Amery, op. cit., footnote page 199.
18 Ibid., footnote page 200.
19 *The Times*, 21st June 1855, page 8.
20 *The Times*, *The Army - Its System and Education*, 10th January 1855, page 10.
21 Bond, B, *The Victorian Army and the Staff College*, Eyre Methuen, 1982, pages 59-60.
22 *The Times*, *The Education of Military Officers*, 12th November 1889, page 12.
23 *The Times*, 22nd April 1902, page 10.
24 *The Spectator*, 1st September 1900, page 20.
25 Quoted in Amery, op. cit., footnote page 198.
26 Beckett, I F W, *Wood, Sir (Henry) Evelyn*, *Oxford Dictionary of National Biography*, OUP, 2004.
27 *Minutes and Evidence taken before the Committee appointed to consider the Education and Training of Officers of the Army*, HMSO, London, 1902, para 2.
28 Ibid., para 4.
29 *The Times*, 9th March 1902, page 4.
30 Ibid.
31 Akers-Douglas, *Report*, op. cit., para 6.
32 Ibid., para 7.
33 Ibid., para 9.
34 *The Times*, 29th December 1903, page 7.
35 *The Times*, 25th December 1903, page 4.
36 *The Times*, 9th March 1902, page 4.
37 Quoted by Brian Holden Reid in a review of The Marquess of Anglesey's *A History of the British Cavalry 1819-1919, Volume 4: 1899-1913* in *History Today*.
38 *The Times*, 9th March 1902, page 4.
39 Ibid.
40 Ibid.
41 Akers-Douglas, *Report* op. cit., para 101.
42 Ibid., para 99.
43 *Hansard*, House of Lords Debates, *Military Education*, op. cit., cc476 and Akers-Douglas, *Report*, para 94.
44 Akers-Douglas, *Report* op. cit., para 95.
45 Ibid., cc477.
46 Ibid., para 108.
47 Ibid., para 111.
48 *The Times*, 9th March 1902, page 4.

49 Akers-Douglas, *Report* op. cit., para 131.
50 Ibid.
51 *The Times*, 9th March 1902, page 4.
52 Akers-Douglas, *Evidence,* page 30, para 698.
53 *The Times*, 9th March 1902, page 4.
54 Akers-Douglas, *Report* op. cit., para. 133.
55 Ibid., para. 132.
56 *The Times*, 9th March 1902, page 4.
57 Akers-Douglas, *Report* op. cit., para. 133.
58 Ibid.
59 Ibid.
60 *The Times*, 9th March 1902, page 4.
61 Akers-Douglas, *Report* op. cit., para. 135.
62 Ibid.
63 Ibid., para. 137.
64 Ibid.
65 *The Times*, Letters to the Editor, page 11, 28th June 1902.
66 Akers-Douglas, *Evidence*, Page 63, paras 1548-64
67 Bowman & Connelly, op. cit., page 20.
68 *The Times*, 20th August 1902, page 9.
69 Ibid.
70 Bowman & Connelly, page 21.
71 Ibid., pages 25-6
72 *The Times*, 16th February 1903, page 10.
73 *The Times*, 14th February 1903, page 11.
74 *The Times*, 5th and 6th April 1906, pages 4 and 11
75 *The Times, The Guards Inquiry*, 19th November to 10th December 1907.
76 Sagona, Prof. A, Atabay, Dr M *et al, Anzac Battlefield: A Gallipoli Landscape of War and Memory*, Cambridge University Press, 2016, pages 63-4.
77 *The Times, Lieutenant Woods's Case*, 11th December 1907, page 8.
78 *The Times, Political Notes*, 3rd February 1908, page 8.
79 *The Times, The Guards Inquiry*, 23rd November 1907, page 7.
80 Brett, op. cit., pages 261-2.
81 Cairnes, W E, *Social Life in the British Army*, John Long, 1900, page 29.
82 *The Times*, 14th February 1900, page 7.
83 Ibid.
84 *The Times*, 14th February, 1900, page 9.
85 *The Times*, 15th February, 1900, page 4.
86 *The Times*, 22nd February, 1900, page 15.
87 Ibid.
88 Ibid.
89 Riedi, E, *Brains or Polo? Equestrian Sports, Army Reform and the Gentlemanly Officer Tradition 1900-14*, Journal of the Society for Army Historical Research, No. 84, 2006, page 240.
90 *The Times*, 8th April 1903, page 11.
91 Ibid.
92 *The Times*, 25th August 1903, page 2.
93 Akers-Douglas, op. cit., and Appendix 42, page 71.
94 Reader, W J, *Professional men: The rise of the professional classes in nineteenth-century England*, Weidenfeld & Nicolson, 1966, page 97-8.
95 Roberts Papers, *NAM*, Roberts to Haig, 10th Jan.1903, in Badsey, S., op. cit., page 158.
96 *The Times, Naval and Military Intelligence*, 4th January 1902, page 10.
97 Ibid., 27th August 1902, page 4.
98 Akers-Douglas, *Report* op. cit., para. 153.
99 *The Times*, Letter from William Trevor, 31st January 1905, page 9.

[100] *The Times*, 24th February 1905, page 6.
[101] Brett, op. cit., pages 183-4.
[102] *Journal of the Royal United Services Institution*, Vol. L, January-June 1906, *The Shortage of Officers in the Army*, page 785.
[103] Ibid., page 788.
[104] Ibid., page 797.
[105] *The Times*, 5th March 1908.
[106] Ibid.
[107] Ibid., 6th February 1908, page 4.
[108] Ibid.
[109] Ibid.
[110] Fontenot, Col. G, *The Modern Major General: Patterns in the Careers of British Army Major Generals on Active Duty at the Time of the Sarajevo Assassinations*, MA Thesis, University of North Carolina, 1980, Page 45.
[111] *The Times*, 6th February 1908, page 4.
[112] Ogilvie, V, *The English Public School*, Batsford, 1957, page 189.
[113] *Conference of General Staff Officers at the Staff College 1908*, HMSO, page 32.
[114] Ibid., page 33.
[115] Ibid., page 34.
[116] *The Times*, 10th February 1908, page 12.
[117] *RUSI Journal*, Vol. LII, July-December 1909, *Readiness or Ruin*, page 1579.
[118] Ibid., page 1593.
[119] *The Times*, 22nd June 1910, page 8.
[120] *Conference of General Staff Officers at the Staff College 1910*, op. cit., page 56.
[121] Ibid., page 59.
[122] Ibid., page 67.
[123] *Conference of General Staff Officers at the Staff College 1911*, HMSO, page 6.
[124] *The Times, Imperial Defence*, 24th May 1912, page 14.
[125] Thompson, F M L, *English Landed Society in the Nineteenth Century*, Routledge, new ed. 2006, pages 110-2.
[126] Duke, R, *The Expense of Officers, The United Service Magazine* 25 (September 1902), page 637, quoted in Fontenot, op. cit., page 22.
[127] Fontenot, op. cit., pages 21-2.
[128] Ibid., page 33.
[129] Robbins, S, *British Generalship on the Western Front 1914-8*, Frankc Cass, 2005, pages 3-4.
[130] Bowman & Connelly, op. cit., page 94.
[131] Ibid., page 9.
[132] Thomas H, *The Story of Sandhurst*, Hutchinson & Co., 1961, page 141.
[133] Otley, C B, *Militarism and militarization in the public schools 1900-1972* in Karsten, P, ed., *The Military-State-Society Symbiosis*, Garland Publishing Inc., 1998.
[134] Seldon A, & Walsh D, *Public Schools and the Great War*, Pen & Sword, page 27.
[135] Beckett, I, Bowman, T & Connelly, M, *The British Army and the First World War*, Cambridge University Press, 2017, page 56.
[136] Spiers, op. cit., pages 97-8.
[137] Fontenot, op. cit., page 63.
[138] *The Times*, 22nd March 1900, page 11.
[139] Ramsay, *Command and Cohesion*, page 64, in Jones, S, *From Boer War to World War*, page 48.
[140] *Statistics of the Military Effort of the British Empire during the Great War 1914-1920*, HMSO, 1922, page 234-5.

8. *Plus ça change, plus c'est la même chose*

"The English people have never awakened to the fact that much has happened in the interval between Blenheim and Mukden"

Lord Esher to the Duchess of Sutherland,
7th September 1906.[1]

SO SERIOUS WERE THE ISSUES revealed by South Africa a Royal Commission was set up to investigate all aspects of the campaign. Chaired by Lord Elgin, ex-viceroy of India, the commission met over fifty times between the autumns of 1902 and 1903 taking submissions from British and South African-based officers. The need for significant structural, technical, and tactical reform emerged from its four-volume report and the baton was taken up by a member of the commission, Lord Esher. Under the auspices of the *War Office (Reconstitution) Committee*, he put forward the essential structural changes which set up the system under which the British Army went to war in 1914.

Despite efforts to suppress publication by such as Kitchener[i], the committee's report was made public in early 1904 and it recommended significant changes to the governance of the Army. Its main points were:

1. The creation of a seven-man Army Council, similar to the Navy's Board of Admiralty, to be made up of the Secretary of State for War, four military[ii] and two additional civilian members;
2. The creation of a General Staff whose head, the Chief of the General Staff (later Chief of the Imperial General Staff or CIGS), was to replace the Commander in Chief, although he would not act as such. The CGS was to be supported by three Directors: a Director of Military Operations, a Director of Staff Duties, and a Director of Military Training; and
3. Changes in the administration of the War Office with duties shared between the CGS, the Adjutant-General, the Quartermaster General and the Master General of the Ordnance.

These recommendations were, in effect, the same as those previously put forward in the handily titled *Report of the Royal Commissioners Appointed to Enquire into the Civil and Professional Administration of the Naval and Military Departments and the Relation of those Departments to Each Other and to the Treasury* published in two parts in 1889 and 1890. The commission was chaired by Spencer Compton Cavendish, Marquess of Hartington (later the 8th Duke of Devonshire). Hartington was twice Secretary of State for War, briefly in 1866 and for three years, 1882-5, under Gladstone. Now a Liberal Unionist he was aided in his enquiries by two other former War ministers: Liberal Henry Campbell-Bannerman[iii], previously Financial

---

[i] Kitchener wrote to Lord Roberts in April 1903 that publication of the report would be 'prejudicial to the interests of Empire', a view firmly rebutted by Lord Elgin [*Source: NA, Kitchener Papers*, PRO30/57/25].

[ii] Chief of the General Staff, Adjutant-General, Quarter-Master General, and Master-General of the Ordnance.

[iii] Liberal MP for Stirling Burghs 1868-1908.

Secretary to the War Office (1871-4 and 1880-2) and briefly Secretary of State for War (1886), and Tory William Henry Smith[i], whose family firm was the high street stationer *W H Smith*. With minor differences, its recommendations were almost identical to those of 1904. The chief stumbling blocks were the Queen, who wished her seventh child and third son, Prince Arthur William Patrick Albert, Duke of Connaught and Strathearn, to be Commander in Chief; and the current CinC, Prince George William Frederick Charles, Duke of Cambridge, who wished neither to stand down nor see the position eliminated in favour of a Chief of Staff. A feeble War Office Council was established in 1890 but to little effect. It took the embarrassments of South Africa to force reform on the more conservative elements of the military establishment.[2] Although the Esher committee's 1904 recommendations were accepted by Arthur Balfour's Tory Government, it fell to the new Secretary of State for War, Richard Haldane, to implement the changes after the sweeping Liberal election victory at the beginning of 1906.

The Rt. Hon. Richard Burdon Haldane, KC, MP,[ii] was, according to Sir Douglas Haig, 'the greatest Secretary of State for War England (*sic*) has ever had'. This was written in a bound copy of Haig's *Despatches* left at Haldane's London house on the evening of 19th July, 1919, the day of the celebratory march past of the Armed Forces. Born in Edinburgh on 30th July 1856, educated at Edinburgh Academy, Göttingen University, and the University of Edinburgh, he was called to the Bar in 1879. Within eleven years he was a QC. A Liberal Imperialist and friend of the future Prime Minister, Herbert Asquith, Haldane was elected MP for Haddingtonshire[iii] in the 1885 General Election and held the seat until 1911 when he went to the Lords as Viscount Haldane of Cloan in the County of Perth.

When the Balfour Conservative government collapsed in December 1905 Haldane hoped to be made Lord Chancellor but was passed over in favour of Sir Robert Threshie Reid, the MP for Dumfries Burghs, and a previous Solicitor and Attorney General. As other candidates for the War Office fell by the wayside, i.e. Lord Esher and Herbert Gladstone, and when it was realised Sir Edward Grey would only join the Cabinet were Haldane in it, the mantle fell on his shoulders.

---

[i] Conservative MP for Westminster 1868-85 (preceded as MP by John Stuart Mill, the Liberal philosopher and economist). He was elected MP for The Strand, 1885-91, in which latter year he died and was succeeded in a by-election by his son, William Frederick Danvers Smith. Previously First Lord of the Admiralty (1877-80) he is believed to have been the inspiration for the character Sir Joseph Porter in Gilbert and Sullivan's *HMS Pinafore*.

[ii] By 1915 The Rt Hon. The Viscount Haldane, KT, OM, PC, KC, FRS, FBA.

[iii] Defeating Lord Hugo Elcho. His family held the seat from 1847 when the previous Lord Elcho (later Earl of Wemyss and March) was elected. *The Representation of the People Act 1884 (Third Reform Act)* and *The Redistribution of Seats Act 1885* increased the electorate. 892 men voted in the 1883 by-election which saw Hugo Elcho elected (492 to 400 for the Liberal), but 5,418 voted in 1885 (Haldane 3,473 votes, Elcho 1,945). The seat became more marginal as middle-class Edinburgh families built villas, but Haldane's successor, John Deans Hope (MP for Fife West 1900 to December 1910), won the seat in the 1911 by-election. He held Berwick and Haddington as a Lloyd George Coalition Liberal in 1918 but came fourth as an Independent Liberal in 1922.

It was a fortunate choice and he assumed office on 13th December 1905. When the Liberals won a historic election victory early in 1906, Haldane was confirmed in his role for the foreseeable future.

Others have more than adequately described Haldane's enormous impact on the British Army in the immediate pre-war period and Haig's later endorsement is wholly justified[i]. Suffice to say, Haldane's changes belatedly brought the administration and structure of the Army into the modern era even if, during his time in office, budgets were constrained and investment in troops, training and equipment limited. Briefly, his key reforms were:

- The creation of a six division Expeditionary Force plus ancillary troops which was created by Special Army Order of 1st January 1907;
- The *Territorial and Reserve Forces Act 1907* of August 1907, implemented on 1st April 1908, which created the Territorial Force for Home Defence and of the Special Reserve from which the Regular Army might draw drafts. These replaced the Volunteers/Yeomanry and the Militia[ii];
- Changes in training based on the various training manuals introduced since 1904 which, under Douglas Haig then the Director of Staff Duties at the War Office, were later codified in *Field Service Regulations 1909*;
- The creation of the Senior and Junior Officer Training Corps based on selected universities and Public Schools respectively. These were organised under Army Orders 160 and 178 of 1908;
- The creation of the Imperial General Staff after the removal of the position of Commander in Chief in 1904 and the creation of the General Staff in 1904. The first Chief of the Imperial General Staff was Field Marshal Sir William Nicholson who assumed this role on 22nd November 1909 (having been CGS since 2nd April 1908).

The previously mentioned changes in the upper echelons of the Army and the War Office were essential and helped in certain ways to shape the highly professional Expeditionary Force which left Great Britain for northern France in August 1914. The Army Council, however, was a committee on which the four military members each had their own separate areas of responsibility and their own individual channel of communication with the Secretary of State for War. As a means of delivering decisive action and a system for generating 'joined up thinking' the Army Council lacked the necessary focus. To quote a paper delivered to the *Land Warfare Studies Centre* in Canberra in 2008:

---

[i] Spiers, E M, *Haldane: Army Reformer*, Edinburgh University Press, 1984, and Chapter 12 onwards in Dunlop, J K, *The development of the British Army 1899–1914*, Methuen, 1938. Also, *Richard Burdon Haldane: an Autobiography*, Hodder & Stoughton, 1929.

[ii] In 1904 a commission, chaired by the Duke of Norfolk and dominated by conscription-favouring politicians and officers, investigated the state of the Militia and Volunteers and called for their abolition as not fit for purpose, i.e. defence against foreign invasion. Their alternative was a Home Defence Army raised by conscription. The Tory Secretary of State for War, Arnold-Foster, rejected the report and its recommendations, accusing the commission of going beyond its terms of reference.

"The stultifying effect of operating as part of a committee meant that no senior officer had responsibility for the (Army's) intellectual development."[3]

Consequently, crucial issues remained about tactics, equipment, training of both officers and other ranks, and the nature of the reserve forces which might be available the next time the Army went to war. There also remained serious questions about the intellect, education, and professional training of the Army's officers and these were of sufficient concern a House of Commons committee was set up to investigate.

The questions about training and the reserves were, in many ways, intertwined and the sweeping reforms introduced by Haldane, although made at a time of swingeing cuts in spending on the Army[i], introduced changes which helped produce a better trained and organised Regular Army, a more effective reserve in the form of the Territorial Force and Special Reserve, and a large source of at least partially trained officers as a result of the introduction of Officer Training Corps (OTCs) in the Public Schools and Universities. In addition, the concept of the Expeditionary Force of six infantry and one cavalry divisions was turned into a reality. The Expeditionary Force was designed to be moved to anywhere in the world where danger threatened the interests of the British Empire, be that the Americas, Africa, India or, as increasingly anticipated, continental Europe.

Of immediate interest to the Army, however, was what might be learnt from the South African experience. Its early months were unrelentingly depressing and embarrassing for Queen Victoria's Army. Leaving to one side the extraordinary tactical incompetence of the senior officers – CinC Sir Redvers Buller[ii], Maj. Gen. Lord Methuen and Maj. Gen. Sir William Gatacre who, between them, supervised the reverses at Ladysmith, Stormberg, Modder River, Magersfontein, Colenso,

---

[i] The Liberal Government cut spending on the Army by 10% between 1906 and 1910. It was nearly back to the 1906 level by 1914 but, during that period, inflation produced a nearly 20% increase in costs meaning that, immediately prior to the war, the 'buying power' of the Army estimates had been reduced by 20% in real terms over eight years.
[ii] Buller tried to blame his inadequacies on his 'rotten staff'. Unfortunately for him, when told who was on his staff, he wrote to Wolseley stating 'If I can't beat the Boers with such a lot of officers as you propose, I ought to be kicked!' [Brett, op. cit., page 261]. Buller somehow survived his ignominious performance to remain in South Africa until the late summer of 1900 and his return to Britain was, remarkably, greeted with something close to acclaim. Wolseley reputedly told his wife that Buller 'had not shown any of the characteristics I had attributed to him: no military genius, no firmness... He seems dazed and dumbfounded' [*Source*: Farwell, B, *Queen Victoria's Little Wars*, Harper and Row, 1972, page 348]. He was eventually summarily sacked by Brodrick and Roberts when he intemperately and publicly responded to a scathing letter in *The Times* of 28th September 1901 written by Leo Amery (under the *nom de plume* of *'Reformer'*) which viciously criticised him, declaring him unfit for command at Aldershot, which post he resumed on his return. Two days before his dismissal on 17th October, Esher wrote 'the man deserves his fate' [Brett, op. cit., page 305]. There is, however, a *Redvers Buller Road* in Aldershot. Whether he is fit to be ranked alongside *Alanbrooke (Road)*, *Slim (Close)* and *O'Connor (Road)* is highly doubtful.

Spion Kop and Vaal Krantz during the winter of 1899-1900 – the Army itself was shown to be deficient in tactics, training and equipment. Indeed, it is fair to say the infection of incompetence, on occasion, touched even the greatest soldiers in the land as Kitchener and Roberts showed at Paardeberg. Furthermore, the Elgin Commission, though critical of the education, training, and performance of junior officers in South Africa, laid most blame on their superiors:

> "... junior officers very rapidly developed in the actual war their natural power of initiative and ... the deleterious effects of a system based upon a passed-away mode of warfare were more apparent among the senior officers."[4]

Kitchener was still more precise, and more scathing:

> "It was found on more than one occasion that the reputation of officers acquired in peace time, and even in other wars, was not sustained under the more modern conditions of South Africa... I should also like to point out, further, that in the higher ranks also there seems to be a want of that professionalism which is essential to thorough efficiency."[5]

Lord Esher expressed the view in September 1902 that:

> "... only two out of every forty regimental officers are any good at all. The rest are loafers... nothing could be more gallant than the regimental officer – but gallantry is not competence".

Overall, very few seemed any good to him and this would remain so 'until the army is looked upon as a profession and not a pastime'.[6] And yet, despite these clear weaknesses amongst the higher and middle 'management' of the Army it was the prospective and the most junior officers of the Army who were made the subject of an inquiry into their intelligence, education and ongoing training.

Esher went on to assert that the 'Staff College men failed in S(outh) A(frica).' For those officers who did well, caught their commander's eye or simply had the right social or military connections, the 'step up' in military education was attendance at the Staff College at Camberley or, from 1905, the Indian Staff College at Quetta now in modern Pakistan. But even the presence of the letters 'p.s.c.', which stood for 'Passed Staff College', did not necessarily mean the officer after whose name they appeared genuinely benefited from the military and technical training which Camberley was supposed to provide. Also, the numbers thus provided were small and the quality not always up to scratch. As a result, the absence of a sufficient number of properly trained staff officers was raised as being of 'supreme importance' to the Army in future. The Army in South Africa had grown rapidly and ended up far larger than anything previously considered likely in an overseas war. Thus, numerous new staff officers experienced the sharp learning curve of 'on the job' training. Afterwards, anyone looking ahead towards a possible European war might have imagined a comparable scenario with a similar shortage of trained staff officers unless dramatic action was taken. It was not.

The creation of the Staff College as an independent entity from Sandhurst in 1858 was a dimly shining light in the Stygian military gloom which surrounded the Army after the debacle of the Crimean War. Its *raison d'être* was to produce men equipped to be staff officers and it was expected to be the career path of the 'brightest and the best' the Army had to offer. The College, however, illuminated the developmental path of the *'élite'* of the Army's officers in an erratic and sometimes misleading manner over the next fifty years.

After 1870 the College's standing was materially enhanced under the guidance of a new commandant, Maj. Gen. Sir Edward Bruce Hamley[i]. The quality of the staff improved, the balance of final examinations was changed, and efforts were made to get students into the field, visiting battlefields and meeting officers from other European Armies. The number of entrants also increased from forty in 1870 to 64 by 1886. Although now Indian Army officers and more than one officer per regiment were able to attend, still 75% of the student places were reserved for the cavalry and infantry meaning more intelligent and better educated gunners and engineers might be refused entry if their small 'quota' was full. On occasion, again because of the quota system, officers from the cavalry and infantry obtained places at the Staff College even though they failed to pass the entrance examination[ii].

Moreover, its limitations on the numbers of Engineers and Gunners who might attend (two of each) meant numerous less qualified and potentially less able infantry and cavalry officers attended Camberley than would have been the case had entrance been strictly on merit.[iii] Later, one of those Engineers fortunate to gain entry (in 1891, having been denied in 1884 as the sixth placed Engineer and fifteenth candidate overall), Col. Frederic Natusch Maude[iv] remarked:

---

[i] Hamley was ADC to Sir Richard Dacres, the commander of the artillery in the Crimean War. Between 1859 and 1866 he was professor of military history at Sandhurst. He later commanded 2nd Division at the Battle of Tel el-Kebir. He was elected the Conservative MP for Birkenhead in 1885. His book *The Operations of War*, published in 1866, was highly thought of by General Helmuth von Moltke, and was used as the only text for the entrance exam at Camberley until 1894.

[ii] Some unlucky officers failed to enter the Staff College because of these rules, some repeatedly. Capt. L H Ducros, RA, scored 2,788 in 1892 which placed him above twelve successful candidates of the 26 who gained entrance, one of whom was Launcelot Kiggell who crept in with 2,003 marks, the third worst. That year four of the top ten were artillerymen and two came from the Indian Staff Corps. Only two cavalrymen featured in the entire list. Capt. H J Du Cane, RA, would also have beaten ten of the successful candidates. The following year, Ducros got in, but Du Cane was again unlucky, losing out to four infantrymen with worse scores. One cavalry officer got in. Du Cane entered the Staff College as a special nomination of the Commander in Chief in 1894.

[iii] In 1882 the top six places in the examination were occupied by four Engineers (1st, 3rd, 4th, and 6th), a Gunner (2nd), and a member of the Bengal Staff Corps (5th). Their marks ranged from 2,712 to 2,464. The 4th and 6th placed Engineers were denied entry and their places taken by a Lt. of the 1st Shropshire Light Infantry (marks: 1,617) and a Major in the 3rd Dragoon Guards (marks: 1,555). This was not an untypical year. The following year, nine of the top thirteen candidates were either Engineers or Gunners and five of them failed to gain entry. The top scoring candidate was Lt., later Lt. Gen., Sir James Moncrieff Grierson, RA [*Source: The Times*, 20th September 1882, page 4].

[iv] Col. Frederic Natusch Maude, RE, was a prolific writer on military history, strategy, and tactics. Born in 1854, he died in 1933. He was educated at Wellington College and

"Instead of making the Staff College into a true University, for experimental and original research, we made it a kind of repetition school for the backward."⁷

Maude, however, went on to excuse the system which gave precedence to less well educated and qualified infantry and cavalry officers, as to allow entry strictly by success in the entrance examination would have filled the Staff College 'exclusively with officers from the Scientific Arms' and this would have upset the other parts of the Army. In short, therefore, the Staff College was not about attracting the 'brightest and the best' but about maintaining a *status quo* within the Army in which the technical arms were of less importance than their social superiors in the infantry and cavalry because, more often than not, it was the less well connected and less wealthy officers who entered the ranks of the engineers and the gunners. The result, as Maude later wrote, was:

> "... the difference between the attainments of the successful candidates at the head of the list and those at the bottom of it was simply immeasurable. Thus in one year I can recall there were fifteen RA and RE officers in order at the head of the list for whom there were only five vacancies, while the last man who qualified from a Line battalion had practically no competition whatsoever.
> How to devise a scheme of instruction to suit such extremes of capacity might have puzzled a Solon[i]."⁸

As a result, all entrants took the same basic first year course irrespective of existing knowledge and experience with, Maude suggests, some of the RA and RE officers having to 'learn up, by heart, the very textbooks which they had, often enough, written themselves'. This waste of a year on basic education for officers was still in place when the likes of Haig, Robertson, Edmonds, Allenby, *et al* attended. It culminated in an examination 'nobody regarded ... seriously'.⁹

Another problem was students 'passed' the Staff College just by taking the final exam. They did not have to attend at all. So, however excellent the staff lectures and battlefield tours, however stimulating and thought provoking the coursework, an officer could graduate without being involved in any of it.¹⁰ For some it was regarded as an interlude between proper jobs, and for others as a chance to achieve something in their 'spare' time, with cleverer officers like Edmonds writing a book on the American Civil War and Macdonogh qualifying as a barrister in London.

The academic rigour of the Staff College paled in comparison with that of the *Kriegsakademie* in Berlin where access was by simple competition in the entrance

---

the RMA, Woolwich, and was commissioned in 1873. He attended the Staff College in 1891. In 1908 Maude was responsible for the belated popularisation in Britain of Clausewitz's seminal work, *Vom Kriege*, when he re-printed (with minor edits) Col. James John Graham's 1873 translation. Graham's work caused barely a ripple in the 1870s. According to Christopher Bassford's figures it sold 69 copies out of 694 printed between 1873 and 1877.
[Source: https://www.clausewitz.com/readings/OnWar1873/Translator.htm#a].

[i] Solon (c. 638 – c. 558 BC), an Athenian philosopher and poet credited with laying the foundations of Athenian Democracy.

examination with no quotas for the various arms. Although some could gain entrance by nomination, if the officer then failed the first-year exam they were out, however august their sponsor. The focus for the examination was on military, not academic, subjects thereby allowing candidates denied the benefit of an excellent school education but with the necessary military skills, experience, and ambition to gain entrance. Examinations were designed to test decision making and problem-solving skills more than the ability to memorise facts which might be absorbed by cramming (a popular activity amongst those aspiring to join Sandhurst, Woolwich, and Camberley). Expected to undertake seventy hours of instruction a week throughout the three-year course,[11] failure to pass any of the end of year exams meant expulsion. This was no place for slackers. And, at the end of their time at the *Kriegsakademie* less than a third of the successful officers were deemed suitable to join the *élite* of the *Großer Generalstab*. The others were placed in less exalted if no less important positions of responsibility in other parts of the Army. In terms of both rigour and focus it was a substantially different establishment to Camberley. It produced officers who shared a common military doctrine but who also had the brain power, discipline, self-confidence, and military knowledge needed to interpret and give orders and then see them through to action. These were officers who expected to give advice to their seniors and be listened to and, if necessary, act without their superiors' approval or even knowledge if the urgency of the situation dictated immediate action.

At Camberley, however, 'p.s.c.' might mean a lot in terms of genuine professional development or, quite possibly, nothing whatsoever. This issue was underlined in South Africa where, according to Esher, having been through the Staff College was no guarantee of success but having previously *served* in a staff position, whether specifically trained for the job or not, was a far better indicator of reasonable achievement against the Boers[i].

Becoming a British staff officer was one thing. Applying one's newly learned skills to the job of a staff officer was another, especially when it came to serving within large units, i.e. an Army Corps, as such organisations existed mainly in name only. But it was these inexperienced staff officers, hurried off to South Africa when the war broke out, who, in the main, then failed in relentless fashion to come to grips with the issues of modern weaponry and radical tactics. But here we talk about trained staff officers with some experience of working as… staff officers. In practice, according to one harsh critic, Capt. William Elliott Cairnes of the Royal Irish Fusiliers and adjutant of the 1st Volunteer Battalion, KOYLI (Militia), in his short and vitriolic book *An Absent-Minded War*, there were few opportunities to practice what was preached at them at Camberley:

> "However, let us suppose that our ambitious friend, having passed through the College course, obtains a staff appointment, let us say as Deputy Assistant Adjutant General in one of the Home Districts, the sort of

---

[i] Barely a quarter of the general and staff officers who served in South Africa attended the Staff College, i.e. 120 out of 460 [*Source*: Stone J, *The Anglo-Boer War and Military Reforms in the United Kingdom* in Stone K & Schmidl E A, *The Boer War and Military Reforms*, University Press of America, 1988, page 108].

appointment usually offered to a graduate in the rank of captain. I ought to postulate here that there is not much chance of our friend getting a staff appointment at all, unless his p.s.c. is backed up by a few friends at court. The Staff College certificate is all very well but there are more graduates than there are appointments, and a number of these graduates will be nominees of the Commander in Chief who have entered the College by favour without passing any examination, and are pretty certain to get the pick of any good appointments going."[12]

It is fair to say this opinion was vigorously challenged by the noted military writer Col. Lonsdale Hale in an exchange of letters in *The Times* at the end of 1900 which, being even fairer, probably concluded in Lonsdale Hale's favour as far as the Staff College was concerned. Having said that, both Cairnes and Lonsdale Hale were highly critical of the educational standards of British Army officers, with Lonsdale Hale giving evidence to that effect to the Akers-Douglas committee which investigated the education and training of officers in 1902. Cairnes went on to be the secretary of that same committee.

There was, however, another issue. Unlike a fully trained German staff officer, his British equivalent was the servant of his commander. Under the guidance of Moltke the elder, the German staff officer reached a status and significance way beyond their notional rank. German staff officers could, indeed were expected to, issue their own orders and directives in their superior's name. Consequently, during the Great War there were staff officers such as Friedrich Karl von Lossberg, a 'mere' *oberst* (colonel), who, after replacing the German *3. Armee's* chief of staff after the initial French success in Champagne in 1915, issued orders to Corps commanders without even having met and consulted his new Army commander, General Karl von Einem. It was *Oberst* Lossberg who was called up to act as the new chief of staff to *2. Armee's* Fritz von Below on the *Somme* on 3rd July when the previous occupant of that role, *Generalmajor* Paul Grünert, was sacked for allowing General Günther von Pannewitz's *XVII Armeekorps* to withdraw in the face of the powerful French attacks south of the *Somme* on 1st July.

German staff officers were trained to assess situations and give orders as part of the devolved system of responsibility within the German Army. British staff officers, however, were there to transmit the orders of their superiors, to collect and assess information and intelligence, to make suggestions (if they dare) but not make decisions. In this respect, they were a more junior version of the General Staff of the Army, the functions of which were described by Brian Bond as:

> "[to] advise on the strategical distribution of the Army; to supervise the education of officers and the training and preparation of the Army for War; to study military schemes, offensive and defensive; to collect and collate military intelligence; and, finally, to direct the general policy in Army matters and to secure continuity of action in the execution of that policy."[13]

That there was no umbrella of understanding as to how war should be fought under which to gather, in other words, no proper British military 'doctrine', revealed itself in the many and various schemes for both defence and attack adopted/adapted at Army, Corps and Divisional level within the BEF. Schemes which subsidiary units, their commanders and staff officers, had either to learn or unlearn as they rotated through different commands on the Western Front. One of the key reasons for this lack of over-arching theory and practice within the British Army was the sheer variety of its responsibilities and the diversity of its garrison locations. The Army, argued Lt. Gen. Robert Stephenson Smyth Baden-Powell at a meeting at *RUSI* in the autumn of 1910, needed to be 'prepared for almost any kind of fighting whether it was against European Powers or against savages'.[14] What appeared appropriate for a continental war might be at odds with requirements on the North-West Frontier or whilst dealing with intermittent disturbances in West Africa or wherever else British troops were based. So went the thinking. The simple answer, therefore, was not to have a doctrine which might constrain an officer's course of action in a particular part of the world and it was this lack of what is now regarded as the essential framework of military planning and action which left so many general and staff officers adrift when war broke out and was then conducted in a way no-one anticipated[i].

But whatever the issues surrounding 'doctrine' and any improvements made to the education of staff officers, the numbers produced proved grossly inadequate to the tasks imposed by the scale of the war to come. Simon Robbins in his 2005 book *British Generalship on the Western Front 1914-8* highlights the extent of the problem: of 447 officers with 'p.s.c' alongside their name in the 1914 Army List a third had no direct staff experience. They learnt on the job and such lessons were hard won and costly, both to their troops and to themselves as just under half of these 447 1914-era staff officers died during the war.[15] There were also question marks over the quality of those staff officers who attended Camberley prior to the Boer War and the tactical and material adaptations which followed on both from the fighting and various inquiries in the succeeding years (a group which included all of the senior officers within the BEF who attended the Staff College in the 1890s). Robbins lists several Divisional and Corps staff officers found to have neither the intelligence nor experience to perform a staff officer's duties.[16] Finally, being a 'p.s.c' was not a prerequisite for high office within the Army. In August 1914, the BEF went to war under a CinC, Sir John French, a CIGS, Gen. Sir Charles Whittingham Horsley Douglas, and an Adjutant General, Lt. Gen. Sir Henry Crichton Sclater, none of whom attended Camberley.[17]

THESE VARIOUS CONCERNS ABOUT THE ARMY were nothing new. Before the South African War, the Conservative Prime Minister, Lord Salisbury, warned an astonished (or extremely unamused) Queen Victoria:

"We have no army capable of meeting even a second-class Continental Power."[18]

Of course, the Boers were far less strong than even a 2nd class European power. But quite why the monarch was surprised is... surprising. Perhaps she was so blinded by the apparent brilliance of 'the sun which never set' on the global British

---

[i] The French Army had similar problems with 'doctrine'. Broadly, each General had their own opinions on the subject that is until a Colonel de Grandmaison imposed his own views on the Army in a manner not challenged until tragically too late.

Empire for her to see the serious flaws inherent in her armed forces. Since the great days of Wellington, the British Army sometimes found defeating even poorly armed tribal troops tricky and anything better armed and trained proved even more problematical. Disasters, usually caused by inadequate generalship, were not uncommon: e.g. the First Afghan War (1839-42) which culminated in the destruction of Maj. Gen. William George Keith Elphinstone's force in the retreat from Kabul; the shambles of the Crimean War (1853-6) which both reinforced the reputation of the stolid, dependable British ordinary soldier and underlined the woefully inadequate quality of his senior officers and the general organisation of the army; and the humiliation of the First Boer War (December 1880 to March 1881) in which British and native troops suffered four defeats in less than ten weeks: Bronkhorstspruit (20th December 1880), Laing's Nek (28th January 1881), Schuinshoogte (8th February 1881) and finally Majuba Hill (26th February 1881), at which the British commander, Maj. Gen. Sir George Pomeroy Colley, was killed, his troops routed and from which nothing was learned when the second South African war broke out in 1899.

Prior to South Africa in 1899, the Army comprised eight components falling under three headings: the Regular Army, the Militia, and the Volunteers[19]:

The Regular Army throughout the Empire	124,000
The Regular Army at home	131,000
The Regular Army Reserve, Section A	5,000
The rest of the Army Reserve	73,000
The Militia	65,000
The Militia Reserve	30,000
The Yeomanry	10,000
The Volunteers	230,000
Total	668,000

The Militia was a reformed version of the part-time force established in the early 18th Century. *The Militia Act* of 1757 formalised affairs in England and Wales and was extended to Scotland in 1797. Protestant-only militias existed in Ireland after 1715 and, after 1793, Catholics could join the 'other ranks' (officers were Protestants). A unified Militia was formed in 1800 after the *Act of Union* created the United Kingdom of Great Britain and Ireland.

By 1899 the Militia was often the province of young men hoping to find a route into the full-time Army as either officer or ranker. About a third of the rankers joined the Regulars whilst another 20% saw out their six years' service and join the Militia Reserve. Another 25% were discharged for various reasons during their six-year service and 20% simply deserted. The overwhelming mass of the 'other ranks' were unskilled men (half under 19[20]) employed in agricultural, industrial or mining labouring for whom the annual training camp represented a 28-day paid holiday and a possible entry into permanent, if not well paid, employment in the army. The *1898 Annual General Return* for the Militia showed 31% of those enrolled were farm labourers, 18% industrial labourers and 12% miners[i].[21]

---

[i] In Ireland, 60% of the men were farm labourers.

The Militia was a home defence force with no overseas service obligation[i]. Infantry only until 1861, when some artillery units were formed and later 1877 when two Fortress Engineer corps were created[ii], there were no support services except for a small Medical Staff Corps. By 1899 123 Militia infantry battalions existed. Because of their history, these tended to be concentrated in areas where agricultural employment was widespread rather than in the fast-expanding cities. Ireland, too, had more than its fair share of Militia units with twelve of the 32 Militia Artillery Brigades (38%) and 25 of the 123 infantry battalions (20%) coming from a country with less than 10% of the entire population.[22] The Militia's artillery units were mainly earmarked for coastal defence with headquarters at ports or seaside towns. They did not represent, therefore, the artillery arm of an embodied Militia force if the country was threatened with invasion. In short, the Militia did not correspond to a Home Defence Army. It was poorly trained and officered, unintegrated with the Regular Army and lacked the artillery, field engineers and other services which would have allowed it to behave like one.

The Yeomanry (38 regiments) was the Militia's cavalry and a completely mainland affair, the Irish Yeomanry being disbanded in 1834[iii]. Again, the Yeomanry was not nationally organised nor did it have the necessary support services which might weld it into a coherent force if invasion threatened. The Yeomanry were locally raised, financed, and led, and owed more to the wealth and prestige of the local commanding officer than the Regular Army. The Queen's Own Oxfordshire Hussars are an excellent example. Based on a troop of volunteers initially formed in 1794, it then fell heavily under the influence of the Spencer-Churchill family – the 5th, 6th, 7th, and 9th Dukes of Marlborough all served in the regiment, two as Colonel, as did Winston Churchill.

The Yeomanry served in large numbers in South Africa under the auspices of the Imperial Yeomanry and gained a chequered reputation. They were also a useful adjunct to domestic forces of law and order in times of social and political unrest. Two of the three cavalry regiments which perpetrated the Peterloo Massacre on 16th August 1819 were from the Yeomanry: the Manchester and Salford Yeomanry[iv] and the Cheshire Yeomanry[v].

The Volunteer Force made up the bulk of the partially trained reserve to be called up if invasion threatened. The Volunteer movement was re-activated in 1859[vi] at a time when war with France seemed a strong possibility. Numerous

---

[i] Some served abroad on garrison duties to free Regular Army units for other uses.
[ii] Anglesey and Monmouthshire.
[iii] With men needed for South Africa six squadrons of horse were raised in Ireland under the provisions of the *Militia and Yeomanry Act, 1901*. The 13th (Irish) Battalion, Imperial Yeomanry, went to South Africa, losing 17 killed, c. 60 wounded and c. 400 as PoWs at Lindley, 27th May 1900. The North of Ireland and South of Ireland Imperial Yeomanry were formed in 1902/3. Under the Haldane Reforms they became Special Reserve units: the North Irish Horse and South Irish Horse respectively.
[iv] The Manchester and Salford Yeomanry was disbanded five years later.
[v] The other cavalry regiment was the 15th (The King's) Hussars with elements of the Royal Field Artillery and 31st and 88th Regiments of Foot.
[vi] Various volunteer units were first raised during the French Revolutionary period.

Volunteer Rifle Corps (VRC) and Artillery Corps were created at the instigation of the Conservative Secretary of State for War, Jonathan Peel, the younger brother of the two-time Prime Minister, Sir Robert Peel[i]. The raising of the VRCs was, like the Yeomanry at this time, restricted to the mainland. It consisted of infantry, artillery, engineers, and medical staff but, as with the Militia and Yeomanry, no services which might provide transport, etc., if and when mobilised.

Traditionally the Volunteers were formed from people with the time and money to… 'volunteer'. They were, therefore, men of substance, men with property and businesses, and men with good local connections. With a stake in society, they were also keen to preserve their version of 'law and order' and they quite often signed up as special constables when radical elements threatened to upset the political *status quo*. Many units charged a subscription to join even as a lowly rifleman[ii], a tradition which continued in certain quarters even after the Volunteers were subsumed into the new Territorial Force in 1908. The Volunteers were, as Dunlop describes, 'essentially *bourgeois*[23] – middle class, professional, the *'nouveau riche'*, more urban and suburban than rural – whereas the Militia and the Yeomanry were based more on the 'county set' – the titled, the landed gentry and gentleman farmers, and their ranks were made up of the young men who laboured in their farms and fields. As a result, large numbers of Volunteer Rifle Corps were formed in the towns and cities which later, through a process of merger and rationalisation, became part of the new Territorial Force in 1908.

Their use was also entirely home-based and was for the purposes of repelling or deterring invasion, but they could also be employed in the case of severe domestic upheaval. Training, and the resulting quality of the units, varied widely and depended much on the enthusiasm and dedication of the senior officers of each corps.

AT THIS TIME, THE MILITARY FORCES OF GREAT BRITAIN were employed according to the dictates of the Stanhope Memorandum. Edward Stanhope was the Conservative Secretary of State for War in Salisbury's administration of 1886-1892. Under pressure from Viscount Wolseley, the Adjutant General of the Forces and victor in Egypt at Tel el Kebir in 1882, for a definitive statement of the strategic role of the Army, the initial version of the memorandum was circulated on 8th December 1888. Five functions were identified, certain of them being conditional on the essential role of the Royal Navy being the first line of defence against domestic invasion.

The five tasks of the Regular Army and Auxiliary Forces were:

1. The support of the civil powers within Great Britain;
2. To supply the numbers of men required by the Government of India for its internal security and defence;
3. To garrison all fortifications and naval coaling stations throughout the

---

[i] They were raised under the provisions of the *Volunteer Act, 1804*, passed to counter the threat of Napoleon.

[ii] The London Rifle Brigade, for example, or 'God's Own' as they were known by some rival London Territorials.

world and to maintain them at levels set for either peace or war-time conditions;
4. To fully mobilise for Home defence two Army Corps of Regular troops and one other made up of Regular and Militia troops whilst organising all remaining Auxiliary troops for the defence of London and key ports;
5. To mobilise two Army Corps, a cavalry division, and Lines of Communication troops for service abroad.

The last paragraph of the memorandum, the final version of which was agreed on 1st June 1891, indicated, however, that it was the belief of those concerned that 'abroad' was unlikely to mean the mainland of Europe:

"But it will be distinctly understood that the probability of the employment of an Army Corps in the field in any European war is sufficiently improbable to make it the primary duty of the military authorities to organise our forces efficiently for the defence of this country."[24]

It was nearly twenty years before this strategic imperative was changed to focus on the probability of a European war in which Great Britain might be involved and, during this period, Britain was, for a time, diplomatically isolated and heartily disliked by most of the other great powers. It was Richard Haldane, as Secretary of State for War, who would effectively tear up the Stanhope Declaration in 1906. He was deeply worried at the prospect of a German attack on France and Belgium and the loss of the key continental Channel ports to a nation desperately trying to compete with the Royal Navy for control over the world's oceans. He decided, therefore, that plans be laid for an Expeditionary Force and for its deployment in northern France, and ordered the military planners to consult with their French equivalents on what might be the best form of intervention by such a force.

Before that, however, the first two priorities set out by Stanhope reflected the most acute current concerns of the Government. In the years preceding the first draft of the memorandum, the Army was used several times in support of the civil powers. In the Scottish Highlands and Islands, a long-standing dispute between landowners and local crofting communities led to the deployment of a navy gunboat, the iron-hulled paddle steamer *HMS Jackal*, off Skye in 1883. Some Marines were landed on the Meanish Pier at Glendale at head of Loch Pooltiel on the north-west of the island. In spite of the government-sponsored Napier Commission which looked into, and reported on, the problems in 1884; the election of five Crofters' Party MPs in the 1885 General Election; and the passing of the *Crofters Holdings (Scotland) Act* in 1886; trouble again erupted and 250 marines were landed on Tiree later that year, brought there by two Royal Naval vessels[i].

In Wales, the enactment of the *Tithe Commutation Act* of 1836, which required the payment in cash of 10% of a person's annual income to the Established Church, caused increasing strife between the predominantly non-conformist

---

[i] Oddly, such a divisive social issue (which besets the Highlands and Islands still) brought the 'benefits' of golf to the honest inhabitants of the island of Tiree. The commander of the marines, Lt. Col. Mackay Heriot, and his officers, helped in the creation of a golf course later known as Scarinish Golf Club. It closed in the 1960s. There is still a golf course on the island at Vaul which has existed since 1911.

residents and the enforcing authorities. Being legally required to contribute to the existing wealth of the Church in Wales became an increasing bone of contention, particularly amongst Welsh farmers. When, in the 1880s, payments started to be taken by the enforced sales of the possessions of non-payers, friction was transformed into violent reaction. Resentment was high in the rural west and north of the country and disturbances took place in both Carmarthenshire and Ceredigion and, most notably, in Denbighshire. Outbreaks of violence in 1887 were followed by the deployment of troops in that and the following year.[i]

Finally, in 1887, both infantry and cavalry were brought into central London to help control a large demonstration led by the *Social Democratic Federation* and the *Irish National League* and other organisations in protest against both long term unemployment and the use of the *Coercion Acts* in Ireland. In consequence, 10,000 demonstrators were opposed by 2,000 policemen in the centre of London on 13th November 1887. In reserve were 400 troops of the Grenadier Guards and the Life Guards. In the subsequent confrontation, which became known as 'Bloody Sunday', 400 demonstrators, including two of their leaders, were arrested and 75 badly injured. In another demonstration on the following weekend at least one demonstrator was fatally injured by Police now reinforced by hundreds of hurriedly sworn in Special Constables, many members of the Army, the Militia, and the Volunteers. With the famous Match Girls' Strike the following year and the successful London Dock's Strike in 1889, it is easy to understand why the Conservative Government placed 'support of the civil power' as one of its highest priorities when calling on the services of the Army.

The maintenance of the armed forces in India was a key priority of the British Government ever since the Mutiny of 1857. Following its suppression, the *Government of India Act* was passed in Westminster in August 1858 and control of the governance of the sub-continent passed from the *East India Company* to the Crown. The impact on the British military presence was considerable. Prior to the Mutiny the Army consisted of both *East India Company* and British Army troops and, within the native contingents, those from Bengal dominated. With the collapse of the rebellion a large part of the Bengal Army was abolished as it was from within these ranks most of the mutineers came. Their replacements were drawn, instead, from a more diverse ethnic and religious grouping of Muslims from the Punjab, Sikhs, Gurkhas, Baluchis and Pathans.

The new army of India was based on the three old Presidencies of the *East India Company*: Bengal, Madras (modern Chennai) and Bombay (Mumbai). Each had its own Commander in Chief although that of the Bengal Army was the overall CinC of the Indian Army. From then onwards the tendency was to centralise and various logistical elements were brought under central control before, after the Second Afghan War (1878-80), a Royal Commission recommended the abolition of the Presidency Armies and the creation of a unified command. In 1886 the Punjab Frontier Force, responsible for the troublesome North-West Frontier, was brought under central control and, five years later, the staffs of the three Armies were combined into the Indian Staff Corps. In 1893 the Madras and Bombay

---

[i] The Church in Wales was disestablished in 1920 by the *Welsh Church Act* of 1914.

Armies lost their Commanders in Chief and, in 1895, all three forces were merged into an Indian Army formed into four commands: Bengal, Bombay, Madras and the Punjab. This process was overseen by Lt. Gen. Sir George Stuart White (CinC India 1893-8) and his predecessor as CinC, Lord Roberts (CinC, 1885-93).

With a triple remit of providing aid to the civil power, controlling the North-West Frontier and any other trouble spots, and deterring Russian aggression through Afghanistan, it was essential the Indian Army was kept up to strength and, increasingly, this demand resulted in a weakening of the numerical strength of home-based units and an undermining of the quality of the residual rank and file. This erosion of the strength of the Regular forces at home was exacerbated by an 1881 War Office regulation which stopped soldiers under twenty, or those with less than a year's service, serving abroad.

This imposed considerable strain on an Army with responsibilities in the Empire's other colonies. 1862 was the only year from the end of the Crimean War in 1856 to the start of the South African War in 1899 in which the British Army did not fight somewhere in the world. Throughout that period, however, the size of the Regular Army fell from 223,000 in 1862 to 184,000 in 1876 before recovering to its highest level of 225,000 just before the South African War started. Over that same period the proportion which served abroad stood at 54% in the late 1860s but fell to just below half in the 1870s. From the latter part of that decade the percentage steadily rose, reaching its peak in 1898 when slightly more than 54% served outside Britain.[25]

The need to sustain the numerous formations serving abroad inevitably caused a dilution in quality of the units formed from the most recent and inexperienced recruits left in Britain. Their instruction was then disrupted by the constant need to introduce to basic training the new and raw recruits whenever and wherever they enlisted. And, with there being no over-arching doctrinal guidance with which to direct their training, these men were left 'betwixt and between' when it came to their military schooling as no-one could tell when and when they might be employed or whether they might face native troops with rudimentary weapons or better trained, armed, and organised soldiers from an industrial or colonial power.

The South African War represented a potentially valuable 'school of hard knocks' with which to beat officers and other ranks into shape. But, in too many ways, any improvements in training, tactics or equipment were not sustained, either through a failure to understand properly what lessons might be learnt or applied; through a conservative-led reversion to out-dated pre-war thinking; or through a belief that, when it came to either traditional colonial policing actions or more conventional European warfare, South Africa was irrelevant.

Taking this latter point first, progressively, any lessons apparently learnt in South Africa were marginalised by the commonly held view the war was an anomalous event from which little might be learnt, especially as it applied to tactics in a European War between the Great Powers. That this attitude was deliberately fostered within the Army is suggested by an exchange between two 'educationalists' as part of the Akers-Douglas committee investigation into the education of officers which reported to Parliament in 1902 (see page 367). Dr Edmond Warre, headmaster of Eton College since 1884, was one of two distinguished Public School 'Heads' on the committee. He questioned a renowned military 'crammer'[i], historian and critic of the system of education of officers, Dr Thomas Miller Maguire[ii], about what lessons the Army learned from South Africa:

> WARRE: Has it not been studiously inculcated in various quarters that the Boer War must not be taken as an example in Tactics, and so on, as everything would be different in a European War?
>
> MAGUIRE: Yes, but its effect has not been to cause more reading about any wars... The younger officers are worse than for a generation.
>
> WARRE: But they have studiously said that... This Boer War is altogether on a different plan from what a war in Europe would be and therefore you will not learn very much by it.
>
> MAGUIRE: That has been said over and over again.[26]

A year later this view was underlined by a review in *The Spectator* of the book *War in Practice* written by Maj. Baden Fletcher Smyth Baden-Powell of the Scots Guards and about whom more later. The review comments:

> "To those who served with him in South Africa the writer recalls certain facts which they might otherwise be apt to forget. We are sure that he is thereby doing good service to the Army; there is too much evidence already that many of the hard lessons we then learnt are being forgotten, in some cases, we fear, wilfully forgotten, particularly the more dis-agreeable of them."[27]

By 1911 Sir John French was bemoaning the fact that the lessons of South Africa had degenerated into 'a mass of theory' and a 'superfluity of literature' rather than a practical system for the benefit of the Army and its leaders.[28]

Ironically, there were signs in the year the war started a possible sea-change in tactical thinking was dawning within the Army, at least in certain quarters. Leading this movement was a Colonel at the Staff College who, earlier, had been an arch exponent of the limiting and centralising ideas which dictated some of the more absurd events of the early months of the war. He taught these redundant ideas to a large number of officers who went on to play vital roles in the conduct of the greater war to come before performing a *volte face* too late to affect the majority of the senior ranks in 1914.

Colonel George Francis Robert Henderson, CB, was born in 1854, the eldest of fourteen children of the Rev. William George Henderson, Headmaster of Victoria School, Jersey. In 1860 Henderson's father was appointed Head at Leeds

---

[i] From 1887 to 1899 two-thirds of the Sandhurst intake attended a crammer, e.g. Kitchener was with George Frost at Woolwich, Ian Hamilton with a Capt. Lendy at Sunbury and Douglas Haig was 'crammed' by a Mr Litchfield of Hampton Court between leaving Brasenose College, Oxford, and entering Sandhurst. By 1910 the percentage 'crammed' into Woolwich fell to 14% from a high of 74% in 1869 though, given the nature of the intake, it is probable the numbers were higher for Sandhurst [*Source*: Leinster-Mackay, D P, *The English private school 1830-1914, with special reference to the private proprietary school*, Durham theses, Durham University, 1971, page 152].

[ii] Dr Miller Maguire wrote, amongst others, two books on the American Civil War and another on the Franco-Prussian War.

Grammar School which school George also attended. He proved, as he moved through his teenage years, an intelligent young man who was also adept at sports, especially cricket. Having captained the School 1st XI, Henderson won a History scholarship to St John's College, Oxford. But his preference was for the Army and, in 1877, he left Oxford to attend Sandhurst at the relatively late age of 23. Again, at Sandhurst, his sporting prowess shone through as he captained the College's cricket team.

77 Col. George Francis Robert Henderson

Commissioned into the 65th Foot (2nd Yorkshire, North Riding Regiment) in 1878, he sailed to India to join them at Dinapur[i]. His sojourn in the sub-continent was brief, however, and he returned to join the 84th Foot, first at Dover and then at the Curragh near Dublin[ii]. In August 1882 his regiment, now the 2nd Battalion, York and Lancaster Regiment, went to Egypt where he saw action in the Egyptian war at El Magfar, Tel-el-Mahouta, Kassassin and Tel-el-Kebir. Throughout the campaign he created an excellent impression, receiving various awards[iii] and a Mention in Despatches. Henderson hoped to serve with the Egyptian Army but, instead, he came home to marry and then followed his regiment to serve in Bermuda and Halifax, Nova Scotia.

In 1885 he and his wife, an Irish lady, Mary Pierce Joyce of Galway, toured the Virginian battlefields of the American Civil War where he studied the campaigns of Robert E Lee's Army of North Virginia and, in particular, the exploits, most especially in the Shenandoah Valley, of the rebel general Thomas *'Stonewall'* Jackson. Later that year he was appointed Deputy Assistant Commissary General in the Ordnance Department based at Fort George in Inverness-shire. Here he started work on his studies of the American Civil War producing, in 1886, an account of the Battle at Fredericksburg (December 1862). His next piece was a description of the Battle of Spicheren from the Franco-Prussian War. To complete

---

[i] Now more commonly known as Danapur, Bihar State.
[ii] In 1881 it merged with the 65th Foot to form the York and Lancaster Regiment, the 84th becoming the 2nd Battalion.
[iii] 5th Class of the Order of the Medjideh, Egyptian Medal & Clasp, and Khedive's Star.

this work, he started to teach himself German to better appreciate the writings of the Prussian victors. His conclusions from the study of these battles, especially Spicheren, was it was essential officers be trained to accept responsibility and show initiative when opportunities presented themselves but their training and practice needed to apply to all so that every officer was 'singing from the same tactical hymn sheet' once in action. This system the Prussian Army rigorously applied in 1870-1 whilst the French, rather as in 1914, believed *élan*, vigour and aggression would suffice to defeat the stolid north Germans.

In 1887 Henderson moved to Gibraltar, a posting which seemed to suggest no great progress in his career but, within two years, he achieved his main objective: a position as an Instructor in Tactics, Military Law and Administration at Sandhurst. In this appointment he was assisted by the good offices of Garnet Wolseley, 1st Viscount Wolseley and the Adjutant-General to the Forces at the War Office. Wolseley, having visited the Army of North Virginia in 1862 and talked to Generals Lee, Jackson, and James Longstreet, noted and approved of Henderson's anonymously published piece on Fredericksburg and this materially assisted Henderson in this significant career progression. Henderson spent three years at Sandhurst and there he embarked upon his most famous work *'Stonewall Jackson and the American Civil War'*, published in 1898. In 1892, he transferred across the road to the Staff College at Camberley where he was appointed Professor of Military Art and History, a position he held for the next seven years.

The Staff College was then a place of moderate reputation. Indeed, so moderate *The Times* posted a lengthy critique of the establishment in its edition of Saturday, 29th December 1894. It started:

> "The Staff College cannot claim a place among our popular military institutions… nor … has the college succeeded in gaining the confidence of the Army as the recruiting ground for the staff which leads it… It is asserted that, on the whole, the officers who have come to the college have not belonged to the class of regimental officers most capable of becoming good staff officers… and … the certificate, PSC, has been granted to many men who, when subsequently put to the proof, have shown themselves to be altogether unfit as staff officers."[29]

Changes were much afoot, however, both in the nature of the entrance examinations and in the nature of the course and Henderson was in at the start of this considerable transformation. Unfortunately, before the Staff College could catch up with the necessary numbers and quality needed, the South African War highlighted the damage which might be caused in the absence of a decent body of adequately trained, as well as experienced, staff officers. But then, many of the Generals commanding were dreadful too.

In 1897 Henderson met and impressed Lord Roberts whilst delivering a talk in Dublin. Later, having read his magisterial *Stonewall Jackson,* Roberts admitted to having applied some of the actions of the Confederate General described by Henderson to his thinking about a possible war in South Africa[i].[30] Thus, after the

---

[i] Though not, one presumes, his religious devotion which led to his men taking no meaningful part on two Sundays during the crucial Seven Days Battle (25th June to 1st

disasters of 'Black Week' in December 1899, and with Roberts asked to take over the conduct of the war, he determined to take Henderson with him to act as his Director of Intelligence. Henderson, however, had not been well for some time but, in spite of this, he went. A brief time in the field broke his health just before the near fiasco at Paardeberg on 18th February 1900 and he was forced to return to England. It took him seven months to recover sufficiently to resume his duties which now included the writing of the official history of the South African War. To achieve this, he returned to the war zone where he visited various battlefields at a breakneck pace. Again, his health failed and he was sent home in early 1902. He continued working on the history but his health was still poor and it was determined an English winter might be the end of him. He sailed, instead, for the eastern Mediterranean in the hope the warm, dry climate of Egypt might help his recovery but he continued to deteriorate and died at Assuan on 5th March 1903.

Henderson was a prolific writer and, in 1905, a volume of essays and articles appeared as *The Science of War*. Within can be found his thoughts on tactics and strategy some of which might well explain the subsequent actions of some of his more significant Sandhurst and Camberley students. The various chapters show that Henderson was an unusual soldier. Unusual in that he was a man prepared to change his mind decisively when what he deemed irrefutable contrary evidence to his current thinking presented itself.

In October 1891, whilst still at Sandhurst, he wrote an article entitled *Criticism and Modern Tactics* for the *United Service Magazine* in which he explained his views on the clear and continuing role of the cavalry on the modern battlefield.[31] Modern breech loading rifles did not make the *arme blanche* obsolete as some claimed, he argued, rather tactics and employment needed to be adapted to take account of these technical changes. He then cited examples from 1870-1 which some interpreted as meaning the end of cavalry in the traditional sense but he re-interpreted them to show that, in fact, cavalry played a significant, if sometimes costly, part in the military successes of both armies.

He then discussed the deployment and use of infantry and, in particular, the issue of formations. Here he argued against what he saw as the injudicious dispersal of units, of giving too much latitude to the initiative of the officers commanding these dispersed units, and of the tendency for these units to scatter still further into isolated groups of skirmishers out of the control of any officer whatsoever. This tendency, he believed, and its resulting loss of control by subordinate officers, was what led to unnecessarily heavy casualties amongst attacking Prussian troops at several of the early battles in Lorraine. Dispersal was the Prussian response to their *Dreyse* 'needle' rifle being outranged by the modern French *Chassepot*. To get close to the enemy to deliver the bayonet charge without suffering crippling casualties, Prussians units tended to a greatly extended attacking line. According to Henderson after the war this resulted in a general acceptance that 'extended order is the rule, close order the exception'.[32] The other

---

July 1862), when his uncharacteristic inaction deprived the Confederacy of, perhaps, their best/only chance of crushing the Union Army of the Potomac and ending the war on favourable terms.

'conclusion' drawn from such dispersal was the unavoidable devolution of decision making to junior officers and even NCOs within reach of the soldiers involved. Encouraging them to take initiative, even at the expense of unit cohesion, was the inevitable conclusion, and tactical training was to change to reflect this new 'truth'.

For Henderson, however, the correct answer lay in the sensible application of the existing British drill books in which:

> "... instead of encouraging excessive exercise of initiative, the paramount importance of order, of the cohesion of the attacking body, and of maintaining the true direction is inculcated on every page."[33]

For Henderson in 1891 this resulted in a new paradigm: 'close order whenever it is possible, extended order only when it is unavoidable.'[34]

Not only was Henderson critical of the Prussian tendency to disperse, but he was also aghast at the men's desire to seek any sort of cover from the long-range fire of the French *Chassepot*. Such a tendency diverted them from the 'true direction' of the attack and could only result in the break-up of the battalion which he regarded as the smallest unit to which initiative might be devolved.

The battalion was the key formation and the role of the commander of such a unit was to oversee the delivery of the frontal attack because it was not the function of subordinate officers to manoeuvre to seek out advantage by flanking fire or flanking charges. The British way was that the overall commander in the field set the dispositions which allowed for such manoeuvres and units were specifically positioned by the commanding general to achieve such a tactical advantage. It was not to be left to the initiative of subordinates to seek out such opportunities because down that road lay disorganisation and failure. The junior officers' *'Bible'*, therefore, was the *Drill Book*. Ideally, Henderson admitted, sufficient latitude might be granted junior officers such that, at the critical moment of the charge, they might micro-manage the battle to advantage. The end product of this approach, Henderson admitted, was that such a strong emphasis on unit cohesion might result in a slavish adherence to drill and an erosion of individual initiative and, as the principles of the *Drill Book* were of overwhelming importance, this became the inevitable result as events in South Africa so expensively proved.

Soon after writing this piece Henderson was appointed to the Staff College and here his teaching was of a practical as well theoretical and academic nature. During his time at Camberley several key officers came under his influence, amongst them Julian Byng, Henry Rawlinson, Launcelot Kiggell and Thomas Snow in 1892, Allenby, Haking, 'Wullie' Robertson and Douglas Haig in 1896, Hunter-Weston in 1897, and Hubert Gough and de Lisle in 1898. Unfortunately, many had already been influenced by the thinking set out by Henderson in *Criticism and Modern Tactics*. It was all the more unfortunate as, seven years after completing this article, Henderson changed his mind.

The explanation for this *volte face* is contained in another article published in *The Science of War* entitled *The Training of Infantry for Attack*. It first appeared in the *United Service Magazine* of August 1899 and, therefore, *after* the officers listed above left Camberley. Posing the question as to how best to train soldiers when the circumstances and geography of their employment were completely unknown, he ventured a brief statement of the two current methods. The first was a traditional response: normal formations, good discipline, good shooting, in other words much as he first suggested in 1891. Then there was an alternative: special formations adapted to special conditions but guided by the dictates of higher authority. But for Henderson this now presented a fundamental problem:

> "All systems, however, which depend on explicit regulations make but small demands on the intelligence of the individual officer, and for that reason, if for no other, they are quite inadequate to the exigencies of modern warfare."[35]

Henderson then gave examples of why 'systems' which depended on higher authority might fail. One was from a battle he studied closely, the Battle of Wœrth on 6th August 1870. He described talking to a German officer who fought there in heavily wooded countryside where 'normal formations' simply could not operate. The officer's view was their training was deficient in that it failed to develop their skirmishing skills and failed to develop the initiative and judgement of the junior officers.

Another was from an officer who fought on the North-West Frontier. Here the fighting was over the steep hills and deep valleys of the Khyber Pass and its surrounds and was against the native Pashtuns, fierce fighters who utilised the terrain to excellent advantage. The ground, by its rugged nature, broke battalion actions down into company, platoon and even sections firefights. Centralised control by 'higher authority' became impossible. Those who could not adapt to the new methods of fighting floundered or perished. The British officer who experienced this fighting now recommended encouraging the development of initiative within all officers; improved physical training for officers and men to allow themselves to move across country and over obstacles; practice using the principles of the light infantry over problematic terrain; and careful training down to the individual soldier.

Finally, Henderson referred to the Light Brigade made famous by Sir John Moore and trained by him at Shorncliffe in Kent during the Napoleonic War. Comprising the 43rd, 52nd and 95th Regiments, the brigade fought independently and later as part of the expanded Light Division at nearly every significant battle of the Peninsular War between 1809 and 1814 and was regarded as the *élite* division of Sir Arthur Wellesley's[i] Army. A close consultation of the memoirs of various officers who trained under Moore revealed the basic training of the Light Brigade was almost precisely that which the officer on the North-West Frontier recommended. Of the greatest importance was the development of junior officers' judgement, decision making and an understanding of the fundamentals of successful devolved and dispersed fighting. These officers would take responsibility and make independent decisions but always with a close understanding of the needs of the entire battalion and brigade. They always had in mind 'the great principle of mutual support'.[36]

---

[i] Following the victory at Talavera, Wellesley was elevated to the Peerage on 26th August 1809 as Viscount Wellington of Talavera and of Wellington, in the County of Somerset, with the subsidiary title of Baron Douro of Wellesley.

From this Henderson drew the conclusions that:

"The conditions of modern warfare render it imperative that all ranks should be taught to think, and subject to general instructions and accepted principles, to act for themselves."[37]

The essential points to be gleaned from the Light Brigade were:

1. troops needed to be flexible and able to adapt to any formation or circumstance which obtained;
2. the general line of any attack needed to be maintained but not at the expense of taking advantage of the lie of land;
3. the section, not the battalion, was the key formation;
4. mutual support was the essence of a successful advance;
5. the advance should take place in whatever manner and at whatever speed the circumstances and ground dictated;
6. cover should be taken advantage of whenever available;
7. volley fire was to be abandoned and the men trained to fire at will and at their own targets;
8. men should work and co-operate with whoever was nearby and not just officers and men of their own battalion or company;
9. they should watch the movements of the enemy carefully in order to be able to inform their superior and act themselves;
10. men should be alert to the need to concentrate when required or support the advance on another group;
11. troops should extend on leaving cover;
12. they needed to be self-sufficient and, if their officer or NCO was killed or wounded, should carry on fighting whilst bearing in mind the need to find colleagues in order to continue the action.

The current, pre-South Africa, training of British troops was almost the complete reverse of these ideas. Henderson quoted a critical foreign observer of some Aldershot manoeuvres:

"I remember one of them saying that our men did not seem to be able to act for themselves, but that they always required someone to tell them what to do; and it is evident that if officers have to look closely after their men, they will have little time to give to a consideration either of the ground or of the enemy."[38]

The changes he sought were not of regulations but by the constant exposure of junior officers to decision making, leadership and independence:

"... the secret of efficiency lies in the self-dependence, the resource, and the resolution of the company and section leaders. How will mere rules assist a commanding officer to instil those habits into his subordinates? Such habits are only to be fostered by constantly placing the company officers in situations where they have to think and act for themselves, by encouraging them to use their wits, to adapt their formation to the ground, to improvise means of overcoming difficulties and to become zealous assistants rather than unreflecting machines."[39]

That Henderson experienced a sea-change in opinion about the way infantry should be trained and used is summed up well by the following quote which damned the idea that regulation piled upon regulation was an answer to the problems of modern warfare:

"... what good can come from laying down a multitude of rules and regulations? Rules and regulations, so far as tactics are concerned, may have a certain amount of value if those who have to carry them out are under the constant supervision of those who make them. Mechanical perfection, to a greater or less degree, can certainly be produced. But mechanical perfection, or rather, the effort made to reach it, ends in paralysing the judgment; it is altogether inimical to the free exercise of an intelligent initiative, and in no way adapted to the needs of war."[40]

His views about drill books also completely changed. He argued officers would be better placed if they knew more about the enemy's tactics and placed greater reliance on their own judgement, knowledge, and common sense rather than '... a mere mechanical obedience to the precepts of the Drill-book'.[41] Not all answers to all questions were to be found in the *Drill Book* as, later, not all answers to all questions could be found in Haig's *Field Service Regulations*. Thus, perhaps, the use of the word 'regulations' in the title was unfortunate because it again created the idea the contents of *FSR* showed the *only* way in which one might fight and any problem newly encountered had an answer in *FSR* if only an officer might find the time to locate it in his well-thumbed copy whilst being shot at and shelled.

Thomas Pilcher (see page 482), who would later perform well in South Africa and who studied under Henderson at Camberley in 1892 when he was still in his 'discipline and control' phase, arrived earlier at Henderson's later conclusions as a result of close study of the German Army at its annual manoeuvres:

"The key-note of the whole German army and the secret of its efficiency is decentralization. This begins from the bottom and works up. From the day an officer joins he is accustomed to responsibility. Commanders of squadrons, batteries and companies are practically independent, their immediate superiors may inspect them, but are forbidden to lay down what parades they shall hold. At manoeuvres I have never seen any interference on the part of battalion or regimental commanders with their subordinates, a man receives his orders and he is allowed to carry them out his own way. An officer is often asked afterwards why he did so-and-so, and is either praised or blamed for his correct or false appreciation of the situation. It is acknowledged that in war a company once committed to action is like an arrow from a bow which can only be gathered when the ground over which it was sent has been won. It is acknowledged that the only way of sending up orders to the firing line will be through reinforcements and when a company is once committed to action the commander is independent.

If an officer is found to be unfit for his responsible position, and every post carries with it a great deal of responsibility, he is retired with a small pension, and this is a matter of every-day occurrence, a great number of compulsory retirements taking place in the lower ranks."[42]

Of course, one of the problems facing an Army which wished to change its methods of training and fighting to one which placed great reliance on the initiative and judgement of junior officers was that these lieutenants, captains, and majors needed the intelligence, education, and knowledge to be able to exercise these responsibilities properly. Given the quality and intellect of many of the young men who chose the Army as a profession and the training provided both at school and Sandhurst, added to the role they then played in their battalion or regiment in peace time, then the prospects for encouraging initiative and judgement were extremely limited. And, in 1914, the elderly 'dug out' officers and NCOs left behind to train Kitchener's volunteers were of an age and attitude which placed discipline and the following of orders far above anything which might encourage individual initiative and personal judgement. These essential attributes were ones hard learned by those who survived the battlefields of the Western Front. Furthermore, had the British Army followed German practice concerning the removal of the inadequate, as explained by Pilcher, one wonders just how many officers might have been left to run the Army.

After only a brief experience in South Africa Henderson was prepared to lay down three key aspects of what he described as a tactical 'revolution' which was taking place because of the radical improvements in range, accuracy, and rate of fire of the new breech loading rifles firing bullets using smokeless propellant. In April 1901, he wrote *My Experiences of the Boer War* in which he responded to the widespread and, to him, ill-informed attacks on the British Army's performance. In *Foreign Criticism* he roundly chastised those European critics who scoffed at the perceived tactical inadequacies of British officers and men. Pointing out that none of these critics had yet faced these new rifles, Henderson set out their impact:

"1. Infantry, attacking over open ground, must move in successive lines of skirmishers extended at wide intervals.
2. Cavalry, armed, trained, and equipped as the cavalry of the Continent, is as obsolete as the crusaders.
3. Reconnaissance, even more important than heretofore, is far more difficult."[43]

Henderson, of course, was not present at the battles of 'Black Week' nor on 'Bloody Sunday' when his first statement was, in the main, completely ignored and at great cost. Lessons were learnt though and an approach using widely spread and deeply aligned waves of skirmishers became, under Lord Roberts, the norm. It was, however, a lesson ignored by the French and Germans in the early months of the 1914 war during which, on too many occasions, masses of men, shoulder to shoulder, fell victim to rifle, machine gun and shrapnel fire. Still later, it was ignored by some in charge on the first day of the *Somme* where rank upon rank of slow moving, heavily laden men walked slowly to their doom in the face of unshaken, entrenched infantry equipped with all the most modern weapons of war then known. Indeed, Henderson made a prescient comment about such tactical inadequacies as were displayed so relentlessly on the Western Front by all involved:

"The most brilliant offensive victories are not those which were mere 'bludgeon work', and cost the most blood; but those which were won by surprise, by adroit manoeuvre, by mystifying and misleading the enemy, by turning the ground to the best account, and of which the butcher's bill was small."[44]

The comment which follows might fittingly sum up every British offensive on the Western Front up to and beyond the *Somme*:

"Too little experience of war and too much experience of field-days have always the same results – rigid and unvarying formations, attacks ruled by regulations instead of common-sense, and the uniformity of the drill-ground in every phase of the soldier's training. Uniformity is simple; it is easily taught, and it is eminently picturesque; it simplifies the task of inspecting officers; it is agreeable to the centralising tendencies of human nature; and when it appears in the guise of well-ordered lines, advancing with mechanical precision, it has a specious appearance of power and discipline, especially when compared with the irregular movements of a swarm of skirmishers. Furthermore, it is far less difficult to train men to work in mass than independently. Thus order, steadiness, and uniformity become a fetish; officers and men are drilled, not trained; and all individuality, however it may be encouraged by regulations, is quietly repressed in practice."[45]

Some of what Henderson wrote after his personal experience of the modern, 'empty' battlefield was either ignored or forgotten in the following years. By 1916, officers like Rawlinson and Haig, who studied under Henderson at Camberley, seemed inclined to remember his pre-1899 views about conformity, discipline, order, and centralisation than the newer and more 'liberal' (or, perhaps, liberating) tactical ideas he expressed between 1899 and his untimely death four years later.

After South Africa, Henderson was asked by Roberts to produce a new version of the *Drill Book*, the value of which he was now so sceptical. It was to be entitled *Infantry Training*. His work became the foundation of the *Combined Training Manual* published in 1905, two years after his death, and was another opportunity for him to press on the Army his reformed views about the value of initiative and flexibility rather than the rigid discipline and formations of previous eras:

"It was mechanical discipline, absorbing all individuality, forbidding either officer or man to move or to fire without a direct command, and throwing no further responsibility on the subordinate leaders than that of merely passing on orders and seeing that they were obeyed ... that was still the ideal of the British army in 1899. The system had certainly been modified. Stereotyped formations in the attack had been abandoned, except by the artillery. It had been attempted to give the lines of infantry skirmishers more elasticity by breaking them up into groups; and a certain measure of independence in action was granted to the company commanders. But the principle was resolutely adhered to of keeping everything in hand by means of precise orders, of formations in which every man acted in accordance with a carefully defined routine, and of a continual looking to, and dependence on, the supreme authority. The infantry, for instance, were taught to move to the attack of a position in regular lines, or by the alternate advances of the units into which it was divided; and the regulation distances between successive bodies of troops were to be as far as possible preserved. In fact there was a constant endeavour to make battle conform to the parade-ground, to apply drill of the most mechanical character to the bullet-swept field, to depend for success on courage and subordination, and to relegate intelligence and individuality to the background."[46]

Again, one could not go far wrong if one used this as a description of the tactical principles employed by the British Army on 1st July 1916 although, in many cases, even the use of skirmishers and the idea of a certain independence at company level had since been abandoned.

Henderson persisted with his idea about junior officers taking the initiative, pursuing flexibility, and taking personal responsibility in his draft of *Infantry Training* which appeared in the *Combined Training Manual* of 1905, and was one of a series of updated manuals: *Cavalry Training* 1904, *Infantry Training* 1905, *Manual of Engineering* 1905, and *Field Artillery Training* 1907.

Infantry Training demanded commanding officers be instructed to:

"... check all practices which interfere with the free exercise of the judgement, and will break down, by every means in their power, the paralysing habit of an unreasoning and mechanical adherence to the letter of orders and to routine, when acting under service conditions."[47]

The central tactical issue to be 'solved' was, as ever, how best to deliver the decisive attack in the face of modern quick-firing and long-range rifles and guns. Henderson came late to the view that dispersal, use of cover, mutually supporting fire, initiative, flexibility, and intelligence were the keys, stating in *The Science of War*:

"... if the new system is dangerous (i.e. dispersed troops) the old (i.e. the massed attacks as to be practised in the manoeuvres) is impossible, except at a cost of life which no army and no nation can afford." [48]

After all, as Henderson wrote in the same book:

"The defender, occupying ingeniously constructed trenches and using smokeless powder, is practically invulnerable to both gun and rifle."[49]

That continental officers (and many in the British Army) refused to accept the new conditions of warfare baffled Henderson:

"... it is with something more than surprise that we note a stubborn refusal to admit that the flat trajectory of the small-bore rifle, together with the invisibility of the man who uses it, has wrought a complete revolution in the art of fighting battles.
To have to confess that the organisation and training of the gigantic armies of the Continent are based on antiquated principles would be more than humiliating: it would be the signal for most costly and laborious reforms. Yet the phenomena of the South African conflict permit no doubt whatever that the revolution is an accomplished fact." [50]

Henderson's death in March 1903 was doubly unfortunate. It not only denied the country the services of one of its best and most flexible military minds, it also closed the path towards a style of offensive warfare which might have placed the

British Army at the forefront of tactical ideas prior to 1914. Thereafter, conservative and conventional thinking was re-asserted.

Lord Esher, so much involved in the development of the Army in the Edwardian era, greatly lamented the early death of Henderson, not only because of his importance to the way the Army might think tactically but also because of the man himself: educated, thoughtful, flexible, academic, and far-sighted. The type of officer, indeed, who according to Esher, was:

> "Exactly what is required, and yet apparently does not exist in the Army."[51]

That Henderson's views had not properly permeated through the ranks of the Army by 1914 can be seen from the worrying comments of Brig. Gen. J E Gough[i], VC, CMG, from the staff at Aldershot, at the final General Staff Officers' conference held before the outbreak of war (12th-15th January 1914). The subject was *Can more be done to render Officers competent Commanders in war?* and he was asked to present the issue by Maj. Gen. Sir William Robertson. Gough, too, referred to Sir John Moore and the Light Brigade/Division and its emphasis on company training and on developing the initiative and knowledge of the junior officer at company level and below. Gough stated that, although the principles were set out in the various training manuals, in practice the company, platoon and section commanders of the infantry were not being given the responsibility and experience they needed in war. He further commented on a recurring problem in the Edwardian army: the often paltry numbers of men, especially amongst the artillery and infantry, available to train on large or small-scale manoeuvres and exercises which rendered these operations irrelevant to what would be experienced in war:

> "Our infantry company commanders… will find a company of 220 or so a very different business to a company of about 80, which is about the strength of their commands during peace training… Many of our senior regimental officers have never handled even a small force of all arms."[52]

LIKE HENDERSON, SOME OFFICERS RECOGNISED these tactical problems even before the salutary experiences of South Africa. Those most concerned were younger officers, the ones likely to be asked to lead charges on entrenched positions against rapid rifle fire. In 1899 the Army crammer Captain Walter Haweis James, RE, (the officers of which Corps often seemed light years ahead of their cavalry and infantry colleagues in appreciating the impact of new technology. See also page 358) wrote in the *RUSI Journal*:

---

[i] Brig. Gen. Sir John 'Johnnie' Edmond Gough VC, KCB, CMG. Born 25th October 1871, Muree, India. Son of Gen. Sir Charles John Stanley Gough VC, GCB, and nephew of Gen. Sir Hugh Henry Gough VC, GCB, both VCs awarded during the Indian Mutiny, 1857. Younger brother of Gen. Sir Hubert Gough, GOC, Reserve Army, later Fifth Army, on the *Somme*. Commissioned, Rifle Brigade, 1891. Won his VC in the Somaliland in 1903. Haig's Chief of Staff, I Corps, during the opening months of the war. Fatally wounded by a sniper on 20th February 1915 whilst visiting 2nd Rifle Brigade, near Fauquissart, just north of Neuve Chapelle. He died in the 25th Field Ambulance and is buried in Estaires Communal Cemetery, Plot II. Row A. Grave 7.

"A defensive line well covered with a clear foreground is almost unassailable in front under modern conditions. It is no good deducing lessons from the days of Frederick, or even from those of Napoleon. In both instances troops could get within distances of their enemy which nowadays would mean annihilation... Now the probability of a man being hit in the open compared with one in a sheltered trench is at least four to one."[53]

By 1907 this favourable defensive multiplier of 4:1 became, in the view of another bright young Engineer, 10:1. In January 1907 Capt. Crofton Edward Pym Sankey[i] wrote an article for the *RE Journal* entitled *The Campaign of the Future*. His vision of modern warfare was positively Blochian. Prolonged sieges – but not of cities and fortresses but 'siege warfare in the field'. Battles, he suggested, would be 'reckoned in weeks' and merge into one continuous and prolonged campaign with each army 'practically ... the garrison of an enormous extended fortress'.[54] Like those of Capt. James, his warnings, redolent of Bloch's forecasts, went unheeded.

Writing after the end of the war in South Africa in 1903, but reinforcing these other points, Maj. Baden Fletcher Smyth Baden-Powell of the Scots Guards (and younger brother of Robert Baden-Powell, then Inspector General of Cavalry and later the guiding light of the Scouting Movement), published *War in Practice*. It was based on his first-hand experience of the fighting in South Africa and he, at least, was determined lessons learnt should not be forgotten. Opening Chapter II (*The Attack*), and underlining James's 1899, prediction, Baden-Powell stated that:

"Recent improvements in firearms, both in rifles and in artillery, have been proved to influence greatly the relative value of attack and defence. Nearly all tend to strengthen the power of the defence."[55]

He then went on to describe the problems facing attacking troops, many of which were simply updated versions of those raised by Bloch. According to Baden-Powell, the long range of the modern rifle meant troops attacking over a fire swept zone of 1,000 yards would take ten minutes to cover this distance (not including any time spent sheltering from the enemy's fire). During this period, every defender would fire at least 100 rounds on men 'fully exposed and unable during that time to fire back'.[56] These advancing troops also had to face the shells of quick-firing field guns and machine guns, which weapon:

"... can open such a terrible rapid and accurate fire on advancing troops as to make certain zones practically impassable."[57]

---

[i] Capt., later Lt. Col., Crofton Edward Pym Sankey, DSO & Bar, RE, was a brilliant mathematician. Born 17th May 1877 (died 1956). Wellington College. Woolwich, 1894. Captain, 1905. Assistant instructor in fortification, School of Military Engineering, Chatham, 1908-1912. Commander, 1st Field Troop, RE, Aldershot, 1912. To France with 3rd Field Squadron, RE, attached 3rd Cavalry Division. Major, 1916, then Bt. Lt. Col. CRE, 1st Division, 1918. Awarded a Bar to his DSO (1915) for his conduct during the crossing of the *Sambre-Oise Canal*, November 1918 (*London Gazette*, 3rd November 1919, page 12217). Member, Institute of Civil Engineers, for 44 years. His son, Lt. Crofton Edmund Peter Sankey, RE, was killed at Arnhem on 23rd September 1944 and is buried in the Arnhem Oosterbeek War Cemetery, grave 23. A. 18.

Baden-Powell assumed the defenders would at least be behind cover and, more likely, entrenched. Thus, whilst the attacking troops were forced to thin their lines to reduce casualties no such restriction imposed itself on the defence which could mass men and weaponry wherever it saw fit. In addition, ammunition supply and distribution to the defender was far easier than across the fire swept zone over which the attack proceeded.

His conclusion was:

> "All this, then, renders the attack generally infinitely less likely to succeed than formerly, and if it be conducted across the open in broad daylight and against well-posted troops, practically impossible of success."[58]

His judgement on the problem facing attacking infantry was accurate and his suggestions of armoured and mobile forts and 'armoured motor cars' at least suggest some creative thought about options for both defence and attack.[59] His comments on artillery, i.e. that 'the importance of artillery fire has not increased to the extent some sanguine gunners seemed to expect', proved substantially wide of the mark when fighting started in 1914. Despite this misjudgement, however, Baden-Powell's concerns about the ability of troops to cross a fire swept zone when facing quick-firing and long-range weaponry were well considered. Well, at least by him and, perhaps, his older brother. Few others appeared to stretch themselves in any way to find a solution to this key battlefield problem.

Others were not so convinced of the virtues of dispersal and the problem of the 'fire swept zone' and these included many now in senior positions taught by Henderson at Camberley when his views were vastly more traditional. The central issue for them was the gaining of 'fire superiority' over the enemy. This superiority, gained by small arms and/or artillery fire, needed to be maintained until the last possible moment before the assault was launched if the attackers were to be protected from the murderous fire of rifles and machine guns defending the area to be attacked. The war in Manchuria provided some evidence that, if the infantry were prepared to accept the risk of friendly fire to gain an advantage, the artillery could still be firing almost as the troops entered the enemy's lines. Some, like Ian Hamilton, harboured the fantasy that the (highly questionable) fanatical, quasi-religious dedication ascribed to Japanese troops might yet be instilled in British soldiers. Most were more realistic but still it was thought possible the infantry might be able to approach to within 100 yards of the enemy's line before the artillery needed to lift onto more remote targets. In this respect, a high-firing howitzer would be beneficial. This gun could fire more accurately and on a plunging trajectory which suggested less risk to the attackers than flat-firing field guns. The new 4.5-in. field howitzer would, it was concluded, provide the answer to this question. Or it might have if British officers truly believed in the efficacy of indirect fire in such circumstances, and this was by no means the case.

How might the infantry help suppress the fire of the enemy? This was a question which, though asked, was rarely answered. The forum for the debate on such issues was the conference held annually by the General Staff at the Staff College. Such a conference was held between 18th and 21st January 1909 at Camberley and the problem was raised by Col. John Philip Du Cane, RA, a man who went on to play a major role in the opening two years of the war, and then assisted Lloyd George in the creation of a British armaments and munitions industry equipped to meet the 'Shell Crisis' of 1915. He then returned to serve in senior roles on the Western Front[i]. Du Cane pointed out current regulations specified superiority of fire was the prerequisite of victory. And yet, he stated, achieving this 'superiority' was something rarely practised at the annual manoeuvres, little understood by either officers or men, and its effect neglected by the umpires.[60] The manner of the movement of units and the delivery of the final assault were the key ingredients at the newly re-introduced autumn manoeuvres but the effects of fire during these exercises was often ignored. That this was still the case was seen in later exercises when the umpires conveniently disregarded the effects of concealed artillery fire on Douglas Haig's troops at Medmenham during the Aldershot Command's exercises in 1913 and again during the large scale Army manoeuvres when Rawlinson's Division was allowed to stand for hours in splendid isolation under heavy 'fire' during the 'Battle of Fawsley' (see page 791).[ii]

Du Cane's view as an artillerist was, of course, that 'fire', either by artillery or infantry support weapons, was of the first importance. It was not enough to rehearse getting attacking troops into position for an assault. They must know what to do once they got there. The debate which followed revealed how little Henderson's views on dispersal and the independence of thought and action of officers permeated the senior officer class of the Army. One Brigadier commented that infantry relied on the artillery to cover their movements rather than providing covering fire themselves. Col., later Gen., Aylmer Haldane, an observer of the

---

[i] Gen. Sir John Philip Du Cane, GCB, RA, (1865–1947), second son of Sir Charles Du Cane; KCMG, of Braxted Park, Essex, and the Hon. Georgiana Susan Lyndhurst, only child of John Singleton Copley, 1st Baron Lyndhurst, three times Lord Chancellor of Great Britain. Wellington College and RMA, Woolwich. Royal Artillery, 1884. Something of a 'golden child', he swanned through early life, with five years spent as adjutant of the Norfolk RGA Militia. Naturally gifted intellectually and physically (he several times opened the batting for the Royal Artillery cricket XI) he served in South Africa, being promoted Lt. Col. Brigade Major, I Corps' artillery, Aldershot 1904. Artillery instructor, Staff College, 1905, an unusual event as he had not attended the College. CGS, III Corps, 1914. Saw action around Armentières in the autumn. Artillery Adviser to Sir John French, January 1915. Promoted Maj. Gen. the following month. Military Adviser, Ministry of Munitions, November 1915. GOC, XV Corps, 1916, again an unusual event. He had never previously commanded even a Brigade. British Representative, Allied Grand HQ, Versailles, March 1918. Lt. Gen., 1919. Master General of the Ordnance (1920-3). GOC, Western Command (1923-4). GOC British Army of the *Rhine* (1924-7). Governor and Commander-in-Chief, Malta (1927–31). ADC General to the King (1926-30). Col. Commandant, RA, 1919. He married Ethel Chapman, widow of Mr Christopher Head, 1914. There were no children.

[ii] Ironically, at the 1909 GSC Rawlinson complained that the effect of the fire of machine guns was given insufficient credit by the umpires during manoeuvres. It was a view supported by Col. F J Davies, from the staff of 1st Division and Smith-Dorrien's representative at the conference [Source: *Report on a Conference of General Staff Officers, 18th to 21st January 1909*, page 67].

Russo-Japanese War, had other, somewhat contradictory views. He had seen at first-hand how machine guns devastated attacking infantry and was of the view the destruction of such guns was essential if an attack was to succeed, later stating:

> "The impression I gained in Manchuria was that it is impossible to take a position which was well defended by machine guns until these guns have been put out of action."[61]

On the other hand, he disagreed with Henderson's statements on the necessary dispersal of attacking infantry. To generate the necessary volume of infantry fire to suppress the opposition, men needed to be in compact units far greater than was the case in South Africa under Roberts. The key to success for Haldane was '… obtaining superiority of fire and not by avoiding loss'. To obtain superiority required men grouped together and therefore vulnerable to counter-fire.

But what might be the nature of the 'fire' thus generated and how did one assess its impact? It was suggested that, though the output might be large, the effect was unknown. Du Cane's view was the same. How did you know, he asked, when sufficient suppressing fire had been delivered to make committing the troops to the assault a reasonable prospect? For Henderson the answer would have lain with well-trained, intelligent officers and NCOs who could make decisions in accordance with their direct observation and experience. But the British Army had not gone down that path. Command was centralised not devolved. This dictated that men were in close enough order to heed orders issued even though close order when faced by quick-firing automatic weapons was a recipe for heavy casualties. Such casualties were, therefore, not only expected, but accepted as the price of victory. Thus, it was of essential importance the men delivering the attack should be highly disciplined, trained to respond automatically to orders, have high morale and, in essence, be ready to die for their country. In other words, except for high morale, it was a list of everything against which Henderson argued between 1899 and 1903. It was not as if no other options were suggested or, indeed, already been tried in the field.

Some advised equipping the infantry with large numbers of lightweight, mobile automatic weapons. The *Lewis Gun*, for example, for which orders were belatedly placed in the autumn of 1914 (see page 642). But a lightweight, mobile automatic rifle already existed and had been tested, and then rejected, by the British Army in 1904. This was the Danish-designed and manufactured *Madsen Light Machine Gun*. Based on an 1883 design by an artillery officer and, later, Danish Minister of War, Captain Vilhelm Herman Oluf Madsen[i], it was built by the newly formed *Compagnie Madsen A/S* and was accepted into the Danish Army in 1902. It was eventually sold to 34 countries in twelve different calibres – but not to Britain. A British officer with the Russian forces in Manchuria paying attention might have seen some of the 1,250 *Madsens* with which their cavalry was equipped in 1904. Indeed, half a dozen *Madsens* fired c. 30,000 rounds repelling a Japanese attack at Mukden in March 1905.[62] The Germans employed the *Madsen Muskete 7.92 mm* from the

---

[i] The *Madsen* was not unlike the later British Bren Gun (itself based on the Czech *ZGB 33* light machine gun). Weight 20 lbs (9.1 Kg), length 45-in. (1.14 metres). With magazines of 25, 30 or 40 bullets it had a notional rate of fire of 450 rpm.

beginning of the war and thirty were used to supplement the defensive firepower of *26. Reserve Division* around Beaumont Hamel and Thiepval on 1st July 1916[i].

Several other similar weapons, such as the Swedish *Kjellman* Light Machine Gun, the Mexican *Mondragon* rifle, the *Smith-Condit* semi-automatic made by the *Standard Arms Company* of the USA, and the French semi-automatic *Fusil Hallé* were also trialled by the Small Arms Committee (set up in 1900) which was charged with investigating all military aspects of small arms and ammunition. None of them were adopted for use.

Now, several years later, the main serious proponent within the British Army of such a weapon was Lt. Col. Norman Reginald McMahon, DSO, of the Royal Fusiliers, who was the Chief Instructor at the School of Musketry at Hythe in Kent[ii]. McMahon appears to have been a man akin to Henderson in his thinking. On 18th December 1907, he gave a lecture at the Prince Consort's Library in Aldershot chaired by Maj. Gen. Grierson. The talk was entitled *Fire Fighting*. In it he made several statements of which Henderson would have approved:

> "Probably the greatest difficulty in the attack is to combine the efforts of all the fire units for a common purpose; control by battalion commanders within the zone of effective rifle fire is almost impossible. Great freedom is now allowed to company officers, who are expected to display individuality and initiative."[63]

In later years, he proselytised on the virtues of 'fire and movement', espousing the principle that fire had but one objective: to facilitate movement. Fire and movement were inseparable elements and, as such, had been formalised in the French Army's *Musketry Regulations* of which he wholeheartedly approved. McMahon argued fire needed to be accurate and not just great in volume[iii]. Furthermore, he argued for the use of concealment and cover in both attack and defence and that movement, once undertaken, needed to be rapid. As one unit moved, another provided covering fire in a system of mutual support. It was the system of Moore's Light Brigade as explained by Henderson (see page 446).[64]

In 1909 the School of Musketry argued each infantry battalion should be

---

[i] A version was believed to be in use with the Brazilian police as late as 2015.

[ii] Lt. Col. Norman Reginald McMahon, DSO, was born in 1866 and was the third son of Gen. Sir Thomas McMahon, 3rd Bt, CB. Eton and Sandhurst. Royal Fusiliers, 1885. Third Anglo-Burmese War in 1886-7. Special Service Officer to the staff in South Africa., 1899. Served for three years, being severely wounded. Instructor at the School of Musketry, 1905, serving for four years. Lt. Col., 1911. CO, 4th Royal Fusiliers (9th Brigade, 3rd Division), August 1914. Mons and le Cateau. GSO1, 4th Division, October 1914. Killed during the 1st Battle of Ypres on 11th November 1914. He is remembered on Panel 1 of the Ploegsteert Memorial.

[iii] McMahon is credited with the 'mad minute' in which British soldiers fired 15 aimed rounds in 60 seconds. Some suggested this was in response to the lack of interest the pre-war British Army had in light automatic weapons. He attracted the nickname of the 'Musketry Maniac' [*Source*: Harlow, N A, *Beyond the Machine Gun Re-interpreting McMahon's 'Fire Fighting' lecture of 1907*, The Journal of the Historical Breechloading Smallarms Association, Vol. 4, No. 8, November 2016, page 30].

equipped with six heavy machine guns rather than the current two as would soon be the case in the German Army. The suggestion was rejected by the authorities partly due to cost but as much because, even then, the use of the machine gun as a defensive and offensive weapon was improperly understood. The Commandant of Hythe at the time was Walter Norris Congreve, later to command the XIII Corps on the *Somme* successfully at Montauban and the Bazentin Ridge in July 1916. Congreve was a long-time advocate of the machine gun and was one of the dozen officers who attended the first ever Maxim machine gun training course at Hythe in 1889. He was convinced of their power in the defence and became frustrated that both the parsimony of the government and the lack of forethought by the General Staff was not only holding back both the use of the machine gun in a defensive role, but also in developing the necessary tactics to overcome the enemy's guns. Clearly, though, under his guidance the School of Musketry developed a more enlightened view about the uses and power of the machine gun well in advance of most of his contemporaries.

Congreve was also a member of the Automatic Rifle Committee set up in October 1909 and chaired by the then Director of Military Operations, Henry Wilson. It was charged with selecting the 'most suitable automatic magazine action for rifles'. It met annually over the next four years and was dissolved in December 1913. Its three volumes of findings were presented on 22nd January 1914. It either tested, or brought forward from earlier, the results for some 25 automatic or semi-automatic rifles. A few received vaguely positive reports, with one designed by the delightfully named Soren Hansen Bang of Denmark being described as having 'performed well'. But not well enough to be bought by the Army.[65] Thus, there was no mobile automatic firepower available to the British Army in August 1914.

The following year the annual General Staff conference was held at the Staff College between 17th and 20th January 1910. Attendees did not face an especially arduous programme. After an hour for breakfast the conference convened each day at 9.45 a.m. Lunch was taken between 1 and 2 p.m. The afternoons and evenings were free with dinner at 7.30 p.m. Gen. Sir William Gustavus Nicholson, GCB, Chief of the Imperial General Staff, was in charge and, amongst many others, it was attended by Maj. Gen. John Ewart, CB, Director of Military Operations, Brig. Gen. Archibald Murray, CVO, CB, DSO, Director of Military Training, Brig. Gen. Launcelot Kiggell, CB, Director of Staff Duties, Brig. Gen. Henry Wilson, CB, DSO, commandant of the Staff College and Brig. Gen. William Robertson, CB, DSO, from the General Staff at Smith-Dorrien's Aldershot Command. Other names stand out for their role in the war or later events: Cols. Du Cane, Hunter-Weston, John Gough and J E Edmonds for example.

The minutes of the conference can be found in a report which, minus brief appendices, covers some eighty pages of which nearly nine are devoted to the subject of *The Offensive Action of Cavalry and other Mounted Troops when Dismounted*. Other subjects covered the training of machine gun detachments, the actions of 'advanced guards' and a full morning was spent on various aspects of the newly formed Territorial Force. The pre-lunch period on Wednesday, 19th January, covered various aspects of training and education within the Regular Army on which more elsewhere.

On Monday, 17th January 1910, McMahon addressed this assemblage of the good and the great. His presentation, agenda item No. 6, was entitled *The Principle that the Object of Fire is to Facilitate Movement in the Direction of the Enemy, and in the Defence, to Prevent the Movement of the attacking Infantry towards the Defender's position*. McMahon opened his address by stating that movement was the essential precursor to success on the battlefield but fire was the enabler of this movement. Whilst accepting there were other secondary reasons for 'fire', e.g. covering fire, demonstration, for its effect on morale, etc., its essential use was to enable the infantry to move towards and then into the enemy's positions. The use of quick-firing and automatic weapons, the use of smokeless powders, the use of cover, extended order, camouflage uniforms, etc., all had an impact on deciding on and controlling the nature and volume of fire placed on the opposing forces. McMahon referred to *FSR* in which there were numerous references to the link between fire and movement quoting such phrases as 'The assault is made possible by the superiority of fire' and 'The object of the artillery is to assist the infantry advance'. All well and good, he suggested, but such generalised statements existed in Training Manuals which pre-dated the South African War and yet neither senior nor junior officers appeared properly to grasp what they meant. The results had been desultory exchanges of fire from which nothing resulted except, perhaps, the exposing of positions (and, possibly, the General's intentions), by the opening of 'purposeless sniping' and a resulting stalemate. McMahon therefore advocated a method of training which instilled in junior officers and other ranks the principles that fire was a signal for movement and movement an urgent call for fire.

He then addressed the subject of the 'automatic rifle'. Every nation thought its arrival imminent but were not prepared to take the first step. It was McMahon's view Britain needed to lead the way, not only in design and production but in determining numbers and use. These latter factors would be based on their ability to affect the enemy in a variety of ways which the School of Musketry had already analysed for the machine gun. This analysis should have given more than a hint to the assembled officers as to the impact heavy machine guns would have on the modern battlefield. Experiments at Hythe explored the ability of machine guns to produce three effects on the enemy: delaying, stopping, and annihilating. As a result, Hythe suggested to *Vickers* and other manufacturers that the heavy machine gun tripod mounting should be sufficiently robust to allow for an annihilating effect on a line of troops 600 yards away, or 'beyond the limit of vision', and extended by two paces between each man. By 'annihilating effect' McMahon meant the loss of 60% of the advancing men within one minute. Currently, the Army's machine guns could produce a 'stopping effect', i.e. 30% losses in a minute. The calculations then needed to be made to determine how many machine guns were required to produce these 'effects' on a set width of front. If one were able to add into the equation the use of the 'automatic rifle', which McMahon envisaged as more akin to a light machine gun to be supplied in a ratio of approximately three to every heavy machine gun, then one could determine the numbers of each required. Tables of fire for these guns could then be determined which would provide the officers in command with the rates of fire needed to produce delaying, stopping and annihilating effects on the battlefield at various ranges.

In response to this point, Lt. Col. William Thomas Furse[i], then a GSO2 at the Staff College, gave an intimation as to the current state of tactical awareness within the Royal Artillery. Agreeing with McMahon, he referred to the 'invisibility of the target' as far as the gunners were concerned and the difficulties this created in supporting the infantry when 3-400 yards away from the enemy. The answer was what, in future, became the Forward Observation Officer (FOO), capable of directly observing the fall of shot or shrapnel burst and communicating the results back to his battery but, according to Furse:

> "I have never seen myself, in the few field-days I have had the chance of attending, a ranging officer sent forward in close and rapid communication with his guns, to range the battery on the target; and I have seen certain cases in field-days where – through the lack of a ranging officer so posted – guns have gone on firing where they might well be of more danger than assistance to their own side."[66]

Neither subject was then taken up by the assembled audience, but it is the final contributions which are so revealing. There is an exchange between Col. Du Cane, one of the brighter intellectual stars in the British military firmament, and the faintly glimmering 'white dwarf' who was Brig. Gen. Launcelot Kiggell, soon to be Haig's right-hand man on the Western Front. A man with no regimental experience since 1893 (when he joined the Staff College) and who, as either a staff officer or administrator, had never been at the 'sharp end' of any fighting, anywhere. Du Cane rather more directly criticised the content of *FSR* on the subject of fire and movement:

> "*Colonel Du Cane*: Major McMahon stated that the *Field Service Regulations* do, as a matter of fact, embody the principle that the object of fire is to facilitate movement by the gaining of fire superiority, and that the object of artillery fire is to facilitate the forward movement of the infantry. But I doubt whether the principle is put into *Field Service Regulations* in a manner which is altogether intelligible to the average intellect of the regimental officer… I doubt whether they do understand that the object of fire in attack is to enable the infantry to get forward… Perhaps for that reason it would be advisable to make some alteration in the *Regulations* in order to bring this point to the fore.

---

[i] Lt. Gen. Sir William Thomas Furse, KCB, KCMG, DSO, RA, (1865–1953) was educated at Eton and the RMA and commissioned into the Royal Artillery in 1884. He was ADC to Lord Roberts, then CinC in India, between 1890–93 and served on his staff in South Africa. Attending the Staff College (1895-6) at the same time as Haig, he served in South Africa as a DAAG and was appointed DAQMG of II Corps in 1902. After three years in the Intelligence Branch at the War Office he joined the staff at Camberley in 1908. In 1911 he took command of 12th (Howitzer) Brigade, RFA, and in 1913 was GSO1, 6th Division. In January 1915 he was appointed BGGS, II Corps, and, in September, GOC, 9th (Scottish) Division on the death of Maj. Gen. Thesiger, killed on the second day of the Battle of Loos. At the end of 1916 he was appointed Master-General of the Ordnance and the fourth Army member of the Army Council. He retired from the Army in 1920.

Brigadier General Kiggell: … After the Boer War the general opinion was that the result of the battle would for the future depend on fire-arms alone, and that the sword and the bayonet were played out. But this idea is erroneous and was proved to be so in the late war in Manchuria. Everyone admits that. Victory is won actually by the bayonet or by the fear of it, which amounts to the same thing so far as the conduct of the attack is concerned. This fact was proved beyond doubt in the late war. I think the whole question rather hangs on that; and if we accept the view that victory is actually won by the bayonet, it settles the point[i].[67]

On which note McMahon's attempted discussion about the relationship between 'fire and movement' and the need for a mobile automatic weapon closed. The result of such attitudes was that the *Lewis* light machine gun was not ordered until *after* the outbreak of war. Indeed, the whole subject of automatic weapons and the best use of the machine gun was one seemingly ignored over the coming years. McMahon's comments about the 'annihilating effect' of a *Vickers* on a line of troops each man two yards apart and 600 yards distant seems not to have been taken on board. Let us examine his assertion in rather more detail.

Before the war, the French estimated that one machine gun firing at a known range had the firepower of 150-200 riflemen. The difference was that one machine gun and its team was more accurate than 200 inexpert soldiers, less prone to nerves or to indecision about which target to select. In short, it was less 'human'. As Basil Liddell Hart expressed it, the machine gun represented 'the concentrated essence of infantry'.

At a range of c. 500 metres, one gun, for example a German *Maschinengewehr 08*, could concentrate something like 450 rounds a minute[ii] into an oval less than 150 metres in length and thirty metres across at its widest point. This oval was called the 'beaten' or 'effective zone' and was the area within which 85% of rounds fell. This distribution was caused by any number of factors: vibration or slight movement in the gun, the heat of the barrel, variable wind along the bullets' path, tiny variations in the quantity of propellant in each bullet case, or the weight of the bullet itself. Thus, bullets would fall in a continuous stream around the true aiming point, some short, some long, some left, some right. Each machine gun bullet entered the 'beaten zone' on a gentle downward parabolic curve from muzzle to ground. But, if fired at short range, the initial flat trajectory meant that sooner or later a bullet entered a zone no more than 1.85 metres above the ground

---

[i] Statistically, Kiggell was barking up the wrong tree. During the Revolutionary and Napoleonic Wars (1792-1815) some 4.5% of French troops were wounded by bladed instruments. In the American Civil War this dropped to 1%. During 1914, 0.9% of French casualties were injured by a bladed instrument, i.e. bayonet, sword or lance. In 1917 no such wounds were reported [*Source*: Clee, Col. F, *Furia francese: representations, limits and reality checks. Or why the French armed forces kept a bayonet on the HK416*, Centre de Doctrine et d'Enseignement de Commandement, June 2019, page 4].

[ii] Firing for this length of time would soon overheat the barrel thereby demanding a barrel change. It is known as cyclic firing. Firing in shorter or slightly longer bursts are described as either 'sustained' or 'rapid'.

(i. e. the average height of a man) where the bullet would either first hit a man in the head or, at the end of its path, in the foot. This is known today as 'first catch' and 'last graze'. This zone is called 'the dangerous space' and the shorter the range at which the machine gun was firing the larger it is. At very short ranges this might be c. 150 metres long, i.e. enough space to contain a line of 75 men two paces apart. According to McMahon, at this range one machine gun, without traversing or otherwise moving the gun, should be able to kill or wound at least 45 of these men in one minute or less.[68]

78 Lt. Gen. Sir Launcelot Edward Kiggell
Believer in the bayonet and direct fire artillery.
Haig's Chief of Staff, BEF

79 Brig. Gen. Norman Reginald McMahon
Chief instructor, School of Musketry, Hythe.
Inventor of the 'Mad Minute'.
Automatic weapons enthusiast.
Killed at 1st Ypres, 11th November 1914

Ideally, the machine gun would be so placed as to take advancing troops in the flank. Flanking fire is described as: fire that is delivered directly against the flank of the target, i.e. the machine gun is firing directly *along* a line/wave of men advancing at right angles to the position of the gun. Next best is enfilade fire which is defined as being: when the long axis of the beaten zone coincides or nearly coincides with the long axis of the target, i.e. the machine gun is firing directly down the line/wave of advancing troops whether they are in line (i.e. firing from the flank) or column (i.e. firing from in front). The next best form of fire is oblique fire: when the long axis of the beaten zone is at an angle other than a right angle to the front of the target. If fired from the flank, in enfilade or obliquely, this constant stream of bullets would hit most things in their path once it enters the 'dangerous space'. In an ideal defensive arrangement, a number of machine guns would be deployed to create interlocking fields of fire creating an extended zone in which the fire of all guns involved would fall.

The most recent example of the effectiveness of the machine gun in a defensive role was with the Russian Army in Manchuria. Here the Russians were mainly equipped with *Maxim-Vickers* Machine Guns (the Japanese used the 1897 *Hotchkiss* machine gun manufactured by the *Société Anonyme des Anciens Etablissements Hotchkiss et Cie* set up by the American Benjamin Hotchkiss in France in 1867).

Often used at remarkably short range, it is suggested a third of Japanese battle casualties fell victim to such guns. At Nanshan, the siege of Port Arthur and Mukden, the Russian *Maxims* caused carnage amongst the attacking infantry, i.e. in both siege and battlefield conditions. The evidence of their brutal effectiveness was plentiful and yet the BEF was equipped with just 108 of these guns when it left for France.

Peter Hart in his book *Fire and Movement: The British Expeditionary Force and the Campaign of 1914* makes the point that the power of the machine gun was clearly appreciated within the senior ranks of the army. After all, he asks, had not Douglas Haig visited the *Royal Ordnance Factory* at Enfield Lock to inspect the *Maxim* in 1898 before employing them to slaughter ill-equipped Dervishes during the Atbara campaign of April of that year? And was not the power of the machine gun written into *Field Service Regulations* authored by Haig? Absolutely, there it is in Section 7 of Chapter 1 of Part I on page 20:

> "The machine gun possesses the power of delivering a volume of concentrated rifle fire which can be rapidly directed against any desired object. Rapid fire cannot be long sustained owing to the expenditure of ammunition involved, and it is therefore necessary that the movements and fire action of these weapons should be regulated so as to enable them to gain their effect by means of short bursts of rapid and accurate fire whenever a favourable opportunity arises. Surprise is an important factor in the employment of machine guns, which should be concealed, and whenever possible provided with cover from fire."[69]

All very good. As *FSR* later shows, this volume of fire was seen to be especially useful as part of the attempt by an attacking force 'to gain superiority of fire' as *FSR* describes on page 136 under the heading *The General Conduct of the Attack*. This was a view widely accepted in armies of all countries. It was part of the widespread belief that automatic weapons mainly enhanced the power of the offensive, which was useful as belief in the power of the offensive was the rock on which most current military thinking and planning was based. Therefore, this section continues:

> "Machine guns will be specially valuable in bringing a sudden fire to bear from such (newly captured) positions, both in order to cover a further advance and to assist in defeating counter-attacks. Machine guns can normally support an attack most efficiently from well concealed positions provided with good cover, and within effective infantry range of the enemy. Occasionally, when good opportunities for a concealed advance present themselves, they may be established within close infantry range of the objective."[70]

This is not to say that *FSR* ignores the role of the machine gun in defence. On page 147 their use is covered:

> "Enfilade fire brought against an enemy's firing line which is already engaged in front will be most effective, and for this machine guns, especially during the later stages of the attack, when firing from positions which have been carefully concealed and prepared beforehand, are of great

value. Machine guns are best utilized to sweep with fire exposed spaces which an enemy must cross, or roads and defiles through which he must advance, and will also be of service to flank salients or advanced posts, and to assist in protecting the flanks."[71]

The point is not that Haig fails to identify the offensive and (rather greater) defensive potential of the machine gun, it is rather that he (along with many colleagues) fails to bring the two points together. i.e. he fails to address how attacking troops might get in position to launch the critical bayonet attack if subject to the interlocking fields of fire of 'carefully concealed' machine guns firing in enfilade into the 'exposed spaces which an enemy must cross'. Sadly, the 'skill, better organization, and training, and above all a firmer determination in all ranks to conquer at any cost' which *FSR* demands in Chapter V, page 126, S. 99, did not make soldiers bullet proof.[72]

We are left then with the pious hope expressed by Sir Ian Hamilton when faced with this quandary:

"I am certain, that an attack can be brought off some-how..."[73]

This was a view given after the South African experience and, seven years later, in the Army's operational 'bible' there were still no solutions. Instead, the answer to how to get to grips with the men firing long-range, modern rifles and machine guns was, according to Launcelot Kiggell, the man who was to spend half of the war as the Chief of the General Staff of Haig's BEF in France and Flanders, the bayonet, the use of which was enshrined in Army training by its inclusion as the key element at the crisis of the battle in the General Staff's manual *Infantry Training 1914*.

That, in 1910, officers should still be arguing about the benefits of the bayonet relative to the rifle is bizarre. *The Times* has never been a newspaper renowned for radicalism on any subject and yet, in 1881, it made definitive statements about bayonets *vis à vis* rifles and the utility of the spade in modern warfare. It followed the shock and dismay the entire Empire experienced after the British humiliations of the First Boer War in 1880-1. In just thirteen weeks, the newly independent Boers of the Transvaal, repeatedly trounced red coated British troops, their tactics of concealment, accurate shooting and independent movement proving too much for the volley-firing, static, inaccurate, bayonet-carrying British. In May 1881, *The Times* published an article entitled *Shooting in the Infantry*. Given Kiggell's devotion to the short, pointy thing on the end of a rifle it is worthy of quotation as, however sensible the comments, they appear to have been forgotten between 1881 and 1899 and, at least by Kiggell, again between 1902 and 1910:

"... only infantry can at the critical moment drive the enemy from its position, put him to rout, and occupy the ground left free by his retreat. It is, moreover, agreed that this important work must be chiefly done by *fire* (*Author's emphasis*). The vast increase of power occasioned by extended range and rapidity of shooting (*note:* this is still the era of single-shot rifles with an effective range of c. 600 yards) has seen no corresponding increase in the power of the bayonet, and the progress of rifle-fire may be expected to continue while the use of the bayonet remains stationary."[74]

The writer went on to reference the British disaster of Majuba Hill on 27th February 1881 after which the Empire remarkably sued for peace with the tiny Boer republic. There, 405 men of the 58th Regiment (later Northamptonshire Regt.), the 92nd Regiment (Gordon Highlanders), and a party from *HMS Dido*[i], all commanded by Maj. Gen. George Pomeroy Colley, were routed by a similar number of Boers with a loss of 70% of their men including Colley who was shot and killed as his troops fled. *The Times* called for British soldiers to become marksmen of the same quality as the Boer (NB this did not happen before 1899). This was needed because:

> "... our soldiers were literally overpowered and their courage quelled by the superior shooting of the Boers. All the accounts of the engagement there show that hand-to-hand fighting (*Note:* i.e. with the bayonet) was impossible, simply because the men could not advance to close quarters with their enemy and live... even in defence the men could not use the bayonet in face of the accurate fire of the Boers."[75]

The writer then stated the view that, if a successful advance was somehow made against troops equipped with modern rifles, then it must be because the shooting of the defenders was abject as, otherwise:

> ".... it will be certain that no troops in the world can approach within 100 yards of them without being, not decimated, but annihilated."[76]

And the reason why British shooting was bad (and would remain so over the next 18 years) was that:

> "The British soldier is the most expensive in the world and there are few of his kind... yet when he has arrived at the end of his training... he is found to fail simply because he is not expert in the use of his weapon. He is perpetually drilled to movements which are never made in close proximity to an enemy. The polish of his buttons and his arms is the object of intense solicitude by day and night, but he does not learn to shoot well."[77]

A few weeks later *The Times*, in an article demanding British infantry be equipped with spades for entrenchment, stated:

> "It is and has been a fashion in every army to believe itself possessed of the true secret of the bayonet charge, and the belief prevails to this day, in spite of the supersession of the bayonet by the rifle, and influences all drill-books."[78]

Spades were not issued and bayonets still beloved. *Plus ça change.* In the British Victorian Army at least.

But back to 1910. Then, a French officer, Capt. Jean-Jules Gaston, *10e bataillon de Chasseurs à Pied*, made his contribution to the bayonet debate. Well, not so much a debate as that requires a counter argument, more a *fait accompli*, as Gaston makes clear, but without any supporting evidence (emphasis below is this writer's):

---

[i] An 1869 *Eclipse*-class wooden screw sloop on the West African station when war broke out. She contributed 50 men and two guns to the force at Majuba.

"The preponderant value of the *arme blanche* (i.e. bladed weapons) in combat is an *undeniable fact and unanimously accepted* at the present time. The Russo-Japanese war brought out the urgent need to give education in the use of the bayonet the greatest possible momentum. Foreign armies have put these lessons to good use; we find that they are seeking to give a new impetus to this branch of education.

France owes itself to its glorious past: once the privileged land of jousting and tournaments, today still an international meeting place for fencers, it must remain the first to use the *arme blanche*, whether it is the foil, an *épée*, a sabre or a bayonet."[79]

J F C Fuller posits the theory that the reason the preference for the use of edged weapons – the sword, the spear/lance and, later, the bayonet – was so deeply engrained within European military society was rooted as far back as the Iron or even Bronze Age: a time when disputes were sometimes settled face-to-face by duels, by a champion such as Achilles. This then translated into the equally up-close-and-personal fighting of, for example, the Spartan or the Alexandrian phalanx, the precursor, if you will, of the Napoleonic column. It was a time when instilling the desire and high morale required to meet the enemy at close quarters was of paramount importance to a European General. But Achilles was killed by a Trojan (Asia Minor) arrow. Thus, whilst Europe continued with the hand-to-hand *melée*, 'the terror of cold steel', the *arme blanche*, from the Middle East and, later, from the depths of Asia, came the bowman, often horsed. Where possible they killed remotely – the Scythians and Parthians, the Persians and Medes, the Huns, the Mongols and the Timurids, the Saracens of the Crusades. In short: a tale of firepower versus morale and short blades.[80]

For the proponents of the *arme blanche* the only problem was that, on the subject of the bayonet's employment in Manchuria, the assertions of Kiggell and Gaston's about the bayonet's 'preponderant value' being '*an undeniable fact and unanimously accepted*' were simply untrue. Not everyone who closely observed the fighting conceded victory was 'won by the bayonet'. Educated at the *Lycée Impérial* at Versailles and the *Gymnasium Friedrich-Wilhelm* in Berlin, and previously military *attaché* in St Petersburg and Berlin, the multi-linguist Col. Wallscourt Hely-Hutchinson Waters, RA, served in South Africa and India and worked in the Intelligence section of War Office under his friend James Grierson. Being without a job in early 1904 he 'sent in his papers'. It was only the personal intervention of a 'firm friend', King Edward VII as it turns out, which persuaded him to stay in the Army. Later that year he was attached to the Russian Army in Manchuria and he subsequently wrote extensive notes for the third volume of *Reports from British Officers attached to the Japanese and Russian Forces in the Field* published in 1908. Waters expressed trenchant views on the relative strengths of 'fire' and the bayonet:

"The Russian Army had been brought up on the idea that shock tactics and close order were the best means by which to win battles… It was the bayonet which was 'to do the trick'. The Russians having failed to grasp the importance of fire attempted to put their old-fashioned theories into practice… the Russians could not understand that their enemy wished to gain victories, and to this end, made use of his modern arms… fire is now, or should be, the all-important factor in a battle... Experience in the field soon taught the Russians that, in the attack, fire was better than the bayonet and extension preferable to the close order in which they had been trained."[81]

Waters was not alone in expressing heretical views about the relative merits of the bayonet and fire in these reports from Manchuria. Maj. James Murray Home, also of the Royal Artillery but now attached to the 4th Goorkha Regiment of the Indian Army, confirmed his colleague's opinion that within the Dragomirov-inspired Russian Army:

"... the importance of fire is not sufficiently insisted upon, the bayonet being generally considered as the most important infantry weapon."[82]

But Home had another point to make and this was about the primacy of artillery on the battlefield. Everything he saw suggested 'artillery is now the decisive arm'. To the average infantry and cavalry officer this might have been bad enough but Home went even further, stating 'all other arms are auxiliary to it'. He then made comments about 'position artillery', or what might be termed siege artillery. Unlike the commonly held view in the French and British Armies, Home saw the virtue of every army having 'guns of position' for the reason:

"... attacks will often have to be made against carefully prepared positions where ample head-cover has been provided."[83]

As amply displayed at Plevna nearly a quarter of a century before, infantry, well dug in, would not suffer from the fire of field artillery and heavier guns would become a 'very important element in a modern battle'. Home's view was that 'other things being equal, the side which is best equipped in this respect will probably win'.[84]

Waters' and Homes' opinions, gained from direct observation of the fighting in Manchuria, were radical in many ways but, on the relative importance of fire and the bayonet, perhaps because they were mere artillery officers or because they observed the defeated Russians rather than the victorious Japanese, they were to be on the 'losing' side. Whatever the explanation, it was still the case that, in the twelve years since the end of the South African War in which time they might determine the solution to the fire swept zone, the leading figures of the Army – Hamilton, Haig in *Field Service Regulations*, Haking in *Company Training*, Altham in *The Principles of War,* Maude in *War and the World's Life* and others too numerous to mention – came to the fundamental conclusion that what was needed was to teach men not to fight better, but to die better. In the offensive, what must be fostered for the final attack was a herd instinct not individualism, an attitude where each man became part of a greater whole and where the emotion of the mass overwhelmed the individual's impulse for self-preservation. Lt. Col. Frederic Natusch Maude described it in terms of the 'automatic regiment'[85] led by a charismatic leader who they would unquestioningly obey and follow. Rather like the Mahdi, perhaps, who's similarly inspired troops were unsparingly slaughtered by modern weapons at Omdurman on 2nd September 1898.

Authoritative voices were even raised against the new orthodoxy, earlier endorsed by Roberts and Henderson, of the dispersal of troops in the advance.

Some suggested this only proved necessary because of the 'peculiar circumstances' found in South Africa, i.e. clear air and wide, unbroken vistas. These would not apply in Europe and, therefore, the key point in the offensive was the massing of sufficient men providing sufficient firepower with which to cover the final assault with the bayonet. Under current thinking this meant waiting whilst support troops came up to thicken the firing line established a few hundred yards in front of the point to be attacked. This caused delay and delay meant casualties and casualties, perhaps, undermined the determination of the troops to press home the attack. Far better, it was suggested, that the mass of troops be present immediately to provide the suppressing fire which would cover the charge. Of course, a mass of troops advancing to the point from which the charge would be launched must attract the enemy's fire and thus cause necessarily extensive loss. These losses, some suggested, were necessary if victory was to be achieved. Spencer Jones in his book *Boer War to World War* quotes an article by Brig. Gen. Francis Charles Carter[i] which appeared in *The Army Review*, an influential publication issued under the *imprimatur* of the Imperial General Staff. The article is dated 1912 and, it should be noted, the author was a man who had not seen action since 1891 and that against Hazara hill tribesman in the Khyber Pakhtunkhwa province on the North-West Frontier. Since then, he had been a staff officer, an administrator in South Africa and commander of 16th Infantry Brigade based at Fermoy in Ireland. He did not fight in the South African War and yet saw fit to criticise the lessons so painfully learned about the effect of rapid rifle and machine gun fire on massed troops. Describing the Roberts/Henderson solution as 'the fetish of 'over-extension which… still claims some devotees amongst our senior officers', Carter went on to urge massed rather than dispersed troops:

> "We must harden our hearts, as did our forefathers of old to the heavy losses that will occur," he argued and be prepared, "to suffer losses… and to snatch victory from the jaws of death."[86]

To harden one's heart it must still be beating which is more than would be the case with those men unfortunate enough to be one of Carter's 'heavy losses'. He, of course, would be well out it. He retired in the same year as his article was published.

---

[i] Brig. Gen. Francis Charles Carter, CB, Royal Berkshire Regt., was born in 1858, the son of Capt. H L Carter, 6th Dragoon Guards. Educated at St Edward's School, Oxford, and Sandhurst, he was commissioned into the 5th (Northumberland Fusiliers) Regiment of Foot in 1878. He served with the 1st Battalion in the 1st Afghan War (1878-80). In 1888 he served in the 1st Hazara Expedition and in 1891 with the 2nd Expedition. Between he saw action in the 1889 Lushai Expedition against Burmese hill tribes on the Assam border. He was CO, 1st Royal Berkshire Regt., 1899-1903 and was then a Brig. Gen. in South Africa between 1906 and 1909. GOC, 16th Brigade based in Fermoy in Ireland he retired in 1912. He returned on the outbreak of war and was GOC, 24th Brigade, 8th Division, during the Battle of Neuve Chapelle, 10th-13th March 1915. After the battle he asked to be relieved on health grounds and was replaced on 17th March. The following month he made a written complaint over the fact he had been passed over for promotion to Maj. Gen. He died in 1931.

As was too often the case, a compromise of sorts was attempted. Soggy or not, steps were taken to reduce extension and dispersion but not to the degree suggested by Carter. Hamilton argued for an advance extended less than suggested post-South Africa but more than that eventually employed by the Japanese in Manchuria. Despite this, however, the trend towards concentration continued and complaints were levelled at the excessive massing of troops in manoeuvres as late as 1913.[87] In the early months of the war, however, the men of the Regular Army proved adept at the practice of defensive dispersed 'fire and movement' tactics. Perhaps being fired at with live ammunition sharpened the senses of the junior officers, NCOs and Privates and reminded them of what was both effective and of what was least likely to cost them their lives[i].

The emphasis laid by *FSR* on 'superiority of fire' prior to the launch of the bayonet charge could, it seemed, only by achieved by the concentration of troops previously in skirmishing order. Progressively, it was suggested, as skirmishers advanced to the launch point, they needed to coalesce into larger and larger groups until such time there was sufficient mass to deliver a heavy volume of fire at relatively short range immediately prior to the charge. Inevitably, larger concentrations of men within full view of an entrenched enemy would provide excellent targets thus the need for high morale, discipline, and officer control.

But what if there was another way of achieving 'superiority of fire', one already tested on the battlefield? By the Japanese, for example, in Manchuria.

Many of the discussions about Manchuria concentrated on the bravery of Japanese attacks pressed whatever the cost. They referred to troops running into friendly fire as they kept up close to the artillery barrage preceding them. What the observers seem to have ignored were the changes made in infantry tactics as the casualty rates suffered became unsustainable, even if attacks were successful. Although victorious, the fighting on the *Yalu River* on 30th April-1st May 1904 suggested that previously recommended long skirmish lines with the men just 1-2 paces apart were likely to result in heavy losses. As the fighting intensified advances were being made by sections, or even one or two men, and at pace with any cover available being used. By the time of the fighting on the *Sha-ho* in October charges were launched from distance by a loose grouping of sections moving as quickly as possible and with no attempt to maintain alignment. Indeed, avoiding linear formations seemed helpful in reducing the effectiveness of Russian machine gun fire. Ian Hamilton witnessed such attacks mounted by the 15th Brigade commanded by Gen. Okasaki on two days on the *Sha-ho* (11th and 12th October). On each day his troops charged across 600 yards of open field, each section advancing on its own initiative and as fast as possible. Both attacks succeeded.

The western reporting of these attacks, however, suggested that observers only saw an apparent maintenance of pre-Boer War 'business as usual' with none of the extremes of dispersal that the fighting in South Africa produced. Though not the tightly bunched columns which came so badly unstuck in the opening months of

---

[i] For an excellent account of the development of British infantry tactics post 1902 see Spencer Jones's *From Boer War to World War: Tactical Reform of the British Army 1902-14*, Chapter 3 *Infantry*. Published by Oklahoma University Press, 2012.

the South Africa War, the Japanese, in the main, reportedly employed frontal attacks conducted by linear formations with gaps between each man of c. 5-6 feet. Supporting fire was delivered by the artillery which maintained its fire on the enemy front line until the moment of the bayonet charge. Then, with the skirmishing line brought together to deliver a sufficient concentration of small arms fire, the charge could be delivered by the disciplined, well-led soldiers, confident in their previous success and thus with high morale. In other words, all the ingredients which many European Army officers believed was needed to get troops across the fire swept zone in the era of high-powered and quick-firing weaponry. All very comforting. For the Generals, at least.

One thing noted in Manchuria, however, suggested that, in the offensive at least, all the work done to improve the accuracy of the average riflemen was not essential. It became apparent that, prior to an attack, *volume* of fire on the enemy position was more important than accuracy. The need was not to pick off individual defenders but to keep their heads down until such time the bayonet-wielding attacker was on top of them. What was helpful, therefore, was a supporting unit able to deposit a considerable volume of fire on the enemy position whilst the assault troops approached. This concept is now known as 'base of fire' and has been standard practice world-wide since introduced in WW1 by German storm troops in 1916. This 'base of fire' could be static if appropriately positioned or, as in classic 'fire and movement' assaults, it might require units leapfrogging one another with the temporarily static group providing covering and suppressing fire whilst the other advanced, and then vice-versa. Nowadays, these ideas have been mainly credited to people like Willy Rohr (see page 833) with his ideas for German *sturmbataillon* tactics developed in 1915-6 but went apparently unnoticed by western observers when they were also employed from time to time by the Japanese in 1904-5.

In his 2002 Master's thesis *Ignoring the Obvious: Combined Arms and Fire and Maneuver Tactics Prior to World War I*, Maj. Thomas Bruno, USMC, quotes various examples of 'base of fire' principles used by the Japanese. At Liaoyang on 31st August 1904 Bruno cites the deployment of a Japanese battalion along a ridge line to give small arms covering fire to the assaulting units. Again, on the *Sha-ho* on 12th October a unit close to the Russian line put down a high volume of fire whilst others mounted a successful if costly flanking attack. The Japanese also used massed machine guns to supplement existing 'base of fire' units as well as sending them forward to provide close support.[88] Whilst it is true that in certain locations Fourth Army used massed machine guns on 1st July 1916, these were for blocking barrages behind the German trenches to be attacked rather than suppressing fire on the trenches themselves[i]. The Japanese, however, found it possible and effective to maintain massed machine gun fire on Russian trenches until their troops were as close as thirty yards from them. Clearly, the availability of lightweight automatic weapons taken forward by the assaulting troops would have assisted in this process but, as shown, the pre-war British Army displayed no great interest, and certainly no urgency, in equipping themselves with such weapons.

---

[i] Employed in this way by 31st and 4th Divisions on VIII Corps' front.

What was shown in Manchuria for those wishing to see was that there was an alternative to the slow-moving linear attacks in which the enemy usually seemed to win the 'race to the parapet', but these were still the tactics widely employed on the *Somme* on 1st July. By the British, at least.

AS WITH CONTINENTAL ARMIES, the emphasis of most senior officers was on the offensive. As Maj. Gen. Sir William George Knox, RA, wrote in 1914:

"The defensive is never an acceptable role to the Briton, and he makes little or no study of it."[89]

Which is ironic as the greatest victory achieved by the British Army in the previous 100 years was at Waterloo[i]; a battle at which Wellington spent the day on the defensive until Prussian reinforcements and the exhaustion of Napoleon's attacking troops produced victory. Take in Quatre Bras, Ligny and Wavre and the entire campaign was fought on the defensive by the Allies. But British officers preferred to explore, and seek to emulate, the rather more dashing earlier victories of the man defeated at Waterloo than learn from the greatest military commander Britain has produced. And their reference point almost always was the twin French victories of 14th October 1806 at which Napoleon at Jena and Davout at Auerstedt routed two substantially larger Prussian/Saxon Armies before marching on Berlin and removing Prussia from the war. Although undoubtedly striking achievements, 66,000 Frenchmen defeating 117,000 Prussians and Saxons (French losses c. 12,000, Prussian/Saxon losses c. 41,000), it should be noted that not everything went swimmingly that day. Martin von Creveld notes that:

"Thus Napoleon at Jena had known nothing about the main action that took place on that day; had forgotten all about two of his corps; did not issue orders to a third, and possibly a fourth; was taken by surprise by the action of a fifth; and, to cap it all, had one of his principal subordinates display the kind of disobedience that would have brought a lesser mortal before a firing squad. Despite all these faults in command, Napoleon won what was probably the great single triumph in his career."[90]

The Napoleonic-era was one of the three wars most studied by officers of the Victorian/Edwardian age. The others were the American Civil War and the Franco-Prussian War. In all three it should be remembered that:

- Black powder was the battlefield-obscuring propellant;
- Single-shot muskets were the norm. In the Napoleonic and Civil War battles they were muzzle-loading[ii] whilst, in 1870-1, both the *Chassepot* and *Dreyse* were breech-loading, but still single-shot, if far more rapid-firing, guns;

---

[i] One might also cite the Battle of Inkerman on 5th November 1854 when heavily outnumbered British and French troops defeated at Russian assault inflicting casualties at a rate of three to one.

[ii] The most commonly used rifles in the Civil War on either side were the muzzle-loading American-made *Springfield Model 1861* rifled musket, the British *Enfield Pattern 1853* rifle-musket and the Austrian *Lorenz Rifle Model 1854*.

- Only the *Chassepot* had an effective range of more than 300 metres; and
- The bayonet charge was regarded as the climactic moment in any battle.

These factors all dictated battlefield tactics though, in the Civil War, the growth of the use of field fortifications with their considerable enhancement of defences was a notable change. None of the four factors listed above would apply in 1914 – smokeless powder was the norm, quick-firing rifles and even quicker firing automatic weapons were ubiquitous with their range having increased many times over, artillery range and power was vastly enhanced and, as a result, the bayonet was a weapon more to strike fear into a less-than-resolute enemy than something with which to kill them.

But so entranced were many British and French officers by Napoleon's great campaigns they seemed prepared to ignore the firepower and technical changes of the subsequent hundred years in favour of romantic ideas about sweeping flanking movements, galloping lancers, and gallant bayonet charges – and of the essential if intangible nature of morale and moral forces in war. Furthermore, they were quite happy to ignore the fact that, in the end, Napoleon lost, his empire was destroyed, and many of the social gains of the Revolution undermined by the return of the monarchy (even if most high-born Army officers in every country would have been more than happy with this aspect of the defeat of 'The Little Corporal').

To understand the importance of these psychological forces in the first part of the nineteenth century (and earlier) one must first understand why the technology of the Napoleonic battlefield made the concepts of discipline, *élan*, mass, and the use of the bayonet, so important. French infantry was equipped with the *fusil Charleville Modèle 1777* designed by Jean-Baptiste de Gribeauval in 1717 and made at the *Manufacture d'armes de Charleville* based in Charleville-Mézières on the *Meuse*[i]. It went through four variants before the 1777 version became available and this weapon was still in use up to the 1840s. This smooth-bore, muzzle-loading, flintlock musket was five feet long (1.53 m.), weighed 10 lbs (4.6 Kg), and fired a .69 in. (16.54 mm) calibre ball. Its bayonet was a 15-inch blade (0.38 m.) and gave the soldier a stabbing 'range' of about five feet (1.5 m.). Nowadays, the Napoleonic-era bayonet might be described as an early-nineteenth century 'force multiplier', i.e. something which allows the General/soldier to do more with it than without it, i.e. the decisive final charge. By 1914, 15-inches of cold steel had been somewhat overtaken in this role by, amongst other things, the heavy machine gun, e.g. the *Maschinengewehr 08* with its maximum range of 3,500 metres.

The *fusil Charleville Modèle 1777's* maximum range was c. 300 metres and its propellant black powder. Its effective range, however, was just 100 metres as, beyond, accuracy fell off dramatically as studies conducted in 1818 by a Capt. Rayne showed.[91] Whereas 75% of balls fired from 100 metres hit a 2-metre target these percentage successes plummeted for every 25 metres distance added: i.e. 59% at 125 metres, 46% at 150 metres, 33% at 175 metres and a wasteful 21% at 200 metres. These are also test results not fired in the fearful chaos of battle

---

[i] Later also manufactured at the royal arsenals at Saint-Étienne, Tulle, Maubeuge, Versailles, Châtellerault, Roanne, Culembourg and Mutzig.

conditions where, anyway, volley fire was the norm not the picking out of individual targets. The *fusil's* output in the hands of an expert might be 4 rounds a minute. In the stress of battle, however, it is questionable how many soldiers might achieve even half this rate when enemy troops came within range and mounted a bayonet charge. All this talk about accuracy, however, becomes increasingly irrelevant as the first volley fired would have obscured the enemy in thick, acrid clouds of smoke (except in very windy conditions). Thereafter, if time allowed, volleys were fired in the general direction of the enemy by troops ready to receive a bayonet charge.

The task of the attacking infantry was to survive this initial volley (or volleys) and then, employing the previously mentioned discipline, *élan*, and mass, get within range for a bayonet attack which might shatter the resolve and morale of the defender. It was such tactics which allowed Napoleon to write to his brother Joseph then embroiled in Spain in 1808: 'In war, moral power is to the physical as three parts out of four'. Or, rather more accurately: "In war, three-quarters turns on personal character and relations; the balance of manpower and materials counts only for the remaining quarter".[92] The briefer version became the convenient, if less accurate and rather more self-serving, short-hand employed by French and British officers before the Great War.

Napoleonic tactics relied on: speed of decision and manoeuvre; feints and distractions; and, in battle, the 'economy of force', a phrase beloved of Foch and which described Bonaparte's ability to concentrate superior numbers against relatively weaker elements of the enemy thus de-stabilising their position.

In this latter aspect, Napoleon was inspired by the intermittent genius of Frederick the Great whose two great victories in the Seven Years War (or Third Silesian War) at Rossbach[i] (5th November 1757) and Leuthen[ii] (5th December 1757), were the concentrated essence of later Napoleonic battlefield tactics[iii]. Such

---

[i] At Rossbach, Frederick (22,000) defeated a Franco-Austrian Army (42,000) using a wide out-flanking movement around the left rear of the Allied Army. Prussian casualties were estimated at c. 1,000, and Allied losses 8,000 to 17,000.

[ii] At Leuthen, Frederick (33,000) used a cavalry distraction to pin the Austrians (66,000) whilst he employed the terrain to conceal the movement of most of his army around a weakened Austrian left wing. Prussian casualties were 6,500. The Austrians lost 22,000, with nearly a quarter of their Army being taken prisoner.

[iii] Frederick was not always, or even usually, successful, and the Third Silesian War could have been a disaster but for several fortunate events. In the first battle, on 1st October 1756 at Lobositz (now Lovosice, Czech Republic) he walked into an Austrian trap and, convinced he had lost, withdrew. The Austrian commander, Maximilian Ulysses Count von Browne, having prevented the attempt to enter Bohemia, left to relieve a Saxon Army besieged at Pirna and allowed Frederick to claim victory. An attempt to take Prague in the summer of 1757 was heavily defeated at the Battle of Kolin (18th June 1757). After the previous year's twin victories, 1758 was a bad year: defeats at Domstadtl (30th June 1758), the inconclusive but expensive Battle of Zorndorf (25th August 1758), and the heavy defeat at Hochkirch (14th October 1758). 1759 saw the crushing defeat by a combined Russian-Austrian army at Kunersdorf (12th August 1759) which threatened Berlin, with only disagreements between the

was Frederick's influence that, after the great victories of the Jena-Auerstedt campaign (14th October 1806) which led to the capture of Berlin, Napoleon paid homage at his tomb in the *Garnisonkirche*, Potsdam, on 26th October, 1806[i].

In all such battles through to Waterloo, however sophisticated the preliminary strategic and tactical manoeuvring, final infantry tactics were crude and relied on mass which, in French terms, was supplied by the column of infantry which attempted to burst their way through the enemy's lines. 'Mass', i.e. sheer numbers, therefore became the final battlefield determinant at the climactic moment. Often they succeeded. Sometimes, as at Waterloo, they failed. There, D'Erlon's *I Corps*, 14,000 men in three columns advancing through clinging mud on a front of 1,000 metres, was held by the Allied infantry and routed by the charge of the Union and Household Brigades. Then some 9,000 French cavalrymen led by Ney failed to puncture the Allied centre. Thirdly, 6,500 infantry from Reille's *II Corps* tried to support the cavalry but were forced to withdraw. And finally, five battalion columns of the *Moyenne Garde* were shattered by Chassé's Dutch-Belgians, Maitland's Foot Guards and Colborne's 1/52nd Light Infantry and the rest of Adam's 3rd Brigade. Up went the cry: *'La Garde recule. Sauve qui peut!'* and Napoleon's career was over.

The defence prevailed over the offence, but not just on the ridge between Hougoumont, La Haye Sainte and Papelotte on 18th June 1815. Equally vital to the Allied success at Waterloo was the defence of Wavre by Johann Adolf, *Freiherr* von Thielmann's Prussian *III. Armeekorps* which allowed the other three Prussian Corps to smash into the French right flank from Papelotte to Plançenoit in the mid-afternoon. Outnumbered two to one by Grouchy's 33,000 French troops, Thielmann's skilful defence of the bridges over the *River Dyle*, until news of Napoleon's disaster at Waterloo allowed him to disengage, was another triumph of the defensive over the offensive. A result, clearly not lost on Thielmann's chief of staff, a certain Carl Philipp Gottfried von Clausewitz, about whom more later.

Allies preventing the city from falling. 1760 saw Frederick victorious at Liegnitz (15th August) but Berlin briefly occupied by Russian and Austrian troops. At Torgau (30th November 1760) Frederick won a truly Pyrrhic victory over the Austrians when two equally matched armies of c. 50,000 clashed. The Prussians held the field but lost more men, c. 17,000 to c. 16,000. Only the death of the Russian Empress Elizabeth and her replacement by the Frederick-besotted Peter III saved Prussia in the 'Miracle of the House of Brandenburg'. Russia withdrew from the coalition and even supplied Frederick with troops, Sweden stopped its campaign in Pomerania, Austria was virtually bankrupt, and France repeatedly lost out to Britain. Unfortunately for Frederick, *Tsar* Peter III did not last long, being replaced by his wife Catherine, later 'the Great'. She took Russia out of the war altogether. A final successful campaign in Silesia ended with Prussia in the ascendant over Austria but more by luck than judgement. The futility of the entire exercise was reinforced by the 1763 Treaty of Hubertusburg in which neither side made territorial gains. Prussia's military reputation, however, was firmly recognised.

[i] An event recorded in the 1810 painting *Napoleon meditating before the Tomb of Frederick II of Prussia in the Crypt of the Garnisonkirche in Potsdam* by Marie Nicolas Ponce-Camus (*Musée national du Château de Versailles*).

Waterloo presented a thorny theoretical problem to French officers heavily invested in the offensive. After all, had not Napoleon attempted what they all advocated – outright and repeated attacks? First, at Quatre Bras on 16th June 1815, but grim defence held up the advance of Ney and prevented him joining the main French Army in an attempt to crush the Prussians at Ligny. This attack, too failed in its main objective of destroying the Prussian Army and, though forced to leave the field, Blücher's troops retreated in decent order north towards Wavre. Then, two days later, two successful defensive actions at Waterloo and Wavre allowed the Allies to concentrate their forces against Napoleon's main army and utterly crush it.

The division of opinion on why this happened was starkly revealed in two articles in the *Revue militaire générale*. The first, entitled *Offensive brutale. Attaque parallèle* was written by a Capt. d'Aubert and appeared in December 1912. D'Aubert was advocating something close to heresy in the French Army – the use of the defensive and even the tactical withdrawal where necessary, and the rejection of the 'blind offensive' as the only means of waging war:

> "To have only one process, one rule, is to be as far from the artist as a house painter is, as far from the scholar as the charlatan in the public square is… So let us not be the followers of a single formula; the French mind is flexible enough to use several depending on the circumstances."

D'Aubert suggested that the Allied success at Waterloo was based on the key principle of 'fix and manoeuvre', in other words, whilst part of your force held the enemy in position with its defence, another moved into position to attack a point of weakness, in other words the Napoleonic theory of 'the economy of force'. This was, explained d'Aubert, the fundamental principle behind Napoleon's great victory at Austerlitz and Frederick the Great's twin victories of Rossbach and Leuthen. His analysis of Waterloo set this out:

> "Waterloo is an example that interests us most particularly. Napoleon did what is proposed to us as the sole rule of success: the parallel offensive, with all his strength. For his part, Wellington confined himself to the pure defence and thus succeeded in keeping him in check.
> Admittedly, the success of the allies was due to the intervention of Blücher and the absence of Grouchy. But, the fact remains that, for a whole day, the defensive allowed the English army to hold their ground, thus giving the Prussian army time to arrive on the battlefield.
> The application of the rule: 'Fix and manoeuvre', due, it is true, to an unforeseen combination of circumstances, had once again given success."[93]

Such a challenge to current orthodoxy could not be allowed to stand and, in June 1913, a '*Lt. H P*' responded in such a manner that Gen Lacroix wrote glowingly how it would be wrong:

> "…not to applaud the vibrant effort made by *Lt. H P* to exalt the offensive and the action of moral forces."[94]

Somewhat predictably (and histrionically) the young Lieutenant's piece was entitled *L'ésprit de sacrifice*. He went straight onto the attack, using, as some political rogues are apt to do nowadays, the word 'science' as an insult:

475

"In an article entitled: *Offensive brutale. Attaque parallèle*, published in December 1912 by the *Revue Militaire Générale*, the author, while recognizing the virtues of the offensive doctrine, claims that we have gone too far in this direction, that it is not necessary to attack thoroughly everywhere, and that, to obtain the defeat of the mass of the enemy forces, the commander will have, in a plan judiciously studied in advance, to combine in a skilful way the offensive, the defensive and the tactical withdrawal.

This scientific and purely intellectual conception of war was, it must be stated, the French doctrine of the past. By studying war in the light of science, it was in science alone that France sought the secret of victory. Of course, we did not deny the power of moral force. The scientific form of war even granted it a high coefficient in its calculations, but once this coefficient was established… it was neglected and then the solution to the problem was sought as one seeks the solution to a mechanical problem; one applied the mechanism of the lever to the mass of the enemy forces, one sought to put victory into formulas:

Offensive x defensive x tactical withdrawal = victory."

The article continues in a similar vein, attacking the use of the defensive in any circumstances, citing example after selective example to support its case until it gets to Waterloo. This decisive battle is simply described:

"Waterloo, a triumph of the defensive, it is said. No!
The arrival of Blucher and the absence of Grouchy saved Wellington."

Lt. H P does not waste time answering questions such as how Wellington fended off repeated attacks in order to give time for the Prussians to intervene; how Blücher got three of his *Armeekorps* into position to slam into Napoleon's right wing; the essential nature of the defence of Wavre against significant odds which prevented Grouchy from assisting his commander-in-chief but which allowed the Prussians to march on La Belle Alliance; let alone the defensive battles at Quatre Bras and Ligny which underpinned events on 18th June 1815.

Perhaps he also needed to explain the results of Crecy (1346), Poitiers (1356), and Agincourt (1415) in which French attackers were devastated by numerically inferior and mainly English and Welsh defenders.

In short, *Lt. H P* was a zealot, and a foolish one at that, but sadly representative of an officer class wedded to a cult-like theory which brooked no criticism and considered no alternatives:

"Let us throw away from us the intellectual fallacies, the causes of all our setbacks. Victory does not reside in the power of weaponry and the means of destruction, nor in the scientific combinations of tactics and strategy, it is in the heart of those who know how to sacrifice themselves to ensure victory."

He ends with the peroration:

"Let us look to the future with confidence, *la furia francese* still exists."

La furia francese was another of those myths to which the French clung as evidence of their special qualities and superior morale. The phrase references the late 15th Century actions of a heavily outnumbered French Army led by Charles VIII which, after seizing Naples, was trying to return to France in the face of a newly formed coalition of Venice, Milan, Mantua, and the Papal States. They met astride the *River Taro* at the small town of Fornovo near Parma on 6th July 1495. Charles's 10,000 men rapidly defeated the 20,000 men led by Francesco II of Gonzaga, Duke of Mantua, in the process suffering just a few hundred casualties whilst their opponents lost many thousands. The reckless and successful charge of the French heavy cavalry was later translated into something altogether more primal and uniquely French – *la furia francese*. What *Lt. H P* neglects to mention with his reference to *la furia francese* is that, as with Napoleon and Waterloo, the French lost that war. Fornovo was a tactical victory but a major strategic defeat. Spain captured Naples the following day, Charles abandoned his conquests in Italy, France was left in huge debt, and Charles, aged just 28, died two years later in an accident after hitting his head on a door. Such an outcome, however, did not quite match up with the narrative the young lieutenant was trying to create.

SINCE THE IDENTIFICATION OF THE IMPORTANCE of the defence in Clausewitz's influential work *Vom Kriege (On War)*, it is, perhaps, ironic that the German Army, having been well ahead of Henderson in espousing dispersal and in encouraging the initiative of junior officers and NCOs, now went into reverse in an imitation of Napoleonic-era battlefield tactics.

Germany took its time to learn lessons from the Franco-Prussian War. It was not until 1888 that new infantry regulations (*Exerzier-Reglement für die Infanterie 1888*) specified the battlefield contest would be decided by 'fire action' and not massed bayonets. In addition, fire would come from dispersed troops and not those in the traditional 'close order' because it was now recognised massed troops within range of the enemy's rifles would rapidly suffer heavy casualties. The objective was to achieve fire superiority over the enemy at which point the final assault might be attempted as, any assault before that point was reached, only invited serious losses and, potentially, defeat.

Progressively, however, this attitude was subtly undermined as conservative opinion moved in line with the *'offensive à outrance'* attitudes prevalent within both the French and British Armies. Increasing emphasis was placed on the importance of high morale, on offensive spirit, and on the human, rather than the material, element again being the dominant force on the battlefield. Thus, in 1906, with the 'evidence' of the war in Manchuria being used to support such changes, the views of people like Grandmaison, Hamilton, Carter and Maude replaced the more circumspect approach of the 1888 regulations. Now, the guiding principle was:

"Forward against the enemy, whatever the cost!"[95]

Paragraph 324 of the 1906 regulations returned German infantry tactics to the ill-conceived European mainstream with its statement:

"The enemy's defeat is completed by the assault with fixed bayonets."[96]

By 1911, the importance of the bayonet was re-established beyond doubt with the infantry encouraged to charge even if fire superiority was not established.[97] Launcelot Kiggell, at least, would have been delighted to read these words.

Kiggell became an important, if controversial, figure at GHQ when appointed Haig's Chief of Staff. He was never a fighting officer, spending almost all his military life behind a desk. Launcelot Edward Kiggell[i] was born on 2nd October 1862 at Wilton House in the tiny and remote village of Ballingarry in the south of County Limerick[ii]. His father, Launcelot John Kiggell, was a local JP and an Honorary major in the local militia, the South Cork Light Infantry[iii]. His wife was Meliora Emily Brown and the younger Launcelot Kiggell was born in his maternal grandfather's house. Educated in Ireland, Kiggell attended Sandhurst before being commissioned into the Royal Warwickshire Regt. in 1882. In 1886, he was appointed Adjutant of the 2nd Battalion, in which role he served until 1890. In 1893, he entered the Staff College, having passed the entrance examination in 1892 24th out of the 26 successful candidates. With 2,003 marks, he was some 401 behind the officer immediately above him in the results and six other unsuccessful candidates each exceeded his total by between 818 and 418 marks[iv]. Here, amongst several other leaders-to-be, he met Douglas Haig. Having graduated from Camberley at the end of 1894 he was appointed an instructor at Sandhurst the following September. In 1897, he was appointed DAAG for Instruction with the staff of the SE District and the following year was promoted Major.

On 13th October 1899, the *London Gazette* announced his appointment as one of four DAAGs on Redvers Buller's staff, the newly appointed CinC, South Africa. He stayed until Buller was sacked by Roberts in October 1901. Kiggell remained in South Africa on the staff at Pretoria and then as AAG in the Harrismith District in the eastern Orange Free State. After the war, Kiggell stayed on as AAG for Natal until, in 1904, he was appointed AAG at the Staff College, Camberley, a role he filled for the three years. Here, he gave early warning of his devotion to the idea the next major European war would be more like the Franco-Prussian War than recent events in Manchuria might suggest. In 1905, he gave a lecture to the Aldershot Military Society during which he referred to 1870 and to Napoleon whilst ignoring events in South Africa and the Far East. Clearly, his views had not changed in the intervening years, but his complete lack of fighting experience did not stop him from making his anachronistic views felt at the highest level within the Army. Sadly, his was not a lone voice in some empty reactionary military wilderness.

On leaving Camberley, his relentless series of staff and administrative jobs continued. He was, between 1907 and March 1909, a GSO1 at Army headquarters before spending seven months, now a Brig. Gen., in charge of administration with Scottish Command. He then followed Haig as Director of Staff Duties at the War

---

[i] For some reason given as Lancelot rather than Launcelot in the *London Gazette*.

[ii] About 11 miles south-west of Tipperary.

[iii] The 3rd (Militia) Battalion, Royal Munster Fusiliers, in 1900 when sent to South Africa.

[iv] Three of them came from infantry regiments already with one successful candidate, two came from the Royal Artillery (three was the RA's quota) and the last from the Indian Staff Corps (again, three was their quota) [*Source: The Times, The Staff College,* 1st September 1892, page 5].

Office, which role he filled for three years, before being appointed the last commandant of the Staff College until its temporary closure on the outbreak of war. Until his call-up to France at Haig's new GHQ, Kiggell spent his time as Director of Home Defence. Then, when Haig's existing Chief of Staff at 1st Army, Maj. Gen. Richard Butler, was deemed too young to be the CinC's right-hand man, Haig called upon Kiggell.

Remarkably, given his complete lack of any command experience, Haig appeared to believe Kiggell capable of commanding a Corps 'after he has been with me 3 or 4 months'.[98] Instead, the 'dyspeptic, gloomy and doleful'[99] Kiggell stayed at GHQ for another two years, during which time, according to Terraine, he 'made little mark on the Army, remaining always a shadowy figure in the background'.[100] His replacement by the more energetic and widely experienced Gen. Herbert Lawrence[i] was undoubtedly a blessing to all concerned: Haig, the BEF, and the exhausted Kiggell.

But, back in 1910, he had enough energy to intervene repeatedly on matters of which he had no direct experience: i.e. fighting. After proselytising on the benefits of the bayonet at a time of long-range, quick-firing weapons, Kiggell was at it again in 1911. The subject was how best the artillery might support the infantry's attack. Despite examples of gun crews and horse teams being shot down in 'close support' of the infantry, e.g. at Colenso, since South Africa several leading officers stated and re-stated their belief in the necessity of direct artillery fire. To justify this, they suggested that the enclosed landscapes of Europe (compared to the wide-open South African *veldt*) would require this tactic to be employed. In 1905 Du Cane

---

[i] Gen. the Hon. Sir Herbert Alexander Lawrence, GCB, 17th Lancers, was a contemporary of Haig's and served with him in South Africa. Unlike many soldiers he had outside interests and resigned from the Army in 1903. Ironically, his resignation was caused by Haig being made Colonel of the 17th Lancers rather than himself. A director of the *Midland Railway*, by 1907 he was also a director of the large private bank, *Glyn, Mills, Currie & Co.*, having married the daughter of the senior partner of the bank, Charles William Mills, 2nd Baron Hillingdon. Recalled to the Army in 1914, he went to Egypt and Gallipoli with 2nd Yeomanry Division. Briefly GOC of both 52nd and 53rd Divisions, he was appointed Deputy Inspector-General of Communications and later oversaw the successful evacuation from Cape Helles. Successful at the Battle of Romani in the Sinai Desert (4th-12th August 1916) he returned to England after disagreeing with strategy towards Palestine. He then took the 66th (2nd East Lancashire) Division to France where it fought at 3rd Ypres. Remarkably, given his possible antipathy towards Haig, Lawrence first replaced Charteris in January 1918 and, a few weeks later, Kiggell. He remained as Haig's Chief of Staff until the end of the war. Post-war he was a member of the *Royal Commission on the Coal Industry* (1925); a trustee of the *Imperial War Graves Commission*, and chairman of *Vickers* (1926); Chairman and Managing Director of *Glyn, Mills & Co.* (1934); and a governor of Wellington College. His two sons were both killed in the war: 2nd Lt. Oliver John Lawrence, 8th London Regiment (Post Office Rifles), died on 26th May 1915 and is buried in the Post Office Rifles Cemetery, Festubert, grave I. C. 9; and Capt. Michael Charles Lawrence, 1st Coldstream Guards, died of wounds on 16th September 1916 and is buried in Grove Town Cemetery, Meaulte, grave I. C. 38. Herbert Lawrence died on 17th January 1943.

and French wrote papers supporting direct fire, with French describing the need for guns to be 'conspicuous'.[101] In 1909 the *Report on Army Manoeuvres* talked about guns of all calibres in close support of infantry. And this despite warnings in a *RUSI* paper presented as far back as 1869 by Charles B Eddy that it was:

"... almost if not altogether out of the question to bring artillery drawn by horses within telling distance of a line of infantry."[102]

Mind, Eddy also commented that the British Army was, in 1869:

"... by a long interval the most ignorant in the art of self-defence against the desolating fire of the breech-loading rifle."[103]

There was, in many ways, a horrible similarity between arguments about tactics and equipment within the higher levels of the British Army as those which beset the French Army before 1914. Whilst the British were not as single-mindedly devoted to a single gun as were the French to the 75 their tactical ideas were not a great deal more up to date as these discussions displayed.

Indirect fire was not a tactic widely accepted in spite of the clear evidence of its adoption by the German Army since the 1890s and its effective use by the Japanese in Manchuria and Russia later in that war[i]. Indeed, according to Maj. Jonathan Bailey[ii], RA, in his 1989 book *Field Artillery and Firepower* so were reluctant were British artillery officers to properly embrace it that the necessary indirect laying instrument was not widely adopted until 1913 with the introduction of the *Number 7 Dial Sight*. The Germans, meanwhile, introduced the *Richtflache*, a gun-mounted sight which, by 1896, was the basis for German indirect fire.[104] This was followed by the Goerz *Panoramafernrohr* (panorama sight) with which all German guns, and most in Europe, were equipped by 1914. The *Number 7 Dial Sight* was a modified version of this sight. It is interesting to note in this context that the British 4.5-in. field howitzer had, in 1914, not just the *Dial Sight* by which to conduct indirect fire but, as described by Brig. Gen. Bethell in 1910 when talking about its predecessor the 5-in. BL howitzer from 1895, it was still equipped with:

"... plain open sights, usually of the arc pattern (N.B. rocking bar sight in the 4.5-in.), for direct laying in an emergency."[105]

The problem this lack of experience and enthusiasm for indirect fire caused was revealed in the early fighting at Mons and Le Cateau where British guns fired from open or only partially covered positions. Martin Farndale described this as the first, and a painful, lesson learned in August 1914:

"... open or semi-covered positions were dangerous; they meant that the

---

[i] Russian gunners were trained in the principles of indirect fire developed by Lt. Col. Karl Georgiyevich Guk (1846-1910) in 1882 and published as *Field Artillery Fire from Covered Positions* (also *Indirect Fire for Field Artillery*) and had an effective sight, the *Uglomer*, but failed to apply them in early fighting in 1904, exposing their guns to Japanese counter-battery artillery firing from defiladed positions. This changed at Liaoyang, 25th August–5th September 1904 [*Source*: Knorr, Maj. M, *The Development of German Doctrine and Command and Control and its Application to Supporting Arms 1832-1945*].

[ii] Bailey served with 5 Brigade in the Falklands, Northern Ireland, and as a battery commander in the BAOR.

guns inevitably became involved in the same fighting as the infantry they were supporting, thus depriving the latter of maximum support at the most critical periods."[106]

Certain Royal Artillery officers were, however, beginning to change their views as the first decade of the Twentieth Century progressed, and were increasingly of the opinion the key to success of artillery support for the infantry was not the proximity and visibility of the guns but the accuracy, weight and control of their fire. Furthermore, they began to promote the utility of the howitzer on the battlefield, citing the need for high-angle fire which could be both damaging to enemy trenches and fortifications and which, if accurate, would also keep the heads of the enemy below their parapets until the attacking infantry were nearly on them. First in the field was an especially bright Royal Artillery lieutenant – Robert Knox Hezlet[i] – who published an article in the *Proceedings of the Royal Artillery Institution* in 1904 about the future role of the field howitzer. His opinion was buttressed in 1906 by that of another scientific gunner, Lt. Col. Henry Arthur Bethell[ii], whose views about the use of concealed howitzers were perhaps even more significant as he changed his mind on the subject after his experiences in South Africa. Thus, in 1910, he wrote:

> "The object of the existence of a field howitzer is to engage a standing target such that field guns cannot reach it. The target may be a position held by troops keeping under cover, or by troops entrenched, or by troops in field-works with overhead cover. Or the target may be shielded artillery, with detachments protected against direct shrapnel fire. In none of these cases is any advantage to be gained by coming into action in the open, and we may therefore safely say that the normal method of opening fire for howitzers is from a covered position… From a gunnery point of view, therefore, the objective of the howitzer battery should be to get as close as possible behind steep cover."[107]

---

[i] Later Maj. Gen. Robert Knox Hezlet, CB, CBE, DSO. Born in Dungannon, Co. Tyrone, in 1879 he attended Clifton and the RMA. He passed the ordnance course and the advanced class at the Ordnance College in 1905/6, becoming an instructor at the college for four years and, in 1913, published a book entitled *Nomography or the Graphic Representation of Formulae*. In South Africa on the outbreak of war, he served for six months on the Western Front before commanding an RFA Brigade in Mesopotamia. In November 1916, he became a member of the Ordnance Committee at the Ministry of Munitions. He went on to become: Superintendent of External Ballistics, Chief Superintendent of the research department, Commandant of the Military College of Science, and, in 1930, Director of Artillery at the War Office. In 1934 he was appointed Director of Artillery in India. He died in 1963.

[ii] Later Brig. Gen. Henry Arthur Bethell, CMG. Born in 1861, he was educated at King's College, London, and the RMA joining the RFA. He was a member of the Howitzer and the Royal Artillery Committees with a special responsibility for Field Howitzer issues and was awarded the Lefroy Medal for Contributions to Artillery Science. He published *Modern Guns and Gunnery* in 1906, re-published in four editions, and *Modern Gunnery in the Field* in 1910. He died in 1939.

Bethell, however, contrary to known German practice of including them in their field army, persisted in describing the 15-cm medium howitzer, then the *15-cm sFH 02*, as a 'siege gun or gun of position'.[108] This trend continued, at least amongst artillery officers, with officers like Budworth, Wood, Du Cane, Furse and Jeudwine all suggesting long-range howitzer fire against dug-in troops would become the norm and represented the best available method of helping the infantry across the 'Fire Swept Zone'.[109]

Ironically, it was a junior infantry officer who earlier championed the general use of 'indirect fire'. Capt. Thomas Pilcher, then a Northumberland Fusilier with no direct experience of war[i], made a presentation at the *Royal Artillery Institute*,

---

[i] Maj. Gen. Thomas David Pilcher, CB, (1858-1928) was an intriguing fellow. Born in Rome (his father, Thomas Webb Pilcher, was curator of a museum) he attended Harrow until his father died in 1874. His mother, Sophia (*née* Robinson) took the family to Celle in Lower Saxony. On her death in 1877, Thomas returned, joining the Dublin City Artillery Militia, the militia being a route by which impoverished or not especially bright young men might then gain a commission in the regular army. This Pilcher did, moving through the Cheshire Regt., Northumberland Fusiliers and, eventually, the Bedfordshire Regt. Pilcher's name was made in South Africa where his aggressive and successful command of the 3rd Battalion, Mounted Infantry, gained him a Brigade command back home. He enjoyed putting pen to paper, his output being considerable if not especially significant. His book *'Some Lessons from the Boer War'*, for example, might have been useful had there been a third Boer War but its application to a European War was marginal in the extreme.

Pilcher was also a gambler and an adulterer. In 1889 he married Kathleen Mary Gonne, daughter of Col. Thomas Gonne, 17th Lancers. Kathleen had a famous/infamous sister, Maud, and a half-sister, Eileen, born from their father's affair with their governess. Maud, born in England of a Scottish father and the muse of the poet W B Yeats, married John MacBride and Eileen his brother, Joseph MacBride. They were all staunch Irish Republicans and John fought with the Boers in South Africa leading the Irish Transvaal Brigade. Estranged from Maud, he was taken prisoner during the Easter Rising and shot in Kilmainham Jail on 5th May 1916. Joseph was arrested but released to go on to be the first Sinn Fein MP for Mayo West. The son of Maud and John MacBride was Seán MacBride later Assistant Secretary General of the United Nations, founder of Amnesty International, and winner of the Nobel and Lenin Peace Prizes for human rights achievements. Pilcher and Kathleen fell out over the behaviour of Maud but also because Pilcher had repeated affairs and used his wife's money to cover his debts. Kathleen eventually divorced him in 1911 when he was named co-respondent in a divorce case involving Capt. James and Mrs Millicent Knight-Bruce. He married the divorced Millicent in 1913.

In 1915, aged 57, he was given command of the 17th (Northern) Division. It was not a happy arrangement. Writing post-war, Col. Walter Norris Nicholson, Suffolk Regt., and the AA&QMG of the division from June 1916, was blisteringly critical of Pilcher and his woeful care of the men under his command finishing 'Thank God he went' [*Source*: W N Nicholson, *Behind the Lines. An Account of Administrative Staffwork in the British Army 1914-1918*, Jonathan Cape, 1939, p. 175]. Pilcher went after, first, the 50th Brigade suffered catastrophic losses on 1st July 1916 in a disorganised and disjointed series of advances near Fricourt, the most notable aspect of which was that the 10th

Woolwich, on 12th March 1896 entitled *'Artillery from an Infantry Officer's Point of View'*. It was later published in the Journal of the Institute[110]. The following year a *critique* by a senior but anonymous German General commented on various aspects of Pilcher's lecture. He was in broad agreement with many of Pilcher's points though he disputed his claim that, in the German Army, indirect fire was the rule not the exception. He did, however, accept, that it was perfectly possible to concentrate artillery fire by indirect laying. In other words, accuracy was not dependent on the guns and gunners being in full sight of the enemy. Indeed, the use of cover was not something to be ignored just because it was widely thought ignoble by officers with more gallantry than brains:

> "Before 1806 some few German officers, more advanced in thought than the rest, advised making use of ground and of cover, but the majority… answered, "What! shall the army of Frederick be made a school for cowardice! No, never." They refused to practise the use of the ground and the result was Jena and Auerstedt.
> To say that to make use of ground in any way destroys *"der geist der waffle"* (the spirit of the arm) is nonsense. I have already said that *"wirkung geht vor deckling"* (effect comes before cover), but this is 1896, not 1870, and the effect of infantry fire must be multiplied by four or by six in comparison with what it was in 1870, and what is the good of artillery coming up close if by doing so the effect of their fire is not greater."[111]

Sound advice then ignored three years later at places like Colenso.

Reinforced by the experience of the Manchurian war, there was also a growing acceptance amongst this type of officer that modern warfare could well assume the form of a prolonged siege as Bloch suggested several years before. The flaw in their various arguments was, however, that the best form of howitzer fire to employ against entrenched troops was shrapnel as it was believed high explosive shells fired from range would be too inaccurate. There were also, pre-South Africa, widespread concern about the safety of firing high explosive shells from the guns then available and this concern may well have lingered[i]. Shrapnel, on the other

---

(Service) Battalion, West Yorkshire Regt., suffered the highest casualties of any unit involved on the day, i.e. 22 officers and 688 other ranks. Then, a week later, after various inept attacks near Mametz Wood insisted upon by Horne in which Pilcher claimed eventually to have used only the minimum force in a hopeless attack, he was sacked on 12th July. He stayed in England thereafter and received no war-time award. Post-war he flirted with extreme right-wing politics, becoming Chairman of the anti-Bolshevik *National Security Union* and joining the *British Fascists*, precursor to Mosley's *British Union of Fascists*, shortly before his death.

[i] Maj. Edward Sinclair May, summing up after Thomas Pilcher's presentation to the *Royal Artillery Institute* in 1896, commented: 'It has been recognized first of all that this high explosive shell, unless fired with a very low velocity, may burst prematurely and that, if such a thing occurred, it would probably shatter and destroy the gun altogether' [*Source*: Transcript of a lecture by Capt. T Pilcher given at the *Royal Artillery Institute* in March 1896 re-printed in the *Journal of the US Military Institute*, 1897, page 147]. This

hand, could be used to keep the defenders' heads down whilst the advance was made and had the added benefit that it was possible to keep up relatively close to the rear edge of a shrapnel barrage as the shell propelled the shrapnel bullets forward and, therefore, in front of the attacking troops. It was, fundamentally, an argument between neutralising the fire of the defending troops with shrapnel fire or destroying them with high explosive. The former argument won pre-war and thus the 4.5-in. field howitzers which accompanied the BEF to France would be mainly supplied with shrapnel shells in the opening months of the war.

Unfortunately, senior infantry and cavalry officers lagged some way behind in this new understanding of the ways in which artillery might be employed.

Launcelot Kiggell, somehow still Director of Staff Duties, was clearly a man who had taken to heart, albeit in the wrong way, Bloch's strictures about the essential importance of a soldier's spade. Always ready to dig a deep hole, jump in and then shovel dirt on his head, he joined in with his usual misreading of how new technology affected the battlefield. He first claimed that, whilst the attacking infantry might accept 'friendly fire' casualties from their artillery if the guns were firing in the open, they would not react so well to shells landing amongst them fired by guns they could not see. Apparently, according to Kiggell, seeing your own guns kill or maim you or your colleagues raised one's morale rather than giving you cause to challenge the reasons for their gross inaccuracy.[112] Kiggell then chimed in again during a lengthy discussion at the 1911 annual General Staff Officers' conference at Camberley on the subject of *Organization and Training of Field Artillery*.

This subject was introduced by the ubiquitous Du Cane who indicated the debate was triggered by feedback from the French manoeuvres contained in a report from Col. William Ernest Fairholme[i], CMG, MVO, who was then the Military *attaché* in Paris, and discussions at the highest levels of the differences between French and British artillery tactics. Fairholme's attendance at the 1910 French manoeuvres convinced him there was much to be learned from the French in many aspects of the use of field guns and, in particular, the shorter ranges at which they preferred to fire. Fairholme advocated the British Army needed to spend more time practising at such ranges.[113]

Du Cane noted that Sir John French, Inspector General of the Forces, wrote in his 1909 annual report that he believed, and it was widely agreed, decisive artillery ranges in a European war would be between 2,000 and 4,000 yards[ii]. It

---

fear was reinforced in WW1 when the first HE shells for the 4.5-in. howitzer were so unreliable the members of batteries firing them became known as 'the suicide club'.

[i] Brig. Gen William Ernest Fairholme, CB, CMG, MVO, RA. A staff officer who spent time in the eastern Mediterranean and Balkans. Military *attaché* in Vienna, Bucharest, Belgrade, Paris, Madrid, Lisbon, Brussels, The Hague, Copenhagen, Christiania, and Athens. He was the CRA, 3rd Division, 1912-3 and GSO1 Salonika Force 1915-6.

[ii] This was disagreed with by various RA contributors to the debate such as Brig. Gen. Neil Douglas Findlay, CB, CRA, 1st Division, and Brig. Gen. Wellesley Lynedoch Henry Paget, MVO, CRA 6th Division, who both argued longer range fire was highly likely. Brig. Gen. Findlay was killed by shrapnel on 10th September 1914 during the Battle of the *Aisne*. He is buried in Vailly British Cemetery, grave IV. A. 53.

should, however, be noted the effective range of the German machine gun, the *Maschinengewehr 08*, was c. 2,200 yards and its maximum range c. 3,800 yards. In other words, French was talking about deploying artillery in the open within range of enemy machine guns! Du Cane then went on at considerable length to discuss the optimum numbers of field guns per battery, i.e. four (the French preference) or six (British/German); the differences between the two main guns, the French 75 and the British 18-pdr; methods of ranging (the French had automatic fuze setters while the British set fuzes by hand); the differences in tactical deployment; and the relative economy in the use of ammunition within the British Army.

In all of this it should be noted he was talking about field guns firing shrapnel. Brig. Gen. Edward Arthur Fanshawe[i], CRA, 5th Division, was prescient in calling for a far greater proportion of high explosive shells versus shrapnel 'which will not kill the infantry in trenches', but he was disagreed with by Brig. Gen. Aylmer Haldane who suggested the use of high explosive in Manchuria was not productive against trenches, a point of view which would have been heartily contradicted by Col. Tretyakov who directly experienced Japanese *Shimose*-powder filled HE shells in the defence of Port Arthur (see page 544).[114]

Responding to both Du Cane and Fairholme, Col. Sydenham Campbell Urquhart Smith[ii], RFA, the Chief Instructor to the RHA and RFA at the School of Gunnery, talked about firing ranges and the concealment of guns:

> "For years it has been impressed on us that in these days of QF guns exposure means annihilation, especially at close ranges. Personally, I am not a great believer in it, but this is what we have been taught."[115]

He then continued to say this too was what the French and German gunners were taught but it was not what they practiced[iii]. But in all other areas Smith demolished Fairholme's arguments about the superiority of the French field gunnery systems and ended by quoting the scathing comments of two officers who attended recent French manoeuvres, one of whom, the then Maj. Budworth, was later Rawlinson's MGRA during the *Somme* offensive.

Spade at the ready, Kiggell then intervened, ever keen to bury himself in filth. He was opposed to applying any lessons from the wide-open spaces of South Africa and Manchuria to a European war:

---

[i] Brig. Gen., later Lt. Gen. Sir, Edward Arthur Fanshawe, KCB. Winchester and RMA, Woolwich. Royal Artillery, 1878. CRA, 1st Division, on the outbreak of war. Commanded 31st and 11th (Northern) Divisions (the latter in Gallipoli) and V Corps during the operation to take Beaumont Hamel in November 1916. Led the Corps through the Third Battle of Ypres. In March 1918 his and Congreve's VII Corps were heavily attacked during the *Michael* phase of the German Spring Offensive. Fanshawe and Congreve were blamed for the enforced withdrawal and sent home.

[ii] Later Maj. Gen. Sydenham Campbell Urquhart Smith, KCMG, CB, RA. He served in Australia, South Africa and was CRA, India, 1911-4. At the beginning of the war, he was the Inspector of the RHA/RFA. He was later attached to GHQ.

[iii] Early experience quickly taught them otherwise. Robert Nivelle, commanding *5e RAC* in the late summer of 1914 wrote: "…visible artillery is doomed to destruction." [Source: *Journal du marche, 5e régiment d'artillerie de campagne*, August-September 1914].

"The battles fought in such a war are not won at long ranges. The crisis of the battle is the time when the infantry wants help and support most urgently, and the crisis will be at short ranges. Will the infantry accept long-range support at that time? Personally, I do not think they will. I think that artillery officers must remember and think of what the infantry will expect from them and demand from them. It is at these short ranges that battles are won and lost and not at long ranges. Artillery can give great help at long ranges, but it cannot win the battle, nor enable the infantry to win it at those ranges. When we study the war of 1870, we find that a tremendous amount of fighting went on at short ranges… (and) was affected by rapid artillery fire, *always* at short ranges.

My own opinion, from an infantry up-bringing, is that the infantry will look to the artillery *then* for direct and rapid support, and if they do not get it, they will not be satisfied with the artillery."[116]

It is as if, in Kiggell's world, the long-range rifle and machine gun ceased to exist and the world returned to the days of the *Dreyse* needle gun with its 650-yard range and, of course, the bayonet, of which Kiggell had proved the previous year he was inordinately fond[i]. Kiggell's conservatism and stupidity is staggering. He would rather cite a war fought forty years earlier in the absence of automatic weapons, quick-firing artillery, and smokeless powder as an example of European wars to come rather than accept the experience of both competing armies and numerous foreign observers in a war just six years earlier and when equipped with such material. Had he knowledge of the Battles of Telissu and *Sha-ho* in June and October of 1904 he would have known that the Russians, having seen their exposed, direct-firing artillery destroyed by indirect firing Japanese guns, broadly abandoned the idea thereafter. That they were then sadly ill-equipped to undertake indirect fire thereafter only compounded their problems[ii].

Thankfully, Lt. Col. William Furse[iii] was there to apply what might have been hoped was a suitable corrective:

"What is this close support and how is it to be given? General Kiggell says the infantry will expect from us, as I understand him, that the guns themselves should be closely supporting the infantry lines. I cannot help

---

[i] Kiggell made constant reference to the conduct of battle during the Franco-Prussian War and the impact of the bayonet, the Germans later stated 85% of casualties were caused by rifle bullets, 14% by artillery shells, and 1% by lances, sabres, and bayonets combined [*Source: The Times, Military Equipment*, 22nd February 1878, page 3].

[ii] Pilcher, in his 1896 address to the *Royal Artillery Institute*, made the additional point that, for guns to closely support the infantry they must cease fire in order to move forward rather than keep the enemy positions under continuous fire. He stated: '…it benefits the infantry but little to have moving targets composed of their comrades of the artillery galloping about behind them, whereas the continuous fire of their guns is of the utmost value to them'. [*Source*: Transcript of Pilcher's 1896 lecture re-printed in the *Journal of the US Military Service Institute*, 1897, page 139].

[iii] Assumed to be (he is not listed) Lt. Col., later Lt. Gen., Sir, William Thomas Furse, KCB, KCMG, DSO, RA. He attended the previous conference.

feeling that when it comes to the real thing they will not care very much where the guns are if they see shells bursting in the face of that infantry which they hope to assault at any moment... I would only like to remind General Kiggell (I am sure he will not mind my doing so) of just two cases – Colenso and Pieters[i]. Our infantry at Pieters (I was not there) never saw a gun at all, and they were getting the closest possible support (*Author's note:* something akin to a creeping barrage), probably the closest given during the whole of the South African war.

Compare this with Colenso; there the guns, having been driven right up, were not able to remain in action. Exactly the same thing happened in Manchuria. On the *Yalu* – Russian artillery up in line with their infantry, and their infantry saw them knocked out."[117]

Brig. Gen. Aylmer Haldane concurred with Furse's views stating artillery was never used in close support in any fighting he witnessed in Manchuria. Haldane also posed the radical idea the artillery could help the infantry forwards by destroying the enemy's machine guns which, it appeared, Kiggell would rather have seen slaughtering British gun teams at relatively short range.

Kiggell, given the opportunity to reply to Furse and Haldane, unfortunately, decided to keep enlarging the hole into which he had dug himself:

"I believe that the crises of future battles in Europe will closely resemble the crises of the battles of 1870... you will find that they were won or lost at short ranges... I cannot see a shadow of doubt that the French methods will be more applicable than will slow and deliberate methods at long ranges... As I understand it, our primary system of training is the slow and deliberate at long ranges... If I am right I think that proceeding should be reversed – that the slow method should be the secondary object and other (i.e. short range, rapid fire) should be the primary... In speaking of close support... I meant fire over the sights at 2,000-2,500 yards."[118]

A rather more junior officer from the East Coast Defences, then made an additional and telling point (already hinted at by Furse's reference to Colenso). Guns in close support had a nasty tendency to suffer heavy casualties amongst the horse teams which then rendered them immovable should they either need to move forward to follow up the infantry or (as at Le Cateau) should they have to retire precipitately. Maj. Reginald Arthur Bright[ii], RA, referred to an incident in the 1909 manoeuvres when some field howitzers were brought up to the infantry firing line (for what conceivable reason he did not explain) where, according to the umpires, and to the fury of the commander, they were forced to remain because their horses had all, metaphorically, been killed.[119]

Du Cane then rendered what should have been the killer blow:

---

[i] Pieters Hill, 27th February 1900, in the campaign which relieved Ladysmith.
[ii] Later Brig. Gen. Reginald Arthur Bright, CB, CBE, he served in South Africa, in Mesopotamia 1916-8, the Afghan War 1919, as CRA Peshawar, 1919-21 and BGRA Northern Command, India, 1921-3.

"It is with the greatest diffidence that I say anything which is in opposition to the views expressed by him (i.e. Kiggell). I hope that I do not again misunderstand him when I take him to say that he thinks we ought to base our tactical ideas largely on the experience of the war of 1870, particularly as regards the decisive phases of the fight; and, further, that in the war for which we are nominally preparing there will probably be a considerable amount of charging and counter-charging at close quarters on the part of the opposing infantry…

In the war of 1870, I think I am right in saying that a great deal of the firing on the part of the infantry took places standing or kneeling. The troops in those days moved, as compared with the present day, in close order, and the charges took place largely by the word of command of officers commanding units.

In these respects the tactics of those days differ largely from the tactics of the present day, and this fact is proved by the experience of South Africa and Manchuria. One of the chief surprises to us at the beginning of the war in South Africa was the manner in which our infantry was glued to the ground by the effect of the Boer fire. We now fire lying down. Movement under heavy fire has been proved to be particularly difficult. This has led to the adoption of extended formations and the development of the initiative of the individual soldier. The officer has much less control.

For these reasons, perhaps, the charges and counter-charges which General Kiggell referred to as taking place in 1870 had very little counterpart in the Boer war and not very much in the war in Manchuria…

Movement at close quarters nowadays, I take it, is only possible as a result of fire superiority. If fire superiority has not been gained it would seem that there is a strong tendency for the combatants to remain lying down shooting at one another."[120]

Du Cane went on to explain that to provide adequate fire support to achieve superiority required weight of fire, accurate observation of fire, and effective fire control and these latter two were far more important than short range. He acidly concluded with the words:

"… to base our tactical ideas too much on rather ancient history and ignore the effect on tactics of the improvements in modern weapons and scientific appliances would be particularly dangerous."[121]

Extraordinarily, the conclusion reached by the presiding 'grandees' (Nicholson, the CIGS, Murray, the Director of Military Training, and… Kiggell, the Director of Staff Duties), and announced on the final day of the conference was that:

"… on the whole there appeared to be a strong opinion that fire at long ranges cannot be decisive, and that it is undesirable to over-emphasise the value of long-range fire, excessive practice in which may be detrimental to the combination of accuracy and rapidity which would be of paramount value in the decisive phases of the fight."[122]

Kiggell was then Director of Staff Duties and later appointed Commandant of the Staff College, the Director of Military Training and Douglas Haig's Chief of

Staff. His first critic, Furse, on the other hand, found himself commanding a field howitzer battery, at least until war broke out. It clearly did not pay to be too wise either before or after the event in the Edwardian Army.

These 'conclusions' drawn about the need for close support by the artillery held good, however, and were reinforced by Haig in 1913. Commenting on Aldershot Command's Training Season in September 1913 he wrote:

> "…artillery must not hesitate to close in towards the enemy so as to give the infantry the best possible support, moral as well as material."[123]

And, so were the guns, even the field howitzers, used in the Army manoeuvres of 1912. This might not be viewed as surprising given the foregoing, as well as the comments on the employment of howitzers made at the Conference of General Staff officers held between 7th and 10th January 1908.

On the final day, Col. Alexander Hamilton-Gordon, RA, a GSO1 at Army Headquarters, raised the issue of the employment of howitzers. He pointed out the obvious fact their plunging fire enabled them to attack both concealed enemy positions and entrenched positions. The fact they could achieve this from defiladed positions Hamilton-Gordon regarded as 'incidental'. They should not mainly be regarded as guns which could 'fire from behind cover', rather they were guns which could 'fire at an enemy behind cover'. This was, for him, the key point and whether they fired from cover 'did not matter nearly so much'. He went on:

> "The field howitzer was essentially a weapon for attack. They need not go into the question of defence, because attack was far more important, and the howitzer was not of much use in defence."[124]

Hamilton-Gordon[i] regarded the field howitzer as an infantry support weapon which, firing shrapnel, covered the infantry attack on enemy trenches.

---

[i] Lt. Gen. Sir Alexander Hamilton-Gordon, KCB, was the paternal grandson of the 4th Earl of Aberdeen, Prime Minister 1852-1856, i.e. the time of the Crimean War, and the maternal grandson of the astronomer Sir William Herschel. His father, Gen. Sir Alexander Hamilton-Gordon, KCB, Grenadier Guards, was an AAG in the Crimea, being present at the Battles of the Alma, Balaklava, Inkerman, and the siege of Sebastopol. Hamilton-Gordon was born in 1859 and attended Winchester College and the RMA, entering the Royal Artillery in 1880. He saw service in the 2nd Afghan War and the South African War and was, for four years, Director of Military Operations in India. In 1914 he was appointed GOC, Aldershot Command, and in 1916 was made GOC, IX Corps. He led the Corps through the Battle of Messines and 3rd Ypres in 1917. The Corps suffered heavy losses during the Battle of the *Lys* in April 1918, part of the German Spring Offensive, and was sent to the Chemin des Dames on the *Aisne* to recuperate. Here they were deployed too far forward by the local French commander, Gen. Denis Auguste Duchêne, *VIe Armée*. On 27th May 1918, the Germans launched a surprise attack with 4,000 guns and 17 divisions which on the exposed British positions completely overwhelming the Allied troops and leading to an advance to within 60 kms of Paris. After nearly continuous fighting for a year Hamilton-Gordon's health suffered and he returned to England in September. He died in 1939.

Whatever their employment, as no formal agreement could be reached as to the best means of infantry/artillery co-operation (i.e. should an artillery officer be at the front to report back, in other words a Forward Observation Officer or FOO, or should it be an infantry officer), the Army embarked upon its first continental war in nearly a century without an agreed system of communication between the gunners and infantry.[125]

These debates concerned the use of field guns and howitzers. Nothing much was ever said about heavier artillery as part of a British field army's arsenal. Thus, apart from the 60-pdr. batteries which accompanied Divisions in the original BEF, there was little or nothing which might constitute 'heavy' artillery, let alone a 'siege train'. That is not to say these issues were being totally ignored, after all the *Coventry Ordnance Works* was asked to bring forward plans for a prototype of a 9.2-in. howitzer in 1910 (though only this one was built before the war). It was unfortunate, therefore, one of the more forwarding thinking contributions to any discussion about heavy artillery was made not in Great Britain but in India. It came in the form of a brief article by the Commandant[i] of the Indian Army's 30 pdr. Field Gun Brigade[ii] in the January 1911 edition of the *Journal of the United Service Institution of India*. Entitled *'The Employment of Heavy Artillery in the Field'* the article was mainly concerned with the application of such *matériel* within India and its borders, however, his comments proved to be of great relevance to the Western Front when siege warfare broke out. He made the point that there never had been a field army within which heavy artillery had a peace time presence (though the Germans might have taken exception to this suggestion) but, he went on, in nearly every recent war, such material had either been brought in to service or extemporised as the fighting went on. This had certainly proved true in both South Africa and Manchuria. The result of this was, he opined:

> "Batteries so improvised with material not specifically designed for employment with the field army and personnel untrained in the tactical and technical training of field artillery could hardly be expected to achieve the results which may be reasonably expected from a permanent organisation with suitable equipment and a highly trained personnel familiar with field operations and directed by Generals accustomed to handle Heavy Artillery with the same confidence as if they were dealing with Field Artillery."[126]

This proved to be an accurate forecast of the state of 'heavy artillery' in the French and British Armies; its command and application early in the war; and of the lack of training of heavy artillery officers in field conditions. Because of this improvised approach, this officer continued, there was no body of experience or learning to which either Generals or heavy artillery officers could easily refer to

---

[i] Believed to be Capt. (later Brig. Gen.) Thomas Mawe Luke, CBE, DSO, RA, who was commandant of the Frontier Garrison Artillery based at Kohat after 1900. He later served as DAAG, AAG, DAG at GHQ, India, and from October 1916 to June 1919 as Director of Administration, General Headquarters, India, with the rank of Brigadier General. His DSO, awarded in 1904, was for service in Tibet.

[ii] The 30 pdr. BL field gun was a gun built specifically for the Indian Army and designed in 1892. It never saw service in Great Britain.

remedy this problem. The applications of Heavy Artillery in *Field Service Regulations, Part I, 1909* (page 14) were then referenced. These were:
1. Engaging otherwise defiladed guns and cover with oblique fire;
2. Seeking to engage at long distance enemy reserves;
3. Destroying buildings and other cover; and
4. Supporting the final infantry assault with converging fire on important targets.

The author then went on to add some functions of his own, mainly in the belief they applied especially to Indian conditions. Interestingly, some of his suggestions, even if adapted, came to form the basis on which heavy artillery was used on the Western Front. They were:
1. To silence at long range enemy guns commanding lines of advance;
2. Destroying villages and houses held by the enemy;
3. To prevent the bringing forward of the enemy's heavy artillery by fire at very distant ranges; and
4. To destroy the enemy's short and medium range guns.

He provided several examples of these applications drawn from South Africa and Manchuria which applied to both suggestions 1 and 2 above, but those from Manchuria (at 1. La Mu Tan and 2. Senkinja) were given as examples of what could have happened *had such artillery been available* to either the Japanese (example 1) or Russians (example 2). He then gave examples from home where 4-ton 8 cwt Mk I 60-pdr. guns were manhandled into difficult to reach positions to participate in field army manoeuvres. Having said that, he concluded somewhat dolefully:

"(at home) heavy batteries attend all manoeuvres and it must be taken as proof of the difficulty that is found in properly using them that they have never yet achieved any great success, nor have they come under criticism at the Conference afterwards. England is not a country for heavy artillery."[127]

Well, not quite yet, anyway.

THE GENERAL STUPIDITY at the General Staff conference of 1911 at Camberley did not come to an end with Kiggell's expressions of faith in a few inches of cold steel stuck on the end of a rifle. Following on, and at the request of Henry Rawlinson, then GOC of 3rd Division, another option was added to those methods under consideration for the effective delivery of the final attack. Intriguingly it was entitled *Consideration of how method of delivering Infantry Assault can be improved. Is it possible to learn something from the French?* It formed Subject No. 3 on the agenda and was presented by Col. Frank Ridley Farrer Boileau[i] of 3rd Division's

---

[i] Col. Frank Ridley Farrer Boileau, RE, 'died of wounds' on 28th August 1914, having been wounded at the Battle of Le Cateau on 26th August. Lt. Col. T S Wollocombe, MC, however, recalled Boileau committed suicide under the immense strain of the retreat [*Source*: Robbins S, *British Generalship*, page 38]. He was GSO1, 3rd Division. Aged 46, he was the son of Col. F. W. Boileau, C.B., and Letitia Bradford. He was married to Mary A. Boileau of Windout Hill House, Exeter. He is buried in Terlincthun British Cemetery, Wimille, grave 16. A.B.1.

staff, a man who had spent the previous four years as a professor at the Staff College at Quetta. Remarkably, Rawlinson's suggestion for a way to get the infantry across the 'fire swept zone' was musical:

> "The General Officer Commanding 3rd Division is of the opinion that the charge as at present carried out by our infantry does not receive sufficient support from the drums and bugles… With our Army, as we all know, directly the charge takes place, one or two bugles blow the 'call' and to the sound of a British cheer the infantry rushes forward. After about 100 yards or so this cheer naturally dies down. It is then that the charge wants the support of, if possible, massed bugles and drums, in fact of anything that in war would help to carry men through a very critical moment."[128]

It was a subject treated with all due seriousness by the assembled officers, all of whom believed Rawly to be on to something. There was a problem that the 'music' for the 'charge' bore, at a distance and disguised by a lot of 'noises off', a passing similarity to the 'stand fast'. Confusion over these signals led to several units on manoeuvres 'going home' rather than charging according to Brig. Gen. Davies, which decision suggests a degree of common sense within these units not currently being displayed by their elders and betters. But regiments pottering off to their barracks a tad early was, apparently, a minor detail.

Now, from this writer's perspective, one might imagine the fire of massed automatic weapons and a creeping barrage (had it yet occurred to anyone) might have been of greater utility than massed drums and bugles. Alternatively, and entering into the spirit of Rawlinson's suggestion rather more actively, as a proud Scot this writer would suggest the enemy might have found the skirl of massed bagpipes far more unnerving, not to say distressing. On a more serious note, however, one wonders whether, while discussing this issue, any of the officers present had regard for Maj. McMahon's disturbing predictions made the previous year about the potentially annihilating effect of heavy machine gun fire on attacking infantry whether supported by the massed bands of the British Army or not. Despite this, Rawlinson's suggestions were taken on board as the following paragraph from *Infantry Training 1914* makes clear:

> "At the appropriate moment the attacking commander would order his bugler to sound the charge, and… the call will be taken up by all buglers, and all neighbouring units will join in the charge as quickly as possible. During the delivery of the assault the men will cheer, bugles be sounded and pipes played."[129]

IN SPITE OF ALL OF THIS NONSENSE, the principle of fire preceding movement was well established within the Regular Army by August 1914. This was allied to the remarkable transformation in the accuracy and rate of fire of the average British infantryman since South Africa. The lessons about targeted rather than volley fire, concealment, and the greater ranges at which fire was effective were some of the main lessons learned and the subject was thoroughly aired during the deliberations of the Elgin Commission. It was generally, though not unanimously, agreed the Boer fired more accurately and over greater distances than most British soldiers and much time was expended in bringing the quality of shooting within the ranks to a far higher pitch of efficiency. Great efforts were made to encourage pride in marksmanship including recognition for the best shots and participation in an ever-growing number of rifle competitions.

80 General Sir Horace Lockwood Smith-Dorrien

One forward thinking officer to actively encourage these improvements was Lt. Gen. Horace Lockwood Smith-Dorrien, GOC, Aldershot Command, 1907. Smith-Dorrien is a tantalising General, whose removal from the Western Front by Sir John French on 6th May 1915 may have been one of French's greatest blunders. Tantalising in as much, by seniority, he was superior to Douglas Haig (who succeeded Smith-Dorrien at Aldershot in 1912) and, had he still been in post at Second Army in December 1915, would have placed the powers-that-be in an interesting position when it came to a choice for the new CinC, Western Front.

Smith-Dorrien was born on 26th May 1858 at Haresfoot near Berkhamsted. He was the sixth son of fifteen children born over a period of seventeen years to Col. Robert Algernon Smith-Dorrien JP (3rd Light Dragoons[i], 16th (The Queen's) Lancers, and the Hertfordshire Militia) and the fecund and, no doubt, long-suffering Mary Ann Drever[ii]. He was a product of Harrow and the RMC, joining the 95th (Derbyshire) Regt. in 1877. Eager to see action and frustrated by his CO's refusal to allow him to be released from battalion duties, he approached the War Office directly with a request to be sent to South Africa in order to serve in the ongoing Zulu War. He was fortunate to be one of the few survivors of the debacle of Isandlwana on 22nd January 1879, escaping on a pony and assisting some others to escape the assegais of the pursuing Zulus. Having evaded the rampaging Zulu *impis* he was, instead, nearly killed by typhoid. He then served with distinction in Egypt (Mentioned in Despatches), briefly in India and, afterwards, the Sudan (DSO 1886). He also attended and passed the Staff College in 1887-9 although he admitted that he:

> "… did not think we were taught as much as we might have been, but there was plenty of sport and not too much work."[130]

---

[i] 13th Hussars as from 1861.
[ii] In spite of her 'labours' she still lived to the ripe old age of 84.

He now returned to India where he broadened his experience by seeking out service with both the cavalry and artillery; served in the Tirah Campaign (1897-8); and returned to Egypt where, as Bt-Lt. Col. of the 13th Sudanese Battalion, he fought at Omdurman on 2nd September 1898. Later in the year he commanded British troops under the overall command of his friend Kitchener during the Fashoda Incident.

On 1st January 1899, he took command of the 1st Sherwood Foresters garrisoning Malta where he organised Brigade manoeuvres in which he led an invasion force supported by British warships. Then, in October 1899, war broke out with the Boers. Smith-Dorrien was despatched to the theatre of war and arrived in South Africa in the middle of the infamous 'Black Week' (10th-17th December 1899) which saw three British armies defeated by much smaller Boer units in quick succession. Smith-Dorrien, promoted Maj. Gen. in February 1900, proved to be one of the few senior officers to enhance his reputation during the war, gaining glowing opinions from both Lord Roberts, Sir Ian Hamilton and, ironically given later events, Sir John French. He was given command of the 19th Brigade, 9th Division (commanded by Sir Henry Colville of whom Smith-Dorrien had a very low opinion), and was involved in the fighting around Paardeberg between 18th and 27th February 1900. There, he spoke out against Kitchener's plan to launch infantry attacks against the entrenched Boer positions. The ensuing fiasco of 'Bloody Sunday' (18th February 1900) in which 83 officers and 1,126 other ranks became casualties only served to bear out Smith-Dorrien's opinions. He then took command of his own independent column during the latter part of the war, a role in which he was conspicuously successful.

Smith-Dorrien then returned to India with Kitchener, taking up the position of Adjutant-General before taking command of 4th (Quetta) Division in Baluchistan which he commanded until 1907. Between these jobs, he returned to England to marry Olive Crofton Schneider[i] in 1902. They bore three sons: Brig. Gen. Grenfell Horace Gerald Smith-Dorrien, killed in action on 13th September 1944 in Italy while commanding the 169th (London) Brigade; Brig. Gen. Peter Lockwood Smith-Dorrien, killed in the Zionist bombing of the King David Hotel in Jerusalem on 22nd July 1946; and Lt. David Pelham Smith-Dorrien (a.k.a. Bromley David Smith-Dorrien), 1st Sherwood Foresters, a Prisoner of War at Tobruk in June 1942[ii].

During his time in India, he helped found the Quetta Staff College and was also responsible for the introduction of the Staff Ride as a means of getting officers out into 'the field' for training purposes[iii]. Ian Hamilton, in Manchuria observing the Japanese side of the Russo-Japanese War, kept Smith-Dorrien in touch with developments there. He took these reports to heart and the digging of complex trench systems, the art of sapping forward towards the enemy's positions, and co-

---

[i] Made Dame Commander, Order of the British Empire in 1916. She died in 1951.
[ii] He died in 2001.
[iii] John Terraine was keen to attribute this new idea to Haig who, then a Colonel, was also in India [*Source*: Terraine J, *Douglas Haig: The Educated Soldier*, Leo Cooper, 1990, page 35].

ordinated attacks using live ammunition became a major part of his Division's autumn 1906 manoeuvres. He, at least, saw which way the military wind was blowing and Bloch would have approved. As S-D wrote:

> "Looking back on it now, it was quite a good forecast of the trench warfare of the Great War."[131]

Smith-Dorrien, throughout his career, showed a remarkable concern for the ordinary soldier. Whilst at Quetta he built sports facilities for the rank and file and a club with bars, baths, and a billiards room. He continued this work at Aldershot. Unlike many of his colleagues, he fraternised freely with junior officers, both native and British, and in the field and at leisure.[132]

Smith-Dorrien took over at Aldershot on 1st December 1907. Amongst his staff and commanders several would go on to prominent positions before and during the war e.g.: William Robertson, his Chief of Staff; Sir James Grierson, commanding 1st Division; Col. Henry Horne, later Lord Horne, his artillery adviser; and Henry Rawlinson commanded a Brigade. On his assumption of command, he brought in a number of reforms[i]. Perhaps the one resented most (and one in direct conflict with his predecessor Sir John French) was his requirement that the 1st Cavalry Brigade attached to Aldershot Command abandon its role as the *arme blanche* with its knee-to-knee sabre or lance charges, and instead focus on a role as well-trained and highly skilled mounted infantry. He was instrumental in improving the health and fitness of the Aldershot command. During his time there he led a programme to significantly expand the availability of sports grounds for cricket, football, hockey, etc., which involved clearing and flattening large areas. By the time he left in 1912 the area available for sports increased by 150%. Barrack rooms were improved, dining rooms introduced (previously men ate in their rooms), the number of baths was increased and showers introduced. In general food standards improved.[133] Large numbers of trees were cut down to expand areas available for training and this also allowed for an aircraft landing strip to be developed near Farnborough Common.

Other changes were of a more direct military application and these included a considerable investment in improving the marksmanship of not only the infantry but the cavalry too. In this he was assisted by Maj. Gen. Charles Munro who had just left Hythe where he was Commandant of the School of Musketry. As part of this process, he instituted the Smith-Dorrien Cup in 1910.

---

[i] According to some these were judged by his predecessor, Sir John French, as implied criticisms of his time in command and this seems to have been the start of the breakdown in relations which eventually led to Smith-Dorrien's sacking in 1915. The final nail in Smith-Dorrien's military coffin came after the German gas attack on the Gravenstafel Ridge on the first day of the Second Battle of Ypres on 22nd April 1915. After the territorial losses Smith-Dorrien recommended withdrawing the line to a more defensible one nearer the town and canal. Sir John French rejected this out of hand and Smith-Dorrien was sacked on 6th May by Sir William Robertson, reputedly with the words "'Orace, yer for 'ome". He was replaced by Plumer who, more or less immediately, recommended withdrawal to the same position. Plumer's advice was accepted. Other than French, no General senior to Haig now remained with the BEF.

The annual Aldershot Rifle Meeting in late summer was started in 1902 but, under Smith-Dorrien (and unlike most other rifle competitions), this competition was increasingly designed to replicate the conditions more likely to be found on a battlefield. *The Times* describes the 1908 meeting thus:

"… the conditions of the ranges approximate more and more closely to those likely to be met with in the fighting line of a belligerent army. Orthoptics, blackened sights, artificial supports, and similar adventitious aids to shooting, permissible at Bisley, are rigorously excluded at Aldershot… In the majority of the competitions which will be decided during the ensuing eight days, success depends as much upon the precautions taken to avoid a suppositious enemy's bullet as upon the actual number of hits registered upon a target. The necessity for rapid as well as accurate fire in actual warfare is emphasised by the number of competitions in which the target exposure is reduced almost to zero, while the possibility of the soldier being at once marksman and target is shown in one match in which falling targets are intended to represent the individual members of rival competing teams."[134]

The Aldershot meeting was open to any serving soldier in the command as well as Sandhurst cadets. Some £1,300 was available in prize money for the 39 different competitions and other events and the whole show culminated in the Aldershot Command Championship involving the 200 best marksmen from the previous days' shooting. Smith-Dorrien was president of the event. Although the 1908 meeting was set back by a storm washing out the first day's shooting the event was greeted as a considerable success with Smith-Dorrien commenting on several aspects. First, he wished to see the 'bull's eye' disappear from rifle training for the British soldier which he later described as only being of use for training recruits 'or possibly for amusing people who take an interest in match shooting'.[135] Instead he wanted to see men asked to judge more precisely variable distances in order to make their firing more accurate. He noted how the Gordon Highlanders and the Buffs had shown this to be both practical and effective. Furthermore, in a precursor to what became known in the Army as the 'mad minute' (i.e. 15 aimed rounds at a target 300 yards or more away within one minute) he commended the performance of the 2nd Scots Guards team which managed to fire twice as many aimed rounds as any other team in eight seconds to win that year's Ash Cup.

The descriptions of some of the competitions show clearly how, under Smith-Dorrien's guidance, the meeting was attuned to the needs of the Army and was not merely an academic exercise in precision accuracy. There was, for example, The Sergeants' Challenge Cup – 200 yards snap shooting in attack; the 500 Yards series – rapid fire, 45 seconds allowed for each firer, unlimited number of rounds fired from any military position; The Goldsmiths and Silversmiths Cup – targets of falling plates at 300 yards; The Marlborough Cup – five rounds from cover on a figure target 200 yards distant with points deducted for undue exposure; and The Bowyers Cup – an attack competition ranged at 200, 300 and 400 yards involving teams of eight with nine falling plates per competitor to be shot down in 45 seconds for each range including any advance. In 1910 a Machine Gun Competition was introduced with teams firing 300 rounds per team at targets 600 and 900 yards distant (the runaway winners being the 1st Leicestershire Regt.).

The Smith-Dorrien Challenge Cup underlined his determination to make rifle competitions more than simple target shooting. His three-day cup was part of a tactical scheme involving 53 officers and men drawn from the brigades which supplied the successful teams drawn from companies or squadrons on day one and battalions and regiments on day two. Each team was part of a *Red Force* engaged in pursuing a smaller *Blue Force* through Farnborough, across the Ash Ranges and the Basingstoke Canal to attack the *Blue* rear-guard entrenched about Scarp and Play Hills. As each team came into action its first view was of mechanical figures apparently digging trenches just below the skyline. They were to open fire, making their own judgements as to the correct range. Next, a *Blue* machine gun 'opened fire' and this was to be engaged and finally a line of skirmishers below the crest of the hill, and represented by falling plates, was their final set of targets. Points were allotted for hits on targets, co-operative fire tactics employed within each team, fire control, distribution of fire between the various targets and the performance of the officer in command.

Thus, Smith-Dorrien and other officers, as well as the instructors at Hythe, helped dramatically improve the accuracy and the firepower of the average soldier to the extent that, in 1914, they proved to be the best defensive infantry anywhere in Europe and the scourge of the still naïve and costly German infantry tactics of the war's opening months.

In March 1912 Smith-Dorrien was succeeded at Aldershot by Haig. He was appointed GOC, Southern Command, which, in the case of war, was the nucleus of II Corps. It comprised the 3rd Division (GOC Henry Rawlinson), the 2nd Cavalry Brigade (GOC Brig. Gen. Henry de Beauvoir De Lisle), and Territorial units from twelve counties with its HQ at Salisbury[i]. He came into regular contact with Territorial Force units, the development of which he encouraged. He also instigated training for fighting withdrawals, which practice no doubt came in handy during the retreat from Mons. His familiarity with the Air Service was further reinforced by the presence of its training centre at Upavon in the heart of Salisbury Plain though frequent, and invariably fatal, accidents somewhat took the gloss of this new and exciting technology.

Smith-Dorrien prepared for war in other ways. In 1909 he, Robertson, and Henry Rawlinson, toured the areas around Charleroi and then east along the *River Sambre* to Namur and Liège then onto eastern Belgium taking in the border region near Eupen before moving south into the Ardennes, and then back to Brussels via Dinant. In other words, the territory through which the German launched their initial great attack designed to take Paris and knock France out of any future war.

IF THE QUALITY OF THE INFANTRY IMPROVED almost out of all recognition after the dark days of 1899 there were still institutional failings within the Army

---

[i] Whilst at Southern Command, Smith-Dorrien and his wife adopted Celia and Frances Gabrielle, the orphaned daughters of his wife's step uncle, Gen. Sir Arthur Power Palmer (d. 1904), and his second wife Constance Gabrielle Richardson Shaw (d. 1912). Power Palmer had been temporary CinC in India between 1900 and 1902 and Smith-Dorrien was Adjutant General for some time in 1902.

which might undermine the effectiveness of these troops. For example, discussions took place at General Staff conferences about how units might signal to one another in order to co-ordinate the sort of fire and movement exemplified by the Smith-Dorrien Challenge Cup. As was then so horribly typical of the British Army it was left to individual Brigades or battalions to determine their means of signalling and each seemed then to come up with its own ideas and train its officers accordingly. The absurdity of this system, or lack of system more correctly, was highlighted by Maj. Gen. Sir Archibald Murray at the General Staff conference of January 1914 in which he set out the systems currently in use. Not only did most Brigades have their own signalling but, within some Brigades, individual battalions had their *own* separate signals. This was the case in 3rd, 4th, 8th, 9th, 15th, 16th and 18th Brigades. There was no standardisation *between* any of the Brigades with agreed Brigade signal systems. The widespread view of the discussions was that such signals were a bad idea and might prevent forward movement of an attack as each unit waited for the other to signal something or other. Broadly, the whole subject smacks of a sorry amateurism amongst the upper reaches of the Army.[136]

The improvement in training and shooting within the Army since South Africa was undoubted, but the tactical changes this allowed for were, in the main, defensive. Though fire and forward movement was still the objective, the prospects for the success of the 'movement' element were still questionable especially as few in the British Army had attempted it whilst under the fire of one or more machine guns (the Boers had some in South Africa).

Apparently, of far great moment was the place of the horse and its rider on the battlefield, and thus there was an intense and prolonged debate about the future, if any, of the cavalry. It was not just the social standing, intellectual quality, military education, and professional development of its officers which were in question. After their varied experiences in South Africa there was a clear disagreement between Lord Roberts and his supporters, amongst them Sir Ian Hamilton, and several senior cavalry offices such as French and Haig about the fundamental role of the cavalry, and the *arme blanche* in particular, in future wars. As early as 1901 Col. Henderson, Director of Intelligence in South Africa, had deplored how small was the number of military men who:

> "... realized that the small-bore and smokeless powder have destroyed the last vestiges of the traditional role of cavalry. Cavalry, armed, trained, and equipped as the cavalry of the Continent, is as obsolete as the crusaders."[137]

Hamilton was in favour of re-arming the cavalry, discarding the lance as 'incompatible with dismounted work', and replacing it with the rifle. He wrote to Roberts in these terms on 30th April 1902.[138] In his view, the cavalry should no longer be the shock troops of the Army but a quicker moving, highly mobile mounted infantry, and he gave evidence to this effect to the Elgin Commission which was looking into the failings of the South African War.

On 10th March 1903, Roberts, no doubt egged on by Hamilton, issued Army Order 39 which stated the lance was forthwith withdrawn from active service, remaining only for ceremonial purposes. The ire of the traditionalists was great. The more so as two leading advocates for the retention of the lance, Generals French and Haig, had not yet been called to give evidence to the Elgin

Commission. Roberts's action looked, therefore, like a pre-emptive strike against these officers and the other advocates of the lance as a weapon still suited to the modern battlefield[i]. Haig, indeed, was not called before the commission until 18th March by which time Roberts's action was a *fait accompli*, but this did not stop him from criticising his Commander in Chief's decision and from confirming his belief in the '*arme blanche* as an effective weapon' according to Esher.[139]

In a manner which might be regarded as unacceptable nowadays, the supporters of the lance, some of them serving officers, fought back vigorously in the media, in Parliament and even at Court. Retired officers in both Houses of Parliament lined up in their droves to condemn the decision. The first to speak on 13th March 1903 was a Colonel of the 9th Lancers and Captain in the Coldstream Guards, Col. The Honourable Heneage Legge, Conservative MP for St George's, Hanover Square, and fifth son of the 4th Earl of Dartmouth. He was followed by another pillar of the establishment and a major in the 16th Lancers, Windham Wyndham-Quin, 5th Earl of Dunraven and Mount-Earl and Conservative MP for South Glamorganshire. Col. Legge had another bite at the cherry on 31st March when he hijacked a debate on the Army Estimates to pursue his personal bugbear. He was supported by Lt. Gen. John Wimburn Laurie, 4th King's Own and Conservative MP for Pembroke and Haverfordwest. He believed his recollection the Boers back in 1881 did not like the lance 'up them' justified its retention in the days of long-range and quick-firing rifles, machine guns and artillery.

From amongst the ranks of serving soldiers several made clear their opposition to the change. One was Douglas Haig who, on 2nd April remarked:

"I think our regiments of cavalry should be armed in equal proportions viz. half the cavalry should have swords, the other half lances – but I believe that a good hog spear would be better than the existing long lance. There is no doubt that the latter is an impediment when scouting and when acting dismounted – but I don't think it is wise to abolish the lance."[140]

This was followed on 3rd April by a man who clearly had his finger on the pulse of modern warfare. Lt. Gen. Sir Drury Curzon Drury-Lowe, GCB, Colonel of the 17th Lancers, was ten years retired and it was 21 years since he last saw action but he nonetheless penned a brief letter to *The Times* describing the removal of the lance as 'the heaviest blow yet dealt at our cavalry'.[141] In these thoughts he was supported on 6th April by Maj. Gen. Sir Leopold Victor Swaine, KCB, CMG, of the Rifle Brigade, who, as the commander of the North-Western military district at Chester, was a serving officer (but not for much longer).

On 14th April, Winston Churchill, MP for Oldham, gave a modernist counterblast in the House of Commons in his own inimitable style:

"He did not understand how anyone who looked at the question impartially could possibly prefer a lance to a rifle. He earnestly hoped that the

---

[i] The soon-to-be ex-Commander in Chief was, however, consistent in his views stating in 1910: "The only possible logical deduction from the history of late wars is, that all attacks can now be carried out far more effectually with the rifle than the sword." [*Source*: Anglesey, op. cit., page 388].

Government would go boldly forward and throw away the ironmongery altogether. If cavalry were to play a great role in the future it would have to be by the use of modern weapons and not the sharp sticks and long irons which were used by savages and medieval chivalry... he earnestly hoped the Government would adhere to their decision to eradicate the lance."[142]

Somewhat late in the pro-lance field was Lt. Gen. Henry Clement Wilkinson, CB, Colonel of the 4th Dragoon Guards, who wrote at length on 23rd April extolling the virtues of a weapon which might, at best, be the cause of the death and wounding of perhaps a few hundred or so of the enemy on the Western Front. That he was a man not quite fully up to speed with modern military technology and tactics can best be seen by his comment:

"We spend millions of money to re-arm our infantry with new rifles and our artillery with new guns that claim to possess some slight advantage over the old ones..."[143]

Slight – but only if significantly increased rates of fire, accuracy and range can be considered 'slight'.

Lord Alwyne Frederick Compton, DSO, DL, 10th Hussars, third son of the 4th Marquis of Northampton, and Liberal Unionist MP for Biggleswade (so a Tory by anyone's standards), was also tempted to join the fray in order to criticise the judgement made by Lord Roberts, his former Commander in Chief in South Africa.[144] Clearly, he believed being a major in the Bedfordshire Imperial Yeomanry, in which he had served, was far better placed than a Field Marshal to make such decisions. Then, on 8th May, there was Lt. Gen. William Godfrey Dunham Massy, 5th Royal Irish Lancers, a hugely brave officer but one who last saw action in 1880. And on and on the campaign went with letters still appearing and questions in Parliament being pursued well into 1908. Roberts was resolutely heretical and, in addition, stated in 1904 'the sword must henceforth be an adjunct to the rifle'. Good grief! What was the world coming to?

One of the highlights of the traditionalists' campaign was a meeting held on 24th December 1904 under the auspices of the *Royal United Services Institution.* Chaired by the letter writing Lt. Gen. Wilkinson, it was addressed by the serving Lt. Col. Charles Blair Mayne, RE, the subject being *'The Lance as a Cavalry Weapon'*. Mayne was critical of the withdrawal the lance, attacking the justifications for its withdrawal given by Lord Roberts (now no longer the CinC as the post was abolished on 12th February 1904 so he was safe enough to do so) as 'a bit of special pleading'.[145] Mayne, though, was not altogether definite in his preference for the lance over the sword (that other essential weapon in the face of a Maxim machine gun) at which point, led by Wilkinson, the audience erupted declaring the lance to be both wondrous and essential. To reinforce the point Wilkinson, the 67-year-old veteran of the Indian Mutiny, produced a dismounted lancer who displayed the full range of manoeuvres by which a cavalryman so armed might swat away Mauser and Maxim bullets fired by an enemy he could not see let alone reach.

Roberts, no liberal himself, knew a blinkered reactionary when he saw one and the officer class of the British Army, both current and retired, was full of them. But Roberts's influence was on the wane and, after his departure as CinC and with

French and Haig in the ascendant, it was not long before the lance was reintroduced for active service.

ANYONE WHO LOOKED TO MANCHURIA for evidence as to the proper application of cavalry was disappointed. The performance of all horsemen was regarded by most as poor and ineffectual. There was, perhaps, an explanation for this which itself should have led to sensible conclusions about the use of cavalry in a modern war. Correlli Barnett explains that cavalry was relegated to the fringes of the fighting because the two armies on contact:

> "…had gone to ground in trenches behind barbed-wire entanglements because of the killing power of machine guns and quick-firing artillery."[146]

In the light of this joint failure it, perhaps, comes as no surprise that certain officers with direct experience of the fighting in Manchuria determined cavalry, in the shock, *arme blanche*, tradition, was now redundant. Such a view was firmly expressed by a Capt. Seki, a Japanese (though admittedly an infantry) officer in an article in the *RUSI Journal* of 1911.[147]

But, with the departure of Roberts, the advancement of Sir John French and the elevation of Haig first to Director of Military Training and then Director of Staff Studies, things soon returned to 'normal' in the cavalry. One aspect of this 'normality' was the reduction, and eventual elimination, of the Mounted Infantry which, after early misfortunes, proved useful in South Africa. But the tide of opinion swiftly turned reactionary, helped by influential voices in the press. Every year *The Times* devoted many column inches to description and criticism of Army manoeuvres not only Britain but also on the continent. Most of the accounts of the annual exercises were written by the military correspondent of *The Times*, the ex-Army officer by way of being an adulterer Charles à Court Repington[i], a man of some influence if his part in bringing down the last ever Liberal Government in 1915 over the shell crisis is anything to go by. He clearly believed himself to be an expert on all issues military and was never reluctant to deliver Olympian assessments of organisational, strategic, and tactical decisions made either in Whitehall or on events unfolding across the trampled fields of whichever unfortunate bit of the country was chosen for the autumn's manoeuvres. Thus, by 1905, Repington was describing as 'heresy' the brief flirtation with cavalry whose main weapon was the rifle, i.e. the time when the lance was temporarily withdrawn before *better* minds than Lord Roberts decided it still had a place on the modern battlefield. By 1910, Repington completely reverted to a pre-South African orthodoxy in which the targets of his ire when talking about cavalry tactics and equipment were the post-war reformers such as Lord Roberts and Erskine Childers and *not* the reactionaries – French and Haig. By then, Repington had determined the use of cavalry and their armaments were decisions best left to

---

[i] He was forced to resign after an affair with Lady Mary, wife of Sir William Garstin, Chief Engineer in Egypt, which, 'upon his honour as a soldier and gentleman' he had declared was ended, only to resume it some years later. Repington was married at the time, to Melloney Catherine Scobell. He later married the now divorced Mary North, previously Lady Garstin.

cavalry officers, though he could not resist advancing the cause of the lance because of its 'longer reach'. Which suggests the cavalry had managed to regain its 'independence' from the other arms of the military rather than being part of a properly integrated and unified force.[148] Or, as Repington wryly stated at the beginning of a comment on the 1908 cavalry manoeuvres:

> "The King's forces have been said to consist of the Army, the Navy, and the Cavalry."[149]

In 1910, approval was given to the German cavalry finally re-equipping all its mounted units with the lance. For Repington, the 'craze' of mounted infantry was over in at least one major continental army:

> "Without entering into the field of controversy on the merits and demerits of the *arme blanche* as the mounted man's weapon, it is safe to say that the Germans have no misgivings as to the superiority of cold steel over the rifle in combats between mounted patrols. All branches of the mounted arm carry the lance. I find now that the *Jäger zu pferde*, which was the nearest concession that the Germans ever made to our Mounted Infantry craze after the South African War, now carry the lance, as well as Cuirassiers, Dragoons, and Hussars."[150]

And a lot of good it did them on the Western Front.

As a devoted cavalryman, Haig believed everything done by Mounted Infantry could be achieved, and more, by well-trained cavalry who, in addition, retained the bonus of 'shock action' with his favoured 'cold steel'. Progressively, mounted infantry schools were closed and the concept of a trained rifleman able to move at speed to a location, there to fight dismounted was allowed to wither on the vine. They were replaced by a 'reformed' cavalry equipped with sword or lance and carbine, and new cyclist units which, it was assumed, might take over many of the roles of the mounted infantry in spite of the horse's obvious 'all terrain' capability. That, in the meantime, aircraft were assuming one of the previous key responsibilities of the cavalry, i.e. long-range reconnaissance, seems to have been lost on the good and the great. It is, perhaps, ironic that one of the early key functions performed by the cavalry on the Western Front (other than a handful of small-scale charges) was to fight dismounted in support of the infantry, for example on the *Aisne*, at Messines, and at First Ypres in 1914. Later in the war this role continued, with the cavalry performing the role of mounted infantry with monotonous regularity. Opportunities to employ their short-range and pennanted pointy sticks were few and far between. The greatest irony about the Haig-inspired retention of lightly armed cavalry against more heavily armed mounted infantry was that, by 1918, to justify the still large number of cavalrymen on the Western Front, he was forced to explain to a sceptical government the cavalry were now more akin to 'highly trained mobile infantry'.[151] Haig's hypocrisy thus exposed on the Western Front, it appears that, even in the wide-open spaces of the Middle East, mounted infantry was more useful than the *arme blanche*. Cavalryman Lt. Gen. Sir Philip Chetwode praised his ANZAC and Yeomanry mounted troops who achieved so much in the liberation of Palestine and the drive towards Damascus as being 'high-class mounted rifles rather than traditional cavalry'.[152]

Dedication to the traditional, and ignoring predictions of the future, has always been the preserve of the conservative and this was well summed up by Anglesey with his comments on the new Haig-drafted edition of the manual *Cavalry Training*:

"In 1907 the 1904 edition of *Cavalry Training* was superseded by a manual which was hardly less conservative than its predecessor... It went so far as to say that 'thorough efficiency in the use of the rifle and in dismounted tactics is an absolute necessity', but it then went on to make it unequivocally clear that 'it must be accepted as a principle that the rifle, effective as it is, cannot replace the effect produced by the speed of the horse, the magnetism of the charge and the terror of cold steel.'"[153]

Now, it must be said that Anglesey's dismissal of the 1904 training manual as 'conservative' in no way reflects the reaction to its introduction at the time because many conservative cavalrymen were outraged. The 1904 manual replaced the 1898 *Cavalry Drill Book* which latter volume extolled the virtues of 'shock tactics' to which Haig returned in his 1907 version. It maintained the close order, knee-to-knee cavalry charge was the cavalry's true *raison d'être* and the employment of a carbine useful only in as much as it alarmed the enemy or deceived them as to the presence of infantry. The 1904 manual was based on the South African experience where, in the main, the *arme blanche* failed and the cavalry/mounted infantry fought mainly dismounted. The 1904 manual's *caveat* remained that shock tactics *might* be appropriate in certain circumstances but that those circumstances would be 'rare'.

Independently, cavalry tactics around the Empire were also adapted in the light of experience in South Africa. In Canada, Lt. Gen. Douglas Mackinnon Baillie Hamilton Cochrane, 12th Earl of Dundonald, KCB, KCVO, and, since April 1902, the General Officer Commanding the Militia of Canada, wrote in the new Canadian cavalry regulations that:

"For all practical purposes the profitable employment of cold steel is over... The intelligent Canadian behind a rifle will be more than a match for any two swordsmen... when they see the enemy preparing to charge with sabre or lance (they) will coolly dismount, form up, and when he gets within range, pour in such a withering fire as will in five minutes kill as many of the enemy as the same enemy with sword or lance would kill in five years of active service."[154]

In India, Kitchener was well in step with this transformation:

"In cavalry the substitution of an accurate long-range rifle for the carbine marks a very distinct change. In the employment and training of this arm the cavalry soldier must have it impressed upon him that, whereas the carbine has hitherto been merely an adjunct to the lance or sword, the old order has now changed, and the lance or sword has become an auxiliary to the rifle."[155]

In Australia, Lt. Gen. Sir Edward Thomas Henry Hutton[i], KCB, KCMG, DL, FRGS, one of Dundonald's predecessors commanding the Canadian Militia,

---

[i] Hutton briefly commanded the 21st (New Army) Division but stood down after a riding accident in 1915, aged 66.

commander of the 1st Mounted Infantry Brigade in South Africa, and now the General Officer Commanding the Australian Military Forces, was, unsurprisingly, completely in line with this approach. *The Times* of 1904 greeted this unanimity with something close to acclaim having complained that:

> "One of the gravest weaknesses of Imperial defence at this moment is that each part of the Empire settles its military organization or its tactics absolutely regardless of every other, a policy, or, rather, an absence of policy, which may have the most disastrous consequences in war."[156]

The 1907 manual was, therefore, a step back in time to an out-moded tradition clear to all but the very blinkered. That the forces of reaction should fight back was inevitable. As *The Times* remarked:

> "The conservatism of the cavalry is intense, and in the case of many of the senior men has already led them to go back upon their war experience."[157]

By 1908 matters were back to what passed for 'normal'. An anonymous letter writer (one *'Ex-I. Y., Ex-M.P.'*, so an ex-Member of Parliament who had been with the Imperial Yeomanry in South Africa) noted:

> "The cavalry has definitely returned to their old role temporarily abandoned after the Boer War and are being exercised on manoeuvres in shock tactics with the *arme blanche*."[158]

As an indication of the re-establishment of the 'old order', in 1908, a new 'thrusting sword' for cavalry troopers was issued (followed by one for officers in 1912). This had a blade 35-in. long which, added to an average arm length of, say, 27-in. gave the 1908 sword a 'range' of just over 5 feet. The 1894 Pattern bamboo or ash lance was 9 ft. long so might have a 'range' of another 2-3 feet. Let us be generous and say 8 feet all told[i]. By comparison, the range of the full metal jacket *Spitzgeschoß* bullet fired by the *Mauser Gewehr 98* rifle was 2,000+ metres. In addition, after a German soldier fired his rifle, it was not ripped from his hands and rendered unusable after a single shot. The 1908 sword, however, thrust into a man's chest whilst the assailant was a full gallop had a tendency of not only remaining in the victim's body but of occasionally dislocating or breaking the wrist of the charging cavalryman who might also be dismounted as well as dis-armed in the collision.

It is quite extraordinary the British Army should spend so much time, money, and energy on debating and re-equipping part of the Army which then played no meaningful role[ii] in the next war and which several senior officers such as Roberts, Henderson and Hamilton believed to be an anachronism. Perhaps one should not

---

[i] The British Army experimented with a steel-shafted lance in 1915. To quote the Royal Armouries' website: 'It is remarkable that even after the experience of trench warfare had begun that improved lance designs for the cavalry were still being explored'. Remarkable is a polite way of putting it. The lance was not withdrawn from service until 1927. [*Source*: https://collections.royalarmouries.org/first-world-war/type/rac-narrative-82.html]

[ii] That is, no meaningful role as traditional 'cavalry' rather than mounted infantry and precious little of that role either on the Western Front.

be too surprised at this commitment to outmoded tradition. Even after the experiences of 1914-18, in June 1925 Haig was still expressing his conviction that, despite automatic weapons, aircraft, tanks, etc., the horse would retain its place on the modern battlefield. Addressing the *Royal College of Veterinary Surgeons* on his award of a Diploma of Honorary Associate membership, he was declared:

> "Some enthusiasts to-day talked about the probability of horses becoming extinct and prophesied that the aeroplane, the tank, and the motor-car would supersede the horse in future wars. But history has always shown that great inventions somehow or other cured themselves; they always produced antidotes, and he believed that the value of the horse and the opportunity for the horse in the future were likely to be as great as ever. How could infantry, piled up with all their equipment, take advantage of a decisive moment created by fire from machine guns at a range of 5,000 to 6,000 yards?[i] It was by utilizing light mounted troops and mounted artillery that advantage could be taken of these modern weapons. He was all for using aeroplanes and tanks, but they were only accessories to the man and the horse, and he felt sure that as time went on they would find just as much use for the horse – the well-bred horse – as they had ever done in the past. Let them (i.e. his audience of vets) not be despondent and think that the day of the horse was over."[159]

TO MAKE MATTERS WORSE, at this time the War Office and the Army was turning down suggestions for equipment which might have assisted in getting men across the 'fire swept zone'. Suggestions which, if pursued, would have placed the British Army well 'ahead of the curve' in terms of the development of tactics and equipment. But rather than pursue the new ideas for tracked, armed, and armoured fighting vehicles, the development of the 1908 Cavalry Sword was clearly far more in tune with military thinking. Which says not a lot about either those thoughts or the men thinking them.

Thus, sadly missing from the debates about fire superiority, morale, cavalry swords and musical support for the final attack were any ideas contained in various works which directly addressed the nature of the modern battlefield and looked at mechanical ways to solve the problem of Bloch's 'fire swept zone'. Notable amongst these was a 1908 article in *Blackwood's Magazine* entitled *The Trenches*.[160] The article is attributed to *'105'* but the author was Capt. C E Vickers of the Royal Engineers then working at the War Office. Atop the article is the following quote:

> "This remains the tactical problem of all ages, how to get men enough together within efficient killing distance of their enemy…"

The quote is taken from page 97 of a book by another Royal Engineer, Col. Frederick Natusch Maude, CB, who published *War and the World's Life* the previous year[ii]. It is interesting to note the solutions of these two officers to this 'tactical

---

[i] The answer was probably by advancing behind the *Vickers Medium Tank Mk I* introduced in 1924 and with a top speed of 15 mph. It was the only modern tank mass-produced anywhere in the world in the 1920s.

[ii] Maude also wrote an invasion scare book in 1900: *The New Battle of Dorking*.

problem' were wildly different. Maude was decidedly *not* a firepower theorist. He regarded morale, discipline, drill, and the power of command as the essentials when asking men to risk their lives in the face of overwhelming firepower. Thus, the full quotation ends:

> "… and of all means to its solution, discipline through drill is the surest and most reliable factor to work upon."[161]

This comes in a page entitled *Dense Columns Cheapest in the End*, which extols the virtues of a formation used by Napoleonic Armies a hundred years earlier.

Writing twelve years earlier in the *Journal of the Royal Artillery Institute* an anonymous German General posited a rather different point of view:

> "There are two ways of training men, you can teach them to be *"dumm dreist"* (bold through stupidity), to disregard cover and to believe there is nothing to fear if they keep a bold heart; the other system is to teach men what dangers there are and how to avoid them, just as a sailor or a steeplejack is taught how to appreciate and how to avoid the dangers of his trade. Men trained on the former system find out on the first day of battle that their teachers have lied and lose all confidence in them. Such training may sound excellent in peace, but will not stand the strain of war. The second will stand any test."[162]

Maude's reference back to anachronistic Napoleonic tactics at a time of quick-firing, long-range weapons should not come as too much of a surprise. An argumentative controversialist, he was responsible in 1908 for the greatly belated introduction to the British military hive mind of the heavily Napoleon-influenced Clausewitz and his book *Vom Kriege*. It is somehow appropriate that the 19th Century's greatest work on the nature of war evaded the overwhelming majority of anti-intellectual and ill-educated British Army officers over the previous seventy years. But, twenty years after the French discovered the man and his work, Maude now popularised the book even if rejecting the German's 'off message' comments about the strength of the defensive in war. Maude 'edited' Col. James John Graham's translation printed in 1873, writing a new introduction (but doing precious little else) and presenting the work in heavily Social Darwinist terms:

> "It reveals 'War', stripped of all accessories, as the exercise of force for the attainment of a political object, unrestrained by any law save that of expediency, and thus gives the key to the interpretation of German political aims, past, present, and future, which is unconditionally necessary for every student of the modern conditions of Europe. Step by step, every event since Waterloo follows with logical consistency from the teachings of Napoleon, formulated for the first time, some twenty years afterwards, by this remarkable thinker.
>
> What Darwin accomplished for Biology generally Clausewitz did for the Life-History of Nations nearly half a century before him, for both have proved the existence of the same law in each case, viz., 'The survival of the fittest' – the 'fittest, as Huxley long since pointed out, not being necessarily synonymous with the ethically 'best'."[163]

Maude then made the case that Germany was the European nation most 'fit' for war and Britain, alone, was weakening its position through a failure greatly to expand its military strength. In a parallel argument, he rails against the German Socialists and rejoiced in the *SPD's* 'defeat' in the 1907 *Reichstag* elections[i] because of what he perceived as their interference with the Army. But Maude is, essentially a 'morale' and a 'leadership' man. His belief was that improvements in firepower and communications gave great leaders with morally inspired troops prepared to sacrifice themselves for the nation an unassailable advantage in modern war. He was proved horribly wrong when fighting broke out and in too many cases leaders rapidly lost complete control of the action:

> "... recent researches of the French General Staff into the records and documents of the Napoleonic period have shown conclusively that Clausewitz had never grasped the essential point of the Great Emperor's strategic method, yet it is admitted that he has completely fathomed the spirit which gave life to the form; and notwithstanding the variations in application which have resulted from the progress of invention in every field of national activity (not in the technical improvements in armament alone), this spirit still remains the essential factor in the whole matter. Indeed, if anything, modern appliances have intensified its importance, for though, with equal armaments on both sides, the form of battles must always remain the same, the facility and certainty of combination which better methods of communicating orders and intelligence have conferred upon the Commanders has rendered the control of great masses immeasurably more certain than it was in the past."[164]

Our young Capt. Vickers, however, was a man of an entirely different stamp to Maude and his ilk. His anonymous piece was intended to propose a technical solution to crossing the 'fire swept zone' rather than one in which, in the middle of some corpse strewn field, human flesh met the 9.9 grams (153 gr), pointed *Spitzgeschoß* round fired by the *Gewehr 98* Mauser rifle. His story concerned the development of a machine which might advance impervious to such bullets. He also made some cutting comments about the process of technological development within the Army perhaps best summed up by these paragraphs:

> "... but you know what a Government Department is, fair to moderately slow taking up new ideas. First of all, they'll want me to report all about it, and refer back two or three times for more particulars; then somebody will suggest referring to a committee, then the committee has to be appointed and to meet, then the committee will talk and may make experiments, and get out volumes of statistics and, finally, they'll find out there isn't any money to buy one till next year...
>
> 'I suppose that means sending it to the Inventions Committee'.

---

[i] Though, with 3,259,029 votes and 29% [down 2.8% since 1903] they still received 10% *more* votes than the next party, the *Deutsche Zentrumspartei*. Through the vagaries of the electoral system, they lost 38 of 81 seats. One wonders how he would have reacted to the 1912 result when the *SPD* became the largest party in the *Reichstag* with 110 seats and 4,250,399 votes [34.8%], more than twice as many as the *Zentrumsparti*.

'To the Grave of Inventions... Do they ever say anything except No further action recommended, or too expensive, or something really solid and British like that?"[165]

The subject of these fictional discussions was an American entrenching machine, one designed to cut a deep ditch into which drainage pipes or the like might be laid. But a bright officer of Engineers seconded to the War Office (such as Vickers) saw a more particular military application – the digging of advanced entrenchments on the battlefield. The tale then moves to some fictitious battle and here Vickers seems, like Bloch, to have grasped the essential nature of modern warfare. The men are entrenched, the lines are static, barbed wire is everywhere, siege warfare is the agenda. Behind woods and hills howitzers are deployed ready to deliver indirect fire on the enemy's lines (Vickers was truly forward thinking). And an attack is planned as an officer tells a journalist:

> "Oh, the same old game, I suppose: going out and getting potted at. What you scribes call 'the hail of lead,' and all that sort of thing: first digging like a mole, and then sitting in a beastly trench, and never getting a chance to draw a bead on the other people. This time they say we're going to make a real dart at 'em, though."[166]

The difference now is that the British Army has a special machine:

> "The machine! . . . But it seems such a simple, almost obvious notion to evolve a machine that shall dig trenches, that shall be able to move unconcernedly across open ground where no man can show himself scatheless, secure under its turtleback of steel, inconspicuous, minding all the hail of lead as little as rain, patient. They have nicknamed it *The Snail*, but it can burrow forward like a mole!"[167]

The Snail digs trenches far beyond the speed of humans equipped with pick and shovel. Protected though not invulnerable, it can do so close to the enemy's lines. Thus, undercover, the attacking infantry could get near enough to stand a chance of entry into the enemy's trenches. Vickers is no rosy optimist, however, and still recognised the likely and awful consequences of close-range fire on exposed infantry. In the story, therefore, the attack stalls and nearly fails until *The Snail* gets to work once more:

> "A machine is at work again. I can see through my glasses a turtle-backed affair pushing out from the advanced trench, something half concealed in a cloud of dust, the same sort of cloud which a motor makes on a dusty day."[168]

Supported by a rudimentary trench mortar, another device ignored by the British Army before the start of the war, *The Snail* and the mortar do their work. Casualties have been high but the key position is taken and held.

Though Vickers's idea is not yet that of the tank, armoured and armed, it did address that key issue of the 'fire swept zone' in a way no General Officer ever contemplated before the outbreak of war. It sought to find a technological answer to the age-old problem of getting men as near as possible to the enemy line before necessarily exposing themselves to the enemy's fire.

And, continuing the theme of good ideas rejected, the trench mortar, too, was a weapon considered and discarded by the British Army, as well as by the French, before 1914, even if several French officers repeatedly tried to interest their Army in such weapons[i]. Most recently experienced when used by Russia in defence of Sebastopol during the Crimean War, numerous extemporised, short-range, 'bombards' were then employed effectively by the Japanese in Manchuria. Before that, however, and considering the French experience in the Crimea and, no doubt, the prolonged siege of Paris in the Franco-Prussian War, in 1880 the prolific Col. de Bange proposed a short-range, high-angle gun for use against permanent and field fortifications. The design was based on a bronze, later steel, 90-mm tube capable of firing a shell 1,930 metres. Weighing in at only 155 Kgs it proved transportable along trenches by only 2 or 3 men. Successfully tested at Calais in 1884, de Bange's novel *lance-mines* (mine launcher) idea was then rejected. After the Manchurian conflict, Gen. Herment, commander of the artillery of the *1er Corps*, demanded this weapon be re-visited. This request, too, was rejected by the powers-that-be. In the meantime, the concept persisted amongst certain French artillery officers. In 1890, at Bourges a *Capitaine* de Place adapted a 75-mm 1873 gun, the *Canon de campagne de 5 de Reffye modèle 1873*, to take a 170 Kg shell to be delivered at short range and with a steep trajectory. This, too, was rejected. In 1912, Col. Arnaud Albert Hirondart, previously the *directeur de l'atelier de construction de Lyon* (previously the *Arsenal de Perrache* built in 1845 and greatly expanded after 1914 for the production of heavy artillery shells), attempted to revive a project he started way back in 1885 when he was a captain at the *Etat-Major particulier d'artillerie* at the *Fonderie de Bourges*. This involved a rifled, 80-mm barrel from a *canon de 80 mm modèle 1877* being re-used as a short-range, high-angle gun. He had no better luck than his predecessors. Within weeks of the outbreak of war, the need for short-range mortars became obvious and the French were obliged to deploy ancient bronze mortars made in the first forty years of the 19th Century in order to fill the armaments gap created by trench warfare. Built in the reign of Louis-Philippe, the last King of France, 104 *mortier lisse en bronze de 15 cm Mle 1838*, which fired a mix of spherical and cylindrical bombs no more than 600 metres, were issued from various eastern garrison towns in October 1914. These were then joined by larger

---

[i] The hand grenade nearly went the same way. Discarded by the British Army officially in 1902 it had to be, unsatisfactorily, re-invented after experience in Manchuria. The *No. 1 Grenade*, akin to the German stick grenade, was developed by the *Royal Laboratory* in 1906 but fewer than 500 were manufactured before 1914. The *No. 2 Grenade* was developed by Frederick Marten Hale, a director of the *Cotton Powder Company* and involved in the *Roburite & Ammonal Explosives Co. Ltd*. This was rejected in 1908 and then temporarily adopted in 1913. Both were percussion-fused, i.e. they had to land on the fuse to trigger a detonation. The downside was that, if in the act of throwing the grenade, the thrower inadvertently hit the fuse on, say, the side of a trench, then both the grenade and thrower would be blown sky high. Only the introduction of the *Mills No. 5* bomb in 1915 provided a relatively safe hand grenade to the British Army. Marten Hale, however, went on to invent and manufacture other weapons such as rifle grenades, aerial bombs (used to destroy the Zeppelins *LZ25* [on the ground] and the *LZ37* [in the air], and the depth charge.

mortiers de 22, 27 and *32-cm Mle 1839,* some of which were still in use in quieter sectors in the autumn of 1915.[169]

As with the field and medium howitzers, one country in Europe did take serious note of developments in this field in Manchuria in 1904-5: Germany. A range of three modern *minenwerfer's* was commissioned in 1907 after work between the German Army's *Ingenieurkomitee* and arms manufacturer *Rheinmetall* resulting, in 1910, in a *25-cm Schwerer Minenwerfer (sMW)*; in 1913 a *17-cm Mittelere Minenwerfer (mMW)*; and, by 1914, a prototype of a *7.6 cm Leichte Minenwerfer (lMW)*. At the beginning of the war, 44 of the *25-cm* version and 116 of the *17-cm* variant were immediately available, giving the German Army a huge advantage when trench warfare became the norm. Manned by the *Pioniers* (engineers) some of these weapons were used as early as 13th August 1914 against the *fort de Fléron* at Liège. By the end of 1915, over 1,200 of these three designs, augmented by newer models, were employed. 16,000 would be built by war's end.

But such novelties had no place in the BEF when deployed in August 1914. At the General Staff conference of January 1912, Brig. Gen. Frederick William Nicholas McCracken of Irish Command raised the idea of a 'bombard' or trench mortar as, after the Russo-Japanese War, trials were conducted in India in 1907 with mortars with a range of some 3-400 yards. Devoted to the idea the next war would be one of manoeuvre, and with the relentless lack of foresight which epitomised pre-war British arms procurement, the idea was soundly rejected, the opposition being led by Brig. Gens. Aylmer Haldane and, surprise, surprise, Launcelot Kiggell. All combatants then designed and built many thousands of trench mortars in a range of different designs and sizes.[170]

But let us return to the notion of what became the Tank. Our visionary young officer, Capt. Charles Ernest Vickers, RE, worked at the War Office up to his untimely death a few weeks after *The Trenches* was published in January 1908 (he died on 6th February 1908 from complications relating to pneumonia). Aged just 35, it is conceivable that, had he lived on, his far-sighted views might have led to his being the name most closely associated with the emergence of the Tank. As it was, it was his immediate superior at the War Office, and the writer of his obituary in the *Royal Engineers' Journal*, Maj. Ernest Dunlop Swinton, who laid claim to this achievement. Swinton clearly knew Vickers intimately. Indeed, they earlier collaborated on a story for *Blackwood's Magazine* in 1907 entitled *An Eddy of War*, a short story about a German invasion of the South of England and the efforts of 'Hun' saboteurs to disrupt the British response[i]. Previously, they both served on the railways in South Africa, Vickers as the Deputy Assistant Director of Railways and Swinton as CO of the 1st Railway Pioneer Regt. They were also appointed Staff Captains at Army Headquarters on the same date: 1st April 1905. Swinton, it appears, helped in the organisation of his friend's funeral, and was still involved

---

[i] The story appears in *The Green Curve and other stories*. It contains articles from *Blackwood's Magazine* and one from *Macmillan's Magazine*. The preface notes 'the latter story (*An Eddy of War*, dated April 1907) was written in collaboration with the late 'CV'.' [Source: Swinton, Lt. Col. E D, *The Green Curve and other stories*, Doubleday, Page & Co., 1914].

with his affairs a year later as he was engaged in the editing of another article by Vickers destined for *Blackwood's* entitled *The Shunting Puzzle*. There is no mention of Vickers, however, in any of Swinton's writings about the development of the Tank, for what reason one can only speculate.[171]

Vickers was the youngest son of a Dublin barrister. He attended Haig's *alma mater*, Clifton College, before joining the Royal Military Academy where he passed out top, and well top, of his class[i]. He was awarded the RMA's Pollock Medal for 'distinguished proficiency' in July 1892, the Pollock Medal being awarded to the best cadet of the class. He was an all-round talent, as his obituary in *The Times* suggests, commenting on his 'success in literature and art… several characteristic specimens of his work were included in the recent exhibition of the *Arts Club* at the Grafton Gallery'.[172] A well-rounded soldier, while at Woolwich Vickers also won prizes for fortification, artillery, chemistry and physics, and landscape drawing. By all appearances, Vickers was more talented and creative than Swinton and, clearly, he was the first of the two to suggest the radical military potential of tracked vehicles. Sadly, his name is now mostly forgotten.

To produce the key technical element of *The Trenches* one imagines Vickers witnessed a display of a British *Hornsby* or American *Holt* 'continuous track' vehicle as the *Hornsby-Ackroyd Caterpillar Tractor* was certainly tested by the *Mechanical Transport Committee*[ii] at the War Office between 1905 and 1908 and was displayed and photographed at Aldershot[iii]. A smaller version was bought by the Army in 1909 but, by 1911, interest in tracked vehicles evaporated.

One assumes Vickers knew about the *Holt* too as the character in *The Trenches* who first presents such a vehicle to the War Office is an American. *The Holt Manufacturing Co* of Stockton, California, was formed in 1892 and was a leader in the production of agricultural machinery and vehicles. For many years, engineers sought to produce an effective continuous track vehicle capable of travelling over broken and/or soft terrain. In 1901 Alvin Orlando Lombard from Maine patented the *Lombard Steam Log Hauler* which utilised a continuous tracking system at the rear. *Holts* negotiated a licencing deal to produce these vehicles in Stockton. Four years later the British company *Hornsby* based in Lincoln developed a tracked vehicle of their own which the British Army tested and rejected over the next five years (a situation perhaps referred to in Vickers' piece). *Holts* was more visionary, however, and bought the patent. Although not directly utilised in the development of the British Tank it seems certain *Holt 'Caterpillar'* tractors (apparently so named after a comment by a British officer on observing one of the machines) influenced their development and were certainly utilised in the development of the French *Renault*, *Schneider* and *Saint-Chamond* tanks. Furthermore, hundreds of *Holt*

---

[i] The then Cpl. Vickers finished top of his class with 8,578 marks. The next best cadet was Cpl. (later Brig. Gen.) Harry Biddulph with 7,914 marks. The margin of 664 marks by which Vickers led Biddulph was the same which covered Biddulph and the next six cadets. Swinton passed out fourth in the Second Class of 1888 winning a prize for landscape drawing.

[ii] Set up in 1900 under various Royal Engineer officers.

[iii] Photographs and an article appeared in the *Daily Mirror* on 19th May 1908.

'*Caterpillars*' were used to draw heavy artillery by the various Allied armies on the Western, Italian and Mesopotamian Fronts.

The attitude of the War Office and the Army to the concept of protecting attacking troops by the employment of an armoured tracked vehicle was not only short-sighted in the extreme but indicative of a lack of care for the junior officers and other ranks who would be ordered into battle against long-range and automatic fire. It was a mind-set later shared by those senior officers in the RFC who declined to equip aircraft pilots and observers with parachutes during the war for fear they might bail out rather than face the enemy. In a way, it was an extension of the belief held in certain quarters that placing soldiers in entrenchments or fortifications eroded their 'offensive spirit'; that the relative comfort, safety, and companionship thus provided would make them increasingly reluctant to leave their subterranean home and face the dangers and horrors of the 'fire swept zone'.[i]

The concept of an armoured and armed all-terrain vehicle had been around for hundreds of years. Leonardo da Vinci, for example, designed something similar as long ago as the late 1480s. Far more recently, the idea of an armoured vehicle used to transport either men or equipment and supplies was realised in 1900 in consequence of the early setbacks in South Africa. It was named the *Fowler B5 Armoured Road Train*. With British supply lines tenuous and vulnerable to rapid hit and run strikes from Boer *kommandos*, Lord Roberts ordered six armoured traction engines, each to be equipped with three armoured wagons. They were built by *John Fowler and Co (Leeds) Ltd.*, at the *Steam Plough Works* at Hunslet. The 7.94-mm armour plate was supplied by *Charles Cammell* of Sheffield and was said to be proof against modern rifle bullets at 20-yard range. These *Road Trains* were huge and ponderous beasts. A *Super Lion Traction Engine* weighing 17½ tons was covered in 4½ tons of armour. It could pull some 55 tons at between two and six miles per hour depending on the surface. And what it pulled were specially designed, 4-wheeled armoured carriages, with sloping sides designed to deflect bullets and able to safely carry men, ammunition, supplies – and even a howitzer or 4.7-in gun. Of the six ordered, four were built in the spring of 1900 and tested near Leeds. Despite some issues on rising ground, two of the *Road Trains* arrived in South Africa in August and the other two in December. By the time of their arrival the tactical situation had changed and their armour plating was no longer required. They were, instead, attached to the *Imperial Military Railways* as ordinary traction engines.[173] Charles Vickers was, of course, the Deputy Assistant Director of Railways in South Africa at the time. Their existence no doubt lingered in his fertile mind. No-one else seems to have noticed their development potential.

In December 1903, in *The Strand Magazine*, H G Wells suggested the prospect of armoured vehicles able to cross trenches in his short story *The Land Ironclads*. Wells was, it seems, trying to solve the problem Bloch posed: how to get sufficient men across the 'fire swept zone' to mount a successful attack. The story starts with the following exchange:

---

[i] One such officer was Russian Gen. Mikhail Ivanovich Dragomirov whose belief in massed infantry bayonet charges would prove costly in the Russo-Japanese War.

"The young lieutenant lay beside the war correspondent and admired the idyllic calm of the enemy's lines through his field glass.

'So far as I can see,' he said, at last, 'one man.'

'What's he doing?' asked the war correspondent.

'Field-glass at us,' said the young lieutenant

'And this is war!'

'No,' said the young lieutenant; 'it's Bloch.'

'The game's a draw.'"

Later, in *The Land Ironclads*, an Army based on science and technology which has the eponymous hardware soundly defeats an Army based on traditional virtues such as personal bravery, physical fitness, and marksmanship.

The modern preoccupation was how to combine armoured design with an all-terrain capability. Wells' ironclads employed a Pedrail system invented in 1903 by Bramah Joseph Diplock. The basic concept was of rubber feet attached by spokes to the rims of metal wheels. Although Diplock abandoned his own system in 1910 in pursuit of a proper 'tracked' system it was still being investigated in Britain in the early years of the war and several tests were mounted by Churchill's *Landships Committee* before the Pedrail was abandoned in favour of the continuous track in mid-1915. What became known as the 'caterpillar track' proved to be the solution but it took dozens if not hundreds of attempts before something which really worked emerged and *Holts* became the world's leading manufacturer.

At least one other officer on the *Mechanical Transport Committee* at the War Office saw the potential of the tracked vehicles tested. Maj. William Edward Donohue of the Army Service Corps was, for some time, an Inspector of Ordnance Machinery with the Royal Artillery. In 1904 he was appointed Inspector of Mechanical Transport, First Class. By 1916 he was Chief Inspector of Mechanical Transport at the War Office with the rank of Colonel. Soon after Vickers' death, Donohue's suggestion of a gun mounted on a tracked and armoured vehicle was rejected.

But even Vickers' concept was not a totally new idea. In 1903, a Capt. Levavasseur of the French Artillery suggested an armed and armoured tracked vehicle in the form of a *Projet de canon autopropulseur*. It involved placing a 75-mm field gun onto a tracked vehicle manned by an officer and three men. It was not a tank in the modern sense of the world in that it had no revolving turret. It was, in fact, a self-propelled gun. It was presented to the *Comité Général d'Artillerie* which, in February 1905, presented the idea to the Army Minister. The main concern was the continuing absence of a reliable system for the continuous track and the idea was rejected. Levavasseur revised his plan and it was re-presented in 1908 to suffer the same fate. Interestingly, one of the officers involved in the second rejection, a Commandant Ferrus, was later involved in the development of the *Saint-Chamond* tank in 1916, a tank which bore a striking resemblance to that proposed by Levavasseur eight years earlier.

Then, in 1911, three different versions of a tracked, all-terrain armoured vehicle were proposed – and all rejected. In Austria Gunther Adolf Burstyn designed a *Motorgeschütz*, or motorised gun, based on *Holt*-designed tracked farm vehicles. Both Austria and Germany ignored his ideas. In Russia, Vasily Mendeleev designed a super-heavy tank which was rejected not least on the grounds of expense. Finally, the War Office and the British Army were given yet another chance to develop an effective tracked vehicle when 31-year-old Australian engineer Lancelot Eldin de Mole designed his own version in 1911 and forwarded his designs to the War Office the following year. It was formally rejected in June 1913 although he tried and failed to generate new interest in 1914. A report by the *Royal Commission on Awards to Inventors* in 1919 later described de Mole's original design as:

> "… a very brilliant invention which anticipated and in some respects surpassed that actually put into use in the year 1916. It was this claimant's misfortune and not his fault that his invention was in advance of his time, and failed to be appreciated and was put aside because the occasion for its use had not then arisen."[174]

'The occasion for its use had not yet arisen'! Tell that to the thousands of young men whose lives were squandered because of the blind stupidity and crippling lack of imagination of the average British General prior to 1914. It is sadly typical that it was only junior officers such as Vickers, the sort of man who might well have been asked to advance under fire rather than order such an advance from a remote and secure distance, who sought to address the problem of the 'fire swept zone' in a way which might help reduce casualties. Officers like Maude, and Hamilton, Haig and Rawlinson, were of the 'cannot make omelettes without breaking eggs' mentality. Or, to put it rather more crudely, the 'mind over matter' attitude, in which the Generals didn't mind, and the men didn't matter.

Sir Ian Hamilton, for example, was regarded by others (and by himself) as something of an intellectual. A military man and a thinking man too, but a man who saw what he wanted to see. His thoughts run thus:

> "Napoleon has told us that the moral is to the physical as three is to one. The Scriptures tell us that 'where there is no vision the people perish'. Clausewitz has said, 'In the combat the loss of moral force is the chief cause of the decision'. Blindness to moral forces and worship of material forces inevitably lead in war to destruction. All that exaggerated reliance placed upon *Chassepots* and *mitrailleuses* by France before '70; all that trash written by M. Bloch before 1904 about zones of fire across which no living thing could pass, heralded nothing but disaster. War is essentially the triumph, not of a *chassepot* over a needle-gun, not of a line of men entrenched behind wire entanglements and fire-swept zones over men exposing themselves in the open, but of one will over another weaker will."[175]

He expressed his views to the Royal Commission on the War in South Africa about the need to produce 'new men' with which to overcome the new weapons. But when asked to explain just how these 'new men' were to cross the fire swept zone to get to grips with the defenders equipped with these new weapons his answer was lame in the extreme:

> "I am certain, that an attack can be brought off some-how…"[176]

Others at least had the brutal honesty to accept that the lack of any means of protecting soldiers as they advanced must result in heavy casualties but argued that, in the end, such sacrifice saved lives. They cited the victorious Japanese in

Manchuria as confirmation of this 'fact of life'. This 'fact of life' was, however, also an attempt to justify and rationalise their own social Darwinist theories in which elites directed and the rest did the decent thing and, if required, died.

Indeed, after his comments to the Royal Commission, Hamilton's views on morale and the power of the offensive were reinforced by his self-serving interpretation of his experiences with the Japanese Army. He regarded the apparent willingness of Japanese troops to die for their Emperor as admirable and wished the average British male might perform in the same way under fire:

"In stark contrast to Bloch's argument of the 'folly of the frontal attack', Hamilton, a highly respected military *attaché*, concluded that the 'offensive spirit', the smashing through every enemy stronghold with brute force generated from the will, courage, and morale of the army was the major lesson to be drawn from his observations of the Russo-Japanese War."[177]

Hamilton wrote of his experiences in Manchuria in *A Staff Officer's Scrapbook*. It is doubtful the views expressed were completely objective. Dr Philip Towle, *Emeritus Reader* in International Relations at Cambridge University, wrote in 1998:

"British anxiety after the Boer War accentuated the Social Darwinist views so fashionable in Britain and elsewhere at the time. Many officers and journalists went to Japan to report on the war determined to show that international life obeyed the law of the jungle, that Britain was becoming decadent and that British education and military training should be revolutionised to meet the dangers ahead. Japan was held up as a country largely immune to the forces making for decadence, so again Britain could learn from its behaviour and successes."[178]

Thus Hamilton, after sexist remarks about the fragrant virtues of Japanese 'femininity' and derogatory comments on 'uppity' American females, concentrated his thoughts on the seemingly debilitated state of Western urbanised manhood:

"It was because of my conviction that up-to-date civilisation is becoming less and less capable of conforming to the antique standards of military virtue, and that the hour is at hand when the modern world must begin to modify its ideals, or prepare to go down before some more natural, less complex and less nervous type. The Boers furnished one example of those primitive peoples whose education and intelligence had just reached the stage at which they could avail themselves of modern rifles and guns. City-bred dollar-hunters are becoming less and less capable of coping with such adversaries as Deer-slayer and his clan."[179]

It was this mentality which led to the disastrous and unproductive casualties at Gallipoli where Hamilton tried, and failed miserably, to command and where the 'will to win' failed in the face of unrelenting Turkish *Mauser* and *Maxim* fire.

A Japanese perspective is, perhaps, instructive – and salutary. In his account of his time in public life, the Foreign Secretary, Lord Grey of Fallodon, recounts an anecdote about a Japanese visiting Britain after the Manchurian War:

"… finding himself and his nation to be objects of admiration, (he) reflected thus upon the course of events: 'Yes', he said, 'we used to be a nation of artists; our art was really very good; you called us barbarians then. Now our art is not so good as it was but we have learnt how to kill, and you say we are civilised'."[180]

Matters were no different in France. The realisation they could not compete with Germany's larger population and higher birth rate led officers to persuade themselves a French soldier's superior morale and fighting spirit would more than compensate. Officer after officer came forward to proclaim their belief in, indeed the necessity of, this self-evident 'truth'. Increased firepower demanded greater patriotism and higher morale if the storm of shot and shell was to be overcome during the assault. Gen. Bazaine-Hayter[i], whose career climaxed with command of *13e* and *4e Corps* (1906 and 1908) when aged 62 to 65, was an influential 'morale' man who believed 'Firepower does not weaken the offensive spirit'.[181]

Langlois (see page 349) suggested history showed the more powerful the weapon, the greater the advantage to the attacker (unless, of course, you were a Frenchman subject to the rapid fire of English and Welsh longbows at Crecy, Poitiers or Agincourt). This became as clear to French officers in Manchuria as it did to Hamilton. There, to their minds, exceptional Japanese morale overcame superior Russian armaments. This thinking allowed French officers to persuade themselves superior morale and offensive spirit would always overcome 'numbers' and 'miraculous machines' as Adolphe Messimy, the ex-infantry officer and twice *Ministre de la Guerre*, stated in 1908[ii].[182] Langlois did admit, however, that even when a position was taken at the point of the bayonet, the attackers would need to 'go to ground' if they were to hold the newly won position in the face of the 'deadly effects of the rapid-loading rifle, which are uncontestable'.[183]

The consequence of this was that many of the key senior officers in both Armies were wedded to the idea the solution to the fire-swept zone lay in elevating troop morale and to imbuing men with an 'offensive spirit' which would keep them pushing forward irrespective of the holes being blown in their ranks. 'Offensive spirit'[iii], or its lack, would become a key indicator of a General's or a unit's abilities and prowess. A perceived lack of such spirit could prove costly to both a commanding officer and his men, as Maj. Gen. Montagu Stuart Wortley, the GOC of 46th (North Midland) Division, found when summarily sacked by Haig for his division's 'lack of offensive spirit' during the 1st July fiasco at Gommecourt to which, in no small measure, Haig contributed.

Higher morale, rather than something bullet proof, was the solution to the problem, the lesson 'learnt' from the past and the Japanese in Manchuria. But the lessons about the nature of the *actual* battlefield appear to have passed them by. Even men close to the pinnacle of their military careers seemed unable to grasp the significance of what Bloch suggested or what happened in war after war since.

---

[i] Gen. George Albert Bazaine-Hayter, nephew of Marshal François Bazaine.
[ii] *Ministre de la Guerre* in the governments of Joseph Caillaux (27th June 1911-14th January 1912) and René Viviani (13th June 1914 to 26th August 1914). He re-joined the Army in December 1914, commanding the *162e Division* at the end of the war.
[iii] A phrase used in Maj. Gen. Edward Altham's 1914 book *The Principles of War*. An an intelligence officer, he spent WW1 in a series of staff jobs, mainly in the Middle East.

Field Marshal Viscount French, 1st Earl of Ypres, is not now regarded as the 'sharpest tool in the military box' available to the Army in 1914 (who was?). He was, however, successful in South Africa, a member of the *Committee of Imperial Defence* for many years, been appointed the Inspector-General of the Army in 1907 and Chief of the Imperial General Staff in 1912. French was, therefore, sufficiently highly regarded within Whitehall and Westminster to be appointed the Commander in Chief of the British Expeditionary Force on the outbreak of war. Here was a man who, on being appointed CIGS, determined to prepare the Army for a continental war. As he wrote later:

"For years past I had regarded a general war in Europe as an eventual certainty."[184]

Having overseen the chaotic retreat from Mons and the advance to the *Aisne* after the German defeat on the *Marne* it was, according to the British *Official History*, French's order of 16th September 1914 for the British to dig-in in front of the Chemin des Dames north of the *Aisne* which represented 'the official notification of the commencement of trench warfare'.[185]

Although without staff training, French was an experienced if flawed senior officer sensible to the mood of Europe's political and military leaders. Sir John Denton Pinkstone[i] French, however, came from a naval background. His father, Commander John Tracy William French, RN, fought in the last great naval battle under sail, Navarino (1827), but, when John French was born on 28th September 1852, his father was retired, serving as a JP and as the Deputy Lieutenant of Kent.

The younger French was named after his grandfather, inheriting all three forenames[ii]. Although born and living in Kent, French junior always clung to some distant Irish connections even though the family had lived at Ripple Vale House[iii] in the village of Ripple near Deal in Kent since the time of his great-grandfather, Fleming French in the second half of the eighteenth century[iv]. Prior to that, the family-owned extensive lands in Roscommon and Sligo in western Ireland which were gained when an ancestor, John *'Tierna More'* French[v], fought on the side of William of Orange at the exceptionally bloody but decisive Battle of Aughrim in 1691, commanding a troop of Enniskillen Dragoons. He went on to purchase lands previously owned by catholic supporters of James II and forfeited to the Crown after the so-called 'Glorious Revolution'.

---

[i] Derived from the earlier family name of Pinkstan. French's great-great grandfather, John French of High Lake, Co. Roscommon, married Eleanora Pinkstan, daughter of Col. Fleming Pinkstan.

[ii] The family was not especially imaginative when it came to Christian names. The Field Marshal's first son was named John (Richard Lowndes). His father, grandfather, great-great grandfather, g-g-g-grandfather and g-g-g-g-grandfather were all named John. The exception was his great grandfather Fleming French.

[iii] Since 1970 Ripplevale School which was, initially, a residential 'approved' school for boys. It is now a school for those with special educational needs.

[iv] He inherited the house on the death of his second wife whose father was Edward Pakenham of Ripple Vale.

[v] *'Tierna More'* – the great landowner.

The older John French died in 1855 and his wife, Margaret Eccles of Glasgow, deeply affected by her husband's death, was eventually confined to an insane asylum where she died in 1867. This left French in the care of his six older sisters[i] who, in 1866, agreed he should follow his father into the Royal Navy. In August of that year, the young John French joined as a cadet aboard the decommissioned 120-gun first rate ship of the line *HMS Britannia*, since 1863 a training ship at Dartmouth. His early reports were not especially favourable and he was sent for a further six-months' training aboard the modern (launched 1861, commissioned 1865) wooden screw frigate *HMS Bristol*. Now a midshipman, he transferred to *HMS Warrior*, the first armour-plated, iron-hulled warship. A cruise in the English Channel and down to the Iberian Peninsula (where he took the opportunity of visiting several of Wellington's battlefields) convinced French that he was no sailor as he suffered both from severe seasickness and a fear of not very great heights (acrophobia) which, given that *Warrior* had three tall masts despite being mainly steam-driven, was a significant disadvantage.

He resigned from the Navy in November 1870 and took a commission in the Suffolk Artillery Militia. From there and having by-passed the need to attend either Sandhurst or Woolwich, he joined the 8th (The King's Royal Irish) Hussars as a lieutenant on 28th February 1874 but, within the month, he transferred to the rather less glamorous and less expensive 19th Hussars. This regiment spent four years in Ireland, in 1880 being embroiled in the Capt. Boycott affair[ii] near Loch

---

[i] Charlotte Despard, Mary Lydall, Caroline French, Margaret Jones, Kate French, and Nellie French. Lest one should imagine that John was the brains of the family, his older sister Charlotte (1844-1939) took a path diametrically opposed to that of her little brother. She was in Paris during the Franco-Prussian War, marrying businessman Maximilian Carden Despard who had interests in India and Asia. He died at sea in 1890 and she devoted her life to increasingly left-wing causes, using her late husband's money to help the working poor in Battersea where she was a *Poor Law Guardian* in 1894. A friend of Karl Marx's youngest daughter, Eleanor, she was a delegate to the *Second International*, supported the *Social Democratic Federation* and the *Independent Labour Party*, opposed the Boer War, was prominent in the *Women's Social and Political Union* and helped found the *Women's Freedom League*. She was imprisoned four times for her activities for women's suffrage. She opposed WWI and conscription, founding the *Women's Peace Crusade* in 1916. She stood for the Labour Party in Battersea North in the 1918 General Election, losing to a Coalition Liberal with 33% of the votes. With her Irish connections she was a supporter of *Sinn Féin*, formed the *Women's Prisoners' Defence League* and was regarded as a radical subversive under the terms of the *1927 Public Safety Act* passed by the Irish Free State. She founded a hospital and school for refugees, was a vegetarian and anti-vivisectionist, supported *Save the Children* and, having met Ghandi, Indian independence. She joined the *Communist Party of Great Britain* and gave anti-Fascist speeches in Trafalgar Square. She died on 10th November 1939 after a fall at her home *Nead-na-Gaoithe*, Whitehead in County Antrim, and is buried in the Republican Plot at Glasnevin Cemetery in Dublin. She sounds like a tremendous lady.

[ii] Charles Boycott was the land agent of John Crichton, 3rd Earl Erne, who tried to evict tenant farmers who refused to pay their rent because of a poor harvest. The estate

Measca[i] which straddles Co. Galway and Co. Mayo (about 90 kms south-west of the historic French family lands around Frenchpark and Carrowduff). In 1881 French was appointed adjutant of the Northumberland (Hussars) Yeomanry Cavalry which role prevented him from accompanying the 19th Hussars to Egypt where they fought at the Battle of Tel el-Kebir in September 1882. He eventually joined them there in 1884 and took part in the failed operation to relieve Gordon in Khartoum.

During this period, French displayed his propensity for two recurring 'loves' in his life: for women, even if married, and of spending money he did not have.

In 1875, aged 23, he married Isabella Soundy even though young officers at the start of their careers were not expected to marry and, in some quarters, a commanding officer's permission was needed. They were soon divorced on the grounds of adultery, with Isabella, it seems, prepared to accept a generous financial settlement from French's brother-in-law, John Lydall, in return for which she was named the co-respondent, i.e. the guilty party. This was not the first time Lydall bailed out French financially but a third approach by the over-stretched French effectively sealed the parting of their ways. Unabashed, French married again in 1880. The spouse on this occasion was Eleanora Selby-Lowndes, one of seven daughters of a wealthy Buckinghamshire landowner. Though this marriage lasted to his death in 1925, French was known to have had multiple affairs including one in India, where he was cited in the divorce case of a brother officer, and another being with a diplomat's wife, Mrs Winifred Bennett, with whom French carried on from 1914 through to his time as Lord Lieutenant of Ireland.

Money was also perennial problem. Having been bailed out of his first and unwise marriage by his brother-in-law, he was severely reduced in his circumstances when placed on half-pay in 1893 (possibly because of the Indian scandal). He was, according to some, unable to afford horses, a bit of drawback for a cavalry officer.[186] In 1899, hours from bankruptcy (and, therefore, resignation from the Army), French was bailed out by a substantial loan, this time from a canny Scottish officer, Douglas Haig, who had the terms set out in writing and an interest rate agreed. The figure borrowed was £2,500 (anything upwards of £276,000 in today's values depending on the measure used). It is not clear if the money was repaid[ii] but it proved a useful long-term investment by French's junior.

Despite his indiscretions and intemperate spending, French was fortunate with his connections. Amongst them were the aptly named Gen. Sir George Luck, Inspector General of Cavalry in both India and at home, Redvers Buller, Adjutant General to the Forces and the first commander in South Africa in 1899, and Gen.

---

staff were persuaded to leave by members of the Nationalist catholic *Land League* and every shop and local supplier refused to deal with Boycott. He now lends his name to the organised blocking of trade, commerce, etc., with an individual, organisation, or community with the intention of bringing pressure to bear for changes in behaviour.
[i] Lough Mask.
[ii] Richard Holmes says 'no', Walter Reid says 'yes' in 1909 [*Sources*: Holmes, R, *The Little Field Marshal: A Life of Sir John French*, Weidenfeld & Nicolson, 2004, pages 50-52, Reid, W. *Architect of Victory: Douglas Haig*, 2006, page 91]

Sir Evelyn Wood, QMG and Adjutant General to the Forces and GOCinC Southern Command, to name but three. All helped to smooth his path to higher office (and, perhaps, to conceal some of the blemishes on his record).

French's name and reputation, warranted or not, was made in South Africa and firmly established by a glamorous, if temporary, tactical victory at Elandslaagte on 21st October 1899. Enjoying a numerical advantage of 3.5:1 against an isolated Boer commando, French was able to reap the benefits of the hard fighting of Ian Hamilton's infantry who dislodged the enemy from their hilltop position. This allowed squadrons of the 5th (Royal Irish) Lancers and 5th Dragoon Guards to get amongst the fleeing irregulars[i]. In overall command at Elandslaagte, French's victory was greeted as a golden shaft of sunlight breaching the generally Stygian gloom which descended upon Great Britain as the opening months of the war rapidly descended into chaos and farce. The success was enjoyed but briefly as, retreating before the advancing Boers, French's men and other units were forced into Ladysmith to be besieged for 118 days before being relieved on 28th February 1900. French and Haig, however, escaped on the last train out of the town, joining the newly arrived Redvers Buller at Capetown on 8th November. French was given command of the Cavalry Division, promoted a local Lt. Gen., and performed with some success in blocking further Boer advances during the winter of 1899-1900.

In early February, French was ordered by the newly arrived Kitchener to relieve Kimberley 'at all costs'. Employing a forced, flanking march to cross the *Modder River* (during which 1 in 10 of his horses either died or were rendered unfit for further work) French achieved another glamorous victory at Klip Drift on 15th February 1900 when, in a South African (but rather more successful) version of the Charge of the Light Brigade, the 9th (The Queen's Royal) and 16th (The Queen's) Lancers galloped up a valley overlooked on either side by Boer-held ridges. Covered by the fire of 56 artillery pieces and resulting in the 'sticking' of just 20 Boers, it was hardly 'the most brilliant stroke of the war', as it was so described by the *Official History* of the War in South Africa. It did, however, clear the way for his arrival in Kimberley later that evening. Her Majesty the Queen and the new commander in South Africa, Lord Roberts, both sent congratulations.

The honeymoon with Roberts was short-lived as French displayed another worrying trait: the ability to fall out with brother officers over perceived slights. A shortage of horses and insufficient fodder weakened French's cavalry and for this he was unfairly criticised by Roberts. A sense of grievance set in, exacerbated by some of the orders given by the less-than exceptionally tactically gifted CinC. Criticism of his superior crept into French's correspondence and arguments erupted with officers from the infantry and mounted infantry. Whilst no-one doubted his personal bravery and his tactical acumen as a cavalry officer in the wide-open spaces of the *veldt,* this tendency to harbour grudges against fellow officers was a recurring and sometimes costly theme: Roberts, Kitchener, Smith-Dorrien and finally Haig all loomed large on French's list of people who, in his mind, had, in some way or another, belittled or undermined his standing.

As the war in South Africa descended into guerrilla warfare French was given

---

[i] Circa sixty became casualties.

command first of the Johannesburg sector and then Cape Colony. He was successful in rounding up Boer combatants who he was ordered to treat with 'severity', an order he followed with, perhaps, too much rigour. Now, however, he fell out with Kitchener, in command after Roberts returned to London after the fall of the Boer capital. Despite this, his star was in the ascendant and Roberts, now the CinC Forces in Whitehall, requested French put together a committee to report on cavalry tactics and equipment and then, on 23rd October 1901 and with the war still dragging on, he was appointed GOC, I Corps, Aldershot Command. Awarded variously the KCB, KCMG and Honorary Oxbridge degrees and confirmed Lt. Gen. he took command at Aldershot on 15th September 1902. In the public's mind, he was now the pre-eminent soldier in the land after Roberts and Kitchener, a remarkable achievement for a man who, three years earlier, was barely a day from bankruptcy and professional ruin.

French's rise was only temporarily set back by the King's decision to veto his elevation to the newly created position of Chief of Staff (the CinC role having been abolished). Edward VII believed French too young (Gen. Sir Neville Gerald Lyttelton, nine years French's senior, was appointed). A mix of moderniser, endorsing the adoption of field howitzers as well as the new 18-pdr., and traditionalist, favouring the retention of the lance and sword, French also fostered diverse strategic concepts: deployments to support the French or at Antwerp; amphibious landings in the Baltic; and moves towards the Dardanelles. Such ideas became even more relevant in the late summer of 1906 when it was confirmed he would command the expeditionary force in the event of a continental war.

Lord Esher took an especial shine to French[i] (referring to him simply as 'The General' in his letters) whilst he commanded at Aldershot, describing him in a letter to Haig on 7th October 1904 as having 'the broadest mind', of displaying 'elasticity and progress' in ideas, and of having 'a high imagination'.[187] A month later, he described him to Balfour as:

"... the best soldier we have got. More 'character' and imagination than any other I have met, although a man recently educated and developed late in life."[188]

On the other hand, his belief that French was '... the best soldier we have got' was sharply put into perspective with the *caveat* previously expressed to Francis Knollys, Private Secretary to Edward VII, that:

"I daresay that he is not the cleverest man, but he is the most successful soldier we could find."[189]

In 1907, French was appointed Inspector-General of the Army and, in 1912, Chief of the Imperial General Staff. His time as CIGS ended abruptly when, naively, he became involved in the Curragh Incident when he co-signed an undertaking that the Army would not be employed to coerce Ulster Protestants into some sort of united Ireland. This declaration was immediately repudiated by

---

[i] But then French did appoint Esher's son, Maurice Vyner Baliol Brett, Coldstream Guards and later 6th Perthshire Battalion, The Black Watch (Royal Highlanders), as his ADC in 1904 in which role he served for eight years.

the Cabinet and the three signatories: Secretary of State for War John Seely, French and the Adjutant General, Sir John Spencer Ewart, were all required to resign on 30th March 1914. Though this seemed at the time a terminal moment in French's career it proved far from it. Within three months he was re-appointed Inspector General of the Forces (26th July) and four days later, as Europe spun headlong into all-out war, he was told he would, after all, command the Expeditionary Force being prepared for Britain's first continental war in nearly 100 years.

He was, however, the wrong man in the wrong job in August 1914 with no sense of the way in which modern armaments might change the face of warfare:

"No previous experience, no conclusion I had been able to draw from campaigns in which I had taken part, or from a close study of the new conditions in which the war of today is waged, had led me to anticipate a war of position. All my thoughts, all my prospective plans, all my possible alternatives of action, were concentrated upon a war of movement and manoeuvre. I knew perfectly well that modern up-to-date inventions would materially influence and modify our previous conceptions as to the employment of the three arms respectively; but I had not realised that this process would work in so drastic a manner as to render all our preconceived ideas of the method of tactical field operations comparatively ineffective and useless. Judged by the course of events in the first three weeks of the war, neither French nor German generals were prepared for the complete transformation of all military ideas which the development of the operations inevitably demonstrated to be imperative for waging war in present conditions.

It is easy to be 'wise after the event'; but I cannot help wondering why none of us realised what the most modern rifle, the machine gun, motor traction, the aeroplane, and wireless telegraphy would bring about. It seems so simple when judged by actual results. The modern rifle and machine gun add tenfold to the relative power of the defence as against the attack. This precludes the use of old methods of attack, and has driven the attack to seek covered entrenchments after every forward rush of at most a few hundred yards."[190]

An elderly Jewish railway man from Russia could not have put it better. Except, that is, for the part about it being 'easy to be wise after the event'. Bloch would not have found such a *caveat* necessary. After all, he and a few others foresaw these developments fifteen years earlier and more. Blinkered, conservative military minds everywhere simply failed to keep up.

To be fair to French, no other British General (perhaps with the exception of Smith-Dorrien) had the prescience to appreciate the changes new technology would bring to the battlefield, and this in spite of the nine month siege of Petersburg in 1864-5 during the American Civil War; the siege of Plevna in the Russo-Turkish War of 1877-8; the extended position warfare along the *Sha Ho River*, and at Port Arthur and Mukden during the Russo-Japanese War of 1904-5; and the defeat of the previously all-conquering Bulgarian Armies in front of the Çatalca lines during the 1st Balkan War of 1912-3.

It is not possible to suggest his successor, Douglas Haig (or any other General) had any better idea as to the way the wind was blowing in modern warfare. Haig was, after all, the main author of the 1909 edition of *Field Service Regulations* (*FSR*), the officer's 'bible' which advised on the way war was to be conducted. Large sections of *FSR*, especially those in Chapter VII *The Battle*, read as though Haig and his assistants were seeking a long-term retirement home for any number of elderly and redundant platitudes. Alternatively, it might simply have been translated from some of the awful French regulations which underpinned their disastrous performance in the early weeks of the war.

Haig's 'advice' starts badly and gets steadily worse:

"Decisive success in battle can be gained only by a vigorous offensive. Every commander who offers battle, therefore, must be determined to assume the offensive sooner or later… Superior numbers on the battlefield are an undoubted advantage, but skill, better organisation and training, and above all, a firmer determination in all ranks to conquer at any cost, are the chief factors of success."[191]

Any hope *FSR* might explain how troops were to get across the 'fire swept zone' is reduced to the statement previously undermined by McMahon:

"The climax of the infantry attack is the assault, which is made possible by superiority of fire."[192]

And that, broadly, was that. Perhaps one should not be surprised at this lack of useful and usable information and explanation, after all, *FSR* more or less opened with the statement that 'The fundamental principles of war are neither very numerous nor in themselves very abstruse' without then going on to set out what these limited and simple principles actually were.[193]

The intellectual void at the heart of the British Army was, indeed, a yawning chasm. Perhaps it was ever thus in all armies. There is an amusing, if apocryphal, story told by J F C Fuller as a preface to his book *Generalship: Its Diseases and Their Cure, A Study of the Personal Factor in Command*.[194] It reads:

"In the summer of 1921 I was lunching at the *Restaurant la Rue*[i] with the Deputy Chief of the French General Staff when he told me the following story:

At the Battle of Waterloo, Colonel Clement, an infantry commander, fought with the most conspicuous bravery; but unfortunately was shot through the head. Napoleon, hearing of his gallantry and misfortune, gave instructions for him to be carried into a farm where Larrey the surgeon-general was operating.

One glance convinced Larrey that his case was desperate so, taking up a saw, he removed the top of his skull and placed his brains on the table.

Just as he had finished, in rushed an *aide-de-camp* shouting: 'Is General Clement here?'

Clement, hearing him, sat up and exclaimed: 'No! But *Colonel* Clement is.'

---

[i] The *Restaurant Larue* in *place de la Madeleine*, owned by Édouard Nignon, one of France's leading chefs and writers. He was previously in charge of the restaurant at Claridge's.

'Oh, *mon général*,' cried the *aide-de-camp*, embracing him, 'the Emperor was overwhelmed when we heard of your gallantry, and has promoted you on the field of battle to the rank of General.'
Clement rubbed his eyes, got off the table, clapped the top of his skull on his head and was about to leave the farm when Larrey shouted after him: '*Mon général* – your brains!' To which the gallant Frenchman, increasing his speed, shouted back: 'Now that I am a General I shall no longer need them!'"[i]

Perhaps more directly pertinent is Fuller's complaint about the impact such an absence of critical and creative thinking had on the tactics employed in the war. If the only solution to increased firepower was an increase in morale and discipline and an acceptance of mass casualties then, by definition, to suffer such casualties one needed to employ an ever-increasing mass of men. As Bloch wrote back in 1899 'Armies of today are not composed of gallant, jovial cavaliers, but of entire peoples…'.[195] The result for Britain was the creation of the largest citizen Army this country has ever seen – and its longest ever casualty list. Indeed, the answer to all military questions became more. More men, more guns, more ammunition – more casualties. Fuller believed this had a deadening, stultifying effect on tactics:

"… when the World War broke out so intellectually unprepared were our higher commanders that they were at once sucked into the vortex of impersonal command which had been rotting generalship on the continent for forty years.

The horde army paralysed generalship, not so much because it changed tactics but because it prevented tactics changing; the one idea being, not to improve the quality of fighting, but to add to the quantity of fighters. New weapons were introduced yearly; but in its essentials the old tactics remained the same, numbers being considered the primary factor, with the result that directly a war was declared, tactics broke down and generalship became ineffective. But more detrimental still, numbers added vastly to the administrative difficulties, that is the handling of the rear services; so much so, that generalship was absorbed into quartermaster generalship, until in the World War all commanders superior to a divisional general were nothing more than commissary generals."[196]

Thus, battles during the middle part of the war 'degenerated into subaltern-led conflicts, just as manufacturing had degenerated into foreman-controlled work.'[197] The consequence was affairs like Passchendaele, 'the most soulless battle fought in the annals of the British Army'.[198] This was the path down which the military wing of conservative thinking in Victorian and Edwardian England led the country. A path characterised by a lack of imagination and creative thought and dominated by the concepts of class in which a narrowly defined 'gentleman' was the natural leader and everyone else was born to follow. And where 'character' and

---

[i] To be fair, Fuller completes the amusing anecdote with the words: 'In this modest study my object is to prove that, though Clement was wrong about his brains, without his courage there can be no true generalship'.

physical prowess were more important than education and intelligence. A mindset which allowed Lt. Col. Arthur Mordaunt Murray, the Assistant Commandant at Woolwich and, therefore, a senior officer involved in the training of young officers, to state to the Akers-Douglas committee in 1902 whilst explaining why science should not be taught to budding gunners and engineers:

> "We would rather have a classically educated boy than one who has very much given up his mind to electricity and physics and those kind of subjects. Power of command and good habits of leadership are not learned in the laboratory. Our great point is character; we care more about that than subjects."[199]

Such a view was again expressed in a House of Commons debate on the Army Estimates for 1903-4 held on 9th March 1903. The proponent was one Col. Thomas Myles Sandys, the Conservative MP for Bootle and the honorary colonel of the 1st Volunteer Battalion of the Loyal North Lancashire Regt. Sandys was a veteran of the Indian Mutiny, an MP since 1885 and the Grand Master of the Orange Lodge of England. He was a man who looked for brawn rather than brain in an aspiring officer. In response to a thoughtful and brief contribution from the soon-to-be Secretary of State for War, Richard Haldane, Sandys remarked:

> "… in their worship of mind for the officers they must not lose sight of the importance of muscle. An efficient officer required, first and foremost, to be strong; secondly to have fair average intelligence and education, and, thirdly, to be a gentleman."[200]

Sadly, Sandys seemed to suggest, there were officers who displayed too much of the second attribute and not enough of the third kind, all to the displeasure of his mess room colleagues who had 'no means of getting rid of him'. This damning view that officers need not be *too* clever was reinforced by another, even older, retired Colonel, Henry Blundell-Hollinshead Blundell, late of the Grenadier Guards and, since 1885, Tory MP for the Lancashire constituency of Ince[i]. Blundell had no time for the concept that educated, university types might make good officers. They would not, he opined, accept the necessary discipline. Nor did he believe in a 'long preparation' for the budding subaltern. 'Throw him in the deep end and let him sink or swim' seemed to be the Colonel's view. And, perhaps, a lack of any heavy grey matter in the skull might help the youngster float rather more easily.

---

[i] He lost his seat handsomely to a Labour candidate in 1906 who beat him with a 40% majority. Blundell died eight months later, aged 75.

ENDNOTES:
[1] Brett, M V, ed., *Journals and Letters of Reginald Viscount Esher*, Vol. II, 1903-10, 1934, page 183.
[2] See Spiers, op. cit., pages 47-8.
[3] Palazzo, A., *From Moltke to Bin Laden: The relevance of doctrine in the contemporary military environment*, Land Warfare Studies Centre, Canberra, 2008, page 20.
[4] *The Times, The Royal Commission on the War in South Africa*, 26th August 1903, page 4 onwards.
[5] Ibid.
[6] Brett, op. cit., page 353.
[7] Maude, Col. F N, *War and the World's Life*, Smith, Elder & Co., 1907, page 171.
[8] Ibid., page 172.
[9] Edmonds J E, unpublished *Reminiscences*, Chapter XIV, *The Staff College 1896-7* quoted in Bond, op. cit.
[10] Spiers, op. cit. page 110.
[11] Samuels, M, *Command or Control? Command, Training and Tactics in the British and German, 1888-1918*, Frank Cass, 1995, page 23.
[12] Cairnes, Capt. W E, *An Absent-Minded War*, John Milne, 1900, page 46.
[13] Bond, B, *The Victorian Army and the Staff College, 1854-1914*, Eyre Methuen, 1972, page 18.
[14] Battine, C W, *The Proposed Changes in Cavalry Tactics*, Journal of the Royal United Service Institution, Vol. 54, No. 393, November 1910, p. 1433.
[15] Robbins, S, *British Generalship on the Western Front 1914-18*, Frank Cass, 2005, pages 35-8.
[16] Ibid., page 38.
[17] Bowman T, & Connelly M, *The Edwardian Army*, OUP, 2012, page 33.
[18] Steele, D, *Salisbury and the Soldiers*, in Gooch, J, *The Boer War: Direction, Experience and Image*, Cass, 2000, page 4.
[19] Dunlop, op. cit., page 89.
[20] Ibid, page 47
[21] Ibid., page 46.
[22] *Hart's Army List 1905*, page xi.
[23] Dunlop, op. cit., page 56.
[24] Ibid. The full memorandum is printed in Dunlop, page 307.
[25] Spiers, op. cit., page 61.
[26] Parliamentary Papers, vol. 10, 1902, *Report of the Committee Appointed to Consider the Education and Training of Officers of the Army*. Command Paper no. 983. p. 101, quoted in Travers, T H, *Technology, Tactics, and Morale: Jean de Bloch, the Boer War, and British Military Theory, 1900-1914*, a paper given at the Institute of Historical Research, London, May 1976.
[27] *The Spectator*, 29th August 1903, page 20.
[28] Quoted in Jones, S, *From Boer War to World War*, University of Oklahoma Press, 2012, pages 51-2.
[29] *The Times, Our Military Correspondent: The Staff College*, 29th December 1894, page 14.
[30] Henderson, G F R, *The Science of War*, Longman, Greens & Co., 1905, page xxiv.
[31] Ibid., page 108 onwards.
[32] Ibid., page 152.
[33] Ibid.
[34] Ibid., page 153.
[35] Ibid., page 344.
[36] Ibid., page 348.
[37] Ibid., page 349.
[38] Ibid., page 355.
[39] Ibid.
[40] Ibid., page 357.
[41] Ibid., page 358.

⁴² Transcript of a lecture by Capt. T Pilcher given at the Royal Artillery Institute in March 1896 re-printed in the *Journal of the US Military Institute*, 1897, page 143.
⁴³ Ibid., page 372.
⁴⁴ Ibid., page 375.
⁴⁵ Ibid.
⁴⁶ Ibid., pages 410-1.
⁴⁷ *Combined Training Manual 1905* quoted in Samuels, M, *Command or Control?*, page 98.
⁴⁸ Henderson, Col. G F R, *The Science of War*, 1905, page 375.
⁴⁹ Ibid., page 159-60.
⁵⁰ Ibid., page 371-2.
⁵¹ Brett, M V, op. cit., page 112.
⁵² *Report on Conference of General Staff Officers, 12th-15th January 1914*, pages 7-8.
⁵³ James, Capt. W H, RE, *Modern Weapons and Their Influence on Tactics and Organisation*, Journal of the Royal United Service Institute, Issue 43/2 (1899), p. 1289–1305.
⁵⁴ Sankey, Capt. C E P, *The Campaign of the Future: A Possible Development*, Royal Engineers' Journal, No. 5, 1907, pages 4-6.
⁵⁵ Baden-Powell, Maj, B F S, *War in Practice*, Isbister & Co., 1903, page 42.
⁵⁶ Ibid.
⁵⁷ Ibid., page 43.
⁵⁸ Ibid., page 44.
⁵⁹ Ibid., pages 187 and 253.
⁶⁰ *Conference of General Staff Officers at the Staff College, Camberley, 18th to 21st January 1908*, pages 9-12.
⁶¹ Ibid., page 68.
⁶² Demaison, G, & Buffetaut, Y, *Honour Bound: Chauchat Machine Rifle*, Collector Grade Publications, Canada, 1995, page 13.
⁶³ *The Times, Naval and Military Intelligence*, 19th December 1907, page 10.
⁶⁴ *The Times, Company Training*, 10th May 1911, page 6.
⁶⁵ The sources of the majority of this material are: *https://www.slideshare.net/tcattermole/early-british-automatic-rifle-trials-a-lecture-to-the-hbsa-of-gb* and *https://www.forgottenweapons.com*.
⁶⁶ *Report of a Conference of General Staff Officers at the Staff College, 17th to 20th January 1910*, HMSO, London, 1910, page 28.
⁶⁷ Ibid.
⁶⁸ MacDonald, A, *Pro Patria Mori*, Iona Books, 2010, page 301.
⁶⁹ *Field Service Regulations 1909 updated 1912*, HMSO, page 20.
⁷⁰ Ibid., page 136.
⁷¹ Ibid., page 147.
⁷² Ibid., page 126.
⁷³ *Royal Commission on the War in South Africa*, pages 107-9.
⁷⁴ *The Times, Shooting in the Infantry*, 21st April 1881, page 4.
⁷⁵ Ibid.
⁷⁶ Ibid.
⁷⁷ Ibid.
⁷⁸ *The Times, Infantry and the Spade*, 7th June 1881, page 10
⁷⁹ Gaston, Capt. J-J, *Manuel d'escrime à la baïonnette: description du fusil d'assaut pour l'étude précise du double jeu et du corps à corps, méthode d'enseignement*, Berger-Levrault, 1920, page V.
⁸⁰ Fuller, J F C, *Decisive Battles of the Western World*, Vol. I, Cassell & Co., 1955.
⁸¹ *The Russo-Japanese War: Reports from British Officers Attached to the Japanese and Russian Armies in the Field*, Volume III, HMSO, 1908, page 202.
⁸² Ibid., page 209.
⁸³ Ibid., page 220.
⁸⁴ Ibid.
⁸⁵ Maude, Lt. Col. F N, *War and the World's Life*, 1907, page 252.
⁸⁶ Jones, S, *From Boer War to World War*, Oklahoma University Press, 2012, page 85.

[87] Ibid., pages 86-7.
[88] Bruno, Maj. T, USMC, *Ignoring the Obvious: Combined Arms and Fire and Maneuver Tactics Prior to World War I*, United States Marine Corps, Command And Staff College, Marine Corps University, 2002, page 21 onwards.
[89] Knox, Maj. Gen. Sir W G, *The Flaw in Our Armour*, 1914, page 31.
[90] Creveld, M van, *Command in War*, Cambridge: Harvard University Press, 1985, page 96.
[91] *Napoléon Ier le magazine du Consulat et de l'Empire*, N° 35, page 15.
[92] Napoleon, *Observations on Spanish Affairs* written on 27th August, 1808.
[93] D'Aubert, Capt., *Offensive brutale. Attaque parallèle*, Revue militaire générale, December 1912, page 808.
[94] Lacroix, Gen. introduction to Lt. H P, *L'esprit de sacrifice*, Revue militaire générale, June 1913, page 737.
[95] *Exerzier-Reglement für die Infanterie 1906*, para 265, quoted in Samuels, M, *Command or Control?* page 76.
[96] Ibid.
[97] Balck, W, *Entwickelung der Taktik im Weltkriege [Development of Tactics in the World War]*, R. Eisenschmidt, 1922, page 33.
[98] Terraine J, *Douglas Haig: The Educated Soldier*, Leo Cooper, 1990, page 176.
[99] Fuller, Maj. Gen. J F C, *Memoirs of an Uncoventional Soldier*, 1936, pages 140-2.
[100] Terraine, op. cit., page 176.
[101] *NA*, WO 27/504, *Memorandum on Military Training, 1905, Aldershot Command*.
[102] Eddy, C B, *Moveable steel mantlet for the protection of artillery and troops*, RUSI Journal, Vol.13, No. LV, 1869, pages 325-336.
[103] Ibid.
[104] Bailey, Maj. J B A, *Field Artillery and Firepower*, The Military Press, Oxford, 1989, page 117 onwards.
[105] Bethell, Brig. Gen. H A B, *Modern guns and gunnery, 1910*, F J Cattermole, 1910, page 171.
[106] Farndale, Gen. Sir M, *History of the Royal Regiment f Artillery, Western Front 1914-1918*, Royal Artillery Institution, 1986, page 22.
[107] Bethell, op. cit., page 246.
[108] Ibid., page 169.
[109] See Bowman and Connelly, op. cit., page 79-81.
[110] *Journal of the Royal Artillery Institute*, No. 6, Vol. XXIII, June 1896.
[111] Ibid, Vol. XXIV, page 47.
[112] Bowman and Connelly, op. cit., page 79.
[113] Ibid., page 57.
[114] *Report on the Conference of General Staff Officers*, 9th-12th January 1911, page 65.
[115] Ibid., page 60.
[116] Ibid., page 65.
[117] Ibid., page 66-7.
[118] Ibid., page 72.
[119] Ibid., page 73.
[120] Ibid., page 74.
[121] Ibid.
[122] Ibid., page 82.
[123] *NA*, WO279/53, *Aldershot Command, Comments on the Training Season, 1913*, page 6.
[124] *Report on the Conference of General Staff Officers, 7th-10th January 1908*, page 44.
[125] For a fuller account of this debate see Bowman and Connelly, op. cit., pages 84-5.
[126] *Journal of the United Service Institution of India, The Employment of Heavy Artillery in the Field*, Vol XL, No. 182, January 1911, page 846.
[127] Ibid., page 448.
[128] *Conference of General Staff Officers 1911*, page 11.
[129] *Infantry Training, 4 Company Orgnization*, HMSO, 1914.
[130] Smith-Dorrien, H L, *Memories*, page 80.

[131] Ibid., page 338.
[132] Seim, R, *Forging the Rapier among Scythes: Lt. Gen. Sir Horace Smith-Dorrien and the Aldershot Command 1907-12*, unpublished MA Thesis, Rice University, Texas, 1980, pages 33-4.
[133] Smith-Dorrien, Sir H L, *Memories of Forty-Eight years' Service*, J Murray, 1925, page 356
[134] *The Times, Naval and Military Intelligence*, 1st September 1908, page 5.
[135] *The Times, Naval and Military Intelligence.*, 25th August 1910, page 5.
[136] *Report of a conference of Staff Officers at the Royal Military College*, 12th-15th January 1914, HMSO, pages 73-8-
[137] Henderson, *The Science of War*, page 372 & *The Times*, 10th September 1901, page 10.
[138] From a House of Commons speech on the Army Estimates made by Lord Stanley, MP for Westhoughton, quoted in *The Times*, 31st March 1903, page 6.
[139] Brett, op. cit., page 391.
[140] Quoted in Anglesey, Marquis of, *A History of the British Cavalry, Vol. 4, 1899-1913*, Pen & Sword, page 394.
[141] *The Times*, 3rd April 1903, page 5.
[142] Ibid., 15th April, page 9.
[143] Ibid., 23rd April 1903, page 10.
[144] Ibid., 4th May 1903, page 12.
[145] Badsey, S, *Doctrine and Reform in the British Cavalry 1880-1918*, Ashgate, 2008, page 172.
[146] Barnett, Correlli, *Britain and her Army 1509-1970*, 1970, page 368, quoted in Anglesey, op. cit., page 405.
[147] Seki, Captain T, *'The value of the Arme Blanche with illustrations from the recent campaign'*, Journal of the Royal United Services Institute, Vol. 55, 1911, pages 885-906.
[148] *The Times, Letters: The Armament of Cavalry by Your Military Correspondent*, 26th March 1910, page 6.
[149] *The Times, The Cavalry Division*, 31st August 1908, page 5.
[150] *The Times*, from our Special Correspondent, *The German Manoeuvres*, 13th September 1910, page 7.
[151] NA CAB 23/13/35 *War Cabinet Minutes, 7 January 1918* quoted in an unpublished PhD thesis by Winrow, A P, *The British Regular Mounted Infantry 1880 – 1913, Cavalry of Poverty or Victorian Paradigm?*, University of Buckingham, 2104, page 336.
[152] Badsey, *Doctrine and Reform in the British Cavalry*, p.285.
[153] Barnett C., op. cit., page 401.
[154] *The Times, The New Cavarly Training I*, 2nd June 1904, page 4.
[155] Ibid.
[156] Ibid.
[157] *The Times, The New Cavalry Training II*, 9th June 1904, page 3.
[158] *The Times, Letters: Cavalry Training*, 24th September 1908, page 5.
[159] *The Times, The Cavalry Arm*, 5th June 1925, page 8.
[160] Vickers, Capt. C E, *The Trenches*, Blackwood's Magazine Vol. CLXXXIII, January 1908.
[161] Maude, Capt. F N, *War and the World's Life*, Smith Elder & Co., 1907, page 97.
[162] *Journal of the Royal Artillery Institute*, Vol. XXIV, page 47.
[163] Clausewitz, C. von, *Vom Kriege (On War)*, trans. by Col G G Graham, (1873), edited by Cold. F N Maude, Kegan Paul, Trench, Trübner & Co., 1908.
[164] Ibid.
[165] Vickers, op. cit., page 42.
[166] Ibid., page 48.
[167] Ibid., page 47.
[168] Ibid., page 51.
[169] François, Gen. G, *Les Canons de la Victoire; Tome 3, L'artillerie de côte et l'artillerie de tranchée*, page 34 onwards.
[170] *Report of a conference of General Staff Officers at the Staff College, 15th to 18th January 1912*, HMSO, Pages 21-2.

[171] See Gannon, Charles E, *Rumors of War and Infernal Machines: Technomilitary Agenda-setting in American and British Speculative Fiction*, Liverpool University Press, 2003, pages 71-3.
[172] *The Times*, 13th February 1908, page 12.
[173] *https://tanks-encyclopedia.com/pre-ww1-uk-fowler-b5-armoured-road-train/*
[174] *The Times*, 28th November 1919, page 14.
[175] Hamilton, Sir I, *Compulsory Service*, John Murray, London, 1911 page 121-2.
[176] *Royal Commission on the War in South Africa*, pages 107-9.
[177] Tohmatsu Haruo, *Approaching Total War: Ivan Bloch's Disturbing Vision* in Wolff, Marks et al, *The Russo-Japanese War in Global Perspective, World War Zero*, Vol. II, Brill, Boston, 2007, page 200.
[178] Towle, P, *British Observers of the Russo-Japanese War* in *Aspects of the Russo-Japanese War*, The Suntory Centre, LSE, London, 1998, page 20.
[179] Hamilton, Sir I, *A Staff Officers Scrapbook during the Russo-Japanese War, Volume 2*, E Arnold, 1907, page 5.
[180] Grey of Fallodon, Viscount, *Twenty-Five Years, 1892-1916*, Vol. 1, Hodder & Stoughton, 1925, pages 114-5
[181] Porch, op. cit., page 226.
[182] Ibid., page 227.
[183] Langlois, H, *Lessons from Two Recent Wars*, Mackie & Co., 1909, page 36.
[184] French, Viscount, *1914*, Houghton Mifflin, 1919, page 1.
[185] Edmonds, J E. *History of the Great War, Military Operations, France and Belgium, 1914*, MacMillan & Co., 1937, page 430.
[186] Reid, W, *Architect of Victory: Douglas Haig*, 2006, page 53.
[187] Esher, *Journal and Letters*, Vol. II, op. cit., page 69.
[188] Ibid., page 70-1.
[189] Royal Archives, W39/21, Esher to Knollys, 16th January 1904
[190] French, op. cit., page 11.
[191] *Field Service Regulations*, page 126.
[192] Ibid., page 138.
[193] Ibid., page 13.
[194] Fuller J F C., *Generalship: Its Diseases and their Cure, A Study of the Personal Factor in Command*, Military Service Publishing Co. Harrisburg, Pa. 1936.
[195] Bloch, *Selected Articles*, page 7.
[196] Fuller J F C., *Generalship*, pages 60-1.
[197] Ibid., page 15.
[198] Ibid., page 17.
[199] Murray, Lt. Col. A M, evidence contained in the *Report of the Committee appointed to consider the education and training of Officers of the Army*, Cmnd Paper 983, 1902, Parliamentary Papers, Vol. 10, page 188.
[200] *The Times*, 10th March, 1903; page 7.

9. More warnings: Manchuria and the Balkans

The Emperor's Army, a million-strong, defeated a powerful foe
The battles and sieges left a mountain of dead
I am ashamed – how can I face their fathers and grandfathers?
A Triumph? But so few men have returned home.

Gen. Count Nogi Maresuke
Triumph, 1905

THE RUSSO-JAPANESE WAR OF 1904-5 was a war which, in various ways, underlined the essential truths of Bloch's predictions for the nature of modern warfare between two industrialised nations with access to modern quick-firing and long-range weapons and almost unlimited supplies of ammunition, but with no rapid means of transporting either men or artillery and with no reliable battlefield communications system.

Tensions between the two countries grew because of conflicting interests in Korea and Inner Manchuria to the west of the *Yalu River* (Korea's north-western border). The contested territories included the Russian port of Port Arthur (now the Lyushunkou District of Dalian and then called by the Japanese Ryojun) at the tip of the Kwantung peninsula (the south-western tip of the larger Liáodōng Peninsula); and the city of Mukden[i], the old capital of the Manchus, the heartland of the Qing Dynasty (1644–1912) and now the capital of Liaoning Province. These cities lay on the southern branch of the *Chinese Eastern Railway* (the *CER*, after 1905 known as the *South Manchurian Railway*). This line cut across outer Manchuria from the Russian city of Chita via Harbin to the port of Vladivostok, thus significantly shortening the distance between the two cities caused by the large loop of the *Trans-Siberian Railway* which ran parallel to, and to the north of, the *Amur River* before turning south at Khabarovsk. The *CER's* extension to Mukden and Port Arthur branched off at Harbin on the *Songhua River*.

There was a problem with the railway as it made the ponderous 5,500-mile journey from Moscow to Port Arthur – a gap in the *Trans-Siberian Railway* of c. 100 miles at the southern end of Lake Baikal. Work on a *Circum-Baikal Railway* started in 1899 but was incredibly challenging, especially in winter, and required digging dozens of tunnels for the single track. 10,000 workers, rising to 13,500 in 1904, were employed and it partially opened on 1st October 1904, by which time the war was eight months old.

In the interim the Lake Baikal gap was bridged by an ice-breaking train ferry, the *Baikal*, and a passenger ferry, the *Angara*[ii]. Even when the *Circum-Baikal Railway* was fully open (after the end of the war in October 1905) these ships were kept available because of regular rock-falls and other disruptions. The Baikal 'gap' and the single-track line meant communications were painfully slow as trains had to wait in sidings to let past others going in the opposite direction. In peacetime, a

---

[i] Now Shenyang, the capital of Liaoning province in China.
[ii] Both built in sections by *Armstrong-Whitworth* in Newcastle-upon-Tyne and assembled near Irkutsk at the mouth of *Angara River* which drains Lake Baikal before joining the *River Yenesi* which then drains into the Arctic Ocean.

battalion took a month to get from Moscow to Port Arthur.[1] Japan, by contrast, had a 700-mile sea-crossing to negotiate in order land troops on the Manchurian-Korean border at the *Yalu River*. Thus, for the Japanese, the strategic essential was control of the Yellow Sea and Korea Bay in order allow the transport and maintenance of its armies in the war zone.

The twelve months of fighting on land between the springs of 1904 and 1905 essentially took place between Port Arthur and Mukden along the line of the railway, though there were initial smaller scale battles along, and to the west of, the *Yalu River*. These land battles grew until the final confrontation around Mukden involving over 600,000 men and which lasted nearly three weeks. It ended with the retreat of the Russians towards Harbin, but at a manpower and financial cost to the Japanese which both army and nation found almost impossible to bear.

The war was characterised by a fundamental dichotomy in the Russian strategic and tactical approach. Their commander, Gen. Alexei Nikolayevich Kuropatkin, was a cautious man akin to Gen. Prince Mikhail Illarionovich Golenishchev-Kutuzov who commanded the Russian Armies during the strategic retreat in the face of Napoleon's 1812 invasion. Thus, Kuropatkin believed a defensive war was the best option, pending the laborious and grindingly slow movement of troops from European Russia through Siberia to Manchuria. With just 83,000 Regular troops (plus 55,000 fortress troops and other units) and 196 guns available east of the Baikal 'gap', opposed by 283,000 Japanese soldiers and 870 guns, this was undoubtedly a prudent view.[2] His preference was to concentrate his forces at Harbin, some 1,000 kms north of Port Arthur, pending the arrival of European reinforcements. However, the importance of Port Arthur as a naval base, it was the home of two-thirds of the Russian Pacific Fleet[i] and, unlike Vladivostok, was ice-free for twelve months of the year, demanded a more advanced position and the town of Liaoyang, 640 kms south of Harbin, was selected.

Tactically, Kuropatkin's more junior commanders were imbued with the offensive ideas of the Russian military theorist, Gen. Mikhail Ivanovich Dragomirov, an officer who enjoyed great success in the Russo-Turkish War of 1877-8 commanding the Russian 4th Division at Plevna and the Shipka Pass. Dragomirov, like many French officers, was absolutely devoted to 'the offensive' and to the irresistible force of the bayonet. He was also greatly committed to the training and efficiency of the individual soldier but, sadly, in the stultifying conservative world of Imperial Russia, this latter point was rather forgotten. And anyway, with insurrection and discontent never far below the surface as the 1905 Revolution showed, the average Russian 5-year conscript was not the most willing or dedicated of soldiers although they fought grimly when challenged.

Writing soon after the war, the German theorist Karl von Donat commented:

"The Russian regulations expected success from obsolete shock tactics without sufficient use of skirmishers and without enough preparation by fire."[3]

---

[i] Seven pre-*Dreadnoughts*, an armoured cruiser and five protected cruisers plus various destroyers, torpedo boats and other lesser ships. One armoured cruiser was at Chemulpo in Korea and four more at Vladivostok.

The art of manoeuvre was also lost thus, in 1904, the Russian Army did not appear to know whether it was coming or going. Having underestimated the tactical acumen of Japan's Generals and bravery and dedication of their soldiers, they were soundly defeated in battle after battle, even though they regularly caused more casualties to the attacking Japanese than they suffered in defence, a moral lost on most Generals prior to 1914.

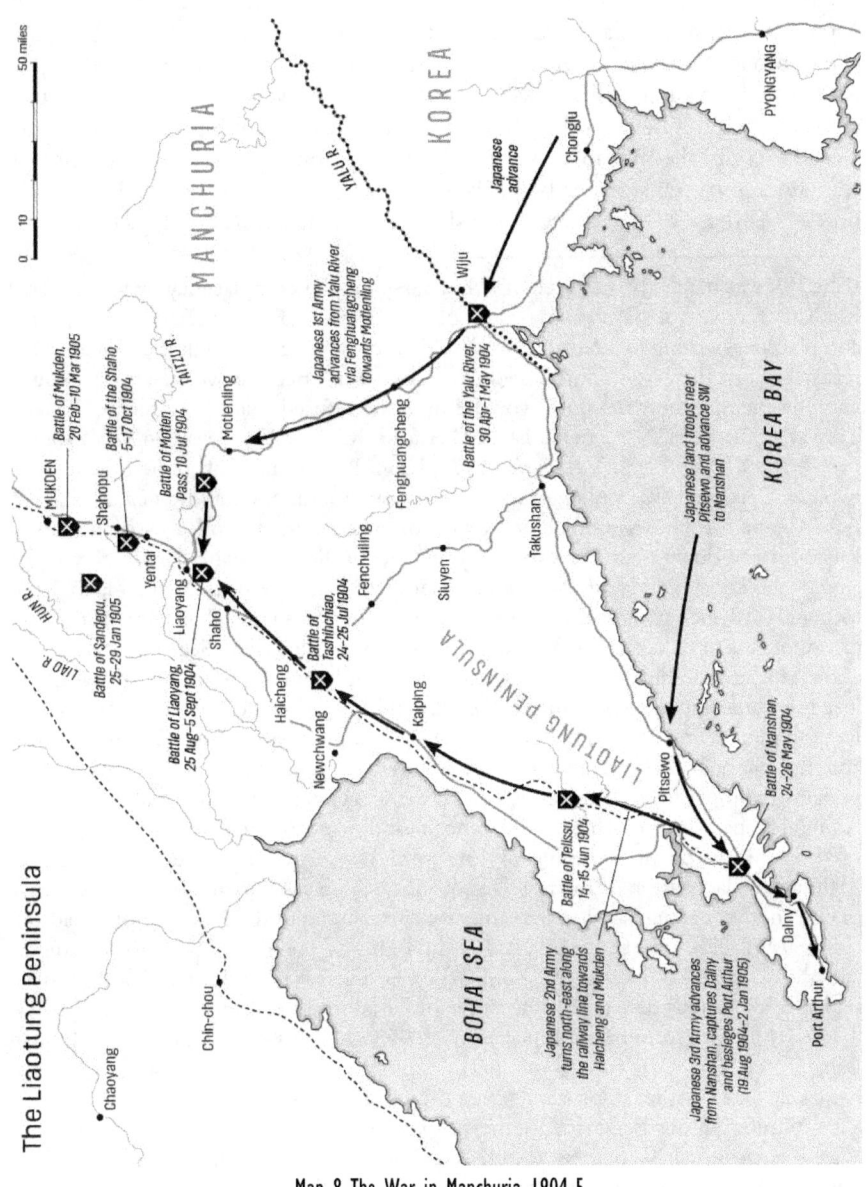

Map 8 The War in Manchuria 1904-5

As was essential to their overall strategy, the Imperial Japanese Navy was even more successful at sea[i]. They first gave warning of their future intentions against the USA at Pearl Harbour in 1941 with pre-emptive strikes on the Russian Pacific Fleet on 8th February 1904, hours *before* they officially declared war. They struck first at the squadron in Port Arthur and then ships at Chemulpo Bay (near Incheon in what is now South Korea). Thereafter, the naval war continued in a one-sided fashion[ii] until the climactic battle in the straits of Tsushima on 27th and 28th May 1905 at which the Russian Baltic Fleet was annihilated[iii]. More than anything, this action brought the war to an end and, within a fortnight, the Tsar agreed to join American-sponsored peace talks. The naval war, however, had less immediate relevance to future events than that of the land fighting. Whilst Admiral Togo's victories established Japan as a major Pacific maritime power, naval technology was about to be transformed by the launching of *HMS Dreadnought* at Portsmouth on 10th February 1906 and few of the slower, pre-*Dreadnought* warships of the type

---

[i] The IJN was helped by a degree of either parsimony or complacency by the Imperial Russian Navy. Col. Tretyakov, one of the heroes of Port Arthur, suspected complacency, writing that naval officers told him: 'Why do you think the Government refused to buy the *Nisshin* and *Kasuga* from Argentina? Because we are strong enough without them; otherwise they would not have refused such a purchase' [*Source*: Tretyakov, Lt. Gen. N A, trans. Lt. A C Alford, RA, *My Experiences at Nan Shan and Port Arthur with the Fifth East Siberian Rifles*, Hugh Rees Ltd., 1911, page 14]. In 1902, two heavily armed *Giuseppe Garibaldi*-class armoured cruisers built by *Gio. Ansaldo & C.* of Genoa for the Argentinian Navy were offered for sale to both Russia and Japan. Russia turned down the offer and they went to join the Imperial Japanese Navy. The ships – the *Kasuga* and *Nisshin* – mounted between them one 10-inch, six 8-inch, 28 6-inch and 20 3-inch guns and with a top speed of 20 knots (faster than any of the pre-dreadnoughts in either navy), fought at the Battles of the Yellow Sea and Tsushima.

[ii] The Japanese dominated the naval campaign but, between 15th and 17th May 1904, lost the battleship *Hatsuse*, cruiser *Yashima* and destroyers *Miyako* and *Akatsuki* to Russian mines. In addition, the cruiser *Yoshino* and gunboat *Oshima* sank in collisions and the gunboat *Tatsuta* ran aground. Mines were a general concern and caused perhaps the most telling Russian loss with the drowning of the unusually competent Admiral Stepan Ossipovich Makarov who went down with the battleship *Petropavlovsk* off Port Arthur on the morning of 13th April 1904. Attempts at sorties from Port Arthur and Vladivostok by the Russian squadrons both came to grief within a few days of one another in August 1904 with the new commander of the Port Arthur squadron, Admiral Wilgelm Vitgeft, being killed at the Battle of the Yellow Sea on 10th August and the *Vladivostok Independent Cruiser Squadron* under Vice Admiral Karl Petrovich Jessen being heavily defeated at the Battle of Ulsan on 14th August.

[iii] The Battle of Tsushima took place on 27th-28th May 1905. The 38-strong Russian Baltic Fleet lost 4,380 men dead, 5,917 captured and six battleships, one coastal battleship and 14 other ships sunk, seven captured and six disarmed. The commander, Vice Admiral Zinovy Petrovich Rozhestvensky, was wounded and made a Prisoner of War. Rear Admiral Nikolai Ivanovich Nebogatov surrendered his squadron and, on repatriation, was court martialled and sentenced to death. The sentence was commuted to ten years in prison but he was released in 1909. Japanese losses were 117 killed, 583 injured and 3 torpedo boats sunk.

which fought around Korea in 1904-5 found a leading role in the naval campaigns of World War One and were cruelly exposed when they tried[i].

Most of the hardware used by the contending armies, however, was present on the battlefields of 1914-18 and their use and effect was of the greatest interest to all of the prospective Western European combatants. As a result, they all sent observers to join the existing military *attachés* in the hope of being embedded with one or other of the armies being deployed in eastern Manchuria. Some of these observers arrived with their own agendas to promote, e.g. Sir Ian Hamilton, and their interpretation of the long-term impact of the weaponry and tactics on display was distinctly coloured by pre-existing opinions. As a result, many of the lessons which might have been learned in Manchuria, and which suggested the correctness of much of Bloch's analysis, were deliberately and even wilfully ignored.

THE JAPANESE PLAN WAS TO LAND three widely spaced Armies in Korea Bay. Count Kuroki Tamemoto's *First Army* landed at Chemulpo (Incheon near Seoul) on the Korean peninsula (9th February) and then drove north towards the *Yalu River* (350 kms). Count Oku Yasukata's *Second Army* then landed at Pitsewo (or Pi-Tzu-Wo now Songjiacun, Pulandian District, Dalian, Liaoning) on 5th May, and then the lead elements of the *Fourth Army* (Marquis Nozu Michitsura) in between. After various minor skirmishes and the deployment of troops by ship (by Japan) and by rail and road (by Russia) the initial heavy fighting near the mouth of the *Yalu River* at the end of April 1904 involved large numbers of men (42,000 Japanese, 25,000 Russian troops) but was marked more by the astute manoeuvring by the Japanese commander Maj. Gen. Kuroki, the stubborn stupidity of the Russian General, Lt. Gen. Mikhail Zasulich, and relatively low casualties – c. 1,000 Japanese killed, wounded and missing against c. 2,000 Russian losses.

This changed at the end of May when the three divisions[ii] of Oku's *Second Army* landed 120 kms north-east of Port Arthur. Access to the land side of the town required an advance along the Liáodōng Peninsula. At its narrowest point, the formidable defences of the 116-metre-high Nanshan Hill[iii] dominated the two-mile-wide isthmus linking the Liáodōng Peninsula to the north-east with the smaller Kwantung peninsula, at the tip of which lay Port Arthur[iv]. Occupied in 1898 as part of a leasing deal with China involving Liáodōng and eastern Manchuria, it was previously fortified by the Russians concerned about threats from the *Militia United in Righteousness* (the *Yihéquán* or *Boxers*) in 1900. Amongst the engineers supervising the work was a Lt. Col. Nikolai Aleksandrovich Tretyakov who, in May 1904, found himself commanding the defenders of the

---

[i] Six British and French pre-*Dreadnoughts* were sunk in the Dardanelles campaign (the *Bouvet* and *HMS Irresistible, Ocean, Goliath, Triumph* and *Majestic*), the German *SMS Pommern* was lost at the Battle of Jutland, the French *Gaulois, Suffren* and *Danton* and *HMS Formidable* and *Britannia* fell to U-boat action, and the Turkish *Barbaros Hayreddin* (previously the *SMS Kurfürst Friedrich Wilhelm*) was sunk by the British submarine *E11*. An unlucky thirteen for these ships and their crews.
[ii] *1st Division* (Tokyo), *3rd Division* (Nagoya), and *4th Division* (Osaka).
[iii] Now part of the Jinzhou District, north of central Dalian, Liaoning, China.
[iv] Two miles at high tide, 2½ miles at low tide.

position. According to the now Col. Tretyakov, commanding *5th East Siberian Rifles*, by February 1904 the Nanshan positions had been grossly neglected:

"...all the trenches and batteries were in a ruined condition, and in the winter ... the ground was as hard as rock[i]."[4]

Employing 5,000 hired Chinese workers the defences were re-built despite the frozen ground. They comprised: five-tiered trench lines, 5,000 metres of barbed wire, land mines, searchlights, and fifteen artillery and ten machine gun positions. It is suggested that the Japanese had first-hand knowledge of the defences as an intelligence officer was one of the workers employed on their construction. If so, such information availed them little.

Nanshan Hill was defended by 3,800 men of the *5th East Siberian Rifles*, two companies of the *14th Rifles* and two scout detachments of the *13th* and *14th Rifles* all commanded by Tretyakov[ii], one of the few Russian officers to emerge from the Manchurian war with any credit. His immediate superior, and commander of the nearest reserves, *4th East Siberian Rifle Division*, was Lt. Gen. Alexander Viktorovich Fok, an artillery officer, ex-security officer from the *Special Corps of Gendarmes* and an individual of such relentless incompetence he was deservedly but unsuccessfully court-martialled after the war. According to Tretyakov, he spent most of the time prior to the Japanese assault on *Nanshan Hill* demanding large extensions to the defences both in depth and width but without at any time offering the additional manpower such work would require or the additional defenders they would need.

His superior, the governor of Kwantung Military District, was Gen. Anatoly Mikhaylovich Stoessel[iii]. Unbelievably, Stoessel was even more of an idiot than

---

[i] Weather in Manchuria can be extreme, from below freezing in winter to 40° C/100° F and more in summer.

[ii] Col., later Lt. Gen., Nikolai Aleksandrovich Tretyakov was born on the 2nd October 1854 in Simbirsk (now Ulyanovsk, renamed after Lenin whose original name was Ulyanov and who was born in this city on the Volga). He graduated from the *2nd Moscow Military Gymnasium* in 1872 and then attended the *Nikolaev Engineering School*. He was commissioned into the *6th Sapper Battalion* in 1875. He served with the *4th Sapper Battalion* during the siege of Plevna. In 1895 he was given command of the *1st East Siberian Demining Brigade* and he was part of the Russian forces deployed during the Boxer Rebellion (1899-1901). In 1901 he took command of the *5th East Siberian Rifles*. After the war he was promoted Maj. Gen. and given command of the *3rd Sapper Brigade* in Kiev. In 1910 he was appointed Inspector of Field Engineering in the Kiev Military District and promoted Lt. Gen. He took command of *10th Siberian Rifle Division* and then *3rd Siberian Infantry Division* in 1911. On the outbreak of war, he was in command of *1st Siberian Infantry Division* and was briefly given command of *23rd Corps* in September 1915. In December 1915 he took command of the *42nd Corps* and, in 1916, *37th Corps*. In December 1916 he was promoted to the rank of Engineer General. He died from pneumonia three months later on 27th February 1917.

[iii] Gen. *Baron* Anatoly Mikhaylovich Stoessel (1848-1915) took part in the Russo-Turkish War of 1877-8 and as a regimental and brigade commander in East Siberia was involved in suppressing the Boxer Rebellion. He took command at Port Arthur, August 1903. Promoted Governor, Kwantung Military District, March 1904. Replaced by Konstantin Smirnov he continued to act as commander at Port Arthur. After a

Fok and it was Stoessel who surrendered Port Arthur without prior consultation with any of his subordinates except Fok. His reward on his return from being held a Prisoner of War was to be court-martialled for cowardice. A death sentence was commuted to ten years in prison. He was pardoned by the Tsar in 1909. Clearly, Tsar Nicholas II had never heard of the principle of shooting failed commanders such as happened to the British Admiral John Byng, executed after his failure to relieve Minorca at the start of the Seven Years War in 1757, and whose fate was immortalised by Voltaire by the comment in *Candide* that the British thought 'it is good to kill an admiral from time to time, to encourage the others'.

In spite of the gross stupidity of Fok and Stoessel, the prolonged and bloody fighting around Port Arthur, starting at Nanshan on 24th May 1904, would reveal the true horror of modern warfare and the lethality of state-of-the-art weapons, especially when allied to inept tactics.

Before this it was the Japanese Army's time to suffer. The Russians at Nanshan, outnumbered ten to one, had the advantage of a hilltop position, trenches, and barbed wire. It is thought ten *Maxim* machine guns on a one-mile front caused most of the Japanese casualties. Unfortunately, the Russians still subscribed to the concept of direct fire artillery and most of the 114 field guns defending Nanshan were put out of action by mid-day either by Japanese fire or a lack of shells.

Preceded by a costly attack on the walled town of Chinchou (now Jinzhou) to the north, three Japanese divisions mounted nine attacks on the Russians on 26th May. In these attacks they were supported by the fire of several gunboats moored off the coast to the north of the hill and able to fire into the rear of the Russian position. By 6 p.m., however, the Japanese attacks were at a standstill and the Russians had inflicted c. 4,300 casualties on the attackers at the cost of 400 men.

Port Arthur was one of the most strongly fortified towns on the Asian mainland but the Japanese commander, now General Count Nogi Maresuke commanding a new *Third Army*[i] (*1st* and *11th Divisions*), foresaw no problems. He commanded the Japanese forces which captured the port (then called Lüshunkou) in two days during the First Sino-Japanese War (1st August 1894 to 17th April

---

series of large mines were detonated under three important forts at the end of December, Stoessel and Fok offered to surrender to Nogi. The surrender was signed on 2nd January 1905 at Shuishiying. Unlike other PoWs, Stoessel was allowed to sail back to St Petersburg. Discharged from the army in September 1906, he was arrested, and put on trial for cowardice and dereliction of duty. Found guilty, he was sentenced to death, then ten years in prison. He was pardoned on 6th May 1909. He re-joined the army, dying in Khmilnyk in the Vinnytsia Oblast, Ukraine, in January 1915.

[i] Oku's *Second Army* (*3rd*, *4th* & *5th Divisions*) advanced north and on 14th-15th June, defeated Lt. Gen. Georgii Stackelberg's *1st Siberian Corps*, sent to re-capture Nanshan and move on Port Arthur, at Te-li-ssu (now Delisi, Wafangdian, 80 kms north-east of Nanshan). This advance, opposed by Kuropatkin, was demanded by Admiral Yevgeni Ivanovich Alekseyev, Viceroy of the Russian Far East and commander-in-chief in Manchuria until recalled on 12th October 1904. Alekseyev was a favourite of the Tsar and rumoured to be the illegitimate son of Emperor Alexander II. He and Kuropatkin fundamentally disagreed on strategy and Alekseyev repeatedly went over the General's head to appeal to the Tsar. Stackelberg's defeat was the result of just such an argument.

1895), and the attack cost 29 killed and 233 wounded. The current siege was another story altogether, it lasted over five months and Japanese casualties totalled c. 60,000 plus another 34,000 sick, some three times the number of Russian casualties (excepting PoWs). Nogi's tactics were crude and expensive perhaps for two reasons: firstly, he wished to deliver Port Arthur as demanded by the Emperor; and, secondly, because his *Third Army* was needed urgently to reinforce the main drive north along the railway towards Liaoyang, Mukden, and Harbin.

As so often happened in this war, Russian incompetence intervened as Tretyakov's superior, the buffoon Fok, refused a request for reinforcements (of which there were some 12,000 available) except to cover a withdrawal, and then ordered a retreat after the Japanese started to send men around the northern end of the Nanshan defences through the shallows of Chin Chou Bay. Tretyakov, ignorant of the order, was left high and dry trying to stem the flood of men to the rear. His regiment lost another 1,000 men, all ten of the machine guns, and 68 field guns in the disorganised evacuation of their unconquered position[i]. The retreat eventually went all the way back to the hills around Port Arthur, some 50 kms, and involved the abandonment of the port of Dalny (now Dalian), thus giving the Japanese an excellent base through which to supply their troops during the forthcoming siege of Port Arthur. By the end of July Port Arthur was invested by Japanese forces and the siege proper began on 1st August 1904.

The Russians, meanwhile, retreated to a range of hills called 'the position of the passes'. Tallest of these rugged hills was 370-metre (1,200 feet) high *Chien-Shan* which, located centrally, gave observation over the Japanese positions almost everywhere to the east. Further north, the steep, rocky hill of *Yu Pil At Zu* was equally significant. From the tops of both hills it was possible to see as far as Dalny and off towards Nanshan. The range of hills ran south-north for eleven miles from the shore of the Yellow Sea before reaching a three-mile-wide coastal plain through which ran the single-track railway line from Harbin down to Port Arthur. Fok was convinced the Japanese would advance along the coastal plain and it was thus heavily fortified whilst the important hill tops were only lightly held and entrenched. *Chien-Shan* was lost to a surprise attack on 25th/26th June and there, bar some desultory exchanges, the lines remained until 26th July though, during this time, Nogi's forces were enhanced by the arrival of the *9th Division*, the *1st* and *4th Kobi Brigades* and a mass of field and siege artillery.

On 26th July an attack was launched along the 'position of the passes' (ignoring the well-fortified coastal plain) and for two days 180 Japanese guns pounded Russian positions from *Yu Pil At Zu hill* in the north down to *Lao-tso Shan hill* by the coast, whilst three divisions and a *Kobi* brigade attacked time after time. *Lao-tso Shan hill* fell in the early afternoon of 28th July and *Yu Pil At Zu hill* soon after. With the 'position of the passes' now untenable, Fok ordered a retreat to the hills immediately surrounding Port Arthur. Japanese losses were some 4,000 against c. 1,400 Russian casualties.

---

[i] Final casualties were: Japanese 4,885 killed and wounded, Russian 1,416 killed, wounded and PoWs. The Russian casualties were all from Tretyakov's command and amounted to 38% of the men involved.

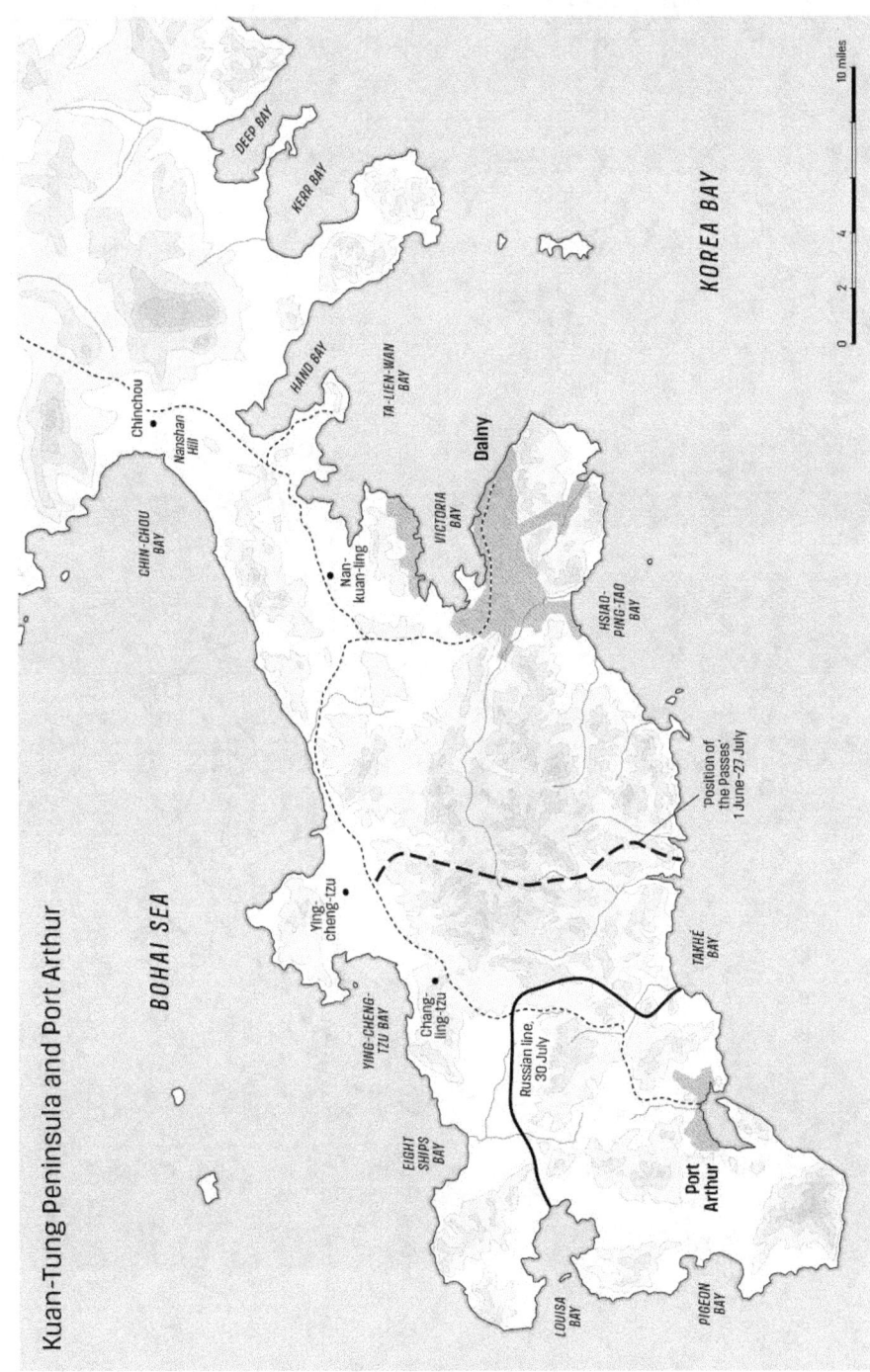

Map 9 Nanshan to Port Arthur

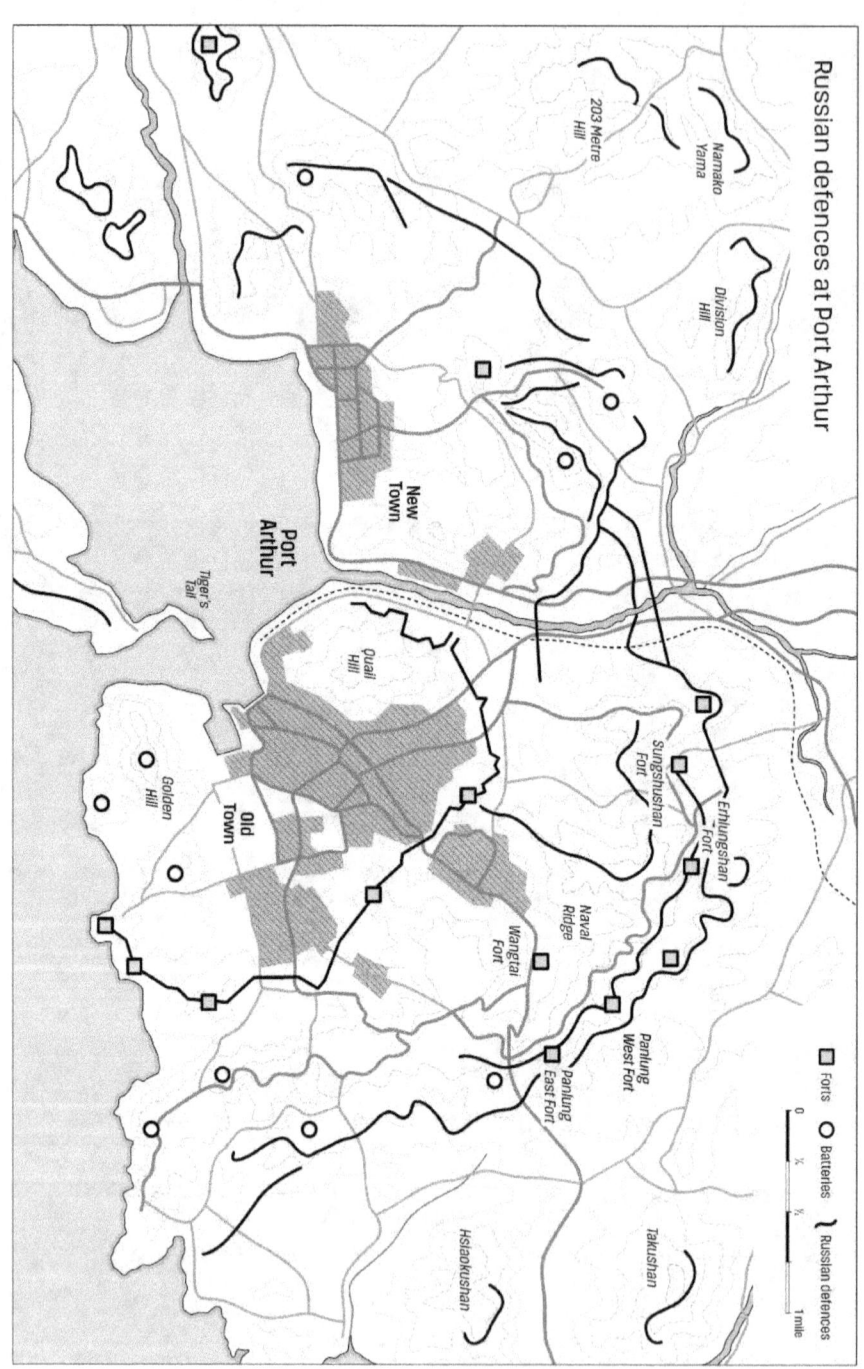

Map 10 The Siege of Port Arthur

The Defeated

81 Gen. Aleksey Nikolayevich Kuropatkin
CinC, Russian Forces, Manchuria

82 Gen. Anatoly Mikhaylovich Stoessel
Governor, Kwantung Military District

83 Gen. Konstantin Nikolaevich Smirnov
Commander, Port Arthur

84 Lt. Gen. Alexander Viktorovich Fok
Commander, 4th East Siberian Rifle Division

85 Lt. Gen. Roman Isidorovich Kondratenko
Commander, 7th E. Siberian Rifle Division

86 Col. Nikolai Aleksandrovich Tretyakov
Commander, 5th East Siberian Rifles

The Victors

87 Field Marshal Prince Ōyama Iwao, CinC Japanese Forces, Manchuria

88 Gen. Viscount Kodama Gentarō, Chief of Staff, Japanese Forces, Manchuria

89 Gen. Count Nogi Maresuke Commander, Third Army (Port Arthur)

90 Gen. Count Oku Yasukata Commander, Second Army (Nanshan)

By 30th July, the Russian lines ran west-east from Louisa Bay in the west, along the *Wolf Hills* before turning south to where the railway line cut through the hills in the *Lun-Ho valley* on its final run into Port Arthur. The position then continued south over the *Big* and *Little Orphan Hills* (*Takushan* and *Hsiaokushan*) to the western end of Ta Ho Bay. The most prominent hill in the north-facing *Wolf Hills* was *Feng-Huang-Shan*, which lay at the centre of a range of hills which were highest in the east but became less prominent the further west they ran towards Louisa Bay. Here, Fok continued with his absurd behaviour by demanding trenches be dug only at the bottom of the hills and irrespective of what was in front of them. He was doing things 'by the book', and thus driving Tretyakov to distraction:

> "These fortifications consisted of deep trenches with hardly any parapet, placed at the very foot of the hills which lay behind them, in accordance with General Fok's system. Right close up to the trenches grew high *kaoliang* (millet) which completely blocked the field of view from the trenches, and, like the plan of the trenches themselves, the positions selected for

them afforded an example of the blind application of a principle in itself sound enough. The man responsible for the defence of the right flank of *Feng-huang Shan* unhappily failed to apply this principle correctly.

In his anxiety to adhere to the principle of a flat trajectory he entirely lost sight of the fact that every small mound, if only two or three feet high, presents an impenetrable barrier to a low-flying bullet. He also quite forgot that the slope of the hill of itself affords an obstacle difficult to surmount; and he, moreover, ignored the difficulties of an eventual retreat from the trenches up the side of the hill, sometimes a very steep one, as was the case at *Feng-huang Shan*.

So the trenches on the right flank of *Feng-huang Shan* were placed at the foot of its northern side. In front of them grew *kao-liang* to the height of 5 feet."[5]

When the Japanese attacked on 30th July, the defending troops had only been able to cut back 50-metres of the millet immediately in front of their trenches. Using the plants as cover the Japanese soon into the inadequate trenches. The *Wolf Hills* position fell to the Japanese who lost just 200 men. As a result, the Russian defences were reduced to the range of forts and redoubts that ran from the coast east of Port Arthur in a semi-circle to a position called the *Temple Redoubts* in front of which lay the small village of Shui-Shih-Ling, and then westwards across the rather more improvised defences (by Tretyakov) of *Division Hill*, *174-metre Hill* and the soon to be infamous *203-metre Hill*. In the meantime, Fok was blaming every failure on treachery rather than incompetent tactics and absurd orders. Clearly, because of his previous role as a secret policeman, paranoia ran deep.

The enclosed harbour at Port Arthur is surrounded from the west, north and around to the east by rugged and steep hills some 2½ miles distant from the centre of the new town. The main defences were either on the eastern hills or facing seaward where 27 hardened coastal batteries were designed to protect the city and the bay. On the western side of the city the hills were higher but less well fortified. Amongst them was a twin-peaked prominence named *203-metre Hill* on the maps. The landward defences, though formidable on paper, were not due to be completed for another five years having been started in 1899 as part of a ten-year programme.

The defence of the city was the responsibility of the recently arrived Lt. Gen. Konstantin Nikolaevich Smirnov[i] whilst the incompetent and complacent Stoessel

---

[i] Konstantin Nikolaevich Smirnov (1854-1930) was born in Odessa. He attended the *Mikhailovsky Artillery School* and the *Nikolaev General Staff Academy*. The commandant of the *Odessa Infantry Cadet school* (1886-1898) he commanded *2nd Infantry Brigade* in 1900. After the siege he accused Stoessel and Fok of cowardice and dereliction of duty of which Stoessel was found guilty. In March 1908, Fok challenged Smirnov to a duel and this was officially sanctioned, it was conducted with pistols at twenty paces at the riding school of the *Chevalier Guard Regt.* in St Petersburg. With his fourth shot, Fok hit Smirnov above the right hip. Smirnov recovered. After the revolution he left Russia, living in Yugoslavia. He died from pneumonia in Pančevo in 1930. Fok then demanded satisfaction from a Gen. Gortbatoffsky who had commanded troops on the western defences at Port Arthur but the War Ministry refused to sanction this one.

remained in overall control of the Liáodōng Peninsula and was thus Smirnov's superior even if the Liáodōng Peninsula command and the Port Arthur command were now one and the same. This was doubly unfortunate as Stoessel was an idiot and Smirnov, though competent, was continuously undermined, his orders over-ridden and his actions criticised in telegrams to the Tsar by Stoessel who had been ordered to leave Port Arthur aboard a destroyer by the overall Russian commander Gen. Kuropatkin but who pocketed the order and ignored it.

The next attacks were on the *Big* and *Little Orphan Hills* (*Takushan* and *Hsiaokushan*) which lay about two miles east of the Old Town of Port Arthur and on the western side of the small *Ta Ho River*. Between *Takushan* to the north and *Hsiaokushan* to the south ran the main road from the newly captured port of Dalny. These attacks over two days, 7th and 8th August 1904, featured costly if successful frontal assaults with the Japanese losing 1,460 men to Russian losses of 450. The main benefit to the Japanese was that the *Tsar* ordered the commander of the Pacific Fleet, Admiral Wilgelm Vitgeft, to escape to Vladivostok. This he tried on 10th August only to run into Togo's battle fleet. The confused and violent Battle of the Yellow Sea left Vitgeft dead, most of his badly damaged ships back in Port Arthur and the rest scattered and later interned in various neutral ports. Tactically inconclusive it was a strategic victory for Japan.

But it was now things began to wrong for Count Nogi and his men.

On 13th/14th August, Nogi attacked towards *174-metre Hill* and *Headquarters Hill* north-west of Port Arthur, a position held by Tretyakov and the *5th* and *13th East Siberian Rifles*. As in previous fighting Japanese artillery fired a mixture of shrapnel and high explosive[i]. After the war British officers were generally dismissive of the effectiveness of high explosive against trenches, believing shrapnel should be employed as long as possible whilst the final bayonet charge went in. As a result, in August 1914, British artillery was almost entirely supplied with shrapnel and the country had little capacity for the manufacture of high explosive. That high explosive *was* effective against entrenched troops can be seen from Tretyakov's comments on the Japanese bombardment on 15th August:

> "Our three hills (*Advanced* and *Headquarters Hills* and *Height 426*) were wreathed in smoke from the enemy's high-explosive and shrapnel shells, and looked like veritable volcanoes in eruption. Though our men had sufficient cover from shrapnel, the high-explosive shells, filled with *Shimose*, caused fearful havoc."[6]

---

[i] The high explosive was *Shimose* powder, a more powerful version of Picric Acid than French *Melinite* or British *Lyddite*, made stable by coating the inside of the shells with wax. This prevented the creation of unstable picrate salts which might lead to premature explosions. *Shimose* was initially developed for the navy by a brilliant graduate of the *Kobu Daigakko* (*Engineering Grand School*), Shimose Masachika (1860-1911), the son of a *samurai* from Hiroshima. He later became director-general of the *Navy Shimose Gunpowder Manufacturing Plant*, 1898. Brought into service in 1893, it was soon applied to all forms of munitions: mines, torpedoes, and naval and army shells. The extreme damage done to Russian warships during the war was, in part, due to the effect of *Shimose* powder.

By mid-day all three hills were lost and Tretyakov withdrew to a new line: *Division Hill* in the east then south-west through *Namako Yama* and *Akasaka Yama* to *203-metre Hill* in the west. *174-metre Hill* was still in his possession. Japanese losses were, however, severe and caused by either rifle or machine gun fire as the Russian artillery was either out of action or unable to locate the indirect firing enemy guns. Tretyakov states the bodies of 432 Japanese soldiers were counted in the barbed wire protecting *Height 426* on the morning of 14th August and fighting there went on until noon the following day.[7] He further states that, in the main, Russian withdrawals were caused by overwhelming Japanese artillery fire using *Shimose*-filled high explosive shells:

> "The fact must be noted that we were driven out of these positions by gun fire, and not by the Japanese infantry. Events here made it clear to everyone what preponderance in artillery really means. The side that silences the enemy's guns can capture his positions without particularly hard fighting, for, having once got the enemy's fire under control, one can choose a point of attack, concentrate the whole of one's artillery on it, and then take it by storm with comparatively small numbers. For this, however, a numerous, well-trained, and efficient artillery is essential."[8]

Points then ignored by both the British and French over the next ten years.

The attack on *174-metre Hill* started on the morning of 19th August. Repeated attacks were made under a hail of unanswered HE and shrapnel. Reinforcements were sent up to replace casualties which were severe on both sides. The fighting went into a second day until, at noon, an urgent request was made for Russian reinforcements of which only one company remained. Tretyakov's superior Gen. Kondratenko, commander of the *7th East Siberian Rifle Division*, was present and agreed to the move. But so was Fok[i] and he compounded his previous errors by countermanding the order. Within an hour *174-metre Hill* was lost forcing Tretyakov to withdraw to *203-metre Hill*. 1,000 Russians were lost defending the hill, a third being killed. And all in a position where no more than 800 defenders could be placed at any one time. Japanese losses are estimated at 1,800.

Further east the Japanese took and lost the *Waterworks Redoubt* east of Shui-Shih-Ling before the launch of a mass attack on 21st August on the robust Russian defences north-east of Port Arthur. In these eastern hills, a first attempt at a creeping barrage was made during an assault on the two *Panlung* forts and, though these were taken, the cost was high[ii] and further progress towards *Wangtai Fort*

---

[i] Fok was relieved of command on 21st August but remained on Stoessel's staff who gave him command of the landward defences when the inspirational Lt. Gen. Roman Isidorovich Kondratenko was killed by a shell on 2nd December 1904. So impressed were the Japanese by Kondratenko they erected a memorial to him where he was killed. Fok urged Stoessel to accept Nogi's surrender terms without consulting the other senior officers in Port Arthur. He later fought with the Bulgarian Army in the First Balkan War, dying in Bulgaria in 1926.

[ii] The *7th Regiment* which took the *East Panlung Fort* lost 1,600 men out of the 1,800 who entered the fighting [*Source*: Connaught, R, *Rising Sun and Tumbling Bear: Russia's War with Japan*, Hachette UK, 2020].

impossible. By 24th August the attack down the *Wangtai* ravine failed at considerable cost with, all told, some 16,000 men having become casualties (and some 20,000 since the siege proper began on 1st August). Afterwards, the Japanese credited the failure of these attacks and the heavy casualties to the work of Russian machine guns.[9] Russian casualties during these attacks are thought to have been c. 3,000.

Heavily reinforced by 20,000 men arriving at Dalny from 3rd September, and with the arrival of the first of the 28-cm (11-inch) coastal howitzers[i], the Japanese campaign now turned to siege warfare with an attempt to properly co-ordinate the work of the artillery and the infantry.

Four key features blocked the way to Port Arthur: the *Temple Redoubt*, the *Waterworks Redoubt* (which fell on 21st September after three costly attacks), and to the west, *203-Metre Hill* and *Namako Yama* (or *180-Metre Hill*). After trenches were dug and saps driven up to their perimeters the two redoubts were overrun in mid-September. Beyond them were two forts: *Erhlungshan* and *Sungshushan*. These proved tougher nuts to crack. The trenches outside fell on 26th October after a six-hour bombardment with shells still falling as the Japanese overran their objectives, but the forts held on. *Erhlungshan* was eventually destroyed by mining on 28th December and *Sungshushan* surrendered on 31st December 1904.

At the same time as the two redoubts were overrun, attacks were launched to the west. The only Japanese success was the capture of the somewhat isolated *Namako Yama* 1,500 yards to the north. At *203 Metre Hill*, however, the dense columns were shot down by the defenders as Nogi reverted to the crude tactics employed earlier. Overall, a third of the 60,000 casualties incurred during the entire siege were killed or wounded in the series of desperate assaults on the key position of *203-Metre Hill*[ii] which started on 20th September and ended on 5th December. This position, stubbornly defended by Col. Tretyakov, was heavily fortified with reinforced concrete redoubts, trenches, searchlights, and electrified barbed wire,

---

[i] The 28-cm (11-inch) *Howitzer L/10* was an 1884 Armstrong-designed coastal defence weapon. Maj. Pompeo Grillo, from an Italian subsidiary, went to the new *Osaka Artillery Arsenal* to assist with their construction and 220 of various calibres were built. From 1892, they were installed around Tokyo and Osaka harbours. Several were dismounted and sent to Port Arthur to assist with the siege. The first group of eighteen was lost when two merchant ships, the *Hitachi Maru* and *Sado Maru*, was attacked by Russian cruisers from Vladivostok on 15th June 1904 in the Straits of Tsushima. The *Hitachi Maru* also carried 700 men of the *1st Reserve Guards Regt*. The *Hitachi Maru* was sunk with the loss of 1,086 of the 1,238 crew and soldiers and the *Sado Maru* was badly damaged and run aground with the loss of 239 passengers and crew. A degree of revenge was achieved at the Battle of Ulsan on 14th August when one of the Russian cruisers from the earlier attack was sunk and two more so badly damaged they could not be repaired in the facilities available in Vladivostok. The *Vladivostok Independent Cruiser Squadron* was thus neutralised for the rest of the war.

[ii] Two linked hills 203 and 210 metres high. Possession of these heights gave observation over the harbour in which sheltered the remains of the Russian Pacific Fleet. Once it fell, 28-cm howitzers were dragged to the summit, and they sank these warships one by one.

and the 1,500 defenders (at any one time) were equipped with machine guns and hand grenades as well as their rifles.

Four major assaults were mounted by Gen. Nogi in September, October, November and December, each one costing the attackers more dead and wounded than the previous one[i]. Indeed, so costly were the attacks on Port Arthur that General Baron Kodama Gentarō[ii], the Chief of the General Staff in Manchuria, went to Port Arthur to advise and possibly replace Nogi. Kodama[iii] arrived at the end of September to oversee matters. There, in mid-October, he met a US journalist, Richard Barry, who reported on the conflict for American, British, and French periodicals such as the *Illustrated London News*, *Scientific American* and the *Westminster Gazette*. The General explained the new form of warfare being explored at Port Arthur. Because of widespread mining of the coastal waters, the naval guns of both sides became redundant thus, as the French were forced to do during WW1 for lack of real alternatives, these guns were being used on land:

> "… they (i.e. the Russians) have turned not only their coast defence, but their navy guns landward. We, in reply, have landed our navy guns and brought from Japan our coast defence artillery. So you will see the spectacle of two great naval equipments fighting on land. I wish I could bring all the tacticians in the world to witness. There will be much to learn for future warfare."[10]

The return of siege warfare and the need for heavy and super heavy guns was a lesson neither Britain nor France would learn over the next nine years.

Eventually, to reduce the Russian fortifications the Japanese employed eighteen 28-cm coastal howitzers as well as mines dug under the two key positions

---

[i] 19th September – losses 3,500, 29th October – losses 3,700, 26th November – losses 4-8,000, 28th November onwards – losses 8,000. Total Japanese losses 19-23,000. The Russians lost c. 6,000 in the defence of *203 Metre Hill*.

[ii] The man who authorised the pre-emptive strikes on the Russian Pacific Fleet made, as in 1941 at Pearl Harbour, before war was officially declared.

[iii] General Viscount Kodama Gentarō was born in 1852 in Tokuyama, Suō Province (now Yamaguchi Prefecture). His was a *samurai* family. He fought in the Boshin War of 1868-9, a Japanese civil war which saw imperial rule replace the Shogunate through the Meiji Restoration. He served in the suppression of the Saga, Shinpūren and Satsuma Rebellions between 1874 and 1877. Promotion was rapid. By 1889, aged 37, he was a Major General. Appointed head of the Army War College (the *Rikugun Daigakkō*) he worked alongside Maj. Klemens Wilhelm Jacob Meckel, a German officer seconded to the Japanese Army. He served in the First Sino-Japanese War of 1894-5. Promoted Lt. Gen. he was Governor–General of Taiwan from 1896 until just before his death in 1906, succeeding Nogi Maresuke. In 1900 he was appointed Minister for the Army and in 1903 was briefly both Minister for Home Affairs and Minister for Education. Promoted full General, June 1904, he went to Manchuria as Chief of Staff. After the war he was Chief of the Imperial Japanese Army General Staff. His sudden death on 23rd July 1906 from a cerebral haemorrhage was viewed as a national calamity. He was added to the ranks of Shinto *kami* or spirits, and shrines exist in his hometown of Tokuyama, now part of Shūnan, *Yamaguchi Prefecture*, and at the site of his summer home on the island of Enoshima, Fujisawa, *Kanagawa Prefecture*.

of *Erhlungshan* and *Sungshushan*. The howitzers fired c. 1,000 230 Kg shells in a single day at the beginning of the final eight-day assault of *203-Metre Hill* and the defences were subjected to a three-day bombardment before the attack on 28th November. Despite this, the attacking Japanese infantry were cut down in their thousands and it took a week's severe, and sometimes hand-to-hand, fighting before the final capture of the summits of *203 Metre Hill* on the late morning of 5th December. During the fighting the gallant Tretyakov was severely wounded. 8,000 Japanese soldiers became casualties and, amongst the many dead, was Gen. Nogi's surviving son, the 23-year-old younger son Yasunori, who died on 30th November. His older brother, Katsunori, died of wounds received at Nanshan on 27th May 1904.

The enormous human cost of the siege grieved Nogi profoundly for the rest of his life. After the war he asked Emperor Meiji to be allowed to commit suicide (or *seppuku*) in atonement. The emperor refused and Nogi spent his days, and money, helping wounded soldiers and erecting memorials to the dead, including seeking to have one erected in memory of the Russians who died in the siege. His request to commit suicide was rejected by the emperor 'whilst he was alive' and, on the day of Meiji's funeral, 13th September 1912, Nogi and his wife Shizuko killed themselves. His final letter explained his death was an act of atonement, partly for the loss of his infantry regiment's colours in the 1877 Satsuma Rebellion, and partly for the enormous losses his Army suffered at Port Arthur.

Nogi[i] was an honourable man desperate to deliver to his emperor the key Russian position on the Manchurian coast. In his desperation, he threw men in human waves numerous times against defences equipped with every modern killing device known to man as well as a few older ones about to enjoy an unexpected revival. The slaughter on the slopes of *203-Metre Hill* was costly to both the Army and Nogi personally. Nogi was literate, sensitive, educated and a noted poet in the *Kanshi* style i.e. using Chinese characters. One poem, *Written*

---

[i] General Count Nogi Maresuke was born in 1849, in Edo (modern Tokyo), the son of a *samurai*. He joined the Army in 1869 and was commissioned into the new Imperial Army as a Major in 1871. He fought in the Satsuma rebellion in which the colours of the *14th Regiment* were lost, a personal disgrace he gave as one reason for his suicide in 1912. His marriage to Shizuko produced two sons: Katsunori and Yasunori. Promoted Maj. Gen., 1885, he visited Germany in 1887 to study strategy and tactics. He commanded the *1st Infantry Brigade* in 1894 during the First Sino-Japanese War, capturing Port Arthur in one day. He was involved in the atrocity of the Port Arthur massacre in which thousands of soldiers and civilians of all ages and both sexes were slaughtered in retaliation for the mutilation and murder of wounded Japanese PoWs. He was promoted Lt. Gen. in 1895 and, after its invasion by Imperial forces during which he commanded the *2nd Division*, he was Governor-General of Taiwan, 1896-1898. He returned to Japan in 1899 to command *11th Brigade*. In 1904 he was recalled to command the *Third Army* in Manchuria. After Port Arthur fell, his troops moved north where they took part in the Battle of Mukden in late February to early March 1905. Between 1906 and 1912 he was President of the *Gakushūin* or Peers' School, in Tokyo which educated the children of Japan's nobility, and he had a profound influence on the young Hirohito, later 124th Emperor of Japan (1926-89).

outside the *Walls of Jinzhou*, was composed after he learnt of the death of his older son, Katsunori, at Nanshan. Another, *Your Souls' Mountain*, was written after Yasunori's death:

Can we say it was easy to climb 203 Hill?
Was it not difficult because men sought their honour?
The mountain has changed shape, covered in iron and blood.
We all now look up in awe at the mountain where your souls lie.

The Chinese characters 2, 0 and 3 are *erh, ling* and *san* (爾 靈 山). In Chinese they are also homonyms for three words: Your Souls' Mountain.

At war's end Nogi wrote a brief despairing poem: *Triumph*. It reads:

The Emperor's Army, a Million-strong, defeated a powerful foe
The battles and sieges left a mountain of dead
I am ashamed – how can I face their fathers and grandfathers?
A Triumph? But so few men have returned home.

His sentiments of regret and loss seem to have passed by his admirers such as Hamilton who saw only that elevated people like Count Nogi could somehow persuade ordinary men in their thousands to give up their lives in war for some vague patrician notion of honour and patriotism.

If the casualties at Port Arthur, especially for the Japanese, were horrific those at the climactic 18-day battle of Mukden were close to unsustainable. Though a tactical victory, it was bordering on the Pyrrhic with over 75,000 Japanese dead and wounded (29% of those involved) against some 66,000 Russians (19% of those involved though plus c. 22,000 Prisoners of War). Intense fighting was not sustained over the 18 days of the battle but was concentrated over some ten days along the 90-mile (140 km) front. In this time, the Japanese fired more rifle bullets (20 million) and artillery shells (280,000) than the German Army throughout the entirety of the Franco-Prussian War of 1870-1 (191 days).[11]

Battle	Japan			Russia		
	Strength	Casualties	%	Strength	Casualties	%
Yalu River, 30.4-1.5.04	42,000	1,000		25,000	2,200	
Nanshan, 24-26.5.04	35,500	6,200	17%	3,800	1,600	42%
Te-li-Ssu, 14-15.6.04	40,000	1,150		33,500	3,500	
Tashihchiao, 24-25.7.04	64,000	1,000		60,000	1,000	
Hsimucheng, 31.7.04	34,000	800		33,000	1,200	
Port Arthur, 1.8.04-2.1.05	150,000	58,000	37%	50,000	31,000	62%*
Liaoyang, 25.8-5.9.04	127,000	24,000	19%	245,000	18,000	7%
Shaho, 5-7.10.04	170,000	20,000	12%	210,000	40,000	19%
Sandepu, 25-29.1.05	220,000	9,000	4%	285,000	14,000	5%
Mukden, 20.2-10.3.05	263,000	75,500	29%	343,000	88,000	26%
Total dead, wounded, missing (exc. PoWs)		196,650			172,500	

Table 14 Strength and casualties, major battles of the Russo-Japanese War 1904-5
N.B. Russian figures include PoWs (except c. 20,000 PoWs at Port Arthur).
Total fatalities: Japan 59,000, Russia c. 34,000–53,000.
27,000 Japanese & 9-18,000 Russian soldiers died of disease

Nor did this vast expenditure of manpower and munitions bring the war to a victorious conclusion. True, Kuropatkin's forces withdrew first to Tieling 53 miles/85 kms to the north, which he then abandoned and set fire to before retreating 60+miles (103 kms) to Hspingkai (modern Siping) which was fortified briefly before the withdrawal began again. Ōyama Iwao's armies, however, were so drained by the fighting and their supply lines so over-stretched their pursuit was half-hearted. Final victory was only achieved when Tōgō Heihachirō's warships crushed the Russian Baltic Fleet at Tsushima on 27th-28th May.

The fact Japan won the war despite these losses was embraced by most in the West as confirmation 'the offensive' was the best, indeed the only, way in which wars were won. Casualties amongst the lower ranks of the Army, who were themselves drawn from the disposable lower ranks of society, were irrelevant. Victory for the nation, for the empire, was all. And yet the cost to the average Japanese soldier was severe, as the table above shows. It should be noted that in three of the four most important battles (i.e. Port Arthur, Liaoyang and Mukden), the numbers of Japanese dead far exceeded that of the Russians and fatal casualties ran at a ratio of two dead Japanese soldiers for every one Russian in these battles.

With Japan's economy buckling, and Russia refusing to pay reparations, the Treaty of Portsmouth[i], signed on 5th September 1905, was poorly received in Japan. The Hibiya riots in Tokyo erupted the day the treaty was signed and were followed by disturbances in Kobe and Yokohama. Such was the political fall-out, Prime Minister Katsura Tarō was forced to resign on 7th January 1906[ii].

With the 1905 Revolution breaking out in Russia, Bloch's predictions about the economic and political impact of war obviously applied to more than just the empires of western Europe. Such non-military outcomes were, though, of no great concern to the western Army officers who witnessed and debated the conduct of the war in technical rather than human and economic terms.

On two things French and German observers agreed: Japanese artillery was obsolete and the modern Russian guns remarkably poorly handled. The Japanese field gun was the 75-mm *Arisaka Type 31*[iii] 1898 model which fired 2-3 rounds per minute to a range of 4,300 metres (4,700 yards). Its recoil system was rudimentary and, by European standards, it was obsolete when introduced. It was replaced at the end of the war by the *Krupp*-designed *Type 38* 75-mm Field Gun which survived into WW2[iv]. The Russians possessed a modern field gun, the 76.2 mm, model 1902, designed at the *Putilovski Works* in St Petersburg. With a range of 4,500

---

[i] Portsmouth, New Hampshire, USA.

[ii] Japan's debt at the end of the war was £192 million or c. £20 billion in current values using RPI inflation. Other, probably more accurate, indices give totals ten times greater. $180 million ($6 billion+ in current values) was raised in the USA through bond sales. It should be remembered that Government spending generally was far lower at this time with few or no social programmes to finance, smaller populations, lower tax revenues, etc., so such debts were relatively far greater than they might appear in modern terms.

[iii] Introduced in the 31st year of the reign of Meiji, 122nd Emperor (1852-1912).

[iv] The Japanese later employed the *Krupp*-designed *Type 38* 12-cm Howitzer, and a 10-cm gun, the *Type 38* 10-cm Cannon, built at the Osaka Arsenal.

metres (4,900 yards), a maximum rate of fire of 10-12 rounds per minute, and a hydro-pneumatic recoil, it was far superior to the Japanese gun and, arguably, to the new German *77 FK 96 (n.A)*. But its crews were poorly trained, tactical application was lamentable and, in most battles, the Japanese gained artillery superiority.

As in the early actions in South Africa and at Le Cateau in 1914, the Russians relentlessly placed their artillery in full view of the Japanese, often on the tops of hills. The Japanese, however, employed indirect fire from defiladed positions using observers equipped with telephones. Their first objective was the destruction or neutralisation of the Russian guns at which they were remarkably successful. In the view of Western observers, the lengthy battles might have been shortened had the Japanese access to a modern QF field gun. Nor need they have employed the suicidal infantry tactics which cost them so dear. On the other hand, these observers relished the way in which Japanese troops 'sacrificed' themselves for their Emperor, and not a few hoped fervently their own citizens might happily martyr themselves in similar fashion.

Which begs the question: which weapon caused most Japanese casualties at Nanshan, Port Arthur and later battles? The general view is that the *Vickers-Maxim* machine guns were the cause, with some suggesting that as many as 50% of all Japanese battle casualties were inflicted by this weapon. Built into protected bunkers, they proved impervious to the Japanese guns even were they lucky enough to hit the position. But the success of the machine gun in a defensive role seems to have escaped senior officers in the British Army with one or two notable exceptions, and these voices were then ignored or belittled by General Officers with no experience of ever having faced the automatic weapons (see page 457). In August 1914, the BEF was provided with 108 machine guns. The German Army possessed 4,900.

In an offensive role as an infantry support weapon the Japanese held the advantage with the French-designed *Hotchkiss Mle 1897*, an air-cooled, gas-actuated, tray-fed machine gun[i]. This was lighter than the *Maxim* and easier to move forward to help the infantry hold any ground gained. The gun of the *Hotchkiss* weighed barely 10 Kgs as opposed to the 70 Kgs (plus water) of the *1904 Vickers-Maxim* which also required a bigger gun team. A truly lightweight automatic weapon would have been useful but, despite arguments being made in favour over several years, nothing was done in the British Army to be so equipped until after the outbreak of war.

---

[i] The *Hotchkiss Mle 1897* was built by the *Société Anonyme des Anciens Etablissements, Hotchkiss et Cie.*, of St Denis, Paris. Benjamin Berkley Hotchkiss, an American gunsmith previously employed by *Colt*, went to France in 1867, moving to Paris in 1875. He died in 1887 and a compatriot, Laurence Benét, took over. In 1893 he was approached by an Austrian Army captain, Baron Adolph von Odkolek, with a design for a gas-actuated automatic gun. *Hotchkiss & Cie* bought the patent which, with the addition of cooling fins on the barrel, produced an air-cooled machine gun. Further improvements in 1903 and 1914 resulted in the *Hotchkiss Mle 1914*, a machine gun preferred over the state-produced *St. Étienne Mle 1907*.

Other more ancient weapons came to the fore during the siege which would re-emerge on the Western Front: the hand grenade and trench mortar. The grenade was discarded by the British Army in 1890 and would have to be re-invented once trench warfare became the norm. As in Manchuria, early efforts on the Western Front would be extemporised weapons created from whatever came to hand, e.g. old shell casings or food cans stuffed with gun cotton and black powder.[12] The same would apply to the trench mortar, the idea of which was raised and dismissed at an annual meeting of General Staff Officers held at Camberley. Within months of the outbreak of the Great War it became an essential part of the armoury of all armies even if every model had to be designed and built from scratch (see page 509).

In general terms the two countries which, perhaps, learnt the *least* from Manchuria were the allies on the Western Front: Britain and France. Neither developed tactically or in terms of equipment in a manner which might have answered any of the questions posed in the Far East. Automatic weapons were left to one side, heavy artillery was ignored, the possibility of trench warfare and, therefore, the need for trench weaponry, dismissed (although almost every war involving one or more industrial nations from the Crimea onwards involved lengthy sieges and extended trench lines). Intelligent men like Foch were so imbued with the concept of wars of manoeuvre and the power of the offensive they dismissed Manchuria, as they dismissed South Africa, as an aberration impossible to replicate in a European War. Foch wrote in the preface of his 1909 book *Conduite de la Guerre*:

"... its lessons are neither complete nor of immediate interest to us; it is not a pattern for us to copy."

Indeed, it was clear from descriptions of France's post-Manchuria manoeuvres in the autumn of 1905 that little was learnt from the various debacles of that war. It seemed the annual exercises were an excuse for garishly uniformed troops to charge around the country playing at soldiers instead of being a serious business in which senior and junior officers honed and/or expanded their skills. *The Times* described them thus:

"In every direction there was a wealth of artillery targets, which are to be seen only in manoeuvres and never in real war.
The infantry of both armies moved in huge masses, within medium ranges and exposed to the view of the hostile batteries. Firing lines advanced in single ranks shoulder to shoulder, and fired, as a rule, standing or kneeling. Supports advanced close behind in line of section columns... The whole country was dotted with these groups, affording objects for shrapnel fire which both Russian and Japanese gunners lived in hopes of seeing but seldom, if ever, saw. As the advance of the opposing firing lines continued, with the rapidity peculiar to manoeuvres, sections, companies, and whole battalions were to be seen blazing in each other's faces at distances of a few hundred yards, or less...
We arrived just in time to see a huge mass of infantry charging up the slopes in the closest formation. Bodies of cuirassiers, dragoons, and chasseurs

were manoeuvring to and fro, all fully exposed to view from the defenders' position. The infantry on the defence were equally exposed; companies stood up shoulder to shoulder to fire, and stayed until the attacking infantry were right on top of them before leisurely retiring. Bugles played, drums beat, bayonets fixed, swords drawn…

The scene on the heights near Chavanges[i] baffles description. Two ridges, the crests of which are about 800 to 1,000 yards apart were covered with masses of men. Batteries in action on the forward slopes blazed at one another, cavalry rode about the field in close formation, infantry charged and counter-charged…

The whole scene reminded one of prints of the battles of 100 years ago, and a British officer present, who had been with the Japanese army, was heard to remark that in no single feature did this sham fight resemble what he had seen of modern war in Manchuria…

The French say that infantry must be trained to advance in any circumstances and cavalry to charge at any odds… yet one left the French fields of mimic battle with the feeling that, to officers and men who have never been under fire, these manoeuvres must be in many ways misleading, and the troops must return to their garrisons with entirely wrong notions of what their arduous training is for."[13]

Little changed over the next nine years either in philosophy, tactics, equipment, or uniform (blue jacketed infantry in red trousers with pale blue trousers for the *Chasseurs à Pied*, gleaming breast plates for cuirassiers, fashionably pale blue tunics for hussars, brass helmets with horsehair plumes for dragoons). The offensive was all. But one should note that in *The Times's* entire four column article, as indeed in nearly every commentary on every country's manoeuvres post-Manchuria up to 1914, there is no mention of the use, effectiveness or impact of the single most destructive weapon in that bloody war in the Far East: the machine gun.

THOUGH VIEWED WITH DISDAIN and dismissed with derision by many military 'experts', Bloch's grim vision of huge, expensive, slow-moving battles on extended fronts was borne out by the Manchurian War and was far more akin to what occurred on the Western Front after the 'race to the sea' than was ever envisaged by any senior General of any of the combatant nations.

There were, however, two other wars involving European powers from which conclusions might be drawn or during which some tactical or technical innovation revealed. The first was the Italian-Turkish War of 1911-12.

Italy, like almost every European country, harboured hopes of empire but its efforts to date had garnered only a poverty stricken, drought-inclined corner of the Horn of Africa – Eritrea and the Somaliland – and an attempt at expansion had proved an utter embarrassment with its humiliating defeat in Ethiopia at the Battle of Adwa on 1st March 1896, the worst ever defeat of a European colonial

---

[i] The manoeuvres took place in the *département de l'Aube* between Troyes and Saint-Dizier in the area where many of Napoleon's battles of early 1814 were fought: Brienne, La Rothière, Montereau, Bar-sur-Aube and Arcis-sur-Aube.

force by native troops. The Italian Army of 17,000 suffered some 80% casualties and lost all its artillery. In the subsequent Treaty of Addis Ababa, Italy recognised Ethiopia as an independent sovereign state. Mussolini sought his revenge on the Ethiopians when Italy invaded without warning in 1935. During the fighting, which extended to 1941, some 600,000 Ethiopian soldiers and civilians died.

As Ottoman power waned, greedy Italian eyes were drawn to territories closer to home. They laid claim to the Ottoman provinces of Tripolitania and Cyrenaica, now Libya. The Italians shipped an expeditionary force across the Mediterranean, landing on 4th October 1911, expecting an easy victory. Despite an overwhelming numerical and technical advantage, they failed to defeat a small number of regular Turkish troops and police units supported by native irregulars[i]. The Italians seized a thin coastal strip around Tripoli, Benghazi, Tobruk, Derana, and Sidi Barrani but, even with the wide-open spaces of the hinterland available, the war bogged down into trench warfare with a few costly infantry assaults punctuated by atrocities and massacres[ii]. It was notable for a few military initiatives: the first use of aircraft for reconnaissance and as bombers[iii], and the use of dirigibles as bombing platforms.

Italy maintained almost complete control of the waters of the central and eastern Mediterranean as well as the Red Sea[iv] throughout the war. In the Red Sea, a force of three protected cruisers[v], a torpedo cruiser[vi] and several destroyers and gunboats, swept the seas and, on 7th January 1912, the *Piemonte* and the destroyers *Artigliere* and *Garibaldino* discovered a Turkish flotilla[vii] in the harbour at Kunfuda (now Al Qunfudhah, Saudi Arabia). Three gunboats were sunk and three driven ashore and destroyed the following day, and an armed yacht sunk. This gave the Italians complete control over the Red Sea which they exploited with intermittent bombardments of the Arabian coastline.

---

[i] Eventually, 100,000 Italian troops faced c. 8,000 Ottomans and 20,000 Libyans.

[ii] Most infamously between 23rd and 26th October 1911. First, at Shar al-Shatt (Italian: Sciara Sciat) near Tripoli, men of the *4ª Compagnia* of the *11° Reggimento bersaglieri* were overrun in the cemetery of Rebab by a mixed force of Ottoman and local troops. 290 men who surrendered were subjected to appalling and grotesque torture and execution; many being crucified. Between 24th and 26th October Italian troops took their revenge, massacring as many as 4,000 Muslim civilians, including women and children, at the Mechiya oasis.

[iii] The first 'bombing' mission was conducted by Italian pilot Guilio Gavotti (1882-1939) when he dropped four 2 Kg grenades from an Italian-built Etrich *Taube* on the oases at Tagiura and Ain Zara on 1st November 1911.

[iv] In the Red Sea to protect their province of Italian Eritrea thought to be under threat from Ottoman troops in the Arabian Peninsula.

[v] The *Armstrong*-built *Piedmonte* (commissioned 1889), and the *Calabria* (built by *Arsenale di La Spezia* and commissioned in 1897) and *Puglia* (built at *Arsenale di Taranto* and commissioned in 1901).

[vi] The *Aretusa*, built by *Cantiere navale fratelli Orlando*, Livorno, commissioned 1892.

[vii] The gunboats *Ordu*, *Bafra*, *Refahiye*, *Gökçedağ*, *Kastamonu*, and *Ayintag*, the armed tugboat *Muha*, and the armed yacht *Şipka*.

On 24th February 1912, two Italian armoured cruisers, the *Giuseppe Garibaldi* and *Francesco Ferruccio*[i], armed with two 10-inch, ten 6-inch and six 4.7-inch guns, bombarded the port of Beirut sinking the elderly corvette *Avnillah* (built 1869) and the modern torpedo boat *Angora*. With the rest of the Ottoman navy tucked up in the Sea of Marmara, this gave total control of the eastern Mediterranean and Aegean Sea to the *Regia Marina* and Italian troops occupied a dozen or so Aegean islands including Rhodes, Kos, Kalymnos and Leros[ii].

A truly relevant, but seemingly ignored, naval event of the war was an incursion on 18th July 1912 by five Italian vessels (the *Spica*, a *Sirio*-class torpedo boat, and four *Pegaso*-class torpedo boats, *Perseo, Astore, Climene* and *Centauro*) 18 miles into the Dardanelles before being stopped by a boom and heavy gun fire from coastal forts and moored ships. The Ottomans claim to have sunk two boats, but none were significantly damaged. They were, however, able to travel at an average of 21 knots, speeds well above anything achieved by the vulnerable and elderly British and French pre-dreadnoughts which tried to force the Dardanelles in early 1915 at such heavy cost. The Italian action led to a significant strengthening of the Dardanelles defences including a narrowing of the channel by the laying of new minefields. This seems to have entirely escaped the Allies in the interim.

The war ended with the Treaty of Lausanne of October 1912 in which the Ottoman Empire conceded defeat. The Italians did not gain complete control over Libya until the late 1920s by which time, through war, famine and emigration, the population of the country halved. The 1911 population was only regained in 1950.

THE OTTOMAN DEFEAT ENCOURAGED Serbia, Montenegro, Bulgaria, and Greece – the Balkan League – to take on the ailing Empire in the First Balkan War, fought between October 1912 and May 1913. All four kingdoms were previously part of the Ottoman Empire. Greece gained independence in 1830 and Serbia and Montenegro in 1869. Bulgaria became an autonomous principality in 1878, declaring full independence in 1908. By 1912 Greece consisted of the Morea (Peloponnese), central Greece and Thessaly. The rest of what is modern Greece, i.e. Epirus, southern Macedonia, and western Thrace, were still part of the Ottoman Empire. Also part of that empire was what are now Albania, Kosovo and North Macedonia and the Sanjak of Novi Pazar, a strip of land between Serbia and tiny Montenegro to the west.

All four members of the Balkan League had territorial ambitions, some of them in direct competition and, for three, hankering back to ancient pre-Ottoman empires: the Byzantine Empire[iii] for the Greeks, the First[iv] and Second Bulgarian

---

[i] Built between 1895 and 1903 by *Gio. Ansaldo & Co.* in Genoa-Sestri Ponente as part of a ten-ship class for the Italian, Spanish, Argentinian and Japanese navies. The *Giuseppe Garibaldi* was launched in 1899 and was sunk by the Austrian submarine *U-4* off Ragusa Vecchia (now Cavtat, Croatia) on 18th July 1915. The *Francesco Ferruccio* was launched in 1902 and decommissioned in 1930.

[ii] The islands were known as the Dodecanese and were ceded to Greece in 1947.

[iii] Dissolved after the Ottoman sack of Constantinople on 29th May 1453.

[iv] Between the 7th and 11th Centuries this ran south from the Carpathians and included Bulgaria and Macedonia, Wallachia, Kosovo, and much of Serbia including Belgrade.

Empires[i]; and the brief Serbian Empire of Stefan Uroš IV Dušan[ii] and his son. The people of the Balkans have always harboured long memories of past glories and bitter defeats and, by 1912, the main protagonists each had their own paramilitary organisations active, especially in Macedonia: the *Vatreshna Makedonska Revolyutsionna Organizatsiya* (*VMRO*, initially founded for an independent Macedonia but then effectively taken over by Bulgarian interests); the Greek *Ethniki Etaireia* later taken over by the *Makedoniko Komitato* (*Hellenic Macedonian Committee*); and the Serbian *Srpska revolucionarna organizacija* (*Serbian Revolutionary Organization* or *Chetniks*).

By 1912 any enlargement of Montenegro was welcome to Nikola I Petrović-Njegoš, the country's first and only king[iii]. He had his eyes mainly on Albania to the south, especially the area around Shkodër. Petar I Karađorđević of Serbia, made king after a military coup in 1903, hankered after several things: access to the Adriatic, the Sanjak, Kosovo and as much of Albania and Macedonia as he could lay his hands on. Bulgaria's Ferdinand I, the Austrian-born Ferdinand Maximilian Karl Leopold Maria of Saxe-Coburg and Gotha-Koháry, looked south to Thrace, Eastern Rumelia[iv] and Macedonia and, most especially, the port of Thessaloniki (Salonika) on the northern shore of the Aegean. Though specifically warned against it by Russia, he also had grandiose ideas about capturing Constantinople thereby dominating access to and from the Black Sea. Greece looked longingly to the north. The country's king was the Danish-born Geórgios I[v], until his assassination in the newly liberated Thessaloniki on 18th March 1913, when he was replaced by his son, Konstantínos I[vi]. The Prime Minister, since a

---

[i] Existed between 1185 and 1396 and included most of the territory mentioned in the footnote above as well as most of Thrace, Thessaly, and Epirus. Already weakened, it came to an end with the defeat of a Crusader Army on the Danube at the Battle of Nicopolis (now Nikopol, Bulgaria) on 25th September 1396.

[ii] Stefan Uroš IV Dušan (the Mighty) was king of Serbia from 1331 and declared *Basileus* and *Autokrator* (Emperor and Autocrat) of the Serbs, Greeks, Bulgarians, and Albanians in 1346. At its peak, the empire consisted of Serbia, Montenegro, Albania, Kosovo, Epirus, Thessaly and Macedonia. Dušan died in 1355 and, with the death of his son, Stefan Uroš V, in 1371 the empire dissolved. Serbia was crushed by the Turks at the Battle of Kosovo, 28th June 1389 (NS), 15th June (OS).

[iii] Nikola was prince of Montenegro from 1860, declaring himself king, 1910. After the Central Powers invaded Serbia in the autumn, 1915, Montenegro was occupied by Austro-Hungarian troops and Nikola fled to France. Post-war, Montenegro was absorbed into the Kingdom of Serbs, Croats and Slovenes, renamed Yugoslavia in 1929. Montenegro regained its independence in 2006.

[iv] Rumelia was part of the Ottoman Empire and an area previously controlled by the Romans and Byzantines. In 1912 it consisted of Eastern Rumelia, i.e. Thrace, and Western Rumelia, i.e. Macedonia, Albania, Kosovo, and Epirus.

[v] Originally Prince Christian William Ferdinand Adolf George of Schleswig-Holstein-Sonderburg-Glücksburg.

[vi] Konstantínos I had the unfortunate record of being commander of the Army of Thessaly in the disastrous Greco-Turkish War of 1897 and then leading the latter part of the campaign in Asia Minor against Turkey in 1920-22 in the equally disastrous

1908 military coup, was Eleftherios Venizelos, a Cretan, a social liberal but a Greek nationalist keen to see Crete[i] and territories to the north absorbed into an enlarged Greece. Their objective was Epirus up to the modern border with Albania, southern Macedonia, and Thrace, including Thessaloniki. Not everyone could emerge with their wish-lists fulfilled.

But, if the conflict was about territory, it was also about ethnicity. In Greece, Pan-Hellenism demanded the reunification of all Greeks, whether they be in Epirus, Macedonia, Crete and the Aegean Islands, or on the coastline of Asia Minor around Smyrna (modern İzmir). Both the Montenegrins and Serbs wished to see the reformation of the old southern Slav empire destroyed by the Ottomans in the 14th Century, though each had their own ideas as to who would lead it. Bulgaria sought to regain the huge swathe of Macedonian territory initially assigned to it by the Treaty of San Stefano which ended the Russo-Turkish War of 1877-8, though this decision was then overtaken by strategic judgements made by the major European powers at the Congress of Berlin in the summer of 1878 which returned these territories to the Ottomans, a verdict very badly received in Bulgaria. The point about these ambitions is that they clashed with one another and with the hopes and aspirations of certain ethnic groups, most particularly the predominantly Muslim Albanians as well as the Muslim communities of Thrace.

In 1878, Albania was divided between four Ottoman administrative areas or *vilayets*. These were Kosovo, Scutari (also Shkodra, modern Shkodër, Albania), Monastir (or Manastir, modern Bitola, North Macedonia) and Janina (modern Ioannina, Greece). The Treaty of San Stefano proposed splitting these Albanian-populated areas between Serbia, Montenegro, and Bulgaria. Although mainly Muslim, Albania had long sought either autonomy or independence from 500 years of rule by the *Sublime Porte* in Constantinople.

Albanian culture and language was from, time to time, actively suppressed by the Ottoman authorities. There was, for example, no standardised Albanian alphabet until the adoption of the *Bashkimi* (unity) alphabet in 1911. In the mid-18th Century two semi-autonomous *Pashaliks* emerged which dominated the territories with Albanian populations: the *Pashaliks* of Shkodra, and of Janina. Shkodra controlled most of what is now Kosovo, Montenegro and Albania, and parts of southern Serbia and western Macedonia. The Pashalik of Janina disappeared with the assassination if its ruler, Ali Pasha, by agents of the *Sublime Porte* in 1822 thus ending a local rebellion against centralised rule. The *Pashalik* of Shkodra disappeared after, first, 4-500 chiefs and their men were slaughtered by the Ottoman General Reşid Mehmed Pasha after being invited to Monastir to be

---

Greco-Turkish War of 1919-22. He resumed the throne, having abdicated in 1917, when his second son, Alexander, died unexpectedly in 1920. He abdicated again on 27th September 1922 and died on 11th January 1923 in Palermo.

[i] Crete became an autonomous region after the bloody revolt of 1897. The revolt precipitated the 1897 Greco-Turkish War (or Thirty Days' War) in which Prince Konstantínos's poorly equipped army was defeated at the Battle of Domokos (*Turkish*: Dömeke) on 17th May. The Turks reached Thermopylae (130 kms short of Athens) before a Russian-negotiated ceasefire ended the war on 19th May 1897.

'rewarded' for their services to the *Sublime Porte* in August 1830, and second, when Rozafa Castle, the base of the *Pashalik*, fell to Reşid Mehmed Pasha in 1831.

Albanians, however, were rarely passive, as revolts in 1833, 1844 and 1847 proved. When, in 1878, it seemed Albania was to be dismembered by the Treaty of San Stefano and shared between Serbia, Montenegro and Greece, armed resistance prevented the largest territorial losses, though some Albanian-populated areas were ceded to their neighbours, with Greece being advantaged by the acquisition of Thessaly. Resistance continued, however, and it was only through the intervention of an Ottoman army that the transfer of territories was confirmed. Demands for autonomy continued, with uprisings taking place in parts of Ottoman-controlled Albania. In 1902, another attack was made on the culture and language when Albanian-language books and periodicals were banned. In addition, the mainly Muslim Albanian communities were coming under attack from the Orthodox Christian Serbian, Bulgarian and Greek terrorist/nationalist groups then very active in neighbouring Macedonia. There were, however, both Catholic and Orthodox believers who were committed to the idea of a secular, independent Albania and they, too, were the targets of Greek, Serbian and Bulgarian aggression. One such was a young Albanian Orthodox priest, *Papa* Kristo Negovani, who dared to conduct the Orthodox Divine Liturgy in the Albanian *Tosk* dialect[i] in front of Germanos Karavangelis, the Metropolitan Bishop of Kastoria. Karavangelis was also a member of the *Makedoniko Komitato* dedicated to the 'liberation' of Greek Macedonia. The psychopathic bishop, ignoring his bible's 6th commandment 'Thou shalt not kill', had the young priest murdered[ii].

In 1908 the *İttihad ve Terakki Cemiyeti* (*Committee for Union and Progress*), better known as the *Young Turks*, instigated a rebellion in Macedonia against the autocratic rule of *Sultan* Abdül Hamid II[iii]. At the same time another uprising broke

---

[i] There are two main dialects spoken in Albania: *Tosk* in the south and *Gheg* in the north and Kosovo. *Tosk* is the basis for standard Albanian. The dividing line is recognised as the *Shkumbin* (aka *Shkembi*) river which enters the Adriatic 30 kms south of the main Albanian port of Durrës (previously Durazzo and Dyrrachium).

[ii] As a reprisal, Albanian nationalists assassinated the metropolitan bishop of Korçë, in Albania, Photios Kalpidis, on 9th September 1906. Negovari was not the first man murdered on the orders of Karavangelis. The Bulgarian/Macedonian revolutionary, Lazar Poptraykov, was decapitated on his instructions and the head photographed on his desk. The picture was published in 1934 in the Bulgarian/Macedonian magazine: Илюстрация Илинден or *Illustration Ilinden*. Poptraykov was a leading figure in the *Vnatrešna Makedonska Revolucionerna Organizacija* or *VMRO* (*Internal Macedonian-Adrianople Revolutionary Organisation*) which had organised the Ilinden–Preobrazhenie Uprising in 1903. After the uprising was crushed, the *VMRO* resorted to simple terrorism, including instigating the Kotchana Massacre on 1st August 1912 which indirectly led to the First Balkan War. There, the *VMRO* planted a bomb in a Muslim market which killed a number of local people. Muslims took reprisals against local Orthodox Christians, murdering 140 of them. The reaction in Bulgaria helped foment the war fever which became irresistible by mid-October.

[iii] Amongst other crimes, Abdül Hamid II instigated what was known as the Hamidian Massacres of Armenians and Assyrians in the eastern Turkish *vilayets* of Bitlis,

out amongst Albanians in Kosovo. Soon, the Army mutinied and the Sultan had to agree to a return to the 1876 constitutional form of government. He was forced to abdicate in April 1909 after a failed counter coup and was replaced by *Sultan Mehmed V Reşâd*. The *Young Turks*, initially dedicated to the preservation of the integrity of the Ottoman Empire, then tried to clamp down on Albanian nationalism generated by the *Rilindja* or Albanian National Awakening. A three-month uprising starting in Kosovo in 1910 resulted in an attempt to crush Albanian culture: schools were closed, and organisations and publications banned whilst villages were razed and many Albanians executed without trial. Another rebellion followed in the spring of 1911 and though defeated, it resulted in limited concessions to the Albanian tribal leaders on issues to do with schools, language, and military service. The key moment, however, was the revolt of 1912 which started in January and ran for eight months. The result, agreed on 4th September 1912, was virtual Albanian autonomy though not as a single entity: administration of the region was still in the hands of the four previously mentioned *vilayets*. By now, however, war between the Ottomans and the Balkan League was almost inevitable and Montenegro, sensing an opportunity, started to advance troops into the area around Shkodër in a pre-emptive action.

IRONICALLY, IT WAS THE SMALLEST of the four combatants which declared war on the Ottoman Empire first, with Montenegro so doing on 8th October 1912. The others followed nine days later, on 17th October.

The Turks were at a severe strategic disadvantage. Their three European armies numbered c. 340,000 whilst Bulgaria alone, which believed itself to be the 'Prussia of the Balkans', could mobilise some 600,000 men, an extraordinary figure for a country with a population of 4.3 million. It deployed some 350,000 men, based in three armies all facing the 450-km long border with Turkey in Macedonia and Thrace. Serbia called up c. 300,000 troops, again formed into three armies, with objectives being the Sanjak, Kosovo, Albania, and parts of northern Macedonia. Greece contributed 125,000 men nominally in the armies of Epirus and Thessaly, but, in practice, 90% of the men were in the latter army. Their objective was to capture Thessaloniki. In addition, Greece, the last to join the Balkan League, possessed a small but modern navy overseen by British naval officers. This successfully blockaded the Turkish coast, preventing reinforcements from being shipped across the Mediterranean from the Levant and the Arabian Peninsula.

In addition, though active army units, the *Nizam*,[i] were well-equipped and trained (mainly by German officers using German armaments), the reserves, the

---

Diyarbekir, Erzurum, Mamuret-ul-Aziz, Sivas, Trebizond, and Van between 1894 and 1897. Up to 300,000 Armenians and 25,000 Assyrians were murdered. After the 1909 counter-coup c. 30,000 Armenians were massacred in Adana. Between 1913 and 1922 the *Young Turks* oversaw the slaughter of up to 900,000 Greeks, 270,000 Assyrians, and 1.8 million Armenians. After that, the main target of Turkish ethnic cleansing was the Kurds who had earlier co-operated in the massacres of Armenians and Assyrians.

[i] Selection for the *Nizam* and *Redif* was made by lottery at aged 20. The *Asakir-i Nizamiye-i Şahane* (Imperial regular soldiers) enlisted for 3 years. They passed to the active reserve, *Ihtiyat*, for 3 years (one 6-week annual training camp). In war-time *Nizam*

Redif, were deficient in training *and* equipment. With every Army Corps containing at least one, and sometimes three, *Redif* divisions (out of three or four), this lack of quality, cohesion and firepower cost them dear. Furthermore, they were defending a large area with a population of 6 million, of which nearly two-thirds were Christian and, until 1909, not trusted to fight on behalf of a Muslim empire[ii].

Finally, they made the cardinal error of trying to defend all their territory, ignoring Frederick the Great's military *dictum*: 'He who defends everything, defends nothing'. Their armies – *Vardar* (west), *Macedonian* (centre), and *Thracian* (east) – were spread almost equally to defend against the Montenegrins, Serbs and Greeks in the west, the Serbs and Greeks in the centre, and Bulgarians in the east. This meant just 120,000 faced the Bulgarians in Thrace whilst 200,000 men defended the rest. To add to the confusion, the High Command ignored existing formations and combined the armies into two: a *Western Army* (*Vardar* and *Macedonian*) commanded by 50-year-old Halepli Zeki Pasha[iii], and *Eastern Army* (*Thracian*) of 66-year-old Kölemen Abdullah Pasha[iv]. It could be said they doubled-down on their error by having two-thirds of their troops far away from their only secure overland supply, reinforcement, and withdrawal route to and from Constantinople into eastern Thrace. To make matters *even* worse, it was this area and these routes which were under threat from the Balkan League's most powerful army, that of Bulgaria. Finally, the icing on the cake came when 64-year-old Hüseyin Nazım Pasha[v], Ottoman Minister of War and a French-trained, Foch-influenced adherent of the offensive, overturned the current defensive strategy defined by Colmar von der Goltz[vi] and implemented by Chief of the General Staff, Ahmed Izzet Pasha[vii], in favour of one of aggressive offensive. It would first knock

---

divisions comprised three, 3-battalion regiments, a rifle battalion, and 6 to 9 field artillery batteries (each of 4 guns). An Army Corps comprised 2-3 divisions, a cavalry brigade, 3 howitzer batteries, 6 mountain batteries and a telegraph company. [*Source*: *The Statesman's Yearbook 1913*, Macmillan & Co., page 1309].

[i] *Asakir-i Redif-i Şahane* (Imperial reserve soldiers) had 30 days bi-annual training which were often missed. There were two classes of *Redif*: the first class made up of the first 5 years of *Redif* service, and the second made up of the remaining 4 years. *Redif* divisions usually consisted of 9 battalions from three regiments, but artillery and engineers were supplied by *Nizam* units. [*Source*: *Ibid*.].

[ii] Rarely in fighting units, as many Muslims disliked the idea of arming the Christian population, several Turkish writers accused them of deserting in large numbers.

[iii] A Kurd, his previous experience had been massacring Armenians in 1894 after the Sasun Rebellion (near Lake Van in eastern Turkey).

[iv] Born in Trabzon (previously Trebizond).

[v] Another Kurd. Trained at St Cyr, he was assassinated by representatives of the *Young Turks* on 23rd January 1913 during the *coup d'état*.

[vi] Goltz went to Turkey in 1883 after their defeat in the Russian War, 1877-8. He spent twelve years there with the titles *Pasha* and *Müshir* (Field Marshal). He trained most of the *Young Turks*, whose 1908 revolution started the transformation of the country.

[vii] Ahmed Izzet Pasha, an Albanian from Nasliç, Monastir Vilayet, was in Yemen dealing with Imam Yahya hamid ed-Din al-Mutawakkil's long-running rebellion in the northern highlands. It resulted in the autonomy of the Zaydi tribes.

out the Serbs before turning its attention on the Bulgarians in Thrace. Nazim Pasha is said to have told his officers to take dress uniforms with them. They would be needed after their victorious entry into Sofia.[14]

Unfortunately, the slow mobilisation of Ottoman forces left the *Vardar Army* facing the Serbs with 50% of the planned numbers, a problem compounded when they misjudged the dispositions of the Bulgarian Army, believing them concentrated west of Adrianople[i] rather than, as was the case, east of that city.

The fighting was brief and disastrous for the Turks. The Montenegrins invested the large town of Shkodër (also known as Scutari and now in northern Albania) on 28th October 1912. The Ottoman forces resisted until 23rd April 1913, initially under the command of Hasan Riza Pasha[ii], but he was murdered by the servants of his second-in-command, Essad Pasha Toptani. Essad Pasha had ambitions to become the king of a newly formed and independent Albania and wished to negotiate the surrender of the town in return for Montenegrin and Serbian support for this move[iii]. Its surrender came after the major European powers had determined it would be part of a new Kingdom of Albania.

The Serbians, meanwhile, drove into the Sanjak of Novi Pazar and Kosovo on 20th October, intent on invading Macedonia. By 22nd October they were near Kumanovo but ignorant of the position and numbers of Halepli Zeki Pasha's *Vardar Army*. Outnumbered two to one, Zeki Pasha determined to attack. In foggy conditions confused but inconclusive fighting continued throughout 23rd October. The Turks missed an opportunity to destroy the Serbian left wing as the Serbian *First Army*, under Crown Prince Aleksandar I Karađorđević[iv], had no real idea what was happening to their advanced units. The fighting resumed the next day and was just as chaotic. Serb reinforcements arrived and, with most of two local Ottoman divisions[v] deserting overnight on hearing the Serbs had occupied Pristina, the battle turned decisively in favour of the Serbs. Under the accurate fire of French-supplied Serbian field guns, the *Redif* divisions started to dissolve and soon their position collapsed. Although casualties were similar, and not especially heavy – some 5,000 in total for each side – the Turks lost two-thirds of their artillery[vi] and

---

[i] Known by the Turkish name of Edirne since 1928.
[ii] Born in 1871, he was the son of a former governor of Baghdad.
[iii] He later formed the Republic of Central Albania which existed between 16th October 1913 and 7th March 1914 when Wilhelm Friedrich Heinrich Prinz zu Wied became Prince Vilhelm I of the Principality of Albania. He went into exile on 3rd September 1914 and a republic was officially declared on 31st January 1925.
[iv] Later King Aleksander I of the Kingdom of the Serbs, Croats, and Slovenes and then Yugoslavia, 1921-34. He was assassinated by a Bulgarian revolutionary, Vlado Chernozemski, in Marseille on 9th October 1934. The French Foreign Minister Louis Barthou was killed in the same incident though by stray police bullet. Chernozemski was stabbed, beaten, and fatally injured by spectators. He was acting on behalf of the Croatian Fascist and ultranationalist *Ustaše* and was trained in Mussolini's Italy.
[v] The *Üsküp Redif Division* and *Priştine Redif Division*.
[vi] The Turks had two bad habits when using their artillery. One was to expose them to give the infantry direct fire support as at Kumanovo. The other was to dig them in and fail to remove them when the tactical situation demanded it which happened both at

were forced to retreat, abandoning Skopje and then withdrawing 150 kms south to Prilep. There, between 3rd and 5th November, they made a stand with their forces reduced to barely 32,000 troops. Though they overwhelmed the Turks by sheer numbers, Serb infantry tactics displayed all the (lack of) subtlety and finesse displayed by the average General on the Western Front, and they managed to lose twice as many men as the Ottoman forces in the extended fighting. Still, however, numbers were remarkably low, the Serbs losing 2,000 dead and wounded.

The Turks withdrew 40+ kms south to the town of Monastir where the final, and conclusive, battle took place between the 16th and 19th November. At the Battle of Monastir, 108,000 Serbs defeated 38,000 Ottoman troops, causing 3,000 casualties and capturing nearly 6,000. Another 5,000 men deserted. Here, again, the Serbian artillery fire was effective in destroying the remaining Turkish artillery and, with that gone, any slight hopes of victory were lost. Ottoman rule in Macedonia, first established in the last quarter of the 14th Century, was at an end.

The Greeks, meanwhile, confounded expectations by mobilising more troops than expected. They then upset Ottoman thinking by directing their main effort not towards Epirus but north-east towards Thessaloniki. The defending Turkish troops were equally split between the two sectors thus giving the 5-division strong *Army of Thessaly* under Crown Prince Konstantínos a numerical advantage of more than 2:1 over the two divisions of 67-year-old Hasan Tahsin Pasha's *VIII Provisional Corps*[i]. They first clashed at the fortified pass of Sarantoporo, 25 kms west of Mount Olympus, on 22nd October. The pass was heavily defended and the Greeks made limited headway, but flanking attacks to west and east were successful. The latter included detachments of the *2nd* and *6th Battalions* of mountain troops – the *Evzones* – commanded by Col. Konstantinos Konstantinopoulos, and the threat of encirclement resulted in the Turkish reserves abandoning their positions. When a neighbouring pass fell, the withdrawal became a rout. On the morning of 23rd October, Greek infantry launched a final assault and the Ottoman defence collapsed, leaving over twenty *Krupp* field guns in Greek hands.

The Turkish retreat took them through Servia, across the *Haliacmon River*[ii] and to Kozani, 55 kms to the north. Before they went, they executed 117 prominent Greek citizens of Servia[iii] whose heads were found lining a road now called *117 ethnomartyron*.[15] An early atrocity in a war in which they became tragically commonplace.

Kumanovo and Monastir. Numerous undamaged field guns were captured by the Serbs. During the war 300 of their 530 field guns were captured by the allies. [*Source*: Morrow, 2nd Lt. N P, 4th Field Artillery, US Army, *The employment of artillery in the Balkan and in the present European War, Field Artillery Journal*, April-June 1915, pages 316-337].

[i] Made up of the *22nd (Nizamiye) Division* and the *Nasliç* and *Aydın (Redif) Divisions*.
[ii] Part of the *Haliacmon River* was flooded to form *Lake Polyphytos* in the 1970s. The bridge over which the Turks withdrew lies submerged in the lake.
[iii] Servia was destroyed by Italian troops after the Battle of Fardykambos, 4th-6th March 1943, when partisans from *ELAS* (*Ellinikós Laïkós Apeleftherotikós Stratós* or *Greek People's Liberation Army*) captured the Italian garrison. In retaliation, the Italian *36ª Divisione di fanteria 'Forlì'* based at Larissa set fire to the town. The Italians abandoned several towns, e.g. Grevena, Karditsa and Metsovo, as their authority evaporated.

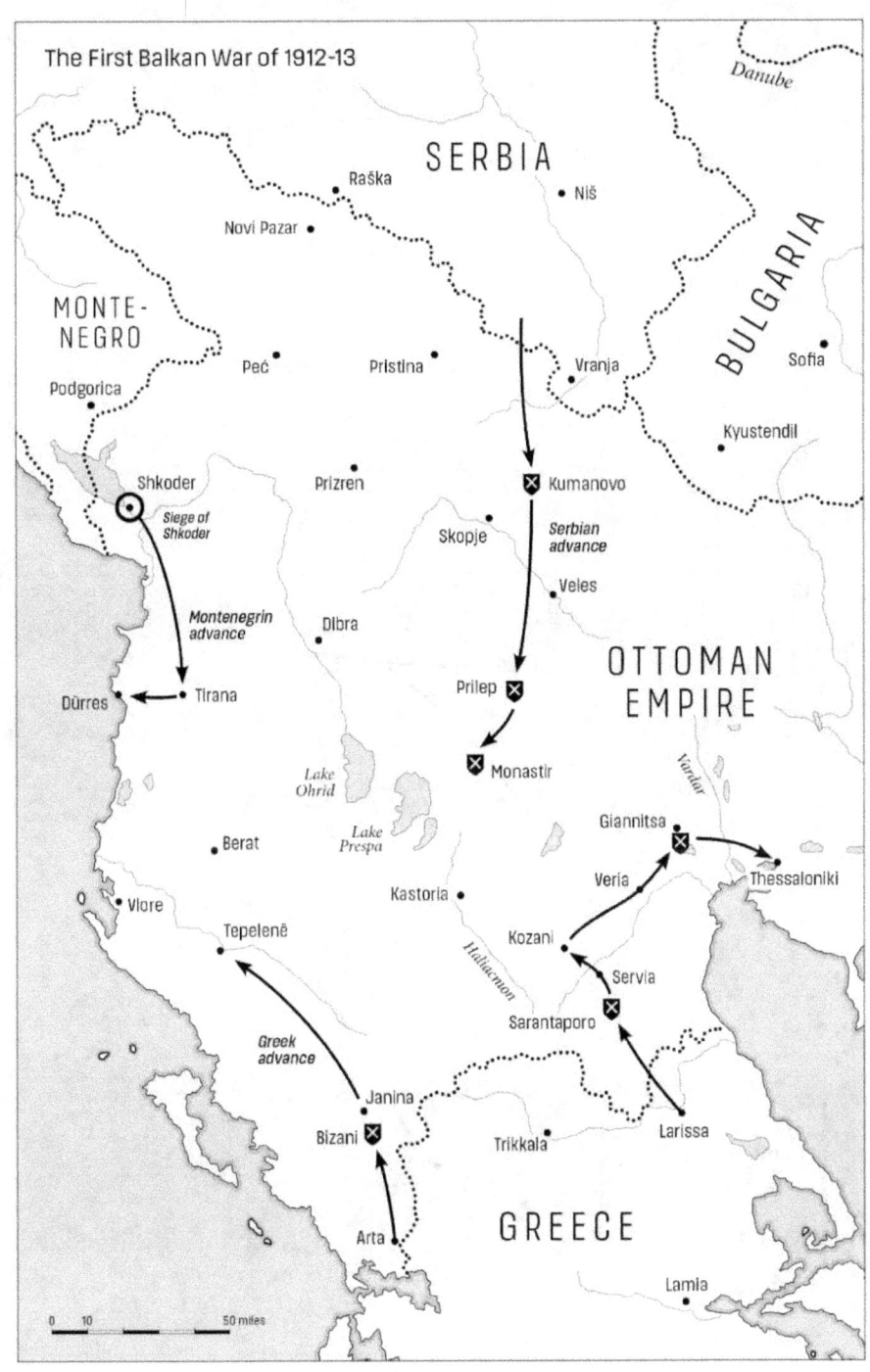

Map 11 First Balkan War: Western theatre

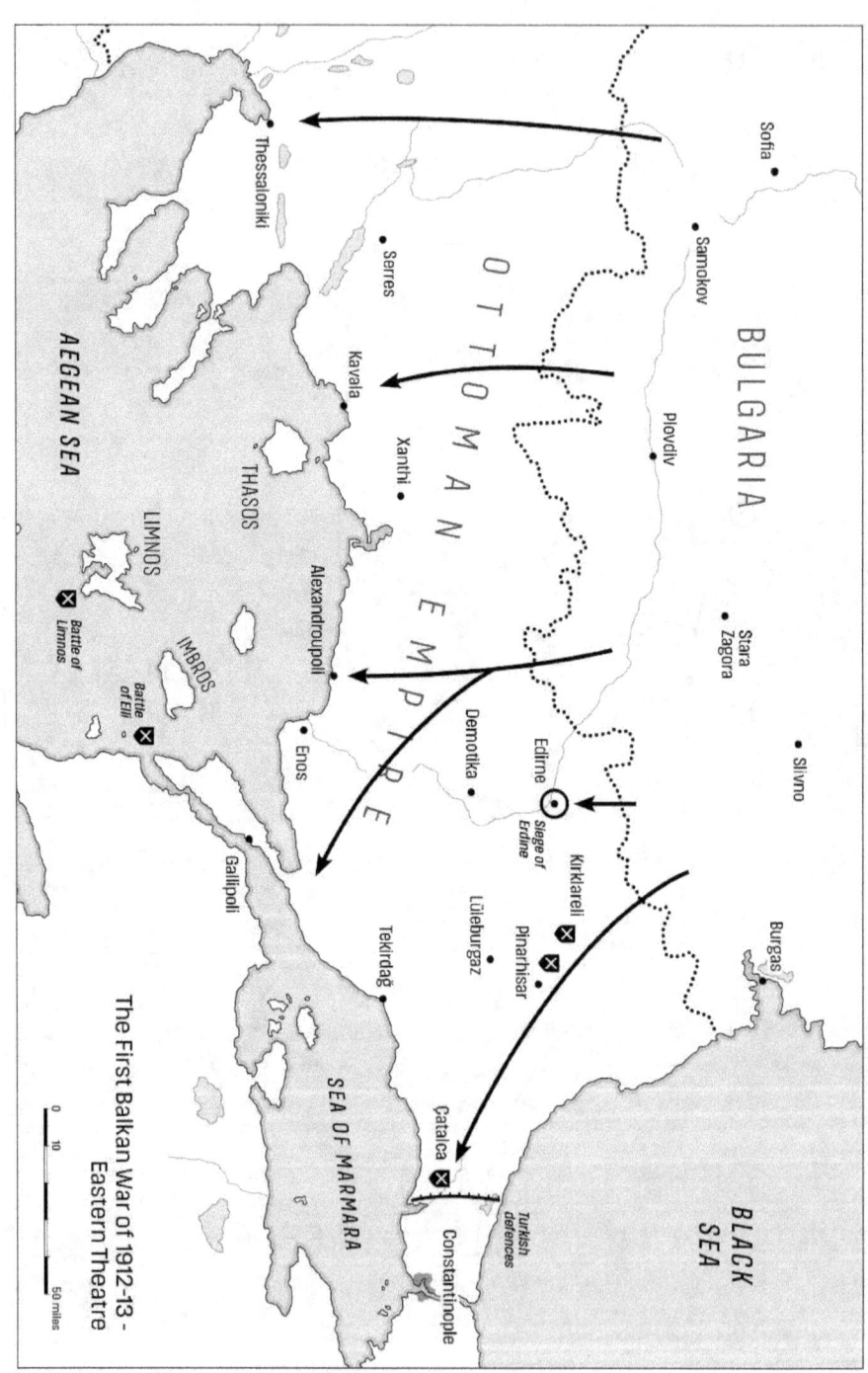

Map 12 First Balkan War: Eastern theatre

Greek cavalry occupied Kozani on 24th October and, two days later, Geórgios I arrived to order the advance on Thessaloniki aware, no doubt, that Bulgarian troops, too, had this essential port as a priority objective. To capture Thessaloniki the Greeks had to advance over the great flood plain of the *Haliacmon, Loudias* and *Vardar Rivers* which descend from the mountains to the north and west and enter the *Thermaic Gulf* to the west of Thessaloniki[i]. This was a vast area of marshland in the centre of which was a large lake at Giannitsa (Turkish: Yenidje)[ii]. Turkish troops were deployed to the north and south of the lake and, in confused fighting over two days, 1st and 2nd November, Tahsin Pasha's 25,000 men were routed, most fleeing into Thessaloniki, 40 kms to the east. Casualties were, again, light, the Greeks losing less than 1,000 men and the Turks some 1,500 and another dozen or so field guns. On 7th November, the *Army of Thessaly* crossed the *Axios River*, 15 kms west of the city, where a delegation from the Turks asked for terms. The following day, with the Greeks insisting on unconditional surrender, 26,000 troops with 70 artillery pieces and large amounts of ammunition and supplies surrendered just before Bulgarian troops arrived. Greek insistence on their continued occupation of the city, and its eventual absorption into a greatly enlarged Greek state would prove a serious bone of contention with Bulgaria and would contribute towards the outbreak of the 2nd Balkan War the following summer.

After the fall of Thessaloniki, a large part of the *Army of Thessaly* was transferred west where it joined in the invasion of Epirus where it helped with the destruction of the *Yanya Corps* at the Battle of Bizani (4th-6th March 1913) in which over 11,000 Ottoman troops were killed or captured at a cost of just 500 Greeks. At Janina, 10 kms further north, 33,000 Turkish troops with 108 guns surrendered on 6th March and, with the fall of Shkodër on 23rd April to the Montenegrins, the war in Western Rumelia was at an end.

Greece's other contribution was through its British-organised navy which effectively tied up the larger and more powerful Turkish fleet and denied them use of sea lanes to transport troops from Arabia and the Levant to Thrace. Two small fleet actions, at Elli on 16th December 1912, and Lemnos on 18th January 1913, ended in the Greek's favour. On both occasions they made better tactical use of their modern armoured cruiser, the Italian-built *Georgios Averof* with a top speed of 23.5 knots, against the Turkish flagship, the 20-year-old but far more heavily armed pre-Dreadnought, *Barbaros Hayreddin* (previously the *SMS Kurfürst Friedrich Wilhelm* with a top speed 16.5 knots), which suffered considerable damage and casualties in both battles. The Greek domination of the Aegean, Ionian and eastern Mediterranean Seas made a major contribution to the success of the Balkan League in the war.

THE HEAVIEST FIGHTING WAS IN EASTERN THRACE where the bulk of the Bulgarian forces faced the Turks across just 120 kms of their common 450 km long border. As mentioned, the Turks believed the main body of the Bulgarian Army would join with the Serbs to attack Macedonia and western Thrace. Thus,

---

[i] An area of 1,500 Km² or 600 Square miles.
[ii] Subsequently drained by engineers from the *New York Foundation Company* between 1928 and 1932.

the *Western Army* was nearly twice as strong as the *Eastern Army*, barely 100,000 strong, which now faced an attack by three Bulgarian Armies of nearly 300,000 men. An attempt to defend a 60 km front between Adrianople and Kırklareli (also known as Kirk Kilise or Lozengrad) 60 kms to the east failed when the *1st* and *3rd Bulgarian Armies* drove the Turks south-east after three days of fighting. (22nd-24th October). Casualties were relatively even but the Turks lost nearly 60 of their field guns in the battle and an increasingly shambolic retreat as the *Eastern Army* disintegrated. To make matters worse, the direction of the Turkish withdrawal isolated Adrianople where over 60,000 troops were now besieged by the *2nd Bulgarian Army*. The *1st* and *3rd Armies*, however, did not immediately follow-up their success giving the Turks time to re-form and bring up new troops.

Kölemen Abdullah Pasha's *Eastern Army* re-established itself 40 kms south-east on a 35 km-long line of hills between the town of Lüleburgaz (also Lule Burgas) and Pinarhisar (also Bunar Hisar) some 150 kms north-west of Constantinople (Kırklareli Province, N-W Turkey). These two towns each lay on the main roads between Adrianople and the capital. The battle, fought on a front of 32 kms, was the largest European battle between 1871 and 1914. There, over five days of heavy fighting starting on 30th October, 108,000 Bulgarians and 360 guns comprehensively defeated 130,000 Turks with 300 guns. Total casualties exceeded 20,000 (20%) on each side. Routed, the Turks retreated in confusion, losing another 50 guns, the Army dissolving in panic. The supply chain having previously collapsed, many men starved to death. Others died from an outbreak of cholera and the dead and dying littered the road towards Constantinople.[16]

The Turks fled chaotically to the Çatalca line protecting Constantinople, which lay c. 45 kms (30 m.) N.W. of the city centre, with the Sea of Marmara to the south and the Black Sea the north. Here, the isthmus is c. 14 miles (23 kms) wide between Bahşayiş at the top of the Büyükçekmece Gölü (Gölü = lake) on the south coast, then north, along the line of the *River Karasudere*, to Yazlık on the Black Sea coast.

The Bulgarians, meanwhile, disorganised and weakened by their losses and then also afflicted by an outbreak of cholera possibly caught from captured Turkish troops, did not immediately follow up and the Turkish defences were able to solidify around the previously and robustly constructed Çatalca line some 30 kms west of Constantinople. Here the Bulgarian advance ground to a halt, the Turkish defences being assisted by fire from Ottoman warships in the Black Sea. It was here that the field guns of the Bulgarians proved useless against well-built and comprehensive Ottoman fortifications. Shrapnel fired at ranges of up to 6,000 metres was no use whatsoever against well-built trenches with excellent head cover. The Turks, meanwhile, brought their field guns up close to the main trench line using communication trenches wide enough to accommodate a gun and its caissons and then provided well entrenched robust positions able to resist the feeble fire of the Bulgarian guns. Thus, the Bulgarian first assault, on 17th and 18th November 1912, failed with the loss of 12,000 men. The Turks had inflicted the first ever defeat on the Bulgarian Army. A harbinger of things to come for the Allies on the Western Front.

On 3rd December, an armistice was agreed, and peace negotiations started in London, but the *Young Turk coup d'état* of 23rd January put an end to the discussions with fighting re-starting in early February. A Turkish offensive out of the Çatalca line and another out of Gallipoli made little headway and just added to the list of the dead and maimed. The Bulgarians, however, strength eroded by cholera and concerned lest the superior Turkish navy might land troops to their rear along the Black Sea coast, withdrew 20 kms to the west to a new defensive position.

To the rear, the siege of Adrianople was ongoing with the Bulgarian *2nd Army* now supported by the *2nd Serbian Army* and some Serb heavy artillery. A two-week bombardment culminated in a successful assault on 11th March in which 150,000 Bulgarians and Serbs overran the 60,000 Turkish defenders.

Serbian-Bulgarian relations, never good, now disintegrated with arguments breaking out over the territorial rewards for the successful military campaigns. A peace treaty was signed in London on 30th May 1913 in which Turkey lost nearly all its European territories, being reduced to a sliver of the continent east of a line running for some 200 kms from Kıyıköy on the Black Sea cost to Enez on the Gulf of Saros and the Aegean Sea[i]. An independent Albania was formed under pressure from the Great Powers and thus Serbian ambitions for access to the Adriatic were thwarted. Greece retained Thessaloniki, much to the irritation of the Bulgarians. Indeed, perhaps only Greece was satisfied with the outcome.

In the areas 'liberated' by the allies their policies towards non-Slav, non-Orthodox communities were soon revealed. The Serbian Army stands accused of murdering upwards of 25,000 Albanian Muslims before the independent state of Albania emerged out of the Treaty of London. Montenegrins massacred 1,800 Albanian Muslims and forcibly converted another 12,000 Muslims and Catholics in the areas of Plav and Gusinje, both now part of south-east Montenegro. The Greeks deliberately burned down the Muslim quarter of Giannitsa amongst other actions. The Bulgarians are said to have murdered or expelled some 150,000 Muslims from Thrace with Muslim refugees across the Balkans exceeding 400,000.

Barely a month later, Bulgaria, its ambitions at Thessaloniki thwarted and unhappy with its gains in Macedonia, attacked its Serbia and Greece. It was an unwise move which led to its first military defeat since the formation of the Bulgarian state in 1878. Not only that but, taking advantage of Bulgarian setbacks, the Ottoman Empire regained some territory in Thrace (including Adrianople) ceded to Bulgaria under the Treaty of London. In the absence of Bulgarian troops fighting to the west and north, the Turkish Army then, as a reprisal for the Bulgarian massacre of Turks during the Edeköy (now Kadıdondurma, Edirne Province, Turkey) Massacre of November 1912, killed or displaced some 200,000 ethnic Bulgarians[ii] in a three-week campaign in July and August 1913.[17]

Meanwhile, on Bulgaria's northern border, Rumania entered the war occupying Southern Dobruja and marching on the capital, Sofia. This second Balkan war,

---

[i] The area around Adrianople, re-taken by the Turks in the 2nd Balkan War, was retained under the terms of the Treaty of Constantinople signed 16th September 1913.
[ii] Turkey and Bulgaria later exchanged c. 50,000 Orthodox Christians and Muslims as the Bulgarian population of eastern Thrace was effectively eliminated [*Source*: Majstorovic, D, *The 1913 Ottoman Military Campaign in Eastern Thrace: A Prelude to Genocide? Journal of Genocide Research*, 21 (1), 2019, pages 25–46.

started on 29th June, ended on 10th August 1913 in a humiliating defeat for the Bulgarians. They did not wait long to get their revenge on the Serbs in 1915 and to see Rumania crushed and mostly occupied by the Central Powers a year later.

The abject failure of the Ottoman forces in the first war until their capital Constantinople was threatened by the Bulgarians is ascribed by various contemporary writers to a variety of causes: military, political, social, ethnic, and religious. The effect it had on the future direction of the empire was stark. Instead of an attempt to hold together its disparate ethnic, religious, and regional elements, the *Young Turks* moved to an Anatolian and Muslim-centred approach in which Christian and other ethnic minorities had little or no place. This strategy inevitably led to the ethnic cleansing of Armenian, Assyrian, Greek and later Kurdish communities and several million deaths over the next ten years, a period during which Turkey was continuously at war.

THE MILITARY IMPLICATIONS OF THE FIGHTING were studied hard, especially by the French whose field guns, the *75*, were in use with the Serbian Army and were opposed by the 77-mm gun supplied by *Krupp* to Turkey. There was also a vigorous debate between those who argued that the *75* had been proved to be the only weapon necessary in the next war against Germany as against those who argued in favour of longer-range guns and, most especially, field, medium and heavy howitzers capable of destroying fortifications from defiladed positions. The argument was lost by those who favoured an expanded arsenal of gun types and the consequences of the over-reliance of the French Army on the *75* would be horribly exposed in the opening weeks of the war.

Though the first war dragged on until May 1913, most of the heavy fighting was over in a few weeks, i.e. until the Bulgarians were stopped in front of the Çatalca line in November 1912. The sieges of Adrianople and Shkodër dragged on into the early Spring of 1913 but, otherwise, most of the fighting was in the nature of mopping up operations punctuated by frequent atrocities. Thus was confirmed in some circles the idea that modern wars must by brief such was their economic and human cost and, in 1914, across Europe, the military, and politicians, went to war expecting a conflict of manoeuvre and relatively quick decision. 'Over by Christmas' indeed. Bloch, however, fifteen years before the outbreak of war, accurately forecast a grinding, costly conflict lasting years. In other words, a Jewish banker and industrialist from Poland forecast the nature, and the end product, of the next great European conflict more accurately than all the Generals and Staff Officers of all the Armies of the Great Powers of Europe. Hardly a ringing endorsement of teachers or students at Sandhurst, Woolwich, or the Staff College, of the *Kriegsakademie* or the *École supérieure de Guerre*, *École Spéciale Militaire de Saint-Cyr* or *École Polytechnique*.

This is not to say all military men rejected Bloch's view of the eventual outcome of a titanic conflict between the major economic and military powers of Europe. He quoted two Generals whose views ran parallel to his in the presentation at the *RUSI* in London in June 1901:

> "The consequence of this increase of the power of the defence is that the duration of a war must be very great. It must be foreseen that any attempt

at invasion would fail infallibly in consequence of the economic and financial perturbations which would follow in its train. The invader, while still having enough men and arms, must conclude peace. In my book on *The War of the Future* I pointed out the reason why this must be, and no serious refutation has yet been attempted. On the contrary, military men in some quarters have begun to declare the same thing. Thus, in the fifth edition of his remarkable book, *The Nation in Arms*, General von der Goltz adopts this view, saying: 'We may predict that wars can only terminate by the complete destruction of one, or the exhaustion of both combatants'. In 1897, another high authority, the Austrian General von Kotié, expressed the same opinion, saying: 'Is it possible to keep for a long time such great numbers of men under arms without plunging the civil population into misery?'"[18]

Bloch's message of the futility of war, its ruinous human and financial cost and the social and political strains placed on the nations involved, fell on deaf ears. But Bloch was an idealist and, in this, a rather poor judge of human nature. War, it turned out, was greatly appealing and, at least initially, regarded as an exciting diversion by a mass of young men who knew nothing about its effects, either political or personal. After 40 years of relative peace in Europe who could have predicted their willingness to follow blindly nationalist politicians abetted, as ever, by ambitious Generals and the greedy corporate leaders of the military-industrial complex who still dominate the world?

Indeed, it was the threat to post-war US democracy from a business sector enriched and empowered by lavish wartime spending which was one reason President Woodrow Wilson was so determined to avoid entering the war in Europe.

According to the Secretary of the Navy, Josephus Daniels[i], Wilson believed:

"We will be dependent in war upon steel, oil, aluminium, ships, and war materials. They are controlled by Big Business. Undoubtedly many captains of industry will be patriotic and serve their country, but when the war is over those whose privileges we have uprooted or started to uproot will gain control of the government and neither you nor I will live to see government returned to the people. Big Business will be in the saddle."[19]

---

[i] Josephus Daniels (1862-1948) was a peculiarly American mix of socially progressive southern Democrat and extreme racist. The son of a Confederate soldier killed in the war, he was proprietor of the *Raleigh News and Observer*, a close friend of Franklin Roosevelt, supported women's suffrage, public works, and robust anti-trust laws, was a white supremacist, *Ku Klux Klan* supporter, and segregationist. He was involved in the 1898 Wilmington insurrection (*aka* the Wilmington Massacre; 300 Black residents were murdered) in which Southern Democrats violently overthrew the Fusionist (a left-wing white agrarian/black populist) administration, and helped a 1900 campaign to disenfranchise black voters in North Carolina, blocking them from public office. Secretary of the Navy, 1913-1921, he was blamed by some for a lack of pre-war preparedness.

His prediction proved horribly accurate and, reinforced by the massive defence spending in WW2, Korea, Vietnam, Iraq, and Afghanistan, has led to the creation of a 'defence' industry on which the US Government spends more money on 'defence' than the next seven countries combined.

Cutting defence spending has never been a policy to which the military have subscribed. Rather, in the early years of the 20th Century (as now), they were concerned to crank up the threat of their prospective opponents to force the hand of politicians and keep turned on the tap of public finance which kept the arms and ammunition makers in business and hugely profitable. Those industrialists with interests in sustained military spending were, as today, appalled at the idea money for guns, warships and ammunition might otherwise be spent on social programmes and economic growth. The response of the French and German governments and their Generals to Bloch's warnings was, instead, to increase the pace of development and the rate of investment in the means of killing the enemy on an increasingly industrial scale. Indeed, in the five years before the outbreak of war military expenditure increased dramatically as the table below shows:

Changes in military expenditure 1908-13[20]
France +69%
Germany +62%
Italy +61%
Russia +49%
Great Britain +31%

The 69% French increase is remarkable in the light of their 1910 national debt of £1,320 million (c. £160 billion in today's values)[i], the largest national debt recorded anywhere and an increase from the £511 million debt in 1870. It, perhaps, helps explain the French enthusiasm for penal reparations against Germany in 1919 in revenge for those imposed on them in 1871.

The increase in British spending was mainly on the Navy. From 1901 to 1911 this budget increased by 43%, up £13.4 million to £44.4 million, whilst, between 1903 and 1913, spending on the Army increased by just £223,000, less than 1%[ii]. German spending on their fleet increased even faster but from a lower base: £9.5 million in 1901 to £22 million[iii] by 1911 (+131%), but spending on the Army in 1911 was nearly 40% higher than on the British Army and most was for the upkeep

---

[i] The National Debts of the other combatant nations in 1910 were: Britain £685 million (c. £84 billion), Russia £956 million (£116 billion), Germany £251 million (£31 billion), Austria-Hungary £253 million (£31 billion) [Source: *Whitaker's Almanac*, 1910]. It baffles this writer where the money borrowed to sustain these debts comes from.

[ii] Naval expenditure 1901 £31 million, 1911 £44.3 million [*Whitaker's Almanac*, 1912]. Army expenditure 1903 £26.7 million, 1913 £26.9 million. Army figures taken from a letter to *The Times* on *The State of the Army* by the Duke of Bedford, *The Times*, 29th August 1913, page 8. By March 1914 Army Estimates of £28.8 million supported a war time establishment of 803,000 men, 75,890 (10.4%) based in India [*Army Estimates, The Times*. 6th March 1914, page 6] but £216,000 was to support the RFC [*The Times*, 23rd February 1914, page 10].

[iii] Equivalent to 185 million Reichsmarks and 450 million Reichsmarks at 1912 values.

and training of home-based troops whilst a sizeable share of the costs of the British Army was incurred maintaining forces overseas, especially in India.

Such military spending and expansion was designed to bring comfort and security to the respective populations. It did not. As Viscount Grey of Fallodon pointed out, all it did was increase concerns that war was inevitable:

> "The increase of armaments, that is intended in each nation to produce a consciousness of strength, and a sense of security, does not produce these effects. On the contrary, it produces a consciousness of the strength of other nations and a sense of fear. Fear begets suspicion and distrust and evil imaginings of all sorts, till each Government feels it would be criminal and a betrayal of its own country not to take every precaution, while every other Government regards every precaution of every other Government as evidence of hostile intent… The enormous growth of armaments in Europe, the sense of insecurity and fear caused by them – it was these that made war inevitable. This, it seems to me, is the truest reading of history, and the lesson that the present should be learning from the past in the interest of future peace…"[21]

It was popular sport amongst the Britain's Generals to blame politicians for most of the problems of the war. It is still popular sport to blame politicians for all our ills but, rather sadly, many contemporary military historians jump on this bandwagon when writing about the Great War. Generals, like Haig, are forgiven their errors because, they say, no-one had ever previously experienced a war of the scale which afflicted Europe between 1914 and 1918. Such latitude is rarely granted to politicians who were also grappling with this unprecedented conflict. Fingers are pointed at the failure of the pre-war Liberal/Labour government to build up the Army. But this government was not elected on a platform of Army expansion but on one of social reform, with the underlying theme of maintaining the pre-eminence of the Royal Navy on the world's oceans. In many ways, this is what they achieved and it seems rather churlish, with all the benefits of a century of hindsight, to now blame them for keeping a rather higher proportion of their pre-election promises than we see currently. Sometimes, it seems, politicians, even dead ones, cannot win.

RETURNING TO THE FAST-INCREASING COST OF WAR, this was highlighted by the dramatic increase in ammunition consumed in each passing conflict:

> "In trying to measure the impact of future conflicts on national economies, Bloch measured the consumption of ammunition as an indicator. First, regarding European Great Power wars prior to the Russo-Japanese War, in the Austro-Prussian War (1866: 3 months), the Prussians consumed 2 million rifle rounds, and in the Franco-Prussian War (1870–71: 7 months), the Prussians consumed 25 million rifle rounds.
> In contrast, regarding the Russo-Japanese War (1904–5: 19 months), in the … Battle of Nanshan (1 day), 2.19 million rifle and machine gun rounds and 34,049 artillery shells were consumed. In the Battle of Liaoyang (9 days), 8.39 million rifle and machine gun rounds and 106,370 shells were consumed. In the first attack on Port Arthur (4 days) 2.68 million rifle and

machine gun rounds and 50,992 shells were consumed. In the Battle of Mukden (11 days), 20.11 million rifle and machine gun rounds and 279,394 shells were consumed. In other words, the ammunition consumed in the 7 months of the Franco-Prussian War was consumed in just over 10 days of fighting at Mukden, and the amount consumed in the entire Austro-Prussian War was consumed in just a single day of fighting at Nanshan."[22]

Such rates of growth continued unabated in the Great War. 279,394 shells were fired in eleven days at Mukden but the French fired 300,000 shells in *24 hours* on 17th June 1915 during the 2nd Battle of Artois. These 300,000 shells weighed 4.5 million kilograms (c. 4,430 tons), took 300 railway trucks and 4,000 six-horse caissons to transport, and cost 9,375,000 *francs* [i].[23]

This incredible rate of increase in the consumption of ammunition was reflected in steadily growing casualty figures as the figures below show.[24]

Austro-Prussian War 1866		
Battle of Königgrätz	Prussian casualties 4%	Austrian casualties 9%
Franco-Prussian War 1870-1		
Battle of Gravelotte	German casualties 10%	French casualties 7%
Battle of Sedan	German casualties 4%	French casualties 14%
Russo-Turkish War 1877		
Siege of Plevna	Russian casualties 11%	Turkish casualties 17%
Russo-Japanese War 1904-5		
Battle of Shaho	Japanese casualties 12%	Russian casualties 19%
Siege of Port Arthur*	Japanese casualties 46%	Russian casualties 30%
Battle of Mukden	Japanese casualties 27%	Russian casualties 19%

Table 15 Increase in percentage casualty rates 1866-1905
* Not including the Battle of Nanshan, 24th-26th May 1904, during which the Japanese lost over 6,000 men (17%) compared to just 1,452 Russians. Russian losses, however, represented 38% of those involved.

And every bullet and every shell fired cost money which ordinary people were encouraged to pay for through bonds, donations, and, literally, through the melting down of the family silver, let alone the taxes they already paid on their incomes and expenditures. It was an excellent way of transferring wealth from the population at large into the pockets of arms manufacturers.

As Bloch suggested, every statistic from every war pointed to a relentless and rapid increase in the human and economic cost of warfare to the point where the states involved found it well-nigh impossible to sustain the necessary levels of expenditure – both human and financial. It has since been estimated that, at 1913 US Dollar prices, WW1 cost $208 billion[ii] ($147 billion for the Allies, and $61 billion for the Central Powers).[25] In human terms it is estimated 9 million soldiers

---

[i] £27.1 million at current prices in simple inflation terms though realistically more likely between five and ten times greater than this figure. The growth of French government spending, and the printing of money to pay for it, reduced the value of the *Franc* by 70% between 1915 and 1920. It fell by a further 43% between 1922 and 1926. The *nouveau franc* replaced it in 1960 (100 old to 1 new *franc*) and the Euro in 2002.
[ii] Anything from $6 Trillion upwards in today's money.

died with another 21 million wounded. In addition, some 12 million civilians perished in the 52 months of the war.

And what about the damage done to the countries fought over? In his post-war book *Le massacre de notre Infanterie*, Gen. Alexandre Percin reports statistics solely for France as published previously in the newspaper *Le Temps* on 24th February and 4th March 1921.[26] The numbers are startling given the relatively small proportion of France over which the war was fought:

Communities entirely destroyed	1,699
Communities 75% destroyed	707
Communities 50% destroyed	1,656
Total:	4,062
Houses completely destroyed	319,269
Houses partially destroyed	313,675
Total:	632,944
Factories destroyed	20,603
Kilometres of railway destroyed	7,985
Bridges destroyed	4,875
Tunnels destroyed	12
Kilometres of road destroyed	52,754
Hectares of uncultivated land destroyed	2.06 million
Hectares of cultivated land destroyed	1.74 million

The financial cost of the damage was calculated as:

Damage to buildings	37 billion *francs*
Damage to other property	22 billion *francs*
Damage to industrial buildings	39 billion *francs*
Damage to fixtures and fittings	25 billion *francs*
Damage to state property	2 billion *francs*
Damage to public works	3 billion *francs*
Other damage	9 billion *francs*
Total	137 billion *francs*

At the exchange rate current in 1921 (i.e. 60.5 *francs* to the £ Sterling), 137 billion *francs* equated to £2.264 billion which, using the Retail Price Index of inflation, gives a current value of c. £103 billion. In Labour value terms, i.e. how much would an employee have to spend to buy one of the commodities on which the RPI was based, then the amount is c. £262 billion in current values. Other economic indices place these costs closer to £1 trillion.

Given the enormous compensation demanded by Germany in 1871 (even though their territory had not been invaded), it is of little wonder that France pursued such penal reparations after the 1914-18 war when a large swathe of their territory was both devastated by the war and picked clean by the occupier. The economic instability these payments created in Germany, however, made for fertile ground for extremists of all hues from which grew, with the more or less enthusiastic help of the Army, the nobility, financiers and industrialists, the regime of Hitler and the Nazis. Thus, an even more devastating conflict would break out just 21 years later.

ENDNOTES

[1] Fuller, J F C, *Decisive Battles of the Western World*, Vol. 3, Cassell, 1956, page 143.
[2] Ibid., page 145.
[3] Donat, K von, *German Account of the Russo-Japanese War: The Yalu*, London, 1908, page 59.
[4] Tretyakov, Lt. Gen. N A, trans. Lt. A C Alford, RA, *My Experiences at Nan Shan and Port Arthur with the Fifth East Siberian Rifles*, Hugh Rees Ltd., 1911, page 5.
[5] Ibid., page 87.
[6] Ibid., page 98.
[7] Ibid., page 109.
[8] Ibid., page 113.
[9] Kinai, M. *The Russo-Japanese War (Official Reports)*, Vol. 1, Kegan Paul, Trench, Taubner and Co. Ltd., page 316.
[10] Barry, R, *Port Arthur: A Monster Heroism*, Moffat, Yard & Co., New York, 1905, page 103
[11] Steinberg J, ed., *The Russo-Japanese War in Global Perspective: World War Zero*, Volume II, Brill Academic Publishing, 2005, pages 191-192.
[12] Collins, C, *Lessons to be Learn from the Siege of Port Arthur as Regards to R.E. Work*, *The Journal of the United Services Institution of India* 179 (April 1910), pages 297-,11.
[13] *The Times, The French Manoeuvres of The East*, 16th September 1905, page 4.
[14] Hall, R C, *The Balkan Wars 1912-1913: Prelude to the First World War*, Routledge, 2000, page 25.
[15] Kargakos, S, *Η Ελλάς κατά τους Βαλκανικούς Πολέμους* (1912-1913) [Greece in the Balkan Wars (1912-1913)] (in Greek). Peritechnon. 2012, pages 58–59
[16] Kılıç, E, *The Balkan war (1912-1913) and visions of the future in Ottoman Turkish Literature*, unpublished PhD dissertation, Universiteit Leiden, 2015, page 31.
[17] Miletich L, *The Destruction of Thracian Bulgarians in 1913*, Bulgarian Academy of Sciences, Sofia, State Printing House, 1918.
[18] Bloch, *Selected Articles*, page 50.
[19] Daniels, J, *The Wilson Era: Years of Peace, 1910-1917*, The University of North Carolina Press, 1944, page 582.
[20] Jacobson, *World Armament Expenditure*, 1935.
[21] Grey of Fallodon, Viscount, *Twenty-Five Years*, Hodder & Stoughton, Vol. I, 1925, pages 87-8.
[22] Oe, *Nichiro senso no gunjishiteki kenkyu*, pp. 412–3, quoted in Tohmatsu Haruo, *Approaching Total War: Ivan Bloch's Disturbing Vision* in Wolff, Marks et al, *The Russo-Japanese War in Global Perspective, World War Zero*, Vol. II, Brill, Boston, 2007, page 191.
[23] *Current Field Artillery Notes: Manufacture and Consumption of Ammunition in France*, article published in the *Fremdenblatt* of April 1st, 1916, *Field Artillery Journal*, Vol. 6, No. 2, April-June 1916, page 331-2.
[24] Oe, op. cit., pages 132–3, quoted by Tohmatsu Haruo, op. cit., page 191.
[25] Fisk, H E, *The Inter-Allied Debts* (1924) pp 13 & 325 reprinted in Horst Menderhausen, *The Economics of War* (1943 edition), appendix table II.
[26] Percin, Gen. A, *Le massacre de notre Infanterie*, Albin Michel, 1921, Annex VIII, page 220.

10. THE ARMY AND CHANGE IN EDWARDIAN SOCIETY

"... thousands of boys and young men, pale, narrow-chested, hunched-up, miserable specimens, smoking endless cigarettes.... One wonders whether this can be the same nation which has gained for itself the reputation of being a stolid, pipe sucking manhood, unmoved by panic or excitement, and reliable in the tightest of places."

Robert Baden-Powell
Scouting for Boys

SOCIAL CHANGE IN BRITAIN ACCELERATED during the latter half of the nineteenth century, but changes within the establishment were far more ponderous and the Army amongst the most resistant to change.

The Crimean War of 1853-6 revealed serious problems with the officer class of the Army, even if the ordinary soldiers displayed the same stubborn, stoic resolve of their Wellingtonian predecessors. It took fifteen years before the Cardwell reforms, instituted between 1868 and 1874, changed the structure, discipline and recruiting processes of the Army. The sale of commissions in the infantry and cavalry, a system which allowed so many 'gentlemen-soldiers' to assume positions of authority far beyond their competence, was abolished. The reforms were not widely welcomed in the Army. It emphasised its innate conservatism by opposing Cardwell's efforts and then, after Gladstone's defeat in the 1874 General Election, attempting to retrospectively overturn them.

Meanwhile, the population expanded at a dramatic rate, growing from 18 million in 1811 to 27.5 million by 1851. Only the collapse of the poverty stricken rural Irish Catholic population caused by emigration and accelerated by the Potato Famine prevented the total topping 30 million[i]. By 1911 the population was 45.2 million. That of England and Wales had doubled.. Scotland had grown by two thirds. But Ireland's fell by a third to 4.4 million.

The population in August 1914 is estimated at 46,089,249 but this raw number conceals enormous shifts in the location of this burgeoning populace. The expansion of cities and towns was remarkable. London more than tripled in size, but others grew even more rapidly as manufacturing and, particularly, service industries drew workers from the countryside to the expanding suburbs and ever-growing slums. Table 1 shows the movement was not just rural to urban. With increasing demand for energy and raw materials, industry spread into sparsely populated areas. The coal mining communities of the Rhondda Valley increased 16-fold between 1851 and 1911. Overall, the population of the cities and towns listed increased threefold between 1851 and 1911 and, as a percentage of the total population, jumped from 20% to 36%.

---

[i] The Irish population fell from 8.2 to 6.6 million from 1841 to 1851 while England and Wales grew by 2.1 million. While Dublin, Belfast and Cork grew, the rural provinces of Connacht and Munster were devastated. Mayo, Sligo, Limerick, Galway and Roscommon lost 30%+ of the population. The current population of the Republic and Ulster is 6.72 million, 1.5 million below the 1841 figure. The Republic's population reached its lowest point, 2.82 million, in 1961 (down from 6.53 million in 1840). Prior to the famine, the population tripled in 100 years.

	1851	1911	% increase
Rhondda	951	153,000	15988%
Cardiff	27,000	210,000	678%
Edinburgh	67,000	401,000	499%
Hull	57,000	282,000	395%
Nottingham	58,000	260,000	348%
Leicester	61,000	227,000	272%
Birmingham	233,000	840,000	261%
Newport	43,000	153,000	256%
Southampton	34,000	119,000	250%
Sheffield	161,000	525,000	226%
Portsmouth	72,000	231,000	221%
Swansea	47,000	151,000	221%
London	2,300,000	7,200,000	213%
Walsall	43,000	128,000	198%
Leeds	250,000	734,000	194%
Stoke	58,000	170,000	193%
Coventry	37,000	107,000	189%
Derby	44,000	124,000	182%
Newcastle	89,000	250,000	181%
Bradford	103,000	288,000	180%
Sunderland	71,000	194,000	173%
Dundee	61,000	165,000	170%
Glasgow	329,000	785,000	139%
Aberdeen	72,000	164,000	128%
Merthyr Tydfil	77,000	174,000	126%
Bristol	160,000	352,000	120%
Plymouth	52,000	112,000	115%
Manchester	340,000	712,000	109%
Liverpool	368,000	746,000	103%
Norwich	68,000	121,000	78%
Wolverhampton	104,000	183,000	76%
	5,486,951	16,261,000	196%

Table 16 Population changes in British cities and towns 1851-1911

The necessary corollary to these shifts was a reduction in both real and proportionate terms of the numbers of people working in, or being otherwise dependent on, agriculture. From 1831, when 50% of the population lived in rural conditions, employment in agriculture steadily declined from over a quarter of the workforce to less than one in ten by 1911. In real terms, by 1871 there was a decline of 500,000 people (mainly men), down from the total of 1.75 million employed in agriculture twenty years earlier. This dramatic decline in the importance of agricultural employment is shown by these figures:

1831	28%
1841	21%
1881	12%
1911	9%

Table 17 Proportion of the workforce in agricultural employment

This relative decline in agricultural employment was not paralleled by an overall increase in employment in manufacturing but rather a move into service industries and mining. Certain sectors, e.g. the cotton, woollen and footwear industries, were already losing workers (to mechanisation and foreign competition) from 1851 onwards and, by 1911, the proportion of the male workforce employed in these industries fell from 15% to 7%. The numbers involved in mining, however, shot up from just over 200,000 in 1851 to 1.05 million by 1911 (or from 4.6% of the male workforce to 8.2%)[i]. Indeed, it was this enormous growth in mining which meant the proportion of the workforce employed in the manufacturing and mining sector remained static between 1851 and 1911 (1851: 50%, 1911: 51%).

The service sector saw by far the biggest increase in employment, growing from 23% (1851) to 38% (1911). The biggest growth areas were in retail and wholesale (up from 3.2% in 1851 to 7.6% in 1911) and transport (mainly the railways) where total employment leaped from 5.1% to 12.5%.

In consequence, Britain was the most urban-centred European nation. The 9% of the British male workforce employed in agriculture must be compared with 43% in France and 33% in Germany[ii]. Although possessing a larger labour force than Britain, only 37% of German workers were employed in industry or mining with 12% involved in trade and transport. One of the main pre-war benefits this brought Germany was that the country produced 90% of its own food. When most of the men of working age were taken off to war, however, this previous self-reliance instead became a severe problem. When the full effect of the Allied naval blockade was brought to bear it became clear the new agricultural workforce of women, children, the elderly and even some prisoners of war, could not sustain the levels of food production the nation needed. And, although the German chemical industry was the most developed and powerful in the world by 1913,

---

[i] Britain produced c. 230 million tons of coal a year in 1914.

[ii] One reason for the continued large scale of German agricultural production was the protectionist policies introduced by Bismarck in 1879, the so-called 'marriage of iron and rye', which shielded German industry and agriculture against cheap foreign, especially US and Russian, grain imports. It helped protect the eastern landowners, the *Junkers*, but antagonised the urban working class who paid more for food. The political impact was neutered by anti-Socialist laws passed in 1878 which prevented Social Democrats from organising effectively between 1878 and 1890. When the laws lapsed the Social Democrats (*Sozialistische Arbeiterpartei Deutschlands* [SAP], later *Sozialdemokratische Partei Deutschlands* [SPD]) won 20% of the vote. Bismarck resigned.

when the German Government diverted chemicals such as ammonium nitrate, which might otherwise have been used for fertiliser, to the manufacture of explosives, food production suffered still further.

There was another problem. Though Germany produced a high percentage of food consumed by the human population this was not so with animal fodder. As the rural population moved into the cities, demand for food, especially meat and meat products (everyone knows how much Germans love sausages), greatly increased. In fifteen years between 1897 and 1912, meat consumption grew from 36 Kgs a head to 52 Kgs, i.e. by 44%. Increasing the quantity of animals needed to supply this huge increase in demand had not been a problem but feeding those animals most certainly was and indicated just how vulnerable Germany was to an interruption of the availability of animal fodder. By the beginning of the war, Germany was spending one billion gold marks a year importing animal fodder, most especially barley from Russia's Ukrainian breadbasket (the amount imported rose by 66% in 35 years) and other fat and protein from outside Europe. Clearly, Russian barley imports would abruptly cease should war break out and an efficient blockade would stop the arrival of other animal foodstuffs from around the world. Germany thus faced a rapid problem with meat, animal fat and milk supply should war break out with both Russia (barley) *and* Great Britain (blockade).[1] The devastating effects on food supply caused by the war and the blockade can be seen from post-war figures on livestock in Austria-Hungary where it was estimated that the pre-war numbers of beef and dairy cattle had fallen 80% (from 17.3 million to 3.5 million) and pigs had nearly completely disappeared, the total falling a staggering 97%, from 7.7 million to just 214,000.[2]

Famine was one of the potential outcomes of a European war predicted by Bloch and, as in so many things, he was again correct. It has been estimated that in Germany alone c. 500,000 civilians died from either malnutrition or from diseases exacerbated by food shortages. Of these, perhaps two-thirds died in 1918-9 when the effects of the allied blockade were at their peak.[3] Post-war in Russia, the collapse of the previous regime, the bitter and prolonged Civil War, and the disruption of much of the industrial and agricultural base led to a famine which cost more than 5 million people their lives in 1921-2.

IN BRITAIN, THE CREATION of this new industrial and urban working class had numerous social and political consequences. Within the upper echelons of society, particularly in the British Army, there was an especially low opinion of the lifestyle, and personal and physical characteristics of the emerging proletariat.[4] Attitudes towards the ill-educated, illiterate, unskilled, often unemployed, labouring class – countrymen drawn to the city in search of work (the sort of man who made up the ranks of the British Army) – were especially dismissive. Social Darwinism determined they were of no account. Eugenics, Galton's 'nature not nurture' argument, determined they were irredeemable. After all, the thinking went, if they had skills or intelligence, they would drag themselves out of abject poverty by their bootstraps. Presuming, of course, they owned boots in the first place.

Even amongst 'enlightened' members of the Victorian/Edwardian *élite* these views were set hard and fast. In *Anticipations*, H G Wells described this part of society as the 'The People of the Abyss'. And joining them, in his assessment, were all peoples with a black, yellow, or brown skin... the Irish catholic, and the Jew. According to Wells, this element of society was the unfortunate by-product of technical and economic progress and, perhaps in former times, was concealed from view amongst the rural peasantry:

> "This second consequence of progress is the appearance of a great number of people without either property or any evident function in the social organism. This new ingredient is most apparent in the towns, it is frequently spoken of as the Urban Poor, but its characteristic traits are to be found also in the rural districts. For the most part its individuals are either criminal, immoral, parasitic in more or less irregular ways upon the more successful classes, or labouring, at something less than a regular bare subsistence wage, in a finally hopeless competition against machinery that is as yet not so cheap as their toil. It is, to borrow a popular phrase, the 'submerged' portion of the social body, a leaderless, aimless multitude, a multitude of people drifting down towards the abyss."[5]

His solution to their existence was one which, one might think, could easily lead to the careless attitude of Generals to the lives of the 'rank and file' in war:

> "The nation that produces in the near future the largest proportional development of educated and intelligent engineers and agriculturists, of doctors, schoolmasters, professional soldiers, and intellectually active people of all sorts; the nation that most resolutely picks over, educates, sterilizes, exports, or poisons its People of the Abyss; the nation that succeeds most subtly in checking gambling and the moral decay of women and homes that gambling inevitably entails; the nation that by wise interventions, death duties and the like, contrives to expropriate and extinguish incompetent rich families while leaving individual ambitions free; the nation, in a word, that turns the greatest proportion of its irresponsible adiposity into social muscle, will certainly be the nation that will be the most powerful in warfare as in peace, will certainly be the ascendant or dominant nation before the year 2000."[6]

To be fair to Wells his opinions changed dramatically in a short time. Thus, the man who wrote in 1902:

> "And how will the new republic treat the inferior races? How will it deal with the black? how will it deal with the yellow man? how will it tackle that alleged termite in the civilized woodwork, the Jew?..."

... was, within a year or so, undergoing a *volte face* on race and skin colour (see *The Tragedy of Colour* in his 1906 book *The Future in America*), declaring in 1916:

> "I hate and despise a shrewish suspicion of foreigners and foreign ways; a man who can look me in the face, laugh with me, speak truth and deal fairly, is my brother, though his skin is as black as ink or as yellow as an evening primrose"[7]

He had already rejected eugenics (in 1904). He stood twice as a Labour candidate, twice coming third in the London University constituency in the 1922 and 1923 General Elections. He was a man who hankered for a meritocratic, classless, peaceful new world order. But, back in 1902, his opinions were indicative of widespread attitudes amongst the 'ruling class' about the uselessness and disposability of the urban poor, left behind by the industrial revolution and impoverished by the unchecked growth of rapacious capitalism. Unfortunately, this opinion fed into an antagonistic view to the British working class in general, especially if, when organised into unions and a political party, they began to threaten the prevailing social order.

THE GERMAN ARMY WAS NOT prejudiced against conscripts from the skilled/educated industrial working class because, as Martin Samuels points out, a man capable of learning an industrial process, the working of a machine tool or lathe for example, should be equally capable of learning the technical elements of being a soldier. But there were considerable reservations about the unskilled proletariat concentrated in cities and towns, attracted by the redistributive policies of the Marxist-influenced *Sozialdemokratische Partei Deutschlands* (*SPD* or Social Democrats)[i]. Already, the German officer class was having to deal with a dramatic shift in its own class base. In the fifty years before the war the 66%/33% ratio of nobility to middle class within the ranks of officers was reversed and the nearly 6 nobility to 1 middle class ratio within the senior ranks, i.e. colonel and above, now reached parity.[8] This brought with it concerns about a weakening of the ultra-conservative attitudes prevalent amongst *Junker* officers who previously dominated and directed attitudes within the Army. Attitudes well summed up by Jonathan Steinberg in his biography of Bismarck, himself a leading *Junker*:

> "Their hatred of free markets, free citizens, free peasants, free movement of capital and labour, free thought, Jews, stock markets, banks, cities, and a free press continued to 1933 and helped to bring about the Nazi dictatorship."[9]

Although a third of Germans still lived in rural areas, this figure was *two thirds* in 1871. Now the cities and large towns held the bulk of the population and with it came a growth in support for the *SPD*. So wary was the government and Army of this urban and left leaning working class that conscription was focussed on calling up young men from less politicised, and more 'reliable' rural communities.

---

[i] In 1863 the *Allgemeinen Deutschen Arbeitervereins* (*ADAV* or *General German Workers' Association*) was formed followed, in 1869, by the *Sozialdemokratischen Arbeiterpartei* (*SDAP* or *Social Democratic Workers' Party*). In 1875 these parties merged to form the *Sozialistische Arbeiterpartei Deutschlands* (*SAP* or *Socialist Workers' Party of Germany*). Betwen 1878 and 1890, at the instigation of Bismarck and others, the *Reichstag* passed the first *Sozialistengesetz*, (or *Socialist Law*) a series of laws banning the promotion of socialism (though candidates for the *SAP* stood and between 9 and 24 were elected in this period). In 1890, after the party doubled its popular vote to 1.4 million and tripled its representation in the *Reichstag*, the laws lapsed and the party was renamed the *Sozialdemokratische Partei Deutschlands* (*SPD*). By 1912 it was the largest party in the *Reichstag* with 4.25 million [or 35%] votes and 110 members out of 397.

In *Germany and the Next War*, Bernhardi sets out the extraordinarily unbalanced social base of German Army conscripts caused by what he saw as the:

"...ever-growing encroachments of a social-democratic, anti-patriotic feeling, and, hand-in-hand with this, the flocking of the population into the large towns, which is unfavourable to physical development."[10]

The result, in terms of the make-up of Other Ranks in the Army was striking:

"This result is clearly shown by the enlistment statistics. At the present day, out of all the German-born military units, over 6.14 per cent. come from the large towns, 7.37 per cent, from the medium-sized towns, 22.34 per cent. from the small or country towns, and 64.15 per cent. from the rural districts; while the distribution of the population between town and country is quite different. According to the census of 1905, the rural population amounted to 42.5 per cent., the small or country towns to 25.5 per cent., the medium-sized towns to 12.9 per cent., and the large towns to 19.1 per cent. of the entire number of inhabitants. The proportion has probably changed since that year still more unfavourably for the rural population, (*Author's note*: the rural population was 33% by 1914) while the large towns have increased in population."[11]

Bernhardi's conclusions were identical to those of senior British officers:

"These figures clearly show the physical deterioration of the town population, and signify a danger to our national life, not merely in respect of physique, but in the intellect and compact unity of the nation. The rural population forms part and parcel of the army. A thousand bonds unite the troops and the families of their members, so far as they come from the country; everyone who studies the inner life of our army is aware of this. The interest felt in the soldier's life is intense. It is the same spirit, transmitted from one to another. The relation of the army to the population of the great cities which send a small and ever-diminishing fraction of their sons into the army is quite different. A certain opposition exists between the population of the great cities and the country-folk, who, from a military point of view, form the backbone of the nation. Similarly, the links between the army and the large towns have loosened, and large sections of the population in the great cities are absolutely hostile to the service."[12]

In almost identical fashion, many British officers believed the national will to fight for the Empire was being fatally sapped by working class drinking, smoking, socialism, and even the increasingly popular professional Association football[i].

---

[i] The first FA Cup Final, Wanderers v. Royal Engineers (16th March 1872, result: 1-0) attracted 2,000 spectators to Kennington Oval. The 1889 Oval Final (Preston North End v. Wolverhampton Wanderers, result: 3-0), was watched by 27,000. In 1893, c. 60,000 are estimated to have seen Wolves beat Everton 1-0 at the Fallowfield Stadium, Manchester. In 1895 the Final took up a long-term residence at Crystal Palace. In 1900, c. 69,000 watched Bury beat Southampton 4-0. The next year 110,820 witnessed Tottenham Hotspur draw 2-2 with Sheffield United (Spurs won the replay 3-1).

Robert Baden-Powell was Inspector General of Cavalry between 1903 and 1907. He was also the man who gave the world the Scouts. His book, *Scouting for Boys*, the unintentionally hilarious collection of 'yarns' which outlined his 'Scouting' philosophy[i], also set out what he was against in modern society. His description of a football crowd says much (including the best way *real* men might inhale tobacco smoke):

"… thousands of boys and young men, pale, narrow-chested, hunched-up, miserable specimens, smoking endless cigarettes, numbers of them betting, all of them learning to be hysterical as they groan or cheer in panic unison with their neighbours – the worst sound of all being the hysterical scream of laughter. One wonders whether this can be the same nation which has gained for itself the reputation of being a stolid, pipe sucking manhood, unmoved by panic or excitement, and reliable in the tightest of places."[13]

As in Germany, such military men hankered after some non-existent stalwart yeoman soldiers from some non-existent halcyon era. They sought solid, stoic, taciturn, disciplined, and dependable country types. Not too intelligent, but with sufficient wit to follow orders unquestioningly, with the temperament to withstand hardship, and able to fire a gun, to hunt – and to kill without qualms[ii].

The perceived differences between this ideal soldier and the smoking, drinking, football-watching working class, or the soft-handed, office-bound city dweller is well summed up in H G Wells' 1903 story *The Land Ironclads* (see page 512). It was set in a war between robust rural types and self-indulgent, unfit city inhabitants in which, unfortunately for the likes of Baden-Powell, the technologically superior 'townies' are victorious. Nevertheless, Wells' description of the urbanites would have had senior Generals wisely nodding in agreement, even if the projected outcome of the war did not coincide with their fondly held beliefs:

"Their men (i.e. the city dwellers) aren't brutes enough; that's the trouble. They're a crowd of devitalized townsmen, and that's the truth of the matter. They're clerks, they're factory hands, they're students, they're civilized men. They can write, they can talk, they can make and do all sorts of things, but they're poor amateurs at war. They've got no physical staying power, and that's the whole thing. They've never slept in the open one night in their lives; they've never drunk anything but the purest water-company water; they've never gone short of three meals a day since they left their devitalizing feeding-bottles. Half their cavalry never cocked leg over horse till it enlisted six months ago. They ride their horses as though they were bicycles - you watch 'em! They're fools at the game, and they know it. Our boys of fourteen can give their grown men points…"[14]

Attendances continued in the 70-80,000 range until 1913 when, on 19th April 1913, 121,919 saw Aston Villa beat Sunderland 1-0.
[i] One doubts whether his suggestion as to how to avoid catching Tuberculosis (breath through your nose not your mouth) has survived the test of time.
[ii] Baden-Powell goes so far as to suggest Scouts visit a slaughterhouse, this being a good preparation for witnessing and, perhaps, inflicting violent death.

In the years following the South African War numerous articles and books written by Army officers deplored the perceived degeneracy and ill-discipline of, most especially, the new urban and industrial working class[i]. It is as if blame for the various setbacks and defeats in that war was being shifted from the men who led the troops so poorly onto the shoulders of what they perceived as an unfit, unreliable, and politically unsound working-class back home.

In addition, a focus developed on the physical fitness of the population, and of the young and the poor especially. Some sought to join the Army as an escape from their current estate both before and after the war but the physical condition of too many was unacceptable. The integration of many reservists and volunteers specifically for service in South Africa was delayed or prevented by their poor physical condition – 40% were found physically unfit, not a few suffering from the effects of rickets[15]. This childhood condition was mainly caused by a Vitamin D deficiency made worse by the living conditions of the urban poor. Neither at work nor at home was there much likelihood of such people being exposed to decent levels of the Ultraviolet B light needed to generate the vitamin. After all, exposure to sunlight was not a priority for employers in factories and mines, and the dreadful insanitary and gloomy housing conditions of many, and the lack of time and space available for out-door recreation, were not conducive to the prevention of this bone-softening condition and the bow-legged appearance which was its common symptom.

In 1902, the Military Correspondent of *The Times* addressed the idea of military training for 14 to 19-year-olds in a series of articles entitled *National Training and National Defence*. It was an idea which the newspaper and others hoped would lead to a National Service/conscription system similar to that adopted on the continent. In the second article concerns were expressed at 'the physical deterioration of the population of our great industrial towns'. The following figures were provided:

> "In the year 1900, out of rather more than 11,000 men who wished to enlist in the city of Manchester 8,000 had to be rejected on account of their lack of stamina and other physical defects, while of the 3,000 who were not rejected only 1,000 could be put into line regiments, 2,000 being placed in the Militia."[16]

The writer then compared unfavourably British and European attitudes towards the physical fitness of their working class. He claimed any improvements in Britain were usually the result of charitable impulses of wealthy philanthropists rather than concerted action by national or local government. The article then debated the 'pros' and 'cons' of National Service with, unsurprisingly given *The*

---

[i] *The United Services Magazine* was a regular vehicle for such pieces, e.g. 'Red Coat', *Concerning Individuality* (October 1903), page 66; Captain Bellairs, *The Educational Value of Universal Service*, (June 1904), 261; Major Pollock in a footnote to *Vicarious Patriotism*, (September 1904), page 594; and before the South African War, Field Marshal Wolseley. *War and Civilisation*, (March 1897), pages 560, 564, and 577 [*Source*: Travers, T H, *Technology, Tactics, and Morale: Jean de Bloch, the Boer War, and British Military Theory, 1900-1914*, 1976].

Times' position on national defence, the 'pros' outweighing the 'cons' by some margin. The article went on to discuss the 'condition of the 'slum' population of our cities', and the need to help 'restore these physically degraded people to a more vigorous state of mind and body'. Apparently, compulsory military training was the answer to the ills of this down-trodden mass of humanity rather than better housing, sanitation, food and education and, perhaps, a shorter working week. The correspondent, however, railed against the government for having reduced by one hour the working week of all textile workers in order to allow 'Lancashire mill hands to stand and watch football matches between professional players'. Instead, he opined, they should be using this hour for military training of some kind.

Nevertheless, the perceived physical (and mental) inadequacies of the industrial working class had been set out in the 'paper of record' and it became a hot topic, discussed under the shorthand title of *Physical Deterioration*. The letters page of *The Times* was immediately, and for some time, filled with observations on the physical state of the nation. The urgent question posed in December 1903 by Dr Robert Farquharson, the Liberal MP for Western Aberdeenshire between 1885 and 1906 and a medical doctor, was whether:

> "… the vital capacity of our race (was) deteriorating, and must we face the disconcerting fact that the battles of the future, whether on the field or in the workshop, must be fought with blunt weapons, with dulled brains, and with stunted forms?"[17]

Being a Liberal or 'enough of a Socialist' to accept the need adequately to feed both children and adults, and decrying the fact that 'nearly one-third of our population are compelled reluctantly to toe the line that separates chronic starvation from sufficient nourishment', the problem of 'physical deterioration' was most pressing when it came to the Army. Quoting Deputy Surgeon General William Gerard Don, the London Medical Officer for Recruiting, Farquharson noted that c. 30% of young men seeking to enlist were rejected on physical grounds and even those thought adequate were 'poor enough specimens' beaten by 'a handful of Dutch peasants… time after time during the last disastrous war'. And, having joined the Army, young recruits were, at least initially, 'denied the messing allowance' needed to 'supply the proper nourishment to the young lad which is absolutely needed to keep body and soul together'. Commenting on the 7,000 Army deserters in the previous year, Farquharson wrote scathingly:

> "… the recruit is compelled to spend every farthing he can scrape together on food; and can one wonder that, bullied by sergeants, swindled by the delusive promise of a free ration, and starved into a condition of continuous weakness and nervous depression, he should seek refuge in flight?"[18]

So concerned was the Conservative Government by the notion of national physical deterioration (and possibly dismayed at the financial implications of remedying such a thing) that Spencer Compton Cavendish[i], 8th Duke of

---

[i] Marquess of Hartington from 1858-1891 when he succeeded as Duke, he served as a Liberal MP until 1886 when he formed the Liberal Unionists over Irish Home Rule.

Devonshire, Leader of the House of Lords and Lord President of the Privy Council, formed an *Inter-Departmental Committee on Physical Deterioration* on 2nd September 1903 which reported in July 1904. It was chaired by one Almeric William FitzRoy[i], the Clerk of the Privy Council[ii], and it was instructed to:

> "... make a preliminary inquiry into the allegations concerning the deterioration of certain classes of the population as shown by the large percentage of rejections for physical causes of recruits from the Army"[19]

Having heard from numerous witnesses, the committee concluded there was no 'trustworthy evidence of the general or extensive degeneration which by some has been supposed to exist'. This was mainly because of the absence of any reliable historic benchmark figures which might be compared to current statistics of which, to be fair, there were not many either. It was suggested a comprehensive system of collecting such data might be worthwhile. That there 'appeared' not be any great decline in the physical condition of the poor of the great urban and industrial centres was put down to significant improvements in sanitation which, amongst other things, reduced the incidence of diseases like cholera which so ravaged London in particular between 1832 and 1866 (even if 'Consumption', i.e. Tuberculosis, was entirely another matter, spread as it was by the movement of untreated raw milk by the ever-expanding railway network[iii]). But, according to the

---

He resigned from Balfour's Conservative administration in 1903 over Free Trade and died in 1908. A government minister for 24 years including Secretary of State for India (1880–1882) and Secretary of State for War (1882–1885) and, at one time or another, led the Liberal, Liberal Unionist and Conservative Parties in either the House of Commons or the Lords. The family seat is a Chatsworth House, Derbyshire, and there are other properties in North Yorkshire and Ireland and, previously, Devonshire House, Piccadilly, one of the great houses of London but demolished in 1924 after its sale to pay death duties and other family debts.

[i] FitzRoy (1851-1935), later KCVO & KCB, was the son of Francis Horatio FitzRoy, Deputy Lieutenant of Hampshire (1823–1900); the grandson of Rear Admiral Lord William FitzRoy (1782-1857), MP for Thetford (and court-martialled and dismissed the Navy in 1811 for corruption, 'tyranny and oppression'); and the great-grandson of Augustus FitzRoy, 3rd Duke of Grafton and Prime Minister 1768-70, a fourth-generation illegitimate offspring of King Charles II and Barbara Palmer *née* Villiers, 1st Duchess of Cleveland and Countess of Castlemaine. Clearly a man unlikely to be in touch with the needs and concerns of the urban poor.

[ii] Other members were Col. G M Fox, Inspector of Physical Training, Board of Education, Mr J G Legge, Inspector of Reformatory and Industrial Schools, Mr H M Lindsell, CB, Principal Assistant Secretary to the Board of Education, Col. G T Onslow, CB, Inspector of Marine Recruiting, Mr J Struthers, CB, Assistant Secretary to the Scottish Education Department, and Dr J F W Tatham, FRCP, of the General Register Office, the only medical doctor involved though acting mainly as a statistician.

[iii] In the 1890s, 90% of the population were infected by the *Tubercle bacillus*, 10% of whom might develop Tuberculosis [*Source*: Condrau F & Worboys M, *Epidemics and Infections in Nineteenth-Century Britain*, Social History of Medicine, 22nd April 2009, pages 165-171]. TB sharply declined in the UK but is on the rise: 'A London Assembly report recently revealed five boroughs in the capital had higher rates of tuberculosis than

self-help ethic popular in Victorian and Edwardian times, these communities of the impoverished had only themselves to blame for their poor living conditions. According to *The Times* they '… had not developed a desire for improvement commensurate with the opportunities offered to them'. Quite what were these 'opportunities' was not specified. Perhaps they only existed in the minds of comfortable middle and upper class conservatively inclined politicians and civil servants. In the absence of any self-improvement, the mass of the urban poor was described as showing this unhappy combination of characteristics:

> "Laziness, want of thrift, ignorance of household management, and particularly of the choice and preparation of food, filth, indifference to parental obligations, drunkenness (which) largely infect adults of both sexes, and press with terrible severity upon the children."[20]

Furthermore, it was apparently not the case an increase in disposable income amongst the lower classes improved their circumstances. Quite the reverse, indeed, as according to the report:

> "… lunacy increases with the rise of wages and the greater spending power of the operative class; while a falling wage-rate is associated with a decrease of drunkenness, crime and lunacy."

It might prove difficult to identify a more self-serving justification for keeping workers' pay rates low than that provided by the *Inter-Departmental Committee on Physical Deterioration* convened by one of the most reactionary Conservative governments in the country's history. More interested in preventing change and preserving status than improving living standards for the mass of the population, it is unsurprising that the desperate conditions of the urban poor should be blamed by Conservatives – on the urban poor.

Others took a contrary view. Reformers such as Seebohm Rowntree, second son of Joseph Rowntree, highlighted the extremes of poverty in Britain and, most particularly, in the ever-expanding urban slums. In 1899 he studied living conditions in York, the results of which he published in 1901 in *Poverty: A Study of Town Life*. He found more than a quarter of the population of the city lived below the poverty line. Furthermore, he argued the main cause of this poverty was low wages and not, as the upper and middle classes liked to believe, the feckless lifestyles of the poor. *Plus ça change*.

Nevertheless, the *Inter-Departmental Committee on Physical Deterioration* came up with no fewer than fifty-three recommendations, some progressive, e.g.:

> Recommendation 4: address overcrowding in the worst slums;
> Recommendation 6: provide open spaces, light, and fresh air to slum dwellers;
> Recommendation 7: strict enforcement of laws on industrial smoke pollution;
> Recommendation 22: setting standards for the purity of food; and
> Recommendation 42: the feeding of elementary school children.

---

parts of Rwanda, Iraq or Eritrea. And last year, TB Alert recorded 6,520 cases of the disease in the UK - of which almost 40 per cent were in London alone.' [*Source*: Buchanan R T, *Tuberculosis in the UK: Being diagnosed with the Victorian disease that never went away*, The Independent, 2nd November 2015].

Others were purely administrative – and some draconian. One example of the latter was recommendation 5 entitled *Labour Colonies and Public Nurseries*. It urged that, when clearing slums, a local authority should have the power:

> "... to take charge of the lives of those who, from whatever cause, are incapable of independent existence up to the standard of decency it (i.e. the local authority) imposes."

Such people were to be placed in 'labour colonies'. It cited as an example the Salvation Army Colony established at Hadleigh[i] in Essex in 1891 where the urban poor were taught farming and other skills. The significant difference between William Booth's concept and that of the Committee was that their suggested Labour Colonies could be populated by dint of 'compulsory detention'. Any children of such detainees would then be taken away, at least temporarily, and placed in public nurseries or farmed out to other establishments. The cost of this temporary 'fostering' was to fall upon the detainee:

> "With a view to the enforcement of parental responsibility, the object would be to make the parent a debtor to society on account of the child, with the liability, in default of his providing the cost of suitable maintenance, of being placed in a labour establishment under State supervision until the debt is worked off."[21]

In other words, the urban poor, probably already in debt, would be placed further in debt and made to work off their debts in state run institutions. So, after the outrage of the concentration camps in South Africa, the British Government was now having recommended to it labour camps for its own citizens in order to solve social problems caused by low or no pay, appalling housing conditions, poor and/or little food, and poor or little education.

Some of these reforms did see the light of day, with Parliament passing laws such as the *Housing of the Working Classes Act 1903*, the *Public Health Act 1904*, and the *Unemployed Workmen Act 1905*, but it fell mainly to the newly elected Liberal Government to deal with many of these issues. Elected in 1906, this Government, initially led by Prime Minister Henry Campbell-Bannerman, won on a platform of Free Trade and social reform. With other issues, such as the impact of the 1902 *Education Act* on non-conformist schools and the use of indentured Chinese labour in South Africa, having driven voters away from the Conservative and Unionist government of Arthur Balfour, the result of the election was a Liberal landslide with the party gaining 214 seats and an overall majority in the House of Commons not reliant on either the Irish Nationalists or the 29 MPs of the Labour Party. Overall, the combined popular votes of the Liberals and the Labour Party gave them a 10% lead over the Tories (54% to 44%). With such a mandate the new government acted radically, and social reform, not spending on the Army, was the focus of its attention. Despite a background of increasing Trade Union militancy, the Liberal/Labour government of 1906-14 proved to be one of the greatest reforming governments of modern times, laying the foundations of what became, after 1945, the welfare state. Amongst the legislation enacted was:

---

[i] Used in 2012 as the site for the Olympic Mountain Biking competitions.

- *The Education (Provision of Meals) Act 1906* (first proposed as a Private Member's Bill by the Labour MP for Westhoughton, William T Wilson);
- *The Workmen's Compensation Act 1906* (compensation for injured workers);
- *The Education (Administrative Provisions) Act 1907* (school medical services);
- *The Matrimonial Causes Act 1907* (helping mothers and children after divorce/separation);
- *The Children Act 1908* (known as the Children's Charter, it kept them out of the Poor/Workhouse, Prison, dangerous trades and generally helped reduce abuse);
- *The Old-Age Pensions Act 1908* (non-contributory old age pensions for people over the age of 70);
- *The Coal Mines Regulation Act 1908* (limited the working day to 8 hours);
- *The Labour Exchanges Act 1909* (helped the unemployed find jobs);
- *The Trade Boards Act 1909* (created boards which could set legally enforceable minimum wages in various industries);
- *The Housing, Town Planning, &c. Act 1909* (stopped the building of 'back-to-back' houses and set minimum house building standards);
- *The Coal Mines Act 1911* (improved mine safety);
- *The National Insurance Act 1911* (health insurance for industrial workers based on contributions from employers, government, and workers);
- *The Shops Act 1911* (early closing, i.e. a weekly half-holiday for staff); and
- *The Coal Mines (Minimum Wage) Act 1912*.

It took years for these reforms to impact on the poorest communities and yet these areas still provided the bulk of the young men who sought to join the British Armed Forces. Improvement in their physical and mental condition was not in any way immediate and, therefore, concerns about the physical and mental state of the potential lower ranks of the Army remained current amongst senior officers.

BY 1905, AFTER THE FIRST MOROCCAN CRISIS, leading officers were again bemoaning the state of the Army and its 'unpreparedness' for war with a 'civilized power', a phrase used by Field Marshal Lord Roberts as 'code' for Germany in a speech to the London Chamber of Commerce at the Mansion House on 1st August 1905. There he called for the establishment of a mass conscript army on the same basis as on the continent. This was the conservative and military answer to the perceived 'failings' of the population: i.e. to instil discipline, character, and high morale by introducing National Service. It was also the way in which aggression from a power like Germany might be diverted if not prevented. Or so the Generals and their political supporters thought. Grey of Fallodon had other ideas. Embroidering upon his pattern of argument that an arms race made war not just more likely but inevitable, the Secretary of State for Foreign Affairs believed, instead, that British conscription with the intention of being able to send an Expeditionary Force of 500,000 men to the continent would have brought forward, not delayed, or prevented, that inevitable war. His riposte to the likes of Roberts was that tit-for-tat developments – one British dreadnought was a precaution but a German dreadnought a threat, one strategic railway line in north-eastern France towards *Lothringen* a precaution, while one through the *Eifel* mountains towards the eastern border of Belgium a threat – only served to ratchet up fear and apprehension on both sides. A conscription-derived half million strong Expeditionary Force able to confront Germany would not generate peace but invite pre-emptive military action. Thus:

> "We should not thereby have prevented the war; we should have precipitated it sooner."[22]

Senior Army officers like Lord Roberts and Douglas Haig supported the aims of the *National Service League (NSL)* formed in February 1902 to further the idea of four year's compulsory service for men aged between 18 and 30. This was a divisive issue within both the country and the Army. Roberts's friend, the influential but sadly late Col. George Henderson, was a stalwart opponent of compulsion and conscription, a fact which might have set him in opposition to Roberts, previously his superior in South Africa, had he survived the illness from which he died on 3rd March 1903. His steadfast view was the morale of a volunteer must always be higher than of a conscript and he cited the performance of the ordinary British soldier in war after war and of the early volunteers to the Federal and Confederate Armies in the 'War of Secession'. Furthermore, amongst people of a liberal or socialist outlook, such a move towards conscription smacked of the European militarism and nationalism they so distrusted.

Initially, *NSL* support was tiny and concentrated amongst a small, if influential, Conservative clique[i]. It steadily grew as the threat of a European War increased but, with a majority Liberal Government elected in 1906 and a Liberal/Labour one elected twice in 1910, there was no prospect of conscription being introduced before the outbreak of war, and for two reasons: first, the Royal Navy, bulwark against invasion, was the overwhelming defence spending priority; and second, with the Army regularly employed in 'assistance to the civil powers', there were many radical Liberal and Labour MPs reluctant to see the size of the Army increased and its power and influence grow within mainland Great Britain.

The aims and objectives of the *NSL* were, however, indicative of the fears of certain classes and institutions that, somehow, the country was slipping beyond their rightful control. Women were agitating for the vote. Trades Unions were striking for shorter hours and higher pay. Overtly socialist politicians were being elected to Parliament and becoming involved in the running of the country. And then, in 1909, Lloyd George introduced *The People's Budget*.

The Welsh Wizard described his budget as a 'War Budget' in a campaign against 'poverty… wretchedness and human degradation'. It introduced a higher rate of income tax and a super-tax, increased death duties, taxes on alcohol and, even more controversially, a variety of land taxes. Money was needed to rein in an

---

[i] Membership of the *NSL* grew from 1,725 in 1904 to 60,000 in 1910. Its magazine, *The Nation in Arms*, claimed over 96,000 subscribers by 1913 [*Sources*: Coetzee, Frans, *For Party or Country. Nationalism and the Dilemmas of Popular Conservatism in Edwardian England*, Oxford University Press, 1990, page 39, and Jeffery, Keith, *Field Marshal Sir Henry Wilson: A Political Soldier*, Oxford University Press, 2006, page 76].

inherited budget deficit[i] and pay for the social reforms enacted, but some was required to help fund the Royal Navy[ii]. The Budget was passed a year later in the face of a fierce battle by conservative vested interests against it in the Lords. The cost to the 'powers that be', however, was the effective loss of the Lords' veto over finance bills as a result of the *Parliament Act* of 1911. Newspaper owners, the wealthy and country landlords railed mightily against the Budget (Lloyd George was especially scathing about the nation's Dukes, such as those of Westminster, Norfolk, and Northumberland). *The Times*, in an article entitled *The Two Voices*[iii], equated it with 'thinly disguised socialism'.[23] Others saw it as the culmination of a sustained attack on the *status quo* and thus as part of a deliberate process of undermining national morale and the Empire's ability to defend itself.

Fears that the man in the street was reluctant to fight and die for his country were not confined to the British military. Similar views were expressed by officers in France and Germany before the war broke out. They, and mainstream politicians, were only too aware of the growth of new political ideas set well outside the traditional Conservative-Liberal axis which dominated European democratic politics for decades and which was underpinned by the franchise being limited for so long to property owning men. Socialism, Marxism, Anarchism and Anarcho-Syndicalism were all philosophies threatening the established order, and concerns these radical ideas were infecting the new and numerous industrial working class only served to increase the establishment's distrust of this growing portion of their various populations. The strikes, riots, and mutinies of the 1905 Russian Revolution did nothing to calm the nerves of the European *élite*.

In Great Britain such left-wing views were only heard at the political margins. Instead, the growth of organised labour preceded that of a Party of the Left. In 1892, Trades Union membership stood at 1.576 million, which figure was to oscillate between 1.6 and 2 million until 1906 when the General Election success of the Liberals under Campbell-Bannerman changed the political landscape. Union membership more than doubled by 1914, from 2 million to 4.15 million, and with it grew working class self-confidence and militancy in the fight for better wages, conditions, and a shorter working week. Such was the level of strike action between 1910 and 1914 that this period became known as *'The Great Unrest'*. Every year there were major industrial disputes and, in spite of the government being a mix of Liberal and Labour politicians, the Army was regularly used to suppress

---

[i] A policy which worked as National Debt was reduced from 30% of GDP in 1900 to 25% in 1914 [*Source: http://www.ukpublicspending.co.uk/debt_history*].

[ii] The outcome of these changes was that whilst in 1905 central government spending on pensions, health, and welfare had been zero and on defence £68 million, by 1913 this changed to £17.8 million spent on pensions, health, and welfare, and £75 million on defence. The effect on Public debt of the increased spending and offsetting taxation between 1905 and 1913 was to reduce it from £707 million to £625 million.
[*Sources: http://www.ukpublicspending.co.uk/uk_year1905_0.html* and
http://www.ukpublicspending.co.uk/piechart_1913_UK_total].

[iii] The 'two voices' were Asquith reassuring men of means no more than necessary was to be taken from them, and Lloyd George who, in his famous Limehouse speech on 30th July 1909, repeatedly and personally attacked the vested interests he threatened.

industrial action even to the extent of using lethal force, a factor which must have loomed large in liberal and socialist opposition to universal Army conscription pre-war and the militaristic aims of the *National Service League*.

1910 started with trouble in the Northumberland, Durham, and South Wales coalfields centring on the workings of the *Coal Mines Regulation Act* of 1908 (also known as the *Eight Hours Act*. Its three-shift pattern was very unpopular with miners and some employers. Other employers viewed it as the only way to make marginal pits pay) and on pay rates which, in South Wales at least, were based on a minimum wage agreement enacted in 1879. Rumblings of discontent continued through the General Election (15th January to 10th February 1910) and stoppages occurred at mines in Lanarkshire, Durham, and Nottinghamshire. On 9th March, a national miners' conference considered a response to the breakdown of negotiations in South Wales with the prospect of a national strike being raised. A general strike by 140,000 miners in South Wales seemed, initially, a near certainty. Negotiations continued throughout March and, by its end, the union recommended acceptance of a new agreement. Feelings at the pit head, however, were more militant but a strike ballot was decisively lost with 25% in favour[i].[24] Within a few days, a ballot of Northumberland miners provided a small majority in favour of a return to work.

Trouble continued to simmer over the summer, however, and, in other sectors, unrest was widespread. There was a lengthy strike in the Newport Docks and another prolonged dispute at Avonmouth. Woollen workers in Huddersfield threatened a large-scale strike and, later, workers in Bradford did withdraw their labour. Bakers demonstrated in central London for a shorter working day. Carters in Newcastle threatened action over pay. Seaman agitated for higher wages. Men of the *North-Eastern Railway* briefly came out on strike over complaints concerning the alleged victimisation of certain workers by the management. There was discontent amongst the employees of the *Great Northern Railway* and *North British Railway*, Violence between strikers and 'blacklegs' broke out at the *Doulton* factory in Rowley, Staffordshire. London taxi drivers struck and threatened to picket their bases for several weeks. And miners in Scotland, Warwickshire and Nottinghamshire were in lengthy disputes with pit owners.

On an almost daily basis *The Times* reported on new or ongoing industrial disputes, often under the heading of *Capital and Labour* which, in many respects, nicely sums up the fundamental basis of the discontent between employers wishing to protect their profits and employees wanting and needing to improve pay and conditions and reduce the working week[ii]. On 2nd September, for example, *Capital and Labour* reported strikes or their threat amongst South Wales miners, seaman, Edinburgh printers, *Great Western* and *Great Northern Railway* employees, and women chainmakers[iii] at Cradley Heath in the Black Country.[25] The following

---

[i] Turnout 92%. Oh, that democracy was so well supported nowadays!
[ii] By mid-September reports were entitled rather more prosaically *Labour Disputes*.
[iii] This strike, involving union and non-union workers, was widely supported especially by wealthy, well-connected women. The Dean of Worcester spoke in favour of the strikers, describing the 'evil conditions of women's labour in the chain trade being

day, shipbuilders on the *Clyde*, *Tyne* and the *Wear*, at Barrow, Birkenhead, Hartlepool and elsewhere declared a 'lock out' of all members of the Boilermakers' Union, affecting some 15,000 men and threatening the livelihoods of another 55,000 working in the shipyards[i]. Two days later, and with the lock-out ongoing, reports came in of a threatened miners' strike[ii] in the Rhondda with 10,000 men potentially involved.[26] On 12th September Lancashire cotton workers were threatened with a lock-out[iii] over a demarcation dispute involving just one man at the *Fern Mill* in Oldham.[27] Truly, industrial relations were at a very low ebb[iv].

By the beginning of November over 30,000 South Wales miners were idle, a resolution of the boilermakers' lock-out rejected, 2,000 carters in Liverpool were threatening strike action, and the *Great Eastern Railway* was facing strike action. Ominously, rumours were spreading that the military might become involved in South Wales as violence against 'scab' labour broke out at the *Powell-Duffryn Coal Company's* pits in Aberdare.[28] These rumours were then confirmed when it was announced the 18th Hussars[v] were under orders to go to South Wales if needed and that trains were being readied to move both infantry and cavalry to mid-Glamorgan.[29] In the light of continuing violence, and at the request of the Chief Constable of Glamorgan, Churchill, as Home Secretary, sent a squadron of the 18th Hussars to Pontypridd, ordered infantry (100 men each of the 1st Loyal North Lancashire Regt., and the 2nd Lancashire Fusiliers) to Newport (though they stopped temporarily at Swindon) and the Metropolitan Police sent down 270 men to help the local constabulary. The troops were placed under the command of Maj. Gen. Cecil Frederick Nevil Macready[vi], CB, the Director of Personal Services at

---

notorious'. Although a pay increase was offered some employers coerced their workers into working at the old rate and 'locked out' 660 women who refused to comply. A visiting German trade unionist, Fritz Kummer, said he have never seen such bad working conditions in any country he had visited. It was eventually resolved on 19th October 1910 [*Source: The Times, Capital and Labour*, 9th September 1910, page 8].

[i] Ballots to resolve the dispute in October and November showed a swing towards greater militancy with the votes for acceptance declining from 9,054 to 5,650 and the votes for rejection growing from 10,212 to 15,563. It was eventually ended by agreement on 14th December [*Sources: The Times, The Shipyard Lock-Out*, 9th November 1910, page 9 and *Shipyard Settlement*, 15th December 1910, page 8].

[ii] By 5th October, 24,000 South Wales miners were idle because of strikes, many of them caused by the continued use of non-union labour [*Source: The Times, The South Wales Coal Trade*, 5th October 1910, page 8].

[iii] The lock-out started at the end of September and was ended on 7th October.

[iv] They were worse in France. A General Strike was called in early October 1910.

[v] Taken prisoner *en masse* at the Battle of Talana Hill, 20th October, 1899, see page 327.

[vi] Gen. Cecil Frederick Nevil Macready, GCMG, KCB, PC, was born in 1862 and died in 1946. His father, William Charles Macready, was an actor as was his grandfather. His mother was granddaughter of the portrait artist Sir William Beechey. He attended the RMC being commissioned into the Gordon Highlanders. He served in Egypt and South Africa and was Assistant Adjutant General in the Directorate of Personal Services at the War Office in 1907, helping to develop the Territorial Force. Having commanded 2nd Brigade, he returned to the War Office as Director of Personal

the War Office and the man responsible for military aid to the civil power.[30] It is possible no more suitable General Officer might have been employed on this task as Macready had liberal instincts, believed workers had a right to strike, and even supported Irish Home Rule. His firm view was that he and the Home Office must retain control of any troops deployed and their use should not be devolved to any overly nervous local authority.

Matters at Tonypandy in the Rhondda were, however, getting out of hand. The three pits of the *Glamorgan Company* were idle and the Llwynypia pit to the north of the small town was in danger of flooding. Only the efforts of men led by the general manager of the *Cambrian Coal Trust*, who kept the boilers of the steam engine driving the pumps, prevented this scenario. These boilers were, though, the target of the strikers, and on the night of Monday 6th, November, a furious battle between police and strikers resulted in free use of the constables' truncheons. 114 injured strikers went to one doctor's surgery alone. The following evening the attacks began again. Similar assaults took place at the *Powell-Duffryn* pits in the Aberdare Valley with reports of over 200 injuries from both locations[i]. The arrival of 1,000 additional police (500 from London) helped quell the rioting in Tonypandy, and Macready deployed two squadrons of the 18th Hussars to the Rhondda and Aberdare valleys, while 200 infantry moved from Swindon to Pontypridd. Five hundred more troops were held in readiness if required. By such methods was the situation calmed, but only briefly. By the last week of November rioting resumed in the Rhondda and Aberdare valleys with events at Penygraig resulting in injuries to over thirty Metropolitan policemen.[31] By early December, however, the mood amongst some of the miners changed as the economics of strike pay hit home. Most of the men were back at work either side of Christmas. The industrial truce was but temporary.

Early in the new year, strikes started to impact the railways with men of the *North-Eastern Railway* coming out on 7th January, returning to work and 'downing tools' again at the beginning of February. Members of the print trades unions soon followed suit with an initially London-based dispute rapidly becoming national. Employers responded with lockouts. Within days, strikes and lockouts took place in cotton factories near Burnley, Northumberland miners showed signs of becoming restless over wages, and trouble was brewing in the shipyards of the *Tyne* and *Wear*. Not long after, indications of possible strike action emerged from the Potteries, the Leicester mines, and the Durham coalfield whilst there were disturbances involving print workers in central London. Then, on 22nd March, there was a renewal of rioting in South Wales, this time in the Clydach Vale just to the west of Tonypandy and disturbances and disputes in the South Wales coalfields would go on for months.

Services in June 1910. After the Curragh Incident he was appointed GOC, Belfast District. In 1914 he was Adjutant General, BEF, and in February 1916 Adjutant General to the Forces in Whitehall. In August 1918 he was appointed the Metropolitan Police Commissioner but, in April 1920, was made GOCinC Ireland during the Irish War of Independence which role he held until the creation of the Irish Free State.

[i] One striker later died of his injuries.

The scene for 1911 was set by the Spring strike of 11,000 workers which started on 22nd March in Scotland's largest industrial concern, *Singer's* Kilbowie, Clydebank, sewing machine factory[i].32 It was followed by strikes in the Southampton docks and by seamen in most British ports, dockers' strikes on the *Clyde*, and carters' and dockers 'strikes in Manchester. Such was the gravity of the situation in Manchester and Salford that C Squadron, Royal Scots Greys, was hurried by train over the Pennines from York and sixteen officers and 400 men of 2nd South Staffordshire Regt. moved north from Lichfield to the same city.33 Then, as a result of serious disorder in Cardiff related to the seamen's strike, two squadrons of cavalry and a battalion of infantry were moved to Bristol on 24th July as a reserve for troops still in South Wales.34 With strikes in the Victoria, Albert and Tilbury Docks in London starting on 1st August and leaving some 27 ships unable to set sail, there was barely a part of the county unaffected by some serious industrial dispute or other.

Most seriously, however, on 14th June a general strike of dockers and transport workers was declared in Liverpool. In the literally over-heated atmosphere of the record-breaking summer of 1911[ii], violence broke out on 13th August when, after the reading of the *Riot Act*, the police charged a large crowd waiting to be addressed by strike leader Tom Mann. This action resulted in 350 injuries. With 2,500 troops stationed in the city, more violence seemed bound to happen and, with the call now for a national transport strike, on 15th August, men from two troops of A Squadron of the 18th (Queen Mary's Own) Hussars commanded by Capt. Noel St Vincent Ramsey Stewart[iii] shot and killed two men and wounded 13 others on the Vauxhall Road when a crowd of 3,000 attacked prison vans taking arrested strikers to Walton Prison[iv]. Only after the intervention by troops from the 2nd Royal

---

[i] A return to work from 7th April was followed by the sacking of 400 strike leaders.

[ii] A heatwave and drought lasted for 2½ months from July to September with a record temperature of 36.7° C (98.1° F) recorded at Raunds, Northamptonshire, and Canterbury on 9th August 1911, a temperature not exceeded until 1990.

[iii] By then a Major he was awarded the DSO and MC in 1915 with the regiment involved at Mons, Le Cateau, the *Marne*, the *Aisne* and Messines. He was seriously wounded on 1st November 1914 near Messines. The citation for his DSO reads: Major N St. V R Stewart. Awarded the D.S.O., June 23rd 1915. 'This Officer commanded the Squadron on the exposed flank of the Brigade during its withdrawal from Messines on November 1st 1914. Under his able leadership and by his personal coolness and bravery his Squadron repulsed several fierce German attacks. His bold defence enabled his comrades to withdraw in good order. During, this time Major Stewart was suffering from a very severe wound in the head.' He did not return to the regiment.

[iv] The inquest heard that the order to shoot was given by Lt. Thomas Gerald Hetherington, 2iC of the 18th Hussars' detachment. Hetherington was later promoted captain and served in the war. The fatalities were John Sutcliffe, a 19-year-old Catholic carter, and Michael Prendergast, a 30-year-old Catholic docker. The inquest recorded verdicts of 'justifiable homicide'. It was suggested by some in authority (and at the inquest) that Prendergast had been fatally wounded by a rioter firing a rifle from behind the crowd [*Source: The Times, The Liverpool Riots*, 1st September 1911, page 6].

Warwickshire Regt., and mounted police did the vans get through[i]. Ironically, *The Times* report of the incident commented favourably on 'the rioters facing with wonderful coolness and courage the police batons'.[35] No doubt many of these 'cool and courageous men' would be fighting for their country across the fields of Picardy as part of the nation's New Armies in less than five years' time.

With a general transport strike imminent, Churchill, now Home Secretary, asked for other troops to be made available if required and both infantry and cavalry units of the Aldershot Command were held in readiness[ii] though there were some concerns that if the strike spread (there was already violence in Sheffield) troops reinforcements would struggle to get north if the railways closed down completely as threatened.[36] The general transport strike was indeed called on 17th August and lasted just two days after which the government agreed to set up a Royal Commission to examine the workings of the 1907 Conciliation Board which was at the root of the problem. Troops began to disperse back to their camps a week later but, even as negotiations to resolve the strike were under way, another fatal incident involving the Army 'in support of the civil power' occurred.

According to newspaper reports, during the afternoon of Saturday, 19th August, 1911, a crowd stopped a train near Llanelli, injured what they viewed as the strike-breaking driver and immobilised the train. Men of the Worcestershire Regt., commanded by Maj. Burleigh Francis Brownlow Stuart, found themselves in a cutting surrounded by stone throwing rioters. They ignored first the reading of the *Riot Act* by local magistrate Thomas Jones, JP; second an advance with fixed bayonets; and third a warning shot from an officer; and continued to pelt the soldiers with whatever came to hand. Though it was later claimed the troops only fired warning shots, in the ensuing fusillade two men were killed outright and three more wounded, two seriously. John Henry 'Jack' John, aged 21, a local tinplate worker, was killed immediately. Leonard Worsell, a 20-year-old labourer originally from London, simply looking over the wall at the bottom of the garden with some mates, was fatally wounded. Jack Francis was seriously injured (his condition described as 'precarious' in *The Times*), and Joseph Hanbury slightly wounded. David Travers, shot in the neck, was 'was not expected to recover'.[37] Later that night, an outraged crowd swarmed through Llanelli attacking the houses of two magistrates and several businesses only to be dispersed by troops and police. The mob then moved onto the *Great Western Railway Company's* goods sheds which they looted, 'liberating' large quantities of alcohol in the process. The shed caught fire setting off a large explosion amongst trucks loaded with a mixture of gunpowder, carbide, and gelatine. Three rioters were killed outright, one fatally injured, and a dozen more wounded. While some strikers ripped up the railway tracks into and out of Llanelli, others were dispersed by bayonet charges by the Worcesters.

---

[i] Commanded by Lt. Gen. Sir Henry Mackinnon: 18th Brigade (Brig. Gen. G F Gorringe): 2nd Royal Warwickshire Regt., 2nd South Staffordshire Regt., 2nd Northumberland Regt., 1st Yorkshire Regt., and the Royal Scots Greys and 18th Hussars [*Source: The Times, Fresh Rioting in Liverpool*, 16th August 1911, page 6].

[ii] In addition, an armoured cruiser, *HMS Antrim*, was moored in the Mersey.

The deaths of John and Worsell were investigated at an inquest held at the end of August. Brownlow Stuart was asked about the order to fire. Telling the coroner the crowd was throwing large numbers of stones at the 70-90 men under his command, he said he gave the crowd a minute to disperse, timing this minute on his watch. Asked about the crowd's response, the Major stated:

"At this time the crowds were daring us to take action and were defying me in every possible way. One man in particular, I noticed, jumped up, bared his chest and dared us to shoot."

Brownlow Stuart then ordered his men to open fire at 'people who were throwing the stones' (i.e. not warning shots as initial reports stated). Asked if he needed instructions or permission to open fire, Brownlow Stuart replied:

"It was my duty. I regretted it, but I had to do it."

Opening fire was, apparently, 'in the interests of the public'. When the lawyer for Jack John pointed out that the *Riot Act* required people to 'depart to their habitations…' and that at least three of dead and wounded were in the garden of their home, Brownlow Stuart replied 'he knew nothing of that'. His orders were explicit – no trains were to be stopped. When asked why the people shot were in one place, in the garden of 'No. 6, the High Street', the Major declined to answer. Later, several witnesses testified no stones were thrown from this garden. Others stated the stones were mainly thrown from the opposite side of the cutting. Their evidence counted for nothing. Another lawyer, a Mr Parfitt on behalf of *ASLEF (The Associated Society of Locomotive Engineers and Firemen)* asked Brownlow Stuart if he was 'at liberty to shoot people?' The reply came: 'I was to use such force as was necessary to ensure the train passing'. Parfitt then asked:

"You admit that the shooting of these people did not effect the object you had in view? *Brownlow Stuart*: The train did not get through."

The Coroner, a Mr J W Nicholas of Carmarthen, summed up:

"… it was immaterial whether these young men were rioters of had thrown any stones or not. They were in the direction from which the stones came, and as there was no evidence that they actually threw stones it was just unfortunate that they were present."

He then 'suggested' to the jury a proper verdict was 'justifiable homicide' although how he arrived at such a verdict after his garbled and illogical statement is difficult to comprehend. Broadly, it seems the young men were innocent bystanders but were shot anyway. 'Collateral damage', their 'fault' was living where they did. The jury, under some pressure, acquiesced but with the *caveat* that:

"We think it would have been better if other means than the order to fire had been adopted by Maj. Stuart for the purpose of dispersing the crowd."[38]

Killing innocent bystanders was no hindrance to the career of Maj., later Brig. Gen., Brownlow Stuart who went on to command the 3rd Worcesters in 1912[i].

---

[i] Served in the retreat from Mons and Le Cateau. Wounded at Ypres, 1915. Commanded a Brigade from 1916. CB, CMG. Died 1952.

The numbers of troops deployed during the industrial unrest of August 1911 are, perhaps, surprising to those unused to seeing the military used to control civilians in Great Britain[i]. These troops were based in seven 'Strike Areas' and their distribution was as follows:[39]

North-West Strike Area – Lt. Gen. Sir W H Mackinnon, KCB, KCVO
12th Brigade (details given above)
2nd Lincolnshire Regt., 2nd Welsh Fusiliers, 1st KRRC, 2nd Wiltshire Regt.
Royal Scots Greys, 18th Hussars, 16th Lancers
Northern Strike Area – Gen. Sir L J Oliphant, KCB, KCVO, 6th Brigade
2nd KRRC, 2nd Oxfordshire and Buckinghamshire Light Infantry
North Midlands Strike Area – Brig. Gen. H N C Heath, CB
1st Gordon Highlanders, 2nd Scottish Rifles, 2nd Durham Light Infantry, 2nd West Yorkshire Regt., 250 men, RFA, 9th Lancers
East Midland Strike Area – Brig. Gen. E R C Graham, CB, 2nd Brigade
2nd Notts & Derby Regt., half battalion Devonshire Regt., 2nd York & Lancaster Regt., 1st Northamptonshire Regt., 2nd Royal Dublin Fusiliers, 1st Dorset Regt., 1st East Lancashire Regt., 1st Royal West Surrey Regt., 2nd Royal Munster Fusiliers, 2nd West Riding Regt., 4th Dragoon Guards
South Midland Strike Area – Brig. Gen. L G Drummond, CB, MVO
1st Worcestershire Regt., 2nd Lancashire Fusiliers, 1st Gloucestershire Regt., 1st Loyal North Lancashire Regt., 4th Hussars, 11th Hussars
South Wales Strike Area – Col. G H B Freeth DSO, Lancashire Fusiliers
2nd Royal Sussex Regt., detachments: 4th Hussars, Worcestershire Regt., Loyal North Lancashire Regt., Somerset Light Infantry, Devon Regt., RFA, RGA.
London Strike Area – Lt. Gen. Sir A H Paget, KCB, KCVO, ADC
1st Brigade, 7th Brigade RHA, 1st Cavalry Brigade

1912 STARTED WITH A COTTON WORKERS' STRIKE in Lancashire, hosiery workers out in Leicestershire, a threat of action by Bradford woolcombers and, most seriously of all, the prospect of a national miners' strike. On Thursday, 18th

---

[i] Bad though industrial relations were in Britain, the number of deaths were as nothing compared to those in the USA where private companies regularly deployed automatic weapons against strikers. Before WW1 this climaxed in the Colorado Coalfield War (September 1913-April 1914). Here, miners and their families lived and worked in appalling conditions. Attempts at unionisation led to a strike organised by the *United Mine Workers of America*. The main company involved was the Rockefeller-owned *Colorado Fuel & Iron Company*. On 20th April 1914, Colorado National Guardsmen and company guards, without either cause or warning, opened fire with a machine gun on an encampment of 1,200 striking miners and their families at Ludlow. An ensuing fire resulted in the deaths by bullet, asphyxiation or burns of between 21 and 55 of the residents, mostly women and children. The strike leader, Louis Tikas, was murdered in cold blood by National Guard Lt. Karl Linderfelt who was found responsible for Tikas's death but acquitted of his murder. Later fighting between strikers and guards raised the death toll to c. 75. President Wilson was forced to deploy Federal troops who disarmed both sides. British industrial relations were, by comparison, positively civilised [*Source*: Ellis, J, *The Social History of the Machine Gun*, Pimlico, 1976, pages 42-5].

January 1912, the result of a strike ballot was announced. There was never any doubt about the outcome and the result was conclusive: for strike action 445,801 (79%), against 115,721 (21%). Only one of the seventeen Miners' Federation districts, the small Cleveland ironstone mining area, voted against a strike. The purpose of the strike was to force agreement to a minimum wage, something miners had demanded and struck over unsuccessfully in 1894. The complex and variable system of payments currently employed made it difficult for some miners to make a living wage on a consistent basis and it was this issue the Miners' Federation was determined to solve once and for all. As negotiations went on during February the authorities decided to act pre-emptively and, on 20th February, Neath Magistrates decided to apply to the Home Office for troops before the strike even started. The Chief Constable of Glamorgan, who was in place during the previous year's confrontations, asked for 3,500 infantry and 500 cavalry to help protect persons and property, and maintain order.[40] Two days later, Rhondda magistrates asked for 1,500 troops to secure law and order in the valleys. In Plymouth, 8th Brigade[i] suspended its spring training and made ready to move at short notice.[41] Meanwhile, concern was expressed about the knock-on effects of the strike at home and abroad, with the Potteries suggesting up to 100,000 workers might be idle a week after the strike started, and the Spanish Minister of the Interior expressing concerns many factories would close without British coal.

The strike started on Friday, 1st March. In general, it proceeded without the violence seen in South Wales and Liverpool the previous year. A half company of the Shropshire Light Infantry was despatched to Chirk, eight miles south-west of Wrexham, towards the end of March when it was feared violence was threatened at the Brynkinallt colliery but, by that time, the *Coal Mines (Minimum Wage) Bill* was on its way through Parliament and the Miners' leadership ordered a new ballot. The strike officially ended on 6th April in a considerable victory for the miners but, in some areas, the reaction to the settlement was negative. Violence in South Lancashire saw troops at Chirk and others from Aldershot and Norwich sent to restore order. Commanded by Maj. Gen. Edward Cecil Bethune, CB, the GOC of the West Lancashire Division, these troops consisted of 450 men from the Suffolk Regt., the 16th Lancers, and the 4th Royal Fusiliers, and they were distributed around Wigan and Leigh. The 2nd Welsh Regt. was also put under orders to move from Pembroke Dock if required.[42] Calm soon returned and the 'revolt', as the newspapers described it, was over within 24 hours.

At the end of May, the mood amongst striking London transport workers resulted in Aldershot Command manning the telephone lines day and night in case 'aid to the civil power' was required.[43] With the strike dragging on, and food and other supplies being maintained through the use of 'free labourers' (or 'scabs'), men of the Dublin Fusiliers were used to maintain order at Tilbury in the middle of July, but this would appear to have been the last time troops were used in this capacity in 1912 or, indeed, into 1913.[44]

---

[i] 2nd Royal Scots, 2nd Sherwood Foresters, 1st Northamptonshire Regt. & 4th Middlesex Regt.

1912 was, though, a record year and provided a sobering insight into the state of industrial relations in pre-war Britain. The number of working days lost in in 1911-2 exceeded the aggregate total for the years 1899 to 1910. In 1912, 31.5 million working days were lost to strike action or 1 in 75 of all working days. 850,000 miners struck over a minimum wage, 121,000 in defence of trades union rights, and 115,000 over wage increases. In all, more working days were lost in 1912 than in any previous year, exceeding even 1910, the worst year since 1893.[45]

An explanation for the increasing unrest can be found in statistics provided by Asquith at a meeting in Downing Street in late June 1912. They showed changes in the prices of food and drink set against the value of wages since 1900. Each index started from a base of 100 and showed wages stagnant for eleven years. Indeed, under the previous Tory government they declined, the index hitting a low of 96.6 in 1904. Wages slowly returned to the levels of 1900, the index reaching a figure of 100.3 in 1911. The food price index, however, rocketed to 111.6 by 1911, with year-on-year increases since 1906. Furthermore, coal costs rose from a base of 100 in 1905 to 110 by 1912.[46] More figures showed that, between 1905 and 1912, the combined changes in retail prices and rents meant costs increased by between 8% in parts of London to 13.3% in Lancashire and Cheshire. In the same period wages for many unskilled workers did not change, though wages for skilled workers in the building and engineering industries increased by 1.9 to 5.5%. This was still not enough to compensate for the eroding impact of inflation.[47] Broadly, therefore, workers were poorer in 1911 than they were in 1900 and their demands for fairer and better pay more than justified.[48]

Such figures continued to impact industrial relations. In the first seven months of 1914, the Board of Trade recorded 937 strikes.[49] Many were small but the figure was indicative of the febrile state of industrial relations in pre-war Great Britain. Of particular concern, as matters in Sarajevo and the Balkans increased Europe-wide nervousness, was the growing agitation amongst the powerful 'Triple Alliance' of miners, railwaymen, and transport workers (many of whom worked in the docks) in response to various historic while more recent events only served to heighten their sense of grievance against both employers and the Government.

For the miners a tipping point was the judgement given against the owners and manager of the *Universal Colliery* at Senghenydd in the Aber Valley near Caerphilly, east Glamorganshire on 18th July 1914 by magistrates at Caerphilly Magistrates Court. On 14th October 1913, a huge underground explosion ripped through the mine with sufficient force to send the cage at the Lancaster pit up the 650-yard-deep shaft and into the pithead gear. Nearby, John Mogridge, a surface worker, was decapitated by a wood splinter. Underground were 950 miners of all ages. 437 perished in the explosion or through asphyxiation from lethal gasses released by an explosion of fire damp (methane) exacerbated by a detonation of coal dust[i].

---

[i] A rescuer also died, William John, bringing the total deaths to 439. It was the worst mining disaster in British history. It was not, however, the first at Senghenydd. Another explosion on Friday, 24th May, 1901 killed 81 of the 82 men underground. [*Source: www.welshcoalmines.co.uk/GlamEast/Senghenydd.htm*].

The Official Court of Enquiry blamed un-insulated electrical signalling equipment, contrary to the requirements of a Home Office circular, and the failure to install a system to reverse the airflow which, by law, should have been installed no later than 1st January 1913. Seventeen charges were brought by the Home Office against the colliery manager, Mr Edward Shaw, and four against the company, the case starting on 5th May 1914. On 18th July, the magistrates rendered their verdict: fines totalling £24 against Shaw or, as stated in a local newspaper headline 'Miners lives at 1s 1¼d each'.[i] The company got off scot-free.

A wave of bitterness swept mining communities and was added to feelings of grievance when their 1912 strike failed to deliver the minimum wage which lay at the heart of the campaigns for improvements to the lives of miners and their families. This bitterness festered. When Thomas Richards, Labour MP for West Monmouthshire and General Secretary of the South Wales Miners' Federation, supported Prime Minister Asquith at a recruiting meeting in Cardiff for a new Welsh Army Corps, it was his bitter reference to Senghenydd[ii] which drew the loudest cheers:

> "Why, it isn't much change when we ask the South Wales collier to go on the battlefield. Many of your working places are dark and dismal, aye, and as dangerous as the trenches at the front. They talk about the Jack Johnsons of the Germans; what about the bombs of Senghenydd? They are not to be compared to them – they swoop 400 of them at a time into eternity."[50]

Amongst railway workers resentment was fuelled by vindictive actions taken against individual union members after the successful strike of 1911. This forced the Government into agreeing to a Royal Commission to investigate the activities of the *Conciliation Board*, set up in 1907 by Lloyd George to resolve issues between employers and employees. Since then, as catalogued in Ramsey MacDonald's 1913 essay *'The Social Unrest'*, union members had been targeted for dismissal, disciplinary action, and denial of pay and time off such that MacDonald described them as 'being goaded into revolt'.

The third arm of the Alliance, the *National Transport Workers' Federation*, was always spoiling for a fight, although, in 1912, it misjudged the mood of its various component unions when a call for a national dock strike in support of a two-month strike by London dockers was ignored in many ports.

In the summer of 1914 strikes and disputes broke out across the country: London building workers struck for months; the shipbuilding and engineering industries fought over the hours in the working day; the *Great Western Railway* confronted their engineers and boilermakers; while the *General Labourers' Union* agitated for a shorter working week.

Government concerns reached fever pitch on 5th July when 7,000 men walked out of the *Royal Arsenal* at Woolwich in a dispute originally over the use of non-union labour but which escalated rapidly when a union member was dismissed for refusing to work as ordered by the Director. Within two days, over 10,000 men were idle and the *Arsenal* closed. The departments affected were the *Royal*

---

[i] £2,000 to £7,500 and £4 to £17 in current values depending on the index used.
[ii] The *Universal Colliery* closed on 30th March 1928 with the loss of 2,500 jobs.

Laboratory, Royal Carriage Department, Royal Gun Factory, the *Mechanical Engineering Department*, the *Building Works Department* and the *Army and Navy Ordnance Department*. It was a dispute requiring an urgent Government climb down, especially when workers at the Portsmouth Dockyard and at *Armstrong and Co.* and *Vickers* came out in sympathetic action.

Thus, with industrial action striking at the heart of Government and the nation's military effectiveness, at a time when mainland Europe was spiralling rapidly into all-out war, it is not surprising concerns about the willingness of the average working man to fight and, if necessary, die for his country were raised at the highest levels of the Army. It is, perhaps, surprising how willing the working class was to respond to the calls for volunteers even from areas where troops had not only been deployed but been in action with bullet or bayonet. As would be revealed in a few short weeks, patriotism, however blinkered, was not the sole preserve of the upper classes. But working men were distrusted and despised by some Army officers and how much such attitudes coloured their training and employment in the autumn of 1914 is an open question. There is little doubt the average intelligence of not just the new officers but of the NCOs and Other Ranks of the New Armies was significantly higher than in the pre-war Regular Army, but concerns about hardiness, fitness for battle, and their reaction to discipline loomed large in the minds of Generals with a distinct vision as to what made a 'real' soldier. This vision did not include soft-handed clerks or radicalised miners.

PRIOR TO SOUTH AFRICA the Army's 'Other Ranks' maintained the traditions which led the Duke of Wellington to describe his own men as 'scum'[i]. Before 1899 rates of pay for ordinary soldiers were so poor they resulted in the lower ranks of the Army attracting men:

"… from those levels of society that were not too particular in their manner of living."[51]

In 1902, Leo Amery drew a more depressing picture of the average recruit:

"Frosty nights are the recruiting sergeant's best allies. Physically, mentally and morally the ordinary Army recruit is a long way below the average standard of his countrymen. In most cases a townsman, he possesses no natural fighting aptitude whatsoever. Initiative he lacks, for the sufficient reason that, if he had not lacked it, he would probably have sought, and found, some more profitable employment than soldiering… he is to all intents and purposes illiterate."[52]

---

[i] The quote, comparing the French and British Armies, reads: "A French army is composed very differently from ours. The conscription calls out a share of every class - no matter whether your son or my son - all must march; but our friends - I may say it in this room - are the very scum of the earth. People talk of their enlisting from their fine military feeling - all stuff - no such thing. Some of our men enlist from having got bastard children - some for minor offences – many more for drink; but you can hardly conceive such a set brought together, and it really is wonderful that we should have made them the fine fellows they are." [*Source*: Stanhope, P H, *Notes of Conversations with the Duke of Wellington*, 1886, Notes, 11th November 1831].

In a letter to Lord Roberts, Gen. Sir William Nicholson, appointed Quartermaster-General to the Forces in December 1905, bemoaned the fact the ranks of the army were only filled by means of the 'compulsion of destitution'.[53] In other words, the lowlier ranks of the pre-war Army were the career choice only of men with no other options in life. Nevertheless, as previously mentioned, not all were successful in their attempts to claim the 'King's shilling' as, in every year between 1903 and 1913, between 20% and 40% of men who attempted to enlist were rejected for medical or physical reasons.[54]

With such material there were few men in the Army who, before South Africa, disagreed with the Duke of Cambridge and Lord Wolseley's belief that discipline – relentless, harsh, and unbending – was the key to the creation of an effective fighting force. The need was to produce men who 'responded to the word of command as the machine answers to the pressing of the button'.[55] And it was this type of man in this type of Army, led by what proved to be, in too many circumstances, an ill-educated and ill-trained Officer Corps, who went to fight in South Africa in 1899 in Britain's first major war for over forty years and the last before the cataclysm of 1914-18.

One means of improving the quality of the 'other ranks' joining the Army might have been by increasing their basic pay which stood at one shilling a day for a private in a Line infantry regiment[i]. At least that was what was nominally paid. The problem was that, from this shilling, all sorts of deductions could be, and were, made: for lost or damaged uniform or kit; damage to barracks; haircuts; repairs; groceries and extra rations, etc. An study of stoppages in 1890 based on 694 men serving at Aldershot showed that, on average, £7 3s 11d per year was deducted from their annual 'pay' of £18 5s thus reducing their *actual* daily pay to 7d a day. It could be much worse, and a regulation was introduced requiring a minimum of 1d a day be left to each private soldier after deductions. Additions to pay were available, but only by extending the working day. The men could become cooks, mess waiters, or an officer's servant, the latter role increasing their pay by some 2½d a day.[56] In spite of this, pay and conditions were generally appalling and gave no encouragement to the sort of men the Army needed.

In 1898, the Inspector of Recruiting, Gen. Thomas Kelly-Kenny[ii], presented a

---

[i] As an indicator of how far one shilling (12d/twelve pence or c. £4 today) might stretch, the *Black Country Living Museum* gives costs for essentials from 1910 as: Loaf of bread 2½d, 1 lb butter 1s 2d, 1 lb sugar 3d, 1 lb tea 1s 6d, 1 lb cheese 6d, and 1 lb bacon 9d. [*Source*: https://www.bclm.co.uk/media/learning/library/witr_costofliving1910.pdf]. Depending on the index used, the rate of pay for a Private/Rifleman of one shilling a day translates into very little nowadays. The average of four different indices gives an equivalent annual income of c. £10,000 with a maximum of c. £17,000.

[ii] Gen. Sir Thomas Kelly-Kenny, GCB, GCVO, was born in Kilrush, Co. Clare in 1840. Eucated St Patrick's College, Carlow, and the RMC. Ensign, 1st Battalion, 2nd (The Queen's Royal) Regiment of Foot, 1858. Served in China and Abyssinia and several staff positions. AAG, Aldershot 1893-96. Inspector-General of Auxiliary Forces and Recruiting. Commanded 6th Division in South Africa. AG of the Forces 1901-04. A man of Liberal sympathies and active in politics and reform in Co. Clare. Also a close friend and confidant of Edward VII. He died in December 1914.

memorandum on the problems of recruiting a better sort of man. It was so radical Lord Lansdowne[i], Secretary of State for War, suppressed the document. It only saw the light of day after the fiascos in South Africa. Kelly-Kenny's message was stark. Having no experience of war 'under modern European conditions', Britain must look to the continent to judge what sort of equipment and what sort of men were required. There, it was found men had a 'high measure of individual intelligence and training, patriotism and self-respect'. But, while the British Army improved its armaments and equipment, the quality of its fundamental component – the private soldier – remained lacking suggested Kelly-Kenny. He then asked and answered three questions:

1. Was the current British recruit up the standards required for a modern European war? Answer: No;
2. Was it possible to induce a better class of man to enlist? Answer: Yes, but only at substantial cost to the taxpayer; and
3. What sort of inducements were required? Answer: 'The pay must be largely increased, larger than ever yet proposed'.

To be fair the Army, prior to 1895, had already put such an idea to the soon-to-be outgoing Liberal Government[ii] but it had not thought such an increase necessary[iii]. Kelly-Kenny now thought even the Army's suggestion inadequate. He proposed increasing the rates of pay for the men in the ranks by 100% to two shillings a day – and, if necessary, by more. Furthermore, he recommended provision be made to ensure ex-soldiers could find decent employment once they left the ranks as another means of encouraging better men to sign up[iv].[57] Sadly, this was a case of 'fine words buttering no parsnips' as pay rates for the private soldier in 1914 were the same as those in 1895 even if the deductions mentioned above were mainly removed.

The question is: did conditions improve between 1902 and 1914? According to Bowman and Connelly in *The Edwardian Army*[58], the answer was: not much. Basic pay did not improve though, by eliminating deductions, 'take home' (or

---

[i] Henry Charles Keith Petty-Fitzmaurice, 5th Marquess of Lansdowne (1845-1927), previously Governor General of Canada, Viceroy of India and later Foreign Secretary.
[ii] The Liberals under Lord Roseberry were heavily defeated by the Conservatives under Lord Salisbury in a General Election held between 13th July and 7th August 1895. Kelly-Kenny's memorandum was dated 12th August 1895.
[iii] One of the justifications being a comparison between the pay rates for the British and German Armies: Private soldier pay, British Army 1s/ day, German Army 4½d/day; Private soldier daily rations, British Army 5d/day, German Army 3½d/day [*Source: The Times, House of Commons*, 17th March 1896, page 6].
[iv] In 1908 it appears to have come as a shock to the Monarch, his Government, senior Army officers and the country at large that surviving veterans of the Crimean War and the Indian Mutiny, men 70 and older, were mainly consigned to the Workhouse. A Veterans Relief Fund was set up with the King as its chief patron and its chief spokesman being Lord Roberts. It was intended 'every veteran should be 'released from the workhouse' and given an allowance in order they might 'spend (their) days in moderate comfort and respectability'. The King donated 1,000 guineas to get the fund going [*Source: The Times, The Veterans' Relief Fund*, 8th January 1908, page 7].

rather 'take to the barracks') pay marginally increased. Leave and basic food improved but accommodation varied hugely depending on where the ranker was lucky, or unlucky, to find himself. Indeed, ten months before the outbreak of war, *The Times* was still bemoaning the state of recruitment[i] and the authorities' failure to 'make military service more attractive'.[59]

Unfortunately, despite Kelly-Kenny's 1898 recommendations, there was no significant improvement in the soldier's career prospects once they left the army and the still current image of the average private soldier as hard drinking and semi-literate did little for their future employment opportunities. Some form of relatively menial public service work in the Post Office, the Prison Service or on the railways was usually the best on offer to the ex-serviceman.

On this the German Army took a different perspective, particularly when it came to attracting and retaining the core of Non-Commissioned Officers which became the bedrock of the Army during the early years of the war. These men undertook to serve for twelve years full-time rather than the two years an ordinary 'ranker' conscript served. After twelve years of satisfactory service, an NCO was awarded his 'civil service certificate' (*Zivilversorgunschein*) which guaranteed a decent job in the public sector. Such a guarantee ensured a constant flow of new NCOs and, in addition, built up a reserve of retired but highly trained and experienced ex-NCOs who might slip back into Army life should circumstances demand.[60]

Within the British Army, recruitment remained a problem and, in the ten years between 1903 and 1913, in only three years did recruit numbers exceed those dying, discharged, deserting or leaving for some other reason. Overall, the number of departures (c. 437,000) far exceeded the new additions (c. 392,000). The one un-looked for virtue of this was that there was a large pool of ex-soldiers, many still of service age, in the country when war broke out.

The training of 'other ranks' continued to be a problem despite all the good post-South African intentions. At the 1909 General Staff Officers' Conference a question was asked: 'Is it possible, under present conditions at home, to carry out a thoroughly progressive training of men?'[61] The question was answered by Col. J P Du Cane from the Army HQ's General Staff, and the answer was 'no'. The problems were multiple. First, unlike the continental conscript armies where every year a new cadre of young men arrived at the barracks at the same time, the British volunteer army recruited men on an *ad hoc* basis. Men joined the ranks 'as and when' and there was a continuous year-round influx, all of whom were at a training disadvantage relative to those who joined before. The first year was especially problematical according to Du Cane and no suggestions as to how this might be resolved worked. One idea was to hold large scale manoeuvres bi-annually or to concentrate company training just before times when a battalion might go to serve abroad. But, as Du Cane pointed out, this might mean the training of the private soldier improved but at the expense of the training of both junior and senior officers. An additional problem was that, compared to the continental armies, it was thought the relative weakness of the British Army was with the performance

---

[i] *The Times* also complained about the lack of a light machine gun, the state of the RFA's 18-pdrs, and the perceived inadequacies of the Lee Enfield Rifle.

of more senior commanders and in the performance of staff duties. Focussing on improving private soldiers at the expense of officers, in Du Cane's estimate, only served to weaken further a part of army where it was already relatively fragile.

In contrast, as with comparisons between the *Kriegsakademie* and the Staff College (see page 431), the training of 'other ranks' within the German Army was similarly far more rigorous, with a ten-hour day being devoted to drill, tactical training, fatigues and lectures all of which imposed a physical and intellectual regime far more taxing and stimulating than the six-hours or so in which the average British soldier was on duty.[62] Furthermore, given the generally lower physical and intellectual quality of the average British volunteer, much time was given either to their drill, in order to instil the necessary sense of discipline, or physical training in order to improve their physique. Their training for war necessarily trailed behind and thus Leo Amery, commenting on the need to improve the quality of NCOs in the Army (because of the dispersal of the firing line found necessary in South Africa), went on to say:

> "Even in the private soldier intelligence has become a factor of the very first importance. If only the same amount of energy were put into the development of the stunted and neglected brains of our recruits as is put into the development of their chests and forearms the result would be an incalculable increase in the fighting value of our forces."[63]

Underlining still further the problems involved in training, Maj. F B Maurice[i] commented that, with approximately half of the infantry serving abroad and with these regularly reinforced by drafts from home, and with 'specialists', e.g. machine gunners, signallers, drivers, etc., being taken away for training, the numbers left to be involved in company, battalion and other training schemes were so small as to render such training pointless. New recruits might be reckoned as representing 30% of more of the men available to be trained and their experience often was to go on some form of manoeuvres before they received any form of more basic training which might inform them what they should do once in the field.[64]

At both officer and 'other rank' level, therefore, the Army was not the career choice of the intelligent, ambitious man anxious to forge a role within a profession of which he could be proud. And both the country and the Army were about to pay a heavy price for these shortcomings.

---

[i] Later Maj. Gen. Sir Frederick Barton Maurice, 1st Baronet, GCB, GCMG, GCVO, DSO, and the son of Maj. Gen. Sir John Frederick Maurice, KCB, mentioned elsewhere as the Chair of the meeting at *RUSI* involving Bloch.

ENDNOTES:
[1] *Der Weltkrieg 1914 bis 1918*, Vol. 1, S Mittler & Sohn, 1925, page 43.
[2] Fuller, *Decisive Battles*, Vol. 3, op. cit., page 319.
[3] Howard, N P, *The Social and Political Consequences of the Allied Food Blockade of Germany, 1918–19*, 1993, pages 161-188.
[4] Samuels, M, *Command or Control?*, op. cit., page 77
[5] Wells, *Anticipations*, op. cit., page 79.
[6] Ibid., page 212.
[7] Wells, H G, *What is Coming? A Forecast of things after the war*, Cassell, 1916, p. 256.
[8] Gat, A, *Development of Military Thought*, op. cit., footnote pages 91-2.
[9] Steinberg, J, *Bismarck a Life*, Oxford University Press, 2011, page 21.
[10] Bernhardi, *Germany and the Next War*, op. cit., pages 243-4.
[11] Ibid.
[12] Ibid.
[13] Baden-Powell, R, *Scouting for Boys*, 1908, page 264.
[14] Wells, H G, *The Land Ironclads*, Strand Magazine, December 1903.
[15] Heffer, S, *The Age of Decadence*, Random House, 2017, page 256.
[16] *The Times, National Training and National Defence*, Saturday, 5th April, 1902, page 14.
[17] *The Times, Letters: Physical Deterioration*, Saturday, 26th December 1903, page 8.
[18] Ibid.
[19] *The Times, Physical Deterioration*, Friday, 29th July 1904, page 12.
[20] Ibid.
[21] Ibid.
[22] Grey of Fallodon, Viscount, *Twenty-Five Years*, Hodder & Stoughton, Vol. II, 1925, page 53.
[23] *The Times, The Two Voices*, 2nd August 1909, page 7.
[24] *The Times*, various reports on the South Wales mining industry February-April 1910.
[25] *The Times, Capital and Labour*, 2nd September 1910, page 6.
[26] *The Times, The Shipyard Lock-Out*, 5th September 1910, page 8.
[27] *The Times, Capital and Labour*, 12th September 1910, page 8.
[28] *The Times, Labour Disputes*, 4th November 1910, page 9.
[29] *The Times, Welsh Strike Riots*, 8th November 1910, page 10.
[30] *The Times, Welsh Strike Riots*, 9th November 1910, page 10.
[31] *The Times, Welsh Strike Riots*, 23rd November 1910, page 12.
[32] *The Times, Strike at Singer's Works*, 23rd March 1911, page 13.
[33] *The Times, Despatch of Troops and London Police*, 6th July 1911, page 9.
[34] *The Times, The Seamen's Strike at Cardiff*, 24th July 1911, page 6.
[35] *The Times, Fresh Rioting in Liverpool*, 16th August 1911, page 6.
[36] *The Times, Spread of The Labour War*, 16th August 1911, page 6.
[37] *The Times, Fatal Riots at Llanelly*, 21st August 1911, page 6.
[38] *The Times, The Llanelly Riots*, 30th August 1911, page 6.
[39] *The Times, Troops and The Strikes*, 23rd August 1911, page 8.
[40] *The Times, Welsh Magistrates' Request for Troops*, 20th February 1912, page10.
[41] *The Times, Troops in Readiness*, 1st March 1912, page 7.
[42] *The Times, The Lancashire Revolt*, 11th April 1912, page 6.
[43] *The Times, Transport Strike*, 27th May 1912, page 6.
[44] *The Times, Strike Negotiations*, 16th July 191, page 6.
[45] *The Times, A Year's Strikes*, 5th November 1913, page 5.
[46] *The Times, Increased Cost of Living*, 3rd March 1913, page 7.
[47] *The Times, The Cost of Living*, 13th August 1913, page 6.
[48] *The Times, Industrial Unrest*, 22nd June 1912, page 9
[49] Dangerfield, G, *'The Strange Death of Liberal England'*, Paladin, 1970, page 347.
[50] *The Times*, Tuesday, 6th October 1914, page 3.

[51] Dunlop, op. cit., page 32.
[52] Amery, op. cit., page 184.
[53] Beckett, I F W, *The Compulsion of Destitution: The British Army and the Dilemma of Imperial Defence, 1870-1914*, in Peter Dennis & Jeffrey Grey (eds.), *Raise, Train and Sustain: Delivering Land Combat Power* (Canberra: Australian Military History Publications, 2010), pages 1-29.
[54] Bowman T, & Connelly M, op. cit., page 48.
[55] MacDonald, Brig. Gen. J H A, *Fifty Years of It – The Experiences and Struggles of a Volunteer of 1859*, Blackwood, 1909, pages 75-6.
[56] Spiers, E, op. cit., pages 134-5.
[57] Amery, op. cit., pages 244-6.
[58] Bowman and Connelly, op. cit., pages 44-5.
[59] *The Times, The State of the Army*, 27th September, 1913, page 7.
[60] Samuels, M, *Command or Control?* page 80.
[61] *Report on the Conference of General Staff Officers, 18th-21st January 1909*, page 44.
[62] Samuels, M, op. cit.
[63] Amery, op. cit., pages 49-50.
[64] *Report on the Conference of General Staff Officers, 18th-21st January 1909*, pages 45-6.

PART FOUR: THE WESTERN FRONT
TRIAL AND, MAINLY, ERROR

"Only the dead have seen the end of war."

George Santayana
Soliloquies in England, Soliloquy 25, Tipperary,
page 102

11. Prologue

"War demands the herding together of peasants and artisans, and then slaughtering them on wholesale lines."

J F C Fuller,
Generalship: Its Diseases and Their Cure, page 89

Monday, 3ʳᵈ August, 1914, was a Bank Holiday in Great Britain and the weather reflected the political and diplomatic atmosphere: over-heated, humid, threatening. On Tuesday, the weather cooled as low pressure moved in from the west bringing with it, appropriately given the febrile state of Europe, the threat of thunder and lightning. Literally, a depression settled over Whitehall. War was inevitable.

After the assassination in Sarajevo of the *Herrschers des Erzherzogtums Österreich* (Archduke of Austria), Franz Ferdinand Carl Ludwig Joseph Maria von Österreich-Este and his wife Sophie Maria Josephine Albina *Gräfin* Chotek von Chotkow und Wognin, Duchess of Hohenberg, by Gavrilo Princip of the *Mlada Bosna (Young Bosnia)* movement on 28ᵗʰ June, not only the diplomatic heat rose rapidly. By Wednesday, 1ˢᵗ July, the temperature at the political heart of Westminster was a sizzling 31.7° C (89° F)[1]. The next day, a blistering temperature of 34.4° C (94° F) was recorded at Greenwich. While the general population perspired in the office, the factory, at school, or at home, politicians, civil servants, and military men sweated metaphorically *and* literally as they wrestled with the diplomatic, economic, and strategic implications of the turmoil in the Balkans.

Most people in Britain seemed unconcerned about events 1,000 miles away in the barely heard of Bosnia-Herzegovina. If there *was* a political event which raised an eyebrow or two outside Westminster it was the recent passing of the third *Home Rule Bill*. Rejected twice by the Lords, it was passed under the provisions of the *Parliament Act, 1911* to become the *Government of Ireland Act, 1914*, when given Royal Assent on 18ᵗʰ September. To those who took an interest, avoiding a civil war between the Ulster Protestants and the Catholic majority was a rather more pressing concern than some confusing Balkans *imbroglio*.

But, as Austria threatened Serbia, and Russia sabre-rattled in Slavic support, so the weather took another turn. With 98% humidity and 25.5° C (78° F) recorded in Westminster on 13ᵗʰ July, thunderstorms were inevitable. Then the weather broke again as another depression settled in from the Atlantic. Heavy rain (40 mm at Clacton!), punctuated by electric storms, drenched the London citizenry. The weather settled into a pattern – warm, humid, uncomfortable – with light winds unable to move the cloud which blanketed the capital. The god of the winds, Aeolus, seemed unwilling to unleash the much-needed westerly zephyrs with which to blow away the glowering low pressure which squatted over the country.

Then, as the Viennese authorities considered an ultimatum to Belgrade they knew must be rejected, temperatures across Europe followed the increase in tension. London basked in 26.7° C (80° F). In Berlin, as the *Kaiser* and his advisers contemplated a war on two fronts, the thermometer reached a baking 32.2° C (90° F). At a time for cool heads, the weather was determined to keep the pot boiling.

The Austrian ultimatum came on 23rd July and with it a sudden and sharp cooling of the weather across Europe. Temperatures plummeted to below 21° C (70° F) in London, Paris, Berlin, and Vienna. Given the grim diplomatic atmosphere it was, again, appropriate that two depressions dominated the continent: one over the North Sea, the other over the Alps. The unseasonably cool weather in no way reflected a cooling of the passions in Vienna, however, where officials demanded 'satisfaction' from Serbia for the murder of the heir to their empire. Over succeeding days nothing changed. The weather and the political mood got chillier, with the thermometer at barely 16° C (60° F) in most of the capitals of Europe, as the continent moved inexorably towards war.

It was only on the last weekend of July that high pressure returned to dominate the weather patterns of Europe. Temperatures started to rise as tempers finally frayed, especially in France and Germany, Russia, and Austria. As atmospheric pressure and the temperature continued to soar, so did the blood pressure of those in power in Paris, Berlin, Vienna, and St Petersburg.

Thus, by the Bank Holiday Monday on 3rd August, the news from Europe was grim. Austria-Hungary was already at war with Serbia, having made the declaration the previous Wednesday (28th July). At 7 p.m. on Saturday, 1st August, Germany declared war on Russia as it mobilised in support of little Serbia. On Sunday, Germany demanded that Belgium, neutral by a treaty of which Prussia was a signatory, allow German armies free access *en route* to an invasion of France. The *Kaiser* declared war on both countries at 6.45 p.m. when the ultimatum was rejected. Meanwhile, after the British government ordered the full mobilisation of the Royal Navy, the country, suddenly alert to the dangers, waited on tenterhooks to see what might happen next.

London was nervous, as *The Times* reported:

"London will spend to-day the strangest Bank Holiday it has ever known… London's streets yesterday afforded a very fair clue of what one may expect to find to-day. Until this week-end there has been little outward indication that the 'man in the street' grasped the extreme gravity of the position. Yesterday, as editions of morning and evening newspapers succeeded one another with bewildering rapidity, each bearing news of an alarming character, things were different and anxious faces and subdued conversation were to be found instead of the light-heartedness that one associates with the Bank Holiday period. Throughout the day Downing Street was a magnet which drew hundreds of spectators to Whitehall…"[2]

On Sunday, 2nd August, the atmosphere in Trafalgar Square was tense. As in France, where the imminence of war brought about socialist and trade union peace demonstrations, so the same took place in Britain. The leading lights of the Labour Party and the Trade Union movement called for anti-war demonstrations. Columns of workers and peace campaigners converged on Trafalgar Square, coming from St. George's Circus, the East India Docks, Kentish Town, and Westminster Cathedral. There they crowded around the base of Nelson's Column to be addressed by Keir Hardie, Labour M.P. for Merthyr Tydfil, Henry Hyndman, Ben Tillett of the *Dock, Wharf, Riverside and General Labourers' Union*, Robert Bontine

Cunninghame Grahame[i], and George Nicoll Barnes[ii], Labour M.P. for Glasgow, Blackfriars and Hutchesontown. As Tillett started to speak, what *The Times* described as a large group of 'anti-socialists' started to chant. The singing of the *Red Flag* was countered with *God Save the King* and *Rule Britannia*. The Union Jack was raised in response to the unfurling of the workers' red flag. While a noisy 'patriotic' counter-meeting developed around Admiralty Arch, at 5 p.m. the other one carried a motion 'in favour of international peace and solidarity', and called upon His Majesty's Government to:

> "...take every step to secure peace on behalf of the British people, and upon the workers of the world to use their industrial and political power in order that the nations shall not be involved in the war."[3]

In Britain, as elsewhere, there was no unanimity about going to war.

Meanwhile, chapels, churches and cathedrals were full of the anxious and concerned in the face of an imminent Europe-wide war, one which threatened to involve Britain for the first time in nearly 100 years.

How had it come to this?

In the afternoon Randall Thomas Davidson, the Archbishop of Canterbury, preached before the congregation in Westminster Abbey. He took as his theme Chapter VI, verse 9 of the gospel according to St Matthew: 'After this manner therefore pray ye: Our Father, which art in Heaven'. His words were both prescient and despairing:

> "What is happening is fearful beyond all words, both in actual fact and in the thought of what it may come to be...
>
> The occasion sets us puzzling and wondering in half a score of different ways. Sixty-three years ago everybody was thinking and talking and hoping about that new departure in human history – the Great Exhibition in Hyde Park, the pioneer endeavour of its kind. The words which great men then spoke, the hopes they deliberately held and expressed, read strangely now. The poet's dream had been realised, the battle-flag was furled.
>
> And what happened? Englishmen must have thought them over with a grim feeling in the icy trenches of Sevastopol or in the noonday glare upon the Ridge at Delhi. Some of the strongest speeches and the rosiest prophecies came from other nationalities than our own. What did those prophets think a little later about Magenta and Solferino? How were their hopes illustrated later still, on the hill-side at Gravelotte or in the cornfields of Sedan? What are we to say of Plevna, of Port Arthur? The strifes were hotter, some of the fields were bloodier than any that our grandsires had known...

---

[i] A radical Liberal MP for North West Lanarkshire 1886-92. Joined the Scottish Labour Party, 1892. President, Scottish Labour Party, 1888-95, and first President of the Scottish National Party, 1934-36.

[ii] Briefly the leader of the Labour Party between 14th February 1910 and 6th February 1911. He served as Minister of Pensions and Minister without Portfolio under Lloyd George, 1916-1920.

This thing which is now astir in Europe is not the work of God but of the Devil. It is not the development of God's purposes, it is the marring of them by the self-will, the sheer wrongness of man. What is happening must be due somewhere, somehow, to the pride, the high-handedness, the stubbornness of man's temper – undoing and thwarting the handiwork and will of God."[4]

Whilst there was no great evident enthusiasm for war – it would take the invasion of Belgium and accusations of German barbarity to trigger that – those who read the 'popular press', and most especially the *Daily Mail*, , had been conditioned over a decade or more to accept that, if war broke out, it would be with Germany. Moreover, such a war would be, indisputably, the fault of German aggression and expansionist ambitions. Germany would then be Britain's implacable enemy. Such newspapers, as well as politicians, Generals and Admirals, and industrialists with a vested interest in 'defence spending', had seen to the creation of this mood over many long years. As is still the case today, scare stories of imminent 'invasion/aggression' were the common currency of the nationalist, the militarist, and the exploitative industrialist hell bent on spending vast sums on preventive 'defence', either as a means of imposing their will on some foreign power or to enrich themselves at the taxpayer and country's expense.

THUS, IN THE LATE SUMMER OF 1914, the warmongers of Europe got their way, and the continent was plunged into its most devastating conflict for 300 years.

Back then, Bohemia was the seat of the appalling religious/political conflict: the Thirty Years War of 1618-48. It was triggered by the infamous incident of the Defenestration of Prague, when representatives of the Habsburg Catholic King of Bohemia and Croatia (and soon Holy Roman Emperor), Ferdinand II, were thrown out of the windows of Prague Castle by Protestants led by Count Jindřich Matyáš Thurn-Valsassina[i].

Some estimates suggest the war resulted in 500,000 combat deaths, 1.35 million soldiers' deaths from disease, and as many as 6.5 million civilian dead.[5] This from amongst the 50 million population of the main combatant nations: the Holy Roman Empire, France, Sweden, etc. But, disproportionately, these savage losses, especially amongst civilians, fell on the c. 20+ million population of Germany – Bavaria and Württemberg in the south and Mecklenburg and Pomerania in the north – and Bohemia.[6] The Thirty Years War left large tracts of what is now Germany and the Czech Republic (Bohemia) a desolate, de-populated wilderness. With populations halved, in places its impact was as devastating as the Black Death of the 1340s and 50s.

J F C Fuller, in *Decisive Battles of the Western World*, cites figures for the wreckage wrought in Bohemia by the war which started and ended there[ii]:

"In Bohemia, of 35,000 villages only 6,000 are said to have survived, the population sank from about 2,000,000 to 700,000."[7]

---

[i] The three men – noblemen Vilém Slavata z Chlumu a Košumberka and Jaroslav Hrabě Bořita z Martinic and their secretary, Filip Fabricius – all survived.
[ii] The final event was the Swedish siege and sack of parts of Prague in July 1648.

The impact of the Thirty Years War clearly left a deep and abiding impression on some Europeans. Fuller cites the German *Staatssekretär des Auswärtigen Amtes* (*State Secretary of the Foreign Office*, 1882-5) and later ambassador to London, Melchior Hubert Paul Gustav *Graf* von Hatzfeldt zu Wildenburg[i]. He told Granville George Leveson-Gower, 2nd Earl Granville, Liberal Leader of the House of Lords and three times Secretary of State for Foreign Affairs (under Gladstone twice and Lord John Russell once), that:

> "Germany has not yet recovered from the effects of the Thirty Years War and the Seven Years War; and a determination to prevent the recurrence of similar disasters ought still to be the keynote of German policy."[8]

Nonetheless, despite such concerns and the peaceful protestations of earlier years, when a pretext was provided Europe's empires rushed to war.

Thus, three hundred years later total military deaths would be c. 8 million. The countries at the seat of the Thirty Years War, Germany, and Austria-Hungary, suffered c. 5 million civilian and military dead and 8 million wounded from a pre-war population of 118 million. Little Serbia, the country which many consider the war's crucible, lost 1.25 million dead, or 28%, of its 4.5 million pre-war population, of which military deaths are estimated at 450,000.[9]

Proportionately, World War One was not as devastating as the Thirty Years War but it is still worth remembering that, according to some figures, 17% of the economically active male population of Austria-Hungary, 15% from Germany, and 11% from France were killed in the war.[10] In addition, some 10 million civilians died, not including those killed in its immediate aftermath through illness, revolution, civil war, ethnic cleansing, anti-Jewish pogroms, and the massacres of some 1.5 million Greeks, Armenians and Assyrians in Turkey.

The assassination of Franz Ferdinand and his wife, Sophie Maria, on 28th June 1914[ii] in Sarajevo, the capital of Bosnia and Herzegovina, was the pretext. And the speed with which Europe collapsed into war was breath-taking, but only if one fails to appreciate the time it took for the various countries to mobilise, arm, equip, and transport their armies to their appointed strategic starting positions. Such was the extended time, especially for a country as vast, and as relatively ill-equipped with railways, as Russia, that setting the process in motion at the earliest moment was the only means by which a country might feel itself able to resist foreign incursions/invasion. And once one state set the mobilisation ball rolling it was very difficult to stop every other country from following suit, presuming they had

---

[i] Aged 32, he married 17-year-old Helen Moulton, daughter of a US landowner, in November 1863. His mother, Sophie *Gräfin* von Hatzfeldt, born *Gräfin* von Hatzfeldt-Schönstein zu Trachenberg, after an unhappy arranged marriage, mixed with Social Democrats and revolutionaries such as Karl Marx and was active in the *Allgemeiner Deutscher Arbeiterverein* (*ADAV* or *General German Workers' Association*), the first working-class political party. Hatzfeldt, described by Edward VII as 'the best representative of the German cause', died in London in 1901.

[ii] The 525th anniversary of the Battle of Kosovo, 28th June 1389 (Gregorian calendar), an important Serbian national/religious date called *Vidovdan* (St. Vitus's day). It ended Serbian independence in the face of Ottoman expansion.

the desire to stop. It is arguable, however, that, by 1914, several of the prospective combatants, particularly the aggrieved Austria-Hungary, the military party in Germany, and numerous French army officers and nationalist politicians, were in no mood for such passivity.

Thus, when Austria-Hungary declared war on Serbia at 11.10 a.m. on 28th July 1914, there was little appetite in many European capitals to prevent a catastrophe, the one which Jan Bogumił Bloch so presciently predicted in 1899.

SINCE THE JAPANESE HAD TWICE taken pre-emptive action against the Russian Navy in 1904 prior to their declaration of war in Manchuria, declarations of war were now governed by the internationally agreed *Laws of War: Convention Relative to the Opening of Hostilities (Hague III)* signed at The Hague on 18th October, 1907, and which, ratified by the signatory states, entered into force on 26th January 1910. Its introductory statement declared:

"… it is important, in order to ensure the maintenance of pacific relations, that hostilities should not commence without previous warning."

Its Article 1 read:

"The Contracting Powers recognize that hostilities between themselves must not commence without previous and explicit warning, in the form either of a reasoned declaration of war or of an ultimatum with conditional declaration of war."

Following this protocol, Austria-Hungary delivered an ultimatum to Serbia on 23rd July, the demands of which, with exceptions involving national sovereignty which Serbia suggested be the subject of arbitration, were accepted on 25th July. The objections to these exceptions, which effectively gave Austrian officials a free hand in any investigation into Serbian involvement in the assassination and in the suppression of all 'subversive elements' in the country, were sufficient of a pretext for the Austria-Hungary government to break off diplomatic relations the same day. In the face of an imminent threat, Serbia ordered its army to mobilise at 3 p.m. and, in response, at 9 p.m., Austria-Hungary ordered its forces to mobilise as from 28th July, declaring war on Serbia just before mid-day on 28th July. The following morning, at the precise time of 3.26 a.m., 26th July, according to *Der Weltkrieg*, Russia declared the start of a 'war preparation period'.

Britain, meanwhile, concentrated the fleet for a trial mobilisation and the various components were set to return to their bases but, on 27th July, this move was cancelled. On the 29th July, a telegram was issued to both the navy and the army warning of the potential imminence of war.

In the meantime, financial markets panicked. The Viennese *Bourse* went into meltdown on 25th July, when the Austrian government broke off diplomatic relations with Serbia. On Monday, 27th July, the bourses of Vienna, Budapest and Brussels closed whilst, in London, shares tumbled. The next day, the American *Exchange Market* closed and banking in London was suspended. Thursday's Bank of England base rate of 4% soared to 8% the next day and 10% on Saturday[i].[11]

---

[i] It fell back to 6% by 6th August and 5% on 8th August.

Acting in defence of Serbia, Russia ordered a partial mobilisation (i.e. the Army Corps facing the Austro-Hungarian border in Galicia, c. 700,000 troops) on 29th July to start the following day. At 6 p.m., 30th July, a full mobilisation was ordered for 31st July. It was joined by tiny Montenegro. Similar orders were immediately given in Berlin and Vienna. The *Hochseeflotte* was put on immediate alert and all ships ordered back to home waters. In Paris, at 7 a.m., 30th July, Joffre asked the government to order full mobilisation, but this was not immediately granted.

The next day, 31st July, Austria-Hungary declared a state of alarm along its border with Russia and, at 12.23 p.m. the full mobilisation of its army, while the navy[i] was to concentrate at Cattaro (now Kotor in Montenegro, then part of the Kingdom of Dalmatia in the Cisleithanian half of Austria-Hungary). Thirty-seven minutes later, at 1 p.m.., Germany declared *Zustand der drohenden Kriegsgefahr*, i.e. an imminent danger of war, which required certain actions on the borders, the requisitioning of transport, horses, etc., etc.

Joffre now demanded a response from the French government, pointing out that even a 24-hour delay risked placing his forces at a severe disadvantage *vis à vis* Germany. Though full mobilisation was still not yet instituted, the process known as *'la couverture'*, in which border forces, especially opposite *Lothringen* and *Elsaß*, (German-held Lorraine and Alsace), were ordered to move into position to both monitor German activity and to screen the eventual deployment of the mass of the army, was set in motion as from 9 p.m., 31st July. This involved the activation of eleven infantry and ten cavalry divisions. Meanwhile, Belgium ordered the mobilisation of its small army.[12]

The German ambassador to France, Wilhelm Eduard *Freiherr* von Schoen, had earlier asked the *Président du Conseil des ministres français*, René Viviani, whether France would remain neutral should war break out in the east. Viviani said he needed time to consider and when, at 11 a.m. on 1st August, Schoen demanded an answer, he was told France would stand by its ally. At 3.45 p.m., France declared a general mobilisation to start on 2nd August and 75 minutes later, at 5 p.m., the *Kaiser* ordered a general German mobilisation.

In a mood of hysterical fervour, reason was rapidly abandoned in capital after capital as war fever spread throughout Europe with dramatic speed:

1st August, 7.00 p.m. – Germany declared war on Russia;

2nd August – Germany demanded Belgium allow free access for its armies *en route* to France; Britain ordered full mobilisation of the Royal Navy;

3rd August – Demands rejected at 6.45 p.m. Germany declared war on France and Belgium;

4th August, 11 p.m. – Britain declared war on Germany;

6th August – Austria-Hungary declared war on Russia and Serbia on Germany;

12th August – Britain and France declared war on Austria-Hungary[ii]

---

[i] A formidable force of four modern *Dreadnoughts*, nine pre-*Dreadnoughts*, three armoured cruisers, 80+ smaller ships (destroyers, torpedo boats, etc.,), and six submarines. The main base was at Pola (now Pula, Istria, Croatia).

[ii] Montenegro declared war on Austria and Germany within a few days. Other countries entered the war progressively. Japan declared war on the Central Powers on

Thus, having rushed into war in haste, Europe was now about to spend nearly 52 months repenting at its leisure as, directly or indirectly, eight countries and their colonies, 877 million men, women and children, came into conflict:

The Allies:
Russia   164 million
Serbia   4 million
Montenegro   400,000
France   37 million (Metropolitan France)
                58 million (Colonial France, 700,000 white colonists)
Total   95 million
Britain   46 million
                434 million (Empire of which 18 million white colonists)
Total   480 million
Belgium   7.5 million
                15 million (Belgian Congo)
Total   23 million
Overall total 747 million

Central Powers:
Germany   67 million
                12 million (Colonies, of which 28,000 white colonists)
Austria-Hungary
                51 million
Overall total 130 million[13]

THE EARLY DAYS OF THE WAR can be but briefly described here for want of space (and time). While, in the first weeks of the war, France launched two wholly unsuccessful invasions into its two lost provinces of Alsace and Lorraine, Germany prepared for the 'great right hook' through Belgium encompassed in the Schlieffen Plan, a strategy Joffre and the French did not believe in until it happened. Meanwhile, Britain's navy flexed its muscles, escorting the BEF across the Channel and seeing off the first U-Boat campaign launched on 6th August which saw two submarines sunk[i] or missing (the unluckily numbered *U-13* believed mined) and no British ships lost or damaged.

The BEF, safely landed, advanced across the Belgium border to be met at Mons by Von Kluck's *1. Armee* on 23rd August. Von Kluck was there because the supposedly robust modern defences of Liège and Namur had been crushed by super heavy howitzers built by *Krupp* and *Skoda*, guns the likes of which simply did

---

23rd/25th August, Russia on the Ottoman Empire on 1st November, and Britain and France on 5th November. The Turks responded on 11th November, declaring war on Serbia/Montenegro in early December. Italy entered the war against Austria-Hungary on 23rd May 1915 (and Germany on 28th August 1916, the day Rumania declared war on Austria-Hungary), and Bulgaria on 14th October 1915. Other smaller nations joined in until, on 6th April 1917, the USA declared war on Germany (and Austria-Hungary on 7th December 1917).

[i] *U-15* rammed and sunk by *HMS Birmingham* on 9th August 1914.

not exist in Allied arsenals. Britain be-wailed the deaths of 1,600 of its soldiers at Mons, but France was reeling from the killing of 21,000 or more of its men 24-hours earlier on 22nd August during the disastrous Battle of the Frontiers.

Then, both allied armies retreated in the face of superior German numbers, tactics and equipment, most especially the field (10.5 cm) and medium (15 cm) howitzers with which they were simply unable to cope.

It was only when Moltke started to lose touch with the German Armies, which had outrun their heavier guns and begun to run short of ammunition; had exhausted their men through forced marches in considerable heat; and unwisely deviated from the plan to extend their lines of march to the west of Paris; that the tables turned on the *Marne* between 6th and 12th September. There, though casualties were nearly even, estimated at 250,000 each, and with French fatalities greater than German (80,000 to 68,000), the tactical advantage lay with the Allies and the German armies withdrew to the north, settling on the right bank of the *Aisne*. It was there, trench warfare as we recognise it on the Western Front between 1914 and 1918 began.

By the end of September, French losses, killed, wounded, and missing, amounted to a staggering 206,515 in August and 213,445 in September. A total of 419,960 or more than 7,000 a day. British losses over the same two months are given as just under 14,000. Such was the impact on France and its armies of the *offensive à outrance*. The French response to the huge casualties suffered in the autumn of 1914 and then, again, in the various failed offensives of 1915 will be examined later.

And, in this volume we shall see how well, or badly, Britain responded to its involvement in its first European war in 99 years. At how well prepared it was for this war, and how well its Generals and ordinary soldiers fared in a war the like of which the country had not seen for nearly century.

BRITAIN HAD AS MUCH NOTICE of a major European war as any other nation. Furthermore, it can be argued that it had one of, if not *the* most highly developed and well-funded armaments industries anywhere in the world. It was an industry with world-wide reach, with greedy fingers in the rich military pies of almost every nation, including some soon to be Britain's sworn enemies. Its major manufacturers had not only contributed materially, but also politically, to the creation of the greatest naval force in World history, its power embodied in the mighty Grand Fleet which dominated home waters from 1914 to 1918. In addition, all the main defence companies had produced, and in the recent past, large quantities of arms and equipment for both the British Army and others around the world.

And yet, when it came to supplying the requirements of the British Empire at war, these defence contractors were unable either to meet the need for an increase in the production of existing equipment, or smoothly move into the production of the new types of material the war in Europe swiftly came to demand. Nor was the established chemical industry in Britain able to cope with the huge increases in production needed to supply a modern army with the vast quantities of ammunition and explosives which soon proved essential.

Whilst France was able to fall back on adaptations of elderly but still serviceable – and very numerous – artillery pieces built since the late 1870s, and had an industrial strategy in place for increases in ammunition and explosives (but which still failed to meet demand), Britain had no such immediate reserves of weaponry, nor did it develop a proper industrial strategy for some months.

It is easy, in these circumstances, to point the finger of blame for such shortages and policy vacuums at politicians and governments. Conservatives, out of office since 1906, of course directed the digit at pacifically-inclined Liberal and, from 1910, Labour politicians, who were originally elected on a platform of peace, retrenchment, and social reform – the three classic pillars of 19th Century Liberal philosophy. These three pillars were inextricably linked. Retrenchment required the cutting of costs and/or spending, and a reduction of the burden on the taxpayer. The major purpose of government defence spending was on maintaining the pre-eminence of the Royal Navy as a means of protecting trade lanes and the Empire. The Army was, by definition, a secondary power reduced, almost, to the status of an Imperial police force able to deal with poorly armed insurgents, guard the borders of India (and keep an eye on rebellious Irish nationalists). The only way in which Government defence spending might be curbed was if the country was at peace with its more powerful neighbours. Therefore, peace and retrenchment went hand in hand. And if, as many Liberal politicians demanded, social reforms were essential to the well-being and economic progress of the mother country, then peace and retrenchment were essential if the funds to spend on social reform were to be found.

It can be argued, therefore, that the constraints placed on the Army's budgets after the South African War were because of Liberal, then Liberal/Labour, governments trying to keep some of their electoral promises, a vanishingly rare event in current times.

The question then arises: did the Army help itself through these relatively lean times by developing tactics, skills, equipment, and material which best suited what many senior officers, such as Sir John French, regarded as an inevitable European War and which would see at least some sort of British military, rather than simply naval, involvement? The answer to this can only be 'yes' if one broadly ignores what is to come in this book, which, of course, readers are free to do.

This writer would contend, however, that:

1. There was more than enough evidence provided by educated civilians and soldiers to suggest precisely how a major European war would develop, i.e, a stalemate involving huge and unwieldy, partially trained citizen armies, with shocking casualty lists and enormous economic costs;
2. Similarly, all the wars involving European powers in the fifteen years before the Great War tended to support this version of how the war would develop;
3. All these previous wars showed that economic costs, military and civilian casualties, ammunition consumption and duration would be far greater than previously anticipated; and
4. Senior officers of all armies exaggerated the power of the offensive rather because it suited their ambitious military plans and not out of any sensible

or prudent investigation into the stopping power of modern weaponry and the protection afforded to the defence by modern fortifications.

Then, as far as Britain specifically was concerned:

1. The training and on-going education of the average British officer in a relatively senior position in 1914 had been seriously deficient over an extended period and this problem was compounded in certain quarters by the basic intelligence of the officers concerned;
2. That, coming from a rural, public-school educated, conservative social class they had little connection with, or sympathy for, the working and urban middle class men who, in vast numbers, would serve in the Army after the creation of Kitchener's New Armies;
3. That, fundamentally, because of the deep social and political divisions which helped create the *'The Great Unrest'* of 1910 to 1914, military men distrusted the patriotism and motivation of the working class and, at the same time, despised the 'soft', bourgeois lifestyles of the emerging middle class, and these attitudes coloured both the ways in which these volunteers were trained and then employed;
4. That the innate conservatism of the British officer class led to the distrust of innovation and creativity within its own ranks which resulted in the failure to adopt vital tools pre-war, amongst them mobile, lightweight automatic guns, what became the Tank, and mobile medium and heavy howitzers, all of which then had to be designed, approved, adopted and manufactured in a rush once the predicted war began and then continued in the predicted fashion;
5. Allied to this was the widely held belief that battles were still won 'at the point of the bayonet' and that this required the infantry to get 'up close and personal' with the enemy with the inevitably high casualties caused by the need to cross the intervening 'fire swept zone' and, for this, a soldier's high morale and a spirit of sacrifice was a prerequisite;
6. That, though the 'fire and movement' infantry tactics practised by the Army post-South Africa provided an excellent tactical defensive base there was no similar investigation into how an army needed to develop its offensive capabilities in the face of modern quick-firing and long-range *matériel*;
7. That a failure to grasp that the enormous increase in firepower made possible by quick-firing weapons also made likely an enormous increase in ammunition consumption (as was shown in immediately previous wars) and the failure of both the Army and the Government to grasp this fact, led to both critical shortages at key times and, as a result, in an increase in casualties as bodies were thrown at a problem rather than high explosive;
8. That a failure to grasp the need for innovation in *matériel* and for a vastly increased capacity for ammunition and explosives production meant that the large and very profitable, British armaments, munitions, and chemical industries were ill-equipped to deal with the demands of the fighting once it became clear the war would not be 'over by Christmas'.

THUS, IN SPITE OF THE SCANDALS, the in-fighting, and the lamentable failure of meaningful tactical development in the face of new technology and the conduct of recent wars, the British Expeditionary Force which left these shores in August 1914 to fight in Belgium and France was regarded at the time and afterwards as the best trained and most suitably equipped force ever to fight on behalf of the country. As the *Official History* wrote:

> "In every respect (the BEF was) incomparably the best trained, best organized, and best equipped British Army which ever went forth to war. Except in the matter of cooperation between artillery and aeroplanes, and the use of machine guns, its training would stand comparison in all respects with that of the Germans."[14]

There are those nowadays who greet this statement as evidence that the senior officers of the British Army were not the 'donkeys' of legend and had planned, equipped and trained their troops correctly and assiduously.[15] In comparison to the two most recent armies sent to large scale wars overseas, i.e. to the Crimea and South Africa, the BEF was, of course, better equipped. How could it not be given the improvements in automatic weapons and artillery and the invention of the aeroplane? Almost any enhancements in the training of officers and men compared to either of the two previous wars *had* to improve their relative performance. But it could equally be said that the BEF which fought in France and Belgium in 1940 was the best equipped and trained army Britain had put in the field to that point. Again, how could it not be relative to what had gone before? It was still swept from the field in a few weeks by the better trained, more appropriately equipped and far better led German Army.

The question is, therefore, more: how *was* the 1914 BEF trained, equipped, and officered, and how suited was it to the style of warfare it soon faced?

It is now claimed the BEF was well-matched to the tasks it encountered between August and November 1914 when the fighting was of the nature anticipated by Generals of all combatant nations. Whilst this might have been true in the various defensive battles fought by the BEF at Mons, le Cateau and Ypres, such claims are totally undermined by the fighting on the *Aisne* in mid to late September. Here, following up the German retreat from the *Marne*, the British needed to attack – and failed at a cost of over 13,000 men. Rather than a temporary setback, this set the trend for British offensives until the summer of 1916 when some partial successes were achieved. This failure on the *Aisne* represented a serious tactical and philosophical problem for the BEF. Haig's *Field Service Regulations*, and the overwhelming sentiment amongst British Generals, was that one could not win a war by defending. The assault with the bayonet was the critical moment when one destroyed the enemy. The *Aisne* proved that the BEF was neither technically equipped nor tactically adept at mounting such an assault on the modern battlefield, especially as here the Germans had done what few British Generals, including the CinC, French, expected (but which had been the norm in all wars of the previous ten years or more) and dug in. Simply put: the devious Hun entrenched and the BEF had no answer. Why? Because in the following paragraphs in that same *Official History* quote there was a serious caveat:

"In heavy guns and howitzers, high-explosive shell, trench mortars, hand-grenades, and much of the subsidiary material required for siege and trench warfare, it was almost wholly deficient. Further, no steps had been taken to instruct the army in a knowledge of the probable theatre of war or of the German army, except by the publication of a handbook of the army and of annual reports on manoeuvres and military changes. Exactly the same, however, was done in the case of the armies of all foreign States. The study of German military organization and methods was specifically forbidden at war games, staff tours, and intelligence classes, which would have provided the best opportunities for such instruction."[16]

In short, whilst the junior officers and men were the best trained men of the best organised and equipped military force ever to leave these shores, they were not appropriately equipped for the fighting to come and their commanders were, in most respects, totally devoid of the necessary tactical training, military intelligence and expertise with which to fight Britain's first major continental war in nearly a century. Whilst, under Haldane, the country committed itself to contributing an effective, if small, fighting force to France and Belgium, little time was spent exploring the necessary tactical control, inter-unit cooperation and other aspects of modern warfare needed in the face of similarly armed and trained, but much larger, enemy armies. Having ignored numerous warnings about the impact of modern firepower, and having trained and equipped themselves to fight a mobile war, the BEF found itself peculiarly ill-equipped to deal with even the rudimentary siege warfare which started on the *Aisne* in mid-September 1914. Here the scales began to fall from military eyes as Sir John French belatedly confessed:

"As day by day the trench fighting developed and I came to realise more and more the much greater relative power which modern weapons have given the defence; as new methods were adopted in the defensive use of machine guns; and as unfamiliar weapons in the shape of 'trench mortars' and 'bombs', hand grenades, etc., began to appear on the battlefield so, day by day, I began dimly to apprehend what the future might have in store for us."[17]

French, however, was not yet convinced 'position warfare' was the norm:

"I finished my part in the Battle of the *Aisne*, however, unconverted, and it required the further and more bitter lesson of my own failure in the north to pass the *Lys River*, during the last days of October, to bring home to my mind a principle in warfare of today which I have held ever since, namely, that given forces fairly equally matched, you can 'bend' but you cannot 'break' your enemy's trench line."[18]

A moral which then clearly eluded his successor.

IN A PAPER WRITTEN AT THE STAFF COLLEGE in 1926 by a team led by Capt. Charles Shearman[i], criticism was levelled at the Army for several important

---

[i] Capt., later Maj. Gen., Charles Edward Gowran Shearman, CBE, DSO, MC, Bedfordshire Regt. (1889-1968). Westminster School. Bedfordshire Regt., 1909. Capt.

failures, these being inadequate infantry and artillery cooperation, the use of machine guns, and the lack of strength and weight within the artillery. Instead, pre-war training centred on mobility. Ignoring the numerous pre-war warnings by Bloch, Esher, Mayer, and others, Shearman explains:

> "As always in peace, the keynote of army training had been mobility. No one, however, had foreseen the effects on mobility of machine gun fire and an artillery preponderant in both shell power and numbers. Mobility had really been divorced from her inevitable and very necessary husband – firepower."[19]

Shearman went on to describe the prevailing attitude of 1914 that:

> "... artillery support was regarded as a luxury rather than an essential adjunct in the development and success of the infantry attack... we failed not only to realise the necessity for weight in artillery but the necessity for intimate cooperation between infantry and artillery".[20]

Which begs the question: just what were the senior officers of the British Army doing before the war if such fundamental issues were not addressed?

The artillery was, in terms of guns, shell types and supplies, experience and expertise, woefully short of the mark for such a war. Its tactics were ludicrously old-fashioned and gave the appearance few lessons had been learned in South Africa. There, in early actions, guns fired from exposed positions in close support of the attacking infantry. As a result, gun teams were shot down by long-range rifle fire and numerous guns lost. As detailed by Gen. Sir Martin Farndale in his *History of the Royal Regiment of Artillery*, such tactics had not changed by 1914:

> "In attack, batteries were employed at close range to support the final stages of the assault – there was no preliminary bombardment... It was also taught that guns must be fought to the last and that it was most important to provide support to the cavalry or infantry to the last possible moment, even if it did mean the loss of the guns. This occurred many times in the opening battles of 1914..."[21]

Such a description could equally have applied to the disastrous Battle of Colenso during Black Week in December 1899 (see page 331). It led to actions like Le Cateau where, on 26th August 1914 and three days into the long retreat from Mons, Brig. Gen. John Headlam, the BGRA of 5th Division and later Artillery Adviser at GHQ during the first six months of Haig's command, insisted on deploying some 42 field guns and howitzers in the open in order to give close support to the infantry. Although they caused heavy casualties amongst the German infantry, they attracted serious retaliatory fire which fell amongst the guns and nearby infantry. 38 guns, 200 officers and men and 257 horses of the seven

---

Bedfordshire and Hertfordshire Regt., 1914. France and Belgium, 1914-1918. GSO3 and Brigade Major, 1917-8. Staff, Irish Command, 1920-2. GSO3, Eastern Command, 1922-1924. Camberley, 1926. GSO3 and GSO2, RAF Co-operation, Aldershot, 1928-1930. DAAQMG, Western Command, 1930-1932. Commanded 1st Bedfordshire & Hertfordshire Regt., 1933-1937. AQMG, Northern Command, 1937-1939. Served in World War Two, retiring in 1945.

RFA Brigades involved were lost during the fighting. This action was later described by Farndale as:

> "... an artillery battle fought with twentieth century weapons by men used to nineteenth century methods."[22]

That Headlam had long thought direct fire and close support an essential element of the role or even ethos of field artillery is, perhaps, underlined by his comments made in 1896 in response to a lecture by the infantryman, Capt. Thomas Pilcher (later GOC 17th Division on the *Somme*), to the members of the Royal Artillery Institute in 1896. Pilcher had described indirect fire methods employed by the German artillery and Headlam's objections were not just to do with accuracy, concentration of fire and shooting at moving targets:

> "There is a very much stronger one and that is the moral objection. If you train field artillery to consider firing from behind cover as 'practically the rule', I believe you will destroy the whole spirit of the arm..."[23]

Little appears to have been learnt between Colenso in 1899 and Le Cateau in 1914. Given that the following advice was given in Para. 5 of Section 156 of the 1914 edition of *Field Artillery Training* it is, perhaps, of no surprise a battery commander might assume oversight of the ground and direct voice control of his guns was more important than firing from cover:

> "To support an attack with success a battery commander must be able to see the ground over which the infantry is advancing and also be able to control the fire of his battery rapidly and effectively, but the more cover that can be obtained compatible with control by voice the better."[24]

The BEF's defensive tactics and skills were certainly more suited to modern warfare than the offensive tactics of either German or France at the outbreak of war. The accuracy and speed of the BEF's rifle fire, and the use made of dispersal and concealment, certainly came as a shock to the masses of German infantry thrown at it in the fighting at Mons, Le Cateau and later at Ypres.

The need to develop such defensive skills were made clear by a series of answers given to the Elgin Commission investigating the South African War. These shared common themes: the good use of ground; and the accuracy of an individual's shooting. As Lord Roberts commented:

> "The intelligent use of ground, combined with accurate shooting is the secret of tactical success".[25]

The Army's trench digging (mainly through lack of practice and a lack of certain tools) and the deployment of its artillery, however, left a lot to be desired. The ability to 'dig in' was supposedly one of the tactical enhancements developed after the South African, Manchurian and Balkans wars. But, on manoeuvres, 'trenches' were indicative (i.e. tape laid on the ground) not real. This issue was raised by Brig. Gen. F J Davies of the Aldershot Command at the General Staff Officers' conference held between 15th and 18th January 1912.[26] He remarked that with, in the main, trenches on manoeuvres being indicated by tapes this lost 'the opportunity of teaching the troops that this irksome labour is part of their normal duty in war'. Thus, when it came to the start of trench warfare on the Western

Front (16th September 1914 on the *Aisne* according to the *Official History*) there was an absence of appropriate tools for much more than slit trenches which might protect from rifle bullets but certainly not from German 15-cm or 10.5-cm howitzer shells.

What was not seriously tested in these opening weeks was the BEF's offensive capability. The question as to how one moved a mass of infantry from its starting point, across the 'fire swept zone' (later, in trench warfare, No Man's Land) and into the enemy's position was not one asked during the great retreat from Belgium to the *River Marne*. And, as the BEF followed up the retreating German forces after the First Battle of the *Marne*, it became clear on the *Aisne* in mid-September 1914 that British tacticians had as little idea as to the solution to this problem as commanders at all levels in all Armies of all countries. Post-war, Shearman suggested this problem was rooted in the thinking that mobility was restricted to the advance rather than to manoeuvre:

> "Movement, too, apparently excluded largely the power of manoeuvre. Fire was produced by rigid, inelastic firing lines and movement was restricted to the advance of those lines. Rigidity of movement naturally tended to impair mobility."[27]

Haig's unimaginative tactics employed in the Aldershot Command manoeuvres of 1912/3 reinforce this point (see page 790) and any reading of Rawlinson's *Tactical Notes* issued as advice prior to 1st July (see *Volume II*) suggests little changed before that date.

Shearman further examined the effectiveness of staff officers produced by various regimes at Camberley. His comments again might have applied in 1916:

> "Yet in the retreat from Mons there were events which pointed to a lack of co-ordination of effort, a tendency to throw in formations piecemeal and little co-operation in forming a combined plan. Such conditions, especially the failure to co-ordinate the work of neighbouring formations, although partly the responsibility of commanders as well as of staff, were bound to engender indecision and stickiness of movement in lower formations."[28]

Though this comment about 'indecision and stickiness' referred specifically to the advance to, and fighting on, the *Aisne* in September 1914, the previous references to 'a lack of co-ordination', the 'piecemeal' use of formations and failures of inter-unit co-operation were still of concern throughout 1916.

FOR THE BEF 1915 WAS A YEAR OF SMALL-SCALE supporting attacks to French offensives, of growing casualty lists, of experimentation in offensive techniques – and of failure. Three major campaigns were embarked upon: at Neuve Chapelle; at Aubers Ridge in support of the French in Artois; and at Loos again in support of the French in Artois. The attacks grew as did the losses but tactical success, let along strategic advantage, eluded the BEF. But what did happen, and this accelerated by the dreadful Spring 1915 fighting around Ypres during which the Germans threw all previous Hague agreements on the conduct of war under the nearest bus, was that the Regular Army all but disappeared, to be followed in large part by the pre-war trained elements of the Territorial Force.

They were replaced by Kitchener's volunteers which formed an army unique in British, indeed, World history. Never had an entirely volunteer citizen force of such size been raised and deployed in the field. In numbers it did not match the vast conscript armies of the European powers, its training was limited and one-dimensional and, even by July 1916, its experience mainly restricted to the nerve-wracking grind of trench warfare. But, green yet enthusiastic, they were on the Western Front and eager to get to grips with the enemy.

The men who responded in tremendous numbers to the recruiting posters, the rallies, the thrill of foreign adventure, came from all walks of life but, in many cases, they represented the country's best and the brightest. They were men who would have never considered joining the Regular Army in peace time. Only the call to fight for King, Empire, and Country brought them from the shop floor, the pithead, the office, the lecture theatre, and the farm to join up. In terms of physical stature, education, and intelligence many easily surpassed the quality of those who filled the Army's ranks before 1914. Sadly, they were then too often trained as if akin to the unemployed, low-skilled, unmotivated men who too commonly enlisted pre-war for want of much else to do.

Peter Simkin's 1988 book *Kitchener's Army*[29] gives a graphic account of the chaos surrounding the billeting, training, feeding, and equipping of the recruits who flocked to the colours in the opening months of the war. Finding officers and NCOs competent to train them was a serious problem. Almost anyone from a public school or University who was a member of an OTC was accepted for a commission but combining inexperienced novice officers with a clueless bunch of civilian 'rankers' was near to a recipe for disaster. The absence of the basic tools for the jobs they were to do was also an enormous problem. There were not enough rifles for the infantry and not enough guns for the artillery, and those available were obsolete and not the ones being employed by the BEF in the field.

In this respect, despite the much-needed re-organisation instigated by Haldane and the reforms at Sandhurst and Woolwich, the Government and the Army were both caught unawares by the demands of a major European war. The scale of this misjudgement is well expressed in the *History of the Ministry of Munitions*:

> "Long before the retreat came to an end in the victory of the *Marne*, indeed, before the first six divisions had been despatched to France, the whole of the pre-war plan had been superseded. To the crisis that had to be met these arrangements were so grotesquely inadequate as to be merely inapplicable. The war formula had to be restated in unfamiliar and indeed as yet indefinable terms; for the war was to be fought out between nations, and not between armies merely."[30]

Had our Jewish banker and railwayman Bloch been alive he would, no doubt, be shaking his head in frustrated bemusement that neither Government nor Military saw this 'war between nations' coming and the way it was to be fought.

But his fears expressed in 1899 about the conduct, outcome and repercussions of a major European War were a small voice in a still greater clamour of those who said war was inevitable. And even that such a war was a good thing.

ENDNOTES:
1. Weather information from: *https://webarchive.nationalarchives.gov.uk/ukgwa/+/ http://www.metoffice.gov.uk/archive/9131*
2. *The Times, Bank Holiday in a New Spirit*, 3rd August 1914, page 3.
3. *The Times, War Protest Meeting*, 3rd August 1914, page 8.
4. *The Times, A Nation at Prayer*, 3rd August 1914, page 8.
5. Wilson, P H, *Europe's Tragedy: A History of the Thirty Years War*, Allen Lane, 2009, page 787.
6. Avakov, A. V. *Two Thousand Years of Economic Statistics*, Volume 1, 2015.
7. Fuller, J F C, *Decisive Battles of the Western World*, Vol. II, Cassell & Co., 1955, page 74.
8. Fuller, op. cit., quoting from *The Cambridge Modern History*, Vol. IV, page vi.
9. Le Moal F, *La Serbie du martyre à la Victoire 1914–1918*, 2008, éditions 14–18, 2013.
10. Kitchen, M, *Europe Between the Wars*, Longman, 1908, page 22.
11. *Unpublished History of the Bank of England*, page 5.
12. *Der Weltkrieg, 1914 bis 1918*, Vol. 1, S Mittler & Sohn, 1925, pages 36-7.
13. Ibid., page 38.
14. *Various, History of the Great War, Military Operations, France and Belgium, France & Belgium 1914*, Vol. 1, page 10.
15. Review of Simon Batten's *Futile Exercises? The British Army's Preparations for War 1902-1914*, Helion, 2019, in *Stand To!* No. 114, page 48.
16. Ibid., pages 10-11.
17. French, Viscount, *1914*, Constable & Co., 1919, page 144.
18. Ibid., page 145.
19. Shearman, Capt. C E G, *Operations, BEF, 1914*, Army Staff College, 1926, page 7.
20. Ibid., page 8.
21. Farndale, Gen. Sir M, *History of the Royal Regiment of Artillery, Western Front 1914-1918*, Royal Artillery Institution, 1986, page 4.
22. Ibid., page 52.
23. Transcript of a lecture by Capt. T Pilcher given at the *Royal Artillery Institute* in March 1896 reprinted in the *Journal of the US Military Institute*, 1897, page 149.
24. *Field Artillery Training 1914*, HMSO, page 249.
25. Quoted in Amery, L S, *The Problem of the Army*, page 179.
26. *Report on Conference of General Staff Officers, 15th-18th January 1912*, page 56.
27. Shearman, op. cit., pages 8 and 8a.
28. Ibid., page 9.
29. See Simkins, P, *Kitchener's Army*, especially Part III *'Enlistment, Equipment and Training'*.
30. *History of the Ministry of Munitions*, Vol. I, Part 1, page 8.

12. The Making of the New Armies

"We must be prepared to put armies of millions in the field, and to maintain them for several years."

Lord Kitchener
Addressing the Cabinet, 7th August 1914

On the outbreak of war the British Army's Regulars, Reserves and Territorials totalled about 691,000, of which 234,000 constituted the Regular Army, 145,000 the Regular Reserve, 56,000 the Special Reserve and 256,000 the Territorial Force. Kitchener's immediate priority was simply more men. The House of Commons voted on 6th August 1914 for 500,000 men to be recruited, with Kitchener issuing an appeal for an immediate 100,000 men aged between 19 and 30 prepared to serve 'for a period of 3 years or until the war is concluded'. Such was the enthusiasm amongst the young men of Britain this total was reached within three weeks. Indeed, such was the flood to the colours that, on 10th September, the House voted to raise another 500,000 troops. By the end of September, as the BEF finished fighting on the *Aisne*, new recruits more than doubled the size of the pre-war Army and reserves. On 16th December, the Commons voted to recruit *another* million men and, finally, on 10th February 1915, voted to maintain land forces of the extraordinary size of 3 million. A recruitment total of 2 million was reached in late July 1915.

On 25th August, Kitchener announced plans for 30 divisions, c. 650,000 men, to be continuously in the field. Volunteers would form New Armies of six divisions. 24 divisions would be added to the six sent to France. Looking forward, a 50-division army of 1,100,000 men was envisaged. Some believed larger numbers necessary and, in February 1915, Lloyd George declared it possible to raise c. 3.5 million men. But, as Table 18 starkly shows, volunteer numbers tailed off sharply as enthusiasm waned, and as the first, heavy, casualty lists were published:

1914	Recruits	Average/week
Aug-Sept	761,824	93,820
Oct-Dec	424,533	32,308
Total	1,186,357	
1915		
Jan-March	358,093	27,867
April-June	369,029	28,386
July	95,413	21,537
Total	822,535	
Grand Total	2,008,892	

Table 18 Recruitment figures August 1914 to July 1915

These reinforcements took some time to reach the BEF in France and Flanders. By the end of the Battle of the *Marne* its six divisions, plus the cavalry, comprised some 150,000 men. By the end of the First Battle of Ypres the BEF had expanded to twelve divisions and 225,000 men. Just prior to the Battle of

Neuve Chapelle in March 1915 the BEF had grown to 407,000 troops, and a figure of 600,000 was reached by the end of May 1915.

When the Ministry of Munitions was formed under Lloyd George in the wake of the shell crisis described in Chapter 1, the BEF was made up of 22 divisions: twelve Regular, six Territorial, three Kitchener New Army divisions, and one Canadian. In addition, there were five cavalry divisions. There were also some 125,000 troops in the eastern Mediterranean at Gallipoli or in Egypt. In total, therefore, there were c. 725,000 British troops in theatres of war by the summer of 1915. At the same time, training in Britain, on garrison duty, etc., were more than twice that number, i.e. 1.5 million. Prior to Loos in September 1915 the overseas Army increased to 41 divisions, of which thirty were in France, eight in the eastern Mediterranean, and three in India.

In the interim, the key issue was how to equip and train these novice troops, and how to provide the artillery, engineering, logistical, and other support services without which no army could function. Ammunition was also a major concern.

THE KITCHENER ARMIES WERE RAISED in several tranches known as K1, K2, K3 and K4 although, technically, there were six 'Armies' in the original arrangements. The first appeal for 100,000 volunteers was issued on 5th August 1914 and, on 21st August, Army Order 324 declared these men would be organised into six divisions, the battalions formed becoming Service Battalions of a parent Regular regiment. These divisions, the K1 Group, were designated 8th–13th Divisions until an 8th Division was formed from Regular battalions returned from overseas and the numbers changed to 9th–14th Divisions.

On 28th August, Kitchener made an appeal for another 100,000 volunteers and, with Army Order 382 (11th September 1914), six new divisions were formed: 15th–20th Divisions, i.e. the K2 Army group.

Such was the response, bolstered by news of the fighting at Mons and Le Cateau and the retreat towards Paris, it was decided to form a K3 Army group – 21st to 26th Divisions – from the surplus.

K4, it was anticipated, would mop up any leftovers and any new volunteers signing on in the meantime, and would be formed ASAP. K4 was to contain divisions number 27 to 32 however, with Regular battalions returning from foreign parts sufficient to fill three new divisions (27th, 28th and 29th Divisions), K4's numbering was changed to run from 30 to 35.

By early December enough men were available to form K5 (37th to 42nd Divisions, 36th Division having been formed out of the Protestant Irish battalions raised in Ulster) but, with the K4 units being broken up into training brigades, the K5 divisions took their place becoming the 30th to 35th Divisions. Another group of divisions was made up by the 36th (Ulster) Division and 38th (Welsh Division), raised in 1914, and four others, some made up of Pals battalions and raised in 1915, and numbered 37th, 39th, 40th and 41st Divisions[i].

Command of these new divisions was a problem given the paucity of available officers with any large unit command experience. The first GOCs of the New

---

[i] Two of these divisions, 35th and 40th, were known as Bantam divisions and utilised men who failed to reach the Army's 5-foot 3-inch minimum height requirement.

Army's divisions were thus a mixed bag of active Regulars, Indian Army officers and other recently retired Lt. and Maj. Generals. Some divisions were lucky, for example the newly formed 18th (Eastern) Division taken over by Ivor Maxse who returned from France after commanding 1st Guards Brigade. Maxse was an outstanding trainer of troops and, at the very least, a decent minor tactician as his division's exploits proved, first at Montauban and later when capturing Thiepval.

Other divisions were not so fortunate. 9th (Scottish) Division, for example, 'enjoyed' the services of no fewer than five commanders from the date of its formation in August 1914 through to its involvement in the Battle of the *Somme*. The first, Maj. Gen. Colin John Mackenzie, Seaforth Highlanders, lasted 45 days. Apart from command of 6th Brigade between 1907 and 1910, Mackenzie was a 'serial' staff officer. Aged 53, he had been Lord Roberts' Director of Intelligence in South Africa, the AQMG, 5th Division, and an AAG at Army HQ before being appointed Chief of the Canadian General Staff. On 3rd March 1914, he was given command of the Highland Division of the Territorial Force. He took over 9th Division on 27th August only to be rushed out to France in mid-October to take over 3rd Division from Maj. Gen. Hubert Hamilton, killed by shrapnel on 14th October at the village of La Couture near Béthune[i]. His successor, Lt. Gen. Sir Charles Fergusson[ii], lasted slightly longer – 66 days. Neither officer can have had much impact on the training of the new civilian soldiers.

Next to try his luck was Maj. Gen. Herman James Shelley Landon of the Royal Warwickshires who went to France as GOC, 3rd Brigade, and who then briefly took command of 1st Division during the First Battle of Ypres. Invalided home he was Inspector of Infantry before taking over the division on 21st January 1915. Landon took the division to France in May but he did not last, being replaced by Haig just over two weeks before the attack at Loos because of illness and bad reports from Hubert Gough, GOC, I Corps. He was replaced by Maj. Gen. George Handcock Thesiger, CB, CMG, Rifle Brigade, on 8th September. Thesiger's tenure was the briefest as he was tragically killed by shellfire on the second day of the Battle of Loos (26th September) whilst inspecting his men's

---

[i] Maj. Gen. Hubert Ion Wetherall Hamilton, CB, CVO, DSO, Queen's Royal Regt., (27th June 1861 – 14th October 1914), was aged 54. Son of the late Lt. Gen. Henry Meade Hamilton, C.B., he was educated at Haileybury, the Imperial Service College and RMC. Originally buried in La Couture churchyard his body was exhumed and is now in St Martin's Church, Cheriton, Kent. His replacement, Mackenzie, lasted barely two weeks before he returned to England, briefly commanding 15th (Scottish) Division before being appointed Director of Staff Duties, a task for which he was better suited. He returned to France as GOC, 61st (2nd South Midland) Division, which he led through the disastrous *Somme* 'diversion' at Fromelles on 19th July 1916.

[ii] Gen. Sir Charles Fergusson, 7th Baronet, GCB, GCMG, DSO, MVO, went to France as commander of 5th Division and returned to take over II Corps from Horace Smith-Dorrien in January 1915. He took command of XVII Corps in 1916 until the end of the war. After WW1 he continued in the 'family business' as Governor General of New Zealand, a role his father and father-in-law both previously fulfilled, with his third son, Bernard, being the last in that position between 1962 and 1967.

forward positions near Fosse 8[i]. Maj. Gen. William Thomas Furse of the Royal Artillery was Thesiger's replacement and he lasted until the end of the Battle of the *Somme* when he returned to England as Master General of the Ordnance, in which role he replaced Stanley von Donop[ii].

10th (Irish) and 11th (Northern) Divisions were both sent to Gallipoli and, therefore, play no further role in the context of these books. Suffice to say, in Lt. Gen. Sir Bryan Thomas Mahon[iii], KCVO, CB, DSO, 8th (King's Royal Irish) Hussars, 10th Division was rather luckier than 11th Division whose commander, the 56-year-old Maj. Gen. Frederick Hammersley, CB, Lancashire Fusiliers, was part of the Akers-Douglas investigation into the education and training of officers a dozen years before (see page 367). Previously GOC, 3rd Brigade, he was removed after a severe nervous breakdown[iv]. In spite of this, he took command of 11th Division in August 1914 and was still in command when it led the landings at Suvla Bay on 6th August 1915. Hammersley was in a state of near collapse when relieved on 23rd August, and the Dardanelles Commission, which investigated the entire campaign, later talked of his 'want of determination and competence'. Describing his leadership as 'not satisfactory' the Commission's report went on to conclude:

> "Major-General Hammersley's health had in the past been such that it was dangerous to select him for a divisional command in the field, although he seemed to have recovered. We think that the defects that we have mentioned in his leading probably arose from this cause."[1]

Command of 12th (Eastern) Division went to Maj. Gen. James Spens, CB, King's Shropshire Light Infantry, aged 61. He had, at least, been commander of a Territorial Force Division, the Lowland Division, in the four years before his retirement early in 1914. He commanded the division until just before it left for France in May 1915.

13th (Western) Division, another Gallipoli-bound unit, was given to the ten-year retired Maj. Gen. Robert George Kekewich, CB, East Kent Regt. Aged 60, Kekewich saw much service in South Africa but was not a well man. Invalided out

---

[i] Maj. Gen. George Handcock Thesiger, CB, CMG, Rifle Brigade, was aged 47. He was the son of Lt. Gen. The Hon. Charles Wemyss Thesiger, and The Hon. Mrs. C W Thesiger. He was the husband of Frances Thesiger, of 13, St. Leonard's Terrace, Chelsea, London. His body was never found and his name is inscribed on the Loos Memorial, Panel 1.

[ii] 9th (Scottish) Division had three further GOCs: Maj. Gen Henry Lukin (until 4th March 1918), Maj. Gen. Cyril Blacklock (for four days before shifting to 39th Division) and lastly, Maj. Gen. Hugh Tudor, who was, perhaps, the most successful but who later achieved notoriety in Ireland as Chief of the Royal Irish Constabulary during the period of the Irish War of Independence (1920-1) during which he formed the infamous 'Black and Tans'. He was the subject of an IRA assassination attempt in the 1950s.

[iii] Lt. Gen. Sir Bryan Thomas Mahon, KCVO, CB, DSO, 8th Hussars, aged 52. South Africa. Commanding 8th (Lucknow) Division, India, 1909–14. CinC Salonika 1915-6. CinC Ireland 1916-8.

[iv] Hammersley was severely wounded in the leg at Talana Hill, 20th October 1899.

of his command and wracked by depression he committed suicide on 5th November 1914[i]. He was replaced by the 60-year-old Maj. Gen. Henry Byron Jeffreys, Royal Artillery, who had retired in 1910.

14th (Light) Division came under the control of Maj. Gen. Thomas Lethbridge Napier Morland (about whom more in *Planning the Big Push*). He had reasonable experience of command (2nd Brigade, 47th (2nd London) Division TF) but only stayed with the division for forty days before being replaced, first by the 56-year-old Brig. Gen. Francis Alexander Fortescue, CB, Rifle Brigade, who was in charge for all of five days before himself being replaced by Brig. Gen. Victor Arthur Couper, also the Rifle Brigade, who had just completed four years as the Inspector of Gymnasia and who now managed two weeks before Fortescue returned. And left again. To be replaced, again, this time until 1918, by Couper.

Apart from the 56-year-old Maj. Gen. Alexander Wallace, Indian Army, who was, until 1913, the GOC of the Jubbelpore Brigade before commanding 15th (Scottish) Division for three months, and the previously mentioned 18th (Eastern) Division commanded by Maxse, the next run of New Army Divisions was all initially commanded by retired officers or 'dugouts'. These were:

- 16th (Irish) Division – Lt. Gen. Sir Lawrence Worthington Parsons, KCB, RA, aged 64, who retired in 1909;
- 17th (Northern) Division – Maj. Gen. Walter Rupert Kenyon-Slaney, Rifle Brigade, aged 63. Brigade commander in India (1909-13). Retired in 1913;
- 19th (Western) Division – Lt. Gen. Sir Charles Grant Mansell Fasken, Bedfordshire Regt., last served in East Africa in 1904 and retired in 1909;
- 20th (Light) Division – Maj. Gen. Edward Owen Fisher Hamilton, Queen's Royal Regt., and Lieutenant Governor of Guernsey since 1911;
- 21st Division – Lt. Gen. Sir Edward Thomas Henry Hutton, KRRC. Commanded mounted infantry in Egypt and South Africa. Aged 66. Retired 1907;
- 22nd Division – 66-year-old Maj. Gen. Robert Arthur Montgomery, RA. Retired 1910. He had seen no active service;
- 23rd Division – Maj. Gen. James Melville Babington, CB, CMG, Colonel, 16th Lancers. Spent time with the New Zealand Defence Force, retiring in 1907. Aged 60;
- 24th Division – Maj. Gen. John George Ramsay, CB. Colonel, 24th Punjabis. Last saw service in the field in Pekin in 1900 before retiring in 1912; and
- 25th Division – Maj. Gen. Francis Ventris, Essex Regt., a Staff College graduate retired since 1909. Last in the field in Sudan in 1886.

Of the above, only Fasken (19th Division) and Babington (23rd Division) took their units to the Western Front. The rest were either already too old, too out of date or so totally lacking in appropriate command experience as to be of no practical use in the training and education of the new enthusiastic officers and men at their command. Indeed, of the eighteen K1, K2 and K3 New Army divisions, only five were initially commanded by a General on the Active List.

---

[i] He is buried in St Martin's Churchyard, Exminster, Devon.

But a divisional commander, unless like Maxse already an enthusiast for training, can only do so much with the type of green volunteers who flooded the recruiting centres in the autumn of 1914. Day to day, the handling of these men and budding officers was the responsibility of Brigadiers[i] and battalion, company, and platoon commanders. And here, too, there was a problem as many of them were also 'dugouts' – officers and NCOs whose knowledge and experience of modern warfare, modern weapons, and modern methods was less than up to date.

An effort was made to supply newly formed battalions with a nucleus of Regular Army officers but, with casualties running at a high level in the BEF, this well soon ran dry. Thus, some, but not all, of the K1 battalions were able to avail themselves of the experience and expertise of serving officers. The difference could be stark. Two battalions of the Border Regt., the 6th (11th (Northern) Division, K1) and 7th (17th (Northern Division), K2) had wildly different experiences. The 6th enjoyed the presence of four Regular officers and three from the Special Reserve in the Officers' Mess, whilst the 7th made do with one officer and one NCO, both from the Special Reserve.[2]

With these new battalions being formed there was no shortage of commissions to be had and no shortage of young and educated candidates. But the social class pool from which they were initially drawn was not significantly different from the one from which pre-war officers emerged. The first port of call was any of the 190 Senior and Junior Officer Training Corps attached to the major universities[ii], the Inns of Court, and the leading public schools, and on 10th August Kitchener called for 2,000 young men from these establishments willing to accept temporary commissions in the Army. Aged from 17 to 30, they were required to have been part of a University OTC. In the months between August 1914 and March 1915,

---

[i] The *London Gazette* of 20th August 1914 listed 105 new Brigadiers such was the need for officers to command both in the New Armies and the Regular Army and Territorial Force. Most were Colonels but four Lt. Cols. were also promoted. One, Col. Frederick Rudolph Lambart, 10th Earl of Cavan, went on to become a Corps commander in 1916, Army commander in 1918, CIGS in 1922 and Field Marshal in 1932. The majority of them were confirmed as Brigade commanders of Territorial Force brigades but several found themselves commanding Regular or New Army brigades, e.g. Brig. Gen. E J Cooper who briefly commanded 46th Brigade, 15th (Scottish) Division; Col R J Pinney (Devonshire and Cornwall Infantry Brigade, TF), to GOC, 23rd Brigade, 8th Division; Col. R Scott-Kerr (2nd London Infantry Brigade, TF), to GOC, 4th (Guards) Brigade, 2nd Division; and Col. D A Macfarlane (Seaforth and Cameron Infantry Brigade, TF), GOC, 81st Brigade, 27th Division. Some were appointed RA commanders in Regular or TF divisions: e.g. Col. E A Fanshawe (Wessex Division, TF), CRA, 1st Division; Col. A W Gay (West Lancashire Division, TF), CRA, 28th Division. New Brig. Gen. E J Phipps-Hornby, VC, was made BGRA, III Corps. Others took on staff roles, e.g. Brig. Gen. F C A Gilpin, GHQ Director of Transport, Brig. Gen. A M Stuart, Director of Works, and Brig. Gen. J H Fowke who became BGRE at GHQ [*Supplement to the London Gazette*, 20th August 1914, page 6581].

[ii] I.e. Oxford, Cambridge, London, Edinburgh, Manchester, Glasgow, Leeds, St Andrews, Bristol, Birmingham, Durham, Sheffield, Queen's Belfast, & university colleges: Nottingham, Aberystwyth, Bangor, and Hartley (now Southampton Univ.).

however, over 20,000 temporary commissions were awarded, with the school OTCs supplying enormous numbers. Just four schools – Charterhouse, Wellington, Marlborough, and Eton – provided the Army with 1,670 new officers. What this did mean, however, was that, at least for some time, if your name did not come with an attachment to one of these institutions the Army was simply not interested in you as officer material.[3] In short, therefore, 'gentlemen' were still in charge but, with their complete lack of experience they were as much learning the ropes as the average Private. The one good thing was most were only too aware of their ignorance and shortcomings and, as some later recorded, talking 'shop' in the mess was no longer an offence which might see you 'ragged' or even forcibly expelled.[4] These officers, at least, understood the knowledge to be found in textbooks and pamphlets was not just useful, it might help keep them and their men alive. It might even help them win the war.

Just over six months were allocated to the training of each division. The first three involved basic training: drill, physical exercise, musketry, etc. The basic musketry course was supposed to be completed within three months but, in the absence of enough Lee-Enfield rifles to equip the units of the Territorial Force, let alone the Kitchener volunteers, it was clear the New Armies had to make do with whatever obsolete hardware was available, this included 'broomsticks and poles' (see also page 641).[5] Ammunition was also in short supply so units fortunate to possess rifles which might fire were unable to practice live firing because there were no bullets. Too often, 'fighting' training was reduced to bayonet practice and the throwing of 'bombs' (grenades). Later, the men became so reliant on the latter that rifles were either poorly used or discarded when it came to trench fighting[i].

As a result, much of the time which should have been spent on shooting was instead devoted to yet more drill and this was overseen only too often by officers and NCOs too old to serve at the front. Quite often these officers and NCOs had been trained in an Army devoted to discipline over initiative, to high morale over battlefield tactics, to close order rather than dispersal, and in an army where automatic weapons, indirect fire and 'fire and movement' were all but unknown. On the other hand, they were dealing with highly motivated, often highly intelligent, and almost certainly better educated men who might well have been receptive to more sophisticated training once the basics had been instilled. A fair few of these elderly officers and NCOs had no genuine idea what the modern 'basics' were and this led to friction and misunderstanding between the 'dugouts' and the recruits not conducive to proper war training. On the other hand, those units fortunate enough to be trained by someone *au fait* with post-Boer War 'fire and movement' tactics would still find themselves at a disadvantage as the war had now moved on to the prolonged and arduous siege tactics of trench warfare. It is for these various reasons so many New Army divisions took so long to be brought up to what was an acceptable level of discipline and training in France.

---

[i] For more detail see Robbins, S, *British Generalship on the Western Front*, pages 91-2. Usually, every man carried bombs to supply trained bombers. The tendency was for the carriers to use them themselves, losing their rifle in the process.

If the 'basics' of drill, musketry and exercise were a considerable problem then the issues surrounding 'specialists', e.g. machine gun teams and the field artillery, were frankly laughable. The modern Vickers machine gun was in extremely short supply and orders for the Lewis gun were not placed until the end of 1914 and, with the production of both weapons lagging way behind contractual agreements, the majority of these guns went to the front rather than to the New Armies. Embarrassed New Army machine gunners were, therefore, reduced to hauling wooden dummy guns around the training grounds, to the amusement of their fellow soldiers and the great British public.

For the field artillery supply of 18-pdrs. and 4.5-in. howitzers was deplorably slow with many K2, K3 and K4 divisions not seeing the genuine article well into 1915 and sometimes only then for but a brief period before they left for the Western Front. With the same applying to the newly raised Heavy and Siege Batteries of the Royal Garrison Artillery it is no surprise Sir Henry Rawlinson was greatly concerned about the abilities of these new gunners to deliver with accuracy the bombardment he thought necessary prior to 1st July. His commander in chief, however, was more sanguine, both about the artillery's capabilities and those of the untried New Army divisions which made up more than 50% of the troops who went 'over the top' at 7.30 a.m. on 1st July.

Even whilst still in Britain, the time it took to train and equip these divisions rarely fell within the allotted programme, as the table below shows. The six divisions of K1 left Britain between seven and nine months after their formation. K2 divisions were, on average, nine months in the training except for one division, 16th (Irish) Division, which did not leave for France until 16 months after its initial formation. The K3 and K4 divisions averaged between 11 and 13 months before they departed for the Western or some other front.

Army	Date raised	Dates left UK	Average time to train
K1	Aug. 1914	9th May–9th July 1915	7-9 months
K2	Sept. 1914	7th–24th July 1915 (16th Division Dec. 1915)	9 months
K3	Sept. 1914	25th Aug.–25th Sept. 1915	11-12 months
K4	Dec. 1914	12th Nov. 1915–28th Jan. 1916	11-13 months

Table 19 The raising and training of Kitchener's New Armies

The slow, and often poor quality, training in Britain, and the generally dilatory manner in which the New Army troops were committed to offensive action once in France, was a consequence of Kitchener's decision his divisions should stand alone rather than act as feeder units to units at the front. This meant a division, once landed, needed many months of additional training and experience before being thought up to the task of participating in a major attack. The catastrophe which befell 21st and 24th Divisions at Loos on 26th September 1915, allied to the enthusiastic attacks and then chaotic withdrawals of the two 9th and 15th (Scottish) New Army divisions, on the first day of that battle, rather confirmed the view the New Armies would take months of training before being of much use. It was the issue of training these green troops which Haig repeatedly raised as a reason for delaying either the BEF's main 1916 offensive, the 'wearing out' attacks supposed to precede it, or the relieving attacks the German assault on Verdun demanded.

An alternative was proposed. When war was declared Gen. Horace Smith-Dorrien moved temporarily from Southern Command in order to head up a Home Defence Army under Sir Ian Hamilton before the death of James Grierson resulted in him taking command of II Corps. In the interval, Smith-Dorrien proposed to Kitchener, the new Secretary of State for War, that, rather than create brand new divisions, the flood of volunteers should be added to the existing Territorial Force units which should themselves be split up so as to accommodate the new recruits and the large number of ex-officers and other ranks who now came forward. Thus, every new unit so created would contain some of the better-trained Territorials, by whom Smith-Dorrien had been impressed when at Southern Command, a leavening of recently returned officers, NCOs and Privates, and the new and utterly raw recruits. His reasoning was that:

> "… this system of expansion would provide efficient units in the shortest time, and would leave available for training purposes a very large number of excellent instructors who would otherwise be merged into the fighting ranks."[6]

Although he invited Smith-Dorrien to draft such a scheme Kitchener then ignored it. Even without the benefits of hindsight Smith-Dorrien's approach would seem to have been more appropriate to the situation.

Of course, the authorities were somewhat constrained by their early commitment to the concept of the Pals battalion in which friends and colleagues might serve together. Although an undoubted success in recruitment terms, it meant units so raised could not then be split up to supply fresh drafts to units already in France and Flanders without reneging on a major and popular policy which, though militarily unsound in some ways, undoubtedly raised the morale as well as the numbers of men who joined such units. These battalions then had to be trained by the few available officers and NCOs with any experience (even if the wrong experience) before being sent off to France where again, kept separate from other divisions, they continued to train before being sent up the line for their first taste of life in the trenches. Here, quite often, they were paired with other New Army divisions who, though they might have been in France for far longer than the newer arrivals, still lacked any direct experience of offensive actions. To cite an example, 32nd Division, a K4 New Army Division arriving in December 1915, was put under the wing of another New Army division, 18th (Eastern) Division, which arrived in late July 1915 but seen no fighting. Together they occupied the area around La Boisselle and Fricourt whilst 32nd Division 'learnt the ropes' of trench warfare in an area neither of which fought over on 1st July 1916.

This system of keeping the New Army divisions as discreet units may have helped maintain morale but, with some exceptions, did nothing to speed their preparedness for the attack. The French Army, meanwhile, took a different view. Whilst, of course, it had a far larger body of trained and partially trained men who had passed their two years of conscript service sometime prior to 1914, its huge casualties also meant it had to absorb and integrate many new, young, green conscripts joining the ranks as part of the annual call-up. These men, however, joined existing regiments within which were a decent number of officers, NCOs and men who had seen action in both offence and defence and who could pass on their knowledge and experience directly to the raw recruits. As a result, few French divisions sat twiddling their thumbs in rear areas or quiet front-line sectors for many months whilst they discovered what it meant to be a soldier under fire.

For example, Ferdinand Foch's first command, *20e Corps*, formed in 1898 and based around the *20e région militaire*, the cities of Nancy and Toul, was involved in heavy fighting from the opening days of the war up until it went over the top between Maricourt and the *Somme* on 1st July. Initially made up of *11e* and *39e Divisions*, *70e Reserve Division*, two *régiments d'infanterie colonial*, two *régiments d'infanterie territorial*, a *régiment de hussards*, a *régiment d'artillerie de campagne* and four companies of *génie* (engineers), it was heavily involved in the Battle of the Frontiers, fighting continuously in the Battles of Morhange and the Grand Couronné (20th August to 13th September) in which it suffered such serious losses *39e Division* was temporarily withdrawn from the front. From 25th September to 2nd November, it was involved in the First Battle of Picardy, becoming familiar with villages such as Gommecourt, Hébuterne, Fricourt and Mametz which the British Third and Fourth Armies were either billeted in or fought over in 1916.

In November, they moved north of Ypres to fight around Poelkapelle and Langemark during the winter. After a relatively quiet few months (and one stresses 'relatively'), the Corps moved south to Artois in April for the first attack of the Second Battle of Artois on 9th May 1915 which again resulted in heavy casualties. It then 'enjoyed' eight weeks rest and training before being shipped east to Champagne where, on 25th September, it was part of the large French offensive which promised so much but delivered only another enormous butcher's bill. *20e Corps* remained at the front for two months before being taken out of the line for rest, and in order assimilate many new recruits. Its quiet life was brief, however, as the attack on Verdun on 21st February saw it rushed into the salient where it was first involved in a week's furious fighting around the fort and village of Douaumont (25th February-4th March 1916) and then, after three weeks' rest, it was committed to the appalling carnage of the fighting around *le Mort Homme* on the left bank of the *Meuse*. Here it remained for nearly a month before being given May to rest and recuperate. On 3rd June, it moved west to take over the line between Maricourt and the *Somme* from which it attacked with great success on 1st July. *20e Corps* then remained on the *Somme*, engaged for seven weeks in the heavy fighting around Hardecourt aux bois, Hem and Maurepas.

Throughout this time *20e Corps* lived up to its nickname as the *Corps de fer*. From the start of the Second Battle of Artois through to 21st August 1916 it rarely had more than two months between bouts of severe fighting and yet it never lost its cohesion and effectiveness irrespective of its heavy casualties. In the BEF every division had at least eight months between the end of the fighting at Loos and the beginning of the Battle of the *Somme* and yet Haig was constantly complaining his units needed more and more training and yet, for six of the New Army divisions involved (17th, 18th, 30th, 31st, 32nd and 34th Divisions), 1st July 1916 was their first taste of offensive action and, on average, these divisions had been training or in quiet sectors on the Western France for some nine months. One can but wonder how much more effective these men might have been had they been immediately integrated into existing and experienced units as was the French practice?

SOMEWHAT PERVERSELY, it was two of the most recent arrivals in France which were thrown into battle quickest. The K3 21st Division (arrived 9th September) and 24th Division (arrived 30th August), were asked to attempt a follow-up attack against unbroken German defences on 26th September 1915, the second day of the Battle of Loos. The result was the loss of over 8,000 officers and men for no gain. This was after two other New Army divisions, the K1 9th (Scottish), which was the first New Army division to arrive in France (in mid-May), and K2 15th (Scottish) Divisions (arrived first week of July) attacked on the opening day with some initial success in both cases. Later, however, shorn of officers and experienced NCOs, both divisions were forced to withdraw in some confusion from locations which, according to Haig's plan, represented but a small staging post on the way to an expected glorious breakthrough.

At first sight, the decision to deploy two completely untried New Army divisions on the second day of a major offensive in manoeuvres which involved a long and arduous march to the British front followed by a complicated advance across the battlefield, up to and through newly won positions to attempt to pursue the supposedly fleeing German troops seems extraordinary enough. Sir John French, because of deployments elsewhere, some of which were designed as diversions to the main attack, only had in general reserve the Cavalry Corps, the Indian Cavalry Corps and Haking's newly formed XI Corps which contained the two New Army divisions, the Guards Division and a new and inexperienced staff which had not previously worked together. To quote the *Official History*:

> "It was apparent that a force of this nature should consist of seasoned troops, as, in the event of a successful assault by First Army, the general reserve might have to participate in open warfare."[7]

Instead, French kept under his hand two raw divisions barely familiar with being in France let alone contemplated being the spearhead of an attempt to return the Western Front to a war of manoeuvre. Extraordinarily, French did not seem remotely perturbed by such a prospect believing, according to Edmonds, these predominantly young and raw volunteers:

> "... would do better for his purpose than divisions which, having been some time in France, had acquired the sedentary habits of trench warfare."[8]

The fact that Douglas Haig, commander of First Army, then allowed these troops to be thrown against unbroken German troops secure in their 2nd Position is, however, something for he which he should have to answer. Instead, the furious argument which later erupted focussed, not on the choice of troops, but on the timing of their release by GHQ to First Army. It was an argument conclusively won by Haig. For once, this writer must agree with Haig: Sir John French was totally unsuited for this vital command on which the fate of the war and the nation depended. He had to go.

Five Kitchener divisions faced their first offensive actions away from the Western Front (10th, 11th, and 13th Divisions in Gallipoli and 22nd and 26th Divisions in Salonika after a brief stay in France). The rest served in France and Flanders and took part in their first offensive actions there (see Table 20). All or part of seven new divisions went 'over the top' on 1st July 1916. Two, 18th and 30th

Divisions, achieved their objectives; one nearly reached its objective but was overwhelmed by counterattacks (36th Division); two gained minor footholds in the German front-line at enormous cost (32nd and 34th Divisions); and two were more or less destroyed as fighting forces (31st Division and 50th Brigade[i] of 17th Division). The demands placed on four of these divisions, 31st, 36th, 32nd, and 34th, were the product of the absurd optimism at GHQ which so infected it during every attempted offensive from 1915 through to the end of 1917.

In the meantime, the British Government, Army, and the armaments industry struggled to come to terms with the demands of Total War. As with the French, the lack of guns and ammunition cost the officers and men of the BEF dear.

---

[i] The 10th West Yorkshire Regt., 50th Brigade, lost more men on 1st July 1916 than any other. 710 officers and men became casualties during the attack.

Division	Army/ date formed	To Western Front	First offensive action	Months before 1st offensive action
9th (Scottish)	K1	12th May 15	Loos, 25th Sept. 15	4
14th (Light)	K1	18th May 15	Bellewaarde, 25th Sept. 15	4
12th (Eastern)	K1	1st June 15	Loos 13th Oct. 15	4½
15th (Scottish)	K2	7th July 15	Loos, 25th Sept. 15	2½
17th (Northern)	K2	12th July, 15	Fricourt, 1st July 16	11½
37th	K6 to K2 Mar. 15	13th July 15	Ancre, 13th Nov. 16	16
19th (Western)	K2	16th July 15	Loos (subsidiary), 25th Sept. 15	2
20th (Light)	K2	20th July 15	Guillemont, 3rd Sept. 16	13½
18th (Eastern)	K2	24th July 15	Montauban, 1st July 16	11
23rd	K3	25th Aug. 15	Contalmaison, 5th July 16	10½
24th	K3	30th Aug. 15	Loos, 26th Sept. 15	¾
21st	K3	9th Sept. 15	Loos, 26th Sept. 15	½
25th	K3	25th Sept. 15	Ovillers, 7th July 16	9½
36th (Ulster)	Aug. 14.	3rd Oct. 15	Schwaben Redoubt, 1st July 16	8
30th	K4	12th Nov. 15	Montauban 1st July 16	7½
33rd	K4	12th Nov. 15	Martinpuich 16th July 16	7½
38th (Welsh)	K4	21st Nov. 15	Mametz Wood, 7th July 16	7
16th (Irish)	K2	Dec. 15	Guillemont, 3rd Sept. 16	8
31st	K4	To Egypt Dec. 15, France March 16	Serre, 1st July 16	7 (4 in France)
32nd	K4	Dec. 15	Thiepval, 1st July 16	7
34th	K4	15th Jan. 16	La Boisselle, 1st July 16	5½
35th	K4	28th Jan. 16	Guillemont, 21st Aug. 16	7
39th	Aug./Oct. 15	29th Feb. 16	Richebourg l'Avoue, 30th Jun. 16	4
41st	Sept. 15	1st May 16	Flers-Courcelette, 15th Sept. 16	3½
40th	Sept./Dec. 15	2nd June 16	Towards Hindenburg Line, Mar. 17	9

Table 20 Deployment of New Army Divisions to the Western Front by date of arrival
(Shaded units involved on 1st July 1916)

ENDNOTES:
[1] NA, CAB 19/1 (1917-18), Paragraphs 108 & 109, Dardanelles Commission final report, 1917.
[2] Simkins, P, *Kitchener's Army: The Raising of the New Armies 1914-16*, Manchester University Press, 1988, page 218.
[3] Ibid., page 221.
[4] Ibid., page 300.
[5] Ibid., page 291.
[6] Smith-Dorrien, op. cit., pages 374-5.
[7] Simkins, op. cit., page 139.
[8] Ibid., page 140.

13. THE BRITISH ARMAMENTS FAILURE

"It had not been the view of the General Staff that the tendency of field operations to approximate towards siege warfare, as manifested under the exceptional conditions of the war in Manchuria, should be accepted as a general tendency."

History of the Ministry of Munitions

ONE ISSUE THE WAR IN 1914 AND 1915 highlighted was that the armaments and ammunition problems facing the French were as bad, if not worse, for the British. Because of its premier role in the defence of the country, much of the British munitions' capability was devoted to the needs of the Royal Navy, the country's first line of defence against invasion. It was no simple task to re-tool factories, and re-train and re-deploy skilled workers for the pressing demands of the Army: rifles and machine guns, bullets and shells, and field and heavy guns and howitzers. Even those companies previously involved in providing rifles, for example, switched their pre-war output to other non-military uses because orders from the Army simply were not forthcoming in sufficient numbers to make continued production economically viable prior to the outbreak of war.

Manufacturing military (as opposed to naval) equipment in Britain was, for some time, a precarious business. The *Birmingham Small Arms Company (BSA)* was a case in point. Birmingham was the centre of small arms manufacturing from the end of the 17th Century, with local businesses receiving their first government contract in 1693. Birmingham's *Gun Quarter* (broadly the area now surrounding the *Birmingham Children's Hospital,* near the junction of the *Birmingham and Fazeley* and *Grand Union canals*) produced large numbers of muskets and pistols throughout the 18th and 19th Centuries for the Army, the *East India Company,* and in support of the slave trade. The Crimean and American Civil Wars saw a huge demand for the products of the numerous (some 578 by 1868) small-scale producers, some fourteen of which came together as the *Birmingham Small Arms Company* in 1861 which received its first Government contract in 1868. In 1879, however, the factory was silent for twelve months due to a lack of orders and, as a result, the business diversified into bicycles (and later motorcycles and cars). This business was suspended in 1887 when it won a contract to supply 1,200 new *Lee-Metford* Rifles every week to the Army. Later, as part of an agreement to supply 25% of the new *Lee-Enfield* rifles to the Army, *BSA* bought the *Sparkbrook Royal Small Arms Factory* from the War Office in 1906. The War Office then failed to deliver their side of the bargain, causing *BSA* significant financial problems. By 1914, companies such as *BSA* still producing weapons for the Army were doing so at a wholly unsatisfactory rate for war-time – 700 rifles a week in the case of *BSA*.[1]

The size of the Expeditionary Force was set at six infantry divisions pre-war but, by October 1914, nine divisions were already in France and Belgium. The calling up of the Territorial Force and the gradual despatch of its battalions overseas revealed the poor state of supply of the fundamental weapons of any Army – rifles. 400,000 rifles were needed by the end of 1914 but only 240,000 were delivered. On the outbreak of war there were only c. 70,000 *Lee-Enfield* and old pattern rifles more than there were men already in the Army. The modern *Lee-*

Enfields were with the Regular Army and older rifles, e.g. *Lee-Metfords*, were with the Territorial Force whilst the rest were available to partially equip the men of Kitchener's First New Army. With its six 17,000-strong divisions being formed this meant the equivalent of at least two divisions did not have access to any sort of rifle for training purposes.

In principle, when the war started there should have been enough rifles for the Regular Army, the Reserve, and the Territorial Force, i.e. 625,000 rifles. Within two months 30,000 rifles had to be replaced on the front-line and 70,000 distributed to the Indian Corps. In consequence, when it came to providing rifles to the Territorial Force of 400,000 as it then totalled, only 240,000 could be found by the end of the year. For the New Armies, whereas 600,000 rifles were needed only 200,000 were available. There were another 200,000 training rifles but these were not useable in action. As a result, orders for a total of 781,000 rifles were placed in late October 1914, to be supplied by 1st July 1915. These numbers were already deemed insufficient and Master General of the Ordnance, Sir Stanley Brenton von Donop, was ordered to increase this number by 400,000.

There were three domestic sources of rifles in August 1914: the *Royal Small Arms Factory* at Enfield Lock, *BSA*, and the *London Small Arms Company* (*LSA*) in Tower Hamlets. Their current capacity was c. 4,000 rifles per week which, with 90,000 men a week turning up to recruiting centres in the first two months of the war, was clearly inadequate. Expansion of existing facilities was not rapid. *BSA* undertook to increase production to 6,000 a week by May 1915 and *London Small Arms* to 1,500 a week by January 1915. To make up the numbers large numbers of older rifles were converted by both *BSA* and Enfield Lock.

It was clear the need to expand small arms manufacture had to parallel that of artillery and shell production if the BEF was to be properly equipped. It was equally clear British suppliers could not meet demand, even with substantial financial incentives to increase production. By the summer of 1915 the five organisations now involved (Enfield Lock, *BSA*, *LSA*, *Vickers* and the *Standard Small Arms Co.*) undertook to produce c. 20,000 rifles a week but even this figure was not enough. 100,000 Canadian *Ross* rifles were bought as a stop-gap in September 1914 but did not arrive until the autumn of 1915 and other contracts for 400,000 rifles were placed in November 1914 with two American companies: the *Winchester Repeating Arms Co.* and the *Remington Arms Union Metallic Cartridge Company*[i]. In 1915 *Remington* received orders for 1.7 million rifles for delivery from November 1915 onwards.[2]

An acute shortage of machine guns was another problem. It had been decided to equip each battalion with two modern machine guns and, in August 1914, the British Army possessed two heavy machine gun types: the older pattern *Maxim-*

---

[i] American arms companies thrived on business generated by the war. The *Remington Arms Union Metallic Cartridge Company's* gross sales soared from $9.7 million in 1913 to $117 million by 1918. The *Winchester Repeating Arms Co.* gross sales increased from $10.5 million to $61 million and *Colt's Patent Fire Arms Company* from $2 million to $32 million over the same period [*Source*: Brandes, S D, *Warhogs: A History of War Profits in America*, The University Press of Kentucky, 1997, pages 284-6).

Vickers guns, a development of the original first seen in the 1880s and first issued in 1890, and the newer *Vickers* gun adopted by the Army in November 1912. On the outbreak of war there were 1,963 machine guns all, except for 106 *Vickers* guns, being obsolete *Maxims*.³

Small scale repair and manufacture of *Maxims* took place at the Enfield *Small Arms Factor*. *Vickers* built the guns at Erith. In the first two months of the war 1,792 machine guns were ordered from *Vickers*, at a rate of 50 guns per week until June 1915. Production rates were poor, however, with every tranche of the contract (it was split into orders of 192, 100, 1,000 and 500) being late. Thus, nearly half (468) of the largest order of 1,000 machine guns was outstanding as of the notional end of the contract in June 1915[i].

Other automatic weaponry was also belatedly under consideration. A new experimental light machine gun was in development, a project based on co-operation between *Armes Automatique Lewis* based in Liège in Belgium and *BSA*. The *Lewis Gun* was the invention of retired US Army Colonel Isaac Newton Lewis (his parents clearly had high hopes he might a scientist) in 1911 who resigned the US Army frustrated by their refusal to adopt his weapon. He set up *Armes Automatique Lewis* in Belgium and worked closely with *BSA* to finalise the design. *BSA* then negotiated a licence to produce the guns in Britain in 1914. By August, this gun was still regarded as experimental and no facilities existed for full scale production. A small number of *Lewis Guns* were ordered on the outbreak of war for use by the RFC and 200 were ordered for delivery in the autumn of 1914. Subsequent orders of 400 (December 1914), 400 (March 1915) and 2,000 (June 1915) were placed. To meet deadlines, *BSA* hoped to be able to manufacture 100 per week but by May 1915 they were only managing 36 a week.⁴

The overall results of these delays in production in heavy and light machine guns was that by July 1915 only 1,022 out of 1,792 *Vickers* Machine Guns had been delivered and just 621 out of 1,500 Lewis Guns.⁵

The next pressing problem was the lack of artillery and ammunition.

BEFORE THE END OF THE SOUTH AFRICAN WAR the Army embarked upon a major programme to bring its field artillery up to date, Lord Roberts having been ordered to send back to Britain several experienced artillery officers for the purpose. Under the chairmanship of Gen. Sir George Marshall, they formed an *Equipment Committee*. Its remit was to decide the parameters for a new generation of guns. Their decisions, in the main, pre-dated the lessons of the Russo-Japanese War as they related to medium and heavy howitzers.

Britain's focus was on re-arming the Horse and Field Artillery. The tactical reasoning was that Britain, like France, and, to a certain extent, Germany still imagined any major continental war would be one of manoeuvre and a few intense, direct fire and, therefore, relatively short-range battles. Unlike the Germans, the British Expeditionary Force did not envisage being involved in any sieges of

---

[i] The French were also given permission to buy *Vickers* Machine Guns and 2,000 were ordered in October 1914. Supply was so slow only 921 had been supplied by the end of 1916 [*Source*: Goldsmith, D L, *The Grand Old Lady of No Man's Land: The Vickers Machinegun*, Coburg, 1993, Appendix V].

modern fortresses as existed on the Franco-German border in *Elsaß* and *Lothringen* or on the Russian border and, therefore, saw no need to transport a siege train across the Channel. As a result, the new programme consisted of three flat-firing field guns: a 13-pdr. for the Royal Horse Artillery, 18-pdr. and 60-pdr. guns for the Royal Field Artillery; plus a light 4.5-in. field howitzer also for the RFA.

To design and build this new range of guns and light howitzers the Army could rely on the services of the *Royal Gun Factory* at the *Royal Arsenal* at Woolwich and the private companies of *Armstrong-Whitworth*, *Vickers*, *Cammell Laird*, *Beardmore* and the *Coventry Ordnance Works*.

Companies were invited to submit designs which were assessed and those deemed suitable turned into prototypes to be tested before approval was given for their mass manufacture. Progress was rapid and, by 1905, orders were placed for all four natures of gun. The programme for the 13 and 60-pdrs. was completed by 1907 and that for the 18-pdrs. by 1909. The field howitzer, the designs for which was the last to be approved, started to come on stream in 1908 and most deliveries were completed by 1911, although guns were still being built at Woolwich up to the outbreak of war. In essence, therefore, with the exception of the field howitzer, no newly designed or, indeed, any significant number of artillery pieces was built in the five years immediately before war started. After the completion of the 18-pdr. contracts in 1909, no new field guns were built in Britain except by Woolwich (for overseas service) and, of the private companies, only *Vickers* was still working on orders but these were for Canada. Thus, *Cammell Laird* had not built any artillery for the Army since 1909 and *Armstrong* and *Coventry* since 1911.

Some larger models were manufactured but on an experimental basis, with *Beardmore* supplying two 9.2-in. guns in March 1913 and *Coventry* designed and built a single 9.2-in. BL (Breech Loading) howitzer approved in July 1914. In addition, a few 6-in. Mk VII naval guns were converted for Army use at Woolwich between 1911 and 1914.[6]

When Britain went to war, therefore, the British problem was not that they had invested too much in just one gun as had the French with the 75. The British did have a range of modern, as well as rather more elderly, guns:

13 and 18-pdr. QF field guns;
4.5-in. QF field howitzers;
60-pdr. BL MK 1 field guns;
one 9.2-in. BL siege howitzer;
some elderly and technically obsolete 4.7-in. QF field guns;
a few elderly 6-in. 30 cwt BL siege howitzers from c. 1896; and
a variety of obsolete weapons such as some 5-in. howitzers (1895)

On the face of it, this was a balanced arsenal providing mobile firepower with the option of flat and high angle fire, long-range high velocity guns capable of hitting the enemy's guns and interdicting their supplies and communications, and medium and heavy howitzers capable of destroying hardened positions and rooting men out of their trenches. Had the numbers of each gun and their shell supplies been adequate then the BEF would have been able to punch its weight in the early days of trench warfare whilst new guns and even more shells were manufactured at home. The fact was neither condition applied.

Gun type	Available August 1914	With BEF 1914 (or delivered by Jan 15)	Deliveries to June 15	Total available June 15
13-pdr QF Field Gun[1]	185	36	0	185
15-pdr QF Field Gun[2]	20*	20	0	20
15-pdr BLC Field Gun[3]	228*	228	0	228
18-pdr QF Field Gun	996	324	802	1798
4.5-in. QF Howitzer	144	108	209	353
4.7-in. QF Field Gun	88*	88	0	88
5-in. BL Howitzer[4]	80*	80	0	80
60-pdr BL Field Gun	38	24	33	71
6-in. Mk VII Gun	16	0 (8 Railway mounted)	6	22
6-in. 30 cwt Howitzer	104	(40)	0	104
8-in. Howitzer	0	0	24	24
9.2-in. Railway Gun	2	0	3	5
9.2-in. BL Siege How.	1	1	18	19
12-in. BL Rail'y How.	0	0	5	5
15-in. BL Siege How.	0	0	5	5

Table 21 Guns available to the Army, August 1914 and June 1915
[1] RHA Gun attached to the Cavalry [2] Not used on Western Front [3] In France then used for training
[4] Replaced by 4.5-in. Some sent to Russia 1916   * Attached to the Territorial Force pre-war

The numbers of these guns, and of other obsolete *matériel* still in use, available in August 1914 and delivered by June 1915, as well as those available to the BEF on the outbreak of war or soon thereafter, can be found in Table 21 above. The demands for new guns were, therefore, focused on equipping the New Army divisions raised by Kitchener with their field artillery: 18-pdrs and 4.5-in. howitzers; whilst the BEF, apparently caught by surprise by the long-range German howitzers and guns, were urgently demanding guns capable of 'keep(ing) down the enemy's long-range artillery fire'.[7] As a result, orders for new artillery ran at a very high level, as Table 22 below shows.

Gun type	Orders 8/14- 6/15	Due by 30th June 1915	Issued to War Office	Balance outstanding
13-pdr QF Field Gun	218	0	0	218
18-pdr QF Field Gun	3628	2338	802[1]	1536
4.5-in. QF Howitzer	530	530	209[1]	321
60-pdr BL Field Gun	160	108	33	75
6-in. 26 cwt Howitzer	16	0	0	0
8-in. Howitzer	24	24	24	0
9.2-in. BL Siege Howitzer	32	24	18	6
12-in. BL Howitzer	32	21	5	16
15-in. BL Siege Howitzer	8	5	5	0

Table 22 Guns ordered before and delivered by 30th June 1915
[1] Some pre-war orders, as were three 9.2-in. & six 6-in. MK VII Beardmore/Woolwich guns.

Government arms factories controlled by the Master General of the Ordnance, von Donop, were: the *Royal Ordnance Factories*, Woolwich, *Royal Gunpowder Factory*, Waltham Abbey, and *Royal Small Arms Factory*, Enfield Lock. The policy was there should be a surplus of capacity which could maintain the six division Expeditionary Force. But, though the plant and machinery existed, a workforce did not. For example, the Woolwich factories required c. 16,000 men to maintain the output needed to keep the Expeditionary Force in the field. The peacetime staffing at Woolwich, a key supplier of guns and shells, was barely half this number – 8,300.[8] Building up to full productivity, therefore, took some time.

Who else then might build these guns other than the Woolwich *Ordnance Factory*? The pre-war experience of the private companies was varied:

Armstrong built 13-pdr., 18-pdr., and 60-pdr. Guns, and 4.5-in. howitzers;
Cammell Laird built 13 and 18-pdrs;
Coventry Ordnance Works was focused on the field howitzer;
Vickers built 13 and 18-pdrs., and field howitzers; and
Beardmore, apart from the 9.2-in. (naval) guns, focussed on naval work.

On the outbreak of war *Cammell Laird* reverted to naval work to be replaced by *Beardmore* for Army work. Contracts for guns were issued rapidly, with Woolwich receiving orders for a significant expansion in the first week of August; *Armstrong, Vickers* and *Coventry* received orders at the end of the month; and *Beardmore* were contracted in October. The companies tended to specialise:

The *Royal Gun Factory* made all guns, except heavy howitzers, but undertook development of new *matériel* and, until 1916, did all repair work;
Coventry specialised in howitzers: 4.5-in., 6-in., 12-in., and its own private initiative, the 15-in. howitzer, briefly adopted by Churchill and the Royal Marine Artillery before reverting to the Army;
Vickers were the sole manufacturers of the 9.2-in. BL howitzer as well as building 6-in., 8-in. and 12-in. howitzers and 18-pdrs;
Armstrong concentrated on 60-pdrs. but also built 8 and 12-in. howitzers, 18-pdrs as well as 6-in. and 9.2-in. long guns; and
Beardmore made large numbers of 18-pdrs. as well as 9.2-in. and 6-in. guns and some 6-in. and 8-in. howitzers.

IT WILL BE USEFUL TO PROVIDE background to the guns mentioned above.

The 18-pdr. QF Mk I field gun

Having been exposed to the quick-firing field guns of *Krupp* in the early months of the South African War it was deemed essential to replace the 1892 *15 pdr. BL 7 cwt* gun. The Director-General of Ordnance, Maj. Gen. Sir Henry Brackenbury, scoured Europe for a modern field gun, finding a 76-mm QF gun built by *Rheinische Metallwaren und Machinenfabrik (Rheinmetall)*. He secretly purchased 108 guns which entered service in June 1901[i] (then passed to the Territorial Force. One battery (Warwickshire Horse Artillery (TF)), went to the Western Front).

---

[i] Roberts later commented on the 'great superiority' of these guns over anything then available in his evidence to the Elgin Commission [Brett, op. cit., page 369].

91 18-pdr. QF Mk I field gun

For a long-term solution an open tendering process was agreed, with submissions requested for new quick-firing field guns for the RFA and RHA. Eight designs were tested in 1902 but none found suitable. The compromise was a composite gun made up of the *Armstrong (Elswick)* tube, a *Vickers'* recoil system and the *Royal Ordnance Factory's* gun sight, elevating gear and caisson. Trials in 1903 proved satisfactory and the gun went into full production. This weapon was to be horse drawn, with a team of ten officers and men. Its shell was an 18½ lb round filled with 375 shrapnel balls fired at a maximum rate of 20 rounds and a sustained rate of 4 rounds per minute. So far, so good.

There were, however, four problems with the gun, none of which manifested themselves until fired regularly and at a rate demanded by battlefield conditions. The first issue was one which in the autumn of 1914 afflicted all British 'guns' (rather than howitzers): all the shells provided were shrapnel. Given the governing notions about how a European war would be fought, i.e. quick manoeuvre over wide areas with a rapid conclusion to hostilities *à la* the Franco-Prussian War, it was determined the main job of the guns was to attack infantry in the open with shrapnel. Shrapnel was the best means of destroying exposed infantry in large bodies (other than a machine gun) and, until war broke out, this was still the way it was imagined the next European war would be fought.

Experience in Manchuria also suggested shrapnel was the best way to suppress enemy fire prior to an infantry assault. In 1906, the War Office published a *précis* of the views of numerous officers who observed the war at first hand entitled *Some Tactical Notes on the Russo-Japanese War*. The considered view was shrapnel forced the enemy into cover and disrupted defensive fire and Japanese gunners fired on Russian positions until their infantry was close to the enemy trenches, even causing some losses through 'friendly fire'. Shrapnel, therefore, seemed to answer most of the needs of the Army as anticipated prior to the outbreak of war.

Not everyone completely agreed with this view. The opinion of Maj. J M Home, RA, concerning the uses of siege guns and high explosive shells has already been referred to on page 467. In addition, Capt. Berkeley Vincent, RA, a *protégé* of Ian Hamilton, commented on the advantage given to Japanese artillery by the availability of HE shells[9], a point remarked upon by Lt. Gen. Sir William Nicholson, also an observer in Manchuria and appointed CIGS in 1908. But all this was seemingly forgotten about in later years. In 1906, Maj. Joseph Kuhn, US Army Corps of Engineers, whilst pointing out the relative weakness of Japanese guns, also suggested that HE shells, which amounted to 25-33% of all Japanese artillery shells, helped make up the difference:

> "This advantage (i.e. the availability of HE shells) turned out to have been a most important one and went far towards maintaining a balance in the artillery equipment of the belligerents. The Russians being nearly always on the defensive and occupying fixed lines with artificial cover or natural cover, the high explosive shells found frequent illustration, both at Port Arthur and in the field battles."[10]

Another American observer, Capt. Peyton March, noted that, like the BEF in 1914, the Russians went to war only armed with shrapnel. He too noted the 'great advantage' the Japanese *Shimose*-powder filled HE shells gave them when dealing with Russian trenches.[11]

With barbed wire and trenches the norm, shrapnel, except for wirecutting (until a new instantaneous fuze was introduced), became far less useful but, with the industrial capacity to produce high explosive shells lacking, shrapnel was, for a long time, the only 18-pdr shell available in large numbers.

The second problem was the gun's maximum elevation. Expecting to be fired in the open with the enemy visible and relatively close by, the maximum elevation of the gun was only 16°. This had two effects:

1. The gun could not fire over anything of any size, i.e. it could only indulge in the most basic and limited forms of indirect fire; and
2. Its range was restricted to just 6,525 yards (5,966 metres).

Thus, it normally had to fire from exposed positions and was out-ranged by the German *10.5-cm Feldhaubitze 98/09* (max. range 6,890 yards/6,300 metres) and by the *15-cm schwere Feldhaubitze 02* and *13* (max. ranges 8,150 yards/7,450 metres and 9,400 yards/8,600 metres respectively). Both these guns could fire from concealed positions which the men of an 18-pdr. could not see let alone reach.

Its other two problems both related to its recoil system, a hydro-spring mechanism[i] (the same as the German *7.7-cm FK 96 n.A.*), in which the gun barrel

---

[i] The hydro-spring recuperation system was invented in Austria-Hungary in 1890: 'The primary recoil braking force is generated by throttling a working fluid. A recuperator system or function, based on a mechanical spring for energy storage, is also provided. The compression of the mechanical spring provides a secondary recoil braking force and the force to return the recoiling mass to its original position' [*Source*: Zepp, William T, *The Designer's Dilemma – Recoil: What to do with it? Armaments Engineering & Technology Center*, Picatinny Arsenal, NJ, 2004, page 4].

was returned to the firing position by a combination of hydraulic recuperation and by buffer springs.¹² There were two issues here. The fluid used in the hydraulic recuperation system was a mixture of water and glycerine. The constant firing of these guns in a long bombardment, as with the *Somme*, generated considerable heat in this liquid which tended to break down the glycerine which then eroded the cylinders thereby creating leaks. Furthermore, it was discovered the buffer springs simply could not deal with the constant pounding of the gun in such battlefield conditions. These buffer springs either broke or became unreliable meaning the gun barrel failed to return to its set position[i]. To get the gun back to its now rather approximate starting position, the whole thing had to be 'run up' by hand by the gun crew, slowing the rate of fire and undermining accuracy.

The impact of this on wire cutting, where the length and height of the shell's detonation were crucial, was significant. The main point of a quick-firing gun was that the barrel should return to within a millimetre or so of the starting position to avoid continuously re-laying the gun. The French *75* avoided these problems through its hydro-pneumatic recoil system which used oil as the basis for the hydraulic recuperation element and compressed air as the return part of the system. A *Vickers* re-design of the 18-pdr. recoil system to one similar to the *75* was embarked upon in 1915 and the first of this type introduced in 1916, with it officially being fitted as from November of that year.¹³

If one added into this mix the problem affecting all guns – barrel wear – then the longer the 18-pdrs. stayed in service the less accurate and quick firing they became[ii]. As the main weapon used for wire cutting in 1916 this was a huge problem for gunners and infantry in the run up to the attack on the *Somme*.

Barrel wear was not only caused by heavy use but also by problems with some ammunition. The copper driving band on certain shells was found to be too hard and this damaged the bore of the gun, undermining a shell's accuracy and range.¹⁴ The only solution during heavy use was to fire more shells to make up for those which missed their target and, of course, this only served to compound the problems of wear and tear on the hard-working 18-pdr. field guns.

1,225 18-pdrs were built in Britain (1,126) and India (99) pre-war by *Armstrong* at *Elswick*, *Vickers*, and at Woolwich. On the outbreak of war, production was increased and an order for 224 placed with Woolwich (68), *Armstrong* (78), and *Vickers* (78). Manufacture was extended to the ship builder and armour plate manufacturer *William Beardmore* at Parkhead, Glasgow[iii]. By the end of October 1914, the various companies had undertaken to construct 2,378 18-pdrs:

---

[i] Supply of springs was a long-term problem, and repairs were of little use. Numerous 18-pdrs. were out of action during the 7-day *Somme* bombardment because of this problem. The effects cannot be quantified except by the numerous reports of uncut wire along VII Corps' and Fourth Army's frontlines.

[ii] The 18-pdr was estimated to have a 'life' of 12,000 rounds [*Source: History of the Ministry of Munitions*, Vol. X, footnote 4, page 75].

[iii] They also built naval *Mk IX* and *X* 9.2-in. guns for the *Cressy*, *Drake* and *Duke of Edinburgh* classes of Armoured Cruisers, the *King Edward VII* class of pre-*Dreadnought* battleships, and four *M15* monitors, and *15-in. Mk I BL* guns. Examples of these are mounted outside the Imperial War Museum

Woolwich 168, *Vickers* 1,010, *Armstrong* 1,000, and *Beardmore* 200. It was hoped these orders would be completed by the summer of 1915. By the end of the year contracts for another 970 were signed: *Vickers* and *Armstrong* to produce 450 each and *Beardmore* another 70.[15] There were delays in fulfilling all orders.

Manufacture of 18-pdrs. extended across the Atlantic, with the *Bethlehem Steel Company* in Pennsylvania getting a contract for 400 guns in two tranches of 200[16] although completion of the order was severely hindered in November 1915 by German sabotage in which many of the guns were destroyed.[17] Overall, 189 were delivered from the USA in 1915 and a further 246 during 1916. In total, 808 18-pdrs. were used by Fourth Army in the preliminary bombardment on the *Somme*.

The 4.5-in. QF Field Howitzer

92 4.5-in. QF Field Howitzer

The 4.5-in. (114 mm) QF field howitzer also emerged from the Equipment Committee's post-South Africa review but at a slower pace than the 18-pdr. Thus, it was possible to incorporate into its development early reports of officers about the use of howitzers in the Russo-Japanese War. Designs were invited from the main companies, but none came up to the standard of a *Krupp 120-mm-Haubitze M1905*. Thought was given to buying this 'off the shelf' but, in 1905, *Vickers*, *Armstrong*, and the *Coventry Ordnance Works*, produced designs and *Coventry's* was selected for trials in 1906. It was recommended for production in 1908 and 192 were completed by the start of the war (fewer than were ordered) of which 144 were on the Western Front. Manufacture was concentrated at *Coventry* but they were also built by the *Ordnance Factory* at Woolwich and, from October 1915, by *Bethlehem Steel* in the USA. The first order for 300 units from *Coventry* was placed in August 1914 to be delivered by the following summer and another order for 200 placed in December. The company struggled to fulfil the contract, and it was only through capital investment via the Ministry of Munitions, the supply of machine tools and other equipment, and by postponing some naval work, that production levels were maintained, though at a lower level than promised. *Bethlehem*, too, failed to produce these guns at the contracted rate.[18]

By 1916 these howitzers (maximum 45° elevation, range of 7,300 yards/6,700 metres), mainly fired high explosive shells[i] but, on the outbreak of war, the shell balance was 70% shrapnel/30% HE. This gun, like the 18-pdr, was equipped with a hydro-spring recoil system although, as it fired far fewer shells, and as howitzers suffered less barrel wear, problems with the recoil system were not so pronounced.

The serious problem with the 4.5-in. came with the rapid expansion in shell manufacture, a reduction in rigorous pre-war testing of shells, and the inevitably lower standards of the munitions supplied. This became especially dangerous for the gun crews during the shift from shrapnel to HE. Poorly manufactured shells contained tiny cracks in the casing which resulted in premature explosions of the shell, either in the barrel or just after leaving it. As a result, the gun teams of the 4.5s became known as the 'suicide club' such was the danger of firing these guns.[19]

Statistics for 'prematures' are telling. With French guns it was estimated there was one per 100,000 rounds fired. With the 18-pdr. it was one in 27,650[20] but the premature was unlikely to be dangerous to the crew as it fired mainly shrapnel. But the 4.5-in. howitzer had a rate of more than one in 5,000.[21] 4 lb 10oz (2.09 kg) of Amatol could do serious damage to the gun, the crew, and to any troops under the shell's path if it exploded early. 202 guns fired 199,905 HE rounds during the *Somme* bombardment suggesting c.40 prematures along Fourth Army's front[ii].

The 4.7-in. BL QF Gun

93 4.7-in. BL QF Gun

The 4.7-in. BL QF gun was designed in 1885 by *Armstrong Whitworth* for the navy, coastal defence, and export, thus the 120-mm calibre. Several were adapted for Army use during the South African War by Capt. Percy Scott, RN. Nearly 90 of these tubes were later mounted either on a 1900 Woolwich carriage or on

---

[i] It was the only British artillery piece with a supply of gas shells on 1st July 1916. These shells were not filled with lethal gas but with tear gas.
[ii] The barrel 'life' of the 4.5-in. howitzer was estimated at 14,000 rounds at full charge [*Source*: *History of the Ministry of Munitions*, Vol. X, footnote 4, page 75].

carriages converted from RML 40 pdr. guns. They were provided with a limited hydro-spring recoil system enhanced by a trail spade and spring case. It had a nominal 10,000 yards (9,100 metre) range at 20° elevation.

In the first two years of the war these guns were deployed on counter battery work, at which they were worse than useless, giving the misleading impression the enemy's guns were being taken under effective fire.

By 1915, the American-made shells of this gun had a narrow copper driving band which was liable to be stripped off as the shell left the tube, thus reducing the range of the shell.[22] The *Official History* reports incidents during the bombardment prior to the attack on Aubers Ridge on 9th May when, because of the stripping of the copper band, the shells started to turn end over end and fell anywhere, some landing 500 yards *behind* the British front-lines.[23] Heavy wear on the barrels also had a significant impact on the accuracy of any shells lucky enough to leave the gun with the driving band intact.

That 48[i] of these guns were still in use prior to 1st July 1916 is indicative of the failings not only of the industrial development programme back in Britain but also of the failure of the Generals to understand the uselessness of such guns in counter battery or, indeed, any battlefield work.

The 60-pdr. (5-in./127 mm) BL Mk I Field Gun

The 60-pdr. BL Mk I field gun emerged out of the post-South African War review conducted by the Heavy Battery Committee under the chairmanship of Col. (later Maj. Gen.) Thomas Perrott, RA, who commanded the siege train in South Africa. It was an *Elswick Ordnance Company* design first investigated in 1903 but which needed several changes to its carriage before being accepted in 1905. Its initial production run of 41 was completed in 1907 but, when it came to war-time production, certain modifications were needed to simplify and speed-up the rate of manufacture. These resulted in two updated versions of the gun, the Mk I$^+$, built by *Elswick*, and the Mk I^{++} built by the *Royal Gun Factory*. In October 1914, an order for 72 guns was placed which was equally split between *Vickers* and *Armstrong* while Woolwich received orders for 76 between October 1914 and March 1915. In 1915, *Armstrong* received two orders: for 400 in July, and for 161 in September. As with many gun orders there were substantial problems with supplies throughout 1915 and early 1916. These were caused by material and machine tool shortages, design issues, and the failures of sub-contractors to deliver components on time.[24]

By 1914, the 60-pdr. came with a shrapnel shell which could be fired out to c. 10,000 yards (9,400 metres) and later 12,000 yards (11,200 metres) with a 9¾ lb Cordite MD charge. These weapons were relatively simple and robust and some of the tubes were still in use as late as 1941[ii].

---

[i] 36 with Fourth Army and twelve with VII Corps, Third Army, at Gommecourt.
[ii] The 60-pdr had a barrel 'life' of 4,000 rounds [*Source*: *History of the Ministry of Munitions*, Vol. X, footnote 4, page 75].

94 A 60-pdr BL Mk I Field Gun at full recoil, Cape Helles, June 1915

Given the limited numbers available in August 1914 it was only possible to provide one four-gun, horse-drawn battery to each of the six BEF divisions. Further adaptations were made, including a Mk 2 carriage using large metal wheels, but the extra weight required these guns to be drawn by tractors. Weight issues necessitated another modification to the carriage resulting in the Mk 3. The recoil system, as with the previous guns, was the hydro-spring combination, with all the attendant issues implied. Rather than upgrade this system, a replacement gun was ordered with a hydro-pneumatic recoil system, the Mk II, but it did not arrive on the scene until the autumn of 1918.

The 60-pdrs. had two main uses: counter battery work (once the supply of HE shells became adequate, although flat-firing guns were of little use against hardened gun positions); and, during the *Somme* bombardment, the 136 guns (124 with Fourth Army and twelve with VII Corps) tried long distance wire-cutting with shrapnel. The concept was frankly absurd as no-one could check its effectiveness and, anyway, no-one reached the wire they were supposed to cut on the opening day. To make matters worse, it was found there was a tendency for the head of the shrapnel shell to come loose whilst in the barrel of the gun leading to dangerous prematures which might occur twice for every 1,000 rounds fired.[25]

The 6-in. MK VII Gun

The 6-in. MK VII gun was a naval gun adapted for Army use. Designed in 1898 it was used in numerous vessels, i.e. pre-*Dreadnoughts* and *Dreadnoughts*, the battlecruiser *HMS Tiger*, armoured and protected cruisers, monitors, and gunboats.

With a need for a long-range gun on the Western Front, some of these guns were placed on improvised carriages designed by Admiral Percy Scott, RN. They first appeared on the Western Front in early 1915. With its range limited by the low elevation provided by the carriage, a new design was introduced in spring, 1916, and the Mark II carriage extended the reach of its 100 lb shell (containing

13 lb 5 oz of *Lyddite*) to 13,700 yards (12,500 metres). Twenty[i] guns were available on the *Somme* and were used mainly for interdiction of supplies and troop reliefs, and the bombardment of rear villages and communications. With a barrel life of just 1,900 rounds, because of its large 23 lb *Cordite MD* charge, and with a hydro-spring recoil this was another gun which tended to suffer from barrel and component wear if over-used.[26]

It was superseded by the far superior, purpose-built Mk XIX. A few of this new gun were again in service in France and Flanders but this time in 1940.

95 6-in. BL Mk VII Field Gun

The 6-in. 30 cwt BL Siege Howitzer

The 6-in. 30 cwt BL siege howitzer was an adaptation of a medium howitzer produced in India in 1896. The gun could be fired either from its carriage with a 35° elevation and a 5,200-yard (4,750 metres) range, or from a fixed mounting on a platform with a 70° elevation and an increased range of 7,000 yards (6,400 metres). Only 120 of these howitzers were produced and, on the outbreak of war, only one siege artillery Brigade was equipped with them. A dozen of these guns were employed in South Africa, where the limited range achieved with its shell weighing 122 lbs 9 oz fired from the carriage was found to be unacceptably short. The production of a lighter 100 lb 6-in. shell increased this range to 7,000 yards. Firing from the fixed platform was not attempted in South Africa, however, as siege conditions never applied. Some eighty guns were still in service in 1914 and most were rushed to France and Flanders and others to Gallipoli where they constituted the bulk of the British Army's siege howitzers until more modern and heavier weaponry started to replace them. This was yet another British artillery piece featuring the hydro-spring recoil system and 52[ii] were employed in the initial bombardment on the *Somme*.

---

[i] 18 with Fourth Army and two with VII Corps.
[ii] 44 with Fourth Army and eight with VII Corps.

96 6-in. 30 cwt BL Siege Howitzer in service with the Greek Army

The 6-in. 26 cwt BL Siege Howitzer

97 6-in. 26 cwt BL Siege Howitzer

The 6-in. 26 cwt BL howitzer was a rapidly developed and built replacement for the elderly 30 cwt version. Designed by *Vickers*, it was tested and proofed within the first seven months of 1915 and large numbers began to come into service at the end of that year. It proved to be the workhorse of the British medium and heavy artillery and remained in service to the end of WW2[i]. Demand for this gun was so great, c. 500 were ordered in 1915 alone, that *Beardmore* was given an

---

[i] *Vickers* produced 1,580 howitzers, June 1916-April 1918 [*Source*: *History of the Ministry of Munitions*, Vol. X, page 70].

order for 200 of them, Woolwich asked to build 100 in January 1916, and, in March 1916, *Coventry* received an order for 120.[27] Farndale, in his history of the Royal Artillery, states the two types of 6-in. howitzers fired c. 22.4 million rounds during the war compared to 7.5 million for the 8, 9.2, 12 and 15-in. howitzers combined.[28]

Equipped with a hydro-pneumatic recoil, its 45° elevation gave it excellent range – 9,500 yards (8,700 metres) – or parity with the *15-cm schwere Feldhaubitze 13*. The gun proved reliable and needed few modifications[i]. Eighty-eight (68, Fourth Army, 20, VII Corps) were used prior to 1st July 1916.

The 8-in. BL Siege Howitzers Mks I – V

98 8-in. BL Siege Howitzer on the Somme

The 8-in. BL Howitzers Mks I through V were improvised guns placed on modified carriages as a short-term answer for the urgent need for more high angle siege guns on the Western Front. Designed by Maj. (later Brig. Gen.) Maurice Lean Wilkinson, the Assistant Superintendent at the Ordnance Factories and previously Chief Instructor at the Ordnance College[ii], they were shortened and bored-out 6-in. Mk II, IV or VI naval guns for which a variety of carriages were constructed. Experiments took place in December 1914 after which 23 6-in. guns were converted with the task being divided between Woolwich (12 units), *Armstrong* and *Vickers* (4 units each) and *Beardmore* (3 units). These guns were delivered in the Spring of 1915. They used the hydro-spring recuperator system widespread amongst British artillery. These were cumbersome, extremely heavy (13½ long tons) and unreliable pieces of kit of which 91 were built before a purpose built 8-

---

[i] Its barrel 'life was c. 5.000 rounds [*Source*: *History of the Ministry of Munitions*, Vol. X, footnote 4, page 75].

[ii] Wilkinson (1873-1946) was later appointed Superintendent of Design at the Woolwich Arsenal between 1921–24; the Commandant of the Artillery College 1924–27 and the Military College of Science, 1927–28; and the Vice-President of the Ordnance Committee between 1928–30.

in. howitzer came into production in 1916. In August 1915, *Vickers* came up with a newmodel, the Mark VI, which was lighter, more mobile, and quicker to build than both its predecessors and the 9.2-in. BL howitzer and the first fifty of these were ordered in March 1916 with the main production centre being *Armstrong* with some orders to *Beardmore*, Woolwich, and *Midvale* in the USA. Manufacturing delays meant none of the new model were available on 1st July 1916.

Sixty-four of the older Marks were employed by Fourth Army, during the preliminary bombardment on the *Somme*, and they were a useful stopgap during the *Somme* fighting. They fired a 200 lb Amatol-filled shell out to a range of 10,500 yards (9,600 metres), however the fuzes employed were unreliable and the sight of unexploded 8-in. shells was commonplace on Western Front battlefields. This could be caused either by the fuze failing to detonate the shell's bursting charge or because the fuze simply unscrewed itself whilst in the air. So commonplace was this the *Official History* talked of the *Somme* battlefield being:

'... in parts... littered with blind shells, now better known as 'duds'.'[29]

Sixteen of these guns were given to the French for a time and were known as the *Obusier Anglais BL Mk VI de 8 pouces (203.2 mm)*. These guns had a barrel 'life' of some 4,500 rounds.[30]

The 9.2-in. BL Mk, I Siege Howitzer

The 9.2-in. BL Mk I siege howitzer was the only heavy howitzer in the British Army designed before the war started, and was the first British gun to use a hydro-pneumatic recuperation system. The gun emerged after the *Coventry Ordnance Works* was asked in 1910 to design a heavy howitzer. What emerged was heavy, weighing over ten tons, and could be fired at elevations of between 15° and 55°. Fired at low elevations, however, the power of the recoil gave it a tendency to rear up and back. To prevent this, a large box was attached to the front of the gun platform into which the gun team had to shovel some 9 tons of earth before firing[i].

A prototype of this gun was first fired at Woolwich and Shoeburyness in the winter of 1913/4 before being sent to the firing range at Rhayader near Llandrindod Wells in central Powys in July 1914. Test firing confirmed its utility and sixteen were immediately ordered from *Vickers* by Maj. Gen. Stanley Brenton von Donop, the Master-General of the Ordnance. Sixteen more were ordered in the third month of the war with the prototype, known as 'Mother', going to France at the end of October 1914. It was employed at Neuve Chapelle in early 1915. *Vickers* received a third order for another sixteen guns in May 1915, partly to keep their production line running and, in July a further 120 were ordered. Elements of an order from *Bethlehem* for 150 guns, placed at the end of 1915 for delivery as from June 1916, were still outstanding in the summer of 1918.

These guns fired a 290 lb shell filled with 34 lbs of Amatol to a maximum range of c. 10,000 yards (9,200 metres) and 84 were involved in the preliminary *Somme* bombardment (Sixty by Fourth Army and 24 by VII Corps). As with the 8-in. howitzer, there were problems with poor quality No. 101 fuzes and there were

---

[i] The howitzer had a barrel 'life' of 4,500 rounds [*Source: History of the Ministry of Munitions*, Vol. X, footnote 4, page 75].

numerous complaints about them not fitting, falling out in flight, or simply failing to detonate on landing (see also page 700[i]). As with the 8-in. shells, large numbers of duds were found on those parts of the battlefield over which the Fourth Army was able to advance after 1st July. There was also an issue with prematures which, with a shell of this size, proved to be a huge threat to the gun teams clustered around the huge howitzer. Indeed, one of these guns burst during the supporting bombardment on 1st July.[31]

99 9.2-in. BL Mk I Siege Howitzer

12-in. BL Siege Howitzers

There were two types of 12-in. BL howitzers prior to the *Somme*: the 12-in. BL Mk I Railway Howitzer built by *Elswick* and first used in March 1916, and a road transported 12-in. BL Mk II Siege Howitzer built by *Vickers*. The first order for 24 rail-mounted (*Armstrong/Elswick*) and 8 road howitzers (*Vickers*) was placed in October 1914. Another 16 rail-mounted guns were ordered from *Armstrong* in August 1915 and ten more from *Coventry* in October.

The *Vickers* guns were effectively scaled up version of the successful 9.2-in. howitzer including a more-than-scaled-up version of the earth box which, this time, required 20 tons of earth to fill it. Its 750 lb shell had a range of 11,340 yards (10,300 metres) at a maximum elevation of 65°. Fourteen of these howitzers were built before a new version was introduced. The railway howitzer enjoyed similar characteristics and fired the same Amatol-filled shell. These howitzers had a barrel 'life' 1,500 rounds.[32]

Six 'road' and seven railway 12-in. howitzers were employed during the preliminary bombardment on the *Somme* – all on Fourth Army's front except two railway howitzers which supported VII Corps' attack on Gommecourt.

---

[i] Also the Artillery chapters in the writer's other books about Gommecourt and the VIII Corps at Beaumont Hamel and Serre.

100 12-in. BL Siege Howitzer

The 15-in. BL Siege Howitzer

101 15-in. BL Siege Howitzer, Polygon Wood, September 1917

The 15-in. Howitzer was the result of a speculative development by *Coventry Ordnance Works* of the successful 9.2-in. siege howitzer. It had not been ordered by the Ordnance Board but a prototype was built which was then touted around Whitehall by one of the directors, Admiral Reginald Bacon, a *protégé* of Jackie Fisher, a technical wizard and a man loathed by many in the Senior Service. Bacon, however, had the right contacts, especially in the Admiralty, and, rather bizarrely, what was clearly an Army gun suddenly joined the arsenal of the Navy. The man responsible for this was the maverick First Lord, Winston Churchill, who rather fancied seeing at least part of the Navy involved on the Western Front or anywhere else they might get their foot in the door. The soon-to-be twelve 15-in. howitzers were, therefore, adopted into the Royal Marine Artillery and were shipped off to France to roam the rear areas, its gun crews dressed, in inclement weather, in rather inappropriate sou'westers.

The guns were monstrously heavy and difficult to transport; and fired, ponderously, an enormous 1,400 lb shell containing 200 lb of Amatol. For some reason (Cost? Profit?), unlike the 9.2-in. howitzer, it utilised a hydro-spring recoil system and its range was a wholly inadequate 10,795-yards (9,870 metres).

Few liked these guns and, by 1916, the Navy, with some relief, handed them over to the Army who, in the main, promptly dismantled them and parked them in locations to the rear. But there was a need for super-heavy howitzers in the run up to the *Somme* offensive and seven[i] were dragged and cajoled into position in time for the bombardment. The sodden ground and muddy conditions made life difficult for all artillerists but some of the 15-in. howitzers were seriously exposed. One on the VIII Corps' front for example, after an equipment failure, slewed around on its platform so far it ended up facing the X Corps' front around Thiepval to the south. Several shells were then fired in this direction in the hope it might persuade the recoil to push the gun back onto the original firing line. Having managed this, it then promptly broke down permanently.

In short, the 15-in. BL Siege Howitzers were the Millwall football fans of the Royal Garrison Artillery. No-one liked them but they didn't care. After all, *Coventry Ordnance Works* had more than made its money back.

KITCHENER LEFT NO STONE UNTURNED in his search for additional production capacity for guns and ammunition. Whilst ensuring the fast-expanding Canadian heavy industry was brought into the process, he also harnessed the massive capacity of the USA (at extortionate cost). In New York was a man only too happy to help – at a price: John Pierpont Morgan Jr. (1867-1943), son of John Snr.[ii], founder of the Wall Street Titan *J P Morgan & Co*. John Jr. was an enthusiastic supporter of the Allies who loaned $12 million to Russia (not a good investment) and, in September 1915, a large consortium of US Banks led by *J P Morgan* organised a $½ billion loan to France and Britain. As a *quid pro quo*, Morgan became official agent for all British purchases from US companies of arms, ammunition, food, clothing, etc., receiving, depending on your source, 1 or 2% of the total value as commission[iii]. It was suggested by Rep. Walter Lewis Hensley, a Democrat from the 13th District of Missouri[iv], in a debate in the House on 15th

---

[i] Five with Fourth Army and two with VII Corps.

[ii] Morgan, Snr, was involved in a Civil War scandal. He financed the sale of 5,000 defective *Hall's Carbines* to the Union Army. Bought by a frontman, Arthur Eastman, in May 1861 for $3.50 each, an arms dealer, Simon Stevens, sold them to Gen. John Frémont, commanding the Union Department of the West, for $22. Many proceeded to blow off the thumbs of soldiers using them. Denied full payment, Morgan went to court and saw a profit of $92,426 (c. $30 million at current prices). [*Source*: Engelbrecht H C & Hanighen F C, *Merchants of Death*, Dodd, Mead & Co., 1934].

[iii] 1% according to Chisholm, H, ed. *Morgan, John Pierpont, Encyclopædia Britannica* (12th ed.), 1922. 2% according to Rep. Hensley.

[iv] Eleven counties south of St Louis, bordered on the east by the *Mississippi River*.

December 1915 that, as of that date, Morgan had made a profit of $40 million (upwards of $2 billion at current prices) based on a 2% commission on the $2 billion already spent.

Armaments and ammunition were the priority and the next five year's output of *Bethlehem Steel* was bought by Britain and its Allies while, *inter alia*, *Midvale Steel and Ordnance Company* of Nicetown, Philadelphia, PA, was used from time to time.. In addition, an officer from Woolwich in the USA was ordered to contact all firms capable of manufacturing guns and/or rifles to ascertain what might be produced monthly between January and July 1915. The number of field guns and rifles the Government hoped to procure was 1,500 guns and 500,000 rifles. Initially they were disappointed as no field guns would be forthcoming before the late summer of 1915, with *Bethlehem Steel* undertaking to produce 200 18-pdrs. by 1st July 1915. A useful number with which 5½ new divisions might be armed.

In April 1915, the *Neue Zürcher Zeitung* re-printed a US newspaper article which underlined the huge expansion in US armaments manufacturing made possible by British and French government cash and US loans:

> "War material destined for the Allies is now shipped by American producers to Canada, from where British ships carry it to England. Goods for France and Russia follow the same route, via England. Through agents or directly, the Allies have contracts with nearly all American armaments factories. Of course, the factories keep this a secret, for fear of having to stop their supplies, because all this material
> is contraband of war.
> Fifty-seven U.S. factories are engaged exclusively in armaments production. They normally employ about 20,000 workers, but now, working two and three shifts, the number is about 50,000. They do not make explosives. These are produced at about 103 factories, whose output has doubled since the outbreak of the war. Many gun-cotton factories are working three shifts. The mass demand has, of course, resulted in higher prices. Thus, in February the French Government ordered 24,000,000 lbs of guncotton at 65 cents per pound, whereas in ordinary times the cost is 24-25 cents.
> In addition, there are items of equipment for troops and animals: footwear, utensils, saddles, tanned leather, etc. For America, the European war means a vast, profitable business."[33]

The problems with US production were price[i], delays, and quality. The big four US arms, ammunition and armour plate companies already had a reputation for price gouging their own government. This was highlighted early in 1915 by Congressman Clyde Howard Tavenner, a 33-year-old Democrat elected in 1912 for the 14th Congressional District of Illinois[ii]. Tavenner unseated an incumbent

---

[i] Between summer 1914 and 1916 the wholesale prices of iron and steel products in the USA increased by 50% to 120% [*Source*: Birkett, M S, *The Iron and Steel Trades During the War*, Journal of the Royal Statistical Society, Vol. 83, No. 3, May 1920, page 386].

[ii] A district 250 kms west of Chicago in western Illinois lying along the *Mississippi River* bordering Iowa, then comprising Rock Island, Mercer, Warren, Henderson, Hancock, and Mc Donough counties. Previously known as the Tri-Cities (Davenport, Iowa, and

Republican in a seat held since 1892 by the GOP and, in his four years in office (he narrowly lost in 1916), he gained a reputation as a vocal critic of big business, monopolies, and what he saw as government corruption in the awarding of large naval and military contracts. One of his prime targets was a group of companies he described as the *War Trust*, 'trust' in the US sense of a monopoly/cartel. They were: the *Bethlehem Steel Co.*, the *Midvale Steel Co.*, the *Carnegie Steel Co.* of Pittsburgh, and *E. I. du Pont de Nemours & Co.*, better known simply as *DuPont*. They all became major suppliers to the British government during the war.

Bethlehem started as the *Saucona Iron Company* in 1857, becoming the *Bethlehem Rolling Mill and Iron Company* in 1860 and *Bethlehem Iron Company* a year later. In 1886, *Bethlehem* signed an agreement with Joseph Whitworth of Manchester in time to take advantage of a major expansion of the US Navy from which they got the contracts to supply armour-plate for two new battleships, the *USS Texas* and *USS Maine*[i]. Four years later it was making guns as well as armour-plate for the US Navy. In 1901, it became *Bethlehem Steel* and, in 1903, fell under the ownership of Charles Michael Schwab, previously president of the *Carnegie Steel Co.* After some complicated re-organisations it appeared, in 1904, as the *Bethlehem Steel and Shipbuilding Company* and then the *Bethlehem Steel Corporation*. In 1913, to reinforce its position as one of the world's largest shipbuilders, it bought the *Fore River Shipbuilding Company* of Quincy, Massachusetts[ii].

To maximise its profits the company paid badly and demanded excessive hours from its workers. As Rep. Tavenner pointed out on 15th December 1915, an official report into *Bethlehem's* labour practices conducted in 1910 revealed:

"That out of every 100 men 29 were working 7 days every week.
That out of every 100 men 43, including these 29, were working some Sundays in the month.
That out of every 100 men 51 were working 12 hours a day.
That out of every 100 men 25 were working 12 hours a day 7 days a week.
That out of every 100 men 46 were earning less than $2 a day."[34]

Midvale started in 1867 as the *William Butcher Steel Works*[iii] but, in 1872, Butcher was forced out and the company renamed the *Midvale Steel Works*. In 1875 *Midvale* made their first guns for the US Navy with an order for 3-inch steel mortars. In 1880 the company name changed to the *Midvale Steel Co.* In 1891 an agreement

---

Rock Island, and Moline, Illinois) but, since the 1930s, as the Quad-Cities with the inclusion of East Moline. Bettendorf in Iowa has since been absorbed into the conurbation but it has remained as the Quad-Cities.

[i] The *Maine* was sunk in Havana Harbour on 15th February 1898 most probably from an internal explosion starting in the coal bunkers. The US Yellow Press, in particular the William Randolph Hearst-owned *New York Journal* and Joseph Pulitzer-owned *New York World*, blamed it on Spain and it contributed to the start of the Spanish-American War two months later. The war ended with the USA gaining Puerto Rico, Guam, the Philippines, and temporary control of Cuba.

[ii] Amongst warships built by this yard were pre-*Dreadnoughts: New Jersey, Rhode Island,* and *Vermont* (1906-7), and *Dreadnoughts: North Dakota* (1910) and *Nevada* (1916).

[iii] Butcher was the son of a Sheffield Steelmaker.

was reached with *Dorian-Holtzer Jackson & Cie* in France for the manufacture of their new chrome-steel alloy tipped, armour-piercing shells. By 1900 *Midvale* was tendering for armour plate for the US Navy as well as marine engines and gun mountings and, as from 1903, *Midvale* was supplying both guns and mountings and was responsible for the installation of many of the disappearing gun mounts used for coastal defence.[35]

The Carnegie Steel Co. was, by 1915, part of the *US Steel Corporation* but the name Carnegie, however badly tarnished, was so well established it was still in use despite the takeover in 1901. Born in Dunfermline in 1835, Andrew Carnegie, having had experience of the railways during the American Civil War and recognising the potential for iron and steel production for the every-expanding railroad system, opened his first steel mill in 1872: the *Edgar Thomson Steel Works* at Braddock, Pennsylvania. Carnegie made excessive profits by the simple expedient of repeatedly driving down wages.

In 1883 he acquired the *Homestead Steel Works* and started to receive lucrative government contracts for arms and armour-plate. Despite this, Carnegie and his associate Henry Clay Frick[i], ever keen to increase profits, decided to take on the *Amalgamated Association of Iron and Steel Workers*, a union which effectively controlled the *Homestead Works*. There had been two previous strikes at the plant, in 1882 and 1889, when, in 1892, Carnegie and Frick decided to break the union. Profits increased (estimated at $4.5 million) but the workforce was offered a significant pay *cut* and were then locked out from a works fortified with barbed wire and armed guards. Frick organised scab labour and 300 armed *Pinkerton* agents to secure their access to the site. The result was 'the Battle of Homestead' along the *Ohio River* on 6th July 1892 in which numerous agents and strikers were killed or wounded. Frick refused to negotiate, hoping the chaos would persuade Robert E Pattison, the Democratic Governor of Pennsylvania elected with the help of Carnegie money, to call out the state militia. After the *Pinkertons* surrendered and were shipped off to Pittsburgh, being roundly and physically abused by the strikers in the process, there was a brief hiatus whilst Pattison decided what to do. On 12th July, 4,000 state militia occupied the works and strike-breakers were brought in. On 18th July martial law was declared. Frick then survived an assassination attempt by the anarchist Alexander Berkmann five days later but, by August, the strike was over and, by September, the union was collapsing. Over the next decade unions in the steel industry disappeared.

---

[i] Frick was a deeply unpleasant, corrupt, and successful businessman. Before joining *Carnegie*, he made a fortune in Pennsylvania coal. With business friends he formed the *South Fork Fishing and Hunting Club* near Johnstown, Pa., taking over a lake, Lake Conemaugh, created by the then largest earth dam in the world. Repairs were neglected, the water level raised and, after heavy rain, the dam collapsed on 31st May 1889. Twenty million tons of water swamped Johnstown, killing 2,209 people, and causing $½ billion's worth of damage (current prices). Frick connived with other members to fend off all legal and other inquiries into the disaster and an official report was undermined, delayed and the true causes suppressed [*Source*: Coleman, N M, *Johnstown's Flood of 1889 - Power Over Truth and the Science Behind the Disaster*, Springer International AG, 2018].

The following year, *Carnegie Steel* was accused of supplying sub-standard armour-plate to the US Government. Found guilty, they were charged a 15% penalty, equivalent to $288,000 ($50-60 million at current prices) although negotiations between Frick and the Navy Department temporarily prevented the details from leaking to the press. Carnegie then went to the White House for a chat with President Grover Cleveland and got the fine reduced by 50%. A later Congressional report condemned Carnegie but the deal was done.[36]

Carnegie's reputation was badly damaged, and all the Carnegie-sponsored libraries and university buildings did not repair it. In 1901 Carnegie divested himself of the company at the modest price of $226 million (c. $6.8 billion in modern terms) when the Wall Street bankers *J P Morgan* formed the *US Steel Corporation* with the forced merger of the *Carnegie Steel Company* with Elbert H. Gary's *Federal Steel Company* and William Henry 'Judge' Moore's *National Steel Company*. It became the single biggest steel producer in the USA and profitable in part through employing black workers on very low wages, and convicts at almost slave-labour rates in many of its southern plants thereby undercutting wages for other employees.

Finally, *DuPont*. Founded in Delaware by the Huguenot *emigré* Éleuthère Irénée du Pont it was, mid-century, the largest supplier of gunpowder to the US Army and Navy. Being in a northern state, it was also the main supplier of explosives to the Civil War Union Armies. Keeping pace with developments, guncotton (Christian Friedrich Schönbein, 1846), dynamite (Alfred Nobel, 1867), smokeless powders (Paul Vieille, 1884) and Ballistite (Alfred Nobel, 1887), and Cordite (Abel, Dewar and Kellner, 1889), DuPont started manufacturing guncotton in New Jersey in 1891, then smokeless powders and, in 1902, bought out the *American Smokeless Powder Company* and, with it, all of the important US patents for smokeless powder. Attempts at foreign competition were dealt with by forming international cartels. So, for example, when the *Vereinigte Köln-Rottweiler Pulverfabriken* of Köln, and the *Nobel Dynamite Trust Company (Ltd.)* of London, attempted to build a powder factory at Jamesburg, New Jersey, a deal was signed in 1897 between *DuPont* and these European interlopers which effectively eliminated the costs and loss of profits brought about through genuine competition.

The arrangement is described in H C Engelbrecht and F C Hanighen's 1934 book *Merchants of Death*:

"1. Neither group was to erect factories in the other's territory;
2. If any government sought bids from a foreign powder manufacturer, the foreigner was obligated to ascertain the price quoted by the home factory and he dare not underbid that price;
3. For the sale of high explosives the world was divided into four sales territories. The United States and its possessions, Central America, Colombia, and Venezuela were exclusive fields of the American powdermakers; the rest of the world (outside of the Americas) was European stamping ground. Certain areas were to be open for free competition."[37]

To reinforce their domestic dominance, *DuPont* gained a near 100% monopoly of explosives supply to the US government through ruthless price-fixing and takeovers (100 competitors were bought out between 1903 and 1907).[38] Investigated under the 1890 Sherman *Anti-Trust Laws* they were forced to divest themselves of some interests in 1912, but hung on to those relating to the military and was thus able to produce (over-priced and sub-standard) explosives for the British government when it became desperate after 1914[i].

These were the members of Tavenner's *War Trust*. Speaking in the House of Representatives on 15th February 1915, he described them as 'Patriots for Profit', in no way meaning it as a compliment.[39] He set out how, since 1887, what he called the *Armour Ring*, i.e. *Bethlehem, Midvale* and *Carnegie*, received $95 million for armour-plate alone ($17+ billion at current prices). By his calculations, based on figures taken from various official estimates, the US taxpayer paid out $35 million ($6 billion) in excess profits to the various companies. Another $55 million ($10 billion) was paid out on other military contracts which included ammunition. *DuPont*, part of an *Ammunition Ring* (which included the other three), was paid $25 million ($4.4 billion) over the previous ten years for smokeless powders of which, Tavenner estimated, some $8-10 million was excess profit ($1.6 to $2 billion). He gave figures which suggested that relative to production costs at US state arsenals, the products supplied cost more than twice as much.[40]

Effectively, Tavenner accused these US companies of acting as a cartel against the interests of the US government and taxpayer. He cited an example involving Josephus Daniels, Secretary of the Navy. Requiring quotes for marine turbine rotary drums he was quoted prices by *Bethlehem* and *Midvale* varying by just 5% of between $160,000 and $170,000. A British company quoted $57,346. On a torpedo contract, *Bethlehem* and *Midvale* miraculously found savings of 44% compared to prices quoted just four months earlier because Daniels got a competitive quote from someone outside the cartel.[41]

On armour-plating, and up against a world-wide steel cartel operating for twenty years, Daniels could do nothing. In 1893, Tavenner stated that, in an unlikely outbreak of international competition between arms manufacturers, *Bethlehem* trod on European toes by selling armour-plate to Russia for $249 a ton (whilst selling to the USA for $616!). As a result:

> "... for a time great consternation prevailed in the ranks of the war trusts of the various nations."[42]

In 1894, representatives of the great arms companies of the world met in Paris to find a solution to the dangers of *real* competition. The only question on the agenda was, according to Tavenner:

> "... why they should cut each other's throats and why it would not be to their advantage to receive $500 or $600 a ton instead of $200 or $300."[43]

And so was formed what he called *The Armour Plate Trust*. Thus, when the battleship, *USS Pennsylvania*, was laid down at the *Newport News Shipbuilding and Drydock Company* on 27th October 1913, Josephus Daniels was forced to admit:

---

[i] *DuPont* supplied c. 40% of the explosive powder used by Allies [*Source*: Engelbrecht H C & Hanighen F C, *Merchants of Death*, Dodd, Mead & Co., 1934].

"Though you cannot establish it in black and white, there is no doubt of an *Armour Plate Trust* all over the world. That is to say, the people abroad who make armour-plate will not come here and submit bids because they know if they do our manufacturers will go abroad and submit bids. They have divided the world, like Gaul, into three parts."[44]

And the basis of this *Trust*, or cartel, was a company recently voluntarily wound-up at two Extraordinary General Meetings in July 1912. The company was the *Harvey United Steel Co.*, of London, formed in 1901, to hold the rights to *Harveyised steel* patents (i.e. armour-plate). They were also licensees for *Krupp* steel. Its international 'Patriots for Profit' membership is instructive:

British representatives:
Albert Vickers (*Vickers Ltd.*), managing director, 2,697 shares;
William Beardmore (*William Beardmore & Co. Ltd.*), director;
John M Falkner[i] (Chairman, *W G Armstrong, Whitworth & Co. Ltd.*), director;
Charles Edward Ellis[ii] (*John Brown & Co. Ltd., Coventry Ordnance Works* and *Thomas Firth & Co. Ltd.*), director, 7,438 shares;
The Fairfield Shipbuilding Co. Ltd.;
Cammell, Laird & Co. Ltd.
USA representatives:
Bethlehem Steel Co., 4,301 shares
French representatives:
Schneider & Cie, 9,862 shares;
La compagnie des Forges et Acieries de la Marine et d'Homécourt (aka *St Chamond*) 150 shares;
Four other French directors each with 2,000 shares.
Italian representatives:
Raffaele Bettini (*Societa degli Alti Forni Fondiere ed Acciaiene di Terni*[iii] and *Vickers-Terni*[iv]), 8,000 shares;
Armstrong Pozzuoli[v] & *Ansaldo-Armstrong & Co.*[vi] (*Armstrong-Whitworth*).

---

[i] Tutor to the family of Sir Andrew Noble, Chairman of *Armstrong Whitworth* 1900-1915, Falkner was chairman 1915-1921. He wrote the novel *Moonfleet* in 1898.
[ii] Joined the Ministry of Munitions, 1915. Later Director-General of Ordnance Supply.
[iii] Formed in 1884 by Vincenzo Breda. The *Societa degli Alti Forni Fondiere ed Acciaiene di Terni* was Italy's first major steelworks. Taken over by shipbuilders Attilio Odero and Guiseppe Orlando in 1903, they built a new armour-plate works.
[iv] A joint venture of *Vickers* and the *Societa degli Alti Forni Fondiere ed Acciaiene di Terni* (*Terni Steelworks*), the *Cantiere navale fratelli Orlando* and *Cantieri navali Odero* formed at the Italian naval base of La Spezia in 1906. A major arms manufacturer for the Italian Navy and Army and now called *OTO* (*Odero Terni Orlando*) *Melara*.
[v] *Armstrong Pozzuoli* was *Armstrong's* first foreign subsidiary. Set up in 1885 west of Naples it became the largest gun factory in Italy, producing the 305-mm (12-inch) guns for three classes (six ships) of *Dreadnoughts* (the *Dante Alighieri, Conte de Cavour and Duilio* classes) laid down before the war.
[vi] *Gio Ansaldo & Co.*, was founded in Genoa in 1853. A joint company with *Armstrong-Whitworth* was formed in 1903 but dissolved in 1912. Taken over in 1904 by

German representatives:

Friedrich Krupp (*Krupp*), 4,731 shares;

Fritz Saeftel (*AG der Dillinger Hüttenwerke* owned by *Deutsche Waffen- und Munitionsfabriken Aktiengesellschaftv*[i]) 2,731 shares.[45]

Bankers:

Ernest Ruffer of *A Ruffer & Sons*, a Franco-German bank founded in Lyon in 1872, holding 6,169 shares

Bougére Frères, Paris, 3,000 shares

Deutsche Bank, Berlin, 1,300 shares

Of course, as Tavenner strongly hinted, for the companies listed the only thing better than an arms race for profits/dividends was a war. Preferably a big one. Tavenner suggested the bounty available in speech in Congress on 15th December 1915: *The Navy League Unmasked*[ii]. The figures quoted are for American companies now, or soon to be, supplying arms and ammunition to the Allied governments:

"I wish to read to the House from a weekly stock-market letter of a New York stock brokerage firm as to the extent of these profits. This is the stock-market letter of the firm of *Gilbert & Elliott Co.*, of New York. I will not read the full circular but only the headlines. It is dated 28th August 1915. It says:

'*Winchester Arms* up 1,000 points. *Colt Arms* up 100 points. *Electric Boat* up 100 points. *Canadian Explosives* up 50 points. *DuPont* declares stock dividend of 200 per cent'.

This is the stock-market report. Now, *Bethlehem Steel* stock at the outbreak of the war could have been bought for $40 and as low as $30. Yesterday *Bethlehem Steel* stock sold for $474. In other words, if you had had an investment of $40 in a share of *Bethlehem Steel* at the beginning of the war, your profit because of war would have been $434. By this we may obtain some idea as to the staggering profits that accrued to the Wall Street *War Trust* magnates who owned millions and millions of dollars' worth of munition stocks. It is not to the financial interest of these men that the European war shall be brought to a speedy close, but that it shall not be brought to a speedy close. It is not to their financial interest that the United States of America shall not become involved in the European war, but that it shall become involved. In one of these stock-market letters it was stated that should the United States become involved in the European war this

---

Ferdinando Maria Perrone (died 1908) and his sons Alessandro Pio Antonio Giovanni Luigi and Luigi Ferdinando Alfonso Giuseppe Mario, it concentrated on shipbuilding, weapons and steel. They also owned newspapers including *Il Messagero* in Rome, using them to argue for a larger Italian navy. They also financed nationalist newspapers such as *L'idea nazionale* and Mussolini's *Il popolo d'Italia*. The company actively lobbied for Italy to enter the war. Its market value grew by over 1500% by 1918 as a result.

[i] Manufacturer of the *Maschinengewehr 08* (German machine gun) and *Mauser* rifle.

[ii] Tavenner was criticising the *Navy League* which was agitating for a $500 million bond issue to finance new US warships. Details of the League's founders and leading members can be found in *Appendix 9: Vested interests: the US Navy League*.

stock would be worth even double its present value, and it held out the hope that there was a pretty good chance of the United States becoming involved."[46]

As has been shown ever since, the power of US economic imperialism knew, and knows, no bounds and the bankrupting and subsequent demise of the British Empire was all part of the process.

THE PRE-WAR ARTILLERY ALLOCATION for each division of the BEF was:
Regular: 54 18-pdr. guns, 18 4.5-in. howitzers, four 60-pdr. guns.
Territorial: 36 15-pdr. BLC guns, eight 5-in. howitzers, four 4.7-in. guns.
The cavalry had the support of the Royal Horse Artillery equipped with 13-pdr. field guns in six-gun batteries and the Territorial Horse Artillery with elderly 15-pdr. QF field guns.
All the TF artillery was obsolete but saw service in 1915 and 1916.

After the outbreak of war, the number of 18-pdrs. per division was reduced from 54 to 48 as a result of reducing the number of guns per battery from six to four but increasing the number of batteries in each RFA Brigade from three to four. Then, in November, the number of machine guns for each battalion was doubled from two to four.

Heavy artillery was the notable absentee from the BEF's initial armoury. The *History of the Ministry of Munitions* explains why:

"It had not been the view of the General Staff that the tendency of field operations to approximate towards siege warfare, as manifested under the exceptional conditions of the war in Manchuria, should be accepted as a general tendency. Nevertheless, it was the experiences of this time which led (1909) to the initiation of experiments with heavy howitzers. These experiments eventuated a few weeks before the outbreak of war in the final approval of a 9.2-in. howitzer. In the meantime, some slight experience had been gained with 6-in. B.L. howitzers."[47]

To address this latter problem, a Siege Committee was formed in mid-September 1914. The members were Maj. Gen. Hugh Palliser Hickman, RA, recently returned from being the Inspector of Coastal Defences in India, Col. Louis Charles Jackson, CMG, an Assistant Director at the War Office and later Director-General of Trench Warfare Supply in the Ministry of Munitions, and Maj. Harry Simonds de Brett, DSO, of the Royal Garrison Artillery and then a GSO2 in the War Office. Sixteen 9.2-in. howitzers had already been ordered from *Vickers* and now this committee came forward with recommendations for a dramatic expansion in the heavy artillery of the BEF. Their programme involved doubling the orders for the 9.2-in. howitzers as well as ordering 32 12-in. howitzers, the plans for which were not yet finalised, and the conversion of a number of 6-in. coastal defence guns into 8-in. howitzers. The recommendations came with the ringing endorsement of Gen. Joffre that the British should deploy – as soon as possible – heavy howitzers to counter the German artillery.

This somewhat prescient committee also suggested on 25th September 1914 a need for specialised 'trench ordnance', i.e. trench mortars. This recommendation emerged a month before GHQ sent a request for such equipment. It was not until mid-1915, however, the first examples of commercially built trench mortars arrived in France. Before that, 4-in. mortars improvised out of 6-in. shells and 3.2-in. mortars devised by the Indian Corps made do. By June 1915 *Vickers* provided 127 units of a 1.57-in. mortar approved for production in January, while the rather more famous 2-in. medium trench mortar, the 'toffee apple', was approved in March and made available in small numbers in June. The 106 trench mortars available to the entirety of the BEF in April 1915 trebled by mid-summer. Shells for these newer weapons were more difficult to come by as they required fuzes needed for other shells and, by June 1915, only 50,000 had been manufactured.[48]

To cover the gap until the fulfilment of the various artillery contracts, elderly weapons were pressed into service and hurried across the Channel. A group of 6-in. 30 cwt pattern howitzers was despatched to join the 24 already there and twenty 4.7-in guns collected from overseas stations and sent to the Western Front. The one modern heavy howitzer, Stanley von Donop's lonely 9.2-in. howitzer soon known as *Mother*, was sent on its way even if, as of October 1914, it was still regarded as 'experimental'. Lastly, a single *Beardmore* 9.2-in. long-range railway-mounted gun was added to the BEF's arsenal.[49]

Von Donop confirmed 892 18-pdrs. had been ordered and 864 were expected by 15th June 1915 (in fact 802 were ready). This was to be sufficient to equip 24 New Army divisions with nine, four-gun, batteries (though it assumed no losses amongst the existing number of guns). At a meeting on 12th October 1914, the Cabinet Committee decided these numbers were grossly inadequate and demanded 3,000 18-pdrs. by 1st May 1915. Management from *Vickers, Armstrong Whitworth, Beardmore* and the *Coventry Ordnance Works* attended a meeting on the following day and they confidently asserted such production figures could in fact be exceeded – so long as the Government gave them a large amount of cash with which to fund the expansion of their factories and the purchase of their products. That these products also included the essential shells, fuzes, propellant charges, etc., seemed not to be a problem either.

By 28th December 1914, the 'heavy' artillery of the BEF consisted of:

Six batteries of 60-pdrs
Ten batteries of 4.7-in. guns
Six batteries of 6-in. 30 cwt howitzers
Two batteries of 6-in. Mk VII guns
One 9.2-in. howitzer

The only guns about which there were good reports were the 60-pdrs. and the 9.2-in. howitzer. The others were inaccurate and/or lacked range.

On 12th January 1915, the War Office advised Sir John French of a large order of heavy howitzers: 32 9.2-in., 24 8-in., and 32 12-in. howitzers, which were expected be with the BEF as from March along with five 15-in. howitzers manned by members of the Royal Marine Artillery in February. Any new pattern 6-in. howitzers were some way off, however, as they were still in the design stage. These, unfortunately, were the guns Sir John desired most, as his 24 elderly 6-in. 30 cwt howitzers were both outnumbered and outranged by the sixteen 15-cm howitzers possessed by *each* German *Armeekorps*.

Not a lot changed after Aubers Ridge and Festubert in May 1915. The heavy howitzers now consisted of fourteen 9.2-in. howitzers, forty elderly 6-in. howitzers and three of 15-in. howitzers of the Royal Marine Artillery.

Gun type	Available to the BEF June 1915	Total Field and Heavy guns/howitzers
18-pdr QF Field Gun	803	968
4.5-in. QF Howitzer	165	
60-pdr BL Mk I Gun	36	105
6-in. Mk VII Gun	8	
6-in. 30 cwt Howitzer	40	
8-in. Howitzer	4	
9.2-in. BL Mk I Siege Howitzer	14	
15-in. BL Siege Howitzer	3	

Table 23 Guns and howitzers available to the BEF, June 1915[50]

In the light of the shortfalls in production highlighted in Table 22, a conference with the French was held on 19th and 20th June 1915 in Boulogne attended by Lloyd George, in his role as Minister of Munitions, and Albert Thomas, *sous-secrétaire d'État à l'artillerie et à l'équipement militaire* (Under Secretary of State for artillery and military equipment, 'munitions' was substituted for military equipment in October 1915). Discussions took place on gun and ammunition supply, and focused on the need for the BEF to receive large numbers of heavy guns and howitzers. The French intended to match the number of field guns, i.e. *75s* and *95s*, with equal numbers of heavy guns and howitzers of 155-mm (6-in.) and larger, because *GQG* was demanding 'more guns... heavier guns and ... more ammunition for heavy guns'. Their current position was that, on active fronts, they had achieved a ratio of one heavy gun to every three field guns. Ammunition supply, however, still lagged, but, as far as shells were concerned, the French argued all heavy guns should fire HE exclusively and fuzes should be a combination of direct action, i.e. exploding on contact, and delayed action.[51]

After the conference Sir John French submitted an outline of what was needed as soon as possible and what would be required in the Spring of 1916. By that time what the CinC wanted to see on the Western Front was:

Per division: 48 18-pdrs, 16 4.5-in. howitzers, 8 60-pdrs, 8 6-in. howitzers
Per Corps: 16 8-in. or 9.2-in. howitzers
Per Army: 8 12-in. or 15-in. howitzers

These proposals were adopted, altered, and finally greatly expanded in the two months after the Boulogne conference.

On 22nd June, Kitchener advised French current plans would produce:

32 12-in. howitzers
48 9.2-in. howitzers
32 8-in. howitzers
80 6-in. 30 cwt & 64 6-in. 26 cwt howitzers
180 60-pdr. guns.

In addition, Kitchener believed it prudent to order a further:

32 9.2-in. howitzers
80 6-in. 26 cwt howitzers
100 60-pdr. guns

Sir John, invited to give his opinions on these numbers, responded by setting out his understanding of the German artillery as of May 1915. This consisted of:

7,150 field guns and howitzers; and
3,350 heavy guns and howitzers (i.e. 5.9-in. [15-cm] and over)[52]

In other words, a ratio of nearly one heavy gun/howitzer for every two field guns/howitzers. This had been achieved since the beginning of the war by, as Sir John understood it, the Germans concentrating on developing their heavy artillery at the expense of the field artillery.

French then invited Kitchener to contemplate the following statement:

"Comparing the above with the situation of the British Army I find that I have at my disposal at the present time:
Guns
Field Guns 1,080
Guns & howitzers between 4.5-in. and 5-in calibre (both inclusive) 336
Guns & howitzers, 6-in. and upwards 71
Total 1,487"

Although it appeared to the British CinC both the German and French Armies were doing away with medium guns equivalent to the 4.5-in. howitzer and 60-pdr. he was reluctant to follow suit unless and until the supply of heavier guns and shells expanded greatly. Guns he was quite happy to see removed were the 15-pdr. BLC field gun, a short-ranged stopgap introduced in 1907, and 4.7-in. gun which, unfortunately, was to remain in service well beyond 1st July 1916.

French then set out his requirements for heavy guns and howitzers:

1. The replacement of the 4.7 with 60-pdrs. by the end of summer 1915;
2. The attachment of a 60-pdr. battery to every newly arrived division;
3. A 6-in. howitzer battery per division as soon as possible, and one attached to every new division sent to the Western Front;
4. Two batteries of either 8-in. or 9.2-in. howitzers for every Army Corps;
5. One battery of 12-in. or 15-in. howitzers be attached to every Army;
6. That these numbers should be doubled by the Spring of 1916; so that
7. By March 1916 a BEF of some 50 divisions would contain:

60-pdrs	400
6-in. howitzers	400
8-in./9.2-in. howitzers	250
12-in./15-in. howitzers	40
Total	1,090

Kitchener forwarded French's letter to Lloyd George at the end of June, adding that more were needed to replace losses. And, as he envisaged a 70-division army, more were needed to equip these divisions too. The final figures were:

Gun type	No. required	In existence or ordered	Balance required
60-pdrs	800	200	600[1]
6-in. howitzers	560	160	400
8-in./9.2-in. howitzers	372	80	292[2]
12-in./15-in. howitzers	60	40	20
Totals	1792	480	1312

Table 24 Numbers of guns required by the BEF, June 1915

[1] It was thought possible 100 4.7-in guns might be 'improved' and included in this figure.
[2] On 13th July 40 6-in. naval guns were made available for conversion to 8-in. howitzers.

In addition, the Director of Artillery also gave figures for the numbers of 18-pdr. and 4.5-in. howitzers required by 30th June 1916. These totalled:

3,407 18-pdrs.
1,284 4.5-in. howitzers

The Director, however, had a larger number fixed for the 60-pdrs, i.e. 752, or 652 if the 4.7-in. guns could be improved sufficiently.

Guns without shells are so much expensive ironmongery and the Director had figures for the number of rounds *per month* needed by July 1916: 2,520,000 rounds of 18-pdr. shell; 672,000 of 4.5-in. shell; and 336,000 of 60-pdr. shell. In meetings with the manufacturers on 5th and 9th July 1915 they were asked to assess how many of each type they might deliver by Spring, 1916. The estimates were then discounted by the Ministry in the light of failings to meet delivery dates for existing orders and went to Kitchener on 13th July. Sir Édouard Percy Cranwill Girouard, managing director at *Elswick*, was then briefly brought in to act as Director General of Munitions (he was unable to work with Lloyd George and left after six weeks). He looked at the numbers and declared that, excepting the 18-pdrs. and 12-in. and 15-in. howitzers, it was impossible to build the numbers required by 31st March 1916. Indeed, they would not be reached even by September 1916. Table 25 shows by how much Girouard's estimates undermined the hoped-for supplies of 60-pdr and medium/heavy howitzers needed for the campaigns of summer 1916:

Gun type	Number required (in addition to stocks as of 30th June 1915)		Estimated deliveries		Shortfall
	By 31.3.16	By 30.6.16	To 31.3.16	To 30.9.16	
18-pdr guns	2680	3407	2680	3407	0
4.5-in. how	1000	1284	667	1284	0
60-pdrs	560	752	247	585	167
6-in. how	474	474	83	327	147
8-in./9.2-in. how	330	330	8	8	158
			48	164	
12-in./15-in. how	55	55	47	47	0
			8	5	

Table 25 Estimated shortfall in gun/howitzer deliveries March & September 1916

Despite these shortfalls, the estimates circulated on 14th July became the basis of 'Gun Programme A'.[53] The concern about these agreed numbers was the 30%

shortfall of medium and heavy howitzers, the types of weapons around which Ferdinand Foch's new ideas about tactics, developed after the summer and autumn 1915 fighting in Artois, were to depend.

Gun type	1915				1916		Max
	Jun	Aug	Oct	Dec	Jan	Mar	
13-pdr	114	145	172	212	242	312	356
15-pdr	228	228	228	228	0	0	0
18-pdr	1700	2200	2780	3420	3740	4380	5107
4.5-in. How.	334	476	596	806	966	1334	1618
5-in. How.	80	80	80	80	80	80	0
60-pdr	68	162	264	408	480	628	820
4.7-in.	88	88	88	88	88	88	0
6-in. Gun	8	20	24	24	24	24	0
6-in. How.	86	64	88	100	108	192	560
8-in. How.	24	24	24	32	40	48	56
9.2-in. How.	18	16	26	30	34	42	53
12-in. How.	1	2	6	12	16	20	28
15-in. How.	4						

Table 26 Gun Programme A, July 1915

With the new guns coming on stream, others were to be withdrawn: all 15-pdr. guns by the end of 1915, and 5-in. howitzers and 4.7-in. guns were to go in 1916.

Before Gun Programme A was even promulgated French asked for changes in the timetable for delivery of certain gun types. On 8th July he wrote to the War Office explaining these variations and suggesting his Artillery Adviser, Maj. Gen John Du Cane, might usefully return to London to join the Ministry of Munitions to explain the new requirements. In the light of these requests Gun Programme B was produced on 28th July (see Table 27 below):

Gun type	1915		1916				Total	By
	Jun	Dec	Mar	Jun	Sept	Dec		
18-pdr	1700	3420	4380	5107	5107	5107	5107	30.6.16
4.5-How	334	709	1001	1301	1618	1618	1618	30.9.16
60-pdr	68	207	339	519	759	801	801	31.10.16
6-How	86	118	198	362	560	560	560	30.9.16
8-How	24	37	52	72	72	72	72	31.5.16
9.2-How	18	42	68	94	174	252	270[1]	31.12.16
12-How	1	33	48	48	48	48	48	30.3.16

Table 27 Gun Programme B, 28th July 1915

[1] Shortfall to revised total of 300 to be made up in early 1917.

This effectively ignored Girouard's concerns about deliveries and now stated that not only could the full delivery of 6-in. howitzers be completed by September 1916, but the number delivered by the end of March 1916 might be 252 instead of 198. Furthermore, it was hoped other programmes for which there were delays – 60-pdrs, 8-in. and 9.2-in. howitzers – might be completed by the end of 1916.

These recommendations still did not meet French's demands of 8th July (although his requirements were still based on a 50 Division Army not the 70 Division Army allowed for in London). The principal difference between Gun Programme A and French's fresh demands lay with medium and heavy howitzers. Gun Programme A allowed for the following numbers by the end of March 1916:

6-in. howitzers	192
8-in. howitzers	56
9.2-in. howitzers	102
12-in. howitzers	44
Total	394

French was asking for 360, 114, 114 and 28 respectively by March (616 guns), an increase of c. 56% including doubling the number of 8-in. howitzers and an 88% increase in 6-in. howitzers.[54] Gun Programme B, therefore, did not come close to answering French's demands for more medium and heavy howitzers.

The discrepancy between the programme's total of 8-in./9.2-in. howitzers and Sir John's demands highlighted a misunderstanding about these guns. The Ministry believed the only source of 8-in. howitzers was converted 6-in. naval guns, whereas specifications and drawings existed for an 8-in. BL Mk VI Howitzer, a wheeled gun with greater range and better mobility than the 9.2-in. Mk I.

Gun Programme B called for 342 of these two howitzers by the end of 1916. Forty-two existed and 300 needed building. The Ministry believed these would be made up of 48 converted 6-in. guns, and the balance by 252 new 9.2-in. howitzers. Contracts for 156 were given to *Vickers* (120) and *Beardmore* (36) while, on 4th August, discussions started with *Bethlehem* for 200 to be supplied from 1st February at a rate of c. one a day[i]. This was described to the company's management as like asking for a 'semi-miracle' but, on 6th August, they replied they would 'undertake anything that is humanly possible'.[55] Their London representative commented 'our friends (in London) expect from you the superhumanly possible'.

It was pointed out a 8-in. Mk VI howitzer was a simpler design than the 9.2-in Mk I and easier and quicker to construct. Shell production would also be 25% quicker. *Armstrong* reckoned they might build 40 8-in. howitzers by 30th June 1916, but only twelve 9.2s by the same date. *Beardmore's* response was similar: 14 8-in. howitzers by the end of March or eight 9.2s. Thereafter, they could build 16 of the new howitzers a month against eight of the older model. It was then suggested the 9.2s ordered from *Bethlehem* should be replaced by 8-in. howitzers. GHQ advised the Ministry they would accept 100 modern 8-in. howitzers and sixty 9.2s if the smaller gun was quicker and easier to build. Tests of a *Vickers* 8-in. howitzer on 20th August proved highly successful and it was immediately incorporated into the programme. It was a good gun but, as things too often turn out in war, it was slow in arriving, the first order for fifty of the guns not being placed until March 1916.

Lloyd George, hyperactive as ever, determined 1916 was to be the war's critical year. 1915 was disastrous for Russia with its collapse during the Gorlice–Tarnów campaign resulting in the Great Retreat from the front running around Warsaw and down through Galicia. In early August, the failure of the attempt to break

---

[i] One every 1½ days to be exact.

open the Gallipoli campaign with the landing at Suvla Bay confirmed L-G of this view and he determined the British should, somehow, put 100 divisions into the field for 1916. As Minister of Munitions he was determined to see they were properly armed and equipped. As a result, he came up with Gun Programme C1.

Encouraged by the counterattack at Hooge on 9th August when a trench lost in the first liquid fire attack on 30th July was regained with support from five 9.2 and 8-in. howitzers. some 60-pdr. and 6-in. guns, and two *'groupes'* of *75s* from the French *36e Corps*, L-G decided success lay with a vast expansion of the BEF's heavy artillery. On 24th August, he asked by how much gun manufacturing capacity might be increased both in Britain and the USA and Canada. The Deputy Director General in the Department of Munitions Supply, Mr Ellis, was pessimistic. What *could* be done was *being* done. Throwing money at the problem would not help if there was no spare capacity into the system. In the USA, *Bethlehem* was already dealing with an order for 400 18-pdr. guns (soon to be substantially delayed by a German-sponsored arson attack) and discussions were ongoing concerning a large order for modern 8-in. and 9.2-in. howitzers. The other US company capable of such large projects, *Midvale Steel*, currently refused to sell ordnance to any combatant. It was not until William Ellis Corey, previously of *Carnegie Steel* heading a consortium funded by New York banks including Percy A Rockefeller, bought the company in September 1915 that it started to bid for these lucrative contracts. Its name was then changed to the *Midvale Steel and Ordnance Co*.

Despite this down-beat assessment L-G was unconvinced and pressed the issue. On 26th August, he unilaterally decided the gun programme must supply a 100-division Army with a 10 to 25% margin to account for future losses and unforeseen eventualities. The numbers involved were substantial:

Gun type	For 100 divisions	Existing pre-war	Ordered/delivered	Balance required
AA Guns	250[1]	0[8]	0	250
18-pdr	6000[2]	897	4210	893
4.5-in. how.	1920[3]	169	1449	302
60-pdr	920[4]	31	769	120
6-in. how.	880[5]	86	474	320
8/9.2-in. how.	580[6]	1	371	208
12/15-in. how.	97[7]	0	60	37
Total	10647	1192	7333	2130

Table 28 Gun Programme C1, 26th August 1915

[1] Included an additional margin of 25%, i.e. 50 guns
[2] Additional margin 25%, 1,200 guns
[3] Additional margin 20%, 320 guns
[4] Additional margin 15%, 120 guns
[5] Additional margin 10%, 80 guns
[6] Additional margin 10%, 52 guns
[7] Additional margin 10%, 9 guns
[8] 114 13-pdr Mk III guns were in use

Negotiations with *Bethlehem* revealed that switching from the 9.2-in. to an 8-in. howitzer could sharply speed up production of the 200 guns ordered. *Midvale Steel's* ownership change opened another avenue of production and approaches to them and other US companies based on a minimum two-year contract were looked at. Huge sums were allocated and the programme submitted for approval but contract delays (1st October for 4.5-in. howitzers and 15th November for 9.2-in. howitzers with *Bethlehem* and 1st April with *Midvale*) undermined deliveries of these guns.

Undaunted, L-G ordered large numbers independent of the War Office and the Army Council. He was not long out on a limb, however, as the War Office swiftly decided Gun Programme B inadequate. As ever, the key concern was the provision of medium and heavy howitzers. The question was: could delivery be speeded up and could yet more be built? If the answer was 'yes', the Army Council wanted 160 more 6-in. howitzers, 112 8-in./9.2-in. howitzers, and 16 12-in. howitzers, or a total of 288 guns. The result was Gun Programme C below:

Gun type								
18-pdr	60-pdr	4.5-in. H	6-in. H	8-in. H	9.2-in. H	12-in. H		Total
4300	852	1586	894	439	359	84		8514

Table 29 Gun Programme C, 8th September 1915
Guns ordered and to be ordered in addition to those in existence as of 1st July 1915

How this affected gun deliveries is shown in Table 30. The delivery of 18-pdrs slowed dramatically after the 1st quarter, 1916, as *Bethlehem Steel's* 4.5-in. howitzer contract disrupted their production. Nevertheless, Gun Programme C suggested a significant firepower increase for the BEF prior to a summer 1916 offensive.

1915	18-pdr	60-pdr	4.5-in. H	6-in. H	8-in. H	9.2-in. H	12-in. H
July	235	8	42	0	0	2	4
Aug.	290	5	43	2	0	4	0
Sept.	334	16	52	8	2	4	5
Oct.	363	24	75	6	3	4	7
Nov.	370	28	75	9	3	4	7
Dec.	370	36	88	16	11	6	6
1916							
Jan.	370	43	111	37	12	8	5
Feb.	370	50	96	58	21	10	5
Mar.	251	52	108	63	31	15	0
April	64	68	127	70	29	16	0
May	70	81	140	70	29	21	0
June	20	81	160	85	29	30	0
Total	3047	492	1177	424	170	124	39
July-Dec.	360	361	467	275	69	163	0
Total	3407	853	1584	694	239[1]	287[2]	39

Table 30 Deliveries under Gun Programme C[56]

[1] Includes 48 converted 6-in. naval guns   [2] 73 more to be delivered by Bethlehem

These guns were to be built by:

Company	Gun type							
	18-pdr	4.5-in. How.	60-pdr	6-in. How.	8-in. How.	9.2-in. How.	12-in. How.	Total
Armstrong	1156	0	597	0	98	0	32	1883
Vickers	1212	0	36	484	1	191	8	1932
Coventry	0	1176	0	0	0	0	0	1176
Beardmore	359	0	0	180	92	0	0	631
Coventry	30	258	220	0	48	0	0	556
Bethlehem	550	150	0	0	0	62	0	762
Total	3307	1584	853	664	239	253	40	6940

Table 31 Companies building guns for Gun Programme C[57]

It should be noted that, in the main, the performance of *Bethlehem Steel* was poor, even making allowances for a German-sponsored arson attack in November 1915 affecting the 18-pdr. and 4.5-in. howitzer contracts. Delivery of nearly every order was late, with most not arriving until 1917. Generally, US prices were far higher and deliveries far worse than British suppliers. Whilst domestic suppliers allowed for a price reduction after the initial investment in plant and machinery was made (often paid for by the British government), US suppliers did not, thereby increasing their already higher profit margins. This plant and machinery was then further exploited when it came to supplying arms to the US Government after the USA entered the war. As in both world wars, and ever since, few US corporations have allowed a world crisis to get in the way of a cynically excessive profit.

IN ORDER TO MAN ALL OF THE GUNS ORDERED the Army would have to find 6,876 officers and 162,328 other ranks, a feat Lord Kitchener later deemed impossible[i], and about which he was unaware at the time as Lloyd George's initiatives had not been passed through the War Office. By the end of September, however, it was clear the Ministry had been unable to place orders for 200 each of the 6-in. and 8-in. howitzers. The number of orders placed still represented a significant surplus over the War Office's estimates and, on 1st October, the Army Council wrote to Lloyd George to suggest some of this surplus might be sent to assist the Russians. Otherwise, they considered the numbers ordered at the end of August to be sufficient for the Army's needs.

During this period, however, the Battle of Loos opened with moderate immediate, if very local, success on the part of Haig's First Army. It had since settled down into a costly and incompetently administered slog with British losses more than double that of the Germans (59,000 v. 26,000). The French attacks in

---

[i] The strength of the RGA stood at 1,174 officers and 26,101 Other Ranks in August 1914. By the beginning of July 1916 this grew to 3,659 officers and 107,361 Other Ranks. The numbers peaked in August 1918 at 9,552 officers and 196,971 Other Ranks, some 7½ times larger than the RGA four years earlier [*Source: Statistics of the Military Effort of the British Empire during the Great War 1914-1920*, HMSO, 1922, page 211].

Champagne and Artois were bogged down in a similar fashion but enjoyed considerably greater success on the opening day of each offensive and been greatly assisted by their heavy artillery in so doing. By now, though, Lloyd George was already looking to the Spring and believed an influx of heavy artillery along the lines he proposed might be the game changer in any new offensive. The War Office, however, was still concerned about where the Army might find the necessary officers with the skills to command this number of guns and Kitchener again argued any spare guns over the current accepted orders be sent to Russia, and these guns be adapted to take Russian ammunition. Russia, after all, had always been beset by a shortage of heavy artillery and this had been substantially exacerbated by the disastrous summer on the Eastern Front.

The issue was raised at the Allied conference in November 1915. Russia had asked for 1,000 4.5-in. howitzers as well as a significant number of heavy howitzers and long guns. The French, however, did not wish to see heavy guns needed for the Western Front sent east where, anyway, defences on both sides of No Man's Land were far less robust than in France and Flanders. Field howitzers were another matter and Britain agreed to supply the Russians with 300 4.5-in. howitzers for delivery between February and April 1916. Furthermore, spare capacity in a contract established with *Midvale* for 200 6-in. and 200 8-in. howitzers was transferred to Russia who placed an order in April.

The fighting at Loos in September and October proved an interesting test for the various guns in the BEF's armoury. It not only tested their abilities but also their limitations over an extended battle. Sir John French was particularly impressed with the 6-in. howitzers. He wanted two batteries each of four guns for every division but currently there were only eighteen batteries and of these 72 guns thirteen, i.e. 18%, were nearly worn out reducing the number of batteries to fifteen. In spite of the BEF's pleas for more of these guns, it was becoming apparent the ambitious plans for the supply of them, and others, were just that – ambitious. A Ministry of Munitions forecast for 11th December suggested only 67 would arrive in France by the end of March 1916. The problem lay with sub-contractors working for *Vickers* who were due to deliver 150 of these pieces. Although the gun tubes themselves were being produced to timetable, there was a problem with the gun carriages others were making. On 13th December, the Army Council advised the soon-to-depart French that, whilst 67 6-in. howitzers would be delivered to the Army by 31st March not all of them would be coming to the BEF but, as yet it was not possible to say with precision how many would arrive, or even when.

On 23rd December 1915 the new CinC, Douglas Haig, heard from the Ministry that gun deliveries in the first nine months of 1916 would be 5% lower than forecast – 7,516 instead of 7,908. The shortfall would mainly be with the much needed 6-in. and new 8-in. howitzers. The cause was a lack of specialist labour in the various factories, exacerbated by skilled workers chasing better pay and conditions around the various arms companies. This problem was eventually resolved by clauses in the *Munitions of War Act 1915*[i] (amended 1916 and 1917).[58]

---

[i] The *Munitions of War Act* was passed in July 1915 bringing private armaments companies under the control of the Ministry of Munitions. It also prevented skilled

In addition, the production of the machine tools needed to allow for the expansion of output was running well behind expectations and this, too, contributed to delays. But there were other problems. There was a substantial lack of accredited inspectors and examiners trained to ensure guns coming off the production line were correctly constructed. Enormous efforts were made throughout 1915 to increase the numbers of such men and, by February 1916, there were 135 inspectors and assistant inspectors and 5,482 examiners and other staff working in the numerous gun factories across the country, an increase from just 365 the year before. In spite of this, however, it was the case certain heavy guns were still issued to the Army without the normal firing proof.[59] There were, in addition, a number of union demarcation disputes and, increasingly, strikes. The introduction of women workers was not universally welcomed by the Trades Unions, nor were unskilled Irish workers or, indeed, military working parties[i]. Such changes provoked demarcation disputes which disrupted production as early as 1916 and in that year Coventry, the heartland of 4.5-in. field howitzer production, was hit by strikes.[60] Thus, even as the initial German success at Verdun was giving added and urgent impetus to the demands for more medium and heavy howitzers, not everyone involved in the work of the war was pulling in the same direction.

ENDNOTES:

[1] Davenport-Hines, R P T, *Dudley Docker: The Life and Times of a Trade Warrior*, Cambridge University Press, 2002, p. 490

[2] *History of the Ministry of Munitions*, Vol. 1, Part 1, page 98.

[3] *BOH, France and Flanders 1915*, Vol. 1, page 58.

[4] *History of the Ministry of Munitions*, Vol. 1, Part 1, page 92.

[5] *BOH, France and Flanders 1915*, Vol. 1, page 58.

[6] *History of the Ministry of Munitions*, Vol. X, Part 1, page 1.

[7] *History of the Ministry of Munitions*, Vol. X, Part 1, page 3.

[8] *BOH, France & Belgium 1914*, Vol. 2, page 12.

[9] Vincent, Capt. B, *Artillery at the Battle of the Yalu, The Russo-Japanese War: Reports from British Officers Attached to the Japanese and Russian Forces in the Field*, HMSO, page 51.

[10] *Reports of Military Observers Attached to the Armies in Manchuria During the Russo-Japanese War* (volume 2) United States War Department: Office of the Chief of Staff (Military Information Division), US Govt. Printing Office, 1906, page 31.

[11] Ibid., Volume I, page 42.

[12] Ibid., page 47.

[13] Ibid., page 47.

[14] *BOH, France & Belgium 1916*, Vol. 1, page 123.

[15] *History of the Ministry of Munitions*, Vol. IX, page 60.

[16] Ibid., page 120.

---

workers from moving from one 'Controlled Establishment' under the Act to another without the agreement of the existing employer, which consent was rarely given.

[i] Industrial relations continued to be fraught during the war. In 1915 there were 707 trades disputes which led to the loss of over 3 million working days. In 1916 disputes led to the loss of more than 2.5 million working days. There were four disputes in munitions factories in 1916 [*Source: BOH, France and Belgium, 1916,* Vol. 1, page 120].

17 *History of the Ministry of Munitions*, Vol. IX, page 64.
18 Ibid., pages 68-9.
19 *BOH, France & Belgium 1916*, Vol. 1, page 122.
20 *History of the Ministry of Munitions*, Vol. X, page 58.
21 Du Cane, *Report on the Effect of Possible Modification of Design of Shells and Fuses*, 7th February 1916, NA.
22 Farndale. Gen. Sir Martin, *History of the Royal Regiment of Artillery, Western Front 1914–18*. London: Royal Artillery Institution, 1986, page 104.
23 *BOH, France & Belgium 1915*, Vol. 2, footnote page 33.
24 *History of the Ministry of Munitions*, Vol. X, pages 67-8.
25 Ibid., page 122.
26 Ibid., page 75
27 *History of the Ministry of Munitions*, Vol. X, pages 70-71.
28 Farndale, op. cit., page 342
29 *BOH, France & Belgium 1915*, Vol. 2, page 122.
30 *History of the Ministry of Munitions*, Vol. X, footnote 4, page 75.
31 Ibid.
32 *History of the Ministry of Munitions*, Vol. X, footnote 4, page 75
33 *Neue Zürcher Zeitung, American Arms Suppliers*, 1915, No. 485, 23rd April, 1915.
34 Tavenner, Hon. C H, *The Navy League Unmasked*, House of Representatives, 15th December 1915, Government Printing Office, 1916, page 6.
35 Midvale Steel Company, *Midvale 1867-1942*, Midvale Steel Company, 1942, pages 11-20.
36 Engelbrecht H C & Hanighen F C, *Merchants of Death*, Dodd, Mead & Co., 1934.
37 Ibid.
38 Ibid.
39 *Congressional Record containing the Proceedings and Debates of the 63rd Congress*, Third Session, Volume LII, Part VI, Appendix and Index, *How the Ear Trust is Robbing the Government while driving us on Toward the Brink* of war, extension of remarks of Hon. Clyde H Tavenner of Illinois in the House of Representatives, 15th February 1915, Govt. Printing Office, 1915, page 417 onwards.
40 Ibid., pages 418-9.
41 Ibid.
42 Ibid., page 420.
43 Ibid.
44 Ibid.
45 Ibid., page 421.
46 Tavenner, Hon. C H, *The Navy League Unmasked*, op. cit., page 2.
47 *History of the Ministry of Munitions*, Vol. I, Part 1, page 16.
48 Ibid., page 34.
49 Ibid., page 25.
50 *BOH, France & Belgium 1915*, Vol. 1, page 55.
51 *Ibid.*, page 29.
52 *History of the Ministry of Munitions*, Vol. X, Part 1, page 6.
53 Ibid., page 10.
54 Ibid., page 12.
55 Ibid., page 14.
56 Ibid., page 22.
57 Ibid., page 23.
58 *History of the Ministry of Munitions*, Vol. X, Part 2, page 85.
59 *History of the Ministry of Munitions*, Vol. X, Part 2, pages 80-1.
60 Ibid., page 86.

14. A Very British Shell Crisis

"When the war broke out France mobilised the whole of her industry in precisely the same way in which she mobilised her troops. Have we done, and are we doing, the same?"

Andrew Bonar Law
House of Commons, 1st March 1915

IF THE NUMBERS OF GUNS WERE INADEQUATE, supplies of ammunition for those guns were equally parlous. Towards the end of the South African War, Sir Francis Mowatt chaired a War Office committee to look into future ammunition provision. The committee's plans were based on maintaining an Expeditionary Force of six infantry and one cavalry division for a war of similar duration to that in South Africa. Its recommendations were accepted in 1904. Despite the adoption of a quick-firing 18-pdr., and the imminent arrival of a quick-firing 4.5-in. howitzer, shell supplies for the Expeditionary Force were not altered, even though the production of small arms ammunition *was* increased in 1912. But the significant costs involved in increasing shell supplies, with the associated costs of transport, etc., was not something politicians were yet ready to address. As a result, pre-war, shell reserves and shell production were at a dangerously low level.[1]

Gun type	Reserves (rounds/gun)	No. of guns	Total reserves	Estimated monthly production
13-pdr	1900	30	57000	10000
18-pdr	1500	324	486000	10000
4.5-in. how.	1200	108	129600	10000
60-pdr	1000	24	24000	100

Table 32 British shells supplies on the outbreak of war

The numbers under 'Reserves (rounds/gun)', do not indicate what was available at the front. 528 rounds went to France with each 18-pdr, of which 176 were immediately available to the gun crew and 472 in reserve on the Lines of Communication. The remaining 500 stayed in Britain.[2] Broadly, therefore, for the opening six months of any Continental war, each 18-pdr had a daily shell allowance of less than ten rounds. Or, to look at it another way, each gun had enough shells immediately available, i.e. 176, to fire for 44 minutes at the 'sustained rate' of 4 rounds per minute (just eight minutes at the maximum rate of fire of 20 rpm).[3] Thereafter, they had enough shells in the system to fire at a 'sustained rate' for another 3 hours and 25 minutes. The reserves from Britain would keep the guns firing for another two hours. Pre-war it was thought these figures, plus an additional supply of 500 rounds per 18-pdr and 400 per field howitzer manufactured in the interim, should be sufficient in a war of movement with occasional and brief battles.[4] Experience suggested allowances five times greater were none too many. It was then found domestic production could not keep up partly because of the huge demands placed on existing production capacity, and partly through the pre-war erosion of capacity and a lack of investment.

Despite evidence from Manchuria and the Balkans of very high consumption, it became obvious every nation grossly underestimated the incredible rate of expenditure of shells. British reaction to the evidence from these wars was to preach economy rather than increase supply and capacity. This parsimonious attitude persisted, with senior officers such as Sir William Robertson laughing up their sleeve at French willingness to bang away at the slightest provocation even in 1916.

The British who, like the French, envisaged a war of manoeuvre and short if intense battles, compounded these shortages by supplying each type of gun wholly, in the case of the 18-pdrs, or mainly, in the case of the field howitzers, with anti-personnel shrapnel. This they believed was the best shell to be used in the artillery's role of supporting the infantry attack through the neutralisation, not destruction, of the enemy's infantry. Then, though not with the same immediate urgency, the call, as in France, was soon for large quantities of high explosive shells, something which the British armaments industry was peculiarly ill-equipped to supply.

At the end of the Battle of the *Aisne*, on 28th September, Sir John French complained his 18-pdr. guns were firing twice as many shells per day as were received in new supplies. In October, he limited guns to 20 rounds per day, but even this meant consumption outran supply. During the month's fierce fighting around Ypres in October and November 1914 some field guns were restricted to just four rounds per day to allow for heavier expenditure at times of 'crisis'.

The solution to this problem took a long time and huge amounts of money to resolve, but the severity of the shell shortage in the opening nine months of the war would bring down the last Liberal government of Great Britain.

Gun type	Shells required/gun/day	Shells/gun/day received in December
13-pdr	50 (25 HE)	0.84
18-pdr	50 (25 HE)	6 (0.24 HE)
4.5-in. how.	40 (35 HE)	4.6 (2.2 HE)
60-pdr	25 (15 HE)	0
6-in. how.	25 (All HE)	4.6 (All HE)
4.7-in. gun	25 (15 HE)	7.6 (4 HE)
6-in. gun	25 (All HE)	6.3 (0.4 HE)
9.2-in. how.	12 (All HE)	5.8 (All HE)

Table 33 BEF daily shell requirements and supply, December 1914

War experience confirmed the fundamental failings of both the current system of arms and ammunition supply as well as the need for a far larger supply of high explosive shells for all natures, particularly the 18-pdrs. which went to war with only shrapnel[i]. The lamentable story of shell supplies for the BEF was, therefore, a smaller scale replica of that of the French Army. By 16th December 1914, the 18-pdrs. had just 648 rounds for each gun (instead of the required 1,000) and the 4.5-in. howitzers just 200 (instead of 800). The reason for this was the almost complete failure of the British shell supply system (see Table 33 above) which meant that the two most numerous guns available to Sir John French, the field guns and

---

[i] 1,000 18-pdr HE shells arrived in France on 19th October 1914 but were for 'trial and report' [*Source: BOH, France & Belgium 1914*, Vol. 2, footnote page 16].

howitzers, were receiving barely 10% of the shells needed, and a fundamental problem in the supply of explosive meant only 9.7% of HE shells ordered were being provided.[5]

A Cabinet *Munitions Committee* was set up in October and, amongst other decisions, large sums of money were committed to the expansion of domestic explosives and ammunition supplies as well as to the placing of large orders for munitions from both British and United States-based private companies.

Basic shell production increased at a phenomenal rate after the outbreak of the war, as the figures for 18-pdr. rounds manufactured per month show:

July 1914 monthly production	8,000 rounds
September 1914 monthly production	10,000 rounds
November 1914 monthly production	45,000 rounds
January 1915 monthly production	93,000 rounds
March 1915 monthly production	174,000 rounds
April 1915 monthly production	225,000 rounds

Of course, the number of divisions on the Western Front and, therefore, the number of attached 18-pdr and 4.5-in. howitzer batteries had also sharply increased so, although the total number of rounds increased significantly, the numbers of rounds per gun per day received was still extremely limited. In April 1915 the number of rounds per gun per day supplied were:

18-pdr.	10.6 rounds per gun per day
4.5-in. howitzer	8.2 per gun per day
9.2-in. howitzer	5 per gun per day
15-in. howitzer	1 per gun per day

The effect was that Sir John French further reduced the daily allowance of 18-pdr. and 4.5-in. howitzer shells from the ten and eight per gun respectively in February 1915 to three in April, none of which were to be high explosive shells.

This elimination of high explosive shells from the daily expenditure of these guns highlighted the extreme problems experienced in the supply of explosive for these shells. The 18-pdr. batteries went to war supplied with 100% shrapnel and the 4.5-in. howitzers with 70% shrapnel (underlining the idea these guns were regarded as anti-personnel weapons rather than ones capable of destroying elements of the enemy's defences). This was despite recent evidence in the Balkans where the Serb and Bulgarian artillery achieved encouraging results using high explosive shells against Turkish trenches and earthworks. The French, meanwhile, swiftly determined high explosive shells were the way forward in modern warfare.

The success of the 1,000 experimental HE 18-pdr. shells sent out in October 1914 underlined the need for a large regular supply and a ratio of 50/50 shrapnel to HE was demanded by the BEF. Manufacturers were in a quandary as to how to meet this demand. Converting existing systems for shrapnel manufacture only reduced the supply of shrapnel without providing any immediate HE shells, and introducing entirely new processes and equipment for the mass manufacture of HE shells only served to delay the delivery of the HE shells for which contracts existed. The result was a lengthy delay in the supply of HE shells for both 18-pdrs. and howitzers and a dramatic failure to fulfil contracts for both. By May 1915, only

52,000 (11%) of the 481,000 18-pdr. HE shells and 73,772 (34%) field howitzer shells out of 220,000 ordered had been delivered. Ironically, although a problem, this was not a disaster as experience of the new German defences had shown HE shell from either of these guns was inadequate to the task of their destruction. Available HE was now to fill medium and heavy howitzers shells and, on 19th April 1915, GHQ determined a ratio of 70/30 shrapnel/HE for 18-pdrs. was the best balance and these proportions applied up to and beyond 1st July 1916. At the same time the demand was for 80% of field howitzer shells to be HE with 50/50 for 4.7-in. guns and 60-pdrs.[6]

Throughout this period the press stirred up the public over the 'shell crisis'. Brought to a head by *The Times'* description of the disastrous attack on Aubers Ridge in early May 1915, it was a crisis triggered by Sir John French's direct contact with military correspondent Charles à Court Repington. Damning correspondence about munitions between French and the War Office was leaked to Lloyd George, Arthur Balfour and Bonar Law by French's military secretary, Lt. Col. Brinsley Fitzgerald[i], and ADC, Capt. Frederick Guest[ii], sent to London for this specific purpose.[7] Fitzgerald and Guest pursued their political targets between 12th and 14th May and Repington's damning piece appeared on 15th May. The crisis brought down the Government and French got his way with the appointment of Lloyd George as Minister of Munitions, he being one of the few army officers to have any time for the Welsh radical. French later suggested his removal as CinC of the BEF was retaliation for his direct interference in the workings of Westminster and Whitehall. His general incompetence, culminating in the fiasco of the use of reserves at Loos on 25th/26th September 1915, was not, as far he was concerned, a factor. French convinced himself he was a martyr to the cause of the successful prosecution of the war though quite how he believed he might continue as CinC after meddling directly in affairs of state when most of the politicians he upset continued in government is anyone's guess. His post-Loos demise in December 1915 was, however, long overdue even if his successor's battlefield track record was no better than his own.

One of the most damaging documents included in the briefs delivered to the three politicians and *The Times* was one entitled *Percentage of high explosive received since first application for it in increased quantities*. It read as follows:

---

[i] Lt. Col. Brinsley Fitzgerald (1859-1931), CB, 2nd Co. of London (Westminster Dragoons) Yeomanry, TF, was the 4th son of Sir Peter FitzGerald, 1st Baronet of Valencia, 19th Knight of Kerry (1808–1880), and Julia Hussey. Educated at Rugby School and University College, Oxford, he joined the 25th Company, 7th Battalion, Imperial Yeomanry, in 1900 and was French's ADC in South Africa.

[ii] Frederick Edward Guest (1875-1937), CBE, DSO, 4th East Surrey Regt., and 1st Life Guards, was the 3rd son of Ivor Guest, 1st Baron Wimborne, and Lady Cornelia Spencer-Churchill. Served Egypt and South Africa. Liberal MP for East Dorset 1910-22. ADC to French before serving in East Africa. Chief Whip, 'Coalition' Liberals, 1917. Privy Council, 1920. Secretary of State for Air 1921-2. Elected Liberal MP for Stroud, 1923, and Bristol North, 1924. Defeated in 1929, he re-joined the Conservative Party (he left in 1904 over Free Trade) and was elected MP for Plymouth Drake, 1931.

Nature of gun	Dec.	Jan.	Feb.	Mar.	Apr.	May
13-pdr	0%	0%	0%	0%	0%	0%
18-pdr	3.8%	6.8%	8.3%	8.2%	6.1%	8%
4.5-in howitzer	44.4%	68.5%	88%	75%	59%	65%
60-pdr	0%	66%	60%	56%	53%	50%
6-in. howitzer	55%	59%	51%	77%	69%	50%

Table 34 Percentage of high explosive shells received by BEF, December 1914-May 1915[8]

These figures are misleading. There was no demand for 13-pdr. high explosive shell, and 18-pdr. HE shell was only effective against flimsy breastworks when fired from exposed positions close to the front. As the *Official History* points out, GHQ had already concluded the issue was *not* a shortage of 18-pdr HE shells. The *real* problem was insufficient numbers of medium and heavy howitzers and *their* HE shells, an issue which would take far longer to solve. The artillery problem was, therefore, more of a 'howitzer shell crisis' and less a generalised 'shell crisis'.

In May, the War Office limited daily rates of fire for the various natures:

Field Artillery (18-pdrs, 15-pdrs, 4.5-in., 60-pdrs): 17 rounds per day;
4.7-in.: 10 rounds per day; and
Medium and heavy howitzers: 5 rounds per day.

Given the activity in May – Aubers Ridge, Festubert and Second Ypres – Sir John French believed these levels to be far too low and, as part of his campaign to increase munitions supplies, it was pointed out to Lloyd George on 10th May 1915 that at Neuve Chapelle the field guns each fired an average of 120 rounds per day or the equivalent of a week's worth at the then prevailing daily rate.[9]

As Table 35 shows, what French thought necessary as a daily allowance and what the War Office allowed differed widely. The BEF's 'needs' were c. 60% above what the War Office thought prudent given the state of supply. The figures given under '*10th May 1915*' are those demanded by French after Aubers Ridge.

Gun type	Shells required per gun per day at various times			
	Requested by CinC BEF, 31st Dec 14	War Office est., 13th April 15	Requested by CinC BEF, 10th May 15	Requested by CinC BEF, 10th June 15
13-pdr	50	17	24	25
18-pdr	50	17	24	25
4.5-in. how.	40	17	20	20
60-pdr	25	17	16	20
6-in. how.	25	5	12	15
4.7-in. gun	25	10	16	15
6-in. gun	25	-	-	12
9.2-in. how.	12	5	12	12

Table 35 Shells requested and allowed 1914-1915

A more detailed breakdown can be found in French's rather self-serving book *1914*:

Gun type	Guns available	Shells required per gun per day		Total rounds required daily*		Total rounds required	
		Shrapnel	HE	Shrapnel	HE	Daily	Monthly
13-pdr	125	12	12	1500	1500	3000	90000
15-pdr	200	12	12	2500	2500	5000	150000
18-pdr	700	12	12	8500	8500	17000	510000
4.7-in. gun	80	8	8	650	650	1300	39000
60-pdr	28	8	8	250	250	500	15000
4.5-in. how.	130	4	16	500	2000	2500	75000
6-in. how.	40		12		500	500	15000
9.2-in. how.	12		12		150	150	450
Total				13900	16800	29950	894450
Grand total daily				30700			
Grand total monthly				921000			

Table 36 Shells requested by CinC BEF, 10th May 1915
French rounds up his figures creating a discrepancy between 'Grand Totals' and 'Total rounds required'

As a first step to increasing shell supplies Kitchener ordered the workforces at the Royal factories be brought up to full establishment. Under existing plans these factories' output should have been sufficient to supply the existing Expeditionary Force then on the Western Front but the Secretary of State for War had ideas for a vast increase in the size of the Army and this would need an equally vast increase in supplies of equipment, armaments, and ammunition.

Given limitations on rapidly increasing output from existing Government armaments factories, attention turned to the large private arms manufacturers based in Britain: e.g. *Vickers, Armstrong Whitworth* and *Beardmore*. The problem here was these companies were committed to the maintenance and expansion of the Royal Navy which, even now, took priority over the Army's needs. Furthermore, to increase supply of existing munitions or to start production of the new weapons, new plant and machinery were required, as was a trained and skilled workforce. The problem was many of these experienced men were, even now, volunteering in large numbers for service in the Army.

The only plant in the country with a government contract to produce explosives was the *Royal Gunpowder Factory* at Waltham Abbey. Unlike in France, where there was both a mobilisation plan for the Army and a mobilisation plan for industry, Britain had no such contingency system in place. Instead, when contracts were placed for the equipping and maintenance of the Expeditionary Force on 10th August these were divided between the Royal factories and seven private companies which then sub-contracted certain works to other, smaller businesses. Because of the lack of essential staff at the War Office, these contracts were, to all intents and purposes, self-managed by each organisation involved.[10] As a recipe for chaos it was as good as any.

This lack of any coherent plan to bring together the needs of industry and the military was vigorously attacked when the problems of a lack of guns and shells persisted into the Spring of 1915. In a House of Commons debate on 1st March 1915 on the subject of the Supplementary Vote of Credit for 1914-15 and the

Estimates for 1915-6, the Leader of the Conservative Party and Leader of the Opposition, Andrew Bonar Law, was acerbic in his criticism of the continuing lack of proper plans, especially as compared to that favourite of British military criticism – France and the French Government:

> "When the war broke out France mobilised the whole of her industry in precisely the same way in which she mobilised her troops. Have we done, and are we doing, the same? The Government know that both this House and the country will give them all the power they ask. We are the greatest manufacturing country in the world. This war has been going on for seven months, and if – I do not say that it is so, for I do not know – after seven months there is a shortage of ammunition, or of the necessary munitions of war, then, in my belief, we have not utilised to the utmost the industrial resources of this country, and I say to the Government now that to bring this war to a close nothing that they can do would be more effective than to look at the industrial position of the country and to consider, though business as usual is wise from the point of view of stopping panic, though business is necessary, that the first necessity is to provide what we need for this war, and it should be done, and other business must wait until the needs of the State have first been met."[11]

IN THE LATE SUMMER OF 1914, shell orders were placed with recognised companies: *Woolwich, Armstrong Whitworth, Vickers, Beardmore, Cammell Laird, Firth, Hadfield.* and the *Projectile Company.* Those 18-pdr. shell were shrapnel and it was not until October the first order for 18-pdr. HE was placed. Orders for 4.5-in. howitzers and 60-pdr. guns contained only 30% HE.

Early fighting revealed how inadequate were both supplies and orders and a Cabinet committee was set up in October to oversee this subject. Contracts were placed in October and November for 10 million shells for guns between the 13-pdr and 5-in. howitzer. Other orders were needed to cover medium and heavy howitzers and for those new guns for which production plans had been agreed.

To allow for this vast expansion in production financial help was given to existing manufacturers. At the same time, details of companies applying to be sub-contractors for elements of shell production were passed to the firms already involved. The Government, wishing to expand the number of direct contractors sent out invitations to tender for certain shells in the opening weeks of the war. Four companies were added to the list of approved contractors: *Messrs J & P Hill* of Sheffield, *Dick, Kerr & Co.* based at Kilmarnock and Preston, the *Rees Roturbo Manufacturing Co. Ltd.* of Wolverhampton, and *Babcock and Wilcox* of Renfrew.[12]

Despite this expansion, labour and machinery shortages, and sub-contractor failures undermined the programmes. A conference with representatives of the shell manufacturers on 21st December revealed the system lacked flexibility. Skilled labour shortages were the most pressing problem. The demand for shells, especially HE, kept rising, however, and it became necessary to widen the net of direct contractors still further with another group of companies being added to the approved list in the first half of 1915.

With British suppliers unlikely to produce the numbers required, the Government looked overseas. Canada was one of the first to be involved and, that country's Shell Committee promised to supply a million unfuzed 18-pdr. shells by the end of 1914. *Bethlehem Steel* also received major orders for 18-pdr. and 4.7-in. shrapnel, and HE shell orders were placed in October. Other contracts went to the *Washington Steel and Ordnance Co.*, and *E W Bliss* of Brooklyn. With overseas expansion secured, significant orders were placed across North America for the shell supply for autumn and winter 1915/6. The Canadian Shell Committee signed a contract in April for five million 18-pdr. shrapnel and HE shells, and 4.5-in. HE, and the various US-based contractors agreed to supply substantial numbers of high explosive shells for the field, medium and heavy howitzers and 60-pdr. guns.[13]

In Britain, consortiums of small engineering companies bid for contracts. The first went to a Leicester-based co-operative with an order for field howitzer shells in March 1915. This model was followed in other parts of the country, with similar co-operatives springing up in Hull, Bradford, Leeds and elsewhere such that more than twenty were eventually formed and these various groups were contributing 9,500 4.5-in. shells and 33,000 18-pdr. HE shells per week by the end of 1915.

Despite contractual promises, at no point did actual deliveries match the numbers ordered. By May 1915, the month of Aubers Ridge and Festubert, only a third of the six million shells which should have been delivered arrived.[14] Overall, 40 million shells had been ordered since the beginning of the war but less than 12% of the 18-pdr. ammunition was delivered by May 1915. It was figures like these which, though not at the heart of battlefield artillery problem, when publicised lay at the heart of the 'shell crisis' which resulted in the collapse of the last ever Liberal Government and its replacement by a coalition in which Lloyd George undertook the role of Minister of Munitions.

In the meantime, unwise shortcuts were applied to shell making. The most serious was a decision to abandon fitting base plates to shells for 4.5-in. howitzers, 4.7-in. guns, and 60-pdrs. Base plates were introduced into the Army and Navy in 1909 as a safety device. They were screwed into the bottom of a shell as a means of ensuring no hot gases from the propellant charge reached the explosive charge in the shell. A guarantee the base plate was properly inserted was an inspector's stamp. Screwing in the base plate was the work of a highly skilled man and, as the number of shells produced increased, the final output became dependent on the fitting of the base plates. Simply put, fitters could not keep pace with the number of shells being produced. Purely as a matter of expediency, it was decided to do away with base plates for the shells of the guns mentioned above. Inspection of some of the shells resulting from this decision revealed such serious flaws that, had they been fired, they would almost certainly have exploded in the barrel of the gun but, despite this, manufacturers, eager to increase output (and profits), argued riveting rather than screwing a base plate would halve the time and cost of production and this process was approved and universally adopted. When dangers with this method became apparent, orders were issued that all HE shells must have screwed base plates and all shells needed to be so fitted within three months of 31st May 1915. By December it became clear some companies were still finishing HE shells without such base plates and eventually, on 9th June 1916, it was decreed no more shells without screwed base plates would be accepted for service. Furthermore, with prematures running at an unacceptable rate with the 4.5-in. howitzers, it was also decided no more empty shells without base plates should be filled and all existing stocks got rid of.[15] There was, of course, an unknown number of potentially unsafe shells in the huge dumps behind the British front lines which might or might not explode prematurely if fired.

By the time Lloyd George became Minister of Munitions some fifteen national shell factories were established, two were being considered, and twelve co-operatives were in action. In addition, several National Projectile Factories were to be opened to increase supplies of shells for larger guns and howitzers. Eight factories were planned, all under the auspices of the larger armaments companies, with two more constructed later. Even so it took time for these factories to have a significant impact on supplies. For example, 500,000 18-pdr. shells were due to be delivered in September 1915 – deliveries totalled 20,000. Labour, skills, machine tool and raw material shortages and the time it took to get new plant on stream hindered production, as did constant changes in specification to shells ordered. These issues were compounded by increasing demand for anti-aircraft shells and small orders for various exotic guns employed away from the Western Front All of this disrupted the production of the main range of shells.

One source of delay was the necessary checks of empty shells by inspectors at Woolwich. Between 19th June and 17th July 1915, 1,064,000 shells went to Woolwich for inspection of which only 711,000 (67%) were issued to the Army, a problem caused by inspection congestion, delays in filling shells, and the return of defective shells[i].[16] An effort was made to solve the inspection congestion by a decision to have the inspections done in the place of production.

The problems with supplies on 29th May 1915 are shown in Table 37. Notable is the virtual absence of medium/heavy howitzer shells delivered by this date. Also, the numbers under *'Shells outstanding'* relate partially to those due by 29th May 1915 and for delivery by the end of the year. The key figures are under *'Delivered'* and *'Arrears'* for 29th May 1915. Broadly, actual deliveries were 50% of War Office estimates, themselves based on 50% of manufacturers' contracted deliveries. The Army received a quarter of what had been ordered for summer 1915.

After the experience of Loos, Du Cane, Artillery Adviser at GHQ, wrote a memorandum stating the proportion of shrapnel for 18-pdrs, 60-pdrs and 4.7-in. guns should be increased. There were a variety of reasons for this, some related to the unpopularity of the HE shells and a lack of appreciation as to their use than to their application. After the fighting of May and June 1915 there was a significant reduction in the quantity of HE used at Loos.

---

[i] The filling of HE shells was production bottleneck. For some time, most shells were filled at the *Woolwich Ordnance Factory*. It filled 5,533,000 shells, or 86% of the 6,466,800 issued by the end of 1915. New National Filling Factories slowly started to come on stream in December 1915 and by April 1916 their output surpassed that of Woolwich.

Gun type and source	Total ordered	Position on 29th May 1915			Shells outstanding
		Due	Delivered	Arrears	
18-pdr HE Home	3915000	303980	59123	224867	3855867
" " Abroad	10191666	445000	27492	417508	10164174
Total	14106666	748980	86615	642375	14020041
18-pdr Sh Home	4377723	1467394	732720	734674	3645003
" " Abroad	11501666	1729684	669166	1060518	10832500
Total	15879389	3197078	1401886	1795192	14477503
4.5-in. HE Home	1087000	278143	91939	186204	995061
" " Abroad	3141666	95000	0	95000	3141666
Total	4228666	373143	91939	281204	4136727
4.5-in. Sh Home	454540	373143	47120	134447	407420
4.7-in. HE Home	235400	71850	2546	69304	232854
" " Abroad	120800	30500	0	30500	120800
Total	356200	102350	2546	99804	353654
4.7-in. Sh Home	24500	9750	0	9750	24500
" " Abroad	30000	28000	14548	13452	15452
Total	54500	37750	14548	23202	39952
60-pdr HE Home	228050	119878	43082	76796	184968
" " Abroad	36000	0	0	0	360000
Total	588050	119878	43082	76796	544968
60-pdr Sh Home	187600	120501	67390	53111	120210
6-in. HE Home	313400	50200	123	50077	313277
" " Abroad	277000	38000	6720	31280	270280
Total	590400	88200	6843	81357	583557
6-in. Sh Home	12000	8280	0	8280	12000
8-in. HE Home	149300	7200	118	9782	149182
" " Abroad	42000	0	0	0	42000
Total	191300	7200	118	9782	191182
9.2-in. HE Home	85775	26075	7082	18993	78693
" " Abroad	42000	0	0	0	42000
Total	127775	26075	7082	18993	120693
12-in. HE Home	32000	7500	0	7500	32000
" " " Abroad	10000	0	0	0	10000
Total	42000	7500	0	7500	42000
Grand total*	38711286	5797274	1968252	3809032	36743034

Table 37 Shells ordered, delivered and due 29th May 1915 (Main natures) 17
* Grand totals include shells ordered/delivered/due for 13-pdrs, 15-pdrs & 5-in. Howitzers.

The reasons for this were:
1. There was a tendency to hoard them given previous shortages;
2. Officers unused to employing HE tended to rely on shrapnel;
3. Accidents 'prejudiced officers against this projectile';

4. Shrapnel was better at wire cutting;
5. Using HE was forbidden during gas releases as it was thought they dissipated the gas cloud;
6. There had been a large amount of fighting in the open over the opening three days of the battle and shrapnel was the better anti-personnel ammunition in these circumstances.[18]

Du Cane further argued that the increasing strength of the enemy's fortifications meant 18-pdr. HE had less effect whilst the increasing depth of their wire defences demanded the use of more shrapnel. Consequently, it was determined HE should not exceed 50% of the field guns' ammunition supply. As it turned out, the ratio of shrapnel to HE used by 18-pdrs. before and during 1st July 1916 was 3 to 1 and with the 60-pdrs. 52% shrapnel to 48% HE. As the 4.7-in. guns were being used mainly on counter battery work these ineffective guns fired HE/shrapnel at a ratio of 20:1. As a result of all of this, shrapnel shell production exceeded HE shell for these natures until April 1916 and the stocks of shrapnel remained much higher than those of HE.

With extreme pressure on the production of HE for howitzer shells, on 16th February 1916 Lloyd George asked Du Cane why so much 18-pdr. HE was produced. He noted the French always used far more field gun HE than the British with their use of instantaneous graze fuzed HE[i] for effective wire cutting being one reason for their greater consumption. The other was they preferred HE when used against bodies of enemy troops whilst the British preferred traditional shrapnel. Du Cane replied by showing the 18-pdr ammunition expenditure by the BEF between September 1915 and January 1916. At no time did the proportion of shrapnel fired fall below 60% and was at that level only in the relatively 'quiet' month of January.

Month	Shrapnel	% of total	HE	% of total
September (Loos)	487789	88	65937	12
October (Loos)	406721	72	163367	28
November	311008	88	42341	12
December	277207	74	100155	26
January	263295	60	178329	40

Table 38 18-pdr. shrapnel and HE use Sept. 15 to Jan. 16

Subsequently, a ratio of 70/30 shrapnel to HE for 18-pdrs. was maintained and large amounts of shrapnel ordered for 60-pdr, 4.7-in. and 6-in. guns. Shortages prevented the maintenance of these levels during summer, 1916. Shell steel was a particular issue as specifications were stringent and, pre-war, only six UK companies had experience in its manufacture. As expertise and experience was spread there were eventually sixty companies capable of producing steel of the

---

[i] The 75 shell was lighter than the 18-pdr but contained more explosive. The 18-pdr. (18½ lbs/8.39 Kgs) contained 13 oz of Amatol. The 75 (12 lb/5.3 Kgs) contained 29 ozs. of *Melinite* (Picric Acid). The 75 had a thin-walled hardened steel shell casing and their fuze and *gaine* occupied less space. [*History of the Ministry of Munitions*, Vol. X, Part 2, page 5].

necessary quality. Whilst average weekly production at the end of 1915 was 20,300 tons, this expanded to 34,500 tons per week by the second quarter of 1916, an increase of 70%. Even so, the demand for shells prior to the Somme offensive meant domestically produced shell steel began to run short in March and April and this shortage became acute by August with the fighting in Picardy intensifying. With British production now more or less static, the situation was eased in 1917 by a more than fourfold increase in the importation of shell steel from the USA and Canada. This was made necessary not just because of the needs of shell producers but also because shipping losses to U-Boats meant more steel had to be diverted to Britain's shipyards. Unfortunately, as with so much of US production, the profit motive overtook quality standards and the rate of rejection of US-produced shell steel was far higher than with home-based production. The increase in the importation of either finished munitions or material from which to manufacture shells from North America was dramatic. In 1915 the USA and Canada exported c. 100,000 tons of finished munitions and c. 710,000 tons of 'ferrous material' to the UK. In 1916, these figures stood at: 950,000 and 720,000 tons respectively and in 1917, 850,000 and 1.57 million tons.[19] Overall, the ratio of domestic to imported shell steel in 1917 was 59%/41%. In 1916 it had been 86%/14%.

Each Gun Programme demanded a parallel increase in shell production.

Gun type	Gun Prog A	Gun Prog B	Gun Prog C	June 1916
18-pdr Sh	29400	170000	383500	420000
18-pdr HE	29400	170000	383500	280000
4.5-in. Sh	31360	10000	50000	0
4.5-in. HE	125440	75000	219000	248500
4.7-in. Sh	4620	2000	4620	6440
4.7-in. HE	4620	2000	4620	6440
60-pdr Sh	39200	28000	56000	49000
60-pdr HE	39200	28000	56000	49000
6-in. MK VII Sh	1010	400	1010	8100
6-in. Mk VII HE	1010	400	1010	8100
6-in. How HE	57820	56000	126000	204000
8-in. How HE	6300	13000	45150	80000
9.2-in. How HE	15290	11000	30070	63500
12-in. How HE	1680	1800	4260	5000
15-in. How HE		200	420	510

Table 39 Maximum weekly requirements for shells under the various programmes[20]

Requirements for 18-pdr field guns under the various programmes were:

Gun Programme A 58,000 shells per week by March 1916; then
Gun Programme B 340,000 shells per week by March 1916; then
Gun Programme C 767,000 shells per week by March 1916.

For the workhorse 6-in. howitzers the changes were:

Gun Programme A 57,820/week; then
Gun Programme B 56,000/week; then

Gun Programme C 126,000/week[21] On 1st January 1916 the Army Council asked the Ministry for Munitions for estimates for weekly shell production to the end of April. Two figures were given:

Estimate A, on which any plans for operations were to be based; and

A more optimistic Estimate B on which transport plans might be based.

Estimate A was not, however, 'a guaranteed figure' but one expected 'if matters went reasonably well'. In fact, January production fell woefully short of even Estimate A, especially for 18-pdr. HE shells, and Lloyd George admitted the Ministry's 'miserably failed in several natures' and the numbers given on 1st January were significantly revised. Even before this failure several queries were raised by the Army Council. The projected weekly figures for May showed, for example, production of 12,000 rounds/week for the obsolete and soon-to-be phased out 5-in. howitzer. Instead, increased production for the 60-pdr. and 4.7-in. guns was demanded. An estimated 1,200 rounds/week of 12-in. howitzer shell was to be produced but the Army Council thought more 9.2-in. shell preferable. Lastly, production of 4.5-in. howitzer HE shells of some 75,000 rounds/week, which provided a daily allowance of just nine rounds/day/gun instead of the twenty rounds/day/gun requested, was deemed totally unacceptable. This problem was exacerbated by the supply of 300 4.5-in. howitzers plus 20 rounds/gun/day to Russia in January. In March the Russians received 180,000 rounds (a month's supply at 20 rounds/gun/day) whilst the BEF received just 97,000 rounds for their 440 guns. The resulting outcry forced Lloyd George to declare Russia would receive 4.5-in HE shells proportionate to the needs of the BEF.

There then ensued an argument between Lloyd George and the Army Council on the latter's suggestion shell production be capped for each nature. L-G stated he understood the numbers of shells being asked for were a minimum whilst a letter from the Army Council dated 5th January suggested the numbers included were to be a maximum. Were this to be the case and were the Army to run short of shells before and during the expected offensive, then, declared L-G, on their own heads be it. In every battle, he went on, the estimated needs of the artillery before the fighting proved too low. His Ministry was going beyond War Office demands to make up for previous deficiencies and to build up an adequate reserve of ammunition. Indeed, he continued, even the Ministry's production figures would not meet the needs of the BEF for the scale of offensive Haig had laid out to him during a recent visit to France, nor would they come close to the numbers of shells Foch planned to expend on his front later in the year.[22]

THERE ARE THREE ESSENTIAL ELEMENTS to an artillery shell if it is to achieve its objective of killing the enemy and/or destroying his fortifications: a propellant charge to send the shell on its way; an initiation agent to ignite the fuze; which then detonates a bursting charge which is either the main element of a high explosive shell or the one which propels shrapnel balls forward either to cut wire or kill enemy troops. In 1914 the British Army used as a:

Propellant charge – *Cordite MD* (i.e. modified); as the

Initiation agent – *Tetryl* (or *2, 4, 6-Trinitrophenylmethylnitramine*), picric powder or powdered *TNT*; and as the

Bursting charge – *Lyddite* (*Picric Acid*) for high explosive or Black Powder for shrapnel.

The British propellant was *Cordite MD*, a smokeless 'low explosive' (as opposed to a high explosive like *TNT*) which produced expanding hot gases sufficient to send the shell on its way but without doing undue damage to the gun tube. In 1889 three members of a government *Explosives Committee* monitoring developments in smokeless explosives – Sir Frederick Abel, Sir James Dewar and Dr Wilhelm Kellner, a chemist in the War Department at Woolwich – patented a new propellant known as *Cordite* because of its look and stringy shape. A 58% *nitro-glycerine*, 37% *guncotton* (*nitrocellulose*) and 5% petroleum jelly mix, which used *acetone* as a solvent, the results were extruded into thin rods for small arms ammunition and thicker rods for shells. As a result of excessive tube wear *Cordite Mk I* was superseded by *Cordite MD*, a formulation of 65% guncotton, 30% *nitro-glycerine* and 5% petroleum jelly.

The problem for *Cordite* production was a war-time shortage of *acetone* needed for the extrusion process. A partial solution was found with the substitution of *collodion*[i] for gun cotton and this became *Cordite RDB* (*Research Department B*), and a longer term solution to the *acetone* shortage was found when the Zionist chemistry professor (and the first President of Israel) Dr Chaim Weizmann of Manchester University found a way of producing large quantities of the chemical through a fermentation process using grain and, during a period of shortage, horse chestnuts, which were collected assiduously by the general public at the time.

Seemingly ignoring the fears of war which swept Europe during the first fourteen years of the 20th Century the British Army laid down no significant reserves of high explosive for the bursting charges of HE shells. The British initially favoured *Lyddite* used in the common shells of many of the obsolete or elderly guns currently employed: the 4.7-in., 60-pdr, 6-in. 30-cwt howitzer. and 6-in. Mk VII gun. *Lyddite* was based on *Picric Acid* and was derived from *Phenol* (or *Carbolic Acid*) itself derived from coal tar. In 1871 a German chemist, Hermann Sprengel, showed *Picric Acid* to have explosive properties. In 1885 a French chemist, Eugène Turpin, patented pressed and cast *Picric Acid* for use in artillery shells, and, in 1887 and mixed with *gun cotton*, the French started its manufacture under the name *Melinite*. A year later Britain started production of a similar explosive at Lydd in Kent naming it *Lyddite*. *Picric Acid* had its dangers, however, as it could react with shell casings or fuzes to form highly unstable picrate salts.

The Navy established a stock of 150,000 lbs of *Lyddite* in 1908 but, in March, it was concluded that, as the Army was going to war with shrapnel-armed artillery, a similarly large reserve was not required for the military. A few small orders were placed with suppliers to ensure they maintained a production capacity and it was confidently believed that, if needed, the explosives trade could supply another 150,000 lbs of *Picric Acid* within a month of the outbreak of war. Having established the principle in 1908 that the Army needed no bulk reserve of high explosive this policy was reviewed in 1910 and 1912 and no change made. In the

---

[i] *Collodion* is a flammable, syrupy solution of pyroxylin (a.k.a. nitrocellulose, cellulose nitrate, flash paper, and gun cotton) in ether and alcohol [*Wikipedia*].

meantime, the size of the Navy, which used *Lyddite* in large quantities, grew year by year and so did its demands for *Lyddite* whilst, at the same time, domestic manufacturing capacity declined. In 1912 a suggestion was made by Capt. B H Chevalier, Superintendent of the Ordnance Stores at Woolwich, to increase stocks but this was ignored.

The Germans started to substitute *Picric Acid* with *TNT* – *trinitrotoluene* – in 1902 as it was less powerful but more stable than *Picric Acid*. *TNT* was first formulated in 1863 and used as a yellow dye but, when a means of detonating was identified, it was widely accepted as preferable to *Picric Acid*. Britain started to experiment with it in shells in 1913-4[i]. The *Ordnance Board* approved it as a replacement for *Lyddite* in larger shells on 11th August 1914. *TNT* is another by-product of coal tar and the result of a three-phase process, the third of which involves the use of *Oleum* or fuming Sulphuric Acid (*Disulphuric Acid*). At this time, the main manufacture of *Oleum* was based at Nordhausen, Braunlage and Tanne in Thuringia in Germany and the product became known as Nordhausen Acid. Sourcing this ingredient would clearly become a problem once war broke out and a way of eking out the supplies of *TNT* became necessary. The solution was twofold. First, in January 1915, Dr William Richard Hodgkinson[ii], Professor of Chemistry and Metallurgy at the Artillery College, Woolwich, found a way of producing *TNT* without the need of *Oleum*. This became known as *RD Process No. 1* and helped boost the domestic production of *TNT* threefold by June. Secondly, supplies were further extended by the addition of 40%-80% *ammonium nitrate* to *TNT* to form *Amatol* of which more later. This mixture maintained most of the destructive power of *TNT* but at a sharply lower cost[iii].

On 30th July 1914, the Chief Superintendent of the Ordnance Stores asked that orders of 504,000 lbs of *Picric Acid* be placed with commercial suppliers. Within two weeks it was realised these companies could not possibly fulfil this order. Since 1908 it had been hoped to maintain domestic capacity with a dribble of orders but commercial pressures led producers to close, convert, or even dismantle plant capable of producing large quantities of *Picric Acid* at short notice.[23] In addition, the basic raw materials needed for its production were not readily available. As a result, two of the seven companies it was assumed would supply *Picric Acid* were unable to tender at all during the opening month of the war.

There was, therefore, a twin problem: a lack of immediate supply *and* a lack of production capacity. The decision was made to address the former and the five companies able to produce were asked to deliver the first consignments of the 504,000 lbs of *Picric Acid* needed within a fortnight. To put this figure into context,

---

[i] *TNT* is toxic and absorbed through the skin causing yellowing. Many of the women who worked with TNT in munitions factories were nicknamed 'canaries'.

[ii] A product of the Royal Grammar School, Sheffield, the Royal School of Mines and Würzburg University. He was previously the Professor of Chemistry and Physics, Royal Marine Artillery, Woolwich. Born 1851, he died in 1935.

[iii] Costs for the various high explosives are given as 1 shilling and 11 pence per lb. for *Lyddite*, 1s 3d per lb. for *TNT* and 7 pence per lb. for 80/20 *Amatol* [*Source: History of the Ministry of Munitions*, Vol. X, Part 4, page 21].

504,000 lbs of *Picric Acid* was enough to fill the Navy's shells for just three weeks. Between the beginning of August and the end of October the weekly production of *Picric Acid* averaged 60,000 lbs. As *Picric Acid* fell out of favour, however, smaller amounts were required and a second order of 320,000 lbs for delivery in September and October 1914 was followed, at this time, by just one more of 260,000 lbs for delivery in January 1916.

Alternative types and sources of high explosive were urgently needed and companies were approached to produce, or be prepared to produce, *TNT*. In addition, some of the major manufacturers of *Picric Acid* were given advance notice the War Department would not be placing any more significant orders for the explosive. At this time, however, *TNT* was only produced by three British companies: *Nobel Industries Limited .)*of Ardeer in North Ayrshire, *John W Leitch and Co Ltd.,* of Milnsbridge near Huddersfield, and the Swiss-owned dye making company, the *Clayton Aniline Co.,* based in Manchester. *Clayton Aniline* was not yet making a product of the standard required and the first 200,000 lb order for *TNT* was divided equally between *Nobel's* and *Leitch* to be followed by another of 162,000 lbs in early September. When, at the end of September, *TNT* was approved for use by 18-pdr. guns demand sky-rocketed and there was a need to place an order for 500,000 lbs as soon as possible[i]. It was at this point, with supplies of the new high explosive also being undermined by the lack of sources of supply,[24] Lord Moulton[ii], the chairman of the Committee on High Explosives formed in November 1914, and his committee determined to pursue other avenues of supply for the artillery. It was a decision reinforced by the demands being placed on Britain by its Allies for supplies of *TNT*. Indeed, so severe was the problem, that the decision to abandon *Picric Acid* was overturned unless or until the quantities of *TNT* being produced was sufficient or a viable alternative found. With an estimated use of 3 million lbs of *Lyddite* by the end of the year, an immediate contract for 500,000 lbs was issued on 15th October which was extended to 2 million lbs by the end of that month. To achieve this total two new companies were given contracts: *R Graesser Ltd.,* of Ruabon near Wrexham, and *Brotherton & Co.,* of Leeds.

In November an estimate was made of the quantities of high explosive needed to keep the Army and Navy going until the end of July 1915. The figures were alarming. Some 304 short tons per month were needed, totalling some 4.9 million

---

[i] Weekly supplies of *TNT* in the first three months of the war averaged 26,000 lbs, i.e. 50,000 lbs short of the total of the first two orders placed.

[ii] John Fletcher Moulton, Baron Moulton, GBE, KCB, PC, FRS, FRAS (18th November 1844-9th March 1921) was a brilliant mathematician, Fellow of St John's College, Cambridge, a barrister, Fellow of the *Royal Society,* first Chair of the *Medical Research Council,* Liberal MP for Clapham, South Hackney, and Launceston, Lord Justice on the Court of Appeal, and a Privy Councillor. Regarded as one the most brilliant minds of his generation, on the outbreak of war he was appointed Chairman of the *Advisory Committee on Chemical Products* then the *Committee on High Explosives* and later Director-General of Explosive Supplies in the War Office (later in the Ministry of Munitions). He was ennobled as Baron Moulton, of Bank in the County of Hampshire in 1912.

lbs.²⁵ 3.1 million lbs of HE was needed by the Army alone during this eight-month period. The orders placed, at least on paper, covered this quantity but not if one factored in the rapidly increasing demand from the Army for HE shells and similarly growing demands from the Allies. Lord Moulton's committee, therefore, revised up the total monthly supply of HE needed from the estimate of 304 tons a month to 1,400 tons per month, i.e. from a total of 4.9 million lbs by the end of July to 22.4 million lbs. This exceeded the total ordered by that date of 4,857 tons (9.7 million lbs) by a factor of more than two. By the end of the year additional orders for 3.5 million lbs were placed, including one for a million lbs from the USA costing three times as much as that produced in Britain.

Renewed efforts were made to increase the production of *TNT* with four more companies being persuaded by generous financial assistance to build the required plant and install the necessary machinery. Rather more draconian methods were also employed when a new factory in Rainham, Essex, was seized by the Government under the provisions of the *Defence of the Realm Act (DORA)* and converted to *TNT* production. In addition, large amounts were purchased at a laughably high price from *du Pont* ., in the USA who insisted on 50% of the price being paid in advance. To add insult to injury, the resulting product had to be re-processed on its arrival in Britain because of its low quality.²⁶ Such was the unreliability of supply the Government determined to take matters into its own hands and in the Spring of 1915 a State-run factory was built at Oldbury in the Black Country. Work started on 8ᵗʰ January and the plant started production in May and was producing 200 tons (400,000 lbs) of *TNT* per month by mid-July. In addition, Canada started producing *TNT*, sending its first shipment in June 1915. A second factory, at Queen's Ferry in Flintshire, was started in June 1915 and a third at Penrhyndeudraeth near Porthmadog soon after.

By the end of May 1915 actual production of *TNT* stood at 152 tons (304,000 lbs) per week and was expected to rise to 612 tons (1.22 million lbs) per week by the end of July. *Picric Acid* production was 110 tons (220,000 lbs) per week and was expected to achieve 317 tons (634,00 lbs) per week by the end of July. An additional 200 tons (400,000 lbs) of *Picric Acid* was expected shortly after the development of a synthetic base for the explosive. *Ammonal* was also produced in large quantities (400 tons, 800,000, lbs per week) and production was expected to double. Few of these figures were reached, with weekly *TNT* production in January 1916 reaching 457 tons (a shortfall of 155 ton/week) and *Picric Acid* 224 tons per week (a shortfall of 93 tons/week).²⁷

Whilst this frantic work went on to increase the production of high explosives, battlefield, and naval experience in the first quarter of 1915 showed actual consumption to have been only 25% of that anticipated. This allowed Britain to transfer nearly 2.5 million lbs of Picric Acid to the Allies as well as to build up a reserve of nearly 900,000 lbs of *TNT.*²⁸ When large numbers of empty 18-pdr. shells started to arrive from the USA in May 1915 this rosy picture started to change.

What did not help were accidents which effectively destroyed two *TNT* production plants. The first was at Penrhyndeudraeth where the *Ergite Company's* works was destroyed on 8ᵗʰ June. They were replaced by the *National Explosives*

Factory built there subsequently. Then, on 30th July, *Nobel's .)TNT* plant at Ardeer was destroyed in another explosion. This plant was not rebuilt but relocated to Pembrey in Carmarthenshire. Added to these problems was the effect of the gun programmes instituted in August and September 1915 which dramatically increased the demand for shells of all types, especially high explosive. Estimates for 1916 showed c. 71,000 tons of high explosive were needed for the year's campaigning and the Navy needed 25,000 tons. The current levels of supply for both *TNT* and *Picric Acid* for that period stood at 58,000 tons, i.e. a shortfall of 38,000 tons. There was provision, however, for the manufacture of 100,000 tons of ammonium nitrate with which to make *Amatol* and that, to make ends meet, both 40/60 and 80/20 *ammonium nitrate* and *TNT* mixtures would be needed (see Table 40 below).

The decision to pursue the various *Amatol* mixes was made by Lord Moulton, in his capacity as chairman of the Committee on High Explosives. He calculated the war would consume the country's entire production of *Lyddite* and *TNT* and still leave a substantial shortfall in high explosive supplies. The issue was: whether to extend the supplies of high explosives by using additives and risk long delays whilst these compounds were tested for effectiveness and safety? Kitchener made the decision in February 1915 that securing supplies was the higher priority and Moulton was given authority to investigate and produce all and any high explosives of which the country was capable.[29] He first considered *Ammonal*, made by the *Roburite and Ammonal Explosives Co. Ltd.* based in Wigan and formed by merger in 1913. *Ammonal* was in use with both the German and Austrian Armies and been widely used in the two Balkan Wars. It was later favoured for employment in many of the huge mines set on the Western Front in places like the *Somme* and Messines. The explosive was a mixture of 65% *ammonium nitrate*, 15% *TNT*, 17% aluminium powder and 3% charcoal. *Ammonal* had been previously considered but there were concerns about its storage but Moulton still pressed its use on von Donop, the Master General of the Ordnance. Tests in June, however, found problems with *Ammonal*-filled shells whilst *Amatol* gave better results and *Ammonal* was forthwith abandoned for shell production.

Another high explosive considered was the French explosive known as *Schneiderite*, a mixture of 88% *ammonium nitrate* and 12% *dinitronaphthalene* (a nitrated version of *naphthalene*, yet another by-product of coal tar, and used for, amongst other things, making mothballs). *Schneiderite* was tested in the form of *Schneiderite tolite*, a mixture of 60% *Schneiderite* and 40% *TNT*, and these experiments suggested it would be suitable for lighter weight shells using the 80/44 Fuze and gaine. The mixture of *Schneiderite tolite* contained such a small amount of *dinitronaphthalene* (7.5%) the Research Department at Woolwich suggested its removal entirely and further investigation was abandoned on 19th March 1915.

Instead, a simple mixture of *ammonium nitrate* and *TNT* was suggested in a ratio of 55/45, amended to a mix of 40/60, to simplify shell filling. By June a new filling plant at Woolwich came on stream and 18-pdr. shells started to be filled with the 40/60 *Amatol* mix instead of pure *TNT* and it was soon approved for several other applications. By August permission was given for the 40/60 mix to be used in howitzer shells from 8-in. howitzers upwards although *Lyddite* could also be used when available. Further experiments were made with different mixes and an 80/20 *ammonium nitrate/TNT* combination was found to be effective with 18-pdr. shells using the No. 18 Fuze and its use was later extended to most types of shell.

Source	1914 Aug-Dec	1915	1916
High Explosive (Picric Acid & TNT) Short tons (1 ton = 2,000 lbs)			
Home	434	9822	58420
Abroad	0	2183	13332
Total	434	12005	71752
Ammonium Nitrate			
Home	0	7101	51158
Abroad	0	1100	4325
Total	0	8201	55483
Total High Explosives	434	20206	127235
Propulsive Explosives (Cordite, Ballistite & NCT)			
Home	5298	12438	29617
Abroad	0	13535	54594
Total	5298	25973	84211

Table 40 Delivery of explosives 1914-6[30]

WHICH BRINGS US NEATLY on to the other element needed for a successful shell – the fuze. In October 1909 the *No. 18 Fuze* was developed for use by coastal defence guns and this was filled with a mixture of *Tetryl* and powdered *TNT*. This fuze was found to detonate both *Lyddite* and *TNT*. Just prior to the war the direct-action *No. 44 Fuze* was developed which could detonate smaller charges of both *Lyddite* and *TNT*. When the decision was made in August 1914 to move over to *TNT* for larger shells the fuze to be employed was the *No. 45 Fuze*, a modified *No. 18*, whilst the *No. 17 Fuze* was to be used with *Lyddite*-filled shells and the *No. 80*, a time and percussion fuze, employed when firing 18-pdr shrapnel. The *Nos. 17, 18* and *45 Fuzes* were all nose impact shells.

There was also a need for a graze fuze, i.e. for flatter firing guns or for things like wire cutting. Initially the *No. 44 Fuze* was the only fuze capable of detonating HE and an adapted version was designed for use with the heavy howitzers. It was a nose impact shell but one which did not work well unless fired at a relatively steep angle. It would take two years of further development before this fuze worked satisfactorily. Other attempts at finding a suitable HE fuze were made with the introductions of the *44/80 Fuze* which was a combination of the *No. 44* and *No. 80 Fuzes* but this too was found not to be the answer to effectively detonating HE shells and was eventually relegated to use as an anti-aircraft fuze. The answer appeared to be the new *No. 100 Fuze* which went from design to production in the space of ten days in the autumn of 1914.

During the late summer of 1915 two problems relating to fuzes began to cause major concern. The first was that less than half of the standard 18-pdr shrapnel fuzes ordered for delivery by May 1915 arrived (870,000 against 1.77 million ordered). These were the *No. 80 Fuze*, a time and percussion fuze based on a *Krupp* design and manufactured under licence by *Vickers*. This translated into a particular problem with fuzes for HE shells. On 25th September, the opening day of the Battle of Loos, there were just 292,000 HE fuzes for 592,000 HE shells.[31] These fuzes, the *Nos. 80* and *100*, were also hugely unreliable, further diluting the potential impact of any British bombardments and barrages. This issue with fuzes was to persist and resulted in the frustration of having rank upon rank of shells lined up in the factories but without the fuzes to detonate them. The *Official History* gives, as an example of this, the fact that in the three months between November 1915 and the end of January 1916 ten million shells were delivered as per contract of which only just over a third could be sent to the Armies complete with fuzes. By August 1916, there were 25 million 18-pdr shells stockpiled lacking fuzes.

Secondly, and more immediately, the combination of 80/20 *Amatol*, the *No. 100 Fuze* and, the *No. 1 Gaine*, an addition to the action of the fuzes, started to receive some seriously bad reports with a large number of 18-pdr. prematures reported. The *No. 100 Fuze* was a graze fuze designed to work with all HE shells for the 18 and 60-pdrs and all natures of howitzers. None of these worked especially well with *Amatol* until new processes for filling were developed in 1917 and the *No. 100 Fuze* caused problems all by itself. Problems like not fitting the shell, falling out in flight, needing to be bashed into a shell with a hammer to fit, as well as the dreaded prematures. So, nothing minor!

By September 1915 prematures in 4.5-in. HE shells on the Western Front were running at one to 5,000 rounds fired. The destruction of guns, and deaths and injuries to the crews, were undermining morale amongst the gunners and making them reluctant to use HE shell even if it was the most appropriate shell for the task in hand. Shells were minutely analysed and found not to be at fault, although some of these prematures may have been caused by shells without base plates still stored in France. Suspicion then fell on the fuzes and the *No. 1 Gaine*.

A *gaine* was an addition to a fuze which amplified the ability of the fuze to set off the HE charge in the shell. It was believed the *No. 1 Gaine* tended to tear away from the fuze when the shell was fired. This led to numerous 'blinds' as well as prematures. The *No. 1 Gaine* was used with HE shells employing the *No. 100 Fuze* or *No. 80/44 Fuze*. The high volume fired during the Loos campaign, and a significant increase in the number of prematures, revealed the *No. 80/44 Fuze* with the *No. 1 Gaine* was too dangerous a combination to employ. This meant every HE shell had to use a *No. 100 Fuze* which not only had its own problems but of which there were insufficient numbers to meet demand. It was then confirmed the *No. 1 Gaine* was the cause of many of the problems and investigations over two months concluded this *gaine* had to be changed. On 2nd December it was ordered no more shells incorporating this *gaine* would be accepted. This meant, in the short term, the heavy shells would have to rely on the old *No. 17* and *No. 44 Fuzes*. The *No. 17 Fuze* was a nose impact fuze designed before the war to work with breech loading and quick-firing *Lyddite*-filled shells, with some made for the Russian Army by *Vickers* but not delivered before the war started. The *No. 44 Fuze* too was a nose impact shell designed for *TNT* (or *Trotyl* to the British) filled shells of the 6-in. and 9.2-in. howitzer shells (a variant, the *44 B*, was designed for the super heavy howitzers). Neither of these fuzes was suitable for 18-pdr. HE and these had to wait for the new *gaine*, the *No. 2 Gaine*, now in the process of production.[32]

The fundamental problem was that the 80/20 mix of *Amatol* was extremely difficult to detonate effectively. Tests took place using a 10-grain mercury fulminate detonator added to the process but problems with both blinds and prematures persisted throughout the autumn, with the blinds being mainly blamed on the *Amatol*.[33] The question of blinds appeared to revolve around the density of the *Amatol* mix and it was thought compressing the mixture of ground *TNT* and *ammonium nitrate* would provide the necessary density of *Amatol* which it would prove possible to detonate. That this still proved highly unreliable could be seen from the number of 'blinds', i.e. unexploded shells, still being fired during the seven-day preliminary bombardment on the *Somme*. There were other reasons for these blinds but it appears the system of compressing the mix to fill the shells was still less than ideal. The need to persist with the 80/20 mix was clear, however, in the light of the enormous expansion in firepower, the need for shells dictated by Gun Programme C, and the shortages of other high explosives.

By February 1916 a new fuze, the *No. 101*, and the *No. 2 Gaine Mk II* had been developed. The *No. 2 Gaine Mk II* used a combination of *tetryl* and a bag of *TNT* to detonate the 80/20 *Amatol* and tests proved satisfactory. The method of filling was still uncertain and operations were set up to deal with either a melting process for 40/60 *Amatol* or pressing the 80/20 mixture direct into the shell. Tests conducted at Chilwell[i] with the pressed 80/20 mix, using, basically, the French method of filling shells, proved effective at the end of January 1916 and large-scale press filling of large shells started at Chilwell on 19th April 1916. This new factory was, using either its 40/60 melt or 80/20 pressing plant, the source of most of the heavy shells used throughout the *Somme* during the summer.[34]

One drawback of the 80/20 *Amatol* mixture was that, instead of the characteristic black smoke left by a German 5.9 in. howitzer shell[ii], *Amatol* detonated with difficult-to-see white/grey smoke. Observation was extremely difficult at medium to long range and partially buried howitzer shells limited any sign of the shell's explosion still further. As a result, it was often associated, perhaps unfairly, with a high rate of blinds, an issue first reported by Sir John French in September 1915. Various solutions were tried but it was not until March 1916 one was found. This required adding a smoke box containing red phosphorus into HE shells and a recommendation to adopt this was made by the Ordnance Committee on 21st March and a design approved by 5th May. As a temporary solution, it was concluded powder-filled shells, which gave off more and darker smoke, should be used for registration purposes. The need for a solution was especially pressing for those guns firing at long range, i.e. the 4.7-in., 60-pdr. and

---

[i] Godfrey John Boyle Chetwynd, 8th Viscount Chetwynd, constructed *National Filling Factory No. 6* at Chilwell, Nottinghamshire, for pressing an 80/20 mix into larger shells, delivery starting in Spring 1916. A 40/60 melt plant was also constructed. Most of the plant was destroyed when 8 tons of *TNT* exploded on 1st July 1918, killing 139 people, of whom 32 were identified, and injuring a further 250. The unidentified bodies were buried in a mass grave in St. Mary's Church, Attenborough. One month later the rebuilt plant broke its own production record.

[ii] The 'Jack Johnson' or 'Coalbox' as the 5.9 was known to the British.

6-in. Mk VII guns, and for counter battery fire where accuracy was crucial. Red phosphorus, an allotrope of ordinary phosphorus, was already in use for smoke bombs, *Stokes* mortar bombs and by the Navy, and was in relative short supply but Du Cane was anxious the BEF should receive shells the explosion of which could be seen at long distance as quickly as possible, but there was a safety issue about the Phosphorus-filled smoke box being placed near the HE as leakage risked premature explosions. The secondary issue was the impact installing the boxes had on the rate of shell production. There was no proper solution prior to 1st July, and it was not until 13th July that a bagged combination of 70% *potassium nitrate* and 30% *aluminium* was approved. Problems with smoke mixtures for heavy howitzer shells persisted, however, and it was not until early 1917 a solution was found.[35]

TAKING THE PRECEDING INTO ACCOUNT, any prudent examination of the quality and quantity of the guns, shells, and fuzes available prior to 1st July 1916 (let alone the lack of experience of many gunners sent out from England) should have led to a conservative assessment of the likely effectiveness of the planned Somme bombardment. Unfortunately, neither Haig nor Rawlinson were gunners by training, unlike their French equivalents Foch and Fayolle. Indeed, only Horne of XV Corps, was a gunner product of the Royal Military Academy. This weakness, perhaps, revealed itself in the ambitious plans of Fourth Army and the lack of focus on such key aspects as the destruction or neutralisation of the enemy's guns, removal of their wire, and the destruction of their forward positions. In this respect, the French 'learning curve' was running far ahead that of Haig and the BEF and the price of this relative lack of education would be sorely felt in the ranks of the infantry on 1st July 1916.

But what of the BEF's new commander? In mid-December, after the relentless offensive failures of 1915, a new man was placed at the helm. The man who, as commander of First Army, oversaw every one of these failures: Sir Douglas Haig.

The men who solved the Shell Crisis

102 Rt. Hon. David Lloyd George

103 Gen. Sir John Philip Du Cane

104 Rt. Hon. John Fletcher Moulton

105 Sir Eric Campbell Geddes

ENDNOTES:

1 *History of the Ministry of Munitions*, Vol. X, Part 1, page 13.
2 Ibid., footnote page 13.
3 Bailey, Maj. J B A, *Field Artillery and Firepower*, The Military Press, Oxford, 1989, page 122.
4 *History of the Ministry of Munitions*, page 21.
5 Ibid., footnote page 16.
6 Ibid., page 29.
7 French, Viscount, *1914*, op. cit., Constable & Co., 1919, page 357-8.
8 Ibid., page 360
9 *History of the Ministry of Munitions*, Vol. I, Part 1, page 25.
10 *History of the Ministry of Munitions*, Vol. X, Part 1, page 15.
11 *The Times,* Tuesday, 2nd March, 1915; page 9, and *History of the Ministry of Munitions*, Vol. I, Part 1, page 132.
12 *History of the Ministry of Munitions*, Vol. X, Part 3, page 2.
13 Ibid., page 3.
14 Ibid., page 5.
15 Ibid., pages 43-4.
16 Ibid., page 19.
17 Ibid., pages 6-7.
18 Ibid., page 3.
19 Birkett, M S, *The Iron and Steel Trades During the War*, *Journal of the Royal Statistical Society*, Vol. 83, No. 3. May, 1920, page 354-5.
20 Ibid., pages 68-9.
21 Ibid., page 8.
22 Ibid., page 10.
23 *History of the Ministry of Munitions*, Vol. X, Part 4, page 38.
24 Ibid., page 40.
25 Ibid., pages 41-2.
26 Ibid., page 45.
27 Ibid., page 74.
28 Ibid., page 52.
29 *History of the Ministry of Munitions*, Vol. X, Part 4, page 9.
30 Ibid., page 138.
31 Ibid., footnote page 22.
32 *History of the Ministry of Munitions*, Vol. X, Part 3, page 23.
33 Ibid., page 14-5.
34 Ibid., page 16.
35 *History of the Ministry of Munitions*, Vol. X, Part 2, page 54-5.

PART FIVE: ACTION AND REACTION

"I believe that a large minority – if not an actual majority – of our generals... simply love the war and would like it to go on for years! They are seldom, if ever, in danger and are having the time of their lives."

Sir Cuthbert Morley Headlam
Letter to his wife, 10th September 1916
The Military Papers of Sir Cuthbert Headlam,
page 136

16. From Mulhouse to the Marne

"... an incessant firing of howitzers which it is impossible to see and therefore to counter battery"

Gen. Émile Edmond Legrand-Girarde
21e Corps d'Armée

THE EARLY FIGHTING AROUND MULHOUSE in Alsace on the 9th and 10th August clearly revealed several significant tactical and command problems for both the French and German armies which resulted in unnecessarily high casualties and several missed opportunities. Then, during the invasion of Lorraine, it was heavily underlined just how disastrous was French prevarication over the use of medium and field howitzers, and how woeful was the underlying strategic plan underpinned by the *offensive à outrance* and adopted by Joffre.

The first glaring point was that commanders on both sides with no actual experience of war were, out of a combination of ignorance, arrogance and/or stupidity, prone to making the most basic and crudest of tactical errors for which their young officers and the Other Ranks were paying a heavy price.

Furthermore, it seems that commanders on both sides either did not care about, or did not understand, the impact the rank and file's physical exertions, i.e. long marches in extremes of heat carrying heavy loads, was having on their morale and ability to fight. This particularly affected the reservists who filled at least a third of every unit's ranks.

Then, perhaps because of the presence of these reservists, infantry commanders, most especially German ones, were initially inclined to send their men forward tightly grouped rather deploying them in skirmishing formations. They thus provided excellent targets to French field and machine guns.

Both sides repeatedly failed to co-ordinate the actions of the available units so they might concentrate the maximum force at a particular time and place – the much quoted, but rarely achieved, Napoleonic concept of 'the economy of force'.

Laughably, it was apparent that cavalry commanders *still* believed the *arme blanche* to be an irresistible battlefield force and, as the French casualties on 19th August at Brunstatt and Tagsdorf during the second French invasion of Alsace revealed[i], they failed to grasp the potential effect of automatic weapons on such an inviting target as a large body of horsemen.

---

[i] At Brunstatt, a charge by the *6e escadron, 19e régiment de Dragons*, up a narrow road in the village resulted in the deaths of the regimental CO, Lt. Col. Paul Louis Touvet, and another officer, the wounding of three officers, the deaths of 25 *Dragons* with five more dying of wounds in the following days. 19 were missing (mainly wounded and PoWs) and seven more wounded. At least 24 of the dead and mortally wounded died in German hands. At Tagsdorf, the commander of the *1er escadron, 4e Régiment de Chasseurs d'Afrique*, Capt. Louis Paul Léon Penet, ignored orders and charged German infantry. Penet, another officer, and 24 *Chasseurs* were killed as were 45 horses. Forty other officers and *Chasseurs* were wounded, and thirty horses captured [*Source*: MacDonald, A, *Liberating Elsaß: The French Invasions of Alsace, August 1914*, Iona Books, 2024].

To add to these French examples were two earlier, and even more costly, German cavalry disasters. The first took place at Lagarde in Lorraine on 11th August. There, two Bavarian *Uhlan* regiments from the *4. (Kgl. Bayerische) Kavallerie Brigade* charged unnecessarily and, on entering the confines of the tiny canal-side village, were duly slaughtered, losing 16 officers, 219 Other Ranks and 304 horses dead or wounded in a few minutes.[1]

Further confirmation of the vulnerability of massed cavalry was provided by the action at Halen (formerly Haelen), Limburg province, Belgium, on 12th August 1914. There, the German *4. Kavallerie Division* from *Höheren Kavallerie-Kommandos Nr. 2* attacked dismounted Belgian cavalry and cyclists supported by field artillery. From the *17. Kavallerie-Brigade* 38 officers and men of *1. Großherzoglich Mecklenburgisches Dragoner-Regiment Nr. 17* were killed, with 40 officers and men from *2. Großherzoglich Mecklenburgisches Dragoner-Regiment Nr. 18* including its commander, Major Viktor Digeon von Monteton, also dying and 84 more being wounded. Overall, the Division lost 501 men and 848 horses. *Oberst* Maximilan von Poseck, the *Chef des Generalstabes* of *Höheren Kavallerie-Kommandos Nr. 2*, is quoted as having stated that:

> "The brigade is destroyed.... Rode in against infantry, artillery, and machine-guns, hung up on the wire, fell into a sunken road, all shot down."[2]

The *2. Kavallerie Division*, also involved, lost a similar number of men with the overall totals being approximately 150 dead, 600 wounded and 300 missing/PoWs.

PERHAPS THE BIGGEST COMPLAINT about the performance on both sides was the failure to co-ordinate the use of the infantry and the artillery with, far too regularly, infantry attacking without either artillery preparation or support.

The gunners or, at least, their commanders, were also overly keen to display themselves in open positions to use direct fire when, eventually, they did come to support the infantry. Exposed, they then suffered badly to counter battery fire from more intelligently located, i.e. defiladed, guns. A particularly egregious example of this took place when eighteen German guns were captured near Brunstatt on 19th August when they were deployed on top of a hill with no cover. Casualties were especially heavy amongst the poor horse teams, and these losses made it impossible for what was left of the crews to remove the guns.

Another point revealed by the fighting was that the availability of the German field (10.5-cm), medium (15-cm) and, at Morhange and Sarrebourg, heavy (21-cm) howitzers gave them a major tactical and firepower advantage which the French, currently, simply could not match. Their pre-war arguments, and a failure to introduce similar *material*, were shown in the opening weeks of the war to have been a dreadful error from which it would take half the war to recover.

The invasion of Lorraine confirmed this in horrific fashion when it climaxed with the disastrous battle of Morhange on 20th August 1914. This action completely unhinged the French offensive and forced both the *1er* and *2e Armées* to retreat in confusion back to, and in places, beyond their starting positions astride the *Meurthe*.

This German firepower advantage was simply not recognised at *GQG*. Indeed, the effectiveness of German howitzers had already been discounted. As of 11th

August 1914, and after a few early and unrepresentative skirmishes, the superiority of the French artillery was not just a matter of faith, according to a secret note sent to all Army commanders, it was a matter of fact:

"The French artillery has everywhere achieved undoubted superiority over the German artillery…"[3]

This declaration of faith was then passed down the chain of command as Dubail and Castelnau included Joffre's comments more or less *verbatim* in a letter sent to Corps and cavalry commanders the following day.[4]

The German experience was not so one-sided. In *Bulletin de renseignements No. 10* issued by *1er Armée* dated 20th August, Dubail's *chef d'état-major*, Demange, cited an order of the day issued by the *1. Bayerisches Armeekorps* at Blâmont on 12th August. This commented that:

"…the French artillery's shrapnel fire often lacks effectiveness because of the excessive bursting height."[5]

This was an issue noted in the fighting around Mulhouse and later confirmed in an action at Cirey on 14th August when *1er Armée's 13e Corps* came badly unstuck against Bavarian troops slowly withdrawing towards Sarrebourg[6].

Certain German artillery practices were identified and this information passed to all Army commanders:

"German artillery firing methods are highlighted by:
a. The constant use of land surveying;
b. Systematic bombardment of ridges to a depth of 400-500 metres as part of the artillery fight.
As for the manner of occupying the positions, it is very variable, from highly defiladed positions to placing batteries almost in the open."

But German howitzers were dismissed out of hand by Joffre and *GQG*.

"The (German) howitzer projectiles produced extremely little effect. They create craters but have little effect on the troops."[7]

Not knowing what he was about to come up against, Castelnau took it one step further stressing to his Corps commanders that they should:

"Take advantage of the superiority of our artillery to gain the upper hand over the enemy artillery from the start of the fight."[8]

These opinions were presumably based mainly on the use of German 77-mm field guns and 10.5-cm field howitzers (*lFH*) around Mulhouse, and reports on small actions at places like Mangiennes, 25 kms south-west of Longwy, on 10th August. The report on that action claimed:

"Our artillery is far superior to the German artillery. The effects of explosive shells are devastating."[9]

It should be pointed out, however, that, unlike *6. Armee*, the *7. Armee* in *Elsaß* had no 21-cm *mörsers* attached. Its heaviest artillery was the 15-cm *sFH* howitzers operated at Corps level which saw little service in that campaign. But, on the occasions when they *did* bring their fire to bear, French troops were appalled by 15-cm *sFH's* destructive power. Then, when the French eventually came up against

21-cm *mörsers* and massed *sFH* batteries at Morhange and Sarrebourg it was an entirely different matter. Not only were the explosions and resulting shell shards hugely damaging, but these guns were being fired from a range which left them untouched by the French guns. The effect was thoroughly demoralising for both infantry and artillerists. The commander of *21e Corps* of Dubail's *Ire Armée*, Gen. Émile Edmond Legrand-Girarde[i], observed during the Battle of Sarrebourg on 20th August 1914, that the attacking enemy infantry was:

> "... reinforced by an incessant firing of howitzers which it is impossible to see and therefore to counter battery."[10]

Even before this engagement, the ability of the German guns to out-range the *75s* was apparent. On 16th August, as the *15e Division* of *8e Corps* advanced towards Sarrebourg, the advanced guard of the *27e* and *10e RI* were taken under long-range fire near the village of Saint-Georges. The German guns were to the south of Sarrebourg and believed to be firing at a range of 10 to 12 kms. When the batteries of the *37e RAC, 8e Corps'* artillery, moved forward in support they were bombarded with the help of a German spotter aircraft. Completely outranged, the regiment lost seven dead and 13 wounded without laying a finger on the German guns.

Three days later, the *JMO* of the *1re Armée* commented that:

> "The characteristic of the day has been the intensive use of German heavy artillery (very large calibre and very long range – 12 kms) which concentrates heavily on batteries, troop concentrations and command posts helped by signals from aircraft or spies, or they fire off-map into specific zones. Our artillery remains unused because of the great ranges."[11]

The following day, during the Battle of Sarrebourg, the effect of German heavy artillery on the retreating *15e Division* was described as 'demoralising and murderous', its *56e RI* having been 'crushed' in the village of Gosselming by 'violent artillery and machine gun fire'.[12] The regiment lost 16 officers and 1,007 Other Ranks (of whom 275 were dead) out of 55 officers and 3,329 ORs, but the casualties were concentrated in the *2e bataillon* which lost its commander, two company commanders and two platoon commanders killed, and was so badly hit it did not reform until a large draft of reservists arrived on 4th September.[13]

---

[i] *Général de division* Émile Edmond Legrand-Girarde, *Grand-Officier*, *Légion d'Honneur*, was born in Saint-Quentin on 16th November 1857, the son of Jules Edmond Legrand and Marie Emélie Angèline Girarde. *École polytechnique*, 1874. *École d'application de l'artillerie et du Génie*, 1876. *Sous-Lt.*, *1er régiment du Génie*, 1878. Youngest captain in the Army 1881.*Professeur adjoint* in fortifications, Sant-Cyr. *État-Major*, *École supérieure de Guerre*, 1885. *Officier d'ordnance*, *Ministre de la Guerre*, 1893. *Chef de bataillon*, attached to the office of the President of the Republic, 1897. Lt. Col., 1899. *Directeur du Génie*, Bastia, then *commandant du Génie*, China, 1900 (Boxer Rebellion). Col., 1901. *Général de Brigade*, *81e Brigade* (1906-10). Deputy Head, *État-Major de l'armée*, 7th August 1913. *21e Corps*, 15th January 1914. He fell out with Gen. Langle de Cary and was dismissed on 13th September 1914. To *18e région militaire* (Bordeaux), he returned to command *27e Division* at Verdun between 3rd November 1915 and 29th May 1916. *État-Majors*, *IIIe* and *IIe Armées* and *GAN* until September 1918. Commandant, *15e région militaire* (Marseille). He died on 23rd December 1924.

Here, the French attack typified the mindless application of the *'offensive à outrance'*. Already exhausted, the regiment marched overnight with nothing to eat and then launched a bayonet attack without artillery support at 3.45 a.m. By 8 a.m. they were in full retreat along with the rest of the division.

With the small number of heavier French guns and howitzers unable to get into action quickly enough to cover the forward deployment of the *75s* and infantry, it was left to these latter two arms alone to try to stop the steady advance of the Germans on 20th August. Gallant French troops attacked *en masse*, led by sword waving officers, flags and even bands, and were mown down in their tens of thousands by rifle and machine gun fire and field and heavy shrapnel. The gun teams of the *75s* were swamped by howitzer and long-range gun fire from batteries they could not see, let alone reach.

Crucially, these errors were compounded by grossly inadequate intelligence gathering, mainly through the misuse of their reconnaissance forces, especially the cavalry, and, in the case of the aerial component, through a combination of uncooperative weather, the limitations of the technology, basic inexperience, and the reluctance of some senior officers to believe what they were told by the aerial observers. On the ground, the French seemed overly keen on keeping their cavalry units in large bodies rather, as the Germans seemed to prefer, to use them in small, discreet units able to penetrate enemy lines to collect useful intelligence.

Another reason for the success of the German artillery, and the comparative failure of the French to respond either accurately or adequately, was that, whilst the Germans developed trusted systems for aerial reconnaissance and observation, the French did not. Writing in the *Field Artillery Journal* in 1916, Lt. Georges Nestler Tricoche[i], from the French *artillerie à pied* (heavy artillery), noted the numerous occasions in which French artillery was surprised and taken under fire by invisible German guns directed by aerial observers. That the French could not do the same is at least partly explained by the *Field Artillery Regulations* for the *75s* then in force which basically stated that using aerial observation to either discover or adjust the fire on enemy batteries was a tactic of last resort.[14] So backward was the thinking, according to Tricoche, that in order to observe where the new French 105-mm long gun's shots fell when it was introduced pre-war:

> "Some of the best known artillerists in France were in favour of adopting a huge, very powerful telescope, drawn on a special vehicle."

It was as late as April 1914 before an officer 'expressed timidly' the opinion that aeroplanes might be useful in both spotting and targeting enemy positions and troop concentrations.[15]

Furthermore, Germany overtook France in the numbers of aerial *matériel* available which, given the pre-eminent pre-war position of French airframes and engines, is remarkable. On the outbreak of war France had immediately available 138 aircraft distributed over 23 *escadrilles*.

---

[i] Born in 1859, he was the son of *Général de Division* Jean Victor Alfred Tricoche and Louise Nathalie Nestler. A prolific writer interested in economics and co-operatives, he lived and travelled extensively in North America. He died in Newfoundland in 1938.

Escadrilles MF2, 5, 8, 16 & 20, flying *Maurice Farman* aircraft powered by *Renault 70 HP* engines;
Escadrilles MF1, 7, 13 & 19, Henri *Farmans* with *Gnôme 80 HP* engines;
Escadrilles V14 & 21, Voisins with *Rhône 80 HP* engines;
Escadrilles BL3, 9, 10 & 18, Blériots with *Gnôme 80 HP* engine;
Escadrilles D4 & 6, Deperdussins with *Gnôme 80 HP* engines;
Escadrille C11, Caudrons with *Gnôme 80 HP* engines;
Escadrille R15, Robert-Esnault-Pelterie or REPs, with *Gnôme 80 HP* engines;
Escadrille N12, Nieuports with *Gnôme 80 HP* engines;
Escadrille B12, Breguets with *Canton-Unné 120 HP* engines;
Escadrilles BL C2 & 5, Blériot cavalerie with *Gnôme 80 HP* engines;

In addition, there were a similar number of aircraft in the *Réserve générale d'aviation*. There were also six airships[i] (*dirigeables*), and four *compagnies d'aérostation de places* (tethered balloons)[ii]. Within eleven days, i.e. by 15th August, four more *escadrilles* were formed:

Escadrille DO22, Dorands with *Anzani 90 HP* engines (3rd August);
Escadrille MS23, Morane-Saulniers with *Gnôme 80 HP* engines (6th August);
Escadrille V24, Voisins with *Canton-Unné 120 HP* engines (6th August); and
Escadrille C25, Caudron Monoplaces with *Gnôme 60 HP* engines (6th August).[16]

Germany, on the other hand could call on: 238 aircraft (33 squadrons of six and ten squadrons of four aircraft), eight airships, and seven companies of *Drachens* (tethered balloons).[17]

Lastly, when heavier and concealed German guns fired on French positions the shock to the men under fire was considerable (as was the case when the small number of Boer long-range guns opened fire on British troops in South Africa in 1899). The *Poilus* were taught to believe in the pre-eminence of the 75 which, they widely believed, would be the king of the battlefield. Thus, when the infantry witnessed batteries of these guns being destroyed as if by a hidden hand, and then when these same remote guns turned with devastating effect on their positions, the consternation, often bordering on panic, was great.

THERE IS NO SPACE HERE to give a detailed account of the campaign in Lorraine. Suffice to say that, most especially at Morhange, it contained, writ large, many of the failings displayed in the Alsace campaign. Add to that the behaviour, reckless and bordering on a dereliction of duty, of Foch, and the disaster which befell the French invasion was almost predictable. It was a defeat which cost thousands of Frenchmen their lives and it undermined the relationship between *2e Armée's* commander, de Castelnau, and Foch, then commanding *20e Corps*.

---

[i] Three type *Clément-Bayard* (*l'Adjudant-Vincenot, Dupuy-de-Lôme,* & *Montgolfier*), one type *Astra* (*Conté*), one type *Zodiac* (*Commandant Coutelle*) and one type *Chalais-Meudon* (*Fleurus*) [Source: *Archives de l'aéronautique militaire de la Première Guerre Mondiale, Archives de la Défense*, Château de Vincennes, 2008, page 18].

[ii] The *Service de l'Aérostation* was set up on 19th May 1886 under the auspices of the *Génie* (Engineers) and, by 1900, formed the *25e bataillon du génie* at Versailles. Its companies were based at Verdun, Toul, Épinal and Belfort.

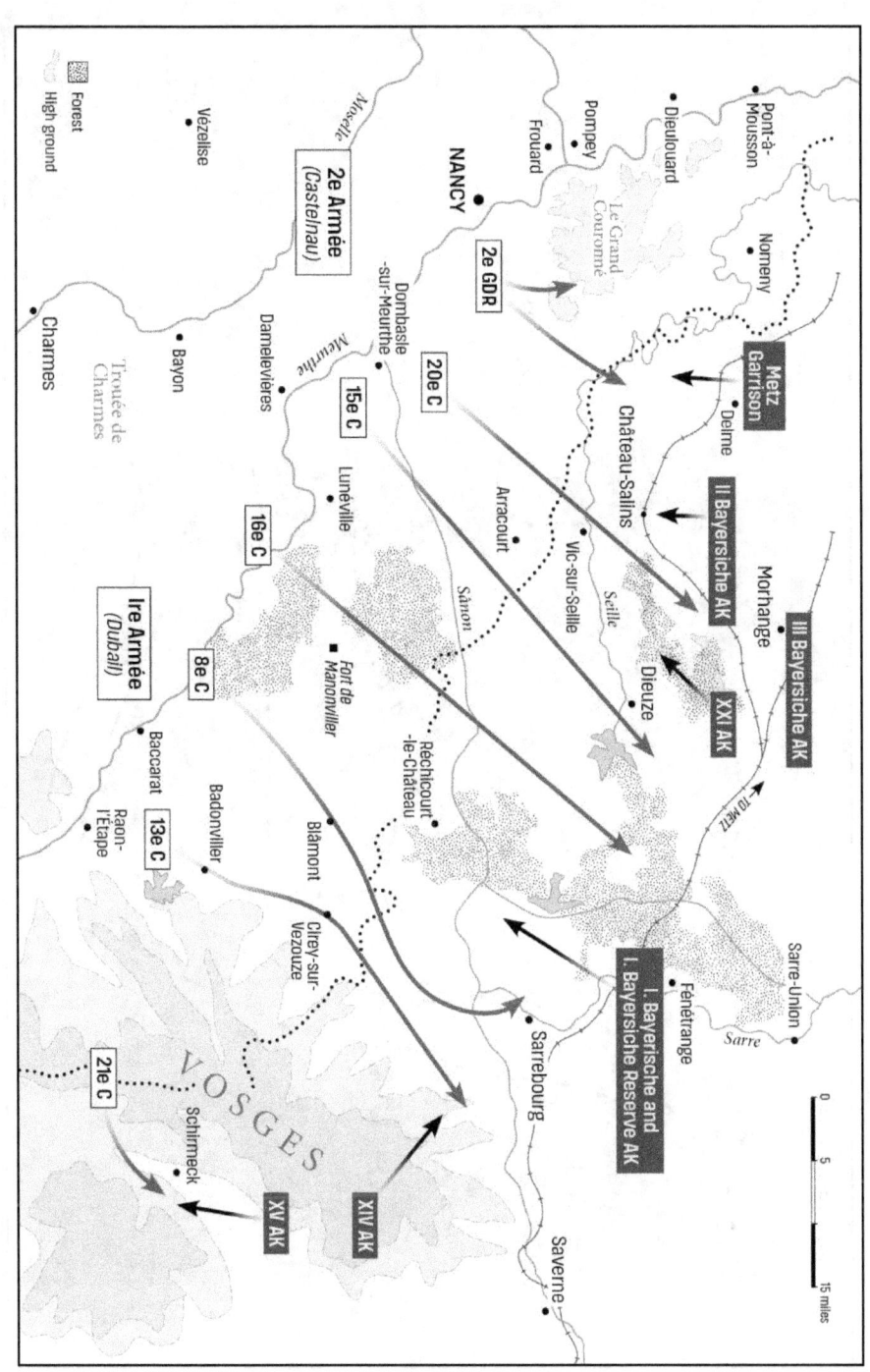

Map 13 The Invasion of Lorraine, August 1914

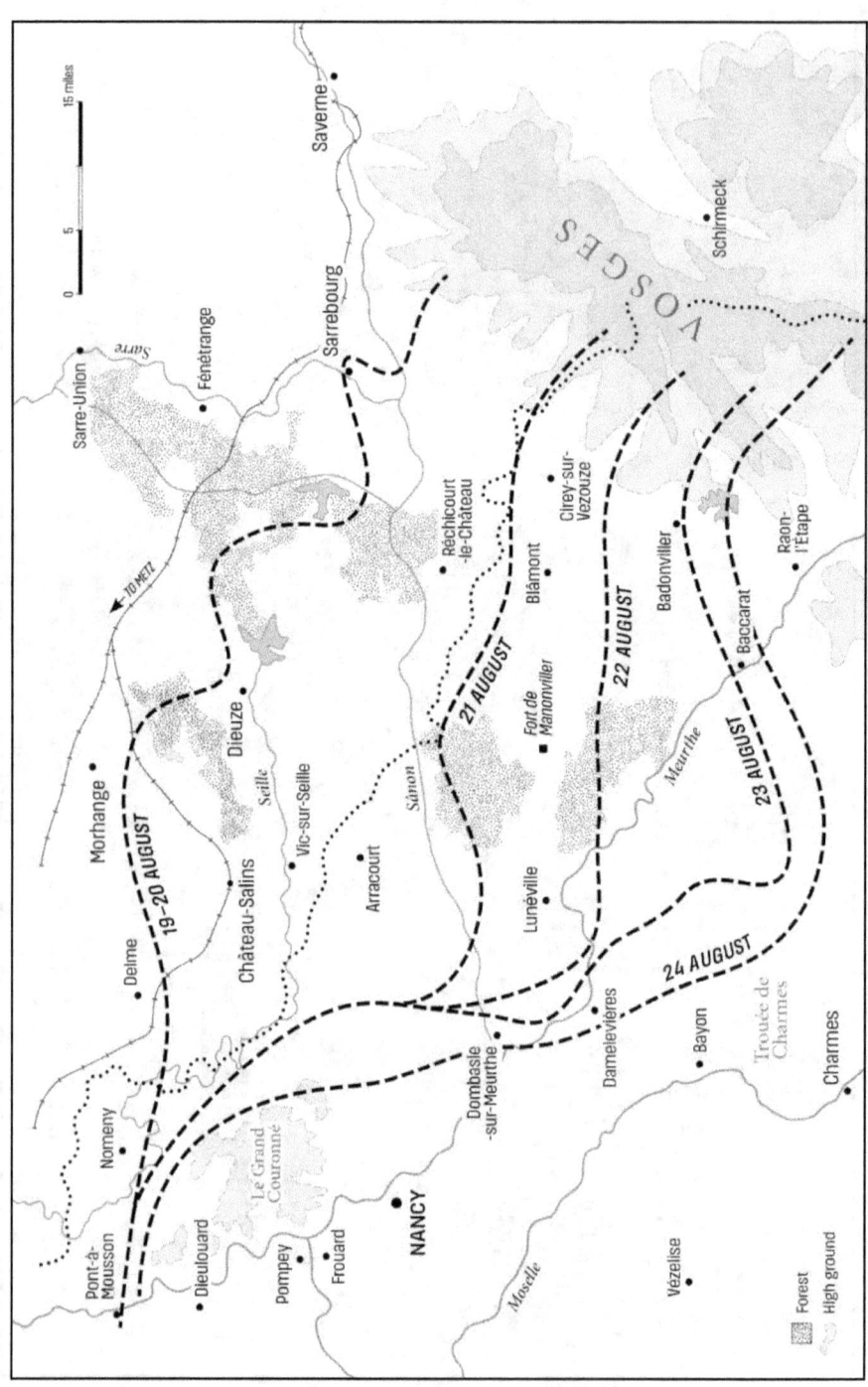

Map 14 The retreat from Morhange and Sarrebourg, 20th to 24th August 1914

The breakdown between the two Generals was caused by Foch's failure to follow Castelnau's orders, and the disaster which ensued can be blamed in part on him. Alternatively, according to Foch, the crucial order never arrived, he was simply pursuing the original campaign plan and, therefore, the defeat and retreat was the fault of Joffre and Castelnau unwisely changing the axis of the advance, and made worse by the inadequacies of the neighbouring *15e* and *16e Corps*.

Briefly, the story is this: after the offensive was launched on 14th August, Dubail entered Sarrebourg on the 18th August but came up against robust defences to the east and north of the city along the line of the *River Saar*. Furthermore, he was threatened by the arrival of the *XIV.* and *XV. Armeekorps* released from around Mulhouse and now approaching through the northern Vosges. Dubail asked Castelnau to ensure that the *2e Armée's 16e Corps* kept in touch with the left of his *8e Corps*. Castelnau, informed that Sarrebourg had been evacuated by the Germans, and convinced they were still retreating, demurred, only offering some infantry and artillery which anyway failed to arrive in the agreed location.

Joffre, meanwhile, ordered the axis of attack of *2e Armée* to switch from the north-east, i.e. parallel to the line of advance of Dubail, to the north, i.e. towards the rear of Metz. This divergence from the north-easterly line of march of *1er Armée* thus threatened to open a gap between the two armies. Meanwhile, Castelnau's *31e Division, 16e Corps*, came up against stern resistance on the 18th August and, generally, the speed of the advance of his *15e* and *16e Corps* slowed relative to that of the *20e Corps* on the northern flank.

Furthermore, *2e Armée* was coming up against the geographical features which made life so difficult for an invading army in Lorraine. *16e Corps*, on the right, was struggling through the marshy terrain surrounding the large *étangs* and negotiating the crossings of the two canals in the region: the *Canal de la Marne et au Rhin* and the *Canal des Houillières de la Sarre*. The *15e Corps* needed to cross the flooded line of the *River Seille* and the *canal des Salines* to approach Dieuze. On the left, *20e Corps* was marching parallel to a line of low hills to the north, stretching from west to east and beyond which lay Morhange and the important railway line from Sarrebourg to Metz. And, crucially, between the *15e Corps* to the south and *20e Corps* to the north was a low ridge covered by the *Fôret de Bride et de Koeking*.

On 18th August, at Joffre's insistence, Castelnau issued orders directing the army to advance north towards the towns of Falquemont and Saint-Avold, the HQ of *Kronprinz* Rupprecht. To achieve this, *2e Armée* would have to cross the fortified *Nied Line*, a position which, at the time, was being garrisoned by troops form the *2.* and *3. Bayerisches Armeekorps* and the *XXI. Armeekorps*. These were bolstered to the west by troops from the garrison of *Festung Metz*, and further strengthened by the installation of heavy *21-cm Mörsers* and long-range guns.

During the day, *15e Corps* fought its way across the line of the *Seille* and the *canal des Salines* with the *30e Division* suffering significant casualties. Meanwhile, *20e Corps* advanced relatively unopposed to a position south of Morhange. Further south, *16e Corps* had a problem as the *31e Division* was 'exhausted' after heavy fighting on the 18th August and the *32e Division* had now to take the lead. This change over further delayed their advance.

Ignoring an aerial reconnaissance report that:

"... the enemy seems to have organized a first line of resistance on the front: Marthil, southern heights of Baronville, Morhange, Rodalben, Bensdorf, and the railway from Bensdorf to Mittersheim"[18]

the conclusion of the staff at *2e Armée* was that:

"...the *2e Armée* has for the moment in front of it strong rear guards composed mainly of infantry and artillery, the latter weapon in a significant proportion, including heavy pieces.
These elements hold seriously organized points of defence in the ground in such a way as to delay our march by obliging us to outflank them or to attack them; the insufficiency of our cavalry, reduced to Corps' regiments[i], prevents us from pursuing them aggressively when they slip away."[19]

In other words, Castelnau expected Rupprecht to continue his withdrawal to the north and east. But, because of the delays experienced by *16e Corps*, allied to Dubail's report he could not at present progress beyond Sarrebourg, Castelnau decided to delay any further advance until 21st August, thus giving *16e Corps* a chance to catch up.

To further confuse the issue, in the afternoon of 19th August, *15e Corps* was prevented from advancing beyond Dieuze by heavy German artillery fire, and the *16e Corps* failed to liaise with *15e Corps* on the arrangements to cross the *canal des Salines* to the east of Dieuze with a view to an advance on Cutting (*Ger.* Kuttingen).

Foch, however, experienced none of these problems and, ever keen to advance and attack the enemy, prepared his Corps for another move northwards on 20th August. Already gaps were opening between the right of the *20e* and the left of the *15e Corps* in the heavily wooded area of the *Fôret de Bride et de Koeking*. There was also a gap between the *15e* and *16e Corps*, and only a tenuous link between the *16e Corps* and the Dubail's *8e Corps*. Taken at face value, it seemed sensible for Castelnau to pause and get his military 'ducks in a row'. Unfortunately, on the same day, Rupprecht ordered an all-out attack by the *6.* and *7. Armees* for the following morning. Even more unfortunately, the morning of 20th August dawned with the ground covered by heavy fog.

In the meantime, at 5 p.m., 19th August, Castelnau issued *Ordre général d'opérations No. 27*. The *15e* and *16e Corps* would resume their northerly advance at 5 a.m. the next day. The *2e groupe de divisions de reserve*, replacing the *9e Corps* as the link between the left of *20e Corps* and the *Moselle* at Pont-à-Mousson, was to extend and fortify their line in case of a German attack out of Metz. Crucially, the *20e Corps* was to:

"... remain on the ground it occupied this evening. It will endeavour to establish its left division (i.e. *39e Division*) in a position allowing it either to continue its offensive towards the northeast, or to face an attack emerging from Metz. Remaining in close contact with the *15e Corps d'Armée*, it should take advantage of the day of the 20th to strengthen its position and to carry out the reconnaissance necessary for the implementation of his artillery and the organization of its attacks."[20]

---

[i] Conneau's recently formed cavalry Corps of three divisions had been notionally attached to Dubail. Dubail, remarkably, had no idea where they were.

This is when accounts diverge. In his memoirs Foch wrote:

> "As I received neither orders nor information from the *2e Armée* during the evening of 19th-20th August, I confined myself to carrying out the spirit of the instructions sent me on 18th August. Accordingly, late in the night, I issued orders from Château-Salins for my Corps to renew its attack at 6 a.m. the following morning. However, when this hour arrived the situation had so changed that the operation was not undertaken."[21]

The *Ordre général d'opérations No. 26, pour la journée du 19 août* to which Foch refers was issued by Castelnau at 2 p.m. on 18th August, and contained no instructions to *20e Corps* other than that, on 19th August, it should:

> "… emerge west of Marsal, inclusive, in the general direction of Château-Salins, Faulquemont (*Ger*: Falkenberg).
> Zone of action limited on the left by the line included Gremecey, Fresnes-en-Saulnois western edge of the forest of Château-Salins, Château-Brehain, Brulange (*Ger*: Brulingen), Mainvillers."[22]

As Elizabeth Greenhalgh suggests in her book *Foch in Command*, in the 'apparent' absence of orders Foch should have first checked with Army command what was required rather than issue orders committing his troops to a continuation of the offensive in the early hours of 20th August.[23] After all, he did not have the complete picture of the progress and problems of the rest of *2e Armée*, nor did he have the most recent intelligence about the actions of the enemy. Instead, he ordered his Corps to attack in the early hours of the next day. One might imagine that the deployment and preparations of *20e Corps* differed in a material way when planning to attack compared to that when assuming a defensive posture.

In his memoirs, Foch accepts that Castelnau, when the problems of the *15e* and *16e Corps* became clear had, indeed, issued new orders for 20th August. A footnote then explains:

> "These orders did not reach either the *20e Corps* or the *68e division de reserve*. It was only during the morning of the 20th, at my advanced headquarters at Burlioncourt, that I was informed of these new instructions, and even then I did not receive the actual text. By that time, the initiative had passed to the enemy, bringing about a radical change in the general situation of the army."[24]

At least part of this statement is provably untrue. The entry for 20th August in the *JMO* of the *68e division de reserve* clearly states:

> "20th August at 1.30 a.m., the *68e DR* receives from the commander of the *2e groupe* (*de divisions de reserve*)[i] the order to maintain their positions of the evening of the 19th August, extending its right to the *Nied* towards Oron to link up with the *20e Corps* (Wiribel detachment[ii])."[25]

---

[i] There is no *JMO* for the *2e groupe de divisions de reserve* which might confirm the time these orders were received from *2e Armée* and forwarded to the *68e DR*.

[ii] The *5e Hussards* and *43e régiment d'infanterie coloniale*. The *5e Hussards* was *20e Corps'* cavalry and commanded by Lt. Col. Hippolyte Raymond de Boutaud de Lavilléon. Its second in command was Lt. Col. Maxime Weygand, who was later Foch's *chef d'état-*

It is also interesting to note that another order issued by *2e Armée* just 20 minutes after the disappearing *Ordre général d'opérations No. 27* somehow *did* arrive at Foch's HQ. This order, specific to *20e* and *15e Corps*, came from Gen. Anthoine, Castelnau's *chef d'état-major*, and read:

> "The General commanding the army orders the General commanding the *20e Corps* to support the elements of the *30e Division* engaged on the northern outlets of the *Fôret de Bride et de Koeking*.
> The *20e Corps* will guard the road from Conthil to Dieuze tonight."[26]

That this order arrived can be confirmed by Foch's reproduction of it in his memoirs where he states it was received at 5.20 p.m. on 19th August.[27] After the event, no-one, including Foch, seems to have thought the arrival of one of these orders but not the other somewhat peculiar.

Castelnau later described Foch's claim not to have received *Ordre général d'opérations No. 27* as 'puerile' and, post-war, it was suggested there had been a cover up as some of *20e Corps'* papers for this period disappeared. Elizabeth Greenhalgh suggests this extends to the *JMO*, or war diary, which, she states, only starts on 28th August when Gen. Balfourier assumed command of *20e Corps*, i. e. after Foch's elevation to command the *9e Armée*. This latter claim is incorrect as the *20e Corps' JMO* for the period 25th July 1914 to 13th March 1915 is available on-line in the form of file *26 N 193/1*.[28]

Whatever the truth – was the order genuinely lost, did a staff officer fail to pass it on, or did Foch simply ignore it – the fall-out led to a breakdown in relations between Castelnau and Foch.

Whatever the case, in the apparent absence of orders to the contrary, Foch issued *Ordre général d'opérations No. 31* in the early hours of 20th August. It committed *20e Corps* to:

> "… a continuation of the general offensive along the entire front."[29]

It is interesting to note Foch's post-war commentary describing the events of the 18th to 20th August. In his memoirs, he reflects on the orders of 18th August which changed the direction of the attack from the north-east to the north. His memoirs question the basis of these orders, especially given that *2e Armée* had been significantly weakened by Joffre's move elsewhere of the *18e* and *9e Corps*:

> "The removal of the *9e* and *18e Corps* greatly reduced the strength of the Army, and consequently its striking power. To protect the left flank, in particular, only the *2e groupe de divisions de reserve* would be available, and these, as the Army advanced, would become stretched out over thirty miles. The protection afforded would be so precarious as to be virtually negligible. On reading these instructions, my first thought was that the General in command (i.e. Castelnau) must have received some very reliable intelligence which caused him to feel justified in ordering this rapid advance with

---

major with *9e Armée*, the *Groupe des armées du Nord* (*GAN*) and, later, when Foch was Supreme Allied Commander. He replaced Gamelin as commander of the French Army in 1940 and was briefly *Ministre de la Défense nationale* in the Vichy Government. He was arrested and interned by the Germans in November 1942. He died in 1965.

objectives as far off the road from Pont-à-Mousson to Saarbrücken. As I saw it, the operation thus far carried out by the *2e Armée* had not constituted an encounter with the enemy so serious in its nature as to have compelled his retreat and much less to have created disorganisation in his ranks. What had taken place had been little more than artillery engagements. Nevertheless, on the very day it had been deprived of two of its Corps and was therefore more weakly protected from the direction of Metz than ever before, this army was ordered to undertake an advance on distant objectives through a country whose dangers have already been described. I presumed that special information from very high sources justifying the enterprise must have been received."[30]

Foch thus tries to pin the blame for the defeat at Morhange on Castelnau, the 'General in command', and Joffre, the 'very high source'. But one must ask, if *2e Armée* had just been placed in a 'precarious' defensive position by the removal of the *9e* and *18e Corps*, if the retreating Germans were in good order, and if the ground to be attacked was known to be dangerous, why did Foch, in the unusual, indeed unique, 'absence' of daily orders from Army command, decide to order an advance without first checking with Castelnau? One must further place all of this into the context of Foch's concerns about any offensive into Lorraine as, again, expressed post-war:

"The Lorraine theatre... was not only a mass of natural obstacles, but its already limited breadth had been further contracted by fortifications. With its flank positions and lateral lines of defence resting on the great fortresses of Strasbourg and Metz-Thionville, and provided as it was with a complete network of railways, it furnished the Germans with a field of battle admirably suited for stopping the adversary with small numbers and then, as occasion arose, inflicting upon him a severe defeat by containing him in front and counter-attacking from the flanks."[31]

These concerns were then reinforced by his unit's first experiences of the German artillery on 14th August. As reported elsewhere, it soon became clear that the heavier German guns outranged the French *75s*. In his *Memoirs*, Foch wrote:

"The superiority of the enemy's armament had already been demonstrated, likewise the advantage he derived from having previously prepared the ground on his side of the frontier. In addition to being numerous, his heavy guns had a longer range than our artillery and could therefore support his troops at a distance impossible for us; moreover, their fire having been ranged beforehand on selected aiming points was extremely accurate."[32]

2e Armée's aerial reconnaissance had already shown the area to be attacked by *20e Corps* was strongly held, well-fortified, and reinforced by heavy artillery. Castelnau therefore knew it was important that this new offensive to the north should employ all his available forces and that, as of the night of the 19th/20th August, they were not suitably located or deployed for a co-ordinated attack to the north. According to Yves Gras, in his 1990 book *Castelnau ou l'art de Commander: 1851-1944*, one of the reconnaissance pilots attempted to report this intelligence to *20e Corps* but was rebuffed by Foch's *chef d'état major*, the 52-year-old Col. Denis

Auguste Duchêne[i]. Duchêne, it seems, was sceptical of the effectiveness of aerial observation and the pilot's request to talk directly to Foch was rejected.[33]

And yet, despite the foregoing, Foch ordered his troops to attack in the early hours of 20th August, and the essence of this order was transmitted to *2e Armée* at 5.15 a.m. In it, Foch informed Castelnau he intended to attack at 6 a.m. On receipt of this message, Castelnau immediately despatched a staff officer, Cdt. Jacquand, to Foch's HQ at Château Salins. He gave precise verbal, and (whatever Foch might claim) probably written[ii], instructions:

"1. Do not advance, do not take the offensive, only local offensives are allowed; install defences strongly.
2. Be able to resist an offensive coming from the area of Metz.
3. In any case, hold the northern edge of the *forêt de Koeking* and link up with *15e Corps*.
4. Help the *15e Corps* not by changing your front, but by drawing on the available troops of the *20e Corps* once your front has been secured."[34]

This message was passed to Foch at 5.30 a.m. At 6.20 a.m., a Capt. d'Amarzit of Antoine's staff telephoned Cdt. Ferry at Foch's HQ with this unequivocal order:

"The *20e Corps* is absolutely prohibited from pursuing its offensive today. You must conform strictly with *Ordre général d'opérations No. 27*."[35]

It was already too late. Overnight, trains busily delivered German troops from the Metz garrison to positions from which to attack the *68e DR*. Even worse, the French had lost track of the *2. and 3. Bayerische Armeekorps* as was made clear in *GQG's Compte rendu de renseignements, No. 49, du 20 Août* issued at 6 a.m.[iii]:

"The *2e Armée* has the impression of having only strong rear guards in front of it. No intelligence on the *2. and 3. Bayerische Armeekorps* reported previously S. E. of Metz."[36]

---

[i] Duchêne experienced a rapid rise,, and even more rapid fall, from grace. Born in 1862, he served in Tonkin 1885-7, before a career as a staff officer. *École supérieure de Guerre*, 1890. Staffs of *4e Division, 9e Corps, 14e Division* and *20e Corps*. Col., *69e RI* in 1912, and *chef d'état-major, 20e Corps* on 23rd March 1914. *Général de brigade*, September 1914. *Chef d'état-major, 2e Armée*, in October then command of *42e Division*. Commander, *Corps*, March 1915, and *2e Corps*, 1916. Command, *10e Armée*, December 1916. A year later he took command of the *6e Armée* holding the *Chemin des Dames* sector. This sector was heavily attacked on 27th May 1918 (3rd Battle of the Aisne, Operation Blücher-Yorck). Duchêne's troops included exhausted British units moved from previously more active fronts. Furthermore, he had not set up a second defensive line as Pétain had demanded and tried to hold the *Chemin des Dames* rather than withdraw beyond the Aisne. His front collapsed and he was forced to retreat to the Marne losing 50,000 PoWs and 800 guns. He was sacked by Pétain on 10th June.
[ii] An unsigned typed copy of the order is in the documents of the *3e Bureau* of *2e Armée*.
[iii] These were not the only 'lost' German units as the same note stated: 'The engagement yesterday on the outskirts of Mulhouse revealed the presence in this region of troops belonging to the *28e Division (XIV. Armeekorps).*' This entire *Armeekorps* was, in fact, about to attack the *1re Armée* south of Sarrebourg.

In fact, these two *Armeekorps* were being moved into positions from which they would overwhelm the over-stretched left wing of Foch's *39e Division*. 'Over-stretched' because this division had advanced well to the north of the line of the *68e DR* and now presented an extended curved flank to the Bavarians whilst, at the same time, it was preparing to push even further north, extending, and exposing this flank still further. The *11e Division* to the east was about to run into the prepared positions of the *XXI. Armeekorps* whilst, at the same time, moving *away* from the left flank of the *15e Corps*. Meanwhile, the *15e Corps* failed to clear the *fôret de Bride et de Koeking* which was, at this time, filling with German troops about to attack the left flank of its *30e Division*. A further complication was that the link between the *15e* and *16e Corps* was, at best, tenuous, as was that between the *16e Corps* and the *8e Corps*, the left wing of the *1re Armée*. It was, overall, a remarkably unhealthy position which, had the Germans pursued the retreat with greater vigour or, indeed, allowed the French to advance still further into the trap laid for them, might have resulted in an even greater catastrophe.

Whatever the German deficiencies in the timing of their offensive, the result still sent both French armies scrambling back to, and in places, beyond the *Meurthe* and even the *Moselle*. There, only desperate French defence at the *Trouée des Charmes* and along the hills above Nancy, the *Grand Couronné*, and absurd tactical errors by Rupprecht and his Generals, prevented a complete collapse of the eastern French armies which almost certainly would have ended the war.

Elizabeth Greenhalgh in *'Foch in Command'* downplays the outcome of Morhange as just a 'bloody nose' and gives casualty figures for *20e Corps* of '4-5,000'. She is wrong on both counts. The *39e Division* alone, with nearly 6,000 dead, wounded and missing, suffered more casualties than those she gives for the entire Corps. As for the 'bloody nose', according to research published by Prof. André Payan-Passeron in 2021, from 18th to 20th August, the two French armies committed 177,000 infantry to the twin battles of Morhange and Sarrebourg. Of these, just over 44,000 (25%) were killed or died of wounds, were wounded, or taken prisoner. 31,000 of these casualties were from the *2e Armée* and c. 13,000 from the *1re Armée*. The heaviest casualties were suffered by the regiments of the *15e Corps* later scapegoated by politicians and the media for the entire disaster.

Payan-Passeron provides the following figures for each Corps:

	Casualties	Percentage loss
2e Armée		
2e groupe de divisions de reserve	3,476	10%
20e Corps	9,572	35%
15e Corps	11,070	41%
16e Corps	7,106	29%
	31,224	
1re Armée		
8e Corps	5,387	22%
13e Corps	4,758	23%
21e Corps	2,697	16%
	12,842	
Grand total	44,066	

The worst hit divisions were the:

29e Division, 15e Corps – 7,113 (948 dead), 44%;
39e Division, 20e Corps – 5,898 (1,400 dead), 41%;
30e Division, 15e Corps – 3,957 (1,504 dead), 29%;
11e Division, 20e Corps – 3,677 (885 dead), 27%.

If one includes the losses suffered by the *15e Corps* on the opening day of the campaign at Moncourt and the *bois du Haut de la Croix* then it was by far the worst hit of Castelnau's three Corps. It lost 15,300 officers and men, or 51% of its strength, between 14th and 21st August. Foch's *20e Corps* suffered 41% losses, the overwhelming majority becoming casualties between the 19th and 21st August.

Despite the chaos and carnage, Foch's reward for his aggressive conduct was to be given command of an army by Joffre.

Immediately after Morhange, another disaster occurred at the small Ardennes village of Rossignol where the French *Corps d'armée colonial*,[i] made up of the *2e* and *3e Divisions d'infanterie coloniale (DIC)* along with the *5e Brigade d'infanterie colonial (BIC)*, already tired and hungry (the history of the *1er Régiment d'Infanterie Coloniale* states 'The men have not eaten for 24 hours, due to constant movement, and the departure is so abrupt that they do not have time to swallow the coffee'), crashed unwittingly into the German *VI Armeekorps* on 22nd August. On a day when more than 21,000 French soldiers were killed in France and Belgium[ii], the men of the *Corps d'armée colonial* suffered casualties of nearly 75% within a few short hours of desperate fighting. By the end of the day nearly 12,000 men were dead, missing, wounded or Prisoners of War from the total of 16,000 who started out the day marching north under the *Tricoleur*. So chaotic was the fighting, and so great the losses amongst officers, the entries for this day and several after are missing from the official war diaries (*Journaux de Marche*) of both *2e* and *3e DIC*.

As an indication of the severity of their losses, *1er BIC* (from *3e DIC*) was only able to collect immediately three or four officers and some 400 men from amongst the six battalions of the *1er* and *2e régiments d'infanterie coloniale (RIC)*. The *1er RIC* alone lost 840 men dead[iii], and 2,000 wounded and missing on this one terrible day and, even having received 150 replacements, was only able to create a single battalion from amongst the survivors[iv]. Forty-one of its 70 officers were killed, wounded, or missing.[37] One of the Corps' cavalry regiments, *3e Régiment de*

---

[i] These units of white Frenchmen served in various French colonies in West, North and Central Africa and Indochina. Black African soldiers, generically named *'Sénégalais'* wherever in West or Sub-Saharan Africa they came from, were not yet present in France.

[ii] Putting this into context, the following day the BEF lost 1,638 killed, wounded and missing in its first major action at the Battle of Mons.

[iii] The regimental history claims 2,000 fatalities plus c. 1,000 wounded and missing [*Source: Historique du 1er Régiment d'Infanterie Coloniale*, page 5].

[iv] After the war, Gen. Alexandre Percin in his 1921 book *Le massacre de notre infanterie, 1914-1918*, stated that a third of the *1er RIC's* casualties, i.e. c. 1,000, were caused by a French 75 battery firing indiscriminately into the edge of the woods from which the regiment was trying to retreat.

Chasseurs d'Afrique, was in the advance guard and heavily involved. After the fighting its losses were: *1er escadron* c. 100%, *2e escadron* 2 officers, *3e escadron* c. 75%, and *4e escadron* c. 50%. Amongst its support units, one officer was the sole survivor of the machine gun section and two officers survived from the regimental train.[38]

WRITING AFTER THE WAR, Joffre blamed two factors for the catastrophic events of August 1914 – his Generals, and a failure by them to understand and apply the 'principles of the offensive'.[39] Given what we have already discovered about the French Regulations for the offensive it seems as though in many cases they were 'just following orders'. But, as far Joffre was concerned:

> "... a large number (of the Generals) had shown they were not equal to their task. Amongst them were some who in time of peace had enjoyed the most brilliant reputation as professors; there were others who, during map exercises, had displayed a fine comprehension of manoeuvre; but now, in the presence of the enemy, these men appeared to be overwhelmed by the burden of their responsibility."[40]

The reference to 'professors' was a barbed comment aimed particularly at Charles Lanrezac, commander of *Ve Armée* based in Charleroi, and, pre-war, regarded as one of the most brilliant intellects in the Army.

Gen. Charles Louis Marie Lanrezac (1852-1925) was born in Pointe-à-Pitre, Guadeloupe. His great grandfather was Colonel de Quinquiry d'Olive, *Marquis* de Cazernal. A member of the Queen's Guard, he was arrested at the *Tuileries* and guillotined on the same day as Marie Antoinette on 16th October, 1793. The family escaped to Guadeloupe via Hamburg changing their name to Lanrezac, an anagram of Cazernal. His father, Auguste, was an officer of Marines and his mother, Marie-Louise Dutau, a *créole* born at Le Moule, Grande-Terre. Returning to France when his father served at Cherbourg, Charles was given a scholarship to the *Prytanée militaire de la Flèche*, a military high school. He joined the *École impériale spéciale militaire de Saint-Cyr* from which he entered the *13e regiment d'infanterie* in 1870. He fought at Coulmiers and Orleans in the Franco-Prussian war before being interned in Switzerland with the remnants of Bourbaki's *Armée de l'Est* in January 1871. He then finished his studies at St Cyr before joining the *30e régiment d'infanterie*. He was appointed a professor at the *École spéciale militaire* in 1880 before spending five years in Tunisia. Promoted *Chef de bataillon* of the *115e régiment d'infanterie* in 1892 he was appointed professor of military history, strategy, and tactics at the *École supérieure de guerre* and its Deputy Director of Studies in 1898. In 1901 he was promoted Colonel and commanded the *119e régiment d'infanterie*. In 1906 he was promoted *général de brigade* and took command of the *43e Brigade*, serving under Joffre in the *6e Division*. In 1911 he was promoted *général de division* with command of *20e Division*. He was then deputy commandant of the *École supérieure de guerre*. In April 1914, on Gallieni's retirement, he was given command of the *Ve Armée* by Joffre and was appointed to the *Conseil supérieur de la guerre* as its youngest member (aged 61).

Immediately before the war Joffre thought very highly of him:

> "... General Lanrezac had attracted my attention by reason of his marked intelligence, activity and initiative, and the skill he had displayed during map

and ground exercises. There was no one who seemed to me more suitable for the command of the *Ve Armée*, the one whose manoeuvres would be the most delicate to carry out, whose movements would be most intricate of all and whose role was essentially dependent on circumstances."[41]

As a professor and second in command at the *École supérieure de guerre*, Lanrezac was renowned as an outstanding lecturer even if impatient, short-tempered, and brusque. He was also a firm opponent of the *offensive a outrance*, stating:

"… if every subordinate commander has the right to ram home an attack on the first opponent he sees, the commander in chief is incapable of exercising any form of direction."[42]

He was thus already at odds with Joffre and his strategy before any fighting began and was highly critical of the reckless nature of *Plan XVII*. Furthermore, and unlike Sir John French and most of the senior officers of the BEF and the French Armies, Lanrezac agreed with Bloch about the nature of the fighting to come. He foresaw 'position warfare' in which:

"… *la pelle et la pioche joueront un role aussi important que le fusil et le canon*."[43]
('the shovel and pickaxe will be as important as the rifle and the cannon')

To complete the heresy, Lanrezac was also an advocate of the defensive and the tactical withdrawal citing Clausewitz and the Russian tactical retreat of 1812 in the face the Napoleon's invasion. That he got to command any unit in the French Army of 1914 is something of a mystery. He did not last long.[44]

Ve Armée formed the left wing of the French Army, with the BEF on its left. Even before Lanrezac took command in April 1914, another distinguished French General, Joseph Gallieni, had questioned the location and purpose of *Ve Armée's* deployment. He resigned rather than accept responsibility for what Joffre had in mind and Lanrezac was moved from *11e Corps* in Nantes and promoted to command *Ve Armée*. Lanrezac then wrote to Joffre explaining he had too few troops to oppose the three German Armies he (correctly) believed were about to sweep through Belgium, but the letter arrived too late for Joffre to respond. Then, before the Battles of the Frontiers, Lanrezac tried to persuade Joffre not to send troops into the Ardennes and to allow his units to face north to oppose the German troops pushing westwards through Belgium. All of this fell on deaf ears.

To make matters worse, Lanrezac and Sir John French formed an instant mutual dislike. After the war, in his book *1914*, French described him as:

"… the most complete example… of the Staff College 'pedant', whose 'superior education' had given him little idea of how to conduct war."[45]

Professional jealousy from French, perhaps, who did not attend the Staff College and then proved to be completely out of his depth as CinC of the BEF.

Lanrezac tried to warn Joffre about the German advance beyond Brussels and wished to withdraw from his advanced position about Charleroi. Attacked, he fought, and lost, the battle (21st-23rd August 1914). He avoided complete disaster by withdrawing *Ve Armée*, saving his command but exposing the BEF. On 29th August Joffre ordered a reluctant Lanrezac to attack at Guise to relieve pressure on the BEF. *Ve Armée* suffered nearly twice as many casualties as the German *2*.

Armée and narrowly escaped the encirclement of which he had warned. Lanrezac then extricated *Ve Armée* in good order but the breakdown of his relationship with Joffre, and his perceived reluctance to attack, persuaded Joffre to sack him before the first Battle of the Marne started. Lanrezac was *limoged* on 3rd September 1914[i].

Lanrezac was not the first, nor the last, General sacked by Joffre in 1914 as grave problems were exposed at all levels in the opening weeks. For example, 61-year-old Gen. Henry Sébastian Sauret[ii], commander, *3e Corps, Ve Armée*, disappeared during the Battle of Charleroi on 23rd August. Replaced by the artillery commander, Gen. Gabriel Rouquerol[iii], Sauret was found the next morning 24 kms to the south in Barbençon. He and eight Corps commanders (40% of the 21 who started the war), André Sordet of *Corps de Cavalerie*, and 33 divisional Generals were sacked. Many were sent to the *12e région militaire métropolitaine* in Limoges. Thus, *'Limoged'* became the French equivalent of the British 'degommed' (unstuck), i.e. sacked.[46]

According to Pierre Rocolle in his 1980 book *L'hécatombe des généraux*: 162 General Officers were *limoged* in the first 150 days of the war.[47] One officer to suffer this sanction was Gen. Louis-Edgard de Trentinian, commander of the *7e Division*. Writing post-war, he estimated at least twenty Generals were sacked in August and another ten before the start of the Battle of the Marne on 5th September.[48]

Senior cavalry officers in particular paid a heavy price for real or perceived failure, with two Corps and five divisional commanders being replaced:

60-year-old Gen. Lescot, *2e Division de Cavalerie*, sacked 13th August 1914

62-year-old Gen. Aubier, *8e Division de Cavalerie*, sacked 16th August 1914

58-year-old Gen. Gillain, *7e Division de Cavalerie*, sacked 25th August 1914

61-year-old Gen. Levillain, *6e Division de Cavalerie*, sacked 27th August 1914

62-year-old Gen. Sordet, *Corps de Cavalerie*, sacked 8th September 1914;

62-year-old Gen. Buisson, *1er Division de Cavalerie* and *Corps de cavalerie*, sacked 30th September 1914; and

60-year-old Gen. Abonneau, *4e Division de Cavalerie*, sacked 13th October 1914

Joffre later wrote about these cavalry officers that:

"While it is true that our cavalry at this period seemed unable to produce generals of first-class ability, capable of managing a mass of three or four

---

[i] He was replaced by Franchet d'Espérey, one of his Corps commanders. After his dismissal he refused offers of further employment. In 1920 he published *Le Plan de campagne français et le premier mois de la guerre, 2 août-3 septembre 1914* (Payot & Cie, Paris), written and revised in 1916-17. He admitted he and Joffre did not share the same strategic or tactical views and that they 'couldn't get along'. He did not attack Joffre, however, because 'I had no right to judge his actions on other parts of the battlefield'.

[ii] Sauret later complained that the raw recruits generated by the *loi des trois ans*, 'had not during this year undergone either instruction in shooting or a sojourn in the instruction camp' [*Source*: Smith, *Between Mutiny and Obedience*, page 31].

[iii] Gen. Gabriel Jean Victor Rouquerol was the second of four sons born to Jean Paul Hippolyte Rouquerol and Jean Marie Gabrielle Ricoux between 1850 and 1854 to reach senior positions in the Artillery. They were all members of the *Légion d'Honneur*.

divisions, it is only fair to say that the division commanders did little to facilitate the task of their chief.

General de Castelnau reported to me on numerous occasions that the cavalry divisions passed whole days without sending him information, even without stating at what places they were to be found[i]. These blunders were confirmed to me by Lt. Col. Brécard, my liaison with Manoury's army. He was a cavalry officer and was deeply humiliated by having to report to me facts which his honesty obliged him to bring to my notice."[49]

Joffre had previously given notice of his dissatisfaction with certain senior officers. Appointed the *Chef d'état-major general* in July 1911, he was immediately critical of certain Generals:

"Many of our General Officers had proved they were incapable of adapting themselves to the conditions of a modern conflict, and for the good of the Army, they ought to be replaced as quickly as possible by younger men with more open minds. The war came on before this important work of regeneration in our higher grades could be accomplished…"[50]

And yet, as was pointed out to the Parliamentary Commission inquiring into the war, all the Corps commanders and two-thirds of the Divisional and Brigade commanders in place in August 1914 had been appointed since July 1911, a fact which begs more than a few questions about Joffre's judgement of personnel.

The subsequent sackings were, legally, beyond Joffre's remit as, technically, only the *Ministre de la Guerre* could sack a General, as Joffre explained after the war:

"In respect of these changes I may as well say here that I was quite conscious of the illegality that I was committing in making them. The general officers whom I removed from their commands had received their *lettres de service* from the *Ministre de la Guerre*, and legally he alone could rescind them."

Joffre, though, covered himself by declaring he was:

"…firmly convinced I was acting in the interests of the country's safety."

He also had the backing of successive *Ministres de la Guerre*, Messimy and Millerand, who happily endorsed all his decisions.

Many of those *limoged* were accused by Joffre of ignoring the 'principles of the offensive'. These failings Joffre described as follows:

"I was told the advanced guards, through a false comprehension of the offensive spirit, were nearly always sent into action without artillery support and occasionally got caught in close formation under the enemy's artillery fire. Sometimes it would be one of the larger units which, moving forward with its flanks unguarded, would suddenly become exposed to unexpected and costly fire. Then infantry was almost always launched to the assault at too great a distance from its objective… Far and beyond all, the co-operation of the infantry and the artillery was constantly neglected."[51]

---

[i] A criticism levelled at Gen. Sordet who commanded the *corps de cavalerie* in the Ardennes in August 1914.

All of this is true as the descriptions of the campaigns in Alsace and Lorraine have amply demonstrated. But Joffre appointed most of the Generals who committed these tactical sins.

Rarely can such egregious errors of judgement over strategy, tactics and equipment have resulted in such catastrophic casualties and overwhelming defeats. Somehow, the French Armies held together as they reeled south and towards the *River Marne* east of Paris. As the speed of the German advance opened temporary gaps between their leading troops and the heavier German guns and howitzers, so the *75s*, under far less pressure from these guns, caused carnage amongst the enemy advance guards. Whenever these long guns and heavier howitzers could take the 75-mm batteries under fire, however, the French retreat started again.

That is until 6th September when, with revised infantry tactics, the support of the heavier elements of the French artillery train, and the massing of the remaining 75 batteries, the French Armies were unleashed on the tired, over-stretched Germans who had out-run the support of their big guns, and whose field artillery was experiencing acute shell shortages. Pressed from the south and, from the west, by Foch's *IXe Armée*, the BEF, and troops from the Paris garrison under Gen. Gallieni (famously driven to the fighting in Parisian taxis), the German Armies withdrew to the *Oise* and the *Aisne*. There the front stabilised.

Now the Allied infantry lost heavily under the fire of the newly replenished German field and heavy artillery while the Allies had neither the means to reply or dislodge the enemy from their new trenches. It was on the *Aisne* that, for the first time, the BEF came under the disconcerting, effective and long-range fire of the *15-cm schwere Feldhaubitze*, guns to which the BEF had no answer in terms of either range or power.

So began the so-called 'Race to the Sea' as each side tried to turn their enemy's open flank to the north. Fighting and movement were hectic, but the French, British, and Belgian forces eventually held the line around Ypres and along the *Yser* as the Germans squandered large numbers of troops in desperate efforts to break the Allied front during the First Battle of Ypres. The cost for all was huge and the result a tactical stalemate. But the strategic advantage lay with Germany.

By the end of January 1915, after the devastating losses of the Battles of the Frontiers, the retreat towards Paris and the 'Miracle of the Marne', followed by the 'Race to the Sea', and the First Battles of Artois and Ypres, the French Armies had permanently lost over ½ million men – dead, missing, died of wounds, and prisoners of war. 330,000, or 66%, of these fell or were captured in just 38 days between 6th August and 13th September 1914. Include the numbers of wounded, 580,000 in six months, and total French casualties by the end of January 1915 were 1.1 million or an average of c. 6,100 per day.[52]

But the fighting in 1914 was not wholly one sided. In the seven months of the Franco-Prussian War the combined German armies lost c. 117,000 killed and wounded, or just 40% of the French total of killed and wounded. In this new war, according to the *Reichsarchiv's* own figures, 171,000 German troops died on the Western Front in the first six months and 119,000 were missing or prisoners of war for a total of 290,000 dead, missing and prisoners.[53] Another 560,000 were wounded. These figures represent nearly 80% of the French casualty numbers for the same period and are double the proportion managed during the same period of the Franco-Prussian War[i]. Clearly, if nothing else, both Armies had, over the intervening period, become far more efficient at killing and maiming one another.

And yet, despite the horrendous French casualties in the opening six months of the war, Paris survived and the German Armies were repulsed. This was now a war France could not afford to lose, whatever the cost, and, with the backing of the Royal Navy, the promise of manpower from Britain and its Empire, huge injections of British, and later American, cash, and with Germany fighting on two fronts against the Triple Entente, plans were laid for the enemy's ejection from French territory. The bloodletting was far from over.

That the French were still fighting twelve months later is remarkable. By the end of January 1916, the French Armies had lost another 423,000 men killed, died of wounds, missing, or as prisoners of war. With over one million permanently lost[ii] and nearly one million wounded in just 18 months it is astonishing that the Armies of France were not only capable of mounting offensives throughout 1915 – the First and Second Battles of Champagne, and the Second and Third Battles of Artois – but, at the end of that year, were also able to propose to the newly appointed CinC of the British Expeditionary Force, General Sir Douglas Haig, yet another, large scale, French-led offensive. But, in December 1915 in the weeks after an Inter-Allied Conference at Chantilly, this is precisely what the French CinC, Gen. Joseph Joffre, suggested – a joint, wide-fronted offensive astride the *River Somme* involving nearly 50 divisions, more than two thirds of them French, to take place concurrently with similar offensives by their Russian and Italian allies. The identified target date for these attacks was to be around 1st July 1916.

As the junior partner of the coalition on land it was a proposal the new British CinC, Douglas Haig, was in no position to reject. Whilst France had lost c. 2 million men dead, wounded or PoWs, British casualties on the Western Front were *just* 404,000[iii]. It was inconceivable the French could be asked to continue carrying the weight of the fighting and the burden of losses for much longer. The British Army in France and Flanders must start pulling its weight and the joint offensive was its main chance to do so in 1916.

---

[i] A proportion of these casualties were caused by the BEF. From August 1914 to end of January 1915, the BEF lost 102,000 killed, wounded, missing and prisoners of war. [*Source:* Churchill, W S, *The World Crisis 1911-1918*, Volume 2, Appendix J, page 1427].
[ii] By 31st December 1915, French casualties amounted to 1,001,271 killed, died, and missing and 1,961,687 in total [*Source: AFdGG*, Tome III, page 602].
[iii] France suffered losses of c. 5% of its pre-war population (41.6 million) against 0.9% of the British/Irish total (45.3 million). Metropolitan France's population fell by 3 million by 1919 through casualties and a falling birth rate partly caused by the number of men killed and disabled. Live births in France, 796,000 in 1913, plummeted to 385,000 in 1916. Low birth rates caused recruiting problems in 1939 when men born between 1914-18 were aged 21-25
[*Source: Developed Countries Demography, Institut National d'Études Démographiques, https://www.ined.fr/en/everything_about_population/data/online-databases/developed-countries-database/*].

Commanding *Les Armées de France* August 1914 – Just One of Them Saw Out the War

106 Maréchal de France Joseph Joffre
Commandant en chef des operations.
Removed 26th December 1916

107 Général d'armée Augustin Dubail
Commander Ier Armée. Sacked March 1916

108 Général d'armée Noël Édouard de Castelnau
Commander IIe Armée, and later GAC and GAE

109 Général de division Pierre Ruffey
Commander IIIe Armée. Sacked 30th August 1914

110 Général de division Fernand de Langle de Cary
Commander IVe Armée. Sacked May 1916

111 Général d'armée Charles Lanrezac
Commander Ve Armée. Sacked 3rd September 1914

ENDNOTES:
[1] MacDonald, A, *The Affair at Lagarde, 11th August 1914*, Iona Books, page 140.
[2] Brose, E D, *The Kaiser's Army: The Politics of Military Technology in Germany during the Machine Age, 1870–1918*, OUP, 2001, page 190.
[3] *AFdGG*, Tome I, Volume 1, Annexes, Annexe 206, page 212-3.
[4] *Ibid.*, and Annexe 208, page 215.
[5] *Ibid.*, Annexe 600, page 536.
[6] Staubwasser, O, *Das Königlich Bayerische 2. Infanterie-Regiment Kronprinz - Erinnerungsblätter*, J. Lindauer, 1924, page 19.
[7] *AFdGG*, Tome I, Volume 1, Annexes, Annexe 180, page 190-1.
[8] *Ibid.*, Annexe 208, page 215.
[9] Ibid., Annexe 219, page 224-7
[10] Ibid., Annexe 791, pages 673-674.
[11] *JMO, 1re Armée*, 26 N 19/1, page 7.
[12] *JMO, 1re Armée*, 26 N 19/1, page 8.
[13] *Historique résumé du 56e Régiment d'Infanterie pendant La Guerre 1914-1918, Imprimerie Berger-Levrault*, pages 8-9.
[14] Tricoche, George Nestler, *Notes on Artillery Aviation and Artillery in Trench Warfare, Field Artillery Journal*, Vol. 6, No. 2, April-June 1916, pages 214-5.
[15] Field Artillery Journal, April-June 1916, page 216
[16] *Archives de l'aéronautique militaire de la Première Guerre Mondiale, Archives de la Défense*, Château de Vincennes, 2008, page 17.
[17] *Musée de Génie, Le redressement militaire de la France 1871-1914*, page 9.
[18] *AFdGG*, Tome I, Volume 1, Annexes, Annex 534, page 489.
[19] Ibid.
[20] *AFdGG*, Tome I, Volume 1, Annexes, Annex 540, page 493.
[21] Foch, F, trans. Mott, *The Memoirs of Marshal Foch*, page 24.
[22] *AFdGG*, Tome I, Volume 1, Annexes, Annex 478, page 444.
[23] Greenhalgh, E, *Foch in Command*, CUP, 2011, page 17.
[24] Foch, F, trans. Mott, *The Memoirs of Marshal Foch*, page 24.
[25] *JMO, 68e division de reserve*, 26 N 390/1.
[26] *AFdGG*, Tome I, Volume 1, Annexes, Annex 541, page 494.
[27] Foch, *Memoirs*, op. cit., page 23.
[28] Greenhalgh, po. cit., page 17.
[29] *AFdGG*, Tome I, Volume 1, Annexes, Annex 673, page 582.
[30] Foch, *Memoirs*, op. cit., pages 20-21.
[31] Ibid., page 13.
[32] Ibid., page 16-7.
[33] Gras, Y, *Castelnau ou l'art de Commander: 1851-1944*, Denoel, 1990, pages 150-3.
[34] *AFdGG*, Tome I, Volume 1, Annexes, Annex 610, page 542.
[35] Ibid., Annex 611, page 543.
[36] Ibid., Annex 580, page 525.
[37] *JMO, 1er régiment d'infanterie colonial*, 26 N 863/1.
[38] *Historique du 3e Régiment de Chasseurs d'Afrique*, Imprimerie Berger-Levrault, pages 23-4.
[39] Joffre, *Memoirs*, page 185.
[40] Ibid., pages183-4.
[41] Joffre, *Memoires*, op. cit., page 111.
[42] Palat, Gen. B E, *La Grande guerre sur le front occidental I: Les éléments du conflit*, Librairie Chapelot, 1917, page 278.
[43] Ibid.
[44] Ibid., page 279.
[45] French, *1914*, op. cit., page 37

[46] Cabanes, B, *August 1914: France, the Great War, and a Month That Changed the World Forever*, Yale University Press, 2016, pages116-7.
[47] Rocolle, P, *L'hécatombe des généraux, Lavauzelle*, coll. L'Histoire, le moment, 1980, page 373.
[48] Trentinian, E de, *L'État-Major en 1914 et la 7e division du 4e corps : 10 août au 22 septembre 1914*, Paris, L. Fournier, 1927, page 83.
[49] Joffre, trans. Mott, Col. T H, *The Memoirs of Marshal Joffre*, Geoffrey Bles, 1932, footnote page 289.
[50] Ibid., page 33.
[51] Joffre., page 185.
[52] *Journal Officiel, Documents parliamentaires, Session Extraordinaire 1920, Annexe 633, Séance du 29 Mars, Pertes des Armées Françaises (Nord-Est and Orient) reparties par periodes.* Quoted in Churchill, W S, *The World Crisis 1911-1918*, Volume 2, Appendix J, page 1428.
[53] Reichsarchiv, *German losses on the Western Front by main operations period.* Quoted in Churchill, W S, *The World Crisis 1911-1918*, Volume 2, Appendix J, page 1429.

17. FRENCH TACTICAL TINKERING

"The purpose of an offensive action is not only to seize a line of enemy trenches, but to drive the enemy from all of its positions and beat him, without giving him time to recover."

But et conditions d'une action offensive d'ensemble
Issued by *GQG*, 16th April 1915

IT IS EASY TO BE CRITICAL OF THE FRENCH ARMY'S infantry-centric tactics and the resulting heavy casualties during 1915. Some British Generals, Haig and Robertson to name but two, expressed scathing views on the subject which, given the BEF's relative inactivity throughout this period, does them little credit. It is easy to reduce casualties if you do not fight. Given the failures of the French armaments industry, added to the need to supply Russia, Serbia, and later Italy, as well as divert men, guns, and ammunition first to Gallipoli and then Salonika, it is clear that, for the first two years of the war, the French Army in France was short of essential firepower and, in the absence of sufficient artillery support, it was the poor *Poilus* who suffered the consequences.

As the fighting developed in 1915, the French started to learn lessons about the need to concentrate artillery and to employ its various natures on tasks appropriate to their characteristics. Concentration was a key issue (and one still not learnt by the British before 1st July 1916). In fighting around Perthes-Lès-Hurlus[i] on the Champagne front on 25th March 1915, for example, the number of heavy guns available was just 109 on a front of 16 km, or one heavy cannon per 146 metres. The attacks were costly failures. Further east at Les Éparges in April, a greater artillery concentration resulted in a markedly improved performance.

The first 'high' point of this new approach was the first day of the Second Battle of Artois on 9th May 1915, an attack made by d'Urbal's *Xe Armée*, part of Foch's *Groupe provisoire du Nord* (later the *Groupe d'Armées du Nord* or *GAN*). A six-day bombardment was carried out using 293 heavy guns along a front of 15 km (one heavy gun/howitzer per 51 metres). The heavy barrage by guns and *mortiers* of 95 to 270-mms was supported by 780 field guns[ii] (one every 19 metres) and an unprecedented quantity of trench mortars and guns. On the same day, Haig's First Army attacked at Aubers Ridge and, whilst French ideas and fortunes showed distinct signs of improvement, Haig's offensive was a lamentable and costly failure.

The artillery strength of the armies is, however, instructive showing both the concentration of *material* achieved by Foch but also its reliance on de Bange, slow-firing guns and howitzers. Whereas 82% of German guns and howitzers defending their positions in Artois were quick-firing, almost 90% of the QF French guns were *75s*. Of the total excluding the *75s*, only 20% were quick firing. 95% of the British QF weapons used at Aubers Ridge were either field guns or howitzers:

---

[i] This village was destroyed and never re-built. It is one of the thirty or so *Village Détruit* around Verdun, on the Aisne, and in Champagne. Perthes' population was 156 in 1911.
[ii] 702 *75s*, 53 *90s* and 25 *80s* [*AFdGG*, Tome III, Vol. III, page 27].

Gun type	German		French		British	
	Total	QF	Total	QF	Total	QF
Field guns	582	554	780	702	450	360
Field Howitzers	156	156	0	0	80	60
Medium Guns (10-15 cm)	36	16	140	48	48	20
Long Guns (15cm+)	16	0	88	0	4	0
Medium Howitzers (155mm)	83	79	80	36	36	0
Heavy Howitzers	20	20	12	0	13	0
Total	893	825	1100	786	631	440

Table 41 German, French and British artillery, Artois, 9th May 1915
[*Source:* Reichsarchiv, *Der Weltkrieg 1914 bis 1918, Die Operationen des Jahres 1915*, Vol. 2, *Die Ereignisse im Westen im Frühjahr und Sommer, im Osten vom Frühjahr bis zum Jahresschluß*, 1932, Annexes]

One of the major improvements was in the quantity of trench mortars now available to the French. In Artois this armament consisted of:

55 *Canon de 37 mm Mle 1885 TR système Hotchkiss* [i].
125 of the various types of 58-mm trench mortar, the *Mortier de 58 T*;
49 *Mortiers Aasen* [ii];
16 *Canon de 80-mm de montagne aménage en lance-mines Gatard* [iii].

To assist with the accuracy of the bombardment *Xe Armée* was supplied with three *groupes de bombardement,* observation aircraft attached to the artillery; a tethered balloon to augment the single *escadrilles* attached to each of the six Army Corps; and three *escadrilles de chasse* to be employed in protecting the observation and reconnaissance flights. In addition, and in response to the German use of *flammenwerfers* (flamethrowers), *Xe Armée* also had attached a *Compagnie Schilt*, equipped with *appareil lance-flammes No. 3*[iv] to assist the infantry when clearing German trenches and dugouts.

By far the most common of these weapons was one of the variants on the *Mortier de 58 Tranchée*. The original 58-mm trench mortar was designed by *chef de*

---

[i] The *Canon de 37 mm Mle 1885 TR système Hotchkiss* was the basis for the later quick-firing (TR) 37 mm gun in service from 1916. The *Hotchkiss* fired a 0.5 Kg round containing 22 grams of explosive to a range of 2,400 m. at a notional rate of 20 rounds per minute. Originally designed for the navy it was used by the Army in Morocco in 1907. 277 guns were handed over to the Army in 1914 [François, op. cit., page 54].

[ii] The *Mortier* (or *Obusier*) *Aasen de 86 mm* utilised an 1874 barrel to fire a *Grenade Excelsior Type B* out to 310 metres. 1,282 were built up to February 1916 and remained in service until early 1917. It was vulnerable both because of its limited range and because it used a black powder propellant charge with gave away its location. It could fire up to 10 rounds a minute [François, Gen. G, op. cit., page 61].

[iii] The *Canon de 80-mm de montagne aménage en lance-mines Gatard* was an adapted mountain gun which could fire a heavy mortar shell, 18-35 Kgs, a short distance (174-480 m.). It was designed by a naval engineer/artillerist and was mainly used in the Vosges and Lorraine [François, op. cit., page 41].

[iv] The *Schilt appareil lance-flammes No. 3* was a portable flamethrower weighing 32 Kg. It had a capacity of 16 litres and a range of 16 metres.

bataillon Duchêne of Fayolle's *70e Division* towards the end of 1914. Called the *Mortier de 58 T (Tranchée) No. 1* 180 were built by *Leflaive-usines de La Chaléassière à Saint-Étienne* between December 1914 and February 1915. They were first employed in Artois in January 1915. It fired a 16 Kg bomb 300 metres.

112 Mortier de 58 T (Tranchée) No. 1

113 Mortier de 58 T (Tranchée) No. 2
Constructed at *Leflaive-usines de La Chaléassière à St Etienne*

A superior version, the No. 2, was then designed and 1,000 were ordered in February 1915 before a further 2,300 were built. This highly effective trench mortar could fire bombs as heavy as 40 Kg to a range of 450 metres, or a 20 Kg bomb as far as 1,450 metres. Whilst these were being manufactured, a simpler upgrade, the *Mortier de 58 T (Tranchée) No. 1 bis*, was ordered with some 1,700 eventually being made. This gun's range was limited to 530 metres but it only took 15 minutes to emplace and weighed a third of the No. 2 (222 Kgs to 600 Kgs). So numerous were these guns by June 1916 that the French *VIe Armée* was able to have a complete 12-gun battery deployed along a front of 200 metres or so in numerous sectors. They represented a major enhancement in the French Army's trench warfare capability and, used *en masse* as they were prior to 1st July 1916, could devastate the front trenches of any German position.[1] An excellent example of such an effect was the almost complete destruction of the German front line north of Maricourt which helped the British take Montauban.

The Second Battle of Artois in May 1915 was in part based on an analysis of the previous fighting and how this might translate into the process of the offensive. This was encapsulated in a note issued by Foch on 3rd February 1915[2]. A *précis* of this was, in turn, issued by GQG under the title of *Extrait d'une note rédigée dans une armée, sur le rôle de'artillerie dans les attaques* on 14th February, and much of this was later incorporated into a document entitled *But et conditions d'une action offensive d'ensemble* and issued by GQG on 16th April 1915.

Based on an attack by two battalions on a four company front some 800 metres wide, Foch's original note comprised nine sections, seven of which dealt with the application of the artillery to the problem of ensuring a successful advance of the infantry, which was given four tasks:

1. *Tir de preparation*: the preparatory bombardment to overcome passive defences such as barbed wire as well as face the heavy rifle and machine gun fire;
2. *Tir de barrage*: barrage (blocking) fire to resist enemy flanking fire and attacks;
3. *Tir de recherche:* Searching/sweeping fire to repulse enemy counterattacks on the captured position; and
4. *Tir de contre-batterie*: counter-battery fire to help hold the position against the inevitably heavy enemy artillery fire which would try to render the lost trenches untenable.

It was the task of the artillery to destroy the passive defences and to either disable or undermine the morale of the defenders so they were either unable to defend their position or, possibly, be forced to abandon it.

Foch was most concerned about the vulnerability of the flanks as it was often infantry counterattacks and heavy machine gun and artillery fire from the flanks which either stopped French attacks or made holding the newly won position impossible. Thus, he suggested a blocking flank barrage some 100 to 200 metres wide on either side of the area to be attacked and as deep as the proposed objective, along with sweeping fire in an area on either wing of at least 7-800 metres wide and 500 metres deep which would search for positions the Germans might use to deploy machine guns or other weapons.

Counter-attacks would be beaten off by an artillery barrage placed 1-200 metres in front of the captured position and 50 to 100 metres from either flank to a depth of 2-300 metres. All of this was illustrated by the graphic below illustrating the necessary artillery preparatory fire, barrage, blocking and counter-battery fire on the right wing of any attack.

Once the objective had been taken, it was the job of the artillery to either destroy or neutralise the enemy guns which would take this newly won position under fire, as in Point 4 above. To achieve this, aircraft and balloons had to be in the air at the time when the infantry left their trenches so observers could spot active enemy batteries and then direct French fire onto them.[3]

Foch then went on to underline the importance of the proper artillery preparation of the first line to be attacked in order to destroy the defences and their garrison. Then, as rapidly as possible, the second position would be similarly prepared for attack. The artillery would then place *'un barrage implacable'* in front of the newly captured trenches and, to achieve this, Foch estimated the need for one gun per 10 metres of front to be barraged. For the flanking 'blocking barrage' he estimated a group of 75s, i.e. twelve guns, would be adequate. Fundamental to the entire plan, however, was the effective counter-battery fire which needed to be unleashed as soon as the infantry left their trenches and which, at the very least, needed to silence, i.e. neutralise, the majority of the enemy's guns.

The penultimate part of Foch's note, section VIII, concerned the actions of the infantry in taking the enemy's first line, securing their flanks, and then taking and consolidating the second line of defences. This second advance might, or might not, take place on the same day. Section VIII, with its suggestion of limited advances, was noticeably absent from the *GQG* version issued on 14th February.

Though hardly revolutionary by later standards, Foch's note was a first attempt at quantifying the numbers, and methodically organising the application of, the artillery needed to prosecute a successful if limited attack. It was this latter point, the limited nature of Foch's ambition, which remained lacking from French, and British, plans for the foreseeable future. As a result, and as with all the Allied battle plans for 1915, *GQG's* April-issued *But et conditions d'une action offensive d'ensemble* was still based on the concept of piercing the German lines and pushing troops through the ruptured position. This was made clear by the opening paragraph:

> "The purpose of an offensive action is not only to seize a line of enemy trenches, but to drive the enemy from all of its positions and beat him, without giving him time to recover." [4]

As a statement of the purpose of an offensive this is, as near as damn it, still what Haig believed prior to the opening of the Somme battle, by which time French offensive tactics had significantly moved on.

Instead of simply throwing good men at organised defences as in the past, there was to be more circumspection to any offensive plan than previously. The important principles were:

- Methodical organisation;
- Complete destruction of the enemy wire;
- A concentrated bombardment of the key parts of the enemy front-line supported by aerial reconnaissance and observation;
- Infiltration tactics with the infantry by-passing enemy strongpoints;
- Sufficient reserves to carry on the action over a prolonged period; and
- Adequate artillery support before and during the attack.

The document contained the first hints of a rolling or creeping barrage to precede the infantry and underlined the importance of counter battery fire. Its ultimate weakness, however, was the distant objectives set to ensure breakthrough. This resulted in the dilution of the planned bombardment and the isolation and disorganisation of any troops who broke deep into the German position.

THE GERMAN POSITION TO BE ATTACKED IN ARTOIS consisted of a large salient in front of Vimy Ridge, the western most part of which occupied the eastern ends of the heights overlooking the valley of the small *River Souchez*. This river was formed by the confluence of two small streams, the *Carency* and *St Nazaire*, at which juncture stood the village of Souchez. The *Souchez* runs away north-east beyond the northern end of Vimy Ridge to become the *canal de Lens* in the middle of that town. It then joins the *canal de la Deûle* which runs north to Lille and south to Douai.

Just behind the German front-line were the ruins of several small villages. These were, from north to south: Angres, Ablain St Nazaire, Carency and Neuville St Vaast. The front-line then bent back southwards near Roclincourt to run to the east of Arras. On the northern flank two ridges running west-east flanked the small *St Nazaire* stream, the northern-most spur being topped by the chapel of *Notre Dame de Lorette*. South of this position, several spurs ran towards the higher ground of Vimy Ridge behind the crest line of which were numerous German artillery batteries. The German defences were complex and comprehensive, most especially on the Lorette spur and in front of Vimy Ridge, where networks of trenches and redoubts formed strongpoints such as the *Ouvrage blanc* near La Targette, and the intricate and deadly warren of the *Labyrinthe*. The villages were fortified, with the houses and cellars connected by tunnels. Dugouts, some 15 metres deep, had been excavated and reinforced, and machine gun posts built at regular intervals into the numerous trench lines. The German 1st Position had a depth of c. 150 metres and contained the strongpoints of the *Notre Dame de Lorette* chapel, Ablain St Nazaire, *bois de la cote 125*, Carency, the *Ouvrage blanc* (NW of la Targette), la Targette itself and the *Labyrinthe* south of Neuville St Vaast. The 2nd Position ran from *bois en Hache* on high ground above Souchez, south around Souchez and along the Cabaret Rouge to the la Targette road, then through Neuville St Vaast and on to Thélus.

Frontal attacks on such strongpoints would be suicidal and thus Foch and Pétain, commanding the *33e Corps* in the centre of the attack, proposed infiltration tactics to avoid such death traps, leaving them to be dealt with by artillery and supporting troops who could attack the German garrisons from flank and rear.

As with so many Western Front battles, the weather did not play ball. The bombardment was extended by two days to complete the job of preparing the way for the infantry. By the morning of the attack, 9th May, there was still uncertainty about the effectiveness of the artillery's work. On 8th May, Gen. Besse, commander of *Xe Armée's* artillery, admitted that, although the first line of German trenches and a large part of the second position was destroyed or badly damaged, the third position (and final objective) along the top of Vimy Ridge (the central highpoint being *côte 140*), south through La Folie (east of Neuville St Vaast) and the village of Thélus (in front of the southern high point *côte 147*) had not been properly bombarded nor could any results be seen. Furthermore, Besse was concerned the Germans were conserving their artillery until the infantry attack went in, as their response to the bombardment had been muted. His main worry was that, if German guns laid down a barrage cutting off the advanced units from their reserves, these forward units would not be strong enough to reach the German gun lines on the reverse slope of Vimy Ridge. Bombarding these guns and the ridge was essential, but it proved impossible to see these positions let alone take them under fire.[5]

The main infantry attack was launched at 10 a.m. on 9th May, but was preceded at 5 p.m. on 8th May by the attempted capture of the *Ouvrage blanc* by the *3e bataillon de chasseurs* in a *coup de main* launched with the springing of five mines under the German front-line at 5 p.m. Within thirty minutes the entire position was occupied. Unfortunately, the officer commanding, *Chef de bataillon* Sébastien Marie Léon Madelin[i] was mortally wounded, and many officers killed or wounded, and severe flanking fire eroded the strength of the troops digging in. A German counterattack at 6 p.m. ejected the disorganised *chasseurs* from their positions and, by the end of the day, all they had to show for their endeavours was the rims of the craters from the five mines. They had lost a third of the battalion of whom 114 were dead[ii]. It was not the most auspicious of beginnings.

After a final intense barrage, the main attack[iii] was launched from north to south by *21e, 33e, 20e, 17e* and *10e Corps* in clear weather at 10 a.m. On the left *21e Corps*, attacking the Lorette spur, captured three lines of trenches but was stopped, partly by a barrage in front of the chapel fired by artillery from the direction of Liévin, but mainly by heavy flanking machine gun fire. They ended the day with a net gain of just 200 metres.[6] On the right, much was expected of the attack by *17e Corps* but here the bombardment of the German defences proved inadequate and the distance between the two frontlines too great. Machine gun fire from behind Roclincourt prevented any progress, except for a temporary hold on the German front-line which was soon ended by a heavy counterattack. On the far right, *10e Corps* suffered a similar fate and attempts to re-launch the attacks in this southern sector only served to increase an already long butcher's bill.

In the centre the attacks were made by *33e* and *20e Corps*. On the southern wing, Foch's old *20e Corps* rapidly took the German 1st Position, overran the hamlet of la Targette and advanced 600 metres beyond. The Neuville St Vaast cemetery was captured but the large defensive work of the *Labyrinthe* proved a step too far and here the attack stopped. An attempt to capture Neuville St Vaast foundered and the French lines solidified around the cemetery.

---

[i] *Chef de bataillon* Sébastien Marie Léon Madelin, *Chevalier, Légion d'Honneur, Croix de guerre avec deux palmes*, was born in Bar-le-Duc on 25th April 1879, the son of Sébastien Amédée Madelin and Félicité *née* Bonnet, and husband of Marie Béchaux. Five children. He died in the *Hôpital temporaire 52*, Nouex-les-Mines, and is buried in the *Carré militaire du cimetière communal*, Nouex-les-Mines, *Tombe 356*.
[ii] Casualties: Eight officers and 411 Other Ranks leaving 16 officers and 1,025 ORs.
[iii] An attack near Loos attack to secure the northern flank was made by *9e Corps*.

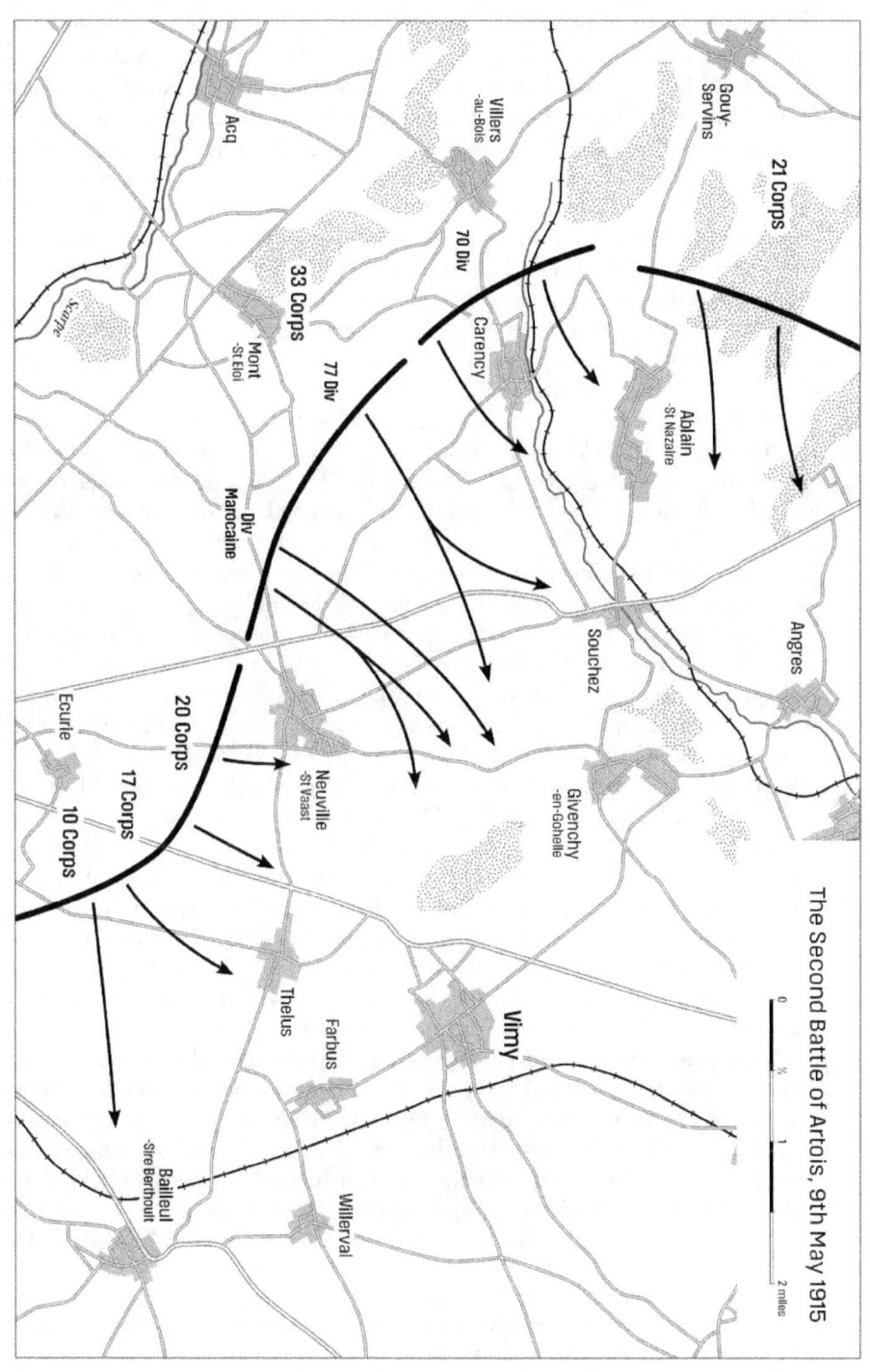

Map 15 The opening attack of the 2nd Battle of Artois, 9th May 1915

It was on the left centre of the attack, where the three divisions of Pétain's *33e Corps* were positioned, remarkable progress was made. From north to south Fayolle's *70e Division*, Gen. Ernest Jacques Barbot's *77e Division* and Gen. Ernest Joseph Blondlat's[i] *Division Marocaine* advanced towards the centre of Vimy Ridge about *côte 140*. The task of *70e Division* was to screen the other divisions from the defences at Ablain St Nazaire and Carency and, at some cost, it took the southern edge of the latter village along with its cemetery. With these defences thus occupied, *77e Division* plunged deep into the German lines taking the chateau at Carleul (just west of Souchez), the southern edge of Souchez, and Cabaret Rouge. Some advanced elements reaching the outskirts of Givenchy en Gohelle. Despite taking 500 prisoners and capturing thirty German machine guns, the Division was unable to hold on to its deepest gains and was forced to withdraw to the Souchez to Neuville St Vaast road later in the day.

The most extraordinary progress was made by the *Division Marocaine*. A little after 11 a.m., its lead elements reached the high point of Vimy Ridge, *côte 140*. Some made it into Givenchy, and a few entered Petit Vimy on the far side of the ridge. In 90 minutes, the Division advanced 4,500 metres for the deepest penetration of German lines anywhere on the Western Front since trench warfare began. It proved too good to be sustainable. Losses[ii], especially amongst officers, a shortage of ammunition and shells, a failure of the artillery's protective barrage, and the collapse of the flow of reserves, caught by artillery and machine gun fire from either flank, left the lead units isolated and vulnerable. The shell shortage was especially acute. The *75s* of *33e Corps* were limited to 400 rounds per gun for 9th May. However, by 11.30 a.m., orders went out not to exceed firing 300 rounds 'no matter what'. Guns were then limited to 60-70 shells for the rest of the day, with 50 kept in reserve in case of enemy counter attacks.[7] Piling mistake on misfortune, shell supplies ordered by d'Urbal arrived late and, in a preview of the problem at Loos on 25th September, reserves were too far away to intervene. The first to arrive, the *8e Zouaves*, marched 8 kms before reaching the original French front-line at 12.20 p.m. A reserve Brigade, 12 kms away at Béthonsart, was still behind the front-line at 5.15 p.m. when it passed Mont Saint Eloi. At 3 p.m. the Germans launched a powerful counterattack on *côte 140*. Unsupported, the *Legionnaires* and *Tirailleurs* of the *Division Marocaine* were forced back on their colleagues of *77e Division* entrenching on the Souchez to Neuville St Vaast road.

This unprecedented advance, on the same day the utter failure of Haig's First Army at Aubers Ridge allowed the Germans to divert two divisions south to Vimy, was, for some, an opportunity missed. Joffre and d'Urbal and, for a time, Pétain saw the opening day as a potential breakthrough let down by a dislocation between the movement of the attacking infantry and their reserves, and a failure of the artillery to cover the glorious advance. They believed if enough men could be constantly fed into the initial breach to widen and deepen the breakthrough then

---

[i] Blondlat was appointed commander of *2e corps d'armée colonial* on 25th June 1915, which unit he commanded until 27th October 1918.

[ii] The *Division Marocaine* lost 155 officers and 7,053 other ranks between 9th and 11th May 1915 [*AFdGG*, Tome III, Vol. III, footnote page 41].

it was possible the German defences might break down over an increasingly wide area leading to a return to mobile warfare and the defeat of the enemy.

For others, such as Foch, it underlined his belief that breakthrough was not yet technically or tactically possible. By advancing too deep, and out of the view of ground-based observers, and by incurring heavy losses especially amongst the officers leading the attack, attacks collapsed because of tiredness, disorganisation, a lack of leadership and an absence of artillery cover. What was needed, *pro tem*, was a steady and methodical wearing down of the enemy's manpower and resources until such time as the balance of power swung in the Allies favour and the military endgame could be pursued.

Others had a more pessimistic view of the outcome of 9th May and beyond. Fayolle, whose *70e Division* fought excellently in awkward conditions around Carency and Ablain Saint Nazaire[i], declared there were simply not enough heavy guns and shells to achieve anything more than costly minor tactical successes. Fayolle was opposed to the style of attack of 9th May, writing in his diary on 21st April such offensives were doomed to costly failure for the simple reason that it always proved impossible to silence the enemy's artillery effectively. Furthermore, the deeper the attempted penetration, the less likely it was the furthest enemy trenches and their garrisons would be sufficiently damaged. Inevitably, those defences which could not be seen from the ground would be damaged the least of all.[8] This led to tired and disorganised troops running into a well-manned, wired, and undamaged obstacle which stopped the offensive cold and was beyond the abilities of the artillery to bombard accurately. Fayolle despaired at the heedless frittering away of his soldiers' lives in attacks of little tactical, let alone strategic, consequence, suggesting *Xe Armée* would 'leave 10,000 men on the ground in order to gain a kilometre'.[9] But, as yet, he was just a lowly divisional commander and it was the conclusions of those in more elevated positions which were acted upon in the campaigns to come[ii].

Overall, though ending in disappointment on 18th June with only minor gains made at huge and disproportionate cost[iii], the opening of the Second Battle of Artois seemed to Joffre to point the way for the autumn campaigns he later proposed at an inter-Allied conference in the chateau at Chantilly on 7th July. Joffre was swift to analyse and draw (incorrect) lessons from the conduct of the battle, with his first comments on the offensive emerging from *GQG* on 20th May.

---

[i] Assisted by the capture of the top of the Lorette spur by *21e Corps* on the night of 11th May, these villages and *bois 125* were taken by Fayolle's troops on 13th May at a cost since 9th May of 2,500 officers and men including seven *chefs de bataillon*. 2,211 Germans were taken prisoner along with seven artillery pieces and numerous machine guns and *minenwerfers* [Fayolle, *Cahiers secret*, page 103].

[ii] Fayolle was either pessimist or realist. On 27th April he forecast the failure of *21e Corps* to progress on the Lorette Spur but was wrong about the prospects for *33e Corps* which he thought grim. He foresaw losses of upwards of 20,000 men for 'diplomatic reasons', i.e. to persuade the neutrals (i.e. Italy and Rumania) to join the Allies [Fayolle, *Cahiers secret*, page 99].

[iii] French casualties were 102,000, the British at Aubers Ridge and Festubert lost 28,000. German casualties amounted to 73,000.

Perhaps unsurprisingly, he announced in the opening paragraph that the fighting in Artois 'confirmed the validity of the principles and methods' contained in his own *But et conditions d'une action offensive d'ensemble* published in mid-April. *Quel surprise!* Joffre stressed the importance of careful preparation for each attack, something which might seem obvious from a contemporary point of view but which, given the emphasis on the *offensive à outrance* which characterised the opening months of the war, had not previously characterised many French attacks in 1915, most especially the appallingly conducted First Battle of Champagne.

His essential conclusion, listed first, could have been drawn straight from Douglas Haig's 1st July 1916 playbook:

> "The key lesson is the need to push forward the reserves as soon as possible. This applies not only to reinforcements and immediate reserves needed to fuel the fight whose deployment is to be organized in advance to allow for a continuous and automatic push, but also to general reserves needed to exploit success. Success can be fleeting and the opportunity may be lost if the reserve troops do not intervene immediately."[10]

Leaving to one side the argument a reserve is not a 'reserve' if it has been assigned an active role in an attack, this interpretation of the initial attack at Vimy proved disastrous to the French troops soon to attack in Champagne. Blinded by ambition, as was the British Fourth Army on 1st July, rather than guided by prudence, it neglected the reasons for the eventual failure of 9th May in favour of the illusion that strategic success was just a few, resolvable, 'if onlys' away.

Joffre then announced future offensives needed to be simultaneous and launched on a wide front to force the enemy to disperse their defensive effort. Narrow attacks, he suggested, led only to the creation of exposed salients vulnerable to enfilade fire from both nearby troops and guns as well as from those whose front was not under attack. The need to attack with width and in depth, however, meant the numbers of men needed were considerable. In other words, attacks *à la* Artois of 15-20 kms width were not big enough. Forty or fifty kilometre fronts of attack were required.

The rest of the document consisted of detailed recommendations about the need to destroy hardened German machine gun posts and deep dugouts and how to deal with strongpoints along with details about the German system of defence in depth within which even communication trenches were arranged as fire trenches and were protected by their own barbed wire, etc.

However sensible these latter points, the damage was done with the first statement about the 'continuous' deep penetration battle. While the French soon learnt how wrong this interpretation was of the events of 9th May, this insight was something which eluded the British High Command who, even after the costly failures during the Battle of Loos, pursued the 'chimera' of breakthrough up to and beyond the catastrophe of 1st July 1916.

AT CHANTILLY ON 7TH JULY JOFFRE PROPOSED a large-scale Franco-British campaign in the autumn, co-ordinated with other offensives on the Serbian and newly opened Italian fronts. The two main French attacks would comprise the Second Battle of Champagne and, in association with the British at Loos, the Third

Battle of Artois. The intention was to collapse the flanks of the huge German salient projecting from Ypres in the north down to Verdun in the south.

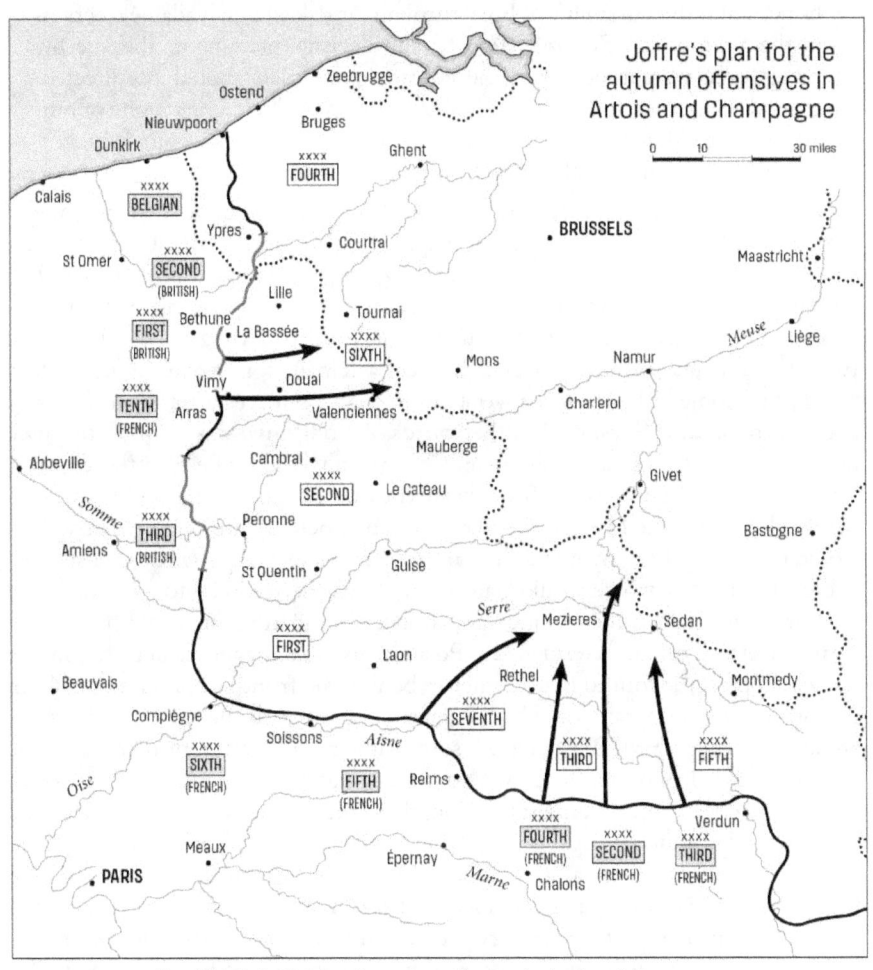

Map 16 Joffre's plan for the autumn offensives in Artois and Champagne
[*Source:* Edmonds, *Military Operations France and Belgium, 1915*, Vol. II, Battles of Aubers Ridge, Festubert, & Loos]

Joffre envisaged the new Champagne battle as one leading to a breakthrough on a broad front. His more optimistic interpretation of the reasons for the eventual failure at Vimy Ridge on 9th May was not that the attack was over-extended and incapable of protection by the available artillery but instead, he argued that, if the reserves had been kept closer to the front and were able to reinforce the *division Marocaine* at the key moment, all would have been well and the ridge taken.

Foch's conclusions were completely different and this divergence of opinion surfaced at an Army Group commanders' meeting at Chantilly on 11th August 1915. Three weeks earlier, on 19th July, he wrote to Joffre to set out his preliminary conclusions drawn from the fighting in Artois in May and June:

"Under the circumstances now prevailing and in the presence of an enemy defensive system long since established, it seems wise not to base all our hopes upon the possibility of breakthrough, or risk all our available reserves in the attempt to effect a victorious and decisive piercing of the line by mere force of numbers. On the contrary, our plan should be directed toward the conquest of certain dominant points of the line; each one of our attacks should have a distinct object, and one whose accomplishment would lead to some further result."[11]

At the Army Group commanders' meeting Foch recommended that, under current conditions and with existing supplies of artillery and shells, the Allies should conduct the Western Front campaign as a prolonged siege, proceeding methodically to wear away at the enemy's defences and its garrisons until such time as the balance of resources – men, guns, shells – swung irrevocably in the Entente's favour. Joffre, supported by de Castelnau, was having none of this, stating their objective was to so weaken the enemy's forces a return to a war of manoeuvre became possible. In other words, the objective was to break through, not just into, the German positions in Champagne. Adding flesh to these bones, it was explained the German front needed to be ruptured on a width and to a depth which gave the French troops room to manoeuvre into open country. This would be achieved not by methodical means but by an *'attaque brusquée'*, a sudden, energetic offensive which would 'gain 10 or 12 kilometres in 24 to 48 hours'.[12]

Foch objected on the grounds any artillery bombardment would have but a marginal effect on the German 2nd Position in Champagne, a line dug into a reverse slope some four to five kilometres behind the front-line and revealed both through aerial photographs and by the interrogation of prisoners. Furthermore, he argued, as for a third line detected some fifteen kilometres further back, the artillery could do nothing as it was so far beyond their reach. In other words, having breached the 1st German position, the same process of bombardment and attack would have to be organised and conducted for each position in turn. There could not, therefore, be any genuine prospect of a complete rupture of the German front. De Castelnau responded by declaring Foch's reasoning only correct if the Germans had sufficient reserves either in place or able to arrive in time to occupy these trench lines. Foch was unconvinced and pronounced prophetically:

"The reserves will occupy the 2nd position. They do not need to be numerous. Machine guns in *points d'appui* will be enough to stop you."[13]

As a result, the attack might capture only the German frontlines and, anyway, experience showed surprise could bring only minimal, transitory benefits and should not be counted on for a major success. Unfortunately, Joffre sided with de Castelnau arguing, rather feebly, 'we must do what we can with the means at our disposal'. If they were to adopt Foch's methodical approach, he went on, there might be a month of fighting which used up all their ammunition and they would still not be ready to launch the decisive offensive. When might that offensive take place? he asked plaintively. He answered his own question by quoting the pre-war tactical regulations which led to the disasters of the attack *à outrance* and the huge casualties of the Battle of the Frontiers:

"Maybe not next year, probably never. Now we must act for ourselves and for our allies. As our regulations say: only inaction is shameful."

But Joffre clearly feared failure as he concluded:

"The tricky part will be how to stop, if we do not get, from the early days, the results that we seek."[14]

The scene was set for another false dawn on bloody fields of Champagne.

FOR THE CHAMPAGNE OFFENSIVE Joffre allocated to the promoted Henri Philippe Benoni Omer Joseph Pétain's *IIe* and Fernand de Langle de Cary's *IVe Armées* a powerful artillery of 1,053 *75s*, 214 obsolete guns of 80 to 95 mm, and 712 heavy guns (*Canon de 105* and larger) and howitzers[15] amongst which were four of the new super-heavy *Mortier de 370-mm Filloux*, each with 100 of their 500 Kg shells.[16] This gave one 75-mm field gun for every 32 metres of front and one heavy piece every 40 metres. Interestingly, this latter statistic approximates closely to the concentration of British heavy guns employed with initial success at Neuve Chapelle where the *break-in* to the enemy position was regarded by Haig as evidence for the possible *rupture* of the German lines. On 22nd September, three days before the attack was due to start Joffre made a decision similar to that made by Haig just before 1st July 1916: the heavy artillery's shells were not just to cover the preparatory bombardment, but also the attack *and* the advance into the enemy position thereby weakening the overall power of the initial bombardment.[17]

The three-day French bombardment culminated in another initially highly successful opening infantry assault of the enemy's lines which were broken into at numerous locations along a front of 14 kilometres and which saw some 14,000 Germans taken prisoner. Success was greatest in the centre where the *2e corps d'armée colonial*[i] of *IVe Armée* drove through the German lines opposite Souain on a frontage of 5 kms and to a depth of 3kms with the *15e Division Coloniale* only being stopped by the German 2nd Position around the infamous *ferme Navarin*. To their right, the *27e* and *28e Divisions* of *14e Corps* set off from the ruined village of Perthes-lès-Hurlus[ii] and, again, were stopped on the German *reserve stellung*. These two advances only served, however, to create two large salients separated by extensive woodland before the area was later taken by the *Division Marocaine*.

---

[i] The *2e corps d'armée colonial* comprised the *10e* and *15e Divisions Coloniale* and was augmented by the *Division Marocaine* for the initial attack.

[ii] Perthes-lès-Hurlus, population 156 in 1911, was not rebuilt and is one of the many *Villages détruits* in the Champagne and Verdun regions. Souhain currently has a population barely half of that of 1911, i.e. 416 then and 238 in 2017. Its peak population was 900 in 1793, its low point 138 in 1975. Both villages were awarded the *Croix de guerre 1914-1918*. The area is surrounded by numerous traces of WW1 as well as memorials and cemeteries. Principle amongst them are the *Monument aux Morts des Armées de Champagne* and the *Ossuaire de Navarin* inaugurated in 1924. The *nécropole nationale de La Crouée* contains the remains of 30,374 French soldiers and a nearby German cemetery those of 13,783 men.

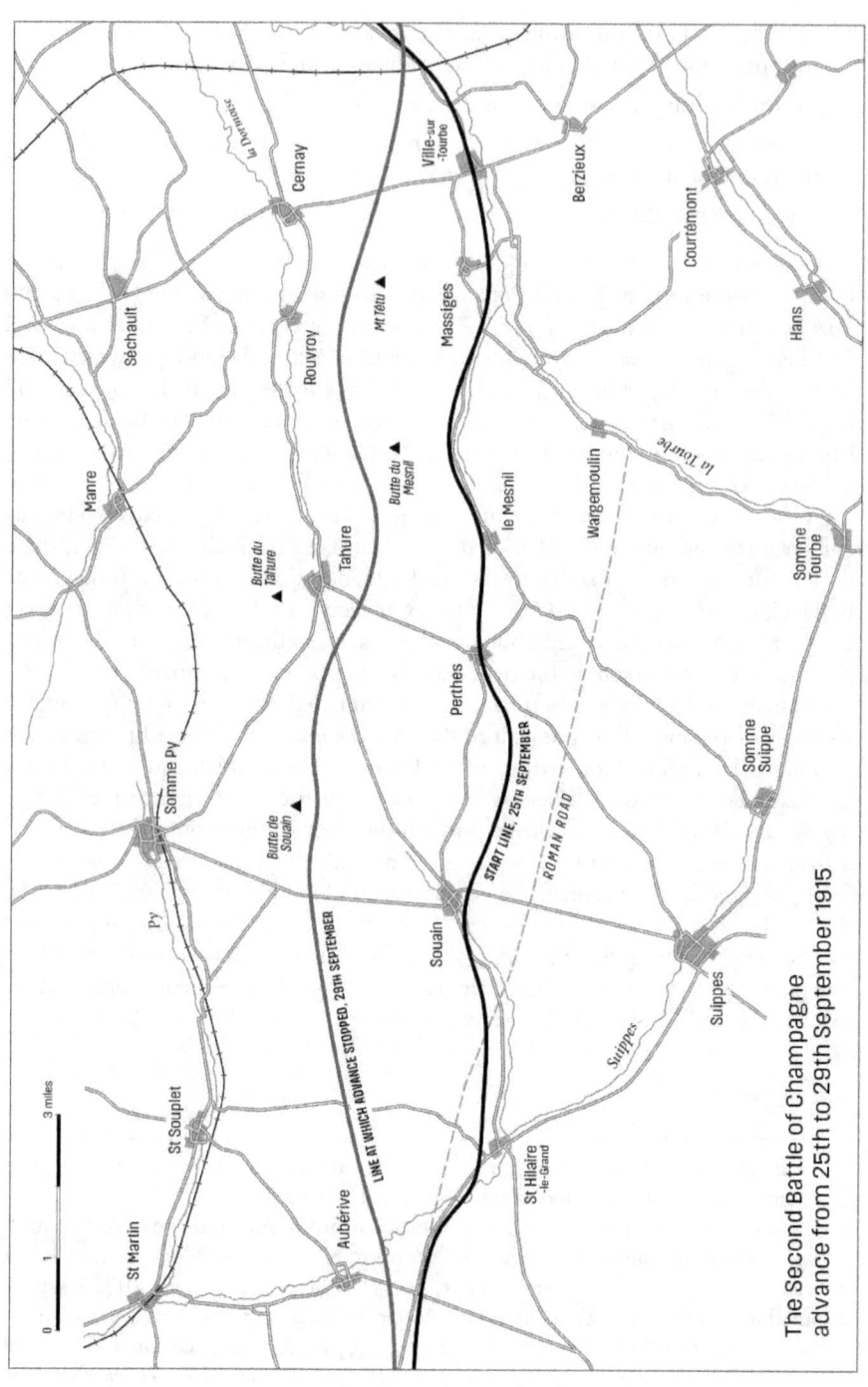

Map 17 The Second Battle of Champagne, advance from 25th to 29th September 1915

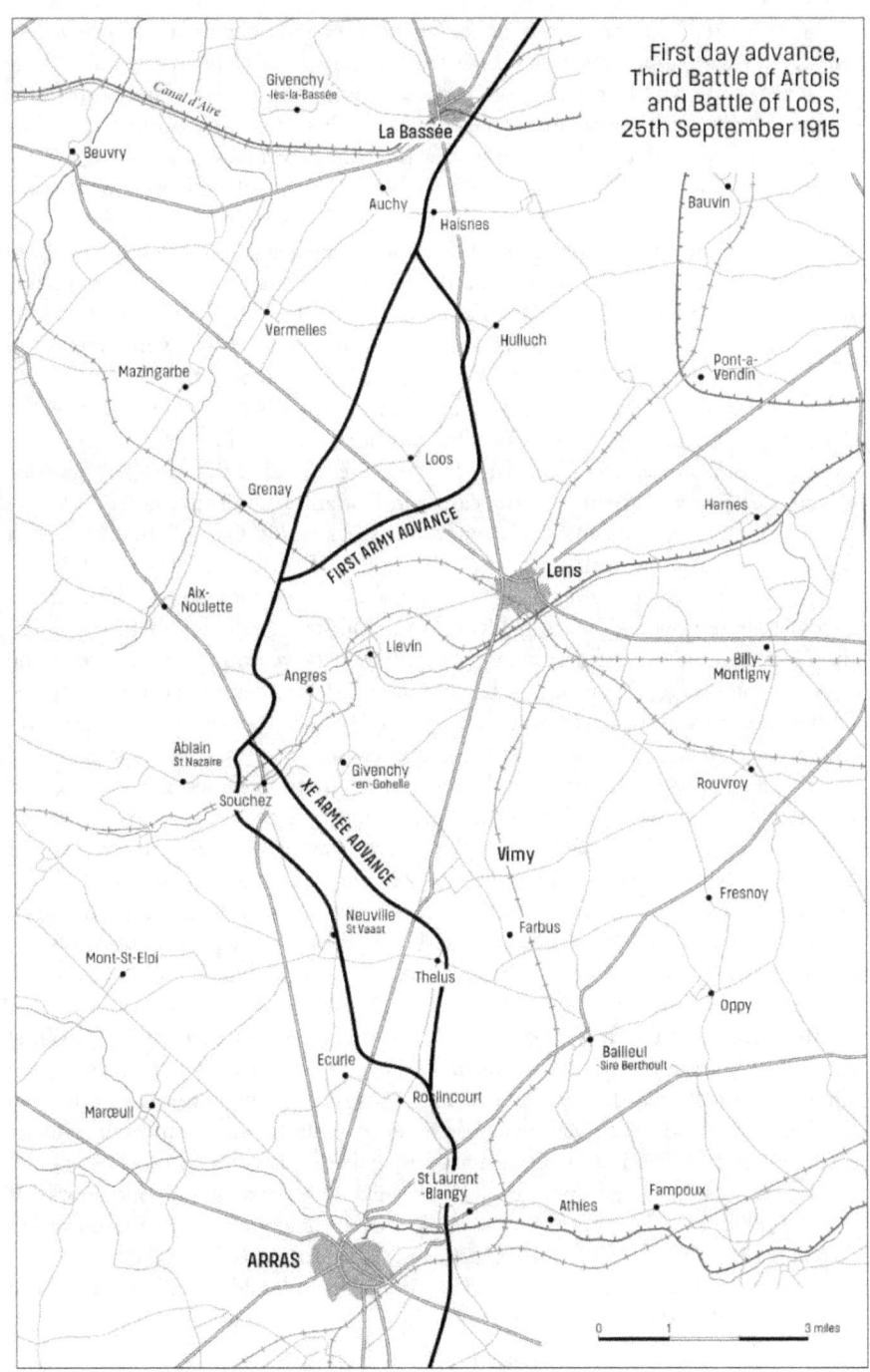

Map 18 First day advance Third Battle of Artois and Battle of Loos, 25th September 1915

As predicted by Foch, however, the German second position, the *reserve stellung*, on the reverse slope was not visible to French artillery observers and, as the excited, enthusiastic but disorganised *poilus* crossed the ridge to attack this line, they were cut down in enormous numbers. High losses amongst officers resulted in a lack of control and direction, and a lack of co-ordination with the artillery meant troops lost their protective artillery shield. The attack collapsed in chaos. A return to the methodical process of the first attack was attempted on 6th October but the Germans were learning as much about defence as the French learnt about the attack and the assault ground to a halt. Again, the result was an unsustainably unbalanced set of casualty lists: the French lost 145,000 men, the Germans 73,000.

Perhaps the only good thing to say is numerous French *Poilus* were saved from death or serious injury by the distribution of the *'casque Adrian'*, the famous French infantry helmet, issued just before the attack started.[18] The *casque Adrian* was designed by Louis Auguste Adrian who was born in Metz in 1859. He left when the city was absorbed into Germany in 1871. He attended the *École Polytechnique*, joined the *Génie* and spent his early career in Brittany and Normandy. In 1907 he was appointed *sous-directeur de l'intendance* at the *ministère de la Guerre*. There he fought fraud and corruption in the Army supply system. He left the Army in 1913, was recalled in 1914 and given responsibility for soldiers' clothing and equipment. He successfully removed 4,000 tons of uniform cloth from Lille just before it fell to the Germans and, in the first winter, he provided *Poilus* with sheepskin tops and trench boots. As tents ran out in the summer of 1915, he arranged for huts to be built in France and the eastern Mediterranean. His most famous contribution was the *casque* or helmet. With 80% of head injuries proving fatal, Adrian suggested a metal skull cap worn under the soldier's *kepi*. He then designed a cheap, easy to manufacture, lightweight (700 gms) steel helmet which took his name. Seven million were manufactured for the French, Belgian, Italian, Serb, Romanian and Russian Armies and reduced fatalities to 22% of head wounds. In 1918 he was asked by Clemenceau to locate by triangulation the German super long-range guns bombarding Paris. He died in 1933 and is buried in the town of Genêts, *Dept. of the Manche*, opposite Mont St Michel near where he worked in the 1890s. His tomb is topped with a replica of the *casque Adrian*.

In Artois, the French *Xe Armée* attacked Vimy Ridge south of Lens whilst First Army took on German positions north of Lens around, and to the north of, the small mining village of Loos. *Xe Armée's* attack was on a much narrower front than in Champagne and the French managed an even greater concentration of artillery: 672 *75s*, 128 *80/90/95s* and 380 heavy guns[19] which translated into one *75* per 30 metres and one heavy gun per 36 metres. Unlike May there was a good supply of shells: 1,000+ rounds per gun for the *75s* and other field guns, and 750 for the *155 C*, 685 for the *155 L*, 470 for the *M220s* and 250 for the *M270s*.

In spite of this, Fayolle, now commanding Pétain's old *33e Corps*, could not understand why attacking Vimy ridge yet again was a good idea:

Was *Xe Armée* stronger than on the days of their two previous major attacks on 9th May and 16th June? he mused. No, was his answer.

Did the Germans still have the advantage in this sector? Yes.

So, why attack at the cost of yet more men with so little prospect of success?

Fayolle was bemused. He was also concerned about the impact of the German artillery if they responded to the increased threat from the French guns in equal measure. Defeat would mean an end to offensive action until the spring of 1916. But Joffre *was* convinced, telling Fayolle on 30th August this would be *the* battle of 1915. The objective was the rupture of the German lines and the destruction of their Field Army in a war of manoeuvre and by 12th September, Joffre was talking about an advance as far as Douai and Valenciennes. Haig talked the same laughable language the following Spring.

But Fayolle asked presciently, and before that grandiose plan unfolded, what about the destruction of the German trenches at Vimy they still could not see? In his view, the best they could hope for was to gain the crest of the ridge. Even Fayolle, the pessimist, would be proved optimistic.[20] As in May the initial advance on the French front was successful but the attacking troops were denied the crest line of the ridge and German reserves and artillery again brought the offensive to a halt. By 5th October both French offensives were at a standstill but fighting dragged on across both the French and British fronts in pointless penny packet affairs which, according to Fayolle, resulted in 'nothing but corpses'.[21]

French casualties in autumn 1915 were severe – 134,000 dead, missing and PoWs, and 279,000 wounded. The British lost 85,000 men in the fighting around Loos and in various diversionary attacks. Fayolle no longer understood the war, bewailing the 'atrocity' which was the current conflict. The Third Battle of Artois was '… a very great failure,' he wrote, perhaps with some grim justification and even satisfaction, 'which demonstrates that breakthrough is not possible'.[22]

For the British, the main outcome of the autumn's fighting was the replacement of Sir John French as CinC of the armies in France and Flanders. By December his replacement was conferring with Joffre over plans for offensives in 1916. Having been previously severely rebuffed at Neuve Chapelle, Aubers Ridge, Festubert and Loos, French's replacement was the less than successful GOC of First Army, Douglas Haig, mainly because, to paraphrase the late and unlamented Margaret Thatcher, 'there was no alternative'.

BEFORE THAT CHANGE WAS CONFIRMED, and while Haig and his then CinC, French, wrangled over the causes of failure in the initial attack at Loos, senior French officers attempted to dissect the lessons to be learnt from the summer and autumn's fighting in Artois and Champagne. Two of these officers had commanded throughout the three Artois campaigns. They were Ferdinand Foch, commander of the *Groupe d'Armées du Nord* or *GAN*, whose sector encompassed Flanders, Artois and Picardy, and Gen. Marie Emile Fayolle, the commander of *33e Corps* and, by February 1916, commander of the French *VIe Armée* based south of the *Somme*. Some of the issues with which they grappled were fundamental to the nature of the warfare in which they were now embroiled. One crucial yet simple problem was the absence of suitable large-scale maps and, as with the BEF, significant resources were put into survey work and cartography. Again, as with the British, the techniques and technology of the artillery started on a sharp, upward, learning curve, although British artillery tactics still lagged for some time. Wind speed, humidity, barometric pressure, and temperature were all found to have significant effects on the range and accuracy of guns of all sizes. As a result, the pre-war range tables for French guns were either significantly revised or thrown away and started from scratch. In addition, Foch analysed the tactics of the artillery in a manner not at the time replicated at GHQ. His conclusions, applied by the *VIe Armée* on 1st July 1916, contributed significantly to the vastly better results enjoyed by the French and the neighbouring British infantry of the XIII Corps on that day.

The main and immediate change, however, was the complete restructuring of French heavy artillery. By the end of July 1915, an army which twelve months before deemed medium and heavy howitzers and long guns an unnecessary intrusion into work which could be entirely conducted by the *75*, had established 272 batteries of heavy artillery. A dozen were made up of the modern *Canon de 105 L modèle 1913 TR Schneider* and slightly more of the not quite so modern *Canon de 155 C modèle 1904 TR Rimailho*. The rest were adapted de Bange tubes from the 1870s and 1880s on improvised carriages and platforms. Indeed, even the *155 C 1904 TR Rimailho* was based on a de Bange howitzer tube from 1881.

Joffre, meanwhile, frustrated by the lack of progress on new *matériel*, placed orders for a wide range of new guns throughout 1915. These included:

- Large numbers of machine guns;
- A range of trench mortars such as the *mortiers de 58 T No. 2*, the *mortier de 75-mm modèle 1915 Type A Schneider*, and the *mortier de 240 CT modèle 1915* (the last to be also used, and later manufactured by, the British);
- On the basis it was better to have two companies vying to supply the French Army, Joffre ordered both the *Schneider* and the *Saint-Chamond* variants of a new *canon de 155 C*, a new, quick-firing 6 in. howitzer (*Saint-Chamond* won that particular race supplying 326 of these guns by the end of 1916 to 136 of the *Schneider* version);
- An upgrade of the *de Bange 155 L modèle 1877* with a long recoil on a new *Schneider* carriage; and, in addition
- A range of new heavy and super heavy guns and howitzers, some to be placed on trains, and which would form the armoury of the *ALGP* – the *Artillerie Lourde à Grande Puissance* – and the *ALVF* – the *Artillerie Lourde sur Voie Ferrée*. Initially employing fortress, coastal and naval guns, these eventually encompassed guns and howitzers of calibre 240-mm, 270-mm, 305-mm, 320-mm, 340-mm, 370-mm, 400-mm and even 520-mm (9.5 in. to 20.5 in.).

After analysis of the battles of 1915, and with 1916 in mind, an attempt was made to turn the results of the successful artillery preparations before the first days of 2nd Artois and 2nd Champagne into something akin to a formula, and this was set out in a directive of 20th November 1915. With divisions and corps being allocated batteries of *155 C* and *155 L* respectively to augment the existing 75, 90 and 95-mm field guns, and with the resulting 'formula' dictating that, in future, divisions should attack on a 1,000-metre frontage and an Army Corps on a 2,000-metre front (on the principle of two divisions attacking and one in reserve), this meant there would be one 155-mm gun or howitzer for every 31 metres of front.

In addition, much time was spent on counter battery work. The destruction or neutralisation of German guns was now seen as a crucial element of any successful advance and the task of control of C/B fire was allotted to the *Corps d'armée*. Within each Corps a *Service Renseignment Artillerie* (*S.R.A.* or Artillery Information Service) was established which was to collect and analyse data on artillery targets and co-ordinate the response. The sources of information were to be: front-line anecdote; the statements of forward artillery observers; information from aerial observers in both balloons and aircraft; and the newly established sound ranging and flash spotting sections, the *Service Renseignement Observation Terrestrial* (or *S.R.O.T.*).

On 16th January 1916, *GQG* issued what was the first update to the French Army's Field Service Regulations of 1914, the ones which caused the infantry and field artillery so much grief during the Battle of the Frontiers. These new regulations were founded on Ferdinand Foch's interpretation of the lessons to be learned from the autumn campaigns and concerned the conduct of a General Offensive. They constituted a major change in tactical doctrine. Offensives were to take place over wide fronts in a series of co-ordinated but limited advances, with the depth of each advance dictated by the ability of the available artillery to properly prepare the way for the infantry. Each advance needed to follow on the previous one as quickly as possible to prevent the enemy from preparing new defences and bring in reserves.

To achieve the necessary artillery support for each stage meant pre-preparing additional forward artillery positions for all types of guns to which they might move and from which they might fire whilst still within existing French territory in order to cover the next phase. In practice, in the early stages of an offensive, this required certain gun crews to prepare two (or more) gun positions and routes between them within the French trench system. As soon as the advance started, designated batteries would move to their new position up close to the old French front-line trench from where they could cover the troops advancing beyond their first objective. Artillery batteries would then leap-frog one another as the advance continued, with one section providing defensive fire for the newly won position while another prepared the way for the next attack.

It was also deemed essential the attacking infantry and supporting artillery be in close contact. With control of certain guns, i.e. batteries of *155 C*, being devolved to the Divisional level it was necessary that liaison between the battery commanders and the infantry was well organised and, above all, speedy. As a result, commanders of both the batteries and the infantry were brought up close to the frontline to minimise the time delays between the infantry asking for a specific supporting artillery action and the gunners delivering it. Though not specifically stated, much of this regulation suggested that, to achieve success in these limited advances, both the objectives and the action needed to be easily observable from the ground (as aerial observation was always subject to the vagaries of the weather). This suggested that limitations on any advance would be dictated by how far the terrain allowed a ground observer to see clearly both the effects of the artillery preparation and the progress of the infantry in the subsequent advance. In most areas of the front, this meant initial attacks would be limited to the German 1st Position. At the Second Battle of Champagne, it was the German 2nd Position hidden on a reverse slope which brought the offensive to a standstill and the French view, especially that of Foch, was if trench lines could not be seen then they should not be attacked until they could be seen and their destruction in detail then observed.

Given their lack of battlefield training pre-war, officers of the French heavy artillery, and those recruited to substantially increase their numbers, went to one of three Heavy Artillery training centres set up at Châlons, Amiens and Toul. These did not just educate artillery officers in the techniques of accurate and effective fire, they disseminated the lessons learned from the experiences in Champagne and Artois. Thus officers from other branches of the army attended as an attempt was made to bridge the long-standing pre-war gap in understanding between the infantry and field artillery, on the one hand, and, on the other, the heavy artillery which had taken little part in Army exercises before 1914.

In spite of all this feverish tactical and instructional work, however, the problems of gearing up French industry to produce the new weapons required meant that, by 1st May 1916, the French Army was still utterly dependent on the 75 and improvised versions of de Bange cannon from the 1870s and 80s.

During the winter of 1915/6 large orders for new guns were placed with the *Schneider* and *Saint-Chamond* factories. Interestingly, every gun ordered was one initially designed for the Russian Army in the years after their disastrous war in Manchuria. Whatever its other grave and persistent military inadequacies, the Russian Army had clearly taken to heart the artillery lessons of the Russo-Japanese War in a far more all-embracing way than either of its Western European allies. The problem was, whilst these guns may have been ordered, getting them delivered to either the French or Russian Armies proved entirely another matter. New plant, new machine tools, new foundries and more workers were all required to furnish the guns now required, and to make up for those lost to the invading Germans in northern France, and everything took longer than planned. Indeed, it is just as well the Russian Government commissioned the design and testing of these guns prior to the outbreak of war as, had their design and trialling started in the autumn of 1914, it is more than likely most of these weapons would not have been available in any significant numbers before the end of 1918. In fact, none of the orders set out in the next programme for the artillery, announced by Joffre on 30th May 1916, were completely fulfilled by 11th November 1918.

The order for the autumn of 1915 comprised:

440 *Canon de 105 M modèle 1914 TR Schneider*, a quick-firing (6-8 rounds per minute), long-range (12,500 metres) gun first shown to the French in February 1912 in a variant being manufactured for the Russian Army. Ordered on 29th August 1913, the initial batch arrived in mid-September 1914 but technical issues, such as an unhappy tendency for the barrel to burst, delayed a general deployment. Manufactured in the *le Creusot* works, it was not until 1917 large numbers of this gun became available. By mid-summer 1916 they numbered less than 70;

500 of the *Canon de 155 C modèle 1915* to be simultaneously manufactured by *Schneider* and *Saint-Chamond*. The equivalent of the British 6 in. howitzer and first developed, again, for the Russian Army in 1907, the first order for 122 of these guns was placed in October 1915 and the first battery to receive these guns took delivery in April 1916. The *Schneider* proved to be the better gun, with a longer range (11,900 metres against the *Saint-Chamond's* 9,300 metres) and a faster rate of

fire (4 rounds/minute against 3 rounds/minute for the *Saint-Chamond*) but large numbers of either gun were not to arrive at the front-line until the end of 1916;

40 *mortier de 220 TR modèle 1915 Schneider*. Another gun first designed for Russia in 1913, this more mobile equivalent of the British 9.2 in. howitzer had a range of 10,800 metres and a rate of fire of 2 rounds/minute. Ordered in October 1915, the first version eventually arrived twelve months later but it was not until June 1917 a significant number of artillery groups were equipped with this weapon. In the meantime, sixteen British 8 in. howitzers, renamed the *Obusier Anglais BL Mk VI de 8 pouces (203.2 mm)* were attached to the French to fill the gap left by the inadequate supply of the *M220 TR modèle 1915 Schneider*;

62 *Mortier de 280 TR Schneider (modèle 1914)*. First built for the Russians in 1909 this was trialled by the Russians in 1912 as part of their intensive artillery testing on the proving grounds around the fortress of Ochakov on the *River Dniepr*. A first, unofficial, French order was placed in November 1913 with the official order arriving in August 1914. The first gun was delivered in June 1915 and, in February 1916, two batteries each of two guns were formed and, prior to the start of the Battle of the Somme, this number had grown to 12 guns. There were only ever 65 of these weapons but it was not until 1917 most of them became available.

114 Artillery modern: the Mortier de 280 TR (modèle 1914)

The ordering of another new gun, the innovative split-trail *Canon de 155 GPF*[i] *(modèle 1917 Filloux)*, from the *le Creusot* works caused knock-on problems. To switch production to this 16,000-metre range gun, all work adapting the *155 L de Bange* tube to a new *Schneider 1914* carriage was stopped. This latter gun, with a range of 13,600 metres and a rate of fire of 3 rounds per minute, was available in small quantities by July 1916 but it was not until the latter half of 1917 its replacement, the *155 GPF*, became available in any numbers.

---

[i] GPF = *Grand Puissance Filloux*.

Two programmes for the development of the artillery were issued by *GQG*, on 14th October 1914 and 5th August 1915. Combined, it was hoped they would result in the availability at the end of Spring 1916 of:

4,500 75-mm guns.
2,500 mobile heavy horse- or tractor-drawn artillery
2,400 cannon manned by the fortress artillery
190 high-powered cannon
60 naval cannon
1,200 58 mm and 150-mm trench mortars
350 240-mm trench mortars[23]

A total of 9,650 guns/howitzers and 1,550 medium/heavy trench mortars.

In fact, by 1st May 1916, 10,054 field and heavy artillery prices were available, however, of these, only 114 were modern guns manufactured since 1913. 9,490 were either 75-mm field guns (4,117) or obsolete, adapted de Bange guns dating from the 1870s and 80s. Other than the *75s*, of the remaining 5,169 guns, 1,600 (31%) were the *90-mm modèle 1877* brought in to cover for the shortage of shells for the *75s* in the autumn of 1914, and 845 (16%) were obsolete *95-mm modèle 1888 de Lahitolle* field guns[24]. Indeed, if one was to add to these figures the various other field and mountain guns of calibre 65 to 100-mm, then just over 70% of all guns within the French arsenal as of 1st May 1916 were lightweight field guns and all had been designed and many manufactured in the previous century with only the 75-mm having a modern or, indeed, any recoil system.

115 Artillery old: the 95-mm modèle 1888 de Lahitolle

As for medium howitzers, there were 515 *155 C*[i] of which 85 had been updated and modified since 1904. In addition, there were 237 *220* or *270 mortiers* designed and built between 1880 and 1891 and just 12 modern *Mortier de 280 TR Schneider (modèle 1914)*. It was this mixture of the elderly and the updated drawn from every

---

[i] According to Touzin and Vauvillier *'Les Canons de la Victoire'*, page 22, but only 480 according to the *AFdGG*, Tome IV, Vol. 1, page 623, footnote 2.

arsenal, fortress, and coastal battery in France which, with a sprinkling of new, quick-firing weapons, was to see the French Army on the Western Front through two of its most severe tests – the Battle of Verdun and the Battle of the Somme[i].

The fighting at Verdun rapidly underlined the importance of quick-firing medium and heavy howitzers and long guns which, in large part, the French lacked. Their significance was not only felt in the ponderous artillery response to the modern German artillery which deluged the French infantry and artillery with shells of all calibres in the hills north of Verdun, but in their inability to launch similar offensives where surprise might play a part. The old, slow firing French guns simply could not match the output of the modern German weapons, thus their artillery preparations had to be protracted and methodical rather than intense and brief. Giving several days' notice of an offensive to the enemy was never likely to lead to them being caught unawares, but the length of the French bombardment prior to the Somme, which was then copied by the British artillery assault, was forced on them by the available *matériel* and not done out of choice. It was the guns now being designed and built, but which would not be available in significant numbers until 1917, which would allow the French Army to reproduce the devastating German preliminary bombardment at Verdun. Until then, however, tactics and timings were entirely dependent on the weapons immediately available.

The other issue limiting the effectiveness of these elderly guns and howitzers was their limited range. The urgent adaptations made to the de Bange cannon's carriages and platforms resulted in significant improvements in range of more than a third, according to Gen. Herr. These improvements, however, still left them short of modern German or British guns and, in many common versions, the adapted French cannons were significantly outranged by both their enemy's and their ally's newer guns. In almost every way, i.e. range, rate of fire and speed of deployment, the French artillery was at a disadvantage but, in some ways, it was the knowledge of this disadvantage and their determination to find ways around it especially when on the offensive, which led to certain tactical developments which, at least initially, served them well in the fighting on the Somme.

One area in which the French excelled was in super heavy guns and howitzers mounted on small barges and railway trucks[ii]. These had the advantage of being able to fire from any location where a river or standard/narrow-gauge railway ran near to the German trenches and rear areas. With their ports protected by the Royal Navy, guns in coastal batteries and some intended for the Navy could be employed in Northern France. The *Commission des Trucs* (*Railway Artillery Board*, later the *Commission de l'ALVF*) was established in October 1914 under *Chef*

---

[i] As of 1st February 1916, the French heavy artillery comprised a total of 3,700 pieces of which 2,904 were long guns (only 83 quick firing), 576 medium howitzers (104 quick firing) and 220 mortiers, of which only six were recent models. The details are: 857 *95-mm*, 83 *105-mm*, 1,335 *120 L*, 143 *120 C*, 629 *155 L*, 329 *155 C*, 104 *155 CTR*, 169 *M 220*, 45 *M 270*, 6 *M 280* [*Source: AFdGG*, Tome IV, Vol. 1, footnote 5, page 71].

[ii] Some were also mounted on fixed platforms which rendered them either redundant or vulnerable should the frontlines move significantly in any direction.

d'Escadron, later Lt. Col., Paul Nicolas Lucas-Girardville[i] to explore the prospects. Three companies, *Schneider-Le Creusot*, *Saint-Chamond*, and the *Société de Construction des Batignolles*, were brought in to examine and manufacture the heavy-duty carriages required to carry cannon of various types of between 200 and 500-mm. The necessarily long-range testing grounds were established on the coast at St Pierre Quiberon in Brittany.

116 A pair of Canon de 32 cm modèle 1870-93 sur affût à glissement Schneider

Some railway-mounted guns were already available or swiftly made ready after the outbreak of war. At the end of the 1880s, a Lt. Col. Peigné in collaboration with Gustave Canet, an engineer with *Schneider*, designed and built a platform capable of mounting a *155 C 1881 de Bange* on a 60-metre railway truck. Sixteen of these were completed by 1893 and were followed in 1897 by another 32 using either *155 C* tubes or ones from *120 L 1878 de Bange* guns. All these medium railway mounted guns were initially deployed in north-eastern France around the fortress cities of Verdun, Toul, Épinal and Belfort. Soon after the outbreak of war, another sixteen *Canon de 95-mm modèle 1888 de côte* were placed on small, armoured, standard gauge trucks and were deployed in 1915, seeing action in Champagne, Artois and around Arras. Lastly, two 200-mm *obusiers* built by *Schneider* for the Peruvian Government were commandeered and mounted on railway trucks. Their use was made somewhat awkward by the limited supplies of 200-mm shells, not a standard size in the French Army, but they were kept going through 1915 with adapted 19-cm shells while new ammunition was manufactured.

By the beginning of January 1915, however, the French Army deployed 52 train-mounted guns and howitzers. These numbers grew dramatically. By 1st July

---

[i] Lucas-Girardville was one of the first students at the flying school at Pau opened by the Wright Brothers in 1908. He was seconded to the *Laboratoire des recherches* at the *Établissement Central de l'Aérostation Militaire* at Chalais-Meudon, south-west of Paris, in 1906 (now the *Office national d'études et de recherches aérospatiales*) and then attached to the aviation section at Vincennes in 1910 (later the *Établissment d'aviation militaire de Vincennes*). He wrote several books on flying and aerial navigation.

1916, there were 121 guns of the *ALGP/ALVF*, with all of the original guns still in use except for the 95-mm versions. In addition, 28 14-cm, and 16-cm naval guns plus two 240-mm coastal guns, also commandeered from the order for Peru, were being manned by naval gunners[i]. All bar two of these were mounted in fixed positions but two *14-cm modèle 1910* naval guns were mounted on small canal barges, or *péniches*. By 1st July, these guns, manned by *Canonniers Marins*, numbered 51. Twelve were *100-mm modèle 1891/3* (4) or *14-cm modèle 1887, 1891* or *1893* guns (8) mounted on a *cannonière*[ii], a partially armoured river boat also equipped with two 47-mm anti-aircraft guns. A number of these guns, river, and land mounted, were employed in the French preliminary bombardment on the *Somme*.

117 *Brutale*, 1er Batterie, Cannonières Fluviales de 14 cm modèle, Paris 1917

The railway mounted guns utilised naval and coastal guns ranging from 16-cm up to 400-mm. The *Canon de 340-mm modèle 1912 sur affût à berceau Saint-Chamond* was able to fire a 465 Kg shell over 30,000 metres or nearly 19 miles. A minimum range of 10 miles was standard for these railway weapons. The Battle of the Somme was the first campaign where these guns were extensively used, as the long planning phase allowed for the construction of special tracks and the necessary accommodation for the guns and their personnel. The powerful and long-range fire of the 56 railway-mounted *mortiers* and 61 guns would be especially effective

---

[i] Seven 14-cm guns, two 16-cm guns, and the two *240-mm de côte 'Perou'* guns were all captured by the Germans at the beginning of the Verdun offensive.
[ii] A vessel capable of negotiating most French canals and displacing 110 tons with a length of 28.5 m, beam of 5 m and draft 1.2 m. It had a maximum speed of 9 knots. The gun was protected by 2 cm of armour plating.

during the fighting and was particularly useful in taking on the larger, long-range German guns, as well as disrupting communications, especially on the bottlenecks where roads needed to cross the river to the north and south of Péronne.

WHILST THESE TACTICAL AND TECHNICAL CHANGES were being pushed forward within the French Army, political upheavals were also changing the balance of power both within the Government and the Army. As in Britain, the French Government was a coalition of sometimes disparate political forces currently led by Prime Minister René Viviani. Viviani was an independent socialist born in Algeria of Italian parents. He previously served twice in the French cabinet when, on 13th June 1914, he was appointed Prime Minister by the then President Poincaré. He remained in office until 29th October 1915 when he was displaced by the flamboyantly moustachioed and 'serial' Prime Minister, Aristide Briand, another independent socialist[i]. The main cause of Viviani's fall was the relentless series of costly French failures experienced on the battlefield and the perceived failure of the Government to provide the Army with the guns and shells with which to deal with the German enemy. But the timing of the collapse of his administration was caused by the resignation of Foreign Minister Théophile Delcassé who was heavily criticised inside and outside Parliament for a failure to prevent Bulgaria declaring for the Central Powers.

Joffre, as CinC, was not absolved from criticism, though his image as the 'Victor of the Marne' helped preserve something of his reputation. He was, however, the man who had overseen the battles of 1914-15 which resulted in the deaths of one million Frenchmen and the wounding of the same number with no apparent successful end to the war yet in sight and thus he was vulnerable.

Under growing political pressure, Viviani's administration collapsed in late October whilst Joffre, too, faced political opposition to his continuing as Commander in Chief. Former PM Georges Clemenceau was amongst those who believed Joffre should be replaced by Gen. Joseph Gallieni, the 66-year-old veteran of the Franco-Prussian War and of various campaigns in far flung French colonies[ii]. Gallieni had been favoured by many to become CinC of the French Army in 1911 but declined on the grounds of age and health. His once junior officer in Madagascar, Joffre, was given the job instead. Now, Gallieni came back to haunt Joffre. Gallieni officially retired in April of 1914 but was rushed back into service as the crisis of the first few weeks of the war grew. He was given command of the Paris garrison and there were some, both at the time and post-war, who awarded him the lion's share of the credit for the defeat of the German at the First

---

[i] Briand formed ten administrations between July 1909 and November 1929. He was, perhaps, the first prominent politician to suggest the idea of a European Federal Union which he proposed in a speech to the League of Nations in 1929. Briand was also an active proponent of the separation of Church and State, the effects of which would be felt within the French Army for some time, especially by active Catholics.

[ii] Another potential rival for Joffre's job, Gen. Maurice Sarrail, was whisked off to Salonika to oversee the actions, or lack of them, of the Franco-British Expeditionary Force, the existence of which was to cause immense and extended *angst* to the soon to be appointed Chief of the Imperial General Staff, Gen. Sir William Robertson.

Battle of the Marne. Now, Briand brought him into the Government as the Minister of War, a role which inevitably brought him into direct contact, if not yet conflict, with Joffre. In addition, Briand gave greater powers to the *Conseil Supérieur de la Défense Nationale,* an inner cabinet consisting initially of Briand, Gallieni and Admiral Marie-Jean-Lucien Lacaze, the Minister of the Navy, and others on an *ad hoc* basis. Overseeing this body was the President of the Republic, the aggressively anti-German conservative politician Raymond Poincaré. As a result, Joffre, though still in place, found his freedom of action severely threatened.

Not to be outdone, Joffre's response was to demand he be made Commander in Chief of all French forces, ostensibly to ensure unity of action but practically as a means of reinforcing his position. One happy by-product would be that he regained control over the 'loose cannon' which was Gen. Sarrail at Salonika in the Eastern Mediterranean. Despite Gallieni's reservations, the Government chose to back Joffre and, on 2nd December, this appointment was officially announced, much to the unhappiness of many left-wingers in the Chamber of Deputies. On 10th December, Noël Édouard Marie Joseph, Vicomte de Curières de Castelnau, currently the commander of the *Groupe d'Armées du Centre (GAC)*, resumed his pre-war role as Joffre's Chief of Staff.

With Briand, however, Joffre now had a Prime Minister wedded to the theory of the 'Easterners' who inhabited the British and French governments and who regarded the war as unwinnable on the Western Front. They favoured attacks on the supposedly 'soft underbelly' of the Central Powers – the Balkans. The first manifestation of this theory was the poorly executed and costly Dardanelles campaign which lacked strategic coherence and competent leadership. Salonika was now the second pillar of this Eastern policy and there were many long, tedious, and unsuccessful attempts by the 'Westerners' led by Robertson and Haig to close what they saw as a wasteful diversion of troops far better employed defeating the main enemy on the main front, i.e. the Germans in France and Flanders.

Joffre's elevation to Commander in Chief over all French forces was, however, also intended to raise his status, and therefore his influence, amongst the Allies. On occasions, it does not seem it took much for Joffre to convince himself he was the Supreme Commander of all the Allied forces, as his Spring-time efforts to dictate both tactics and strategy to both Cadorna, the CinC of the Italian Army, and Douglas Haig showed. He was now, however, about to take the lead in determining the coalition's overall strategy for 1916, a strategy which led, eventually, to the British catastrophe of the first day of the Battle of the Somme.

The French, well before war started, tried to increase the British commitment to a war on the mainland of Europe. Sir Henry Wilson, then a Major General, told of a conversation with Foch in 1910 in which he asked the Frenchman what was the smallest British force which might be of genuine assistance in a war with Germany. Foch is said to have replied 'one single Private soldier (or one corporal and four private soldiers depending on the source) and we would take good care that he was (they were) killed'.[25] In other words, France would do whatever it could to draw Britain further and further into a large-scale continental war.

Joffre had some small success in pursuance of this policy when Sir John French agreed to the offensive at Loos in late September 1915. There the first Kitchener

New Army divisions were flung casually into battle. The heavy Allied casualties of that autumn, however, brought a new realism to *GQG*, a realism founded on the worsening French manpower problem and on the unrealised potential, in numbers if not experience, of their British Allies. These related subjects were the themes of two papers produced at *GQG* in the first half of October 1915.

The first of these, written by Joffre and dated 7th October 1915, was entitled *'Note on the employment of English (sic) Forces in the winter campaign 1915-16'*.[26] It began by referring to certain Allied tactical successes which then failed to produce the breakthrough which was the objective of their offensives. The result was a combination of heavy French losses and the need to bring in and train new troops and to re-stock ammunition and shell stores which meant the French were facing a long period on the defensive. Since the beginning of the war France bore the brunt of the fighting and it was France which sacrificed its best men in the Allied cause without counting the cost. This simply could not continue and it was time the other Allies, with large manpower reserves at their disposal, undertook the task of wearing down the resources of the enemy. France needed to conserve its last men to be able to participate in the final victory. They could not be thrown away prematurely. Russia, when its Armies were properly equipped and up to strength, had the means to take the leading role in this fight but, the point was made, the New Armies of Lord Kitchener must play an important part.

If the Russians were left to face the Germans and Austrians on their own, while the French were on the defensive as they rebuilt, then the Central Powers would be free either to shift their forces east to defeat Russia or could use the time on the Western Front to build up their strength unhindered. This could not be allowed to happen. The German Army on the Western Front had to be pinned to that front and worn down by concerted action. The French Army was in no state to do this and it was up to the BEF to undertake this role. Throughout 1915, the note pointedly stated, it was the French who attacked whilst, for the most part, the British remained on the defensive. During the coming winter, these roles had to be reversed. Joffre's conclusions were:

- The British Government must send to the Western Front as quickly as possible most of the forces at its disposal; and
- A powerful British offensive needed to be launched during the coming winter to which the French would contribute with artillery.

Such ideas were already under consideration by the British, according to Joffre, who accepted it was time British troops took the fight to the enemy.

These were words which needed saying to the British Government and its military commanders but there was no chance of the BEF being committed to a winter offensive however benign the weather. British casualties at Loos were significant and the deficiencies of New Army troops harshly exposed. More guns were needed for the BEF, more training was needed by the men and, as the new CinC Douglas Haig repeated throughout the first half of 1916, more men were needed too. It was only to be hoped the Germans would not pre-empt the efforts to rebuild the French Army and build-up the BEF by launching a major offensive on the Western Front of their own at a time and a place of their choosing.

The issues confronting the French Army and the Coalition were laid bare by the second document also dated 7th October.[27] It was a note on the general state of the war prepared by the *3e Bureau* at *GQG*. It started by setting out the three main events of the year. These were that the Allied offensives had achieved local tactical successes which not been translated into major strategic advances. Blame for this was laid mainly on the lack of artillery ammunition. Secondly, although the Central Powers had enjoyed real success in Poland and Western Russia, they had been forced to suspend their campaign without achieving the result they desired, i.e. knocking the Russians out of the war. Lastly, Bulgaria, no doubt seeking revenge for its losses in the Second Balkan War, had joined the Central Powers and was preparing to join in an attack on Serbia.

As a result of their efforts in 1915, the Franco-British forces in France and Flanders were in no position to resume offensive actions against Germany. On the Eastern Front, the Russians had avoided disaster by mounting a fighting withdrawal but now needed to be re-equipped, reorganised and brought up to full strength by large drafts from their depots and enormous material help from France and Britain. Rather optimistically, the document suggested the Russian Army might be ready to resume fighting in about six weeks, i.e. by the end of November, which, with 'General Winter' on their side, was the classic time during which the Russians traditionally counter-attacked invaders.

As far as the Central Powers were concerned it appeared as if, at least temporarily, they had given up the pursuit of their main objectives in France and Russia and were, instead, preparing, with the connivance of Bulgaria to go for easier secondary targets in the Balkans. This might help open the way to direct contact with the Ottoman Empire to pursue strategies in the Middle East and put pressure on British links with India and Australasia.

The document then went on to ask how the Coalition should pursue its objectives and concluded that decisive results could only be obtained by concentrating on the main theatres of war. The Central Powers' main enemies were France, Russia, and Britain and, therefore, the main theatres were the Western Front and Russia. Italy and the Balkans were secondary theatres and, whatever happened there, could not bring decisive results. It was then argued the Franco-British forces had just made a considerable and partially successful effort on the Western Front which showed the enemy's positions were vulnerable to attacks conducted in the right way. Furthermore, the intensity of these attacks had stretched the enemy such that, in the view of *GQG*, they had been close to breaking point. Despite this, however, neither the French nor British Army was in a condition to renew the offensive in the immediate future. Attacks on defences such as those constructed on the Western Front by the German Army were extremely costly in terms of both men and ammunition and, before the fighting could resume, reinforcements, and more guns and ammunition were required.

The French Army was close to the end of its immediate manpower supplies. The classes of 1916 and 1917 (some 270,000 men) were its total reserve for any fighting in 1916. Furthermore, the campaigns in Artois and Champagne in the autumn had used up a significant proportion of French shell supplies and it was essential the French Army should enter the next campaign with enough ammunition so that the Commander in Chief need not worry about potential shortages. Lastly, the paper concluded, the autumn fighting had shown up clearly the deficiencies within the French Army in the forms of equipment most essential in modern warfare, i.e. large numbers of modern heavy artillery, modern and powerful trench mortars, gas shells, and infantry support weapons such as light (i.e. portable) machine guns and automatic rifles. The result of all this was that it was now essential to assume a defensive posture on the Western Front, but one which allowed the Allies to deliver powerful counterattacks should the enemy assume the offensive. How long this defensive posture would have to be maintained was unclear and a lot depended on what might happen elsewhere, especially on the Russian front. It was expected, however, that a minimum of three to four months would pass before the French Army was ready to go over to the offensive and, with winter intervening, this delay might well extend until the spring. The benefit of this was it would allow time for the incorporation of drafts from the Classes of 1916 and 1917 and to re-build ammunition supplies.

It was accepted the BEF also needed time to rebuild, although it was felt the issues of manpower and ammunition were not as pressing as in the French Army. It was thought the BEF had sufficient troops in France adequately to maintain their defensive line whilst six New Army divisions were expected imminently in France and nineteen more were being formed. Furthermore, the proportion of the manpower pool currently enrolled in the British Army was considerably less than in either France or Germany and, as a result, its reserves were significantly larger. Another advantage was that, unlike France, Britain had lost none of its major industrial centres to the enemy and its capacity to produce ammunition and guns was in no way diminished. In these circumstances it was thought the BEF ought to be able to resume active operations somewhat earlier than the French. On the other hand, *GQG* believed 1915 showed the BEF had limited offensive capability and it was best they should postpone any major offensives until it was possible to do so alongside French troops and guns. In the interim, a lot depended on the abilities of the Russians and, to an extent, the Serbs to carry on the fight whilst the Western Allies made ready their next offensive. To pin enemy units to this front during this hiatus limited attacks in France and Flanders were needed. These the BEF must undertake.

Having established large-scale operation on the Western Front were out of the question for the foreseeable future, the paper then looked at whether it might be useful to conduct limited operations in secondary theatres. It was accepted the Coalition could not stand by and see Serbia crushed by the German, Austrian and Bulgarian troops currently massing on its border and the question arose as to what size of Franco-British Expeditionary Force might be sent to support them. The appearance of such a force might also usefully solidify support within both Greece and Rumania which were currently prevaricating in deciding which side they might join. The problem again was only Britain was in a position, in terms of manpower and, crucially, shipping, to move large bodies of troops around the Mediterranean. The only two sources for such troops were Gallipoli, where the campaign was deadlocked, and the Western Front, which had implications for the BEF's ability to take over more of the front-line and participate in any grand offensive in 1916.

These questions were pre-empted when German and Austrian troops crossed the *Rivers Danube* and *Sava* on 6th October 1915 to attack Serbia. The first of six Divisions[i] (four French, two British) committed to support Serbia at a conference in Calais on 11th September arrived in Salonika from Gallipoli on 5th October. The appearance of these divisions close to the border was not enough to deter Bulgaria. On 14th October they sided with the Central Powers, declaring war on its Slav neighbour. Greece, Serbia's ally in the Balkan Wars, announced it would not intervene on 7th October. Bulgarian troops advanced into Macedonia as Serbia was attacked simultaneously on two fronts and Britain (15th October) and France (16th October) declared war on Bulgaria. The additional units the two western Allies agreed to send on 5th October did not arrive in time to prevent the Bulgarian offensive cutting off Serbian communications with Salonika. Unable to resist this triple attack, the Serbian Army was forced into a painful and costly retreat over the mountains to the Adriatic coast from where they were evacuated to Corfu.

At a Calais conference on the same day the first two divisions arrived in Salonika, France agreed to send the *57e* and *122e Divisions* plus two cavalry divisions to Salonika while Britain agreed to send three infantry divisions from France and divert another recently sent from France to Egypt[ii]. In order to provide these divisions, and with the Loos campaign ongoing, it was deemed necessary the French relieve two British divisions occupying a part of the front south of the Somme they had taken over in mid-September and, on 14th October, Kitchener wrote to Alexandre Millerand, the French Minister for War, requesting this should take place.[28] Unhappy though he was about losing yet more French troops, Joffre was hardly in a position to say no, although he did try. Only the day before, Sir Henry Wilson discussed the Balkans issue with Joffre at Chantilly and the French CinC voiced the deep concern that, if Serbia was not supported and Salonika not occupied by the Allies, then the German would continue their advance into northern Greece and take the port themselves.[29] With the Germans in control of Salonika and directly connected with Constantinople the campaign at Gallipoli would have to end and the threat to the Middle East substantially increased.

Joffre's immediate response to Millerand was to argue the BEF could easily make these divisions available, not only without the French relieving British units but also without affecting the Loos offensive. He pointed out that the French held 650 kms of front-line with 90 divisions (one division per 7.2 kms), the British just 100 kms with 36 divisions (one division per 2.8 kms).[30] He had no troops available, he argued testily, partly because he had taken over Haig's front between Angres and Loos to assist with *his* offensive. If he was forced to reduce the level of the Champagne offensive he could not do this without first taking a key feature – the *Butte de Mesnil* salient. This required a significant commitment of troops. Lastly, in response to the Champagne offensive, the Germans had built up forces locally and Joffre feared the threat of an imminent counter-offensive. He concluded with an untypically acerbic swipe at the BEF and its performance saying:

---

[i] 10th Division & *2e Division d'infanterie du Corps Expéditionnaire d'Orient* now *156e Division*.
[ii] 22nd and 26th Divisions, (arrived in France, September 1915, and Salonika mid to late November), the experienced 27th, and 28th Division, initially directed to Egypt.

"Due to the plight of the Serbian Army and the lack of results from the English (*sic*) offensive I do not mind if it (i.e. the 'English offensive') is closed down if this helps in the sending of divisions to Salonika".

Joffre was then placed in a dilemma by a telegram from Sir John French which stated that, based on an assumption they were to be relieved by French divisions, the 22nd and 27th Divisions (XII Corps, Third Army), now in the front-line south of the Somme, were to leave for Egypt. Six divisions were to follow. Joffre was forced to write again to Millerand explaining he simply did not have the troops available to undertake these reliefs and this had been explained to Sir John.[31] He stated bluntly any French divisions for Serbia had already been withdrawn and, as the BEF possessed more reserves than did the French, any additional divisions for Salonika must be drawn from amongst British formations. Joffre pointed out to Millerand that, anyway, the British CinC had indicated the 22nd and 27th Divisions were destined not for Salonika but Egypt and it was not clear whether this destination was temporary or permanent. Joffre made it perfectly clear he did not believe the British were living up to their part of the agreement on troops for Salonika and it was about time they did.

Huguet, liaison at GHQ and no admirer of Sir John French[i], attempted an intervention. He supplied Joffre with three additional pieces of information:

1. The British Government had decided not to send immediately any troops to Salonika except, perhaps, one division from Gallipoli;
2. Instead, they had decided to remove from the Western Front two Corps, each of three Divisions, plus the two divisions of the Indian Corps[ii] and these eight divisions were to be sent to Egypt from where they might be go either to Gallipoli, Salonika or even India, though they might well remain in Egypt; and

---

[i] Post-war Huguet wrote *'Britain and the War: A French Indictment'* (Cassell, 1928). Written in 1921-2, but uncorrected or amended before translation and publication in 1928, it was a scathing indictment of the personality and qualities of Sir John French who, according to a review in the Catholic weekly *The Tablet*, was described as 'touchy, vain, irresolute, always looking out for offence and with the mentality of a child; passing in a moment from the extremes of confidence to the depths of depression; he was incalculable and unreliable as an ally, and never really happy in attack unless he knew he had a large French army on each flank and a big French reserve in his rear'. However accurate a description of French's character and performance, the reviewer described the book as a 'sorry exhibition of mingled spite and stupidity'. This, one imagines, particularly refers to the *Epilogue* which reveals Huguet's profound post-war antagonism towards Great Britain, his raging anti-Semitism and reactionary Catholicism. It appears the only Englishman he had time for was Sir Henry Wilson, the scheming Francophile so heartily disliked and distrusted by the likes of Haig and Robertson and assassinated by the IRA in 1922.

[ii] In October the Indian Corps was broken up. The *Meerut* and *Lahore Divisions* (minus British battalions and RFA brigades) went from the freezing winter of France to the warmer climes of Mesopotamia. Relieved on 6th November they began a snail-like progress to Basra, arriving in April 1916, in time to hear of the fall of Kut-al-Amara.

3. It was for this reason French had asked Joffre first to relieve the two British divisions south of the *Somme* and then all or part of the front currently occupied by the six other British divisions to be sent east.

On 17th October, a revised estimate of the strength and responsibilities of the various Allied Armies and the details of the German forces opposing them was produced by *GQG*.[32] This showed 90 French divisions opposed by 77 German divisions. A ratio of 1.17 French divisions to 1 German division. On the British front the numbers were 37 divisions against 18 German divisions. A ratio of 2:1 in favour of the BEF. In addition, six Belgian divisions were opposed by four German divisions for a ratio of 1.5:1. The paper then deducted from the equation the eight British divisions to be removed and sent east. This reduced the ratio of British to German troops from 2:1 to 1.6 to 1 but still resulted in an advantage significantly better than any enjoyed by the average French division. In the light of these numbers Joffre held fast to his belief he would not supply any more divisions either for Salonika or to cover the withdrawal of British ones. A telegram to the Ministry of War stated the two divisions already agreed to were all he could afford to send to Greece. Cavalry had also been asked for, with some *Chasseurs d'Afrique* and a group of *artillerie à pied* (heavy artillery) selected. Joffre wondered whether these were the most appropriate troops for a mountainous region.

In order to resolve this dispute a conference at Chantilly at 10.30 a.m. on 18th October, was attended by Joffre, Pellé[i], Huguet, French, Robertson and Wilson.[33] French stated that, in London, he had been told Joffre had agreed to relieve two divisions south of the *Somme*. Joffre replied the British Government was poorly informed, to which Sir John replied that, nonetheless, he had been ordered to withdraw the 22nd and 27th Divisions and send them to Marseille to be shipped to the eastern Mediterranean. Joffre then showed French a telegram from Millerand received the previous afternoon. It made three points:

1. The British Government accepted the need to send two divisions east;
2. That if Sir John French could not replace them from his reserves, then Joffre would relieve the two nominated divisions; and, importantly,
3. Any such relief was purely temporary.

In these circumstances Joffre undertook to relieve these divisions but stated the relief would take at least eight days and the British divisions could not be ready to go to sea for some twelve days. As a result, Joffre agreed to relieve the divisions immediately but suggested two British reserve divisions which could depart for Marseille more quickly be sent instead of the 22nd and 27th Divisions. French, with

---

[i] Gen. Maurice César Joseph Pellé (1863-1924) attended the *École Polytechnique* in 1882 and the *École d'application de l'artillerie* in 1886. An artillery instructor 1889-91, he attended the *École supérieure de guerre*, 1893. 1896, attached to *Ministre de la Guerre*. 1900-03, Chief of staff to Joffre in Madagascar. Military *attaché*, Berlin, (1909-12). Served in Morocco, 1913. 1914, commanded *2e brigade de tirailleurs, division marocaine*. On 21st August 1914 to *GQG*, serving until December 1916. Commanded *153e Division* on the *Chemin des Dames* and *5e Corps* to the end of the war. 1919-20, headed the military mission to Bohemia. First Chief of Staff of the new Czechoslovak Army. In 1921 he was appointed ambassador to Turkey.

the Loos offensive still spluttering along, but with the disaster of 46th Division's attack on the Hohenzollern Redoubt no doubt firmly on his mind, answered he was not sure he could use reserve divisions and, although he understood the need to get troops to Salonika urgently, he needed time to study this proposal. Encouraged by Joffre to make a quick decision, French then agreed to send one division immediately and the other once relieved. In this way, both divisions would be at sea within a fortnight or less. This having been agreed, a definition of 'temporary', as specified in Point 3 above, was sought by Joffre. French was not able to be specific but did say he would do everything possible to replace the French divisions south of the *Somme* as soon as he could without jeopardising other parts of his front, but in a manner which worked in the best interests of both Armies. On this basis Joffre agreed, but only so long as the two British divisions were sent directly to Salonika rather than Gallipoli or Egypt.

It was on this basis the issue was resolved but, for Joffre, on a purely *pro tem* basis. The repercussions from these decisions were felt for months, however, as time after time successive British CinCs sought to renege on the agreement, much to the frustration and irritation of Joffre.

THE ALLIED OFFENSIVES WERE SHUT DOWN by the beginning of November. 1915 proved an acute disappointment. France suffered significant casualties which called into question their ability to sustain the effort needed to eject the enemy from France. The fighting in 1914 was bad enough. According to a Parliamentary debate on 29th March 1920, France lost 528,000 men dead, missing or prisoners of war, with another 580,000 wounded and sick that year. This figure did not include officers.[34] 329,000 of these fatal/prisoner casualties occurred between 6th August and 13th September, i.e. the Battles of the Frontiers and the Marne, a daily attrition rate of c. 7,500 officers and men. The devastating impact of the Battle of the Frontiers is underlined by its average daily losses of c. 16,000. For the rest of 1914 the average daily rate was c. 3,500.

The French were then on the offensive through much of 1915. Casualties were huge, with a daily average of more than the c. 2,000 suggested in Table 42 as the figures do not include daily 'wastage'. During the year the French launched two large offensives in Champagne and two in Artois. There was continuous heavy fighting on secondary fronts, especially Lorraine and Alsace. The French harboured high hopes for their planned offensives in the autumn of the year but they ended in frustration and casualty lists of just over 143,000 in Champagne and over 48,000 in Artois and all for advances of, at most, a few kilometres[i].[35]

The BEF, meanwhile, mounted three small and one medium scale offensives (Neuve Chapelle, Aubers Ridge, Festubert and Loos) and one large defensive action (Second Battle of Ypres), as well as minor actions at Givenchy and around Ypres. In the period between the beginning of the war and the end of 1914, British

---

[i] A French Parliamentary debate of 29th March 1920 gave higher figures for some campaigns: 1st Battle of Champagne 69,000 killed/missing/PoW, 171,000 wounded, total 240,000; 2nd Battle of Artois 143,000 killed, etc., 306,000 wounded, total 449,000; 2nd Battle of Champagne & 3rd Battle of Artois 134,000 killed, etc., 279,000 wounded, total 413,000. This excludes c. 9,000 officers.

losses on the Western Front have been calculated at around 94,000 (28,000 fatal). Of these, c. 58,000 were suffered during the five weeks' fighting of the First Battle of Ypres (44% dead or missing). Between 1st January and 31st December 1915, total British casualties on the Western Front were 285,000 of which some 86,000 were fatal. Their major losses were incurred in the actions listed in Table 43 below.

Battle & Army involved	Period of campaign	Casualties		Total losses
		Officers	ORs	
First Battle of Champagne				
IVe Armée	Dec. 14-Mar 15	1646	91786	93432
St Mihiel				
IIIe Armée	15th Jan-end March	486	26564	27050
Woëvre				
Ier & IIIe Armées	26th March-30th April	1200	64000	65200
Alsace				
VIIe Armée	Jan-April	300	20000	20300
Second Battle of Ypres				
IIe Armée	22nd April-25th May	?	10000	10000
Woëvre				
Ire Armée	1st May-20th June	200	16000	16200
Second Battle of Artois				
Xe Armée	9th May-18th June	2260	100240	102500
Alsace				
VIIe Armée	May-June	164	6502	6666
Toutvent Ferme				
IIe Armée	7th-15th June	174	10176	10350
Soissons				
VIe Armée	June	134	7771	7905
Argonne				
IIIe Armée	20th June-20th July	183	11409	11592
Woëvre				
Ire Armée	June-July	222	12800	13022
Alsace				
VIIe Armée	22nd June-22nd July	60	23000	23060
Second Battle of Champagne				
IIe, IIIe & IVe Armées	25th Sept-7th Oct	3743	139824	143567
Third Battle of Artois				
Xe Armée	25th Sept-13th Oct	1250	46980	48230
Alsace				
VIIe Armée	21st Dec 15-8th Jan 16	165	7300	7465
Frise, Somme				
VIe Armée	Jan-Feb 16	56	3500	3556
Total				612795

Table 42 French casualties in major actions 1915 to early 1916 [*Sources: AFdGG*, Tomes II and III]

British casualties were running at a rate of 1 to 3½ French soldiers lost. Yes, the French Army dwarfed the BEF at this time and it was to be expected French losses would be greater. The disparity in losses and the sheer volume of French casualties from 4th August 1914 to 31st December 1915, i.e. c. 2 million, needs to be borne in mind, however, when the disputes between the two high commands over each army's responsibilities in 1916 were debated.

Battle & Army involved	Period of campaign	Casualties		Total losses
		Officers	ORs	
Neuve Chapelle				
1st Army	10th-13th March	554	11108	11662
Second Battle of Ypres				
2nd Army	22nd April-25th May	2150	57125	59275
Aubers Ridge				
1st Army	9th May	451	11046	11497
Festubert				
1st Army	15th-25th May	710	15777	16487
Givenchy				
1st Army	15th-21st June	?	4311	4500 approx.
Bellewaarde & Hooge				
2nd Army	June-July	318	7828	8146
Loos				
1st Army	25th Sept-13th Oct	2466	59247	61713
Total				173280

Table 43 British casualties in major actions 1915
[Source: British Official History, Military Operations, France and Belgium 1915, Vols 1 & 2]

Furthermore, according to Churchill, the French caused 4.6 German casualties for every 1 caused by the BEF[i]. Based on these figures during the autumn of 1915, when the French were fighting the Second Battle of Champagne and Third Battle of Artois and the BEF the Battle of Loos, the French lost five men for every four German casualties. The British, however, lost eight men for every four German soldiers killed, captured or wounded[ii].

The British Expeditionary Force had lost a high proportion of its immediately available front-line resources, however, and was still recovering, albeit slowly, from

---

[i] Figures showed the French/Belgian Armies caused 534,000 German casualties during between 1st February 1915 and 31st January 1916. The BEF is estimated as causing 115,000 German casualties in the same period. The figures show the BEF caused more German casualties than the French only between August 1917 and June 1918. During the approximate period of the Battle of the Somme (July to the end of 1916), the French caused 394,000 casualties (including those at Verdun) and the British 236,000. In addition, the French caused c. 278,000 German casualties in the Verdun fighting before 1st July 1916 [Churchill, *The World Crisis*, Appendix J of Volume 2, page 1429].
[ii] 192,000 French casualties versus 154,000 German and 62,000 British & Empire versus 32,000 German casualties.

the destruction of the original professional army despatched in August 1914 to its first western European war in nearly 100 years. Bolstered by the 'part time soldiers' of the Territorial Force, reinforced by some of the remaining Regular battalions withdrawn from far flung parts of the Empire, and now beginning to see the arrival of the newly recruited, hurriedly trained, enthusiastic and completely inexperienced 'Kitchener's Army' volunteers, the BEF was slowly building its strength. Too slowly for some at *GQG*, who read their Army's casualty figures and counted the numbers of Frenchmen in uniform and wondered for how much longer their country should or could carry the main burden of the war on its shoulders.

The BEF, on the other hand, suffered setback after setback as it tried to come to grips with the offensive in industrial warfare. The Battle of Loos which, at least in part, promised much in its opening hours, ended in costly failure with the British *Official History*, usually circumspect in its criticism of 'higher authority', describing the last, futile attacks as nothing more than the 'useless slaughter of infantry'.[36] 62,000[37] (or 23%) of the BEF's 285,000 casualties in 1915 came in the month's fighting at Loos[i]. As mentioned, in a move, elements of which were to cause increasing friction between the French and British Commanders in Chief, several experienced Divisions were sent to the eastern Mediterranean to be replaced by inexperienced troops of lesser value. In consequence, during September 1915, the total number of troops available to the BEF declined and it would need the closing down of the Gallipoli campaign and the influx of many of the New Army Divisions now training at home to build up the expeditionary force to the extent it would be able to conduct a protracted campaign with the resulting losses which fighting in France and Flanders required.

Between them, the Allied Armies on the Western Front suffered 253,000 casualties after the beginning of the Champagne and Artois offensives in the last week of September 1915. On the other side of No Man's Land, German losses during this same period amounted to 141,000[38], meaning these battles created a net loss to the Allies of 112,000 men.[ii] Such unbalanced casualty rates were simply not sustainable, especially for the French.

Moreover, there was little good to say about the campaigns in the East. The poorly led, ill-equipped, badly trained and under-educated armies of the Tsar suffering reverse after reverse in East Prussia, Poland, and the western fringes of Russia-proper, had been forced back to the line between Riga on the Baltic to Tarnopol to the north of Rumania. Not only were casualties severe but losses in equipment seriously undermined the Russian Army's ability to wage war. As a result, French industry, already suffering from the loss of some of its main areas of production now occupied by the Germans, was also trying to re-equip Russia

---

[i] German casualties in this fighting were around 20,000.
[ii] Details of German losses were: 30,673 killed, 73,333 wounded, 37,427 missing. Total 141,433. Of the missing 23,955 were in Allied hands meaning 13,472 were, in fact dead giving 44,145 fatal casualties. Of these casualties 85,032 occurred in Champagne, 26,765 in Artois and 29,366 during the British attacks on Loos and elsewhere [*Source: AFdGG*, Tome III, Annexes Vol. 4, Annexe 3240, page 588].

with rifles, ammunition, artillery, and aircraft. In the Balkans, Bulgaria, noting any lack of military activity on the part of the Greeks and Rumanians, took advantage by declaring for the Central Powers and joined in a three-way attack on Serbia.

The slowly growing Expeditionary Force (or *Armée de l'Orient* as its commander Gen. Sarrail named it) in Salonika was a serious bone of contention between Britain and its Allies. It was regarded as either a waste of valuable troops best used on the Western Front (Robertson/Haig), or the only military force preventing the collapse of the Allied position in the entire eastern Mediterranean (according to every other Ally). The continental members of the Allied coalition believed it to be the main reason why Greece and Rumania did not declare for the Central Powers and, at the same time, it was the only military force preventing the Central Powers and Turkey improving their geographical links and it blocked any possible German naval expansion in the eastern Mediterranean. Indirectly, therefore, in the opinion of the French and Russians, the Salonika Force helped protect essential British trade, military, and naval links with Egypt, India, and the Far East.

What was not disputed by any of the Allies, was the failure of the Gallipoli expedition and, as a result, the evacuation and redeployment of the troops tied up there was a priority. Some would be used to protect the vital Suez Canal against interference by the Turks, and others returned to France for the campaigns of 1916. One division had already been sent to Salonika.

Lastly, the entry of Italy into the war on the side the Triple Entente on 25th May 1915 proved a disappointment to all involved. Italy's hopes of easy victories against the Austro-Hungarian Army, and thus a quick end to the European War, proved ill-founded. Italian manpower was slow to be mobilised and the fighting in the Alps and along the *Isonzo River* was as grim and unproductive as anything on the Western Front.

In short, 1915 produced nothing more than a series of uncoordinated, unsuccessful, and hugely expensive campaigns for the Allies. The cause of this was analysed by Gen. Pellé, Joffre's Chief of Staff, as coming from a:

"... lack of unity of views which resulted in the dispersion of effort".[39]

As the Armies took advantage of the winter to rest, re-equip, and increase their manpower, Joffre and the French Government decided to act to improve the prospects of the coalition in the coming year. There were three key areas: military, diplomatic, and economic; and the French took the lead on all of them in an effort to improve the co-ordination and, therefore, the results of all Allied activity.

The French and British started the ball rolling by convening a series of meetings which addressed various significant points. On 17th November 1915, a conference was held in Paris between the new Prime Minister, Briand, who came to power in late October, and Asquith. This adopted, in the presence of Gen. Joffre, resolutions about how to proceed in the eastern Mediterranean. These discussions were, said Monsieur Briand, to be 'the first of a series continuing until the complete victory of the allies', and were followed the same day by a meeting, chaired by Poincaré, which approved the principle of a permanent joint committee to co-ordinate the work of the coalition.

The French Government then signed a decree on 2nd December 1915 (see page 756) allowing Gen. Joffre to speak on behalf of all French Armies in Europe, and adopted the French plan to be put forward to the Chantilly Conference on 6th, 7th, and 8th December 1915. They also gave assent to the proposals for the 'direction of the war', i.e. there should be constant liaison between the Commanders-in-Chief of the Allied Armies, to be ensured by regular conferences (easier to convene now the Russian Tsar had a permanent military representative at GQG), using military *attachés*, and through the exchange of liaison officers. In addition, the political and diplomatic relations between Governments would be assured by permanent liaison and, eventually, by conferences of the Prime Ministers involved.

THE NEXT STEP ALONG THE ROAD to improved and, it was hoped, successful coordination of military, diplomatic and economic activities was to be the Chantilly conference starting on 6th December and convened by Joffre.

Joffre had been considering the options for a resumption of Allied offensives on the Western Front since October, aware that, on occasions, both the French and British Armies had achieved some local tactical successes but nowhere had it proved possible to translate these into advances of strategic significance. Joffre, was undismayed. He was convinced he could break the German lines with properly organised offensives supported by the necessary weight of artillery and manpower, and if conducted over a wide enough front. To combine this increase in military power with weather suitable for the offensive meant waiting until, at the earliest, the Spring of 1916 before his concept of simultaneous or, at least, concurrent offensives on all fronts was possible. Joffre wanted to integrate two new annual classes of conscripts into the French Army and to ensure stocks of ammunition should be such that 'in the next battle, the question of munitions ceases to be a permanent concern of the High Command'.[40] The key offensives were those in France and Russia and it was here breakthroughs would be sought. Italy's attacks were designed more to pin Austro-Hungarian forces to this front, thereby preventing them from interfering with any Russian offensive.

There was one issue about any offensive on the Western Front. Senior French officers were impressed by the defensive abilities of British soldiers but harboured serious doubts about their offensive capability. This, indeed, was one of the reasons why the Somme was eventually selected for the next great attack – here the French *poilu* would fight side by side with the British Tommy, hopefully in a manner designed to bring out the best characteristics of each. On the other hand, it also meant that, whenever possible, Joffre was keen to release experienced French units to use in offensive action. One such unit, *Xe Armée*, currently resided around Arras and Vimy, stuck between the British Third Army to the south and First Army to the north. *Xe Armée* had been involved in the heavy fighting in Artois in 1915 and Joffre now wished to see them moved to an area where they might be more gainfully employed on the main French front. Were *Xe Armée* withdrawn from the front-line about Arras it was realised British units would have to cover this gap, thereby reducing any reserves available for any British offensive action. But, given the previously mentioned French opinion on the attributes of the British soldier – stubborn, stolid, calm, all good qualities while defending but lacking the French flair and exuberance in the attack – having the British defend more front-line in order to release French troops for an assault somewhere seemed like a fair deal. Life was not so simple and the issue of *Xe Armée* became something of running sore between Joffre and Haig and an irritation only finally salved when events at Verdun forced Haig's reluctant hand.

Joffre first broached the subject of the relief of *Xe Armée* with Sir John French in a letter of 2nd December 1915.[41] The issue was bound up in the frantic manoeuvrings triggered by the attack on Serbia in early October. France not only sent troops to Salonika to assist the Serbs, it also relieved British troops sent to do the same, having already relieved other units to help the faltering campaign at Loos. The relief of these troops had, on 18th October, been agreed as a temporary measure which Sir John French undertook to reverse as soon as possible. Since that date, however, there had been no move to alter deployments in such a way the French troops occupying previously British trenches might be relieved.

Four divisions left the BEF for Salonika and two more were on the move towards Mesopotamia. These changes were confirmed on 21st November by a note from Lt. Col. Clive, the liaison at *GQG*.[42] On the debit side it showed three divisions had already left, one was getting ready to leave and the departure of two more was anticipated. In addition, one Indian Division had left and the other was to leave soon. In the credit column was one new Division from Britain with another about to arrive in France, but these new divisions had only recently received their rifles and, Clive thought, they needed a month's training before they were ready to go anywhere near the front-line. Furthermore, the divisional artillery of these units would not be ready until the middle of December at the earliest.

As a result of these comings and goings *GQG* decided it needed an analysis of the current state of the BEF in France. This document was dated 23rd November.[43] Prior to the departure of the various divisions for Salonika and Mesopotamia, the BEF held 120 kms. of front with 37 divisions. Since then, six divisions had gone east whilst eight had either arrived or were due imminently. In addition, *Xe Armée* had taken over 5 kms. of British front in First Army's sector towards Loos and other troops some 13 kms. of front south of the *River Somme*. As a result of this, by December the BEF would hold 102 kms. of front with 39 divisions. The paper accepted two of the divisions sent east, 27th and 28th Divisions, were good and experienced units and were being replaced with mediocre divisions in need of both training and experience of trench life. Nevertheless, with an anticipated strength of 39 divisions, *GQG* believed the BEF should be more than capable of holding at least another 20 kms of front, i.e. between 120 and 130 kms[i], and, as new divisions arrived in France, the BEF should take over an increasing part of the Allied front-line[ii].

---

[i] The BEF never held a length of front proportionate to its strength. By the end of 1915 it quadrupled in strength, the front doubled. In 1917, with 62 divisions it occupied 190 kms of front (3 kms/division). The French, 110 divisions, occupied 630 kms (5.7 kms/division) [Huguet, *Britain and the War: A French Indictment*, page 173].

[ii] Current estimates of the strength of the various armies on the Western Front were given in a *GQG* document dated 24th November 1915. These were:
France 2,039,000 combatants (104 Divisions and 110 Territorial battalions)
Great Britain 740,000 combatants (35 Divisions)

The question was: which parts of the front currently held by French troops should the British take over? *GQG* was aware Foch believed the front immediately about Arras and Vimy Ridge to be a good place for further offensives and he might wish to keep a certain part of the current *Xe Armée* in position to pursue this aim. Fighting in this area, however, had proved difficult and extremely costly. In the view of *GQG*, to be truly successful local offensives required the inclusion of attacks along a wide front including the area in front of Lens-Liévin to the north. This, they thought, was best done under a unified command. Previous experience at Loos somewhat coloured French views against close co-operation between French and British troops in an offensive. Loos revealed the considerable difficulties in attempting to co-ordinate joint offensives in which French and British tactical, planning and fighting methods were significantly different. Retaining the old part of the British First Army's front above Lens now occupied by the French *9e Corps* to make an attack on Vimy Ridge an all-French affair was simply not possible. The current need was to reduce rather than expand the French front to relieve and rest units and to create a reserve for future actions. Consequently, it made more sense to ignore Foch's interest in this sector and to pass the entire front of *Xe Armée* over to the British who could then attack in this area if they so wished.

There were, however, other parts of the front currently occupied by French troops the BEF might usefully relieve as new divisions arrived from Britain:

The *Yser*: this was dismissed because, as the document cryptically comments, 'Political interests require the avoidance of direct contact between Belgian and British forces'. It was also deemed necessary for French forces to cover the important area of the French-garrisoned *Region Fortifiée de Dunkerque*;

South of the *Somme*: any extension of Third Army south of the river would have to be limited to no more than two or three divisions as had previously been the case. The reason was *GQG* believed it essential French forces held all direct routes to Paris from the front-line which here was the main road south from Compiègne. Similarly, it was thought this principle might also apply to the important city of Amiens which sat at the hub of essential road, railway and river routes. In addition, were *GAN* to consider an attack between the *Somme* and the *Oise*, the presence of British divisions south of the *Somme* would bring the same problems of co-ordinating attacks between armies of different nationalities as had been experienced around Loos; and

On the *Aisne*: this was thought impractical because of the great distance between any such British units and the majority of the BEF. In addition, the majority of French troops on the *Aisne* front were Territorials and, if relieved, of no genuine offensive value in any French attack.

Summing up, *GQG* believed it was best the BEF should occupy one continuous zone. As their strength increased it was thought they might prefer to

---

Belgium 86,000 combatants (6 Divisions)
Total 2,865,000 combatants (or 537,000 men/23 Divisions more than Germany)
Germany 2,328,000 combatants (122 Divisions and 130 Battalions)
[*Source*: AFdGG, Tome III, Annexes, Vol. IV, Annexe 3099, page 323].

retain complete freedom of action which would be restricted if divisions were scattered along the front-line in Northern France. Additionally, GHQ repeatedly expressed the wish to have the BEF operate *en bloc*. And, although this would change in the new year, the current thinking at *GQG* was the British and French offensives, whilst they might be co-ordinated in terms of time, could not be co-ordinated tactically. As a result of this, *GQG* concluded the only sensible outcome was the BEF should relieve some and, possibly all, of *Xe Armée* around Arras.

The BEF would thus hold the 146 kms front between Boesinghe, just north of Ypres, down to the *Somme*. This had the disadvantage of so stretching the BEF (assuming 39 Divisions) they would be unable to launch an effective offensive. To avoid this it seemed sensible for *Xe Armée* to temporarily retain the front of c. 20 kms from Arras to Notre Dame de Lorette which French troops fought for at substantial cost twice in 1915 and which Foch might wish to attack again. The paper therefore suggested the relief of *Xe Armée* should start in the sectors south of Arras, and between Notre Dame de Lorette and Loos, though the aim should be the complete relief of *Xe Armée* and a unified British front. This would take place either after new British divisions arrived or if French troops took over some part of the front north of the *Somme*. After this, part of the new reserve created by the relief of *Xe Armée* could be kept around Frévent and St Pol against any emergencies in Picardy or Artois. In this manner, the paper concluded, the French achieved the relief of *Xe Armée*, the British obtained the single front they wished for, and operations by each Army could then proceed independently as current French thinking believed to be for the best.

This document was further discussed in a note from Maj. Gen. Ferdinand Auguste Pont[i] to Joffre on 24th November which raised the prospect of retaining the area between Lens and Loos.[44] The relief of *Xe Armée* by the British seemed to Pont to depend on the future activities of Foch at *GAN* who was planning a large offensive with *GQG's* approval. Lt. Col. Clive indicated that, currently, Sir John French favoured the next British attack being south of Arras, between Ransart and the *River Ancre*. If this were to happen then, Pont suggested, *Xe Armée* should not get involved, allowing the British Third Army to attack when and where it wished. Furthermore, to give them greater room to manoeuvre, Third Army should take over some of *Xe Armée's* front to the south of Arras. If, however, it was decided to go ahead with a French attack towards Vimy Ridge then it would prove useful for *Xe Armée* to hold onto the area to the north, as this allowed the artillery to fire from the Loos Salient into the rear of Vimy Ridge. Were this to happen then Pont suggested asking the British to take back the stretch of line south of the *Somme* they had previously temporarily occupied and which was the subject of such frantic negotiation in mid-October.

Based on this, Joffre's letter to French of 2nd December explained that the reasons why the French had taken over parts of the British line on the fronts of

---

[i] Previously the head of the *3e Bureau* at *GQG* and now a Maj. Gen. with responsibility for operations in Northern France. He later went on to Brigade, Divisional and Corps command leading *4e Corps* through the Fourth Battle of Champagne and Second Battle of the Marne in 1918. An artillery officer he was born in 1865 and died in 1926.

the First and Third Armies no longer held good. The First Army was no longer involved in offensive activity at Loos[i] and the divisions sent to the eastern Mediterranean and beyond were now being replaced by a larger number of new divisions from Britain[ii]. He accepted these new divisions needed training, but felt sure that, under French's guidance, this process would be both speedy and effective and that, soon, these divisions would be suitable to hold the line in relatively quiet parts of the British front. Furthermore, Joffre suggested that were it the case the British Third Army went on to the offensive in the following year, then it would be useful for this Army to take over more of the line towards Arras thus giving them a much wider area from which to select a suitable front for this attack. He thus suggested that, rather than take over the trenches south of the *Somme* occupied by elements of Third Army during the early autumn, Third Army should, instead, shift its left wing northwards some 14 kms to the Arras to Beaurains road, taking over this frontage from the *1er corps de cavalerie*, *88e division d'infanterie territoriale* and one regiment of *17e Corps*, all part of the French *Xe Armée*. Joffre suggested further arrangements be made directly with Foch at *GAN* but asked to be kept informed of progress he hoped would be speedy.

Believing these movements to be in hand, Joffre's attention now turned to the forthcoming conference which, he hoped, would point the way forward to a successful and, possibly, a victorious 1916. The conference would be at Chantilly, home to the famous horse racetrack and of the *Grand Quartier Général*.

---

[i] Haig informed Sir John French of the closure of the Loos campaign on 4th November.
[ii] 36th (Ulster) Division arrived in France in October, 30th, 32nd, 33rd and 38th (Welsh) Divisions during November and 16th (Irish) and 31st Divisions in December 1915.

ENDNOTES:
1. *Source:* François, Gen. G, *Les Canons de la Victoire 1914-18, Tome 3, L'Artillerie de côte et l'artillerie de tranchée*, Histoire et Collections, Paris, 2010, pages 42-4
2. *Les Armées Française dans La Grande*, Tome II, Annexes Vol. 2, Annexe 792, page 24.
3. Ibid., page 26
4. *AFdGG*, Tome III, Annexes Vol. 1, Annexe 52, page 94.
5. Ibid., Annexe 146, page 230.
6. *AFdGG*, Tome III, Vol. III, page 40.
7. Ibid., page 42.
8. Fayolle, M E, ed. Contamine H, *Cahiers secrets de la grand guerre*, Plon, 1964, page 98.
9. Ibid.
10. *AFdGG*, Tome III, Annexes, Vol. I, Annexe 297, page 400.
11. Foch, F, *The Memoirs of Marshal Foch*, W Heinemann Ltd., 1931, page 238.
12. *AFdGG*, Tome III, page 275.
13. Ibid.
14. Ibid.
15. *AFdGG*, Tome III, Annexes Vol. 2, Annexe 1535, page 1128.
16. Ibid., Annexe 1334, page 803.
17. *AFdGG*, Tome III, page 282.
18. Ibid., page 289.
19. *AFdGG*, Tome III, Annexes Vol. 2, Annexe 1535, page 1128.
20. Fayolle, pages 127-8.
21. Ibid., page 134.
22. Ibid., page 133.
23. Herr, op cit., Part 2, *Field Artillery Journal*, July-August 1927, page 338.
24. Touzin, P & Vauvillier, F, *Les Canons de la Victoire 1914-18, Histoires & Collections*, pp 22.
25. Calwell, Maj. Gen. C E, *Field Marshal Sir Henry Wilson: His Life and Diaries*, Cassell & Co., 1927, Vol. 1, page 28 ('One private soldier'). Jeffrey, K. *Field Marshal Sir Henry Wilson: A Political Soldier*, OUP, 2006, page 86 ('One corporal and four private soldiers').
26. *AFdGG*, Tome III, Annexes Vol. 3, Annexe 2792, page 1023.
27. Ibid., Annexe 2793, page 1024.
28. Ibid., Annexe 2931, page 1211.
29. Ibid., Annexe 2953, page 1244.
30. Ibid., Annexe 2955, page 1249.
31. Ibid., Annexe 2956, page 1250.
32. *AFdGG*, Tome III, Annexes Vol. 4, Annexe 2976, page 13.
33. Ibid., Annexe 2982, page 22.
34. *Journal Officiel, Documents parliamentaires, Session Extraordinaire 1920*, Annexe 633, *Séance du 29 Mars*, 1920.
35. *AFdGG*, Tome III, Volume III, pages 539-540.
36. *Official History of the War, Military Operations, France and Belgium 1915*, Vol II, page 388.
37. *BOH*, 1915, Vol II, page 392
38. Ibid. See footnote 1.
39. *AFdGG*, Tome IV, Vol 1, page 2. *GQG, Note on unified action by the Franco-British forces*, Gen Pellé, Chief of Staff, 7th October 1915.
40. *AFdGG*, Tome IV, Vol 1, page 6. *GQG*, Letter to Minister for War, 3rd October 1915.
41. *AFdGG*, Tome III, Annexes Vol. IV, Annexe 3112, page 357.
42. Ibid., Annexe 3095, page 314.
43. Ibid., Annexe 3096, page 314.
44. Ibid., Annexe 3100, page 325.

18. SIR DOUGLAS HAIG TAKES OVER

'Haig... had a single track mind, intensely and narrowly concentrated, like a telescope, on one object; except his profession of soldiering, and later his family, he had no real interests of any kind, and little knowledge; nor had he any desire for knowledge, unless it bore on his own special subject... Haig, secure in his own self-confidence, seldom listened to the opinion of others.'

Field Marshal Archibald Percival Wavell,
Allenby – A Study in Greatness

THE APPOINTMENT OF SIR DOUGLAS HAIG as the new C-in-C of the BEF on 19th December was, perhaps, the most significant event of the winter of 1915/6 and one which profoundly impacted on the conduct of the war over the next 25 months. The reputations of few military commanders have seen so many ups and downs as those which have buffeted Haig. Amongst British historians and military commentators, he moved from being the man who won the war, to the status of a bungling butcher. Since the 1960s, his reputation has been steadily re-built, first by John Terraine and latterly by others who following his lead. There is no doubt Haig trained and studied assiduously for this essential job throughout his career. The fact Terraine should entitle his rehabilitative biography of Haig *The Educated Soldier* is indicative not only of the fact he attended to his studies, learnt his trade and was a dedicated officer. It is, perhaps, also suggestive of the fact such behaviour in the Victorian-era Army was, of itself, unusual and led him to stand out from his peers. It would, perhaps, be unkind to suggest 'in the land of the blind, the one-eyed man is king'. Perhaps.

Born on 19th June 1861 to the wealthy whiskey distiller John Haig and his wife Rachel Mackerras Veitch, Douglas was the ninth and youngest survivor of eleven children. He was the 5th son and had no hope of inheriting *Haig & Haig Distillers*, his father's lucrative business. This inheritance fell to the first son, Hugh Veitch Haig, who took control of the Cameronbridge Distillery on their father's death in 1878[i]. Douglas, like many of his Army contemporaries, was, therefore, at something of a loose end when it came to a career. He was also the offspring of a man in 'trade', unlike the mass of his military brethren who were born into the aristocracy, the landed gentry or came from an existing military family. His later obsession with gentlemanly conduct, or its absence, might almost be seen as an over-compensation for his father's mercantile background. His other three older brothers – William, John, and George – all attended either Oxford or Cambridge[ii] and, after attending Clifton College near Bristol, it seemed Douglas would follow in his brothers' footsteps when he entered Brasenose College, Oxford, in 1880. He had, however, set his heart on a career in the Army.

---

[i] C. 70% of UK gin production comes from Cameronbridge, including the well-known brands of *Gordon's*, *Booth's* and *Tanqueray*. Though all described as 'London Dry Gin', the word 'London' refers to the process rather than the location.

[ii] William gained an MA at *University College, Oxford*; John (who out-lived Douglas) a BA at *Trinity College, Cambridge*; and George went to *Magdalene College, Cambridge*.

Denied a degree on a technicality, Haig crammed heavily to enter Sandhurst just within the age limit for officer training. He was thus some five years older than most of his contemporaries at the Royal Military College. His mother is said to have instilled in him a strong work and religious ethic. His work ethic set him apart from many of his contemporaries, not a few of whom regarded the Army as a pastime rather than a profession. Perhaps being the youngest in a large family in which it might have been the case of 'sinking or swimming' in rivalry with his siblings, Douglas chose to 'swim' – as well as ride, being a keen huntsman and an excellent polo player. The cavalry was always going to be his chosen berth, and in 1885 he was commissioned into the 7th (Queen's Own) Hussars. Before that, he passed out first in his class and been awarded the Anson Memorial Sword.

Service in India saw him promoted Captain before he came home at the end of 1892 to prepare for the 1893 Staff College entrance examination for entry in 1894. Much has been made of Haig's delayed arrival at Camberley in 1896. He first sat the entrance exam in the summer of 1893 but, failed the mathematics paper with 182 marks out of 400 (200 was the required pass mark), and did not qualify. Recently, Gary Mead[1] has sought to suggest Haig was unjustly disqualified in 1893. Haig, with an overall mark of 2,642 against a minimum pass mark of 1,600, was 27th out of 67 candidates. According to Mead, there were 28 places. Haig thus should have won an automatic place. According to *The Times*, however, this is not accurate. In its edition of Thursday, 10th August 1893 (page 4), it records the names, units, and marks of the successful candidates, as well as those who achieved a pass but for whom there were no places. This lists 25 (not 28) successful candidates and eleven who qualified but were denied a place for various reasons. The top score was 3,363 (Capt. C E Keith, 2nd Northumberland Fusiliers). The lowest qualifying score was 2,503. Four of the candidates denied a place scored more than 2,503 but, with places limited for the R.A., R.E. and Indian Staff, and with one successful candidate already from the Argyll and Sutherland Highlanders, these four were excluded. All bar three of the 25 successful candidates scored more than Haig's 2,642 as did four of the six excluded. 'Justice', as Mead would have it, should have still excluded Haig as 26 candidates scored more than he for the 25 (not 28) places available. In addition, the lowest qualifying score for entry was, in this case, 2,252 and not 1,600.

Mead makes a further argument. The 1893 mathematics paper, set by a new examiner on the death of his predecessor, was more difficult than normal. This exam, it is claimed, was *so* difficult 'candidates might well not be able to do anything at all'.[2] As an explanation for Haig's failure this surely holds good if he were the only one who sat this exam. Every candidate took the paper, 36 passed. As it was known passing this paper was a requirement for entry, one might suggest Mead's arguments are a case of special, and not especially accurate, pleading.

Despite his failure, Haig entered Camberley by nomination of the Commander in Chief in 1896. Normally a nomination should have been for 1895 but, for whatever reason, a special case was made. According to James Edmonds, a contemporary at Camberley and compiler of the *Official History*, Haig did not admit to his failure in the entrance examination but instead put about a story suggesting he asked for his nomination to be postponed because of 'private reasons'.[3]

Edmonds and George Macdonogh, later the BEF's Chief of Intelligence who then went to London as Director of Military Intelligence at the War Office, were by a long way the two 'brightest sparks' in the 1896 intake to Camberley. So far ahead were their entrance examination totals, indeed, efforts were made to conceal the wide gap between their results and the rest. Neither officer, both Royal Engineers, found their time at the Staff College especially taxing. Edmonds honed his writing skills by producing a lengthy history of the American Civil War published in 1905 in conjunction with Lt. W Birkbeck Wood, MA (and the Devon Regt.), under the title of *A History of the Civil War in the United States, 1861-5*. Macdonogh merely spent his time qualifying as a barrister at Lincoln's Inn.

According to Edmonds, apart from himself and Macdonogh, the outstanding officers at the Staff College during his tenure were Capt., later Maj. Gen., Henry Newport Charles Heath, 1st South Staffordshire Regt., and later of the KOYLI[i], Capt., later Gen., Sir Richard Cyril Byrne Haking, Hampshire Regt.,[ii] and Capt., later Maj. Gen., Sir Thompson 'Tommy' Capper, East Lancashire Regt.[iii].4 Not on his list were two men due to become Field Marshals – Edmund Henry Hynman Allenby and Douglas Haig. Edmonds thought Allenby 'out of his depth' but, failing to note his wide interests in music, reading and wildlife, especially birds (which led him in later life to become a Fellow of the Zoological Society), he perhaps misjudged and stereotyped him as a simple 'typical English fox-hunting squire'[iv]. This view might have been reinforced by the popular Allenby's elevation

---

[i] Heath took command of 48th (South Midland) Division TF in 1914, taking it to France in March 1915. According to Edmonds he wore himself out 'knocking the division into shape' and he died after a short illness on 29th July 1915. Maj. Gen., Henry Newport Charles Heath, CB, 1st South Staffordshire Regt. and the KOYLI, was aged 55. He was the son of Maj. Gen. Alfred Heath and the husband of Harriet Heath, of 25 Ovington St., Chelsea, London. He is buried in Brookwood Cemetery, grave I. 176242.

[ii] Haking later commanded, with no little controversy but also some success, the XI Corps at Loos, at Fromelles, during the German Georgette offensive of March 1918, and throughout the 100 Days offensive at the end of the war.

[iii] Capper died the day after being shot on 26th September 1915, the second day of the Battle of Loos. Commanding 7th Division, he was fatally wounded in the front-line by a sniper. Maj. Gen. Sir Thompson Capper, KCMG, CB, DSO, East Lancashire Regt., was aged 51. He was the husband of Mary Capper, of 67, Portland Court, Marylebone, London. He is buried in Lillers Communal Cemetery, grave in front of II. A.

[iv] This misjudgement is, perhaps, best expressed by the sensitive proclamation he made to the citizens of Jerusalem after it was captured by his forces on 9th December 1917: "To the Inhabitants of Jerusalem the Blessed and the People Dwelling in Its Vicinity: The defeat inflicted upon the Turks by the troops under my command has resulted in the occupation of your city by my forces. I, therefore, here now proclaim it to be under martial law, under which form of administration it will remain so long as military considerations make necessary. However, lest any of you be alarmed by reason of your experience at the hands of the enemy who has retired, I hereby inform you that it is my desire that every person pursue his lawful business without fear of interruption. Furthermore, since your city is regarded with affection by the adherents of three of

to Master of the Camberley Drag Hunt, a post Haig, the superior horsemen, was expected to fill but, relatively unpopular with his fellow students, he was beaten by Allenby in the election.[5]

Allenby had no inflated view as to his intellectual abilities. He twice failed the entrance examination for the Indian Civil Service and reverted to Sandhurst and the Army 'because he was too big a fool for anything else'[i]. Although, like most, he failed to solve the conundrum of the Western Front, his performance in Palestine, both as general and 'diplomatic administrator', displayed a creative intelligence greater than he himself might admit[ii]. Certainly, the conception, planning and execution of the climactic Battle of Megiddo (19th-25th September 1918) which Allenby oversaw was perhaps the most brilliant of any action between 1914 and 1918 by any General and its co-ordinated 'all arms' approach as close to the overwhelming World War Two German *Blitzkrieg* tactics as was possible given the current level of technology.

Haig was altogether another kettle of rather silent Lowland Scottish fish. Here was a man devoted to his studies (and his horses) perhaps to the exclusion of other interests which might have developed a more rounded character. Capt., later Gen., Sir George de Symons Barrow, initially of the Connaught Rangers and later the 35th Scinde Horse, was a year behind Allenby and Haig at Camberley and, according to Brian Bond, his view of the two was at odds with that of Edmonds. Allenby he regarded as more imaginative and with a more liberal set of interests.

---

the great religions of mankind and its soil has been consecrated by the prayers and pilgrimages of multitudes of devout people of these three religions for many centuries, therefore, do I make it known to you that every sacred building, monument, holy spot, shrine, traditional site, endowment, pious bequest, or customary place of prayer of whatsoever form of the three religions will be maintained and protected according to the existing customs and beliefs of those to whose faith they are sacred. Guardians have been established at Bethlehem and on Rachel's Tomb. The tomb at Hebron has been placed under exclusive Moslem control. The hereditary custodians at the gates of the Holy Sepulchre have been requested to take up their accustomed duties in remembrance of the magnanimous act of the Caliph Omar, who protected that church." [Horne, C F, ed., *Records of the Great War*, Vol. V, National Alumni 1923].

[i] His own description of himself made in a speech and recorded in R. Savage, *Allenby of Armageddon*, 1925, page 24.

[ii] Haig and Allenby did not get on and this became increasingly apparent after Haig became CinC. Both were shy, inarticulate men and Wavell tells of an incident when, left alone in a room together, they said not one word before parting with an unspoken agreement they would never again be in the same room without at least one member of their respective staffs. Wavell also records that at Army commanders' meetings Haig often invited others to speak whilst Allenby was still putting forward his views, the more so if that person happened to be the Haig favourite and commander of Fifth Army – Gough. Wavell suggests an element of jealousy on Haig's behalf given it was known the new Prime Minister (Lloyd George took over from Asquith on 6th December 1916) was considering what options there were for a new CinC on the Western Front [*Source:* Wavell, Gen. Sir A P, *Allenby: A Study in Greatness*, Harrap, 1940, pages 63 and 170].

Haig, though, 'carried the habit of concentration on professional studies to excess' thereby narrowing his horizons and 'stunting his imagination'.[6] Haig had been regarded as somewhat stand-offish at Sandhurst and he continued this tendency next door at Camberley. Again, his maternally ingrained work ethic set him apart from all but one other officer, Capt., later Brig. Gen., Arthur Blair of the King's Own Scottish Borderers, with whom he socialised. Otherwise, Haig, according to Edmonds:

"... worked harder than anyone else, was seldom seen in the mess except for meals (and) kept himself to himself."

The distinguished World War Two commander, Gen. Archibald Wavell, served as the BGGS of XX Corps during 1918, part of the Egyptian Expeditionary Force commanded so successfully by Allenby. Wavell, a huge admirer of Allenby, wrote an early biography of his erstwhile CinC first published in 1940. Within it he gives a revealing comparative assessment of the personalities and characters of Allenby and Haig. His comments on Haig are illuminating:

"Haig... had a single-track mind, intensely and narrowly concentrated, like a telescope, on one object; except his profession of soldiering, and later his family, he had no real interests of any kind, and little knowledge; nor had he any desire for knowledge, unless it bore on his own special subject... Haig, secure in his own self-confidence, seldom listened to the opinion of others... Haig had a deeply religious strain, and was a regular churchgoer... To sum up, Allenby was the more broad-minded and the more human; Haig, by virtue of concentration, the more technically efficient."[7]

Except for Macdonogh, Edmonds regarded all other students at the Staff College as his intellectual inferiors. The Camberley professor Col. Henderson, however, often paired Edmonds and Haig (and, thereby, Blair too) which, Barrow later suggested, was because of their different natures: Edmonds a man who rejoiced in detail and complexity; Haig a generalist with a simpler view of military affairs. The 'staff officer' and the 'general officer' as Andrew Green suggests in his book about Edmonds and the writing of the *Official History*.[8] Edmonds, however, found Haig 'terribly slow on the uptake' and, on one occasion, abandoned Haig and his Borderer friend on a three-day Staff Exercise because, as he later told Haig, he 'could not afford to be handicapped by you and Blair any longer'.[9] Edmonds would later relate to Liddell Hart concerns about Haig's 'lack of intellectual clarity'.

Haig was not about to let the low opinions of a colleague get in the way of his ambitions to rise far and fast. In this, he was assisted by the connections of his older sister, Henrietta Frances, who married William George Jameson in 1876. Jameson was a scion of the Irish whiskey family (founded by the Scot John Jameson), and the families were intimate. Henrietta became almost a substitute mother to her youngest brother on the death of their mother in 1879. But, apart from support and counsel, Henrietta brought with her another advantage – her husband was a yachting friend of the Prince of Wales, the future King Edward VII. It was not a connection to be ignored and was sufficiently close that, on his arrival at Camberley, Haig immediately requested three days' leave 'to shoot, to meet the Prince of Wales'.[10] This did not impress his new colleagues at the College as a social opening gambit, some of whom might already have been wondering at his unusually favourable treatment at the hands of the Commander in Chief, Garnet Wolesley, in granting him a postponed place against previous precedent.

Perhaps, as Haig strongly believed during the war, his god was on his side. From this distance, the religious convictions of the officers and men from all armies seem difficult to fathom. It is one of the human race's deepest absurdities that one's god is always on one's side in war, even when that god is the same one to which the enemy is equally devoted. Then, when one side loses, it is either because someone, somehow had angered their god or, rather more conveniently, because someone or some group, almost always of another racial or religious background, has stabbed the righteous in the back, as many in Germany decided must have been the case in 1918.

Haig was raised a Presbyterian by a devout mother who demanded he regularly send her his response to, and interpretation of, different passages of the bible whilst a schoolboy. On the death of his mother, sister Henrietta stepped in acting, quite literally, as his spiritual guide by encouraging him towards the spiritualism then hugely popular within late Victorian and Edwardian society. Some modern writers, for example Douglas Scott (the editor of Haig's pre-war diaries and letters), regard his dalliance with spiritualism as an amusing interlude during which he took *séances* 'in a light-hearted spirit'.[11] Not so Gerard de Groot in 1988 who placed Haig's involvement firmly in the context of the great explosion of interest in the spirit world which took place after the importation of the concept from the United States in the 1850s.

Spiritualism at this point was not simply the province of the desperate or the fraudulent. Genuine scientists such as Alfred Russel Wallace, naturalist, explorer, geographer, anthropologist, biologist and the joint if independent originator of the theory of evolution with Darwin in the 1850s, argued the possibility of spirits existing should not be ignored by science in his book *The Scientific Aspect of the Supernatural* in 1886. More famously, Arthur Conan Doyle of Sherlock Holmes fame joined the *Society for Psychical Research* in 1893 and investigated and promoted spiritualism even before the death of his son from pneumonia in 1918, an event which stoked the fires of his interests with his second book on the subject, *The Vital Message*, appearing soon after in 1919. Spiritualism was, therefore, a widely accepted element of religious belief, even if on the fringes of Christianity, and there is no particular reason why the religiously devout Henrietta and Douglas Haig should not have found attending *séances* and receiving messages from 'the beyond' an accepted and reasonable activity in Edwardian society. Indeed, they both attended one such *séance* on 20th September 1906 and another in November. At the first of these, the medium, one Miss McCreadie, suggested she had contacted a 'small man named Napoleon' (one of Haig's military heroes, especially when it came to the use of Murat's cavalry during the Jena-Auerstedt campaign of 1806) who might help Haig if he so wanted. Interestingly, Haig's account of this *séance* is reported in various biographies of the Field Marshal. Rather like the somewhat favourable editing of his war-time diaries which have appeared over the years, none of them report precisely the same account of this event (or, as is the case of Duff Cooper and Terraine, mention it at all). Sixsmith and Sheffield mention it 'in passing' and as of little consequence. Reid, Mead, and Scott regard it as 'a bit of lark' done to support his sister Henrietta, a view later 'confirmed' by Haig's widow, but her comments, made at a time when the fad of spiritualism was fast fading, tempt one to paraphrase the late Mandy Rice-Davis with 'she would say that, wouldn't she'.

Reid, Mead, and Scott all quote Haig's account of the *séance*. Or, rather, quote parts of the account of that afternoon's events. Haig, during the war at least, was a great one for underlining sections of reports or plans and Mead and Reid keep Haig's underlining (or emphasis) in their quotations. One of these phrases so highlighted, however, suggests, at least to this writer, Haig was taking McCreadie's words rather more seriously than modern historians might like to believe. The three accounts read as follows:

Douglas Scott (*Douglas Haig, Diaries and Letters 1861-1914*)

"… was influenced by several spirits: notably a small man named Napoléon aided me. That it was in my power to be helped by him for good affairs but I might repel him if his influence was for bad, tho' he had become changed for the better in the spirit world. I was destined to do much good and to benefit my country. Asked by me how to ensure the Territorial Army Scheme being a success, she said thought governed the world. Think out the scheme thoroughly, one's thoughts would then be put in so convincing a manner that the people would respond (without any compulsion) and the National Army would be a reality. She c'd not bring Napoléon to me when I wanted but I must think of him & try & get his aid as he was always near me."

Walter Reid (*Architect of Victory: Douglas Haig*)

"[a]t 3pm went with Henrietta to see a *médium*, Miss McCreadie … [she said that] I had come recently from abroad and was now settling down. Seemed to be drawing a great force around me which would be of assistance in the new Scheme… She thought a 'company basis' better than a 'battalion basis' for expansion of Territorial Army. Then I gave her a letter from Mr. Haldane (the S of S). She said he was a 'very clever man'. Honest and far seeing and would fight to bring people around to his opinions. Asked by Henrietta about me (before she went under control) she said she felt I wanted magnetism and had been unwell but was getting better. It seems as if I would go abroad for some special object of a wide and important nature. Much would depend on me. Then when under control by a little native girl 'Sunshine' she said that I was influenced by several spirits: notably a small man named Napoléon aided me. That it was in my power to be helped by him for good affairs but I might repel him if his influence was for bad, tho' he had become changed for the better in the spirit world. I was destined to do much good and to benefit my country. Asked by me how to ensure the Territorial Army Scheme being a success, she said *thought governed the world*."

Gary Mead (*The Good Soldier: The Biography of Douglas Haig*)

"… little native girl 'Sunshine', said that I was influenced by several spirits - notably a small man named Napoléon aided me. That it was in my power to be helped by him for good affairs but I might repel him if his influence was for bad tho' he had become changed for better in the spirit world. I was destined to do much good & to benefit my country. Asked by me how to ensure the Territorial Army Scheme being a success, she said <u>thought governed the world</u>. Think out the scheme thoroughly, one's thoughts would then be put in so convincing a manner that the people would respond (<u>without any compulsion</u>) and the National Army would be a reality. She cd not bring Napoléon to me when I wanted but I must think of him & try & get his aid as he was always near me. My mother too was close to me and a sister Lally. My mother threw a light round me, and Henrietta, & placed on my breast a star which illuminated all about me. Hugo also sent me a message. So did George but latter feeble."

Given that, promoted by Lord Roberts under the auspices of the *National Service League* and supported by Haig and many other Army officers, compulsory army service was a red-hot topic, the fact Haig should underline the phrase 'without any compulsion' in reference to the creation of a National Army is… intriguing. Furthermore, Haig's dutiful account of the 'contacts' with his deceased mother and a sister Lally (presumed to be Rachel Alice Haig, born in 1849) and his recently dead older brother George Ogilvy Haig (who died the previous December) is not suggestive of one who disbelieves what they are hearing. Douglas Scott's suggestion, therefore, that Haig was pulling Miss McCreadie's leg with his questions and comments seem, at least to this writer, to be rather wide of the mark.

Now, this writer is not suggesting Douglas Haig determined strategy and tactics whilst communing with mediums or over a Ouija board. His increasing belief in the guidance of a 'higher power' and of being an instrument of god, however, is worrying, particularly at a time when representatives of the church continued to spout sermons on the need for 'sacrifice', which sacrifice tended to be the lives of the young men either enlisted or conscripted into the Army.

LIKE NEARLY EVERY OTHER OFFICER of every army Haig failed adequately to address, and certainly did not solve, the key tactical issue which so concerned Bloch: how to get men in sufficient numbers across 'the fire swept zone' and into the enemy's positions. His previous experience was as a staff officer rather than as a leader of troops in the field and there were doubts about his tactical, rather than his organisational, skills before the war.

Much is made in certain circles of the apparent failures of Haig at the last two Army manoeuvres conducted before the outbreak of war in 1912 and 1913. Of the two, the 1912 manoeuvres are more often cited as examples of Haig's tactical failings and, erroneously, of his failure to grasp the potential of the new technology of air power. This latter charge is hinted at by the Marquis of Anglesey in his *History of the Cavalry*:

> "It is interesting to note that Haig, who took the chief command at Aldershot in 1911, failed miserably in the 1912 manoeuvres. One staff officer remarked that he 'was so completely outmanoeuvred that the operations were brought to a premature end'. This seems to have been

chiefly because his opponent made clever use of the new air arm. In 1913 he was no more successful. His dispositions were said to have left a three-mile gap in the 'British' centre. On the other hand, Haig much criticised French, who himself conceded that 'the manoeuvres taught us all many lessons'."[12]

Unlike France and Germany, Britain was not used to, nor especially suitable for, the large-scale military manoeuvres which were an annual feature of the two continental powers' training and planning[i]. The previous British manoeuvres took place in September 1910 on Salisbury Plain and was the first time aircraft were employed when Capt. Bertram Dickson, RHA,[ii] and the actor and later squadron commander Robert Bilcliffe Loraine (later DSO & MC) flew *Bristol Boxkites* Nos. 7 and 8. Dickson flew for the *Red Force* and successfully located *Blue Force's* positions but, on landing to telephone the news, his aircraft was 'captured' by *Blue's* cavalry[iii]. Loraine, in the meantime, transmitted the first successful British airborne wireless signal.

The manoeuvres planned for 1911 between Hertford and King's Lynn were cancelled in August because of a record heatwave and severe drought[iv], though it is suggested Haldane in fact cancelled them in order to free up money to complete preparations for the Expeditionary Force at a time when foreign affairs were in danger of over-heating as a result of the Agadir incident in Morocco. Also preying on the government's mind was, no doubt, the violence and disorder in Liverpool surrounding the transport workers' strike which resulted in the deployment of troops to the city; the suspension of a move by 12th Brigade from Dover to Aldershot for manoeuvres; the readying of the 11th (Prince Albert's Own) Hussars and other units at Shorncliffe to be deployed to strike areas; and the cancellation of the Aldershot Command Rifle Meeting.[13]

The manoeuvres for 1912, scheduled for September, took place in an area just east of that planned for 1911, with Cambridge being one of the early objectives

---

[i] The 1912 manoeuvres involved 51 battalions, 33 cavalry squadrons and ancillary units. The previous week German manoeuvres in Saxony involved 110 battalions and 129 cavalry squadrons [*Source: Report on Foreign Manoeuvres 1912, NA*, WO33/618 quoted in Batten, S, 'A School for the Leaders': What did the British Army learn from the 1912 Army Manoeuvres?, *Journal of the Society for Army Historical Research*, Vol. 93, No. 373 (Spring 2015), pages 25-47].

[ii] Dickson was badly injured when his *Farman* biplane collided with an *Antoinette* monoplane piloted by the French motor racing champion René Thomas (he won the 1914 Indianapolis 500) in Milan on 1st October 1910. Both men survived but Dickson's injuries let to his early death on 28th September 1913, aged 40. Thomas died in 1975, aged 89.

[iii] The Air Battalion was formed in 1911 and the Royal Flying Corps on 13th April 1912. The Air Battalion contained two companies: No. 1 Company (airships) at Farnborough and No. 2 Company (aircraft) at Larkhill, Salisbury Plain. The RFC initially consisted of No. 1 Airship and Flying Squadron, and Nos 2, 3 and 4 Aeroplane Squadrons.

[iv] The July/September heatwave was a record until 1990. A temperature of 98° F (36.7° C) was recorded at Raunds, Northamptonshire, on 9th August 1911.

for the 'invading' troops of the *Red Force* which was then to threaten London. Haig commanded the invading force. His opponent was the clever, but unfit and portly, Sir James Grierson. Chief Umpire was Sir John French, now flying high in the military firmament and regarded by many as the premier soldier in the country.

Although broadly balanced, Haig's *Red Force* enjoyed significant advantages over Grierson's *Blues*. Each force consisted of a cavalry division, two infantry divisions, army troops, two aeroplane flights, and an airship, although the decision not to use monoplanes[i] in the manoeuvres denied *Blue Force* the use of these aircraft and gave Haig's army an advantage of seven aircraft to four[ii]. Haig's army was also a more homogeneous force than that of Grierson and consisted mainly of the Aldershot Command, of which Haig had taken command in 1911 and which became his I Corps on the outbreak of war. This gave *Red Force* the advantage of having trained together and of a unified staff structure. Furthermore, its cavalry[iii] had been involved in their own manoeuvres earlier in the month and the infantry divisions had been working between 9th and 13th September in the area to be used for the manoeuvres. Its two infantry divisions were both based at Aldershot whereas *Blue Force* employed one from Southern Command (3rd Division) and one from Eastern Command (4th Division). In addition, Haig's cavalry force of three brigades was both larger than that of *Blue Force* and was entirely made up of Regular Army units. *Blue Force*, however, did have attached a Brigade of Liverpool Territorial infantry which was, initially, to garrison and 'fortify' Cambridge.

Red Force enjoyed another major advantage over *Blue Force* as it was already concentrated, having 'invaded' the north coast of East Anglia before driving south to positions north-east of Cambridge. *Blue Force* had to mobilise and move its men by train to various stations between Bedford and Hitchin.

---

[i] This resulted from a War Office decision, made on 12th September 1912, to suspend the use of monoplanes after an accident on 6th September 1912 just north of Stevenage. On that day the pilot of a *Deperdussin* monoplane, Capt. Patrick Hamilton, Worcestershire Regt. and No. 3 Squadron, RFC, took off from Wallingford as part of the ongoing cavalry manoeuvres. He was accompanied by Lt. Athole Wyness-Stuart, RFA and RFC, as observer. Heading for a landing ground near the village of Willian (now on the southern edge of Letchworth) the aircraft broke up, killing both men. The aircraft was a product of the *Société pour les Appareils Deperdussin (SPAD)*, set up by silk merchant, Armand Deperdussin near Reims. An inquest found the accident occurred because of the failure of an engine component. Both men were aged thirty and their funerals were held at St Saviour's Church in Radcliffe Road, Hitchin. Deperdussin's name disappeared from aviation history when the company joined with that of Blériot to become *Blériot-SPAD (Société pour l'aviation et ses dérivés)* in 1914. *SPAD* was responsible for a series of well-known fighter aircraft for the French air force and employed by all the main Allies. For more see: http://homepage.ntlworld.com/frank.cooke/the_aviators.htm.

[ii] *Red Force*: two 100 h.p. *Breguets*, two *Maurice Farman Biplanes* and one *BE1*, *BE4* and *BE5 Biplane* plus airship *'Delta'*. *Blue Force*: One each of *BE2* and *BE3* Biplanes, a *Short Tractor Biplane* and one other *Aircraft Factory Biplane* plus airship *'Gamma'*. Every aircraft used French-built (either *Gnome* or *Renault*) engines.

[iii] Three cavalry brigades with *Red* and the Regular Mounted Brigade with *Blue*.

The composition of the two forces was as follows:

Red Army – Lt. Gen. Sir Douglas Haig
Cavalry: Maj. Gen. Edmund Allenby
1st (Kavanagh), 2nd (de Lisle) and 4th (Bingham) Cavalry Brigades
1st Infantry Division: Maj. Gen. Samuel Lomax
1st (Maxse), 2nd (Morland) and 3rd (Landon) Brigades
2nd Infantry Division: Maj. Gen. Henry Lawson
4th (Cavan), 5th (Haking) and 6th (R H Davies) Brigades
Two airplane flights and one airship.

Blue Army – Lt. Gen. Sir James Grierson
Cavalry: Col. Charles Briggs
Regular Mounted Brigade[i] (Brown-Synge-Hutchinson) and 1st South Western Mounted Brigade (TF) (Le Roy Lewis)
Three battalions, Territorial cyclists
3rd Infantry Division: Maj. Gen. Henry Rawlinson
7th (Drummond), 8th (Doran) and 9th (Burney) Brigades
4th Infantry Division: Maj. Gen. Thomas D'Oyly Snow
10th (Haldane), 11th (Heath) and 12th (Wilson) Brigades
Territorial detachment, Maj. Gen. W F L Lindsay
Liverpool Infantry Brigade (TF), Col. A R Gilbert
Two airplane flights and one airship

THE 1912 MANOEUVRES ARE INTERESTING not just because of questions raised over Haig's performance but also because they were conducted in a manner suggesting wars like Manchuria never happened. For example, artillery was dragged out into the open to conduct direct fire in close support of attacking infantry. It was still thus at Le Cateau two years later and this is, perhaps, of no surprise when people such as Douglas Haig were still advocating these tactics as late as 1913.

Operations were scheduled to run for four days from 6 a.m. on the morning of 16th September but were curtailed in the late afternoon of 18th September. By this point, Grierson's troops stopped the advance of *Red Force* and with an entire infantry Brigade, 10th Brigade, uncommitted. It was also about to launch an attack by the Liverpool Brigade on *Red's* 2nd Brigade when a halt was called to proceedings.

The consensus was Grierson's force got the better of Haig's men. True, Allenby's cavalry worked their way around the southern flank of *Blue Force* but they were not engaged and were held up by the intelligent employment of detachments of the *Blue* cavalry. Indeed, the success of the *Blue* mounted units under Col. Charles Briggs was, perhaps, the highlight of the entire event and the virtues of both the units and their commander were extolled in *The Times'* account of the manoeuvres. Not only did they cleverly exploit the terrain to mask their movements, they massed at a crucial moment to capture the village of Camps Green and, by so doing, placed Haig's 2nd Division in difficulties.

---

[i] Composite Household Cavalry, Royal Scots Greys, and a Mounted Infantry Battalion.

There were a few trenches 'dug' (i.e. taped out) by *Blue Force* around Cambridge and on higher ground further to the south-east but no indications of barbed wire. To the pleasure of the traditionalists there was, however, a cavalry charge by 2nd Cavalry Brigade of *Red Force* at Mutlow Hill near Saffron Walden which captured half a company of *Blue* Territorials. Afterwards, though, Allenby withdrew his three brigades fifteen miles north-eastwards thus losing touch with both the *Blue* cavalry and the 'enemy's' 4th Division.

According to a report made by some Canadian observers:

"A gallant charge was made *'en masse'* by the whole of General Allenby's Cavalry Division across several fields separated by hedges which were cleared in great style; unfortunately it proved to be a blow in the air, as the only adversaries encountered were a few cyclists holding advanced positions. Disappointed in the results of the great charge and being beyond the reach of support of his infantry and guns at Brinkley, General Allenby broke off the fight, and moved across the front of the opposing line of outposts to Great Bradley without being molested."

It has been suggested Grierson's 'success' was based on a better appreciation and exploitation of the aircraft available to him. In fact, both sides used their aircraft successfully and, in the early part of the manoeuvres, each had precise details as to the location of the opposing units. According to Grierson's own diary, he was able to stay 'in camp all day receiving reports and very soon locating all the lines of march and halting places of the *Red* forces'. Haig remarked 'The aeroplanes and dirigibles brought comfort and balm to his soul' which suggests he was more than happy with their performance and the intelligence so gathered. Indeed, it would have been somewhat incredible had Haig not appreciated the potential use of airpower as it was regularly discussed at senior levels ever since the Army manoeuvres of 1910. A *Memorandum on Army Training* issued after these manoeuvres stated '… considerable developments will take place in the immediate future in the direction of reconnaissance by aircraft' and, a few months later, a meeting at the Staff College, Camberley, suggested more work needed to be done on conducting troop movements by night, as day-time marches would invariably be spotted by observers in either aircraft or airships.

Recently, at the Aldershot cavalry manoeuvres, starting on 2nd September, the opposing forces each deployed four aircraft to assist with reconnaissance, although poor weather prevented much flying and previous heavy rain and flooding disguised usual river landmarks on the *Thames*.[14] Prior to the main manoeuvres, however, the War Office issued a statement entitled *'Employment of Royal Flying Corps on Army Manoeuvres'* which stated unequivocally:

"There can no longer be any doubt as to the value of airships and aeroplanes in locating an enemy on land and obtaining information which could otherwise only be obtained by force. All the principal Powers, therefore, are expending much energy and money in the development of an air service for employment with their land and sea forces in war."[15]

We can, therefore, set aside the notion Haig was somehow caught unawares by the potential of aerial observation. It is simply not true. Indeed, his movement of Allenby's cavalry from his right wing to the left was based on evidence supplied from aeroplane observers, one of them being Major Hugh Trenchard, later the commander of the RFC and Marshal of the RAF. This intelligence suggested Grierson's force failed to occupy this area thus exposing one of his divisions to an attack from the flank and rear.

On the other hand, there is evidence Grierson sensibly applied one of the suggestions made at Camberley in February 1911. He instructed his 4th Division, which arrived somewhat late on the battlefield and caused Haig's 2nd Division significant trouble, to avoid aerial observation as far was possible. It was to march after dusk and, at the sound of any approaching aircraft, the troops were to conceal themselves in any available hedgerows and woodland. The result for Haig was an incomplete picture of the deployment of *Blue Force* and, despite efforts to check the locations of *Blue's* units being partly hampered by mist, he determined a scheme of attack based on this inaccurate intelligence and thus exposed his 2nd Division to damaging attacks from both 4th Division and Briggs's cavalry.

Writing afterwards, Haig was somewhat despondent at this error saying:

'…the information brought in [by aerial reconnaissance] was, as a rule, so reliable that there seems a danger in taking it for granted that if no enemy are seen by the observers none are there'.[16]

Haig was not a man afraid to deploy new technology. The problem was, rather, he placed too great a reliance on its effectiveness as his optimism about the use of gas at Loos and impatience to employ tanks on the *Somme* later confirmed.

More galling for Haig must have been Sir John French's criticism of his tactics, use of intelligence, and deployments, all reported *verbatim* in *The Times*. His criticisms were that: Haig missed an opportunity to destroy the detached Liverpool Territorials at Cambridge; mis-used and rather wasted Allenby's numerically stronger and qualitatively better cavalry; and embarked upon a potentially risky movement with 2nd Division in the absence of definitive information about the deployment and lines of march of the opposition's forces. French's criticisms were not one-way traffic. Grierson, too, came in for a dressing down because of the extended nature of his deployment but, overall, whatever might have been said publicly, privately most officers accepted Grierson 'won' the 1912 war games.

The post-manoeuvres de-brief took place at Trinity College, Cambridge[i]. To add to Haig's discomfort the King was present. Haig and then Grierson explained their plans and the resulting operations. According to *The Times*, Haig's account was 'full and clear', Grierson's 'concise and lucid'. Haig's diary entry records he thought his remarks were 'well received'. He dismissed French's later criticisms as 'not much thought of' by the assembled good and great.[17]

Surprisingly, Haig's *protégé*, John Charteris, was not remotely so kind:

"Although Haig had written out a clear and convincing statement of his views, and held the paper in his hand throughout the conference, he did

---

[i] Trinity College according to *The Times*, *The Spectator* and Charteris, Trinity Hall in Haig's diary and several dependent biographies, e.g. Reid, *Architect of Victory: Douglas Haig*, page 160.

not refer to it when he spoke, but to the dismay of his staff attempted to extemporize. In the effort he became completely unintelligible and unbearably dull. The university dignitaries soon fell asleep. Haig's friends became more and more uncomfortable, only he himself seemed totally unconscious of his failure".[18]

One wonders whether French then took advantage of the 'unintelligible' nature of Haig's commentary when he responded by quoting Haig and disagreeing with him on what was then a fundamental point of military principle: i.e., the currently indisputable power of the offensive. The *Red* commander, stated French, had said:

"… the enclosed nature of the country and the practical equality of *Blue's* and *Red's* field force indicate that that force which can force its opponent to attack it will have the greatest chance of decisive success."

French was having none of this:

"This may read to some as if the *Red* Commander's view was that, as a general principle, when the country is close and when opposing forces are equal, the defensive is to be preferred to the offensive. This, it is presumed, is not what he meant."[19]

French was not finished as he then criticised Haig for developing a strategy based on what he expected rather than on the situation facing him:

"I cannot gather that the *Red* Commander formed any very definite plan, because by his orders he appeared to be endeavouring to meet a situation which he expected would exist in the next morning instead of the situation – very favourable to him – which actually faced him."[20]

None of Haig's many biographers have a good word to say about this incident or his performance in the manoeuvres (or, in the case of Duff Cooper, any word at all. The entire event is ignored). Philip Warner describes the manoeuvres as 'a disaster and a humiliation'.[21] Some contemporary critics were especially acerbic, with the military correspondent of the *Westminster Gazette*[i] writing:

"With regard to General Haig's strategy, no particular brilliance could be claimed. He worked almost entirely by the training manuals, and his every move could be foreseen and met."

It appears to this writer that French's comment below was a recurring theme in Haig's battles, i.e. that he:

"…appeared to be endeavouring to meet a situation which he expected would exist … instead of the situation … which actually faced him"

Thus, Aubers Ridge was a battle to defeat the German defences First Army came up against two months earlier at Neuve Chapelle. The disastrous advance of the 21st and 24th Divisions on 26th September 1915 at Loos was against defences which appeared weak on the first day of the battle but which the Germans, as

---

[i] The *Westminster Gazette* was a small circulation though influential Liberal evening paper founded in 1893 and edited by J A Spender, the uncle of poet/novelist Stephen Spender.

should have been expected, had rushed to reinforce. The first day on the *Somme* was an attack on positions and defenders it was believed on scant evidence had been overwhelmed by the artillery bombardment but with no genuine plan should this prove otherwise. As would further be suggested by the 1913 Aldershot Command exercise, nimbleness of thought and anticipating the actions of the enemy seem not to have been amongst Haig's strongpoints.

One aspect of post-manoeuvre fiasco was Haig's difficulty in expressing himself verbally. He was, at best, inarticulate, especially amongst people not personal friends and close colleagues. Verbal communication, in every language it later turned out, was a problem. The Marquis of Anglesey describes this problem thus:

"Haig's chief drawback, which dogged him throughout his career, was a combination of ineptitude when it came to expressing himself verbally and a propensity for blunt brusquerie with those that disagreed with him."[22]

Or, as Viscount Esher wrote of him in 1909:

"On paper he is hard to beat, although he is so obscure in speech."[23]

Such disconcerting command problems were not isolated to the British Army. It should have come as no comfort to the Governments of either Britain or France that the French manoeuvres of the same year were regarded by the British observers as displaying the 'marked inferiority' of French infantry when it came to minor tactics. Ironically, given the way British tactics developed after the South African experience, it seemed to observers that:

"The infantry, and the cavalry, did not seem to realize what modern rifle fire was like"[24]

The annual French manoeuvres were regarded by many, including some French officers, as a farce[i]. Porch in *The March to the Marne* records that, between 1909 and 1914, at least one of the two Generals involved was past retirement age and was, therefore, unlikely to feature prominently in any forthcoming war.[25] In 1913, for example, the two commanders, Gen. Paul Pau and Gen. Nicolas Charles Chomer, both retired soon after, with Chomer dying in 1915. Furthermore, and to put it politely, not all involved were competent. The 1912 *'grandes manœuvres'* took place along the *Loire* and the *Vienne* and involved five Army Corps. They were conducted under the direction of the new *chef d'État-Major*, Joffre, and were due to run from 11th to 17th September. Early in the proceedings (13th September) and, perhaps, anxious to get back to more useful activities, Gen. Galliéni, commanding *Blue Force*, captured his opposite number, Gen. Marion, his headquarters staff, a Corps commander, and Marion's entire artillery as well as

---

[i] Divisions were involved in *grandes manoeuvres* every four years. Between these Army-based exercises, Divisions spent two years on brigade manoeuvres and the third year on Corps manoeuvres. These lower-level manoeuvres were, it seems, even more absurd than Army *grandes manoeuvres*. For a description of the Normandy and *Seine*-basin based *5e Division's* involvement in *3e Corps'* manoeuvres of September 1913 see Leonard Smith's *From Mutiny to Obedience*, pages 31-4. *Ve Armée's* commander, Galliéni, wrote a scathing report on *3e Corps'* efforts which had few, if any, redeeming features.

four aircraft. This was achieved by the simple expedient of sending two brigades of cavalry from the *1er Division de cavalerie* commanded by a Gen. Dubois unobserved through some woods to descend on Marion and his men from the rear. As *The Times* reported:

> "The influence of this skilfully conducted enterprise on the fortunes of the day could only be surmised, for the 'Cease Fire' was sounded before its results could be felt in other parts of the battlefield."[26]

Clearly the impact of *Red Force* losing their commander, staff and artillery was not regarded as severe as the manoeuvres continued until 17th September when, under the eyes of Joffre and the French President Armand Fallières, Galliéni's troops launched a gallant, unrealistic but successful frontal attack on Marion's entrenched positions in the 'Battle of Ste Maure'.

IN 1913 THE BRITISH ARMY CONDUCTED what was termed an 'exercise' rather than 'manoeuvres'. The reason for this differentiation was that the actions of the defending *White Force* were mainly prescribed in advance. The interest lay in how the attacking *Brown Forces* dealt with what was in front of them and how well the staff of the various senior units conducted themselves.

Before the main exercise, Aldershot Command (Haig) conducted manoeuvres in which Haig's *Brown Force* (2 infantry divisions minus 4th (Guards) Brigade) pursued Charles Briggs's *White Force* 'rear-guard' (4th Guards Brigade plus 1st Cavalry Brigade, minus 5th Dragoon Guards which was attached to Brown Force), both with attached aircraft. The area to be 'fought over' was north of the *Thames* between Henley and Marlow and started with Brown Force trying to cross the river. Haig ordered 1st Division to cross the *Thames* at Medmenham and gave them a bridging train to achieve this objective. Briggs cannily arranged his artillery to take this location under close fire from concealed positions. Haig, however, so deployed his two divisions (1st and 2nd) that 2nd Division was unable to assist 1st Division in the crossing. Somehow, despite *White's* artillery fire, the 2nd Royal Sussex Regt. was deemed by the umpires to have crossed the river and seized the ferry on the north bank. Pontoons were then brought up and the division proceeded to cross. But, under close range 'artillery fire' throughout. All well and good, one might think. The report in *The Times*, however, cast the enterprise in a rather different light:

> "During this performance (i.e. seizing the ferry and bringing up the pontoons) at least four batteries were engaged in shelling them from concealed positions at effective ranges and, although this fire was eventually replied to, it is well known that the neutralization of guns thus situated presents difficulties in which success can only be reaped with the assistance of a considerable amount of luck. This, however, was presumably supplied by the umpires who, doubtless in ignorance of the artillery conditions, allowed the Royal Sussex to hold their own against the opposing infantry and the bridge building to progress."[27]

Unfortunately, this was not the umpires' only error as, that evening, having advised the Guards Brigade the day's events were over and they might bivouac, they were then 'attacked' after the event by 5th Brigade. The umpires' decision in the face of their own error was to ask the Guards to do the decent thing and withdraw an additional five miles instead of sitting down to their evening meal[i].

On day two of the event, Haig ordered 1st Division to 'advance more or less frontally against the opposing rearguard'. *The Times* described the attack as:

> "…sledgehammer operations designed for the discomfiture of General Briggs's small force. The latter, however, had the satisfaction of fulfilling the primary object of its existence and, in the absence of any attempt of the pursuing enemy to manoeuvre it out of its position, to be able to check effectually the Brown advance."[28]

In general, the description is hardly a ringing endorsement of the tactical acumen of the commander of the Aldershot Command who appears, yet again, to have been out-thought and out-fought by that cavalry gadfly Briggs[ii].

Affairs hardly improved during the large-scale Army Exercise then conducted in an area between the Chilterns and Daventry. Here, *Brown Force*, commanded by Sir John French and comprising two 'Armies' under Haig (1st Army) and Gen. Sir Arthur Paget (2nd Army) and the cavalry division under Allenby, was to pursue and drive away *White Force*, a motley collection of mainly Territorials and Yeomanry commanded by Maj. Gen. Sir Charles Monro. Monro's men were to undertake a fighting withdrawal before eventually giving battle on a ridge and some detached hills between the villages of Hellidon and Everdon. The centre of the position was about the village of Fawsley and the newspaper reports of the exercise culminated in a none too flattering account of the 'Battle of Fawsley'.

Minor criticisms of the organisation of the advance of *Brown Force* can be left to one side, although they generally reflect badly on the skills of the staff officers

---

[i] 'Umpiring' at manoeuvres was not a popular role and umpires were often ill-trained and picked more or less at random from the units involved. Ill-equipped to judge properly events witnessed, they were required to complete numerous reports on a function many failed to understand. The Inspector General's Report for 1912 highlighted one of the key problems which was the 'inability of the senior umpires to grasp a tactical situation as a whole', hardly a ringing endorsement of the system of Army exercises and manoeuvres and even less so of the Army offices so described [*NA*, WO275/508, *Inspector General's Report 1912*, page 12].

[ii] Col., later Lt. Gen., Sir Charles James Briggs, GCMG, KCB, 1st King's Dragoon Guards, was highly thought of in certain circles and widely praised for his work with the Yeomanry, having been appointed commander of the South Eastern Mounted Brigade in 1910. *The Times* devoted two complimentary articles to his training of the brigade in 1911. He commanded 1st Cavalry Brigade in France before taking command of 3rd Cavalry Division in May 1915. In October 1915 he was shunted off to Salonika to command 28th Division, and later XVI Corps until the end of the war. John Bourne, in his biography of Briggs on the *Centre for First World War Studies* web site, suggests his 1912 performance embarrassing the future commander of the BEF 'may not have been a wise career move'.

[*http://www.birmingham.ac.uk/research/activity/warstudies/research/projects/lionsdonkeys/b.aspx*].

involved and the commanders directing them. An example, however, was the 'ambush' near the village of Canons Ashby (just north of what was then the *Stratford on Avon and Midland Junction Railway*[i]) whilst in marching order of Maxse's 1st Brigade, which constituted the advance guard of Haig's 1st Army. The attack by one of Hubert Gough's three Yeomanry Cavalry Brigades was but one unexpected incident suggestive of a lack of 'intelligence' at all levels and of all types within *Brown Force*.

The fighting at Fawsley, however, was altogether another matter in which, yet again, the umpires necessarily heavily favoured the 'big battalions' of *Brown Force*, perhaps because it was an 'exercise' and not 'manoeuvres', and possibly because Sir John French was not only in command of *Brown Force* but was the Director and in overall control of the entire exercise. After all, as Bloch observed ten years' earlier, it did not pay to embarrass one's senior officers by exposing their inadequacies during high profile manoeuvres.

French, however, as in 1912, wasted no opportunity to denigrate his subordinates, even if some of the problems which arose could be squarely laid at his door. Variously, the problems he observed were:

> Rawlinson's 3rd Division, part of Paget's force, was forced to fight isolated for several hours because of a lack of proper co-ordination of the two 'Armies' by French's staff. That the division was allowed to stay on the field was a generous decision by the umpires as, in a genuine fight, many thought they would have been, at best, forced to withdraw and, at worst, destroyed. Perhaps typically, in the light of events in 1915 at Loos, French blamed Rawlinson for this error rather than accept he and his staff were at fault;
>
> Haig left a large gap between 1st Army's right wing and the left of the exposed 3rd Division which, in different circumstances, might have proved costly;
>
> Haig's arrangements for the co-ordination of the attacks of his 1st and 2nd Divisions, regarded as the crucial moment of the exercise were described by French as 'disjointed'. He complained the 2nd Division was not 'sufficiently in hand and did not sufficiently observe the principles which should govern the close attack of infantry on a defended position';[29] and
>
> The slowness with which 1st Army's artillery came up to support the infantry.

All this no doubt accentuated the friction between Haig and the putative commander of the BEF, and this would come to a head after Loos in September 1915 and lead to French's removal as CinC. Haig was, it seems, a man to bear a grudge and his irritation at French's criticisms can be seen in a diary entry which gives his side of events (although the wording clearly indicates this entry was written some considerable time after the event):

> "Sir John French's instructions for moving along the front of his enemy (then halted on a fortified position) and subsequently attacking the latter's

---

[i] Formed in 1909 by a merger of the *East & West Junction Railway*, the *Evesham, Redditch, & Stratford-upon-Avon Junction Railway*, and the *Stratford-upon-Avon, Towcester, & Midland Junction Railway*. Passenger traffic ceased in 1951 and freight traffic in 1965. Its last vestige is the Fenny Compton to Kineton Ministry of Defence Establishment line.

distant flank, were of such an unpractical nature that his Chief of the General Staff demurred. Some slight modifications in the orders were permitted, but Grierson ceased to be his CGS on mobilization, and was very soon transferred to another appointment in the BEF."[30]

Brown's were not the only errors. Congreve's 10th 'skeleton' Division mounted a vigorous defence of the important Sharman's Hill against Haig's attack, however Congreve made the same error as the Boers in early fighting in South Africa by 'digging' his trenches[i] along the top of the hill rather than at the base. This did not so much cause his phantom riflemen a problem with their accuracy but made them visible to the *Brown* artillery which, unlike in South Africa, was able to 'pummel' them with, one assumes, field howitzer fire.

Allenby's cavalry was also unable to perform mounted in the lanes and hedgerows of rural Northamptonshire and they predominantly fought dismounted in support of Haig's 'Army'. Criticism centred on the tendency to collect the horses in large groups in exposed positions close to the fighting line. French demanded more attention be paid to the prospect of 'tremendous losses amongst the horses from hostile artillery fire'. With good cause but to little effect. On one of the few occasions when cavalry of Brigade strength and upwards were employed during the war, i.e. at Monchy le Preux during the Battle of Arras in 1917, this problem was replicated, with one division alone losing nearly 1,000 horses from shell fire whilst they were held in large concentrations at the rear of that village.

Later criticisms were mainly directed at French's, Haig's and Paget's staffs. The Military Correspondent of *The Times* particularly complained about the lateness of the issuance of orders for lower units, a problem which still prevailed well into the Battle of the *Somme* and beyond and led to numerous poorly organised and costly attacks taking place at ludicrously short notice. Most criticism was, worryingly, directed at French and his staff and especially his complaints about the conduct of both 3rd and 2nd Divisions which *The Times* rebutted robustly, instead blaming General Headquarters for failing to co-ordinate the work of the two Armies.[31]

Overall, therefore, the last sets of manoeuvres and exercises conducted by the Army immediately prior to the outbreak of war exposed some serious limitations in the offensive capabilities of both men who went onto become the Commanders in Chief of the BEF during the war.

Of those who came out with some credit, Grierson and Briggs in 1912, and Briggs again in the Aldershot Command manoeuvres of 1913, much might have been expected but little materialised. Grierson, due to command the BEF's II Corps, died from an aneurism on a train near Amiens at 7:00 a.m. on 17th August 1914, whilst travelling to join his troops, a victim to his high blood pressure and excessive weight. Briggs briefly commanded 3rd Cavalry Division on the Western Front before being shunted off to a command in the relative backwater of Salonika.

---

[i] Canvass strips laid across the hillside.

SUBSEQUENTLY, HAIG'S DIRECT EXPERIENCE of large formation leadership was that gained during the fighting in France and Flanders in 1914 and 1915 and, as with many, his performance was, at best, mixed. His defensive skills, as displayed at Ypres in 1914 for example, far exceeded those displayed when asked to attack. As an offensive tactician he was repeatedly found wanting throughout 1915. The question is: what did he learn from the repeated and costly defeats from Neuve Chapelle to Loos, and how were these lessons applied to the start of the *Somme* battle? In addition, it is interesting to note that, as will be shown later, his interpretation of the Allied failings of 1915 and how they might be avoided in 1916, was at odds with almost every leading commander within both British and French Armies on the Western Front, not that this would have undermined his certainty in the correctness of his views.

Haig was not a man to entertain doubts. In some respects, this was a great strength when faced with the overwhelming problems of the modern battlefield where defensive technology, so far, had relentlessly overpowered that of the offence. He was steadfast, and correct, in his strategic vision as to how the war would be won. Germany had to be defeated first and foremost, then the remaining elements of the coalition of the Central Powers would capitulate. But his vision about the tactical means of defeating the enemy was limited, although, as mentioned, accusations of a reluctance to embrace new technology are well wide of the mark. Instead, he often placed too much reliance on 'new technology' (as with the aircraft in the 1912 manoeuvres) such as poison gas and the tank and was in too great a rush to employ them before their limitations and proper application were adequately assessed. This suggests a degree of impatience, a strange word to apply to such a solid, dependable, and even dour Lowland Scot. But impatience and ambition were bound together and manifested themselves in a repeated groundless optimism about outcomes which then failed to be achieved[i]. Haig was convinced the British Army under his guidance was the weapon which would win the war. A deeply religious man, this belief extended to the idea only he could achieve this end. Brig. Gen. John Charteris, in his book *'Field Marshal Earl Haig'*, gives a revealing insight into his character:

> "He (Haig) was genuinely convinced that the position to which he had now been called was one which he, and he alone in the British Army, could fill. It was not conceit; there was no man who was less inclined to over-estimate his own value or capacity.

---

[i] Charteris states that, after long and careful consideration, Haig concluded the Western Front was the sphere in which the war must be won and it was here the great majority of the forces of the British Empire should be concentrated. Charteris goes on to write: "With due concentration on the Western Front, with full co-operation between the Allied commanders, and a carefully thought-out and energetically executed plan of campaign, the resistance of Germany might reasonably be overcome *before the lapse of twelve months.*" It was, perhaps, Haig's conviction this could be achieved which led him to impose on Rawlinson the high-risk tactics which were the cause of the disaster on the northern and central sectors of Fourth Army's attack on 1st July [*Source*: Charteris, J, *'Field Marshal Earl Haig'*, page 185].

It was a considered opinion based upon a dispassionate consideration of all the factors that he could discern. He came to regard himself with almost Calvinistic faith as the predestined instrument of Providence for the achievement of victory for the British Armies. His abundant self-reliance was reinforced by this conception of himself as the child of destiny."[32]

Charteris was, undoubtedly, devoted to his 'Chief' and, perhaps, he was 'over-egging' the spiritual pudding somewhat in this description of Haig's quasi-religious certainty over the inevitability of his elevation and eventual success. Such certainty can lead to delusions of infallibility, sometimes described in organisations like the Army 'as everyone being out of step but me'. The tactics Haig was about to impose on Fourth Army on the *Somme* were 'out of step' with most other tactical thinking based on any serious analysis of the experiences of 1915. The consequences for the untested men of the New Armies would be profound and too often fatal[i].

IT IS SENSIBLE NOW TO LOOK at Haig's track record in France and Flanders.

Douglas Haig was fond of referring to, and drawing lessons from, the initial success of the attack at Neuve Chapelle on 10th March 1915, where, after a brief bombardment on a narrow front, British and Indian troops succeeded in breaking into the German trenches along most of the line before capturing the village of Neuve Chapelle and some land to the east. There they were stopped by a combination of German resistance, a lack of artillery support, the collapse of communication systems, and failures of attacks on either flank. The fighting carried on for four inconclusive days before a shortage of shells and worn-out troops forced an ending. During the fighting Rawlinson's IV Corps and two divisions of the Indian Corps suffered 11,200 casualties out of c. 40,000 men, or some 28%, fairly low by the standards of future offensives.

Haig still referred to this initial success and the short preliminary bombardment employed during the run up to the *Somme*, and the surprise element of the short, i.e. 35-minute, bombardment was something Fourth Army should replicate[ii]. The German preliminary bombardment at Verdun was also held up as an example of relatively brief but intense bombardments demoralising the opposition and opening the way for the infantry. The lengthy debate which ensued between Rawlinson and his commander in chief concerning the *Somme* bombardment is indicative of the grip these 'short' bombardments gained on Haig's imagination.

---

[i] In an interesting insight into Haig's priorities, Charteris quotes a letter to Churchill, apparently written in 1927, which purports to show how little Haig was 'inclined to over-estimate his own value or capacity'. It reads: "No one knows as well as I do how far short of the ideal my own conduct both of the I Corps and the First Army was, as well as of the British Expeditionary Force when Commander-in-Chief. But I do take credit for this, that it was owing to the decisions which I took in August and September 1918 that the war ended in November and, thereby, to say the least, saved the country many millions of money". Not men's lives, money.

[ii] Maj. Gen. Harvey Frederick Mercer, RA, the MGRA of First Army, initially proposed a four-day bombardment at Neuve Chapelle. Haig suggested a three-hour bombardment to retain 'the element of surprise' [*Source*: Sheffield & Bourne, eds., *Douglas Haig: War Diaries and Letters 1914-1918*, Orion Books, 2005, page 99].

What Haig seems to have failed to recollect by Spring 1916 was that the circumstances of the Neuve Chapelle attack did not obtain on the *Somme* and, indeed, had not done so on the British front within a few weeks of the end of the failed offensive. In short, there were a variety of reasons not then repeated why the German defensive front-line was so rapidly overrun on 10th March 1915.

Firstly, the area was relatively weakly held, with just two German divisions in this sector opposing the entire First Army. These units, *13.* and *14. Divisions*, had each been weakened by the removal of a three-battalion regiment to assist with the formation of a new division in the Champagne sector, the equivalent of a 25% reduction in strength. Their parent corps, *VII Armeekorps*, was defending a frontage of 21 kms (13 miles). Thus, in the area to be attacked by the fifteen battalions of the IV and Indian Corps, the best the defence could muster was ten companies drawn from three different regiments, with a further two companies in reserve some 3,000 yards behind the German front-line[i]. The arithmetic, therefore, was simple: the British attackers outnumbered the German defenders 10 to 1.

One of the reasons for this disparity was the Germans had no great belief in the offensive effectiveness of the BEF and left their lines relatively weakly held. Neuve Chapelle changed that opinion and lead to far greater difficulties for the BEF in subsequent attacks as the Germans hurriedly improved their defences opposite British units. Secondly, there was the nature of the German defences. Because of the high water table locally the 'trenches' consisted of a breastworks four feet high (1.2 m.) and five to six feet wide, behind which lay a 3-foot deep (0.91 m.) trench. Protecting these breast works was a belt of barbed wire 6-15 yards (1.8-4.6 m.) deep arranged in two to three rows of knife rests. There was a support trench behind the front-line trench, but this was so badly flooded the Germans did not use it. In all, therefore, the state of the forward defences and the numbers of men defending them were fairly feeble.

The actual front to be attacked was 1,790 yards (1,635 metres) but, wing to wing, the width of the attack was 2,480 yards (2,270 metres). This was because there was a 690-metre gap between the divisions of IV Corps (785 m. front) and the Indian Corps (850 m. front). Thus, these Corps were to attack in a pincer movement to cut out the village of Neuve Chapelle in the initial advance before then driving south-east towards the deeper objectives.

The bombardment was provided by ninety 18-pdr guns, which cut lanes in the wire, and another 90 18-pdrs, 36 4.5-in. howitzers, eight 4.7-in. guns and 24 6-in. 30-cwt howitzers[ii] which bombarded the breastworks[iii]. In addition, eight 2.75-in.

---

[i] These companies were, from north to south, *10* and *11/Infanterie-Regiment Herwarth von Bittenfeld (1. Westfälisches) Nr. 13, 25. Infanterie-Brigade, 13. Infanterie-Division, 1* and *3/Kurhessisches Jägerbataillon Nr. 11,* and *9, 12, 11, 10, 8* and *5/Infanterie-Regiment Freiherr von Sparr (3. Westfälisches) Nr. 16, 27. Infanterie-Brigade, 14. Infanterie-Division*. The two reserve companies were *12/IR 13* and the *7/IR 16*.

[ii] 59th and 81st Siege Batteries, VII Siege Brigade, arrived the day before the attack.

[iii] 50 RHA 13-pdrs and the 18-pdrs later formed a protective barrage 400 yards east of Neuve Chapelle. Other guns (4.7-in., 6-in. guns, the 9.2-in. howitzer, etc.,) were used for counter battery work or bombarded strong points further to the German rear.

mountain guns were manhandled into the front lines to provide direct fire support, with two being attached to the Indian Corps and the other six attached to the 8th Division. These guns, however, only had shrapnel shells and were, therefore, of little use in their allotted task of destroying German machine guns[i]. For counter battery and interdiction purposes there were:

1 – 15-in. howitzer	3 – 9.2-in. howitzers
4 – 6-in. guns	24 – 4.7-in. guns
HM Armoured Train *Churchill*: 1 – 6-in., 1 – 4.7-in. and 1 – 4-in. gun	

To breakdown the breastworks there was one medium gun or field/medium howitzer for every 26 yards of trench to be attacked, one howitzer for every 30 yards and one medium howitzer for every 75 yards of trench. These heavier guns also only fired at the German front-line position (by mistake in the case of the empty German support trench) and were not being scattered over numerous and distant trench lines as was the case on the *Somme*. Ironically then, despite the relative paucity of both guns and shells employed, this *concentration* of howitzers was by far the greatest achieved by the BEF in any of the offensives of 1915 and greater even than was managed by the far greater number of guns available on the *Somme*. The 18-pdrs found little trouble in cutting the wire and the breastwork was rapidly demolished by the fire mainly of the 4.5-in howitzers so flimsy were these defences[ii]. The problems of the battle emerged as the infantry advanced and the fighting slipped out of the control of the Generals behind the lines.

What then is peculiar to later battles involving the BEF, in fact involving Haig's First Army which was the one predominantly employed, is that, as the Germans concentrated more troops, and strengthened and deepened their defences, the weight of British preliminary bombardments in successive offensives got progressively weaker. Indeed, by the time of Loos on 25th September 1915, the concentration of medium and heavy howitzers per yard of front was barely a third of that employed at Neuve Chapelle. The details can be seen in Table 44 below.

	Width of front (yards)	No. of Guns (medium/heavy howitzers)	No. of yards per guns (All guns/howitzers)	No of yards per medium/heavy howitzer*
Neuve Chapelle	1790	60 (24)	30	75
Aubers Ridge	3800	102 (36)	37	106
Festubert	5000	121 (36)	41	139
Loos	11200	145 (65)	77	172

Table 44 Guns/howitzers used for trench bombardment British offensives 1915[33]
* 6-in. howitzers and heavier.

---

[i] Three mountain gun batteries went to France in autumn 1914: 2nd, 5th, and 7th Mountain Batteries. They formed III Pack Artillery Brigade, then attached: 2nd Battery to 4th Division, 5th Battery to 3rd Division, and 7th Battery to 8th Division. They were later deemed unsuited to the Western Front and went to Salonika in December 1915.

[ii] Some 3,000 howitzer shells were fired during the 35-minute bombardment with the 4.5-in. howitzers firing c. 2,520 (84%) and the 6-in. howitzers c. 420 (16%) [*Source: BOH, France and Belgium 1915*, Vol. 1, footnote page 92].

Neuve Chapelle was the first offensive action undertaken by the BEF in 1915 and, as with most of the others conducted by First Army, after an initially limited set of objectives was identified, Haig began to believe a breakthrough was a distinct possibility. Haig originally instructed Rawlinson to prepare plans for an operation to eliminate the shallow salient about the German-held village of Neuve Chapelle on 6th February. This idea resulted from a meeting and lunch held the previous day at Sir John French's HQ in St Omer attended by both Haig and Joffre. Joffre was planning to make two large scale attacks as soon as the terrain and weather improved. One was to be undertaken by Maud'huy's *Xe Armée* at Arras and the second in the Champagne/Argonne region. Some sort of British attack in support of this was, therefore, in order and Sir John favoured Haig and First Army over Smith-Dorrien's Second Army for such an action.

There was no obvious reason for this apparent favouritism, but it proved the thin end of the wedge for Smith-Dorrien's tenure as commander of Second Army. As mentioned, there have been suggestions French was no fan of Smith-Dorrien's, asking for Plumer not S-D on the sudden death of Grierson, and he neglected no opportunity to denigrate him in front of his brother officers. At the meeting mentioned above he confided to Haig that:

> "Smith-Dorrien is a weak spot, and that he ought not to be where he is in command of an Army."[34]

Smith-Dorrien himself sensed a change at GHQ in February 1915 though he was at a loss, both then and after the war, to explain it. Regrettably for the modern reader, in his memoirs S-D honourably determined not to comment on matters 'which might be interpreted as imputing blame to others'. What was clear, however, was that now 'I and the II Army could do nothing right'. He soon narrowed that down to himself. He was the problem and 'until he went the Army would be handicapped and the cause jeopardised'.[35]

After the near disaster of the first German gas attack at Ypres on 22nd April 1915 and the rapid contraction of the Allied salient east of that town S-D wrote to French on 1st May asking for an interview. His letter was ignored. He wrote again on 6th May. Some sections are especially pertinent:

> "My Dear Field Marshal,
> ... Whatever may be the reason, there can be no question that your attitude to me for some time past has tended to show that you had, for some reason or other unknown to me, ceased to trust me...
> My position as Army Commander has become impossible, and I regard my remaining in command with a cloud hanging over me ready to burst at any moment, as a positive danger to the cause for which we are fighting.
> Plenty of complicated situations have arisen on the last few months and the difficulty of dealing with them has been greatly enhanced by the knowledge that unless I was successful, I and the 2nd Army would be blamed – *in fact, I have had more to fear from the rear than from the front* (S-D's emphasis).
> We have got to win this war, and to do so there must be no weak links in the chain. Your attitude to me constitutes a very seriously weak link, and I feel sure that, trying as that attitude has been to me, you have not wished

to carry it quite so far as to appoint someone else to command the 2nd Army in my place.

This step is, however, the only one which to my mind will strengthen up the chain again, and it is to render it more easy for you to take it without further delay that I am writing this letter…"

Again, French did not reply. Instead, Smith-Dorrien received a note from the Adjutant General to the BEF, Maj. Gen. Cecil Frederick Nevil Macready, advising him to leave for London on the following day. Plumer would take his place. On his appearance in front of Kitchener at the War Office, the Secretary of State for War expressed surprise at S-D's physical state as GHQ informed him that the health of the ex-commander of Second Army had broken down[i].

Questions remain to this day as to the reasons for the sudden and then terminal breakdown of relations between two such close colleagues. French, though, was a vainglorious, insecure little man whose public reputation, at least, was mainly based on two brief but glamorous cavalry charges in South Africa at Elandslaagte and Klip Drift. That he was in position to achieve even this he had to thank Douglas Haig for his timely bailout of French's recurring financial problems. Smith-Dorrien's achievements, both on the battlefield and as commander of troops, were perhaps more mundane but, at least to this writer, of far great significance to both the well-being, training, and performance of the British and Indian Armies and, therefore, to the BEF in France and Flanders in 1914-5.

In his book *1914*, French explained away his glowing endorsement of Smith-Dorrien's conduct in the retreat from Mons as one based on false information. He then inflated his lies by more than doubling the losses II Corps suffered at Le Cateau. His book was later privately described by Smith-Dorrien as 'mostly a work of fiction and a foolish one too'.[36]

To remind the reader of French's original thoughts about Smith-Dorrien's conduct in the retreat from Mons one should refer to his Official Despatch published in the Third Supplement of the *London Gazette* of 8th September 1914:

> "I cannot close the brief account of this glorious stand of the British troops without putting on record my deep appreciation of the valuable services rendered by General Sir Horace Smith-Dorrien. I say without hesitation that the saving of the left wing of the Army under my command on the morning of the 26th August could never have been accomplished unless a commander of rare and unusual coolness, intrepidity, and determination had been present to personally conduct the operation."

Whatever the true reason, Smith Dorrien, senior to Douglas Haig in the Army List, was now no obstacle to promotion should a vacancy as the BEF's CinC occur.

BUT, BACK TO THE ATTACK ON NEUVE CHAPELLE and its planning. Meeting with Rawlinson on 6th February Haig told him:

---

[i] Smith-Dorrien was commander of the 1st Home Defence Army based in East Anglia. Appointed to command troops in German East Africa his health broke down on the voyage to South Africa. He was seriously ill for several months. He was appointed Lieutenant of the Tower of London, 1917, and Governor of Gibraltar, 1918.

"... to prepare a scheme and put forward proposals for the capture of Neuve Chapelle, I hoped to be ready for this operation in about 10 days' time."[37]

That Haig should ask for such an undertaking to be ready in just '10 days' time' is of itself an indication of just how much a lack of experience in offensive actions coloured aspects of the planning of this and subsequent operations. Rawlinson, with knowledge of the ground to be attacked, appeared to understand little could be achieved until it dried out and this might take at least four weeks. During that four weeks, and in a harbinger of things to come, Haig's concept of the potential of IV Corps/Indian Corps' attack became increasingly grandiose. But, in parallel, a far more detailed understanding of the nature of the German position was achieved by a detailed mapping programme undertaken both from higher ground to the rear of the British lines but also by observers in aircraft from the RFC. Haig later (22nd February) described the 'wonderful map' of the German trenches which resulted in it being possible 'to make our plans very carefully beforehand'.[38]

Six days after Haig asked Rawlinson to prepare a plan for the attack, i.e. 12th February, Haig forwarded to French an outline of what he believed was possible. It involved an initial move to the line of an old trench to the east of Neuve Chapelle called the Smith-Dorrien trench, Rawlinson's IV Corps attacking on the left (northern) wing and the Indian Corps on the right (southern) wing. The old Smith-Dorrien trench position had been lost by II Corps in heavy fighting on 26th and 27th October and resulted in the creation of the German salient which ran from the position called Port Arthur on the Estaires to La Bassée road in the south and then north-east, 500 yards to the west of Neuve Chapelle, to another position called the Moated Grange (the *ferme Vanbesien*). For some distance on the eastern side of the Smith-Dorrien trench ran a small but significant stream called the *Layes Brook* which, according to Gen. Willcocks, GOC, Indian Corps, was:

"... from six to ten feet wide and from three to five feet deep, and along this stream the Germans had constructed strong bridgeheads and trenches."[39]

In other words, the objective was no longer simply 'the capture of Neuve Chapelle', it had gained a far wider and more strategic remit: the advance was to take Aubers Ridge between the villages of Herlies and Illies, some 3.4 miles distant (5.4 kms). Such a move would not only threaten to outflank the German positions around La Bassée to the south-west, if pushed further east towards Don on the *canal de la Deûle* (another 3.5 miles/5.7 kms), it threatened the rail, road, and waterway communications between the conurbations of Lens to the south-west and Lille to the north-east. If combined with the expected French drive eastwards out positions north of Arras, this would so de-stabilise the German positions a major realignment of their front would be forced on them. And that was the minimum ambition. Potentially, according to Haig, still more exciting prospects beckoned to those who dared.

The ambition involved is highlighted by the language used in a First Army memorandum issued after the attack.[40] Its opening paragraphs read:

"It was proposed to undertake operations which should the attack on the enemy's trenches succeed, offered a possibility of a definite advance with a view to breaking the enemy's line.

It was considered that, if the Aubers-Haut Pommereau ridge could be secured, far reaching effects might be obtained. With this high ground in our possession it was possible that the German line N of La Bassée might break, that La Bassée itself might fall, and that in any case a considerable portion of the German line north of Givenchy must give way."

This expansive thinking was generated from the top. A First Army conference was held on the morning of 5th March in Bethune and the notes (attached as Appendix A to the memorandum) make it clear what Haig had in mind:

"The advance to be made is not a minor operation. It must be understood that we are embarking on a serious offensive movement with the object of breaking the German line, and consequently our advance is to be pushed vigorously. Very likely an operation of considerable magnitude may result. The idea is not to capture a trench here, or a trench there, but to carry the operation right through; in a sense surprise the Germans, carry them right off their legs, push forward to the Aubers-Haut Pommereau ridge with as little delays as possible, and exploit the success thus gained by pushing forward mounted troops forthwith."

Haig's objectives were:

1. To break the German line;
2. To reach Aubers Ridge as soon as possible;
3. To then send the cavalry towards La Bassée;
4. To use I Corps and 7th Division of IV Corps to push through any gap created; and, at the very least
5. Cut off German troops on the line from Neuve Chapelle to La Bassée.

A week before the attack Haig asked for and was given by 'Wullie' Robertson (then French's Chief of Staff), a cavalry division with which to exploit any 'suitable opportunity which might arise'.[41]

The GOC of IV Corps, Henry Rawlinson, as in later battles, was of a more conservative opinion and, it appears, rather laid back about the planning of the entire operation. On 21st February, he forwarded to Haig plans for the attack prepared by his two Divisional GOCs, Davies of 8th Division and Capper of 7th Division. It came with several pages of Rawlinson's hand-written comments which ran to twenty paragraphs, paragraph 18 of which read:

"The scheme put forward by Gen'l Davies may seem somewhat complicated. The actual details must be left largely in the hands of the Brigadiers who are selected to command the respective columns but they must nevertheless be gone into and settled before hand by higher commanders for on them the success of the enterprise very largely depends."[42]

In all, a rather remarkable abdication of responsibility by the Corps commander, who finished his comments by advising his Army commander:

"… until the condition of the soil has become such that fresh trenches can be dug, and old ones made use of, it would be unwise to undertake that attack of Neuve Chapelle."[43]

This did not go down well with Haig who told him both to 'get his finger out' and that, furthermore, he was not content with *just* taking the village of Neuve Chapelle, as 'our existing line was just as satisfactory for me as if we were in Neuve Chapelle!'[44] No, Haig planned to 'break the Enemy's front'.[45] The commander of First Army sought a rapid advance 'in the hope of starting a *general advance*'.[46] Ambitious offensives seemed never far from Haig's thinking and, as a result, this affected the nature of the planning of each successive attack. And, as fronts grew broader and resources were increasingly stretched to meet them, the results tended to be an increase in casualties without any obvious increase in performance.

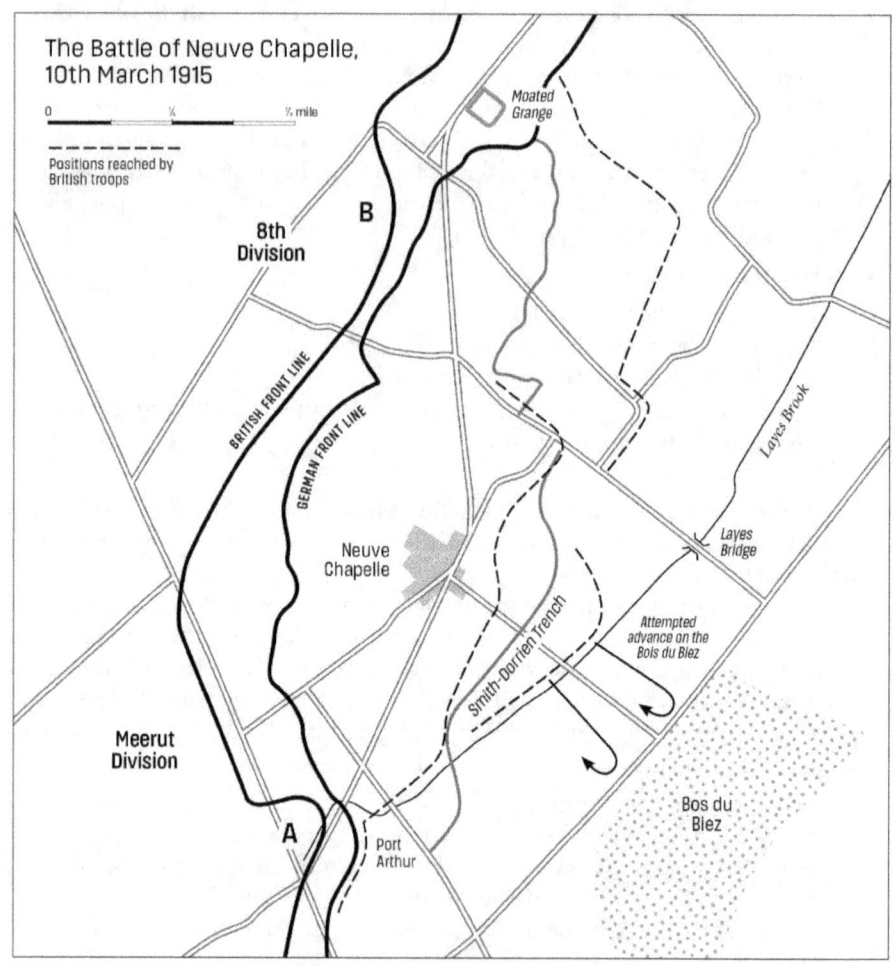

Map 19 Battle of Neuve Chapelle, 10th March 1915
The dotted line shows the limit of the first day's advance
[*Source*: British Official History, Military Operations France & Belgium, 1915, Volume I]

The commanders on the ground, Rawlinson of IV Corps, and Davies of 8th Division, were in favour of pausing on the eastern side of the village before resuming the attack the following morning with fresh troops and with some guns moved forward to cover any further advance. This idea was over-ruled, with Haig citing a popular theme of his that the enemy, demoralised by the bombardment, should be pressed hard before they could recover. This idea ground might be taken in the first rush which might otherwise prove more difficult and costly to capture if the enemy was given time to recover was a constant refrain of Haig's and would loom large in his thoughts on the planning of the *Somme* attack and, before that, the Battle of Loos. It was also the current tactical thinking of Joffre and most of his Generals though, in their case, this changed significantly during 1915.

As it turned out, the initial attack on the somewhat feeble German defences west of Neuve Chapelle on 10th March achieved some immediate success before the advance ran out of steam on the far side of the village as the German defences hardened. The breastwork was mainly flattened by the howitzers and the wire well cut. There were problems, however, on the right of the Garwhal Brigade and the left of the 23rd Brigade. The lead companies of the right-hand battalion of the Garwhal Brigade, 1/39th Garwhal Rifles, lost direction and attacked trenches unaffected by the bombardment (see location A in Map 19). On 23rd Brigade's front the late arrival of the two 6-in. howitzer batteries meant the breastworks in front of the 2nd Middlesex was undamaged and heavy casualties ensued and progress was temporarily stopped (see location B on Map 19). Generally, though, an advance beyond Neuve Chapelle was achieved. But one of the key problems for the attackers was the almost immediate loss of control which befell the battalions once they left their trenches. It was almost impossible to identify their locations and, therefore, to direct supporting artillery fire or reserves. There was also a lengthy delay in launching the second phase of the attack, which did not start until late in the afternoon and under gathering clouds which reduced visibility. This phase of the operation failed to advance further.

After the first day, the weather prevented adequate observation of supporting artillery fire and German reserves, including large numbers of machine gun, stabilised their front stopping any further advances and causing heavy casualties. German counterattacks too met with costly failure. On the afternoon of 12th March, Army HQ came to the conclusion (presumably based on a false report from 7th Division) success was imminent and Rawlinson and Willcocks[i] were

---

[i] Gen. Sir James Willcocks, GCB, GCMG, KCSI, DSO, was born in Baraut, Meerut District, on 1st April 1857, 4th son of Capt. William W Willcocks, Honourable East India Company Service, and Mary Martin. Educated at Easton, Somerset. Entered Sandhurst at the 3rd attempt. 100th Foot (later, after merger with the 109th Foot, the Prince of Wales's Leinster Regt.) at Jullundur, Punjab. Attached to Transport Dept. during the latter part of the 2nd Afghan War. MiD. Married Winifred, 2nd daughter of Col. George Augustus Way, CB, 7th Duke of Connaught's Own Rajputs, 1889. A variety of staff appointments, many to do with transport. Several campaigns on the North-West Frontier. 2iC then commandant, West African Field Force, 1898. Commanded the Ashanti Field Force in the relief of Kumasi. After three months in South Africa, 1902, returned to India to command a brigade. Maj. Gen., 1906. GOC,

ordered to press the attacks of the IV and Indian Corps 'with the utmost vigour regardless of fire' and 5th Cavalry Brigade and 2nd Cavalry Division were ordered forward to press through in support of an anticipated breakthrough by 7th Division.[47] Such an advance had not, as it turned out, materialised. By 13th March it was decided to hold the gains made and to dig in and properly fortify these positions. Casualties were: Meerut Division 2,353, Lahore Division 1,694, 7th Division 2,791, and 8th Division 4,814. Total: 544 officers and 11,108 Other Ranks. Seven battalion COs were killed or died of wounds. German casualties are estimated at 8,500 to 12,000.

After the failure Rawlinson, in a crass attempt to pass the buck, blamed the breakdown on 8th Division's Maj. Gen. Francis Davies[i]. He demanded a replacement, an action with which Haig was initially only too happy to agree[ii]. It was only when Davies objected to criticism that he was responsible for the failure of the attack to push on past the village that Rawlinson was forced to climb down and accept responsibility for his decision to involve the available reserve battalions early in the fighting thus making them unavailable for the later planned push towards Aubers Ridge. As a result, Haig was required to withdraw his letter to Sir John French demanding Davies's sacking, an embarrassment for both him and Rawlinson, especially as the decision to remove Davies had already reached, and been endorsed by, Prime Minister Asquith.

Soon after the fighting ended, attention turned away from Davies to focus on Rawlinson. His performance during the brief battle was, in many ways, replicated in larger form on the *Somme*. Initially wanting to fight a limited battle (restricted to capturing Neuve Chapelle and straightening the line), by the time the offensive started he had the same mind-set as Haig, believing bigger things to be possible and, as a result, he ordered (or tried to order) additional attacks which would have done little but add to the substantial casualty lists. Within days, however,

---

Peshawar Division, 1908. Led Mohmand Field Force, 1908. Lt. Gen., commander, Northern Army, 1910 (1st (Peshawar), 2nd (Rawalpindi), 3rd (Lahore), 7th (Meerut), and 8th (Lucknow) Divisions). Commander, Indian Corps (Lahore and Meerut Divisions), August 1914. Haig, junior in terms of seniority, was no fan. After a breakdown in their relationship, he was replaced on 5th September 1915. Later, Col., Loyal North Lancashire Regt., and Governor of Bermuda, 1916. Willcocks published three books: *From Kabul to Kumassi* (1904), *With the Indians in France* (1920), and *The Romance of Soldiering and Sport* (1925). Died, 18th December 1926, in the Moti Hahal Palace, Bharatpur.

[i] Maj. Gen. (later Gen.) Sir Francis John Davies, KCB, KCMG, KCVO (1864–1948). Worcestershire Militia, 1881. 2nd Grenadier Guards. DAAG Intelligence, South Africa. DAQMG, War Office, 1902. Assistant Director of Military Operations, 1904. GOC, 1st Guards Brigade, 1909. BGGS. Aldershot Command 1910-1913. Director of Staff Duties, 1913. GOC, 8th Division, August 1914. GOC VIII Corps after Aylmer Hunter-Weston invalided home from Gallipoli, August 1915. In command during the successful evacuation of the peninsula. Military Secretary, War Office, June 1916. GOC, Scottish Command. ADC to the King.

[ii] "I thought that he (i.e. Davies) was unfit to command a Division at this critical period of the operations in France" [Sheffield & Bourne, op. cit., page 110].

Rawlinson was telling all who might listen this was not his fault. Others were to blame for the over-ambition which undermined the original plan. According to Rawlinson this was the fault of 'our leaders, all cavalry officers' (i.e. French and Haig) who demanded too much and who, by pursuing the idea of 'pushing through the cavalry', undermined the potential of a limited, if significant, success in which:

> "… our losses would have been one quarter of what they were & we would have gained just as much ground."[48]

However true this might have been, the fact was Rawlinson, as was his tendency, was drawn into the optimistic euphoria which so infected senior British officers before every offensive up to the end of 1917 and resulted in unrealistically ambitious plans and the excessive casualties which then ensued.

This trait of Rawlinson's to try to blame others when things went wrong was one of which Haig was aware and of which he was highly critical ('I am afraid Rawlinson is unsatisfactory in this respect, loyalty to his subordinates'[49]) and, for a time, Rawlinson's future on the Western Front hung in the balance. The long-term support of Haig, however, persuaded French not to send the embarrassed General back to London but left him forever obliged to his immediate superior for the saving of his reputation and, perhaps, career[i].

Whatever its outcome, the initial advance of c. 1,500 metres at Neuve Chapelle had an influence on Allied commanders disproportionate to the results. The loss of 10,000 men on the last two days of the battle with no discernible improvement in their position was ignored. Clutching at whatever straws were to hand, the tantalising prospects of the first morning's attack were clung to as evidence breakthrough *was* possible with minor tweaks of the plan (and, more usefully perhaps, a few hundred thousand extra shells). Instead of wallowing in failure, First Army and its commander basked in the undeserved glow of near success.

After the war, Gen. Huguet, head of the Military Mission at GHQ, wrote:

> "The brilliant success of the opening phase, far from being considered a piece of good fortune, due to surprise and the luck of an attack on a little or badly guarded sector, was, on the contrary, attributed solely to excellent preparation. General Joffre sent to all French Staffs a translation of General Haig's orders as an example of how things should be done."[50]

Joffre, however, would also later comment that Neuve Chapelle was a success which led to nothing (*'Mais ce fut un succès sans lendemain'*) and, at the time, suggested Huguet, the numerous failures on all three days were erroneously regarded as 'mistake of detail or of manoeuvre' and 'easily remedied in the future'.

The next attack by First Army was to prove otherwise.

Two months elapsed between the partial success at Neuve Chapelle and the total disaster of the attack on Aubers Ridge on 9th May. This latter attack was designed to support the main French offensive around Vimy made by *Xe*

---

[i] When asked by the new CIGS, Sir William Robertson, for a recommendation for the new commander of First Army on his promotion to CinC, Haig suggested Rawlinson describing him as 'though not a sincere man, he has brains and experience' [Source: *NA*, WO256/6, entry for 12th December 1915].

Armée as part of the Second Battle of Artois, a French attack which was to make significant initial leeway before floundering to a standstill when the infantry again lost their artillery support by attempting too deep a penetration.

During this eight-week interval, the British convinced themselves their plans at Neuve Chapelle were basically correct and there were only a few minor details to address to be completely successful. That the Germans might change their form of defence seems not to have weighed heavy on Haig's thinking. The irony of Haig's lack of foresight is revealed in his diary entry of 24th April, in which he took Foch and his generals to task for their failure to foresee the German gas attack at Ypres two days earlier[i]. Here he described his Allied colleagues as:

> "A mixture of fair ability (not more than fair) and ignorance of the practical side of war. They are not built for it by nature. They are too excitable, and they never seem to think of what the enemy may do."[51]

They were clearly not alone as, while Haig simply tinkered with his tactics, the Germans fundamentally altered the nature of the battlefield to their advantage and, thereby, changed the rules of 'the game'. In its way, and in so many actions in which Haig was involved, this represented a flaw in his make-up. Edward Luttwak is a distinguished academic and author amongst whose many books is *Strategy: The Logic of War and Peace*, a much-used text in universities and war colleges. He developed a theory about what he called linear decision makers and paradoxical decision makers. Col. Fabrice Clee of the *Centre de Doctrine et d'Enseignment du Commandement* described these concepts in an article entitled *The Foundations of the Operational Decision-Making Culture in France* in 2019:

> "The linear decision-maker identifies problems, describes them, develops the solution according to their nature and implements it. However, according to Luttwak, the linear decision-maker does not take into account the fundamental aspect of war, i.e. the dialectic of wills, the contrary intention and the opponent's reactions to a decision taken. Thus, operational decision-making does not only consist in matching resources

---

[i] Sir John French was more charitable: 'I would only express my firm conviction that, if any troops in the world had been able to hold their trenches in the face of such a treacherous and altogether *unexpected* (writer's emphasis) onslaught, the French Division would have stood firm'. Interestingly Haig's previous views on the use of lethal gas were rather dismissive, suggesting both he and the BEF too would have regarded the gas attack as 'unexpected'. On 11th March he was visited by Gen. Douglas Mackinnon Baillie Hamilton Cochrane, 12th Earl of Dundonald and Chairman of the Admiralty Committee on Smoke Screens. Cochrane was looking into exploiting an idea developed by his great-grandfather, Archibald Cochrane, 9th Earl of Dundonald FRSE (1st January 1748 – 1st July 1831) for using sulphur fumes to 'drive a garrison out of a fort'. Archibald Cochrane, who served in both the Army and Navy, developed a system for the mass production of coal tar, amongst other inventions. Haig's sarcastic responses was: 'I asked him how he arranged to have a favourable wind'. By 25th September 1915, however, Haig regarded lethal gas as the secret weapon which would lead to a breakthrough at Loos [*Sources:* Sir John French's despatch, *Supplement to the London Gazette* 29225, 10th July 1915, page 6788; Blake, op. cit., page 87].

to achieve objectives, but also and above all, in making the opponent's reaction support our goals. Otherwise, the chosen solution remains ineffective or even counterproductive. Against the linear decision-maker, Luttwak puts forward the paradoxical decision-maker who, in turn, integrates this dialectic of wills into his manoeuvre and takes into account one of the main requirements of operational decision-making, i.e. acting to degrade the other's decision-making capacity. Finally, since uncertainty is the same for both sides, the winner is the one who, through his bounded rationality, his 'eye' and his intuition, will be able to take the best decision-making initiative quickly by concealing his goals and his potential, by understanding those of the opponent, and thus by acting against his will."

Haig was, and remained, a linear decision-maker who, perhaps until the enforced staff changes at the beginning of 1918, saw only as far as the end of his plans, and never looked beyond or thought through how an enemy might respond or anticipate his next ponderous move. The planning for Aubers Ridge, etc., was a classic example of this tendency to do essentially the same thing over and over again in the expectation that, at some point and at whatever cost, it would be successful. The *Somme* and Third Ypres were these ideas writ large.

So, what, precisely, did the Germans do to change the game? First, they increased the number of troops opposite Haig's First Army by 66% by adding a new four-regiment division, *6. Königlich Bayerische Reserve-Division*, to *VII Armeekorps*. This division occupied the sector previously held by *13. Division* in front of Fromelles, the area to be attacked by IV Corps on 9th May. This redistribution of men reduced the front defended by each regiment from 3,000 yards to just 2,000 yards. The net effect of this was a considerable thickening of the German defensive line and an enhancement in the number of machine guns and supporting artillery. Furthermore, the increased number of troops allowed for the creation of large numbers of working parties. These working parties then made a considerable effort to improve and deepen their defences, though all this activity appears to have been invisible to British observers. The four-foot-high and six-foot-wide sandbagged breastwork which proved so vulnerable at Neuve Chapelle was now rebuilt to be six to seven feet high and fifteen to twenty feet deep. The wire defences were also deepened and strengthened, and the depression in front of the breastworks from which earth had been dug to fill the new sandbags (and was, therefore, invisible from the British lines) was also filled with barbed wire. Wooden and sandbag covered shelters were built into the parapet or parados every few yards to protect small groups of men and, every twenty yards, a new wood and iron rail reinforced machine gun post was built into the base of the breastworks. These were believed to be safe from all but a direct hit from a howitzer shell. The front-line was also reinforced with a series of strongpoints which allowed machine guns to take No Man's Land in enfilade. The previously flooded and uninhabitable support line was reconstructed and turned into a useable defensive line with a wire barrier between it and the front-line trench. Communication trenches were increased in number, strengthened, and often concealed from view with screens or entirely covered over. As a result of the reinforcements and the re-shaped and strengthened defences in front of Aubers

Ridge, the area to be attacked by First Army now bore little resemblance to that attacked on 10th March.

The existence of the machine gun positions and strongpoints seems to have escaped GHQ and First Army. Furthermore, the strength of the German breastworks was still under-estimated. This led to a decision to employ 18-pdr. HE to break them down, an idea based on an experiment conducted on 20th April at the *ferme de Verbois* between the *Forêt de Nieppe* and Merville. Haig attended and was most impressed:

> "A very strong breastwork seven to eight feet high, six feet at top, and about 14 to 15 feet at the base was built up with rammed earth and was revetted with sandbags... On examining the breastwork... many said ... it was much stronger than any breastwork which the Germans had erected on our front."[52]

Three HE shells fired from 1,500 yards then made a breach 15-ft. wide. Haig declared this was the equivalent of '1 shell per yard of front!'[53] and concluded this meant the 18-pdrs could be added to the howitzers when it came to demolishing the German frontlines. Unfortunately, of course, these defences were now a third or more thicker than the breastwork on which the tests took place. In addition, such rosy forecasts of shell expenditure and effect took no account of barrel and gun wear, fuzing and detonation problems, and the effects on accuracy and activity caused by being heavily shelled by an enemy unlikely to ignore the enticing prospect of firing on field guns just 1,200 to 1,500 yards behind the British front. In addition, the accuracy of these field guns and howitzers was not excellent. For example, a 4.5-in. howitzer firing at 4,000 yards range could expect only 50% of its shells to fall within a zone of c. 24 yards long by 3 yards wide square (approx. 72 square yards). The 18-pdr. was considerably less accurate in terms of length, i.e. 50% of shells fired from this range fell in a zone 38 yards by 3 yards square (114 square yards). When trying to demolish a specific target where accurate range was essential, e.g. wire, a breastwork, a machine gun post, etc., this meant far more than one shell per yard of front would be needed to have the desired effect.

As with Neuve Chapelle, the attack on Aubers Ridge involved two simultaneous flank attacks on a shallow German salient. The difference was that, instead of a gap of 700 yards between the inner flanks of IV Corps on the left and the Indian Corps and I Corps on the right, the gap was nearly ten times greater. Whilst the number of howitzers available to bombard the German trenches nearly doubled, this increase consisted mainly of additional field howitzers and some obsolete 5-in. howitzers. On the other hand, the front to be bombarded more than doubled in length, from 1,450 yards at Neuve Chapelle to 3,800 yards. To have maintained the ratio of howitzers per yard as achieved at Neuve Chapelle the Aubers Ridge bombardment needed 147 howitzers rather than the 102 available, of which 63, not 36, should have been 6-in. howitzers. According to Prior and Wilson, the combination of the width and depth of the area to be bombarded and the relatively limited supply of additional guns compared to Neuve Chapelle meant that, whereas 5 lbs of shell per yard of German front was fired at Neuve Chapelle (N.B. fired at, not landed on), this was reduced to 2 lbs per yard at Aubers Ridge.[54]

Such was the relative weakness of the artillery on this extended front

Rawlinson, commanding IV Corps on the northern flank, later wrote privately to Kitchener lamenting the lack of howitzers, and explaining it was the absence of a suitable number of these guns, rather than simply a lack of high explosive shells, which undermined the prospects of success[i].[55] That, and the tactics employed overall, but he made no mention of this latter issue.

	Neuve Chapelle	Aubers Ridge
4.5-in. howitzers	24	50
5-in. howitzers	0	16
6-in. 30 cwt howitzers	24	36
4.7-in. guns	8	0
Total	56	102

Table 45 Bombardment groups Neuve Chapelle and Aubers Ridge

The tactics of this attack reveal an apparent fixation with simultaneous but separate attacks. Leaving aside the issue of co-ordinating such attacks (and the difficult position troops might find themselves in if one attack failed and the other succeeded), the main problem was that each attack offered two open flanks to be fired on by defending troops not otherwise engaged. Such schemes were not easily abandoned, it seems, as they were used during the battle of Festubert a few days after the initial attack on Aubers Ridge and, on 1st July 1916, the Third Army at Gommecourt (four open flanks) and Fourth Army (one open flank and several gaps not directly attacked) both indulged themselves in such tactics.

On 27th April Haig explained to his Corps and Divisional commanders that the plan was to break through the German lines to make a 'general advance' towards Herlies and Illies (the hoped-for objectives at Neuve Chapelle) and then to Don, a town on the *Canal de la Deûle*. This required an advance of more than six miles, something not achieved on the Western Front since trench warfare began.

Some astute minds assessed the defeat at Neuve Chapelle not as one snatched from the jaws of victory but as a necessary and salutary learning experience which showed breakthroughs were not yet possible. As Foch later argued, and Rawlinson suggested and then failed to persist with, what was needed were limited assaults which invited costly German counterattacks and which, following on one after the other, would so exhaust the enemy's reserves that, at some point, the war on the Western Front would reach a decisive phase. One such voice crying in the British tactical wilderness was John Philip Du Cane, currently the MGRA at GHQ and Sir John French's Artillery Adviser. Writing soon after the failure at Neuve

---

[i] It was about this shortage *The Times* war correspondent, Col. Charles à Court Repington made such a fuss in his article 'Need for shells: British attacks checked: Limited supply the cause: A Lesson from France' (*The Times*, Friday, 14th May 1915, page 8). This precipitated the Shell Crisis which led to the formation of the Coalition Government and appointment of Lloyd George as Minister for Munitions. Kitchener, as Secretary of State for War, was blamed for the 'Shell Crisis'. At the heart of the critics was an unholy alliance of Sir John French, Lloyd George, Bonar Law, and Lord Northcliffe, owner of *The Times* and the *Daily Mail*, which latter newspaper stirred the pot a week later with a piece entitled *'The Shells Scandal: Lord Kitchener's Tragic Blunder'*.

Chapelle[56] he suggested an approach later to be wholeheartedly adopted by Foch and Fayolle in the early attacks on the *Somme*. Allied attacks '... should not be pressed so far as to carry the infantry beyond the range of artillery support', or, as Foch later demanded, beyond the ability of the artillery to support the infantry by *direct* observation. Having taken the first and necessarily limited objective, Du Cane advocated effective consolidation which, with the artillery's support, would allow German counter measures to be repulsed. The next phase, also limited in its extent but already planned for, would then take place 'as soon as possible' and be repeated as many times as needed to exhaust the enemy and render him unable to resist a decisive attack. This concept of limited but repeated attacks during which German casualties incurred during counterattacks weighed more heavily in the balance than did Allied losses in the advance was the policy adopted by the French for the early parts of the *Somme* fighting and was the policy Rawlinson would have liked to adopt for the Fourth Army in the same campaign. In this, though, he was over-ruled by Haig and his expansionist ideas.

The attack on Aubers Ridge was a disaster waiting to happen, made all the worse by the absurd optimism which accompanied the preparations. Haig seems to have believed his own positive publicity after Neuve Chapelle, and, clinging to the notion surprise was somehow better than a proper artillery preparation, a mere forty minutes was allocated to this essential preliminary activity. Whilst Foch and *Xe Armée* ignored the 'lessons' of Neuve Chapelle and delivered a heavy, deliberate and targeted artillery preparation stretching over several days on the German positions in front of Vimy Ridge, First Army started firing its brief bombardment at 5 a.m., an hour before the four-hour final French bombardment began. At 5.40 a.m. the British and Indian infantry left their trenches to be greeted by scything machine gun and rifle fire. By the end of the day First Army had lost over 11,000 men. German casualties were barely 1,000.

The southern attack by 1st Division and the Meerut Division was almost entirely stopped in No Man's Land, but heavy casualties were suffered on a British parapet swept relentlessly by concealed machine guns. Several efforts were made to re-start the attack in the afternoon, but this only increased the already severe losses. By the end of the day, losses were 250 officers and 6,300 other ranks and some battalions of 1st Division suffered 60% casualties.

8th Division's attack, helped by two mines sprung on their left, enjoyed initial success. But the break-in was contained, and its support units caught in the flimsy jump-off trenches by heavy artillery fire. The assault ground to a standstill. At Haig's order, futile efforts were made to resume the attack but to no avail. 8th Division's casualties, 4,700 officers and men, were even worse than those of 1st and Meerut Divisions. The 1/13th London Regt., (Kensingtons), lost 70% of its strength.

Aubers Ridge was a fiasco with no redeeming features. Its strategic purpose of pinning enemy units was utterly ineffective as German troop movements opposite the First Army involved sending *away*, with the *58.* and *115. Divisions* helping contain the French attack at Vimy. It showed that, though the BEF might have worked out how to remedy the shortcomings of Neuve Chapelle, it had not occurred to them that the Germans would spend the intervening period designing new puzzles with which to bamboozle the attackers. No-one at either GHQ or First Army appears to have put themselves into the enemy's shoes and asked how they might defend against current British tactics. For rather too long, senior British commanders kept answering questions which were no longer relevant. It was the 'Poor Bloody Infantry' who paid the price of this complete absence of creative forethought.

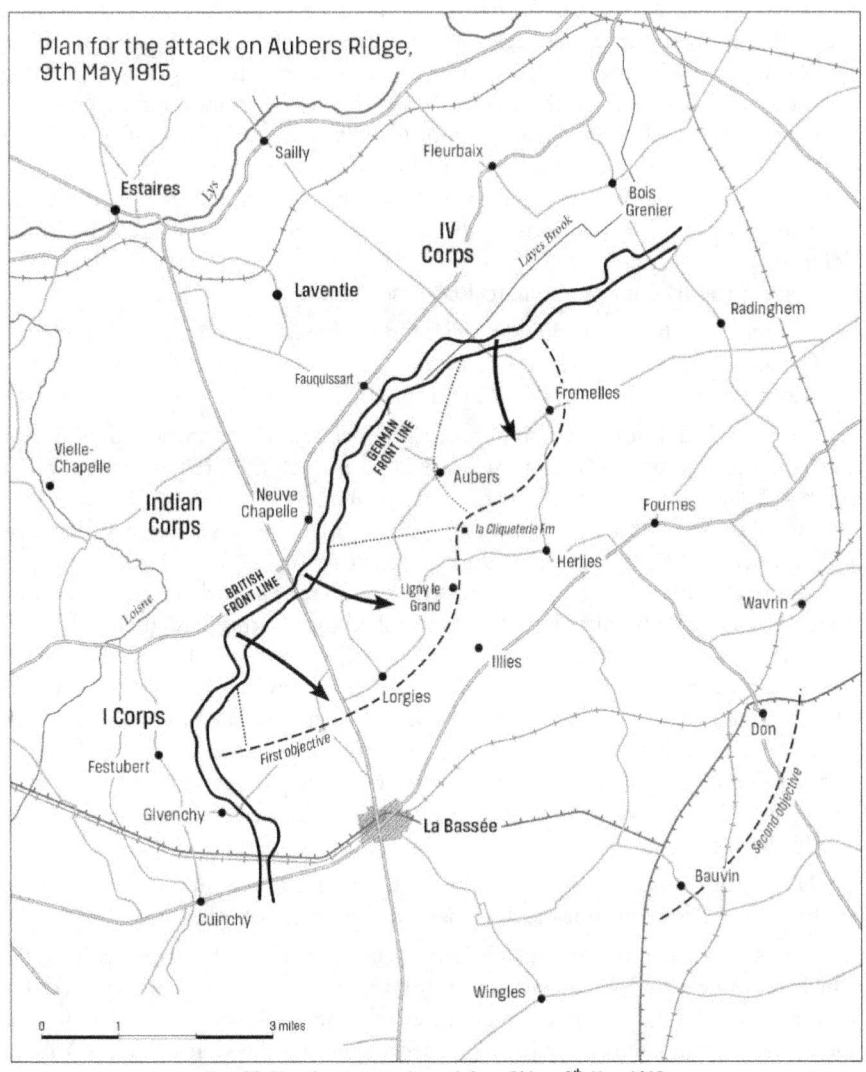

Map 20 Plan for the attack on Aubers Ridge, 9th May 1915
The final objective was the line of the *Haute Deule Canal* between Don and Bauvin, far right
[*Source*: British Official History, Military Operations France & Belgium, 1915, Volume II]

Aubers Ridge was the third severe check for the Allies on various fronts within a few days. At Gallipoli, between 6th and 8th May, Hunter-Weston oversaw the killing and wounding in several pointless daylight attacks of nearly a third of the

British, Australian and New Zealand troops committed to the criminally badly planned Second Battle of Krithia for which both Hunter-Weston and Hamilton deserved the sack. On the Russian front, the German-Austrian offensive at Gorlice–Tarnów was launched on 2nd May with devastating results for the Russian Army. All of Galicia, including the hard-fought for passes through the Carpathians, was lost. Mackensen's *11. Armee* advanced c. 80 miles in four weeks and, by late June, the Russian 3rd Army, commanded by the ex-patriate Bulgarian, Gen. Radko Dimitriev, was destroyed, losing c. 80% of its strength. This depressing news led Kitchener to the idea the Germans might soon release experienced divisions from the Eastern Front for use in France and Flanders or, even, an invasion of Britain in an attempt to slow or stop the flow of New Army divisions to the Western Front. Just this threat was sufficient to persuade Kitchener to tell the War Council on 14th May he was not currently prepared to send more New Army divisions to the continent if it meant undermining home defence.

It also provoked him to write to Robertson stating:

"… the French have an almost unlimited supply of ammunition including HE and 14 divisions in reserve so if they cannot break through we may take it as proved that the lines cannot be forced."[57]

The French did not 'have an almost unlimited supply of ammunition', but it was believed true by the British for some time. In fact, the French experienced a grave shortage of both howitzers and shells well into 1916.

With the French heavily engaged at Vimy, a meeting was convened between Joffre, Foch and French at Bryas on the afternoon of 12th May. French excused the failure at Aubers Ridge by blaming a lack of shells rather than the operational plan and the feeble bombardment. Joffre replied that, in this case, the First Army might as well stop fighting if they lacked the means to do so effectively. Instead, Joffre suggested, the BEF might relieve three French divisions, *58e, 152e* and *153e Divisions*, the latter two being tied up north of Ypres since they were rushed there after the first gas attack on 22nd April. Sir John French refused to agree to lose the units at Ypres (a reluctance to relieve French troops was a common theme amongst both commanders of the BEF) worried as he was by the threat to Ypres and his lines of communication in Flanders. Joffre's reply was damning:

"Then, British co-operation in the battle is limited to the relief of one French division; it is not much. What will they think of it in England?"[58]

It was only the intervention of Henry Wilson, the British liaison with *GQG*, which redeemed Sir John French from total humiliation when he suggested, on their return to GHQ, the situation be reviewed. The result was, rather than relieve the French around Ypres, Sir John decided to resume the attack around Aubers Ridge, and Haig was ordered to do his utmost to assist the French to the south over whatever period was required.

The campaign recommenced on 15th May with the attack at Festubert, a battle which eventually dragged on for ten days at a cost of nearly 17,000 British casualties against just 5,000 German. The fighting took place initially in the area where 1st Division failed on 9th May in the southern end of the Aubers Ridge battlefield, and eventually extended further south to take in the entire shallow German salient, the tip of which lay 500 yards east of the village of Festubert and which was bordered by Neuve Chapelle in the north and Givenchy in the south. The major advantage to the British of attacking this area again was that, except for *13.* and *14. Divisions*, the Germans had no appreciable reserves within reach of the sector to be attacked, as the two divisions which might have been made available, *58.* and *115. Divisions*, were sent to Vimy to counter the continuing attacks of the French *Xe Armée*.

In some ways, the approach to the battle was a complete change from the first attack on 9th May and, in others, it was sadly similar to that event and even more so to Neuve Chapelle back in March. Yet again the attack was to be made in two locations separated, this time, by just six hundred yards. But these attacks were to be separated by more than just distance, they were also separated by time, with the first attack by two brigades of 2nd Division and one from the Meerut Division leaving their trenches at 11.30 p.m. for the first British night attack of the war. This attack was to be followed 3¾ hours later by one made by two brigades of 7th Division who were to go over the top at 3.15 a.m. The three northern brigades, from left to right the Garhwal Brigade (Meerut Division), 5th Brigade and 6th Brigade (2nd Division), were to attack on a frontage of 1,600 yards. The later, southern, attack by 20th and 22nd Brigades of 7th Division went in on a front of 850 yards. In another change from the 9th May attack, the immediate objectives of which were 3,000 yards distant, the initial attack on the night of 15th/16th May was to progress no further than 1,000 yards in the first advance.

Even this was not the only innovation. Learning something from the initially successful French attacks around Vimy Ridge on 9th May, Haig decided to follow their pattern of a long and deliberate artillery preparation[i]. The *Official History* explains Haig's thinking behind this major tactical change:

> "... he had drawn the conclusions that the German defences were so strongly built, and the machine guns so well placed that a rapid infantry assault with distant objectives, preceded by merely a short, sudden and intensive burst of artillery fire, was no longer a practicable operation. He now proposed to follow the French method of a long methodical bombardment of the German defences by a heavy artillery, chiefly 9.2-inch, 6-inch and 5-inch howitzers, in order to ensure the destruction of the enemy's wire and the demolition of the machine gun emplacements and strong points before the infantry was sent forward."[59]

This methodical bombardment was to stretch 5,000 yards between Festubert in the south to Port Arthur, which lay just the north of the La Bassée to Estaires

---

[i] Sheffield and Bourne (page 122) make much of Haig's analysis of the Aubers Ridge failure stating it 'had an important influence on his plans for the *Somme*'. The first point in his 11th May diary entry was the need for a 'long methodical bombardment' to destroy German defences. As Haig, overly influenced by the initial German success at Verdun, argued strenuously against Rawlinson's plan for a 'long methodical bombardment' on the *Somme* and then reduced it in scale a few days before the attack it is difficult to see what they mean.

Road. Starting on 13th May it continued unabated throughout the 14th and, because of the weather, 15th May and involved 433 guns and howitzers including 18 French 75s. This artillery consisted of:

Field Guns		Howitzers	
13-pdrs	48	4.5-in. howitzers	54
15-pdrs	16	5-in. howitzers	20
18-pdrs	210	6-in. howitzers	36
4.7-in. guns	4	9.2-in. howitzers	9
60-pdrs	12	15-in. howitzers	2
6-in. Mk VII guns	4		
75-mm	18		
Total	312		121

Table 46 British artillery at Festubert, 15th May 1915

For the bombardment of the German trenches and strongpoints there were, nominally, 47 medium and heavy howitzers and 74 light/field howitzers or one howitzer for every 41 yards of front and one medium howitzer every 139 yards. These simple numbers conceal a degree of greater complexity and further dilution of the overall power of the British bombardment. Evidence from the first attack suggested the 4.5-in. howitzers shell was of little use against the far more robust breastworks built since Neuve Chapelle and, therefore, these guns were not to be used on the front-line but on the support line, communication trenches and other specially selected targets. The two 15-in. howitzers were tasked with bombarding the villages of Violaines and Beau Pits as well as a location called the Distillery which lay 1,000 yards behind the right wing of the German defences on the La Bassée to Estaires road. The 9.2-in. howitzers took on selected points in the German defences, meaning it was left to the 6-in. howitzers to demolish the front-line breastworks. Each gun was given a stretch of breastwork 250 yards wide[60] and, on average, each gun fired 186 rounds during the bombardment[61] which theoretically meant one shell should have landed on every 1.3 yards of German front-line trench. To achieve this would have required 100% accuracy, which was impossible given the nature of the technology, the rudimentary artillery techniques then employed, and the increasingly worn state of the guns. It also needed all the shells to detonate, which they did not.

The dire effects wear could have on the range and accuracy of the artillery had previously been highlighted by the performance of the 4.7-in. guns at Aubers Ridge. The *Official History* reports incidents during the bombardment prior to 9th May when, because of the stripping of the copper driving band from the American manufactured shells, some started to turn end over end and, as a result, fell anywhere – with some landing 500 yards *behind* the British frontlines![62] Barrel wear only served to increase these guns' inaccuracy, and this problem was widespread if less severe amongst the other guns. The life span of howitzers was generally longer than that of a gun. A 6-in. howitzer, for example, could fire as many as 5,000 rounds during its lifespan whilst the barrel of a 6-in. MK VII gun lasted for just 1,200 rounds.[63] The muzzle velocity of the 6-in. Mk VII gun was some 2,500 feet per second as against a 6-in. 26 cwt howitzer which was just 1,409 feet per second. The propellant charge for each piece was also substantially different: the Mk VII gun employed a 23 lb Cordite charge against a 4lb 12 oz. Cordite MD charge for the howitzer. This all contributed to the greater wear on the gun (as opposed to howitzer) barrel and its reduced life. At the rates of fire which became the norm on the Western Front these numbers meant most guns' barrel life did not exceed twelve months and often considerably less. The average barrel lives of the various natures are given below:

18-pdr. 12,000 rounds
4.5-in. howitzer 14,000 rounds
60-pdr. 4,000 rounds
6-in Mk VII 1,200 rounds
6-in 30 cwt howitzer 5,000 rounds
6-in. 26 cwt howitzer 5,000 rounds*
8-in. howitzer 4,500 rounds*
9.2-in. howitzer 4,500 rounds
9.2-in, Mk X railway gun 500 rounds
12-in. howitzer 1,500 rounds*
15-in. howitzer 3,500 rounds[64]
(* These howitzers were not yet available to the BEF)

As previously mentioned, barrel life was only one of the issues which could affect the accuracy and rate of fire of these guns. Issues with the recoil systems were also causing problems. Of the guns listed above all, except for the modern 6-in. 26 cwt, 9.2-in. and 12-in. howitzers, used a hydro-spring recoil system, i.e. a hydraulic system initially based on a water and glycerine mix supplemented by springs. The constant firing of these guns in a long bombardment, as with the *Somme*, generated considerable heat in this liquid which tended to break down the glycerine which then eroded the cylinders thereby creating leaks. Furthermore, it was discovered the buffer springs simply could not deal with the constant pounding of the gun in such battlefield conditions.

Added to these problems of wear and tear were the numerous issues with the quality of the shells, the detonation of their explosive filling and the reliability of the fuzes used. In short, nowhere near one 6-inch shell per 1.3 yards was effectively delivered onto the German front-line opposite Festubert.

With the introduction of the lengthy deliberate bombardment, a great deal of effort was expended to properly observe both the fall and effect of the shells fired. In addition to the observers watching from the British trenches, officer patrols were also sent out to inspect the German wire and the state of the defensive works. These produced numerous reports of unexploded 6-in. howitzer shells lying in and about the German wire and trenches.

The night attack on the northern flank commenced at 11.30 p.m. on 15th May with the three attacking Brigades crossing the breastworks and laying bridges across a dyke (12 ft. wide and containing 4 ft. of water) before starting across No Man's Land. On the right of the attack, 6th Brigade successfully gained the German front-line with few losses and then headed towards the German support line. The other two brigades were not so fortunate. On the northern edge of the attack the

Jullundur Brigade of the Lahore Division was engaged in an ill-advised attempt at confusing the enemy about British intentions. Someone had the bright idea of ordering them to open fire for five minutes at intervals four times during the evening, the last occasion being at 10.30 p.m. just an hour before the attack was due. Unsurprisingly, instead of confusing the Germans, it only served to place them on the alert and the men of the 5th and Garhwal Brigades were spotted leaving the British lines to lay the bridges over the dyke. Swept by rifle and machine gun fire, and illuminated by numerous flares, the attacks of the Garhwal Brigade and the left battalion of 5th Brigade (2nd Worcestershire Regt.) collapsed. Only the right-hand battalion, 2nd Royal Inniskilling Fusiliers, managed to get some men of their right-hand platoons into the German trenches. There they were eventually joined by ten platoons of the support battalion, 2nd Oxfordshire Regt. An attempt was made to renew the attack to coincide with the southern attack of 7th Division at 3.15 a.m. but this failed to materialise. The four British battalions involved lost 53 officers and 1,610 other ranks and 39th Garhwal Rifles 154 of all ranks.

7th Division's attack was initially more successful. For tactical reasons, the bombardment of the German front-line was extended to the breastworks to the north and south of the 850 yards frontage to be attacked and this helped prevent the enemy from enfilading the attacking infantry. In addition, six field guns[i] were dragged into the front-line from where they fired high explosive shells directly into the German breastworks. This was a novelty which proved highly useful. The 2nd Queen's and 1st Royal Welsh Fusiliers of 22nd Brigade on the right, in spite of suffering heavy casualties in No Man's Land, attained their objectives, but only at a cost of 57% and 70% casualties respectively and with both COs killed. On their left, the two lead battalions of 20th Brigade, 2nd Scots Guards and 2nd Border Regt., advancing early in the hope of taking advantage of the British bombardment, instead ran into it, suffering heavy casualties from 'friendly fire'. Despite this, they too pressed on and gained their objectives, however F Company, 2nd Scots Guards, was overwhelmed and wiped out by a German counterattack.

The battle then degenerated into mainly pointless skirmishes, although another significant attack was launched on 18th May by 3rd Canadian and 4th Guards Brigades. A typical shambles, the Guards were left to attack on their own and got nowhere. 2nd and 7th Divisions were withdrawn, having suffered over 9,000 casualties, to be replaced by 47th (2nd London) Division TF, the Canadian Division, and 51st (Highland) Division TF. The final attacks took place on 24th and 25th May. 142nd Brigade, 47th Division, gained a few hundred yards of mud-filled German breastwork at a cost of 1,000 men[ii]. By the end of the battle, Haig's troops lost 710 officers and 15,938 men against an estimated 5,000 German casualties.[65] In addition, his artillery nearly exhausted their shell supplies, the 18-pdrs having just 40 rounds per gun left and the 4.5-in. howitzers twelve. Unconsciously it seems, the British *Official History* summed up the battle by damning it with faint praise:

---

[i] Four 13-pdrs of T and U Batteries, RHA, and two 18-pdrs of 12th Battery, RFA.

[ii] The battle was to be closed down anyway as, sensitive to the nth degree about Ypres, Sir John French responded to a heavy gas attack on the night of 23rd and 24th May by starting to move guns and shells north to protect the salient.

"Units in some case had reached the objectives assigned to them."[66]

The troops were given far more limited objectives than previously, and the artillery concentrated on particular targets even if more widely spread even than at Aubers Ridge. A greater effort was made to assess the progress of the bombardment and some initiatives were introduced. The bravery and commitment of the infantry, many of them new to fighting of any sort, was undoubted. Furthermore, an effort had to be sustained to support the French further south. In short, however, the cost of three British casualties to one German hardly made this a sustainable long-term strategy or set of tactics.

The final Haig/Rawlinson-led disaster of the summer (if on a smaller scale) occurred on 15th June just to the north of Givenchy-lès-la-Bassée, which village gave the action its name. It was designed to eliminate a shallow German salient in front of Rue d'Ouvert, a stretch of road along which several houses and other buildings were scattered. The distance to be covered was modest, about ¼ of a mile, but the task difficult as Rawlinson soon appreciated. After re-organisation he was to use 7th Division on the right of the attack and 51st (Highland) Division TF on the left where No Man's Land was considerably wider. In reserve was the Canadian Division.

Rawlinson immediately took against the place describing it as 'a pretty stiff nut for us to crack' and forecasting the loss of 'many thousands of lives' when the attack went in.[67] Designed to support a renewal of the French offensive in Artois, it was supposed to be a limited exercise of line straightening, though Haig, as the day of the attack drew near, asked Rawlinson to prepare plans for further advances once Rue d'Ouvert was taken. This he did in half-hearted fashion, and this downbeat attitude towards the operation was heavily reinforced in his diary entry for 13th June, the day the slow and deliberate two-day bombardment started:

"I wrote out some orders at night and showed them to him in the morning. They are in the form of a pious aspiration rather than anything that is likely to be actually carried into effect for we are not going to capture the Rue d'Ouvert as easily as he appears to think... My opinion is that we shall be very lucky if we get the Rue d'Ouvert after three days hard fighting and 5,000 casualties."[68]

He was partially correct. The wire was badly cut and, on 15th June, the few men who entered the German front line were quickly expelled, killed, or captured. Rue d'Ouvert was not reached. At Haig's insistence (he visited Rawlinson to so instruct him) the attack was renewed the following day, this time with some of the Canadians involved. The results were a repeat of the previous assault: a few entries into the German line and heavy losses. Further attacks were ordered for 18th June, but postponed to the following day and then cancelled when it became apparent Foch had called off the French attacks around Vimy. Casualties for the three divisions involved were c. 4,000.

No-one emerges with any credit for the fiasco at Givenchy. Rawlinson did not want to attack but was in no position to refuse Haig's orders. Haig, again, had grossly optimistic ideas as to the prospects for success and even an additional exploitation of ground gained.

In his private diary, Rawlinson dare not speak this publicly, he fulminated:

"It is a thousand pities that we were allowed to attack the Rue d'Ouvert for any sensible person would have known that we should not take it! We lost 3,000 men, fired off a lot of ammunition and did harm to our morale."[69]

'Any sensible person'? Only two people were able to stop this attack: Sir John French and Douglas Haig. Neither did.

There was no silver lining in this glowering cloud of doom. Those men who entered the German trenches and lived to return brought news of their construction. They were 7-10 feet deep but of far greater concern were the new shell-proof dugouts excavated 5-6 feet further down. Rawlinson made a special note in his report on the action of 21st June. His conclusion should have been a cause for unease for anyone planning an attack on the German lines:

"I much doubt if any kind of artillery fire however accurate and well sustained will have the desired effect unless it is sufficient to bury the garrisons in the deep dug-outs they have now constructed, and this is a matter of chance."[70]

Forewarned is forearmed so they say. But not, as far as 1st July 1916 was concerned, in the case of the BEF.

THESE ATTACKS SET THE SCENE for the last British offensive of 1915 at Loos launched on 25th September. Like the attacks at Aubers Ridge and Festubert, the Battle of Loos was designed to support a French attack, the Third Battle of Artois, and augment an even larger one in Champagne (Second Battle of Champagne). Overall, the French intended to attack on two fronts with 46 divisions (29 under de Castelnau in Champagne and 17 under Foch north of Arras) and Joffre asked the BEF to mount as large an operation in support as was possible. Sir John French was undecided where best to attack with the BEF, which by this time numbered 28 divisions. There was a debate concerning the merits of Ypres, Messines, or Loos, which lay immediately to the north of the planned French attack in front of Vimy. The preference of Foch and Joffre was for the area around Loos and Hulluch and Sir John therefore agreed to commit eight divisions to an offensive in the area, again under the command of Haig.

It was the largest British offensive of the war to date, on the widest front and with the largest number of supporting guns. The campaign technically lasted six weeks (it was formally closed down by Haig on 4th November) but was effectively over after twenty days with the failure of 46th Division's attack on the Hohenzollern Redoubt on 13th/14th October. Within this six-week period British casualties amounted to nearly 62,000 – over 50,000 immediately around Loos and over 11,000 in subsidiary supporting operations. German casualties amounted to less than half those of Haig's First Army, again an unacceptable 'return on investment' of British lives.

It is not the purpose of this book to provide a detailed account of the fighting at Loos (anyone wishing to pursue this should avail themselves of a copy of Niall Cherry's 2005 book *Most Unfavourable Ground*) but rather to look at the planning of the battle and the possible lessons which might, or should, have been learned.

It is fair to say neither French nor Haig were especially keen on fighting over the Lens coalfield. On 20th June, with an attack at Loos under consideration, Haig visited the area. It was littered with pit heads, slag heaps and small, mean mining villages. He concluded 'the problem of an attack in this area (is) very difficult'.[71] Two days later he went into greater detail:

> "Since the French attacked at Loos the Enemy has greatly strengthened his position. A second line with wire entanglement is distinctly visible here… I came to the conclusion that it would be possible to capture the Enemy's first line of trenches (say a length of 1,200 yards) opposite Maroc but it would not be possible to advance beyond, because our own artillery could not support us, as ground immediately in our front cannot be seen from any part of the front. On the other hand the Enemy has excellent observation for his artillery… The Enemy's defences are now so strong that they can only be taken by siege methods… the ground above is so swept by gun and machine gun and rifle fire that an advance in the open, except by night, is impossible."[72]

In all, an excellent summation of the problems to be encountered at Loos, with the issues identified being the ones Fayolle and later Foch identified from the fighting at Vimy: unseen lines of German trenches towards the rear being difficult to bombard, strong defences, and the likelihood of a heavy German barrage on the British positions.

On 7th July Haig discussed with Lt. Col. Fowkes, RE, the prospects for the first British use of poison gas in response to the German attack in April. His comments, in the light of his rush to use another technical innovation – the tank – in whatever limited numbers were available, are interesting:

> "I said better wait until we can use it on a large scale, because the element of surprise is always greater on the first occasion."[73]

His preference, however, was to employ gas for the first time in yet another attack on Aubers Ridge, which area he preferred to the French-favoured Loos.[74] Haig pursued his preference for another extensive attack on Aubers Ridge throughout July and early August but it was Foch who applied the pressure for First Army to attack between the La Bassée canal down to the left of *Xe Armée* near Lens in support of their new attack on Vimy Ridge. Haig, however, seemed to think it possible such support might only require 'small infantry attacks',[75] but this idea was partly scotched when Joffre weighed in with support for Foch's plans. In response Haig was asked to produce a plan for a limited action 'made chiefly with artillery'. He was:

> "… not to launch a large force of infantry to the attack of objectives which are so strongly held as to be liable to result only in the sacrifice of many lives. That is to say, I am to assist the French by neutralising the Enemy's artillery, and by holding the hostile infantry on my front."[76]

By 13th August this circumspect approach was underlined at a conference with Rawlinson (IV Corps) and Gough (I Corps). Though the long-term objective was stated to be to turn the German defences around Lens from the north whilst the French did the same after taking Vimy Ridge, the initial plan was extremely limited and reflected Haig's opinion stated on 22nd June 'that it would be possible to capture the Enemy's first line of trenches'. Again, Haig stated the intention was to hold the German defenders in place and attack their artillery. British troops were to be 'held in readiness' should an opportunity for a successful attack present itself. In case of this eventuality, Rawlinson was asked to submit a plan to take the German front-line to the west of the village of Loos and Gough was asked for proposals for an attack on the Hohenzollern Redoubt and some neighbouring defences. Additional work was to be done on arrangements for further advances by IV Corps on Loos itself and on Hill 70 behind it, and by I Corps for an attack on Hulluch. These latter advances, however, depended on the success of the French at Vimy. It was thought gas might be employed in the initial attacks and the support of some additional guns and howitzers was to be expected.[77]

Joffre, however, was not content with the idea the British might mount a small scale and limited attack north of Lens at the same time as the French were going all-out to break through at Vimy and, on an even larger scale, in Champagne. An additional issue was the possible collapse of the Russian Armies already reeling from the heavy blows inflicted throughout the summer in the Gorlice–Tarnów offensive which resulted in the complete loss of its Polish territories along with nearly two million men. Kitchener expressed the view to Haig on 19th August that, to relieve pressure on the Russians, the BEF needed to join with the French in *major* offensives on the Western Front. In consequence, the BEF would have to attack vigorously, even if this meant suffering heavy casualties.[78]

Over the following days Haig spent some time investigating the uses and supply of asphyxiating gas, in this case chlorine, with a demonstration of its release from gas canisters taking place on 22nd August at Helfaut just south of St Omer. Haig, Rawlinson, and the Divisional commanders present were impressed by the demonstration to such an extent that, after Haig received definite orders for a large-scale attack, it was decided a gas discharge would precede the simultaneous attack of six divisions between the La Bassée canal and Lens. It was hoped a forty-minute release of chlorine on a favourable breeze would enable First Army 'to advance through the German defences without any serious opposition'.[79]

With the deployment of lethal gas on a wide front, Haig's initial scepticism about the prospects for an attack about Loos evaporated. No doubt thinking of the collapse of the French troops at Ypres at the end of April, he believed the potential effects of the gas would enable him to spread his artillery more thinly than before and yet still achieve the necessary breach in the enemy's lines. In many respects, this optimism shared some similarities with his over-confident approach to the Aubers Ridge attack in May. Then, minor tinkering with his own tactics failed to consider a major change in defensive German thinking and planning. Now, it appeared, an assumption was made that a gas attack *à la* Ypres on 22nd April would generate the same panicked collapse amongst the Germans that the first ever gas attack on the Western Front achieved amongst utterly unprepared French troops.

> "Decisive results are likely to be obtained. The gas… will be carried by the wind in front of the assaulting divisions and create a panic in the German ranks, or, at least, incapacitate them for a prolonged resistance."[80]

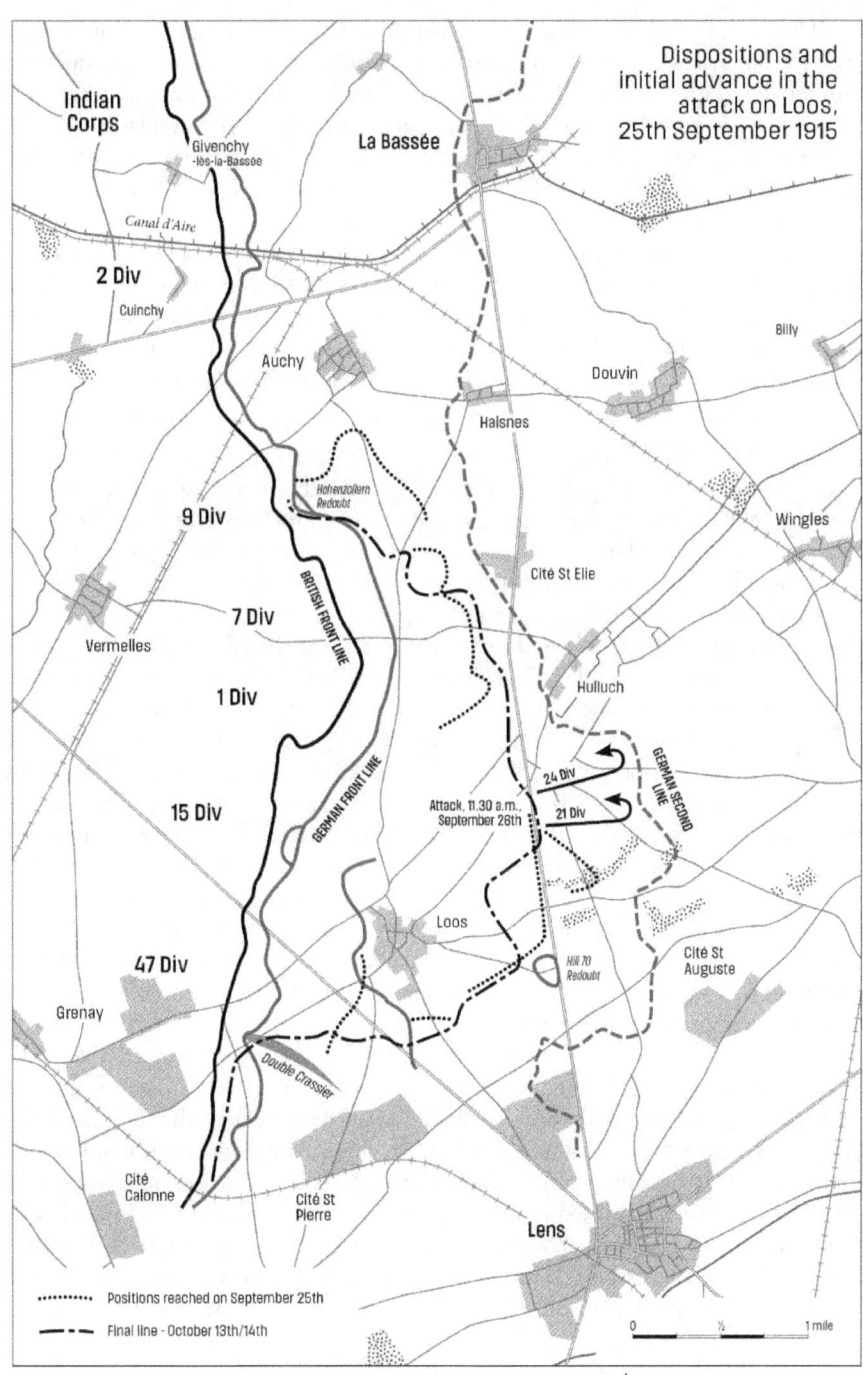

Map 21 Dispositions and initial advance in the attack on Loos, 25th September 1915 and the attack of the 21st and 24th Divisions, 26th September 1915

That, at least, was the theory but, unsurprisingly, counter measures against gas moved on in the next six months. The Germans had recently introduced a rubberized cloth gas mask, known as *Gummimasken*, with the first, and not very effective, *Linienmaske* (introduced late summer 1915) being replaced by the *Bandmaske*. These contained chemical filters and seem to have been slightly more advanced than the early British idea for an effective mask, the 'Hypo helmet', a hood impregnated with thiosulfate, sodium bicarbonate, and glycerine.

As with so many other promises on the supply of munitions, the quantity of gas demanded proved beyond the manufacturer's capabilities in the time available and, a month before the attack was due, it seemed barely 50% of the supply would arrive in France in time. In these circumstances, Haig believed either the front to be attacked had to narrow or the date of the attack put back, again arguing:

"... 'surprise' is always greatest on the first occasion of having some new instrument of war!"[81]

Delays in French preparations for the main offensive in Champagne came to the rescue, with Joffre twice being forced to postpone the start date. Despite a 'break down' at the chlorine gas producing plant, of which Haig was notified on 2nd September[82], it appeared enough gas would be available by the new date to cover the entire front to be attacked.

So encouraged was Haig by the availability of lethal gas he, like Joffre, anticipated punching a hole straight through the German lines. This was in spite of the fact there was a recognition the available British artillery and their shell supply was insufficient to destroy the German wire and defensive strongpoints, a fact already recognised by Haig.[83] On 18th September he met Sir John French to discuss the attack and he explained that, were the supply of gas to fall short or were the weather uncooperative, then he 'only had enough guns to cover the attack of 2 divisions'.[84] In either circumstance, therefore, the attack would have to be limited to assaults on the Hohenzollern Redoubt and the area around Loos. But so different were the conditions expected to be after the gas release, Haig had already abandoned the phased and limited approach belatedly adopted at Festubert in favour of a rapid and unlimited advance which would take the infantry through both the German 1st and 2nd Positions before any German reserves could arrive.[85]

First Army's offensive was part of a grand strategic concept to attack the flanks of the great German salient running through Artois, Picardy and Champagne, the apex of which thrust south-west towards Paris. Once through the German lines, hordes of cavalry were to be unleashed and a triumphant drive north-east towards the Belgian fortress towns of Liège and Namur would see the German Armies on the Western Front shattered beyond repair. At a conference at Chantilly on 14th September, de Castelnau, commanding the largest of the various offensives, explained the plan of attack. It was based on the misinterpretations of First Army's 'success' at Neuve Chapelle on 10th March, compounded by the general misreading of the events of 9th May on the front of *33e Corps* at Vimy:

"The attack would take place in depth, by successive waves without a stop, night and day, in order to ensure continual effort until a breakthrough was accomplished. It would be preceded by a storm of shells on the enemy lines, followed by the uninterrupted advance of the infantry in assault formation; then by a drive through of all the cavalry, who would take distant points as objectives, such as road junctions, railway lines, bridges, telegraph and telephone lines, etc…'[86]

The baseless optimism on which all of this was founded was to be a recurring theme amongst certain Allied commanders over the next two years. This absurd positivity, a true triumph of hope over experience, was repeated prior to the *Somme* and again before the Nivelle offensive in the Spring of 1917 and would cost the Allied Armies hundreds of thousands of casualties.

Privately, always privately, one man demurred from this view. The divisions of Henry Rawlinson's IV Corps, 1st, 15th (Scottish) and 47th (2nd London) Divisions, were to attack the southern end of the battlefield including the village of Loos, the important Hill 70 to the east, and the re-entrant in the German 2nd Position between Hulluch and Cité St Auguste. Noting the strengthening of this second line he wrote in his diary that his men would be 'very fortunate indeed if (they) manage to penetrate there'. He then gloomily speculated 'It looks to me as if we may be here for the winter'.[87] And two winters more, Henry, two winters more.

The tactical plan for Loos was different from the previous main attacks of 1915 in that it was to take place on one continuous front. Two divisions, 47th (2nd London) Division in the south and 2nd Division in the north, were to provide flank guards to a four-division thrust through the centre of the German position between Lens and the La Bassée Canal. These central divisions were instructed to 'push on eastwards… to the extreme limit of their power'.[88]

Everything, however, depended on wind strength and direction. Its vagaries would dictate success or failure of the gas release. It was a plan the success of which lay outside the control of ordinary man – or, even with his god on his side, the General Officer Commanding, First Army.

THE OPENING DAYS OF THE LOOS FIGHTING are simply told.[89] An artillery sufficient for a two-division attack did what it could, spread, as it was, over a six-division frontage. The 18-pdrs took on the task of cutting wire ten to twenty yards deep in front of the German 1st line trench. Beyond that, wire in front of the second line was barely touched, being out of range of the 18-pdrs and too distant (5-7,000 yards) to be properly observed in any case. To make matters worse the weather, on which so much depended, steadfastly refused to play ball. The first two days of the bombardment were dry but an easterly wind blew dust and smoke back across the battlefield rendering observation extremely difficult. On day three, 23rd September, the weather broke bringing mist and low cloud. Again, observation was problematic. The following night a thunderstorm flooded the trenches. Being lined with chalk they became 'nearly impossible' to move along.[90] On the final day, rain swept the battlefield and the winds, never especially strong, continually veered from south to east-south-east and then back to the west.

Such weather caused problems for the counter-battery programme. In addition, the German batteries were found to have ceased firing if a British shell fell nearby. This created an impression they had been neutralised or destroyed, an idea which proved to be completely wrong when the infantry left the trenches.

In general, the British artillery bombardment was so scattered and so thin the Germans concluded only the French to the south were going to mount a serious attack, with First Army mounting diversions and feints. In many ways, this idea was reinforced by the results of the bombardment which left large amounts of German wire along their front-line uncut, the wire in front of their 2nd position mainly untouched, and the various strongpoints, villages, and the network of trenches relatively undamaged. Casualties amongst the defenders were also light, with the 25-foot-deep dugouts excavated from the underlying chalk keeping the German front-line troops safe as did those on the *Somme* just over eight months later. Attempts at cutting these troops off from supplies and reliefs through intermittent night firing failed in almost every respect.

In all, the artillery programme was a failure compounded by spreading the guns over a wide area. Ironically, however, it was this failure which helped lull the Germans into a sense of false security and, not having detected the preparations for the gas release, led to some partial initial success when the attack was launched.

By 3 a.m. on 25th September the local wind speed around Haig's HQ fell to 1 mph[i]. Haig consulted the RFC's meteorologist, Capt. Ernest Gold, a Fellow of St John's College, Cambridge, and previously the Schuster Reader in Dynamical Meteorology, who was appointed in 1910 the Superintendent of the Statistical and Library Section of the Meteorological Office, then part of the Board of Trade[ii]. Gold's only thought was the wind would 'probably' be stronger after sunrise (which was at 5.30 a.m. and an hour before the infantry attack was due) than later in the day. Otherwise, he was reluctant to commit himself. At 5 a.m. Haig described the wind as 'almost a calm', but some cigarette smoke drifted slowly north-east. This was sufficient for Haig to give the order at 5.15 a.m. for the full-scale attack, although he expressed concerns about the gas blowing back over the waiting British troops. Were this to happen, the heavier-than-air chlorine would pool in the bottom of the trenches.[91] Such was the concern, one of Haig's staff phoned Gough at I Corps to ask whether the gas release could be stopped, but by then it was too late.

There was, of course, the 'Plan B' of the two-division attack on which to fall back. In this case the final intense bombardment to be delivered on all of the divisions' fronts would have been concentrated on the two areas to be attacked. Had Haig opted for this reduced frontage without the concealment effect of the

---

[i] The *British Official History* expends six pages on the arrangements for monitoring the wind and on the numerous and various reports on the wind speeds on 24th and 25th September [*Military Operations, France and Flanders, 1915*, Vol. 2, pages 168-173].

[ii] Major, later Lt. Col., Ernest Gold, CB, DSO, OBE, FRA, RE, was born in 1881, the son of the late John Gold and Ellen Peckett. He was educated at Coleshill Grammar School, Warwickshire; Mason's College, Birmingham; and St John's College, Cambridge, where he studied Natural Sciences. He was the Schuster Reader in Dynamical Meteorology between 1907 and 1910 when he joined the Meteorological Office. After the war he was the President of the International Commission for Synoptic Weather Information 1919-47, President of the Meteorological Sub-committee of the International Commission for Aerial Navigation 1922-46, and President of the Royal Meteorological Society 1934-6. He died on 30th January 1976.

smoke and the surprise impact of the gas the likelihood is the results would have been similar to, if not far worse, than those experienced at Aubers Ridge. Most of the artillery would not have previously registered the area being attacked, the wire was at best partially cut, and the defences relatively undamaged. Troops advancing over the open plain in full view of the enemy would have presented an unmissable target. It is, perhaps, for this reason Haig risked all on the gas.

So light and variable was the breeze that when the smoke and gas was released it moved in different directions in different sectors and at different speeds. From the Hohenzollern redoubt southwards it drifted slowly over towards the German trenches, although in places it was the smoke which concealed and aided the advancing infantry more than the gas. Generally, however, although effective where it moved in the right direction, the gas/smoke cloud was neither thick enough nor did it move quickly enough to achieve everything hoped.

On 2nd Division's front on the extreme left the wind was such the gas had to be turned off immediately as it hung over the British trenches and causing casualties amongst the attacking troops. Here the attack failed, with the failure compounded by the fact two mines were inexplicably blown ten minutes before the advance, giving the defenders ample time to man their fire-steps. Such stupidity clearly escaped most senior officers as, in a replica of this attack, VIII Corps was allowed to spring the huge mine under the Hawthorn Ridge redoubt ten minutes before zero on 1st July 1916.

Elsewhere the attack, covered by the slow-moving gas and smoke cloud, was clearly unexpected and defenders in many areas were caught unawares and, in some places, rendered incapable of defence by the gas and the panic caused. As instructed, where possible, British troops pushed forward as far as they could whether it was tactically sensible or not. Most notable was the experience of the enthusiastic battalions of 9th (Scottish) and 15th (Scottish) Divisions.

9th Division was given an extremely tough task: taking the soon infamous Hohenzollern Redoubt; as well as The Dump, a 20-foot-high slag heap giving good observation over the flat terrain to the north of Loos; and the mine buildings of Fosse 8. They were then to advance to take the German 2nd Position between the villages of Haisnes and the Cité St Elie, before advancing to the western bank of the *Canal de la Haute Deûle*. In all, this was advance of some five miles (8 kms). Haking's new XI Corps (the New Army 21st and 24th Divisions plus the Guards Division) would then pass through this new position to continue the advance.

9th Division's right unit, 26th Brigade, captured its objectives and pushed parties on to the unoccupied and partially completed German 2nd line (Pekin Trench) between Haisnes and the Cité St Elie. There they were joined by men of the reserve, 27th Brigade. Unfortunately, 28th Brigade on the left, affected by British gas drifting back into their trenches and a strong German artillery barrage, was stopped in No Man's Land with devastating casualties. The temporarily successful troops of 26th and 27th Brigades in the 2nd Position were then subject to heavy flanking bombing attacks and eventually forced to withdraw. Whilst some men rejoined their units, the mass fell back in confusion through the advanced British positions to the original German front-line. Total losses were c. 3,000.

15th Division attacked further south. Its objectives were the fortified village of

Loos and the important Hill 70 and redoubt. Then, ignoring the Cité St Laurent (the northern edge of Lens) to the south, it was to drive east through the Cité St Auguste to a line between Annay in the north (just south of the point where the *Canal de la Haute Deûle* changes direction east-west to south-north) and Loison-sous-Lens: an advance of 4.6 miles (7.4 kms).

With great vigour, 15th Division pushed through Loos and up the north-western slope of Hill 70. The 'summit' gave views over the German 2nd line in front of Cité St Laurent to the south and Cité St Auguste to the east. So great was the enthusiasm, and so lacking the control that, having reached the summit of Hill 70, the men flooded down the *southern* slope of the little hill towards Cité St Laurent rather than *east* towards Cité St Auguste. They were caught in the open and pinned down by rifle and machine gun fire from the relatively undamaged German 2nd line. German counterattacks after midday re-took the hill. The attacking units, 44th and 46th Brigades, lost 145 officers and 4,176 Other Ranks.

At the end of the day First Army's troops were not advancing rampantly towards the *Canal de la Haute Deûle*, but were, to quote the *Official History*:

> "… in extemporized positions, broken by gaps. Worse than this, it was much exhausted by fighting and had suffered very heavy casualties, amounting in total to 470 officers and 15,000 other ranks, nearly a sixth of its forces engaged."92

Affairs did not improve on 26th September. After a long, grossly mishandled advance through heavy traffic in poor weather, 21st Division (in France 17 days) and 24th Division[i] (in France 27 days) were casually thrown into the heavily defended re-entrant between Hulluch and the Cité St Auguste. Having marched throughout the night in pouring rain, their orders from a poorly informed Haig were to push through the German reserve line to occupy the crossings of the *Canal de la Haute Deûle,* some three miles further on, and the area between Harnes and Pont à Vendin. A supporting attack by 1st Division on Hulluch on their left was, unknown to these divisions, postponed, and an attempt to take Hill 70 on their right failed. The Corps commander, Haking, four miles behind the lines at Noeux-les-Mines, remained oblivious of these facts until it was too late. Thus, the inexperienced officers[ii] and men marched stolidly forward to the amazement of the German defenders who, significantly reinforced, behind unbroken wire, and in practically undamaged trenches, took them in enfilade from both flanks. Shot down in their thousands, these New Army divisions broke. Some, in what is now known in combat training as *Condition Black*[iii], fled:

---

[i] The Division was not helped by the fact none of its Staff Officers had any experience in the field in that role [*Source*: Robbins S, *British Generalship*, page 40].

[ii] In 21st Division most of the battalion commanders were retired, many from the Indian Army. No battalion had more than one other Regular Army officer in its ranks (*Source:* Robbins, op. cit., page 87).

[iii] *Condition Black* – overwhelmed by fear, was a US Marine Corps addition to a combat readiness code developed by ex-US Marine Lt. Col. John Dean 'Jeff' Cooper (1920–2006). He developed a 4-level combat readiness code: *White* – unaware/vulnerable; *Yellow* – alert/relaxed; *Orange* – alert to a specific threat; *Red* – fighting.

"…when the heart rate gets above 175 beats per minute because of the influx of adrenaline from stress. At this point vasoconstriction, the tightening of the blood vessels, allows less oxygen to the brain. The midbrain, the part we share with animals like dogs and bears, takes over. Rational thought goes out the window."[93]

'Auditory exclusion' mutes the sounds of battle, 'tunnel vision' impacts peripheral vision, pain from wounds is masked by adrenaline, memory loss results in repeated, futile, actions, distance perception is distorted, control over bowels and bladder may be lost. In other words, blind panic.

Casualties totalled 385 officers and 7,844 Other Ranks. Seven battalions lost 400+ officers and men. 72nd Brigade (24th Division) suffered over 2,000 casualties. It might have been worse had the Germans not ceased firing at the retreating survivors. According to the history of *Reserve Infanterie Regiment Nr. 15* the defenders were so 'nauseated by the sight of the massacre on what they called the *'leichenfeld von Loos'*, the 'Corpse Field of Loos', they allowed these men to escape.[94]

As the *Official History* says:

"Without sufficient artillery support, they went forward under terrific fire into a re-entrant held on three sides by the enemy, their flanks completely open… Gravely handicapped by having no previous initiation into the nature of war and by being kept too far back in general reserve, they were, as it turned out, asked to do the nearly impossible."[95]

'Nearly impossible'!? Let us call a spade a spade. This was a disgracefully incompetent sacrifice of thousands of young, naïve, novices in the art of war for which the commanders of the BEF, First Army, and XI Corps must all bear their share of responsibility. Just because Sir John French was the only one removed a few months later does not mean he was solely at fault.

This outcome was the cause of the most bitter, and final, dispute between French and Haig, which row the Scot won hands down. The positioning of these reserves, and their retention under French's hand until too late, were undoubtedly grave errors, but the bile directed by Haig against French in his diary suggests this costly fiasco was but the culmination of a series of crass errors of judgement made by French for a year (or more?). On 28th September, sensing a great opportunity had slipped through his fingers, Haig wrote:

"When the CinC remains blind to the lessons of the war in this important matter (handling of reserves) we hardly deserve to win."[96]

Such was Haig's anger he wrote to Kitchener the next day to complain vigorously about French's errors. Rather than dissipate, Haig's irritation seemed to concentrate and ferment. On 2nd October he reacted to a comment by French to Robertson that 'the second day of the battle was the correct time to put them in (i.e. Haking's Corps)' with:

"It seems impossible to discuss military problems with an unreasoning brain of this kind! At any rate, no good result is to be hoped from so doing."[97]

Two days later and Haig was complaining that:

"Sir John is very ignorant of the nature of the fighting which has taken place ever since Neuve Chapelle!"[98]

The next day it was:

"The fact is Sir John seems incapable of realising the nature of the fighting which has been going on."[99]

Finally, on 9th October, Haig was visited by Haldane, come to investigate the disaster of 26th September. Haig recited his litany of complaints about the handling of the reserves and, at long last, confirmed the two divisions should not have been used for this crucial advance in the first place:

"But the 21st and 24th Divisions, having only recently arrived in France, with staffs and commanders inexperienced in war, should not have been detailed for this work. It was courting disaster to employ them at once in fighting of this nature…"[100]

If this was so, why did Haig, at 2 p.m. on 25th September blithely order Haking:

"… to advance between Hulluch and Cité St Auguste, and occupy the high ground between Pont à Vendin and Haisnes[i] with the crossings over the Canal to the east and south of that line."[101]

Twenty-four hours later his diary entry (inaccurately) records:

"About lunch-time reports arrived that the 21st (Ramsay) and 24th (Forestier-Walker) which had been ordered to attack on the line Hulluch-Hill 70 had broken, and were coming back in great disorder."[102]

Leaving to one side that Ramsay[ii] was commander of 24th Division and Forester-Walker[iii] that of 21st Division, the attack started around 11.30 a.m., at a

---

[i] Actually Harnes. Haisnes is a village c. 1 mile south of La Bassée and was just behind the German 2nd line. It is two miles north of where the attack was made.

[ii] Maj. Gen. Sir John George Ramsay, CB, (1856-1920), 2nd son of Cdr John Douglas Ramsay, RN, and Harriet Young. Educated Queen Elizabeth's School, Ipswich, and Stubbington House, Hampshire, (a noted crammer for prospective naval officers). Sub-lieutenant, 14th (Buckinghamshire) Regiment, 1875. Joined Bengal Staff Corps, 1877. Afghan War 1878-80. Promoted Capt., 1886. Hazara Expedition, 1888. DAAG, Bengal, 1890-5. NW Frontier 1897-8 including defence of Malakand. Relief of Pekin, 1900. AAG 2nd Division, Northern Army Corps, India, 1904-5. Commanded Rawalpindi Brigade, 1907, Jhelum Brigade 1907-8, 3rd Brigade, Mohmand Field Force 1908, Kohat Brigade 1908-9 and Bangalore Brigade 1909-11. Colonel, 24th Punjabis. Maj. Gen., 1910. Retired, 1912. He married Ethel Cave, third daughter of Maj. Gen. George Noble Cave, Bengal Staff Corps, in 1878.

[iii] Maj. Gen. Sir George Townshend Forestier-Walker KCB (1866–1939), 3rd son of George Edmund Lushington Walker and Camilla Georgina Calder. Educated Rugby and the RMA, Woolwich. Commissioned, Royal Artillery, 1884. DAAG, staff in South Africa 1899-1900. At *Modder River*, Magersfontein, Paardeberg, etc. East Africa 1900-02. Chief Staff Officer in operations in Somaliland in 1903. ADC, King George V, 1907-15. AAG Southern Command, 1910. Brig. Gen. General Staff, Irish Command, 1912. Chief of Staff, II Corps, 1914. GOC, 21st Division, April 1915. GOC, 65th (2nd Lowland) Division and 63rd (2nd Northumbrian) Division, 1916. GOC, 27th Division

time when there was already evidence of a hardening of the German defences as reinforcements rushed into position. It was over by 2 p.m. and the remnants of the two divisions were, by then, in full retreat. The delay in making these troops available was French's fault as was the selection of such green units for such an important role. Haig, however, committed the troops knowing of their inexperience but not, apparently, taking due note of the inevitable strengthening of the enemy defences. Ordering them forward to the crossings on the *Canal de la Haute Deûle* seems a decision made based on the status of the fighting in the afternoon of the 25th September and not the reality of the situation in the late morning of the 26th. The lion's share of culpability may well be laid at French's door. Haig, however, cannot escape scot-free.

Ironically, given the attitudes of certain British Generals to the tactical acumen of their French equivalents, that this entire episode was a serious mistake in the making had been previously recognised by Joffre and Foch. A French paper, dated 12th September 1915 and written after a meeting of French Army Group commanders and Joffre and reflecting on the problems of the reserves on the first day of the Second Battle of Artois, had identified the positioning and control of these two completely inexperienced divisions and the Guards Divisions as a significant weakness in the British plan of attack. Commenting on French's plan to retain control of the reserve until the last minute, the report stated 'these divisions risked arriving too late to exploit the initial success'. It then said these Divisions needed to pass under Haig's control *before* the attack started, not after.[103]

Sir John French was a liability the BEF simply could not afford and his return to England in December was long overdue. Haig, however, cannot escape criticism for the conduct of the advance of these troops and for committing them to a hopeless attack against a German 2nd position still heavily wired and relatively undamaged but which had also been recently reinforced. Exhausted and hungry and, no doubt, nervous and unsure, these first elements of Kitchener's Citizen Army were squandered in an attack which would not have taken place were it not been for Haig's belief that this breakthrough battle, which in his mind Loos had now become, could still be won. Kitchener demanded the BEF support the French attack in Artois to the utmost. He had not demanded First Army breakthrough the German lines. Indeed, in early 1916, he would make it clear to Haig and others that he, like Foch, did not believe it possible to breakthrough, something Haig simply did not accept. Writing after the war, and in response to the initial draft of the volume of the *Official History* describing Loos, one of the key participants, Hubert Gough commanding I Corps, was highly critical of the attempt to break through the German defences. What was essential was First Army should pin German reserves in their front to give the French to the south the best opportunity for a major advance. Instead, and despite his initial views about the Loos sector, Haig's plans became increasingly ambitious, a trend seen at many battles both before and after. Gough, indeed, described the operation as 'very ambitious'. He then went on:

BEF then Salonika. Retired 1920. Col. Cdt. RA, 1931. Married Lady Mary Maud Diana Liddell, daughter of Henry George Liddell, 2nd Earl of Ravensworth, 1892.

"Should not the attack have been strictly limited in its objectives? Such an attack, if successful, would have drawn as many reserves as it actually did. It would not have caused such heavy casualties and such disappointment. If the French had met with some marked success in our vicinity it would then not have been difficult to organise and launch fresh attacks on our front. If they failed, as turned out to be the case, heavy casualties in attempting to get forward would have been avoided.
Haig's optimism in these operations, as in many others, obscured his judgement and led to heavy casualties in attempts to advance and decisively defeat the German Army, with very insufficient means." [104]

As on the *Somme*, the fighting now disintegrated into a series of desultory but costly penny packet attacks, punctuated by more major assaults notable only by the proportionately greater casualties incurred. The battle effectively ended with yet another appallingly costly attack by the Territorials of 46th (North Midland) Division, recently brought down from Ypres. This attack on the Hohenzollern redoubt on 13th October (the last part of which was lost to German counterattacks ten days earlier) was, perhaps, the low-water mark. Shamefully badly organised and supported, the men of the North Midlands were hung out to dry in an attack as pointless as it was costly. The severe losses in officers and NCOs, 180 officers and 3,583 other ranks, undermined the abilities of this unit for months to come. It had not recovered by the time it was carelessly flung against the northern flank of the Gommecourt salient on 1st July, a setback nearly as severe.

The *Official History's* description of the later fighting at Loos as nothing more than the 'useless slaughter of infantry' is unusually, but correctly, critical.[105] The 62,000 casualties incurred during the main fighting (50,370) and subsidiary operations (11,333) testify to this statement. The ratio of British to German casualties of c. three to one reinforces it.

What was learned from these unhappy experiences, and would the next British offensive be any more successful? If Haig's diary comment written on Sunday, 7th November 1915, shortly after the end of the Battle of Loos, is anything to go by then the answer to this question is, perhaps, 'not a lot':

"Sunday, 7th November 1915
If we only act methodically and after full consideration of the situation, we must win without much difficulty."[106]

Or, rather, something might have been learned (i.e. being methodical) but this was then forgotten as, once more, the tantalising prospect of breakthrough re-asserted itself in Sir Douglas's mind.

The other vital issue was: who would be in command of the BEF by that time? The answer to this essential question was: Sir Douglas Haig.

IT IS INSTRUCTIVE TO NOTE THE DIFFERING RESPONSES to the fighting of 1915 on either side of No Man's Land. Whilst Foch and Pétain developed their artillery-based theories involving repeated but limited attacks with the intention of conserving their infantry whilst wearing down the enemy, the BEF clung on to pre-war notions about the essential nature of the bayonet and of linear (wave) assault formations, only now they were preceded by the heaviest possible artillery preparation (but without the necessary emphasis on counter battery work).

During the various battles in 1915, the BEF flirted with, and retreated from, novelty. At Neuve Chapelle it was the use of 2.75-in. mountain guns dragged into the front lines and tasked with the destruction of German machine guns. Armed only with shrapnel this tactic failed. At Aubers Ridge two 18-pdrs from 104th Battery, RFA, were placed 350 yards from the German breastworks from where they fired over open sights. One blasted a six-yard hole in the breastworks through which a small party of infantry from 24th Brigade made a temporary entry whilst nearly everywhere else the attackers were cut down on their own parapet or in No Man's Land. Although never employed at Aubers Ridge because of the general failure, some ancillary units were attached to the lead Brigades, the purpose of which was to deal with the type of German strongpoints which prevented further advances after the initial break-in at Neuve Chapelle. These consisted of 'infantry artillery' to be man-handled forward to provide direct fire support against obstructions. Thus, trench mortars and mountain guns were made available to the troops should they advance. Had the attack been significantly successful then 7th Division, ready to exploit a breakthrough, had a fully mobile force available to deal with problems deeper into the German lines. A squadron of cavalry, mobile machine guns, trench mortars, Royal Engineer companies, four field guns and a Hotchkiss gun mounted on a lorry, were all waiting behind the lines ready to exploit a German collapse. They were never employed at Aubers Ridge.

At Festubert six 18-pdrs fired into the German breastworks from the British front line causing considerable damage. But the German machine guns and artillery went unsuppressed and, again, the infantry attacks broke down. Had they succeeded, however, mountain guns, trench mortars and two RE companies were ready to move to the support of the infantry in the event direct fire support was required. They did not advance.

Finally, at Loos, where Haig placed so much faith in the first use of asphyxiating gas, four 2.75-in. mountain guns were deployed in the front line tasked, as at Neuve Chapelle, with destroying enemy machine guns. The problem was that failing in this task inevitably led to heavy infantry casualties and, on the 47th (2nd London) Division's front, two German MGs survived to cause heavy casualties as the men advanced.

The repeated failures of such initiatives, even if most never saw action, persuaded GHQ that the old ways were the best. Somehow, if they could get men into the enemy's trenches with the bayonet, all would be well. Man, rifle and bayonet following on a prolonged bombardment was both metaphorically and literally the way forward. Linear tactical formations also meant that direct fire infantry support weapons, unless always at the leading edge of the advance, were of no use. An Inventions Committee formed at GHQ in June 1915 tasked with investigating new ideas for trench warfare soon subsided into an under-manned and unofficial Experimental Section, RE. Novelty within the BEF was at an end.

The German response was different. At *OHL* was *Oberst* Max Hermann Bauer, a pre-war *protegé* of Erich Ludendorff and one of the most significant staff officers of the war. By 1915, Bauer was aged 46. He planned to study law but his father's financial woes led him to join the army as an *Offiziersaspirant* in *Fußartillerie-Regiment von Hindersin (1. Pommersches) Nr. 2.* He attended the *Kriegsschule* in Hannover before serving with various heavy artillery regiments (*Fußartillerie*) in Gdansk, Swinemünde, and Metz. In 1899 he was attached to the *Artillerieprüfungskommission*, the *Artillery Examination Commission*[i]. Between 1902 and 1907 he commanded a battery of the *Westfälischen Fußartillerie-Regiment Nr. 7* before, in October 1907, joining the *Großer Generalstab* as an artillery specialist. Such an elevation was highly unusual as Bauer had not attended the *Kriegsakademie*, the normal route for such appointments. Bauer made a special study of trench warfare in the Russo-Japanese War focussing much on the siege of Port Arthur. In this he was helped by the fact that *Krupp* partially developed the town's defences in the 1880s when it was still under Chinese rule. Prior to this, Bauer indulged in a little espionage, spending time in Poland masquerading as a timber merchant to investigate Russia's fortifications around Vilnius and Kaunas in Lithuania, Grodno (now Belarus), and Lomza (eastern Poland). Then, acting as a journalist for the German magazine *Die Woche*, he further researched developments in Russian artillery as well as visiting the fortress cities of Liège, Namur, and Antwerp in Belgium.

Bauer's research on Port Arthur led him to place an unauthorised order for a new heavy *Mörser* with *Krupp*. He noted the effectiveness of the 28 cm (11-inch) coastal howitzers in the final bombardment prior to the fall of the port and believed even larger weapons were needed to deal with the European defences he had recently investigated. Instead of the sack, such high-handed actions received official approval when the new weapons proved highly successful. The end product, in 1912, was the *kurze Marinekanone 14 L/12*, or the *Minenwerfer-Gerät*, a 42 cm *Mörser* which, at the beginning of the war, helped crush the forts around Liège and opened the way for the invasion of Belgium.

On the outbreak of war Bauer was attached to *OHL* as head of Section II, responsible for heavy artillery, mortars, fortifications, and munitions. Amongst various 'innovations' Bauer suggested to von Falkenhayn was that chemical weapons be tested. He then worked closely with chemist Fritz Haber in the development and deployment of asphyxiating gas, an act contrary to the 1907 Hague Convention of which Germany was a signatory.

But Bauer did not just develop and test new munitions and equipment[ii]. New tactics were also his field. Early in 1915 he formed three new units called collectively *Front Versuchtruppen der Oberste Heeresleitung* or 'Front line experimental units of the Supreme Command'. These involved different infantry support weapons: flamethrowers (a *Flammenwerfer-Abteilung* commanded by *Hauptmann*

---

[i] The *Artillerieprüfungskommission* was founded in 1809 and combined elements of the field and foot artillery and the Navy. Since 1875 they used a firing range comprising 911 hectares on the Kummersdorf estate 45 kms south of Berlin.

[ii] Bauer involved himself in the machinations which brought the removal of Erich von Falkenhayn and replacement by Hindenburg and his pre-war mentor Ludendorff, as well as the removal of the Chancellor, Theobald von Bethmann Hollweg. Post-war he was involved alongside Ludendorff in the failed Kapp Putsch in March 1920 which sought to overthrow the Weimar Republic and he was forced to leave Germany for five years. In 1927 he became Chang Kai-shek's military adviser in China. He died from smallpox on 6th May 1929.

Hermann Reddemann[i]), trench mortars (a *Grabenmörser-Abteilung* commanded by Maj. Lothes), and assault guns (a *Sturmkanonen-Abteilung* commanded by Maj. Calsow[ii] and equipped with 3.7 cm *Krupp* field guns).

Sturmabteilung Calsow was formed in early March and comprised two companies of engineers and twenty guns. They tested both their equipment and their tactics over realistic trench systems with the idea being the guns would help breach the front-line defences and then advance alongside the infantry in order to deal with hardened defences to the rear, and any infantry reserves being brought up. That was the theory, but, in practice, either the innate conservatism of the commander or a misunderstanding as to their purpose by more senior commanders, led to the guns being established in front line positions built for them by *Pioniers* around Notre Dame de Lorette in Artois. They then became part of the static defences and lost heavily as the guns were easily spotted by the enemy and retaliatory fire was heavy. Casualties amongst guns and men reached 50%.

Only when Calsow was replaced in September 1915 by *Hauptmann* Willy Rohr[iii], a company commander from the *Garde-Schützen-Bataillon*; the ineffective 3.7 cm guns replaced by cut down 7.62 mm Russian field guns; and the unit reinforced with machine guns, trench mortars and *flammenwerfers* did matters improve. Without interference from above and working closely with Reddemann and his newly established *Garde-Reserve-Pionier-Bataillon 3*, Rohr rapidly developed a new theory of infantry tactics based on *Stosstruppgedanke* (assault squads), small groups which infiltrated at speed, in depth and with a variety of weapons. *Sturmabteilung Rohr* then proved its worth at the *Schratzmännele* (part of a range of four hills in the Vosges c. 4 kms north of Munster[iv]) in October 1915 and at *Hartmannsweilerkopf* in the southern Vosges on 22nd December and 10th January 1916. On 22nd February 1916 Rohr's unit was attached to the *6. Division* of the *III Armeekorps* and fought at Azannes, Herbebois, and Fort Douaumont in the Battle of Verdun. On 1st April 1916 it became a *Sturmbataillon* of four companies with a special training ground constructed at Beuveille, near the village of Doncourt-lès-Longuyon, south-west of Longwy. Here, the unit conducted two-week training courses in the new tactics as they were disseminated throughout the German Army and on to the Austrian,

---

[i] Formerly chief of the Leipzig Fire Brigade and a *Landwehr* officer. Reddemann read accounts of the Japanese using flamethrowers at Port Arthur and simulated the use of them with his unit in peace time. He developed a two-man back-pack flamethrower first employed with great success against the French at Malancourt in February 1915.

[ii] An engineer from *Samländisches Pionier Bataillon Nr. 18*. Samland is a Baltic peninsula north of Koenigsberg/Kaliningrad in what was East Prussia.

[iii] Wilhelm Martin Ernst Rohr was born in Metz in 1877. Joined *3. Magdeburgische Infanterie-Regiment Nr. 66*, 1896. Later a battalion and regimental adjutant. Promoted *Oberleutnant* in 1906 he was an instructor at the *Infanterie-Schießschule* in Wünsdorf in 1911-2. Promoted captain he joined the *10. Rheinischen Infanterie-Regiment Nr. 161* in Trier. In 1913 he took command of the *3. Kompanie* of the *Garde-Schützen-Bataillon*. He served on the *Aisne* and in Champagne before taking over the *Sturmabteilung*.

[iv] The museum at the *Mémorial du Linge*, the northern most of the hills, retains trench systems and dugouts from the fighting in this area: *Collet du Linge*, 68370 Orbey, France [http://www.linge1915.com/en/home/]

Bulgarian and Ottoman Armies. Another fifteen *Sturmbataillons* were formed by the end of 1916 as Rohr's tactical ideas established themselves. They would form the basis of German assault tactics through to the end of World War Two[i].

There was no similar British technical and tactical development during this time. The devolved system of command in the German Army lent itself well to the tactics Rohr developed but such an approach found no echo within the BEF where an absence of suitably trained junior officers and NCOs, a distrust of the New Armies, and a stultifying hierarchical and conservative approach to modern industrial war and its demands led to the hopelessly inept tactics adopted by Rawlinson and Haig throughout 1915 and 1916.

ACCORDING TO THE *BRITISH OFFICIAL HISTORY*, once it was decided Sir John French must go, and with Sir Horace Smith-Dorrien conveniently out of the way, only two people were under serious consideration or the post of commander of the BEF: Haig and Gen. Sir William Robertson, who was French's Chief of Staff throughout 1915. Robertson, however, had never commanded any large force in the field and did not seriously entertain becoming CinC, believing Haig to be the better man for the job. That is, if Haig's diary is taken at face value:

> "Thursday 25th November 1915
> Sir William Robertson came to see me about 9.30... He told me Lord Esher was going to France tomorrow to break the news to Sir John that he is to be recalled. R. (Robertson) said he was going back to St Omer in case he might be required by Sir John. He added that the selection of a successor lay between me and him, but he of course was out of the question and that there was no one in it but me!"[107]

Robertson is the only man in the history of the British Army to rise from the ranks to become a Field Marshal, but his lack of a significant command in the field perhaps counted against him. Although he lost out to Haig in this appointment, within a few days he was installed in another essential role – Chief of the Imperial General Staff. Here he became Haig's close ally, if not his friend. This appointment was confirmed on 23rd December, with Robertson succeeding Lt. Gen. Sir Archibald Murray as the CIGS.

Robertson was to play an increasingly influential role in the conduct of the war. At the time of his appointment as CIGS he was one-month short of his 56th birthday[ii]. Born in 1860, an underage Robertson, having spent the previous four years in domestic service, enlisted in the 16th (Queen's) Lancers in 1877, to his mother's severe disapproval. By dint of extremely hard work, study and practice he was promoted Troop Sergeant Major in 1885 and, so impressed were his superiors by his diligence and intelligence, he was recommended for a commission.

---

[i] Rohr's unit became *Sturmbataillon Nr. 5* in February 1917.
[ii] He was born on 29th January 1860 in Welbourn, a small village (pop. c. 700) in North Kesteven District, Lincolnshire, eldest son of the tailor and postmaster Thomas Robertson and his wife Ann. There is a large memorial on a wall in the parish church, St Chad's. He gives his name to the local secondary school, the Sir William Robertson Academy (previously the Sir William Robertson High School).

Having passed the necessary examinations he was promoted 2nd Lieutenant in the 3rd Dragoon Guards in 1888 with which unit he went to India. Being prevented by his lack of wealth and social standing from participating in the popular interests of the average cavalry officer, these being polo, pigsticking, drinking and other officers' wives, he spent his spare time learning six languages: Urdu, Hindi, Persian, Pushtu, Punjabi, and Gurkhali. Such dedication saw him gain a role in the intelligence department at Simla. In 1895, he accompanied the Chitral Expedition, during which he caught dysentery and was nearly murdered by traitorous native guides. He ended the campaign with a Mention in Despatches and, later, the DSO.

The year before, Robertson made a useful marriage to Mildred Adelaide Palin, second daughter of Lt. Gen. Charles Palin, Indian Army. Having gained a degree of much needed, and highly useful, 'social standing', Robertson's career took another upward swing in 1896 when he was nominated to attend the Staff College by the then CinC India, Gen. Sir George White[i]. Robertson thus became the first 'ranker' ever to attend the Staff College. To pass the examinations he received special early morning tuition in mathematics, French and German before performing his normal daytime functions. At Camberley, he came under the influence of Col. G F R Henderson, and he rubbed shoulders with numerous officers who went on to prominence, if not success, in the World War. One Douglas Haig was amongst his new colleagues.

Early in the South African War, Robertson gained a place in the intelligence section of Lord Roberts' HQ under his mentor, Henderson. After nine months, he returned to the War Office where he started to work with politicians and civil servants – an activity he loathed. Head of the foreign section of the intelligence department of the War Office until 1907, he travelled extensively in Western Europe and the Balkans, broadening his knowledge of the military and strategic situations in these areas. Between 1907 and 1910 he undertook various roles at Aldershot under Smith-Dorrien and it was here he first met the future King George V. He then added to his list of 'firsts' by becoming the first man from the ranks to be appointed Commandant of the Staff College. Here he aimed at a practical education for the officers attending, teaching, usefully as it turned out in the autumn of 1914, the finer points of the withdrawal as well as of the advance. At the end of his time at Camberley he was appointed Director of Military Training at the War Office on 9th October 1913. During this time, he played a significant role in the near mutiny of certain cavalry units during the Curragh Incident from which imbroglio he managed to emerge with his reputation unscathed.

On the outbreak of war, he was almost immediately ordered to replace

---

[i] Gen. Sir George Stuart White, VC, GCB, OM, GCSI, GCMG, GCIE, GCVO, won his VC during the Second Afghan War at the Battle of Charasiab in October 1879 and was commander at the siege of Ladysmith, 1899-1900. Promoted Field Marshal, 1903 he died in 1912. His son, 'Jack' White, DSO, fought in South Africa, campaigned against the Protestant cause in Ulster, helping found the Irish Citizen Army in 1913, was a colleague of Roger Casement's, and was in Pentonville on the day of Casement's execution. He espoused socialism and came into contact with Anarchists whilst in Spain during the Spanish Civil War. He died in 1946.

Archibald Murray as the Quartermaster General of the BEF, in which role his organisation of the logistics of the Expeditionary Force did much to help it through the trying times of the retreat from Mons. At the end of January 1915, he was appointed Chief of Staff of the BEF, despite knowing he was not French's first choice and, more pointedly, despite having no faith in French as CinC. In this he shared the views of Douglas Haig, commander of the BEF's First Army. Robertson, typically, was not backward in coming forward with his opinions of French, and his views were regularly transmitted to key figures in London. In addition, he made it quite clear to his contacts in the UK the strengthening of the role of the Imperial General Staff was crucial to counter-act both the meddling, as he saw it, of politicians and also the less than useful strategic recommendations of that fading 'Titan' of the late Victorian Army, Lord Kitchener.

His predecessor as QMG in the BEF, Archibald Murray, was appointed CIGS in September 1915 but Robertson was not satisfied with his appointment. When, in December 1915, French was ousted by Haig as CinC, the 'Palace Coup' was completed by Robertson's installation as CIGS on 23rd December 1916. The partnership of Haig as CinC and Robertson as CIGS took the Army through three of its largest and bloodiest campaigns on the Western Front over the next two years. In public, Robertson supported Haig in everything he did. In private, his concerns about Haig's tactics were shrewdly judged but never voiced to a wider audience. A case of mis-placed loyalty, perhaps.

That Robertson took with him Brig. Gen. George Macdonogh, the BEF's excellent intelligence chief, to become Director of Military Intelligence (DMI) was almost as damaging[i]. Macdonogh's inadequate replacement was the untrained sometime fantasist and often incompetent John Charteris, later described by Macdonogh as 'a dangerous fool'.[108] Sadly, Haig too often distrusted the usually cautious and well-founded advice and information provided by the DMI. When Macdonogh's assessment of German morale contradicted Charteris's optimistic views, Haig exposed his religious bias[ii] when he wrote on 15th October 1917:

---

[i] Brig. Gen., later Lt. Gen., Sir George Mark Watson Macdonogh, GBE, KCB, KCMG, was born in 1865, the son of G V MacDonogh, Deputy Inspector of Hospitals, Royal Navy. RMA, Woolwich. Commissioned, Royal Engineers, 1884. He passed into the Staff College 2nd, 1895. DAAG, RE, Dublin, 1898. Brigade Major, School of Military Engineering, Chatham, 1901. DAQMG, Thames District, 1903 before re-joining the RE to serve in Gibraltar. GSO3, War Office, and GSO2, 1908. In 1910 he was appointed to lead a new counter-espionage unit called MO5 (later MI5).and was responsible for much of the Defence of the Realm Act (DORA) which was enacted on 8th August 1914. On the outbreak of war he was put in charge of the Intelligence Section at GHQ. In January 1916 he was made head of a new Directorate of Military Intelligence at the War Office. In September 1918 he was appointed Adjutant General, with the rank of Lt. Gen., and supervised the bulk of the demobilisation of the Army. He retired in 1925 and was a member of the Imperial War Graves Commission (later the CWGC) and of various company boards and associations, and a Royal Commission on Local Government. He died on 10th July 1942. Macdonogh was not wholly trusted by Haig because he converted from Methodism to Catholicism.
[ii] Haig and Charteris were Scots, Presbyterian, and Freemasons.

"I cannot think why the War Office Intelligence Department gives such a wrong picture of the situation except that General Macdonogh (DMI) is a Roman Catholic and is (unconsciously) influenced by information which doubtless reaches him from tainted [that is, Catholic] sources."[109]

But back to 'Wullie' Robertson. Eventually, his bad temper, ungracious behaviour, and a tendency to 'cook the books' lost him favour with Prime Minister, Lloyd George, and other key cabinet figures. He was even abandoned by Haig who, asked if he would have him as an Army commander, replied he 'was quite unfitted to command troops'.[110] Given control of Eastern Command and then made CinC Home Forces, Robertson was never far from rumours of political intrigue to unseat the much-loathed Lloyd George. It would take more than the alleged efforts of a ragbag of failed politicians, Asquith amongst them, journalists, and ex-military men, e.g. Trenchard and Jellicoe, to unseat the 'Welsh Wizard'.

In the meantime, if there was one thing above all which unified Haig and Robertson, other than their dislike of the Salonika Force and their commitment to the Western Front as the key arena of the war, it was their negative attitude, at times bordering on contempt, towards the majority of French Generals. Charteris takes this attitude a step further, using the word 'distrust' in his biography of Haig:

"Thus it was not the French Army and nation which Haig mistrusted: he believed they would rise to the occasion. But he was not equally convinced of the military capacity of the leaders in the field. Haig did not share the belief held by some of our soldiers and many prominent civilians in the infallibility of French military leadership. He could not forget that French leadership had been at fault in the initial appreciation of the situation in August 1914; that a French general had inspired the Salonika Expedition in the face of convinced opposition and advice from all of the British authorities."[111]

It is extraordinary to imagine Haig might damn Foch, Pétain and Fayolle because Sarrail had been despatched to Salonika. Furthermore, if there was an Allied General with a correct appreciation of the military situation on either the Western or Eastern Fronts in August 1914 then we have yet to hear of them. Had Haig, since that date, covered himself in glory at even one of the offensives over which he presided then, yes, he would have been in a position of professional and moral superiority over his French colleagues. Unfortunately, his brow was not yet crowned with a victor's laurels. His failures, indeed, proved relatively costlier, casualty for casualty, than those of the French in 1915. The need for the British to learn lessons from their experiences was just as great as for the French but, whilst the likes of Foch, Pétain and Fayolle did appear to have correctly analysed many of their failings against *current* German defensive tactics it, perhaps, comes as no surprise that Haig, with his dismissive attitude towards senior French officers, chose to learn different and, it turned out, disastrously incorrect lessons from the wreckage of the attacks he led.

Another question was: did he yet have the tools to finish the job? And the answer, in spite of all of the warnings, the pre-war planning, the examples from earlier wars and the massive growth of the British defence industry was: no.

Out with the Old — In with the Nearly New

118 Field Marshal Sir John French
CinC, BEF, Aug. 1914-Dec. 1915

119 Gen. Sir Douglas Haig
CinC, BEF, Dec. 1915-Nov. 1918

120 Gen. Sir Archibald James Murray
CIGS, Feb-Dec. 1915

121 Lt. Gen. Sir William Robert Robertson, CIGS, Dec. 1915-Feb. 1918

122 Lt. Gen. Sir George Mark Watson Macdonogh, GSO1 (Intelligence) BEF 1914-5

123 Brig. Gen. John Charteris
GSO1 (Intelligence) I Corps, First Army, BEF, 1914-8

ENDNOTES

[1] Mead, G, *The Good Soldier: The Biography of Douglas Haig*, Atlantic Books, 2014, page 74.
[2] Ibid., pages 67-8.
[3] Green, Andrew, *Writing the Great War: Sir James Edmonds and the Official Histories, 1915-1948*, Routledge, 2003, page 24.
[4] Bond, B, *The Victorian Army and the Staff College*, Eyre Methuen, 1972, page 163.
[5] Ibid.
[6] Ibid.
[7] Wavell, Gen Sir A P, *Allenby: A Study in Greatness*, G G Harrap & Co., 1940, pages 62-3.
[8] Green, op. cit., page 25.
[9] Bond, op. cit., page 164, and Green, op. cit., page 25.
[10] Ibid.
[11] Scott, D, ed., *The Preparatory Prologue: Douglas Haig Diaries and Letters 1861-1914*, Pen & Sword, 2006, page 260.
[12] Anglesey, op. cit., page 422.
[13] *The Times, Spread of the Labour War*, 16th August 1911, page 6.
[14] *The Times*, 3rd September 1912, page 2.
[15] Ibid., 13th September 1912, page 13.
[16] NA, WO 279/47, 'Report on Army Manoeuvres, 1912', p.162, quoted in Whitmarsh, A, *Far from a "Useless and Expensive Fad". Aircraft at the British Army Manoeuvres, 1910-13'*.
[17] Haig. D., ed. Scott, D, *Diaries and Letters 1861-1914*, Pen & Sword, 2006, page 319.
[18] Charteris, J,
[19] *The Times*, 21st September 1912, page 7.
[20] Ibid., page 8.
[21] Warner P, *Field Marshal Earl Haig*, The Bodley Head, 1991, page 107.
[22] Anglesey, op. cit., page 383.
[23] Brett, M V, ed. *The Letters and Journals of Reginald, Viscount Esher*, Vol. II, Nicholson & Watons, 1934, page 401.
[24] NA, WO33/618, *Report on French Manoeuvres 1912*, page 20.
[25] Porch, op. cit., *The March to the Marne*, page 178.
[26] *The Times, French Army Manoeuvre*, 2nd October 1912, page 5.
[27] *The Aldershot Command Manoeuvres, The Times*, 16th September, 1913, page 3.
[28] *The Aldershot Command Manoeuvres, The Times*, 17th September, 1913, page 4.
[29] *The Times*, 27th September, 1913, page 6.
[30] Quoted in Warner, P, *Field-Marshal Earl Haig*, Bodley Head, 1991 and Cassell, 2001, pages 110–111
[31] *The Times*, 10th October, pages 7 and 8, and 16th October 1913, page 9.
[32] Charteris, John, *Field Marshal Earl Haig*, Cassell & Co., 1929, page 181.
[33] Edmonds, *Official History, 1915*, Vol. 1, pages 81-5, & Vol. II, pages 18-9, 52-5 & 163-7.
[34] Sheffield & Bourne, op. cit., page 98
[35] Smith Dorrien, *Memories*, op. cit., page 479.
[36] Holmes, R, *The Little Field Marshal: A Life of Sir John French*, Weidenfeld & Nicolson, 2004, page 223.
[37] Sheffield & Bourne, op. cit., page 98-9.
[38] Ibid., page 102.
[39] Willcocks, Gen. Sir J, *With the Indians in France*, Constable & Co., 1920, page 203.
[40] NA, WO95/708, *Memorandum on the Attack on Neuve Chapelle by First Army*.
[41] Sheffield & Bourne, op, cit.,
[42] NA, WO95/708, *IV Corps, March 1915, The attack of Neuve Chapelle*.
[43] Ibid.
[44] Sheffield & Bourne, op, cit., page 105.
[45] Ibid.
[46] Ibid. Emphasis in Sheffield & Bourne's text.

[47] *NA*, WO95/708, *Report on Operations of IV Corps from 8th to 14th March 1915*.
[48] *Rawlinson Papers*, Rawlinson to Kitchener, 1st April 1915.
[49] Sheffield & Bourne, op, cit., page 111.
[50] Huguet, Gen., *Britain and the War: A French Indictment*, Cassell & Co., 1928, page 179.
[51] Blake, op. cit., page 91.
[52] Sheffield & Bourne, op. cit., page 116.
[53] Ibid.
[54] Prior R, Wilson T, *Command on the Western Front*, Pen & Sword 2004, page 85.
[55] *NA*, PRO30/57/51.
[56] *NA*, WO158/17, *General Staff: Notes on operations. 15th March 1915*.
[57] *BOH, France and Belgium 1915*, Vol. 2, page 46.
[58] Huguet, op. cit., page 188.
[59] *BOH, France and Belgium 1915*, Vol. 2, page 47.
[60] Ibid., page 53.
[61] Ibid., footnote, page 53.
[62] *BOH, France & Belgium 1915*, Vol. 2, footnote page 33.
[63] Ibid., pages 47 and 53.
[64] Ibid., footnote page 75.
[65] Ibid., footnote page 76.
[66] Ibid., page 78.
[67] *Rawlinson Diaries*, 4th June 1915.
[68] Ibid., 13th June 1915.
[69] Ibid., 24th June 1915.
[70] *NA*, WO95/710, *IV Corps report, 21st June 1915*.
[71] Sheffield & Bourne, op. cit., page 128.
[72] Ibid., pages 128-9.
[73] Blake, op. cit., page 96.
[74] Sheffield & Bourne, page 121.
[75] Ibid., page 133.
[76] Ibid., page 134.
[77] Ibid., page 135.
[78] Blake, op. cit., page 101-2.
[79] *BOH, France and Belgium 1915*, Vol. 2, page 153.
[80] *BOH, France and Belgium 1915*, Vol. 2, page 153-4.
[81] Sheffield & Bourne, op. cit., page 139.
[82] Ibid., page 141.
[83] See *BOH, France and Belgium 1915*, Vol. 2, page 136.
[84] Sheffield & Bourne, page 149.
[85] *BOH, France and Belgium 1915*, Vol. 2, page 154.
[86] Huguet, op. cit., page 193.
[87] *Rawlinson Diaries*, 17th September 1915.
[88] *BOH, France and Belgium 1915*, Vol. 2, page 155.
[89] For the complete story see either Niall Cherry's *Most Unfavourable Ground* (Helion, 2005), Nick Lloyd's *Loos 1915* (The History Press, 2008), or Philp Warner's *The Battle of Loos* (re-printed by Pen & Sword, 2009). For detailed accounts for parts of the battlefield see the *Battleground Europe – French Flanders* series by Pen & Sword.
[90] Ibid., page 166.
[91] Sheffield & Bourne, page 153.
[92] *BOH, France and Belgium 1915*, Vol. 2, page 267.
[93] From a summary by S McKinney, School of Conflict Analysis and Resolution, George Mason University of Grossman, D & Christensen L W, *On Combat: The Psychology and Physiology of Deadly Conflict in War and Peace*. 2nd ed. PPCT Research Publications, 2007.
[94] Forstner, *Das Reserve Infanterie Regiment 15*, Berlin, 1929, pages 226-32.
[95] *BOH*, 1915, Vol. 2, page 344.

96 Sheffield & Bourne, op. cit., page 159.
97 Ibid., page 161.
98 Ibid., page 162.
99 Blake, op. cit., page 106.
100 Ibid., page 107.
101 Sheffield & Bourne, op. cit., page 154.
102 Ibid., page 155.
103 *AFdGG*, Tome III, Annexes Vol. 2, Annexe 1386, page 888
104 *NA*, CAB 45/120, General Sir H. Gough to Edmonds, 23rd July 1926
105 *BOH, France and Belgium 1915*, Vol II, page 388.
106 *NA*, WO256/6.
107 Ibid.
108 Imperial War Museum, *Kirke manuscript*.
109 Sheffield and Bourne, pages 337-7.
110 Jeffery, K, *Field Marshal Sir Henry Wilson*, op. cit., page 218.
111 Charteris, *Haig*, op. cit. page 187.

ALSO AVAILABLE:
THE LONG ROAD TO THE SOMME
VOLUME II:
PLANNING THE BIG PUSH

The Chantilly Conference
The planning of the French and British campaigns
The relationships between *GQG* and GHQ
The impact of Verdun on French planning
The effect of the Austrian and Russian offensives on the war
The tactical development of the French and British Armies
prior to 1st July 1916
Reasons for success and failure

Glossary

Military Ranks and abbreviations

Britain	France	Germany
Field Marshal	Maréchal de France	Generalfeldmarschall
General	Général d'Armée	Generaloberst
Lieutenant General	Général de Corps d'Armée	General der Infanterie[1]
Major General	Général de Division	Generalleutnant
Brigadier General	Général de Brigade	Generalmajor
Colonel	Colonel	Oberst
Lieutenant Colonel	Lieutenant-Colonel	Oberstleutnant
Major	Commandant	Major
Captain	Capitaine	Hauptmann
Lieutenant	Lieutenant	Oberleutnant
Second Lieutenant	Sous-Lieutenant	Leutnant
	Aspirant	Fähnrich/Kadett
Regimental Sergeant Major	Adjutant-Chef[2]	Feldwebel-Leutnant
Company Sergeant Major	Adjutant[3]	Vizefeldwebel
Sergeant	Sergent-Major/Sergent	Feldwebel
Lance Sergeant		
Corporal	Caporal	Unteroffizer
Lance Corporal		
Private/Rifleman	Soldat 1/2.eme classe	Gefreiter

[1] Or General der Kavallerie/Artillerie [2] Maréchal de Logis-Chef (Artillery/Cavalry)
[3] Maréchal de Logis (Artillery/Cavalry)

British Military Organisation
British Expeditionary Force:
Army – made up of Corps and other services. There were four Armies plus a Reserve Army (soon to be renumbered Fifth Army) in June 1916. Commanded by a full General.
Corps – Numbered I to XVII Corps. In addition, I and II Anzac Corps and the Canadian Corps. Normally three Divisions. Corps controlled the siege and heavy artillery. Commanded by a Lt. Gen.
Divisions – three infantry Brigades, Pioneer battalion, Royal Field Artillery Brigades (inc. heavy trench mortar batteries), Field Companies, Royal Engineers, Field Ambulances, RAMC, other services. Divisions mainly controlled the field artillery. Commanded by a Maj. Gen.
Brigades – four infantry battalions, light trench mortar battery, machine gun company, and ancillary units. Commanded by a Brig. Gen.
Battalions – four companies of infantry, a Battalion headquarters with transport, stretcher bearers, etc., Lewis Gun teams, and Battalion bombers. 1,000 men of whom 800 might take part in an assault. Sometimes 700 men or less. with just 550 or so 'effectives. Normally commanded by a Lt. Col. but often by Majors and even Captains.
Companies – four Platoons of 200 men but sometimes half that number. Usual company designation A, B C and D, but sometimes W, X, Y and Z, or 1, 2, 3 and 4. Commanded by a Captain, Lieutenant, 2nd Lieutenant or, in extremis, by the CSM.
Platoons – numbered 1 to 16 and made up of Sections. Anything from 50 to 25 men commanded by a 2nd Lieutenant, a senior sergeant or, *in extremis*, whoever was available.

British Military Terms and Positions
CIGS – Chief of the Imperial General Staff
GHQ – General Headquarters (France & Flanders)
AG – Adjutant General
AAG – Assistant Adjutant General
DAAG – Deputy Assistant Adjutant General
QMG – Quartermaster General
DQMG – Deputy Quartermaster General
GOC – General Officer Commanding (Brigade upwards)
MGGS – Major General, General Staff (Corps)
BGGS – Brigadier General, General Staff (Division)
MGRA – Major General, Royal Artillery (Army)
BGRA – Brigadier General, Royal Artillery (Corps)
GSO – General Staff Officer (Grades 1 to 3, e.g. GSO1)
RMA – Royal Military Academy, Woolwich
RMC – Royal Military College, Sandhurst

French military abbreviations
GQG – Grand Quartier Général
GAN – Groupe d'Armées du Nord
GAC – Groupe d'Armées du Centre
GAE – Groupe d'Armées de l'Est
RfV – Région fortifiée de Verdun
RfD – Région fortifiée de Dunkerque
CAC – Corps d'Armée Colonial
CC – Corps de Cavalerie
DI – Division d'Infanterie
DC – Division de Cavalerie
DIC – Division d'Infanterie Coloniale
BIC – Brigade d'Infanterie Coloniale
RI – Régiment d'Infanterie
RIC – Régiment d'Infanterie Colonial
DIT – Division d'Infanterie Territoriale
RIT – Régiment d'Infanterie Territorial
BCP – Bataillon de Chasseurs à Pied
BCA – Bataillon de Chasseurs Alpin
RAL – Régiment d'Artillerie Lourde (Heavy artillery)
RALH– Régiment d'Artillerie Lourde Hippomobile (Heavy artillery horse drawn)
RALT– Régiment d'Artillerie Lourde Tracteur (Heavy artillery tractor drawn)
RAP – Régiment d'Artillerie à Pied (Heavy and super heavy artillery)
RAC– Régiment d'Artillerie de Campagne (Field artillery and trench artillery)

Appendix 1: The Virginia Campaigns 1864-5

Action	Union Strength	Union Casualties	Rebel Strength	Rebel Casualties	Winner
Overland Campaign May-June 1864					
Wilderness, 5th-7th May	124000	17700	65000	11000	Inconclusive
Spotsylvania Court House, 8th-21st May	110000	18400	63000	12700	Inconclusive
Yellow Tavern (cavalry), 11th May	12000	625	5000	300	Union
North Anna, 23rd-26th May	100000	4000	53000	1550	Inconclusive
Haw's Shop (cavalry), 28th May	4000	365	4500	378	Inconclusive
Totopotomoy Creek, 28th-30th May		730		1600	Union
Cold Harbor, 31st May-12th June	117000	12700	62000	5300	Rebel
Trevilian Station (cavalry), 11th-12th June	9300	1500	6800	810	Rebel
Saint Mary's Church, 24th June	2150	350	4000	250	Inconclusive
Richmond-Petersburg-Appomattox Campaigns June 1864-April 1865					
Assault on Petersburg, 15th-18th June	62000	11400	38000	4000	Rebel
Jerusalem Plank Road, 21st-23rd June	27000	2960	8000	570	Inconclusive
First Deep Bottom, 27th-29th July		488		679	Rebel
Battle of the Crater, 30th July	8500	3800	6100	1490	Rebel
Second Deep Bottom, 14th-20th Aug.	28000	2900	20000	1500	Rebel
Globe Tavern, 18th-21st Aug.	20000	4300	15000	1620	Union
Second Ream's Station, 25th Aug.	9000	2750	10000	814	Rebel
Chaffin's Farm, 29th-30th Sept.	26600	3380	14500	2000	Union
Peebles's Farm, 30th Sept.-2nd Oct.	29800	2890	10000	1240	Union
Boydton Plank Road, 27th-28th Oct.	30000	1760	11700	1300	Inconclusive
Hatcher's Run, 5th-7th Feb. 1865	34500	1540	13800	1160	Union
White Oak Road, 31st Mar.	22000	1870	8000	800	Union
Dinwiddie Court House (cavalry), 31st Mar.	9000	350	10600	760	Rebel
Fort Stedman, 25th Mar.	14900	1040	10000	4000	Union
Five Forks, 1st Apr.	22000	830	10600	2950	Union
Third Petersburg, 2nd Apr.	114000	3940	45000	5000	Union
Sailor's Creek, 6th Apr.	26000	1150	18500	7700	Union
Appomattox Court House, 9th Apr.	150000	164	28000	All	Union

Appendix 2: The Franco-Prussian War 1870-1

Action	French Strength	French Casualties	German Strength	German Casualties	Winner
Wissembourg, 4th Aug. 1870	8000	2300	25000	1550	Germany
Spicheren, 6th Aug.	29000	4000	37000	4880	Germany
Wœrth, 6th Aug.	50000	20000	75000	10600	Germany
Borny—Colombey, 14th Aug.	83500	3500	67500	4900	Inconclusive
Siege of Strasbourg, 15th Aug.-28th Sept.	23000	All	40000	930	Germany
Mars-la-Tour, 16th Aug.	80000	17000	80000	15800	Germany
Siege of Toul, 16th Aug.-23rd Sept.	2400	All	13000	?	Germany
Gravelotte, 18th Aug.	113000	28000	250000	20000	Germany

Action					
Siege of Metz, 19th Aug.-27th Oct.	154500	All	168000	5700	Germany
Beaumont, 30th Aug.	21000	4800	80000	3400	Germany
Noisseville, 31st Aug.-1st Sept.	96000	3500	69000	3000	Germany
Bazeilles, 1st Sept.		2600		4100	Bavarian
Sedan, 1st-2nd Sept.	130000	122000	200000	9900	Germany
Siege of Montmédy, 4th Sept.-14th Dec.	3000	All			Germany
Siege of Soissons, 11th Sept.-16th Oct.	4400	All	9000		Germany
Siege of Paris*, 19th Sept. 1870-28th Jan. 1871	400000	170000	240000	12000	Germany
Bellevue, 7th Oct. 1870		1800		1400	Germany
Châteaudun, 18th Oct.	1200	340	12000	3000	Germany
1st Dijon, 29th-30th Oct.					Germany
Siege of Belfort, 3rd Nov.1870-18th Feb. 1871	17700	All	40000	2000	Germany
Siege of La Fère, 5th-27th Nov. 1870	2800	2400			Germany
Coulmiers, 9th Nov.	70000	1500	20000	2100	France
Siege of Thionville, 13th-24th Nov.	4000	All			
Amiens, 27th Nov.	25000	2400	30000	1300	Germany
Beaune-la-Rolande, 28th Nov.	60000	8100	12000	850	Germany
Villepion, 1st Dec.	15000	1100	7000	1000	France
Loigny—Poupry, 2nd Dec.	45000	7000	35000	4100	Germany
Orléans, 3rd-4th Dec.	62000	20000	86000	1700	Germany
Beaugency, 8th-10th Dec.	110000		27000		Germany
2nd Dijon, 18th Dec.		1200		100	Germany
Hallue, 23rd-24th Dec.	40000	2300	22500	1000	Minor French
Bapaume, 3rd Jan. 1871	33000	1600	18000	800	Germany
Villersexel, 9th Jan.	20000	1350	15000	600	France
Le Mans, 10th-12th Jan.	100000	44200	73000	3600	Germany
3rd Dijon, 14th Jan.	4000		4000		Minor French
Lisaine, 15th-17th Jan.	110000	6000	40000	1900	Germany
St. Quentin, 19th Jan.	40000	12500	33000	2400	Germany
* Siege of Paris includes these actions:					
Chevilly, 30th Sept. 1870		2100		440	Germany
1st Buzenval, 21st Oct.	11000	440			Germany
Le Bourget, 27th-30th Oct.		3000		380	Germany
Villiers, 29th Nov.-3rd Dec.	80000	9500		3500	Germany
2nd Buzenval, 19th-20th Jan. 1871	90000	4100	12000	600	Germany

Appendix 3: 2ND South African War 1899-1902

Action	British Strength	British Casualties	Boer Strength	Boer Casualties	Winner
Kraaipan, 12th Oct. 1899			800		Boer
Siege of Mafeking, 13th Oct. 1899-17th May 1900	1500	812	8000	2000	British
Siege of Kimberley, 14th Oct. 1899-15th Feb. 1900	1600	187	3-6500	?	British
Talana Hill, 20th Oct. 1899	4000	440	3000	110	British tactical
Elandslaagte, 21st Oct.	3500	260	1000	330	British tactical
1st Ladysmith, 30th Oct.	12500	1200	21000	200	Boer
Siege of Ladysmith, 2nd Nov. 1899-28th Feb. 1900	12500	1650	21000	?	British
Belmont, 23rd Nov.	8000	308	2000	133	British tactical
Graspan, 25th Nov.	9000	185	3000	220	British
Modder River, 28th Nov.	8000	450	9000	75	British tactical
Stormberg, 10th Dec.	2050	780	2300	c. 30	Boer
Magersfontein, 11th Dec.	15000	950	8500	236	Boer
Colenso, 15th Dec.	16700	1140	4500	40	Boer
Spion Kop, 23rd-24th Jan. 1900	20000	1500	8000	350	Boer
Vaal Krantz, 5th-7th Feb.	20000	333	5000	80	Boer
Paardeberg, 18th-27th Feb.	15000	1290	7000	4400	British
Tugela Heights, 14th-27th Feb.	20000	2300	5000	200+	British
Poplar Grove, 7th Mar.	5000	57	5000	2	British
Driefontein, 10th Mar.		424	1500	100	British
Sanna's Post, 31st Mar.	2000	580	400	8	Boer
Boshof, 5th Apr.	750	13	120	75	British
Diamond Hill, 11th-12th June	20000	173	6000	30+	British
Eland's River, 4th-16th Aug.	505	48	2-3000		British
Bergendal, 21st-27th Aug.	19000	385	7000	78	British
Bothaville, 6th Nov.	600	38	800	170	British
Nooitgedacht, 13th Dec.	1500	650	2100	30	Boer
Groenkloof, 5th Sept.	1100	10	130	120	British
Blood River Poort, 17th Sept.	750	285	1000	Few	Boer
Elands River, 17th Sept.	130	130	250	7	Boer
Moedwil, 30th Sept.	930	219	500	56	British tactical
Kleinfontein, 24th Oct.	680	90	500	51	British tactical
Bakenlaagte, 30th Oct.	210	207	900	62	Boer
Groenkop, 25th Dec.	550	351	600	41	Boer
Ysterspruit, 25th Feb. 1902	600	178			Boer
Tweebosch, 7th Mar.	1250	392	2000	51	Boer
Rooiwal, 11th Apr.	3000	70	1700	230	British

Appendix 4: Russo-Japanese War 1904-5

Action	Russian Strength	Russian Casualties	Japanese Strength	Japanese Casualties	Winner
1904					
Yalu River, 30th Apr-1st May	25000	2200	42000	1000	Japan
Nanshan, 24th-26th May	3800	1400	35500	6200	Japan
Te-li-Ssu, 14th-15th Jun.	45000	c.5000	40000	c. 1200	Japan
Tashihchiao, 24th-25th Jul.	60000	1000	64000	1000	Japan
Siege of Port Arthur, 1st Aug. 1904-2nd Jan. 1905	55000	All	150000	58000	Japan
Hsimucheng, 31st Jul.	33000	1200	34000	800	Japan
Liaoyang, 25th Aug.-5th Sept.	245000	19000	127000	23000	Japan
Shaho, 5th-17th Oct.	210000	41300	170000	21100	Japan
1905					
Sandepu, 25th-29th Jan.	75000	14000	40000	9500	Inconclusive
Mukden, 20th Feb.-10th Mar.	340000	88300	263000	75500	Japan

Appendix 5: First Balkan War 1912-3

Bulgarian Front	Bulgarian Strength	Bulgarian Casualties	Turkish Strength	Turkish Casualties	Winner
Kırklareli, 24th Oct. 1912	154000	5700	98000	4500	Bulgaria
Lule Burgas, 28th Oct.-2nd Nov.	108000	19500	130000	25000	Bulgaria
Siege of Adrianople 3rd Nov. 1912-26th Mar. 1913	106000+ 47000 Serb	10500	c. 60000	All	Bulgaria/ Serb
Merhamli, 27th Nov.			10000	9600	Bulgaria
First Çatalca, 17th-18th Nov.	176000	12000	140500	5-10000	Turkey
Bulair, 26th Jan.1913	10000	500	37000	16000	Bulgaria
Şarköy, 9th-11th Feb.			20000	2700	Bulgaria
Second Çatalca, 3rd Feb.-3rd Apr.					Inconclusive
Serbian/Montenegrin Front	Serbian Strength	Serbian Casualties	Turkish Strength	Turkish Casualties	
Kumanovo, 23rd-24th Oct. 1912	132000	4500	65000	4500	Serbia
Siege of Scutari 28th Oct. 1912-23rd Apr. 1913	40000	15000	20000	All	Montenegro/ Serb victory
Prilep, 3rd-5th Nov. 1912		2000		1300	Serbia
Monastir, 16th-19th Nov.	108000	2600	38000	8600	Serbia
Greek Front	Greek Strength	Greek Casualties	Turkish Strength	Turkish Casualties	
Sarantaporo, 9th-10th Oct. 1912		c. 1500		1500	Greece
Giannitsa, 2nd Nov.	65000	c. 1000	25000	1450	Greece
Pente Pigadia, 21st-23rd Oct.	8000	250	14000	?	Greece
Bizani, 4th-6th Mar. 1913	41000	500	35000	14400	Greece

Bibliography

Various, *History of the Great War, Military Operations, France and Belgium, 1914, 1915, 1916*
Various, *Les Armées Française dans La Grande Guerre*, Tomes I-IV
Various, *History of the Ministry of Munitions*
Various, *The Russo-Japanese War: Reports from British Officers Attached to the Japanese and Russian Armies in the Field*, Volume III, HMSO, 1908
Various, *Statistics of the Military Effort of the British Empire during the Great War 1914-1920*, HMSO, 1922
Anon., *The British Officer: Leading the Army from 1660 to the present*, Pearson Education Ltd., 2006
Anon., *Field Artillery Training 1914*, HMSO
Anon., *Infantry Training, 4 Company Organization*, HMSO
Anon., *Manufacture and Consumption of Ammunition in France*, The Field Artillery Journal, April-June 1916
Anon., *Official Records of the Guards' Brigade in South Africa*, 1904
Anon., *Report on a Conference of General Staff Officers at the Staff College 1906*, HMSO
Anon., *Report on a Conference of General Staff Officers at the Staff College 1908*, HMSO
Anon., *Report on a Conference of General Staff Officers at the Staff College 1909*, HMSO
Anon., *Report on a Conference of General Staff Officers at the Staff College 1910*, HMSO
Anon., *Report on a Conference of General Staff Officers at the Staff College 1911*, HMSO
Anon., *Report on a Conference of General Staff Officers at the Staff College 1912*, HMSO
Anon, *Annales du Bureau central météorologique de France, 1914*, Gauthier-Villars & Cie, 1919.
Anon, United States Congressional Serial Set, House Documents, 4th December 1911-26th August 1912, Volume 141.
Alvin, Capt. P, trans. by Lt. H R Odell, 3rd Field Artillery, *The Field Artillery in the Balkans*, Field Artillery Journal, Vol. IV, No. 2, Apr-June 1914
Altmayer, Capt. M-R, *Je Veux, Revue militaire générale*, tome XII, 1912
Amery, L S, *The Problem of the Army*, Edward Arnold, 1903
d'Andurain, J, *Verdun, ou le tournant de la doctrine française*, Revue Défense Nationale 2016/2 (No. 787)
Angell, N., *Europe's Optical Illusion*, Simpkin, Marshall, Hamilton, Kent & Co., 1909
Anglesey, Marquis of, *A History of the British Cavalry, Vol. 4, 1899-1913*, Pen & Sword
Baden-Powell, Maj, B F S, *War in Practice*, Isbister & Co., 1903
Baden-Powell, R, *Scouting for Boys*, 1908
Badsey, S, *Doctrine and Reform in the British Cavalry 1880-1918*, Ashgate, 2008
Bailey, Maj. J B A, *Field Artillery and Firepower*, The Military Press, Oxford, 1989
Baillot, Capt. R, *Le Général Maillard et les Origines de la Doctrine de Guerre Actuelle*, Revue militaire Générale, November 1923
Baquet, Hen. L H, *Souvenirs d'un directeur d'artillerie*, Charles-Lavauzelle, 1921
Baring, M, *With the Russians in Manchuria*, Methuen, 1905
Barry, R, *Port Arthur: A Monster Heroism*, Moffat, Yard & Co., New York, 1905
Batten, S, *Futile Exercises? The British Army's Preparations for War 1902-1914*, Helion, 2019
Battine, C W, *The Proposed Changes in Cavalry Tactics*, Journal of the Royal United Service Institution, Vol. 54, No. 393
Bauer E, *Jan Gottlieb Bloch: Polish Cosmopolitism versus Jewish Universalism* in Miller, M L & Ury, S (eds), *Cosmopolitanism, Nationalism and the Jews of East Central Europe*, Routledge, 2016
Beach J, ed., *The Military Papers of Sir Cuthbert Headlam*, Army Records Society, 2010
Beckett, I F W, *The Compulsion of Destitution: The British Army and the Dilemma of Imperial Defence, 1870-1914*, in Peter Dennis & Jeffrey Grey (eds.), *Raise, Train and Sustain: Delivering Land Combat Power* (Canberra: Australian Military History Publications, 2010)
Bellenger, Capt. G., trans. by Maj. W S McNair, 6th Field Artillery, *Notes on the employment of artillery in the Balkan campaign*, Field Artillery Journal, Vol. IV, No. 1, Jan-Mar 1914
Berglund, A, *The Iron-Ore Problem of Lorraine*, The Quarterly Journal of Economics, Vol. 33, No. 3 (May, 1919)

Berthaut, Gen. H M A, *L"Erreur" de 1914: réponse aux critiques*, G. Van Oest et Cie, 1919
Billard, Capt. *breveté, Éducation de l'infanterie*, Librarie Chapelot, 1913
Bloch, J de, *Selected Articles*, U.S. Army Command & General Staff College, 1993
Bloch, J de, *The Future of War: in its Technical, Economic and Political Relations*, Trans. by R C Long, The World Peace Foundation, Boston 1914
Bond, B, *The Victorian Army and the Staff College*, Eyre Methuen, 1982
Bornemann, K, *Das Infanterie-Regiment Nr 99 im Weltkrieg 1914-1918*, Wien-Znaim 1929
Boucher, Col. A, *L'Offensive contre L'Allemagne*, Berger-Levrault, 1911
Bourcart, J, PhD thesis: *Lunéville: une garnison de cavalerie dans l'espace frontalier lorrain, 1873-1921. Représentation et évolution d'une division de cavalerie aux avants-postes, Annexes*, Université de Lorraine, 2013
Bowman T, & Connelly M, *The Edwardian Army*, OUP, 2012
Brett, M V, ed., *Journals and Letters of Viscount Esher*, Vol. 1, 1870-1903, Ivor Nicholson & Watson, 1934
Bruno, Maj. T A, *Ignoring the Obvious: Combined Arms and Fire and Maneuver Tactics prior to World War One*, US Marine Corps Command & Staff College, Marine Corps University, 2002 and Verdun Press 2015
Buat, Gen. E, *L'artillerie de campagne : son histoire, son évolution, son état actuel*, F Alcan, 1911
Bugnet, Cdt. C, *En écoutant le Maréchal Foch*, Grasset, 1929
Cabanes, B, *August 1914: France, the Great War, and a Month That Changed the World Forever*, Yale University Press, 2016
Cairnes, Capt. W E, *An Absent Minded War*, John Milne, 1900
Cairnes, Capt. W E, *Social Life in the British Army*, John Long, 1900
Callies, A, *Carnets de guerre d'Alexis Callies, (1914-1918)*, retranscrits et commentés par Eric Labayle, E/L éditions, 1999
Calwell, Maj. Gen. C E, *Field Marshal Sir Henry Wilson: His Life and Diaries*, Cassell & Co., 1927
Cardot, L, *Hérésies et apostasies militaires de notre temps*, Berger-Levrault et Cie, 1908
Caron, F, *An Economic History of France*, Routledge, 2012
Cebro, Cdt,, *Les Conditions de L'offensive, Journal des sciences militaires*, March 1914
Cerf, Col. A, *La guerre aux frontières du Jura*, Payot & Co., Lausanne, 1930
Chambe, Gen. R, *Adieu, Cavalerie! La Marne, Bataille gagnée – Victoire perdue*, Plon, 1979
Charteris, J, *Field Marshal Earl Haig*, Cassell & Co., 1929
Chesney, Gen. G T, *The Battle of Dorking*, Grant Richards Ltd., London, 1914
Challeat, Gen. J, *L'Artillerie de terre en France pendant un Siècle, Histoire Technique (1816-1919), Tome Second (1880-1910)*, Charles Lavauzelle et Cie, 1935
Challéat, *Chef d'escadron* J M J, *La question de l'obusier léger, Revue d'artillerie*, January 1912
Childers, E, Amery, L S ed., *The Times History of the War in South Africa 1899-1902*, Vol V, Sampson, Low, Marston & Co., London, 1907
Churchill, W S, *My Early Life*, Fontana, 1957
Churchill, W S, *The World Crisis 1911-1918*,
Clausewitz, C von trans. by Lt. Col. de Vatry, *Théorie de la Grande Guerre*, Librarie Militaire de L Baudouin et Cie, Paris 1886
Clausewitz, C von, trans. by Howard, M, & Paret, P, *On War*, David Campbell Publishers Ltd., 1993
Clément-Grandcourt, Capt. A J E, *La Question de l'uniforme de l'infanterie, Revue militaire Générale*, June 1914
Clery, Capt. C F, *Minor Tactics*, 1875
Coetzee, F, *For Party or Country. Nationalism and the Dilemmas of Popular Conservatism in Edwardian England*, Oxford University Press, 1990
Comparato F E, *Age of Great Guns*, Stackpole Co., 1965
Condrau F & Worboys M,, *Epidemics and Infections in Nineteenth-Century Britain, Social History of Medicine*, 2009
Congressional Record containing the Proceedings and Debates of the 63rd Congress, Third Session, Volume LII, Part VI, Appendix and Index, *How the Ear Trust is Robbing the Government while driving us on*

Toward the Brink of war, extension of remarks of Hon. Clyde H Tavenner of Illinois in the House of Representatives, 15th February 1915, Government Printing Office, Washinton, 1915

Connaught, R, *Rising Sun and Tumbling Bear: Russia's War with Japan*, Hachette UK, 2020

Creveld, M van, *Command in War*, Cambridge: Harvard University Press, 1985

Creuzinger P, *Geschichte des Königlich Preussischen Jäger Regiments zu Pferde Nr. 5*, Bernhard Sporn, 1932.

Dangerfield, G, *'The Strange Death of Liberal England'*, Paladin, 1970

Daniels, J, *The Wilson Era: Years of Peace, 1910-1917*, The University of North Carolina Press, 1944

Davenport-Hines, R P T, *Dudley Docker: The Life and Times of a Trade Warrior*, Cambridge University Press, 2002

Dennis, P & Grey J (eds.), *Raise, Train and Sustain: Delivering Land Combat Power* Australian Military History Publications, 2010

Descols, L, *La Genèse du drap Bleu Horizon*, Eguzon, Point d'Ancrage, 2014

de Syon, G, *Zeppelin!: Germany and the Airship, 1900–1939*, Johns Hopkins University Press, 2007

De Tarlé, Cdt. A, *La Préparais Industrielle de la Guerre en France et en Allemagne*, Revue Militiare Françcaise, 1st July 1921

Détrie, J-F, *Le général Arthur Boucher (1847-1933): une carrière atypique, une oeuvre erudite*, Unpublished PhD thesis, Université Paul Valéry - Montpellier III

Deuringer K, trans. Zuber, T, *The First Battle of the First World War: Alsace-Lorraine*, The History Press, 2014

Donat, K von, *German Account of the Russo-Japanese War: The Yalu*, London, 1908

Dosse, Capt. E., *Tactical Notes, Field Artillery Journal*, Vol. IV, No. 1, Jan-Mar 1914

Doughty, R A, *Pyrrhic Victory: French Strategy and Operations in the Great War*, Harvard University Press, 2008

Doughty, R A, *The Seeds of Disaster: The Development of French Army Doctrine, 1919-39*, Stackpole Books, 2014

Doyle, A C, *The Great Boer War: a two years' record, 1899–1901*, 15th ed., 1901

Dragomirov, Gen. M I, *Uchenie o voine Klauzevitsa - osnovnye polozheniia*, in the journal *Voennyi sbornik*

Dragomirov, *Manuel de préparation des troupes au combat, Préparation de la compagnie*, Librairie militaire de L. Baudoin et Cie, 1885

Dubail, Gen. A, *Quatre années de commandement, 1914-1918 (1re armée, groupe d'armées de l'Est, armées de Paris):* journal de campagne, Tome 1, L. Fournier, 1921-2

Du Cane, *Report on the Effect of Possible Modification of Design of Shells and Fuses*, 7th February 1916

Dunlop, Col. J K, *The Development of the British Army 1899-1914*, Methuen, 1938

Du Picq, Col. C J J J A, *Etudes sur les combat: Combat antique et moderne*, Hachette, 1880

Earle, E M, *Maker of Modern Strategy*, Princeton, 1948

Eddy, C B, *Moveable steel mantlet for the protection of artillery and troops, RUSI Journal,* Vol.13, No. LV, 1869.

Edmonds J E, unpublished *Reminiscences*, Chapter XIV, *The Staff College 1896-7*

Ellis, J, *The Social History of the Machine Gun*, Pimlico, 1976

Engelbrecht H C & Hanighen F C, *Merchants of Death*, Dodd, Mead & Co., 1934

Evans, N, *From drill to doctrine: forging the British Army's tactics 1897-1909*, unpublished PhD thesis, King's College, London

Farndale, Gen. Sir M, *History of the Royal Regiment of Artillery, Western Front 1914-1918*, Royal Artillery Institution, 1986

Farwell, B, *Queen Victoria's Little Wars*, Harper and Row, 1972

Fayolle, M E, ed. Contamine H, *Cahiers secrets de la grand guerre*, Plon, 1964

Foch, F, trans. Belloc, H, *Principles of War*, Henry Holt & Co., 1920

Foch, F, *De la Conduite de la Guerre*, Berger-Levrault & Cie., 1919

Foch, F, trans. Belloc, H, *Precepts and Judgements*, Chapman & Hall Ltd, 1919

Foch, F, trans. Bentley Mott, Col T, *The Memoirs of Marshal Foch*, W Heinemann Ltd., 1931
Fontenot, Col. G, *The Modern Major General: Patterns in the Careers of British Army Major Generals on Active Duty at the Time of the Sarajevo Assassinations*, MA Thesis, University of North Carolina, 1980
Fortescue, Sir J W, *The History of the British Army*, Vol. XIII, MacMillan, 1899
Forstner, *Das Reserve Infanterie Regiment 15*, Berlin, 1929
Fraser W H & Maver, I *Glasgow: 1830 to 1912,* Manchester University Press, 1996
French, Viscount, *1914,* Constable & Co., 1919
Freydorf, R von, *Das 1. Badische Leib-Grenadier-Regiment Nr. 109 im Weltkrieg 1914-1918*, Verlag C.F. Müller, 1927
Fuller J F C., *Generalship: Its Diseases and Their Cure, A Study of the Personal Factor in Command*, Military Service Publishing Co. Harrisburg, Pa. 1936
Fuller, J F C, *The Dragon's Teeth: A Study of War and Peace*, London, 1932
Fuller, J F C, *The Decisive Battles of the Western World,* London. 1956
Galton, F, *On men of science, their nature and their nurture*, Proceedings of the Royal Institution of Great Britain, 1874
Gannon, Charles E, *Rumors of War and Infernal Machines: Technomilitary Agenda-setting in American and British Speculative Fiction*, Liverpool University Press, 2003
Gat, A, *The Development of Military Thought: The Nineteenth Century*, Clarendon Press, 1992
Gawler, Col. G, 2nd edition (1852) to *The Essentials of Good Skirmishing*, Savill & Edwards, originally published 1837
Gebsattel, Ludwig Frh. von, *Das K. B. 1. Ulanen-Regiment 'Kaiser Wilhelm II. König von Preußen'*, J. P. Himmer, 1924
Gilbert, Capt. G, *La Guerre sud-africaine*, Berger-Levrault, 1902
Globowski, Oberlt. D Res., *Das Kgl. Sächsische 6. Infanterie-Regiment König Wilhelm II. von Württemberg Nr. 105*, Baensch, 1929
Gluck, *Generalmajor,* & Wald, *Generalmajor, Das 8. Württembergisches Infanterie-Regiment Nr. 126 Großherzog Friedrich von Baden im Weltkrieg 1914-1918*, Belser, 1929
Glück, Capt. G-L, *Obusiers de campagne et Artillerie lourde, Journal des sciences militaires*, July 1913
Gooch, J, ed., *The Boer War: Direction, Experience and Image*, Routledge, 2000
Grandmaison, Cdt. L, *Dressage de l'infanterie en vue du combat offensive*, Berger-Levrault 1906
Gras, Gen. Y, *Castelnau ou l'art de commander*, Denoël, 1990
Green, A, *Writing the Great War: Sir James Edmonds and the Official Histories, 1915-1948*, Routledge, 2003
Grey of Fallodon, Viscount, *Twenty-Five Years*, Vols I & II, Hodder & Stoughton, 1925
Grossman, D & Christensen L W, *On Combat: The Psychology and Physiology of Deadly Conflict in War and Peace.* 2nd ed. PPCT Research Publications, 2007
Grouard, A, *France Allemagne. La guerre éventuelle*, Chapelot, 1913
Guide Michelin des champs de bataille: Artois-Arras-Lens-Douai
Guggisberg, F E, *Modern Warfare or How our Soldiers Fight*, Thomas Nelson & Sons, 1903
H, *Les Uniformes de l'Armée, Criminelle Impuissance,* La France Militaire, 16th July 1912
Haberman, Prof. F W, ed., *Nobel Lectures, Peace 1901-25*, Nobel Foundation, 1995
Hall, R C, *The Balkan Wars, 1912–1913: Prelude to the First World War*, Routledge, 2000
Hamilton, Sir I, *A Staff Officers Scrapbook during the Russo-Japanese War, Volume 2*, E Arnold, 1907
Hanotaux, G, *Histoire illustrée de la guerre de 1914*, Tome 3, 1915-7
Harlow, N A, *Beyond the Machine Gun Re-interpreting McMahon's 'Fire Fighting' lecture of 1907, The Journal of the Historical Breechloading Smallarms Association*, Vol. 4, No. 8, November 2016
Haruo, T, *Approaching Total War: Ivan Bloch's Disturbing Vision* in Wolff, Marks et al, *The Russo-Japanese War in Global Perspective, World War Zero*, Vol. II, Brill, Boston, 2007
Haußner, K, *Das Feldgeschütz mit langem Rohrrücklauf: Geschichte meiner Erfindung*, R. Oldenbourg, 1928
Hayes, M H, *Horses on board ship: a guide to their management*, Hurst & Blackett, 1902
Heffer, S, *The Age of Decadence*, Random House, 2017

Held, K, *Das Königl.Preuss.Infanterie-Regt.Graf Barfuss (4.Westf.) Nr.17 im Weltkriege 1914/1918*, Verlag Bernard & Graefe, 1934

Henderson, G F R, *The Science of War*, Longman, Greens & Co., 1905

Herment, Gen. G, *Considérations sur la défense de la frontière du Nord, Journal des sciences militaires*, 1st January 1913

Herr, Gen F-G, *L'Artillerie, ce qu'elle a été, ce qu'elle est, ce qu'elle doit être* Berger Levrault, 1924

Herrmann, D G, *The Arming of Europe and the Making of the First World War*, Princeton University, 1996

Heuser, B, *Reading Clausewitz*, Pimlico, 2002

Holley, L A, *A treatise on ordnance and armor: embracing descriptions, discussions, and professional opinions concerning the material, fabrication, requirements, capabilities, and endurance of European and American guns for naval, sea-coast, and iron-clad warfare, and their rifling, projectiles and breech-loading*, Van Nostrand, 1865.

Holmes, R, *The Little Field Marshal: A Life of Sir John French*, Weidenfeld & Nicolson, 2004

Horne, A, *The Price of Glory*, 1962

Horne, C F, ed., *Records of the Great War, Vol. V*, National Alumni 1923

Howard, M, *Men Against Fire – Expectations of War in 1914*, International Security, Vol. 9, No. 1, Harvard University & MIT, Summer 1984

Huguet, Gen. V, *Britain and the War: A French Indictment*, Cassell & Co., 1928

Immerwahr D, *How to Hide an Empire: A Short History of the Greater United States*, Bodley Head, 2019

Jacobson, *World Armament Expenditure*, 1935

Jager, Herbert, *German Artillery of World War One*, Crowood Press, 2001

James, Capt. W H, RE, *Modern Weapons and Their Influence on Tactics and Organisation*, Journal of the Royal United Service Institute, Issue 43/2 (1899)

Jeffrey, K, *Field Marshal Sir Henry Wilson: A Political Soldier*, Oxford University Press, 2006

Joffre, J J C, *The Memoirs of Marshal Joffre*, trans. Capt. Bentley-Mott, Geoffrey Bles, 1932

Joffre, J J C, *La préparation de la guerre & la conduite des opérations: 1914-1915*, Chiron, 1920

Jones, S, *From Boer War to World War*, University of Oklahoma Press, 2012

Kaufmann H E and J W, *The Forts and Fortifications of Europe 1815-1945- The Central States*, Pen and Sword Military, 2014

Kessler, Gen. C, *Tactique des Trois Armes, Libraire Militaire R Chapelot*, 1902

Kinai, M. *The Russo-Japanese War (Official Reports)*, Vol. 1, Kegan Paul, Trench, Taubner and Co. Ltd

King, J W, *Report of Chief Engineer J. W. King, USN, on European ships of war and their armament, naval administration and economy, marine constructions and appliances, dockyards, etc., etc.* Government Printing Office, Washington D.C, 1877

Knox, Maj. Gen. Sir W G *The Flaw in Our Armour*, 1914

Krause, J, *Early Trench Tactics in the French Army: The Second Battle of Artois, May-June 1915*, Ashgate Studies in First World War History, 2013

Kruger, Rayne. *Goodbye Dolly Grey: The Story of the Boer War*, Four Square Books, 1964

Kuhn J, *Reports of Military Observers Attached to the Armies in Manchuria During the Russo-Japanese War*, United States War Department: Office of the Chief of Staff (Military Information Division), US Government Printing Office, 1906

Laffaye, H A, *The Evolution of Polo*, McFarland & Co., 2009

Langlois, Gen, H, *Enseignements de deux guerres récentes: Guerres Turco-russe et Anglo-Boer*, Lavauzelle, 1904

Langlois, H, *Le Haut Commandmant, Revue des deux mondes*, 1st September 1911

Langlois, Gen. H, *L'artillerie de campagne en liaison avec les autres armes*

Lanrezac, C., *Le plan de campagne français et le premier mois de la guerre (2 août-3 septembre 1914)*, Paris, Payot, 1920

Lasch, Lt. W, *3. Unterelsässisches Infanterie-Regiment Nr. 138*, Stalling, 1921

Laure, Gen. A M E, *L'Offensive française*, Berger-Levrault, 1912

Lavisse, E, *La tenue de campagne de l'infanterie. Comment l'améliorer?*, Chapelot, Paris, 1913

Lavisse, É, *Sac au dos, études comparées de la tenue de campagne des fantassins des armées française et étrangères*, Paris, Hachette, 1902
Le Hallé, Guy, *Le système Séré de Rivières ou le témoignage des pierres*, Ysec Editions, 2001
Lerner, H, *Le colonel Emile Mayer et son cercle d'amis*, Revue Historique, Tome CCLXVI, Presses Universitaires De France, 1981
Leroy, Capt., *Historique et Organisation de l'Artillerie, Ecole Militaire de l'Artillerie*, 1922
Liddell Hart, B, *Foch: The Man of Orleans*, Penguin, 1931
Liddell Hart, B, *The British Way in Warfare*, London, 1932
Loboda, Y O, *French Military Strategy of the End of XIX – First Half of XX Centuries: between Descartes and Bergson?* University of North Carolina at Greensboro
Lone, Dr S, *The Japanese Military during the Russo-Japanese War, 1904-05: A Reconsideration of Command Politics and Public Images* in *Aspects of the Russo-Japanese War*, The Suntory Centre, LSE, London, 1998
Lucas, Lt. Col. P M H, trans. Kieffer, Maj. P V, *The Evolution of Tactical Ideas in France and Germany During the War of 1914-1918*, Berger-Levrault, 1923
Macbean, Col. W A, *The French Plan of Concentration and the Collapse of 1914*, The Journal of the Royal Artillery, April 1923
MacDonald, Brig. Gen. J H A, *Fifty Years of It – The Experiences and Struggles of a Volunteer of 1859*, Blackwood, 1909
Maillard, Maj. L A G d, *Éléments de la Guerre*, Paris 1891
Maistre J-M de, *Considérations sur la France*, 1797
Maistre, *The Evenings of St. Petersburg or Talks on the Temporal Government of Providence*, 1821
Mandeles, M D, *The Future of War: Organizations as Weapons*, Potomac Books, 2005
Marchal, Capt. C-J, *La VIIe Armée Allemande en Couverture en Aout 1914*, Revue Militaire Française, Tome Trente-Deuxième, April-June/July-September 1929, Librairie Militaire Berger-Levrault
Marder, A, *From the Dreadnought to Scapa Flow*, Naval Institute Press, 2015
Masson, *Chef d'Escadron, Historique du 47e Régiment d'Artillerie de Campagne*, Schmitt Frères
Maude, Col. F N, *War and the World's Life*, Smith, Elder & Co., 1907
Maud'huy, L-E de, *Manœuvre, étude théorique (1911), précédée du testament militaire du colonel de Maud'huy à son régiment, Belfort 27 Mai 1912*, Berger-Levrault
Maurice, Maj. Gen Sir F & Grant, Capt. M H, *Official History of the War in South Africa 1899-1902*, vol. II, HMSO
Maurice, Lt. F., *The System of Field Manoeuvres Best Adapted for Enabling Our Troops to Meet a Continental Army*, Wellington Prize Essay, Blackwood & Sons, 1872
May, E R, *Knowing One's Enemies*, Princeton Legacy Library, 1986
Mayer, Col. E, under the name Manceau E, *Un vieil article du lieutenant-colonel Émile Mayer (Émile Manceau) sur la guerre actuelle.... 1915*, Revue Militaire Suisse, 1915
Mayer, Col. E, *Prophéties sur la guerre de 1914-1918*, Revue Militaire Suisse, 1935
Mayer, E, *L'artillerie lourde de campagne avant la guerre*, Revue Militaire Suisse, LXIII, No. 8, August, and No. 9, September 1918.
Mead, G, *The Good Soldier: The Biography of Douglas Haig*, Atlantic Books, 2014
Menne B, *Blood and Steel - The Rise of the House of Krupp*, Menne Press, 2007
Menu, Col., *Le Fabrication de Guerre*, Revue Militaire Française, October-December, 1933
Messimy, A, *Mes Souvenirs*, 1935
Midvale Steel Company, *Midvale 1867-1942*, Midvale Steel Company, 1942
Miller, M L & Ury, S (eds), *Cosmopolitanism, Nationalism and the Jews of East Central Europe*, Routledge, 2016
Ministère de la Guerre, *Règlement sur la conduite des grandes unites*, 1913
Ministère de la Guerre, *Article 313, Règlement de manœuvre d'infanterie*, 1914
Minutes and Evidence taken before the Committee appointed to consider the Education and Training of Officers of the Army, HMSO, London, 1902
Moltke, *Generaloberst H von, Erinnerungen, Brefe und Documente 1877-1916*, A. S. Verlag 1922
Mondésir, Col J F L P de, *Siège et Prise d'Adrianople*, Librairie Chapelot, 1914
Montaigne, Lt. Col. J-B, *Vaincre - Esquisse d'une Doctrine de la Guerre basée sur la Connaissance de*

l'Homme et de la Morale, Berger-Levrault, 1913

Murray, N A A, *The Theory and Practice of Field Fortification from 1877-1914,* D. Phil Thesis, St Antony's College, Oxford, 2007

Musée du Génie, *Le redressement militaire de la France 1871-1914*

Musée du Génie, *Août 1914 - La mobilisation et la concentration des forces*

Musée de Génie, *Le redressement militaire de la France 1871-1914*

Négrier, Gen. F O, *L'évolution actuelle de la tactique, Revue des Deux Mondes,* 1904

Nigote, C C, J, *La Bataille de la Vesles,* Librairie Militaire de L. Baudoin, 1894

O.B., *Questions d'artillerie d'actualité, Journal des Sciences Militaire,* December 1912

O.B., *The Question of the Light Field Howitzer, Journal des sciences militaires,* 19th March 1912

Obkircher, H, *Jäger-Regiment zu Pferde Nr. 3 im Frieden und im Kriege,* Verlag G. Stalling, 1923

Ogilvie, V, *The English Public School,* Batsford, 1957

Pakenham, Thomas, *The Boer War,* Johannesburg: Jonathan Ball, 1979

Palat, Gen., B E, *La Grande guerre sur le front occidental I: Les éléments du conflit,* Librairie Chapelot, 1917

Palat, Gen., B E, *La Grande Guerre sur le front occidental II: Liège, Mulhouse, Sarrebourg, Morhange,* Librairie Chapelot, 1917

Palazzo, A., *From Moltke to Bin Laden: The relevance of doctrine in the contemporary military environment,* Land Warfare Studies Centre, Canberra, 2008

Paloque, Col. J H, *Artillerie de campagne,* Octave Doin et Fils, 1909.

Parliamentary Papers, vol. 10, 1902, *Report of the Committee Appointed to Consider the Education and Training of Officers of the Army.* Command Paper no. 983

Pastre, J.-L. G, *Trois ans de front : Belgique, Aisne et Champagne, Verdun, Argonne, Lorraine : notes et impressions d'un artilleur,* Berger-Levrault, 1918

Paulus, Oberst K, *Kgl. Bayer. Jäger Regiment* Nr. *1.,* Bayerische Kriegsarchiv, 1925

Peloux, Capt., *Matériels de campagne et de siège à tir rapide de gros calibres, Revue d'artillerie,* April 1912, page 5 onwards.

Percin, Gen. A, *1914,* Albin Michel 1919

Percin, Gen. A, *Le massacre de notre Infanterie,* Albin Michel, 1921

Percin, Gen. A., *Le combat,* Alcan, *Nouvelle collection scientifique,* 1914

Persson, G, *The Russian Army 1859-1871,* PhD thesis, London School of Economics and Political Science, 1999

Petri, H, *2. Oberrheinisches Infanterie-Regiment 99,* Stalling, 1925

Philpotts, Maj. A H C, RA, trans. *Activity of Field Artillery in the Russo-Japanese Campaign and the influence of the war experience on the use of artillery, Field Artillery Journal,* Vol. III, No. 4, Oct-Dec 1913

Pierrefeu J de, *Plutarch Lied.* 1924

Pilcher, T D, *Some Lessons from the Boer War,* Isbister & Co., 1902

Porch, D, *The March to the Marne,* Cambridge University Press, 1981

Prior R, & Wilson T, *Command on the Western Front,* Pen & Sword 2004

Ramsay, M A, *Command and Cohesion: The Citizen Soldier and Minor Tactics in the British Army 1870-1918,* Praeger, 2002

Reader, W J, *Professional men: The rise of the professional classes in nineteenth-century England,* Weidenfeld & Nicolson, 1966

Reichsarchiv, *Der Weltkrieg 1914 bis 1918, Die Operationen des Jahres 1914-6*

Reichsarchiv, *German losses on the Western Front by main operations period.* Quoted in Churchill, W S, *The World Crisis 1911-1918*

Reid, W. *Architect of Victory: Douglas Haig,* 2006

Renoult, P, *Les munitions de l'artillerie française de la Grande Guerre* in Aubagnac, Berlemont, Boutet *et al., Un milliard d'obus, des millions d'hommes: l'artillerie en 14/18,* Paris, Lienart éditions, 2016

Rhone, Lt. Gen., trans. by Spaulding, Col. O L, *Artillery Statistics from the World War, Field Artillery Journal,* Sept.-Oct. 1924

Riedi, E, *Brains or Polo? Equestrian Sports, Army Reform and the Gentlemanly Officer Tradition 1900-*

14, Journal of the Society for Army Historical Research, No. 84
Rimailho, Lt. Col. E, *Artillerie de campagne*, Gauthier-Villars, 1924
Robbins, S, *British Generalship on the Western Front 1914-8*, Frankc Cass, 2005
Roberts, A, *Salisbury: Victorian Titan*, Faber & Faber, 2012
Rose, A, *Waiting for Armageddon? British Military Journals and the Images of Future War (1900–1914)*, 2011, *Veröffentlichungen des Deutschen Historischen Instituts*
Rosny, J-H, *La Guerre Anglo-Boër*, 1902
Sagona, Prof. A, Atabay, Dr M *et al*, *Anzac Battlefield: A Gallipoli Landscape of War and Memory*, Cambridge University Press, 2016
Samuels, M, *Command Or Control?: Command, Training and Tactics in the British and German, 1888-1918*, Routledge, 1996
Sanders, C W, *No Other Law: The French Army and the Doctrine of the Offensive*, Rand, 1987
Schiel, Oblt. O, *Das 4. Badisches Infanterie-Regiment Prinz Wilhelm Nr. 112 im Weltkrieg*, Oldenburg, 1927
Schirmer, Generalleutnant H, *Das Gerät der schweren Artillerie vor, in und nach dem Weltkrieg*, Vol 1, Bernard und Graefe, 1937.
Schmidt, W, *Das 7. Badische Infanterie-Regiment Nr. 142 im Weltkrieg 1914/18*, Oldenburg, 1927
Scott, D, ed., *The Preparatory Prologue: Douglas Haig Diaries and Letters 1861-1914*, Pen & Sword, 2006
Seim, R, *Forging the Rapier among Scythes: Lt. Gen. Sir Horace Smith-Dorrien and the Aldershot Command 1907-12*, unpublished MA Thesis, Rice University, Texas, 1980
Seldon A, & Walsh D, *Public Schools and the Great War*, Pen & Sword
Seltzen, J A, *The Doctrine of the Offensive in the French Army on the Eve of World War One*, PhD dissertation, University of Chicago, 1972
Shearman, Capt. C E G (and syndicate), *Operations, BEF, 1914*, Army Staff College, 1926
Sheffield G & Bourne J, *Douglas Haig: War Diaries and Letters 1914-18*, Weidenfeld & Nicholson, 2005
Shimazu, N, *Japanese Society at War: Death, Memory and the Russo-Japanese War*, Cambridge University Press, 2009
Simkins, P, *Kitchener's Army: The Raising of the New Armies 1914-16*, Manchester University Press, 1988
Smith, L V, *From Mutiny to Obedience*, Princeton Legacy Library, 1994
Smith-Dorrien, Sir H, *Memories of Forty-Eight years' Service*, J Murray, 1925
Snyder J, *The Ideology of the Offensive: Military Decision Making and the Disasters of 1914*, Cornell University Press, 2013
Sondhaus, L, *Franz Conrad Von Hötzendorf: Architect of the Apocalypse*, Brill, 2000
Spiers, E M, *Haldane: Army Reformer*, Edinburgh University Press, 1984
Spiers, Edward M., *The Late Victorian Army 1868-1902*, Manchester University Press, 1992,
Stanhope, Philip H, *Notes of Conversations with the Duke of Wellington*, 1886
Staubwasser, O, *Das Königlich Bayerische 2. Infanterie-Regiment Kronprinz - Erinnerungsblätter*, J. Lindauer, 1924
Strachan, H, *European Armies and the Conduct of War*, Routledge, 1983
Stevenson, D., *Armaments and the Coming of War: Europe, 1904-1914*, Oxford University Press
Stoker D J, *Clausewitz: His Life and Work*, Oxford University Press, 2014
Stone J, *The Anglo-Boer War and Military Reforms in the United Kingdom* in Stone K & Schmidl E A, *The Boer War and Military Reforms*, University Press of America, 1988
Swinton, Lt. Col. E D, *The Green Curve and other stories*, Doubleday, Page & Co., 1914
Tanenbaum J K, *French Estimates of German Operational War Plans* in May, Ernest R, *Knowing One's Enemies*, Princeton Legacy Library, 1986
Tavenner, Hon. C H, *The Navy League Unmasked*, House of Representatives, 15th December 1915, US Government Printing Office, 1916
Terraine J, *Douglas Haig: The Educated Soldier*, Leo Cooper, 1990
Thévenet, Gen. C-M-F, *La Place de Belfort et la pénétration française dans le sud de l'Alsace en 1914*, Berger-Levrault, 1919

Thevenet, Gen., *Le Role de Belfort en 1914, Revue militaire générale*, January 1920.
Thomas H, *The Story of Sandhurst*, Hutchinson & Co., 1961
Thompson, F M L, *English Landed Society in the Nineteenth Century*, Routledge, new ed. 2006
Thooris, M-C & Billoux, C, *École polytechnique: une grande école dans la Grande Guerre*, Palaiseau, École polytechnique, 2004
Touzin, P & Vauvillier, F, *Les Canons de la Victoire 1914-18*, Histoires & Collections, Paris, 2006
Towle, P, *British Observers of the Russo-Japanese War* in *Aspects of the Russo-Japanese War*, The Suntory Centre, LSE, London, 1998
Travers, T H, *Technology, Tactics, and Morale: Jean de Bloch, the Boer War, and British Military Theory, 1900-1914*, Institute of Historical Research, London, May 1976
Tretyakov, Lt. Gen. N A, *My Experiences at Nan Shan and Port Arthur with the Fifth East Siberian Rifles*, Hugh Rees Ltd, 1911
Tricoche, G N, *Notes on Artillery Aviation and Artillery in Trench Warfare*, Field Artillery Journal, Vol. 6, No. 2, April-June 1916
Treitschke, H von, *Politics*, Vol. 1, 1898
Trotha, T von, *Tactical Studies on the Battles around Plevna*, trans. by 1st Lt. Carl Reichmann, US Army, Hudson-Kimberley Publishing Co., Kansas, 1896
Vickers Capt. C E, *The Trenches*, Blackwood's Magazine Vol. CLXXXIII, January 1908
Vincent, Capt. B, *Artillery at the Battle of the Yalu, The Russo-Japanese War: Reports from British Officers Attached to the Japanese and Russian Forces in the Field*, HMSO
Warner P, *Field Marshal Earl Haig*, The Bodley Head, 1991
Warren, K, *Steel, Ships and Men: Cammell Laird, 1824-1993*, Liverpool University Press, 1998
Wavell, Gen Sir A P, *Allenby: A Study in Greatness*, G G Harrap & Co., 1940
Weber, Thomas, *British War Propaganda and the Thesis of German Militarism. Friedrich von Bernhardi's Germany and the Next War reconsidered*. Unpublished thesis quoted in Rose, A, *Waiting for Armageddon? British Military Journals and the Images of Future War (1900–1914)*, 2011, Veröffentlichungen des Deutschen Historischen Instituts
Wells, H G, *Anticipations of the Reaction of Mechanical and Scientific Progress upon Human Life and Thought*, Chapman & Hall, 1902
Wells, H G, *What is Coming? A Forecast of things after the war*, Cassell, 1916
Wells, H G, *The Land Ironclads*, Strand Magazine, December 1903
Whitaker's Almanac, various years
Willcocks, Gen. Sir J, *With the Indians in France*, Constable & Co., 1920
Wilkinson, S, *Killing No Murder: An Examination of Some New Theories of War*, Army Quarterly, v.14, 1927
Wilson, A N, *The Victorians*, W W Norton, New York, 2003
Zepp, W T, *The Designer's Dilemma – Recoil: What to do with it?* Armaments Engineering & Technology Center, Picatinny Arsenal, NJ, USA, 2004
Zuber, T., *The Real German War Plan 1904-14*, The History Press, 2011

INDEX

1st Balkan War, 1912-3, 555
   Atrocities and massacres, 567
   Battles
      Çatalca, 252, 254, 566
      Fall of Thessaloniki, 565
      Giannitsa, 565
      Janina, 565
      Kirk Kilise, 566
      Kumanovo, 250, 561
      Lüleburgaz, 566
      Monastir, 251, 254, 562
      Sarantoporo, 562
      Siege of Adrianople, 567
      Siege of Shkodër, 561, 565
   Naval battles
      Elli, 565
      Lemnos, 565
   Treaty of London, 567
2nd Balkan War, 1913, 567
1st South African War, 435
   Battles
      Bronkhorstspruit, 435
      Laing's Nek, 435
      Majuba Hill, 369, 435, 465
      Schuinshoogte, 435
2nd South African War, 311
   Battles
      Belmont, 328
      Colenso, 50, 331, 622
      Elandslaagte, 322, 520
      Graspan, 328
      Klip Drift, 520
      Lindley, 338
      Magersfontein, 35, 50, 327, 329-31
      Modder River, 328
      Moedwil, 340
      Nooitgedacht, 339
      Paardeberg, 336
      Renoster River Bridge, 338
      Rooiwal, 340
      Sanna's Post, 338
      Stormberg, 50, 327
      Talana Hill, 321
      Tugela Heights, 335
      Tweebosch, 331, 340
      Yzerspruit, 340
   Casualties, 340
   Costs, 342
Adrian, L A, 746
   Casque Adrian, 746

Adwa, Battle 1896, 62, 118, 553
Aerial League of The British Empire, 14
Affaire des fiches, 111
Agadir crisis 1911, 119
Akers-Douglas, A, 363, 369
Aldershot Rifle Meeting, 496
Allenby, Gen. E H H, 372, 411-2, 431, 445, 777-9, 785-7, 791, 793
Altmayer, Gen. M-R, 152, 160
Alvin, Capt. P, 252, 255-7
American Civil War
   Overland Campaign, 51
   Siege of Petersburg, 52
Amery, L, 347, 605
   Army recruiting, 601
   The Problem of the Army, 346
André, Gen. L, 99, 111, 120
Angell, N
   Europe's Optical Illusion, 21
Anti-Semitism
   France, 107
   Germany, 66
Ardant du Picq, Col. C J J J, 151, 160
Army Council, 425, 427
Artois, 2nd Battle of, 735-9
Artois, 3rd Battle, 746
Asquith, H H, 426, 599-600, 804, 837
Asquith, R, 388
Aubers Ridge, Battle, 805
   Bombardment, 808
   Casualties, 810
Austrian arms manufacturers
   Skoda, 138, 255
Austro-Hungarian Army
   Strength 1912, 94
Automatic and semi-automatic weapons
   Fusil Hallé, 457
   Kjellman Light Machine Gun, 457
   Lewis Gun, vi, 456, 642
   Madsen Light Machine Gun, 456
   Maxim Machine Gun, 458, 500
   Mondragon rifle, 457
   Smith-Condit semi-automatic rifle, 457
   Vickers Machine Gun, 634
Automatic Rifle Committee, 458
Babington, Maj. Gen. J M, 631
Bacon, Rear Admiral Sir R, 658
Baden-Powell, Lt. Gen. R S S, 434
   Scouting for Boys, 582

Baden-Powell, Maj. B F S
 War in Practice, 441, 453
Balfour, Arthur, 426
Bange, C T M V R de, 231
Barbot, Gen. E J, 738
Barthou, J L, 127
Base of fire tactics, 470
Bazaine, Maréchal de France F A, 79, 81, 83, 86, 146, 165, 261, 267, 330
Bazaine-Hayter, Gen. G, 516
Bellenger, Capt. G, 250, 252-5
Bergson, H L, 162, 163, 205
Bernhardi, Gen. F A J von, 63, 137, 156
 Deutschland und der Nächste Krieg (Germany's Next War), 18, 68, 106, 581
Berteaux, H M, 96, 111, 120, 196
Bethell, Brig. Gen. H A, 222, 480-1
Bethmann Hollweg, T T F A von, 69
Billard, Lt. Col. M M A
 Éducation de l'Infanterie, 154
Bloch, Jean de, 23, 25, 28-9, 45-7, 51, 53-7, 89, 125, 171, 253, 257, 292, 311, 335, 343, 345, 349, 453, 483-4, 505, 508, 512, 514-6, 524, 526, 531, 535, 550, 553, 570-2, 583, 605, 625, 782, 792
 Is War Now Impossible?, 32
 Talk at RUSI 1901, 48-9, 55, 63, 348
Blücher, Gen. G L von, 149, 475-6
Board of Ordnance, 410
Bonar Law, A, 686
Bonnal, Gen. A B E H, 105, 134, 165, 168, 174, 349-50
Bosnia-Herzegovina, annexation by Austria 1908, 118
Boucher, Col. E A
 Etudes stratégique, 138
Bourbaki, Gen. C, 82, 90, 278, 721
Brackenbury, Gen. Sir H, 220, 645
Brailsford, H N
 The War of Steel & Gold, 59
Bredow, Maj. Gen. F W A von, 88
Brett, M V B, 34
Brett, R B (2nd Viscount Esher), 25, 34, 54, 341, 384, 392, 401-3, 425-6, 429, 432, 452, 499, 622, 834
 On Sir John French, 521
Brex, J T
 Scaremongering from the Daily Mail 1896-1914, The paper that foretold the war, 8
Briand, A, 299, 756-7, 768
Briggs, Lt. Gen. Sir C J, 785, 791, 793
Bright, Brig. Gen. R A, 487

British Arms Manufacturers
 Armes Automatique Lewis, 642
 Babcock and Wilcox, 686
 Birmingham Small Arms Co., 640-2
 Cammell Laird & Co. Ltd., 512, 643, 645, 665, 686
 Coventry Ordnance Works, 490, 643, 645, 649, 656, 658-9, 668, 678
 Dick, Kerr & Co., 686
 Fairfield Shipbuilding and Engineering Co. Ltd., 665
 Hadfield's Foundry Co. Ltd., 686
 John Brown & Co. Ltd., 665
 London Small Arms Co., 641
 Messrs J & P Hill, 686
 Nobel Dynamite Trust Company (Ltd.), 663
 Nobel Industries Ltd.), 695, 697
 Projectile Company, 686
 Rees Roturbo Manufacturing Co. Ltd, 686
 Royal Gun Factory, 601, 643, 645-6, 649, 651, 688
 Royal Gunpowder Factory, 645, 685
 Royal Small Arms Factory, 640-1, 645
 Sir W G Armstrong Whitworth & Co Ltd, 20, 646, 648, 650-1, 657, 668, 671, 685, 686
 Standard Small Arms Co., 641
 Thomas Firth & Co. Ltd., 686
 Vickers Ltd, 20, 459, 601, 641-3, 645-6, 648-9, 654, 657, 667-8, 673, 677, 685-6, 698-9
 William Beardmore & Co., 20, 643, 645, 648-9, 654, 656, 665, 668, 673, 685-6
British Army
 BEF
  First Army, 637, 676, 730, 738, 746-7, 769-70, 773, 796-7, 800, 802, 805, 810, 812, 818-20, 824, 826, 829, 836
  Second Army, 798
  Third Army, 762, 769, 771, 773
  Fourth Army, 795, 809
  I Corps, 784, 801, 808, 820, 824, 829
  II Corps, 635, 793, 799-800
  Indian Corps, 641, 668, 762, 795-6, 800, 804, 808
  IV Corps, 795-6, 800, 803, 807-8, 820, 823
 India, 439
 Other Ranks
  Conditions and Pay, 603
  Recruitment and Retention, 604

859

Training, 604
Preparedness for war, 620
Support of the civil powers, 438
The Militia, 435
The Volunteer Force, 436
The Yeomanry, 436
British Army manoeuvres
1895, 313
1898, 315
1912, 785
1913, 790
Aldershot Command exercise 1913, 455, 489, 790
British rifles
Lee-Enfield, 312, 633, 640
Lee-Metford, 312
Martini-Henry, 312
Brodrick, St J, 363, 384-5
Broqueville, C M P, Comte de, 137
Brownlow Stuart, Brig. Gen. B F, 595
Brugère, Gen. H J, 99
Brühl, M A Grafin von, 149
Brun, Gen. J J, 180, 196
Buat, Gen. E A L, 135-6, 266, 268, 270, 280
Budworth, Maj. Gen. C E D, 482, 485
Buller, Gen. Sir R, 48, 316, 320, 323, 331, 333, 345, 366, 428, 478
Bushidō, 182
Caillaux, J-M-A, 120, 122, 128
Cairnes, Capt. W E
An Absent-Minded War, 49, 366, 432
Campbell-Bannerman, Sir H, 21, 101, 587, 590
Methods of Barbarism, 341
Canadian Shell Committee, 687
Canal de la Haute Deûle, 825, 826, 829
Capper, Maj.Gen. Sir T, 390, 777, 801
Cardot, Gen. L, 147, 158-9, 164, 173, 175, 178
Hérésies et apostasies militaires de *notre temps*, 155
Cardwell, E
Army reforms, 4, 369, 384, 575
Carnot, Count L N M, 30
Carter, Brig. Gen. F C, 468
Castelnau, Gen. E de C de, 91, 115, 131, 158, 257, 713, 715, 742, 757, 818, 822
Cavalry
Its future, 344
Training 1907, 503
Use and equipment, 498
Cavalry actions
Brunstatt, 705

Halen, 706
Lagarde, 706
Tagsdorf, 705
Cavendish, S C, Marquess of Hartington, later 8th Duke of Devonshire, 425
Cébro, Cdt.
Les Conditions de l'offensive, 155
Chamberlain, H S
The Foundations of the Nineteenth Century, 70
Champagne, 2nd Battle, 743
Chanzy, Gen. A, 4, 82
Charleroi, Battle of, 722
Charteris, Brig. Gen. J, 416, 421, 787, 794-5, 836-7, 841
Chesney, Gen. G T, 3, 4
Chetwode, Lt. Gen. Sir P, 502
Chief of the Imperial General Staff, 425
Childers, R E, 344
The Riddle of the Sands, 7
Children Act 1908, 588
Churchill, W S, 436
Army and industrial disputes, 592, 595
Landships Committee, 513
On cavalry, 499
President, Board of Trade, 22
Royal Marine Artillery, 645, 658
The World Crisis, 766
Cissey, Gen. E C de, 93, 96
Cité St Auguste, 823, 826, 828
Cité St Elie, 825
Cité St Laurent, 826
Clark-Kennedy, 2nd Lt. R W S, 386
Clausewitz, P G von, 81, 137, 146-7, 149-51, 157, 159, 164-5, 175, 360, 431, 474, 477, 506-7, 514, 529
Clemenceau, G B, 86, 108-9, 174, 756
Clément-Grandcourt, Capt. A J E, 200
Clery, Maj. Gen. Sir C F, 51, 54
Coal Mines (Minimum Wage) Act 1912, 588
Coal Mines Act 1911, 588
Coal Mines Regulation Act 1908, 588
Cochrane, Rear Admiral B E, 384
Colley, Maj. Gen. G P, 369, 435, 465
Colonisation
Belgium and the Congo, 62
Germany and the Slavs, 64
Germany in Africa and the Pacific, 67
Italy, the Horn of Africa and Libya, 62
The British Empire, 60
USA and the Philippines, etc., 62
Colvile, Maj. Gen. Sir H E, 329, 331, 337
Combes, E, 111, 120
Combined Training Manual 1905, 450

Comité central de l'artillerie, 257
Committee on the Education and Training of Officers 1901, 363
Compton, Lord A F, MP, 500
Congreve, Lt. Gen. Sir W N, 416, 458, 793
Connaught, Lt. Gen. HRH Duke, 74, 313, 316-8, 359, 426
Conseil supérieur de la guerre, 129, 257
Couper, Brig. Gen. V A, 631
Crise de l'obus-torpille, 92
Hamilton, Gen. Sir I S M, 403
Crofters Holdings (Scotland) Act, 1886, 438
Culmann, Gen. F, 204
d'Amade, Gen. A G L, 100
Daily Mail, 1, 8, 10, 15, 17, 612, 809
Daniels, J, Secretary of the Navy, 569, 664
Darwin, C
  On the Origin of Species, 71
Davidson, Archbishop R T, 611
Davies, Brig. Gen. F J, 623
Davies, Gen. Sir F J, 801, 804
Debeney, Gen. M-E, 184, 193
Defenestration of Prague, 612
Delcassé, T, 756
Demange, Gen. M-G, 124, 707
Deport, Col. J A, 223-5, 228, 259, 267-9
Déroulède, P, 94
Detaille, E B, 198-9
Deutschsoziale antisemitische Partei, 67
Deville, Capt. E S-C, 221, 225-6, 228, 269
Diedenhofen (Thionville), 99, 132, 134, 208-9
Donop, S B von, 340, 630, 641, 645, 656, 668, 697
Doughty, R
  Seeds of Disaster, 202
Douglas, Gen. Sir C W H, 434
Dragomirov, Gen. M I, 158-9, 532
Dreyfus, Capt. A, vi, 78, 107-9, 111, 116-7, 120, 128
Drumont, E, 110
Drury-Lowe, Lt. Gen. Sir D C, 499
Du Cane, Maj. Gen. Sir J P, 408-9, 454, 458, 460, 479, 482, 604, 672, 688, 701, 809
Du Maurier, G L B
  An Englishman's Home, 11
Duchêne, Gen. D A, 718
Dulitz, Gen. O F F von, 279
Edmonds, Brig. Gen. Sir J E, 53, 403, 407, 431, 458, 637, 776, 778
Education (Administrative Provisions) Act 1907, 588

Education (Provision of Meals) Act 1906, 588
Education Act, 1902, 8
Elementary Education Act, 1870, 8
Elgin Commission, v, 342, 347, 367, 429, 492, 498
Elgin, Lord, 425, 623, 645
Esterházy, Maj. C M F W, 109-10
Étienne, E, 129, 196
Ewart, Lt. Gen. Sir J S, 102, 458, 522
Faidherbe, Gen. L L C, 83
Fairholme, Brig. Gen. W E, 484
Fanshawe, Lt. Gen. Sir E A, 485
Farndale, Sir M
  History of the Royal Regiment of Artillery, 622
Fasken, Lt. Gen. Sir C G M, 631
Faure, F, 109
Favre, J C G, 81
Fayolle, Gen. M E, *173*, 184, 193, 259, 701, 732, 738-9, 746-7, 774, 810, 819, 837
Fergusson, Lt. Gen. Sir C, 629
Festubert, Battle, 812
  Bombardment, 813
  Casualties, 816
Field Service Regulations 1909, 491, 523
Filloux, Col. L J F, 259
First Afghan War, 435
Foch, Marshal F, 40, 103, 151
  20e Corps, 636
  2nd Battle of Artois, 302
  Affaire des fiches, 260
  Army career, 173
  Background, 172
  Battle of the Marne, 725
  Borny-Colombey 1870, 165
  Des Principes de la Guerre, 177, 191
  Dragomirov, 158
  French superiority, 162
  Groupe provisoire du Nord, 730
  Henry Wilson, 105
  Invasion of Lorraine, 184, 710, 714
  Jesuit teaching, 155
  Maistre, 66, 156
  On de Grandmaison, 185
  On Manchuria, 552
  On offensives, 733
  Teachings, 175
Fok, Gen. A V, 536, 538, 545
Forestier-Walker, Maj. Gen. Sir G T, 828
Fortescue, Brig. Gen. F A, 631
Foster, Sir M, 367
Franco-Prussian War, 47
  Battles
    Borny-Colombey, 165

861

Gravelotte, 79, 165
Gravelotte, 330
Le Mans, 82
Lisaine, *27*, 82, 90, 278
Mars le Tour, 51, 88
Mars-le-Tour, 165
Sedan, 93
Spicheren, 173
Wissembourg, 173
Wœrth, 173, 446
Franz Ferdinand, Archduke, 32, 351, 609, 613
French airpower, 1914, 709
French Arms Manufacturers
  Atelier de Construction de Bourges, 231
  Atelier de Construction de Puteaux (APX), 223
  Atelier de Précision, 231
  Leflaive-usines de La Chaléassière à St Etienne, 732
  Manufacture d'armes de Châtellerault, 231
  Saint-Chamond (Compagnie des forges et aciéries de la marine et d'Homécourt (FAMH)), 244, 259, 750, 754
  Schneider et Cie, 20, 244, 247, 249, 259, 313, 343, 750, 754
  Société Anonyme des Anciens Etablissements Cail, 232
  Société de Construction des Batignolles, 754
  Société des Automobiles Renault, 784
French Army
  Armée de l'Orient, 768
  Artillery
    Artillerie lourde à grande puissance - ALGP, 748, 755
    Artillerie lourde sur voie ferrée - ALVF, 748, 755
  Groupe d'Armées de l'Est (GAE), 115
  Groupe d'Armées du Centre (GAC), 115, 234, 757
  Groupe d'Armées du Nord (GAN), 730, 747, 771-3
  Ire Armée, 131, 708
  IIe Armée, 131, *210*, 743
  IIIe Armée, 131, *209*
  IVe Armée, 132, 743
  Ve Armée, 132, 721, 722
  VIe Armée, *489*, 747
  IXe Armée, 725
  Xe Armée, 301, 730-1, 739, 746, 769, 772, 798, 810, 819
  Officer and NCO shortages, 128
  Region Fortifiée de Dunkerque, 771
  Région fortifiée de Verdun, 234

Shell supplies, 292
Strength 1912, 94
Strength 1914, 97
Terms of service, 95
French Army manoeuvres
  1901, 55
  1905, 552
  1910, 484
  1912, 789
  1913, 789
French Army uniforms
  La Tenue Reseda, 196
  Le Bleu Horizon, 202
  Le Pantalon Rouge, 193
French artillery
  Canon de campagne de 75-mm modèle 1897, ii, vi, 31, 86, 88, 101, 134, 137, 216, 228, 230, 232-3, 236-7, 239-40, 242-3, 247, 250, 252, 257-8, 292, 297-8, 300-2, 331, 340, 390, 430, 485, 525, 590, 643, 648, 690, 710, 720, 725, 746, 750, 797, 814
  Canon de campagne de 80-mm de Bange Modèle 1877, 232
  Canon de montagne de 80-mm de Bange Mle 1878, 232
  Canon de campagne de 90-mm de Bange modèle 1877, 232, 293, 298
  Canon de campagne de 95-mm modèle 1875 de Lahitolle, 231
  Canon de campagne 95-mm modèle 1888 de Lahitolle, 294, 752
  Canon de 105 L modèle 1913 TR Schneider, 249, 257, 748
  Canon de 105 M modèle 1914 TR Schneider, 750
  Canon de 120 Long de Bange Mle 1878, 232
  Canon de 120 mm Schneider-Canet M1897, 251, 254
  Canon de 155 C de Bange modèle 1881, 232, 291
  Canon de 155 C modèle 1904 TR Rimailho, 291, 748
  Canon de 155 C modèle 1915 Saint-Chamond, 750
  Canon de 155 C modèle 1915 Schneider, 292, 750
  Canon de 155 GPF (*modèle 1917 Filloux*), 303, 751
  Canon de 155 L modèle 1877/1914 sur affût Schneider, 248, 292
  Canon de 155 Long de Bange Mle 1877, 232

Canon de 194 GPF sur affût chenilles Saint-Chamond, 303
Canon de 240 de côte de Bange Mle 1884, 232
Mortier de 150-mm Schneider-Canet M1897, 252
Mortier de 220-mm de Bange Mle 1880, 232
Mortier de 220 TR modèle 1915 Schneider, 751
Mortier de 270-mm de Bange Mle 1885, 232
Mortier de 280 sur affût chenilles Saint-Chamond, 303
Mortier de 280 TR Schneider modèle 1914, 249, 292, 751, 752
Mortier de 370-mm Filloux, 291-2, 303, 743
Obusier Anglais BL Mk VI de 8 pouces (203.2 mm), 751
Plaquette Malandrin, 247
Schneider-Canet Canon de Campagne de 75-mm Mle 1904, 255
Schneider-Creusot modèle 1907 75-mm TR, 251
Système La Hitte, 87
French Infantry Weapons
  Automatic & Semi-automatic
    canon de 37 à tir rapide, 731
  Flamethrowers
    appareil lance-flammes No. 3, 731
  Trench Mortars
    Canon de 37 mm Mle 1885 TR système Hotchkiss, 731
    Canon de 80-mm de montagne aménage en lance-mines Gatard, 731
    Mortier Aasen, 731
    Mortier de 240 CT Mle 1915, 748
    Mortier de 58 T, 731
    Mortier de 75-mm Mle 1915 type A Schneider, 748
French Military Laws
  loi de 27 juillet 1872 (loi Cissey), 96
  loi des cadres de l'infanterie 1912, 128
  loi des cadres de la cavalerie 1913, 129
  loi des trois ans 1913, 96, 127, 259
  loi du 15 juillet 1889 (loi Freycinet), 96
  loi du 19 juillet 1892, 96
  loi du 21 mars 1905 (loi Berteaux), 96, 259
French railway development, 113
French rifles
  Chassepot rifle, Fusil modèle 1866, 86
  Fusil Modèle 1886, Lebel, 312

French Tanks
  Renault FT, 304
French War Plans
  Plan XI, 174
  Plan XIV, 94, 99
  Plan XV, 99, 100
  Plan XVI, 100, 103, 121-2, 126, 129
  Plan XVII, 91, 129, 132, 134
French, Field Marshal Sir J D P, 25, 316, 434, 441, 484, 517, 621, 804, 812
  Cavalry lance, 345
  Loos aftermath, 827
  On Gen. Lanrezac, 722
  Resignation and the Curragh, 521
  South Africa, 322
Freycinet, C de, 82, 92, 96, 113
Fuller, Maj. Gen. J F C, 57, 523
Furse, Lt. Gen. Sir W T, 460, 486, 630
Gallieni, Gen. J, 114, 134, 234, 725, 756
Galton, F
  Africa for the Chinese, 72
  Eugenics, 71
Gambetta, L, 81
Gatacre, Maj. Gen. W, 323, 327, 428
Gathorne-Hardy, Gen. the Hon. Sir J F, 389
Gawler, Col. G, 330
General Staff Officers' conference 1908, 489
General Staff Officers' conference 1909, 454
General Staff Officers' conference 1910, 458
General Staff Officers' conference 1911, 484, 491
General Staff Officers' conference 1912, 623
General Staff Officers' conference 1914, 452, 498
Gentarō, Gen. Baron K, 547
German airpower, 1914, 710
German Arms Manufacturers
  Krupp (Fried. Krupp Grusonwerk AG.), 20, 87, 212, 231, 243, 245, 249, 255, 313, 343, 550, 645, 649, 698
  Rheinmetall Rheinische Metallwaaren und Maschinenfabrik AG, 20, 243, 645
German Army
  1. Armee, 132
  2. Armee, 132, 433, 723
  Strength 1912, 94
  Taxation and effects, 125
  Terms of service, 95
German Army Law
  1912, 125
  1913, 125
German border fortifications, 208
  Breuschstellung, 209

863

Moselstellung, 209
German gas mask development, 822
German Naval Law
   1912, 125
German Navy
   Costs of High Seas Fleet, 98
German rifles
   Dreyse needle rifle, leichtes Perkussionsgewehr Model 1841, 86
   Mauser Gewehr 88, 312
   Mauser Gewehr 98, 312, 504, 507
   Mauser Modell 95, 311, 312, 320
Gilbert, Capt. G, 350
Gilbert, Capt. J-F-G, 158, 164
Gilmour, Col. G, 388
Girouard, Col. Sir P, 671-2
Givenchy, Battle, 817
   Casualties, 817
Glück, Capt. G L
   Obusiers de campagne et Artillerie lourde, 277
Gneisenau, Gen. A W A von, 148
Goiran, Gen. F L A, 120
Gold, Capt. E, 824
Goltz, W L C von der, 53, 54, 67, 147, 161, 351-2, 569
   Das Volk in Waffen (The Nation in Arms), 67
Gommecourt, iv, 516, 636, 651, 657, 809, 830
Gough, Brig. Gen. J E, 452
Gough, Gen. Sir H
   Loos, 819
Government of India Act, 1858, 439
Government of Ireland Act, 1914, 609
Government social reforms, 587
GQG Publications
   But et conditions d'une action offensive d'ensemble, 733, 734, 740
   Extrait d'une note rédigée dans une armée, sur le rôle de'artillerie dans les attaques, 733
Grand Couronné, 92
Grandmaison, Col. F-J L de, 112, 121, 130, 134, 152, 178, 180, 182-5, 250, 434, 477
Graves, Brig. Gen. F J, 348
Greenhalgh, E
   Foch in Command, 715, 719
Grey of Fallodon, Viscount, 101, 515, 571
Grierson, Lt. Gen. Sir J M, 101-2, 389, 430, 457, 466, 495, 635, 784-7, 793, 798
Grouard, Col.

Mission de couverture du 3e corps d'arméee, 138
Grouard, Lt. Col. A A
   France et Allemagne, 188
Groupe antijuif, 41, 110
Grünert, Gen. Maj. P F A, 433
Guggisberg, Brig. Gen. F, 5
Guise, Battle of, 722
Haeckel, E H P A, 70
Hagron, Gen. A A R, 100
Hague Convention 1899, 31
Haig, Gen. Sir D, 12, 501, 589, 726
   Aldershot Command exercise 1913, 455, 489, 624
   Army manoeuvres 1912, 782
   At Ladysmith, 520
   Aubers Ridge, 806
   Cavalry lance, 345
   Cavalry Training 1907, 503
   Conflict with Sir John French, 520
   Elgin Commission, 498
   Elgin Commission evidence, 347
   Entrance to the Staff College, 776
   Family background, 775
   Field Service Regulations, 427, 467, 522
   Influence of Henderson, 445
   Loan to Sir John French, 519
   Loos aftermath, 827
   Loos planning, 819
   Neuve Chapelle, 795
   On cavalry, 498
   On cavalry and lances, 499
   On 'gentlemen', 395
   On Haldane, 426
   On Kiggell, 479
   On Sir Evelyn Wood, 369
   Sacking Stuart-Wortley, 516
   Spiritualism, 780
   Staff College, 431
   Staff Officers' Conference 1908, 403
   Understanding and speaking French, 375
Haisnes, 825, 828
Haking, Gen. Sir R C B, 403, 445, 467, 637, 777, 785, 825-8
Haldane, Gen. Sir A, 455, 485, 487
   Criticism of Public Schools, 404
Haldane, R B, 101-3, 402, 405, 416, 426, 428, 438, 525, 621, 625, 781, 783, 828
Hale, Col. L A, 48, 336, 433
Hamilton, Gen. Sir I S M, 181, 340, 389, 454, 467, 469, 477, 498, 504, 514, 535, 549

South Africa, 322
Hamilton, Maj. Gen. E O F, 631
Hamilton, Maj. Gen. H I W, 629
Hamilton-Gordon, Lt. Gen. Sir A, 489
Hamley, Maj. Gen. Sir E B, 430
Hammersley, Maj. Gen. F, 367, 630
Hardecourt-aux-bois, 636
Hardie, Keir, 610
Harmsworth, A (1st Viscount Northcliffe), 8, 15
Harnes, 826, 828
Hart, Maj. Gen. A F, 333
Hatzfeldt zu Wildenburg, M H P G *Graf* von, 613
Haußner, K, 216, 228
Headlam, Gen. Sir J E W, 622
Headlam, Lt. Col. C, 348
Heath, Maj. Gen. H N C, 777
Henderson, Col. G F R, 53, 55, 346, 361, 388, 441, 456, 498, 504
   Criticism and Modern Tactics, 444
   Infantry Training, 450
   My Experiences of the Boer War, 449
   The Science of War, 444, 451
   The Training of Infantry *for Attack*, 445
Herment, Gen. G J, 140, 509
Herr, Gen. F G, 101, 137, 233-8, 242, 250-2, 254-7, 292-3, 753
Hezlet, Maj. Gen. R K, 481
Hill 70 (Loos), 820, 823, 826, 828
Hohenzollern Redoubt, 764, 818, 820, 825
Home, Maj. J M
   War in Manchuria, 467
Honourable war death (*meiyo no senshi*), 182
Horne, Lt. Gen. H S, 701
Hötzendorf, Conrad von, 351
Housing of the Working Classes Act 1903, 587
Housing, Town Planning, &c. Act 1909, 588
Howard, Michael, 26
Huguet, Gen. V J M, 100-3, 762-3, 770, 805
Hulluch, 818, 820, 823, 826, 828
Hunter-Weston, Lt. Gen. A, 403, 412, 419, 445, 458, 804, 811
Hutton, Lt. Gen. Sir E T H, 631
Infantry Training 1914, 492
Invasion scares, 1
   A history of the sudden and terrible invasion of England by the French, in the month of May, 1852, 3
   An Englishman's Home, 11

involving a Channel Tunnel, 5
involving food shortages, 5
involving Germany, 5
involving Irish independence, 5
involving Russia or France, 5
involving the USA & Canada, 5
Modern warfare or, How our soldiers fight, 5
The Battle of Dorking, 3
The Invasion of 1883, 5
The Invasion of 1910, 11
The Riddle of the Sands, 7
Isaacs, R D, 387
Italy-Austrian relations, 133
James, Capt. W H, 452
Jameson, Henrietta Frances (née Haig), 779
Janson, Gen. R von, 56
Japanese militarism
   Myth of, 181
   The honourable war death, 183
Jaurès, J, 127
Jelf, Maj. Gen. R H, 367, 373
Joffre, Marshal J J C, ii, iii, 103, 112, 114-6, 119, 121-3, 126, 129-30, 132, 134, 172, 181, 184, 234, 249-50, 257, 293, 298, 300-3, 375, 420, 667, 721-4, 726, 738-43, 747-8, 750, 756-8, 761, 763, 768-9, 772, 789-90, 798, 803, 805, 812, 818-20, 822, 829
Jones, S
   Boer War to World War, 468
Kekewich, Maj. Gen. R G, 321, 339-40, 630
Kelly-Kenny, Gen. Sir T, 336, 602
Kenyon-Slaney, Maj. Gen. W R, 631
Kessler, Gen. C
   Tactique des Trois Armes, 168
Kiggell, Lt. Gen. Sir L E, 171, 403, 430, 445, 458, 460-1, 466, 477-9, 484-5, 487-8, 491
Kinloch, Lt. Col. D, 384
Kipling, R, 7
Kitchener, Field Marshal Lord, 6-7, 336-7, 339-40, 363, 369, 421, 425, 429, 449, 494, 520-1, 625, 627-8, 632-5, 637, 639, 641, 644, 669-71, 676-7, 685, 697, 757, 761, 767, 799, 809, 812, 820, 827, 829, 836
Kitson, Col. G C, 382
Knox, Maj. Gen. Sir W G, 471
Kondratenko, Lt. Gen. R I, 545
Krantz, C, 42, 92, 429, 847
Kuropatkin, Gen. A N, 210, 532
La Boisselle, 635
Labour Exchanges Act 1909, 588

Lacroix, Gen. H de, 160, 200
Lahitolle, H P de, 231
Lamothe, Gen. L J B de, 243, 248, 257, 291
Landon, Maj. Gen. H J S, 629
Langlois, Gen. H, 56, 105, 138, 157, 165, 175, 180, 266-7, 269-70, 279-80, 349, 516
Lanrezac, Gen. C L M, 134, 163, 193, 721-2
Lansdowne, Lord, 48, 331, 603
Laure, Gen. A M E
   L'Offensive française, 153
Laurie, Lt. Gen. J W, MP, 341, 499
Lavisse, Gen. E-C, 193, 197
Lawrence, Gen. the Hon. Sir H A, 479
Laws of War: Convention Relative to the Opening of Hostilities, 614
Le Cateau, Battle of, 622
Le Queux, W T
   The Invasion of 1910, 11
Lee, Capt. A H, 367, 374
Legge, Col. the Hon. H, MP, 499
Legrand-Girarde, Gen. E E, 708
Levée en masse, 30
Leveson-Gower, 2nd Lt J H, 384
Lewal, Gen. J L, 146
Liberal Government 1906, 587
Liddell Hart, B, 57, 150, 184
Moore, Sir J, 446
Lloyd George, D, 455, 589, *590*, 600, 627-8, 669-1, 673, 676, 677, 684, 687-8, 690, 692, *778*, *809*, 837
Lloyd, H H E, 2
Lone, Dr S, 182
Loos, Battle
   Bombardment, 823
   Casualties, 818
   First day, 825
   Second day, 826
      Casualties, 827
   Use of gas, 820, 824
Lorraine, French invasion, 713
Lossberg, Col. F K von, 433
Lucas, Lt. Col. P M H, 189, 192
Macdonogh, Lt. Gen. Sir G M W, 431, 777, 779, 836
Mackenzie, Maj. Gen. C J, 629
MacMahon, Maréchal de France M E P M de, 37, 79, 93, 321
Macready, Maj. Gen. C F N, 592, 799
Madsen, Capt. V H O, 456
Mahon, Lt. Gen. Sir B T, 630
Maillard, Gen. A G dit, 164
Maistre, J M Comte de, 66, 156, 157, 164

Considérations sur la France, 156
Maitrot, Gen. C A E X
   Nos frontières de l'Est et du Nord, 138
Mametz, 636
Maresuke, Gen. N, 537, 544, 546, 548-9
Margueritte, Gen. J-A, 88
Markham, Lt. Gen. Sir E, 373, 388
Marne, Battle of the, 617
Martin, Rudolf
   Zeppelin scare, 15
Massy, Lt. Gen. W G D, 500
Matrimonial Causes Act 1907, 588
Maud'huy, Gen. L E de, 184, 193, 798
Maude, Col. F N, 430, 467, 477, 505, 514, 526
Maurice, Maj. Gen. Sir F B, 605
Maurice, Maj. Gen. Sir J F, 47, 330
Mayer, E, 277, 278
Mayer, Emile, 39, 43
   Comment on pouvait prévoir l'immobilisation des fronts, 42
   Evolution de la Tactique, 41
Mayne, Lt. Col. C B
   The Lance as a Cavalry Weapon, 500
McCracken, Brig. Gen. F W N
   On trench mortars, 1912, *510*
McMahon, Lt. Col. N R, 457, 459-61, 492, 523
Mead, G
   The Good Soldier, 776, 781
Meckel, Maj. K W J, 183
Messimy, A M, 105, 112, 115, 121, 196, 202, 516
Methuen, Lt. Gen. Lord, 49, 323, 327, 329, 331, 340, 366, 428, 526
Metz, 99, 122, 130, 131, 132, 134, 173, 208, 209, 246, 846
Michel, Gen. V C, 103, 112
Military expenditure, 570
Military Manoeuvres Act. 1897, 315
Miller Maguire, Dr T, 356, 361, 371-2, 405, 422, 441
Millerand, A, 121, 135, 202, 298, 761-3
Millet, Gen. C-F, 173
Milyutin, Count D A, 56
Miribel, Gen. J de, 174
Möller, Lt Col B D, 322
Moltke, H von (The Elder), 56, 65
Moltke, Helmuth von (The Elder), 81
Monis, A E E, 120
Mons, Battle of, 616
Montaigne, Col. Jean-Baptiste
   Vaincre, 44, 153
Montaigne, Lt. Col. J-B, 182

Montauban, 114, 629
Montgomery, Maj. Gen. R A, 631
Moore, Sir J
    Light Brigade, 452
Morgan, J P, Snr, 659
Morgan, Lt. Gen. Sir F E, 383
Morhange, Battle of, 717
    Casualties, 719
Morland, Lt. Gen. Sir T L N, 631, 785
Morocco crisis 1905, 117
Mulliner, H H, 14
Murray, Gen. Sir A J, 458, 498, 834, 836
Museum of War and Peace, 32
Mutzig, 209
National Debts of combattant nations, 98
National Insurance Act 1911, 588
National Miners' Strike 1912, 597
National Service League, 589, 591, 782
Négrier, Gen. F O de, 164, 167, 168, 350
Neuve Chapelle, Battle, 803
    Casualties, *804*
    Planning, 799
Nicholson, Field Marshal Sir W G, 407, 420, 427, 458, 602, 647
Nivelle, Gen. R G, 112, 115, 823
Nobel Peace Prize, 20-1, 32, 50
Nobel, A B, 20, 663
Noble, Sir A, 665
Nord-Pas de Calais Mining Basin, 85
Ochakov, testing grounds, 751
Officer Training Corps, 427
Oku, Gen. Y, 535
Old-Age Pensions Act 1908, 588
Palikao. C G comte de, 79
Paloque, Col. H J
    Artillerie de Campagne, 280
Pannewitz, Gen. G L F von, 433
Paris Commune, 83
Parliament Act 1911, 590
Parsons, Lt. Gen. Sir L W, 631
Pau, Gen. P, 116, 754, 789
Pellé, Gen. M C J, 763, 768, 774
Perceval, Maj. Gen. Sir E M
    Education of officers 1910, 406
Percin, Gen. A, 179-80, 260, 37-6, 573
Pétain, Gen. H P B O J, 184, 193, 234, 735, 738, 743, 746, 837
Picquart, Col. M-G, 109
Pierrefeu, J de
    Plutarque a menti, 162
Pierron, Gen. E, 147
Pilcher, Maj. Gen. T D, 416, 418, 448-9, 482-3, *486*, 623
Poincaré, R, 117, 123, 126,7, 756-7, 768

Pont à Vendin, 826, 828
Princip, Gavrilo, 609
Public Health Act 1904, 587
Pulteney, Lt. Gen. Sir W P, 412, 418
Queen Victoria
    Spread of haemophilia in Europe's Royal families, 73
Ramsay, Maj. Gen. Sir J G, 631, 828
Rawlinson, Gen. Sir H S, 184, 340, 403, 412, 445, 450, 491-2, 495, 514, 624, 634, 785, 792, 798
    Givenchy, 817
    Loos, 819, 823
    Neuve Chapelle, 795, 799, 801
    Aftermath, 804
Reffye, Gen. J-B V de, *87*
Règlement de manœuvre d'infanterie, 191, 207, 233
Règlement sur la conduite des grandes unités, 185
Règlement sur le service des armées en campagne, 166, 191, 232
Reichstag elections
    1903, 118
Reid, W
    Architect of Victory - Douglas Haig, 781
Re-Insurance Treaty (1887), *29*
Rhodes, C, 331
Rimailho, Capt. E, 129, 228, 243, 259, 292
Rimington, Brig. Gen. M F, 346
Robbins, S
    British Generalship on the Western Front 1914-8, 434
Roberts, Lord, 12, 55, 327, 333, 337, 344, 352, 364, 368, 385, 440, 443, 498, 500, 504, 602
    Mansion House speech 1905, 588
Robertson, J M, MP, 18
Rocolle P
    L'hécatombe des généraux, 723
Rosny, J H
    La Guerre Anglo-Boer, 36
Rossignol, Battle, 720
Rouquerol, Gen. G, 723
Rouvier, M, 107, 111
Rowntree, J
    Poverty, A Study of Town Life, 586
Royal Commission on the Defence of the United Kingdom 1859, 3
Ruggles-Brise, Maj. H G, 381
Russian Army
    Strength 1912, 94
Russian border fortifications, 208
Russo-Japanese War, 531

Battles
    Liaoyang, 34, 571
    Mukden, 34, 210, 531, 550, 572
    Nanshan, 210, 535, 571
    Port Arthur, 537
    Shaho, 34, 469
    Siege of Port Arthur, 34
    Tsushima, 534
    Yalu River, 469, 535
    Treaty of Portsmouth, 550
Russo-Turkish War, 26, 59, 532
    Battles
        Plevna, 27, 54, 210, 243, 522
Saar-Warndt coal mining basin, 84
Salisbury, Lord, 434
Sandys, Col. T M, 525
Sankey, Capt. C E P
    The Campaign of the Future, 453
Sarrebourg, Battle of, 708
    Casualties, 719
Sauret, Gen. H S, 723
Scharnhorst, Gen. G J D von, 148
Schirmer, GenLt. H, 276
Schoen, W E *Freiherr* von, 615
School of Musketry, 458
Schubert, Gen. R T L von, 279
Schwab, C M, 661
Sclater, Lt. Gen. Sir H C, 434
Scott, D
    Douglas Haig - Diaries and Letters, 781
Select Committee on the Royal Military College, Sandhurst, 1855, 364
Serbia. Invasion, 761
Séré de Rivières fortifications, 90, 93, 94, 134, 146, 208
Séré de Rivières, Gen. R A, 89
Serre, 657
Service Renseignement Observation Terrestrial (S.R.O.T.), 749
Service Renseignment Artillerie (S.R.A.), 749
Shearman, Capt. C, 621, 622, 624, 626
Sheldon, Jack, xi
Shimazu, Prof. N, 183
Shimose Powder, 485, 544, 545, 647
Shops Act 1911, 588
Simkin, P
    Kitchener's Army, 625
Smirnov, Lt. Gen. K N, 543
Smith, Maj. Gen. S C U, 485
Smith, W H, 426
Smith-Dorrien, Lt. Gen. Sir H L, 409, 421, 458, 493, 496-7, 798, 835
    Education of officers 1910, 407
    South Africa, 337

Snow, Lt. Gen. Sir T D'O, 445, 785
Some Tactical Notes on the Russo-Japanese War, 646
Somerville, A A, 368, 371
Sordet, Gen. A, 723
Spanish-American War (1898)
    Battles
        El Caney, 311
        San Juan Heights, 311
Spencer, H, 162
    Principles of Biology, 71
Spens, Maj. Gen. J, 630
Staff College
    Comparisons with *Kriegsakademie*, 431
    Performance in South Africa, 429
    Quality of graduates, 432
Stanhope Memorandum, 437
Stead, W T, 50
Stoessel, Gen. A M, 536, 543
Strachan, H
    European Armies and the Conduct of War, 171
Strassburg (Strasbourg), 131, 134, 208, 209
Stuart Wortley, Maj. Gen. M, 516
Stucley, Maj. H StL, 388
Suttner, Baroness Bertha von, 20, 32
    La Thèse de Jean Bloch, 31
Suvorov, Gen. A V, 159
Swaine, Maj. Gen. Sir L V, 499
Symons, Gen Sir W P, 321
Talbot, Lt. Col. J S, 373
Tank development
    Burstyn, G A, *Motorgeschütz*, 513
    Diplock, B J, Pedrail, 513
    Donohue, Maj. W E, 513
    Ferrus, Cdt., *Saint-Chamond*, 513
    Fowler B5 Armoured Road Train, 512
    Hornsby Ackroyd Caterpillar Tractor, 511
    Landships Committee, 513
    Levavasseur, Capt., *Projet de canon autopropulseur*, 513
    Lombard Steam Log Hauler, 511
    Mechanical Transport Committee, 511, 513
    Mendeleev, V,, 513
    Mole, L E de, 514
    Saint-Chamond, 511
    Schneider et Cie, 511
    Société des Automobiles Renault, 511
    Swinton, Maj. E D, 510
    The Holt Manufacturing Co., Stockton, 511
    Vickers, Capt. C E, 510, 513
    Wells, H G, *The Land Ironclads*, 512

Terraine, J
  The Educated Soldier, 775
Territorial and Reserve Forces Act 1907, 427
Teutonic Order, 64
The Great Unrest, 590, 619
The People's Budget, 589
Thesiger, Maj. Gen. G H, 629
Thiepval, 629, 659
Thirty Years War, 612, 613
Thomas, Albert, 298
Tithe Commutation Act, 1836, 438
Tottleben, Gen. F E von, 28, 54
Towle, Dr P, 515
Trade Boards Act 1909, 588
Trades Union Agitation
  Liverpool General Strike 1911, 594
  Llanelli Riots 1911, 595
  Royal Arsenal strike 1914, 600
  South Wales Miners' Strike 1910, 592
  Strikes 1910, 591
  Strikes 1911, 594
  Strikes 1912, 597
  Strikes 1914, 599
Trades Union Membership, 590
Treaty of Frankfurt, 83
Treitschke, H G von
  A Word about Our Jews (Ein Wort über unser Judenthum), 66
  The Origins of Prussianism, 65
Tretyakov, Col. N, 536, 538, 542, 545-6
Tricoche, Lt. G N, 709
Trimmel, Haptm R, 351
Trochu, Gen. L-J, 81
Trouée de Charmes, 90-1, 124
Turco-Italian War 1911-12, 50, 62, 119, 554
Turpin, E
  Picric Acid, 92
UK employment changes, 576
UK physical deterioration, 583
  Army recruitment, 584
  Inter-Departmental Committee on Physical Deterioration, 585, 586
  Recommendations, 586
UK population growth
  Ireland, 575
  Urban growth, 575
Unemployed Workmen Act 1905, 587
Universal Colliery, Senghenydd, disaster 1913, 599
US Arms Manufacturers
  Bethlehem Steel Company, 649, 656, 660-1, 664, 666, 673-4, 676, 687

  E. I. du Pont de Nemours & Co., 661, 663, 696
  Midvale Steel and Ordnance Company, 656, 660-1, 664, 674, 677
  Remington Arms Union Metallic Cartridge Company, 641
  Washington Steel and Ordnance Co., 687
  Winchester Arms Co., 641
US Navy League, 666
Vengeur documents, 99
Ventris, Maj. Gen. F, 631
Vickers, Capt. C E
  The Trenches 1908, 505
Vieille, P
  Smokeless powder, 92
Vincent, Capt. B, 647
Viviani, R, 121, 298, 299, 516, 615, 756
Wallace, Maj. Gen. A, 631
War Office (Reconstitution) Committee, 425
Warre, Dr E, 367, 440
Warren, Maj Gen Sir C, 333
Waters, Col. W H H
  War in Manchuria, 466
Wauchope, Maj. Gen. A G, 35, 327, 330, 333
Wavell, Field Marshal A P, 775, 778-9
Wells, H G
  Anticipations of Mechanical & Scientific Progress upon Human Life & Thought, 35
  The Land Ironclads, 36, 582
  The War in the Air, 15, 36
Werder, Gen. K von, 278
White, Lt. Gen. Sir G S, 321, 323, 440
Wilkinson, H S, 150
Wilkinson, Lt. Gen. H C, 500
Willcocks, Gen. Sir J, 803
Wilson, Field Marshal Sir H H, 102, , 458, 757
Wilson, President W, 569
Wimpffen, Gen. Baron E F de, 79
Wolseley, Field Marshal Sir G, 316, 331, 367, 369, 437, 443, 602
Wood, Gen. Sir E, 368, 373, 379
Woods, Lt. H C, 387
Workmen's Compensation Act 1906, 588
Wyndham-Quin, Maj. W, MP, 499
Ypres, First Battle of, 725
Yule, Brig Gen J H, 322
Zeppelin scare (1909), 15
Zola, E, 109

www.ingramcontent.com/pod-product-compliance
Lightning Source LLC
Chambersburg PA
CBHW070855300426
44113CB00008B/843